Testimony on the Influence of J. Thomas Looney's *"Shakespeare" Identified*

Once having read [*"Shakespeare" Identified*], I doubt if anyone, friend or foe, will ever forget it. . . . I have been fascinated beyond measure. . . . If [**Looney's**] conclusions are accepted by posterity, it chronicles the most important literary pursuit and discovery ever given to the world.

> *Gelett Burgess*
> *Novelist and short story writer*

I no longer believe that . . . the actor from Stratford was the author of the works that have been ascribed to him. Since reading *"Shakespeare" Identified* by **J. Thomas Looney**, I am almost convinced that the assumed name conceals the personality of Edward de Vere, Earl of Oxford. . . . The man of Stratford seems to have nothing at all to justify his claim, whereas Oxford has almost everything.

> *Sigmund Freud*
> *Psychoanalyst*

I myself have become sufficiently convinced that Lord Oxford is the author of Prince Hamlet's tragedy, and highly recommend a reading of **J. Thomas Looney's** treatise, *"Shakespeare" Identified in the 17th Earl of Oxford, Edward de Vere*. It is one of the 20th Century classics.

> *Mortimer J. Adler*
> *Philosopher and Educator*

J. Thomas Looney's *"Shakespeare" Identified* is a sane, dignified, arresting contribution to the abused and sadly discredited Shakespeare controversy. It is one of the most ingenious pieces of minute, circumstantial evidence extant in literary criticism. . . . Every right-minded scholar who seriously cares for the welfare of letters in the bigger sense should face the problem that this book presents and argue it to a finish.

> *Frederick Taber Cooper*
> *Former Editor, Forum*
> *Professor of Literature*
> *Columbia University*

"Shakespeare" Identified is not only a fascinating book, it is clear and convincing argument that cannot be ignored or disbelieved by a thinking reader. . . . Anyone who has read **Mr. Looney's** book with an open mind, has an open mind no longer; he is a disciple of Mr. Looney.

> *Carolyn Wells*
> *Novelist and short story writer*

Testimony on Resistance to Changing Long-Held Beliefs

All great truths begin as blasphemies.

George Bernard Shaw

A settled scholarly tradition can inhibit free thought.

Hugh Trevor-Roper

A foolish faith in authority is the worst enemy of truth.

Albert Einstein

A genuinely unfashionable opinion is almost never given a fair hearing.

George Orwell

Nothing is so likely as a false theory to blind the eyes to existing evidence.

S. R. Gardiner

A traditional guild belief is more preciously guarded than any other treasure.

John Kenneth Galbraith

The declining culture refuses to change, clinging ever more rigidly to its outdated ideas.

Fritjof Capra

Whenever you seek a new path to truth, you must expect to find it blocked by expert opinion.

Albert Guerard

Contempt prior to examination is an intellectual vice, from which the greatest faculties of mind are not free.

William Paley

At any moment we are prisoners caught in the framework of our theories, our expectations, our past experiences.

Karl Popper

The greatest enemy of Knowledge is the Goliath of Authority, received opinion and the inbred feeling that the older a statement is, the nearer it approaches to the fountain of Truth.

Sir Thomas Browne

There is a principle which is a bar to all information, which is proof against all arguments, and which cannot fail to keep a man in everlasting ignorance; this principle is contempt prior to investigation.

Herbert Spencer

Most men can seldom accept even the simplest and most obvious truth if it would oblige them to admit the falsity of conclusions which they have delighted in explaining to colleagues, have proudly taught to others, and have woven thread by thread into the fabric of their lives.

Leo Tolstoy

SHAKESPEARE REVOLUTIONIZED

The First Hundred Years of J. Thomas Looney's *"Shakespeare" Identified*

by
James A. Warren

Published by
VERITAS PUBLICATIONS
BRINGING HIDDEN TRUTHS TO LIGHT
CARY, NORTH CAROLINA

Published by
VERITAS PUBLICATIONS
CARY, NORTH CAROLINA
www.veritaspublications.net

ISBN: 978-1-7335894-3-7

The Shakespeare cube on the cover was designed by Frank Lawler,
who retains the rights to it.

The *Funky Winkerbean* comic strip reproduced on page 500
is used with permission from Tom Batiuk and King Features.

Published July 2021

This book is dedicated to three extraordinary scholars
whose work to call attention to the history of the Shakespeare authorship question
led directly to my own fascination with the subject.

Paul H. Altrocchi, MD

whose ten anthologies, *Building the Case for Edward de Vere as Shakespeare*
(the first five volumes co-edited by Hank Whittemore),
brought the most important Oxfordian research from the past century
to the attention of today's scholars.

Warren Hope, Ph.D.

whose *The Shakespeare Controversy* guided me and so many others
through the history of the Shakespeare authorship question.

Hank Whittemore

whose *The Monument* presented his profoundly inspiring insights
into the true meaning of *Shake-speares Sonnets*
and the real-life events that lay behind them.

CONTENTS

PART TWO:
THE CONTINUING INFLUENCE OF *"SHAKESPEARE" IDENTIFIED*

PART THREE:
PROSPECTS FOR THE OXFORDIAN IDEA

Biographical Text Boxes

Preface

When I first encountered the idea that Edward de Vere, 17th Earl of Oxford, had written the works usually attributed to William Shakespeare, it made me angry. I wondered why the person who had brought it to my attention—someone I hadn't known long but for whom I had a great deal of respect—was wasting my time with this nonsense. How could he possibly believe this idea to be true?

But now that the idea was in my head I began to see references to it everywhere I looked, sometimes in the most unexpected places. Among the more usual places were discussion programs, such as *Firing Line*, which examined the issue at least twice, NPR's *Morning Edition*, which addressed it several times, and PBS's *Frontline* documentary "The Shakespeare Mystery."

Among the more surprising places were TV shows such as *Granite Flats*, a sitcom with a character who was an Oxfordian (a believer in authorship by the 17th Earl of Oxford, Edward de Vere) portrayed by Christopher Lloyd, and the popular game show *Jeopardy!* on which host Alex Trebek brought up the subject on at least three episodes. Even cartoonists believed their readers were familiar enough with the name Edward de Vere that they could mention it in their cartoons, as Tom Batiuk did in *Funky Winkerbean* (see p. 500).

The idea of Edward de Vere as Shakespeare has been the subject of cover stories in *The Atlantic*, *Harper's* and *U.S. News & World Report*, and examined by three law reviews. It has gained credibility among people with no vested interest in the subject either way. Michael Hart, for instance, in his book ranking the one hundred most influential persons in history, listed Edward de Vere, not William Shakespeare, at position thirty-one.

Actors who have come to believe that Edward de Vere was Shakespeare include Orson Welles, Derek Jacobi and Keanu Reeves. Author Anne Rice concluded that Edward de Vere was Shakespeare, as did ambassador Paul H. Nitze and historian David McCullough. And so did Friend W. Richardson, former governor of California, who wrote an op-ed piece about it for a local newspaper.

And, I learned, five Justices of the U.S. Supreme Court had examined the authorship issue and concluded that the man from Stratford did not write the works attributed to him. At least three of them publicly stated their belief that Edward de Vere was the real author: Harry A. Blackmun, Antonin Scalia and John Paul Stevens.

The idea of Edward de Vere, 17th Earl of Oxford, as "Shakespeare" was introduced by J. Thomas Looney in his book *"Shakespeare" Identified*, which was published on March 4, 1920, just over one hundred years ago. The Oxfordian claim has rocked the study of William Shakespeare and his works ever since; even literary scholars who don't address it directly show distinct signs of having been influenced by it.

But ideas come and go. What is it about this one that accounts for its having lasted one hundred years, and for its having every prospect of replacing the Stratfordian paradigm?

One reason is the persuasiveness of Mr. Looney's book. Among the many persons who were convinced by the case made in *"Shakespeare" Identified* were the founder of psychoanalysis Sigmund Freud, novelist and humorist Gelett Burgess, and philosopher and educator Mortimer J. Adler. Freud wrote that "Since reading *"Shakespeare" Identified* by J. Thomas Looney, I am almost convinced that the assumed name conceals the personality of Edward de Vere, Earl of Oxford." He later stated his definite conviction that Oxford was Shakespeare. Burgess wrote, "Once having read *"Shakespeare" Identified*, I doubt if anyone, friend or foe, will ever forget it. I have been fascinated beyond measure." Adler wrote that he "had become sufficiently convinced" that Oxford was Shakespeare, and "highly recommended a reading of J. Thomas Looney's *'Shakespeare' Identified,*" which he called "a 20th century classic."

Another reason is the stark contrast between the improbabilities of the traditional story of authorship by William Shakspere[1] and the natural way the literary works flow from the life and pen of Edward de Vere in Mr. Looney's telling.

In the traditional story, a young man from Stratford with no known education—someone who spoke a dialect of English difficult to understand outside his native area—went to London, where he soon wrote two lengthy poems in the most sophisticated London English, and then followed them up with plays showing a deep understanding of politics, diplomacy, Italy and the law as well as intimate familiarity with the interactions of courtiers at the highest levels of that hierarchical society, without leaving behind a single trace of how he did it. He was uninvolved with the publication of his works, and in his mid-forties, so the story goes, abandoned his career to return to Stratford to engage in small-time commercial transactions for the rest of his life.

In Mr. Looney's story, the author was one of the most highly educated people of his time, and, as the highest-ranking earl in the kingdom, was someone intimately involved with the Queen, her court and the political and diplomatic events of the time. He had traveled extensively in Italy and France, and was acclaimed by his contemporaries as a gifted poet and dramatist. He was deeply involved with the publication of "Shakespeare's" works, which stopped in 1604, the year of his death.

The results of the two stories are, on one hand, literary works that have no connection to the life or times of the man who supposedly wrote them, and, on the other, works that are deeply personal portrayals of events and people important in the life of Edward de Vere and of the political and diplomatic events of his time.

In one story, the works were the products of fantasy and genius; in the other they arose from concrete realities imaginatively recreated by genius.

One story led to doubts: Ralph Waldo Emerson spoke for many in saying that he "could not marry" Shakspere's life to his verse. The other led to convictions: Gerald H. Rendall, one of the founders of the University of Liverpool, observed that "[t]he plays reveal numerous and arresting coincidences with recorded incidents and traits in the career of Edward de Vere."

So it's not a matter of simply plucking one man out and putting another in his place. The consequences of the change in author flow in unrelenting waves outward, altering our understanding of many subjects, some only tangentially related to the study of literature. The Oxfordian idea has endured and spread because it gives us a deeper understanding of Shakespeare's plays and poems, the Elizabethan Era, the nature of genius and literary creativity, and the personality of the true author and the central place

---

[1] A note on page x explains the spelling of "Shakspere."

he occupied in the time. These four subjects, like many others addressed in this book, have been greatly misunderstood over the past 400 years because "Shakespeare" has been misidentified.

- - - - -

Shakespeare Revolutionized: The First Hundred Years of J. Thomas Looney's "Shakespeare" Identified tells the story of how Mr. Looney came to write his book and how he promoted the Oxfordian claim afterwards. It chronicles the rise of an Oxfordian movement during the first quarter-century after the book was published: from 1920 to 1945 in England and from 1920 to 1948 in the United States. It also explores the wider effects that the introduction of the Oxfordian idea has had on public opinion, on Shakespeare Studies within academia and on scholars working in related fields.

This book opens with a chapter describing the state of "the Shakespeare Mystery" at the time Mr. Looney began to investigate the authorship question. It shows the publications and ideas he encountered as he surveyed the authorship landscape. The second chapter examines why Mr. Looney decided to examine the issue and lays out the process he used to conduct his investigation. The next two chapters describe how the book came to be published by Cecil Palmer and the responses to it. Chapter 5 explains why it was so difficult for many people to accept the Oxfordian thesis at the time: it lays out the dozen Mental Revolutions that readers had to go through to fully buy into the new paradigm.

Chapters 6-10 examine the rise of an Oxfordian movement under the umbrella of the Shakespeare Fellowship and trace its activities through 1936. Chapters 11-13 report how academia and traditional Shakespeare scholars responded to the Oxfordian challenge. Chapters 14-18 examine the activities of the Oxfordian movement in Britain through the summer of 1945 and in North America through the end of 1948.

Much of the material in these first eighteen chapters could have been presented in summary form, resulting in a shorter book. I did not go that route in part because I viewed my role, to some extent, as that of a tour guide. I often had in mind Maurice Ravel's orchestration of Modest Mussorgsky's *Pictures at an Exhibition*, in which listeners are treated to musical portrayals of pictures they might have seen while strolling through an art exhibition. I wanted to showcase the first generations of Oxfordian scholars just as artists' works are showcased in an art gallery. I wanted to give a sense of the richness of their thought, the brilliance of their writing, and the persuasiveness of their presentations. That was best done by allowing them to speak for themselves.

In Part Two (chapters 19-24) I assess the state of the Oxfordian claim today: the activities of the Oxfordian movement, the degree to which the general public has become aware of the Oxfordian idea and academia's response to it. Part Three (chapters 25-26) provides some analysis. I examine why it matters who wrote Shakespeare's works, and in the final chapter I draw on the experiences of the first generations of Oxfordians to construct a strategy for completing the Oxfordian revolution launched by J. Thomas Looney one hundred years ago.

Appendices include a list of Mr. Looney's Oxfordian writings, short excerpts commenting on *"Shakespeare" Identified*, a comparison of the five editions of the book published so far, a list of Shakespeare Fellowship officers and events from 1922 to 1945, and a chronological listing of every known Oxfordian event and publication from 1920 to mid-1945 in Britain and through 1948 in North America.

- - - - -

This book is one result of six years of research, which included examining thousands of long-forgotten books, articles, reviews, letters to editors, and personal letters. In addition to scouring online databases and print and microfiche holdings at several large research libraries in the United States, my effort to locate older Oxfordian materials included four trips to England for research in the British Library and in archives at the University of London, Brunel University and the University of Liverpool.

That research also resulted in the publication of the Centenary Edition of *"Shakespeare" Identified* in 2018, which brought J. Thomas Looney's revolutionary book back into print in a modern typesetting. It also included all material omitted from the three previous U.S. editions and 230 footnotes identifying the source of hundreds of passages that Mr. Looney quoted.

A third result was the publication, early in 2019, of *"Shakespeare" Revealed: The Collected Articles and Published Letters of J. Thomas Looney*, which consists of fifty-three shorter pieces he published on the Oxfordian idea after *"Shakespeare" Identified.* Among them are more than forty articles and letters to editors written in response to reviews critical of his book which had never been reprinted and, indeed, were unknown to anyone alive today until I uncovered them. They provide a fascinating look into the activities of the founding father of the Oxfordian claim after publication of his book.

Yet another publication resulting from my research was the Fourth Edition of *An Index to Oxfordian Publications*, designed to serve as a guide to the 9,000 Oxfordian books and articles published from 1920 through 2017. It's intended for both general readers interested in learning more about the extent of research into the Oxfordian case and as a reference tool for scholars needing information on specific books or articles. The fifth edition of the *Index*, with several thousand additional listings, will be published soon.

To my surprise I found in the archives references to more than 500 letters that Oxfordian scholars had written to each other and to Stratfordian scholars during the first twenty-five years of the Oxfordian era. More than half are from or to Mr. Looney. I intend to bring them out in an annotated volume, *"Shakespeare" Discovered: The Oxfordian Correspondence of John Thomas Looney and Other Early Oxfordians, 1920-1945.*

The most exciting moment in my research came when I learned through Kathryn Sharpe of the existence of some of J. Thomas Looney's papers. That this cache of papers had survived, and had been discovered by his grandson, Alan Bodell, in 2019, seventy-five years after Mr. Looney's death, were themselves minor miracles. I am grateful to Alan for entrusting them to me. They consist of 386 items totaling 1,940 pages. Though they are only a fraction of what would have been in Mr. Looney's possession at the time of his death in 1944, they are a goldmine of information about the first decades of the Oxfordian era. Among them are copies of some of his published articles I had not known about, a dozen or so short manuscripts in varying stages of completeness, and correspondence. A collection of them relating to the Oxfordian thesis, properly introduced and annotated, will, at some point, be published.

Many of the papers provide information about J. Thomas Looney himself, including unpublished accounts of him by people who had known him, as well as correspondence on non-Oxfordian matters. The information in those papers is substantial enough to show that a full biography is warranted, and I am now at work on it.

The text box below contains a list of the publications resulting from my Oxfordian research, showing where this current book fits into the stream. Like the others on the list, it contains much newly discovered information that will, I hope, bring to the Oxfordian claim and the Oxfordian movement—and to the man who discovered Oxford's authorship—the prominence they and he deserve.

<u>Publications Resulting from Six Years' Research into J. Thomas Looney and the Early Years of the Oxfordian Movement</u>

2017   *An Index to Oxfordian Publications*, Fourth Edition.

2018   *"Shakespeare" Identified* — Centenary Edition of J. Thomas Looney's book.

       "J. Thomas Looney in *The Bookman's Journal*: Five Letters (1920-1921)" [Introduction and annotated editions of Looney's five letters], *The Oxfordian*, vol. 20: 131-156.

2019   *"Shakespeare" Revealed: The Collected Articles and Published Letters of J. Thomas Looney.*

       Shakespearian Fantasias — Modern Edition of Esther Singleton's novel, first published in 1929.

       Oxfordian Archives in England: A Database of Oxfordian Ephemera in the Special Collections of Brunel University, the University of London and the University of Liverpool.

2020   "Comparisons of Oxford's Poetry with Shakespeare's: Five Letters from J. Thomas Looney to *The New Age* (1920-1921) and *The Outlook* (1921)," *The Oxfordian*, vol. 22: 103-120.

2021   ***Shakespeare Revolutionized: The First Hundred Years of J. Thomas Looney's "Shakespeare" Identified***

○   *"Shakespeare" Investigated: The Oxfordian Letters of J. Thomas Looney and Other Early Oxfordians, 1920-1945.*

○   *"Shakespeare" Explained: Shakespeare Fellowship Circulars and Articles in The Hackney Spectator, The Shakespeare Pictorial and The East Anglian Magazine, 1922-1940.*

○   *An Index to Oxfordian Publications*, Fifth Edition.

○   "The First Hundred Years of the Oxfordian Movement: The Middle Years (1945-1984)."

○   A biography of J. Thomas Looney.

Editorial Notes

The book is written in modern American English, but I have retained British English spellings (e.g., "theatre," "organisation," "characterised," "connexion," "travellers") in passages quoted from British publications and letters. Antiquated words such as "whilst" have likewise been retained to give readers a sense of the style of the original publications, but hyphenated words such as "to-day" and "no-one" have been modernized. Punctuation has also been modified—punctuation marks have been placed inside quotation marks and the blank space before quotation marks, colons and semicolons eliminated—to increase readability for modern eyes.

"Shakespeare" Identified is consistently spelled with the first word inside quotation marks as Looney intended, regardless of how it appears in texts quoted. I have also standardized the capitalization of *Sonnets*: when individual sonnets are referred to the word is not capitalized, but when the publication *Shake-speares Sonnets* is referred to the word is capitalized and italicized.

Titles of periodicals are also standardized with "The" capitalized, as in *The New York Times* and *The Hackney Spectator*, except in footnotes, where "the" is omitted.

"Edward de Vere," "the Earl of Oxford" and "Oxford" are used interchangeably. The "de" has been changed to lower case in those instances when authors used "De."

In distinguishing between the names "Shakespeare" and "Shakspere" I am following the practice explained by Sir George Greenwood and used by J. Thomas Looney in *"Shakespeare" Identified*:

> In discussing the authorship the word SHAKESPEARE is used to refer to the author. The word SHAKSPERE is used to refer to the person from Stratford hitherto credited with the authorship, with the Christian name "William" occasionally added to accentuate the distinction. In immaterial connections and in quotations "Shakespeare" is usually employed.

Text boxes contain supplementary information for readers who want additional information on the specific subjects addressed in them.

In order to keep the number of footnotes to a minimum, when more than one passage from the same page of another publication is quoted, only the first passage is cited. Readers can assume that all following quoted passages are from the same source and page just cited until the next footnote appears.

Titles of publications are sometimes shortened in footnotes; full titles are listed in the Bibliography.

Abbreviations Used in Footnotes

BTC	*Building the Case* – The ten volumes of anthologies of Oxfordian articles edited by Paul H. Altrocchi (Hank Whittemore served as co-editor of the first five volumes)
HS	*The Hackney Spectator*
SF	The Shakespeare Fellowship
SFA	*The Shakespeare Fellowship News-Letter* (published by the American branch, 1939-1943)
SFE	*The Shakespeare Fellowship News-Letter* (published by the English branch, 1937-1958)
SFQ	*The Shakespeare Fellowship Quarterly* (published by the American branch, 1944-1948)
SP	*The Shakespeare Pictorial*

Acknowledgements

I am grateful to many people for their contributions to this book:

+ **Alex McNeil**, editor *extraordinaire* and one of the unsung heroes of the Oxfordian movement, whose stylistic improvements immeasurably improved the readability of the book;

+ **Kathryn Sharpe** for the title, for engaging a group of Oxfordians in Michigan and Washington who came up with the design of the cover, and for proofreading many chapters;

+ **Frank Lawler** for the design of the intriguing Shakespeare cube on the cover;

+ **Mike A'Dair** for making available a full set of legal documents related to the Barrell-Dawson lawsuit;

+ **Paul H. Altrocchi** and **Hank Whittemore** for guidance and encouragement throughout the research and writing of this project;

+ **Warren Hope** for commenting on early drafts and for proofreading the nearly final draft;

+ **Bill Boyle** and **Kathryn Sharpe** for comments that helped me sharpen points not made clearly enough in early drafts;

+ **Milee Grace Marasigan Jabon** for improving the quality of images in the text.

Needless to say, I am solely responsible for any remaining errors.

+ I am especially grateful to **Alan Bodell**, J. Thomas Looney's grandson, for entrusting his grandfather's papers to me.

+ My deepest appreciation must go to my wife, the lovely **Naiyana**, for her steadfast support for a project that took her husband from her for so many lengthy periods of time.

1

Setting the Stage

What Looney Saw

In 1920 a bombshell exploded over Shakespeare Studies from which it has yet to recover; a bombshell—in the form of J. Thomas Looney's *"Shakespeare" Identified*—so powerful that even a hundred years later orthodox Shakespeare scholars haven't yet found a credible way of responding to its thesis that Edward de Vere, 17th Earl of Oxford, was the real author of the plays and poems attributed to William Shakspere of Stratford-upon-Avon. Even now, most scholars either ignore the book or attempt to change the subject by attacking those who are convinced that its thesis is correct. Even after a span of one hundred years scholars have not conducted an objective, scholarly examination of the Oxfordian claim, either to confirm it or to show where its evidence is wrong or misinterpreted or its logic faulty. And yet scholars have been influenced by it, and much of their work today is a reaction to it even if they do not say so openly.

The bombshell's power came not from its presentation of doubts about authorship by the man from Stratford but from its identification, for the first time, of a credible candidate for authorship. Its power came from the multifaceted range of evidence Looney presented, much of it drawn from the work of Stratfordian scholars, supplemented by his extensive knowledge of the literature of the Elizabethan era and the historical and political contexts in which it had been written.

In this chapter our task is to understand what Looney would have observed regarding "the Shakespeare Mystery," as it was often called at the time, as he became interested in it. What publications and ideas on the subject were being discussed at the beginning of the second decade of the twentieth century? Why had so many individuals come to doubt William Shakspere's authorship? What arguments had they presented that convinced him that someone else was the author?

Looney saw that modern doubts about Shakspere's authorship arose currently with the rise of modern scholarly practices in the study of literature during the middle and later years of the nineteenth century.[1] He observed that,

> "Shakespeare" had to wait until the Nineteenth Century for his full literary appreciation: and this was essential to the mere raising of the problem. "Not until two centuries had passed after his death," says Emerson, "did any criticism which we think adequate begin to appear."[2]

Throughout the eighteenth and nineteenth centuries Shakespearean scholars laid the groundwork for a more sophisticated appreciation of Shakespeare's works by standardizing the texts of the plays and poems, attempting to determine the order in

---

[1] For a discussion of earlier doubts, arising as far back as the first use of the name William Shakespeare in 1593, see Bryan H. Wildenthal's *Early Shakespeare Authorship Doubts* (2019).
[2] J. Thomas Looney, *"Shakespeare" Identified* (2018), p. 78.

which they had been written and acquiring a broader understanding of the development of the public theater. They established the basic facts of William Shakspere's life, identified the literary and historical works on which Shakespeare had drawn, and identified earlier plays on which they believed he had based his own.

Those scholarly activities also brought to light, almost from the time they began, doubts about Shakspere's authorship. "The rapid undermining of that belief," Looney later wrote, was due "mainly to two movements . . . [arising in] the nineteenth century." The first was the marked interest in practical historical research, which "brought to light the disconcerting fact that the English writer most distinguished by the brilliancy of his powers was, paradoxically, separated from all his fellows by a glaring deficiency of relevant personal records." The second was the development of a scientific study of literature, which "yielded a truer measure of the culture represented by the works." These two developments "produced in many minds a definite conviction that . . . a school of literature of the first rank had been allowed to grow up around a personality having no title whatever to the honour."[3]

Shakespearean scholarship had laid bare the petty and boorish nature of the man from Stratford and the widespread learning and aristocratic mien characteristic of the plays. Scholars had shown that they were based in part on literary works written in Greek, Latin, French and Italian that had not yet been translated into English. They demonstrated the seemingly unavoidable fact that not every work—or not every part of every work—included in the First Folio had actually been written by Shakespeare, whoever he was.

By the late nineteenth century, doubts about Shakspere's authorship had become widespread, especially among those whose own experiences gave them insight into the process of literary creation or knowledge of specialized subjects such as Italy or the law portrayed in the plays. Creative writers of fiction, who knew firsthand how literary works were created and how that process affected writers' lives, were among the first to challenge the traditional story. Among them were:

Samuel Taylor Coleridge (1772-1834): "What? . . . does God choose idiots by whom / To convey divine truth to men?"[4]

Ralph Waldo Emerson (1803-1882): The "verdict of the Shakespeare Societies comes to mind, that he was a jovial actor and manager. I cannot marry this fact to his verse. Other admirable men have led lives in some sort of keeping with their thought; but this man, in wide contrast."[5]

John Greenleaf Whittier (1807-1892): "Whether Bacon wrote the wonderful plays or not, I am quite sure the man Shakspere neither did nor could."[6]

Walt Whitman (1819-1892): "I know what will become of Master Shaksper the actor—what has already become of him. He has gone for good."[7]

Mark Twain (1835-1910): "I only *believed* Bacon wrote Shakespeare, whereas I *knew*

---

[3] J. Thomas Looney, "The Earl of Oxford as Shakespeare: New Evidence," *The Golden Hind*, vol. 1/1 (Oct. 1922): 23-24.
[4] Samuel Taylor Coleridge, quoted in Sir Edwin Durning-Lawrence, *Bacon is Shakespeare* (1910), p. 179.
[5] Ralph Waldo Emerson, *Representative Men*, in *Works*, vol. IV, p. 218.
[6] John Greenleaf Whittier, quoted in Sir Edwin Durning-Lawrence, *Bacon is Shakespeare* (1910), p. 179.
[7] Walt Whitman, in conversation with Horace Traubel, quoted in Traubel's *With Walt Whitman in Camden* (1908), p. 170.

Shakespeare didn't. . . . You can trace the life histories of the whole of [the world's celebrities] save one—far and away the most colossal prodigy of the entire accumulation—Shakespeare. About him you can find out . . . nothing of even the slightest importance. Nothing worth the trouble of stowing away in your memory."[8]

Henry James (1843-1916): "I am 'a sort of' haunted by the conviction that the divine William is the biggest and most successful fraud ever practised on a patient world. The more I turn him round and round the more he so affects me."[9]

Politicians and statesmen were another special category of doubters because of Shakespeare's obsession with portraying political developments in his plays. Prominent politicians who publicly expressed doubt include:

Prime Minister Lord Palmerston (1779-1848): "[I] rejoiced to have lived to see . . . the explosion of the Shakespearean illusion."[10]

Prime Minister Benjamin Disraeli (1804-1881): "And who is Shakespeare? We know as much of him as we do of Homer. Did he write half the plays attributed to him? Did he write a single whole play? I doubt it."[11]

British Statesman and Lord Rector, University of Glasgow John Bright (1811-1889): "Any man who believes that William Shakespeare of Stratford wrote *Hamlet* or *Lear* is a fool."[12]

German Chancellor Otto von Bismarck (1815-1898): "I could not understand how it were possible that a man, however gifted with the intuition of genius, could have written what was attributed to Shakespeare, unless he had been in touch with the great affairs of state, behind the scenes of political life, and also intimate with all the social courtesies, and refinements of thought, which, in Shakespeare's time, were only to be met with in the highest circles. . . . [It is not believable] that a man who had written the greatest dramas in the world's literature, could, of his own free will, whilst in the prime of life, have retired to such a place as Stratford-on-Avon, and lived for years cut off from the intellectual society and out of touch with the world."[13]

Prominent members of the legal profession, impressed by Shakespeare's legal knowledge and use of legal imagery, formed yet another specialized group that publicly expressed doubts about the traditional story.

Judge Thomas E. Webb (1821-1903): "For well nigh three hundred years the world has believed the author to be the young man who . . . came up from Stratford. . . . At the present moment there is much doubt and misgiving on the subject among

---

[8] Mark Twain, *Is Shakespeare Dead?* (1909), pp. 11, 142.

[9] Henry James, letter to Miss Violet Hunt dated Aug. 26, 1903, in *Letters of Henry James*, selected and edited by Percy Lubbock (1948).

[10] Lord Palmerston, quoted in Sir Edwin Durning-Lawrence, *Bacon is Shakespeare* (1910), p. 178.

[11] Benjamin Disraeli (Lord Beaconsfield), *Venetia*, Book 6, chap. viii, quoted in Sir Edwin Durning-Lawrence, "Bacon is Shakespeare," in *The Shakespeare Myth* (1914), p. 3.

[12] John Bright, quoted in Sir Edwin Durning-Lawrence, *Bacon is Shakespeare* (1910), p. 179.

[13] Sidney Whitman, *Personal Reminiscences of Prince Bismarck* (1903), p. 152.

serious men, and its discussion can no longer be tabooed as fit only for the lunatic, the faddist, and the fool."[14]

James Wilde, 1st Lord Penzance (1816-1899): "What a monster then is this that the defendants would present to us! The butcher's apprentice transformed at short notice into the philosopher and poet! Why, it is almost contrary to nature. Well, to be sure, the grub turns into the butterfly . . . but who ever heard of the butterfly turning back again into the grub? Yet nothing less than this is offered to our belief. From the moment he got back to Stratford he dropped his butterfly wings—tilling his own land, wholly occupied in the making and selling of malt, and other agricultural pursuits. If it was difficult to believe in William Shakespeare's transformation, it is harder still to give credit to his relapse."[15]

United States Supreme Court Justice Oliver Wendell Holmes (1841-1935): Sir George Greenwood cited Holmes, along with Lord Penzance and Judge Webb, as being "supporters of the 'Baconian' theory."[16]

Two other prominent doubters that Looney surely would have been aware of were:

American scholar William Henry Furness (1802-1896), who wrote that "I am one of the many who have never been able to bring the life of William Shakespeare [i.e., Shakspere] and the plays of Shakespeare within planetary space of each other. Are there any two things in the world more incongruous?"[17]

Helen Keller (1880-1968): "[Research into the playwright's life] led me to the conclusion that Shakespeare of Stratford is not to be even thought of as a possible author of the most wonderful plays of the world. The question now remains: Who was William Shakespeare?"[18] She later wrote a thirty-four page manuscript entitled "A Concealed Poet Disclosed," in which she argued that Bacon secretly wrote Shakespeare's plays.

The poem by Edmund C. Steadman in the nearby text box shows the degree of public interest in the authorship question in the early years of the twentieth century.

Reasons for Doubt

Looney would have seen that doubts about William Shakspere's authorship could be sorted into several categories. First were those questioning how the man from Stratford could have acquired the depth of knowledge exhibited in the literary works in so many fields—the law, Italy and France, music, literature in foreign languages, politics as practiced in the Elizabethan court and government, diplomacy, the intimate behavior of courtiers, and activities such as horsemanship, fencing and hawking practiced only by the upper classes—without leaving any trace of how he acquired it. Mastery of these subjects, and the ease with which they are presented in the plays, bespeaks of long familiarity with them, not mere book learning over the short period of time between Shakspere's

---

[14] Judge Thomas E. Webb, *The Mystery of William Shakespeare: A Summary of the Evidence* (1902), p. 232.

[15] James Wilde, 1st Baron of Penzance, *Lord Penzance on the Bacon-Shakespeare Controversy: A Judicial Summing-Up* (1902), p. 146.

[16] Sir George Greenwood, *Shakespeare's Law* (1920), p. 16.

[17] Dr. W. H. Furness, quoted in Sir Edwin Durning-Lawrence, *Bacon is Shakespeare* (1910), p. 180.

[18] Helen Keller, in *Matilda Ziegler Magazine*, January 1909. See https://www.perkins.org/ stories/helen-keller-shakespeare-skeptic.

departure from Stratford and the supposed launching of his literary career.

Other doubts arose from the absence of any documentation attesting to Shakspere's theatrical or literary activities during his lifetime; all references to Shakespeare were to the works or to the name of the man who wrote them, not to the man from Stratford unless he was the author, the very point in dispute. There is no mention of Shakspere as an actor or dramatist in any private papers; no diary or letter in which anybody connected him with the famous writer William Shakespeare. Nobody in Stratford, down through two generations after he died, ever mentioned that he had been a famous writer. His son-in-law, a medical doctor who commented in his diary on a famous writer he had treated, Michael Drayton, made no mention of his father-in-law. William Camden's chapter on Stratford in *Britannia*, his history of England, made no mention of Shakspere even though he discussed other prominent people in the town.[19]

Oddly, there is no mention of Shakespeare, either, as an actor or dramatist in London's theatrical records, no mention in the provincial records, and, with the exception of one or two questionable instances, no mention of him in the records of the court Revels. There

---

Advice to English Schoolboys Who Want to Become Shakespeare

Edmund C. Steadman

To gain command of English words and every grammar rule,
'Tis best to be a butcher's son and never go to school.
To form good plays in perfect style, and full of classic knowledge,
'Tis best to be a poacher boy, and never go to college.

To write of ladies, lords and dukes, of kings and kingly sport,
'Tis best to be a common man and never go to court.
To write about philosophy and law and medicine,
'Tis best to stand at horses' heads, and never read a line.

To treat of foreign lands in strains that all men must applaud,
'Tis best to stay in England and never go abroad.
To scale the heights of human bliss and sound the depths of woe,
'Tis best to make a steady "pile" and never let it go.

If come to ripe maturity when genius has full play,
'Tis best to lead an easy life and lay the pen away.
To show that "knowledge is the wing wherewith we fly to Heaven,"
'Tis best that to your own dear child no lessons should be given.

To surely earn immortal fame as England's greatest bard,
'Tis best to leave no manuscripts and die of "drinking hard."

Bacon:
To win injustice and contempt from every biased mind,
'Tis best to be "the wisest and the brightest of mankind."

Shake-Speare:
To warn the strong, to teach the proud, to give new knowledge scope,
'Twas best to use a nom-de-plume, and write in faith and hope,
That future ages, wiser grown, would learn the royal rule,
That knowledge does not come to those who never go to school.

From *The Literary World*, vol. 63 (1901): 327.

---

[19] Ramon Jiménez, "Shakspere in Stratford and London: Ten Eyewitnesses Who Saw Nothing," in *Shakespeare Beyond Doubt?* edited by John M. Shahan and Alexander Waugh (2013), pp. 47-57.

is no mention of Shakspere or Shakespeare in Philip Henslowe's Diary. Henslowe, owner of the Rose and Fortune Theaters, kept meticulous records of plays performed, gate receipts and payments made to actors and playwrights. His records indicate that half a dozen of Shakespeare's plays were performed in his theaters during the 1592-97 period, yet not one payment was made to Shakspere as an actor, a playwright or a reviser of plays. No payments were recorded for the purchase of any of Shakespeare's plays—the only plays he produced for which no payments were made.

There is no record that Shakspere made a personal impact on any of the other literary figures or great intellects of his time; if indeed he was Shakespeare, he was the only famous playwright for whom no eulogies were written at the time of his death. Again, the contemporary references to Shakespeare are to the name of the writer (whoever he may have been) or to the works.

Perhaps most important were doubts arising from the disconnect between what was known of Shakspere's mundane, shallow and uncultured life and the cultured and sophisticated milieu of so many of Shakespeare's plays. Emerson's statement that he

---

Looney was familiar with Sir Sidney Lee's listing for William Shakspere in the *Dictionary of National Biography*. The excerpts below show that the paucity of verifiable facts required Lee to use repeatedly the qualifiers noted.

-- -- -- -- --

"SHAKESPEARE, WILLIAM," *Dictionary of National Biography*, **11th Edition (1910)**

"Shakespeare, William (1564-1616), dramatist and poet . . . undoubtedly . . . no doubt . . . may be assumed to have . . . he may have been . . . doubtless . . . suggested that he was . . . seems to have been . . . doubtless . . . is generally accepted as . . . probably . . . perhaps . . . cannot be reasonably contested . . . doubtless caused . . . It is possible that . . . may have been . . . there is little doubt . . . undoubtedly . . . probably . . . doubtless . . . might have . . . assumption . . . cannot reasonably be identified . . . may well have been . . . the theory that . . . is quite untenable . . . it is unsafe to assume . . . it is unlikely . . . implies . . . doubtless . . . according to a credible tradition . . . . probably . . . doubtless . . . seems pure invention . . . reported to have . . . beyond doubt . . . seems possible that . . . suggestion . . . doubtless . . . tradition points to . . . we may suppose . . . likely to have been known . . . the theory . . . tradition and common-sense . . . according to the compiler . . . . no inherent improbability . . . every indication . . . doubtless . . . probably . . . there seems no doubt . . . it is fair to infer that . . . seem to have been . . . doubtless . . . doubtless . . . it is not certain . . . may be credited . . . were doubtless . . . there is nothing to indicate . . . doubtless . . . is not known to have been . . . appears . . . probably . . . perhaps . . . must be credited . . . doubtless . . . doubtless . . . possibly . . . suggests that . . . every likelihood . . . doubtless . . . may have been . . . in all probability . . . probably . . . it is possible that . . . can only owe to . . . were doubtless . . . perhaps . . . the theory that . . . much can be said . . . was clearly suggested . . . suggests . . . doubtless . . . was probably . . . no doubt . . . was doubtless . . . may be . . . there is little doubt . . . little doubt . . . seems to allude . . . doubtless . . . there is no ground for assuming . . . possibly due . . . doubtful . . . . may be reasonably included . . . was probably . . . would well apply . . . allusions have been detected . . . no direct proof that he didn't . . . no improbability . . . there is no ground for supposing . . . wholly erroneous premises . . . practically confers . . . have assumed . . . therefore probable . . . . doubtless . . . suggests that . . . there is no evidence . . . seems . . . unlikely that . . . seems . . . doubtless . . . there seems ground for the assumption that . . . it may well have been . . . may be tentatively assigned . . . doubtless . . . probably . . . probably . . . beyond doubt . . . credible tradition . . . thenceforth . . . probably . . . no doubt . . . does not seem to . . . does not appear . . . doubtless . . . . puzzling problem . . . doubtless . . . doubtless . . . a likelihood that . . . wholly in harmony with . . . . perhaps . . . doubtless . . . doubtless . . . perhaps . . . there seems some ground for the belief . . . may safely be credited . . . been suspected . . . probably . . . probably . . . possibly . . . probably . . . probably . . . doubtless . . . doubtless . . . doubtless . . ."

could not "marry" the man to the works and Furness's on his inability "to bring the life . . . and the plays of Shakespeare within planetary space of each other" attest to the unbridgeable gap between the glories of the literary works on one hand and, on the other, the life of a man born to illiterate parents who had no known education, who did not educate his own daughters, who had no known exposure to courtly life, who never claimed to have written any literary works, who never sent any letters even though he was supposedly conducting commercial transactions in Stratford while living in London, who was in Stratford at just those moments when his plays were being performed at court, who retired to Stratford while still in the prime of his life, who showed no interest in the commercial value of his plays, whether published or still in manuscript, after his departure from London, and who made no mention of books or manuscripts or any reference to literary or intellectual possessions in his will.

Even before beginning his investigations, Looney saw that the man from Stratford did not have the background or experiences that the literary works show their author to have had. Looney may also have been aware of the work of the American lecturer and educator Delia Bacon, who in 1856 was among the first modern scholars to comment on this gap and to recognize that Shakespeare was "habitually practiced in the refinements."

> How could we have failed to recognize . . . the poet whose habits and perceptions have been moulded in the atmosphere of these subtle social influences? He cannot shake off this influence when he will. He carries the court perfume with him, unconsciously, wherever he goes, among mobs of artisans . . . into country feasts and merrymakings. . . . He looks into the Arden and into Eastcheap from the court standpoint, not from these into the court.[20]

Looney was certainly aware of Walt Whitman's doubts and of the speculations that had brought him to the very brink of identifying the true author:

> We all know how much mythus there is in the Shakespeare question as it stands today. Beneath a few foundations of proved facts are certainly engulf'd far more dim and elusive ones of deepest importance—tantalizing and half suspected— suggesting explanations that one dare not put into plain statement. But coming at once to the point, the English historical plays are to me not only the most eminent as dramatic performances . . . but form, as we get it all, the chief in a complexity of puzzles.
>
> Conceiv'd out of the fullest heat and pulse of European feudalism—personifying in unparallel'd ways the medieval aristocracy, its towering spirit of ruthless and gigantic caste, its own peculiar air and arrogance (no mere imitation)—only one of the 'wolfish earls' so plenteous in the plays themselves, or some born descendent and knower, might seem to be the true author of those amazing works—works in some respects greater than anything else in recorded literature.[21]

The Split Between Academia and Others

An examination of the Shakespeare authorship landscape by an observer as astute as J. Thomas Looney would have revealed three splits of importance: 1) Between scholars within academia and those outside it; 2) Within academia, between Departments of History and Departments of Literature; and 3) Outside of academia, between doubters

---

[20] Delia Bacon, "William Shakespeare and His Plays," *Putnam's Monthly*, Jan. 1956, p. 14.
[21] Walt Whitman, "What Lurks Behind Shakspere's Historical Plays," *November Boughs* (1888), p. 390.

who professed not to know who wrote the works and those who were convinced that Sir Francis Bacon was the real author.

This situation of doubts expressed openly outside of academia but denied within was well established before Looney began his investigations. All the doubters mentioned above were active outside academia; orthodox scholars within the walls were confident in their belief in the man from Stratford and maintained a hostile attitude toward doubters when they couldn't ignore them.

Academic scholars defended their position in one of two ways. Some, including the eminent Shakespeare scholar Sir Sidney Lee, denied that any reason for doubt existed.

> Contemporaries whose trustworthiness and access to the facts cannot be questioned knew Shakespeare of Stratford-on-Avon as "the famous seenicke poet" and "the admirable dramatic poet" whose comedies and tragedies were "the glory of the stage." Only obstinate habits of doubt, divorced from full knowledge, or lacking the power of testing literary evidence, can challenge their inexorable verdict.[22]

French scholar Abel Lefranc, observing academia's defense of the traditional story, wrote in 1918 that,

> Not only does it defend with all its soul the articles of the credo of which it constitutes itself the guardian and is its right, but refuses, under any circumstances, to admit the most legitimate doubts and reservations. In its eyes the innumerable difficulties attaching to the Shakespearian problem are as if null and void. Not a reservation, not an objection; these things appear to it, in general, quite simple and easy to explain . . . the beautiful faith of the coal-man . . . faith stalwart, complete, contemptuous of all pernicious attacks and denials which might shake it. [T]here is something religious in this manner of conceiving things . . . [and in] the near unanimity of the well-known critics and historians of this present time.[23]

Others attempted to minimize the apparent gap between the man and the works. This was the approach of English scholar, author and poet Sir Walter Raleigh, who attacked the gap at both ends: by denying the learned nature of the plays while claiming that Shakspere had a more sophisticated education than the record indicated. The knowledge shown in the plays was so superficial, he believed, that it could have been acquired through casual conversation. "In this age of cheap printed information we are too apt to forget how large a part of [Shakspere's] knowledge he must have gathered in talk. Books were licensed and guarded; but in talk there was free trade. . . . [T]he knowledge that he gained from such talk, if it was sometimes remote and curious, was neither systematic nor accurate, and this is the knowledge reflected in the plays."[24]

If traditional scholars within academia had ventured to examine the authorship issue in an objective, academic manner—as their professional duties required—they could, perhaps, have cleared up many of the matters that had led doubters to doubt.

> ➤ They might have tried to explain—rather than dismiss—the absence of evidence that anyone ever referred to Shakspere as a playwright during his lifetime. They might have tried to explain the fact that Shakspere was the only noted playwright

---

[22] Sir Sidney Lee, "More Doubts About Shakespeare," *Quarterly Review*, July 1919, p. 206.
[23] Abel Lefranc, *Under the Mask of William Shakespeare* (1988), p. 27-28.
[24] Sir Walter Raleigh, *Shakespeare* (1907), p. 58.

of the time for whom no one wrote commemoratory verses at the time of his death.

➤ They might have recognized that "William Shakespeare" was a pseudonym, as the man from Stratford was christened "Gulielmus Shakspere." Although he and other family members spelled their last name in various ways, none ever spelled it "Shakespeare." "Shak" and "Shake" were similar, but they had different roots and different meanings. The same was true for "spere" and "speare." And no member of his family ever hyphenated his name.

➤ They might have tried to answer—rather than ignore—the puzzling questions raised by the absence of any mention of the name of Shakspere (or Shakespeare) in Henslowe's Diary. The Diary was edited and published by W. W. Greg, between 1904 and 1908, yet scholars turned away from asking obvious questions.

➤ They might have tried to explain—instead of explain away—why the First Folio, the first collection of Shakespeare's plays published in 1623, some seven years after Shakspere's death, contained no biographical information about him. Not even his coat of arms was printed in it. The closest it came to stating that the man from Stratford was the author were references to "thy Stratford Moniment" and "sweet swan of Avon" in the lengthy prefatory material. But why do those phrases appear several pages apart, in statements by two different persons? Why was there no unequivocal statement that the man from Stratford was the author in a large and expensive book that was supposedly compiled to honor him and his works?

➤ They might have noticed—and sought an answer as to why—the monument to Shakspere in Holy Trinity Church in Stratford gave no indication of where exactly he was buried, nor any indication that whoever was buried there was a writer. Why was there no reference on the monument to any literary works, let alone a statement that Shakspere had written them?

➤ They might have wondered—and investigated to explain—why those who sought to gather together Shakspere's documents after the Shakespeare Jubilee in 1769 couldn't find any. Not only had Shakspere himself apparently never sent or received a letter, but no surviving documents from his lifetime contained any reference to the author as a distinct person living at the time the works were written. There were many references to the name "Shakespeare," but no one appeared to have ever stated in writing that he had known or even met the writer.

➤ They might have tried to explain why, even in Stratford, in the century and a half between the publication of the First Folio in 1623 and the Shakespeare Jubilee held in 1769, not one person had ever referred to Shakspere as a famous poet or dramatist. Why had contemporary descriptions of Stratford and its noted inhabitants by such well-known historians as William Camden made no mention of such a famous author as having come from that town?

The Split Within Academia Between Departments of History and Literature

The second split of importance was the rise of separate Departments of History and Literature with minimal interaction between them, a development of great importance for subjects such as the Shakespeare authorship question that draw on scholarly work conducted in both fields. It's worth pausing to consider just how that division between the two fields came about and why it remains so strong even today.

The rise of modern scholarly practices in the study of literature in the late nineteenth century was mirrored by similar developments in other fields. This development led in many fields, including history, to the establishment of formal departments within universities. The development of a "robust understanding of the stature and distinctiveness of History as a form of scholarly enquiry," Stefan Collini, Professor of English and Intellectual History at the University of Cambridge, explained, included formulation of a methodology that "brought together elements of German historicism, ideals of scientific accuracy and disinterestedness, and an inherited focus on the political, administrative, diplomatic, and legal machinery of the state." This amalgam, characterized by "the marriage of 'scientific' method and largely political subject matter... shaped academic historians' conception of their role ... [and] defined what counted as 'serious' history."[25]

Literature, initially, was not one of the fields for which formal departments were created. In the later nineteenth century, the study of English literature, to the extent that it took place within universities at all, was within Departments of History, with emphasis placed on areas with the greatest overlap, such as literary history. "Attempts to legitimate the academic study of English literature had reflected some of the same ideals [as in the study of history]: the enterprise had to be historical, factual, 'objective', and hence—this was a crucial requirement in the celebrated debate at Oxford over introducing English as a subject—examinable." Although this "pairing of History and English was not uncommon," it was obvious to many scholars that literature was a poor fit within Departments of History and considerable opposition existed at many universities to it. In the view of William Stubbs, Regius Professor of Modern History at Oxford, "to have the History School hampered with dilettante teaching, such as the teaching of English Literature, must necessarily do great harm to the School. ... There is no special connection between English Literature and Modern History."[26]

The more scholarly the study of literature became—the more that programs tried to emphasize those aspects of the subject most unique to literature rather than those with the greatest overlap with history—the poorer the fit. Eventually a point was reached where the study of literature broke away and independent Departments were established. Afterward both fields withdrew into their core areas. Departments of History focused even more intensely on political, diplomatic and military history, studied through an impersonal, archive-based methodology in order to cleanse themselves of any remnants of the literature studies they had recently regurgitated. "The sprit of Stubbs survived," Collini reported, "notably among Oxford-trained historians, for many decades after this gruff rebuff, and not the least part of that legacy was the conviction, more a matter of professional habit than intellectual contention, [that] there is no special connection between English Literature and Modern History" (7).

Seeking to establish themselves as fully legitimate and independent entities, Departments of Literature moved to set up courses of study and methodologies emphasizing those aspects of their field having little or nothing to do with history. Thus,

---

[25] Stefan Collini, *The Nostalgic Imagination: History in English Criticism* (2019), p. 7.
[26] Quoted in Collini (2019), p. 7

Collini explained,

> A strong and largely shared conception of what counted as serious scholarship
> was well established in both disciplines. Those who found their sense of their
> professional and disciplinary identities adequately represented by, on the one
> side the *English Historical Review* or the *Transactions of the Royal Historical
> Society*, and, on the other, *Notes and Queries* or (from 1925) *The Review of English
> Studies*, could equally give their allegiance to a similar notion of respectable
> academic work, where "respectable" suggests both the prevailing canons of
> propriety and an anxiety about falling into some derogated lower or more
> popular category. (8)

From one perspective, the separation of literature from history was legitimate;
because they studied different subjects, they needed different approaches and
methodologies, and each benefited by maintaining high scholarly standards in their
respective areas. But the Departments' move away from each other was unfortunate for
subjects that drew on scholarly work in both fields. Such subjects, including the
Shakespeare authorship question, were orphaned in the new Departments of Literature
just as the study of literature had been orphaned within the Departments of History.

A few professors regretted the extreme nature of the split between the two fields. One
English professor at Oxford, lamenting the consequences for his students, wrote that,
"The weak point of our students of English lit is that they have no adequate knowledge of
English history, or European literature and history" (7). But it was too late to do much
about it. The Departments had hardened into distinct fields of study with little common
ground.

The Split Outside Academia Between Baconians and Other Doubters

The third important split that Looney observed occurred outside academia, between
doubters who championed Sir Francis Bacon as the true author of Shakespeare's works
and those who did not. The Baconians, as they came to be called, were the first to offer an
alternative candidate for authorship. They made significant contributions to the case
against the man from Stratford, showing that he couldn't have, and hadn't, written the
works attributed to him. Looney was particularly impressed by the evidence in support
of that conclusion in the first section of *The Great Cryptogram: Francis Bacon's Cipher in
Shakespeare's Plays* (1888) by Ignatius L. Donnelly, an American who had served three
terms as a Congressman from Minnesota.

The idea of Bacon as Shakespeare had some plausibility because of what was known
of the brilliance of Bacon's mind and writings. Further study showed, however, just how
different his logical and scientific mind was from Shakespeare's poetic sensibilities, and
hence the second section of Donnelly's book, in which the case for Bacon was made, was
less persuasive than the first. As the title of the book indicated, some of the more fanatical
Baconians, unable to make a persuasive case based on the available evidence, relied on
complex cryptograms and codes they claimed were hidden within Shakespeare's works
to prove Bacon's authorship. Reliance on such spurious "evidence" undermined not just
the case for Bacon, but the entire case for authorship doubt. The Baconians, being louder
and shriller in their insistence on Bacon's authorship than other doubters, overshadowed
them in the public mind.

Thus the Baconian cause was a godsend for traditional scholars. They could, and did,
distract attention away from the weakness of their own case by pointing to the ludicrous

nature of some of the "evidence" presented. Much of the general public agreed that the Baconian evidence was obscure and unconvincing. With the non-Baconian doubters' case obscured, the public remained largely committed to the traditional Stratfordian story.

All that changed in 1908 with the publication of Sir George G. Greenwood's *The Shakespeare Problem Restated*. The book, Greenwood later wrote, "was simply an attempt to put together, in something like rational form and sequence, the arguments, or some of the arguments, which appeared to me to cast doubt upon the received belief that the Stratford player . . . was the author of the Plays and Poems of Shakespeare."[27] He also added that he had no "thought of making any attempt, to say who the author may have been supposing 'Will' was not really the author" (2).

The Shakespeare Problem Restated was one of the most important books ever published on Shakespeare. By presenting the reasons for doubt while refraining from addressing who the author might have been, Greenwood freed the doubters' case from the Baconian wackiness; by presenting the mass of evidence against Shakspere in such persuasive form, he made the case impossible to ignore.

One reason that *The Shakespeare Problem Restated* was so persuasive was Greenwood's clear presentation of how his doubts had developed. He described his fascination with *Macbeth* and *As You Like It* as a student and his initial "unquestioning faith" in the traditional story. He then recounted his reaction, after he had turned "with eager interest, to read the life of the great poet as set forth by one of his numerous 'biographers'":

> I shall never forget the feeling of blank amazement and bitter disappointment with which I read it. Was *this* the man who had called into existence those marvellous works of fancy and imagination, those masterpieces of poesy, and wisdom, and philosophy? It is true that little was known about him; but how much better would it have been if that little had never been revealed! . . . [F]or, try to disguise the fact as you may, the plain truth is that in all that is known about Shakspere of Stratford . . . there is . . . absolutely nothing to inspire, nothing to warm our hearts towards him. Nay more, there is not one single generous act, not one single even creditable act, recorded to his credit. . . . As it is, though we know so little, we know, alas, so much too much. (181-82)

Born in 1850, Greenwood would have been about eighteen when he read that biography of Shakspere. Over the following forty years he completed his education, was called to the Bar by the Middle Temple, served in Parliament, and continued to investigate the authorship question. By 1908 he was one of the leading barristers in England and one of the sharpest Shakespearean scholars of the time. He brought the full force of his training, experience and knowledge to bear in his presentation of the mass of facts documenting the gap between the man and the work—between the mundane nature of Shakspere's small-time commercial activities and the learned and poetic nature of the plays—in such a way that readers could become well briefed on the reasons for doubt without becoming overwhelmed by a mass of details.

The Shakespeare Problem Restated spurred Mark Twain to record his own thoughts on the authorship question, published in 1909 as *Is Shakespeare Dead?* It was also the work that led the writer Henry James to exclaim, "That fellow Greenwood has finally

---

[27] Sir George Greenwood, *Is There a Shakespeare Problem?* (1916), p. 2.

settled the business!"[28] And in a letter to Mrs. Hunt he stated that "a fellow called Greenwood . . . [has written] an extremely erudite, fair, and discriminating piece of work."[29]

The book was widely reviewed. Greenwood observed that *Restated* "has met with more success than I had ventured to anticipate, both in this country and the United States."[30] *The Manchester Guardian* said that "On the destructive side his book is so strong, that merely to call it the ablest extant argument against the identity of the Stratford-born actor with the author of the poems and plays does not give the full measure of its strength."[31] *The Sunday Times* observed that the traditional story is an "almost inconceivable hypothesis" and that "Mr. Greenwood has exposed the weaknesses of the 'Stratfordian' position with splendid lucidity and cogency."[32] Excerpts from other reviews in major newspapers and literary journals are included in a text box to show the openness to the authorship question generated by Greenwood's book.

Professor Louis P. Bénézet, only thirty years old in 1908, recalled forty years later that Greenwood's *The Shakespeare Problem Restated*

literally rocked the foundations of the whole orthodox Shakespearean edifice like

---

Sir George G. Greenwood

Birth: January 3, 1850. Death: October 27, 1928.

Age when *"Shakespeare" Identified* was published: 70

Shakespeare Fellowship President: 1920-1928

Studied at Eton and Trinity College, Cambridge. Received a First Class in Classical Studies in 1873.

Called to the Bar by the Middle Temple in 1876

Member of the House of Commons, 1906-1918

Knighted in 1916

Supporter of measures for the protection of animals; served on the Council of the Royal Society for the Prevention of Cruelty to Animals.

Tribute paid to Greenwood at his death: "'As a controversialist he was merciless to his opponents, but his gift of humour always made him interesting, and his literary style made his fencing bouts a joy to onlookers. From his first book, *The Shakespeare Problem Restated*, published in 1908, to his last book, *The Shakespeare Signatures and 'Sir Thomas More,'* published in 1924, we find the same finished style, and no diminution in the flashes of humour that conceal the ruthlessness of the attack.'"*

Looney on Greenwood: "It is quite safe to say that but for the works of Sir George Greenwood my own books would not have come into being.'"*

*"Origin and Achievements of the Shakespeare Fellowship," *Shakespeare Fellowship News-Letter* (American), vol. 1, no. 1 (Dec. 1939).

---

[28] Quoted in Col. Montagu Douglas, "Editorial," *Shakespeare Fellowship News-Letter*, no. 1 (Jan. 1937): 1.
[29] Quoted in Charlton Ogburn, *The Mysterious William Shakespeare* (1992), p. 181.
[30] Sir George Greenwood, *The Vindicators of Shakespeare* (1911), p. 11.
[31] *Manchester Guardian*, review of *Revisited*, from quotes at end of *Is There a Shakespeare Problem?*
[32] *Sunday Times*, review of *Revisited*, from quotes at end of *Is There a Shakespeare Problem?*

the explosion of a ton of TNT. The complacent little professors, who had so long sent forth their synthetic compilations of fabulous fancy and approved guesswork on the alleged genius of the Avonside, floundered and stuttered under the impact of Greenwood's hammering attack.... In the end, those who profit by maintenance of the Stratford myths, decided that if they could not openly argue Greenwood out of the court of public opinion, they could at least ignore his bill of particulars.[33]

The response from academic scholars was a mixture of disdainful silence peppered with occasional hostility. Greenwood observed that the book "has received the abuse of those whose abuse I value, and, what is still better, the praise of those whose praise I

Additional Prominent Reviews of Sir George G. Greenwood's
The Shakespeare Problem Restated

The Academy: "What he means to do, and what he does very well ... is to set out the case against Shakespeare. It is a pretty strong case of course; it always was."

The Bookman: "It is a book which cannot by any possibility be ignored. It is not based upon assertion, but upon argument. It hits hard at accredited 'Stratfordian pundits,' as Mr. Greenwood calls the orthodox, all round.... The point is, however, that having entered this book in a spirit of sanctimonious orthodoxy, we have emerged from it sick and sore at heart, our deepest convictions bleeding and battered, for the time being, at any rate, in a hardened, unrepentant, agnostic frame of mind."

The Bristol Times: "Mr. Greenwood does not attempt to solve the problem; he simply sets out the evidence for and against the claims of William Shakespeare, of Stratford-on-Avon, and his verdict, as that of all unprejudiced persons must be, is that the claimant was not, and could not possibly have been, the poet whose works are so justly admired and revered by the whole civilised world."

Mr. Thomas Secombe, in *The Daily News*: "Let the biographers begin by confuting Mr. Greenwood. I cannot."

The Liverpool Courier: "A serviceable book of incalculable value to a reader who wishes to become an expert on the Shakespeare problem, and most assuredly he has spoiled the complacency with which so many have held the old traditional faith."

The Nation: "We would recommend all who care for Elizabethan literature to acquire it and read *The Shakespeare Problem Restated*. For Mr. Greenwood is no faddist.... [H]e gives evidence of a wide and close study, a critical temper, and a general mastery of his subject which may not carry conviction, but must at least compel attention. Indeed, we doubt whether the case has ever been stated more persuasively or with greater force.... Mr. Greenwood has produced a carefully reasoned, scholarly, and interesting book."

The Outlook: "Mr. Greenwood is a lawyer and a scholar; he has mastered his brief thoroughly and marshalled his evidence cleverly; and it calls for a tougher article of orthodoxy than we have at command to deny that he makes out a case, even stronger than the cases made out before, for a Shakespeare not at all like the Shakespeare of whom the biographers tell us."

The Scotsman: "A book of sober and elaborate research, a study of which should not only instruct the ignorant, but also refresh the memory and the understanding of the most erudite Shakespearean."

The Star: "It is a tempting and tantalising book.... It stirs up all sorts of doubts in your mind. It rouses your scepticism and stimulates your incredulity. It spurs you into rebellion against authority. It breeds in you irreverence for literary mandarins."

From the back pages of *Is There a Shakespeare Problem?* (1916) (pages not numbered)

estimate even more highly than that stimulating abuse."[34] The case was made so expertly and so convincingly—by one of England's most respected barristers—that it could hardly be argued with. Most senior scholars did not even try. "The leviathans of literature," Greenwood wrote, "left the battle to the small fry" (12).

Among the first of the small fry to critique the book and its author was Canon H. C. Beeching of Norwich, who delivered an ill-informed attack in the form of a lengthy paper read before the Royal Society of Literature. Greenwood described Beeching's speech as "a mere travesty" of his arguments, and was later to write that, "He has put into my mouth arguments which I never uttered, and which I should not dream of uttering, and has proceeded to demolish them with great self-satisfaction and with the most entire success."[35] Beeching later combined his speech with two others and published them in book form, to which Greenwood responded with his own book, *In re Shakespeare: Beeching v. Greenwood: Rejoinder on Behalf of the Defendant*. Thus was launched a decade-long public battle between Greenwood and his critics that established him as the most prominent spokesman for the case against Shakspere.

An important new front in the battle was opened in the spring of 1909 in the monthly journal *The Nineteenth Century and After*, which in March and April published two long articles by Sir Edward Sullivan under the title "The Defamers of Shakespeare." They were, Greenwood wrote, "directed . . . almost entirely against my humble self. . . . Thereupon I tendered a request to the Editor for a like amount of space for a reply. This was not granted to me, but I was graciously allowed one article wherein to answer Sir Edward's double-barrelled onslaught."[36] Greenwood's article, "The Vindicators of Shakespeare," appeared in the June issue. It was followed by two more attacks on him and the doubters' case in the August issue by Sir Edward Sullivan and Canon Beeching. Greenwood was given no further space in which to reply. The demonstrated hostility with which doubts about Shakspere's authorship were met by academics and their allies in this exchange should be kept in mind so that it can be compared with another multi-part exchange of views on the same subject that would take place in the same periodical eight years later, in 1917.

Although Greenwood wasn't given space to reply to the August attacks, he combined his response to them with his June response and published it in book form in 1911 under the title *The Vindicators of Shakespeare*. In it, Greenwood defended his views and renewed the case against Shakspere with his usual effective blend of facts and reasoning. He also acknowledged that he had known he was "baring my devoted head to the thunderbolts of Olympian orthodoxy," and that he had been "fully prepared to receive hard knocks, and of the hard knocks of honest criticism I should be the last to complain" (144). However, he continued, it had caught him by surprise that so "many of the reviewing confraternity . . . seem to have no conception [of their duty] to read, and endeavour to understand, the arguments upon which it is his duty to comment."[37]

> They lead out, like wretched sheep for the slaughter, a whole row of ridiculous arguments and suggestions, which they attribute to the unhappy author whose work they are employed to criticise, but which are, in reality, mere phantoms of

---

[34] Sir George Greenwood, *The Vindicators of Shakespeare* (1911), p. 11.
[35] Sir George Greenwood, *In re Shakespeare* (1909), p. vii.
[36] Sir George Greenwood, *The Vindicators of Shakespeare* (1911), p. 12-13.
[37] Sir George Greenwood, *The Vindicators of Shakespeare* (1909), p. 144.

their own imagination. . . . The anonymous critic who gives rein to spleen and personal malice has been well compared to the assassin who takes advantage of the darkness to stab his fellow-man in the back.

Nevertheless, he concluded, he had "gratefully . . . received much generous treatment both in the Press and in numerous letters from correspondents in the Old World, and in the New. The views which I have endeavoured to expound are, evidently, gaining ground day by day" (146). With that statement Greenwood demonstrated his understanding that presenting sound views on the authorship question and having them examined and accepted by thoughtful readers was the goal. Whatever unpleasantness occurred along the way was beside the point.

The dust hadn't settled for long before attacks on doubters in general and Greenwood specifically came from Andrew Lang in 1912, in *Shakespeare, Bacon, and the Great Unknown*, and from J. M. Robertson in 1913, in *The Baconian Heresy, a Confutation*. Greenwood responded in 1916 with another large book; at more than 580 pages, *Is There a Shakespeare Problem? — With a Reply to Mr. J. M. Robertson and Mr. Andrew Lang*, was even longer than *The Shakespeare Problem Restated*.

Greenwood accomplished several things with *Problem?* He updated many of the arguments laid out in *Restated*: Shakspere's small-time commercial activities and Shakespeare's learning, knowledge of the law and intimate familiarity with the details of courtier life were re-examined in light of new information uncovered in the eight intervening years. He also took on new subjects: Shakspere's Will and handwriting, the Preface materials in the First Folio, the Stratford monument, and portraits of Shakespeare

---

**Sir George G. Greenwood, Selected Pre-1920 Publications
Defending Disbelief in the Man from Stratford**

1908	Sir George Greenwood, *The Shakespeare Problem Restated*
	Criticism: 1908, H. C. Beeching, "William Shakespeare, Player, Play-Maker, and Poet: A Reply to Mr. George Greenwood, M.P." [A speech given at the Royal Society of Literature] 1909, Sir Edward Sullivan, "The Defamers of Shakespeare I & II," ***The Nineteenth Century and After***, nos. 385, 386 (March, April): 419-34, 631-47.
1909	Sir George Greenwood, "The Vindicators of Shakespeare," ***The Nineteenth Century and After***, no. 388 (June): 1038-55.
	Criticism: 1909, Sir Edward Sullivan, "Francis Bacon as a Poet," ***The Nineteenth Century and After***, no. 390 (August): 267-82. 1909, H. C. Beeching, "A Last Word to Mr. George Greenwood," ***The Nineteenth Century and After***, no. 390 (August): 283-93. 1909, H.C. Beeching's book, *William Shakespeare, Player, Play-Maker, and Poet: A Reply to Mr. George Greenwood*.
1909	Sir George Greenwood, *In re Shakespeare: Beeching v. Greenwood: Rejoinder on Behalf of the Defendant*.
1911	Sir George Greenwood, *The Vindicators of Shakespeare*.
	Criticism: 1912, Andrew Lang, *Shakespeare, Bacon, and the Great Unknown*. 1913, J. M. Robertson, *Baconian Heresy, a Confutation*.
1916	Sir George Greenwood, *Is There a Shakespeare Problem?—With a Reply to Mr. J. M. Robertson and Mr. Andrew Lang*.

were all examined for the light they shed on the authorship question. Two of Greenwood's most famous phrases made their first appearance in this book. "Professor Dryasdust" is introduced to characterize "those doctrinaire exponents of the orthodox Stratfordian creed" who lack the imagination "which enables a man to put himself in the place of another, even after the lapse of many generations, and . . . [that is needed] to appreciate all that is required to make a 'Shakespeare.'"[38] And "Many pens and one Mastermind," which encapsulated the "group theory" of Shakespearean authorship formulated to account for indications that Shakespeare, whoever he was, had not written everything in the First Folio.

The most important parts of the book were two chapters titled "The Real Shakespeare Problem." That problem, Greenwood wrote, was not the question of how a man with Shakspere's background could have acquired any of the many specific bodies of knowledge—such as the law, Italy, or hawking—exhibited in the plays. Rather,

> [i]t is the knowledge of life in all its aspects, knowledge of men, knowledge of human nature, knowledge of society, knowledge of the philosophy of life, and, above all, it is the manner in which he has embodied that knowledge in immortal poetry, which has raised doubts and difficulties in the minds of the sceptics.

> The lawyer or the journalist can, indeed, 'get up' a large amount of technical knowledge at short notice . . . but he cannot 'get up' all that is denoted by the term 'culture' if he does not happen to be possessed of it. Ask a vulgarian half-educated barrister to make himself a refined and highly cultured man at a few days' notice, or at any notice for the matter of that. You might as well ask him to make a silk purse out of a sow's ear. (183-84)

Greenwood then advised his readers to

> [r]ead some of the Shakespearean masterpieces again. . . . Then meditate on what has been handed down to us concerning the life of William Shakspere . . . about whom we know so little, and yet so much, too much! Search all the wide world over for analogies—for men of such birth, such breeding, such environment, such ignoble life-history, who have yet put forth . . . a series of noble, priceless, and immortal poems or plays, and I say no such analogies can be found. . . . [B]ut for me, and for those who feel as I do, and reason as I do—and their number is not small and is, undoubtedly, on the increase—it is this fact which constitutes the real "Shakespeare Problem." (281-82)

Frank Harris and *The Man Shakespeare* (1909)

Another book that perhaps steered Looney toward the idea of inferring the life and personality of the true author from Shakespeare's works themselves must be noted: Frank Harris's *The Man Shakespeare*, published in 1909. Looney credited Harris with having "done much to destroy the old notion that there is no character in the plays who can be identified with Shakespeare."[39] He further praised Harris's argument that "the old conception of a writer creating everything by the vigour of his imagination" needed to be set aside, and that it was essential, when considering Shakespeare, "to regard the writings as reflecting the personality and experiences of their author" (7).

Harris must surely have set Looney's mind spinning, judging from passages in *"Shakespeare" Identified* where he credited Harris with asserting that "Shakespeare

---

[38] Sir George Greenwood, *Is There a Shakespeare Problem?* (1916), p. 283.
[39] J. Thomas Looney, *"Shakespeare" Identified* (2018), p. 245.

usually represents himself as a lord or a king" (245) and claiming that "[i]n *Hamlet* Shakespeare has discovered too much of himself," that "Brutus [is] an idealized portrait of himself," that "Edgar is peculiarly Shakespeare's mouthpiece," and that "it can hardly be denied that Shakespeare identified himself as far as he could with Henry V."[40] He also noted Harris's observation that all these characters hid their true nature or true intentions from other characters.

Looney quoted Harris's observation that "Shakespeare did not understand the middle classes. . . . He utterly missed what a knowledge of the middle classes would have given him. . . . [I]n all his writings he praises lords and gentlemen."[41] And yet Harris, who lived until 1931, eleven years after *"Shakespeare" Identified* was published, remained an adamant believer in the Stratfordian story. How did he square this circle? How did he align Shakspere from Stratford with Shakespeare the author, who did not understand the middle class or lower classes and who identified himself with courtiers and the nobility and who "discovered too much of himself" in *Hamlet*? He couldn't; his effort to shoehorn his brilliant inferences about the author into the life of the man from Stratford was the great flaw in his book.

Why did Harris hold to his belief in the man from Stratford when it conflicted so dramatically with his own brilliant inferences about the nature of the author? The answer might come from his experiences. As a self-made man from a dirt-poor childhood, it was only by the sheer force of his personality and the brilliance of his literary talents, combined with great ambition, that Harris pulled himself up to the heights of the editorship of *The Saturday Review* and other periodicals, not to mention his glittering literary productions. He identified with the man from Stratford who, he thought, had done something similar.

Harris's inability to give up his illusions when confronted by his own insights and discoveries might have served as a warning to Looney as to how hard it would be to win support for his discovery of Edward de Vere's authorship from those with an emotional or professional commitment to the traditional story. Several dozen instances of this very situation—Shakespeare scholars whose own findings undercut the traditional story of Shakspere's authorship but held to it anyway—will be discussed in Chapter 13.

This, then, was the authorship landscape during the years when Looney was busy working out the solution to the authorship mystery. It was characterized by recognition of the disconnect between the life of the uneducated small-time businessman from Stratford and the literary works showing great erudition and intimate familiarity with the life of the nobility. That gap was widely recognized by many educated readers outside of academia, but not generally acknowledged within. Investigation into the authorship question was made more difficult by the creation of separate university Departments of History and Literature, with little overlap in their subject matters. Outside academia, the Baconian idea had almost overwhelmed the authorship subject until independent scholars, principally Sir George Greenwood, rescued it by bringing back into public view the possibility of a non-Baconian, non-Stratfordian solution to the problem.

Two surprising developments occurred during the years when *"Shakespeare" Identified* was being written and prepared for publication that affected attitudes toward the authorship question. The first Looney would have been aware of; the second he did

---

[40] Frank Harris, *The Man Shakespeare (1909)*, p. 142. Paraphrased in Looney (2018), p. 255.
[41] Looney (2018), p. 184.

not know about until after his book was finished.

New Development 1: *The Nineteenth Century and After* Redux

The first surprising development, in 1917, was the publication of three articles on the authorship question in *The Nineteenth Century and After* following the journal's eight-year silence on the issue. Refreshingly, they bore none of the hostility that had characterized the earlier series of articles. The first piece, by Gordon Crosse in June, was titled "The Real Shakespeare Problem"—the same title Greenwood had given to the most important chapters in *Is There a Shakespeare Problem?* The second was a response to Crosse by Sir George Greenwood, in June. The third—an amazing article—was a reply to both Crosse and Greenwood by H. B. Simpson.

Crosse's article reads as though he expected it to put the authorship issue to rest forever, which might explain his magnanimous tone. Though a Stratfordian, he began by admitting that "[t]here really is a Shakespeare problem."[42] He didn't deny that any problem existed as had Sir Sidney Lee, nor did he try to explain away the gap between the man and the works as had Sir Walter Raleigh. He readily acknowledged

> the difficulties which lie in the way of accepting William Shakespeare of Stratford as the author of the plays and poems usually known by his name. These difficulties are considerable, but they by no means exhaust the problem, which, in fact, consists in a balance of probabilities, or rather of improbabilities. Granted that it seems improbable that Shakespeare wrote the plays, can it be shown to be equally or more improbable that any other person or group of persons did so? That is the real Shakespeare problem, and in his failure to face it lies the deficiency of Sir George Greenwood's work.

This was quite an admission! No other Stratfordian had dared to admit in a widely read literary journal that William Shakspere's authorship was improbable. "But," Crosse continued,

> until a similar test has been applied to at any rate some other possible authorships, we have not only failed to solve the problem, but we are not even in a position to say that Sir George Greenwood has proved his own negative case. He cannot say "never mind who actually was the author, I have at least cleared one competitor off the field." He has not even done that, because the reader cannot appreciate the force of the arguments against Shakespeare until he sees how the same or similar arguments would affect other candidatures for the authorship. I venture to suggest that if these were subjected to as keen and searching a test as Sir George has applied to the Shakespearean theory they would appear even more improbable. And, therefore, on the balance of probabilities, Shakespeare would after all come out as a less unlikely author than any other who could be suggested. (884)

This is a potent argument. Yes, Shakspere's authorship is improbable, but it is less so than any other candidate who has been or might be proposed. It was a direct challenge to this statement Greenwood had made in *Is There a Shakespeare Problem?*

> Who was the author of *Hamlet*, and *Lear*, and *Othello*, and *Macbeth*? That is a question which I make no attempt to answer. . . . The subject is full of difficulty, and life is too short—in my case at any rate—to pursue it. . . . I must be content to rest upon the negative case. "Very unsatisfactory," of course. The same is said

---

[42] Gordon Crosse, "The Real Shakespeare Problem," *Nineteenth Century and After*, vol. 81 (April 1917): 883.

of the Agnostic attitude in theological matters. But, after all, in matters of belief, it is not what is satisfactory that we seek, but what is true.[43]

Greenwood was sixty-six years old at that time, so it is understandable that he felt he didn't have the time needed to search for the true author.[44] But Crosse wouldn't let the wider community of doubters off the hook. "Merely to show at however great length, that there are difficulties in accepting the 'orthodox' theory is an achievement of little value if the obstacles in the way of any other solution are as great or greater."[45] He thus turned Greenwood's argument on its head and challenged doubters to put up or shut up: propose a candidate more likely than our Stratford man, or cease and desist.

Crosse then advanced a second argument.

> The real case against what Sir George Greenwood calls the Stratfordian authorship may be summed up in the phrase of Emerson "I cannot marry [his life] to his verse." In other words the facts of William Shakespeare's life, as far as we know them from record or tradition, make it appear very unlikely that he was the author.... It is on this apparent inconsistency between the life of the man and his reputed works that their case rests. When that is said all is said. There is no other evidence that the traditional authorship is not also the true one. (887)

This, too, is a potent argument. No fact presented by doubters made it impossible that Shakspere was the author. But Crosse weakened the impact of that point by stating speculations as facts and making the elementary mistake that all references to the name William Shakespeare were references to the man from Stratford. However, as irritating as those ill-informed statements are, they do not detract from the challenge he had issued to doubters.

How did Greenwood respond? In an article published two months later, he began by acknowledging

> the debt of gratitude which I feel I owe to [Crosse]. His criticism, effective though I must own it to be, is perfectly courteous, and admirably fair. He neither travesties nor misrepresents my arguments. That is, indeed, something to be grateful for in these days; and when I call in mind certain other articles which have appeared upon the same subject, both in this Review and elsewhere, my gratitude is increased in threefold measure.[46]

He also acknowledged that Crosse's "weighty piece of criticism still remains to be answered" and agreed that the problem will "'be found to consist in a balancing of probabilities'" (1347).

Greenwood proceeded to demonstrate that the probability of Shakspere being the author was lower than Crosse believed and that the likelihood of the author being someone else was higher than orthodox scholars believed. He accomplished the first by calling attention "to the fact that 'orthodox' Shakespearean writers and critics differ fundamentally among themselves upon various important matters" in a story supposedly settled in all its major points.

---

[43] Sir George Greenwood, *Is There a Shakespeare Problem?* (1916), pp. 470-71.

[44] This was, as most readers are already aware, only four years before Looney would announce his solution to the world.

[45] Gordon Crosse, "The Real Shakespeare Problem," *Nineteenth Century and After*, vol. 81 (April 1917): 884.

[46] Sir George Greenwood, "The Real Shakespeare Problem: A Reply to Mr. Gordon Crosse," *The Nineteenth Century and After*, vol. 82 (June 1917), p. 1340.

> Some high Shakespearean authorities have maintained not only that Shakespeare was a man of excellent education, much learning, and high culture, but also that he was endowed with a singularly accurate knowledge of law and of legal life generally. . . . [But] exponents of another school of Shakespearean orthodoxy [hold that] . . . Shakespeare had only a smattering of education, no learning, and no legal knowledge at all. (1341)

If orthodox scholars are "in hopeless disagreement . . . on a matter of the highest importance to all students of Shakespeare, and one which has a very direct bearing upon the question . . . of the authorship of the Plays and Poems," then, Greenwood concluded, "the fort which they defend would soon, I think, have to surrender to their assailants" (1342).

As to the likelihood that someone other than Shakspere wrote the works and kept his authorship hidden, there is, Greenwood noted, "abundant evidence to show that it was considered contemptible and degrading for any man of position at that time to publish plays for the theatre. . . . No man who aspired to rise in high place in the State could afford to come before the public as a playwright." In these circumstances, "many men of position published their works under a pseudonym, and I see no improbability, still less absurdity, in the supposition that, the name of 'Shakespeare' having 'caught on' . . . dramatists who wished to preserve their anonymity might have published plays . . . by arrangement with the actor-manager" (1349).

Regarding the Bacon-Shakspere case specifically, Greenwood asked which has the higher probability: that the plays were written by Shakspere, of whose life so many "banal" details have become known, or by Bacon, of whom Macaulay said "he possessed 'the most exquisitely constructed intellect that has ever been bestowed on any of the children of men.'" Greenwood quickly clarified that "I am not a 'Baconian," for several reasons, one being that "that term implies a belief that Bacon wrote the plays, or some of them, and my mental attitude towards that suggestion is not one of belief, but of suspension of judgment. In fact, I am an 'Agnostic' on that as on many other questions. I have not, so far, seen sufficient evidence upon which to found belief." "Nevertheless," he continued, "if I should be asked whether I think it more probable that Francis Bacon or Will Shakspere of Stratford might have written the works in question, I must say again that I, for my part, weighing the problem as 'a balance of probabilities, or, rather, of improbabilities,' should not hesitate as to my answer. To me the balance of improbability appears to be strongly against 'Will'" (1351).

Greenwood noted that this conclusion was not held only by himself, and asked:

> Why it is that in "Shakespeare's" case, and in "Shakespeare's" case only, so many thinking and intelligent men and women, not only in this country, but in America and, indeed, throughout the world, have come to the conclusion that the traditional ascription of authorship must be rejected? . . . It is simply because the sceptics, among whom many distinguished names might be cited, have found, on "balance," that the "improbabilities" are too strong for them. (1354)

He concluded by quoting David Hume's observation that "'It is contrary to experience that miracles should be true: it is not contrary to experience that testimony [or tradition] should be false.'"

Six months later came H. B. Simpson's groundbreaking response to both Crosse and Greenwood, "Shakspere, Bacon and a 'Tertium Quid.'" Simpson began by stating that he "finds it equally impossible to believe that Shakespeare's plays and poems were written by Bacon or by Shakspere."[47] Guided by the idea of the "middle course" (the English translation of the Latin phrase in the title of his article), he speculated about the characteristics that the author of the plays must have possessed *by inferring them from the literary works themselves.* This step is, of course, the same method that Looney had already been following for several years in his search for the real author.

Simpson's surmises about the author are quite remarkable and are quoted at length so that they can be compared with J. Thomas Looney's more formal list of criteria to be discussed in the next chapter.

> We will image the younger son of some noble family, born to affluence and high social position, but to few responsibilities, a lover of horsemanship and field sports, and [an] even more ardent lover of books, but above all a man with a passionate interest in his fellow-men. With ample leisure to indulge his tastes he is known to his associates for his nimble wit, his genius for friendship, the keenness of his apprehension, but most of all for his eager curiosity in the diverse ways in which men feel, think and earn their living.
>
> The profundities of his mind, the imaginative power with which Nature has endowed him, are unknown to them and probably unsuspected even by himself; he thinks of himself as a fair specimen of the well-nurtured and well-educated youth of Elizabethan England; he may even be regarded by some and possibly by himself as something of a trifler—a man of gentle and generous disposition, but without any aim in life beyond the acquisition of knowledge which he is not disposed to turn to any practical purpose. Trained to the law in early life he has taken an intellectual delight in mastering all its intricacies and familiarising himself with its artificial jargon, but he has found neither need nor inclination to practice it. He is essentially a looker-on at life, though he has an intense sympathy with all who struggle with its difficulties.
>
> While his heart is in the country and the life of the country, he finds in London the most diverse food for his intellectual curiosity. In London taverns, among the students of the Temple, at the docks where seafaring folk resort, as well as in the abodes of the rich and powerful, he finds meat for his inquiring mind. Most of all he is attracted by the company of actors. There is something in their gaiety and irresponsibility, their disregard of the conventions, the difference in their mode of life from that to which his own home has accustomed him, which especially takes his fancy. (1258-59)

For Simpson, however, compiling his list of qualities was the end of the road. He did not develop it further or take steps to ferret out the identity of the true author, tasks Looney was already engaged in. Instead, he concluded that "The hypothesis I have sketched out" is of "one who is known to us only through his writings and whose very name and life-history are likely, except for some totally unexpected chance, to remain for ever unknown" (1262-63).

New Development 2: Abel Lefranc and Derby

The second surprising development to occur while Looney was researching and writing *"Shakespeare" Identified* was the publication of Professor Abel Lefranc's *Sous le Masque de William Shakespeare* (*Behind the Mask of William Shakespeare*), which presented the case for William Stanley, Sixth Earl of Derby, as the real author of

---

[47] H. B. Simpson, "Shakspere, Bacon and a 'Tertium Quid,'" *The Nineteenth Century and After*, vol. 85 (Dec. 1917): 1248.

"Shakespeare's" works. Though the book was published in two volumes in French in 1918 and 1919, reviews did not appear in English publications until spring 1919, when the manuscript of Looney's book was already in the hands of potential publishers in London.

Like many others, Lefranc, professor at the Collége de France and a respected scholar of Renaissance literature, had been struck by the disconnect between the ordinariness of the life of the man from Stratford and the sophisticated nature of the literary works attributed to him. He was impressed, negatively, by absences: the absence of any writings by Shakspere other than, supposedly, the literary works; the absence of any mention in public records during Shakspere's lifetime of him as an actor or playwright; the absence in Shakspere's Will of any mention of books or manuscripts or anything at all relating to a literary life; the absence of any records explaining how he had acquired knowledge of Italy, of the law, or of how he had managed to base many of his plays and poems on works written in Latin or Greek but not yet translated into English; the absence of any eulogies written for him at the time of his death; his lack of concern when pirated and mangled copies of his plays were published; the absence of any records mentioning his social rise or accounting for his understanding of politics and diplomacy at the highest levels; and the absence of any biographical records indicating experiences reflected in Shakespeare's darkening view of humanity.

Nowhere was this disconnect more striking for Lefranc than between the mundane life of the man from Stratford and the flowing passages in *Love's Labour's Lost* depicting so intimately the glittery, witty, flirtatious interactions between men and women in a court setting. How, Lefranc wondered, could a man from an isolated small town—a three-days' horse ride from London—have acquired so sophisticated an understanding of courtly life without having actually been raised in such a milieu? It's a question not of knowledge, Lefranc thought, but of the character or disposition of the man himself; not of what Shakspere knew but of who he was.

Lefranc firmly believed that

> [b]etween the writers' lives and their literary productions there exist definite links. No work, worthy of consideration, could come into existence without letting one catch some impress of actual circumstance, as well as reflection of ideas, feelings, preoccupations, struggles, passions, joys, trials—in a word, without leaving trace of the author's soul. . . . Even in works where fantasy and imagination are turned loose to romp as they please, the rein of reality whips through in multiple instances.[48]

Writing of the mystery that arises if Shakespeare is conflated with Shakspere, Lefranc was incredulous that any thinking person could accept that

> [t]his unique soul, one of the most vibrant, the most embracing that ever put in its appearance in this world, is only revealed to us, outside of his works, by acts which are not only bereft of any greatness but conform even to the level only of mediocre feelings and flatness of character. Not a voice raised to speak of him in his quality of thinking man, in his capacity for love and suffering. In the midst of the miraculous blossoming forth of great men which saw the opening up of Queen Elizabeth's reign, he remains isolated, as though inaccessible. This poet who spoke so eloquently of friendship appears not to have had one real friend, worthy of his range of intelligence and treasures of his tenderness which his plays let us see in the creator of Horatio and Mercutio. . . . Not one of those "special friends"

---

[48] Abel Lefranc, *Under the Mask of William Shakespeare*, tr. by Cecil Cragg (1988), pp. 15-16.

among whom he is supposed to have circulated his "sugar'd sonnets" is known to us. . . . No recollection of Shakespeare's conversation, of his turn of wit, his intellectual presence, his distinctive manners, no recollection of his opinions, of his shafts: . . . Not the briefest note written by him. (21-22)

Having eliminated the man from Stratford from contention, Lefranc then introduced William Stanley, Sixth Earl of Derby, who was raised in just the kind of educated, cultivated courtly society that would have enabled him to easily absorb the sensibilities portrayed in *Love's Labour's Lost*. Upon this basis, Lefranc made the case for Derby as Shakespeare. Although this idea was not entirely new—James Greenstreet had proposed it in 1891—Lefranc brought new levels of public attention to it, and it formed part of the intellectual firmament into which Looney's book was launched.

Sir Sidney Lee's Response

Sir Sidney Lee, editor of *The Dictionary of National Biography* and one of the most stalwart defenders of the Stratfordian claim, responded to Lefranc's book and the idea of the Earl of Derby as Shakespeare in *The Quarterly Review* in July 1919. Ten months later, in May 1920—two months after *"Shakespeare" Identified* had been published—Lee stated that the arguments he had used in that article against Lefranc's claims for Derby were also applicable to Looney's for Oxford.[49]

Lee rejected outright Lefranc's conclusion that the man from Stratford could not have written the works of Shakespeare. He did not allow any room for doubt about it. "It is useless even if space allowed, to detail the omissions which leave M. Lefranc's account of Shakespeare's career a virtual blank. The gist of the matter is that our author is unconcerned with the facts of biography or bibliography or literary history."[50] Space did allow, though, and Lee filled it not with examples of Shakspere's experiences or disposition that might have made him a suitable candidate for authorship, but with suppositions presented as fact, and with outright falsehoods—that Shakspere's "epitaph in Stratford Church presents him . . . as the greatest man of letters of his or any other day" (203); actually, it made no mention of him as an author at all—all the while studiously avoiding any admission of the difficulties with the case for Shakspere that Crosse and Simpson had noted in their *Nineteenth Century* articles two years earlier.

Lee rejected any similarities between Derby's experiences at the Court of Navarre— the court that almost all other Shakespeare scholars agreed served as the model for the fictional court setting in *Love's Labor's Lost*—writing, "One cannot admit any substantive justification that *Love's Labour's Lost* is an embodiment of the political and social observations which Lord Derby had made while a sojourner in the hospitable little kingdom [of Navarre]" (199-200).

He then turned to a subject of great importance for consideration of Looney's claims on behalf of the Earl of Oxford. Considering the nature of literary creativity, Lee gave great weight to the unfettered imagination. He supported "the assertion that supreme literature is mainly the creation of the imagination working on and transmuting anything and everything in heaven or earth. We deny that the function of supreme literatures is the reporting or the chronicling of private experience" (204-05). Lee interpreted Lefranc to be saying "that all literature is to be judged as autobiographic portraiture of the writer; and that a writer's eminence varies according to the fullness and literalness with which

---

[49] Sir Sidney Lee, "To the Editor," *Bookman's Journal*, vol. 2/30 (May 21, 1920): 58.
[50] Sir Sidney Lee, "More Doubts About Shakespeare," *Quarterly Review*, July 1919, p. 203.

he puts into his work '*ses sentiments intimes*.'" He accused Lefranc of ignoring, "in a great writer's equipment, the creative faculty, the faculty of the imagination." "The poet's eye," Lee believed, "ranges far beyond the always comparatively puny scope of his personal experiences or private sentiment" (204).

Aside from Lee's having attributed beliefs to Lefranc that he never expressed, he is only half right in his understanding of the nature of literary creativity. He is right about the importance of "the creative faculty, the faculty of the imagination," and also that "it transmutes anything and everything in heaven and earth." But he is mistaken in thinking that it regards anything and everything in heaven and earth equally. The imagination is not freely floating in space, triggered by random phenomena. It must have some substance to work with, some starting point, and that starting point is the life of the writer: his personal experiences, perceptions and disposition. The imaginative faculty is open-ended on only one end.

Elsewhere Lee wrote that "it is dangerous to read into Shakespeare's dramatic utterances allusions to his personal experience. . . . An unquestionable characteristic of Shakespeare's art is its impersonality."[51] In this he profoundly misunderstood the works of William Shakespeare. As will be made clear in later chapters, Edward de Vere, the author of the works attributed to William Shakespeare, was one of the most autobiographical writers who ever lived.

- - - - -

To sum up, in surveying the authorship landscape early in the second decade of the twentieth century, J. Thomas Looney was aware of doubts expressed over half a century or more concerning William Shakspere's authorship. He understood the historical reasons why doubts had arisen, and knew that doubters were more likely to be found outside academia than within. He knew that doubters were split between those who favored Sir Francis Bacon and those agnostic about the author's identity, whose principal spokesman was Sir George Greenwood.

With this understanding of what Looney would have seen in hand, we can now turn to his investigations into "the Shakespeare Mystery."

---

[51] Sir Sidney Lee, *A Life of William Shakespeare* (1915), p. 33.

PART ONE:
THE FIRST DECADES
OF *"SHAKESPEARE" IDENTIFIED*

2

J. Thomas Looney and His Investigations

Mr. Looney Begins His Investigations

On several occasions J. Thomas Looney described how he came to solve "the Shakespeare Mystery"—how he became interested in the question of Shakespearean authorship, how he devised the logical process that guided his investigations, how he first encountered the name "Edward de Vere," and how he uncovered the literary and biographical evidence that convinced him that de Vere had indeed been the real author of "Shakespeare's" works. In addition to his accounts in *"Shakespeare" Identified* and in several letters, the most intriguing description was probably in an article titled "The Solving of the Shakespeare Problem." Looney and Cecil Palmer, his publisher, attempted without success to place it with several literary journals; no copy of it is known to have survived.[1]

Looney became interested in the authorship question after repeated readings of *The Merchant of Venice* brought home to him the disconnect between the open-hearted qualities he inferred of the author on one hand and what he knew of the grasping nature of the man to whom the works were attributed on the other. Shakspere had been involved in moneylending and had sued neighbors for small debts; he had hoarded grain and enclosed public lands for personal profit. The writer, though, Looney had inferred, possessed such a magnanimous nature that he would sacrifice his own life to help a friend in need. He "had no great respect for money and business . . . [M]aterial possessions would be in the nature of an encumbrance to be easily and lightly disposed of."[2] Looney was also puzzled by indications that the author had firsthand knowledge of Italy, though the man from Stratford was not known to have ever left England. In sum,

> [t]his long-continued familiarity with the contents of one play induced a peculiar
> sense of intimacy with the mind and disposition of its author and his outlook

---

[1] Looney's article is mentioned in a letter from Cecil Palmer to Looney dated April 8, 1920.

[2] J. Thomas Looney, *"Shakespeare" Identified* (2018), p. 2. Hereafter passages cited from *"Shakespeare" Identified* will be identified by page numbers listed after the passage.

> upon life. The personality which seemed to run through the pages of the drama I felt to be altogether out of relationship with what was taught of the reputed author and the ascertained facts of his career. (2)

Looney knew that he was not the first to doubt that William Shakspere had written the works attributed to him. Sir George Greenwood's two large books had "convinced me that the opponents of the orthodox view had made good their case to this extent, that there was no sufficient evidence that the man William Shakspere had written the works with which he was credited, whilst there was a very strong *prima facie* presumption that he had not." He concluded that "the greatest literary treasures of England, ranked by universal consent amongst the highest literary achievements of mankind [were] to all intents and purposes of unknown origin" (3).

Looney initially approached the authorship question as a matter of purely personal interest. "At the beginning it was mainly the fascination of an interesting enquiry that held me, and the matter was pursued in the spirit of simple research." He had no inkling of how consuming the subject would become for him or that he would be the one to discover the missing author. The issue increasingly gripped him, though.

> As the case developed, however, it has tended increasingly to assume the form of a serious purpose, aiming at a long overdue act of justice and reparation to an unappreciated genius who, we believe, ought now to be put in possession of his rightful honours; and to whose memory should be accorded a gratitude proportionate to the benefits he has conferred upon mankind in general, and the lustre he has shed upon England in particular. (3)

He found that "[a]mongst all the literature on the subject, we have so far been able to discover no attempt, starting from an assumed anonymity of the plays, to institute a systematic search for the author. Yet surely this is the point towards which the modern movement of Shakespearean study has been tending; and once instituted it must continue until either the author is discovered or the attempt abandoned as hopeless" (78).

As Looney put it, "We have before us a piece of human work of the most exceptional character, and the problem is to find the man who did it" (71). The process he devised to find him was a "common sense method" consisting of two steps. The first was "simply to examine closely the work itself, to draw from the examination as definite a conception as possible of the man who did it, to form some idea of where he would be likely to be found." The second was "to go and look for a man who answers to the supposed description" (80).

This process would be made all the easier by the extraordinary nature of Shakespeare's work.

> The more distinctive the work the more limited becomes the number of men capable of performing it, and the easier ought it, therefore, to be to discover its author. In this case . . . the work is of so unusual a character that every competent judge would say that the man who actually did it was the only man living at the time who was capable of doing it. (72-73)

At the same time it would be harder because the author had made a deliberate effort to conceal his identity.

> Special obstacles have intentionally and most carefully been laid in the way of the discovery. There is no mere accident in the obscurity which hangs round the authorship, and the very greatness of the work itself is a testimony to the thoroughness of the steps taken to avoid disclosure. . . . It is not merely a question of finding out the man who did a piece of work, but of circumventing a scheme of

self-concealment devised by one of the most capable of intellects. (73)

Looney recognized that he would not be looking for obvious clues as to the author's identity, but must infer it "from more or less unconscious indications of himself in the writings" (73). Like Frank Harris and H. B. Simpson, he sought to infer from the plays and poems what the author had inadvertently revealed about himself, but he did so more systematically, compiling lists of what he believed to be the author's qualities and characteristics. He read all of Shakespeare's works repeatedly to become as familiar with them as possible, and added qualities he inferred the author to have possessed to those he had already deduced from his readings of *Merchant*. He found that traditional scholars had also drawn ideas about such qualities from the literary works; paradoxically, they often did not fit with what was known about the man from Stratford. Combining his own insights with those of other scholars, he constructed two formal lists, one of nine general inferences about the broader features of the author's life and character and the other of nine more specific qualities and distinctive characteristics (see the nearby text box).

The second step—looking for the man who fit the supposed description—was more complicated. Looney divided it into several logical and sequential sub-steps: select one outstanding feature as a clue; search for a man (or men) with that feature; then see if he (or they) possessed the other distinguishing characteristics. If a suitable candidate were found, it would be necessary to reverse the process. "Having worked from Shakespeare's writings to the new man, we should then begin with the man; taking new and outstanding facts about his performances and personality, we should have to enquire to what extent these were reflected in Shakespeare's works" (120). He would also seek to determine what connections the candidate(s) had with other writers of the time.

Looney selected "a lyric poet of recognized talent" as the feature to begin with because he already had a body of Shakespeare's work in that vein with which to compare whatever works he might find. He reasoned that the man who used the name Shakespeare had already written under his own name poems with the same formal structure as "Shakespeare's" first published work, the long narrative poem *Venus and Adonis*. All that was necessary "was to observe the number and length of the lines—six lines, each of ten syllables—and the order of the rhymes: alternate rhymes for the first four lines, the whole finishing with a rhymed couplet" (107).

He found fewer such poems than he had anticipated; after eliminating those that seemed unsuitable, he was

---

Looney's Two Lists

General Inferences

1. A matured man of recognized genius.
2. Apparently eccentric and mysterious.
3. Of intense sensibility—a man apart.
4. Unconventional.
5. Not adequately appreciated.
6. Of pronounced and known literary tastes.
7. An enthusiast in the world of drama.
8. A lyric poet of recognized talent.
9. Of superior education—classical—the habitual associate of educated people.

Specific Qualities

1. A man with feudal connections.
2. A member of the higher aristocracy.
3. Connected with Lancastrian supporters.
4. An enthusiast for Italy.
5. A follower of sport (including falconry).
6. A lover of music.
7. Loose and improvident in money matters.
8. Doubtful and somewhat conflicting in his attitude to woman [sic].
9. Of probable Catholic leanings, but touched with scepticism.

left with only one poem: "Women," by Edward de Vere, Earl of Oxford, someone he didn't recall ever having heard of. The poem had "the same succinctness of expression, the same compactness and cohesion of ideas, the same smoothness of diction, the same idiomatic wording which we associate with 'Shakespeare'; there was the characteristic simile of the hawks, and finally that peculiar touch in relation to women that I had noted in the sonnets" (110).

Investigating further, he found that,

> [c]ompetent literary authorities, in testifying to the distinctive qualities of [de Vere's] work, spoke of his poems in terms appropriate to "Shakespeare." An examination of his position in the history of Elizabethan poetry showed him to be a possible source of the Shakespeare literature, whilst an examination of his lyrics revealed a most remarkable correspondence both in general qualities and in important details with the other literary work which we now attribute to him. (420-21)

Seeking to learn more about the life of Edward de Vere, Looney turned to Sir Sidney

---

Oxford's Biography Confirmed Looney's "Nine Specific Qualities"

<u>1. A man with feudal connections</u> — Oxford was the 17th in the lineage of the Earls of Oxford that stretched back five hundred years, deep into England's feudal past.

<u>2. A member of the higher aristocracy</u> — As the Great Lord Chamberlain in Queen Elizabeth's court, Oxford was a senior member of the higher aristocracy.

<u>3. Connected with Lancastrian supporters</u> — Looney reported that "we are assured by several writers that he was proud of his ancient lineage," and quoted a passage noting that John the 11th Earl of Oxford was beheaded for his loyalty to the Lancastrian line (118).

<u>4. An enthusiast for Italy</u> — Oxford lived in Italy for more than a year, in just those cities in which many of Shakespeare's plays are set. Looney noted that "so permanent upon him was the effect of his stay there, that he was lampooned afterwards as an 'Italianated Englishman'" (116).

<u>5. A follower of sport (including falconry)</u> — Looney writes that Oxford's father, the 16th Earl, had quite a reputation as a sportsman, and that Oxford's own poems use words or phrases associated with courtly sports involving animals, including "the haggard hawk, the stricken deer, the greyhound, the mastiff, the fowling nets and bush-beating" (117). He won championships in the tilt games at court three times, and a famous quarrel with Philip Sidney involved tennis, a sport played only by the nobility.

<u>6. A lover of music</u> — The entry for Oxford in the *Dictionary of National Biography* states that he "evinced a genuine taste in music and wrote verse of much lyric beauty" (112). The most accomplished musicians of the times, William Byrd and John Farmer, praised Oxford's musicianship, with Farmer writing that although using music only "as a recreation, your Lordship [has] overgone most of them that make it a profession." By some accounts *The Earl of Oxford's March* was written by the earl himself.

<u>7. Loose and improvident in money matters</u> — "His looseness in money matters, and what appears like a complete indifference to material possessions, is undoubtedly one of the most marked features of his character . . . [F]rom being one of the foremost and wealthiest of English noblemen he found himself ultimately in straitened circumstances" (115).

<u>8. Doubtful and somewhat conflicting in his attitude to woman [sic]</u> — In a passage of the greatest importance, Looney observed that Oxford's poems show "[j]ust that deficiency of faith which we have pointed out as marking the Shakespeare sonnets; the very terms employed being as nearly identical as Shakespeare ever allowed himself in two separate utterances on one topic" (418-19).

<u>9. Of probable Catholic leanings, but touched with scepticism</u> — "Oxford's name appears at the head of a list of noblemen who professed to be reconciled to the old faith shows his leanings sufficiently well . . . [and] further, we find that his father had professed Catholicism" (119).

Lee's entry on him in *The Dictionary of National Biography*, and later described the elation he felt on reading one key passage, "every word of which, in view of the conception I had formed of 'Shakespeare,' read like a complete justification of the selection I had made" (111). That passage (on pages 111-112 of *"Shakespeare" Identified*) cited contemporary opinion referring to Oxford as "the best of the courtier poets," and noted that a modern authority—Sir Sidney Lee—corroborated it, writing that Oxford "evinced a genuine taste in music and wrote verse of much lyric beauty" (111).

Lee's entry in *The Dictionary of National Biography* confirmed thirteen of the points on Looney's lists; after investigating further he concluded that Edward de Vere satisfied all eighteen. A summary of his findings regarding the nine Specific Qualities is in the nearby textbox. At that point Looney was confident "that if we have not actually discovered the author of Shakespeare's works we have at any rate alighted upon a most exceptional set of resemblances" (111-12).

The subsequent steps in Looney's process reversed the direction and worked from the man to the works—a key step because it was one Stratfordians could not duplicate with their candidate. Before describing those steps it is worth pausing to consider several qualities that Looney himself possessed that contributed to his success.

Personal Factors

Born in South Shields in 1870, Looney lived his entire life in the Newcastle area. He worked as an English teacher or as Deputy Head Master at several schools set up by the Durham County Board of Education before moving to serve in the same capacities at its largest school, the Sheriff Hill Board School in Gateshead, just south of Newcastle, around 1910.[3] He is known to have left the United Kingdom only once, for a vacation in Belgium in the summer of 1924.

Raised in a religious (Episcopalian) home, Looney trained to be a missionary before losing his faith in the literal truth of the Bible and abandoning his training. When he was seventeen years old the real estate development on the River Tyne that his father and uncle had recently launched and invested heavily in went bankrupt due to the economic depression that hit northern England at that time, disrupting his educational plans and leaving him at loose ends. He later enrolled at Chester Diocesan College, which prepared him for a career as a teacher.

Even as a young man, Looney had broad philosophical, religious and literary interests and was well read in English poetry. The thinkers who "exercised the greatest influence over me," he later wrote to Charles Wisner Barrell, "were Channing, Carlyle, Emerson, John Stuart Mill, and Herbert Spencer. . . . The greater poets, Shakespeare, Wordsworth, Tennyson, Byron and Burns were my constant companion."[4] "It was then, too," he added, "that I contracted the habit of stating my problems very definitely to myself and seeking for these problems some definite and satisfactory solution." His dominant interest beginning around age twenty-six was the Positivist philosophy of Auguste Comte. The core of that philosophy, as distilled by the British Positivist movement during the final decades of the nineteenth century, was faith in progress, which could be assisted through

---

[3] Although the Durham County Board of Education no longer ran the schools after 1902 when local education authorities took over management of them, they were still referred to as Board schools.

[4] J. Thomas Looney, letter to Charles Wisner Barrell, June 6, 1937. Reprinted in *SF Quarterly*, vol. V/2 (April 1944): 22-23.

the correct application of human reason. Human beings had first made sense of their place in the universe by invoking gods, then through metaphysics, but had now entered a third phase, an age in which human beings, relying on their reason and common sense, would be responsible for their own destinies.

Guided by these ideas, Looney became a member of the Temple of Humanity in Liverpool established by Richard Congreve and other leaders of the British Positivist movement. His commitment to Positivist ideas was noticed by Congreve himself, who sponsored Looney's induction into the Church of Humanity when he was only twenty-eight years old, the youngest age at which entry was permitted. Positivism gave Looney an approach to intellectual and social issues that influenced his thinking for the rest of his life. Of particular importance was Positivism's emphasis on using one's mind to distinguish between permanent truths and ephemeral appearances, and then of learning to live in accordance with those truths to improve one's own life and society as a whole. The application of that approach, he later wrote, aided him in his examination of the question of Shakespearean authorship.

The Church of Humanity went into sudden decline in 1913, when its newly constructed building in Liverpool burned to the ground in mysterious circumstances. It was around that time that Looney turned his attention to the authorship question. William McFee wrote that Looney "had been working on the mystery for a long time when the First World War intervened,"[5] and Charles Wisner Barrell stated that "'*Shakespeare*' *Identified* was completed by Mr. Looney before 1914, but its publication was delayed for

---

John Thomas Looney: Major Events in His Life

Born: August 14, 1870. Died: January 17, 1944

Age when *"Shakespeare" Identified* was published: 49

Family: Married Elizabeth Campbell (February 27, 1866-December 29, 1950) on September 23, 1893, when he was 23 years old and teaching in South Shields. They had two children, Evelyn and Gladys. Evelyn's son, born in the mid-1930s, was given the middle name of De Vere.

During the years he was researching and writing *"Shakespeare" Identified*, Looney was Deputy Headmaster of the Sheriff Hill School, the largest of the schools founded by the Durham County Board of Education.

In 1939, aged 69, he and Elizabeth left their home in Gateshead to live with their daughter and grandson in Swadlincote, near Burton-on-Trent, after anticipating the heavy German bombing of the Newcastle area that would take place during the Blitz.

Looney's health began to fail by the spring of 1942, close to two years before his death. He was already very ill by his fiftieth wedding anniversary on September 23, 1943.

A list of Looney's known Oxfordian publications is in Appendix 1.

---

[5] William McFee, "The Master Mystery," in J. Thomas Looney, *"Shakespeare" Identified* (1948), p. xvii

six years by World War I and its aftermath."[6]

Neither statement appears to be correct, however. Looney himself wrote in the preface to *"Shakespeare" Identified* that "The solution to the Shakespeare problem . . . was worked out whilst the Great European War was in progress; and my wish was to give the matter full publicity immediately upon the cessation of hostilities."[7] That timing is supported by two documents. One is the sealed envelope containing a description of his solution to the Shakespeare problem that Looney delivered to the Director of the British Museum in mid-December 1918.[8] The second was a letter from an editor at Wm. Heinemann, Publisher, to Looney dated May 1, 1919, in which he acknowledged receiving the "extra chapter" that Looney had sent him a day or two earlier.[9] That was almost certainly what is now Chapter 1 in *"Shakespeare" Identified*, "The Stratfordian View." The publisher must have had the full manuscript, minus that chapter, well in advance of that date. That would mean that the manuscript of the book (except for that one chapter), was completed around the end of 1918.

Whenever it was that his investigation began, Looney brought to it a number of personal qualities that contributed to his success, among them a dedication to truth, courage and modesty.

He Sought Truth, Not Debating Points

From an early age, Looney had sought to distinguish between what was true and what only had the appearance of truth, and his Positivist training had strengthened his independence of mind and spirit. He later wrote that in his search for the real author of Shakespeare's works he was driven by a "serious desire to discover the truth and a willingness to take some trouble to arrive at it" (6). His aim was not to score mere debating points but to discover how "Shakespeare's" works had really come to be written, a point he addressed again in a letter to a reviewer of *"Shakespeare" Identified*:

> The "honesty" which the reviewer attributes to my work, I must point out, is not a matter of personal choice, but is forced upon me by the logic of the situation. My object being to solve definitely a great problem, it would have been fatal to my purpose to pass over its difficulties, or to try to conceal weaknesses either in the case itself, or in the conditions of my researches.[10]

He was Courageous

Although always temperate in his actions and words, Looney was courageous, not backing away from a fight even when he knew he would be outnumbered. As will be seen, *Mr.* Looney did not hesitate to challenge the findings and beliefs of *Sir* Sidney Lee and *Sir* Edmund Chambers, the two most respected Shakespeare scholars of the day. He had no illusions about the severity of the test to which his ideas would be put, but anticipating the storm of criticism that was to come did not stop him.

> I was well aware that, in propounding a new theory of Shakespearean authorship, I was exposing myself to as severe an ordeal as any writer has been called upon to face: that the work would be rigorously overhauled in none too indulgent a spirit by men who know the subject in all its minutiae; and that, if the

---

[6] Charles Wisner Barrell, "Afterwords," in J. Thomas Looney, *"Shakespeare" Identified* (1948), p. 466.

[7] J. Thomas Looney, *"Shakespeare" Identified* (2018), p. v.

[8] *"Shakespeare" Identified: A Preliminary Notice* is dated Dec. 14, 1918.

[9] See Chapter 3 for further discussion.

[10] J. Thomas Looney, "Shakespeare's Identity: Case for Lord Oxford," *Western Mail*, May 6, 1920, p. 7.

argument contained any fatal flaw, this would be detected immediately and the theory overthrown.[11]

The courage to publish his findings was the most obvious form of courage. Another was demonstrated by his determination to investigate the Stratfordian myth in the first place. It would have been all too easy to dismiss the problem as a mystery that would never be fully explained—exactly what H. B. Simpson had done in his December 1917 article.

A more personal aspect of Looney's courage can be seen by considering the ideas of Romain Rolland, the French man of letters awarded the Nobel Prize for Literature in 1915. In his article "Shakespeare the Truthteller," published in August 1920, five months after Looney's book, Rolland wrote that although all men at all times profess a Platonic love of Truth, they also "have [a] very real fear of it. This fear they manifest by showing they do not wish to recognize it, and by their ingratitude toward those who point it out."[12] It's not known whether Rolland had Looney's book in mind, but the statement is apt considering the hostility of most of the responses to the Oxfordian claim, as will be seen in Chapter 3.

Rolland stated that thinkers and writers, whom we rely on to tell us the truth,

> would need for this as much courage as intelligence. And if the latter is not common the former is exceptional. One does not realize this at first, when one enters the career of letters as an enthusiastic and confident novice who believes the only difficulty to be that of finding the exact artistic expression of what one thinks. But one discovers, little by little, that the greatest difficulty is to wish to say what one thinks—still more, to dare to think it.

"Daring to think it"—daring to breech social convention and reject blind belief in the traditional story. That is the courage Looney demonstrated in launching and carrying out his search for the real Shakespeare. Looney the man might have possessed a gentleness that was apparent to all, but his mind was anything but gentle. It was rigorous and sought the truth of any matter it considered. Looney is to be admired for his discovery, but honored for his courage. To break away from conventional belief *and* be right is true greatness.

He was Modest

Looney remained modest and self-effacing throughout his life. He was described by one and all as "a true gentleman." During his Shakespearean research and writing, he generally did not mention his work to others. One to whom he did mention it, in a low-key way, was his former student V. A. Demant, who later became Canon and Chancellor of St. Paul's Cathedral.

> He was not in the least like many supporters of minority movements with a cause, going about with a chip on the shoulder and an obsessional neurosis. You would never know from his general conversation that he was producing a shattering contribution to the authorship question. . . . The appearance of *"Shakespeare" Identified* in 1920 surprised his acquaintances. He had dropped hints to me towards the end of the 1914-18 war, that the Stratfordian authorship was impossible to hold, and that he was setting about deliberately to find, if possible, the true author.[13]

---

[11] J. Thomas Looney, "The Identity of Shakespeare," *Bookman's Journal*, May 21, 1920, p. 58.

[12] Romain Rolland, *"Shakespeare the Truthteller," Dial*, August 1920, p. 109.

[13] Rev. V. A. Demant, "John Thomas Looney," *Shakespearean Authorship Review*, no. 8 (Autumn 1962): 9.

Even after the publication, Looney never brought up the "Shakespeare" question spontaneously in my conversations with him. But when I asked he was ready to answer questions and explain. (8)

Factors Related to His Investigations

In addition to the personal qualities Looney brought to his search and which enabled him to design the commonsensical, two-step investigatory process he used, several other factors contributed to his success.

An Outsider's Independence

Looney wasn't part of academia; he didn't have a position at a university and wasn't a literary scholar by profession. He hadn't spent his life in study of the Elizabethan era or British literature in preparation for his examination of the authorship question. A schoolteacher and Deputy Headmaster at the Sheriff Hill Board School in Gateshead—located just south of Newcastle-upon-Tyne in northern England—Looney lived in the city in England farthest from London.

It is not uncommon for the greatest scientific and scholarly discoveries and innovations to be made by outsiders: Albert Einstein made his great discovery of relativity while working as a patent clerk. Ben Franklin, an amateur tinkerer, invented bifocals and conducted a series of experiments proving that lightning is a form of electricity.

As an outsider, Looney was not bound by the division of knowledge and scholarly pursuits into segregated fields such as history and literature. He could draw freely on findings in all areas and pursue leads wherever they took him. He was free of institutional pressures to profess belief in the Stratfordian story. Living so far from the intellectual capital of England, he was aware of, but not as susceptible to, the informal pressures on those living in London's intellectual and literary center to adhere to tradition.

As chance would have it, in Newcastle Looney had access to the same books and periodicals as professors at the most prestigious universities in England. The Literary and Philosophical Society, commonly referred to as the Lit & Phil, was, and still is, located in Newcastle. As the largest independent library outside London, the Lit & Phil made it possible for a schoolteacher who couldn't afford to purchase many books to conduct in-depth research. That the library was located next to the train station was also a godsend. He later recognized his good fortune, writing that "[o]ne of the greatest debts I have to acknowledge is . . . to the Library of the Literary and Philosophical Society, Newcastle-upon-Tyne. The unique system upon which this institution is conducted has rendered possible an ease and rapidity of work that would probably have been impossible in any other institution in the country" (vi).

An Amateur's Broad Perspective

As an amateur scholar, Looney was able to bring to his investigation a broader approach than most specialists could, given the intensity of their focus on their areas of specialization. From the very beginning he recognized that the authorship problem "is not, at bottom, purely literary. . . . Its solution does not depend wholly upon the extent of the investigator's knowledge of literature nor upon the soundness of his literary judgment." The problem had not yet been solved "because it has been left mainly in the hands of literary men, whereas its solution required the application of methods of research which are not, strictly speaking, literary methods" (4). Experts in literature may, therefore, "be unfitted for prosecuting . . . an investigation" into the authorship question, "whilst a mind constituted for this kind of enquiry may have had only an inferior preparation as far as purely literary matters are concerned." Therefore, he concluded, "the imperfection of my own literary equipment [was] no reason why I should not attempt the task" (4).

Looney brought to his investigation a broad knowledge of literary, cultural and historical matters acquired through the wide reading referred to earlier in this chapter, and a common sense approach and astute judgment sharpened by his Positivist training. He could turn to expert opinion when needed and felt competent to evaluate its relevance and reliability. He compared his work with "the kind of enquiry with which lawyers and juries are faced every day."

> They are called upon to examine questions involving highly technical matters with which they are not themselves conversant. Their method is naturally to separate what belongs to the specialist from what is matter of common sense and simple judgment; to rely upon the expert in purely technical matters, and to use their own discrimination in the sifting of evidence, at the same time allowing its full weight to any particular knowledge they may chance to possess in those things that pertain specially to the expert's domain. (72)

Such a non-specialist mindset was just the approach needed to solve the Shakespeare authorship question that had stumped the "experts." Still, he recognized, amateur investigators such as himself must eventually "submit the result of their labours very largely to the judgment of literary men" (71).

Because Looney had compared his methods to those used by scientists, it is appropriate, even at the risk of stepping outside the Looney time frame, to consider the degree to which several prominent scientists attributed their success to having employed the "Looney method."

Michael Berridge, a cell biologist, explained that,

> [t]o be a successful scientist you need to be able to make connections. If I was thinking of any single gift that one needs it's this ability to make connections between a lot of disparate facts. That's what I enjoy—particularly going into libraries, sitting down and reading, and trying to collate different pieces of information. The gifted scientists that I meet and enjoy talking to do have this facility. They have a very broad view of what's going on and they're able to make connections between different ideas, different disciplines.[14]

Theoretical physicist Murray Gell-Mann and physical anthropologist David Pilbeam likewise attributed their successes to having brought knowledge from relevant fields to bear on their work. Gell-Mann explained that "I do have a tendency to take a very broad view; to try to see the big picture and connect a lot of things together" (161). Pilbeam explained that "right from the start of picking up a fossil you can't make any sense at all out of it unless you have an understanding of anatomy, particularly comparative anatomy, unless you also have some understanding of functional anatomy, behavioural ecology, the ecological context, and so on. These are not facts that speak for themselves, they're facts that you have to put a lot into" (205).

Evolutionary biologist Jared Diamond also believed that experts must have the ability to synthesize information from many fields. "To understand the jungle you can't operate narrowly. . . . In order to understand ecological problems, there are lots of things to fit

---

[14] Michael Berridge, quoted in Lewis Wolpert and Alison Richards, *Passionate Minds* (1997), p. 146.

together. . . . You have to have a breadth of knowledge and be able to synthesize it." He went on to explain the institutional pressures that work to keep scientists—like professors of history and literature—from the broad view they need to be successful.

> It's very hard for a scientist to make a go of it in more than one area. The cards are just so heavily stacked against you. First of all, there is the prejudice that if you work in a second area, you're just a dilettante. Secondly, there are the realistic difficulties. How are you going to get grant funding in a second area where you don't yet have any indications of ability? There's also a question of the outlook. In scientific papers we are forced to trim speculation from our papers, we are forced to write them in a dull style and we're prevented from making connections. So we're prevented from working in a field other than our own. (33)

These scientists recognized that being an expert did not mean closing the doors and barricading their field against knowledge from outside. It meant doing just the opposite: having more knowledge than others, integrating knowledge from whatever source it may come, if it can be used to explain historical events, aid in the creation of works of literature or history, or result in scientific discoveries.

Familiarity with Works of Stratfordian Specialists

Looney not only turned to Stratfordian scholars for information about specialized literary matters; he constructed the Oxfordian claim largely on their work. He brought together facts already uncovered by orthodox scholars and viewed them, in combination, from a new vantage point that revealed their true significance.

> It will be found that nothing important in the argument rests upon newly unearthed data. Everything has been accessible for years to anyone who might have been on the lookout for the facts, and was prepared to take trouble to ascertain them. . . . The case has been made to rest at almost every critical stage, not upon my own judgment alone, but upon the statements of writers of recognized standing and authority whose works have for some time been before the public. (6)

What had been missing, but was in place now, was a structure on which to hang the isolated facts so that the connections between them could be easily seen.

> The basic facts of [George Greenwood's] discoveries have usually been well known for some time before. What has been of special consequence has been the perception, sometimes purely accidental, of a relationship amongst these facts hitherto not noticed. Once detected, however, other facts have become grouped and coordinated by it, and the resultant discovery . . . appears at last so natural and obvious, that men wonder that it had not been thought of before. (7)

In forming his argument in *"Shakespeare" Identified*, Looney drew on more than 230 passages from dozens of works by Stratfordian scholars. Those drawn on most heavily are shown in the nearby text box.

Looney remarked that "both by his biography of Edward de Vere in the [*Dictionary of National Biography*] article . . . as well as by his invaluable work, *A Life of William Shakespeare*, Sir Sidney Lee, convinced Stratfordian though he is, has furnished more material in support of my constructive argument than any other single modern writer" (111). Almost as important was Halliwell-Phillipps's *Outlines of the Life of Shakespeare*. Looney added an interesting comment that explained why Halliwell-Phillipps had no concerns about revealing so much information that undercut the case for Stratfordian authorship.

> Writing in 1882, . . . the problem of Shakespearean authorship seems never to have touched him; and therefore, undoubting Stratfordian though he was, he writes with perfect freedom and openness, glozing over nothing, and not shrinking from making admissions which some later Baconians or sceptic might use against the subject of his biography. . . . [W]e may describe [his *Outlines*] as the most honest biography of William Shakspere yet written. (15)

Most-Cited Sources Quoted in *"Shakespeare" Identified*	Number of Citations
Sir Sidney Lee, *A Life of William Shakespeare* (1898)	57
J. O. Halliwell-Phillipps. *Outlines of the Life of Shakespeare* (1883)	21
Richard William Church. *Spenser* (1879)	13
R. Warwick Bond. *The Complete Works of John Lyly* (1902)	12
Charlotte Stopes. *Burbage and Shakespeare's Stage* (1913)	9
Sir Sidney Lee. "Vere, Edward," *Dictionary of National Biography* (1898)	9
Frank Harris, *The Man Shakespeare and His Tragic Life-Story* (1909)	5
Rev. Ronald Bayne. "Lesser Elizabethan Dramatists," *Cambridge History of English Literature* (1907)	5

Looney's list of eighteen inferred qualities that the author must have had was itself drawn up largely from findings by Stratfordian scholars. "The various points are, indeed, the outcome of the labours and criticisms of many minds spread over a number of years, and it may be that the only thing original about the statement is the gathering together and tabulating of the various old points" (104).

> There is scarcely a single point that is not more or less in contradiction to that [Stratfordian] tradition. . . . [M]ost, if not all, of the points we have been urging have been pointed out at one time or other by different writers; . . . If, then, it be urged that there is not a single original observation in the whole of these two chapters [discussing the inferences about the author], then so much the better for the argument. (103)

Looney also quoted dozens of literary works from the Elizabethan era in his discussions of Oxford's poetry, including the plays or poems of Daniels, Davison, Drayton, Greene, Lyly, Jonson, Marlowe, Munday, Sidney, Spenser and Lord Vaux, as well as anonymous works such as the Parnassus plays. Though Looney was too modest to say so directly, by the time he finished his investigation he was as familiar with the political and literary history of the Elizabethan era as any scholar in the field.

In sum, Looney succeeded in answering the authorship question in large part by reversing the three splits between scholars identified in Chapter 1. He drew on the work of historical *and* literary scholars—and those from other fields, too—something that was discouraged by the methodologies in place in Departments of History and Literature in the universities. He drew on the works of scholars within *and* outside of academia. And he drew on the works of both Baconian scholars *and* those such as George Greenwood who did not claim to know who the real author had been.

An Informed Imagination

In his pursuit of the truth of the matter of Shakespearean authorship, Looney went beyond the bare facts he uncovered. He cultivated what might be called an informed intuition or an informed imagination—what historian H. J. Elliott described as "the ability to enter imaginatively into the life of a society remote in time or place, and produce a plausible explanation of why its inhabitants thought and behaved as they did."[15] He was bound by the facts, but he was not limited to them. He sought to fill in the cracks between them to understand the life and times of Edward de Vere.

An informed imagination is the opposite of fantasy, in which anything is possible. The capacity for an informed imagination is the critical quality Sir Sidney Lee showed that he lacked when he stated that works of fiction were either completely autobiographical or completely the result of imagination. His definition of imagination, unbound by a writer's personality and experiences, or a historian's regard for the facts he has uncovered, is equivalent to an uninformed imagination, or fantasy. Lee would not, perhaps could not, acknowledge the wide middle ground between autobiographical writing and purely imaginative works.

Looney, in his capacity as a historian, used his imagination, informed by the facts he uncovered, to understand the conditions in which Shakespeare's works had been written. He knew he didn't have all the answers, but he presented what he had found, along with his understanding of the implications of his findings, thereby enabling readers to grasp what had happened. Two examples illustrate this point.

On the question of why Oxford hid his authorship, Looney wrote, "We may justly wonder why the author of such works should prefer to remain unknown.... Difficult as it is to penetrate and appreciate the private motives even of people circumstanced like ourselves, the difficulty is immeasurably increased when the entire social circumstances are different, as is the case before us" (46). We must try to understand "the Shakespeare problem in its relationship to the age to which it belongs." He cited Halliwell-Phillipps's statement that "'[i]t is difficult to realize a period when ... the great poet, notwithstanding the immense popularity of some of his works, was held in no general reverence. It must be borne in mind that actors then occupied an inferior position in society, and that even the vocation of a dramatic writer was considered scarcely respectable.' ... To have laid claim to the authorship of even 'Shakespeare's' plays would therefore have been of no assistance to any man seeking to obtain, preserve, or recover the social dignity and eminence of himself and his family" (47).[16]

Nor did Looney pretend to have a complete explanation for how the secret could have remained secret; he was "quite unable to offer a satisfactory explanation of the complete success of the 'blind,' just as we may stand puzzled before the other mysteries of history. This again is a difficulty which is greatly magnified by giving it a modern setting. In 'Shakespeare's' day, however, according to Halliwell-Phillipps, 'no interest was taken in the events of the lives of authors ... non-political correspondence was rarely preserved, [and] elaborate diaries were not the fashion'" (47).

Drawing on his informed imagination, Looney understood the significance for the authorship question of the secrecy practiced in the society in which "Shakespeare" lived and wrote. "[I]n those times no important secret would be imparted to anyone without first of all receiving the most solemn assurances that no risk of disclosure should be run. Certainly the writer of *Hamlet* was not the man to neglect any precaution. The carefully framed oaths by which Hamlet binds Horatio and Marcellus to secrecy, and the final

---

[15] H. J. Elliott, *History in the Making* (2012), p. xi.
[16] Internal quote is from J. O. Halliwell-Phillipps, *Outlines* (1883), pp. v-vi.

caution he administers, is clearly the work of a man who knew how to ensure secrecy so far as it was humanly possible to do so. And we do know, as a matter of actual human experience, that when a superior intelligence is combined with what may be called a faculty for secrecy and a sound instinct in judging and choosing agents, secret purposes are carried through successfully in a way that is amazing and mystifying to simpler minds" (48).

Factors Related to the Presentation of His Case

Beyond these factors related to Looney's personal qualities and the nature of his investigation, the manner in which he presented his findings contributed to the powerful effect of *"Shakespeare" Identified*.

Told the Story of His Investigations

Recognizing that "the force of a conviction is frequently due as much to the manner in which the evidence presents itself, as to the intrinsic value of the evidence" (4), Looney didn't just present a summary of his finding, though presentation of the Oxfordian claim in any form would have been revolutionary; instead, he pulled readers in by taking them along as he moved through each step in designing and carrying out his investigative plan. By showing them the information uncovered at each step and sharing with them the excitement of each new discovery, he enabled them to experience the same surprise and delight that he had felt as the case for de Vere's authorship strengthened with each newly-uncovered piece of evidence.

The success of his approach is shown by comments from several of his first readers:

John Galsworthy: "The most fascinating detective story [I have] ever read."[17]

Gelett Burgess: "It has all the charm, all the excitement of the most thrilling detective story. Indeed, it is a detective story."[18]

Charles H. Herford: "Mr. Looney . . . has written a book which has the fascination of a detective romance."[19]

William McFee: "The Looney method, [is that] of a detective methodically and relentlessly closing in on the author, not of a crime but of a mystery . . . His book is a combination of a detective thriller, a mystery story, and a historical narrative built solely from authentic historical data."[20]

Oliver Herford: "Mr. Looney's book is fascinating reading, more thrilling even than the best detective story by . . . Edgar Allan Poe."[21]

Gilbert Slater: "The method Mr. Looney adopted to find . . . Shakespeare was similar to that used by Scotland Yard when called upon to investigate a burglary or a forgery."[22]

"Shakespeare" Identified was indeed laid out as a detective story. It posited a mystery and unfolded with a distinctive and relentless logic. It began with a large number of unknown candidates that Looney narrowed down as evidence long hidden or not properly understood came to light. The case was built on both negative evidence

---

[17] The source of this quote attributed to the British novelist and playwright John Galsworthy is unknown.

[18] Gelett Burgess, letter to Frederick Stokes, Publisher, May 19, 1920, who passed it on to J. Thomas Looney.

[19] C. H. H. [Charles H. Herford], "Sh. Deposed Again," *Manchester Guardian*, March 19, 1920, p. 7.

[20] William McFee, "The Master Mystery," in Looney (1948), pp. xvii, xx.

[21] Oliver Herford, review in *Leslie's Weekly*, Summer 1920, quoted in *Literary Digest*, Aug. 14, 1920.

[22] Gilbert Slater, *Seven Shakespeares* (1931), p. 176.

regarding William Shakspere's authorship and positive evidence in support of Oxford's. In the end the evidence narrowed the field to the only person who could have been the author.[23]

Looney's presentation did not descend into mere sensationalism or entertainment because of the seriousness with which he conducted his investigation and his recognition of the great importance of the issue, as shown by this statement from the very first page of his book: "The transference of the honour of writing the immortal Shakespeare dramas from one man to another is not merely a national or contemporary event, but a world event of permanent importance, destined to leave a mark as enduring as human literature and the human race itself" (1). He explained that no one "who has a due sense of these things is likely to embark upon an enterprise of this kind in a spirit of levity or adventure;" that "however much the writer of a work like the present might wish to keep himself in the background he is bound to implicate himself so deeply as to stake publicly his reputation for sane and sober judgment, and thus to imperil the credit of his opinion on every other subject."

Looney's recognition that he was staking his good name on the validity of his findings reassured his readers that they were in the hands of someone who truly valued and respected the greatest of England's literary treasures. On this point, one reviewer quoted above, Charles H. Herford, opened his review with this favorable assessment of J. Thomas Looney, even though the book had not convinced him of Edward de Vere's authorship: "It is impossible not to like, and even to admire, Mr. Looney. He has written a book which has the fascination of a detective romance, and we follow the chase with yet keener zest in view of the solemnity with which the detective at the outset assures us of the enormous gravity of the issues involved."[24]

Powerful Takedown of William Shakspere

Looney's book was also effective because he prefaced it with a powerful takedown of the man from Stratford. The chapter on the weakness of the evidence supporting the Stratfordian story is an effective piece of work by itself. Looney did not take the easy route of simply providing readers with a summary of the case against William Shakspere found in books by Sir George Greenwood and others. Instead, he explained, as "great as are my obligations specially to Sir George Greenwood's work, I have purposely refrained from quoting from it when I might often have done so with advantage to my own argument, and preferred resting upon the authority of writers of the opposite school" (6-7). Drawing on the facts uncovered by Stratfordian scholars, he built the case against Shakspere from the ground up in his own inimitable way, pointing out new implications, and in doing so made a more persuasive case than anyone had yet made.

In one of his most powerful arguments, Looney demonstrated the incompatibility of the first and third of the three periods of Shakspere's life with the supposed middle period: "[T]he coarse and illiterate circumstances of his early life" and the "closing period spent, like the first, in the unwholesome intellectual atmosphere of Stratford" did not fit with "the middle period during which he is supposed to have resided mainly in London

---

[23] Looney's grandson reported that his grandfather liked to read detective novels by E. Phillips Oppenheim on the train—books with titles such as *The Great Secret*, *The Magnificent Hoax*, and *The Great Impersonation*. Could it be that he was primed to write *"Shakespeare" Identified* in the manner he did by books such as these?

[24] C. H. H. [Charles H. Herford] (1920), p. 7.

and produced the remarkable literature to which he owes his fame" (21). Looney found it difficult to conceive that a young man from a small, isolated provincial town—where a dialect of English difficult to understand in London was spoken and where most people were illiterate—could have "produced at the age of twenty-nine a lengthy and elaborate poem in the most polished English of the period, evincing a large and accurate knowledge of the classics, and later the superb Shakespearean dramas." If he had done so, Looney continued,

> he accomplished one of the greatest if not actually the greatest work of self-development and self-realization that genius has ever enabled any man to perform. On the other hand, if, after having performed so miraculous a work, this same genius retired to Stratford to devote himself to houses, lands, orchards, money and malt, leaving no traces of a single intellectual or literary interest, he achieved without a doubt the greatest work of self-stultification in the annals of mankind. (36)

Then came the point that made Shakspere's authorship impossible for him.

> It is *difficult* to believe that with such a beginning he could have attained to such heights as he is supposed to have done; it is *more difficult* to believe that with such glorious achievements in his middle period he could have fallen to the level of his closing period; and in time it will be fully recognized that it is *impossible* to believe that the same man could have accomplished two such stupendous and mutually nullifying feats. Briefly, the first and last periods at Stratford are too much in harmony with one another, and too antagonistic to the supposed middle period for all three to be creditable. The situation represented by the whole stands altogether outside general human experience. The perfect unity of the two extremes justifies the conclusion that the middle period is an illusion; in other words William Shakspere did not write the plays attributed to him. (36-37)

A second example of the effectiveness of Looney's reasoning was how he systematically eliminated the man from Stratford from consideration as the author by continually whittling down the period of time in which he could be placed in London. At one end, there was no record of any literary activity by Shakspere (assuming he was Shakespeare) from the time of his birth until 1593; and at the other end of his life, all but one of the existing records place him in Stratford from 1604 onward. It seemed impossible, Looney had reasoned, that even a genius of the highest order could have written thirty-seven of the greatest works in English drama in the impossibly short period of eleven years. Looney later reduced Shakspere's actual time in London "to a mere matter of four years (1592-1596)" (43).

Having shown that Shakspere was actively involved in business and personal matters in Stratford almost every year from 1597 to 1604, Looney concluded that if he had been charged with the "crime" of being "the author and directing genius of the magnificent stream of dramatic literature which in those very years was bursting upon London," then, "the business record we have just presented would in almost any court in the land be deemed to have proved an *alibi*" (44).

The key point for Looney—a point he stressed repeatedly—was the need for an author whose life and work cohere, for an author whose work arises from a "natural relationship with human experience and normal probabilities" (67).

Looney later speculated about why Oxford should have selected a third-rate actor—as he believed Shakspere to have been—as his cover, as he also believed him to have been.

"Shakespeare," whoever he was, . . . would certainly select for such a purpose the most reliable agent available. The success of the "blind" is the best testimony to the soundness of his choice. It was probably, too, just because he was third-rate that he was chosen. A second-rate man who talked and wrote letters would have "given the show away": a single letter left behind would have betrayed him; and, of course, a first-rate man would not have accepted a role which involved his own literary self-effacement. William [Shakspere's] social and dramatic career, it must not be forgotten, is purely hypothetical. Everything points to his being safely out of the way, living in Stratford, in what are regarded as the years of his London triumph.[25]

To make the blind stick, all evidence that contradicted it had to be destroyed, if any had ever existed. Shakspere, or somebody else, destroyed all evidence of his literary activities in the first and third segments of his life. He or they "deliberately reduced to a minimum all that kind of evidence which might have placed his title beyond question. For, as we have seen, neither that part of his life prior to his appearance in the London theatre, nor that subsequent to his retirement from the stage, nor a single word in his will, shows any mark of those dominating literary interests to which the writings bear witness. . . . [H]e must have actually gone out of his way to remove the normal traces of his literary pursuits" (69).

Looney concluded that Shakspere played a role in the subterfuge and didn't begrudge him the rewards he received for it. But, Looney added, "that he was himself the author of the great poems and dramas stands altogether outside the region of natural probabilities, and he must now yield for the adornment of a worthier brow the laurels he has worn so long" (67).

Careful Not to State More Than He Knew

Looney knew that he hadn't answered all questions that could be raised about the subject of Edward de Vere's use of the William Shakespeare pseudonym. He called attention to many areas where additional research was needed.

➢ On Oxford's poems: "The necessity of knowing the poems themselves and of subjecting them to a very careful examination, for this must form the crux of a very great deal of future investigation" (123).

➢ On comparing de Vere's poetry with Shakespeare's: "This decisive step is to bring the writings of Edward de Vere alongside the Shakespearean writings. . . . As this has never been done before, . . . all we can hope to do is to submit such points for consideration as may give a lead in this new line of investigation, by which eventually, we believe, our case will either stand or fall" (135).

➢ On the crisis of 1576: "At this point we approach a great crisis in his life which, when his biography comes to be written, will require much patient research, and the most careful weighing of facts, before a straight story can be made of it or the events placed in a clear light" (227).

➢ On Anne Cecil: "Her father had created a situation in which she must choose definitely between father and husband. The unravelling of the facts and their proper interpretation must, however, form matter for future investigations" (232).

---

[25] J. Thomas Looney, "Shakespeare's Identity: Case for Lord Oxford," *Western Mail*, May 6, 1920, p. 7.

➤ On Oxford's dramatic activities: "Research will probably furnish fuller details and dates of Edward de Vere's connection with the stage; sufficient has, however, already been established to show that by the year 1580 he was already deeply committed" (256).

➤ On Oxford's spiritual experiences: "This faculty of observation must have compelled him to subject his own nature to a rigorous examination and analysis. Consequently, when the author is better known, it will doubtless be found that his works are packed with delineations and studies of his own spiritual experiences. The working out of this department of Shakespearean enquiry belongs largely to the future (391).

➤ On portrayals of Oxford's contemporaries in the plays: "If our identification of Oxford and Harvey with Berowne and Holofernes be accepted, an interesting point for future investigation will be the identification of other contemporaries with other characters in [*Love's Labour's Lost*]" (248).

"The plays of Shakespeare contain possible pen portraits of men with whom the Earl of Oxford had dealings, representing them, not as tradition has preserved them, but as they stood in relation to Oxford himself. It is no necessary part of our argument that these identifications should be fully accepted. They bear rather on a branch of Shakespearean study that must receive a special development once our main thesis is adopted" (251).

"[Again, just as] the erudite have interested themselves in endeavours to identify the original literary and historical sources of his work, so may we, once it has become possible, occupy ourselves with the more fascinating task of identifying his contemporary materials and the human models for his characters."[26]

➤ On additional evidence: "It would not in the least surprise us, moreover, if particular items of evidence much more conclusive than any single argument we have offered, should be forthcoming, or even if it should be pointed out that we have blunderingly overlooked some vital matter" (422).

➤ On things "standing thus unknown": "To reinterpret the known facts by the light of the Shakespearean literature, in which work we have made the first essay, will doubtless yield larger and truer results when others have taken up the task. There is also the possibility that new data may be unearthed, and this, together with the gathering together and unifying of facts scattered through the diverse records of other men, may bring to light the things 'standing yet unknown' which were in his mind" (414).

➤ On the Dark Lady of the *Sonnets*: "The other personal relationship with which these poems deal . . . presents a problem not yet solved, and which may remain unsolved for all time. . . . [T]he set of sonnets (beginning 127) namely, that to him was a matter of the heart, of a most intense and sincere character, but to the lady a much more equivocal affair. Nothing but an overwhelming heart hunger could ever have induced any man of spirit to maintain the attitude described" (127).

"Nor is it necessary to solve the mystery of the Dark Lady, for it is not in the nature of things for such a man to pass away and leave no insoluble mysteries; . . . neither

---

[26] J. Thomas Looney, *The Poems of Edward de Vere* (1921), p. xiii-xiv.

is it necessary to penetrate all the disguises which 'Shakespeare' himself . . . thought right to adopt" (385).

Looney realized that with the identification of Shakespeare as Edward de Vere, the real work of Shakespeare Studies was only just beginning. "With Oxford as the key, this literature, which for over three centuries has been regarded as wholly impersonal, is found to be packed with delineations of Elizabethan personalities, and the study of it undergoes a profound revolution. Indeed, we may say that, furnished for the first time with the key principle of interpretation, the real study of 'Shakespeare,' as distinct from the merely literary and academic, is only now in its early stages."[27]

The Main Argument, I: Literary Linkages

Once Looney had established that Edward de Vere met all eighteen criteria he inferred "Shakespeare" to have had, he turned to an in-depth comparison of de Vere's poetry with Shakespeare's. Up to this point he had considered only a single poem by Oxford and only one by Shakespeare. He now sought out other poems by each as well as other opinions of Oxford's poetry beyond the two complimentary assessments he had seen in the *The Dictionary of National Biography*. His comparison of the "two" poets' work filled more than fifty pages of *"Shakespeare" Identified*, and he regarded this examination in Chapter VIII as "the most decisive section of the argument" (121).

With *"Shakespeare" Identified* now back in print, it is not necessary to recount in great detail Looney's fascinating comparison of the two bodies of work in order to judge "whether or not the former contain the natural seeds and clear promise of the latter" (135). Readers can examine it for themselves. Mention should be made, though, of a few points that weighed heavily with Looney. One is that "Women," Oxford's poem that Looney had stumbled on first, was not Oxford's only poem in the same stanza form as *Venus and Adonis*. It was, Looney discovered, "a familiar and practised form in which [Oxford] . . . excelled" (123). He also found a striking parallel in theme between another poem of Oxford's and several of Shakespeare's sonnets.

> Edward de Vere's poem on the loss of his good name, and Shakespeare's sonnets on the same theme, are the only poems of their kind with which we have met in our reading of Elizabethan poetry—the only poems of their kind, we believe, to be found in English literature. . . . Personally, I find it utterly impossible to read this poem of Edward de Vere's and the sonnets in which "Shakespeare" harps upon the same theme, without an overwhelming sense of there being but one mind behind the two utterances. (159, 158)

Similarities of themes, subject matter, tone, style, formal structure, phrasing and word use, meter and rhyming scheme, and quality struck Looney so strongly because, he recalled, when he selected de Vere as the possible author he "had no knowledge whatever of these poems of his, almost every line of which we now find paralleled in Shakespeare. To discover such a correspondence in the poems under such circumstances furnishes, to the discoverer at any rate, a much greater weight of evidence than if he had been acquainted with the writings at the outset" (166).

Looney was equally impressed by the "coincidence" that only Oxford's early work had survived, even though "the continuance, or rather the intensification of his literary interests in later years has been amply proved" (126), while with Shakespeare only his

---

[27] J. Thomas Looney, "'Shakespeare's' Identity" [letter], *Sydney Morning Herald*, July 15, 1921, p. 12.

mature work is known of today, even though he must have produced juvenile works as he developed his literary talents.

> These two facts alone, in work of such exceptional character, . . . constitute . . . one of the most remarkable coincidences in the history of literature. When to this we add the fact that the dates in the respective cases are such as to fit in exactly with the theory of one work being but the continuation of the other, . . . [i]t is difficult to resist the conviction, on this ground alone, that it is indeed but one writer with whom we are dealing. (126-27)

The Main Arguments, II: Biographical Linkages with the Plays and Poems

After announcing at the end of Chapter VIII his conclusion that Oxford had written "Shakespeare's" works, Looney proceeded "to examine, in whatever detail possible, the life and circumstances of the man in order to ascertain how far they, too, relate themselves to the contents of, and the task of producing, the Shakespearean plays and poems."

> Here our task is one of special difficulty, for our theory presupposes a man who had deliberately planned his self-concealment. Our material is bound, therefore, to be as scanty as he could make it, and, at the outset, probably misleading. We shall, therefore, be under the necessity of reconstructing a personality from the most meagre of data, with the added disadvantage of a large amount of contemporary misrepresentation, which it will be necessary to correct. (173)

In the fifty pages of Chapter XI, which he described as "of extreme importance" (294), Looney documented how he found "fully reflected in the dramas . . . pronounced marks of all the outstanding incidents and personal relationships of [Oxford's] career, whilst the special conditions of his life when these plays were being produced were just such as accorded with the issuing of the works" (420-21). In sum, "The chapter in which we deal with the lyric poetry of Edward de Vere, and this chapter in which his dramatic relationships are examined, must, by the nature of the case, form the principal foundations of our constructive argument" (294).

The biographical material in Looney's chapter is cumulative and should be read in its entirety. Here is a brief rundown of some of the most important linkages between the man and the works that will be important in the following chapters of this book.

"The long-accepted notion that the author has not given us a representation of himself in his plays breaks down completely," Looney observed, citing "the case of Lord Berowne in *Love's Labour's Lost*" and "a most striking parallel between Edward de Vere and . . . Bertram in *All's Well*" (391). But there is no better play to cite for correspondences between Oxford's life and his works than *Hamlet*. Looney showed in great detail how the external circumstances and the internal or personal aspects of Oxford's life come together in that play. Looney also established that a half-dozen other characters had their inspiration in people intimately involved in Oxford's life.

> The essential objectivity of Shakespeare's work, with its foundations fixed in observation, is assurance enough that his characters would be taken from his own experience of the men and women about him. Mere photographic reproduction, of course, such a genius would not offer us; but actually living men and women, artistically modified and adjusted to fit them for the part they had to perform, are what we may be sure the plays contain. (390)

This same facility resulted in Oxford's portrayal of himself as the title character in

Hamlet.

> Such a faculty of observation as we have noticed in him, leading him to fix his attention specially upon those whose lives pressed directly upon his own . . . is certain to have made his work much more a record of his own personal relationships than has hitherto been supposed. His special domain, moreover, being the study of the human soul, this faculty of observation must have compelled him to subject his own nature to a rigorous examination and analysis. Consequently, when the author is better known, it will doubtless be found that his works are packed with delineations and studies of his own spiritual experiences. The working out of this department of Shakespearean enquiry belongs largely to the future. (391)

Having determined that "*Hamlet* is the play which . . . is entitled to be regarded as 'Shakespeare's' special work of self-delineation," Looney provided a twenty-four page account of his investigations into whether the play did indeed have "a marked and peculiar applicability to the case of Edward de Vere" (395).

Vivid portrayals of powerful personages in Queen Elizabeth's court and government provided a second reason for Oxford's authorship to have been hidden—the first having been the disrespect in which writers and the stage were held by the highest social classes. Prominent persons in the court could not have enjoyed seeing characters modeled on themselves mocked on stage in court productions, but they couldn't prevent it given how thoroughly the queen enjoyed entertainment of that sort. But it would have been beyond tolerable for them if public audiences had realized that the pretentious or foolish or evil characters at which they laughed were modeled after themselves. Cutting the connection between Oxford and the plays through the use of a pseudonym, and, perhaps, a stand-in, would have made the connection between the plays and the court and government less likely. Such a step protected not only the reputations of individual politicians and courtiers but also respect for the entire nobility in what was a very class-conscious society.

Looney recognized that "when a theory that we have formed from a consideration of certain facts leads us to suppose that certain other facts will exist, the later discovery that the facts are actually in accordance with our inferences becomes a much stronger confirmation of our theory than if we had known these additional facts at the outset" (4). One example of such a predicted fact is the swordfight between the Montagues and the Capulets in *Romeo and Juliet*, which mirrored a real-life swordfight between Oxford and Sir Thomas Knyvet in which both were wounded, Oxford seriously. When *"Shakespeare" Identified* was published, Knyvet was believed to have been a lover of Anne Vavasour, with whom Oxford had an affair and by whom he fathered an illegitimate son. But, based on the relationship between Tybalt and Juliet in the play, Looney predicted that it would be discovered that Knyvet was not Anne's lover but her relative. It was indeed later discovered that Knyvet was Anne's uncle.

In another example tying Oxford to the plays, if Oberon in *A Midsummer Night's Dream* is partially a stand-in for Oxford, then the fight between Oberon and Titania over the changeling boy mirrors the fight between Oxford and Queen Elizabeth over his illegitimate son by Anne Vavasour. The mother of the boy in the play is described as "a votress" of a queen, and Vavasour was a lady of Queen Elizabeth's bedchamber. Elizabeth had thrown Oxford and Vavasour into the Tower upon the birth of the child (in separate cells) and he was not allowed to see her or his son for several years.[28]

Looney also uncovered the important linkage between Oxford's life, Shakespeare's plays and the court at Windsor. As a ward of the Queen under the care of her chief minister William Cecil after his father died when he was twelve years old, Oxford spent much of his youth at Elizabeth's court at Windsor.

> It is not without significance that the "Shakespeare" play which contains the fullest and most precise English topography is *The Merry Wives of Windsor*: a play which certainly exhibits much greater familiarity with Berkshire, Windsor, and its environs than any other shows respecting Warwickshire, Stratford, and its neighborhood. Indeed . . . it is the only drama from the master pen in which precise local detail is made predominant: an intimacy embracing the Royal Park and its traditions, and extending even to the rooms of the Castle and the Royal Chapel.[29]

In a final linkage to be mentioned here, a robbery perpetrated by several of young Edward de Vere's servants in real life in the Gad's Hill area "between Rochester and Gravesend" is mirrored by a robbery perpetrated by Prince Hal, Falstaff and others in Shakespeare's *1 Henry IV*. The event in the play is stated to have taken place at just the number of years and months into the king's reign that the real-life event occurred into Queen Elizabeth's. Either Shakespeare had extraordinarily detailed information about the Earl of Oxford's youth, or Oxford was Shakespeare.

Looney also demonstrated that the nature of the literary evidence changed with the *Sonnets*. In the plays, the search had been "for indirect and unconscious self-expression on the part of 'Shakespeare.' Anything like deliberate and complete direct self-disclosure is not to be expected; otherwise there would have been no problem for us to solve" (369). With the *Sonnets* it was otherwise. They are "Shakespeare's work of poetic self-expression. . . . The idea that these poems are fantastic dramatic inventions with mystic meanings we feel to be a violation of all normal probabilities and precedents. Accepting them, therefore, as autobiographical, our next step must be to see how these poems, as a whole, stand related to the authorship question we are now advancing" (369-70). At the end of a chapter in which he showed how closely the *Sonnets* reflect sentiments natural to one in Oxford's position and situation, Looney concluded that "[t]he supposition that Edward de Vere is 'Shakespeare' places the appearance of this literature for the first time within the category of natural and human achievements" (422).

Correspondences and Circumstantial Evidence

The biographical case for Oxford's authorship is necessarily built on circumstantial evidence. This must be so because direct evidence, to the extent that it ever existed, was destroyed as part of the deliberate effort to conceal his authorship. Circumstantial evidence is, Looney observed, "mistakenly supposed by some to be evidence of an inferior order, but in practice the most reliable form of proof we have" (80).[30] "The predominating

---

[28] An alternative interpretation of this scene is discussed in Chapter 10.

[29] J. Thomas Looney, *The Poems of Edward de Vere* (1921), p. 64.

[30] Circumstantial evidence is regularly accepted as valid in the American legal system. Lawyer Tom Regnier confirmed that "Circumstantial evidence may be conclusive evidence in certain situations, depending on the issue and the quality and quantity of the evidence." (personal communication, May 2018). Law professor Bryan H. Wildenthal concurred, explaining that "Many non-lawyers use 'conclusive' and 'direct' as synonyms, as if 'direct' evidence were always (or even usually) 'strong' evidence. But of course highly explicit and direct

element" in circumstantial evidence, he explained, is that of coincidences. A few coincidences we may treat as simply interesting; a number of coincidences we regard as remarkable; a vast accumulation of extraordinary coincidences we accept as conclusive proof." If nothing "of an unusual character appears" to contradict "a vast accumulation of coincidences," then the conclusion supported by the coincidences can be "accepted as a permanently established truth" (80).

The Oxfordian case is supported by such a mass of literary similarities and biographical "coincidences" that, Looney believed, it can be accepted as proved. "It is the perfect harmony, consistency and convergence of all the various lines of argument employed, and the overwhelming mass of coincidences that they involve, that give to our results the appearance of a case fully and, we believe, unimpeachably proven" (422). In fact, what Looney called coincidences aren't "coincidences"—chance happenings—at all; they are linkages arising directly out of the fact that Oxford was Shakespeare and that his works in large part arose from personal experiences and concerns.

Looney contrasted the mass of linkages between Oxford's life and Shakespeare's works with the absence of any such evidence in support of Shakspere's authorship. If there is no direct evidence of Oxford's authorship, there is also none for Shakspere's from within his lifetime. The First Folio, the collection of Shakespeare's works, with its preface materials providing ambiguous direct evidence, was not published until 1623, seven years after Shakspere's death.

Looney also considered what he termed "incredibilities"—a line of reasoning similar to Crosse's improbabilities noted in Chapter 1 of this book. "Difficulties do not kill truth," he wrote, but "incredibilities"—things that fly in the face of "general human experience"— "are fatal" (49). One "incredibility" inherent in—and destructive of—the case for the Stratford man is

> the belief that the author of the finest literature lets others do just as they please during his own lifetime in the matter of publishing his works but does nothing himself. . . . He is thus represented as creating and casting forth his immortal works with all the indifference of a mere spawning process, and turning his attention to houses, land, malt and money at the very moment when the printed issue of these great triumphs of his own creative spirit begins. This is the fundamental incredibility which along with the incredible reversion represented by Shakespeare's second Stratford period, and a succession of other incredibilities ought to dissolve completely the Stratfordian hypothesis, once it has become possible to put a more reasonable hypothesis in its place. (48-49)

Oxford and the Literary Renaissance

Looney provided a more comprehensive and believable picture of the English Renaissance than scholars had provided up to that time by showing the critical role that Edward de Vere, Earl of Oxford, played in it. Looney filled in the blanks, showing that Oxford was the missing link between the literary publications of the 1550s and the literary and linguistic revolutions that began in the second half of the 1570s, immediately

---

testimony (whether oral or in writing) can be very unreliable or outright false. At the same time, 'circumstantial' evidence can be extremely powerful and convincing, and is often not prey to the well-known weaknesses affecting 'direct' evidence (e.g., that people often lie, that they often convince themselves to believe untrue things, biases of perception, etc.)" (personal communication, May 26, 2018).

following Oxford's return from Italy. The most important work of English literature since Chaucer (and before the Elizabethan reign) was the collection of poems published in 1557 known as *Tottel's Miscellany: Songs and Sonnets written by the right Honourable Lord Henry Howard the late Earle of Surrey and Others*. In *The Merry Wives of Windsor* a character says, "I had rather than forty shillings I had my Book of Songs and Sonnets here," thereby establishing a link between Shakespeare and *Tottel's Miscellany*. Looney established the connection between the Earl of Surrey, the principal author of that book, and Oxford; Surrey had married Oxford's father's sister and so was Oxford's uncle by marriage. He strengthened that connection by noting that "Surrey's life was associated with Windsor Castle, where Oxford had been brought to court as a royal ward in 1562," and by noting that *Merry Wives*, "the play which furnishes the most precise Shakespearean topography gives not the environment of William Shakspere's early poetic life, but of Edward de Vere's, and the poetry to which direct reference is made is not of William Shakspere's period, but of the period of the Earl of Oxford."[31]

Surrey was also the creator of the form of the English sonnet known as "Shakespeare's," establishing yet another link between Shakespeare and Oxford, and between Oxford and the birth of the English Renaissance.

The revival of literary activities in the 1570s was marked by the publication in 1573 of Bedingfield's translation of *Cardanus Comforte* and George Gascoigne's *A Hundreth Sundrie Flowers*, the first collection of poetry published in the Elizabethan era. Bedingfield's translation was published "by commaundement of the right honourable the Earle of Oxenford," and Oxfordian scholar Capt. Bernard M. Ward made a persuasive case that Oxford, not Gascoigne, was the publisher, editor and principal author of *A Hundreth Sundrie Flowers*. Ward also documented that Oxford was the producer of theatrical entertainment in Queen Elizabeth's court, and that the first public theaters, built on the Italian model, were constructed in London soon after Oxford's return from Italy in 1576. Other Oxfordian scholars established that Oxford was the patron of more writers of literary and historical works, and composers, than any other Elizabethan courtier.

Oxford, then, was the literary sun around whom the English Renaissance began and flourished. He was not merely a courtier with poetic tendencies, as Sir Sidney Lee would have it, but someone who stood at the heart of the intellectual and literary and artistic life of the Elizabethan Age. As Gerald Rendall, one of the preeminent scholars in England at the time *"Shakespeare" Identified* was published, would write a decade later, "Only lately has it become plain how central a place belongs to Edward de Vere, 17th Earl of Oxford, at the confluence of the various currents of literary activity—poetic, dramatic, exotic, and academic—which combine to form the product known as 'Elizabethan.' Student, poet, playwright, and patron of the drama, he was in touch with the most versatile spirits of the age, and in the judgment of his best-informed contemporaries his own compositions were second to none in excellence."[32]

IX

Restoration of Oxford's Character and Reputation

In identifying Edward de Vere, 17th Earl of Oxford, as Shakespeare and in bringing the details of his life to light, Looney corrected a great injustice. "The discovery of the author

---

[31] J. Thomas Looney (editor), *The Poems of Edward de Vere* (1921), p. xlvii.
[32] Gerald H. Rendall, *Shakespeare Sonnets and Edward de Vere* (1930), pp. 291-92.

and the establishing of his just claims to honour is," he wrote, "a duty which mankind owes to one of the most illustrious of men" (71). "Many generous pronouncements on 'Shakespeare' already made, being almost wholly inferred from the plays he has left us, must in all honesty be passed on to Edward de Vere when he is accepted as the author. They are his by right. We cannot go back upon the judgments that have been so passed upon 'Shakespeare,' simply because it transpires that the Stratford man is not he. . . . What the world has written in this connection it has written, and must be prepared to stand by" (343-44).

Concluding *"Shakespeare" Identified*, Looney stated that he had no doubt that when the Oxfordian claim is "tried in public by means of a discussion in which expert opinion must play a large part in the formation of a definitive judgment, the ultimate verdict will be to proclaim Edward de Vere, Seventeenth Earl of Oxford, as the real author of the greatest masterpieces in English literature" (423).

3

"Shakespeare" Identified:
Launching and First Impact, Spring, 1920

Shaping the Manuscript for Publication

By the middle of 1918 J. Thomas Looney had the manuscript of *"Shakespeare" Identified* complete enough to submit to publishers. Among those to whom he sent it was "one of the foremost English publishers." That publisher, "foreseeing the handle" Looney's "patronymic . . . would provide for the critics," wanted him "to adopt a nom-de-plume." Friends had also made the same recommendation. He "declined very decidedly," later explaining why to Charles Wisner Barrell:

> One of my chief reasons for refusing to make the concession was that the people for whom I write are not the kind of people to whom the mere name of a writer would make any difference: & I think the high standard of the first converts to my views has justified the stand I took. Another reason was the great respect I felt for others who have borne the name, & for whom I had no reason to be ashamed, either for their wisdom or probity.[1]

After the manuscript was considered and refused by several publishers, Looney, wanting "to ensure that the results achieved would not be lost, and also to safeguard what I believed to be my priority of discovery" (v) of Edward de Vere's authorship, deposited a sealed envelope describing his discovery with Frederick G. Kenyon, Librarian of the British Museum, in mid-December 1918. He also had printed a two-page statement titled *"Shakespeare" Identified: A Preliminary Notice*. Dated December 14, 1918, it stated, in part:

> As a result of special investigations conducted during the war, I have every reason to believe that I have succeeded in discovering the actual writer of the plays hitherto attributed to William Shakespeare of Stratford. The evidence having been collected and put together, all questions of publication were put aside until the end of the war. Being unable, however, to proceed immediately with the publication, I have deemed it advisable to make an *ad interim* announcement of the bare fact of the discovery; any incomplete statement of particulars being for several reasons undesirable.[2]

The *Notice* also included excerpts from Looney's correspondence with Kenyon in which the latter stated that while he could not take custody of the sealed envelope in an official capacity, he had "no objection to keeping it in a safe place" and also told him that

---

[1] J. Thomas Looney, letter to Charles Wisner Barrell, June 6, 1937. Since the 1940s, Looney's family name has been pronounced in the United States as "Lōny," to rhyme with Sony or Tony. The correct pronunciation, though, rhymes with the names of the actors Mickey Rooney and George Clooney. That is the way that Looney and his family pronounced it then, and it is the way that his descendants pronounce it today. Given Looney's insistence on publishing his findings under his real name regardless of the drawbacks of doing so, it would be a sign of respect to him to pronounce his name the way he did.

[2] Two copies of this *Preliminary Notice* are known to exist. One is in the British Library, tucked inside its copy of *"Shakespeare" Identified*. The other is in the library at Cambridge University.

"You are quite at liberty to mention the fact and date of the deposit of your statement in my hands." In concluding the *Notice*, Looney stated: "In making this announcement, my first duty is to thank Sir F. G. Kenyon for his kind assistance in the matter, and to assure the public that there will be no unnecessary delay in publishing the full statement." In *"Shakespeare" Identified* he further expressed his indebtedness to Kenyon "for the freedom from anxiety that I have enjoyed whilst further developing the argument and carrying through its publication" (v).

Then, probably early in 1919, William Heinemann, Publisher, expressed interest in the manuscript. After examining it he asked Looney to write another chapter describing the weakness of the case for William Shakspere's authorship. Looney submitted the new chapter at the end of April 1919. Its receipt was acknowledged by C. S. Evans, who explained that he could not tell him "whether our firm will undertake the publication of the book or not . . . until I have consulted Mr. Heinemann. This I propose to do without delay, and will let you know the decision as soon as may be."[3]

Evans also stated his objections to the book, which demonstrated how resistant many people were to be to Looney's position. "Personally," Evans wrote, "I have always thought that all normal probabilities are in support of the Stratfordian hypothesis and the chief argument in favour of Shakespeare being the author of his own works seems to be the mere fact that the contrary assumption is against probability." Evans appeared not to have read the manuscript carefully, as he believed that Shakspere was widely known as a playwright during his lifetime and that Looney's theory was that he had presented work "not his own" in the same manner that a schoolboy might submit as his own work a paper written by somebody else.

Evans went on to say that "I confess that I am hardly convinced by your arguments, although it certainly seems to me that you have established a body of circumstantial evidence which ought not lightly to be brushed aside. . . . Whether they are more than coincidences, I frankly confess that I do not consider myself competent to judge." He also raised two concerns that would later be raised by many readers and reviewers: "The motive for the disguise—if disguise there was—must have been a strong one, and it does not seem to me that you have made out your case in this connection;" and, as the "knowledge of this deception must have been shared by a considerable number of persons," how could it be that "no contemporary hint is given of the mystery surrounding the authorship?" These "why" and "how" questions would arise repeatedly, and even today remain the subjects of the greatest controversy among Oxfordians.

Evans said that the company "will probably [need to consult with] an expert on Elizabethan literature" before a decision on the book could be made.

In the end, Heinemann decided not to publish *"Shakespeare" Identified*; it was published ten months later, in March 1920, by Cecil Palmer.

Enter Cecil Palmer

It wasn't until thirty-two years later that an account surfaced of how the book reached Cecil Palmer's hands. Speaking to a group of Oxfordians in 1951, Palmer explained that he had been rung up by William Heinemann, who'd informed him that he had a manuscript which he thought was very good. Heinemann could hardly publish it, though,

---

[3] C. S. Evans, letter to J. Thomas Looney, May 1, 1919. The signature is hard to read; "Evans" is my best guess as to the writer's name.

because of his associations, his principal reader being Sir Edmund Gosse, a prominent English poet, author and critic, and staunch Stratfordian. Heinemann thought that nobody would give Looney's manuscript more sympathetic consideration than Mr. Palmer.[4]

Palmer read it at once, and wrote to Looney describing it as "a lovely book—one of the best Anti-Stratfordian books" he had ever read. He had found a few things to correct—a rather pedestrian style and other errors that only a schoolmaster could commit is how he explained it to his audience, though it's not known exactly how he phrased it to Looney—and asked if he would like a revision to be made. Looney replied that Palmer could do what he liked; Palmer then revised it without changing any of the arguments. It was, he told his audience, now less like a schoolboy's essay and more resembling an undergraduate's thesis. Concerning Palmer's preparation of the book for publication, Looney later wrote that Palmer's relationship "to the undertaking has been much more than that of publisher. When the case was laid before him he adopted its conclusions with enthusiasm and made the case his own. My personal obligations to him are therefore very considerable" (6).

Sir William Richmond, K.C.B., R.A., a friend to whom Palmer gave a copy of the book shortly after it was published, commented that "I think the man's right, but why has he got such an awful name. Is it a hoax? Did you write it?" Palmer denied writing it, but had difficulty in persuading Richmond that his denial was genuine, and, he told his audience, he had never been able to live down the moment when he became unorthodox. Palmer had indeed gained some renown or notoriety as the publisher of Looney's book. An obituary observed that "he came early to public repute as a young publisher of vision and enterprise, and [was] especially interested in the Shakespearian contro-versies."[5] In a letter to Sir Sidney Lee in 1921 he asked if Lee knew that he was the

---

Cecil Clifford Palmer

Born: 1887. Died: January 18, 1952.
Age when *"Shakespeare" Identified* was published: 37

Publisher, lecturer, author, translator.
Published most of the first dozen Oxfordian books.
Founder and executive officer of The Society of Individualists.

Notable Books by Palmer
1932: *Post Office Reform*
1938: *The Truth About Writing*
1944: *The Debit Side of the Beveridge Report*
1943: *Implications of the Catering Wages Bill*
1952: *The British Socialist Ill-fare State*

Works Translated
1915: *National Proverbs: Holland* (tr. With Frank Palmer}
1946: Diego Valer's *A Sentimental Guide to Venice*
1947: Imre Reiner's *Woodcut Engraving, A Contribution to the History of the Art*
1951: Fritz Ernest's *European Switzerland, Historically Considered*

---

[4] "Cecil Palmer," *Shakespeare Fellowship News-Letter*, March 1952, p. 4.
[5] Obituary of Cecil Palmer, *Truth*, January 1952, quoted in "Cecil Palmer," *SF News-Letter* (English), March 1952, p. 4.

publisher of *"Shakespeare" Identified*. Lee replied, "Of course I know that you are the publisher of Mr. Looney's book."[6]

Why did Cecil Palmer, British publisher, author, and lecturer decide to publish *"Shakespeare" Identified* when other publishers had decided not to? The profit motive played a part, certainly, but perhaps also he was receptive to a book on such a controversial subject because he was already infused with the ideas that led him to become, in 1942, a founder and executive officer of the Society of Individualists, an organization dedicated to independent thought and individual freedom.

After *"Shakespeare" Identified*, Palmer went on to publish another twenty-five books on the authorship question, many of them supporting the Oxfordian claim.

Books About Shakespeare Published by Cecil Palmer		
1920	J. Thomas Looney	*"Shakespeare" Identified*
1921	Sir George Greenwood	*Ben Jonson and Shakespeare*
1921	J. Thomas Looney, J. (ed.)	*The Poems of Edward de Vere*
1921	Colin Still	*Shakespeare's Mystery Play; a Study of The Tempest*
1923	Sir George Greenwood	*Lee, Shakespeare and a Tertium Quid*
1923	Capt. Hubert H. Holland	*Shakespeare Through Oxford Glasses*
1923	Col. Bernard R. Ward	*The Mystery of "Mr. W. H."*
1925	Edward Ge. Harman	*The Impersonality of Shakespeare*
1927	Georges A. Connes	*The Shakespeare Mystery*
1928	Percy Allen	*Shakespeare, Jonson and Wilkins as Borrowers*
1929	Percy Allen	*Shakespeare and Chapman as Topical Dramatists*
1929	Alfred Mudie	*Self-named William Shakespeare*
1929	Bertram Theobald	*Shake-speare's Sonnets Unmasked*
1930	Percy Allen	*The Case for Edward de Vere as "William Shakespeare"*
1930	Eva Turner Clark	*Shakespeare's Plays in the Order of Their Writing*
1930	Roderick Eagle	*Shakespeare: New Views for Old*
1930	Gilbert Standen	*Shakespeare Authorship*
1930	Bertram Theobald	*Francis Bacon Concealed and Revealed*
1931	Percy Allen	*The Oxford-Shakespeare Case Corroborated*
1931	Col. Montagu W. Douglas	*The Earl of Oxford as "Shakespeare"*
1931	George Frisbee	*Edward de Vere*
1931	Gerald H. Rendall	*Shake-speare: Handwriting and Spelling*
1931	Gilbert Slater	*Seven Shakespeares*
1931	Bertram Theobald	*Exit Shakespeare*
1932	Percy Allen	*The Life Story of Edward de Vere as "William Shakespeare"*
1932	Edward D. Johnson	*The First Folio of Shake-speare*
1932	George W. Phillips	*The Tragic Story of "Shakespeare" Disclosed in the Sonnets*
1932	Bertram Theobald	*Enter Francis Bacon*

Palmer's Marketing Strategy

"Shakespeare" Identified in Edward de Vere, Seventeenth Earl of Oxford was published by Cecil Palmer in London on March 4, 1920. Three printings are known. The two printings for general sale are almost identical and can be distinguished only by the gold or black lettering on the cover and spine. A third printing was prepared specially for the Times Book Club. This edition, with a dark blue cover and slightly smaller outer dimensions (the pages inside are exactly the same except for slightly small margins) was apparently prepared for sale by the Times Book Club to its members through subscription

---

[6] Sir Sidney Lee, letter to Cecil Palmer, June 13, 1921.

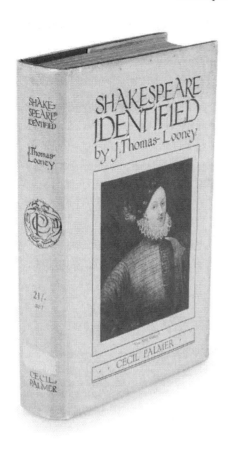

and to members and non-members at its two London stores.[7]

Palmer went all-out to promote Looney's book. Review copies were sent to all the principal critics and bookstores in Great Britain; full-page ads were placed in trade publications such as *Publishers' Circular, Books of Today, Books of the Month* and *Menzies Monthly Book List*. Large ads were placed in the *Times Literary Supplement* and *The Bookman* on March 4. In a letter ten days before the book was released, Palmer told Looney that, "It is with very great pleasure that I am able to send your six presentation copies of *"Shakespeare" Identified*. You would have had them a day or two earlier but for the fact that the whole office has been preoccupied with an immense amount of advance propaganda work in connection with the book."[8]

Palmer continued to place ads in literary journals through the spring. He even placed full page advertisements on the end pages of several books he published on other subjects. His extraordinary efforts to promote Looney's book were recognized at the time. *The Publishers' Circular* commented that,

> [i]t is always a good thing for an author when he can get his publisher to take a personal interest in his work, and from the Preface to Mr. Looney's book, as well as from Palmer's letter to us, it is evident that [Palmer] is convinced that Mr. L. has discovered, uncovered, and covered with glory the name of Edward de Vere, 17th Earl of Oxford."[9]

Cecil Palmer's Advertising of *"Shakespeare" Identified* in 1920	
(only the first appearance in each publication is listed)	
February 28	*The Publishers' Circular* — Cecil Palmer ad for SI
March	*The Bookseller* — Cecil Palmer ad for SI
March 4	*The Times Literary Supplement* — Cecil Palmer ad for SI
May 8	*The Publishers' Circular* — Cecil Palmer ad
June	*The Bookman* — Cecil Palmer ad
June 19	*Notes and Queries* — Times Book Club ad lists SI third
August 14	*The Publisher's Circular* — Cecil Palmer ad
December	*The Bookman* — Cecil Palmer ad

[7] In a similar practice, the Book of the Month Club and the Literary Guild in the United States sold special printings of selected books to their members when I subscribed to those services in the early 1980s.

[8] Cecil Palmer, letter to J. Thomas Looney, Feb. 23, 1920.

[9] "'Shakespeare' Identified in Edward de Vere," *Publishers' Circular*, March 6, 1920, p. 233.

The *Circular* also published the letter Palmer sent to it and other trade publications along with review copies.

> Dear Sir,—I am sending for your acceptance a copy of a work entitled *"Shakespeare" Identified*, which I venture to think will repay your consideration and notice. It is my intention to publish the book on Thursday, March 5th,[10] and I shall be glad therefore, if you will be good enough to withhold from publication any review you may write until that date. My object in sending this advance copy is, obviously, in order that you may have full opportunity to read the book at leisure, since I am conscious that your task as critic of a work of scholarship of this nature is a peculiarly responsible one. If there is any additional information which would prove of assistance I shall be glad to give it on hearing from you.— I am, with compliments, faithfully you.   CECIL PALMER.

The Circular granted Palmer's request and held its review until the March 6 issue. Its reviewer stated that he had "read Mr. Looney's book with much interest" and found that his arguments "furnish us with many apt comparisons and parallels." But, he concluded, "before that legitimate doubt can be converted into the belief that Shakespeare was only the adopted name of another writer, much more must be done."[11] For him, Looney's arguments "are as nothing compared with . . . the testimony of Shakespeare's contemporaries. [We cannot throw] Jonson's testimony overboard."

H. D. S., the reviewer for another trade publication, *The Bookseller: A Newspaper of British and Foreign Literature*, initially appeared to admire Looney's book.

> The preparation of this book has obviously entailed much labour. . . . His style is lucid, the arrangement of his book leaves nothing to be desired, and his points are clearly and forcibly put. He has spared himself no pains in the pursuit of his investigation, and nowhere lays himself open to the charge of having wilfully distorted the evidence. . . . There can be no question as to the sincerity of the author's belief that

CECIL PALMER.

AN IMPORTANT ANNOUNCEMENT.

SHAKESPEARE IDENTIFIED

By J. THOMAS LOONEY.

Demy 8vo. Cloth. 552 pages. 21s. net. ILLUSTRATED.

PUBLISHED TO-DAY OF ALL Booksellers and Libraries.

For the first time the methods of what may be called *practical scientific investigation* have been applied to the search for the ACTUAL AUTHOR of the works hitherto attributed to WILLIAM SHAKESPEARE of Stratford-on-Avon.

A NEW THEORY and a new method of research have produced evidence which in the mind of the author, and in the minds of others to whom the evidence has been submitted, leaves no reasonable doubt that the problem has at last been solved.

OAKLEY HOUSE, BLOOMSBURY ST., W.C.1.

---

[10] The date was later changed to Wednesday, March 4.
[11] "'Shakespeare' Identified in Edward de Vere, the 17th Earl of Oxford," *Publishers' Circular*, March 6, 1920, p. 233.

he has at last solved "the Shakespeare problem," nor can there be any doubt of his conviction that he has here produced evidence in support of his candidate's claims so overwhelming that it needs must prove as irresistible to others as it has to himself.[12]

In the end, though, he reached a negative verdict not only about Looney's conclusions, but also concerning the validity of almost every point of his evidence and reasoning.

> Nevertheless, nothing appears to us less likely than the realisation of his confident anticipation that the world will henceforth proclaim Edward de Vere "the real author of the greatest masterpieces in English literature."
>
> [Looney's] knowledge of the Elizabethan drama and of Elizabethan literature generally is of the most superficial sort. . . . [W]hen he comes to the documentary evidence upon which he rests his identification of Shakespeare with de Vere, his lack of expert knowledge becomes painfully evident. The value of "parallels" as a clue to authorship cannot be gainsaid; in the hands of a judicious critic they frequently yield most valuable results. But without a wide reading of Elizabethan authors, no critic can hope to be able to distinguish between parallels that are significant (whether of plagiarism or identity of authorship) and those merely casual and accidental. The resemblances between de Vere's poems and Shakespeare's plays triumphantly cited by Mr. Looney as proof of their common authorship are utterly worthless, being no more remarkable than a comparison of the work of any two Elizabethan poets, chosen at random, would afford.

That such a review by a reviewer clearly less knowledgeable about Elizabethan literature than Looney could appear in *The Bookseller* must have alerted Looney and Palmer to the uphill battle they faced.

First Reviews of *"Shakespeare" Identified*

Cecil Palmer's publicity campaign resulted in sixty reviews of *"Shakespeare" Identified* in England, Scotland, Wales and Ireland in 1920. Most of them ran in the first three months after its publication. Eight appeared on Wednesday, March 4, the day of publication, with another ten coming out the following two days. By one account it was "reviewed at greater length than any other book recently published."[13]

Reviews were mostly of two types. First were general reviews that appeared in newspapers; they were mostly unsigned and written by staff reviewers without special knowledge of Shakespeare. They appeared in papers throughout the British Isles—a testament to the thoroughness of Cecil Palmer's publicity effort—including *The Times*, *The Sunday Times*, *The Scotsman*, *The Yorkshire Post and Leeds Intelligencer* and *The Irish Times*—and are representative of the reaction by the general public to the Oxfordian idea. The second were critical assessments of the book by literary scholars, often Shakespeare specialists, which appeared in weekly literary magazines, including *The Times Literary Supplement*, *The Athenaeum*, *The Spectator* and *The Bookman's Journal*, as well as in newspapers. The Oxfordian idea was also mentioned in many other places—articles, letters to editors, notices of recently published or acquired books—throughout the final nine months of 1920.

Many reviewers were puzzled by *"Shakespeare" Identified*. Was the author serious? Was "Looney" his real name? How could the author of Shakespeare's works be someone

---

[12] H. D. S., [review of *"Shakespeare" Identified*], *The Bookseller*, March 1920, p. 147-48.
[13] Cecil Palmer advertisement, *Publishers' Circular*, Aug. 14, 1920, p. 160.

nobody had ever heard of? Many felt they lacked the expertise to evaluate Looney's claims. Some had examined and rejected the Baconian claim, or, worse, had accepted it only to see the case for Bacon collapse. Once burned, twice shy was their approach to the authorship question. If Oxford had indeed been Shakespeare, many wondered, why had he hidden his authorship, and how could it have remained hidden for more than 300 years? Many thought Looney's answers to these questions not entirely persuasive.

Other reviewers, principally those with more specialized knowledge of Shakespeare's works, were dismissive of Looney's claims. Thus arose a paradox: Those most knowledgeable and thus most capable of judging the Oxfordian claim were also those with the most significant vested interests in the traditional Stratfordian story and with the most to lose if the Oxfordian claim turned out to be correct. Others remained staunch believers in Shakspere's authorship, their beliefs unshaken by the case made against him by Sir George Greenwood or Looney. Not all reviewers were cordial; some were quite the opposite: dismissive, ill-informed, and condescending as they attacked Looney's conclusion, evidence and reasoning. Even many of those who maintained a higher degree of civility appeared not to have read the book carefully (if at all) before reviewing it.

There were also those precious few who were largely convinced by the evidence presented in *"Shakespeare" Identified*. The short notice in *The Hull Daily Mail* on the day of publication, for instance, stated that, "Mr. J. Thomas Cooney [sic] . . . almost proves that Shakespeare's works were written by Edward de Vere, the 17th Earl of Oxford."[14] *The Halifax Evening Courier* believed that "Mr. Looney certainly makes out a far stronger case for Oxford than has ever been made out for Bacon. . . . It will be interesting to see what the Stratfordian stalwarts have to say."[15] The beginning of the review in the *Manchester Guardian*—"It is impossible not to like, and even to admire, Mr. Looney"—was unusual for the admiration it expressed for him even while doubting the soundness of his conclusion.

Looney carefully monitored reactions to the book, and during the spring of 1920 responded with a dozen letters to editors or articles correcting ill-informed reviewers and defending the Oxfordian claim. By the time of his death in January 1944 he had written more than fifty such pieces, some quite lengthy.[16] A nearby text box lists a dozen reviews in nine publications to which Looney responded in the spring of 1920.

One mistake or misunderstanding common to many reviewers was that "Shakespeare = Shakspere," i.e., that all references to the writer William Shakespeare were references to William Shakspere of Stratford-upon-Avon. Another was the "Shakespeare didn't write his own plays" line, in which reviewers incorrectly believed Looney to be saying that William Shakespeare had presented work "not his own" in the same way that a schoolboy might submit as his own work a paper written by somebody else. Another is the "coincidences" line, as though the depiction in the plays of events that had actually occurred in the life of Edward de Vere could not be more than similarities arising through mere chance. Yet another common theme was the "doubters are snobs" charge—that doubters who posited candidates for authorship who were members of the nobility did so because they believed that someone of yeoman stock could not have written the works.

---

[14] *Hull Daily Mail*, March 4, 1920, p. 4. The notice is untitled.
[15] "The Real Shakespeare," *Halifax Evening Courier*, March 4, 1920, p. 4.
[16] For the full text of these letters and articles, as well as a description of how they were uncovered, see *"Shakespeare" Revealed: The Collected Articles and Published Letters of J. Thomas Looney* (2019), edited by the author of this book.

Text of the ads in *The Publishers' Circular* and *The Bookseller*

The problem of the authorship of the plays and poems hitherto known as Shakespeare's has of late been forcing itself to the front and the number of people who have abandoned the old ideas on the subject forms now a large and growing section of the reading public. For the first time, however, the methods of what may be called practical scientific investigation have been applied to the search for the actual author: and with surprising results. Feeling his way at first with great caution and much diffidence, but according to a pre-arranged plan, Mr. J. Thomas Looney chose lyric poetry as his guide in the great quest, and was led to the selection of one of the best of the Elizabethan poets as the probable author of our great national dramas. The way in which evidence immediately poured in justifying this selection, forming as it did so many converging lines of argument, produced in his own mind and has since produced in the mind of others to whom the evidence has been submitted, so decided a conviction that it seems hardly possible to doubt that the problem with which he deals has at last been solved.

If this be so the publication of this work will constitute a landmark in the history of the world's literature, and its importance from this point of view has determined the form in which the author presents his argument. It is given, that is to say primarily, as a work of research, intended to represent something of the actual process of investigation and to be judged mainly from the standpoint of its central idea: a contingent object, however, being to secure fitting national recognition and a more accurate judgment of the character and personality of the man whose work will be England's most enduring glory. Recognising the fact that this is not merely a literary man's question, the author of "SHAKESPEARE" IDENTIFIED, whilst avoiding the artifices of "popular exposition," has addressed himself to the general reader and sought to satisfy the requirements of research rather than the demands of literary criteria.

Still another was the magic wand of genius—that sophisticated understandings of Italy, the law and courtly pursuits portrayed in the plays could have been acquired almost overnight through the magic of "genius."

And there were jibes at Looney's family name; many recognized that it was beside the point, but sheepishly couldn't stop themselves. *The Scotsman*, for instance, observed that "Mr. Looney's name invites a play on words which the Elizabethan author could not have resisted."[17] Still another was the dismissal of the entire authorship question with the "we have the plays" line, claiming that it didn't matter much who wrote them.

Two other common criticisms merit further discussion; both had been addressed in *"Shakespeare" Identified*.

The 1604 Issue

Many reviewers raised the "1604" issue, claiming that Oxford could not have been Shakespeare because he died in 1604, before some of the plays were written. Had they read *"Shakespeare" Identified* carefully they would have known that Looney had explained that the "1604" issue is actually one of the strongest pieces of evidence supporting Oxford's authorship because the publication of Shakespeare's plays largely ceased in that very year.

> We have a flood of Shakespearean plays being published authentically right up to the year . . . [of] the death of Edward de Vere, then a sudden stop and nothing more published with any appearance of proper authorization for nearly twenty

---

Reviews of *"Shakespeare" Identified* in 1920 to which Looney Responded

The Athenaeum
Review (April 2) → Looney's Response (April 30)

The Bookman's Journal
Review (March 19) → Looney Response (April 9)
Reviewer's Reply (April 16)) → Looney Response (April 23)
Letters by Lee and Robertson (May 21) → Looney's Response (May 21, May 28)

The Daily Telegraph
Review (March 19) → Looney's Response (April 1)

The Saturday Review of Politics, Literature, Science, and Art
Review (March 27) → Looney's Response (April 17)
→ Reviewer's Reply (April 24)

The Scotsman
Review (March 4) → Looney's Response (March 20)

The Spectator
Review (March 27) → Looney's Response (April 10)

The Times Literary Supplement
Review (March 4) → Looney's Response (March 25)

The Western Mail
Review (April 23) → Looney's Response (May 6)

The Yorkshire Post and Leeds Intelligencer
Review (March 4, 5, 6) → Looney's Response (March 11)
Review (March 11) → Looney's Response (April 1)

---

[17] "Shakespeare Identified," *The Scotsman*, March 4, 1920, p. 2.

years. . . . We have no hesitation in saying that the simple fact we have enunciated in our last sentence furnishes an argument it is hardly possible to strengthen further. (357)

Looney also cited Stratfordian scholars who believed that 1604 marked a crisis of some sort in Shakspere's life.

> Not only does the time of the death of de Vere mark an arrest in the publication of "Shakespeare's" works, it also marks, according to orthodox authorities, some kind of a crisis in the affairs of William Shakspere. Charles and Mary Cowden Clarke, in the "Life of Shakspere" published in their edition of the plays, date his retirement to Stratford in the year 1604 precisely. After pointing out that in 1605 he is described as "William Shakspere, Gentleman, of Stratford-on-Avon," they continued: 'Several things conduced to make him resolve upon ceasing to be an actor, and 1604 has generally been considered the date when he did so." (359-60)

He noted further that "Several other writers, less well known, repeat this date; and works of reference, written for the most part some years ago, place his retirement in the same year: 'There is no doubt he never meant to return to London, except for business visits after 1604' (*National Encyclopedia*)" (360).

Looney emphasized that no one knows when Shakespeare's plays were actually written. The usual dates are those devised by Edmond Malone and Sir Edmund Chambers, who assigned dates of composition that would fit easily into the lifetime of William Shakspere. But if he wasn't the author, then their timeline is of little value. Furthermore, Stratfordian scholar Sir Walter Raleigh had already stated that many of Shakespeare's plays were finished by other hands after his death, which could easily account for references to events taking place after 1604:

> At the beginning of his career Shakespeare made very free use of the work of other men. . . . Towards the end of his career his work is once more found mixed with the work of other men, but this time there is generally reason to suspect that it is these others that have laid him under contribution, altering his completed plays, or completing his unfinished work by additions of their own.[18]

The Tempest

Why were so many reviewers unable to understand what Looney wrote? A case in point is the Appendix in *"Shakespeare" Identified* dealing with *The Tempest*. The reviewer of *The Publishers' Circular*, making a mistake that many others were to make, wrote that, "Mr. Looney, unable to find a place for it without upsetting his galley, calmly throws *The Tempest* overboard."[19] The *Aberdeen Daily Journal* made the same claim, adding, "For by almost universal consent *The Tempest* is the most genuinely Shakespearean of all the Shakespeare plays."[20] Their common belief was that Looney's conclusion that Oxford hadn't written *The Tempest* was an evasion designed to sweep under the rug a fact that didn't fit with the Oxfordian timeline.

Looney had, however, cited four respected scholars who placed the play before 1604. He had rejected the play as Shakespeare's not because of the supposed date of composition but because of what he saw as its "un-Shakespearean" elements.

---

[18] Sir Walter Raleigh, *Shakespeare* (1907), p. 109, quoted in *"Shakespeare" Identified* (2018), p. 454.

[19] *The Publishers' Circular*, "'Shakespeare' Identified in Edward de Vere," March 6, 1920, p. 237.

[20] "Shakespeare," *Aberdeen Daily Journal*, April 5, 1920, p. 5.

We are prepared to maintain, then, on the strength of the various points indicated, that *The Tempest* is no play of "Shakespeare's." It is not the absence of an odd Shakespearean characteristic, but the absence of so many dominant marks of his work, along with the presence of several features which are quite contrary to his style, that compels us to reject it. (452)

Reviews in Three Important Publications

We now turn to three representative reviews and Looney's responses to them.

The Times Literary Supplement's First Response

The Times Literary Supplement, the most important literary journal in England, ran more pieces—forty—mentioning the Oxfordian idea than any other publication during the 1920s, and its coverage grew increasingly respectful over time. It never really accepted the idea of Edward de Vere as Shakespeare, though; its coverage became more favorable over time only because it started with outright rejection of the Oxfordian idea. One sentence in its March 4 review—written by Alfred W. Pollard, one of the most prominent Shakespeare scholars of the day—captured the spirit of orthodox Shakespearean scholarly opinion: "Fundamentally it is a sad waste of print and paper."[21]

Reviews of and Commentary on *"Shakespeare" Identified* in Great Britain, 1920

March	*Bookseller* – H. D. S.	March 20	*New Statesman*
March 4	*Halifax Evening Courier*		*Saturday Westminster Gazette*
	Liverpool Echo	March 27	*Saturday Review*
	Pall Mall Gazette		*Spectator*
	Scotsman	April 1	*Essex Review*—W. Gurney
	Sunderland Daily Echo		Benham
	Times Literary Supplement —		*Morning Post*
	Alfred W. Pollard	April 2	*Athenaeum*
	Yorkshire Evening Post	April 4	*Sunday Times*—H. C. Minchin
	Yorkshire Post and Leeds	April 5	*Aberdeen Daily Journal*
	Intelligencer [two reviews]	April 10	*Christian Science Monitor*
March 5	*Derby Daily Telegraph*	April 12	*Birmingham Daily Gazette*
	Newcastle Daily Chronicle		*Nottingham Evening Post* — C. B.
	Yorkshire Post and Leeds		*Sheffield Daily Telegraph*
	Intelligencer — J. M. Robertson	April 13	*Yorkshire Post and Leeds Int.*
March 6	*Aberdeen Press and Journal*	April 16	*Bookman's Journal*
	Burnley Express and Advertiser	April 17	*Boston Guardian*
	Coventry Herald	April 22	*Nottingham Journal*
	Hull Daily Mail	April 23	*Western Mail* — C. B.
	Publishers' Circular	May 7	*Christian Science Monitor*
	Sheffield Evening Telegraph		*Irish Times*
	Yorkshire Post and Leeds Int.	May 21	*Bookman's Journal* — Sir Sidney
March 12	*Derbyshire Advertiser and Journal*		Lee, J. M. Robertson [letters]
March 13	*Derbyshire Advertiser and Journal*	May 24	*Sheffield Daily Telegraph*
March 15	*Evening Telegraph*	June	*Baconiana* — J. R.
March 17	*Sketch* — Keble Howard	Sept. 2	*Western Daily Press*
March 19	*Bookman's Journal*	Sept. 4	*Town Talk*
	Daily Telegraph — W. L. Courtney	October	*Commonwealth* — Gordon
	Manchester Guardian — C. H. Herford		Crosse
	Nottingham Journal		*New Forest Magazine*
		Dec. 2	*New Age* – R. H. C.

---

[21] Alfred W. Pollard, "Another 'Identification' of Shakespeare," *Times Literary Sup.*, March 4, 1920, p. 149.

After describing Looney's method of setting out to find what he believed to be the true author, Pollard attacked Looney for something Looney had never said and made a series of statements that no scholar should have made. One was citing Looney's modest acknowledgment that when he began his study of the authorship question he had little knowledge of Elizabethan literature, implying that the case was being presented by someone who did not know what he was talking about. The reality is that regardless of the level of Looney's knowledge when he began his investigation, no one without expert knowledge of the period could possibly have written the detailed analysis and comparisons of Oxford's poetry with that of Shakespeare, Lyly, Munday and other writers whose works were discussed in *"Shakespeare" Identified*.

Another of Pollard's nonsensical statements was that "Almost any man's life could be illustrated from Shakespeare's plays, and Mr. Looney makes them illustrate the life of the Earl of Oxford." If that is so, Looney responded in a letter to the *Supplement*, please explain why "It has been impossible to do anything of the kind for either William Shakespeare or Francis Bacon."[22] Continuing, Pollard wrote that "There was a wealth of thought and phrases and tricks of style common to most of the Elizabethan verse-writers; and Mr. Looney has no difficulty in finding parallels between the handful of poems attributed to the Earl of Oxford and Shakespeare's."[23] Looney responded by noting that "Those on the loss of his good name, which are vital, are certainly not common; there is probably no other similar example."[24] He returned to the subject at greater length in his *The Poems of Edward de Vere* issued a year later, demonstrating that the phrases to which Pollard referred became stock in trade only after being introduced by Edward de Vere. He was the earliest and best of the courtier poets, who preceded the non-courtier poets.

Pollard then nitpicked at a few points, including the "1604" issue, while ignoring the massive evidence from multiple lines of investigation—poetic, biographical, chronological—that Looney had accumulated. The review appeared on March 4, 1920, the day the book was published, thus setting the tone for academia's coverage of it and its dismissal of the Oxfordian idea. Given its initial harsh assessment, the *Supplement*'s softening stance over the next two decades is an untold story. So, too, is the snap back to intolerance as shown by its reprinting of the initial review on March 4, 2020, exactly one hundred years after it had first appeared, without also reprinting Looney's response, thereby denying him the same chance to respond that it had given him one hundred years earlier.

The Yorkshire Post and Leeds Intelligencer

This publication, the largest-circulation newspaper in northern England, ran six pieces on *"Shakespeare" Identified* within a week of its being published—coverage extensive enough to range from hostile to puzzling to accepting of the Oxfordian claim. It had the second most coverage of the thesis in 1920 and the fourth most throughout the decade. It was the only publication other than *The Bookman's Journal* to run more than one letter from Looney.

The first review began with a comment that was on target and would, at the same time, prove to be something of an understatement: "There is published today a book which is likely to make a stir, not only in the professional ranks of Stratfordians and

---

[22] J. Thomas Looney, "'Shakespeare' Identified," *Times Literary Supplement*, March 25, 1920, p. 201.
[23] Pollard (1920), p. 149.
[24] Looney, *Times Literary Supplement* (1920), p. 201.

Baconians . . . but among the public generally."[25] The review noted public skepticism of both Stratfordian and Baconian authorship, observing that the "dissatisfaction so commonly felt with the orthodox theory of Shakespeare's life and art has grown considerably in the last twenty years, and has been felt by many who are not Baconians."

Drawing on information in *"Shakespeare" Identified* it showed how Oxford as Shakespeare solved several anomalies: how a child of an illiterate household could have written Shakespeare's plays (the author wasn't from an illiterate household); how the creator could have walked away from his work and his works at the height of his powers (he didn't); how one man could have had the mind of a small-time commercial operator and the mind that created *Hamlet* and *A Midsummer Night's Dream* (they were two different people); and how it could be that no records of Shakspere's social rise and literary career have survived (he wasn't the author).

The reviewer provided a decent introduction to Looney's investigative process and urged readers to examine the full case in the book before making up their minds about his conclusions. "But the true value of the book lies elsewhere," he continued. "The first test of an hypothesis is not whether it is true, but how many isolated facts it correlates and explains. De Vere was actively connected with playwriting and dramatic production from 1580. He was intimate with Anthony Munday, and may very well have written some of his better works. . . . To all who find it impossible to accept William Shakespeare of Stratford, we recommend Mr. Looney's candidate for international fame."

Here, then, was a responsible, informed review by someone who had read and absorbed the information in the book. A day later came something very different in the same newspaper by someone who clearly had not read the book. The Rt. Hon. J. M. Robertson, a member of Parliament and a well-known literary critic. He rightly observed that, having questioned orthodox opinions and attacked vested interests,

> Mr. Looney was doomed to have a hundred critics. . . . His problem will be, not the usual problem, how to avoid neglect, but how to escape from the paddock alive. It is unfortunate for him, of course, that he is not a trained scholar. The scaffolding of his theory will be ripped like cardboard. . . . His pages are strewn with guesses. . . . His scholarship is weak. . . . But there is room, and will always be room, for the innocent among the doctors. We consider it by no means impossible for a bad but enthusiastic scholar to hit, now and then, on the truth.[26]

Robertson was surely right that what mattered was not Looney's scholarly background and prior scholarly attainments, but whether his conclusions were correct. In one of the more positive passages of the review he stated that,

> Mr. Looney, it is true, . . . [has drawn] attention to a very remarkable nobleman and writer hitherto neglected by Elizabethan research. That a man so interesting as this Earl of Oxford, with a character and a career so temptingly illustrative of the whole gamut of Shakespearean emotion, from Mercutio to Hamlet, from laughter to despair; a known writer also of fine lyrics and fine drama, and a leader of the boldest tastes of his day—that such a personality, in this world of thesis writers, should have escaped the net, is a matter for legitimate surprise, and justifies any wonder that Mr. Looney may have felt when he found William Shakespeare, of Stratford, changing to Oxford in his hands.

---

[25] "The Real Shakespeare: Edward de Vere, Earl of Oxford," *Yorkshire Post and Leeds Intelligencer*, March 4, 1920, p. 6.

[26] J. M. Robertson, "New Shakespeare Claim," *Yorkshire Post and Leeds Intelligencer*," March 6, 1920, p. 6.

But Robertson went on to viciously attack Looney's methods, scholarship and findings. Looney responded in a letter printed the following week. It shows just how capably and succinctly he dispensed with Robertson's ill-informed criticism.

> Sir,—I shall not attempt to characterize the tissue of misrepresentations which Mr. J. M. Robertson has permitted to go forth in his name; but as illustrating how much he knows of the book he is criticizing I shall quote one sentence.
>
> "Of the Rutland theory, he (Mr. Looney) summarily disposes, by pointing out that in 1590, when, as he hardily alleges, all the Shakespeare sonnets were written," etc.
>
> Now, not in one place only, but throughout the book, whenever the question of the dates of the sonnets arises, I treat these poems as having been written throughout the period of 1590 to 1604. Indeed, one of the strongest arguments in the work gives an important place to the fact that the last of the series was written in 1603 or 1604. (See pp. 438 and 491.)
>
> If Mr. Robertson had even taken the trouble to read the whole of the sentence from which he quotes he could not have so misrepresented me, for I there say that "in 1590 Roger Manners was only fourteen years of age, and the entire series of Shakespeare's sonnets was brought to a close before he had reached the age of twenty-seven." (Page 443.)
>
> The public may accept this as a fair specimen of Mr. Robertson's knowledge of the contents of my work.—Yours, etc.   J. THOMAS LOONEY[27]

On April 1 the paper printed a letter from a reader critical of Robertson and supporting Looney. "I hope I shall not be thought to belong to Mr. Looney's critics. On the contrary, I hope his book will be widely read, and his claim discussed by competent critics; criticisms of the style of that of Mr. J. M. Robertson, in your issue of the 5th, are singularly ineffective."[28]

On April 1 the *Yorkshire Post* printed a much longer response by Looney to all of its coverage of the book titled "A Reply to Critics and Some New Facts." In it he expressed "a very warm appreciation" to the *Yorkshire Post* for its extensive coverage of the authorship question, which, he wrote,

> indicates clearly a recognition that something more than the mere fate of a book is at stake; that a large national and international issue has been raised which far transcends all questions of literary rivalry. The critics, unfortunately, have not always grasped this view of the matter; hence the acrimonious attacks upon the author as an author, and the book as a book, in the place of an examination of the evidence as evidence.[29]

He also defended his methods and depth of knowledge—"It is, of course, a matter of indifference to the public what may have been the extent of my interest in Elizabethan literature before I began the researches, or even the precise extent of my knowledge when I finished. What does matter is the accuracy of the facts stated, and the question of whether increase of knowledge strengthens or weakens belief in the theory I propound." He then presented newly uncovered evidence in support of the Oxfordian claim in a

---

[27] J. Thomas Looney, "*Shakespeare Identified*," *Yorkshire Post and Leeds Intelligencer*, March 11, 1920, p. 4. Robertson and Looney will tangle again, in *The Bookman's Journal*. See below.

[28] H. E. Thornley, letter, *Yorkshire Post and Leeds Intelligencer*, March 11, 1920, p. 4.

[29] J. Thomas Looney, "Shakespeare Identified: A Reply to Critics and Some New Facts," *Yorkshire Post and Leeds Intelligencer*, April 1, 1920, p. 8.

passage linking Hamlet's stepfather with Oxford's.

> Hamlet, it will be remembered, utters a rhyme in reference to his step-father which ought to have finished with the word "ass." Instead, however, he pauses, and substitutes the word "pajock," a term of contempt for a peacock. Our scholarly Shakespeareans have written much in seeking a reasonable explanation of the substitution, but not with much success. When, however, it is remembered that Oxford's step-father was Sir Charles Tyrrel, and that the peacock's tail is the distinctive feature in the Tyrrel crest, the obscurity disappears under the new theory of authorship.

Looney concluded with a rebuke to orthodox Shakespeare scholars which is as relevant today as it was in 1920.

> The point that matters, however, is that all my study of the personalities and literature of the period has added confirmation to the theory I expound, whilst nothing I have discovered, and nothing my critics have yet pointed out, has disclosed a single serious objection to the theory. . . . I must, however, protest most strongly against the tactics of certain reviewers even in reputable journals who have searched the work for its trivialities, and have put a few of these forward mockingly as constituting the body of the argument, their evident object being to secure the neglect of the work.

> What I aim at presenting is a synthetic argument, the force of which depends upon the reader's knowing all the particulars, and, by an effort on his own part, bringing all these into their right relationship to one another. In the words of the writer who reviewed the work in these columns: "The first test of a theory is the number of isolated facts it correlates and explains." And when a theory so tested survives the test of synthesis; when, that is to say, it is found to be in harmony with all the facts, correlating under every aspect all the phenomena with which it deals, we speak of it as being true. How nearly the de Vere theory comes to this completeness can only be appreciated by those who have taken the necessary time and trouble to learn the particulars, and to assimilate the argument as a whole. Those who have come nearest to such an understanding of it are also those who have come nearest accepting it. The future, therefore, I am confident, is ours. Only let us have the matter properly examined by men who are more anxious for truth than for the defense of their own over-confident past dogmatism.

The Oxfordian Idea in *The Bookman's Journal*

The weekly *Bookman's Journal* ran more coverage of the Oxfordian idea in the months after *"Shakespeare" Identified* was published than any other publication, including a review, excerpts from reviews in four other publications, letters from two well-known Shakespeare scholars, and four letters from Looney—the most he wrote to any publication.[30]

With pieces ranging from positive to actively hostile to the Oxfordian idea, the *Bookman's Journal* coverage is a microcosm of the impact the Oxfordian idea had in its first year. The first piece on the subject, a review of *"Shakespeare" Identified* on March 19, was one of the most welcoming pieces to appear anywhere.

> This is a remarkable book. . . . Mr. Looney has awakened in us a curiosity . . . as to the real author of the plays, the authorship of which we had taken for granted,

---

[30] *The Bookman's Journal* published a fifth letter from Looney in 1921, written in response to its review of his collection of the poems of Edward de Vere.

and a conviction that the matter cannot now be allowed to stand where it is. Briefly, although we are satisfied that Shakespeare, as presented by Mr. Looney, did not write the plays, we are not at all satisfied that they were written, as Mr. Looney avers, by the Earl of Oxford.

This is not to dismiss his attempt lightly. The book should be in the hands of all who are interested in the identity of the author known to us as Shakespeare. It is to be hoped that those who have preconceived opinions will attempt to put them aside and judge the work without prejudice.[31]

Three weeks later *The Bookman's Journal* printed Looney's response to its review. That issue, dated April 9, 1920, had a special banner at the top of the cover reading "IS SHAKESPEARE IDENTIFIED? Mr. Looney's New Clue." Inside, along with his letter, was an introduction by the editor and excerpts from reviews in four other publications, giving readers a broader overview of reactions to Looney's book than was available elsewhere. All four reviews were far less favorable than *The Bookman's Journal's* own. An advertisement for that issue was placed in *The Guardian's* April 8 issue.

Though now forgotten (it has never been indexed, and the British Library does not have copies of its issues), *The Bookman's Journal* was so highly regarded at the time that its April 9 spread was reprinted in six newspapers in England.[32]

A week later came a reply by the reviewer, in which he, following the lead of reviewers in other publications, was much more cautious in his praise of *"Shakespeare" Identified* and much more guarded in his opinion of Oxford's authorship. A week later it ran Looney's response.

A month later, on May 21, *The Bookman's Journal* again outdid all other literary journals by running a special section on "The Identity of Shakespeare" that included short pieces by Sir Sidney Lee and the Rt. Hon. J. M. Robertson requested by the *Journal*, as well as a third letter by "Mr. J. Thomas Looney." *The Bookman's Journal* not only highlighted the special section on the front cover but also ran advertisements for it in *The National Review, Westminster Gazette* and the *Times Literary Supplement* (see image nearby). Its Oxfordian coverage continued in the following issue with another letter by Looney, his fourth, in which he responded to Lee's and Robertson's critical comments. Coverage then dropped off until its review of Looney's edition of *The Poems of Edward de Vere* in March 1921.

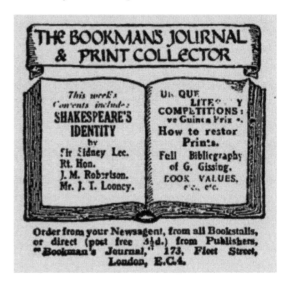

In the May 21 special section, Sir Sidney Lee wrote that,

---

[31] "A New Mask for Shakespeare," *Bookman's Journal*, March 19, 1920, p. 408.

[32] Publications reprinting *The Bookman Journal's* April 9 review included *Nottingham Evening Post, Birmingham Daily Gazette* and *Sheffield Daily Telegraph* (all on April 12); *Yorkshire Post and Leeds Intelligencer* (April 13); *Boston Guardian* (April 17); *Christian Science Monitor* (May 18).

> I have had some correspondence with Mr. Looney, and have examined his book. His theory seems to me to present difficulties which are quite insuperable. The author ignores Ben Jonson's apostrophe "of his friend, the author," as "sweet swan of Avon," which seems to me a rather serious inadequacy. I wrote on M. Abel Lefranc's attempt to identify the author of the plays with the Earl of Derby in last July's *Quarterly*, and much of what I said of the French professor's theory applies equally well to Mr. Looney's. I took account in that article of the general point of view which Mr. Henry James expresses as to the inevitable appearance of discrepancies between the proofs of supreme genius and the mundane facts of the biographies of men possessing supreme genius. Yours truly, SIDNEY LEE.[33]

Looney's responses to critics—in *The Bookman's Journal* and elsewhere—were eminently reasoned and reasonable. He sought to set the record straight by correcting misperceptions and filling in gaps in the reviewer's knowledge. On one occasion he also gave us something more—his thoughts on the ordeal he was undergoing. He had, he explained, been under no illusions about the severity of the test to which his ideas would be put.

> I was well aware that, in propounding a new theory of Shakespearean authorship, I was exposing myself to as severe an ordeal as any writer has been called upon to face: that the work would be rigorously overhauled in none too indulgent a spirit by men who know the subject in all its minutiae; and that, if the argument contained any fatal flaw, this would be detected immediately and the theory overthrown.[34]

He had, perhaps, expected to engage in what has been called "the great conversation" that people of good will engage in as they seek to discover the truth of a subject. He had hoped "that English literary journals . . . [would] throw open their columns to such a discussion as will let in the fullest light upon the question." He further hoped that "the arguments will . . . be most carefully weighed before [readers] precipitate themselves into debate upon the question."[35]

Given these hopes, Looney must have been surprised by the hostility exhibited by so many reviewers and readers. He must have been taken aback by attacks that weren't in line with "the spirit of impartiality and truth by which alone any problem can be solved." The editor of *The Bookman's Journal* informed readers that "Mr. Looney's book was extensively reviewed . . . [and] provoked in nearly every case hostile criticism."[36] Looney himself observed that "certain sections of the 'orthodox' [in America] have assailed my work with a hostility quite equal to what it has aroused in England."[37] He had assumed that critics would read his book before critiquing it, and that they would state his findings accurately before taking issue with them.

The personal nature of the attacks must also have been a surprise: J. M. Robertson's charge of "prepossession,"[38] for instance—the charge that Looney had the idea of authorship by the nobleman Edward de Vere in mind from the beginning and set out to find evidence to support it—directly challenged the veracity of Looney's description of his actual methods. Robertson had, in short, called him a liar. It would have been

---

[33] Sir Sidney Lee, "The Identity of Shakespeare," *Bookman's Journal*, May 21, 1920, p. 58.

[34] J. Thomas Looney, "Stratford and Stony Stratford," *Bookman's Journal*, March 25, 1921, p. 388.

[35] J. Thomas Looney, "Is Shakespeare Identified?" *Bookman's Journal*, April 9, 1920, p. 452.

[36] Editor, "Is Shakespeare Identified?" *Bookman's Journal*, April 9, 1920, p. 452.

[37] J. Thomas Looney, "Stratford and Stony Stratford," *Bookman's Journal*, March 25, 1921, p. 388.

[38] J. Thomas Looney, "The Identity of Shakespeare," *Bookman's Journal*, May 21, 1920, p. 59.

impossible for Looney to have anticipated the ludicrousness of Robertson's statement that, "It is precisely because the data for the Stratford actor alone gives an intelligible biographical substratum for the plays that I hold to it."[39] It is not hard to imagine Looney's puzzling over that statement, given that it was exactly the unintelligibility of the biographical substratum that had led to doubts about Shakspere's authorship in the first place.

In the face of such hostility, Looney had no choice but to respond. "However distasteful the matter," he wrote, "no man can ignore a challenge of this nature, from whatever source it may come."[40] His letters, invariably measured in content and reasonable in tone, are extraordinary for a man who throughout his life sought to avoid controversy and confrontation. He responded to Robertson rather sternly: "As this is a complete misrepresentation of the view of the sonnets maintained throughout [my] book, . . . it was at once evident that Mr. Robertson had merely dipped here and there into the work, in so hurried and perturbed a manner as to have missed not only the whole of important arguments, but even the sense of the sentence from which he was actually quoting." Further, it is "impossible for even a superficial reading of the book to result in so complete a misunderstanding. It will be noticed that he even takes me to task . . . for saying something contrary to what I had repeated with almost wearisome reiterations."

The very nature of those attacks enabled Looney, drawing on his historical knowledge and intellectual adroitness, to turn the tables on many of his critics. To those who stated that similarities between events in the works and events in Oxford's life were an illegitimate form of evidence of authorship, he pointed out that "critics who are standing out staunchly against my solution of the Shakespeare problem, are already admitting that Shakespeare must have been well acquainted with the Earl of Oxford, and very probably made him his model for 'Hamlet.'"[41] To those who pointed out the difficulties inherent in

	The Bookman's Journal's **Selected Coverage of the Oxfordian Idea in Spring 1920**
1920, March 19	"A New Mask for Shakespeare" [review of *"Shakespeare" Identified*]
1920, April 9	**J. Thomas Looney**, "Is 'Shakespeare Identified'?" [Response to the March 19 review] [Preceded by editor's introduction and followed by excerpts from reviews in *The Spectator* (March 27), *The Saturday Westminster* (March 20), *The Times Literary Supplement* (March 4), and *The Sunday Times* (April 4)] [Banner at the top of the cover reads "IS SHAKESPEARE IDENTIFIED? Mr. Looney's New Clue"]
1920, April 16	[Reviewer's reply to Looney's April 9 response]
1920, April 23	**J. Thomas Looney**, "The Shakespeare Controversy: Mr. Thomas Looney and 'Oxford's Boys'" [letter: additional response to the April 9 review]
1920, May 21	Sir Sidney Lee, J. M. Robertson, **J. Thomas Looney**, "The Identity of Shakespeare" [Three letters preceded by editor's introduction]
1920, May 28	**J. Thomas Looney**, "The Identity of Shakespeare" [letter: Response to Robertson's May 21 letter]
1920, June 4	R. Atkinson, "The Identity of Shakespeare" [letter, with note from editor]

[39] J. M. Robertson, "The Identity of Shakespeare," *Bookman's Journal*, May 21, 1920, p. 59.
[40] J. Thomas Looney, "The Identity of Shakespeare," *Bookman's Journal*, May 28, 1920, p. 68.
[41] J. Thomas Looney, "Is Shakespeare Identified?" *Bookman's Journal*, April 9, 1920, p. 452.

hiding Oxford's authorship—a point he readily acknowledged—Looney pointed out that "the maintaining of secrecy has been phenomenal . . . whoever the author may have been. . . . If the Stratford man were the author, the silence of contemporary documents in reference to all his literary and dramatic dealings with other people is as pronounced as if he had been in hiding. Under any hypothesis, then, we are bound to admit a most extraordinary avoidance of leakage." In other words, the same argument made against de Vere could be made against the man from Stratford: no documents during his lifetime connect him directly to the plays and poems.

Looney also incorporated Sir Walter Raleigh's finding—that toward the end of Shakespeare's career "his work is once more found mixed with the work of other men . . . altering his completed plays, or completing his unfinished work by additions of their own"—to make Oxford uniquely qualified to have been the author. "Is such a state of things more consistent with an author who had passed away leaving his unfinished writings in other hands, or with one who was still alive, intellectually vigorous, at the summit of his profession as a playwright, and but forty-three years of age?"[42] Looney's answer was that the later plays, "instead of presenting a difficulty, add their own peculiar quota of evidence in support of the theory that Edward de Vere was the author." "The "flood of publications which started in 1597 . . . continued up to the publication of *Hamlet* in 1604 (the year of Oxford's death). . . . There was then a complete stoppage. . . . This year of 1604 was for long held to be the identical year of William Shakespeare's retirement to Stratford."[43] "Surely," he concluded, "it is not too much to claim that the date of Oxford's death, instead of being a weakness, is one of the strongest links in the chain of evidence."[44]

Another point of special importance was the effectiveness of Looney's response to one critic's inane statement that "I cannot see that the question of whether Shakespeare's works were written by Shakespeare, or Bacon, or the Earl of Oxford, or by any other man of the period, is of the least importance." Looney set things straight, noting that "doubtless 'the play's the thing;' but these, I am convinced, will never be fully understood apart from the personality of the man who has left a permanent record and monument of himself in the great 'Shakespeare' dramas."[45]

Reviewing the criticism of the first ten weeks, Looney must have felt a degree of satisfaction from seeing that the Oxfordian claim had withstood all attacks. He was able to write that "The ordeal has been passed through; I have watched anxiously every criticism and suggestion that has been made, and what is the result? . . . [N]ot a single really formidable or destructive objection to the theory has yet put in an appearance." To the contrary, he continued, "those critics and reviewers who have made themselves most intimate with the many-sidedness of the evidence, have confessed themselves most impressed and 'almost persuaded,' sometimes apparently against their evident wish."[46] His five letters in *The Bookman's Journal* show that during that difficult first year Looney responded to criticism and hostility with courage, steadfastness, perseverance and grace—all qualities that are required of Oxfordians today as they face a similar intellectual climate.

---

[42] J. Thomas Looney, "The Identity of Shakespeare," *Bookman's Journal*, May 21, 1920, p. 59.
[43] For a fuller discussion of this point, see *"Shakespeare" Identified* (2018), p. 424.
[44] J. Thomas Looney, "The Identity of Shakespeare," *Bookman's Journal*, May 21, 1920, p. 59.
[45] J. Thomas Looney, "The Shakespeare Controversy," *Bookman's Journal*, April 23, 1920, p. 484.
[46] J. Thomas Looney, "The Identity of Shakespeare," *Bookman's Journal*, May 21, 1920, p. 17.

Roundup of Other Reviews from London

Other reviews sometimes raised points especially surprising or unusual.

The New Statesman's reviewer, after disparaging Looney, his methods and his findings, noted the similarities between events in de Vere's life and plot developments in *All's Well That Ends Well* and asked a startling question: "How does [Looney] know that Shakespeare did not adapt to his purpose the story of Oxford's career?"[47] The reviewer didn't even hazard a guess, though, as to how a commoner from the sticks could possibly have known so much about the life of the Earl of Oxford.

The Spectator's reviewer, in a review that Looney called "fair and helpful," asked, "Could an Elizabethan actor know the heart of an Englishman from the King to the peasant?" and answered the question with, "Genius would not be the miracle that it is if it were accountable. That he should have known every class from within is a mystery, and out of that mystery spring the two others which never cease to agitate the less balanced of his worshippers, that of his identity and his personality. Even for the latter it is useless to search in his work. The universality of his sympathies forbids us to discover its outline."[48] In other words, the Shakespeare mystery is beyond human understanding.

The reviewer for *The Sunday Times* acknowledged that "the candid reader may admit that there do exist certain coincidences which may with some degree of plausibility connect Oxford with the coveted authorship . . . [including] some remarkable parallels to the experiences of Bertram in *All's Well that Ends Well*, several of which did not occur in the story by Boccaccio on which the play is based. Conceivably, then, *All's Well* might be a piece of autobiography."[49] And yet, he continued, it is all easily explained, through genius and "every-day hearsay and observation."

Given the many pieces supportive of the Oxfordian claim to appear in *The Christian Science Monitor* later in the 1920s and 1930s, the paper's first take on the subject was surprisingly negative. Its reviewer observed that "Mr. Looney . . . is at no pains to cover his complete ignorance of Elizabethan literature; he tells us that when he first made his discovery he had read no one save Spenser, Sidney and Shakespeare,"[50] failing to notice that the second half of his sentence contradicts the first: nobody who has read Spenser, Sidney and Shakespeare is "completely ignorant" of Elizabethan literature. Beyond that, what matters is not a scholar's starting point but the depth of his knowledge at the end of his investigations; ignorance is not a word at all applicable to the author of the *tour de force* that is *"Shakespeare" Identified*. The reviewer failed to notice the contradiction between his claim that the man from Stratford was able to educate himself to the heights shown in the Shakespeare plays while denying the same capacity of self-education to the author of the book he was reviewing.

The Morning Post, another publication that would later become a forum for discussion of the authorship question, got off to a bad start. Its reviewer was one of those who did not read Looney's thoughts on *The Tempest* carefully, writing that "There was not room for it in the theory, and it simply had to go."[51] He then swept aside all authorship doubts—"There is the strongest evidence in favour of . . . the Stratford man's authorship"—before

---

[47] "The Latest Shakespeare," *New Statesman*, March 20, 1920, p. 713.

[48] "A Sleepless Shakespeare," *Spectator*, March 7, 1920, p. 416.

[49] H. C. Minchin, "Who Was Shakespeare?" *Sunday Times*, April 4, 1920, p. 5.

[50] "Shakespeare and Bacon Again," *Christian Science Monitor*, May 7, 1920, p. 3.

[51] "A New Round Game," *Morning Post*, April 1, 1920, p. 5.

declaring that the "parallel passages" that Looney documented between Oxford's poems and Shakespeare's "are to be found in almost any two writers of the period." He didn't name any such writers or cite any such passages, however.

W. L. Courtney, reviewer for *The Daily Telegraph*, exhibited an extreme level of misunderstanding. He stated that "there were a great number of contemporary writers who, under an Italian influence, wrote poems of much the same order"[52] as Oxford's, without naming any. He declared that Shakspere's authorship of Shakespeare's plays was "strongly held by [his] contemporaries" without citing any evidence for that assertion. After claiming that Looney rejected *The Tempest* because it didn't fit his timing scheme he stated that "the play . . . contains a love scene almost as magical as the inspired colloquy of *Romeo and Juliet* in the warm southern night under the watchful stars."[53] Looney wrote a long letter in rebuttal to Courtney, but *The Telegraph* printed only a small portion of it.

The reviewer for *The Athenaeum* also hadn't read *"Shakespeare" Identified* carefully, for he saw Looney as merely recapitulating the negative arguments of the Baconians. He stated that "One cannot read this book without feeling, in spite of all impatience, a real sympathy with the author. He is so transparently honest and serious, so evidently oppressed by the magnitude of his discovery that Shakespeare was really Edward de Vere, 17th Earl of Oxford, so manifestly ignorant of the conditions of Elizabethan literature as a whole, so obviously unfitted to pass an opinion upon any one of the more intimate problems of literary psychology."[54] Looney's response correcting several ill-informed statements was supported by letters from two other readers. One stated that "The article in question has no value to the reader who desires to know whether the book reviewed is worth the buying and the reading, and the writer, therefore, appears to have failed in his proper function as a reviewer."[55] Prominent Baconian Roderick L. Eagle also wrote in to correct several of the reviewer's misinformed statements. The *Athenaeum* gave itself the final word: "We hold that it [Mr. Looney's book] is a waste of time and energy, and an abuse of our readers' patience."[56]

The reviewer for *The Saturday Review of Politics, Literature, Science and Art* got just about everything backward. He believed that "it is the common people in the plays who are the most realistic. . . . They and their kind are breathing actualities,"[57] whereas royalty and couriers in the plays are mere idealized images—an opinion contrary to almost every Shakespearean scholar. He wrote that Looney was of "limited intelligence" and that "his arrogance is amazing, but it is probably a waste of time to argue" with him given the "great defects . . . in his reasoning." Looney began his response by noting that "It is almost as unbecoming to notice an ill-natured anonymous attack as to make one;" nevertheless he went on to correct many of the reviewer's grossest misrepresentations before asking that "the public should weigh well the terms and the spirit of this attack."[58]

Another item, a spoof in *Punch* on May 19, 1920, showed that the paper's editors believed that the Oxfordian idea had become widely enough known that their readers

---

[52] W. L. Courtney, "Shakespeare Identified," *Daily Telegraph*, March 19, 1920, p. 16.

[53] The Reviewer was surely thinking of a scene in *The Merchant of Venice* (V.1), not *The Tempest*.

[54] "Another Shakespeare," *Athenaeum*, April 2, 1920, p. 450.

[55] Francis Clarke, "Correspondence: 'Shakespeare' Identified," *Athenaeum*, April 16, 1920, p. 521.

[56] Editor, "Correspondence: 'Shakespeare' Identified," *Athenaeum*, April 16, 1920, p. 521.

[57] "Shakespeare: A New Folly," *Saturday Review*, March 27, 1920, p. 309-10.

[58] J. Thomas Looney, "Edward de Vere and Shakespeare" [letter], *Saturday Review*, vol. 129 (April 9, 1920): 370.

would appreciate the humor in the following satirical passage, which purported to be an interview with a "Mr. Blinkingham, a well-known publisher:"

> Nor shall we overlook the earlier masters. Professor Chamberlin, whose thrilling lectures on Queen Elizabeth and Lord Leicester have been the talk of the town for the last fortnight, has kindly undertaken to organise a new variorum version of the *Plays of Shakespeare*, with the assistance of Mr. Looney, the writer of the recently-published and final work on the authorship of the plays.[59]

Roundup of Reviews from Outside London

Two reviews in regional papers give the impression that the reviewers had been persuaded by Looney's arguments but on second thought couldn't admit it to themselves, resulting in self-contradictory, confused assessments.

The reviewer for *The Essex Review* accepted "Mr. Looney's contention that there exists a 'main mystery' about William Shakespeare, of Stratford-on-Avon, and an equal mystery about Edward de Vere, and that this identification theory reconciles and solves these two mysteries." Yet he couldn't accept the conclusion that flowed so logically from that reconciliation. "The evidence for the 'Stratford man' is not to be despised. To me, at any rate, it outweighs all the coincidences and all the ingenious inferences which Mr. Looney has collected and woven together so effectively."[60] If the works had been discovered with no author's name on them, this reviewer would, apparently, have had no difficulty at all in attributing them to Oxford; only his existing beliefs stood in the way.

The Nottingham Journal and Express's reviewer, after a careful reading of *"Shakespeare" Identified* stated that "I am bound to admit that I am almost persuaded; but I am not convinced."[61] This is surely one of the pieces to which Looney referred when he wrote in *The Bookman's Journal* that "some critics . . . have confessed themselves most impressed and 'almost persuaded,' sometimes apparently against their evident wish."[62] The reviewer acknowledged that Looney "does present an amazing chain of parallels from Oxford's life showing that the text of the plays is based upon the experiences of this man."[63] But, he concluded, "We remain sceptical . . . while not negating Mr. Looney's claim . . . because he has no conclusive proof." And yet, he admitted, "Mr. Looney does present a case deserving serious consideration, and one that Shakespeare students should study carefully." All in all, this reviewer gave the impression of being convinced by Looney's evidence, arguments and reasoning, but of not being able to admit it.

The reviewer for the *Aberdeen Daily Journal* also wrote of the difficulty of accepting the Oxfordian claim because the newness of it was so unsettling. "Here is a brand new proposition in reference to the authenticity of Shakespeare's Plays and Poems. In some respects it outreaches all former efforts. . . . It is not easy to read such a book with an open mind; . . . All the same, the question is of immense literary interest, and it is not necessary to agree with all or any of the arguments here propounded to appreciate the merit of the book as a work entitled to fair and careful consideration."[64] He saw that "the Stratfordian

---

[59] "Bridging the Literary Gulf," *Punch, or the London Charivari*, May 19, 1920, p. 396.

[60] W. Gurney Benham, "Edward de Vere, Earl of Oxford, 'Identified' as Shakespeare," *Essex Review*, vol. 29 (April 1, 1920): 95-100.

[61] C. R.., "Shakespeare: Was He Edward de Vere, Lord Oxford?" *Nottingham Journal*, April 22, 1920, p. 4.

[62] J. Thomas Looney, "Stratford and Stony Stratford," *Bookman's Journal*, March 25, 1921, p. 388.

[63] C. R.., "Shakespeare: Was He Edward de Vere, Lord Oxford?" *Nottingham Journal*, April 22, 1920, p. 4.

[64] "Shakespeare," *Aberdeen Daily Journal*, April 5, 1920, p. 5.

view still holds the field," but predicted that "If there is anything in this ever arising Shakespeare problem, and if it is ever finally solved, this book will probably do as much as any other of its kind in helping competent scholars to arrive at definite conclusions."

C. H. H. [Charles H. Herford], in a review in *The Manchester Guardian* already noted, found that Looney had a "curious blend of immense . . . erudition in a narrow field," and concluded by advising him to "cut out of his book, ruthlessly, all the nonsense about Shakespeare and make it what with some reshaping it might become, a serviceable, if not brilliant, life of Edward de Vere."[65]

The reviewer for *The Western Mail* (Cardiff, Wales) acknowledged that "a satisfactory life of Shakespeare has yet to be written" but doubted the validity of the literary correspondences Looney documented—"most of the parallels in phrase between de Vere and Shakespeare are valueless, as they are Elizabethan commonplaces"—without understanding that those commonplaces originated in de Vere's work. He noted gaps in Looney's case—the "why" and "how" gaps that many others commented on—"Mr. Looney never shows us clearly why the Earl of Oxford should wish to conceal his authorship . . . or how the secret was completely kept till the twentieth century." Still, he concluded, "We need a life of Shakespeare on similar broad principles; and we shall have it from honesty like Mr. Looney's, joined to the scholarship and acumen which he has not."[66]

Responding, Looney noted that "Your reviewer's desire for a more satisfactory biography of William Shakespeare is, I fear, doomed to disappointment. The amazing industry of very capable men for many years has only yielded a harvest of a few facts which, it has been said, even by believers, could be written on a single sheet of notepaper—and not one of these indicates a trace of literary interests or the capacity even to write a letter."

The tenor of the review in *The Irish Times* is shown by its final paragraph. "We have written enough to show the argument of the book, which is full, copious, and abounding in interest. It is a pity that the author's talent, researches, and enthusiasm have been expended on what we honestly feel can only be a lost cause."[67]

The Scotsman's review was the most jarring exception to the trend of more favorable assessments appearing in publications outside of London. Its reviewer stated that "certain grave objections [must] be removed before" Mr. Looney's claim can "overturn the fabric of Shakespearean criticism and speculations." His objections, though, dissolve upon examination: that Shakspere was widely acknowledged as a dramatist during his lifetime, that many plays were written after Oxford's death, that literary correspondences between Oxford's poetry and Shakespeare's are imaginary, and that correspondences between events in Oxford's life and events in the plays are mostly imaginary. Looney had addressed all of these points in his book; a closer reading of it would have shown the reviewer that Looney based his case not on "assumptions," but on historical facts long known to Shakespeare scholars. The reviewer is right, though, that "No [thorough and convincing] explanation that can hold water is suggested of how and why the 'mystery' was invented, or why the many who must have been in the secret kept absolute silence after as well as before 1604."[68]

---

[65] C. H. H., "Shakespeare Deposed Again," *Manchester Guardian*, March 19, 1920, p. 7.
[66] C.B., "Shakespeare's Identity," *Western Mail*, April 23, 1920, p. 7.
[67] "'Shakespeare' Identified," *Irish Times*, May 7, 1920, p. 7.
[68] "Shakespeare Identified," *Scotsman*, March 4, 1920, p. 2.

Looney responded forcefully. *The Scotsman's* review "ought not to pass unchallenged. . . . Such articles . . . are calculated to mislead readers respecting the nature of the work, and cause it to be neglected." He then invited readers to "study my work, and place the matter it contains alongside of the criticism" before forming their own opinions about "the character of my argument as a whole." After explaining Ben Jonson's part in the "subterfuge of the First Folio publication" he announced new information discovered since the publication of *"Shakespeare" Identified* that firmly tied Oxford to Shakespeare.

> Permit me . . . to point out publicly now, for the first time, that of the two men to whom the First Folio was dedicated, one, Philip Herbert, was an actual son-in-law of the Earl of Oxford; and the other, William Herbert, had been engaged to Oxford's daughter, and Oxford had written approvingly of him, although the engagement was broken off. In brief, the very reference given by the critic makes against the Stratfordian view, and brings its own quota of evidence in favour of the authorship theory I proposed.[69]

Another Distant Review

Reviews of *"Shakespeare" Identified* outside of London were far more favorable to Looney's presentation of the Oxfordian claim those in the capital city. With only a few exceptions, the farther away from London the city in which the publication was based, the greater the receptivity to the new Oxfordian claim. As noted, *The Scotsman* was the most extreme exception to this general trend.

In line with the trend, *The Times of India* (Bombay) ran one of the most judicious and perceptive reviews of *"Shakespeare" Identified* to appear anywhere. Perhaps, just as J. Thomas Looney was successful in part because he was an outsider, so too the *Times of India*—based in far Bombay, half a world away from the pressures toward conformity with the Stratfordian story in London—was able to take an objective look at the authorship mystery and Looney's proposed solution to it.

After appreciatively and succinctly presenting the reasons Looney gave for believing that Edward de Vere was Shakespeare, this remarkable review concluded:

> It is impossible to do Mr. Looney justice in a summary, since the effect of his argument is cumulative and in driblets is easily reduced to absurdity. On the other hand he does himself such ample justice that a little less from a reviewer cannot impair his sublime consciousness of having achieved "not merely a rational or contemporary event, but a world-event of permanent importance destined to leave a mark as enduring as human literature, or the human race itself." . . . Even our old familiar William does not come out of it so badly, since from having been the most stupendous dramatist, he has become the most stupendous fraud in history. He deceived not some of the people some of the time, but all the people all the time.[70]

---

[69] J. Thomas Looney, "Shakespeare Identified" [letter], *Scotsman*, March 20, 1920, p. 11. Looney presented the same new information five weeks later in a letter to *The Bookman's Journal*: "I may, at any rate, point out here, what I had missed in writing the book, that, although no relative or representative of the Stratford man's family appears in connection with the publication of the First Folio of 'Shakespeare,' that work is dedicated to the husband of one of Oxford's daughters, Philip Herbert, and to one who had been engaged to another daughter, William Herbert." J. Thomas Looney, "Is 'Shakespeare Identified'?" *Bookman's Journal*, April 9, 1920, p. 453.

[70] "The Latest Shakespeare," *Times of India*, May 26, 1920, p. 11.

4

J. Thomas Looney and the Oxfordian Claim, Summer, 1920-1922

"Shakespeare" Identified in the United States

"Shakespeare" Identified was published in the United States by Frederick A. Stokes Co. on May 8, 1920, two months after the Cecil Palmer edition came out in London. Like Palmer, Stokes publicized it widely, with advertisements placed in trade publications: *Publishers' Weekly* (May 8), *Weekly Review* (May 22); in literary magazines: *The New York Times Book Review* (May 30), *Atlantic Monthly* (June), *The Library Journal* (June 1, June 14); and in newspapers: *The New York Times* (June 6).

Although full reviews of the book did not appear in American periodicals until after the launching of the U.S. edition, several American newspapers ran short notices about the London edition before May 8. The first to appear was in the *Chicago Daily Tribune* on March 24. It cheekily dismissed the book and its author: "A reviewer [in England] remarks that the redeeming feature of the book is its honesty. And this honesty, we should say, is contained in the name of the author, who is J. Thomas Looney. He is."[1] The paper ran a similar piece a few months later:

> An American [!] named J. Thomas Looney has written a book to prove that Shakespeare was really the Earl of Oxford. We can not help thinking that Shakespeare, who went out of his way to prove that Ophelia was one of the original Looneys, has brought this on himself.[2]

Don't write off Chicago, though. A short review by Fanny Butcher in June concluded that,

> [I]f one can keep one's self from being too amused by the fact of his name the book will be most interesting. They say that Walt Whitman, Oliver Wendell Holmes, Whittier, and Emerson were all certain that Shakespeare didn't write his own stuff, and Lowell, Byron, Hallam, Disraeli, and . . . Bismarck, were frankly skeptical. Prof. Looney makes out a good case for his candidate, one must submit.[3]

Apart from the "Shakespeare didn't write his own stuff" line, a misunderstanding of Looney's argument, this wasn't a bad short review. Quite different in tone was John Corbin's much longer review in *The New York Times*. It would be hard to find another review in a leading paper with so many misstatements that could easily have been avoided if the reviewer had read the book. Inaccuracies include the 1604 issue—"the fact that when Oxford died in 1604 some dozen of the plays were, according to the best

---

[1] "A Line o' Type or Two," *Chicago Daily Tribune*, March 24, 1920, p. 8.
[2] "A Line o' Type or Two," *Chicago Daily Tribune*, Aug. 8, 1920, p. 8.
[3] Fanny Butcher, "Tabloid Reviews," *Chicago Daily Tribune*, June 13, 1920, p. 9.

knowledge and belief, unwritten"; the "snob" charge—"the aristocratic or snobbish assumption that supreme genius cannot arise from yeoman stock, but may be easily credited in the son of the sixteenth Earl"; and the false testimony belief—"the superabundant evidence set down by Shakespeare's contemporaries— intimate and lifelong friends—that he was a man of rare honesty and gentility of spirit, a resident of Stratford and author of the plays." In Corbin's view, "the argument connecting Oxford and the Shakespearean plays has the abundance of strained literary and personal analogies, and the amazing absence of common sense which characterize most Baconian endeavors. No shadow of a reason is given why this harum-scarum Earl . . . should conceal the fact" of his authorship. He does find one praiseworthy aspect of the book: "The chief value and interest in Mr. Looney's book consists in the fact that it assembles what can be discovered with regard to the life of an Elizabethan nobleman and poet who seems to have possessed, and been possessed by, a full measure of the wilding, colorful spirit of his time."[4]

Convincing Evidence on the Shakespeare Problem

"SHAKESPEARE" IDENTIFIED

By J. THOMAS LOONEY

Newly discovered evidence which strongly points to the Seventeenth Earl of Oxford as the real author of the Shakespeare plays is here presented logically, without recourse to cipher, cryptogram or mystery. *Gelett Burgess* says "I have been fascinated beyond measure. . . . If the author's conclusions are accepted by posterity, it chronicles the most important literary pursuit and discovery ever given to the world." *Net $5.00*

New York Times, June 6, 1920

Looney respond to Corbin, but his letter to *The New York Times* was rejected. Stokes reported back to him that "I have not yet succeeded in getting publication for your reply to Mr. Corbin. *The Times* declined to print it without giving reasons. . . . *The New York Evening Post* and *The New York Tribune* refused [it] because they did not want to appear to be criticizing a rival paper."[5]

Other publications were more open to the idea of Edward de Vere as Shakespeare, or rather became more open to it over time. The New York-based *The Bookman: A Review of Books and Life* (not to be confused with *The Bookman's Journal* in England) ran three reviews of *"Shakespeare" Identified* in 1920, the first negative in tone, the second neutral and the third thoughtfully positive.

The first review, in May, which bore the interesting title of "Shakespeare and the Liliputians," competed with Corbin's piece for the largest number of misunderstandings in a single review. Like Corbin, the reviewer misunderstood the nature of the authorship question—"What first led Mr. Looney to believe that Shakespeare did not do his own work;" the fallacy that genius could do anything and everything—"The fatal error in all Mr. Looney's argument is that he makes no allowance whatever for genius;" the phrasings-common-to-the-era fallacy—"references in it to hawks and hawking, and with comparisons of a woman's face with roses and lilies, and so forth, and, apparently unaware that all this sort of thing was part of the conventional stock-in-trade of the poets

---

[4] John Corbin, "Who is 'Baconian' Now?" *New York Times*, June 27, 1920, p. 58.
[5] Frederick A. Stokes, letter to J. Thomas Looney, Oct. 29.

of the time;" and the 1604 canard—"the plays that did not make their appearance till after his death are a stumbling-block which Mr. Looney's specious explanations will not carry him over."[6]

The second review, in June, by the publishers of *The Bookman*, recognized the possibility that Looney might be on to something. It noted the continuing interest in the actual identity of "Shakespeare," and acknowledged "the weakness of the Stratfordian theory." Regarding the author of *"Shakespeare" Identified*, they wrote "His conclusions are as unusual and startling as his investigations have been complete. . . . Mr. Looney has carried his investigations to the point where they deserve the serious consideration of experts."[7]

The third review, in August, "Shakespeare?" by Swedish-American novelist, poet, literary critic and essayist Edwin Björkman, was one of the most thoughtful and favorable to appear in any publication in 1920. Björkman readily acknowledged "that some sort of mystery has been connected with the authorship of those plays ever since the days when Shakespeare still lived."

> What I believe quite humbly, and have believed for years, is that certain mysterious circumstances attach to the reputed authorship of those plays, and that the problem . . . will continue to challenge every open-minded student of English literature until it is settled by some discovery of documents or facts hitherto unknown. For this reason I hold that every sincere effort like that of Mr. Looney's must be welcomed . . . as a starting point for new, and maybe more fruitful research.

The final two paragraphs must surely have warmed Looney's heart after six months of mostly hostile criticism.

> It is impossible in an article like this to do justice to the wealth of evidence collected by Mr. Looney, or to the ingenuity displayed by him in its coordination. Perhaps the most remarkable aspect of his labors is that they affect not only the central problem of William Shakespeare's relation to the work named after him, but a whole series of literary enigmas that have puzzled every painstaking student of this period for nearly two hundred years. . . . The peculiar thing is that all these problems seem to fall into place and form a consistent picture the moment you accept the theory of Oxford's connection with the Shakespeare plays.
>
> Mr. Looney thinks he has proved this theory. Of course, he has not. But he has opened most promising vistas, and it is to be hoped that his leads will be followed up. The days are past when a new Shakespearian theory can be laughed out of court. . . . In this as in all other cases, we should be moved solely by a desire for truth, and nothing that may be helpful in finding it should be despised.[8]

Björkman also brought to light a contemporary reference to Oxford that Looney had overlooked. From *The Arte of English Poesie*, published in 1589 and dedicated to Queen Elizabeth and Lord Treasurer Burghley, it read "and in Her Majesty's time that now is are sprung up another crew of Courtly makers (poets). Noblemen and Gentlemen of Her Majesty's own servants, who have written excellently well as it would appear if their doings could be found out and made public with the rest, of which number is first that

---

[6] A. Sr. J. A., "Shakespeare and the Liliputians," *Bookman*, vol. 51/3 (May 1920): 84.
[7] "Looking Ahead with the Publishers," *Bookman*, vol. 51/4 (June 1920): 499.
[8] Edwin Björkman, "Shakespeare?" *Bookman*, vol. 51/6 (Aug. 1920): 677.

noble gentleman Edward Earl of Oxford." Later in the same work, in a passage listing various writers and their areas of greatest accomplishment, "the Earl of Oxford and Master Edwards of Her Majesty's Chapel" are given "the highest praise ... for Comedy and Interlude."

Björkman's review, with its measured response to the thoroughness and fruitfulness of Looney's investigations, should have served as a model for others to emulate.

Roundup of Reviews in North American Publications

The Literary Digest quoted extensively from Oliver Herford's review *in Leslie's Weekly* and John Corbin's in *The New York Times*. Herford (1860-1935) had clearly joined the ranks of the Oxfordians. Though British born, he was an American writer, playwright, artist and illustrator sometimes called "The American Oscar Wilde." As far back as 1899 he had described William Shakespeare as the "Stratford imposter whose fantastic usurpation of the throne of genius has befuddled the world for over three hundred years."[9] Of *"Shakespeare" Identified* he wrote, "Whether you believe that Shakespeare was the author, or whether you agree with Emerson, Holmes, Whittier, Whitman, Coleridge, Mark Twain, and many others that he was no more than a human dummy or personal alibi for some great unknown—or whether you have no views of any sort on the matter and don't care a hang who wrote the Shakespeare plays and sonnets, Mr. Looney's book is fascinating reading, more thrilling even than the best detective story by . . . Edgar Allan Poe." *The Literary Digest* commented that "In Mr. Herford's way of putting it, Mr. Looney gives the poets of Elizabeth's court the 'once over,' and 'points an accusing mental finger at Edward de Vere, seventeenth Earl of Oxford, as the 'guilty party." From that moment, we are told, 'items of evidence seemed to fly from every direction as if eager to confirm what at first seemed scarcely more than a guess—fitting together and interlocking with all the satisfying nicety of a 'jigsaw puzzle.'"[10]

From Corbin's review, *The Literary Digest* reprinted his opinion that Looney's evidence "has abundance of strained

Reviews of *"Shakespeare" Identified* in North America, 1920	
March 24	*The Chicago Daily Tribune* [short notice]
April 4	*The New York Times* [brief comment]
April 24	*The Nation*
May	*The Bookman* — A. Sr. J. A.
May 1	*The Globe and Mail* [Toronto]
	The Weekly Review [short notice]
June	*The Bookman* — The Publishers
June 10	*Reedy's Mirror* — William M. Reedy
June 13	*The Chicago Daily Tribune* — Fanny Butcher
	The New York Times [brief description]
June 27	*The Courier-Journal* [Louisville, KY]
	The Montgomery Advertiser
	The New York Times – John Corbin
Summer	*Leslie's Weekly* — Oliver Herford
July 17	*The Billboard*
August	*The Bookman* — Edwin Björkman
August 4	*The Outlook*
August 8	*The Chicago Daily Tribute* [short notice]
August 14	*The Literary Digest*
August 28	*The Nation* — Joseph Krutch
August 29	*The San Francisco Chronicle*
August 9	*Life* — F. E. Schelling [poem]
September 30	*Life* — Arthur Guiterman [Rhymed review]

---

[9] Oliver Herford, *An Alphabet of Celebrities* (1899).
[10] Oliver Herford, "'Shakespeare' Identified Again," *Leslie's Weekly*, quoted in *Literary Digest*, Aug. 14, 1920, pp. 32-33.

literary and personal analogies and the amazing absence of common sense which characterize most Baconian endeavors." It also gave readers a large picture of the Welbeck Abbey portrait of Edward de Vere from the frontispiece of *"Shakespeare" Identified*. Between the digests of the reviews, it presented a summary of Looney's plan of investigation and findings from the "Conclusion" to *"Shakespeare" Identified*.

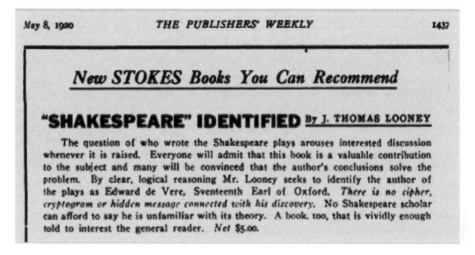

Others couldn't make up their minds about what they thought. The reviewer for *The Globe and Mail* in Toronto drew from the first chapter of *"Shakespeare" Identified* to make a case for doubting Shakspere's authorship:

> There is this mystery about Shakespeare: that a man born of illiterate parents and brought up in dirt and ignorance in Stratford, who was forced into marriage at the age of eighteen with a woman eight years his senior, and who, on the birth of twins, deserted his family, could produce in London, at the age of twenty-nine, an elaborate poem in the best English of the period, showing accurate knowledge of the classics, and follow it up with the superb Shakespearian dramas. Then, after a few years, this genius retired to Stratford to devote himself to houses, lands, orchards, malt, leaving no traces of a single intellectual or literary interest.[11]

And yet, even after accepting the disconnect between Shakspere's life and supposed literary achievements—and even after acknowledging that "Looney has taken great pains to investigate everything connected with the life of Oxford, and has found many curious and interesting bits of evidence in support of his claim," and that "he has made a contribution to Shakespeariana which is worth reading"—he continued to accept Shakspere's authorship.

On August 23, 1920, *The San Francisco Chronicle* printed a letter from Shafter Howard (with whom J. Thomas Looney was to correspond in 1926) that quoted an unnamed paper commenting that "while [Looney] may prove nothing, yet he brings the novelty of scholarship and modesty to what has been made for the first time an interesting dispute."[12] Perhaps spurred by Howard's letter, the *Chronicle* ran a review of *"Shakespeare" Identified* a week later. The reviewer's blanket acceptance of Sir Sidney

---

[11] "Life and Letters" [review of *"Shakespeare" Identified*], *Globe and Mail*, May 1, 1920, p. 13.
[12] Shafter Howard. "Scholarship and the Baconian Controversy," *San Francisco Chronicle*, Aug. 21, 1920, p. 16, quoting an unknown editorial titled "Who's Looney Now?"

Lee's statement that "no fact of literary history is better authenticated than the authorship of Shakespeare's plays" set the tone of the review. He informed readers that "it is impossible to examine in detail all the arguments contained in these 458 large pages," before proceeding to examine only a few of the lightest of Looney's arguments while ignoring his weightiest. He concluded with the nonsensical question, "we have the plays—does anything else really matter?"[13]

Others had a hard time making up their minds. William M. Reedy reported in his lengthy, thoughtful review in *Reedy's Mirror* (St. Louis) that *"Shakespeare" Identified* is "the best I have read . . . of all the books purporting to reveal the identity of the author of the Shakespeare plays and poems. . . . Mr. Looney almost persuades one to his plausible theory." He was held back by two things. One was the litany of widely believed "facts" that were simply not so: that "the plays were rewritten from older plays by Dekker and others," that Shakespeare "was not more learned than others," that "Jonson and Greene and Meres and others . . . have seen Shakespeare do the work," and so on. Second was Looney's incomplete answers to the "why" and "how" questions: "I don't quite make out exactly why it is that Oxford should have hid himself behind Shakespeare," and the difficulty of believing that "All of the men of the time were in a conspiracy to help the concealment of some really able, distinguished man under the name of Shakespeare."[14] He concluded, though, that "if I have to think of anyone other than Shakespeare being Shakespeare, I prefer Edward de Vere, seventeenth Earl of Oxford, to . . . any of the others who have been nominated for a vacancy that has not been proved to exist."

The following week Henry Watterson weighed in on the pages of *Reedy's Mirror* with the view "that William Shakespeare of Stratford-on-Avon did not write them—could by no reasonable conjecture have written them—ought to be, and is, clear to intelligent, unbiased minds."[15] His "guess" was that the true author was Christopher Marlowe. Reedy responded in the same issue by retracting his comments in the earlier issue and agreeing with Watterson that Marlowe was "the one powerful genius of the age of Shakespeare who surely could have written the plays, if Shakespeare did not write them." Why this switch? Because of his personal association with Watterson, a poet, journalist and

STOKES

BOOKS

"SHAKESPEARE" IDENTIFIED

By J. THOMAS LOONEY

There is no cipher, no cryptogram, no mystery in this important treatment of the Shakespearean controversy. Its straightforward attitude must appeal to all intelligent readers, whether Shakespeare scholars or not. The growing doubts regarding the claims of William Shakespeare of Stratford are here crystallized, and a logical presentment of the known facts, backed by newly discovered evidence, strongly points to Edward de Vere, Seventeenth Earl of Oxford, as the real author of the plays. *Net $5.00.*

Frederick A. Stokes advertisement in *The Atlantic Monthly*, June 1920

---

[13] "Shakespeare is Again Unmasked," *San Francisco Chronicle*, Aug. 29, 1920, p. E2.

[14] William M. Reedy, "Another Shakespeare," *Reedy's Mirror*, vol. 29/24 (June 10, 1920): 474.

[15] Henry Watterson, "The Shakespeare Myth," *Reedy's Mirror*, vol. 29/25 (June 17, 1920): 498.

Congressman "whose opinion . . . has more weight with me than that of any of the men who have written books to prove that Shakespeare was someone else than Shakespeare."[16] The Watterson-Reedy exchange was reprinted in the *Montgomery Advertiser* on June 27 and *The New York Times* on July 18.

Frederick Taber Cooper, Columbia University professor and former editor of the New York based literary periodical *The Forum*, wrote a very favorable assessment of *"Shakespeare" Identified.*

> Here at last is a sane, dignified, arresting contribution to the much abused and sadly discredited Shakespeare controversy. It is one of the most ingenious pieces of minute, circumstantial evidence extant in literary criticism. . . . Every right-minded scholar who seriously cares for the welfare of letters in the bigger sense should face the problem that this book presents and argue it to a finish.[17]

In January 1946 Forrest Rutherford wrote an article describing how his uncle, the dean of American stage producers Daniel Frohman, had enchanted him and other dinner guests with the story of J. Thomas Looney's great discovery shortly after *"Shakespeare" Identified* was published. It is a fascinating story, made more so by the fact that other guests included actress Alma Gluck, writer Fannie Hurst and violinist Efrem Zimbalist. Rutherford ended his account of the evening with the comment that "Emerson said 'Shakespeare is the only biographer of Shakespeare' and that is but partly true now. J. Thomas Looney is the first one to break through the fog of legend and disclose acceptable biographic material about the greatest literary personality of all time."[18] A fuller excerpt from Rutherford's account of the evening is reprinted below.

Forrest Rutherford: Daniel Frohman Introduces *"Shakespeare" Identified*

Excerpt from Rutherford's account of how Daniel Frohman introduced him to *"Shakespeare" Identified* in Frohman's apartment in New York in the early 1920s.

During dinner Mr. Daniel Frohman, then Dean of American stage producers and a wise old authority on plays and theatrical history, enchanted us with the story of J. Thomas Looney's great discovery as given in his *"Shakespeare" Identified.*

"Read it," said Uncle Dan, "and you will never again believe the old Stratford legend. 'Shakespeare' was Edward de Vere, the 17th Earl of Oxford."

He, himself, was so convinced and genuinely excited as he regaled us with incidents of proof from the book, that I am sure, his enthusiasm infected us all. Speaking for myself, I returned to Denver, secured the book, and true to Mr. Frohman's prophecy, could not but believe intensely in the Looney discovery. I became fascinated with the great figure that emerged from the mists surrounding this most elusive (until now) of all literary mysteries. Certainly I feel as did John Galsworthy that the book *"Shakespeare" Identified* is the greatest detective story I have ever read, and to a lover of creative genius, it is an emotional adventure one can never forget.

I loaned the book to a distinguished lawyer friend in Denver, Mr. Peter H. Holme, and his reactions were similar to my own. We purchased about thirty of the books and presented them to friends. We had great pleasure in the result. A few became as convinced as were we, and a few were mildly interested. One scholarly friend of mine would not even read the book. However, most of them, including the beloved William H. Smiley, then superintendent of schools and a great educator, were so fascinated by what might prove the greatest literary discovery of the ages, that several club dinners were largely devoted to discussion of the book.

---

[16] William M. Reedy, "The Shakespeare Myth," *Reedy's Mirror*, vol. 29/25 (June 17, 1920): 493.

[17] Although often quoted, the source of Cooper's assessment remains unknown.

[18] Forrest Rutherford, "Daniel Frohman Introduces the Great Unknown," *SF Quarterly*, vol. VII/1 (Jan. 1946): 1-2.

The prize for the most unusual reviews goes to *Life*, which ran a rhymed commentary on the authorship question by F. E. Schelling on September 9 and a "Rhymed Review" of *"Shakespeare" Identified* by Arthur Guiterman on September 30.

At least six American public libraries—in Boston, Chicago, Cleveland, Los Angeles, New York and St. Louis—held copies of *"Shakespeare" Identified* in 1920, as evidenced by their bulletins. The description of the book in the *Chicago Public Library Book Bulletin* was quite even handed:

> Critics differ on the value of this book. *The Times* says it is "unencumbered by any knowledge at first hand," *The Bookman*, "Impossible to do justice to the wealth of evidence collected . . . [I]t is to be hoped that [Mr. Looney's] leads will be followed

---

Who Wrote Shakespeare?

M'sieur Lefranc, who hails from Paris
Following a Mr. Harris
    More or less,
Believes that Shakespeare's dramas are by
William Stanley, Earl of Derby:
    That's his guess.

M'sieur Demblon, who likewise French is,
Holds, of dates and facts, such wrenches
    Under ban:
Sure as Elsinore's not Jutland,
Roger Manners, Earl of Rutland,
    Is the man.

These are foreign theories, Gaully;
A New Yorker thought that Raleigh
    Filled the myth;
Colonel Watterson says "Marlowe,"
And a certain Mr. Barlow
    Thinks 'twas Smith.

Was it Wilson, Harding, Cox, Ford?
Mr. Looney swears Lord Oxford
    Slung the ink.
"J. T. Looney," though illumey,
Sounds a wee bit nom de plumey,
    Don't you think?

You may believe it Oxford, Lyly,
Rutland—that some other Willy
    Writ these plays;
But you mustn't think that Bacon
Was a poet or could take on
    Such bad ways.

Francis really had no eye for
Drama; what he loved was cipher,
    Low—and pelf.
Yet these plays got written. Come now!
Could it be Will cribbed them, somehow,
    From himself?

F. E. Schelling

    [*Life*, vol. 76/1975 (Sept. 9, 1920)]

Rhymed Reviews
"Shakespeare" Identified
(By J. Thomas Looney. Frederick A. Stokes Co.)

Stay, Reader, stay! and listen here
    Before you take your journey bedward,
For I was "Oxford's famed De Vere,"
    Her Earl (the Seventeenth), named Edward.

In Gloriana's gorgeous age
    In joyous joust I couched and brake spear;
I patronized the British stage
    And wrote the plays of "William Shakespeare"!

The Sonnets bare the soul of me,
    And all that's any good in Lyly
Is also mine; for I am he
    Whom Spenser call, "Our pleasant Willie."

A royal ward, constrained and penned
    In court, my life was blighted early
By one who should have been my friend—
    My dad-in-law, the great Lord Burleigh.

For reasons not precisely sure
    (But faults I had, and fears and quarrels),
I made the stupid Stratford boor
    Who yet retains them, wear my laurels.

That mocker, Jonson, praised the lout!
    Bad Ben! for while, perchance, I bound him
To guard the facts from leaking out,
    He kept his word too well, confound him!

Alas! a sorry joke I played
    Upon myself, alone, in masking!
For still I see the Player's shade
    In all my rightful glory basking.

Yet I was Bertram, naughty youth,
    And princely Hamlet, sad and moony;
So if you want to learn the Truth,
    'Tis all worked out by **Mr. Looney**.

Arthur Guiterman.

    [*Life*, vol. 76/1978 (Sept. 30, 1920): 590]

up;" *The Nation* questions the validity of the evidence.[19]

Perhaps due to the preponderance of unfavorable reviews, sales of *"Shakespeare" Identified* were not what Looney nor Stokes would have wished. In October 1920, five months after it was published in the United States, William Morrow of Frederick A. Stokes Co. reported that "The book is going rather slowly at present, but interest may again revive."[20] Interest apparently did not revive, because Stokes later remaindered the book. It was out of print by spring 1927.

Meanwhile, Back in England . . . and in Australia and New Zealand

In England reviews of *"Shakespeare" Identified* continued to appear from time to time during the second half of 1920. An advertisement placed by Cecil Palmer in *Publishers' Circular* stated that "The publication of Mr. Looney's book has caused immense controversy in the press. . . . It has been reviewed at greater length than any other book recently published."[21]

Of greatest interest among reviews was Gordon Crosse's long review in *The Commonwealth*, a Christian social magazine. Crosse, whose article "The Real Shakespeare Problem" had launched the Crosse-Greenwood-Simpson exchange of authorship articles in *The Nineteenth Century and After* in 1917 (see Chapter 1), was not impressed. In his view, Looney had been "carried away by the force of his plausible array of misapprehensions, assumptions, guess-work, and coincidences," and lacked the "literary judgment, the power of weighing evidence, and some knowledge of the conditions under which Elizabethan literature was produced [which] are requisite for the profitable study [and] much more for the solution of a question of this kind."[22] Crosse, apparently, confused Looney's limited knowledge when he began his investigations with the depth of knowledge and acuity of judgment he had acquired by the time his book was completed.

Of greater interest are Looney's responses to several key parts of Crosse's review. These responses, handwritten on his personal copy of it, have never been published and are transcribed here for the first time. In response to Crosse's statement "Nor is it easy to explain why an author who wished to remain concealed should invite detection by choosing an illiterate as the putative father of his work," Looney wrote:

> It was practically the only way of doing it. Suppose he had chosen a man of some literary ability, say Lyly or Jonson or Munday. He would have to get them in to suppress themselves entirely in his interest. Secure an illiterate man, enforce complete silence and keep him out of sight. A single fragment of correspondence from the pen of his mask might have upset the whole scheme. In this case all we have are suppositions and they support the plan.

Ignoring the fact that nobody during Shakspere's lifetime ever attributed the plays to him, Crosse restated thoughts he had earlier expressed in his *Nineteenth Century and After* article: "There is no reason whatever to suppose that Shakespeare of Stratford did not write the plays attributed to him by all his contemporaries who have said anything positive on the subject, and by the universal opinion of more than two centuries, except that certain facts or alleged facts of his life have been thought to be inconsistent with his

---

[19] "Literature," *Chicago Public Library Book Bulletin*, December 1920, p. 157.
[20] William Morrow [Frederick A. Stokes, Publisher], letter to J. Thomas Looney, Oct. 29, 1920.
[21] Cecil Palmer advertisement, *Publishers' Circular*, Aug. 14, 1920, p. 160.
[22] Gordon Crosse, "Yet Another Shakespeare," *Commonwealth*, Oct. 1920, p. 289.

authorship" (290). The correspondences between Oxford's life and characters and events in the plays Crosse dismissed as "superficial." Looney's handwritten response:

> The truth is that beyond the fact that the plays are attributed to him, there is nothing to connect the actual publishing with Shakspere of Stratford. Nothing in his will, nothing of his being impacts the publication [of the First Folio]: no suggestion that anyone was acting on instructions either from his family or his executors.

Turning to Oxford, Crosse wrote that "there is nothing but conjecture . . . to connect his name with the publication of Shakespeare's plays nearly twenty years later [in the First Folio]," to which Looney handily wrote, "The plays are dedicated to Oxford's son-in-law and an intended son-in-law," thereby showing that it was Oxford's family, not that of the man from Stratford, who was directly connected to the publication of Shakespeare's collected works. Crosse then turned to *The Tempest* and, disagreeing with Looney's belief that the play is un-Shakespearean, cited Sir Arthur Quiller-Couch's belief that *The Tempest* was "one of the brightest jewels in Shakespeare's crown" (291). Nearby Looney penciled in: "The late plays represent the crowning achievement of the great genius," but by late plays he was referring to the great tragedies, which he identified in *"Shakespeare" Identified* as Oxford's final plays, not the "Romances" that are usually referred to as "late" plays. He then commented:

> Mr. Crosse appeals to Sir Arthur Quiller-Couch, especially his work on *Shakespeare's Workmanship*.[23] I accept his court of appeal and ask the reader to consider this fully . . . .

The final words after "fully" are illegible, but I interpret Looney's meaning to be a request that readers ask themselves whether or not *The Tempest* is one of Shakespeare's "brightest jewels" or "crowning achievements" in the sense that his other late plays—the great tragedies—were. He also could have intended to direct readers to Quiller-Couch's conclusion that in 1604 "something happened" with Shakespeare, as discussed later in this chapter.

Meanwhile, halfway around the world from London, an edition of *"Shakespeare" Identified* was scheduled to be published in Sydney, Australia on May 12, 1920 by Angus and Robertson Co. Unlike the Cecil Palmer edition in London published on March 4 and the U.S. edition published by Frederick Stokes on May 8, the Australian edition was unknown until several articles and advertisements mentioning it were recently discovered. As of December 2020, no copies of the Australian edition have been found, and it is possible that no such edition was actually published.[24]

> "Shakespeare Identified," by J. Thomas Looney; London, Cecil Palmer; Sydney, Angus and Robertson.
> • • • • •

More than a dozen reviews of *"Shakespeare" Identified* appeared in Australian newspapers, and at least four in New Zealand. Most early reviews were positive and more forward-looking in thinking through the consequences of acceptance of the Oxfordian claim. The reviewer for the *Avon Gazette and York Times* got it exactly right: "A book has

---

[23] Sir Arthur Quiller-Couch, *Shakespeare's Workmanship, From Lectures by Sir Arthur Quiller-Couch* (1918/1924).
[24] This image mentioning the Australian edition is from *The Sun* (Sydney) on June 17, 1920.

just been published in London which is going to set the whole literary world by the ears, and this time shake the foundations of Shakespeare's claims to immortality."[25] *"Shakespeare" Identified*, he continued, "throws overboard all previous theories and breaks entirely new ground. . . . Looney re-states the problem and advances new answers and solutions that will win adherents."

Henry Corder, in *The Advocate* (Melbourne), wrote that "The new theory has been set out with great ingenuity and with a mass of detail . . . that, though separately slight, when taken together make a strong argument." He found de Vere a "more attractive claimant than Bacon," in part because "his extant poems show clear resemblances to Shakespeare" and because "he is known to have had a close connection with theatrical affairs. . . . Moreover, his familiarity with Court life is thoroughly in keeping with that minute and vivid portraiture of kings and their courts which is so prominent in nearly all those plays."

He observed that "many writers on this subject display a heat and fervour of contentiousness which would hardly be justified [even] if the gravest principles were at stake," and concluded that "it should be entirely a matter of evidence, and not at all of personal feeling." "[26]

Corder's review had one blemish—the statement that "However interesting it may be, the question of who wrote the plays is not of any practical importance." Yet he went on to speculate "about the probable results which would follow general recognition" of the Oxfordian claim, thereby undermining his own prior statement.

The Oxfordian Thesis in the Australian and New Zealand Media, 1920-1922	
"Shakespeare" Identified published in Australia, 1920, May 12, by Angus and Robertson (Sydney)	
Reviews in Australia	
1920, May 1	*Daily Telegraph* (Sydney)
1920, May 12	*Sun* (Sydney)
1920, May 15	*Telegraph* (Brisbane)
1920, May 20	*Advocate* (Melbourne) — Henry Corder
1920, May 22	*Avon Gazette and York Times* – The Rambler
1920, May	*The Bulletin* — David McKee Wright
1920, June 17	*Sun* (Sydney)
1920, November 11	*Freeman's Journal* (Sydney)
1920, December 5	*Sun* (Sydney)
1921, April 23	*Sydney Morning Herald* [Mentions *"Shakespeare" Identified*]
1921, July 15	*Sydney Morning Herald* [Response by **J. Thomas Looney**]
1921, October 27	*The Bulletin* — Athos
1922, December 30	*Daily Telegraph* — W. J. P. Fitzgerald
Reviews in New Zealand	
1920, May 12	*Oamaru Mail* — Louis J. McQuilland
1920, June 5	*Southland Times*
1920, October 19	*Oamaru Mail*
1922, December 16	*Otago Daily Times*

> A fresh zest would no doubt be imparted to the study of the plays, and a new and fascinating world of research would be opened up to commentators. What numerous points of contact would be established between the personages of the plays and those of the Court! Hamlet's friend Horatio, for instance, has already been identified with Horace de Vere, the Earl of Oxford's cousin and a famous

---

[25] "Out and About," *Avon Gazette and York Times* (Australia), May 22, 1920, p. 2.
[26] "Who Wrote Shakespeare?" *Advocate* (Melbourne, Australia), May 20, 1920, p. 3.

soldier of the day. On the other hand, as hinted above, the unmasking of this greatest hoax of history would lead to a gradual waning in the popularity of Stratford, the Birthplace, and Anne Hathaway's Cottage would cease to be famous shrines and become merely picturesque houses, and the throngs of tourists would betake themselves elsewhere.

In *The Daily Telegraph* (Sydney) at the end of 1922, W. J. P. Fitzgerald provided another partial answer to the question of why it matters: "If Oxford really be the prototype of several leading Shakespeare characters—and there seems little doubt that he was—a vast field is opened to Shakespearean students. . . . The two men, Oxford and Shakespeare, must have been known to one another. It will be more than interesting to have the connection traced."[27]

The Freeman's Journal declared itself "unconvinced by Mr. Looney's arguments" because—in one of the most singular explanations put into print—"the most modern research shows" that Shakspere's work was simply "editorial: it dealt with masses of learned material, selected and arranged . . . by the brains of numerous playwrights who had preceded him. It was no more necessary for Shakespeare to be learned, in any true sense of the word, than it was necessary for an ordinary newspaper editor to be learned, however learned and comprehensively learned the contents of his newspaper."[28]

The first review to appear in New Zealand, in the *Oamaru Mail* on May 12, 1920, stated that "Mr. J. Thomas Looney makes out an extremely strong case against Shakespeare as author, but is only fantastically plausible in his substitution of the Earl of Oxford," before concluding that "the mystery of the making of the plays is almost an insoluble one."[29]

In a lengthy review, *The Southland Times* made a telling point: "At a time when literary men inferior to Shakespeare were the regular correspondents of the aristocratic patrons of literature there is no evidence that Shakspere ever corresponded with a single soul." Regarding Looney's book, his judgment was that,

> The process is ingenious, the reasoning plausible. The conclusions are not always convincing but they cannot be lightly thrust aside. A comparison of the work of the two men reveals amazing similarity in mentality and literary style. A remarkable series of coincidences is established, not only between the literary works, but also between the circumstances of Edward de Vere and the conditions essential to the wrier of the Shakespearian dramas. . . . The synchrony is too sustained and harmonious to be dismissed as fancy. The life facts are even more confirmatory than the literary facts.
>
> The book merits the attention of the Shakespearian student, and is certain to revive interest in an old and seemingly endless problem.[30]

A review of special interest was in the Sydney-based *The Bulletin*. It was by David McKee Wright, an Irish poet and journalist who lived and worked in Australia. "I came to the book full of prejudice and with a distinct bias against anyone who would attempt to rob the great dramatist of his laurels," he stated, "yet by the sheer hard logic of facts

---

[27] W. J. P. Fitzgerald, "Forgotten Celebrity of Elizabeth's Day," *Daily Telegraph* (Sydney), Dec. 30, 1922, p. 14.

[28] "Shakespeare Identified," *Freeman's Journal*, Nov. 11, 1920, p. 11.

[29] Louis J. McQuilland, "The Mystery of William Shakespeare." *Oamaru Mail*, May 12, 1920.

[30] "A Literary Log," *Southland Times* (New Zealand), issue 18840, June 5, 1920.

advanced he proved his case to me, a reader most unwilling to be convinced."[31] Wright's influence was so pervasive in Australia at the time that his positive review was mentioned by three other reviewers. One, Athos, told readers in the same publication a year later that he almost became convinced of the Oxfordian claim by Wright's review before reading the book. After presenting his own assessment of *"Shakespeare" Identified*—the book "unfolded in a logical, temperate and convincing manner . . . [and] I rose from it a convert"[32]—he shared reactions to the authorship issue by friends of his in the fall of 1921.

> When I have discussed the matter with any of my friends who I thought might be interested they nearly all took one or other of two attitudes. The first, and the commonest, is one that I think unworthy of any genuine lover of literature, or indeed of any seeker after truth. They ask: 'What matters it who wrote them? We have the stuff and don't care who was the author." . . . For these we have no hope.
>
> The other illogical and irrelevant reply is to this effect: "All sorts of cranks have said that Bacon and others wrote the plays, and no one has taken them seriously but themselves; Looney is probably just one more." It is characteristic of the shallow-brained of all ages to stigmatise as "cranks" all who first state opinions differing from the ordinary and the orthodox. Galileo, Newton, Einstein—all cranks!

Athos concluded with a call for an examination of the issue guided only by the desire to uncover the truth of the matter.

> If Looney's solution of the mystery is a bubble, let us by all means prick it: but at any rate let it be examined with fairness. Truth will prevail. But the earnest seeker after it must be prepared to follow the light of evidence even to the most unwelcome conclusions; to emancipate the mind from early prejudices; to resist the current of the desires and the refracting influence of the passions; to proportion on all occasions conviction to evidence, and to be ready, if need be, to exchange the calm of assurance for all the suffering of a perplexed and disturbed mind. To do this is very difficult and painful, but it is clearly involved in the notion of an earnest love of truth. By such methods and such only will the problem of the real Shakespeare, like every other mystery, be solved.

Two and a half months later *The Bulletin* ran a short notice stating that "Enough has reached us on the Looney-Shakespeare-de Vere matter to fill at least 20 *Bulletins*," though it didn't print any of the letters.

The Sydney Morning Herald was the only newspaper outside the United Kingdom to run an original piece by Looney. His fascinating letter, written in response to an article that had mentioned *"Shakespeare" Identified*, is worth noting for several reasons. One is his provocative statement that one scholar and author had told him that "'Even if your identification of de Vere with Shakespeare were wrong, it would still stand clear that you have made the most important discovery re the Shakespearean literature that has yet come to light; for here (in de Vere) is a poet who, if not Shakespeare, was Shakespeare's Model, and exercised, indubitably, the most profound influence on his style and thought.'" If only he had identified that scholar!

Looney also made clear that the Oxfordian thesis went far beyond merely claiming

---

[31] David McKee Wright, review in *The Bulletin*, date not known, quoted in "Out and About," *Avon Gazette and York Times* (Australia), May 22, 1920, p. 2.

[32] Athos, "The Real Shakespeare," *Bulletin*, Oct. 27, 1921, p. 25.

that Oxford wrote Shakespeare plays; it also claimed that Oxford was the actual prototype for "outstanding characters like Hamlet, Othello, Romeo, Berowne, Bertram, Prince Hal, Timon, and King Lear." Once that insight is accepted, Looney stated, the study of Shakespeare's plays "undergoes a profound revolution. . . . Furnished for the first time with the key principle of interpretation, the real study of 'Shakespeare,' as distinct from the merely literary and academic, is only now in its early stages."[33] The full passage with Looney's psychological insights is reprinted nearby.

Passage from J. Thomas Looney's Letter to *The Sydney Morning Herald*, printed as "Shakespeare's Identity," July 15, 1921, p. 12.

Shakespearean study has of late all tended to show that a certain psychological unity, a single personality under different moods and aspects, with many variations of external detail, runs through outstanding characters like Hamlet, Othello, Romeo, Berowne, Bertram, Prince Hal, Timon, and King Lear, along with the general assumption that this personality represents "Shakespeare" himself. Now, the singular fact in that this personality corresponds psychologically with the mentality revealed in Edward de Vere's poems; and the known details of Oxford's life are represented in such combinations in the plays that, on a simple mathematical calculation of probabilities, he may be proved the actual prototype. Then, with Oxford as the key, this literature, which for over three centuries has been regarded as wholly impersonal, is found to be packed with delineations of Elisabethan personalities, and the study of it undergoes a profound revolution. Indeed, we may say that, furnished for the first time with the key principle of interpretation, the real study of "Shakespeare," as distinct from the merely literary and academic, is only now in its early stages.

Roderick L. Eagle and the Baconian Idea after *"Shakespeare" Identified*

The first scholar, professional or amateur, known to have corresponded with Looney on the Oxfordian claim was Roderick L. Eagle, a prominent Baconian. Like Looney, Eagle was not a Shakespeare scholar by profession. His day job with the Marine Insurance Co. began in 1904; he retired as claims adjustor in 1947 and died at age eighty-nine in 1977, fifty-six years after his review of *"Shakespeare" Identified* was published in 1921. He also wrote several books on Bacon as the author of Shakespeare's works, including *Shakespeare: New Views for Old* (1930), published by Cecil Palmer.

Eagle had written to Palmer on April 1, 1920, to thank him for a review copy and to get Looney's address. He declared that, "[a]lthough a Baconian, I shall not be prejudiced against Mr. Looney's theory. All we seek is the truth, no matter how that may leave our most cherished beliefs." Palmer promptly forwarded the letter to Looney, and a correspondence ensued that included at least four letters in each direction over the next few months.[34]

In his first letter, Eagle informed Looney that he was reading *"Shakespeare" Identified* with the object of drawing up a review of it for *Baconiana*, the official organ of the Bacon Society, and had a number of questions for him. If only all reviewers were so concerned with understanding what an author had to say before writing their reviews! His first "questions," however, were transparent attempts to persuade Looney that Bacon wrote "Shakespeare." *Venus and Adonis* was the work of a youthful genius; why would Oxford have stayed its publication for so many years? Isn't it more likely that the younger Bacon was its author? Who revised *Othello* in 1611 and added 160 new lines to the 1622 edition?

---

[33] J. Thomas Looney, "'Shakespeare's' Identity," *Sydney Morning Herald*, July 15, 1921, p. 12.
[34] Of the nine letters they exchanged, only the five to Looney are known to exist today.

Isn't this evidence that the author was alive then, as Bacon was and Oxford wasn't? Eagle raised seventeen additional points, citing statements Looney made on specific pages of his book, and suggested several books on Bacon for him to read.

In his next letter Eagle thanked Looney for replying and stated that "The Baconians will welcome your labours because they will recognize the difficulties and disappointments which every pioneer is bound to face." He explained that "Our experience is that it is a waste of time to correct the errors and expose the ignorance of pressmen and journalists. Their work is to bolster up the Stratfordian tradition and the interests vested in its maintenance." Given his experience over the previous six weeks, Looney must surely have had some sympathy with that assessment.

Eagle remained a Baconian even after reading *"Shakespeare" Identified*, writing that "While I admit that there is a case for the Earl of Oxford that is entitled to be submitted, it is, in my opinion, too weak in many vital points to shake my conviction that the plays and poems of Shakespeare are due, in the main, to the penmanship of Francis Bacon. Still, your work, especially as it is the first presentation of a new theory, is wonderful, and I hope you will not be discouraged because the critics are against you."

Eagle's review of *"Shakespeare" Identified* was submitted to *Baconiana* by early August, but it did not appear until March 1921 because of the reduction in the number of issues produced each year—a development showing the fading appeal of the Baconian claim. The review repeated the same arguments for Bacon's authorship that Eagle had presented in his letters, and made the odd claim that "After the death of Oxford, in 1604, there is no trace of any falling off in the output of plays,"[35] by which he meant that plays such as *Lear*, *Othello*, *Antony and Cleopatra* were written, and other plays revised, after Oxford's death—issues that Looney had addressed in *"Shakespeare" Identified*. Eagle also failed to grapple with Looney's wealth of examples linking Oxford's early poetry with Shakespeare's, and events in his life to developments and characters in the plays.

The insubstantial nature of the review and the absence of any mention of Looney or Edward de Vere in Eagle's 1930 book, *Shakespeare: New Views for Old*, were indicative of Baconians' inability to compete with the Oxfordian claim. Many authorship doubters in the latter decades of the nineteenth century had attributed the greatest literary works of the Elizabethan era to one of the greatest intellects of the period, Sir Francis Bacon, as a stopgap measure in spite of the absence of any substantive evidence for his authorship. Baconians had been quick to acknowledge the support the Oxfordian idea gave to the doubter movement, but were slower to realize how effectively it would sink their own ship. The Baconian idea had been foundering well before the end of the nineteenth century. It still has a few adherents even today, but the death blow came in 1920 with the publication of *"Shakespeare Identified*.

The Poems of Edward de Vere

J. Thomas Looney's second book, *The Poems of Edward de Vere*, was published by Cecil Palmer on February 12, 1921,[36] almost a year after *"Shakespeare" Identified*. It brought

---

[35] Roderick L. Eagle, "Shakespeare and the Earl of Oxford," *Baconiana*, vol. XVI/63 (March 1921): 84-85.
[36] The exact date of publication is uncertain. Looney wrote "12-2-21" [February 12, 1921] in his personal copy of the book, but that could have been the date he received an advance copy rather than the release date. *The Yorkshire Post and Leeds Intelligencer*, in its review on February 16, stated that the book "was published today," but the paper could have delayed printing the review for several days after it left the reviewer's hands. I use the date Looney wrote in his copy.

together forty-eight poems, consisting of twenty-four accepted as authentic by Dr. Alexander B. Grosart in 1876, thirteen songs from the plays of John Lyly that Looney believed were written by de Vere, and eleven poems signed "Ignoto" in *England's Helicon* (1600) that Looney attributed to him. The book also includes a lengthy "Biographical Outline" of de Vere and an even longer "Introduction to the Poems," as well as annotations to them.

In the "Biographical Outline" Looney presented the most important discoveries supporting the Oxfordian claim uncovered since publication of *"Shakespeare" Identified*. Among them were newly established linkages between important events in Oxford's life and the Fenton-Anne Page-Slender storyline in *The Merry Wives of Windsor*, and his discovery that orthodox Shakespeare scholars had tied "Shakespeare" closely to Windsor Castle and its environs, the setting for that play. Looney also provided a fuller statement on the absence of ties between William Shakspere's family and the publication of the First Folio, on the subterfuge involved in the statements by Heminges, Condell and Ben Jonson in its prefatory materials, and on the direct ties between Edward de Vere's family and the publication of the Folio.

Looney reproduced Arthur Quiller-Couch's statement that "The longer we consider these later plays that fall to be dated between the great tragedies and *The Tempest*, the more we are forced to feel that something had happened . . . [resulting in] the sublime confusion of dates and places . . . the laxities of construction . . . the tours de force mixed up with other men's botch work . . . [and] serious scamping of artistry."[37] Looney also reprinted the passages concerning "the gentleman Edward Earle of Oxforde" from Puttenham's *Arte of Poesie* (1589) that had been discovered by Edwin Björkman.

In the "Introduction to the *Poems*" Looney further established the vital and unique position Edward de Vere occupied in the literary life of Elizabethan England:

> The Elizabethan period was the time of the great outburst of our national song literature; and Edward de Vere's work stands at the beginning of that period, the time of the early courtier poets, and before the movement had passed into the wider social area in which it gained the vigour and reality of the later Elizabethan poetry and drama. Of these early courtier poets he was one of the first; he was recognized as 'the best'; he is the only one whose work foreshadowed the spirit of the later work; the only one of whom it could possibly be said that he wrote poetry which 'Shakespeare' might have written; and he, too, was the only one whose life passed from the circle of the royal court to become immersed in that larger Bohemian society, in which the poetic and dramatic developments of Elizabeth's later years were elaborated.
>
> Personally, then, he represents the source of the movement, and a vital connecting link between the two periods. Under any conception of Shakespearean authorship, and under any unified theory of Elizabethan literature, his position is central and commanding, and the failure to perceive this means that the sixteenth century poetry has not yet been fully understood.[38]

Oxford "is the key to understanding Elizabethan literature," Looney continued. "From the lyrics of Surrey, through the courtier poets of Elizabeth's early years, to the playhouses and dissolute acting companies of the succeeding years, and on to the great Shakespeare dramas culminating in *Hamlet*—for which it is now being admitted that he

---

[37] Arthur Quiller-Couch, *Shakespeare's Workmanship* (1917), p. 296, quoted in J. Thomas Looney (editor), *The Poems of Edward de Vere* (1921), p. xxxvii.

[38] J. Thomas Looney, *The Poems of Edward de Vere* (1921), pp. xlii-xliii.

was the model—the Earl of Oxford is the personal thread which unifies all" (lxxvi).

Looney then built on the similarities between Oxford's early poetry and Shakespeare's mature works that he had introduced in *"Shakespeare" Identified*. He called on readers to make their own detailed examinations of both sets of poems, such an effort being necessary because, "like the biographical argument, the poetical argument can be burlesqued by representing minor points as constituting the whole; but this is not the way of those who want the truth." Such an examination would also help them "in discriminating between what is distinctive and personal, and what was common to the poetic fashions or stock of the times. Even conventional forms and phrases were not conventional to the first men who employed them, and a study of dates will probably show how much of what ultimately became common stock actually had its source in the Earl of Oxford" (lxxiii).

Reviews of *The Poems of Edward de Vere*

The Poems of Edward de Vere was reviewed in at least ten publications in Britain but none at all in North America, where no edition was issued. Looney responded to three reviews. In two cases—*The New Age* and *The Outlook*—this resulted in extended back and forth with the reviewer.

In December 1920, after the rush of interest in *"Shakespeare" Identified* had died away, *The New Age: A Weekly Review of Politics, Literature and Art* ran a review that differed from all others in the nature of its criticism. The review, by A. R. Orage, owner and editor of *The New Age* writing under the name R. H. C., generated

Reviews of *The Poems of Edward de Vere*, 1921	
February 16	*Yorkshire Post and Leeds Intelligencer*
February 17	*The Scotsman*
February 24	*Times Literary Supplement*
March 4	*The Bookman's Journal*
April 1	*Irish Times*
May	*The Bookman*
June 4	*New Statesman*
August 27	*The Spectator*
See below for reviews and exchanges of letters in *The New Age* and *The Outlook*.	

a series of letters between Looney and Orage that became a seven-part exchange of views.

Orage wrote that he, like Looney, was convinced "that neither the Stratford man nor Bacon wrote the plays," and he conceded that "the parallels Looney draws from his researches into the history of the 17th Earl of Oxford are certainly striking."[39] But he could not accept de Vere as Shakespeare, he explained, because he did not see in his poems, as Looney did, the "natural seeds and clear promise" of Shakespeare's mature works. Edward de Vere, he concluded, "could not have possibly written a single true Shakespearian line." Looney's response captured his surprise at this judgment.

> Most of my critics have been writers acquainted with all the leading facts of the Shakespeare controversy, who have yet been able to preserve a steadfast orthodoxy. From them I feel separated by a wall of *constitutional* mental difference—not of knowledge or of capacity—against which argument would be unavailing. My critic in the *New Age* stands, however, in a totally different relationship, both to the problem and to my researches. He rejects alike the Stratfordian and the Baconian theory: and is therefore predisposed to adopt a reasonable alternative; he frankly admits that the general mass of my evidence

---

[39] R. H. C., "Readers and Writers," *New Age*, Dec. 2, 1920, p. 56.

is 'striking,' but he feels obligated to reject the De Vere solution absolutely on very definite grounds. He presents, therefore, a case which calls for a serious answer.[40]

Looney's response was two-pronged: first, to urge consideration of the nature of all the evidence, and second to challenge the reviewer's judgment about Oxford's early poetry and the potential it showed for him, decades later, to have written Shakespeare's. On the first point, he wrote that "when many distinct lines of evidence, involving a vast accumulation of details, all support in a 'striking' way a given solution to any problem, whilst one point raises a difficulty, the presumption is against the one; not until that one point has been exhaustively investigated, and the matter placed beyond dispute, is it sound wisdom, or scientific, to set aside 'for ever and ever' a conclusion otherwise so well supported?" And on the second,

> For such an investigation in this case certain things are necessary: it is necessary to know the poetry of Edward de Vere as a whole; . . . it is necessary to know whether a given passage was written at the age of 15 or 50; whether during the conventional period of the early court poets, or the vigorous realistic period of the later dramatic poets; and whether it was written before or after the writer had passed through his stimulating experiences in the Bohemian world of Elizabethan drama. As little or none of this material is yet available, a definite rejection of all the other evidence on the grounds of poetic incompatibility is at any rate premature, and places the whole issue at the mercy of mere caprice. (91)

He noted that "other competent literary men have not only praised the poetry in terms appropriate to Shakespeare, but have gone as far as to admit that the poetry is 'such as Shakespeare might have written.'"

Exchanges about parallel passages and the quality of Oxford's lyrics consumed the next four letters. Looney then concluded that, "The whole conception, imagery, and workmanship are so similar [in the passages being considered] that they might easily have been taken for two parts of one poem; and in this case the parallel is actually strengthened by a common inversion of the natural or spoken order of words."[41]

The second extended exchange between Looney and a reviewer over the quality of Oxford's poems was with John C. Squire, editor of *The Observer*, writing in *The Outlook*

J. Thomas Looney-R. H. C. (A. R. Orage) Exchange of Views	
in *The New Age: A Weekly Review of Politics, Literature and Art*	
1920, Dec. 2	
R. H. C.	Readers and Writers [Review of *"Shakespeare" Identified*]
1920, Dec. 23	
J. Thomas Looney	Readers and Writers [Response to the Dec. 2 review]
R. H. C.	Reviewer's reply to Looney
1921, Jan. 20	
J. Thomas Looney	Readers and Writers [Response to reviewer]
R. H. C.	Reviewer's second reply to Looney
1921, Jan. 27	
R. H. C.	Readers and Writers. [Reviewer's additional reply]
1921, Feb. 17	
J. Thomas Looney	Shakespeare Identified [Looney's response to reviewer]

---

[40] J. Thomas Looney, "Readers and Writers, *New Age*, Dec. 23, 1920, p. 91.
[41] J. Thomas Looney, "Readers and Writers," *New Age*, Jan. 20, 1921, p. 138.

under the name Solomon Eagle. Looney and Squire would engage again two years later when Squire's review of Col. Bernard R. Ward's *The Mystery of "Mr. W. H."* was answered by Looney (see Chapter 6).

The series was launched by Squire's review on March 12. Looney responded at length, Squire responded at even greater length, and the result was a fascinating discussion of just the kind that Looney must have envisioned when he'd previously expressed his hope "that English literary journals . . . [would] throw open their columns to such a discussion as will let in the fullest light upon the question."[42]

In his review Squire acknowledged that Looney "has a much more presentable candidate than most have had," and stated that "I have read every line of both his books." Nevertheless, he continued, "I am still quite unshaken in my belief that Oxford did not write Shakespeare, and still fairly established in my opinion that Shakespeare did. What slight weakening there may have been on my part when I was reading the introduction soon disappeared when I was confronted with Oxford's intermittently convincing but often lame poems."[43] He went on to say that whenever Looney "prints a footnote with a 'parallel passage' from Shakespeare what strikes me invariably is not the resemblance, sometimes interesting, between the conceptions of the two men, but the vast gulf between their styles."

In response, Looney cited the "identity of conception" and "parallels in phrasing" in support of his belief that the two bodies of work came from the same pen. The differences were just what should be expected, he explained, given several factors. One was that Oxford's early poems were for the most part "hasty ephemeral products of his dilettante courtier days," and as such would surely differ from "Shakespeare's," which "had undergone a lengthy process of most exacting revision and vast enrichment."

Another factor, even more decisive, was "historical." "It was absolutely impossible for the greatest genius to have produced, in 1576, literature at all resembling, either in form or quality, the work which came from Shakespeare's pen eighteen years later," because:

> In the whole history of England there never has been, and there never can be again, anything like the phenomenally rapid expansion, that took place at that time, in literary craftsmanship, and even in the English language itself. . . . The rich veins of phrase and figure created by two abnormal decades of national poetical enthusiasm, the intense stimulus given to many phases of intellectual

---

J. Thomas Looney-John C. Squire (Solomon Eagle) Exchanges in
The Outlook: A Weekly Review of Politics, Art, Literature and Finance

1921, March 12
    Solomon Eagle   "Mr. Looney and Lord Oxford"
                               [Review of *The Poems of Edward de Vere*]

1921, June 25
    J. Thomas Looney   Shakespeare, Lord Oxford, and Mr. Looney
                               [Response to the March 12 review]

1921, July 2
    Solomon Eagle   The Critic at Large: A Voice from the Past
                               [Reply to Looney's June 25 response]

1921, July 16
    J. Thomas Looney   Mr. Looney Replies [Response to Eagle's July 2 reply]

---

[42] J. Thomas Looney, "Is Shakespeare Identified?" *Bookman's Journal*, April 9, 1920, p. 452.

[43] John Collins Squire (as Solomon Eagle), "Mr. Looney and Lord Oxford," *Outlook*, March 12, 1921, p. 231.

interest, the free and even licentious probing of life and human nature, furnished the 'nineties with literary powers and possibilities far beyond the highest hopes of the 'seventies.[44]

Roundup of Other Reviews of *The Poems of Edward de Vere*

Other reviews were almost unanimously unfavorable as to the quality of Edward de Vere's poems and their "evidence" as to his authorship of Shakespeare's works.

The Scotsman wrote that "Adverse criticism, and the neglect that is still harder to bear, has not discouraged Mr. Looney in his belief that the Seventeenth Earl of Oxford was the 'real Shakespeare.'"[45] Still, it found that "These verses, whatever their merits, have singularly little in them to suggest a great dramatist in the making; and the reader must feel that Mr. Looney has, by their citation, done more to disprove than to advance his theory." It also repeated the 1604 canard that "some of Shakespeare's greatest work kept appearing on the boards and in print for years after Oxford was dead," thereby ignoring not only Looney's explanations on that point but also the testimony of respected orthodox scholars.

The Irish Times "remain[ed] entirely sceptical and held fast to the recognised Shakespearian creed."[46] *The Spectator* similarly concluded that "the present volume does not affect the opinion of the inadequacy"[47] of the Oxfordian claim that it expressed in its review of *"Shakespeare" Identified* a year earlier. *The Bookman*, retreating from the perceptiveness of Björkman's review nine months earlier wrote that "Before one wastes space in discussing Mr. Looney's transparent sophistries one would like him to explain why de Vere produced his feeblest work under his own name, and his best (assuming it was his) under the name of Shakespeare. But the whole contention is the idlest nonsense."[48] *The New Statesman*, after committing the sin Looney warned against of pulling out and critiquing only the weakest examples from a complex cumulative argument, did admit that "de Vere found time to write very reasonable poetry. His place is secure in any limited anthology."[49]

The lengthy review in the *Yorkshire Post and Leeds Intelligencer* was notable. The reviewer recognized that "the most competent critics . . . acknowledged that Edward de Vere wrote some very beautiful lyrics—some lines that Shakespeare himself might have written," but that "doesn't get us very far." He found that Looney's "analysis of the poems is not the strongest or most stimulating part of his case," and that "there is more matter in his introduction, in which he supplements his previous book by producing his 'new material.'"[50] He recounted many of the "impressive" linkages Looney presented between Oxford and Shakespeare without being convinced by them, and concluded that "In

---

[44] J. Thomas Looney, "Shakespeare, Lord Oxford, Solomon Eagle and Mr. Looney," *The Outlook*, June 25, 1921, pp. 543-45.

[45] "Poetry," *Scotsman*, February 17, 1921, p. 2.

[46] "Elizabethan Poems," *Irish Times*, April 1, 1921, p. 2.

[47] "The Poems of Edward de Vere," *Spectator*, Aug. 27, 1921, p. 278.

[48] "Notes on New Books," *Bookman*, May 1921, p. 78.

[49] "New Poems of Shakespeare," *New Statesman*, June 4, 1921, p. 252.

[50] "Mr. Looney's Solution of 'Shakespeare:' Edward de Vere's Poems," *Yorkshire Post and Leeds Intelligencer*, Feb. 16, 1921, p. 4. The reviewer's statement made it even more unfortunate that much of the introductory material in *The Poems of Edward de Vere* was omitted in the 1975 reprinting of the book. The full text of that introductory material has since been reprinted in *"Shakespeare" Revealed: the Collected Articles and Published Letters of J. Thomas Looney* (2019), compiled and edited by the author of this book.

statements of fact Mr. Looney has been careful; it is in his deductions that he is exposed to, as he invites, criticism. The largest deduction[s] . . . [are] that Oxford wrote the plays secretly, that Shakespeare was a nonentity, and that Shakespeare's friend Ben Jonson was a party to the subterfuge." The reviewer seemed to want to make the case for Oxford as Shakespeare without openly stating that he agreed with it.

The review in *The Bookman's Journal* provided Looney an opportunity to express his reflections on responses to the Oxfordian claim over the past year. The reviewer, S., presumably the same reviewer of *"Shakespeare" Identified* a year earlier, wrote that Looney "has done a good service in reprinting Oxford's poems, which indeed were not hitherto easily accessible. He is also to be thanked for collecting here Lyly's poems and the Ignoto poems from *England's Helicon*—both of which books are difficult to get hold of and should certainly be reprinted. But not for one moment can I accept his theory that Oxford was responsible for these last." He went on to make the obtuse statement that "For myself, I may be wrong, but I cannot see that the question whether Shakespeare's works were written by Shakespeare, or Bacon, or the Earl of Oxford, or by any other man of the period, is of the least importance."[51]

Responding, Looney addressed the last point first:

> What I am unable to understand is his view that the importance of "Shakespeare's" identity requires to be proved. If historic research has any value, if it is important that we should know the truth and form a just appreciation of any man whose labours have gone to shape the life and thought of his fellows, surely it is of importance to Englishmen that the truth should be known and justice should be done to the memory of the one Englishman who, more than any other, has established himself permanently in the intellectual life of mankind.[52]

He went on to say that he "was not optimistic about the future of British intellectual life. The attacks on the Oxfordian idea did not reflect well on "the intellectual credit of England." "The present-day handling by the 'intellectual classes' of all problems requiring *thought* rather than erudition and literary style [gave him] an uneasy feeling that the initiative which England held in the latter half of the nineteenth century is passing into other hands."

In America, he continued, although "certain sections of the 'orthodox' have assailed my work with a hostility quite equal to what it has aroused in England . . . there have been people of standing who have risen to the requirements of the problem." But in England, "not a single writer of equal standing has been big enough to do the same."[53] He named one literary and oriental scholar and author, the Rev. W. A. L. Elmslie, formerly a lecturer at Cambridge and a Fellow of Christ's College, who had, "by public lecture rather than by his pen, shown a courage and independence of judgment in respect to my theories quite equal to that of the better-known American writers." In writing to Looney, Elmslie had stated "'I do not know what our literature experts are dreaming about that your book has not been the talk of the year.'" That, Looney responded, "is but confirmation of my fears respecting the intellectual credit of England."

Francis Clarke submitted a letter to the editor disparaging the reviewer's dismissal of

---

[51] S. "Stratford and Stony Stratford," *Bookman's Journal*, March 4, 1921.

[52] J. Thomas Looney, "Stratford and Stony Stratford," *Bookman's Journal*, March 25, 1921, p. 388.

[53] Looney could also have mentioned the British novelist John Galsworthy. Or perhaps his well-known comment was made after March 25, 1921.

the Oxfordian claim that perhaps eased Looney's concerns slightly.

> I forget all the good things that have appeared in *The Bookman's Journal* since its inception (and there are many) when I read articles like [the review of *The Poems of Edward de Vere*] in your issue on March 4. It cannot be called a review, but poses as one. . . . You will be doing your journal more justice, Sir, if the next time you have an article for that reviewer that you ascertain whether he has some comprehension of the subject, for the man who says *it does not matter* has no interest, and therefore no understanding.[54]

**Early Literary Supporters Mentioned by J. Thomas Looney
in *The Bookman's Journal*, March 25, 1921**

In the United States:

Gelett Burgess (1866-1951). A San Francisco based artist, art critic and writer. In 1947-1949 Burgess would publish a number of important letters and articles supportive of Oxford's authorship in *The New York Herald Tribune*, *The Washington Post* and *The Saturday Review*. He and Looney exchanged letters in 1920 and 1927. (See text box in Chapter 18.)

Oliver Hereford (1860-1935). British-born, but American, writer, illustrator and poet.

Eric Schuler (1889-1937). Worked in the copyright office in the Library of Congress. Served as secretary and treasurer of the Author's League of America (now The Authors Guild).

Edwin Björkman (1866-1951). In the August 1920 issue of *The Bookman* (vol. 51/9: 677-682) (not to be confused with *The Bookman's Journal*), he wrote one of the longest and most favorable reviews of *"Shakespeare" Identified*.

Frederick Taber Cooper (1864-1937). Writer, professor at Columbia University, and former editor of *The Forum*.

Carolyn Wells (1862-1942). A prolific writer noted for humor, poetry, and children's books. (See text box in Chapter 16.)

In England:

Rev. Walter Angus L. Elmslie (1856-1935). A Scottish missionary, former lecturer at Cambridge, Fellow at Christ's Church.

Looney's Oxfordian Correspondence

J. Thomas Looney carried on extensive correspondence with many people who had become interested in the Oxfordian idea after reading *"Shakespeare" Identified*. As of the end of 2020, more than 500 letters between early Oxfordians are known of—surely only a small fraction of those that were sent—with more than half from or to Looney. More than 400 of them have been found and transcribed; I plan to prepare an annotated collection for publication.

Sir George G. Greenwood, whose books and articles had made such a strong case against William Shakspere's authorship in the dozen years before *"Shakespeare" Identified* was published, wrote to Looney in April 1921 asking about sources for some of the passages Looney had quoted from the works of traditional Shakespeare scholars. They were to exchange at least nine letters in each direction over the following twenty-seven months. Although ten of Greenwood's letters have survived, only three of Looney's are known to exist. (Greenwood's papers, which may contain the other letters Looney sent to him, have not yet been located).

---

[54] Francis Clarke, "Stratford and Stony Stratford," *Bookman's Journal*, March 25, 1921, p. 388.

A typical question posed to Looney by Greenwood—from his first letter—showed the nature of their interactions.

> At p. 74 of your *"Shakespeare" Identified* you give a quotation from Halliwell-Phillipps concerning his searches of municipal records. Would you very kindly send me the reference? I presume the passage is in the *Outlines*. If so would you please state what is the edition you quote.[55]

Greenwood's questions had been necessary because Looney seldom provided complete information for the passages he quoted in *"Shakespeare" Identified*. He usually gave either an author's name or a book's title, but not both, and he rarely provided page numbers or mentioned which edition a quotation came from. He included only a handful of footnotes and no bibliography.[56] In his letter of April 6, Looney explained why such information had not been included.

> Let me assure you that I feel it a pleasure to be able to furnish you with these particulars: indeed it helps me to make good certain deficiencies in my book. In working up an argument with so many sides to it I found it imperative to press on somewhat rapidly at times with the work of committing conceptions to paper & was obliged to perforce frequently to neglect the matter of references, & sometimes to trust my memory more than was desirable. I felt, however, that I was only marking out foundations upon which others were destined to build. I must thank you therefore for affording me an opportunity of filling up a few of the small gaps.

Their correspondence also addressed works by other scholars. Their extensive discussion of George Hookham's article in *The National Review*—his reasons for believing that "Shakespeare" may have been alive at the time the First Folio was published in 1623—filled several long letters. *The Tempest* was also discussed extensively, launched by Greenwood's comment in support of Looney's position on the play: "In my humble opinion . . . your arguments are very strong. . . . Have you any idea as to who the author may have been?"[57] Looney's 1,000-word reply, in one of the few letters to Greenwood that have surfaced, was that,

> The view to which I am increasingly inclined is that the work, as a whole, is one of those composite productions, upon which it was not uncommon to employ a group of court writers and stage experts, when an impressive dramatic novelty was required for some special occasion. . . . The question then is: who supplied the central core and was thus regarded as the author? . . . [William Stanley, the Earl of] Derby, it seemed to me . . . was just the man to have had a foremost hand in the editing of the Folio, and to have been the author of some of the non-Shakespearean parts of it.[58]

Katharine E. Eggar, perhaps the least known of the first generation of Oxfordians, had more extensive surviving correspondence with Looney than anybody else. Seventeen of

---

[55] Sir George G. Greenwood, letter to J. Thomas Looney, April 3, 1921. One of the few Looney-Greenwood letters to have been found so far is the one dated April 6, 1921, in which Looney answered Greenwood's question. The source he gave is "the Preface (pp. XIV and XV) Second Edition (1852)" of Halliwell-Phillipps's *Outlines*. The same quotation can also be found in the Third Edition (1883), p. 281.

[56] The Centenary edition of *"Shakespeare" Identified* (2018) which I edited, provides full bibliographical information for more than 230 quoted passages.

[57] Sir George G. Greenwood, letter to J. Thomas Looney, Feb. 19, 1922.

[58] J. Thomas Looney, letter to Sir George Greenwood, March 14, 1922.

her letters to him have survived, as have twenty-nine of his to her. Their communications began early in 1922 and continued—with several lengthy gaps—until at least 1938. From start to finish they focused almost exclusively on Oxfordian matters. Some letters are quite lengthy. They serve as a record of how their research and publishing interests changed over time, and provide unique and extensive commentary on developments within the Oxfordian movement over that critical early decade and a half.

Eggar first inquired about the possibility of Looney's giving a talk to a group in London of which she was vice president. After stating that he rarely traveled to London, Looney expressed his view that

> [t]he fact that your societies are not specifically literary is no reason why the question of Shakespearean authorship should not be laid before them. Indeed, I think I should prefer for audiences those whose interests are wide, and whose inclination is to examine problems from the standpoint of common sense, rather than those who are more exclusively literary.[59]

He updated her on his current work linking events in Oxford's life with developments in *The Merry Wives of Windsor* that would form the bulk of his article in *The Golden Hind* seven months later. He also passed on information about two letters of Oxford's that had just come to light, one brought to his attention by "an American lady who is following the subject with considerable skill and enthusiasm" (Margaret L. Knapp of Hartford, Connecticut). Eggar responded with a letter describing her own work on similarities between Oxford's poetry and Shakespeare's, and Looney, in his next letter, informed her of the discovery of the house—Brooke House, also known as King's Place—in which Oxford had lived during the last years of his life.

Correspondence with American Oxfordians

Looney was in correspondence with several Americans as early as the spring of 1920, including Gelett Burgess as early as May, Carolyn Wells beginning in June, and Margaret L. Knapp from November onwards. These three, all noted writers and all known to each other, formed the first nucleus of support for the Oxfordian claim in North America.

Gelett Burgess's first letter, dated May 19, 1920, was addressed to Frederick A. Stokes, Inc., the American publisher, who sent it on to Looney.

> I have been fascinated beyond measure by *"Shakespeare" Identified*. It has all the charm, all the excitement of the most thrilling detective story. Indeed, it is a detective story; and, if the author's conclusions are accepted by posterity, it chronicles the most important literary pursuit and discovery ever given to the world....
>
> No one, whatever his conventional prejudices in favor of the Man of Stratford, can read it without being impressed by the fairness of view, the logical pursuance of the inquiry, and the elegance of clarity of Mr. Looney's style....
>
> One cannot help being moved and inspired by this extraordinary and sincere attempt to solve the greatest literary mystery of modern times. Once having read the book, I doubt if anyone, friend or foe, will ever forget it.[60]

This letter was an unparalleled act of courage and magnanimity by a writer of national stature willing to use his good name and reputation to help the Oxfordian cause in the

---

[59] J. Thomas Looney, letter to Katharine E. Eggar, March 4, 1922.
[60] Gelett Burgess, letter to Frederick A. Stokes, May 19, 1920.

face of the often hostile criticism that *"Shakespeare" Identified* had received in many publications. In his response, Looney was overflowing with gratitude.

American novelist <u>Margaret L. Knapp</u>, writing to Looney on Armistice Day 1920, related her great interest in *"Shakespeare" Identified* and offered the provocative idea that "If Oxford is Shakespeare, we should in all probability never have had the best of his plays had he remained in favor with the Queen."[61] In her second letter she raised another interesting point not followed up on, to my knowledge, for more than twenty years. "Has any connection ever been traced between the Edward Vere who was in the Netherlands with the other Fighting Veres? . . . [H]e left a large volume of manuscript translations."[62] In the same letter she made another observation of great perceptiveness not developed further by Oxfordians for more than half a century.

> It would be a gain if the circumstances attending the publication of the First Folio could be cleared up a little more. . . . Henry Vere [Oxford's son and the 18th Earl of Oxford] was in the Tower all through 1623, which might have been the reason why the psychological moment for revealing the authorship was allowed to pass. If Southampton was still in disgrace at that time, it would not have done to dedicate the Folio to him. The next best thing would have been what was actually done—to dedicate them to the two Herberts, one of whom was Lord Chamberlain, and the other was married to Oxford's daughter.[63]

Knapp proposed that efforts be made to trace the copies of the First Folio that would have been in the possession of Oxford's daughters. "I cannot help thinking that some item in a catalogue of one of the libraries of the great private families may yet come to light."

Her five long letters to Looney that still survive document that sophisticated interest in the Oxfordian claim existed in North America even at that early date. Every effort must be made to determine whether her papers have survived, and if so whether Looney's letters to her are among them.

The National Review, 1921-1922

Between November 1921 and October 1922 *The National Review*[64] ran five important articles on the Shakespeare authorship question that were to lead to far-reaching developments. The trigger was R. MacDonald Lucas's article in the November 1921 issue, "Did Lord Derby Write Shakespeare?" In it, Lucas reviewed the case for de Vere's authorship—as stated by Looney in *"Shakespeare" Identified* (1920)—and the case for William Stanley, Earl of Derby's—as stated by Abel Lefranc in *Sous le Masque de William Shakespeare: William Stanley, VI Comte de Derby* (1918, 1919)—and decided in favor of Derby.

Looney's response to Lucas, "'Shakespeare:' Lord Oxford or Lord Derby?"—his longest article on the Oxfordian claim since his two books were published—ran in the February 1922 issue. Looney had considered Derby's role in *"Shakespeare" Identified*, where he wrote, "Seeing, then, that the Derby theory arose from the simple fact that in

---

[61] Margaret L. Knapp, letter to J. Thomas Looney, Nov. 11, 1920.

[62] Margaret L. Knapp, letter to J. Thomas Looney, Jan. 10, 1921.

[63] See related discussion on this point in Chapter 6.

[64] Leopold James Maxse (1864-1932), editor of *The National Review*, was an early supporter of the Oxfordian thesis. He became one of the three original vice presidents of the Shakespeare Fellowship founded in November 1922 to promote study of the Shakespeare authorship question, the other two being J. Thomas Looney and Abel Lefranc (see Chapter 6).

1599 the Earl of Derby had been occupied in 'penning' plays, whilst nothing is known of his composing them, it is not an unreasonable supposition that, as husband to Oxford's favourite daughter, he may have been assisting his father-in-law in the actual penning of 'Shakespeare's' plays" (448-49).

Looney responded to Lucas's criticism with criticism of his own, in part aimed at correcting his misunderstanding of the significance of the 1604 date. Lucas had written: "All lovers of literature must, however, be grateful to Mr. Looney for the scholarly care with which he has connected certain facts of Oxford's life . . . with 'Shakespeare's' Works, but must also regret that he has passed beyond the true mark in an endeavor to set up a theory that is— *hopeless*. There is no other word for it. *Oxford died in 1604*."[65] Looney laid out the correct understanding, as he had in *"Shakespeare" Identified* and elsewhere, that 1604 had indeed been a significant date—the year in which the steady stream of publications of Shakespeare's plays ceased and the date at which several orthodox scholars had concluded that "something happened" with regard to Shakespeare. He then turned the tables on Lucas, pointing out that real significance of the 1604 date: if Derby had been Shakespeare, why is it that he, living until 1642, never wrote another play during the remaining thirty-eight years of his life?

Having run articles by proponents of Derby's and Oxford's authorship, *The National Review* apparently felt it was time to run one on Bacon's. For this it turned to George Hookham. Hookham, however, did not push the Baconian theory *per se*, but instead cited evidence indicating that "Shakespeare" was alive when the First Folio was published in 1623, thus disqualifying both Shakspere and Oxford. His evidence was the insertion of 193 new lines and 2,000 emendations in the text of *Richard III* in the First Folio that were not in the Sixth Quarto, published in 1622. Hookham believed that they could have been made only by Shakespeare, thereby establishing that the author had to have been alive in 1623. He closed his article with "Mr. Looney may have found the answer

Advertisement in the Feb. 11, 1922 issue of *The Outlook* for the February 1922 issue of *National Review*.

---

[65] R. Macdonald Lucas, "Did Lord Derby Write Shakespeare?" *National Review*, vol. 78 (Nov. 1921): 364.

to this riddle. If so, it would be extremely interesting to hear it."[66]

The Oxfordian Claim in *The National Review*, 1921-1922	
1921, November	
R. Macdonald Lucas	Did Lord Derby Write Shakespeare?
1922, February	
J. Thomas Looney	'Shakespeare:' Lord Oxford or Lord Derby?
1922, March	
George Hookham	Edward de Vere and the Shakespeare Plays
1922, September	
Col. Bernard R. Ward	"Mr. W. H." and "Our Ever-Living Poet"
1922, October	
Col. Bernard R. Ward	Edward de Vere and William Shakespeare — A Dual Mystery

Consequences of the *National Review* Articles

Of greatest importance for the Oxfordian cause was the effect Looney's piece had on Col. Bernard R. Ward. It inspired him to conduct his own research into the Oxfordian claim—research that was published in articles in the *National Review* in September and October and that formed the basis for his book published the following year. It also led him to found the Shakespeare Fellowship in November 1922 to provide institutional support for the Oxfordian thesis and to encourage research to further substantiate it (see Chapter 6).

Looney's article resulted in his corresponding with Lucas and Hookham. The known Looney-Lucas correspondence, February through June 1922, consisted of three letters from Looney and five to him, though only those to Looney have been found. The reasoned discourse in Lucas's letters was surely the kind of cordial interaction in the pursuit of truth that Looney championed, and the pleasant tone that began Lucas's first letter must surely have pleased him.

> I have read with great interest and pleasure your article in the *National Review* replying to mine on the subject of the Shakespeare authorship. It is most refreshing to find an opponent who expresses views, although incompatible with one's own, without the least unfairness. The subject has by no means always been so treated.[67]

The pleasant tone did not mean that Lucas had backed away from his Derbyite leanings, though. On the contrary, he claimed that certain facts uncovered by Looney actually supported Derby's claim. Among them was the paternity trick in *All's Well*, something Lucas imagined that the victim wouldn't recount against himself, but that Derby might well tell about his father-in-law. He also saw no problem with Derby ceasing to write literary works thirty years before his death. How Looney responded to Derby's letter is not known exactly, but he surely reciprocated the good will expressed in the closing sentence in Lucas's letter:

> I trust, and will do my best to insure, that should I reply in a published article, you will have no reason to complain of anything I write in respect of the fairness

---

[66] George Hookham, "Edward de Vere and the Shakespeare Plays," *National Review*, March 1922, p. 96. One obvious response, which Looney may have made in a letter that has been lost, is that both the 1622 and 1623 versions came from Oxford's pen before his death in 1604.

[67] R. Macdonald Lucas, letter to J. Thomas Looney, February 14, 1922.

and courtesy, as I should be sorry to treat your work, though I may keenly dispute its correctness, as a silly Stratford parrot treated Professor Lefranc's.[68]

In his third letter, Lucas passed on information about Lefranc that is of great interest for Oxfordians today in the absence of any known direct communication between Looney and Lefranc.

> I showed your letter to Professor Lefranc, and he handed to me for you a little pamphlet he has just published which he thought would interest you on the origin of Ariel. He does not feel that your discoveries and researches on the connection of the Earl of Oxford with the plays really affect his theory of the Derby authorship except as I have pointed out to strengthen it; and I still hold entirely to all I wrote in *The National Review*.

Lucas thanked Looney for having directed his attention to characters resembling in important ways Philip Sidney and Anne Cecil in *The Merry Wives of Windsor*; that letter was dated April 6, 1922, a full six months before Looney published his article on that subject in *The Golden Hind*.

On April 15, 1922, Lucas concluded that,

> I am afraid we are never likely to agree upon certain matters, one of these being the difficulty of harmonizing the character of de Vere with the character of "Shakespeare." The two go as badly together as Shaksper and "Shakespeare." De Vere was clever and had a fine literary sense, but it can hardly be denied that he was more known as a fop than anything else. Also, unless history has wholly misrepresented him, he was a mean unprincipled scoundrel.[69]

This statement must have caused Looney great dismay, given the efforts he made in *"Shakespeare" Identified* to resurrect Oxford's good name and to clarify the circumstances in which the slanders against him had arisen. That Lucas continued to hold such a negative view of Oxford showed that much still needed to be done to resurrect Oxford's reputation, work that would be undertaken by Capt. Bernard M. Ward in his biography of Oxford published six years later. Another point of interest was Lucas's statement that he had translated into English Lefranc's *Sous le Masques de Shakespeare* and hoped to get it accepted by a publisher later in the year. It appears he was unsuccessful.[70]

The Looney-Hookham correspondence, from June to November 1922, consisted of at least three letters from Looney and at least four to him, though only Hookham's letters have been located. They dealt with Hookham's *National Review* article, which he expanded into a book, *Will o' the Wisp, or The Elusive Shakespeare*, published later in 1922. Hookham, like Lucas and Looney, was an "amateur" scholar.

Looney in *The Golden Hind*

The next important Oxfordian publication to reach the public was Looney's "The Earl of Oxford as 'Shakespeare:' New Evidence," an article in the October 1922 issue of *The Golden Hind*. Cecil Palmer, the publisher of *"Shakespeare" Identified*, was one of the subscribers to *The Golden Hind*, which had a print run of only 400, a link that perhaps

---

[68] R. Macdonald Lucas, letter to J. Thomas Looney, February 14, 1922.
[69] R. Macdonald Lucas, letter to J. Thomas Looney, April 15, 1922.
[70] That translation, along with copies of Looney's letters to Lucas, is ample justification for a continued effort to find Lucas's papers.

explained the appearance of Looney's article in the quarterly's inaugural issue.[71]

In a letter to early American Oxfordian researcher Eva Turner Clark in 1926, Looney described this article as containing his most important findings since *"Shakespeare" Identified* had been published. Of particular importance were his thoughts on why the authorship question rose to prominence in the middle of the nineteenth century and the presentation of newly discovered information showing just how extensively "Oxford's career and personal relationships have been distinctly embodied in the Shakespeare writings." The most striking examples were drawn from *The Merry Wives of Windsor*, and show an "almost exact parallel" between the financial aspects of the marriage contract between Anne Page and Slender arranged by Mr. Page and Mr. Shallow in the play, and the arrangements made by Lord Burghley and the Earl of Leicester for the marriage of Anne Cecil to Philip Sidney in real life. "The story of Slender's intended marriage to Anne Page being upset by her marriage to Fenton," Looney observed, is "in all essentials analogous to that of Sidney, Anne Cecil, and the Earl of Oxford."[72]

Looney concluded with thoughts on how such linkages supported the case for Edward de Vere and how recognition of them could increase readers' understanding and enjoyment of the plays. "It is because the Shakespeare literature embodies work representing all periods of Oxford's lifetime, sometimes in a single play, that efforts to fix a Shakespeare canon on the basis of an author younger than the Earl of Oxford have proved so inconclusive." Readers willing to accept that embodiment will "find in Oxford

The Earl of Oxford as "Shakespeare"
New Evidence
BY J. THOMAS LOONEY

HE strongest single argument in favour of William Shakespeare's authorship of the plays attributed to him is that the belief in it went unchallenged for over two hundred years. What is far from generally understood is that the rapid undermining of that belief in recent years is due mainly to two movements belonging specially to the nineteenth century.

First, there was the marked interest in practical historical research. The merely traditional was laid aside; all kinds of archives were ransacked; everywhere search was made for original sources of information. Applied to "Shakespeare" matters, this movement brought to light the disconcerting fact that the English writer most distinguished by the brilliancy of his powers was, paradoxically, separated from all his fellows by a glaring deficiency of relevant personal records.

The second movement was the development of a scientific study of literature. This threw up sounder criteria of literary criticism, which, applied to the "Shakespeare" writings, completely reversed the established opinion respecting the mental equipment of the dramatist. In the previous century, David Hume could write, without misgivings, of Shakespeare's lack of "instruction from the world or from books," and of the unfitness of the plays for "a refined and intelligent audience," even of "the reproach of bar-

---

[71] Looney's article was not reprinted in full until the 2015 issue of *The Oxfordian*, and was reprinted again in *"Shakespeare" Revealed: The Collected Articles and Published Letters of J. Thomas Looney*, edited by the author of this book. It had been partially reprinted in a heavily edited version in 1975 in *Oxfordian Vistas*, a collection of Oxfordian articles edited by Ruth Loyd Miller.

[72] J. Thomas Looney, "The Earl of Oxford as Shakespeare: New Evidence," *The Golden Hind*, vol. 1, no. 1 (Oct. 1922): 23-30.

an author whose presence illuminates each page and transforms the literature from the most impersonal to the most personal documents in the English tongue. We have, in fact, become possessors of a new literature: a merriment heightened by personal touch with the great laughter-maker; the eternal human tragedy reinforced by a sense of the shadows that gathered around his life" (30).

Looney in *The Freethinker*

In 1923, to celebrate the tricentennial of the publication of the First Folio, *The Freethinker* ran an article with the subtitle "Dethroning Shakespeare—Anti-Stratfordian Scepticism" by George Underwood. Underwood stated that "as a more or less educated Freethinker with no vested interest in Stratford-on-Avon, I have a sort of natural sympathy with the sceptics." That approach was in line with the sceptical thought predominant at the weekly periodical, which billed itself as a "secular humanist magazine." Though initially anti-religious in character, it sought "to do its best to employ the resources of Science, Scholarship, Philosophy and Ethics" to combat beliefs held because of "Divine Revelation." It sought to rely on common sense, and eschewed the weapons of ridicule and sarcasm.

Underwood noted, though, that "for the average man scepticism is an uncomfortable position. He must have something positive, something to fill up the gap left by the clearing out of the Stratford yokel. . . . Oxford is the latest claimant put forward, but I am afraid the ingenious framer of the theory has spoilt his chance of convincing us by reprinting Oxford's verse."[73] Looney wrote two pieces in response to Underwood (the second ran in two consecutive issues). Although he found much to agree with in Underwood's "very interesting" article, he set much of it aside in his first piece, challenging Underwood's conclusion that "strict application of the principles of historical criticism to the problem of the Shakespearean authorship" led to the orthodox belief in the man from Stratford.

> In relation to the problem of "Shakespeare" authorship the only questions that matter are whether William Shakespeare of Stratford did or did not write the plays and poems attributed to him, and, if he did not write them who did? It is a matter of no consequence, then, whether this or that disputant is the most scholarly or entertaining, or which controversial method we may happen to like best. The one important question is: Who comes nearest to the truth?[74]

Turning to Shakespeare, Looney noted that "there does not exist a parallel case in the whole of modern history" to compare with the "dead silence of the contemporary records so far as concerns a visible personality. Not a single incident or interview; no conversation, correspondence or obituary notice" has survived. "Comparing then the contemporary claims, implied by the published works . . . only one explanation seems possible, namely, that false claims were entered on his behalf, and very deliberate steps taken to back those claims with fictitious credentials." He suggested that it was the peculiar psychological nature of the English that accounts for some of the difficulty Oxfordians had faced since *"Shakespeare" Identified* had been published three years earlier. "The English mind does not take kindly to plots, and therefore finds it difficult to believe in successful plotting. Our intelligence is affronted at the suggestion that we, at

---

[73] George Underwood, "Readers and Writers: Dethroning Shakespeare—Anti-Stratfordian Scepticism," *The Freethinker*, vol. 43/20 (May 20, 1923): 316.

[74] J. Thomas Looney, "The Shakespeare Problem," *The Freethinker*, vol. 42/33 (June 10, 1923): 364.

any rate, could be imposed upon—and by our own greatest writer himself—but sooner or later we shall have to face the facts and swallow our humiliation with as good a grace as may be."

In the second article, Looney dispensed with the 1604 "problem" for Oxfordian authorship, noting that "it is common knowledge that when the First Folio appeared it contained very many plays universally admitted to have been written before those published in 1598, proving that the publications from the 1593-1604 period were from a large accumulated stock, and that the work of publication was stopped short suddenly in 1604, with a number of plays on hand awaiting their turn to be trimmed up for printing." The same was true of the *Sonnets*: "the latest are understood to have been written immediately after the death of Queen Elizabeth. So that 'Shakespeare,' having composed sonnets for many years, stopped suddenly and forever at the exact time of the death of the Earl of Oxford."[75] Sir Arthur Quiller-Couch was correct to conclude, Looney said, that "something had happened"[76] in 1604; what had happened was the death of the real "Shakespeare."

He then presented to *The Freethinker's* readers a point made in *"Shakespeare" Identified* that held the key to the solution of the Shakespeare mystery. Oxford "is the only dramatist mentioned by any of these authorities [Webbe, Puttenham, Meres] no trace of whose plays can be found. The two outstanding mysteries of Elizabethan drama are, in fact, the Oxford mystery and the Shakespeare mystery; and these . . . fit into and explain one another."[77]

These were the last short items that Looney would publish independently. The next twenty-five or so were all published in conjunction with the Shakespeare Fellowship, either in its regular columns in other periodicals or in the *News-Letters* of the American branch.

After Three Years: A Status Report and a Look Ahead

"Shakespeare" Identified and the Oxfordian idea had made a splash in 1920. In 1922 the idea popped up here and there, but those isolated mentions of the Oxfordian claim were not part of a sustained campaign to bring the idea to public attention or to persuade scholars of its validity. Looney had succeeded in solving the Shakespeare mystery but not in gaining widespread acceptance of his solution.

The story of the Oxfordian idea from 1920 to 1922 was largely the story of one man's efforts. The originator of the Oxfordian claim was its sole active promoter. He was David fighting the Stratfordian Goliath.

A new burst of energy was needed to promote the Oxfordian idea. One would come with Col. Bernard R. Ward and the formation of the Shakespeare Fellowship, a development recounted in Chapter 6. But first it is necessary to examine why so many people—readers, reviewers, critics and scholars—found it difficult, if not impossible, to accept the idea of Edward de Vere as Shakespeare.

---

[75] J. Thomas Looney, "Shakespeare: Was it Oxford, Bacon, or Derby? I," *The Freethinker*, vol. 43/26 (July 1, 1923): 412.

[76] Internal quote is from Sir Arthur Quiller-Couch, *Shakespeare's Workmanship*, p. 296-97.

[77] J. Thomas Looney, "Was it Oxford, Bacon, or Derby? II," *The Freethinker*, vol. 43/27 (July 8, 1923): 428.

5

The Dozen Mental Revolutions

The Difficulty of Changing Beliefs

Accepting Edward de Vere as "Shakespeare" was not easy for most early readers of *"Shakespeare Identified.* Many probably thought that although the evidence Looney brought to bear on the authorship question seemed valid, there must be a flaw in it, somewhere, even if they couldn't quite see what it was. Any idea that clashed so completely with something everybody already believed couldn't possibly be true, could it?

One reviewer said as much, conceding that Looney "does present an amazing chain of parallels from [Edward de Vere's] life showing that the text of the plays is based upon the experiences of this man.... His parallels are too remarkable to be ... mere coincidences." Yet, he found himself only "almost persuaded, but ... not convinced."[1] Another accepted "Mr. Looney's contention ... that there is a 'main mystery' about William Shakespeare, of Stratford-on-Avon, and an equal mystery about Edward de Vere, and that this identification theory reconciles and solves these two mysteries," but continued to believe that "the evidence for the 'Stratford man' ... outweighs all the coincidences and all the ingenious inferences which Mr. Looney has collected and woven together so effectively."[2]

Why was it so difficult for so many persons (then and now) to accept the conclusion toward which Looney's evidence, arguments and reasoning led? If Shakespeare's works had been newly discovered with no author's name on them, Oxford would be at or near the top of anyone's short list of possible candidates. Looney's evidence matching the man with the works, linking Edward de Vere with *Hamlet, All's Well That Ends Well* and the *Sonnets* was so strong that just about everybody would have been convinced once the facts of his life became known.

But that was not the task that Looney faced. He had to convince people that works already attributed to William Shakspere for more than 300 years had really been written by somebody else. That pre-existing belief was the problem.

Looney knew he faced an uphill battle, but he believed he was well prepared for it because of the multifaceted nature of the evidence he had accumulated and presented. The battle was far harder than he expected, though, because of multiple layers of resistance that had to be overcome: Human Resistance, Cognitive Resistance and Institutional Resistance. The first two are discussed here, the third in later chapters.

---

[1] C. R.., "Shakespeare: Was He Edward de Vere, Lord Oxford?" *Nottingham Journal and Express*, April 22, 1920, p. 4.

[2] W. Gurney Benham, Edward de Vere, Earl of Oxford, 'Identified' as Shakespeare," *Essex Review*, vol. 29 (April 1, 1920): 95-100.

Human Resistance

Human Resistance is common to all people. It's simply the natural human resistance to changing any long-held belief. It's easier to go straight ahead than to turn, and especially to do a U-turn. Most people accept as true ideas prevalent in the society around them. Very few have the time or inclination to think things through for themselves. Thinking is difficult, and the brain, like all other physical objects—so we learned in high school physics—remains at rest (or in constant motion) until acted upon by external forces. For most people, the emotional and social benefits of fitting in, of being part of the group, of following the leader, are greater than those gained from thinking for themselves. Most see accepting society's beliefs and practices as the right thing to do. Those who would change them face a twofold challenge: convincing others of the *legitimacy* of challenging or opposing existing beliefs and practices and the *validity* of the new ones.

The first level of resistance incorporates both individual and social aspects of human psychology. Walter Bagehot, the prominent British economist and critic, whom Looney quoted in *"Shakespeare" Identified*, recognized this situation 150 years ago. "Unbelief far oftener needs a reason and requires an effort than belief. Naturally, and if man were made according to the pattern of the logicians, he would say: 'When I see a valid argument I will believe, and till I see such argument I will not believe.' But, in fact, every idea vividly before us soon appears to us to be true, unless we keep up our perceptions of the arguments which prove it untrue, and voluntarily coerce our minds to remember its falsehood."[3]

After surveying the development of societies over all of recorded history, Bagehot concluded that "The great difficulty which history records is not that of the first step, but that of the second step. What is most evident is not the difficulty of getting a fixed law, but getting out of a fixed law; not of cementing . . . a cake of custom, but of breaking the cake of custom" (53). This individual emotional commitment to existing beliefs makes for stability and continuity in a society. Breaking the cake of custom is disruptive, and purposeful disruption is avoided by most people most of the time.

The American historian Frederick Jackson Turner, in attempting to explain the unique American character, noted that it was "at the frontier [that] the bonds of custom are [most easily] broken."[4] This "freedom of the frontier" perhaps played into the discovery of Oxford's authorship, with the idea arising in Looney's Newcastle—the city in England farthest from London—and in reviews of *"Shakespeare" Identified* becoming, on average, more favorable as one moved farther afield from London, into northern England, Wales and Scotland, and into Bombay and Australia and New Zealand. In North America, the media in cities farther from New York City—in Canada and San Francisco, for instance— were more open to the Oxfordian idea than those in the Big Apple.

Another factor working against the Oxfordian claim was the bias in this democratic age in favor of the idyllic story of an everyman rising from modest origins to great heights through his own effort. As noted earlier, this bias may have limited Frank Harris's receptiveness to the authorship question. William Shakspere, from distant Stratford-on-Avon, fit the bill. Edward de Vere, Earl of Oxford and the Queen's Lord Great Chamberlain, decidedly did not. William Shakespeare's status as a national icon of Great Britain makes the situation all the worse; dethroning him could not help but tarnish the image of the

---

[3] Walter Bagehot, *Physics and Politics* (1912), p. 94.
[4] Frederick Jackson Turner, *The Frontier in American History* (1976), p. 37-38.

union, making Britain appear a bit less Great.

Cognitive Resistance

The second level of resistance, Cognitive Resistance, arises from the need to change the specific beliefs involved in the subject of Shakespearean authorship. There are two parts to it. One arises from the complexities of the Oxfordian claim itself, the other from the consequences that flow from it. The weight of the two is so heavy that it's hard for the human mind to process it all. It wants to shut down when faced with such difficulties. Multiple attempts may be required to understand it and absorb its ramifications.

Looney knew that acceptance of the Oxfordian thesis would be neither easy or instantaneous. "Everything depends on the willingness of the reader to familiarize himself with all the particulars, and by a mental effort of his own, to bring them together, so as to judge of their total weight as evidence. This requires time and an open mind."[5]

Because of its complexity, many of the consequences of the Oxfordian claim are not immediately apparent; the more it is investigated the more complex it seems. It is not merely a matter of simply plucking one man out and putting another in his place. Change in the overarching belief about who the author was logically leads to overthrowing another dozen major beliefs, and these in turn lead to changes in dozens of subsidiary beliefs. If Shakspere wasn't the playwright, was he still to be regarded as an actor? What was his relationship with the real Shakespeare? Was the Earl of Southampton the patron of the real Shakespeare? If not, what was the nature of their relationship? The list of issues to be rethought is seemingly endless.

The older beliefs, like the newer ones, all hang together as a coherent package. Readers couldn't pick and choose which ones to change. Accepting the Oxfordian thesis required abandoning not mere isolated beliefs, but a tapestry of tightly woven beliefs. Cognitive resistance—the shutting down of the brain—comes when the number of beliefs to be changed become overwhelming. It's so much easier to back up and reject the change in that one overarching belief about who the author was than to engage in the mental effort to change so many other subsidiary beliefs.

The Dozen Mental Revolutions

Looney recognized that accepting the Oxfordian thesis required a mental revolution. "We have labored the point because of the difficulty of the mental revolution involved" (321). "Revolutions" might be more accurate. I have identified a dozen major beliefs that must be changed. They are so substantial that each requires its own Mental Revolution.

Each of these twelve beliefs has been researched extensively by other scholars, Stratfordian and Oxfordian. My aim here is to show through representative examples how markedly the old Stratfordian and new Oxfordian views differ, and, therefore, how aptly the term Mental Revolutions captures the depth of the intellectual reorienting needed to move from the older to the newer understandings.

Readers who want to avoid an extended break in the narrative can skip over the following text boxes with details of the dozen Mental Revolutions and fifty subsidiary beliefs. The text resumes on the final page of this chapter.

---

[5] J. Thomas Looney, *The Poems of Edward de Vere* (1921), p. xvii.

The Dozen Mental Revolutions and Fifty Subsidiary Beliefs

1. Change in Identity of Author
   --Identity of the dramatist
   --The authorship story
   --The authorship mystery
   --Southampton as patron
2. External Aspects of Shakespeare's Plays
   --Dates of composition
   --Venues where first performed
   --Adaptations of older plays
   --*Hamlet* I
   --Collaborations
3. Internal Aspects of Shakespeare's Plays
   --Topicality of Shakespeare's plays
   --Contemporaneous nature of the plays
   --Personal allusions in the plays
   --*Hamlet* II
4. Chains of Influence on Shakespeare
   --Chains of influence: Lyly
   --Chains of influence: Munday
   --Chains of influence: Others
5. Shakespeare's Knowledge
   --Bodies of knowledge I: Italy
   --Bodies of knowledge II: The law
   --Bodies of knowledge II: Courtly life
   --Bodies of knowledge III: Politics
   --Bodies of knowledge IV: Latin and Greek
6. The Elizabethan Era
   --Contemporaneous allusions
   --Merrie olde Englande
   --War, hard times and famine

7. Development of Elizabethan Drama
   --Elizabethan era literary transformation
   --Direction of the Chamberlain's Men
8. The Nature of Genius
   --Explanatory power of genius
   --Development of genius I: development
   --Development of genius II: knowledge
   --Geniuses are absorbed with their work
   --Geniuses care about their works
9. The Nature of Literary Creativity
   --Literary creativity in general
   --Literary imagery
   --Motivations for writing literary works
10. The Inner Emotional Life of Shakespeare
    --Shakespeare's inner emotional life
    --The Sonnets
    --Shakespeare's darkening view
11. Edward de Vere, Earl of Oxford
    --Oxford's reputation
    --Oxford as representative of his class
    --Oxford as "the soul of the age"
    --Oxford's life history in the plays
    --Academia's views of Oxford's poems
    --Oxford/Shakespeare as revisionist
12. William Shakspere
    --Shakspere as actor
    --Shakspere as playwright
    --Shakspere's retirement
    --Silences about Shakspere the man
    --Shakspere's Will

Mental Revolution 1: Change in Identity of Author

Identity of the dramatist

Old view: William Shakspere of Stratford-upon-Avon wrote the plays.

> Sir Sidney Lee: "Shakespeare, William (1564-1616), dramatist and poet."[1]

New view: Edward de Vere, 17th Earl of Oxford, was the author.

> J. Thomas Looney: "It has become impossible to hesitate any longer in proclaiming Edward de Vere, Seventeenth Earl of Oxford, as the real author of 'Shakespeare's works." (171)

The authorship story

Old view: A young man from the provinces, speaking a dialect of English difficult to understand outside his native Warwickshire and with no known education nor any known connection to any member of Queen Elizabeth's court, transformed himself within a few short years through sheer genius and hard work into the greatest poet and dramatist in English history.

> Lee: "The scantiness of contemporary records of Shakespeare's career has been much exaggerated. . . . Nevertheless many important links are missing, and at many critical points appeal to conjecture is inevitable."[2]

New view: The highest ranking earl in Queen Elizabeth's court and one of the richest men in England bankrupted himself to finance his literary and theatrical activities and to sponsor so many other writers that he almost singlehandedly sparked the English Literary Renaissance.

> Looney: "The supposition that Edward de Vere is 'Shakespeare' places the appearance of this literature for the first time within the category of natural and human achievements." (321-22)

The nature of the authorship mystery

Old view: The core of the old authorship mystery was the gap between the mundane details known of William Shakspere's life and Shakespeare's learned plays easily portraying intimate relations between royalty and courtiers and evincing a deep understanding of high-level governmental and diplomatic undertakings.

> Lee: "The apparent contrast between the homeliness of Shakespeare's Stratford career and the breadth of observation and knowledge displayed in his literary work has evoked the fantastic theory that Shakespeare was not the author of the literature that passes under his name."

New view: The new authorship mystery is the two-sided enigma of why Edward de Vere decided to conceal his authorship of "Shakespeare's" works and how such an effort could have been kept secret.

> Looney: I am quite prepared to admit that the success of the secrecy both during Oxford's lifetime and after his death is very remarkable. . . . If the Stratford man were the author, the silence of contemporary documents in reference to all his literary and dramatic dealings with other people is as pronounced as if he had been in hiding.

---

[1] Sir Sidney Lee, "Shakespeare, William," *Dictionary of National Biography*, 11th ed. (1910), p. 348, and Sir Sidney Lee, *A Life of William Shakespeare* (1915), p. 651.
[2] Sir Sidney Lee (1910), p. 395 and (1915), p. 651.

... and, of course, such a state of things is much more compatible with a planned secrecy than with a secrecy without aim or intention.

Southampton as patron

Old view: Henry Wriothesley, Third Earl of Southampton (1573-1624), was Shakespeare's patron.

> Lee: "Shakespeare appended his full signature to the dedication [of *Venus and Adonis*], which he addressed in conventional terms to Henry Wriothesley, third earl of Southampton. . . . He had vast possessions, was well educated, loved literature, and through life extended to men of letters a generous patronage. . . . Shakespeare [also] dedicated his second volume of poetry [*Lucrece*] to [him]."[3]

New view: Southampton was not Shakespeare's patron. Scholar Charlotte Stopes searched the records for many years for connections between Southampton and Shakspere and came up empty-handed. He was still a minor when *Venus and Adonis* and *Lucrece* were published and therefore had no money of his own with which to sponsor literary publications.

> Looney: "Oxford was a nobleman of the same high rank as Southampton . . . [but] a generation older. . . . Just at the time when these sonnets were being written urging Southampton to marry, he was actually being urged into a marriage with a daughter of the Earl of Oxford. . . . This furnishes the vital connection between the Earl of Southampton and the Earl of Oxford." (378)

Mental Revolution 2: External Aspects of Shakespeare's Plays

Dates of composition

Old view: Shakespeare's plays were written between 1592 and 1611, the latest date to which scholars attribute his retirement and return to Stratford.

> Lee: "There is no external evidence to prove that any piece in which Shakespeare had a hand was produced before the spring of 1592." (102)

> Lee: "With the year 1611 . . . Shakespeare's regular home would seem to have shifted for the rest of his life to his native place." (450)

New view: Orthodox scholars had dated the plays to fit neatly into the known facts of the life of William Shakspere. Using dates based on other external and internal factors, the plays were seen to have been written and revised from the mid-1570s until 1604, the year of Edward de Vere's death. Revisions after his death were made to some plays by other hands.

> Looney: "The dating of the plays is largely guesswork or inference, based upon the assumption that the Stratford actor was the author, and may demand drastic modifications when another author is supposed."[4]

> Looney: "Dates of publication have no necessary correspondence with dates of writing, and makes us realize how completely all inferences with regard to the years in which the several plays were written may be upset by the substitution of another author for William Shakspere of Stratford." (318)

---

[3] Sir Sidney Lee, *A Life of William Shakespeare* (1915), pp. 141, 147.
[4] J. Thomas Looney, "Shakespeare's Identity: Case for Lord Oxford," *Western Mail*, May 6, 1920, p. 7.

Venues where first performed

Old view: The plays were written for performances in the public theaters.

> Lee: "It was for the public theaters that most of Shakespeare's work both as actor and dramatist was done.... The dramas which the Sovereign witnessed were seldom written for the occasions. They had already won the public ear in the theatre."[5]

> J. O. Halliwell-Phillipps: Shakespeare's "sole aim was to please an audience, most of whom, be it remembered, were not only illiterate but unable either to read or write."[6]

New view: Many of the plays were originally written for performances in the court or for educated audiences in small private venues, and only later performed in the public theaters. Sir Edmund K. Chambers was one of the first Stratfordian scholars to recognize the importance of performances in the court.

> Chambers: Oxford's group of players "are traceable" in the period 1579-1583, and "it is natural to suppose that he wrote comedies for his own men."[7]

> Chambers: "The Palace was the point of vantage from which the stage won its way, against the linked opposition of an alienated pulpit and an alienated municipality.... It is worthwhile, therefore, to attempt to recover something of the atmosphere of the Tudor court, and to define the conditions under which the presentation of plays formed a recurring interest in its bustling many-coloured life."[8]

Shakespeare adopted older plays by other writers

Old view: Shakespeare adapted rather ordinary older plays by other writers and infused them with his genius. *The Taming of a Shrew*, by an anonymous author, became Shakespeare's *The Taming of the Shrew*, and the anonymous *The Troublesome Raigne of King John* became Shakespeare's *King John*.

> Lee: "Shakespeare gained much early experience as a dramatist by revising or rewriting behind the scenes plays that had become the property of his manager."[9]

> Lee: "It was doubtless with the calculated aim of ministering to the public taste that he unceasingly adapted, as his genius dictated, themes which had already, in the hands of inferior authors or playwrights, proved capable of arresting public attention." (99)

New view: Edward de Vere was the author of those older plays, which he revised and updated before they were presented as the work of "William Shakespeare."

> Looney: "With his artistic striving after perfection it was natural that he should work long and laboriously at any literary task he undertook, and that in the process of transforming his plays they should undergo such changes that the original work of Oxford should not have been detected in the finished plays of 'Shakespeare.'" (282)

Hamlet

Old view: References in the 1580s to a play with a character named Hamlet, before

---

[5] Sir Sidney Lee, *A Life of William Shakespeare* (1915), p. 68, 71.

[6] J. O. Halliwell-Phillipps, *Outlines of the Life of Shakespeare* (1907), p. 117.

[7] Sir Edmund K. Chambers, *The Elizabethan Stage*, vol. 2 (1923), pp. 99, 102.

[8] Sir Edmund K. Chambers, *The Elizabethan Stage*, vol. 1 (1923), prefatory material, page not numbered.

[9] Sir Sidney Lee, *A Life of William Shakespeare* (1915), p. 114.

it would have been possible for Shakspere to have written it, are to a different play by another writer. Scholars have designated that play *ur-Hamlet*, and believe that Shakespeare based his play on it.

> Lee: "An old piece called *Hamlet* was in existence in 1589—soon after Shakespeare joined the theatrical profession. In that year the pamphleteer Tom Nashe credited a writer whom he called 'English Seneca' with the capacity of penning 'whole Hamlets, I should say handfuls of tragical speeches.'" (357)

New view: The early references to *Hamlet* are to a version written by Edward de Vere no later than 1589 and probably by 1583. There is no independent justification for the existence of an earlier play with the same name by another writer. Speculation about such a play is mere special pleading by scholars desperate to overcome the difficulty that the earlier date for *Hamlet* creates for Shakspere's authorship.

> Sir George Greenwood, quoting Edwin Reed: "That this early *Hamlet* was Shake-speare's no unprejudiced person can entertain a doubt, for we are able to trace it in contemporary notices all along from 1589 . . . to its appearance in print in the Shakespearean Quarto of 1603."[10]

> Looney: "The play and the character of *Hamlet* may therefore be accepted as being in a peculiar sense the dramatic self-revelation of the author, if such a revelation exists anywhere." (393)

Later plays written in collaboration with other writers

Old view: Shakespeare collaborated with other writers on many plays at the end of his career (when he was still in his mid-forties).

> Lee: "Although Shakespeare's powers were unexhausted, . . . he reverted in the following year [1608] to earlier habits of collaboration."[11]

New view: There is no corroborative evidence for collaboration. Oxford's unfinished works, or earlier works not yet revised for the public stage or for publication, were finished or updated by others after his death in 1604. Collaboration is a myth invented by orthodox scholars in their attempts to explain how Shakespeare's "final plays" came to contain passages and scenes written in un-Shakespearean style even though Shakspere was in London and writing.

> Looney: "To suppose that 'Shakespeare,' having attained the highest rank as a play-writer whilst still in the heyday of his powers, should, on approaching his zenith, have reverted to his earlier practice of collaboration with others—the master-hand in the craft returning to the expedients of his prentice days—is to deny to him the possession of ordinary common sense." (346)

> Looney: "The general stamp . . . of this later work is greatness, suggestive of unfailing powers; and defects suggestive of unfinished workmanship and the intervention of inferior pens: a combination which we claim can only be explained by the death of the dramatist." (351)

---

[10] Edwin Reed, *Francis Bacon our Shakespeare* (1902), p. 97, quoted in Sir George Greenwood, *The Shakespeare Problem Restated* (1908), pp. 501-02.
[11] Sir Sidney Lee, *A Life of William Shakespeare* (1915), p. 402.

Mental Revolution 3: Internal Aspects of Shakespeare's Plays

Topicality of Shakespeare's plays

Old view: Shakespeare's plays were works of the imagination; references or allusions to contemporary events were few and general in nature. With only one exception (*Merry Wives*), none of the plays had contemporary English settings, and none addressed contemporaneous events.

> Chambers: "Shakespeare does not seem to have been greatly given to 'topical allusions,' and the hunt for them is dangerous."[12]

> Lee: "A topical allusion of a different kind and one rare in Shakespearean drama is made in some detail at the end of [*Merry Wives*]."[13] [Note: this is the only time that Lee used the word *topical* in his 780-page book.]

New view: Shakespeare's plays were intensely topical, full of allusions to contemporary political and social events and the people involved in them— some from the time the plays were first written, others from the times when they were revised.

> Looney: "The fact that the authorship we are now urging brings 'Shakespeare's' plays into line with the literature of the times, as a dramatic representation of contemporary events and personalities, and at the same time gives the works a firm root, like all the other great achievements of mankind, in the direct social intercourse of men possessing common tastes and interests, is not the least of the arguments in its favour" (276).

> Adm. Hubert H. Holland: "The number of [topical] allusions in the plays are now as follows: *Midsummer Night's Dream*, 16; . . . *Merchant of Venice*, 28; . . . *Hamlet*, 50; . . . Total 433."[14] Of the fifty topical references in *Hamlet*, forty-four tie the play to the early 1580s.

> Julia Altrocchi: One of the references in *Hamlet* is to magnetism. When Gertrude tells Hamlet "Sit here," and he replies "No, Mother, here is metal more attractive," and then sits down next to Ophelia, the author is making a topical reference to a new book on magnetism that was the subject of discussion in court circles in the early 1580s.[15]

Personal or autobiographical content in Shakespeare plays

Old view: Shakespeare's plays are works of the imagination with little autobiographical content.

> Lee: "An unquestionable characteristic of Shakespeare's art is its impersonality. The plain and positive references in the plays to Shakespeare's personal experiences . . . are rare and fragmentary, and nowhere else can we point with any confidence to any autobiographic revelations. . . . We seek in vain for any self-evident revelation of personal experience of emotion or passion."[16]

---

[12] E. K. Chambers, *William Shakespeare: A Study of Facts and Problems* (1930), p. 246.

[13] Sir Sidney Lee, *A Life of William Shakespeare* (1915), p. 248.

[14] Adm. Hubert. H. Holland, "Shake-Spear 1573-1593: A Short Report on Latest Research into Internal Evidence by Topical Allusions," *Shakespeare Fellowship News-Letter*, April 1942, p. 2.

[15] This allusion was discovered by Julia Cooley Altrocchi, "From Mrs. Julia Cooley Altrocchi," *Shakespeare Oxford Society Newsletter*, vol. 7/1 (March 30, 1971): 3. See also Paul Altrocchi and Hank Whittemore (editors), *My Name Be Buried* (2009), pp. 419-20.

[16] Sir Sidney Lee, *A Life of William Shakespeare* (1915), pp. 634-35.

Halliwell-Phillipps: "The higher the genius the more complete will be the severance from the personality."[17]

New view: Shakespeare's plays are intensely personal. Many plays have characters resembling Edward de Vere and others close to him, and many storylines portray real-life events from his life.

Looney: "'Shakespeare' made very free use of literary and historical material which lay ready to his hand. . . . It would be inconsistent . . . to suppose that he did not make a similar use of the human material immediately in front of him, and of the incidents and relationships of his own life." It is necessary "to put aside the old conception of a writer creating everything by the vigour of his imagination, and to regard the writing as reflecting the personality and experience of the author."[18]

Looney: "Shakespeare's work is much more a record of his own personal relationships than has hitherto been supposed. . . . Shakespeare's characters were taken from his own experience of the men and women about him. . . . Actually living men and women, artistically modified and adjusted to fit them for the part they had to perform, are what we may be sure the plays contain." (391, 390)

Hamlet

Old view: *Hamlet* is a work of fantasy, built on a plot that Shakspere read about. It is neither topical nor has anything to do with the author's biography.

Lee: "It is dangerous to read into Shakespeare's dramatic utterances allusions to his personal experience."[19]

New view: *Hamlet* is not only topical, it is Oxford's most direct portrayal of himself.

Looney: In *Hamlet*, "[Oxford] was actually striving most consciously and earnestly . . . to represent himself. . . . Every line of Hamlet's speeches . . . pulsates with the heart and spirit of Oxford." (393-94, 396)

Looney: "More than one critic . . . has admitted that 'Shakespeare' must have been well acquainted with the Earl of Oxford, have been furnished by the Earl with biographical material for his plays, and made him his model for Hamlet."[20]

Looney: "Whilst some critics are acknowledging that Oxford is probably Hamlet, others are just as freely admitting that *Hamlet* has long been suspected of being the author's work of special self-revelation. Let the two parties join forces and the new theory will have made notable progress." (xvi)

Mental Revolution 4: Chains of Influence on Shakespeare

Chains of influence: John Lyly (c. 1553-1606)

Old view: The playwright John Lyly influenced Shakespeare.

Lee: "It was when the first reformers of the crude infant drama, Lyly, Greene, Peele, Kyd, and Marlowe, were busy with their

---

[17] J. O. Halliwell-Phillipps, *Outlines of the Life of Shakespeare* (1907), vol. 1, p. xii.

[18] J. Thomas Looney, *The Poems of Edward de Vere* (1921), pp. viii, 7.

[19] Sir Sidney Lee, *A Life of William Shakespeare* (1915), p. 32, and "Shakespeare, William," *Dictionary of National Biography*, 11th edition (1910): 352.

[20] J. Thomas Looney, *The Poems of Edward de Vere* (1921), p. xv.

experiments that Shakespeare joined the ranks of English dramatists. As he set out on his road he profited by the lessons which these men were teaching. . . . Lyly in comedy and Marlowe in tragedy may be reckoned the masters to whom he stood in the relation of disciple on the threshold of his career."[21]

Bond: "Lyly taught him something in the matter of unity and coherence of plot construction, in the introduction of songs and fairies."[22]

Feuillerat: "Yet [Shakespeare] is an author in whom we find numerous traces of Lyly's influence. When we read Shakespeare's plays, at every instant we have the growing conviction that the great dramatist had studied the works of his predecessor and set out to copy his manner."[23]

New view: Lyly was a servant of the Earl of Oxford and managed an acting company and even a theater for him. Lyly's most famous prose work, *Euphues* (1578), whose main character is largely modeled on the Earl of Oxford, was entered in the Stationers' Register as "compiled by John Lyllie," not "written" by him. The inventiveness and dramatic form and dialogue that characterize Lyly's plays was due to the influence of Edward de Vere, whose own plays are "lost." The correct order of influence is: *Edward De Vere → Lyly → "Shakespeare."*

Looney: "Lyly and his work constitute a most important link in the chain of evidence connecting the work of 'Shakespeare' with the Earl of Oxford; only, under the influence of the Stratfordian theory, cause is mistaken for effect." (269)

Looney: "The dramas of Edward de Vere form the source from which sprang Lyly's dramatic conceptions and enterprises, and Lyly's dramas appear as the chief model, in comedy the only model, upon which 'Shakespeare' worked. . . . The dramatic activities of Edward de Vere stands in almost immediate productive or causal relationship of a most distinctive character with the dramatic work of 'Shakespeare.'" (272)

Chains of influence: Anthony Munday (c. 1560-1633)

Old view: The playwright Anthony Munday influenced Shakespeare.

Rev. Ronald Bayne: "Munday in 1580 and in his earliest published works is anxious to proclaim himself 'servant of the Earl of Oxford' . . . [One of] Munday's plays is a humble variation of the dramatic type of *A Midsummer Night's Dream* . . . and we find in [another of Munday's plays] phrases that may have rested in the mind of Shakespeare."[24]

New view: Munday, like Lyly, was a servant of the Earl of Oxford. The correct line of influence is: *Edward De Vere → Munday → "Shakespeare."*

Looney: "Munday's plays contain passages not written by himself: passages which 'might have rested in the mind of Shakespeare.'" (417)

Looney: "One peculiar fact about Munday has been the attributing to him both of dramatic and poetic compositions of a superior order, which competent authorities now assert could not have been written

---

[21] Sir Sidney Lee, *A Life of William Shakespeare* (1915), p. 634-35.
[22] J. Thomas Looney, *"Shakespeare" Identified*, p. 269, quoting Bond.
[23] Feuillerat, quoted in Abel Lefranc, *Under the Mask of William Shakespeare* (1988), pp. 227.
[24] Rev. Ronald Bayne, "Lesser Elizabethan Dramatists," *Cambridge History of English Literature*, vol. 5, pp. 315, 318.

by him." (257)

> Looney: "Two men, and two men only, Anthony Munday and John Lyly, are directly and actively associated with [Oxford] in his dramatic enterprises. Both men have work attributed to them which is evidently not theirs, and it is this work which links them on . . . to the work of 'Shakespeare,' thus forming a direct bridge between the . . . dramas of Edward de Vere and 'the greatest literature of the world.'" (283)

Chains of influence: Others

Old view: Drayton, Daniels, Marlowe and other playwrights and poets influenced Shakespeare.

> Lee: "Shakespeare shared with other men of genius that receptivity of mind which impelled them to assimilate much of the intellectual energy of their contemporaries. . . . The lyric and narrative verse of Thomas Watson, Samuel Daniels, Michael Drayton, Sir Philip Sidney, and Thomas Lodge, were among the rills which fed the mighty river of his lyric invention. But in all directions he rapidly bettered the instruction of fellow-workers. Much of their work was unvalued ore, which he absorbed and transmuted into gold in the process. By the magic of his genius English drama was finally lifted to heights above the reach of any forerunner or contemporary."[25]

New View: The same refashioning of chains of influence is also true for other writers who, under the old view, were thought to have influenced Shakespeare. Instead, it was Oxford who influenced writers such as Drayton, Daniels, and Marlowe, and likely many others.

> Looney: "[Sharp] points out . . . that when Shakespeare used this form of sonnet in the last years of the sixteenth century, he was using a form 'made thoroughly ready for his use by Daniels and Drayton.' Now, as Daniel was twelve years, and Drayton thirteen years younger than Edward de Vere, and as the last named . . . it is clear that his early lyrics come before those of either of the other two men." (386)

Mental Revolution 5: Shakespeare's Knowledge

Italy

Old view: Shakespeare's plays embody no significant knowledge of Italy. References to Italy inserted to give flavor to scenes and settings and characters were acquired through reading and conversations with those who had visited the country.

> Lee: "To Italy, it is true, and especially to the northern towns of Venice, Padua, Verona, Mantua, and Milan, he makes frequent and familiar reference, and he supplied many a realistic portrayal of Italian life and sentiment. . . . He doubtless owed all to the verbal reports of travelled friends or to books, the contents of which he had a rare power of assimilating and vitalising."[26]

New view: The plays embody deep knowledge of those places in Italy where Edward de Vere visited and/or lived during the sixteen months he spent on the continent in 1575-76.

> Looney: *"The Merchant of Venice . . .* bespoke a writer who knew

---

[25] Sir Sidney Lee, *A Life of William Shakespeare* (1915), p. 95.
[26] Sir Sidney Lee, "Shakespeare, William," *Dictionary of National Biography*, 11th edition (1910): 356.

Italy at first hand and was touched with the life and spirit of the country. . . . Those who know Italy . . . tell us that there are clear indications that Shakespeare knew Venice and Milan personally. . . . There is thrown about these plays an Italian atmosphere suggestive of one who knew and felt attracted towards the country. Everything bespeaks an Italian enthusiast." (96-97)

Looney: Oxford's "stay in Italy . . . had so marked an influence over him as to affect his dress and manners and cause him to be lampooned as an "Italianated Englishman." (242)

Law

Old view: Shakespeare's plays show no in-depth knowledge of the law. Whatever legal knowledge is shown in them was acquired through conversations or reading, not through formal education or personal experience.

Lee: "The poet's legal knowledge is a mingled skein of accuracy and inaccuracy, and the errors are far too numerous and important to justify on sober inquiry the plea of technical experience. . . . Moreover the legal terms which Shakespeare favoured were common forms of speech among contemporary men of letters and are not peculiar to his literary or poetic vocabulary. Legal phraseology in Shakespeare's vein was widely distributed over the dramatic and poetic literature of his day."[27]

New view: The plays reveal such a depth of understanding of the law that legal analogies are part and parcel of the author's thought.

Looney: "Three eminent English lawyers tell us that the plays of Shakespeare display an expert knowledge of law such as William Shakspere could hardly be expected to possess." (14)

Looney: "It seems clear that the study of law had proceeded along with study of the classics. Oxford's letters of a later date show, moreover, an intimate acquaintance with a large range of legal precedents. . . . Throughout his life Edward de Vere was involved in legal matters dealing with the tenure and disposal of lands, and . . . [he] participate[d] in several important trials: that of Mary Queen of Scots in 1586, of Philip Howard, Earl of Arundel, in 1589, and of the Earls of Essex and Southampton in 1601." (68-69)

Courtly life, manners, sports

Old view: Shakespeare's knowledge of courtly life was acquired through reading and through imagination.

Lee: "To assume that [Shakspere] wrote all or any [of his plays] from practical experience, unless the direct evidence be conclusive, is to underrate his intuitive power of realising life under almost every aspect by force of his imagination."[28]

New view: Oxford placed his plays within the social milieu in which he was raised and lived as the highest ranking earl in Elizabeth's court. The plays show him at home in an environment that lower classes would never have been allowed to enter.

Looney: "[Shakespeare] does this best when he shows us that human nature at work in the classes with which he is most intimate.

---

[27] Sir Sidney Lee, *A Life of William Shakespeare* (1915), p. 43.
[28] Sir Sidney Lee, *A Life of William Shakespeare* (1915), p. 36.

The suggestion of an aristocratic author for the plays is, therefore, the simple common sense of the situation." (95)

Looney: "The plays which are recognized as having the most distinct marks of aristocracy about them, are supposed to have been produced by the playwright furthest removed from aristocracy in his origin and antecedents." (95)

Politics and diplomacy

Old view: Shakespeare's plays contain few, if any, references to contemporary political events.

Alfred F. Pollard: "No period of English literature has less to do with politics than that during which English letters reached their zenith; and no English writer's attitude towards the questions, with which alone political history is concerned, is more obscure or less important than Shakespeare. . . . Shakespeare himself, whose genius was less circumscribed than any other's, shuns the problems of contemporary politics."[29]

New view: Almost all the plays have royal settings and portray kings, courtiers and government ministers—in whatever country the settings are purported to be—absorbed in political activities and issues important during Queen Elizabeth's reign. Many of the plays portray the sensitive political issue that dominated all others during the last decade of Elizabeth's life (she turned sixty years old in 1593): succession to her throne. As the Queen's Lord Great Chamberlain, Oxford was intimately familiar with these developments.

Hart: Shakespeare's plays form "a series of simple lessons on the fundamental principles of Tudor politics. . . . Shakespeare outdoes every dramatist of his time in the number and variety of the allusions made to those issues. References are scattered through at least twenty plays, including the comedies as well as the histories and tragedies."[30]

Hart: "What is peculiar to Shakespeare is that he treats the politico-theological doctrines of divine right, non-resistance, passive obedience and the sin of rebellion, as the accepted and immutable law of almost every land in every age. He has adroitly woven into the fabric of his plays so many and varied references, direct and indirect, to these doctrines, that we may extract from them an excellent digest of the main articles of the . . . political creed of the Tudors concerning the constitution of the body politic in general and the relation of ruler to subject in particular." (28)

Latin and Greek language and literature

Old view: Shakespeare had "little Latin and lesse Greek." Shakespeare was not familiar with much classical literature, and what little he knew was acquired at the Stratford Grammar School.

Lee: "A lack of exact scholarship fully accounts for the 'small Latin and less Greek' with which he was credited by his scholarly friend, Ben Jonson. But Aubrey's report that 'he understood Latin pretty well' is incontestable."[31]

---

[29] A. F. Pollard, *The History of England, 1547-1603* (London, 1919), p. 440, quoted in Lily B. Campbell, *Shakespeare's "Histories:" Mirrors of Elizabethan Policy* (1947), pp. 4-5.
[30] Alfred Hart, *Shakespeare and the Homilies* (1934), pp. 27-28, 29.
[31] Sir Sidney Lee, *A Life of William Shakespeare* (1915), p. 22.

New view: Shakespeare was fluent in Latin and Greek (and French, Italian and Spanish) and was extensively well read in literature in those languages, including works he drew on that weren't translated until years later. Oxford had private tutors in those languages—the records of his education still exist—as do letters he wrote in fluent French and Latin.

> Looney: Oxford was "thoroughly grounded in French and Latin." (200)

Mental Revolution 6: The Elizabethan Era

Merrie Olde Englande

Old view: Good Queen Bess presided over a Golden Age in English history.

> John Guy: "'England was economically healthier, more expansive, and more optimistic under the Tudors' than at any time in a thousand years."[32]

> *Encyclopedia Britannica*: "The long reign of Elizabeth I, 1558–1603, was England's Golden Age. The Renaissance . . . at last reached the northern island. 'Merry England,' in love with life, expressed itself in music and literature, in architecture, and in adventurous seafaring. William Shakespeare, poet and dramatist, mirrored the age in verse that lifted the English language to its fullest beauty."[33]

New view: England under the Tudors was a police state, with Star Chamber trials, secret police and torture. Ben Jonson was branded and Kyd thought to have been tortured. Discretion was needed in all written communications, resulting in veiled allusions rather than open statements; this was as true for personal letters as it was for stage productions and publications.

> Looney: "Mystery and concerted secrecy were moreover characteristic not only of the literary life of the times, but even more so of the general social and political life. Plots and counterplots, extreme caution and reservation in writing letters—men habitually writing to friends as if suspicious that their letters would be shown to their enemies." (48)

> Looney: The careful manner in which Hamlet swears his friends to secrecy is "clearly the work of a man who knew how to ensure secrecy so far as it was humanely possible to do so. And we do know, as a matter of actual human experience, that when a superior intelligence is combined with what may be called a faculty for secrecy and a sound instinct in judging and choosing agents, secret purposes are carried through successfully in a way that is amazing and mystifying to simpler minds." (48)

War, hard times and famine

Old view: The Elizabethan era was a peaceful time, a Golden Age, a time of prosperity and plenty, broken only by the approach and quick defeat of the Spanish Armada in 1588.

> Wikipedia: "The Elizabethan age contrasts sharply with the previous and following reigns. It was a brief period of internal peace between the English Reformation and the religious battles between Protestants and Catholics and then the political battles between

---

[32] John Guy, *Tudor England* (1988), p. 32.
[33] "Elizabeth I and England's Golden Age," *Encyclopedia Britannica Online*, accessed June 26, 2020. https://web.archive.org/web/20061112031836/http://www.britannica.com/ebi/article-200261.

parliament and the monarchy."[34]

> Lee: The word *famine*" does not appear in his *A Life of William Shakespeare.*

New view: Protestant England was at war with Catholic Spain from 1585 until 1604. The effects of the war were as severe on England as World War I almost 400 years later. A quadrupling of taxes and near famine as a result of the Anglo-Spanish War made the second half of Elizabeth's reign a time of great hardship for many. These facts were uncovered and brought to the attention of other scholars by the first generation of Oxfordians. (See Chapter 7.)

> Hugh Kingsmill: "Owing to its dramatic nature, the victory over the Armada has come to be looked upon as ending the war with Spain. But ...1588 marks the opening of hostilities which were to continue during the rest of the Queen's life."[35]

> Col. Bernard R. Ward: "During the seventeen years that the war lasted, the annual direct expenditure on the Army and Navy alone exceeded 80 percent of the total revenue of the country on no fewer than seven occasions; and at the time of the Armada crisis—1587 and 1588—the figures are 95 percent and 101 percent, respectively."[36]

> Col. Montagu W. Douglas: "From 1558, the date of the Queen's accession, to 1588, the date of the Spanish Armada . . . taxation had remained at a fairly constant level. In 1589 it was doubled, in 1593 it was trebled, and in 1601 it was quadrupled. This fourfold increase in taxation occurred also during the Napoleonic War, and our [Great War]."[37]

> Col. Montagu W. Douglas: "Between 1593 and 1596 the price of wheat was nearly trebled. During the Napoleonic War food prices were also trebled, and the same phenomenon was repeated in our own recent experience between 1914 and 1920. In 1596 and 1597 there was a scarcity of foodstuffs amounting almost to a famine. The same threat of famine recurred during the Napoleonic War, and again in 1917 when the submarine menace was at its highest point."

Mental Revolution 7: Development of Drama and the Theater

The great Elizabethan era literary transformation

Old view: Shakespeare benefited from a decades-long development of the English literary Renaissance.

> Lee: "Shakespeare shared with other men of genius that receptivity of mind which impelled them to assimilate much of the intellectual energy of their contemporaries.... Much of their work was unvalued ore, which he absorbed and transmuted into gold in the process. By the magic of his genius English drama was finally lifted to heights above the reach of any forerunner or contemporary."[38]

---

[34] "Elizabethan Era," Wikipedia. Accessed June 26, 2020. This fanciful view survives even into the 2020s.

[35] Hugh Kingsmill, *The Poisoned Crown* (1944), p. 44.

[36] Col. Bernard R. Ward, "Shakespeare and Elizabethan War Propaganda," *Royal Engineers Journal*, Dec. 1928, p. 472.

[37] Col. Montagu W. Douglas, "First of England's Three Fights Against Famine" [letter], *Morning Post*, Sept. 19, 1929, p. 9.

[38] Sir Sidney Lee, *A Life of William Shakespeare* (1915), p. 95.

New view: From the early 1570s Edward de Vere was the driving force behind the rise of the English Renaissance. Creation of the first public theaters began within weeks of his return from Italy and France, and they were modeled after the theaters he saw there.

> Looney: Oxford "is the personal embodiment of the great literary transition by which the lyric poetry of the earlier days of Queen Elizabeth's reign merged into the drama of her later years. Thus we get a sense both of the literary unity of the times, and of the great and consistent unity of his own career." (292)

> Looney: "The Elizabethan period was the time of the great outburst of our national song literature; and Edward de Vere's work stands at the beginning of that period. . . . He was the only one whose life passed from the circle of the royal court to become immersed in that larger Bohemian society, in which the poetic and dramatic developments of Elizabeth's later years were elaborated. . . . [His] position is central and commanding, and the failure to perceive this means that the sixteenth century poetry has not yet been fully understood."[39]

Direction of the Lord Chamberlain's Men ("Shakespeare's" Company)

Old view: Shakespeare worked for the Lord Chamberlain's Men as an actor and writer, and became part owner of it; hence it is often referred to as "Shakespeare's Company." Sir Sidney Lee, in his *A Life of Shakespeare*, uses the term "Shakespeare's Company" sixty-three times to refer to the "Lord Chamberlain's Men."

> Lee: "Jonson . . . was soon writing for Shakespeare's company . . . When the Lord Chamberlain's men, Shakespeare's company, were cooperating there with the Lord Admiral's men . . . On Boxing Day 1600 and on the succeeding *Twelfth Night*, Shakespeare's company was at Whitehall. . . ."[40]

New view: The Lord Chamberlain's Company was not "William Shakespeare's Company," but Edward de Vere's. "The Lord Chamberlain" was a term often used to refer to "The Lord Great Chamberlain," an office filled by the Earl of Oxford. The company was under his direction from start to finish.

> Charles Wisner Barrell: "Proof secured from recently printed transcripts of the Cecil family correspondence [shows] that Oxford's official title of 'Lord Great Chamberlain of England' was frequently shortened to "Lord Chamberlain.' . . . Oxford, actually the only permanent 'Lord Chamberlain' of the whole period, was commonly designated by the shortened, distinctively Shakespearean title."[41]

Mental Revolution 8: The Nature of Genius

Explanatory power of genius

Old view: Shakespeare's genius explains everything, It enabled him to overcome all obstacles.

> Lee: "The infinite difference between his endeavours and those of

---

[39] J. Thomas Looney, *The Poems of Edward de Vere* (1921), pp. xlii-xliii.
[40] Sir Sidney Lee, *A Life of William Shakespeare* (1915), pp. 358, 368, 374.
[41] Charles Wisner Barrell, "Afterwords," in J. Thomas Looney, *"Shakespeare" Identified* (1948), pp. 461-62.

his fellows was due to the magical and involuntary working of genius, which, since the birth of poetry, has owned as large a charter as the wind to blow on whom it pleases."[42]

Lee: "His literary practices and aims were those of contemporary men of letters, and the difference in the quality of his work and theirs was due to no conscious endeavour on his part to act otherwise than they, but to the magic and involuntary working of his genius. He seemed unconscious of his marvellous superiority to his professional comrades." (503)

New view: Claims for Shakspere's genius violate psychologists' understanding of the phenomenon and the well-established conditions necessary for its full flowering.

Looney: "There is a frequent assumption that the possession of what we call genius renders its owner capable of doing almost anything. Now William Shakspere is the one [and only] stock illustration of this contention. In all other cases, where the whole of the circumstances are well known, we may connect the achievements of a genius with what may be called the external accidents of his life. Though social environment is not the source of genius, it certainly has always determined the forms in which the faculty has clothed itself. . . . A vast disparity or incompatibility between the man and the work must always justify a measure of doubt as to the genuineness of his pretensions and make us cast about for a more likely agent." (73-74)

Development of genius I: Development of abilities

Old view: Genius springs to life spontaneously. It doesn't develop, nor do geniuses produce works of lower quality. It was only natural that Shakespeare's first piece would be *Venus and Adonis*, a poem full of classical references and written in the most polished London English.

Keble Howard: "Mr. Looney evidently has failed to understand the brain of a genius. He thinks that a genius goes through a course of learning and preparation before he can write a work of genius. Precisely the opposite, of course, is the fact. The one thing genius does not require is learning, preparation, or the cultivation of any particular style. The brain of a genius is like a sensitive record on which impressions and emotions crowd at every waking moment without any effort or desire on the part of the owner of that brain, and he must express himself or go mad."[43]

Lee approvingly quotes a poem from 1693 conveying the message that Shakespeare was born, not made:

> "Shackspear whose fruitfull Genius, happy wit
> Was fram'd and finisht at a lucky hit,
> The pride of Nature, and the shame of Schools,
> Born to Create, and not to Learn from Rules."[44]

New view: Psychologists tell us that creative individuals need ten years of intense involvement to master the subject matter of their field. During that period, the developing genius will spin off works of genius but also works of inferior quality as his skills develop.

---

[42] Sir Sidney Lee, *A Life of William Shakespeare* (1915), p. 634.
[43] Keble Howard, "Mr. Looney on Shakespeare," *Sketch*, March 17, 1920, p. 4.
[44] Sir Sidney Lee (1915), p. 594.

Looney: "Genius must be supplemented by a wide and intense experience of life and much practice in the technical work of staging plays. Poetic geniuses who have not had this experience, and have cast their work in dramatic form, may have produced great literature, but not great dramas." (76)

Looney: "Most of the other poets differ from Shakespeare in that they furnish us with collections of their juvenile productions in which, though often enough poor stuff, we may trace the promise of their maturer genius. . . . Masterpieces, however, are the fruits of matured powers." (75-76)

Ben Jonson's poetic statement that Shakespeare's art was made, that is, developed; it was not entirely the result of innate genius:

"Shakespeare
Yet must I not give Nature all; thy Art,
My gentle Shakespeare, must enjoy a part.
For a good Poet's made, as well as born,
And such wert thou."

Development of genius II: Acquisition of knowledge

Old view: Shakspere acquired such knowledge as is incorporated into the plays through reading and conversations, though no record of either exists.

Lee: "He doubtless owed all to the verbal reports of travelled friends or to books, the contents of which he had a rare power of assimilating and vitalising."[45]

New View: Oxford was tutored by the most learned scholars in England in those subjects in which Shakespeare shows a great depth of knowledge.

Looney: "In no matter has the hitherto accepted view of the authorship of the Shakespearean writings played such sad havoc with common sense as in the matter of the relationship of genius to learning. . . . Everything indicates a man in contact at every point with life itself, and to whom books were but the adjunct to an habitual intercourse with men of intellectual interests similar to his own. His is the learning which belonged to a man who added to the advantages of a first-class education at the start, a continued association with the best educated people of his day." (91-92)

Looney: "If we find that a man knows a thing we must assume that he had it to learn. If he handles his knowledge readily and appropriately we must assume an intimacy born of an habitual interest, woven into the texture of his mind. If he shows himself skillful in doing something we must assume that he attained his skill by practice. And therefore, if he first comes before the world with a masterpiece in any art, exhibiting an easy familiarity with the technique of the craft and a large fund of precise information in any department, we may conclude that preceding all this there must have lain years of secret preparation, during which he was accumulating knowledge, and by practice in his art, gaining skill and strength for the decisive plunge; storing up, elaborating and perfecting his productions so as to make them in some degree worthy of that ideal which ever haunts the imagination of the supreme artist." (75)

---

[45] Sir Sidney Lee, "Shakespeare, William," *Dictionary of National Biography*, 11th edition (1910): 356.

Geniuses are absorbed with their work

Old view: Geniuses have no special emotional or personal involvement with their work and can easily move between it and other more mundane activities. Shakspere walked away from his literary activities at the height of his powers to spend the final dozen years in Stratford engaged in brewing malt, speculating in grain and suing his neighbors for petty sums.

> Lee: "Shakespeare, in middle life, brought to practical affairs a singularly sane and sober temperament. . . . As soon as his position in his profession was assured, he devoted his energies to re-establishing the fallen fortunes of his family in his native place, and to acquiring for himself and his successors the status of gentlefolk."[46]

New view: Geniuses are intensely absorbed in their work and can barely stand to be away from it. They will sacrifice their time and resources to their work beyond all prudent measure, and continue to do so until their death. Oxford bankrupted himself, selling one estate after another to finance his theatrical activities.

> Looney: "An intense, even passionate devotion to the special form of art in which his masterpieces are produced is invariably characteristic of a genius. . . . We are entitled, therefore, to expect that 'Shakespeare' appeared to his contemporaries as a man over whom the theatre and all that pertained to play-acting exercised an irresistible fascination." (88)

> Looney: "To think of him as one who made an excursion into literature in order to win a competency for himself, and who retired from literary pursuits when that purpose had been served, is to contradict everything that is known of the production of such masterpieces." (87-88)

Geniuses care about what happens to their works

Old view: Geniuses don't care much about what happens to their works. Shakspere was not involved in publishing his plays, did not respond when they were published surreptitiously and in mutilated form by literary pirates, and walked away from many half-finished plays at the time of his retirement.

> Lee, quoting Jusserand: "The same genius who could create *Othello* and *Macbeth* gave no thought at all to preserving them for a posterity for which he had no concern; it is a remarkable thing to see the same man risk the disappearance of these masterpieces and go to the greatest pains to exact payment of a bond or to recover a debt."[47]

> Lee: "It is questionable whether any [of the plays] were published under his supervision. . . . But if in 1611 Shakespeare finally abandoned dramatic composition, there seems little doubt that he left with the manager of his company unfinished drafts of more than one play which others were summoned at a later date to complete."[48]

New view: Geniuses are intensely concerned with protecting their finished work. They don't leave unfinished work behind without some thought as to what will happen to it. The greater the genius, the greater the care that is taken to ensure the work will survive.

---

[46] Sir Sidney Lee, "Shakespeare, William," *Dictionary of National Biography*, 11th edition (1910): 369.

[47] Jusserand, quoted in Abel Lefranc, *Under the Mask of William Shakespeare* (1988), pp. 42-43.

[48] Sir Sidney Lee, "Shakespeare, William," *Dictionary of National Biography*, 11th edition (1910): 257, 379.

Looney: "Sir Sidney Lee's statement that Shakspere had no hand in these various publishing operations we accept. The idea that the author had no hand in them we reject entirely, as almost an outrage upon common sense." (317)

Looney: "Unfinished performances of great geniuses are not unknown in the world, but when they appear one explanation alone accounts for them—an utter inability to proceed: usually death." (345)

Looney: "In the case of Edward de Vere alone do we get the natural explanation that the writer was cut off in the midst of his work, leaving unpublished some plays that he may have considered finished, and others published later, either unfinished or as they had been finished by other writers." (346)

Looney: "When we find that certain plays, issued after that date, were completed by other writers, the situation involves no such anomaly as belongs to the Stratfordian view: that a living writer of the first rank could so allow his own creations to be marred." (317-18)

Mental Revolution 9: Literary Creativity

Source of Literary creativity

Old view: Literary creativity is open-ended, the result of the free play of imagination and fantasy on any and all subjects. It has no necessary connection with the life of the author.

Sir Sidney Lee: "Supreme literature is mainly the creation of the imagination working on and transmuting anything and everything in heaven or earth. We deny that the function of supreme literature is the reporting or the chronicling of private experience. . . . [If not, then] all literature is to be judged as autobiographic portraiture of the writer; and that a writer's eminence varies according to the fullness and literalness with which he puts into his work 'ses sentiments intimes.'"[49]

New view: Literary creativity grows out of the life of the author. It is open-ended on one end only. On the other it is bounded by a writer's experiences, temperament and personality, and by the subjects he knows about and cares about. The greater the work, the stronger the connection between it and the life and mind of its author.

Looney: We must "put aside the old conception of a writer creating everything by the vigour of his imagination, and to regard the writings as reflecting the personality and experiences of their author." (7)

Looney: "Plays and the personality of their authors are . . . complementary: their lives and characters form the natural key to the literature: the literature throws light into the obscure corners of the lives. . . . The importance of the personality of a writer is . . . in direct proportion to the recognized importance of his work."[50]

Looney: "Truly great dramatic literature can only come from the pens of writers who are accustomed to look closely into their own souls and make free use of their secret experiences; and it may be doubted whether a single line of living literature ever came from pure

---

[49] Sir Sidney Lee, "More Doubts About Shakespeare," *Quarterly Review* (July 1919), p. 204.
[50] J. Thomas Looney, "Shakespeare: A Missing Author, Part 1," *SF News-Letter* (American), vol. 2/2 (Feb. 1941): 13.

imagination or mere dramatic pose." (13)

Literary imagery

Old view: The mind consciously constructs images, metaphors and similes. Shakespeare had no depth of knowledge and needed none. He needed just enough to include in the plays to give flavor to scenes, settings and characters.

> Lee: "The knowledge of a soldier's life which Shakespeare exhibited in his plays is no greater and no less than that which he displayed of almost all other spheres of human activity, and to assume that he wrote of all or of any from practical experience, unless the evidence is conclusive, is to underrate his intuitive power of realising life in almost every aspect by force of his imagination."[51]

New view: Artistic creativity consists largely in the preconscious forming of new combinations of existing materials and selecting from them the ones that work best in a particular context. It is critical for a writer to possess an associative richness, a wealth of knowledge to draw on. Only a mind already filled with such riches could form surprising new combinations and put them into truly creative works of literature, music and art.

> Spurgeon: Shakespeare "gives himself away" through his images. He "unwittingly lays bare his own innermost likes and dislikes, observations and interests, associations of thought, attitudes of mind and beliefs, in and through the images, the verbal pictures he draws to illuminate something quite different in the speech and thought of his characters."[52]

> Looney: "In reading the poems of de Vere, as in reading the works of Shakespeare, one lives in a world of similes and metaphors. In both cases there is a wealth of appropriate classical allusions; but this is mingled harmoniously with an equal wealth of illustration drawn from the common experiences and what appear like the personal pursuits of life." (131)

Motivation for writing

Old view: Shakespeare wrote the plays solely to earn a living. After he was paid, he had no further interest in his literary creations.

> Lee: "With his literary power and sociability there clearly went the shrewd capacity of a man of business. His literary attainments and successes were chiefly valued as serving the prosaic end of providing permanently for himself and his children. His highest ambition was to restore among his fellow-townsmen the family repute which his father's misfortunes had imperiled."[53]

> Lee: "It was doubtless with calculated aim of exploiting public taste to the utmost that he unceasingly adapted, as his genius dictated, themes which had already, in the hands of inferior writers or dramatists, proved capable of arresting public attention." (356-57)

New view: Shakespeare/Oxford wrote the plays for reasons personal and political.

> Looney: "Do they look like the work of one whose chief interest was to keep a theatre business going, or of one who was primarily a poet? . . . Everything is much more suggestive of a poet creating his

---

[51] Sir Sidney Lee, "Shakespeare, William," *Dictionary of National Biography*, 11th edition (1910): 354.
[52] Caroline Spurgeon, *Shakespeare's Imagery, and What It Tells Us* (1935), p. 4.
[53] Sir Sidney Lee, "Shakespeare, William," *Dictionary of National Biography*, 11th edition (1910): 384.

varied passages out of the multiplicity of his own moods and experiences, and incorporating these into suitable parts of his different plays: afterwards putting them through a final process of adjusting the parts, and trimming and enriching the verse." (327)

Mental Revolution 10: Shakespeare's Inner Life

Shakespeare's inner life and emotional experience

Old view: Shakespeare's emotional and intellectual responses to the events of his life are not reflected in his plays or poems, which are based on literary and historical sources, modified for dramatic effect on stage.

>Lee: "Ultimately, tragedy rather than comedy gave him the requisite scope for the full exercise of his matured endowments, by virtue of the inevitable laws governing the development of dramatic genius. To seek in the necessarily narrow range of his personal experience the key to Shakespeare's triumphant conquest of the topmost peaks of tragedy is to underrate his creative faculty and to disparage the force of its magic." (418)

New view: Great works come from the depths of great souls. Shakespeare's literary works are highly artistic gems—the results of intellectual and emotional stimuli. The plays portray events and people important in Oxford's life, and, even more intensely, his emotional and intellectual reactions to them, configured to the demands of the dramatic storyline. His rocky life and career contained the requisite experiences for generating, by all normal human standards, the wide range of human responses portrayed in Shakespeare's plays.

>Looney: "What distinguishes Oxford's work from contemporary verse is its strength, reality, and true refinement. . . . [E]very line written by the poet is a direct and real expression of himself in terms at once forceful and choice and no mere reflection of some fashionable pose." (129)

>Looney: "The plays of Shakespeare contain possible pen portraits of men with whom the Earl of Oxford had dealings, representing them, not as tradition has preserved them, but as they stood in relation to Oxford himself." (251)

>Lefranc: "Certainly, the greater the writer the more he puts into his works his closest feelings, his personal ideas, his experience of life, in a word his soul and his own psychology."[54]

>Lefranc: "How suppose that Shakespeare, alone, among mankind's torch-bearers, could escape the general law, by entirely separating his works from his life? . . . The intellectual life of the author, and his emotional life, his affliction—for he certainly knew some—the particular events of his life, his experience of men, his animosities, his travels, his dreams, the turn of his insatiable curiosity, his innumerable observations, his own place: that ought all to reflect in his plays." (41)

The Sonnets

Old view: The *Sonnets* are mere poetry, the result of literary imagination with no personal content.

>Lee: "The conviction [is] that Shakespeare's collection of sonnets has no reasonable title to be regarded as a personal or autobiographical

---

[54] Abel Lefranc, *Under the Mask of William Shakespeare* (1988), p. 40.

narrative."[55]

> Lee: "The claim that has been advanced in their behalf to rank as autobiographical documents can only be accepted with many qualifications. The fact that they create in many minds the illusion of a series of earnest personal confessions does not justify their treatment by the biographer as self-evident excerpts from the poet's autobiography" (168).

> Halliwell-Phillipps: "The Sonnets [are] . . . entirely impersonal."[56]

New view: Shakespeare's *Sonnets* are the most deeply personal poems Oxford ever wrote.

> Looney: "The sonnet, possibly more than any other form of composition, has been the vehicle for the expression of the most intimate thoughts and feelings of poets. Almost infallibly . . . do a man's sonnets directly reveal his soul. The sonnets of 'Shakespeare,' especially, have a ring of reality about them quite inconsistent with the fanciful non-biographical interpretation which Stratfordianism would attach to them." (100)

> Looney: "Shakespeare's work of poetic self-expression is, of course, the *Sonnets*. The idea that these poems are fantastic dramatic inventions with mystic meanings we feel to be a violation of all normal probabilities and precedents" (369-70).

Darkening of Shakespeare's view

Old view: We know of no events in the life of the modest businessman from Stratford that would account for the darkening view of human beings and human society in Shakespeare's great tragedies.

> Lee: "The commonly accepted theory that traces in this change of tone [reflect] a corresponding development in the author's own emotions ignores the objectivity of Shakespeare's dramatic work. Every phase of feeling lay within the scope of his intuition, and the successive order in which he approached them bore no explicable relation to the course of his private life or experience."[57]

> Lee: "A popular theory presumes that Shakespeare's decade of tragedy was the outcome of some spiritual calamity, of some episode of tragic gloom in his private life. No tangible evidence supports the allegation. The external facts of Shakespeare's biography through the main epoch of his tragic energy show an unbroken progress of prosperity, a final farewell to pecuniary anxieties, and the general recognition of his towering genius by contemporary opinion. The biographic record lends no support to the suggestion of a prolonged personal experience of tragic suffering. Nor does the general trend of his literary activities countenance the nebulous theory."[58]

New view: Shakespeare's darkening view was a direct result of the difficult and tragic events occurring in the life of Edward de Vere.

> Looney: "We have in Oxford the same moral trait that we have in Hamlet, that we have parallel external circumstances tending towards its production, and that these external circumstances are just such as

---

[55] Sir Sidney Lee, *A Life of William Shakespeare* (1915), p. xi.
[56] J. O. Halliwell-Phillipps, *Outlines of the Life of Shakespeare* (1907), vol. 1, p. viii.
[57] Sir Sidney Lee, "Shakespeare, William," *Dictionary of National Biography*, 11th edition (1910): 378.
[58] Sir Sidney Lee, *A Life of William Shakespeare* (1915), p. 417.

might lead to all the tragic developments which succeeded in both instances." (400)

Lefranc: "Critics are unanimous in discerning in the poet's dramas during the waning years of the sixteenth century and into the first seven or eight years of the seventeenth, indications of a deep mental disturbance of a pessimistic nature, of a deep discouragement: this would be the epoch of *Hamlet*, of *Macbeth*, *King Lear*, *Timon*, *Troilus*, etc.: now, nothing, absolutely nothing like, shows up in the life of the man of Stratford."[59]

Mental Revolution 11: Oxford and his life and literary work

Oxford's reputation

Old view (the pre-*"Shakespeare" Identified* view): Edward de Vere was a man of violent temper and a spendthrift, yet also wrote poetry and was patron of a company of players.

Encyclopedia Britannica: "Hitherto the earls, in spite of their vicissitudes, had retained possession of their ancient seat and great estates; but Edward, the son of Earl John, was a spendthrift. A brilliant, gifted courtier, in whom Elizabeth delighted, he quarreled with his father-in-law, Burghley, 'sent his patrimony flying,' patronized players, poets and musicians, and wrote excellent verse himself."[60]

Lee: "He was thoroughly grounded in French and Latin, but at the same time learnt to dance, ride, and shoot. While manifesting a natural taste for music and literature, the youth developed a waywardness of temper which led him into every form of extravagance, and into violent quarrels with other members of his guardian's household. . . . Oxford had squandered some part of his fortune upon men of letters whose bohemian mode of life attracted him. He was patron of a company of players who gave performances at Ipswich, Cambridge . . . and other places. . . . Among men of letters who acknowledged Oxford's patronage the chief were John Lyly . . . and Edmund Spenser."[61]

New view: Many slanders about Oxford were made by traitors to England trying to destroy the reputation of a chief witness against them. They must be set aside, and all the wonderous things said about Shakespeare transferred to Oxford.

Looney: "One of the most serious hindrances to the formation of correct views will be the necessity of reversing judgments that have had a long standing social sanction. We shall first have to dissociate from the writings the conception of such an author as the steady, complacent, businesslike man-of-the-world, suggested by the Stratford Shakspere." (86)

Looney: "Add to that the reputation of the 17th Earl of Oxford as an unlikeable, arrogant spendthrift that has come down to us, and the task is more difficult still. . . . We shall therefore be called upon in his case radically to modify and correct a judgment of three hundred years' standing." (87)

---

[59] Abel Lefranc, *Under the Mask of William Shakespeare*, tr. by Cecil Cragg (1988), pp. 22-23.
[60] "Vere," *Encyclopedia Britannica* (1910-11), p. 1020.
[61] Sir Sidney Lee, "Vere, Edward," *Dictionary of National Biography* (1885-1901), pp. 225-228.

Oxford as representative of his class

Old view: As the seventeenth earl in the Oxfordian line, Oxford was the highest ranking earl in the kingdom.

> Encyclopedia Britannica: The de Veres were "the family of which is extolled by Macaulay as 'the longest and most illustrious line of nobles that England has seen.'"[62]

New view: As the highest ranking member of the nobility in a society with a vertically-oriented class structure, Oxford was engaged in an ultimately unsuccessful holding action to preserve the status of his class against the rise of the new commercial class.

> Looney: "Only as we realize [Oxford's] spontaneous hostility to the social and political tendencies represented by Burleigh, Walsingham, Sidney, Raleigh and Fulke Greville shall we be able to judge him accurately or adjust ourselves properly to the Shakespeare problem." (300)

> Looney: "Hamlet's cry, therefore, that 'the time is out of joint,' points to something deeper than his personal misfortunes and the tragedy of his private life. They are much more like the outburst of a writer, himself suffering from a keen sense of the unsatisfactory character of his whole social environment: one out of rapport with the age in which he lived; an age of social and spiritual disruption incapable of satisfying either his ideals of social order or the poet's need of a full, rich and harmonious spiritual life. All this personal dissatisfaction that the poet expresses through *Hamlet* is quite what was to be expected from one placed as was Edward de Vere in his relations to the men and movements of his day." (410)

Oxford as the "Soul of the Age"

Old view: The Earl of Oxford was a foppish courtier with poetic tendencies.

> Lee: "While manifesting a natural taste for music and literature, the youth developed a waywardness of temper which led him into every form of extravagance.... He evinced a genuine interest in music, and wrote verse of much lyric beauty."[63]

New view: The Earl of Oxford was "the Soul of the Age" who stood at the heart of the intellectual and literary and artistic life of Elizabethan society. He was a principal conduit of the ideas flowing in from Italy and France, and was at the forefront of the literary and linguistic revolutions taking place from the 1570s onward in England.

> Looney: "When as a young man de Vere began to write poetry he was strongly under the influence of Lord Vaux' work . . . Now, by a curious chance, the last poem in the 'Vaux" collection . . . is the identical song of Lord Vaux' which 'Shakespeare' adopts for the use of the gravedigger in *Hamlet.*" (137)

> Gerald H. Rendall: "Only lately has it become plain how central a place belongs to Edward de Vere, seventeenth Earl of Oxford, at the confluence of the various currents of literary activity—poetic, dramatic, exotic, and academic—which combine to form the product known as 'Elizabethan.' Student, poet, playwright, and patron of the drama, he was in touch with the most versatile spirits of the age, and in

---

[62] "Vere," *Encyclopedia Britannica* (1910-11), p. 1019.
[63] Sir Sidney Lee, "Vere, Edward," *Dictionary of National Biography* (1899): 226.

the judgment of his best-informed contemporaries his own compositions were second to none in excellence."[64]

Oxford's life history and his theatrical works

Old view: The Earl of Oxford published a few poems as a young man and also organized theatrical performances for the court, but all his dramatic works have been lost.

> Lee: "Puttenham and Meres reckon him among 'the best for comedy' in his day; but, although he was a patron of a company of players, no specimens of his dramatic productions survive."[65]

New view 1: The plays as we know them today were written in two phases, first as dramas to be performed, and then as literature to be read. The first produced the works for which de Vere was known during most of his life; the second produced the works now known as Shakespeare's.

> Looney: "The Shakespearean dramas, as we have them now, are not to be regarded as plays written specially to meet the demands of a company of actors. They are stage plays that have been converted into literature. This we hold to be their distinctive character, demanding in their author two distinct phases of activity, if not two completely separate periods of life for their production." (310)

> Looney: "For it is upon their merits as literature that the fame and immortality of Shakespeare's dramas rest. Though the writer's first aim may have been to produce a perfect drama for stage purposes, in the course of his labours, by dint of infinite pains and the nature of his own genius, he produced a literature which has over-shadowed the stage play." (326)

> Ranson: "[T]he plays passed through several distinct phases: (1) They were *originally written* during the fifteen-seventies and early eighties for *private* performance as Court Masques; (2) They were *adapted* during the late eighties and nineties for performance in the *public theatres*. Each play, therefore, has two dates—its first composition for performance at Court, and its revision and adaptation for performance in the public theatres. Moreover, certain plays—e.g., *Hamlet*—went through yet another revision before publication."[66]

New view 2: Many of Oxford's plays and poems survive under the name of William Shakespeare. Others survive as anonymous or under other pseudonyms or the names of other known writers. Oxford disappeared from the literary record just as Shakespeare's works began to be performed on the public stage.

> Looney: "If such a dramatic and literary outburst had had no original connection with de Vere it must inevitably have swept him within its influence. But the very man who had the greatest affinities with this particular type of production, and who, up to within a year or two of the first appearance of William Shakspere, had been amongst the foremost to encourage and patronize literary men, is never once heard of either in connection with William Shakspere or the Shakespearean drama. So far as these momentous happenings in his own peculiar domain are concerned, he might have been supposed to have been already dead." (311-12)

---

[64] Gerald H. Rendall, *Shakespeare Sonnets and Edward de Vere* (1930), pp. 291-92.
[65] Sir Sidney Lee (1899): 228.
[66] F. Lingard Ranson, "Shakespearean Page," *East Anglian Magazine*, vol. 3/7 (May 1938): 351.

> Looney: "We have, therefore, a most remarkable combination of silences; a silence as to his own occupations during these important years, and a silence as to any manifestation of interest in a work which, under any circumstances, must have touched him deeply. We can only suppose that he did not wish to be seen in the matter; and the only feasible explanation of such a wish is the theory of authorship we are now urging." (312)

Academic opinion of Oxford's early poems

Old view, before 1920: Scholars praised Oxford's poems before the Oxfordian thesis was proposed.

> Lee: "Oxford, despite his violent and perverse temper, his eccentric taste in dress, and his reckless waste of his substance, evinced a genuine interest in music, and wrote verse of much lyric beauty. . . . A sufficient number of his poems is extant, however, to corroborate Webbe's comment that he was the best of the courtier-poets in the early years of Elizabeth's reign, and 'that in the rare devices of poetry, he may challenge to himself the title of the most excellent among the rest.'"[67]

> Grosart: De Vere's poems "are not without touches of the true Singer and there is an atmosphere of graciousness and culture about them that is graceful."[68]

Revised view among academics: After Oxford had been proposed as the real "Shakespeare," opinion of his poems changed. What had been praised was now disparaged.

> Alfred R. Orage: "Not in three lives . . . could Edward de Vere have learned to write a true Shakespearean line, let alone some hundreds of them. . . . While it is true that circumstantial evidence lays him under suspicion of having been Shakespeare, his own works constitute a perfect alibi."[69]

New view: Oxford's poetry came before any of the better known poets between him and Shakespeare. The so-called clichés that Oxford employed were his innovations that were copied by others.

> Looney: "A comparison of these two verses . . . entitles us to say that 'Shakespeare' was either a kind of literary understudy of de Vere's, guilty of a most unseemly plagiarism from his chief, or he was none other than the Earl of Oxford himself."[70]

> Looney: "Even conventional forms and phrases were not conventional to the first men who employed them, and a study of dates will probably show how much of what ultimately became common stock actually had its source in the Earl of Oxford." (lxxiii)

> Looney: "His poems are by far the most Shakespearean in quality and form of any of that time. His dramatic record places him in the forefront of play writers. Then a silence of an additional twelve years . . . *and this twelve years of comfort and seclusion exactly corresponds to the period of the amazing outpouring of the great Shakespearean dramas.*" (311) [emphasis in original]

---

[67] Sir Sidney Lee, "Vere, Edward," *Dictionary of National Biography* (1885-1901), pp. 225-228.
[68] Alexander B. Grosart, *Fuller Worthies' Library*, vol. 4, p. 359.
[69] Alfred R. Orage [R. H. C.], "Readers and Writers," *New Age*, Dec. 23, 1920, pp. 91, 92.
[70] J. Thomas Looney, *The Poems of Edward de Vere* (1921), p. 156.

Shakespeare as revisionist and precisionist

Old view: Shakespeare wrote rapidly and never revised.

> Lee: "Ben Jonson was often told by the players that 'whatsoever he penned he never blotted a line.' The editors of the First Folio attested that 'what he thought he uttered with that easiness that we have scarce received from him a blot in his papers.' Signs of hasty workmanship are not lacking, but they are few when it is considered how rapidly his numerous compositions came from his pen, and in the aggregate they are unimportant."[71]

New view: Shakespeare/Oxford often revised his works. The title pages of many of Shakespeare's plays state that they were newly revised.

> Looney: "Everything points to 'Shakespeare' being given to storing, elaborating, and steadily perfecting his productions before issuing them, when his mind was bent on producing something worthy of his powers.... How it could ever have been believed that the finished lines of Shakespeare were the rapid and enforced production of a man immersed in many affairs, will probably be one of the wonders of the future. Everything bespeaks the loving and leisurely revision of a writer free from all external pressure; and this, combined with the amazing rapidity of issue, confirms the impression of 'a long foreground somewhere.'" (322)

> Looney: We "have found in Shakespeare's compression a clear evidence of the latter's careful and persistent elaboration of his lines. Now this tendency to revert to his work in order to further improve it is typical of Edward de Vere. Variant copies of his small lyrics are extant, and these furnish unquestionable proof that he was accustomed to turn back to poems, even after their publication, in order to enrich and perfect them. He was a precisionist; the very ease and lucidity of whose lines was the consummation of an art which hid its own laboriousness." (323)

Mental Revolution 12: Shakspere and his life

Shakspere as actor

Old view: Shakspere was widely recognized as an actor during his lifetime and he is almost universally referred to as "the Stratford actor."

> Lee: "Shakespeare's earliest reputation was made as an actor, and, although his work as a dramatist soon eclipsed his histrionic fame, he remained a prominent member of the actor's profession till near the end of his life." (46)

> Lee: "There is little doubt that at an early period Shakespeare joined this eminent company of actors which in due time won the favour of King James. From 1592, some six years after the dramatist's arrival in London, until the close of his professional career more than twenty years later, such an association is well attested." (54)

New view: Neither the records of theatrical performances in London nor those in the provinces contain any mention of an actor named Shakespeare or Shakspere.

> Looney: "[T]he whole of the municipal records of the acting companies are silent with regard to William Shakspere, and the whole

---

[71] Sir Sidney Lee, *A Life of William Shakespeare* (1915), pp. 97-98.

of the Treasurer of the Chamber's records, with the one irregular exception. . . . If the reader still persists in believing that William Shakspere was a well-known figure on the stage, or a prominent member of the Lord Chamberlain's company of actors, or in any way much in evidence in connection with the doings of that company, we would respectfully suggest that his time could not be more profitably spent than reading the remainder of these pages." (58)

Shakspere recognized as playwright

Old view: Shakspere was widely recognized as a playwright during his lifetime.

> Lee: Shakspere's "genius as dramatist and poet had been acknowledged by critics and playgoers alike, and his social and professional position had become considerable. Inside the theatre his influence was supreme."[72]

New view: Not one record exists from during Shakspere's lifetime of anyone claiming that the man from Stratford was a playwright.

> Looney: "Shakespeare's work if viewed without reference to any personality would never have been taken to be the work of a genius who had emerged from an uncultured milieu." (18)

Shakespeare's "retirement"

Old view: After having become wealthy, Shakspere retired to Stratford, where he busied himself in the non-literary activities of hoarding grain and suing his neighbors for small amounts of money.

> Lee: "With the year 1611 . . . Shakespeare's regular home would seem to have shifted for the rest of his life to his native place. . . . We may accept without serious qualification the assurance of his earliest biographer Nicholas Rowe that 'the latter part of life was spent, as all men of good sense will wish theirs may be, in ease, retirement, and the conversation of his friends.'"[73]

New View: For Shakspere, if he had been Shakespeare, the production of literary works would have been an all-consuming purpose right up to the moment of his death. There is no record of any literary or intellectual activities by Shakspere after his retirement to Stratford.

> Looney: "For we are assured that the greatest genius that has appeared in English literature, when he had reached his maturity, and when there was no sign of failing powers, having lined his pockets well with money, retired from his literary labours, leaving in the hands of stage managers the manuscripts of uncompleted plays, that others, at a later date, were called upon to finish." (345)

Silences about Shakspere the man during his lifetime and at his death

Old view: Shakspere was widely known during his lifetime and his genius recognized after his death.

> Lee: "Shakespeare was gaining personal esteem outside the circles of actors and men of letters. His genius and 'civil demeanour' of which Chettle wrote arrested the notice of noble patrons of literature and the drama. His summons to act at court with the most famous actors of the day at the Christmas of 1594 was possibly due in part to personal interest in himself. Elizabeth quickly showed him special favour. Until

---

[72] Sir Sidney Lee, "Shakespeare, William," *Dictionary of National Biography*, 11th edition (1910): 368.
[73] Sir Sidney Lee, *A Life of William Shakespeare* (1915), p. 450.

the end of her reign his plays were repeatedly acted in her presence."[74]

Lee: Except for Ben Jonson years after "Shakespeare's" death, "no other contemporary left on record any impression of Shakespeare's personal character" (383).

New view: Shakspere as an educated or literary figure was invisible to contemporaries.

Looney: "Not during these years is there the slightest record of any of those things by which a genius impresses his personality upon his contemporaries. Outside the printed works nothing but blank negation meets us whenever we seek to connect this man with any of those things by which eminent literary men have left incidental impressions of themselves upon contemporary life." (52-53)

Looney: "The death of William Shakspere passed quite unnoticed by the nation. No fellow poet poured forth mourning. The Earl of Southampton whom he is supposed to have immortalized showed no interest. . . . Mrs. Stopes attributes this neglect to his retirement." (37)

Shakspere's Will

Old view: Although in his will Shakspere was "precise" with the disposition of every item he owned, he made no mention of any manuscripts, books, papers or anything else connected to an intellectual or literary life.

Lee: Lee insists "[t]he precision with which the will accounts for and disposes of every known item of his property refutes . . . the conjecture that he had provided for his wife under a previous settlement or jointure." (383)

New view: Shakspere's Will made no mention of any intellectual or theatrical or poetic interests because he was not William Shakespeare.

Looney: "From the first word of this will to the last, there is nothing which suggests that the testator ever had an interest either in the sixteen plays that had already appeared in print or in the twenty that had yet to be published or in anything else of a literary nature. . . . The omission from the will of all mention of books . . . confirms the impression that William Shakspere had never owned any." (26, 30)

---

[74] Sir Sidney Lee, "Shakespeare, William," *Dictionary of National Biography*, 11th edition (1910): 363.

A New Basis for Understanding the Works, the Man and the Era

For those with the courage, time and mental energy to pass through the dozen Mental Revolutions, a new vista lay before them. Deeper and better informed readings of the plays were suddenly possible. Recognizing the real identity of the author deepened their appreciation of the struggles that lay behind the works, and recognizing his critical role in launching the English Renaissance in the 1570s radically changed their understanding of the history of the era. The nature of genius and literary creativity was freed from the distortions that Shakespeare Studies had forced on them.

Looney had recognized the importance of "getting the problem into the right perspective and on the same plane of vision as the other problems and interests of life. We must free the problem from illogical entanglements and miraculous assumptions, and look for scientific relationship between cause and effect" (77). He believed he had done that.

> Contrasted with the Stratfordian view or any other theory of authorship yet propounded, the supposition that Edward de Vere is "Shakespeare" places the appearance of this literature for the first time within the category of natural and human achievements. (81)

For those not up to the challenge, it is easier to defer to the experts. The experts, though, were not the unbiased scientific authorities they professed to be. As comforting as it was to assume that they had conducted an objective examination of the authorship of Shakespeare's works—this is what they were paid to do, after all—and concluded that the man from Stratford was indeed the author, that is not what happened. For experts, with their own interests to defend, the idea that someone other than Shakspere had written the works was simply impossible to grasp.

For several years after *"Shakespeare" Identified* was released, those convinced by its evidence in support of Oxford's authorship had remained isolated, mostly unaware of each other. That situation was about to change.

6

Founding of the Shakespeare Fellowship, 1922-1925

Col. Bernard R. Ward and the Founding of the Shakespeare Fellowship

"Shakespeare" Identified convinced many people that Edward de Vere had written the literary works attributed to William Shakspere of Stratford-upon-Avon. But for two and a half years those individuals remained, for the most part, isolated from each other. That began to change in November 1922, with the founding of the Shakespeare Fellowship.

The Fellowship was launched by Col. Bernard Rowland Ward, a retired military officer who had been in charge of the air defenses of London during the Great War. He had become aware of the Oxfordian claim in February 1922:

> On the 13th February, 1922, I was invited to lecture to a literary society in Gillingham, Kent, on "The Sonnet in English Literature." I went down to Gillingham by an afternoon train from Victoria, and while looking at the magazines on W. H. Smith's bookstall for something to read on the train, I noticed an article in the *The National Review* entitled "Shakespeare: Lord Oxford or Lord Derby?" by J. Thomas Looney. I bought the magazine and read it on my way down.

> I had been familiar for many years with the Baconian controversy, but had never been a convinced Baconian, as the evidence has not satisfied me that he could have been the actual author, although I thought he might possibly have been the editor of the plays. I was, therefore, a Stratfordian—not an enthusiastic one, but a Stratfordian for want of a better hypothesis.

> The reading of Mr. Looney's article did not convert me, but it decided me to go into the question later on. During my lecture I quoted several of Shakespeare's sonnets in illustration of my theme, and spoke of the author as the actor who came up to London from Stratford in 1586 or thereabouts.... A Frenchman came up to me and said ... the Earl of Derby wrote the plays.... I said 'Yes, I know about that, and intend to read what he has to say.[1]

Upon returning to London, Col. Ward purchased both of J. Thomas Looney's books—

---

[1] Col. Bernard R. Ward, *The Mystery of "Mr. W. H."* (1923), pp. v-vi.

"Shakespeare" Identified and *The Poems of Edward de Vere*—and both volumes of Professor Abel Lefranc's *Sous le Masque de William Shakespeare, William Stanley 6th Comte de Derby*. He read *"Shakespeare" Identified* first, and, "by the time I had got through about a third of it, I felt convinced that he had practically proved his case."[2] After reading the other volumes he came to these conclusions:

1. That Mr. Looney had proved his case as regards the authorship of *Venus and Adonis*; and that with reference to the authorship of *All's Well, Troilus, Hamlet* and the *Sonnets* his arguments, if not constituting an absolute proof, pointed at least to a high degree of probability.

2. That Professor Lefranc had conclusively shown that Derby was concerned in the composition of *Love's Labour's Lost*, and that his authorship of *The Tempest* was highly probable.

3. That Looney and Lefranc corroborated one another, probably owing to the fact that Derby, who married Oxford's daughter Elizabeth, had on occasions assisted his father-in-law. Lefranc, indeed, made this suggestion in the case of *A Midsummer Night's Dream*. At the same time, Looney argued against Oxford's authorship of *The Tempest*, to that extent supporting Professor Lefranc's case.

Having learned that Edward de Vere had lived the final decade or so of his life at King's Place, later known as Brooke House, in Hackney (which by 1922 had become a borough of London), Col. Ward "determined to make some searches in that locality in order to find out . . . other details about his life there."[3] He thus became the first Oxfordian researcher after Looney himself. His researches were "more fruitful than I ever anticipated." He found "a remarkable series of correspondences between Oxford's life and residence at Hackney and the dates and circumstances of publication of the Shakespeare Quartos," and was amazed at "how strikingly they confirm Mr. Looney's hypothesis as to the identity of Edward de Vere and William Shakespeare" (vii).

Col. Ward published his findings in an article in *The National Review*,[4] concluding that "I cannot but think that a careful weighing of the evidence now brought forward will result in a powerful reinforcement of the case so ably put forward by Mr. Looney in his *"Shakespeare" Identified*, that not only the sonnets but also the great majority of the plays are in all probability the work of the Earl of Oxford."[5]

What happened next was that nothing happened, and that lack of response to his findings spurred him to found the Shakespeare Fellowship. "Although the evidence put forward in the *National Review* is far from being negligible in character, no attempt has so far been made to explain it away. . . . 'La consigne est de tout ignorer,' [The response is to ignore everything,] as Professor Lefranc expressed it. . . . [The subject is] taboo to the editors of all decent journals'" (vii).

> After two months of complete silence, broken only by a very kind and appreciative article in *The Hackney Spectator* on the 8th September, 1922, I came to the conclusion that this curious attitude on the part of all "decent journals" could only be dealt with by means of group action, which might serve to encourage some of the many thousands of doubters that exist up and down the

---

[2] Col. Bernard R. Ward, "'Mr. W. H.' and 'Our Ever-Living Poet,'" *Nat. Review*, vol. 80 (Sept. 1922): 81.
[3] Col. Bernard R. Ward, *The Mystery of "Mr. W. H.,"* (1923), pp. vi-vii.
[4] Col. Bernard R. Ward, "'Mr. W. H.' and 'Our Ever-Living Poet,'" *Nat. Review*, vol. 80 (Sept. 1922): 81-93.
[5] Col. Bernard R. Ward, *The Mystery of "Mr. W. H.,"* (1923), p. 23.

country to join a society definitely founded on the basis of free research. (vii-viii)

In setting out to organize what became known as the Shakespeare Fellowship, Col. Ward recruited his friend Sir George Greenwood to serve as its first president and called "upon all Shakespeare students who set a higher value on truth than on orthodoxy to join [it] and to judge all questions of evidence upon the oaths of judgment and reason" (viii).

The Fellowship held its founding meeting on November 6, 1922, at the Central Library in Hackney, following visits to Brooke House and to the parish church of St. Augustine where Oxford and Elizabeth Trentham, his second wife, were believed to have been buried. The names of those who attended are listed in the textbox on the following page.

Colonel Ward opened the meeting by describing his researches at Hackney and explaining why a new society was necessary. He then proposed that Sir George Greenwood take the chair. The motion was seconded and carried unanimously.[6] A vote was then held to select the officers of the Fellowship with the unanimous result that Greenwood was confirmed as president; Professor Abel Lefranc, Mr. J. Thomas Looney, and Mr. L. J. Maxse (editor of *The National Review*) as vice presidents, and Col. Ward as Hon. Secretary and Treasurer. The Hon. Sir John Cockburn, MD, and Mr. William T. Smedley were later added as additional vice presidents.

At its founding the Fellowship included "the originators of the Derby and Oxford hypotheses, two distinguished Baconians, as well as Shakespeare students who are dissatisfied with Stratfordian orthodoxy."[7] Although Maxse, Lefranc and Looney were not present, all later expressed their pleasure at having been selected as vice presidents. Maxse stated that "I will gladly become a Vice-President of your new society, and appreciate the compliment."[8] Lefranc wrote that "I received your kind letter just as I was about to leave for Belgium where I shall be lecturing in the universities. It will be a great pleasure to me to work alongside of Sir George Greenwood, whom I look upon as a friend, although I have never met him, and for whose works I have so high an opinion. . . . I therefore accept the honour which you are kind enough to offer me, of having my name forward as one of the Vice-Presidents of the new Society." Looney wrote to Greenwood to express

> the great delight it has given me to learn of your willingness to undertake the presiding of the Shakespeare Fellowship. My great hope now is that, under your leadership, the greatest literary issue that has ever been raised in the world's history will be placed upon a solid basis of competent co-operative effort, and may I venture to hope also, carried forward to something like a general settlement. If the ultimate verdict is in favour of the Earl of Oxford—and, personally, I cannot see any other possibility—then the triumph must belong in an especial degree to yourself; for, but for your work, I do not think I should ever have taken up the case in the way I did.[9]

Almost immediately the Shakespeare Fellowship launched two series of publications, both at the initiative of Col. Ward, who prepared and edited them. One was the regular Shakespeare Fellowship column in the weekly *Hackney Spectator*, which had been

---

[6] *Hackney Spectator*, Nov. 17, 1922, p. 7, and Col. Bernard R. Ward, *The Mystery of "Mr. W. H."* (1923), pp. 122-26.

[7] Col. Bernard R. Ward, *The Mystery of "Mr. W. H.,"* (1923), p. viii.

[8] Col. Bernard R. Ward, "'Shakespeare' at Hackney," *Hackney Spectator*, Nov. 24, 1922, p. 14.

[9] J. Thomas Looney, letter to Sir George Greenwood, Nov. 3, 1922, excerpt quoted in Col. Bernard R. Ward, "'Shakespeare' at Hackney," *Hackney Spectator*, Nov. 24, 1922, p. 14.

SHAKESPEARE FELLOWSHIP FOUNDATION MEETING AND OBJECTS
REPRINTED FROM *THE HACKNEY SPECTATOR*, NOVEMBER 17, 1922
SHAKESPEARE AT HACKNEY

The following party drove, on Monday the 6th November, to Hackney and visited Brooke House and the old tower of St. Augustine's Church, before having lunch at "The Pembury Arms," in Amhurst Road: Mr. Francis Clarke, Lieutenant R. Dubau, Sir George Greenwood, Rev. and Mrs. Hobart-Hampden, Colonel B. R. Ward. The following gentlemen joined them at luncheon: Mr. T. Alfred, Chief Librarian, Central Library, Hackney; Mr. A. Hester, St. Kilda's Studio, Clapton, E.5; and Mr. C. W. Slade, representing *The Hackney Spectator*.

The party afterwards proceeded to the Central Library, where Mr. A. Walrond Clarke showed drawings of the old church and of a tomb of grey marble which he thought had been erected to the Earl and Countess of Oxford after the death of the latter in 1612. There were two coats of arms on the tomb at one time, but the brasses had been removed. Mr. Clarke thought these two coats were probably those of Vere and Trentham. There is, however, no written evidence about this, and in any case the tomb was not erected until after 1612.

A meeting was subsequently held, attended by the foregoing, and, in addition, by Mr. Thurkill Cooke and Colonel M. W. Douglas, C.S.I., C.I.E. Miss G. Mellor, Mr. Cecil Palmer, and Brig.-Gen. E. M. Paul, C. B., C.B.E., expressed their regrets at being unable to attend the meeting.

Colonel Ward opened the proceedings by a description of his researches at Hackney, and gave reasons why a new Shakespeare Society was necessary for research and propaganda. He then proposed that Sir George Greenwood take the chair. This was seconded by Lieutenant R. Dubau and carried unanimously.

The Shakespeare Fellowship was named. It was next proposed by Mr. Albert Hester, and seconded by Mr. C. W. Slade, that the officers of the Fellowship be as follows: President: Sir George Greenwood; vice-Presidents: Professor Abel Lefranc, Mr. J. Thomas Looney, and Mr. L. J. Maxse; Hon. Secretary and Treasurer: Colonel B. R. Ward. . . . The above resolution was then carried unanimously.

The *Hackney Spectator* was designated the official organ of the Fellowship.

OBJECTS OF THE FELLOWSHIP

The fellowship was founded at Hackney on the 6th November, 1922, with the following objects:

(1) To unite in one brotherhood all lovers of Shakespeare who are dissatisfied with the prevailing Stratfordian orthodoxy, and who desire to see the principles of scientific historical criticism applied to the problem of Shakespearean authorship.

(2) To encourage and to organise research among parish registers, wills, and other documents likely to throw light on the subject.

(3) To form the nucleus of a Shakespeare reference library, and to collect lantern slides to be issued on loan for lecturing purposes.

Membership

Membership is open to all persons who sympathise with the objects of the Fellowship, as detailed above.

Officers for 1923

President: Sir George Greenwood.

Vice-Presidents: The Hon. Sir John Cockburn, K.C.M.G., M.D.; Professor Abel Lefranc; Mr. J. Thomas Looney; Mr. L. J. Maxse; Mr. William T. Smedley. Additional Vice-Presidents for 1923 may be elected by the Executive Committee.

Executive Committee: Sir George Greenwood; Mr. Francis Clarke; Colonel M. W. Douglas, C.S.I., C.I.E.; Colonel B. R. Ward, C.M.G.

Hon. Secretary and Treasurer: Colonel B. R. Ward.

designated the "official organ of the Fellowship" at the inaugural meeting. The column, reporting on Fellowship events and research for members and the public, continued for more than 152 weeks, until the newspaper ceased publication in March 1925. The other publication was a series of *Shakespeare Fellowship Circulars* sent to members. More than sixty issues were produced on an irregular basis for more than fourteen years, until the *Shakespeare Fellowship News-letter* was begun in 1937.

Col. Bernard R. Ward

Col. Bernard Rowland Ward, C.M.G.,[10] was the first Oxfordian researcher after J. Thomas Looney and the first to publish an Oxfordian book. He was the driving force behind the founding of the Shakespeare Fellowship; without him there would have been no institutional support for the Oxfordian idea. He created the first real Oxfordian community through his extensive correspondence with others intrigued by the Oxfordian idea and by bringing them into contact with each other. In short, he was the founder not just of the Shakespeare Fellowship, but of the Oxfordian movement that continues to this day even as various Oxfordian organizations fall by the wayside. For almost a decade, until he was hospitalized early in 1932, he was the indispensable man. It is impossible to overstate his contributions to the Oxfordian cause.

Col. Ward was a man of extraordinary accomplishments. As a member of the Royal Engineers, in the Great War he served on the Western Front, where he was awarded the 1914 Star, before being entrusted with command of aerial defenses of London from 1914 to 1918.[11] He was a poet as well as a distinguished military officer. Phyllis Carrington reported that "Poetry was his chief delight, and among the poets, Shakespeare, especially the Sonnets, took first place."[12]

After retiring from the Air Force, Col. Ward moved to Farnham Royal in Buckinghamshire, which at that time was a lovely unspoiled village on the edge of Burnham Beeches. "His home," Carrington wrote, "became an operational headquarters from which he launched a crusade for the vindication of Oxford's character and the truth of his authorship of the Shakespeare plays." In his work editing the Fellowship column in *The Hackney Spectator* (1922-1925), and its page in *The Shakespeare Pictorial* (1929-1933), he was "an ideal editor; absolutely impartial, fearless, bringing out the best in each contributor, encouraging, praising, inspiring, writing many of the articles himself. He was the most modest of men, playing down his own contribution and encouraging the work of his fellow members."

Carrington described him as being "a man of middle height and—when I first met him in 1931 [when he was sixty-eight years old]—greying hair and moustache, a pleasant, friendly smile and charming courteous manner, which quickly put one at one's ease. Anyone who met him could not but recognize in him a man of ability and resource, no

---

[10] C.M.G. is the designation of the Order of St Michael and St George, started in 1818 to honor those who made extraordinary contributions to the British Commonwealth. Given the impact of the Great War on the Commonwealth, those appointed to the Order were accorded great respect by the British people in the following decades.

[11] Phyllis Carrington, "Col. B. R. Ward," *Shakespearean Authorship Review*, no. 8 (Autumn 1962): 5. Although Carrington was an American, she lived in England. She died in 1945, but her pieces on several early Oxfordians were not published until 1962. She was a niece of Esther Singleton, and the unsold copies of her aunt's novel, *Shakespearian Fantasias*, were shipped to her after Singleton's death in 1930.

[12] "Origin and Achievements of the Shakespeare Fellowship," *Shakespeare Fellowship News-Letter* (American), vol. 1/1 (Dec. 1939): 5.

matter what subject he might be dealing with." To Col. Ward, she continued, "we owe a deep debt of gratitude, for without his untiring efforts and hard work, and encouragement of his friends and collaborators, we should not have had any Shakespeare Fellowship and so the question of the Oxfordian authorship of the Shakespeare Plays might have died an early death."

COLONEL B. R. WARD, C.M.G.

In his research, Col. Ward spent much time examining parish registers and local histories. He discovered that in 1608, the year before the *Sonnets* were published, Elizabeth Trentham, Oxford's widow, had sold King's Place in Hackney, where she and Oxford had lived during the final years of his life (1596-1604). Ward surmised that the original manuscript of the *Sonnets* "had been found at King's Place when the house was sold and Lady Oxford's effects cleared out of it in 1609."[13]

In seeking to explain how the *Sonnets* had come to be published, Ward was guided by comments made by two other Shakespeare scholars. Sir Sidney Lee had written that "Mr.

Col. Bernard Rowland Ward, C.M.G.

Born: 1863. Died: April 30, 1933.

Age when *"Shakespeare" Identified* was published: 57

One of the first Oxfordian researchers.

Author of the first Oxfordian book after Looney, *The Mysterious "Mr. W.H."* (March, 1923)

The leading force behind the founding of the Shakespeare Fellowship in November, 1922.

Sent out scores of Shakespeare Fellowship *Circulars* to keep members aware of research and publications. Edited the Fellowship column in *The Hackney Spectator*, 1922-1925, and the Fellowship page in *The Shakespeare Pictorial*, 1929-1933.

Published dozens of articles. Major findings: Oxford received funding of £1,000 a year from Secret Service funds from mid-1586 until his death in 1604. Expenditures on the Anglo-Spanish War (1585-1604) were comparable to the cost of England's war with France, 1793 to 1815, and the war with Germany, 1914-1918.

Military service in the Royal Engineers. In command of air defenses for London during the Great War. From a military family; the eldest son of Col. Bernard E. Ward, of the 60th Rifles. Educated at Winchester, Woolwich and Balliol College, Oxford. Commissioned in 1882.

Military publications
   Regimental Rhymes (1893)
   Manual of Military Ballooning (1896)
   Notes on Fortifications (1902)
   School of Military Engineering (1908)
   Pasley's Military Policy (1914) (editor)
   "Col. Coote Manningham," Regimental Song of the Rifle Brigade (composer)

His first wife, Jeanie Duffield, daughter of John Milner Duffield of the British Civil Government of Gibraltar, died in April, 1925. He married Amy Margaret Nelson eighteen months later, in November 1926. Upon his marriage he moved from 28 Fitz George Avenue in London to Wyvenhoe, Farnham Royal, twenty-five miles west of the city.

---

[13] Col. Bernard R. Ward, "Edward de Vere and William Shakspere—A Dual Mystery," *National Review*, vol. 81 (Oct. 1922): 267.

W. H.," the "onlie begetter" of Shakespeare's *Sonnets* named in Thomas Thorpe's dedication, referred to Mr. William Hall, an obscure stationer. "William Hall was in this period filling, like Thorpe, the irresponsible role of procurer of manuscripts."[14] Second, Charlotte Carmichael Stopes had conjectured that the dedication seemed to present the *Sonnets* to Mr. Hall "somewhat as a wedding present."[15] "It is clear that they were not published by the poet himself," she stated, "or it would have read 'Sonnets by William Shakespeare.' It is equally evident that they were not published by the Earl of Southampton. Thomas Thorpe takes the responsibility of editing them. He dares not *dedicate* them to anybody, but he 'wishes' something, which, read in ordinary prose, is quite clear" (343).

Putting those comments together, Col. Ward concluded that the sonnets had made their way into the possession of William Hall, who conveyed them to Thomas Thorpe, who then published them with the dedication offering the publication to Hall as a wedding gift. To confirm this supposition, Col. Ward searched parish records and discovered a record of the marriage of William Hall to Margery Gryffyn at Hackney on August 4, 1608. So, Ward wrote, "what more suitable wedding present for him than the volume of sonnets which open with 'From fairest creatures we desire increase.'"[16]

The discovery was the final link in a long and complicated chain of circumstantial

---

Col. Bernard R. Ward's Oxfordian Publications, 1922-1925

1922, Sept.	"'Mr. W. H.' and "Our Ever-Living Poet,'" *National Review*, vol. 80: 81-93.
1922, Sept. 1	"Shakespeare's Mysterious 'W. H.' a Hackney Man?" [letter], *The Hackney Spectator*, p. 12.
1922, Oct.	"Edward de Vere and William Shakespeare – A Dual Mystery," *National Review*, vol. 81: 267-76.
1922, Nov. 24	"Shakespeare at Hackney," *The Hackney Spectator*, p. 14
1922-1925	152 Shakespeare Fellowship columns in *The Hackney Spectator* (editor)

1923, March	*The Mystery of "Mr. W. H."*

Reviews
"Yet Another 'Shakespeare,'" *Aberdeen Press and Journal*, March 26, 1923, p. 2.
"Shakespeareana," *Church Times*, June 29, 1923, p. 27.
    [responses by J. Thomas Looney, *Hackney Spectator*, Sept. 7 and 14.]
[No title], *Glasgow Herald*," Mar/Apr, 1923.
"The Mystery of 'Mr. W. H.," *The Saturday Review*, vol. 135 (April 28, 1923): 570-71.
[No title], *The Scotsman*, March 19, 1923, p. 2.
"The Mystery of 'Mr. W. H.,'" *Spectator*, vol. 130 (June 23, 1923): 1049.
[No title], *Times Literary Supplement*, issue 1108 (April 12, 1923): 248-50.
Col. Montagu W. Douglas, "The Mystery of 'Mr. W. H.,' I," *Hackney Spectator*, March 23, 1923, p. 2. [continued on March 28, p. 2]
Col. Montagu W. Douglas, "The Mystery of 'Mr. H. H.,' *Royal Engineers Journal*, March 1923, pp. 154-56.
Charles H. Herford, "Mr. W. H.," *Manchester Guardian*, June 5, 1923, p. 7.
John C. Squire, "The Oxford Movement," *Observer*, March 25, 1923, p. 4.
    [response by J. Thomas Looney, *Hackney Spectator*, April 23, 1923, p. 8.]

---

[14] Sir Sidney Lee, "Thomas Thorpe," *Dictionary of National Biography*, quoted in Col. Bernard R. Ward, *The Mystery of "Mr. W. H."* (1923), p. 11.
[15] Charlotte Carmichael Stopes, *The Life of Henry, Third Earl of Southampton* (1922), p. 344.
[16] Col. Bernard R. Ward, "'Mr. W. H.' and 'Our Ever-Living Poet,'" Sept. 1922, p. 92.

evidence, the cumulative effect of which was to conform the supposition . . . that the Earl of Oxford was the author of the *Sonnets*.[17]

A careful weighing of the evidence now brought forward will result in a powerful reinforcement of the case so ably put forward by Mr. Looney in his *"Shakespeare" Identified*, that not only the *Sonnets* but also the great majority of the plays are in all probability the work of the Earl of Oxford.[18]

Col. Ward reported on his research in two articles in the *National Review* and in several columns in *The Hackney Spectator* in the fall of 1922. He compiled his findings into a book *The Mystery of "Mr. W. H."*, published by Cecil Palmer in March, 1923. His conclusions were viewed sympathetically by Oxfordian and even by orthodox Shakespeare scholars of the times. Charles Herford—the same reviewer who wrote that "It is impossible not to like, and even to admire, Mr. Looney"—opined that, "The author of the present volume . . . is neither the most erudite nor the most dogmatic; he repudiates both the doctrine of the 'Baconians' and their strident tones. But few have approached him in the union of charming amiability of manner with the gift of taking impalpable grossamers of possibility for strong cords of proof."[19]

Reviewers also noted Ward's leading role in the founding of the Shakespeare Fellowship. J. C. Squire, writing in *The Observer*, wryly observed that

> A Government may . . . if it be sufficiently strong and disdainful, unite even the most incompatible of opponents into a Coalition. . . . This is the position which has now been reached as between the Stratfordians and their enemies. These latter, tired of the small impression made by uncoordinated attacks on various parts of the front, have come together to frame a common offensive policy. They have agreed on their principal War Aims and decided in favour of a Unified Command. On November 6 last year the Shakespeare Fellowship was founded.[20]

Squire found the record of William Hall's marriage to Margery Gryffyn to be "Colonel Ward's main contribution to the documentary evidence." But "[i]t cannot, I think, be called very substantial. . . . Half the parishes in England may have given birth to, or even seen the nuptials of, William Halls in the period in question. So far as it goes, however, the discovery is a link, if a small and defective one, in Mr. Looney's chain. For the rest Colonel Ward produces circumstantial evidence of an indirectly contributory kind." He could have pointed out, though didn't, that although Hall was married on August 4, 1608, the *Sonnets* were not registered until May 20, 1609, nine and a half months later, and were not published until sometime thereafter—hardly the right timing for a wedding gift.

Though appearing to be open to the idea of someone other than Shakspere as Shakespeare, Squire was unable to accept Edward de Vere as the author for the reasons he had expressed in his back and forth with Looney in *The Outlook* back in 1921. He could not marry Oxford's verse with Shakespeare's (see Chapter 4).

The Aberdeen Press and Journal also noted that the Shakespeare Fellowship was founded in order "to unite in one brotherhood all lovers of Shakespeare who are dissatisfied with the prevailing Stratfordian orthodoxy." In its judgment, "the chapters in Col. Ward's book which deal with Oxford are ingenious and well knit, presenting a solution of the 'W. H.' mystery, and erecting a plausible case for Oxford's authorship—

---

[17] Col. Bernard R. Ward, "Edward de Vere and William Shakspere—A Dual Mystery," Oct. 1922, p. 267.

[18] Col. Bernard R. Ward, "'Mr. W. H.' and 'Our Ever-Living Poet,'" Sept. 1922, p. 93.

[19] C. H. H. [Charles H. Herford], "New Books: "Mr. W. H.," *Manchester Guardian*, June 5, 1923, p. 7.

[20] J. C. Squire, "The Oxford Movement," *Observer*, March 25, 1923, p. 4.

plausible, that is, so long as we bear in mind that all the data is merely probability and provided we do not give heed to such internal evidence as the style, language, and method of the plays."[21]

The Times Literary Supplement in its review also noted the founding and aims of the Shakespeare Fellowship. "We wish it well, since all investigation of the Shakespeare period is valuable, and there is no knowing what luck it may have in discovery. But it must be very careful about the meaning of 'conclusive.'"[22]

Whether or not his findings were correct, Ward had the courage to publicize them and to launch the Shakespeare Fellowship, thereby calling attention to the Oxfordian claim and his belief in it even though, as he explained in the preface to *The Mystery of "Mr. W. H.,"* "To proclaim oneself a supporter of the de Vere theory of authorship is, under present conditions, equivalent in the opinion of a large number of people to a confession either of mental deficiency or of moral obliquity."[23]

Sir George Greenwood

Although management of the Shakespeare Fellowship resided largely with Col. Ward, that such a prominent person as Sir George Greenwood served as president helped to draw attention to it and the Oxfordian claim. This was the case even though Greenwood was careful never to express an opinion about the identity of the true author of Shakespeare's works. As he explained in an interview, "That is a question which I have never attempted to answer. It has been quite sufficient for me to confine my arguments to the negative side of the Shakespeare problem. The positive, or constructive, side I have hitherto been content to leave to others."[24] The interviewer then expressed the frustration felt by many at having no author to put in Shakspere's place:

> But what are poor mortals to do in the matter? Professor Lefranc . . . has credited William Stanley, sixth Earl of Derby. . . . He is a competent scholar. Mr. Looney has broached the claims of Edward de Vere, 17th Earl of Oxford. . . . What *are* we to do, if we would keep sane?

It was perhaps that question and the Fellowship's stated mission to get to the bottom of the authorship mystery that convinced Greenwood, at age seventy-two, to accept the presidency. Whether he was truly agnostic on the authorship question may never be known. Some Fellowship members doubted that he believed Oxford was the author. J. Thomas Looney recorded his assessment of the situation in a draft of a letter to Katharine Eggar around the end of 1923.

> The activities of the Fellowship being dominantly Oxfordian, I cannot but think that if, as you suspect, our President is definitely anti-Oxfordian, his resignation will be only a matter of time, unless his views undergo a change. This would certainly prove a blow for the time being to the movement; though I have little fear but that we should rally again in more definitely Oxfordian lines. In any case I am confident that we have hold of the truth of the Shakespeare business, and whoever may be with us or against us now in the end our cause will win.

---

[21] "Yet Another 'Shakespeare,'" *Aberdeen Press and Journal*, March 26, 1923, p. 2.

[22] Review of *The Mystery of "Mr. W. H.", Times Literary Supplement*, April 12, 1923, pp. 248-50.

[23] Col. Bernard R. Ward, *The Mystery of "Mr. W. H.",* p. v.

[24] "Bacon-Shakespeare Controversy," *Aberdeen Press and Journal*, October 23, 1922, p. 2.

Of Greenwood's eight authorship publications after Looney's book was published—see the nearby text box—only two made any mention of Looney, *"Shakespeare" Identified*, or the Oxfordian claim. In *Baconian Essays* he mentioned Looney's book in a brief footnote: "As for the claims of Edward de Vere, 17th Earl of Oxford, see *"Shakespeare" Identified* by J. Thomas Looney (Cecil Palmer, 1920)." In *Ben Jonson and Shakespeare*, he cited *"Shakespeare" Identified* repeatedly in a ten-page span as a source of information for Shakspere's residences and business activities, but never once mentioned the Oxfordian thesis. In many of his writings Greenwood referred to the Baconian claim and to Lefranc's claim on behalf of the Earl of Derby, but never allowed his name to be associated with the idea of Edward de Vere as Shakespeare.

**Sir George Greenwood's Post-*"Shakespeare" Identified*
Shakespeare Authorship Publications**

1920   *Shakespeare's Law* [London: Cecil Palmer]
1920   *Shakespeare's Handwriting* [London: John Lane]
1922   *Ben Jonson and Shakespeare* (Hartford, CT: Edwin, Valentine, Mitchell]
1922   *Baconian Essays* (by E. W. Smithson, with an Introduction and two essays by
           Greenwood) [London: Cecil Palmer]
1923   *Lee, Shakespeare and a Tertium Quid* [London: Cecil Palmer]
1924   *Shakespeare's Signatures and "Sir Thomas More"* [London: Cecil Palmer]
1925   *The Stratford Bust and the Droeshout Engraving* [London: Cecil Palmer]
1926   "A Cambridge Scholar on Shakespeare," *National Review*, vol. 87 (March): 898-910

In 1926, Greenwood inched forward on the idea of what characteristics the author must have had, while still not venturing an opinion on his identity, in response to criticism of his agnostic position by Mr. Arthur Gray, Master of Jesus College, Cambridge. In his book, *A Chapter in the Early Life of Shakespeare*, Gray had begun by agreeing with much of Greenwood's position: "The Stratford legend has no fact to go upon, and it is utterly improbable."[25] For Shakspere to have been the author we would be forced to assume that he "stood apart from all the conditions which govern the rest of humanity, and that in the preparation for his life's work he neither had nor required the help and suggestions without which the celestial fire cannot in other men be fanned into flame" (898). Greenwood's response was that "*The Shakespeare Problem Restated* . . . has been either scoffed at, or—more especially of late—simply ignored, as though under a *taboo*, by the Highbrows and High Priests of the Orthodox Faith, wherefore it is a cause of sincere pleasure to me that the Master of Jesus College, in my own University of Cambridge, is, at least up to this point, in entire agreement with me" (899-900).

But, Gray continued, "Sir George offers us only an unknown and neuter *Tertium Quid*. What I want, and what in reason everybody demands, is a *Tertius Quid*. . . . In the dual Shakspere-Shakespeare of his begetting, Sir George, by not confounding the persons but dividing their substance, imperils my faith in human individuality. I confess myself so far an orthodox Shakespearean that I must clothe his unessential dramatist in some likeness of a man. Somewhere in this breathing world there lived a man, whose name may or may not have been Shakespeare, but who wrote plays, which were Shakespeare's Works" (898, 900). It was that statement that nudged Greenwood a bit, drawing from him the following

---

[25] Arthur Gray, *A Chapter in the Early Life of Shakespeare* (1926), p. 63, quoted in George G. Greenwood, "A Cambridge Scholar on Shakespeare," *National Review*, vol. 87 (March 1926): 900.

characteristics that the author must have had.

> I can feel no doubt whatever that the name "Shakespeare," affixed to that dedication to the Earl of Southampton, was the maskname of some man of high position, and also of high culture, who wished to conceal his identity, though he was, assuredly, well known to the Earl, and, in fact, an intimate friend of his. That an obscure player of the period should have dared to dedicate his first poem, in such terms as we find in the dedication of *Venus and Adonis*, to the most brilliant young nobleman of the time, is an assumption entirely beyond my belief. We may be quite sure, however, that Southampton well knew who the real author was, and would not have cared "a twopenny button-top" even if the authorship was, in course of time, ascribed to an almost unknown player. (903)

Activities of the Shakespeare Fellowship

In November 1922, the same month the Shakespeare Fellowship was founded, one of its members—Mr. M. Gompertz, Headmaster of Leytonstone County Higher School and Looney's brother-in-law—gave two public lectures on the Oxfordian thesis. In the first, he "spoke to a large audience on the difficulties that existed in . . . accepting the Stratford Player as the author" before noting that "what gives [*"Shakespeare" Identified*] special local interest is that the Earl of Oxford was an Essex man, born at Hedingham, who lived part of his life at Earl's Colne, . . . and who spent the last eight years of his life just over the border at Brooke House, in Hackney, where he died in 1604."[26]

Only one previous public lecture on the Oxfordian claim is known to have occurred. It was given at the Nottingham Shakespeare Society on March 18, 1920, by Councillor C. Foulds, who held up a copy of *"Shakespeare" Identified* for the audience to see and examine.[27]

The founding of the Shakespeare Fellowship was noted by *The Evening Standard*, which commented that "Now, however, there is to be a Shakespeare Fellowship, but it appears to be promoted by people who think that Shakespeare's works were either written by somebody else of the same name, or may have been written by Bacon, or possibly by some contemporary member of the House of Lords."[28]

Two days later the same paper ran another notice titled "Under the Greenwood Tree":

> I wrote something the other day about the Shakespeare Fellowship, and I understand from the friend who told me about it that Sir George Greenwood, who is one of the leading spirits of the Fellowship, was hurt by my suggesting that it is going to make Shakespeare a pretext for eating and drinking.
>
> Well, I gather from my valued contemporary, *The Hackney Spectator*, that the Fellowship was inaugurated at a lunch, and I am sure that Shakespeare himself, if he had survived the formidable attacks made by Sir George on the claim that he wrote his own works, would certainly have insisted on a little refreshment, if not at Hackney, at least at the Mermaid Tavern.[29]

The Fellowship held its first Annual General Meeting on October 30, 1923, in the flat of Canon A. K. Hobart-Hampden and his wife in Roland Gardens.[30] Membership stood at

---

[26] Col. Bernard R. Ward, "Report of a Lecture," *Hackney Spectator*, Dec. 8, 1922, p. 11.

[27] "Interesting Half Hour Talk at Carrington," *Nottingham Journal*, March 19, 1920, p. 5.

[28] "The Shakespeare Fellowship," *Evening Standard*, November 23, 1922.

[29] "Under the Greenwood Tree," *Evening Standard*, November 25, 1922.

[30] Capt. Bernard M. Ward, "Notices: The Late Canon A. K. Hobart-Hampden," *Shakespeare Pictorial*, Nov. 1935, p. 176.

forty-two. A year later, in July 1924, Col. Ward reported that "over fifty members have joined the Fellowship since its foundation.... We have made steady, slow, progress in this country, and our membership abroad is going ahead very satisfactorily. We have members in France, Belgium, and Holland, and our three last-joined members (Nos. 51, 52, 53) hail from America."[31]

In the Fellowship's "Report of Our First Year's Work," sent to members in a *Shakespeare Fellowship Circular* on December 14, 1923 (and also printed in *The Hackney Spectator*), Col. Ward reported that "much of our first year's research work was mainly concerned with transcribing documents relating to the Earls of Oxford and Derby from the Lansdowne and Harleian MSS in the British Museum" and that "[t]his particular line of research is now approaching completion."[32]

He also noted that "what may be called the group theory of Shakespearean authorship" had been much discussed in *The Hackney Spectator* column over the past year and "may be said to be developing gradually in the minds of many of our members."[33] The idea had been first broached in the January 19 column by member Francis Clarke, who observed that evidence appeared "to be accumulating from all directions to show that Shakespearean literature was the work of a group of noblemen at the Court of Queen Elizabeth," and that "Francis Bacon was the great organising genius who coordinated the work of them all."[34]

Appearing to agree with Clarke's first contention, Looney—in an article in *The Hackney Spectator* on August 14—described how "the suddenness and brilliancy of the great literary outburst of the latter half of Queen Elizabeth's reign, which had puzzled students of literature," resulted from

The Shakespeare Fellowship's report on its First Year's Work in *The Hackney Spectator*, December 14, 1923.

---

[31] Col. Bernard R. Ward, "Recent Progress," *Hackney Spectator*, July 25, 1924, p. 9.

[32] Montagu W. Douglas, "Recent Research," *Hackney Spectator*, June 27, 1924, p. 2.

[33] Col. Bernard R. Ward, "Report of Our First Year's Work," *Hackney Spectator*, Dec. 14, 1923, pp. 8, 18.

[34] Francis Clarke, [letter], *Hackney Spectator*, Jan. 19, 1923, p. 2.

"the active association of representatives of the intellectual movement with people educated by the refinements of the court." It was only through such "group activity," led by "the soul of the (great Elizabethan) age," Edward de Vere, that "the Shakespeare dramas could have been made to embody, as they do, the whole culture of the age."[35]

Greenwood had written in *Is There a Shakespeare Problem?* (1911) of "Many pens, one Master Mind," without venturing to speculate about who that mastermind might have been. Members of the Fellowship appeared to be moving toward consensus that there was indeed a mastermind and that it was Edward de Vere. In Col. Ward's recounting,

> The constructive or positive case has made considerable strides. . . . The Fellowship has already collected a certain amount of evidence which points in the direction of 'a crew of courtly makers' (poets), as Puttenham expressed it in 1588, 'of which number is first that noble gentleman Edward Earl of Oxford' with Derby, Willoughby, Rutland, and others in close attendance. The positive case may be said to be developing gradually in the minds of many of our members into what may be called the group theory of Shakespearean authorship.[36]

The Fellowship's second Annual General Meeting, on October 24, 1924, was attended by Sir George Greenwood, Katharine Eggar, Mrs. Hunter, Miss Ursula Smithers, Col. Montagu W. Douglas and Col. Bernard R. Ward. Issues addressed in the second year of the *Hackney Spectator* column included the political implications of the changeling in *A Midsummer Night's Dream* and a comparison of "Hand D" in *Sir Thomas More* with Shakspere's signatures.

Viewing those early Oxfordian activities from a distance of almost ninety years, two observers wrote that "[i]t was a heady time and Oxfordians had every right to feel confident that the sheer weight of new circumstantial evidence in favor of de Vere would force Stratfordians to capitulate and leap on the Oxfordian bandwagon. . . . The powerful resistance to change by entrenched ideational guilds was a phenomenon not yet understood by enthusiastic Oxfordians."[37]

Shakespeare Fellowship Publications and Additional Media Coverage

The Fellowship's columns in *The Hackney Spectator* were hugely important, and a subscription to the paper was included with membership. The first few columns, all by Col. Ward, introduced readers to the authorship question and took them through the evidence and reasoning that led Looney to his extraordinary conclusions:

> It is not too much to say that [*"Shakespeare" Identified*] is the most remarkable and convincing book on the Shakespearean question which has been published since doubts concerning the authorship of the famous dramas first arose in the minds of a few Shakespeare students about 75 years ago.[38]

Another column documented academia's response:

> As might have been expected, the book was not received with a chorus of praise. Not to put too fine a point upon it, it may be said that, for the first eighteen months subsequent to its publication, it was received with a chilling silence, varied only by a very contemptuous reference. The last edition of Sir Sidney Lee's *Life of*

---

[35] J. Thomas Looney, "An Elizabethan Literary Group II," *Hackney Spectator*, Aug. 14, 1923, p. 9.

[36] Col. Bernard R. Ward, "Report of Our First Year's Work," *Hackney Spectator*, Dec. 14, 1923, pp. 8, 18.

[37] Paul H. Altrocchi and Hank Whittemore, editors, *The Great Shakespeare Hoax* (2009), p. 241. [Volume 1 in a series of ten anthologies with the overall title of *Building the Case for Edward de Vere as Shakespeare.*]

[38] Col. Bernard R. Ward, "'Shakespeare' at Hackney," *Hackney Spectator*, Oct. 27, 1922, p. 3.

> *William Shakespeare* goes so far, however, as to acknowledge the existence of the
> book in a footnote to an Appendix on the Bacon-Shakespeare controversy; and
> further evidence which has been accumulating during the last six months is
> beginning to produce an impression upon minds hitherto impermeable to doubts
> concerning William Shakspere or Shaxper of Stratford-on-Avon.[39]

The first column in 1923 contained a message from President Greenwood
encouraging members "to put forth our best endeavours as a Fellowship to help clear up
the greatest and most interesting of literary mysteries" as the 300th anniversary of the
First Folio approached.

> The time of individual action is over, and an organised corporate effort is at last
> being made to reach a solution of the question.
>
> For 75 years, individual students have attacked the problem, and have published
> hundreds of books, pamphlets, and magazine articles on the subject. Now, at last,
> group action is being brought to bear, and we may, I think, confidently look
> forward to great results.[40]

Noting that members Smedley and Cockburn were stout Baconians, Looney was
Oxfordian, and Lefranc was in favor of authorship by Derby, he concluded that "truth is
greater than any single personality, and it is the truth underlying all these theories that it
is our business to discover and our determination to attain."

On the American side of the Atlantic, *The Washington Post* got around to noticing the
Shakespeare authorship issue in March 1924. It rejected the Derby thesis while making
no comment on the Oxfordian: "A candid opinion of Mr. Lefranc's loudly proclaimed
'discoveries' is that they in no way weaken faith in the accepted authorship of the plays in
question and that neither wholly nor partly is Shakespeare dethroned."[41]

Perhaps it was with that article in mind that Col. Ward, in the Fellowship column on
August 1, 1924, noted the closed-mind attitude of the media. "The number of journals and
magazines in sympathy with the aims of the Fellowship is not so great that we can afford
to disregard the assistance of any one of them. *The Galleon* in America and *The National
Review* and *The Hackney Spectator* in England are the only periodicals at present which
do not look askance on our aims and objects. It is up to individual members of the
Fellowship to respond by ensuring that—so far as they are concerned—the Shakespeare
friendly periodicals shall be continued."[42]

Later the same month came an important article in *The English Review*, "The
Shakespeare Myth: A Challenge," in which two Baconian scholars, Lord Sydenham and H.
Crouch Batchelor, expressed their incredulity that a belief with such flimsy foundations
could have endured for so many years.

> For three and a half centuries the belief that the greatest poet of all time was a
> Warwickshire rustic, who deserted the illiterate wife he was forced to marry and
> three children about 1585 and went to London to seek his fortune, has been
> cherished and disseminated. This great myth is unique in the long and painful
> history of human credulity, because there is not a shred of valid evidence to
> connect the man from Stratford with the authorship of the immortal plays, which

---

[39] Col. Bernard R. Ward, "'Shakespeare' in Hackney," *Hackney Spectator*, Nov. 3, 1922, p. 11. Col. Ward is
referring to the 1922 edition of Sir Sidney Lee's book, which will be discussed in Chapter 11.
[40] George G. Greenwood, "The Shakespeare Fellowship," *Hackney Spectator*, Jan. 5, 1923, p. 11.
[41] "A New Rival to Shakespeare," *The Washington Post*, March 10, 1924, p. 6.
[42] Col. Bernard R. Ward, "Fellowship Notes," *Hackney Spectator*, August 1, 1924, p. 10.

bear a name that was not his.[43]

The lengthy article generated much comment. Among the first to respond was Col. Ward, who echoed the authors' challenge to traditional Shakespearean scholars to conduct an objective examination of the authorship question.

> Lord Sydenham and Mr. Crouch Batchelor have issued a resounding challenge to the Shakespearean experts "to descend from their pedestals, to abandon the pose of disdain, and, quitting vague generalities, to take up the challenges now thrown down by supplying—if they can—rational explanations of simple facts."
>
> To ascertain truth must be the first object of mankind if civilization is to endure, and the persistence of a myth, which has not even the lure of probability, is doubly unfortunate. It inflicts shameful injustice upon the greatest genius England has produced, and the belief that an illiterate person could surreptitiously absorb all the learning of the Elizabethan age and transmute it into immortal verse is intellectual degrading.
>
> What is likely to be the effect of Lord Sydenham's challenge? Will it be seriously taken up, or will it be passed by as unworthy of serious notice? It is always dangerous to prophesy, but this, at any rate, may be said. Lord Sydenham's article represents an attempt to transfer the question from the purely literary sphere to the region of common sense.
>
> If it be true that civilization and make-believe cannot indefinitely co-exist, and that intellectual degradation must be the inevitable consequence of juggling with historical evidence, our literary leaders must some day be forced to face the facts that historical researches have been collecting for the last 50 years. The change of front will no doubt be made gradually, but in the end—unless civilization is destroyed in the meanwhile—truth is bound to prevail.[44]

On November 7 he ruefully noted that when it came to the issue of Shakespearean authorship critics were "three quarters subjective and one quarter or less objective." But, he continued, "it is not for us . . . to complain of the subjectivity of reviewers, for it is to that very subjectivity that we owe our existence, our aim being to accustom ourselves and those who are in touch with us to a less subjective attitude in the matter."[45] He went on to affirm the Fellowship's "avowed object being to unite in one brotherhood all lovers of Shakespeare who are dissatisfied with the prevailing Stratfordian orthodoxy, and who desire to see the principles of scientific historical criticism applied to the problem of Shakespearean authorship."

A year later came a favorable review of *"Shakespeare" Identified* in the United States by Clement Wood, who described how he overcame his initial bias against the Oxfordian idea. It appeared in the *New Leader* in September 1925.

> We turned to this book . . . with a bias against it. But that mood could not continue; for here, for the first time, we have a study of the authorship of the "Shakespeare" literature that is written by a man of compelling intellect, skillful in the marshalling of his facts, and fair in stating evidence even when it mitigates against his theory. The book is practically conclusive, to any fair-minded reader. . . . As a presentation of a legal case, as a masterly marshalling of evidence, I have

---

[43] Lord Sydenham of Combe and H. Crouch Batchelor, "The 'Shakespeare' Myth: A Challenge," *English Review*, August 1924, p. 225. Lord Sydenham, like Col. Bernard R. Ward, had been an officer with the Royal Engineers.

[44] Col. Bernard R. Ward, "The 'Shakespeare' Myth," *Hackney Spectator*, August 15, 1924, p. 11.

[45] Col. B. R. Ward, "The Shakespeare Signatures and *Sir Thomas More*," *Hackney Sp.*, Nov. 7, 1924, p. 4.

encountered few books in my life than can compete with this.[46]

Wood also mentioned the issue in his book *The Outline of Man's Knowledge*, published two years later. After dismissing the possibility of authorship by the businessman from Stratford and the weak case supporting Bacon's, he stated that, "with far more cogent logic,"

> J. Thomas Looney and others have identified the real author as Edward de Vere, 17th Earl of Oxford, and a member of what Macaulay calls the noblest house that ever dwelt in England. The surviving poems of de Vere (who bested Sir Philip Sidney in his youth repeatedly, and was hailed as the chief court poet) are strangely like young experiments of the genius that blossomed in Shakespeare. The few contemporary records that laud Shakespeare call de Vere 'the best for comedy' in his day, and 'best of the courtier poets' of the early days of Elizabeth. The sonnets, and indeed the plays, tell de Vere's story, and not the Stratford actor's. The case identifying the nobleman with the author of the plays can only be grasped in its entirety from Looney's treatise. Perhaps future discoveries will settle for all time the vexing problem.[47]

If only all reviewers were as sensible and open-minded as Clement Wood!

Col. Ward and the Development of an Oxfordian Community

The growth of the Shakespeare Fellowship throughout the 1920s was due in large part to Col. Ward's efforts to draw in those who had been intrigued or convinced by Looney's arguments in *"Shakespeare" Identified*. He welcomed letters and carried on an extensive correspondence, passing on information and putting newly-minted Oxfordians in contact with each other. He encouraged his correspondents—ordinary people who were not necessarily writers—to organize their thoughts and perhaps write a piece or two for the column. To help them get started, he often printed a paragraph or two from their letters. Some of the biggest future names in the Oxfordian movement got their start in this manner, including his son, Capt. Bernard M. Ward, Katharine E. Eggar and future Fellowship president Col. Montagu W. Douglas. He also published pieces by such luminaries as Looney and Greenwood, as well as by less prominent members of the Oxfordian community, including Margaret L. Knapp and Quincy Ewing in the United States and Ursula Smithers in England.

Margaret L. Knapp

Margaret Knapp, who had corresponded with Looney as early as November 1920, became one of the earliest American members of the Shakespeare Fellowship. She was a writer of detective stories and novels of some repute, and lived across the street from the Mark Twain House in Hartford, Connecticut. Col. Ward published two letters and an article by her in *The Hackney Spectator*. Her article of June 13, 1924, is especially delightful, in part because of the list she compiled of the "extraordinary number of coincidences" tying real-life people, places and events related to Oxford to the plays, which she extracted from *"Shakespeare" Identified*.

> He [Oxford] was a royal ward like Bertram [*All's Well*], ran wild like Prince Hal [*Henry IV*], was a spendthrift like Bassanio [*Merchant of Venice*], a poet-courtier like Biron [*Love's Labour's Lost*], a patron of players like Hamlet, made enemies

---

[46] Clement Wood, "The Shakespeare Riddle: Has It at Last Been Solved," *New Leader*, Sept. 26, 1925, p. 9.
[47] Clement Wood, *The Outline of Man's Knowledge* (1927), pp. 414-15.

by his pride like Coriolanus, was banished from Court like the Duke [*As You Like It*], lived apart from his three daughters like Lear, and in his last years, was poor, obscure, and a despiser of parasites like Timon of Athens.[48]

Even more important was Knapp's perception that the political events surrounding the publication of the First Folio tied it to Edward de Vere's family. Her letter is the first known published notice of this connection:

> When the First Folio was going through the press, Oxford's son, Henry Vere, was for political reasons a prisoner at the Tower, and Southampton was out of favor at court. If then Oxford was author or part author of the historical plays, the time was not propitious for making the fact known, nor for associating Southampton with its publication.

The historical setting for the First Folio and how it involved the de Vere family was independently discovered and more fully developed by historian and scholar Peter W. Dickson many decades later.[49]

Quincy Ewing

A letter from Louisianan Quincy Ewing, published on July 25, 1924, showed the pleasure that connecting with the Oxfordian community had given him and the quality of his own thinking on the issue. It's reprinted almost in full in a nearby textbox.

Ursula Smithers

Col. Ward brought Ursula Smithers into the Oxfordian fold through correspondence and by publishing her two-part article, "Oxford and Jonson." She cited two plays by Jonson in which she believed Oxford's influence can be felt. The first was *Every Man Out of his Humour* and Jonson's statement about his decision to publish not the original version of the play, but a new version

---

Quincy Ewing Letter to Col. Bernard R. Ward, From *The Hackney Spectator*, July 25, 1924

Dear Sir,

I cannot tell you how very much I appreciate your kind letter of April 29th with enclosures! The authorship of Shakespeare is one of the things that interests me most intensely, and I am heartily glad to be put into touch with you and the other members of the Shakespeare Fellowship, in spite of the many separating miles of land and sea....

I have read Mr. Looney's *Shakespeare Identified* twice. It seems to me a fine piece of constructive work. He makes his points with great clearness, and does not overstrain them. As a "destructionist" Sir George Greenwood hardly leaves anything to be desired. Surely, if any array of facts, brilliantly and tellingly put, can ever disprove an alleged fact, he I should say, has disproved that William Shagsper of Stratford was the author of *Hamlet, Lear* and the *Sonnets*. I sometimes am moved to doubt the quite sane sense of people who see no gaunt contradiction between the *Sonnets* and the life and personality as we have them of the Stratford man!

There is one matter connected with the career of William Shaxpur on which I very much want light: viz., his acquiring of considerable wealth in so short a time. Certainly he was never notable as an actor. Was playwriting so remunerative an occupation in his day that it enabled him to retire from work when just in his prime, and be known as one of the most prosperous citizens of his native town? ...

Please convey assurances of my regard to the members of the Fellowship at their next meeting. It may interest them to know that their work is being watched with applause in far away Louisiana in the U.S.A.!

Again thank you, and with all best wishes,

Quincy Ewing.

---

[48] Margaret L. Knapp, "Oxford Theory Coincidences," *Hackney Spectator*, June 13, 1924, p. 10.

[49] See, for instance, Peter W. Dickson, *Bardgate: Shake-speare and the Royalists Who Stole the Bard* (2011), and "Are British Scholars Erasing Two Heroic Earls from Jacobean History to Protect the Shakespeare Industry?" *Shakespeare Oxford Newsletter*, vol. 35/1 (Spring 1999): 8-9, 24.

which he said was weaker than the first, but which was entirely his own.

> From Jonson's preface to the published version of the play: "This book in all numbers is not the same with that which was acted on the public stage, wherein a second pen had a good share; in place of which I have chosen rather to put weaker, and, no doubt, less pleasing of mine own, rather than defraud so happy a genius of his right, by my loathed usurpation."[50]

She speculated, not without good reason, that Oxford was the "second pen." In the second play Smithers saw Jonson honoring Oxford soon after his death.

> One of the most interesting passages in Jonson's tragedy of *Sejanus* is the eulogy, in the first act, of the Emperor Germanicus. Germanicus is already dead, and has nothing to do with the development of the play, and I think no one can read the passage without feeling convinced that it was written by Jonson in memory of someone he himself had loved.

> I can think of only two men to whom this passage could possibly apply, and they are the Earls of Essex and Oxford.... [A]s there is an undoubted portrait of that Earl [Essex] later in the play, it seems more than likely that these lines were written by Jonson on Oxford.... The passage begins with a description of the fairness of both body and mind of the dead prince, and a touch of intimacy is given.[51]

These were just a few of the many interesting letters and ideas further substantiating Looney's Oxfordian thesis that first appeared in the Shakespeare Fellowship's column in *The Hackney Spectator*. A collection of all columns is currently being prepared for publication.

Captain Hubert H. Holland

Naval Captain Hubert H. Holland, was the third person to write an Oxfordian book. *Shakespeare Through Oxford Glasses*, published in May 1923, two months after Col. Ward's book, examined Shakespeare's works from a topical point of view. Noting that the Earl of Oxford was born fourteen years before William Shakspere, and recognizing that "[f]ourteen years is a long time when plays contain topical references," he concluded that "[i]f the Earl of Oxford be the author of the plays ... and topical events are alluded to, they will be events of much earlier date than are usually looked for."[52] "This does prove to be the case," he continued, "if the allusions pointed out ... are real." After placing the plays chronologically by topical events in them, Holland provided evidence showing "continual personal allusions to the Earl of Oxford himself, incidents of his life, punning allusions to names, birthdays of his family and references to his own age. Whenever an age of any importance is referred to it will be found (with three exceptions) to coincide with the Earl of Oxford's age at the time of writing the play (as discovered by topical events)" (11).

Like Looney, Holland argued that the weight of his evidence is cumulative. Individually, allusions could "be illusions or mere coincidences. It is the quantity rather than the quality which makes them so extraordinary. In thirty plays there appear to be about 150 references which either point to the dates of the plays being quite different from those ordinarily accepted, or which point to incidents connected with the Earl of

---

[50] Quoted in Ursula Smithers, "Oxford and Jonson," *Hackney Spectator*, February 29, 1924, p. 4.

[51] Ursula Smithers, "Oxford and Jonson, II" *Hackney Spectator*, March 14, 1924. This piece, scheduled for the March 14, 1924 issue, was apparently inadvertently omitted. A copy exists in the Oxfordian archives at Brunel University.

[52] Capt. Hubert H. Holland, *Shakespeare Through Oxford Glasses* (1923), p. 10.

Oxford's life."

Holland did not initially assume that Oxford was the author of "Shakespeare's" plays, but instead aimed "to draw attention to certain curious facts, and to leave the reader to form an opinion about whether they are illusions, coincidences or definite allusions to the Earl of Oxford. If the last, then the problem to be solved is, 'Why are there all these allusions to the Earl of Oxford?'" (10). At the end of the book Holland asked if the historical events could have been referred to years after they occurred; if so, they would not be reliable indicators as to when the plays were written. He rejected that possibility as unlikely.

> Taking one play, or even two plays, individually there is no reason why this should not be done, if the events are of sufficient interest. But it appears to be a very different matter when year after year this occurs. Why should the author, writing ten or fifteen years later, select all the events of 1574 or 1589 to write about? . . . Is this likely to be done at any time but the period itself?

And, he asked:

> Why do new moons and May-days, leap years and Ash Wednesdays, eclipses, comets, meteoric displays, heavy falls of snow . . . all fit in so well with the rest of the topical allusions? Are they only coincidences? (122)

Rear Admiral Hubert H. Holland, C.B.*

Born: March 3, 1873. Died: August 19, 1957.

Age when *"Shakespeare" Identified* was published: 47

President of the Shakespeare Fellowship, Sept. 1946 to Oct. 1955

<u>Books</u>

    1923 (May)   *Shakespeare Through Oxford Glasses: Topical Allusions in Shakespeare's Plays*
        <u>Reviews</u>
        1923, June 5   *Aberdeen Press and Journal*
        1923, May 14   *Scotsman*
        1923, June 7   *Times Literary Supplement*
        1923, June 21   *Daily News* — George Sampson
        1923, July   *London Mercury* — Edward Shanks
        1923, Sept. 21   *Hackney Spectator* — Col. Bernard R. Ward [continued on Sept. 28
            and Oct. 19.]

    1933 (Oct.)   *Shakespeare, Oxford and Elizabethan Times*

    Unpub.   *Shakespeare, Oxford and Elizabethan Times II* [The hand-written MSS dated
          1946 is in the Oxfordian Archives at Brunel University.]

<u>Articles and Published Letters</u>

    1933, June 17   "Oxfordian Rejoinder," *Christian Science Monitor*
    1933-1958   More than thirty articles on the Fellowship page in *Shakespeare Pictorial*
          and in the Fellowship's *News-Letter*
    1931-1950   At least nine letters to editors of *The Morning Post, The Times Literary
          Supplement,* and *The Daily Telegraph*

*C.B. — Companion in the Most Honorable Order of the Bath, the fourth most senior of the British Orders of Chivalry.

Though Holland did not explicitly state that Oxford was Shakespeare, the questions he asked led the reader toward that answer. "The Earl of Oxford has come down to history as one of the best writers of comedy of his day. Are the plays written before 1588 the ones referred to?" Even more intriguing, "Could remarks be made about Shakespeare which were intended to refer to the Earl of Oxford, by those who knew his identity, in the same way as one now talks of George Eliot?" If so, "and it does not appear an unreasonable possibility," later generations, not realizing this, would assume they referred "to William Shakespeare of Stratford, and so the Stratfordian theory would gain ground."

Captain Holland then disappeared from the Oxfordian story for a decade, reappearing as Rear Admiral Holland and the author of a new Oxfordian book, *Shakespeare, Oxford and Elizabethan Times* (see Chapter 9).

In a short but fair review of *Shakespeare Through Oxford Glasses*, *The Aberdeen Press and Journal* noted that "the internal evidence" of the plays "when read in the light of the biographical sketch which he gives of the Earl of Oxford . . . certainly unveils curious parallelisms or coincidences."[53] *The Times Literary Supplement* noted that "[t]he book good-humouredly and thoroughly does what it sets out to do; it does not . . . explain why Oxford, wishing to keep his authorship a secret, should have loaded the plays with references to himself, his wife, his daughters, and everything that was his."[54] In Col. Ward's assessment, "it would be difficult for anyone to read this book with an open mind without acknowledging that the author has made out a strong case for the thesis . . . that the self-revelation disclosed in the Plays points, with greater or less clearness, to the personality . . . of the earl of Oxford."[55]

J. Thomas Looney's Contributions to *The Hackney Spectator*

J. Thomas Looney wrote about twenty pieces for the Shakespeare Fellowship columns in *The Hackney Spectator*, from November 1922 through February 1924.

The first, in response to the March 25th review of Col. Ward's book in *The Observer* by John C. Squire, now editor of the *Mercury*, can serve as a status report of sorts on the Stratfordian response to the Oxfordian claim. Looney recognized that although Squire remained unconvinced that Oxford wrote Shakespeare's plays (even after their back and forth in *The Outlook* in 1921), "he has done what some of our opponents have not done: he has read the whole of our case. He has not joined in any conspiracy of silence respecting our propaganda. He has not treated the 'antis' as legitimate objects of discourtesy. . . . All these are healthy signs."[56] Looney readily acknowledged the mental effort needed to

---

[53] "Shakespeare and Oxford," *Aberdeen Press and Journal*, June 5, 1923, p. 5.

[54] "Shakespeare Through Oxford Glasses," *Times Literary Supplement*, June 7, 1923, p. 389.

[55] Col. Bernard R. Ward, "Shakespeare Through Oxford Glasses," *Hackney Spectator*, Sept. 21, 1923, p. 2.

[56] J. Thomas Looney, "The Oxford Movement," *Hackney Spectator*, April 13, 1923, p. 8.

grasp the full Oxfordian thesis; even for those whose minds are receptive to it "conviction depends upon rather a big effort of synthetic coordination and the careful weighing of probabilities that are frequently slow to form. . . . We are not without hope that the able pen of the editor of the *Mercury* may yet be enlisted on behalf of the Earl of Oxford."

Squire reported that the Oxfordian idea "has made only a slight impression" on Shakespeare scholars and the literary press. Looney disagreed:

> From all parts of the world, and from a variety of students we are hearing of the abandonment of the old position. . . . The affected blindness to this of the "respectable" literary press furnishes no means of gauging the actual position, and cannot be persisted in much longer without completely discrediting literary journalism.

Having heard from an enthusiastic and vocal minority, Looney had perhaps overestimated the impact of the Oxfordian idea. His assessment of its impact on the "respectable" literary press must have been dampened on seeing J. L. Garvin's article in *The Observer* ten days after Squire's. Garvin, who would go on to serve as editor of the new edition of *The Encyclopedia Britannica* published in 1929, focused mostly on Abel Lefranc and made the colossal blunder of thinking that Lefranc had attributed authorship of Shakespeare's works to Ferdinando Stanley, Fifth Earl of Derby, when his attribution had clearly been to William Stanley, the Sixth Earl. What must have weighed most heavily on Looney's hopes of progress in convincing editors were Garvin's continuing beliefs that

> Shakespeare himself was as well known in London as the Globe Theatre; that his literary contemporaries and fellow actors working with him in the closest intimacy had no doubt about him; that they knew him in the faults and the qualities of his writing and in his ways of work; that he was famous in his early career; that afterwards for twenty years and more he was regarded as a man of surpassing genius in an age of genius; and that at his death, and so long as any personal memory of his generation endured, he was praised without question as the glory of the land.[57]

It must have shocked Looney that such ill-informed statements could be made as late as April of 1923; his response in *The Hackney Spectator* took apart Garvin's fantastical portrait.

> Every competent Shakespearean knows that the records reveal neither incident, interview, conversation, correspondence, obituary notice, nor a single example of the thousand and one distinctive things that must inevitably have attended so prolonged and brilliant a publicity. . . . If Shakspere had been what [Garvin] claimed, he would have had the personal notoriety described by Mr. Garvin. That the distinctive personal elements are wholly absent is evidence of the false claims entered on his behalf.[58]

Looney's next three pieces also responded to media coverage. One was a rebuttal to George Sampson's review of both Col. Ward's and Adm. Holland's books in *The Daily News*. Two decades later Sampson would become the compiler of the *Concise Cambridge History of English Literature*. Looney challenged Sampson's dismissal of the authorship question as one of only minor importance. "All other problems are subordinate to this one," to knowing who the author was, Looney argued, because,

---

[57] J. L. Garvin, "Who Shakespeare Was: The Comedy of Doubt," *The Observer*, April 22, 1923, p. 12.
[58] J. Thomas Looney, "How *The Observer* Observes," *Hackney Spectator*, May 11, 1923, p. 2.

> All great art grows out of the personality of the artist. The schools may teach him the tricks of manipulation, . . . but only by shaping . . . in moulds of intense personality some portions of the vast amorphous mass of living thought and passion can he produce enduring masterpieces of art. The key to all great art is to be found then in the personality of the artist, just as the key to the real personality of the artist is to be found in his art. Each is complementary and explanatory of the other.[59]

Looney expressed his "considerable sympathy with those whose livelihood or vocation has happened to be linked with Stratfordian interests. We ought not to forget . . . that to the professional littérateur, his 'Shakespeare' lore is a large business asset, of constantly recurring utility; and that, in consequence, to ask him to admit the possibility of an entirely new point of view, is to ask him to re-value his stock in trade, and possibly to write off a large percentage for depreciation."

In June 1923 *The Church Times* ran a critical review of Col. Ward's *The Mystery of "Mr. W. H."* Looney's response, correcting several factual errors, was rejected with no explanation. Col. Ward then ran it along with his observation that,

> We are clearly, in this matter, up against forces that are resolved that our case shall not be seriously examined so long as they can prevent it. There is in it not even a pretense of impartiality and truth seeking: merely an unqualified resistance which only stiffens the more, the stronger our evidence becomes.
>
> What we now need is one man of letters, sufficiently well established to be independent of the literary press, clear in judgment, strong in courage, willing, for truth's sake, to face the derision of smaller men and help to redress a wronged memory.[60]

These reviews revealed the strength of opposition to the Oxfordian claim and showed how assiduous Looney and Col. Ward were in responding to them.

Among the most provocative of Looney's other pieces in *The Hackney Spectator* was the article titled "An Elizabethan Literary Group," published over three columns in August 1923. He provided the context in which a group of playwrights might have come together to write jointly under the overall direction of the Earl of Oxford (as noted earlier in this chapter). Col. Ward and his son, Capt. Ward, would later bring new discoveries to bear on the idea of group authorship (see Chapter 7).

Looney's *Hackney Spectator* article on who wrote *Hamlet* was built around a syllogism: 1. Prince Hamlet is "Shakespeare" himself. 2. Hamlet is the Earl of Oxford. Therefore, 3. The Earl of Oxford is "Shakespeare."

Percy Allen, the drama critic for *The Christian Science Monitor* who would become the most active and influential Oxfordian of the 1930s, first addressed Oxfordian subjects one month after Looney's "*Hamlet*" article in a review of *"Shakespeare" Identified* that largely focused on the same play.

> It is almost a commonplace among Shakespearean students, that Hamlet, the man, is not wholly imagined, but had, somewhere, a prototype in history, our reason for thinking so being that the prince's mental processes are revealed with an intimacy so complete and so sympathetic that, in most of us, no other conclusion is possible. We say with conviction, "This man once lived"; and the only question remaining is, "Who was he?" . . . The instinctive, and no doubt partly

---

[59] J. Thomas Looney, "A *Daily News* Critic," *Hackney Spectator*, August 31, 1923, p. 4.
[60] J. Thomas Looney, "*The Church Times* and a Rejected Letter, II," *Hackney Spectator*, Sept. 14, 1923, p. 4.

true answer comes, "Shakespeare himself!"[61]

After reading both of Looney's books, Allen concluded that "without going all the way with Mr. Looney, he was probably right in identifying the historic Hamlet with Edward de Vere. . . . That here is Hamlet in the original, is a conclusion I cannot easily set aside. The parallel is astonishingly close. . . . [S]uch parallels . . . show how strong the grounds for supposing that, when Shakespeare wrote *Hamlet*, he had Edward de Vere, seventeenth Earl of Oxford, 'in his mind's eye.'"

Allen's observation might bring to mind Looney's comment in *The Bookman's Journal*:

> Critics who are standing out staunchly against my solution of the Shakespeare problem are already admitting that Shakespeare must have been well acquainted with the Earl of Oxford, and very probably made him his model for Hamlet—an admission which, if at all general, would, I believe, carry us forward very rapidly towards the acceptance of my theory.[62]

Looney had repeated the claim in his piece in the *National Review* in February 1922. "One of the best supported identifications—one which several hostile critics have been inclined to concede—is that of Oxford with Hamlet."[63] When making that claim he might have had in mind the following statements made by critics of the Oxfordian idea:

✓ "It is thinkable that Bacon, so near and so aware of Oxford's history, may have in a manner dramatized it in *Hamlet* instead of Oxford himself having dramatized himself."[64]

✓ "The writer's interpretation of *Hamlet* shows to what extent Shakespeare may have drawn upon his knowledge of the household of the Earl of Oxford."[65]

✓ "How does he [Looney] know that Shakespeare did not adapt to his purpose the story of Oxford's career?"[66]

✓ "Mr. Looney . . . does present an amazing chain of parallels from [Oxford's] life showing that the text of the plays is based upon the experiences of this man, who was a ward of Cecil, the first Lord Burghley. . . . His parallels are too remarkable to be . . . mere coincidences, and there is much in the material of the plays which certainly reads like a paraphrase of the events in de Vere's own life."[67]

✓ "'Even if your identification of de Vere with Shakespeare were wrong, it would still stand clear that you have made the most important discovery re the Shakespearean literature that has yet come to light; for here (in de Vere) is a poet who, if not Shakespeare, was Shakespeare's Model, and exercised, indubitably, the most profound influence on his style and thought.'"[68]

---

[61] P.A., "Hamlet's Identity With an Elizabethan," *Christian Science Monitor*, May 19, 1923, p. 17.

[62] J. Thomas Looney, "Is 'Shakespeare Identified'?" *Bookman's Journal*, vol. 1/24 (April 9, 1920): 452-53.

[63] J. Thomas Looney, "'Shakespeare'—Lord Oxford or Lord Derby?" *National Review*, Feb. 1922, p. 804.

[64] Claude Bragdon, letter to William Morrow (Literary Advisor to Scribner's Sons), Sept. 24, 1920. Morrow forwarded the letter to Looney.

[65] "Shakespeare," *Aberdeen Daily Journal*, April 5, 1920, p. 5.

[66] "The Latest Shakespeare," *New Statesman*, March 20, 1920, p. 713.

[67] C. R.., "Shakespeare: Was He Edward de Vere, Lord Oxford?" *Nottingham Journal*, April 22, 1920, p. 4.

[68] Letter to Looney from an unnamed writer quoted in J. Thomas Looney, "'Shakespeare's' Identity," *Sydney Morning Herald*, July 15, 1921, p. 12.

Other critics would later made the same point.

✓ Ivor Brown, in a hostile review of Percy Allen's *Shakespeare and Chapman as Topical Dramatists*, acknowledged that: "It may be that Lord Oxford sat as an unwitting model for Lord Hamlet and that . . . Ophelia is Anne Cecil-cum-Anne Vavasour."[69]

✓ B. H. N., reviewing the same book, noted that "Mr. Allen gives us some grounds for believing that the figure and character of Oxford were present in Shakespeare, subconsciously, if not indeed consciously, when he was creating Hamlet."[70]

Percy Allen would not write about the Oxfordian idea again for more than five years, so we part ways with him, as we did with Capt./Adm. Hubert Holland, until Chapter 8.

Looney wrote nine additional pieces for *The Hackney Spectator*, discussing research in Hackney and Southwark and offering advice on how Oxfordians might best make use of the facts they had found. They were the last pieces he would publish anywhere for more than a decade.

In the November 21, 1924 column, Col. Ward noted in his annual report that Looney had been "incapacitated owing to ill-health for the greater part of the year. . . . The last letter I have received from him is dated the 9th March." A resolution sending the Fellowship's best wishes for an early restoration of health was unanimously passed at the annual meeting and Col. Ward passed it on to Looney.[71]

Oxfordian Correspondence: A Wondrous Time?

Judging from correspondence between Col. Ward and other Oxfordians, they found the middle 1920s a wondrous time—wondrous and difficult and full of promise and frustration all jumbled together. In March 1925 he told Katharine Eggar that "I was beginning to fear that we had got to the end of Oxfordian discoveries,"[72] but nine months later was able to report to Gilbert Standen that "I hope our members will be pleased with the result of our efforts by this time next year. All the omens are favourable and I think we are only at the beginning of real successes. Discoveries are simply tumbling over one another."[73]

At some moments it seemed as if the Oxfordian idea was on the verge of being widely accepted. In April 1925 Ward reported to Eggar that "I am inclined to think that the work of the Shakespeare Fellowship as an organised body is over now that *The Review of English Studies* has been started and the material for a Life of Oxford all got together. I feel rather inclined to issue a winding up *Circular* advising our members to take in McVernon's *Review*. Having caused a split in the Stratfordian camp, all we have to do is join the deserters."[74] But he was less optimistic in December, writing to Standen that "My son [Capt. Bernard M. Ward] has an article on George Gascoigne and his Circle for the January number of *The Review of English Studies* and has written another on *Twelfth Night* for the April number. Will the editor take it? That is the problem. He has carefully camouflaged

---

[69] Ivor Brown, "The Muse on Loan," *Saturday Review*, February 23, 1929, vol. 147: 252.
[70] B. H. N., [review of *Shakespeare and Chapman as Topical Dramatists*], *Shakespeare Pictorial*, March 1929, p. 8.
[71] Col. Bernard R. Ward, "The Annual Report 1923-24," *Hackney Spectator*, Nov. 21, 1924, p. 2.
[72] Col. Bernard R. Ward, letter to Katharine E. Eggar, March 26, 1925.
[73] Col. Bernard R. Ward, letter to Gilbert Standen, December 14, 1925.
[74] Col. Bernard R. Ward, letter to Katharine E. Eggar, April 4, 1925.

his unorthodoxy, but the true inwardness of it is fairly obvious, and if it is taken it will mean that a real panic has taken place in the Stratfordian camp."[75]

In April 1927 Col. Ward was again brimming with hopeful expectations.

> It is wonderful what a lot of ramifications the Oxford Theory leads one into! J. M. Robertson's *Problems of the Shakespeare Sonnets* published last year is interesting from our point of view, as showing how genuinely frightened the orthodox are of the Oxford Theory. Sidney Lee's theory of "Mr. W. H." being William Hall is ridiculed (no doubt in consequence of my *Mystery of "Mr. W. H."*). Elizabeth Vere is alluded to as Lord Burghley's grand-daughter, and the epithet "scoundrelly" is applied to the Bertram of *All's Well* no doubt because of his being thought to be a representation of the hated peer whose name must not even be mentioned by sensible Shakespeareans. A chapter on "Fantastic Theories" includes the Baconian theory but not the Oxford theory. It is evidently too dangerous to be alluded to.[76]

The implications of these observations will be explored in Chapter 12.

---

[75] Col. Bernard R. Ward, letter to Gilbert Standen, December 14, 1925.
[76] Col. Bernard R. Ward, letter to Katharine E. Eggar, April 13, 1927.

Further Achievements of Col. Bernard R. Ward
and Capt. Bernard M. Ward, 1925-1931

The Seventeenth Earl of Oxford 1550-1604

The closing in March 1925 of *The Hackney Spectator*—the periodical most open to articles on the Oxfordian claim—resulted in a lull in presentations of it reaching the public. All that changed in April 1928 with the publication of Capt. Bernard M. Ward's biography *The Seventeenth Earl of Oxford 1550-1604.* Even though Capt. Ward (the son of Col. Bernard R. Ward) studiously avoided any mention of the Shakespeare authorship question, his book generated more extensive media attention to the Oxfordian thesis than any Oxfordian book published in the 1920s other than *"Shakespeare" Identified.*

And yet, the span between the closing of *The Hackney Spectator* and the publication of Capt. Ward's book was not a wasteland; articles touching on the Oxfordian claim were published, with several of them later issues as pamphlets. That important work must be examined before turning to Capt. Ward's biography.

The Rise of Capt. Bernard M. Ward

Like his father, Capt. Ward was a military officer. He was educated at Winchester and the Royal Military College at Sandhurst, but his "brilliant record in scholarship"[1] was interrupted when he was called to service in the Great War. He later studied Elizabethan literature under Prof. Charles J. Sisson at the University of London. At the end of the 1920s he entered the world of business, opening an inn and a hotel with a fellow officer. In the early 1930s he edited the memoirs of Dr. Cecil Reddie, founder and headmaster of the Abbotsholme School, of which he served as a Trustee. It was published as *Reddie of Abbotsholme* in 1934. He was recalled to active military service at age forty-six in 1939, shortly after the outbreak of the Second World War. He served for four years in the Royal Observer Corps and participated in the D-Day invasion of Normandy. He was released from military service early in 1945 and died in October of that year.[2]

Like many other early Oxfordians, Capt. Ward's first published pieces appeared in the Shakespeare Fellowship's column in *The Hackney Spectator* edited by his father. He soon developed into a prominent Oxfordian scholar, publishing several important papers in *The Review of English Studies* in the mid-1920s and bringing back into print one of the first literary collections of the Elizabethan era, *A Hundreth Sundrie Flowers*, long attributed to George Gascoigne. After his father's death in April 1933, Capt. Ward replaced him as the Fellowship's Hon. Secretary and Treasurer, and took on editing its page in *The Shakespeare Pictorial*. He also served as the first editor of *The Shakespeare Fellowship*

---

[1] Charles Wisner Barrell, "Afterwords," in J. Thomas Looney, *"Shakespeare" Identified* (1948), p. 456.
[2] "Oxford-Shakespeare Case Loses Brilliant Advocate," *SF Quarterly*, vol. VI/44 (Oct. 1945), p. 50.

News-Letter when it was launched in 1937.

In his first article in *The Review of English Studies*, Capt. Ward challenged the traditional attribution of *The Arte of English Poesie*, published in 1589, to George Puttenham. After showing that "it is absolutely impossible for either Richard or George Puttenham to have written the book,"[3] Ward examined "the internal evidence provided by the *Arte*" for clues to the real author and prepared lists of five general characteristics and nine "particular" references before proceeding to search for a candidate—a process closely resembling that designed by J. Thomas Looney in his search for the true author of "Shakespeare's" works. He concluded that John, Lord Lumley (1532-1609 had been the real author.

Even more interesting was his description of how a courtier who wished to publish a work of his own without revealing his identity might have proceeded—steps that closely align with those that the Earl of Oxford might have taken four years later in publishing *Venus and Adonis*; both works were published the same publisher, Richard Field.[4]

> Let us suppose that the author—some courtier unknown to us but not to Field [the publisher]—was alive in 1588, and wished to publish his MS., which is really a defence of poets and poetry against the Puritan attacks. This author being by hypothesis a courtier, cannot bring out the book under his own name. Now, if the book were published anonymously, and no hint as to authorship given, it would surely not be long before people reading it would guess whence it originated.
>
> I suggest, therefore, that our author went to Richard Field and asked him to publish the book anonymously, but, at the same time, told him to give out vague and undefined hints that the book, as far as he knew, "was by a fellow called Putnam, or something of the sort," adding, in a confidential whisper, "a bit of a bad hat, you know; got into trouble some years ago, and is now in prison." A hint

---

Capt. Bernard Mordaunt Ward

Born: January 20, 1893. Died: October 12, 1945.

Age when *"Shakespeare" Identified* was published: 27

Shakespeare Fellowship Honorary Secretary and Treasurer, 1933-1939

His biography of Edward de Vere, *The Seventeenth Earl of Oxford 1550-1604*, was published in March 1928, after five years of research in original records at great pains and expense. That research also resulted in a dozen important articles that he and his father published at the end of the 1920s.

Editor, Shakespeare Fellowship page in *The Shakespeare Pictorial*, 1933-1936.

Editor, *The Shakespeare Fellowship News-Letter*, 1937-1939.

Resided at Welwyn Garden City, Hertfordshire.

He was born in Madras, India, the only child of Col. Bernard R. Ward and Jeanie Duffield. Educated at Winchester and the Royal Military College at Sandhurst. Called to service during the First World War. Later studied Elizabethan literature under Prof. Charles J. Sisson at the University of London.

Returned to active duty in the military in mid-1939. Served until early in 1945 in the Royal Observer Crops and participated in the D-Day landing in Normandy.

---

[3] Capt. Bernard M. Ward, "The Authorship of *The Arte of English Poesie*: A Suggestion," *Review of English Studies*, vol. 1, no. 3 (July 1925): 293.

[4] In this description and in his challenge to the traditional assumption of Puttenham's authorship, Capt. Ward showed himself to be as audacious in challenging conventional scholarly beliefs as Beethoven had been in challenging traditional musical practices by opening his first symphony with a dominant seventh chord.

of this kind would have been quite sufficient to stop too many inquiries about the author.

Ward achieved more notice by editing and publishing a new edition of *A Hundreth Sundrie Flowers*, a collection of poems published in 1573 that had never been reprinted. Though the work had long been attributed entirely to George Gascoigne, Capt. Ward made the case that the book was actually a collection of poems and prose pieces by several people and thus one of the first literary anthologies published during Queen Elizabeth's reign. He further argued that it had been prepared not by Gascoigne, but by Edward de Vere, who published Bedingfield's translation of *Cardanus Comforte* the same year. In attempting to identify the actual authors of the poems in the collection, Ward speculated that de Vere was the author of the sixteen poems signed "Meritum petere," the Latin posy that also appeared on the title page in the space usually reserved for the author's name. He attributed others to Christopher Hatton and George Gascoigne, and showed that the work was published at a time when both Hatton and Gascoigne were traveling outside England. He further showed that *The Poesies of George Gascoigne* (1576) was a revised version of *A Hundreth Sundrie Flowers* published three years later when de Vere himself was traveling abroad.

Reviews of Capt. Ward's edition ranged from cautious acceptance of his claims to outright hostility. In a review in *The Times Literary Supplement*, Harold H. Child stated that, "On the whole argument it is impossible yet to pronounce a definite decision, Mr. Ward has a way of making one suspicious about the whole of his case by leaning too much on conjecture and possibility in minor points. . . . [B]ut certain internal evidence would incline one to believe that he may be right." Child fully supported Ward on one important point concerning *Poesies*: "Mr. Ward is right in claiming that the authentic and original text is that of the *Flowers* and that the *Posies* show a revision not made for poetical reasons alone."[5] Another well-known scholar, George Saintsbury, in a review in a literary journal, *The Nation and the Athenaeum*, also recommended Capt. Ward's edition of *Flowers* while disagreeing with him on some points:

> This, as has been said, does not seem to the present reviewer to have been proved: though here is great expenditure of ingenious suggestion— chronological, coincidental, acrostical, with other varieties of the usual kind. But disagreement here [and there] need by no means bar recommendation of the book itself, which is and deserves to be one of the beautiful "Haslewood" volumes.[6]

A third noted scholar, W. W. Greg, welcomed the reprinting of *A Hundreth Sundrie Flowers*, but in his review in *The Library* was less than enthusiastic about Ward's introduction, which is "full of the grossest blunders." He directly challenged Ward's identification of Christopher Hatton as author of several pieces in the collection, and rejected "Mr. Ward's ingenious theory respecting the *Flowers*,"[7] by which he meant Ward's belief that Oxford was behind the publication of the book and the author of sixteen poems in it. He also expressed his "deep regret" that several lengthy parts of the original book were not included in Ward's edition.

---

[5] Harold H. Child, [review of *A Hundreth Sundrie Flowers by George Gascoigne*, Edited by Capt. Bernard M. Ward], *Times Literary Supplement*, June 10, 1926, p. 391.
[6] George Saintsbury, "The Hundred Flowers," *Nation and the Athenaeum*, vol. 39/10 (June 12, 1926): 295.
[7] W. W. Greg, "A Hundreth Sundry Flowers," *Library*, December 1926, p. 281.

Three respected literary scholars, then, found Capt. Ward's first major work of literary scholarship worthy of serious examination, and two were cautiously accepting of Ward's startling conclusions—the first acceptance by academia of a significant contribution by an Oxfordian to an area of literary scholarship only indirectly related to the Shakespeare authorship question.

Capt. Bernard M. Ward — Important Early Oxfordian Writings and Responses to Them

Articles

"The Authorship of *The Arte of English Poesie*: A Suggestion," *Review of English Studies*, vol. 1, no. 3 (July 1925):284-308. [Later published as a pamphlet.]

"George Gascoigne and His Circle," *Review of English Studies*, vol. 2/5 (Jan. 1926): 32-41. [Later published as a pamphlet.]

"The Death of George Gascoigne," *Review of English Studies*, vol. 2/6 (April 1926): 169-72.

"Further Research on *A Hundreth Sundrie Flowers*," *Review of English Studies*, vol. 4/13 (Jan. 1928): 35-48.

Books

A Hundreth Sundrie Flowers From the Original Edition. Ed. by Capt. Bernard M. Ward (1926)

Reviews

[Review of *A Hundreth Sundrie Flowers*], *New Statesman*, vol. 27 (June 19, 1926): 266.

Ambrose, Genevieve, [Review of *A Hundreth Sundrie Flowers*], *Modern Language Review*, vol. 22 (Jan. 1, 1927): 214-20.

Child, Harold H., [Review of *A Hundreth Sundrie Flowers*], *Times Literary Supplement*, issue 1271 (June 10, 1926): 391.

Greg, W. W., "A Hundreth Sundrie Flowers," *Library*, vol. VII (Dec. 1926): 269-82. Response by Capt. Ward, *Library*, June 1927.

Saintsbury, George, "The Hundred Flowers," *Nation and Athenaeum*, vol. 39/10 (June 1926).

Georges Connes and *The Shakespeare Mystery* (1926, 1927)

George Connes's *Le Mystere Shakespearian*, published in French in 1926, was published in English in 1927 in an abridged version translated "by a member of the Shakespeare Fellowship."[8] It made a splash in literary circles, and was reviewed in at least ten publications. *The Times Literary Supplement* described it as a "useful and interesting contribution to Shakespeare literature."[9] In the introduction Connes informed readers that he spent a year of his life studying the authorship question and the claims made on behalf of five men before writing the book. He presented the claims for each of the contenders—Bacon, Rutland, Derby, Oxford and Shakspere—as though they had been

---

[8] In a Shakespeare Fellowship *Circular* dated March 27, 1928, the translator was identified as "Mrs. Ward." She could not have been Col. Ward's first wife, Jeannie Duffield Ward, who died in April, 1925, before Connes's book was published in France. Capt. Ward was unmarried at the time. Col. Ward married a second time, in November 1926, to Amy Margaret Nelson Ward. Was she the translator?

A "Miss Ward" attended the Fifth Annual Meeting on October 7, 1927. Capt. Ward was an only child and had no children of his own. Did Col. Ward have an unmarried sister known as "Miss Ward"? But even if he did, she could not suddenly have become "Mrs. Ward" because her last name would have changed.

The situation becomes more complicated when a notice in the June 1942 American *News-Letter* (vol. 3/4, p. 54) is considered. It states that the first Mrs. Bernard Rowland Ward, widow of the Col., died in 1942. If that notice is correct and genealogical records incorrect, then she had not died in 1925. If so, she could have been the translator. And, if the "Miss" had been a mistake and "Mrs." had been intended, then she could also have been a member of the Shakespeare Fellowship.

This matter, like so many larger issues, will surely be resolved when the Wards' papers are found.

[9] "Le Mystere Shakespearien," *Times Literary Supplement*, July 8, 1926, p. 464.

written by ardent believers in each candidate's authorship. The chapter on Oxford is largely drawn from *"Shakespeare" Identified. The Shakespeare Mystery* was perhaps the first book to present arguments for more than one candidate, and Connes succeeded in presenting fairly the evidence for each. In the final chapter, though, he disappoints—not just by coming out in favor of Shakspere ("things are quite satisfactorily explained if we accept the Stratford man, and indeed are much more easily explained than by the substitution of any other personality"[10]), but also by making a number of odd statements: "It is not possible to obtain any useful results in attempting to identify the author by comparing facts and historical allusions in the plays with the events and circumstances of his life;" and "I believe that Shakespeare was recognised by his contemporaries as the author of the Shakespearean work, and the best proof so far as I can see of this is that they [the other candidates] never denied it" (277).

Connes was a young man when he wrote his book. Almost forty years later, in 1964, he explained that he could not have written it in the middle of his career; his explanation serves as a marker for academia's resistance even to acknowledging the existence of the authorship issue during the middle decades of the century.

> Anybody who expressed the slightest doubt would instantly be condemned and annihilated by half-a-dozen British pundits, and would terribly damage the chances of success in his career. To risk this one must either be a young man who is afraid of nothing, as I was 40 years ago, or an old one who has nothing more to fear, as I am today. Furthermore, any student who expressed the least doubt would be condemned and annihilated by his professor.

> Simply for having dared to make a circular tour round the question forty years ago, although my conclusions were then orthodox, I got a bad reputation, I was thought to be bringing grist to the mill of the heretics by paying them any attention. If you attempt even today, to express any uncertainty among the orthodox die-hards, you will at once find that faces are closed, expressions harden, or else you are treated with ironic condescension or mourned over, more or less sincerely—with "Ah! a touch of the Baconian disease!" One of the five or six great ones said this to me himself.[11]

The Seventeenth Earl of Oxford 1550-1604 Redux

Capt. Ward completed a draft of *The Seventeenth Earl of Oxford 1550-1604* by the end of 1926 after five years of extensive research in various State Papers and Public Records, including the Lansdowne, Harleian and Rawlinson collections in the British Museum, the Bodleian Library and the Hatfield House archives. As of October he had not found a publisher; it was eventually published by John Murray on April 17, 1928.[12]

By bringing to light much long-buried information about Edward de Vere, Ward's biography accomplished many things, among them documenting Oxford's role in directing theatrical entertainment at the court and establishing that he had served as patron for many scholars, writers and musicians. The book enhanced Looney's pioneering effort to resurrect Oxford's reputation by showing the slanders made against him for what they were—hollow charges flung by two men desperately trying to save their own lives

---

[10] Georges Connes, *The Shakespeare Mystery* (1927), p. 267.
[11] Georges Connes, "I Have Changed My Mind: Some Afterthoughts by Georges Connes," *Shakespearean Authorship Review*, Autumn 1964, p. 4. [Article in the French media translated by R. M. D. Wainewright.]
[12] Col. Ward wrote to Gilbert Standen in a letter dated October 9, 1926, that "My son's *Life of the Earl of Oxford* has been finished, but so far we have not been able to find a publisher."

after Oxford had exposed their planned treasons against the Queen and the country. As summed up in an obituary, Capt. Ward presented "the authentic records of Edward de Vere's remarkable career as courtier, soldier, scholar, poet, dramatist, literary patron and theatrical entrepreneur."[13]

What Ward did not do in his biography was claim that Edward de Vere had used "William Shakespeare" as a pseudonym. He made only two brief references to J. Thomas Looney, and in the text of his book made no mention of *"Shakespeare" Identified in Edward de Vere, Seventeenth Earl of Oxford.* According to the obituary, the authorship subject was avoided partly "to keep the size of his book within reasonable bounds," and partly at the insistence of the publisher, "one of the oldest and most conservative publishing houses in London, [where] editorial opinion was . . . against bringing out the Shakespeare parallels as part of the biography." In this connection, the writer observed, "it is only fair to admit that to have done so would have entailed the issuance of at least a two-volume study."

Of the two references to J. Thomas Looney and *"Shakespeare" Identified* in Ward's biography, one is in a brief footnote near the end:

> A theory has recently been advanced that the Earls of Oxford and Derby are in some way connected with the authorship of Shakespeare's plays. . . . I have refrained from comment on what the conservative element among literary critics is wont to stigmatise as a "fantastic theory" [for two reasons]. In the first place, adequate space could not be afforded to the subject without devoting many chapters to its consideration, and, in the second place, the treatment of controversial matters that cannot be definitely settled by contemporary documents and evidence is outside the scope of this biography.[14]

> *Lefranc, Sous le Masque* (cit.); and J. T. Looney, *"Shakespeare" Identified.* [Footnote is in original]

The other is a carefully worded passage in the annotated bibliography:

> *Shakespeare Identified*, by J. Thomas Looney. Cecil Palmer. 1920. A long and carefully worked out argument, in which the author claims most of the Shakespeare plays and poems for the Earl of Oxford.

> *The Poems of Edward de Vere*, by J. Thomas Looney, 1921. In addition to the 23 poems published by Dr. Grosart in 1872, Mr. Looney included 13 of the songs contained in the 1632 edition of Lyly's plays, and 11 poems which appeared in *England's Helicon* (1600 and 1614) signed "Ignoto." With regard to the latter it seems more probable that the pseudonym "Ignoto" belongs not to Lord Oxford, but to his cousin and friend Lord Lumley. (390)

Although Ward avoided directly tying Edward de Vere to Shakespeare, he did show that de Vere's experiences and personality up to the time that "William Shakespeare" appeared were just what a thoughtful observer would expect the great dramatist's life and nature to have been like. Charles Wisner Barrell made the same point twenty years later.

> While obliged to forego direct application of the great mass of new and illuminating information on Oxford's character, personal interests, and associations to the "Shakespeare" identification . . . Ward achieves in his

---

[13] "Oxford-Shakespeare Case Loses Brilliant Advocate," *SF Quarterly*, vol. VI/4 (Oct. 1945), p. 49.

[14] Capt. Bernard M. Ward, *The Seventeenth Earl of Oxford 1550-1604* (1928), p. 328. Passages quoted from Ward's biography are indicated by page numbers in the text for the rest of this chapter.

biography the same effect by implication. It is the essential companion volume to *"Shakespeare" Identified.*

The factual record which it presents of Oxford's intellectual development; his hunger for knowledge of men and affairs; his boredom with the trivialities of Court life and politics; his achievements as a champion "spear-shaker" of the tiltyard; his predilection for creative arts in varying forms, particularly those having to do with writing, acting, and music; his familiar association with a numerous group of professional poets, playwrights, and story-writers; his tragic love affairs and their disgracefully costly consequences; and—of paramount significance—the detailed account which Ward gives of this brilliant but unfortunate nobleman's lifelong interest in stage affairs, combine to verify him as the one best-qualified man to fulfill the obligations of a real-life "Shakespeare."[15]

Drawing on a wider range of information than had been available to Looney in two important areas—Oxford's relationships with Lord Burghley and Sir Philip Sidney—Ward reached conclusions at variance with his.

Regarding Oxford's relationship with Burghley (his father-in-law and, as Queen Elizabeth's Secretary of State and Lord High Treasurer, the most powerful man in England), the prevailing view among "all historians who have written about Lord Burghley and his son-in-law" was that they had "become bitter and irreconcilable enemies . . . from the moment the Duke of Norfolk was executed in 1572." But, Capt. Ward concluded, "the utter falsity of such a view has been so clearly demonstrated . . . that further argument is unnecessary" (331). He cited "the affectionate tone of Lord Oxford's letters to his father-in-law," and showed that "the few letters we possess that passed between the Earl of Oxford and Lord Burghley [even] after the death of the Countess show both men to have been on quite friendly terms" (303). Although recognizing that "it is clear that two such men as Burghley and Oxford could not live in close proximity and at the same time in complete harmony with one another for more than a very short period" (76-77), Ward described "Lord Burghley's unfailing kindness to Lord Oxford, often in very difficult circumstances" as "one of the most striking features of this biography" (331).

Regarding the Oxford-Sidney relationship, Ward corrected the view of Sidney's biographers, who, he observed, "start with the preconceived idea . . . that anybody who dared to quarrel with Sidney must *ipso facto* be a 'brute' and a 'scoundrel' and entirely to blame" (165). He showed that most historians exclude from their biographies of Sidney much information that casts a negative light on him in his interactions with Oxford. As for the infamous tennis-court quarrel, Ward showed that even one of Sidney's closest friends, Hubert Languet, criticized Sidney's handling of it. He provided the first-ever publication in English translation of a passage in a letter long suppressed by historians who quote other sections of it. Ward showed that although Oxford's and Sidney's lives "ran curiously at cross purposes"—they were rivals for the hand of Anne Cecil (so Ward claims), they clashed over the Anjou marriage and they were literary rivals—"it would be wrong . . . to exaggerate the importance of these incidents, and to argue therefrom that throughout their lives they were hostile to each other" (284).

Not all of Ward's findings have withstood ninety years of scrutiny. A. Bronson Feldman subjected them to scholarly examination and presented a detailed analysis in an

---

[15] Charles Wisner Barrell, "Afterwords," in J. Thomas Looney, *"Shakespeare" Identified* (1948), p. 457.

article published in *The Bard* in 1984.[16] Among the most important of Ward's many findings that have withstood scrutiny are:

About Edward de Vere's Life, Reputation and Literary Activities:

> Oxford served on the Privy Council: He was appointed to King James's Privy Council in July 1604, which "has not hitherto been suspected" (344).

> The £1,000 Annuity: Capt. Ward discovered that Queen Elizabeth awarded Oxford a grant of £1,000 annually beginning in June 1586. He speculated that the Queen, "fully alive to the importance of masques and similar entertainments in promoting the well-being of the Court," and recognizing that Oxford "was instrumental, by means of his brain, his servants, and his purse in providing the Court with dramatic entertainment" (282), and further recognizing that Oxford no longer had the private means to fund such entertainment, ... issued the grant so that "well-organised recreation ... [something] as essential to herself and her courtiers as a plentifully supplied supper-table," would continue. Ward was right about the existence of the grant but wrong in his first guess as to its purpose. Further research by himself and his father would reveal the true purpose of the grant only a few months after the book was published.

> Praise for Oxford from Other Writers: Adding to praise by William Webbe, Harvey and Meres already known, Capt. Ward showed that literary men found in Oxford not "merely a patron willing to be the passive recipient of a dedication, but one who took a keen interest in reading their manuscripts" (90). He also brought to light additional contemporary praise for Oxford's own literary works.

> John Marston, *The Scourge of Villanie* (9th Satire) (1599): References to a concealed poet in phrases that fit the Earl of Oxford:

> > Far fly thy fame
> > Most, most of me belov'd, whose silent name
> > One letter abounds. Thy true judicial style
> > I ever honour, and if my love beguile
> > Not much my hopes, then thy unvalued worth
> > Shall mount fair place, when Apes are turnèd forth.

> Thomas Underdowne also honored the earl, in *To the Earl of Oxford* (1569):

> > Such virtues be in your honour, so haughty courage joined with great skill, such sufficiency in learning, so good nature and common sense, that in your honour is, I think, expressed the right pattern of a noble gentleman.[17]

> Praise of Oxford in the Harleian Manuscripts:

> > Edward de Vere, only son of John, born the 12th day of April 1550, Earl of Oxenford, High Chamberlain, Lord Bolbec, Sandford, and Badlesmere, Steward of the Forest in Essex, and of the Privy Council to the King's Magesty that now is. Of whom I will only speak what all men's voices

---

[16] A. Bronson Feldman, "Amendments to Bernard M. Ward's *The Seventeenth Earl of Oxford*," *Bard*, vol. 4/2 (1984): 53-67.

[17] Thomas Underdowne to the E of O (1569), quoted in Capt. Bernard M. Ward, *The Seventeenth Earl of Oxford*, p. 14.

confirm: he was a man in mind and body absolutely accomplished with honourable endowments. (348)

➤ Oxford's Interactions with Other Writers: Ward brought to light much new information about the nature of the literary life of the Elizabethan era.

> These fleeting vignettes, sketched by the literary underworld of London, give us a vivid glimpse of Lord Oxford and his Bohemian friends and foes. We may perhaps be surprised at the familiar tone in which men like Harvey, Nashe, and Riche spoke of the Lord Great Chamberlain; but the fraternity of letters has always broken down the artificial barriers of caste, and we shall undoubtedly miss the light-hearted buffoonery of these quips if we attempt to analyse them without a sense of humour.

> The Elizabethans were not grave, solemn scholars who issued learned treatises from the seclusion of their studies. They were first and foremost men of action, full of *joie de vivre*, and bubbling over with the irrepressible spirits of over-grown schoolboys. . . . To them life, literature, and war were indissolubly mixed, and could only be enjoyed to the full after a liberal admixture of fun and adventure. No one who fails to appreciate this can catch the true spirit of Elizabethan England. (194)

➤ Context for the Slanders Against Oxford: Ward showed the "charges" by Charles Arundel and Henry Howard in January 1581 for what they were: "We must remember that [Arundel] was fighting for his life. Oxford had accused him of complicity with Spain, an accusation that proved in the end to be correct. By bringing a host of frivolous counter-charges, mostly imaginary, against his accuser he secured for himself breathing space; and so contrived to escape to Paris, where he joined the English fugitives and was paid as a spy by the King of Spain" (100). "But it is, unfortunately, the case that many modern historians have accepted at their face value the preposterous slanders written by [Arundel and Howard] about the Earls of Leicester and Oxford. Whatever faults these two Earls may have had they were never guilty of any unpatriotic action. . . . It is to be hoped that in future all right-minded historians will follow the example of King James, and will never again advance the disgusting lies of the 'suborned informer' Charles Arundel as reliable historical evidence" (222-23).

➤ The Crisis of 1576 and Anne Cecil's Pregnancy: Capt. Ward noted that "the entire blame for the tragedy of 1576 has, without any justification, been placed wholly on Lord Oxford's shoulders" (331). Ward laid out the chronology for this perplexing episode. On one side were Oxford's statements that he did not regard Anne Cecil's child as his, and statements by Queen Elizabeth, Anne Cecil's doctor and Anne herself showing that she was distraught on learning that she was pregnant and that she doubted whether her husband would accept the child as his. Oxford's behavior after his return to England—having nothing to do with his wife for five years—is harsh but in line with someone who believed all these statements to be true.[18] On the other side are two letters from Oxford expressing his pleasure at hearing the news that his wife was expecting and, later, had given birth to a girl. Ward noted that "Both [letters] express his whole-hearted joy at

---

[18] See pp. 114-116, 142 and 331 in Ward's book.

the news. There is no hint of suspicion or mistrust from beginning to end" (113). He then asked, "How can we reconcile the statement made by Dr. Masters that Lord Oxford had denied the parentage of the child with the Earl's own obvious pleasure when he heard a few days later that the Countess was about to become a mother?" It did not occur to Ward to question the authenticity of the two letters from Oxford that stand in opposition to all other evidence. They exist only in handwritten versions prepared by Lord Burghley, Anne Cecil's father. Why Burghley would have made copies in his own hand of letters addressed to him and in his possession has been left unexplained.

➢ Oxford and Lyly: Capt. Ward laid out six reasons why the literary works attributed to Lyly were either by Oxford or by the two together. Among them are that "all his plays were written and acted while he was in Lord Oxford's employ. . . . [Although he] lived for at least another twelve years, he never wrote another play" (274) after leaving Oxford's service. Further, all "the quartos of Lyly's plays were published anonymously. This is most odd if we are to understand that Lyly himself was the sole author . . . but if he could not claim them as entirely his own the matter becomes quite different" (278). Given the strong connections that existed between Lyly and Oxford, what are we to think, Ward asked, when we see that in *The Encyclopedia Britannica's* article on Lyly, "which occupies over two pages . . . Lord Oxford is not mentioned! Incredible as this may seem it is really scarcely more than typical of the treatment the Earl has received at the hands of historians and literary critics" (279).

About Elizabethan Times and the Theater:

➢ Status of Acting Companies: Ward made clear the real nature of the nobility's sponsorship of acting companies. "Sir Sidney Lee would have us believe that Elizabethan companies of actors were under the 'nominal' patronage of noblemen; implying that as soon as a company had persuaded a nobleman to grant them the use of his name all connexion between patron and player ceased. So far from this being the case . . . the patron occupied the essential position of paymaster; and that but for his financial support the company would have been quite unable to carry on. In brief, it was the demand at Court for theatrical entertainments that brought the companies into existence, and so it was naturally the courtiers themselves who had to foot the bill for the maintenance by 'retaining them in their services'" (267).

➢ Change in Elizabeth's Policy Toward Catholics: Capt. Ward brought to light the key role played by the Earl of Oxford in Queen Elizabeth's reversal of her toleration toward Catholics in England. Oxford had "observed among his friends [such as Charles Arundel and Henry Howard] the growth of [Spain's] influence, and it would seem that in his opinion it had by December 1580 reached a point of actual disloyalty and treason" (210). Oxford's revealing that disloyalty and treason to Queen Elizabeth resulted in her Proclamation on January 12, 1581—only three weeks later—which "marks the turning point of Elizabeth's policy towards her Catholic subjects."

> For twenty-three years she had striven to win their loyalty by leniency and tolerance. But Lord Oxford had opened her eyes. From this time

forward Jesuits who ventured into England were remorselessly hunted down, persecuted, and executed; and the law imposing fines on Catholics for non-attendance at Protestant services, which had remained practically a dead-letter since it received the royal assent at the beginning of Elizbeth's reign, was resuscitated and put into rigorous execution. It . . . [was] Lord Oxford's dramatic interview that induced the Queen to take the first decided step against her Catholic subjects—a step that Burghley, Walsingham, and the House of Commons had vainly urged upon her over and over again in the past. (214)

Oxfordian Reactions to *The Seventeenth Earl of Oxford 1550-1604*

In writing his biography of Edward de Vere Capt. Ward had "stood on the shoulders of genius," as Sir Isaac Newton had said in praise of his predecessors. One would have expected from Ward an acknowledgement of Looney's pioneering work in rescuing the brilliant courtier from obscurity. Yet he remained silent, mentioning Looney and his work in only the most cursory manner.

Looney must have been appalled that Capt. Ward had made no mention in the text or the index of himself or of *"Shakespeare" Identified*. Scores of examples could be cited of how Ward's research had expanded findings originally made by Looney. One importance instance was Ward's placing the "influence" of John Lyly on "Shakespeare" in the correct context of *Edward de Vere → John Lyly → "William Shakespeare"* without noting Looney's priority in reversing that chain of influence.

In a letter to Eggar, Col. Ward (Capt. Ward's father) commented that, "I think *The 17th Earl of Oxford* rather upset [Looney] by giving him so little acknowledgment. I pointed out to him beforehand the reason for this and the necessity for a Life without any 'Shakespeare' argumentation, but he did not see it and the result was a considerable coolness. Things are more satisfactory now—especially since Percy Allen's acknowledgments[19]—but if you see him do try and smooth down his ruffled feathers and assure him that no one is more conscious of his almost miraculous achievement than the Hon. Sec. of the Fellowship."[20]

On very few occasions did Looney express any criticism of the work of other Oxfordian scholars. On the contrary, he was unfailingly supportive of their work and courteous in his comments even on work he thought was misguided. Nor did he often express any direct emotional reaction to ill-informed statements by critics and reviewers. His response to Ward's biography, however, was both: critical and tinged with emotion. He acknowledged to Katharine Eggar that he was feeling "somewhat sore" that Ward included no acknowledgement of the importance of his work to resurrect Oxford's reputation.

Looney's comments in a letter to Katharine Eggar show that he was a man of great maturity and restraint, even when he had every reason to feel slighted.

> It is quite true, as you say, that I have felt somewhat sore that Capt. Ward's biography of the Earl of Oxford contains no acknowledgment of its own parentage. I may, however, be wrong in this. Perhaps some remnant of the old Adam of vanity in me lies at the bottom of my feelings on the matter. Perhaps, too, having been somewhat remorseless in "cutting prejudice against the grain" I am less sympathetic than I ought to be towards those who practice a greater

---

[19] This refers to Percy Allen's co-called "Manifesto of Conversion" discussed in Chapter 8.
[20] Col. Bernard R. Ward, letter to Katharine E. Eggar, June 21, 1929.

reserve.

A full biography of the Earl of Oxford following upon the work of investigation set out in *"Shakespeare" Identified* was what I had pointed out in that book as being necessary; and the knowledge that Captain Ward had undertaken a life of Oxford seemed, in this view of the whole of its antecedents, to promise an early realization of great hope. From this point of view the attitude of the work to my own could not be otherwise than a disappointment. Indeed Colonel Ward himself realized this before the work appeared and wrote preparing me. Frankly, under similar circumstances I could not imagine myself adopting a like course; preferring always to overstate rather than to understate a literary indebtedness. Still, each of us has to do his own work according to his own conception of it; and, as I have said, I may be wrong; and the course followed by Capt. Ward may prove more fruitful in the long run. We all, I am sure, agree in hoping that it may be so.[21]

Percy Allen, the most prominent and active Oxfordian in the 1930s, wrote two reviews of Ward's book, both published in *The Christian Science Monitor*, where he served as drama critic, in June and July 1928, one year before he publicly announced his acceptance of the Oxfordian claim. In the second review he noted that the two most comprehensive accounts of Oxford prior to Ward's, by Sir Sidney Lee and Looney, were based not on original sources but on "already printed records." Capt. Ward, though, "after five years' search among the unpublished MSS. of the period . . . gives us a documented, valuable and interesting book, in which, at last, we can see comprehensively before us the actual career and character of one of the most remarkable men even of his astonishing age."[22]

Roundup of Reviews of Ward's Book

More than twenty-five publications ran reviews of *The Seventeenth Earl of Oxford 1550-1604*. Most praised Capt. Ward for bringing back to scholarly notice a colorful and important but overlooked courtier. Many praised him for his scholarly approach and for the mass of information he found in original records. Most did not refer even indirectly to Looney's having, eight years earlier, made the claim that Edward de Vere wrote "Shakespeare." Several were critical of Ward's scholarship.

Reviewing Ward's biography for the American *Saturday Review*, Esther Singleton, well-known American author (and not yet publicly acknowledged Oxfordian), praised the book for restoring Oxford's reputation: "Happily the truth regarding this most distinguished member of a most distinguished race has at last triumphed over calumny and has been put forward in a book that will rank high both as a biography and as a picture of the Elizabethan period."[23] *The New York Sun* also reviewed the book on May 23; Col. Ward described it as "the best so far." It was "printed on the editorial page which gives it unusual importance. Mrs. [Eva Turner] Clark, one of our New York members, writes that she is delighted that the book should have got such a fine introduction to the American Public."[24]

In a review that Col. Ward called "one of the best," *The Daily Telegraph* judged the book "a sound and scholarly piece of work. . . . The result of his researches is a notable reconstruction of a somewhat forgotten reputation. . . . Mr. Ward goes far towards

---

[21] J. Thomas Looney, letter to Katherine E. Eggar, August 25, 1929.

[22] P. A. [Percy Allen], "Versatile Elizabethan," *Christian Science Monitor*, July 3, 1928, p. 12.

[23] Esther Singleton, "A Great Courtier," *Saturday Review* [American], July 21, 1928, p. 1049.

[24] Col. Bernard R. Ward, letter to Gilbert Standen, June 7, 1928.

removing the uglier features of suspicion and scandal. Oxford may have given opportunities to his detractors, but he was held in high esteem by the best of his contemporaries; and in those days few men of any eminence succeeded in escaping calumny."[25] The reviewer for *The Guardian* agreed. "It has been Mr. Ward's pleasant task to restore to favour Edward de Vere Lord Great Chamberlain of England in the reign of Queen Elizabeth, and one of the outstanding figures in that age of famous men."[26] Several others expressed similar positive judgments, including *The English Review*, which regarded the book as "a contribution to Elizabethan biography of first-rate importance, for Mr. Ward has used unpublished and hitherto undiscovered documents to do justice to Edward de Vere, who has been misrepresented."[27] *The New Statesman* observed that "Mr. Ward's biography is most exhaustive. . . . [H]is book throws an entirely fresh light on the facts already known and adds considerably to previous knowledge. This is no mere summary of work done before. Mr. Ward has examined and brought to light an immense amount of interesting material. . . . He has certainly established the Earl as a person of supreme importance at the court of Queen Elizabeth."[28]

Other reviewers sounded notes of caution. Writing in *The Library*, Muriel St. Clare Byrne regretted that "Mr. Ward's work should be marred by two really grave defects. Firstly . . . his transcripts of original material are inaccurate and unreliable. Secondly, his whole view of Oxford's character and achievements is continually open to question because he treats his evidence, whatever its provenance or nature, as equally valuable."[29]

G. C. Moore Smith, in *The Review of English Studies*, while giving Ward credit "for flair, freshness of approach, and considerable industry," questioned whether he had "a scholar's open mind to all sides of truth, a scholar's caution in drawing conclusions, and a scholar's accuracy. . . . He seems to consider that he holds a brief for Lord Oxford and must defend or excuse all his actions. He is ready to draw conclusions from insufficient evidence, and then to deal with these conclusions as facts. He is hopelessly inaccurate in transcribing sixteenth century manuscripts, and produces versions which often make havoc of the writer's meaning."[30] Moore Smith went on to document, and provide corrections to, more than one hundred mistranslations or mistranscriptions. It is indeed unfortunate that those mistakes occurred, but none affect the substance of the biography.

The review by J. C. Squire, editor of *The Mercury*, must have been puzzling to Ward and other Oxfordian scholars as it showed that Squire, who had sparred with Looney in a lengthy exchange of views in *The Outlook* in 1921, hadn't learned much from it. Although his review began on a positive note—"It is here that the reader must look for whatever information he wants about one of the most brilliant and fascinating figures of the English Renaissance"[31]—it was characterized by misstatements and unwarranted assumptions. That "Shakespeare's father was Mayor of Stratford,"[32] and that "the Stratford Grammar

---

[25] A. W., "A Forgotten Elizabethan," *Daily Telegraph*, May 4, 1928, p. 6.

[26] "The Seventeenth Earl of Oxford," *Guardian*, April 27, 1928, p. 258.

[27] V. R., "Biography," *English Review*, June 1928, p. 735.

[28] "The Seventeenth Earl of Oxford," *New Statesman*, June 2, 1928, pp. 268-69.

[29] Muriel St. Clare Byrne, "Reviews and Notices," *Library*, vol. 9/2 (Sept.): 211.

[30] G. C. Moore Smith, "The Seventeenth Earl of Oxford," *Review of English Studies*, vol. 5/17 (Jan. 1929): 92, 93.

[31] J. C. Squire, "Lord Oxford," *Observer*, May 6, 1928, p. 6.

[32] Some accounts state that bailiff, the position John Shakspere held, was equivalent to that of mayor today. Even if so, it should be remembered that he held the position for only one year (in 1568, when Shakspere was

School was in Elizabeth's day a very good and important school" are only two of the many claims that go far beyond the facts known to historians and scholars.[33]

It must have been especially disheartening for Looney and other Oxfordians to see

---

Reviews (in chronological order) of

The Seventeenth Earl of Oxford 1550-1604 (1928) by Capt. Bernard M. Ward

<u>1928, April</u>

"An Elizabethan Dark Horse," *Birmingham Daily Post*, April 27.

"The Seventeenth Earl of Oxford," *The Guardian*, April 27.

<u>1928, May</u>

A. W., "A Forgotten Elizabethan," *Daily Telegraph*, May 4.

J. C. Squire, "Lord Oxford," *Observer*, May 6, p. 6.

F. G. Bettany, "A Favourite of Elizabeth," *Sunday Times*, May 6, p. 8.

"A Misjudged Elizabethan," *Scotsman*, May 10, p. 2.

"The Elizabethan Earl of Oxford," *Saturday Review* (London), vol. 145 (May 19): 636.
  Response by Capt. Ward, June 2, p. 297.

"The Seventeenth Earl of Oxford," *New York Daily Sun*, May 23.

H. W. C. D., "Books of the Day," *Manchester Guardian*, May 22, p. 9.

<u>1928, June</u>

V. R., "The Seventeenth Earl of Oxford," *English Review*, June, pp. 735-36.

"The Seventeenth Earl of Oxford," *New Statesman*, June 2, pp. 268-69.

Percy Allen, "With Hamlet in Hackney," *Christian Science Monitor*, June 15, 1928.

"Edward de Vere, Earl of Oxford," *Times Literary Supplement*, issue 1282 (June 21,): 461.
  Response by Capt. Ward, issue 1289 (June 28): 486.
  Reply by reviewer, issue 1379 (July 5): 504.
  Response by Ward, issue 1383 (Aug. 2): 568.
  See also W. W. Greg's response to Ward's Aug. 2 response in the *Modern Language Review*, Jan. 1929.

"Renaissance Courtier and Patron of Letters" *T.P.'s and Cassel's Weekly*, June 23.

Clennell Wilkinson, "Seventeenth Earl of Oxford," *London Mercury*.
  Response by Capt. B. M. Ward, with reply by reviewer in the July issue.

<u>1928, July</u>

"Terse Reviews of Latest Books," *Washington Post*, July 1, p. S9.

Percy Allen, "Versatile Elizabethan," *Christian Science Monitor*, July 3, p. 12.

Esther Singleton, [Review not titled.], *Saturday Review of Literature*, July 21, p. 1049.

<u>1928, Sept.</u>

Muriel St. Clare Byrne, "The Seventeenth Earl of Oxford," *Library*, vol. IX/2 (Sept.): 211-14.

<u>1928, Oct.</u>

Georges Connes, "Du nouveau sur De Vere, Part I," *Revue Anglo-Américaine*, vol. 6/2: 145-54.
  "Du nouveau sur De Vere, Part II," vol. 6/3 (Feb. 1929): 241-57.

<u>1929</u>

W. W. Greg, "The Seventeenth Earl of Oxford," *Modern Lang. Review*, vol. 24/2 (Jan.): 216-21.
  [In response to Capt. Ward's response in the Aug. 2 *Times Literary Supplement*.]

Edwin Greenlaw, "The Seventeenth Earl of Oxford," *Modern Language Notes*, vol. 44/3 (Mar.): 202.

G. C. Moore Smith, "The Seventeenth Earl of Oxford," *Review of English Studies*, vol. 5/17 (Jan.): 92-103.

Baldwin Maxwell, [Review not titled.], *Philological Quarterly*, Jan. 1, p. 233.

---

four years old) and that it was in a town of only 1,500 people. Stated without this context gives a misleading impression.

[33] Squire mistakenly referred to Capt. Ward with a female pronoun: "This requires more proof than Miss Ward offers. Beyond this, she is cautious." The same mistake was made by the reviewer in *The Saturday Review*: "Miss Ward has put a tremendous amount of work into this book. She has weighed and examined every fact even remotely connected with Lord Oxford and his family." ["The Elizabethan Earl of Oxford," *Saturday Review*, May 19, 1928, p. 66.]

Squire so misstate the nature of the authorship question eight years after publication of *"Shakespeare" Identified*: "It at any rate appears that many Englishmen love to think that a lord wrote the works of Shakespeare. The assumption with which they begin is that Shakespeare could not have written his own works"[34]—implying yet again that Oxfordians were motivated by snobbery and that their thesis was that Shakspere had submitted work written by somebody else in the manner of a student turning in work that wasn't his own.

Two Important Reviews: *The Times Literary Supplement* and *The Modern Language Review* (W. W. Greg)

The unsigned review of *The Seventeenth Earl of Oxford* in *The Times Literary Supplement* is of special note because it generated responses by Capt. Ward and others. Although the reviewer found Ward "an able and resourceful investigator," he also found him to be "uncritically speculative," and an "impenitent believer in his own speculations." Especially unsettling to the reviewer was that Ward "is apparently working towards what may be called an 'Oxford-Derby theory' somewhat on the lines of Lefranc and Looney, with whose general attitude towards the authenticity of Shakespearian works he is sympathetic without very definitely saying so." Here, finally, the cards are laid on the table: the authorship question is directly acknowledged as the source of many reviewers' unease about Ward's book. "No responsible critic," the reviewer continued, "can allow his work on the Earl of Oxford to be much more than an ingenious attempt to invest him with a significance in the history of English poetry and drama to which he has no obvious claim."[35]

Thus began the sparring over Ward's statement that "Men like Harvey, William Webbe, Francis Meres and others are unanimous in testifying that [Oxford] stood supreme from 1578 till 1598 both as poet and dramatist."[36] Ward, the reviewer stated, "is misusing his evidences in the interests of his theory. These men nowhere make such a statement. . . . When Ward suggests that the reason for our neglect of Oxford is that his writings were not printed under his own name, one has the uncomfortable feeling that claims are going to be made for him of which confirmation will be impossible."[37]

Capt. Ward's response, printed a week later, was to "protest emphatically" and to declare the reviewer's statement on the disputed passage "a piece of unfair criticism and misrepresentation,"[38] and he quoted the full text of Harvey's, Webbe's and Meres's praise of Oxford. The reviewer responded on July 5 with the claim that those statements were mere "ingenious and elaborate flattery." He continued, though, by reassuring Capt. Ward that "the results of his five years of able and resourceful research have gained for him many admirers. His book on Edward de Vere is full of curious interest as a picture of the various activities of courtier life in Elizabethan England."

Ward responded on August 2, noting that "The effect of this [exchange] has been to obscure the main object of the book, which is the rehabilitation of [Oxford's] character. . . . No one would imagine—from your reviewer's account of my book—that it has definitely proved the falsity of all the scandals and defamatory legends that have dogged Lord

---

[34] J. C. Squire, "Lord Oxford," *Observer*, May 6, 1928, p. 6.
[35] "Edward de Vere, Earl of Oxford," *Times Literary Supplement*, June 21, 1928, p. 461.
[36] Capt. Bernard M. Ward, *The Seventeenth Earl of Oxford*, p. 144.
[37] "Edward de Vere, Earl of Oxford," *Times Literary Supplement*, June 21, 1928, p. 461.
[38] Capt. Bernard M. Ward, "Edward de Vere" [letter], *Times Literary Supplement*, June 28, 1928, p. 486.

Oxford's memory for over 300 years."[39] He continued with a point that drew nearer to the authorship question.

> A researcher is not responsible for the facts which he unearths in the course of his investigations. . . . Investigations among old documents may lead to the unearthing of facts that are unpalatable to existing authorities, and this has undoubtedly happened in the case of my investigations into the life of the seventeenth Earl of Oxford. . . . Many facts have been brought to light connecting both Oxford and Derby with the Shakespeare literature. The effect of this has been to concentrate the weight of "authority" against both these noblemen.

Ward urged scholars to conduct their own investigations into the Oxfordian claim and honestly accept whatever conclusion the evidence supported.

> Now . . . that the scandals that have pursued his memory up to the present time have been cleared out of the way, I can assure your reviewer and all other "authorities" who are content to rely upon that broken reed the printed book that the sooner they climb down from their high horse of infallibility on the subject of Shakespeare and his contemporaries the better will it be for their peace of mind, and the more likely will it be that they will be able to retain with credit some fragment of that "authority" which is seriously endangered by their present Olympian attitude.

Although the exchange of letters in *The Times Literary Supplement* ended with Ward's August 2 letter, the discussion did not stop there. W. W. Greg, who had written a review critical of Ward's edition of *A Hundreth Sundrie Flowers* two years earlier, responded to Ward's August 2 letter with a lengthy piece in the *Modern Language Review* charging Ward with the same faulty methodology and lack of professionalism that Ward had leveled against traditional scholars such as Greg.

It's worth asking why Greg's response to Ward's August 2 letter appeared in the *Modern Language Review*, rather than *The Times Literary Supplement*. A hint toward the answer can be found in the letter from Col. Ward (Capt. Ward's father) to Gilbert Standen on August 10: "Do you think the Stratfordians will be able to get over that knock of the 2nd August in the T.L.S.? They must know—and in any case they will soon find out—that it was delivered with the full concurrence of the Editor."[40] So, the editor either refused to run Greg's response or insisted on so many changes to it that Greg pulled it back.

The editor of *The Times Literary Supplement* might have objected to the following paragraph in Greg's piece.

> [Ward] belongs to the tribe of mystery-mongers, who, out of the inevitable puzzles of history, seek to construct a system that shall overthrow and replace generally accepted views—a tribe familiar everywhere, but particularly numerous in the entourage of Shakespeare. It is eminently desirable that the puzzles should be examined and every legitimate implication of the evidence carefully considered. What these gentlemen appear never to understand is that the objection of the ordinary student is far less to their conclusions than to their methods, the construction of fantastic explanations of what often needs no explanation at all.[41]

---

[39] Bernard M. Ward, "Edward de Vere," *Times Literary Supplement*, Aug. 2, 1928, p. 568.
[40] Col. Bernard R. Ward, letter to Gilbert Standen, August 10, 1928.
[41] W. W. Greg, Review of *The Seventeenth Earl of Oxford, 1550-1604*, *Modern Language Review*, vol. 24 (Jan. 1, 1929): 217.

Or he might have objected to Greg's declaration that "as critical biography Mr. Ward's book is worthless; . . . The trouble is that Mr. Ward lacks any sense of evidence." Greg provided examples related to Oxford's birth and education in which, he claimed, Ward "only proves what nobody is likely to have questioned" while ignoring the most pertinent points for which solid evidence is needed.

Greg was careful to find fault with Ward's methodology, not his findings. Ward had proceeded intuitively, and intuitive insights are not always logical. Scholars in academia have intuitive insights, too—or should. What scholars often do is disguise such leaps of understanding by returning to them later to fill in the blanks so as to present their findings as resulting from a sequence of many small steps, each undertaken as the result of careful reasoning. Ward was perhaps not as careful in covering his tracks, but that in no way invalidated his conclusions, something that Greg knew or should have known.

Greg went into a lengthy examination of the circumstances related to Oxford's doubting the paternity of the daughter born to Anne Cecil while he was abroad, a point of particular importance. He recited the many reasons in support of Oxford's doubts noted earlier in this chapter, but then swept them all aside to reach the conclusion that "[i]t is evident that so long as Oxford was looking to Burghley's favour and assistance to prosecute his travels he was willing to show a polite interest in his wife's pregnancy and confinement; while as soon as the withdrawal of leave and supplies forced his unwilling return he vented his anger against Burghley by smirching the honour of his daughter. . . . [His behavior] was execrable." Greg seemed unable to consider the possibility that the two letters of Oxford's that exist only in Burghley's handwriting and that contradict the mass of evidence on the other side of the issue might be forgeries.

There is indeed a mystery surrounding Anne Cecil's pregnancy in 1574-75. Half a century after Ward's biography was published, Charlton Ogburn offered his own explanation in *The Mysterious William Shakespeare* (1984).[42]

Death of Sir George Greenwood, and New Fellowship President Col. Montagu W. Douglas

Shakespeare Fellowship president Sir George G. Greenwood died on October 27, 1928. Although Col. Ward had in effect run the organization since its founding in 1922, Greenwood had brought luster and recognition to it during his tenure as president. He had done much to disentangle the Shakespeare authorship question from the Baconian thesis. Doubts about Shakspere's authorship had been entwined so thoroughly with the Baconian idea, however, that Greenwood's neutral public stance on the identity of the real author was often overlooked. *The Washington Post* opened its ill-informed obituary by stating that "No more earnest or persistent advocate of the Baconian authorship of the plays usually attributed to Shakespeare ever existed than Sir George Greenwood, whose death, in his seventy-ninth year, has recently been announced."[43]

Greenwood's passing gave his many friends and admirers the opportunity to express their respect and admiration for him, as did The Rt. Hon. T. P. O'Connor, M.P., in *The Sunday Times*.

> He was an eager and enthusiastic soul. I have scarcely ever seen a face which
> reflected so much goodness of heart and eagerness of temperament. With his

---

[42] Charlton Ogburn, Jr., *The Mysterious William Shakespeare* (1984), pp. 574-575.
[43] "A Noted Baconian," *Washington Post*, November 15, 1928, p. 6.

short form and his gleaming eyes, palpable eagerness and incessant enthusiasm were written in his face, his gestures, and his acts.

Three things mainly interested him in life: his Liberal principles, his pity for animals, and his enthusiasm in the constant controversy over the authorship of Shakespeare's plays. What was most delightful in him was, that keen, incessant, eager as was his advocacy of these three causes, he always put them forward with a persuasive gentleness that demanded and obtained immediate attention. I can still see those wistful, sweet eyes of his as he urged his causes. . . . His country never, in my experience, produced a more characteristic and a nobler spirit.[44]

Col. Ward attended the funeral for Greenwood at Golden Green Crematorium "as the representative of members of the Fellowship all over the world," and "deposited in their name a wreath in memory of our first President in the beautiful colonnade overlooking the Garden of Rest."[45]

Col. Montagu W. Douglas

Col. Douglas was elected president of the Shakespeare Fellowship in November 1928. He remained president until 1945, and chaired numerous lectures and public events organized to bring awareness of the Oxfordian thesis to wider public attention. In the 1930s he authored a number of important Fellowship *Circulars*, published two important Oxfordian books, and wrote more than fifty articles and letters for various Fellowship publications.

The Shakespeare Fellowship was fortunate in having a respected barrister serve as its first president; it was equally fortunate in having as his successor a man who commanded respect for his strength of character and his insistence on seeking the truth

---

Col. Montagu W. Douglas

Born: 1863. Died: February 24, 1957.

Age when *"Shakespeare" Identified* was published: 57

Shakespeare Fellowship President: 1928-1944

Douglas was an accomplished draftsman and painter in water colors and his works were frequently shown in London exhibitions. Some of his sketches of the keep of Castle Hedingham were reprinted in his books.

Much of his career was spent in India, where he held many important posts, including Commissioner or Deputy Commissioner of many districts. From 1913-1920 he served as High Commissioner of the Andaman and Nicobar Islands.

As a student at Sandhurst he played rugby football and captained the varsity team.

Books
1931	*The Earl of Oxford as "Shakespeare:" An Outline of the Case.* Forward by Gerald H. Rendall.
1934	*Lord Oxford was "Shakespeare:" A Summing Up.* Forward by Gerald H. Rendall. [2nd edition, considerably amended.]
1952	*Lord Oxford and the Shakespeare Group: A Summary of Evidence Presented by J. T. Looney, G. H. Rendall and Gilbert Slater.* Introduction by Gerald H. Rendall.

Articles
52 articles and letters, almost all in Shakespeare Fellowship publications.

---

[44] Rt. Hon. T. P. O'Connor, M.P., "Sir George Greenwood" [letter], *Sunday Times*, Nov. 4, 1928.
[45] Col. Bernard R. Ward, "Sir George Greenwood," *Shakespeare Fellowship Circular*, Nov. 6, 1928.

of any matter that came before him. An example of how these qualities led to his becoming known as "the just Pontius Pilate" throughout the Andaman Islands in 1907 is recounted in a nearby text box.

Col. Douglas's perceptive understanding of the realities before him in that case were demonstrated again when, as Fellowship president, he guided the organization through the crisis it faced in 1936 that will be described in Chapter 10. In his obituary, T. M. Aitken wrote that "During his term of office he gave a great deal of his time to the affairs of the Fellowship, taking the chair at nearly all meetings. He was a first-rate chairman, fair

Col. Douglas and Nazrat Sherali in 1936.

and impartial and always prepared to give a hearing to views he did not share. In fact he endeared himself to all members.... We mourn the passing of an indomitable champion of our cause and trust that his work will act as an inspiration to some of our younger members."[46] His most important book on the Oxfordian claim was *Lord Oxford as*

"Judge Meets Witness After Forty Years"

While serving as High Commissioner of the Andamans—the island territory in the Indian Ocean between India and Burma (as it was called then)—Col. Montagu Douglas presided as judge at a trial of a controversial religious figure in 1907. Thirty-nine years after the event Douglas met with Nazrat Maulvi Sherali, a companion of Mitra Gholam Ahmad, the accused, in London. The following are excerpts from *The Daily Sketch*'s report on that meeting.

> Col. Douglas is known to more than a million and a half of the Ahmadiyya community in India as 'the just Pontius Pilate,'" Sherali told the reporter after meeting with Douglas. "He is very much loved by the community. He set a fine example of British justice."
>
> "For some years previously, Ahmad [the defendant] had been hailed by his followers as the promised Messiah, and his teachings had caused great controversy among the Hindus and other religious sects in India. Many allegations were made against him, and he was generally regarded with suspicion. . . . An Indian boy of 16, the chief witness for the prosecution, declared that Ahmad had instructed him to murder the missionary, but he made several conflicting statements," Douglas explained to the reporter. "I quickly reached the conclusion that there was no case against Ahmad and acquitted him. Later it was learned that the boy had been coerced to tell a story that was completely false. As far as I was concerned, the acquittal of Ahmad was simply a matter of judicial procedure. But the trial became famous and Ahmad's adherents grew to immense proportions, and the community has chosen to describe me as "the just Pontius Pilate."

"Judge Meets Witness After Forty Years," *Daily Sketch*, April 13, 1936, p. 10.

"Shakespeare:" A Summing Up, in which he presented a convincing summary of the evidence for the Oxfordian thesis as well as his own opinion that Shakespeare's plays had been written by various members of the aristocracy who shared the name Shakespeare.

In a later book Col. Douglas stated the group theory this way:

> The Earl of Oxford was the Leader and Inspiration of a Group of Dramatists who

---

[46] T. M. Aitken, "Obituary: Lieut.-Col. Montagu W. Douglas," *SF News-Letter*, Spring 1957, p. 11.

were responsible for the Plays attributed to Shakspere of Stratford. It was known that Lord Oxford employed professional dramatists at times, whom he probably remunerated from his state allowance. He collaborated with his son-in-law the Earl of Derby, a recognized playwright, and possibly with his cousin, Francis Bacon. Professor Slater and Captain Ward see traces of "a woman's hand," in certain plays, and includes the Countess of Pembroke.... Mr. J. M. Robertson finds "disparity in styles" and traces the handiwork of Peele, Green, and Chapman in the plays. This is, in the circumstances, probable."[47]

More New Discoveries by the Wards

Throughout the second half of the 1920s Col. Ward and Capt. Ward continued to sift through official records in pursuit of a deeper understanding of the political and social conditions in which "Shakespeare's" works had been written, performed and published. Their intense research was necessary, Col. Ward explained in a *Shakespeare Fellowship Circular* in 1925, "to provide a suitable foundation for further literary research. The period between Froude and Gardiner—between 1588 and 1603—has been much neglected by historians, and it is at the same time a most important period in Shakespeare publication. Froude's *History* ends with the Defeat of the Spanish Armada in 1588, and Gardiner's commences with the accession of James I in 1603.[48] In order to get at the facts of this intermediate period, 1588-1603, constant reference has had to be made to original documents, and no time is really available for carrying on weekly articles."[49]

Col. Ward explained elsewhere that research was needed "in order to throw light on the many Shakespeare problems that still await solution." We have "for the last three years extended the field of its researches so as to include the general history of the time. Literary problems, we have found, cannot be studied apart from questions of social environment; and the results of our investigation will, we believe, throw a new and interesting light on a period which has been hitherto much misunderstood.[50]

The Wards' findings revolutionized scholarly understanding of conditions in England during the final eighteen years of Elizabeth's reign (1585-1603), which in turn led them to new understandings of the plays themselves and how Oxford had come to write them. They reported on their findings in more than a dozen important articles during the two-year period from mid-1928 through mid-1930 in mainstream academic publications and on the Shakespeare Fellowship Page in *The Shakespeare Pictorial*.

The Heavy Burden Imposed by the War with Spain

The Wards' research revealed the enormity of the burden imposed on the government during the nineteen years of the War with Spain (1585-1604). Contrary to popular belief that the military threat from Spain had ended after the defeat of the Armada in 1588, "The Anglo-Spanish War of 1585 to 1604 was a 'Great War' in precisely the same sense as our recent struggle with Germany from 1914 to 1918 was a 'Great War.'"[51] The

---

[47] Col. Montagu W. Douglas, *Lord Oxford and the Shakespeare Group* (1953), p. 33.

[48] James Anthony Froude, *History of England from the Fall of Wolsey to the Defeat of the Spanish Armada*, in 12 volumes (1893). Samuel Rawson Gardiner, *History of England from the Accession of James I to the Outbreak of the Civil War, 1603-1642*, in 10 volumes (1883-1908).

[49] Col. Bernard R. Ward, "Annual Report for 1925," *Hackney and Stoke Newington Recorder*, Nov. 20, 1925.

[50] Col. Bernard R. Ward, "Shakespeare and Elizabethan War Propaganda," *Royal Engineers Journal*, Dec. 1928, p. 470.

[51] Capt. Bernard M. Ward, "Shakespeare and the Anglo-Spanish War, 1585-1604, I," *Revue Anglo-Américaine*, vol. 6/4 (April 1929): 302.

records they uncovered showed that the direct cost of the War was so heavy that "during the seventeen years that the war lasted, the annual direct expenditure on the Army and Navy alone exceeded 70 percent of the total revenue of the country on no fewer than seven occasions; and at the time of the Armada crisis—1587 and 1588—the figures are 95 percent and 101 percent, respectively. In one year only—1595—did the naval and military expenditure drop below 50 per cent of the revenue. These figures, moreover, do not take into consideration extraordinary expenditure due indirectly to the war."[52]

Their findings overturned the commonly accepted view of the second half of Elizabeth's reign as a time of peace, and therefore changed, or should have changed, scholars' understanding of the character of the Elizabethan era itself.

Percentage of Government Revenues Consumed by the Royal Navy and the Field Armies in the War with Spain, 1585-1602					
1585	44%	1591	80%	1597	88%
1586	51%	1592	55%	1598	71%
1587	95%	1593	53%	1599	78%
1588	101%	1594	62%	1600	87%
1589	69%	1595	47%	1601	87%
1590	50%	1596	87%	1602	72%

The traditional "before" understanding, Col. Ward explained, "is one of a prosperous and a 'merrie England'; a great theatrical boom; a young, aspiring playwright quick to seize his opportunity; a brief period of competition with his rivals to secure supremacy among the theatre-going public; his complete triumph; his great financial success; and finally his retirement and comfortable old age."

But, Capt. Ward asked,

> Is this a correct picture of the theatrical conditions under which the Shakespeare plays were written? Were these plays—most of which were admittedly written during the reign of Elizabeth—produced under the normal competitive conditions of peace, and at a time when England was enjoying a great boom in national prosperity? Emphatically no. The plays were produced during the stress and strain of a great war: a war that is comparable in every respect to the war of 1914-1918, save that it lasted nearly a generation instead of four years: a war in which the distress and sufferings of the English civil population were on a par with our own recent experiences, with those of our great-grandfathers during the Napoleonic Wars.[53]

He cited the example of historian Lytton Strachey, who, in *Elizabeth and Essex*, stated that the War with Spain had effectively ended in 1588. "The Spanish War," Strachey wrote in his consideration of the year 1599, "drifted on, in complete ambiguity, while peace was indefinitely talked of, with no fighting and no expense, a war that was no war in fact— precisely what was most to her (i.e., the Queen's) liking."[54] The actual situation in 1599 was that "the total expenditure on national defence amounted to £463,000, or 78% of the total revenue, which came to £590,000."[55]

---

[52] Col. Bernard R. Ward, "Shakespeare and Elizabethan War Propaganda," *Royal Engineers Journal*, Dec. 1928, p. 472.

[53] Capt. Bernard M. Ward, "Shakespeare and the Anglo-Spanish War 1585-1604," *Revue Anglo-Américaine*, vol. 6/4 (April 1929): 298.

[54] Lytton Strachey, *Elizabeth and Essex* (1922), p. 192. Also quoted by Col. Bernard R. Ward, "Queen Elizabeth's Patrimony," *Shakespeare Pictorial*, June 1929, p. 20.

[55] Col. Bernard R. Ward, "Queen Elizabeth's Parsimony," *Shakespeare Pictorial*, June 1929, p. 20.

Capt. Ward went on to express his—and his readers'—surprise and dismay at how incorrectly the situation had been portrayed in historical and literary accounts of the time.

> "How is this possible?" the reader will exclaim. "I have read many lives of Shakespeare, I have read many books about the Elizabethan stage, but never once has this war even been mentioned!" Exactly; that is just what I said to myself when I came across the proofs about the great Anglo-Spanish War that I will now place before the reader.[56]

> What a very different background to the writing and acting of the Shakespeare plays is here presented from the "peace, prosperity and Merrie England" picture that biographers of Shakespeare would have us believe! (303)

The Wards' findings corrected the prevailing view of the Queen's parsimony in her failing to support her armed forces adequately.

> The discovery that the average annual expenditure on the Navy and Expeditionary Forces throughout the whole of the Anglo-Spanish War (1585-1604) amounted to 70% of the Revenue, supplies a complete answer to the charges of neglect of her fighting forces, so commonly levelled against Queen Elizabeth.[57]

No biographer of Shakespeare has so much as hinted that there was a war in

---

Col. Bernard R. Ward and Capt. Bernard M. Ward
Publications Announcing Significant Discoveries, 1928-1930

<u>Captain Bernard M. Ward</u>

[1] 1928, July   "The Famous Victories of *Henry V*: Its Place in Elizabethan Dramatic Literature," *Review of English Studies*, vol. 4/15: 270-94.

[3] 1929, Jan.   "Queen Elizabeth and William Davison," *English Historical Rev.*, vol. 44: 104-06.

[4] 1929, Jan.   "John Lyly and the Office of the Revels," *Rev. of English Studies*, vol. 5/17: 57-59.

[8] 1929, April   "Shakespeare and the Anglo-Spanish War, 1585-1604, Part 1," *Revue Anglo-Américaine*, vol. 6/4: 297-311.

[14] 1930, April   "Shakespeare and the Anglo-Spanish War, 1585-1604, Part 2," *Revue Anglo-Américaine*, vol. 7/4: 298-311.

<u>Col. Bernard R. Ward</u>

[2] 1928, Dec.   "Shakespeare and Elizabethan War Propaganda,: *Royal Engineers Journal*, vol. 42/4: 658. [Later released as a pamphlet.]

[5] 1929, Jan.   "1928: An Important Year," *Shakespeare Pictorial*, p. 16.

[6] 1929, Feb.   "Elizabethan Secret Service; Propaganda in Plays," *Shakespeare Pictorial*, p. 16.

[7] 1929, March "Elizabethan Exchequer Figures," *Shakespeare Pictorial*, p. 16.

[9] 1929, June   "Queen Elizabeth's 'Parsimony,'" *Shakespeare Pictorial*, p. 20.

[10] 1929, July   "Queen Elizabeth and Secretary Davison; Fine of £10,000 Unpaid," *Shakespeare Pictorial*, p. 19.

[11] 1929, Sept.   "What Lurks Behind Shakespeare's Historical Plays," *Sh. Pictorial*, p. 16.

[12] 1929-30, Winter   "Shakespeare and the Sonnets: A Suggested Interpretation," *Poetry and the Play*, pp. 10-13. [Later released as a pamphlet.]

[13] 1930, March "The Elizabethan Chronicle Play as War Propaganda," *Royal Engineers Journal*, pp. 14-16. [Later released as a pamphlet.]

[15] 1930, May   "A Government Propaganda Department," *Shakespeare Pictorial*, p. 20.

[16] 1930, June   "Captain Ward's Researches," *Shakespeare Pictorial*, p. 20.

---

[56] Capt. Bernard M. Ward, "Shakespeare and the Anglo-Spanish War 1585-1604, I" *Revue Anglo-Américaine*, vol. 6/4 (April 1929): 298.

[57] Col. Bernard R. Ward, "Queen Elizabeth and Secretary Davison," *Shakespeare Pictorial*, July 1929, p. 19.

progress while the plays were being written and acted, and all historians have unanimously asserted that the Queen persistently starved her Army and Navy of money. One modern authority actually goes so far as to say that it is a "misnomer" to call the Anglo-Spanish War a war at all! Need we wonder that all historians and biographers have given us a picture of the last seventeen years of Elizabeth's reign that is utterly false and meaningless from beginning to end?[58]

Taxes, Hardship and Famine Imposed on the People of England

Equally significant was the Wards' discovery of the true burden of the war on the people of England in terms of taxes, economic hardship and famine—and hence on the conditions in which Shakespeare's plays were written and performed. Col. Ward found that "From 1558 to 1588 taxation had remained at a fairly constant level; in 1589 it was doubled; in 1593 it was trebled; and in 1601 it was quadrupled. Between 1593 and 1596, the price of wheat was very nearly trebled, and in the latter year the scarcity of food stuffs amounted almost to a famine."[59] Laying out the significance of this finding, Capt. Ward showed that,

> The condition of the civil population of England during the last seventeen years of Elizabeth's reign, so far from being "peaceful and prosperous," was exactly the reverse. All the nightmares that inevitably follow in the wake of a Great War— crushing taxation, soaring food prices, and famine—are here found in just the same degree of intensity as in the England of 1914-1918. We must therefore rid our minds of all our existing conceptions about "Shakespeare's England" and substitute a picture of suffering, hunger, want, and penury—a picture that we of this present generation can fully comprehend and appreciate because we have just undergone exactly the same sufferings and experiences as our ancestors did in the days of "Shakespeare's England." (298)

He then related these conditions to scholars' misunderstanding of the context in which Shakespeare's works had been written and performed,

> We are now able to understand the complete failure of all Shakespeare's biographers and critics. They have taken a man who was essentially a war-time dramatist writing under the stress and strain of a Great War: they have entirely obscured his historical setting by surrounding him with a purely imaginary atmosphere of peace and prosperity: and they have then endeavoured to persuade us that their interpretation of him as a normal, competitive, peace-time dramatist is perfectly natural, straightforward, and intelligible! Need we wonder at the ever-growing body of opinion that, having read these conclusions, refuses to accept them, and instinctively believes that the "Shakespeare Mystery" is a fact and not a fancy? (303-04)

Further Understanding of the £1,000 Annuity

How did Queen Elizabeth "hold together and inspire her war-worn subjects, who were labouring under so great a strain of taxation, high prices, and scarcity"?[60] The answer became apparent during research conducted later in 1928, after Capt. Ward's biography had been published. The annuity was not, as he had speculated in his book, funding for theatrical entertainment within the court, but for an informal "propaganda

---

[58] Capt. Bernard M. Ward, "Shakespeare and the Anglo-Spanish War 1585-1604, I" *Revue Anglo-Américaine*, vol. 6/4 (April 1929): 301-02.

[59] Col. Bernard R. Ward, "Shakespeare and Elizabethan War Propaganda," *Royal Engineers Journal*, Dec. 1928, p. 471.

[60] Col. Bernard R. Ward, "Shakespeare and Elizabethan War Propaganda," *Royal Engineers Journal*, Dec. 1928, p. 474.

department" run by the Earl of Oxford, whose mission was to produce plays for public audiences designed to maintain the morale of the British people during the war. In Capt. Ward's new understanding, "The suggestion I now offer is that Lord Oxford was placed in charge of a Secret Service Department of State which was responsible for producing war propaganda plays in order to encourage the patriotism and loyalty of the civil population of England during the Anglo-Spanish War" (308).

As Col. Ward explained,

> The evidence we have succeeded in accumulating shows quite conclusively that a Government Propaganda Department was instituted in 1586, and that stage plays in the public theatres were made use of during the remaining years of Queen Elizabeth's reign in order to infuse a warlike spirit into the English people and to inculcate the virtue of loyalty to the Tudor dynasty.[61]

> The wording of this warrant was couched in the same phraseology as that employed in the case of Secret Service money, the Exchequer officials being expressly forbidden to call for any account as to its expenditure. We know, moreover, that it was granted for some State service because it is not included with the ordinary annuities in Part I of the Exchequer accounts, but is entered in Part XIII, which consists of payments to the heads of the various State departments.[62]

Capt. Ward explained further that,

> At the outbreak of the war, recognising the propaganda value of the stage, the Queen set up a Department of State to foster and encourage war propaganda plays: that this Department worked secretly, partly because propaganda cannot be labelled "propaganda" or it loses its whole effect, and partly because no record of such a Department has survived: and that this Department, having subsidised playwrights (both professional and amateur) took over their plays, inserted war propaganda into the first and last scenes, got them acted by the various noblemen's companies, and finally had them printed anonymously.[63]

These steps, Col. Ward found, were similar to those taken during the two other major crises faced by the English government in the three centuries since then. The use of the theater to maintain public morale was accompanied by a renewed effort to censor all printed documents. A Star Chamber decree issued on June 23, 1586—the same month the grant to Oxford was first paid—restricted printing only to London, Oxford and Cambridge and required that all presses be registered and all publications approved in advance of publication.[64]

> Queen Elizabeth took the same two steps that were taken by Lord Kitchener and the Prime Minister soon after the declaration of war in 1914. That is to say, she established a severe and rigid control over the Printing Press by a Star Chamber Decree of 23rd June, 1586, and three days later she sanctioned a grant of £1,000 a year to the Earl of Oxford as the head of a Secret Service Department of State.

---

[61] Col. Bernard R. Ward, "Shakespeare and Richard III: A Tudor Government Propaganda Dept.," *Morning Post*, Sept. 3, 1929.

[62] Col. Bernard R. Ward, "Shakespeare and Elizabethan War Propaganda," *Royal Engineers Journal*, Dec. 1928, p. 476.

[63] Capt. Bernard M. Ward, "Shakespeare and the Anglo-Spanish War, 1585-1604, II," *Revue Anglo-Américaine*, vol. 7/4 (April 1930): 304.

[64] Col. Bernard R. Ward, "Shakespeare and Elizabethan War Propaganda," *Royal Engineers Journal*, Dec. 1928, p. 475.

This could hardly have been anything but a War Propaganda Department. Oxford drew this £1,000 a year until his death in 1604, the year which marked the close of the long Anglo-Spanish War.[65]

Capt. Ward emphasized that this information was not previously known to historians.

> Owing to their neglect of this war, all orthodox historians and biographers of Shakespeare have been completely misled as to the conditions under which the chronicle plays of Shakespeare, Marlowe, Peele, and other anonymous dramatists were written and acted. . . . Nashe, writing in 1592, says quite definitely that the plays then being acted contain war-propaganda intended to rouse the patriotism, loyalty, and war-spirit among the civil population of England.

> Rather than being a spontaneous outburst, the patriotic plays were "the result of a deliberate piece of policy secretly arranged and organised by the Queen and her Government." "The war brought about a nearly *five-fold* increase in the total number of plays, with a *nine-fold* increase in the number of anonymous plays; while the post-war period shows a slight decrease in the number of plays, with *only a quarter* of the number of anonymous plays. I submit that there must have been some unknown influence at work which led to such an enormously increased output of plays, *and especially of anonymous plays*, during the war period. What was this influence?[66]

The range of "war-like propaganda to be found in the Chronicle plays"—that is, in the patriotic plays produced between 1587 and 1600—Col. Ward found, include: "1. The invincibility of English arms . . . 2. The encouragement of patriotism . . . 3. The fate of disloyalty . . . 4. Loyalty to the reigning house . . . 5. The inevitable fate of rebels . . . and 6. Anti-Spanish propaganda."[67]

These findings were later supported by Australian scholar Alfred Hart, who noticed that many of Shakespeare's plays have royal settings and portray kings, courtiers and governments—in whatever the settings are purported to be—absorbed in political activities and issues important during Queen Elizabeth's reign. Taken as a whole they form "a series of simple lessons on the fundamental principles of Tudor politics. . . . Shakespeare outdoes every dramatist of his time in the number and variety of the allusions made to those issues. References are scattered through at least twenty plays, including the comedies as well as the histories and tragedies." "What is peculiar to Shakespeare," Hart continued,

> is that he treats the politico-theological doctrines of divine right, non-resistance, passive obedience and the sin of rebellion, as the accepted and immutable law of almost every land in every age. He has adroitly woven into the fabric of his plays so many and varied references, direct and indirect, to these doctrines, that we may extract from them an excellent digest of the main articles of the . . . political creed of the Tudors concerning the constitution of the body politic in general and the relation of ruler to subject in particular.[68]

Capt. Ward then showed how the annuity produced not only the propaganda plays

---

[65] Col. Bernard R. Ward, "Elizabethan Exchequer Figures," *Shakespeare Pictorial*, March 1929, p. 16.

[66] Capt. Bernard M. Ward, "Shakespeare and the Anglo-Spanish War, 1585-1604, II," *Revue Anglo-Américaine*, vol. 7/4 (April 1930): 301.

[67] Col. Bernard R. Ward, "Shakespeare and Elizabethan War Propaganda," *Royal Engineers Journal*, Dec. 1928, p. 49.

[68] Alfred Hart, *Shakespeare and the Homilies* (1934), pp. 29, 27-28, 28.

but also what is now referred to as the group theory of authorship of Shakespeare's plays due to the team of writers that Oxford assembled to draft dozens of plays, some of which are now attributed to Shakespeare.

> Perhaps it is not too much to hope that a new era is opening up in the history of Shakespeare controversy. It ... follows as a direct result of these discoveries that many apparently irreconcilable opinions are now harmonised by the Group Theory of Shakespeare authorship which follows quite naturally from the hypothesis of a Government Propaganda Department.
>
> We have grown so accustomed to thinking of the Elizabethan dramatists as independent playwrights working under the normal competitive conditions of peace time, with one eye on the box office receipts and a finger on the public pulse, that time will be required to enable us to rid our minds of this misapprehension, and to study the plays in their true war-time setting.
>
> There is no longer any need to suppose that one man wrote all these plays. . . . [T]he war-propaganda dramas were initiated by Queen Elizabeth as a deliberate piece of policy: that she created a Secret Service Department of State to carry this policy into effect: that she placed the Earl of Oxford at the head of this Department: that Oxford gathered round him a group of helpers: and that this group comprised on the one hand his son-in-law Lord Derby and his cousin Francis Bacon, and on the other hand "University wits" and actors like Marlowe, Peele, and William Shakspere of Stratford, who formed a link between him and the public theatres.[69]

Other Findings by the Wards

In addition to these astounding findings about the Elizabethan era, the Wards' research also uncovered information that changed—or should have changed—the way scholars understood other developments.

> ➢ *The Famous Victories of Henry V* (1594) was probably written by the Earl of Oxford. In Capt. Ward's view, "I can hardly conceive of anybody else not only making use of the Gad's Hill incident—which was so personally connected with the Earl—but also writing up one of his ancestors in order to show him, in defiance of history, to have been the chief warrior-courtier of King Henry V."[70]

> ➢ "The charges against Richard III are based on Tudor government propaganda, and have no relation to actual fact."[71]

> ➢ The commonly accepted understanding of the relationship between Queen Elizabeth and William Davison, a Privy Counsellor and her Secretary, was wrong. Davison had not been "punished" for allegedly attaching the seal to the death warrant for Mary Queen of Scots and forwarding it to Burghley without her approval. The punishment was only *pro forma*. The fine imposed on him—one of the largest fines ever imposed during Elizabeth's reign—was never paid, and Davison's salary—one of the highest of any government official—was paid throughout the time he was in the Tower. Therefore, Ward concluded, only the

---

[69] Capt. Bernard M. Ward, "Shakespeare and the Anglo-Spanish War 1585-1604, I" *Revue Anglo-Américaine*, vol. 6/4 (April 1929): 311.

[70] Capt. Bernard M. Ward, "The Famous Victories of Henry V," *Review of English Studies*, vol. 4 (July 1928): 87.

[71] Col. Bernard R. Ward, "Shakespeare and Richard III: A Tudor Government Propaganda Department," *Morning Post*, Sept. 3, 1929, p. 5.

appearance of "punishment" existed in order to protect the queen from blame for Mary's execution."[72]

➤ Oxford "'loaned' Lyly to the "the Office of the Revels"[73] for several years, thus establishing a connection between himself and that office. Cecil Palmer was so impressed by Capt. Ward's discoveries that he wrote to Col. Ward to tell him so. The Colonel, proud of his son's successes, reprinted most of Palmer's letter in one of the Shakespeare Fellowship pages in *The Shakespeare Pictorial*.

> Allow me to congratulate you on the completeness of your son's researches. Your short comments on the various books and articles indicate quite clearly, to my mind, that the Oxford theory has definitely ceased to be a hypothesis, and is now an established fact.
>
> What orthodoxy awaits before it will even consider the Oxford theory is some definite evidence connecting Oxford with the public theatres or with the Revels Office. This is exactly what Captain Ward's discovery of the death of [Acting Master of the Revels] Thomas Blagrave in 1590 provides us with.
>
> If this latest discovery connecting Oxford's manager with the Revels Office from 1586, when the holder of the Clerkship was promoted Surveyor of the Works, does not prove Oxford's close connection with stage performances from that time onwards, it is difficult to imagine what discovery could do so more clearly.[74]

The Shakespeare Fellowship in the Late 1920s and Early 1930s

The Shakespeare Fellowship held annual general meetings and organized special events throughout the middle and late 1920s. Appendix 4 shows the continuity in those attending the Fellowship's gatherings and in the organization's leadership over more than two decades. The Fellowship's *Circulars* and its page in the *Pictorial*, and correspondence between Fellowship officers, provide information on other developments of interest during the later 1920s and early 1930s, including:

✓ The annual meeting on September 18, 1926, which was held at Col. Ward's house on Fitz George Avenue. That was the final Fellowship gathering that he hosted there before moving on November 12 to Wyvenhoe, Farnham Royal, Bucks, located about twenty miles west of London. The Fellowship library was transferred to his new house at the time of his move.

✓ Abel Lefranc was elected to the Academe des Inscriptiones et Belles-Letters on April 1, 1927.

✓ Members of the Fellowship, including Col. Ward, Capt. Ward and Percy Allen (Katharine Eggar and Gilbert Standen were also invited) took a trip to de Vere country in the early summer of 1928. They visited Lavenham, Earl's Colne, Castle Hedingham, St. Augustine's Church and Belchamp St. Paul, all important places in

---

[72] Capt. Bernard M. Ward, "Queen Elizabeth and William Davison," *English Historical Review*," vol. 44 (Jan. 1929): 104.

[73] Capt. Bernard M. Ward, "John Lyly and the Office of the Revels," *Review of English Studies*, vol. 5/17 (Jan. 1929): 57-59.

[74] Cecil Palmer, "John Lyly and the Office of the Revels" [letter to Col. Bernard R. Ward], *Shakespeare Pictorial*, August 1930, p. 16.

an area where the 16th Earl of Oxford owned many large estates that the 17th Earl later sold. They also visited the Gad's Hill area, scene of the infamous hold up by the Earl of Oxford's men in May 1573. F. Lingard Ranson, who served as their guide, would go on to play an important role in the Oxfordian movement in the later 1930s.[75]

✓ The Fellowship organized an Oxford-Bacon Debate on November 29, 1928. Percy Allen and B. S. Theobald were the principal speakers.

✓ Katharine E. Eggar was elected to the Executive Committee of the Fellowship at the Annual General Meeting in September 1929. Marjorie Bowen, the well-known novelist, joined the organization around the same time.

✓ A two-part article by Professor Georges Connes of the University of Dijon reporting on the work of the Shakespeare Fellowship over the previous six years, "De nouveau sur de Vere," ran in the *Revue Anglo-Américaine* in December 1928 and February 1929.

✓ Capt. Ward had "taken to hotel keeping with a brother officer."[76] In the middle of 1929 they opened the Angel Inn, at Midhurst, Sussex. Col. Ward reported to Katharine Eggar on July 2 that the hotel's fifteen rooms were all occupied, and that *The Shakespeare Pictorial* "is one of the papers on the table in the lounge." A few years later Capt. Ward launched a second venture, the Black Swan Hotel, in Hemersfield, Halaston, Norfolk, close to Long Melford, Lavenham and other places of interest to Oxfordians.[77]

The Angel Inn (recent image)

Surviving Fellowship publications and correspondence reveal the thinking of the Fellowship's leadership at key moments. The closure of *The Hackney Spectator* in March 1925, together with the launching of *The Review of English Studies*, for instance, led Col. Ward to ask whether the Shakespeare Fellowship still served a useful purpose. In a *Circular* on August 14, 1925, he expressed his supreme confidence that the battle had already been won.

> This [the closure of *The Hackney Spectator*] leaves us of the Shakespeare Fellowship without an official organ of our own. Seeing, however, that the new quarterly review—*The Review of English Studies*—has already published an article by one of our members, and that it is definitely founded for the encouragement of research, the question arises as to whether an official publication of our own is really wanted.
>
> It is in order that this question may be considered, and also the further question

---

[75] Col. Bernard R. Ward, "De Vere Country," *Shakespeare Fellowship Circular*, July 5, 1928.
[76] Col. Bernard R. Ward, letter to Katharine E. Eggar, July 2, 1929.
[77] Col. Bernard R. Ward, letter to Gilbert Standen, Nov. 18, 1932.

whether it is necessary or desirable for the Shakespeare Fellowship to continue its activities for another year that a special general meeting of members and their friends who are interested in the association founded at Hackney nearly three years ago, is hereby announced to take place . . . [on] 14th October, at 3 p.m.[78]

At the meeting Sir George Greenwood asked whether the Fellowship should continue. Cecil Palmer pointed out that in both "the London and Provincial Press the anti-orthodox view was now much more in evidence than it had been before the formation of the Shakespeare Fellowship. For this reason he thought that the Fellowship should, if possible, continue. All present were in favor."[79]

The *Circulars* and correspondence also provide information on the steps leading toward publication of Capt. Ward's *The Seventeenth Earl of Oxford* and his and his father's research after it was published. In the fourth annual report on September 7, 1926, Col. Ward reported that after several years of research, "[T]he materials are now complete for a fairly full biography of the Earl of Oxford, and it is hoped that a Publisher will be found for this important work in the course of the next few months."[80] Yet a year later, in the Fifth Annual Report on December 21, 1927, he reported that their research at Hatfield House has "been opening fresh ground," that they "have found much useful material for the Life of the Seventeenth Earl of Oxford. The discoveries made have been sufficiently important to necessitate considerable alterations in and additions to the manuscript. The completion of the work has thus been considerably delayed, but on the other hand the value of the book, which it is hoped will come out in March or April next, will be materially increased thereby."[81]

Six months after the biography was published Col. Ward explained more about why it had not addressed various topics.

> No attempt has been made in this book to prove Oxford's authorship of the Shakespeare literature. All the available facts of his life as recorded in letters and State Papers have been woven into a continuous and fully documented history. The object of the work is to provide a reliable point of departure from which students may be able to form reasonable opinions as to his life and literary activities. In view of the financial discoveries (detailed later) it is fortunate that no Shakespeare hypotheses were put forward in this book. If this had been done such hypotheses must necessarily have become obsolete already.[82]

That last sentence referred to the articles published by the father and son from mid-1928 through mid-1930. Their research, to recap, had shown that,

➢ The Anglo-Spanish War lasted nineteen years, from 1585 until 1604, the year after James became king.;

➢ The War consumed a large part of the government's budget during that entire period;

➢ The War resulted in great hardships and near famine for the people of England during the latter decade of Elizabeth's reign;

➢ The Earl of Oxford received payments of £1,000 a year from mid-1586 until his

---

[78] Col. Bernard R. Ward, *Shakespeare Fellowship Circular*, Aug. 14, 1925.

[79] Col. Bernard R. Ward, Annual Report for 1925," *Hackney and Stoke Newington Recorder*, Nov. 20, 1925.

[80] Col. Bernard R. Ward, "Fourth Annual Report," *Shakespeare Fellowship Circular*, Sept. 7, 1926.

[81] Col. Bernard R. Ward, "Fifth Annual Report, 1927," *Shakespeare Fellowship Circular*, Dec. 21, 1927.

[82] Col. Bernard R. Ward, *Shakespeare Fellowship Circular*, Oct. 29, 1928, p. 82.

death in 1604 to run a propaganda unit that produced plays designed to increase support for Elizabeth's reign and to sustain morale during the War.

Col. Ward shared these discoveries—highlighted in the Sixth Annual Report in a *Circular* on October 29, 1928—with Greenwood before it was distributed to other members, and heard back from him only a week before the latter's death on October 27.

> My Dear Ward,
>
> I am sorry that I have not been able to return the copy of the Annual Report before this.
>
> I have read it with interest and almost the only criticism which I have to make is that you have been too kind to your "President," and not sufficiently appreciative of the excellent research work done by your son!
>
>   . . .
>
> I have not much strength for writing just now.
>
> Yours sincerely,
George Greenwood.[83]

Commenting on Greenwood's letter in a *Circular*, Col. Ward noted his satisfaction in learning that,

> The last and most important of our Annual Reports—announcing the discovery of the Elizabethan Exchequer figures of Revenue and Expenditure during the Anglo-Spanish War of 1585 to 1604 with its accompanying hypothesis of a War Propaganda Department under the guidance of the Earl of Oxford—was examined and criticised so sympathetically by Sir George Greenwood.
>
> That our latest hypothesis should have received the stamp of his approval speaks loudly for its plausibility and general likelihood.
>
> Members of the Fellowship will be glad to see that before he died this indefatigable critic of hitherto accepted opinions had an opportunity of examining, and did sympathetically examine, what may turn out to be the key destined to unlock the long-debated Shakespeare mystery.[84]

Greenwood's letter further raised Col. Ward's confidence and optimism about the eventual triumph of the Oxfordian claim. In May he had reported to Katharine Eggar that "One of the straws showing the way the wind is blowing occurred yesterday, when my son returned the corrected proof of an article 25 pages in length to the editor of *The Review of English Studies*. My son's thesis is to this effect, that Oxford presented a masque before the Queen at Christmas 1574 which afterwards developed into the play acted by the Queen's players in the '80's and was published for the first time in 1594 as *The Famous Victorie of Henry V!* . . . Until yesterday we felt that editorial regrets and explanations might cancel it at the last minute."[85]

With another of his son's articles set to appear in *Le Revue Anglo-Américaine*, Col. Ward's hopes for the coming year soared further. "I do not see how a big landslide in public opinion about Shakespeare can be put off much later than early in 1930."[86] Three weeks later, he wrote to Gilbert Standen that "I think research work is now pretty well finished. What is now wanted is what the French call 'vulgarisation.' In this work every

---

[83] Sir George G. Greenwood, letter to Col. Bernard R. Ward, Oct. 20, 1928, quoted in *Shakespeare Fellowship Circular*, Nov. 6, 1928.

[84] Col. Bernard R. Ward, "Sir George Greenwood," *Shakespeare Fellowship Circular*, Nov. 6, 1928.

[85] Col. Bernard R. Ward, letter to Katharine E. Eggar, May 17, 1928.

[86] Col. Bernard R. Ward, letter to Gilbert Standen, Dec. 7, 1928.

member of the 'S.F.' can do his or her 'bit.' It will be a good day for English letters when we have succeeded in loosening the Stratfordian strangle-hold."[87] In other words, it was not more research that was needed but a public awareness campaign, a key part of which would consist of working to convince editors that Stratfordian scholars didn't have all the answers and that alternative candidates deserved consideration in their pages.

He reaffirmed his optimism to Standen in March 1929.

> I think we are going to have some fun with "our friend the enemy" this year. Their position is such an awkward one that one cannot help feeling some sympathy for them. They possess the true British courage which never knows when it is beaten, for their thick skills will take a lot more hammering before they cry: "Hold, enough!"[88]

Writing to Eggar in July he referred to the continuing strained relationship with J. Thomas Looney and expressed great confidence that the stream of articles he and his son were publishing would put the Oxfordian claim over the top.

> I am sorry you did not see Looney. I am sure it would have cheered him up to have had a talk with you about the "Oxford Movement." His name is "writ large" in the history of English literature but his fame is not due just yet. He will probably have to wait until after his death, but there is no reason why he should not in his present incarnation enjoy it by anticipation.
>
> The historical approach to the problem is quite as important as the literary approach. Our historical discoveries have—in my judgment—made our final victory over public opinion certain. Without these historical discoveries—which as you may have noticed I keep rubbing in all the time in *The Shakespeare Pictorial*—I am not so sure that Looney with his *"Shakespeare" Identified*, Holland with his *Shakespeare Through Oxford Glasses* and I with my *"Mr. W. H."* would have carried the enemy's position.
>
> Percy Allen with the historical discoveries in addition to his own literary discoveries (Ben Jonson, Chapman, and *The Sonnets*) will, I believe, carry the "mullet agent" to victory next year.[89]

He expressed similar confidence in another letter to her on September. 4.

> By the way did you see my letter in yesterday's *Morning Post* about the Elizabethan historical plays in general and *Richard III* in particular? It was honoured by having a leading article all to itself—our biggest success in publicity up to date!
>
> I wonder whether you would mind sending it to Looney? It would come better from you and would perhaps give you a chance of rubbing in the importance of our Exchequer discoveries. Like most people he looks upon our problem as a purely literary one. As a matter of fact our discoveries in general history are far more important than any literary discoveries which people in general simply won't look at.[90]

Katharine E. Eggar

Katharine Eggar was unique among the first generation of Oxfordians in that she

---

[87] Col. Bernard R. Ward, letter to Gilbert Standen, Dec. 25, 1928.
[88] Col. Bernard R. Ward, letter to Gilbert Standen, March 22, 1929.
[89] Col. Bernard R. Ward, letter to Katharine E. Eggar, July 2, 1929.
[90] Col. Bernard R. Ward, letter to Katharine E. Eggar, Sept. 4, 1929. The letters in *The Morning Post* are discussed in Chapter 14.

remained active in the Oxfordian movement and in the Shakespeare Fellowship for almost forty years (although was a break from 1936 to the later 1940s), until shortly before her death in 1961 at age eighty-seven. She had been in correspondence with Looney as early as February 1922, a correspondence that lasted more than sixteen years and included more than sixty letters in both directions. She also corresponded with many noted Oxfordians during the 1920s and 1930s, with her letters to and from Col. Ward from early 1923 until early 1930 as numerous as her exchanges with Looney. Fortunately, her Oxfordian papers have survived and are located in the Katharine E. Eggar Archives in the Special Collections room in the Senate House Library at the University of London. Those papers, which fill twenty-eight boxes, document important developments during the first decades of the Oxfordian movement that would be otherwise unknown.

Eggar began adult life as a pianist and composer, achieving public notice for her performances, which included the first public concert in England at which a woman performed one of her own chamber music compositions. She was active in promoting opportunities for women in music, helping found the Society of Women Musicians in 1911 and serving briefly as its president.

She was bitten by the Oxfordian bug while reading *"Shakespeare" Identified* around the end of 1921; she soon wrote to Looney and began her own research. She got in touch with Col. Ward shortly after the founding of the Fellowship, and her first Oxfordian articles appeared in the Fellowship column in *The Hackney Spectator* in June 1923. One of her most important contributions, "The Seventeenth Earl of Oxford as Musician, Poet, and Controller of the Queen's Revels," printed in *The Proceedings of the British Musical Association* in the mid-1930s, greatly impressed Looney.

> Dear Miss Eggar,
>
> I feel that I cannot wait until I have more carefully studied your paper on "Oxford and the Queen's Revels" to say how very deeply I have been impressed by the first reading of it.
>
> You have certainly struck a vein of research of the utmost importance and worked it with exceptional skill. You seem to carry investigation into the wonderful phenomenon of Elizabethan dramatic literature right to its roots, as it has never been done before. For the first time we see the seed and seedling stages of a great tree that all other writers have presented to us as a kind of miraculous

---

Katharine Eggar

Born: January 5, 1874. Died: August 15, 1961.

Age when *"Shakespeare" Identified* was published: 46

A noted pianist and composer of works for piano, voice and chamber groups.

Eggar served on the Executive Committee of the Shakespeare Fellowship from 1929 until 1936, when her resignation from the Committee and the Fellowship reflected the deepening crisis within the organization. She rejoined the Fellowship at the end of the 1940s, and led its Study Group during much of the 1950s.

She corresponded extensively with J. Thomas Looney, Col. Bernard Ward and a dozen other important Oxfordians, wrote two articles and several pamphlets, and gave dozens of public talks on Oxfordian subjects. She spent decades working on a biography of Edward de Vere that was never published.

Drafts of her speeches, the book on Edward de Vere and many other Oxfordian papers are housed in the Katharine E. Eggar Archives, Senate House Library, University of London.

sudden appearance of a full grown plant of huge dimensions.[91]

Eggar went on to publish several pamphlets and two dozen articles on Oxfordian topics. She also gave dozens of public lectures, most of which weren't published. She spent decades writing a biography of Edward de Vere that was left unpublished at the time of her death.[92] She also played a consequential role during the crisis that hit the Fellowship in 1936 (see Chapter 10).

The Shakespeare Fellowship Page in the *Shakespeare Pictorial*, 1929-1936

Col. Ward scored yet another coup by convincing the *Shakespeare Pictorial: A Monthly Illustrated Chronicle of Events in Shakespeareland* based in Stratford-on-Avon, to make one page of each issue available to the Shakespeare Fellowship. The Fellowship page began with the January 1929 issue and continued through the end of 1936. The *Pictorial* occasionally ran additional Oxfordian content on other pages. Each Fellowship page was prefaced with this statement: "In the interest of Shakespearean research this page is placed at the disposal of the Shakespeare Fellowship who alone are responsible for the opinions expressed therein." The page was edited by Col. Ward until he was incapacitated by illness in 1932. Capt. Ward served as temporary editor during his illness and replaced his father as editor after his death in April 1933.

How did Col. Ward convince a publication based in Stratford-on-Avon, territory presumably hostile to the Oxfordian claim, to run an Oxfordian page? The initiative apparently came from Mr. E. P. Ray, publisher of the *Pictorial*, Councillor of the Borough and Executive of the Board of Trade of Stratford. Col. Ward explained to Fellowship member Gilbert Standen that,

> I have had an offer of a column every month in *The Shakespeare Pictorial*, a two-penny Stratford monthly magazine. I have accepted, and my first column will appear in the January number. The annual subscription of the "SF" will include a copy to all members. It will of course be much cheaper than printing *Circulars*. Colonel Douglas, our Acting President, thinks that it offers a golden opportunity for us to get our foot firmly planted in the enemy's camp![93]

A year later Col. Ward wrote to Katharine Eggar that "it is doubtful whether Ray will allow us to continue for another year with the *Shakespeare Pictorial*. Up to date he has allowed us a column free but now he wants us to pay for advertising space. I am now haggling as to terms and hope to be able to report something satisfactory at the Annual Meeting."[94] Ten days later he wrote that he had reached an agreement with Ray, and that he, Ward, would try to get advertisers for the column to help defray the cost.

Col. Ward edited the page in the same fashion as he had the Fellowship's column in *The Hackney Spectator*, by writing many of the pages himself but also by bringing in many other contributors. The very first Page, in the January 1929 issue, noted the issuance of the Fellowship's Annual Report for 1928, the death of Sir George Greenwood, and the publication of *The Seventeenth Earl of Oxford*. It also mentioned two of the momentous discoveries Col. Ward and Capt. Ward had recently made: the reason for the £1,000 paid to Oxford annually, and that the War with Spain that raged from 1585 to 1604 was

---

[91] J. Thomas Looney, letter to Katharine E. Eggar, Sept. 19, 1935.
[92] The Archives contain multiple drafts of the chapters of the book, with what appears to be the final draft of each chapter stored in the last two of the twenty-eight boxes.
[93] Col. Bernard R. Ward, letter to Gilbert Standen, Dec. 25, 1928.
[94] Col. Bernard R. Ward, letter to Katharine E. Eggar, Sept. 4, 1929.

comparable in importance and effect to the Great War.

Another important column, "What Lurks Behind Shakespeare's Historical Plays" by Col. Ward, gave readers a fuller look at Walt Whitman's remarks on Shakespeare. Beyond his well known statement that the plays, "conceiv'd out of the fullest heat and pulse of European feudalism," could only have been written by "one of the 'wolfish earls' so plenteous in the plays themselves," Ward cited other perceptive passages, including one hinting that the plays had been written by someone other than William Shakspere:

> We all know how much mythus there is in the Shakespeare question as it stands today. Beneath a few foundations of proved facts are certainly engulf'd far more dim and elusive ones, of deepest importance—tantalizing and half suspected—suggesting explanations that one dare not put in plain statement.[95]

Lesser known, but perhaps of equal interest was Whitman's intuitive grasp that the plays aided in "some ulterior design."

> But coming at once to the point, the English historical plays are to me not only the most eminent as dramatic performances [my mature judgment confirming the impressions of my early years, that the distinctiveness and glory of the Poet reside not in his vaunted dramas of the passions, but those founded on the contests of English dynasties, and the French wars,] but form, as we get in all, the chief in a complexity of puzzles.

> It is impossible to grasp the whole cluster of these plays . . . without thinking of them as, in a free sense, the result of an essentially controlling plan. What was that plan? Or, rather, what was veil'd behind it?—for to me there was certainly something so veil'd.

> All the foregoing is premise to a brief statement of how and where I get my new light on Shakespeare. Speaking of the special English plays, my friend William O'Connor says: "They seem simply and rudely historical in their motive, as aiming to give in the rough a tableau of warring dynasties—and carry to me a lurking sense of being in aid of some ulterior design, probably well enough understood in that age, which perhaps time and criticism will reveal."

In a partial answer, Ward recalled his and his son's recent researches showing that

> The Elizabethan historical plays were produced under the auspices of a Government Propaganda Department presided over by one of Walt Whitman's "wolfish earls." Not only was the Earl of Oxford head of a Secret Service Department of State, but as Captain Ward showed in an article published in July last year in *The Review of English Studies*—he was also almost certainly the author of the *Famous Victories of Henry V*, if not the actual author of the three plays that grew out of it—*I.* and *II. Henry IV,* and *Henry V.* Thus we see that Walt Whitman's intuition as to the true author being a 'wolfish earl,'" and William O'Connor's impression as to an ulterior design lurking behind Shakespeare's historical plays have both been amply justified by our recent researches and discoveries.

Ward also called attention to two lengthy items by Edith Rickert that had appeared in 1923 "showing that *Dream* contained political propaganda on the Succession question in favour of Lord Beauchamp, grandson of the duke of Suffolk and nephew of Lady Jane Grey, as against the claim of James VI, King of Scots, who is caricatured as Bottom." Whether

---

[95] Walt Whitman, quoted in Col. Bernard R. Ward, "What Lurks Behind Shakespeare's Historical Plays," *Shakespeare Pictorial*, Sept., 1929, p. 16.

Rickert's interpretation is correct or not, "If political propaganda on the Succession question—a very dangerous question to raise in Elizabethan days—could be insinuated into a stage play," Col. Ward commented, "there is every reason to suppose that anti-Spanish, anti-Catholic, and war propaganda generally would occur with considerable frequency. This we find to be the case, and many Elizabethan plays produced during the Anglo-Spanish war contain such propaganda."[96]

Although E. P. Ray, editor of *The Shakespeare Pictorial*, received frequent complaints about running an Oxfordian page in a publication based in Stratford-upon-Avon and dedicated to reporting on events in Shakespeareland, he took the heat and let the page continue for a full eight years. The Fellowship was charged full advertising rates for it after the first year, much of which was recouped from advertising by Cecil Palmer and other publishers. The page apparently did Ray little irreparable harm; he was elected Mayor of Stratford for 1937, the year after the column ended.

The Importance of Individuals

This examination of the first decade of the Oxfordian era showed the keen importance of individuals. J. Thomas Looney wrote *"Shakespeare" Identified* as an individual, and waged the struggle for recognition of the Oxfordian claim over the next two and a half years almost alone.

He was joined in his efforts in November 1922 by the Shakespeare Fellowship, which was itself largely the initiative of one person, Col. Bernard R. Ward. Even after it was founded Oxfordian research and public outreach were carried on largely by a small number of people as individuals, not by the Fellowship itself. That was true even for the Fellowship's column in *The Hackney Spectator* and page in *The Shakespeare Pictorial*, which were largely the work of Col. Ward.

Although a vice president of the Fellowship, Looney remained largely apart from it. He attended none of its meetings or other special events. There is no record that he ever met any of its members other than those already known to him. He resisted all requests from Oxfordians to call on him when they were in northern England—written requests exist from Katharine Eggar, Charles Wisner Barrell, Eva Turner Clark and others—usually citing illness. He went so far as to refer to himself as "a recluse," as in this letter to Katharine Eggar:

> It was a great pleasure, I assure you, to receive your letter of July 18th and to know that my own remissness in the matter of letter writing had not put me out of your good graces. It was news altogether to me that you had been lecturing at the North East Coast Exhibition; otherwise, although an incorrigible recluse, I think I should have had at least a surreptitious peek at you.[97]

At the same time, he was immensely grateful to Col. Ward for undertaking the work of publicizing the Oxfordian claim for which he was so temperamentally unsuited. In the letter just noted he was not as optimistic about a quick acceptance of the Oxfordian thesis as Col. Ward appeared to be. He returned to that subject in another letter to Eggar dated January 12, 1930 that provides further insights into his temperament and thinking as the new decade began.

---

[96] Col. Bernard R. Ward, "Propaganda in Plays," *Shakespeare Pictorial*, Feb. 1929, p. 16. The reference is to Edith Rickert, "Political Propaganda and Satire in *A Midsummer Night's Dream, Parts 1 and 2*," *Modern Philology*, vol. 21/1 and 21/2 (Aug. and Nov. 1923).

[97] J. Thomas Looney, letter to Katharine E. Eggar, Aug. 25, 1929.

Col. Ward's optimism—which I earnestly hope may be justified in the event, but which, I am afraid, I do not altogether share—is a valuable and refreshing asset. For some years, owing largely to indifferent health and the pressure of other calls, I have myself done very little in the way of propaganda, and have been only too glad that others were taking this work upon themselves. My own special task was to seek out "Shakespeare" and to present, in outline, the evidence of his authorship. Later, this developed into presenting, in a general way, the case for a retrial of Edward de Vere—to obtain a correct judgment upon his life and character. With the publication of *"Shakespeare" Identified* I felt that my special task had been, on the whole, carried out, and that the rest lay mainly with others.

Being grateful, therefore, that others were taking up the work, and recognising that each one must naturally be responsible for what he did, I have been quite content to stand aside and leave a clear field for other workers to win their honours. In doing this I have not sought to enter into judgment upon the wisdom of their methods—for, as to propagandist methods, I am afraid I [am] not a competent judge. Indeed, my only method is simple, to state, as clearly as I can, the truth as I see it, and leave it to take its course; and this—the method of the solitary thinker rather than of the man of affairs—may not be the wisest way; but, as Touchstone would put it, "an ill-favoured thing (maybe) but mine own." And, of course, it is from the standpoint of this somewhat unsophisticated method, that the failure of Captain Ward to state, in his *Life of Edward de Vere*, the actual genesis of that *Life*, does not quite fit in with my mentality.

However, as I have already said, the responsibility is not mine; but as you suggest that there are "methods of spreading the idea" which may possibly retard the recognition of Oxford as "Shakespeare," I should be glad to have a line or two from you upon the point. It may be that I ought to be less passive than I have been.

Another point that becomes obvious when looking over the first decade of the Oxfordian era is that the individuals who were active in the movement all came from outside academia. One observer, in a facetious piece on the authorship question that nevertheless had more truth to it than he realized, stated:

> It is discreditable to our so-called men of letters that the students who have cleared up this mystery and proved that, first, Bacon, and now the Earl of Oxford wrote the works with which the Stratford man is credited, are not themselves professed literary critics, or even poets, who might be supposed able to feel the difference in quality between Bacon's and Oxford's acknowledged verse and the far greater verse ascribed to Shakespeare—it has been left to barristers, judges, Members of Parliament and military officers to make these important discoveries in the world of poetry.[98]

But individuals do not live forever. The Wards, father and son, entered the first year of the new decade on a roll, but it was to end all too soon. Col. Ward was forced to withdraw from much Oxfordian activity early in 1932 due to health problems and died in April 1933. Capt. Ward would take on his duties with the Fellowship, including that of editing the Fellowship page in *The Shakespeare Pictorial*, but the era of the major research findings and publications by the Wards was over.

---

[98] A. Sr. J. A., "Shakespeare's Ghosts," *The Bookman*, April 1923, p. 35.

The Oxfordians, 1929-1936, I:
Percy Allen and Gerald Rendall

A New Decade

The Oxfordian movement entered the 1930s on a roll. Capt. Ward's *The Seventeenth Earl of Oxford* had given new visibility to the Oxfordian claim in the first half of 1928, and the dozen articles by Capt. Ward and Col. Ward beginning in the middle of that year drew more attention to it. The launching of the Shakespeare Fellowship page in *The Shakespeare Pictorial* at the beginning of 1929 gave the Fellowship a platform through which to broadcast further developments. Several extraordinary scholars became active in the movement at that time, including Percy Allen and Gerald H. Rendall in England and Eva Turner Clark in the United States. Bringing extraordinary energy and spirit and enthusiasm, Allen would become the animating force of the Oxfordian movement throughout the 1930s.

Enter Percy Allen

By the spring of 1930 Percy Allen had joined Col. Ward and Capt. Ward as one of the three key people working on behalf of the Oxfordian cause. He was indefatigable, writing more books and articles, sending more letters to editors to correct misstatements in their reviews and giving more public lectures than anybody else. In two years—1930 and 1936—almost half of all public notices about the Oxfordian cause were due to Allen.[1] He found so many opportunities to promote the Oxfordian idea, and did so in so convincing a manner, that he might have directly convinced more people of Oxford's authorship during the first decades of the Oxfordian era than anyone besides J. Thomas Looney.

Handsome in a chiseled-marble kind of way, Allen was, by every account, a mesmerizing speaker, capturing audiences in person as completely as he did readers with his books and articles. So great were his output and so effective his presentations that *The Western Morning News* aptly wrote that "The great protagonist for the Oxfordian cause is Mr. Percy Allen."[2] He could, perhaps, have been called "Looney's Bulldog" for his promotion of the Oxfordian idea as aggressively as Thomas Huxley, known as "Darwin's Bulldog," had promoted Darwin's idea of evolution through natural selection.

From 1928 to 1933 Allen published a stream of books and pamphlets presenting the evidence and reasoning that led him to two controversial conclusions. The first, which infused all his books, was that "Shakespeare was, from the beginning, in some degree, a topical and satirical dramatist.... Even the sonnets ... contain many topical allusions."[3] We have already seen that a mental revolution was needed to accept this idea, and that

---

[1] They included Allen's books and articles, reviews of them, letters to editors he wrote in response to the reviews, public lectures he gave and media coverage of them.

[2] T. H. L. Hony, "Oxford or Bacon?" *Western Morning News*, July 15, 1939, p. 13.

[3] Percy Allen, *Shakespeare as a Topical Dramatist*, p. 1. A pamphlet published by the Poetry League, 1928.

this particular revolution was one of the most difficult to pass through.

The second was that Edward de Vere, Earl of Oxford, was the real author of the Shakespeare works. The evolution of Allen's private and public stance on that idea is fascinating. In his first book, *Shakespeare, Jonson and Wilkins as Borrowers*, published in 1928, he established, according to one reviewer, that "Any real knowledge of Shakespeare must be founded on an acquaintance with the historical events and personages about which and whom he wrote."[4] A year later Allen moved the ball forward in *Shakespeare and Chapman as Topical Dramatists* by focusing mostly on one topical subject, the character of Hamlet, whom he presented as modeled on the life and personality of the 17th Earl of Oxford. He mentioned J. Thomas Looney and quoted from his book, but never mentioned its title. He never broached the idea of Oxford as Shakespeare, but was carefully bringing his readers along step by step.

Then, early in 1930, Allen finally made the argument for Oxford's authorship in *The Case for Edward de Vere as "Shakespeare."* He reaffirmed his conviction a year later, in *The Oxford-Shakespeare Case Corroborated*. By the time *The Plays of Shakespeare and Chapman in Relation to French History* appeared in 1933, Oxford's authorship was simply assumed.

Allen's gradual approach to the Oxfordian claim led one critic, G. B. Harrison, to charge him with having been an Oxfordian all along. Not so, countered Allen. He was simply recording his findings as he understood them at the time. In support

---

Percy Allen
"The great protagonist of the Oxfordian cause is Mr. Percy Allen."

Born: October 13, 1872. Died: February 3, 1959.
Age when *"Shakespeare" Identified* was published: 45

Drama Critic for *The Christian Science Monitor*.

Grandson of Mrs. Stirling, a notable Victorian actress, whose life he had written. From the age of 15 until the opening of the Second World War he made frequent trips to France, which gave him the knowledge of French history and culture needed to write his first books.

Principal address: 99 Corringham Road, N.W. 11, London

Most Active Period: 1928-1946
- ❖   14 Books and pamphlets
- ❖   153 Articles and reviews
- ❖   104 Lectures on Edward de Vere as Shakespeare
- ❖   59 Letters to editors in response to articles or reviews that misstated the facts

Editor, *The Shakespeare Fellowship News-Letter* 1939-1945
President, Shakespeare Fellowship, 1945-1946

His lecture tour of eastern North America in the fall of 1936 sparked the rise of the Oxfordian movement in Canada and the United States.

---

[4] B.E.S.S.," Shakespeare and Chapman," *The Stage*, October 11, 1928, p. 17.

of his claim of gradual acceptance of Oxford's authorship, Allen prepared a so-called seven-page *Manifesto of Conversion* in which he recounted the steps through which his thinking changed. Col. Ward published it in a *Shakespeare Fellowship Circular* and as a pamphlet in June 1929. In it Allen explained that "The process of my conversion, or heresy, contains nothing of the sudden, or of the sensational; but is the slow, and gradual, outcome of study, and meditation, extending over the past six years."[5]

The process had begun in 1923, when he attended performances of a number of Shakespeare's plays staged in celebration of the tercentenary of the First Folio. He had become convinced, he wrote,

> that the commentators generally had not yet probed to the bottom of the matter; had failed altogether to take sufficient account of the inveterate tendency of the Elizabethan dramatists towards the use of hidden clues and secret double meanings; and had not detected the trick constantly practised by Shakespeare and his fellows, of weaving into their plays, under more or less transparent disguises, allusions, not only to rival writers and to their works, but also to forbidden political matters, then of living interest to the theatre-going public. To these were added eulogies of, and daring satires upon prominent personalities of the day.
>
> The Elizabethan drama, I began to perceive, had never yet been properly correlated with the intensely active inner life of a period in which—because freedom of speech, and of pen, were denied—the stage, necessarily, became, to some extent, the newspaper, and the debating platform, of its day. It became clear to me that underground methods afforded, moreover, peculiar delight to the Elizabethan mind; and I became absolutely certain that a closer examination, and collation, of the texts of Elizabethan poems, and plays, would reveal inner, and, hitherto, concealed, meanings, of enormous literary interest and import. In what direction my projected studies were likely to lead me, I had no idea whatever. Without any preconceived theory, I began to follow simply what seemed to me the internal guidance of the texts.

That passage is the clearest statement I have found of Allen's thinking on the topical nature of the plays that guided his research and writings over the following decades.

Then came a key moment.

> About 1925,[6] my attention was called to Mr. J. T. Looney's book, *"Shakespeare" Identified*, which seeks to shew that Edward de Vere was, in fact, the author of the works usually attributed to William Shakespeare. That book I read, with some care; and though unwilling, at the finish, to admit that its author's case was fully established, I could not withhold assent from his proposition that Lord Oxford was, in some ways, intimately connected with the Shakespearean plays; and that he provided, almost beyond question, Shakespeare's historic original for the Prince of Denmark, as also for Bertram in *All's Well that Ends Well*.[7]

After studying the Oxford poems and songs that were interpolated into Lyly's plays, Allen agreed with Looney's contention that they "were, very probably, written by the Earl, in whose service Lyly had been.... One could not but be struck by the repeated analogies

---

[5] Percy Allen, *Manifesto of Conversion* (June 1929), p. 1.
[6] Allen is mistaken about the date, which should be 1923. In his review of *"Shakespeare" Identified* in *The Christian Science Monitor* on May 19, 1923, he stated that "I read Mr. J. T. Looney's books, *"Shakespeare" Identified*, and *Poems of the Seventeenth Earl of Oxford* . . . and I concluded that, without going all the way with Mr. Looney, he was probably right in identifying the historic Hamlet with Edward de Vere."
[7] Percy Allen, *Manifesto of Conversion*, p. 2.

of mentality, outlook, thought, and expression, between the Oxford (and Lyly) poems, and certain poems, songs, and lyrical speeches of Shakespeare." Comparing Oxford's poems with *Venus and Adonis* and *Lucrece*, he found "many, and striking, Oxford motives, and linkings of phrase and expression with the Oxford poems, on the one hand, and with the Shakespearean sonnets and plays, on the other."

Allen explained how

> [a] continued examination of [Shakespeare's] plays was confronting me with insistent problems and difficulties, which I could logically dispose of only upon the double assumption that the works were written by a man considerably older than the Stratford actor, and by a nobleman of high rank. The nothing-but-courtier theme and manner of *Love's Labour's Lost*, and the apparently constant preoccupation of Shakespeare with events of the early fifteen-seventies, . . . together with the deep and intimate concern shewn by the dramatist in important political and historic events, at the courts of England and Scotland, during the sixties and seventies, seemed, in my judgment, wholly incompatible with the coming of Shakespeare to London, as a young rustic from Stratford, in or about 1585—supposing that he were the author of the plays. (3)

Addressing the process of his conversion in relation to the publication of his books, he observed that, "Critics of my book, *Shakespeare and Chapman as Topical Dramatists*, have gently pointed out this glaring improbability, of which I was, of course, aware; though I deliberately refrained from raising the Oxford theory, in a volume which was already unusually controversial." Apparently Allen was not yet a full Oxfordian when he published *Shakespeare, Jonson and Wilkins as Borrowers* in March 1928, but he was a non-public Oxfordian by February 1929, when *Shakespeare and Chapman as Topical Dramatists* appeared. He publicly declared that he was an Oxfordian in *The Case for Edward de Vere as "Shakespeare"* published in February 1930.

The decisive facts for Allen were those discovered by Col. Ward and Capt. Ward and described in Chapter 7: the £1,000 annuity paid to Oxford by Queen Elizabeth and continued by King James; the revelation that a significant portion of Elizabethan drama created during the War with Spain was produced under the auspices of a secret government committee of which Oxford was the head; and that the War was a "vastly more serious and costly undertaking, and imposed far more severe sufferings, and sacrifices, upon the nation, than historians hitherto, have led us to believe."

The final paragraph of the *Manifesto* showed how confident Allen was in his new belief.

> Temperamentally conservative though I am, the case for Oxford seems to me to be made out; and I am, therefore, forced to the conclusions here set down, from which intellectually, I see no possible escape. The reasons, and process of argument, briefly indicated in this letter, will be more fully set forth in a book, upon which I am now at work, and which will appear, I hope, in the spring of 1930. Meantime, should you think it worth while, I ask you to be kind enough while noting my considered opinion, to suspend final judgment upon the conclusions at which I have arrived.

Allen's Careful Monitoring of the Press and Defense of His Ideas

The seven books Allen published from 1928 to 1933 generated more than seventy reviews, many appearing in important literary publications such as *The Times Literary Supplement*, *The Saturday Review* and *Notes and Queries*, thereby giving readers repeated exposure to the ideas of topicality in Shakespeare's plays and Edward de Vere's authorship of them. Allen relentlessly monitored the press for mention of his books and made a point of responding to reviews he felt did not present his findings in an accurate or fair light. The nearby text box shows seven of Allen's books and pamphlets, selected reviews of them, and his responses.

Shakespeare, Jonson and Wilkins as Borrowers (1928)

Allen must have been pleased that T. S. Eliot, one of the most respected literary critics, commented favorably on his first book on Shakespeare in *The Times Literary Supplement.*

> Mr. Percy Allen, a dramatic critic who modestly professes no special skill in Elizabethan scholarship, has written an intelligent and interesting book which should be of service to students of Elizabethan drama, whether they accept his particular conclusions or not. His subject lies slightly outside the field of exact Elizabethan scholarship, but is one which the scholars should not ignore.... Mr. Allen has hit upon a line of inquiry which should interest literary critics as much as scholars. To our mind, the most important point that Mr. Allen makes is the borrowings of writers from themselves.[8]

He must also have been pleased with the review in *Notes and Queries.* "This is an exhilarating book, which, by the methods of the newer criticism, tends to give a novel interest to the Elizabethan drama, even if it does not command assent altogether.... Mr. Allen [is] concerned more with the action and the stage qualities of the plays than with the verbal resemblances, but it is still verbal resemblances that bears away the palm."[9] The reviewer judged the most convincing chapter to be the one on the connection between Jonson's *Every Man Out of His Humour* and *Twelfth Night*, and praised "Mr. Allen's treatment of Wilkins's authorship of *Pericles*" as a "delightful and clever suggestion of how a play in general, and this play in particular, may have been pieced together from an author's works so as to acquire an air of having been written by him."

The Manchester Guardian's reviewer, after justly remarking that, "to cite isolated cases is always held to be unfair to a method which relies on cumulative effect," straightaway proceeded to do just that. Allen responded forcefully.

> This, as any careful reader of my book can, I hope, verify for himself, is a mere travesty of what I wrote.... [Y]our reviewer omits to inform the readers that ... dozens of verbal and other resemblances and analogies between *Every Man Out of His Humour* and *Twelfth Night* are very carefully set forth, all pointing, with almost monotonous insistence, to the same conclusion—a conclusion vital to my argument—that Jonson's mind, while writing his play, was filled with the scenes and dialogue of *Twelfth Night.*[10]

The "cumulative effect" argument was featured prominently in Allen's responses to many reviewers, who had attacked isolated weaker parallels while ignoring the stronger ones.

Another common charge by reviewers was that the similarities among passages in the plays of Shakespeare, Jonson and Wilkins were merely coincidental, a tack taken by Ivor Brown—a critic Allen would tussle with repeatedly in the coming decade—in *The Saturday Review.* "When Mr. Allen starts to expose the stolen goods, his sense of evidence

---

[8] T. S. Eliot, "Poets' Borrowings," *Times Literary Supplement*, April 5, 1928, p. 255.
[9] "Shakespeare, Jonson and Wilkins as Borrowers," *Notes and Queries*, vol. 154 (March 24, 1928): 215.
[10] Percy Allen, "Shakespeare, Jonson, and Wilkins as Borrowers," *Manchester Guardian*, Apr. 4, 1928, p. 5.

**Percy Allen – Books and Pamphlets, 1928-1933
and his responses to reviews of them**

Shakespeare, Jonson and Wilkins as Borrowers (March 1928)
    15 reviews, including:
    -----. *Manchester Guardian*, March 20, 1928
        Response by Allen on April 4
    Ivor Brown. *Saturday Review*, March 24, 1928
        Response by Allen, March 31; reply by Brown, April 7
        Response by Allen, April 14
    A. S. Ferguson. *Times Literary Supplement*, Sept. 19, 1929
        Response by Allen, Sept. 26, 1929

Shakespeare and Chapman as Topical Dramatists (Feb. 1929)
    14 reviews, including:
    Ivor Brown. *Saturday Review*, Feb. 23, 1929
        Response by Allen and reply by Brown, March 2
    Muriel St. Clare Byrne. *Times Literary Supplement*, March 21, 1929
        Response by Allen. March 28, 1929
        Additional Response by Allen, April 4, 1929
    G. B. Harrison. *Review of English Studies*, Jan. 1930
        Response by Allen and reply by Harrison, April, 1930
    -----. *The Stage*, May 23, 1929
        Response by Allen, May 30, 1929
    G. B. Harrison. *London Mercury*, Aug. 1929
        Response by Allen, Sept. 1929

The Case for Edward de Vere as "Shakespeare" (pamphlet) (Feb. 1930)
    4 reviews, including:
    -----. *Eastbourne Gazette*, March 12, 1930
        Response and reply by Allen, April 2, 1930

The Case for Edward de Vere as "Shakespeare" (book) (April 1930)
    20 reviews, including:
    -----. *Saturday Review*, May 10, 1930
        Response by Allen, May 17, 1930
        Reply by Reviewer, May 24, 1930
    Muriel St. Clare Byrne, *Times Literary Supplement*, Sept. 11, 1930
        Response by Allen, Sept. 18, 1930

The Oxford-Shakespeare Case Corroborated (March 1931)
    11 reviews, including:
    -----. *Notes and Queries*, March 7, 1931
        Response by Allen, March 28, 1931
    C.F.A. *Christian Science Monitor*, April 25, 1931
        Response by Allen, June 5, 1931

The Life-Story of Edward de Vere as "William Shakespeare" (March 1932)
    5 reviews, including:
    -----. *Saturday Review*, June 4, 1932
        Response by Allen, June 11, 1932
    Arthur Clutton-Brock. *Times Literary Supplement*, June 23, 1932
        Response by Allen, June 30, 1932

The Plays of Shakespeare and Chapman in Relation to French History
(July 1933)
    6 reviews, including:
    Harold H. Child. *Times Literary Supplement*, Aug. 3, 1933
        Response by Allen, Aug. 10, 1933

becomes fantastic. After all, the store of English words . . . is limited and all minds do occasionally think alike, without either the purpose or the performance of mental larceny'"[11]

That criticism, Allen responded, "breaks down before the single fact that these abounding parallels occur only as between certain plays, dozens of borrowings from *Twelfth Night* being visible in *Every Man Out of His Humour*, and in *The Silent Woman*, whereas you may seek them in vain in, e.g., *Every Man in His Humour* and *The Alchemist*. . . . The coincidence theory, then, is in my judgment, far more 'fantastic' than my own simple and logical explanation, namely, that Shakespeare's rivals imitated, for obvious reasons, the most popular dramatist of his time."[12]

Brown replied, again taking examples out of context, to which Allen promptly responded.

> Mr. Ivor Brown's . . . argument fails because he has omitted, somewhat strangely, to take into account a truth vital to the issue, namely, that all such theses as those which my book seeks to prove, are, and must be, based upon *cumulative effect*. . . . The problem, moreover, goes deeper than mere textual resemblances. As an astute London reviewer wrote, of these very passages: "Here we are over the frontier beyond literary scholarship. . . . [T]he rest is really a matter for psychologists to take up."[13] [a paraphrase of T. S. Eliot's review, noted above]

Allen raised what was to become a third theme in his exchanges with critics: the need for "imaginative mental contact" to understand a society that existed several hundred years in the past.

> The question to be determined is, whether I have, or have not, across 300 years, made some genuine imaginative contact with the mental inter-relations of variously coupled Elizabethan dramatists? Dangerous! urges Mr. Brown. I grant him; and claim no infallibility; but what pioneer work, I ask, literary or other, has ever been exempt from danger? Orthodoxy is safer—and easier. . . . That my able opponent has allowed me "grace for grace," I am gratefully mindful; for these are among the pleasures of controversy. (463)

The last sentence revealed another aspect of Allen's personality that would become increasingly apparent: his love of spirited engagement with his critics in print and with audiences in the many lectures he gave on the Oxfordian theme. Brown's response to that point was probably characteristic of many critics who did not usually venture to discuss their personal preferences or beliefs. "Mr. Allen's argument by cumulation still affrights me and I must confess myself a timid shelterer behind what he calls orthodoxy, and I, common sense. I cannot agree that if you pile up a quantity of bad reasons for believing a thing you make one good reason. The value of evidence is surely a matter of quality, not of quantity, and I am not attracted by the *cumulus*."[14]

Another review worth noting was George Sampson's in *The Bookman*. In 1923 Sampson had blithely rejected Looney's theory as one of little importance and had been rebuked by Looney in turn. Sampson's review of Allen's book began, surprisingly, by noting that he had gone through at least a few of the "Mental Revolutions" (see Chapter

---

[11] Ivor Brown, "The Theatre: Merchandise Marks," *Saturday Review*," March 14, 1928, pp. 215-16.

[12] Percy Allen, "Shakespeare, Jonson and Wilkins," *Saturday Review*, March 31, 1928, p. 388.

[13] Percy Allen, "Shakespeare, Jonson and Wilkins," *Saturday Review*, April 14, 1928, p. 463.

[14] Ivor Brown, in a paragraph following Percy Allen's rebuttal, "Shakespeare, Jonson and Wilkins," *Saturday Review*, April 14, 1928, p. 463.

5) necessary to fully buy into the Oxfordian idea.

> We have not only much to learn but much to unlearn. The accident of time gave us Shakespeare at a period when language, press, theatre, state and church itself were in the very act of turning sharply in new directions, and within a few years of his death Shakespeare had become part of a vanished past, and could be recaptured only with labour and devotion, well meant but sometimes ill considered. Many people are still in the grip of a Shakespeare legend created in the eighteenth and nineteenth centuries.[15]

Sampson, however, closed his review by dismissing those doubting Shakspere's authorship. "Baconians and their like are not people to be argued with. They have a kink in their minds. It is quite useless to argue with people who believe that the earth is flat... . The only thing to do with them is to let them alone. Argument is too great a compliment to pay to monomania."

Shakespeare and Chapman as Topical Dramatists (1929)

A friendly review by Col. Bernard R. Ward showed just how important this book was and still is.

> Last year Mr. Percy Allen showed ... that Ben Jonson was a persistent imitator of Shakespeare's work, his *Sejanus* being written as a counterblast to *Julius Caesar* and in rivalry with it. *The Silent Woman* being in the same way a copy or rather a parody of *Twelfth Night*. Ben Jonson was a realist who could not stand Shakespeare's fantastic romanticism, while at the same time he could not help admitting that there was "ever more in him to be praised than pardoned." This grudging admission ... was by no means surprising in the case of so confirmed an egoist as Ben Jonson was. No one, however, had any idea that in spite of his patronising tone his borrowings from the older dramatist were carried out on an absolutely colossal scale.
>
> Now Mr. Percy Allen has followed up his study of Ben Jonson by one on George Chapman, and has shown in his new book with equal conclusiveness that the famous translator of Homer was no less indebted to Shakespeare than Ben Jonson was. Here is an entirely new field of Shakespeare study opened up to us in these two books.[16]

Col. Ward was right: Allen had opened up a new field of Shakespeare study by documenting the degree to which Jonson and Chapman were influenced by, and indeed, wrote in direct imitation of, Shakespeare's plays. Here we see yet another mental revolution that must be overcome to fully accept the Oxfordian paradigm.

But, Col. Ward asked, "How is it that this has never been found out before? Many scholars have studied the plays written by Ben Jonson and George Chapman, whole editions of their works have been brought out by painstaking and no doubt learned men, but this obvious fact—obvious at least now that Mr. Allen has pointed it out to us—has never struck one of them." One reason, he suggested, is that "although scholars read the plays they edit, they seldom or never see them on the stage. Mr. Allen is a dramatic critic, and the revival of old plays ... has afforded him an opportunity which he has seized with both hands."

Ward recounted many examples showing how much more interesting Jonson's and Chapman's plays become when viewed from this new perspective.

---

[15] George Sampson, "More About Shakespeare," *Bookman*, May 1928, p. 113.
[16] Col. Bernard R. Ward, "Shakespeare and Chapman," *Shakespeare Pictorial*, May 1929, p. 24.

> Mr. Percy Allen . . . has increased enormously the interest with which the Jonson and Chapman plays will in future be read, for he has shown how dependent they both are on Shakespeare in spite of their attacks and criticism. Lastly, by a wonderful effort of constructive imagination, he has succeeded in laying bare—not once but many times—the secret opinion that these two dramatists held of their great forerunner and contemporary.

Reviews in *The Bookman* and *The Christian Science Monitor* were largely in agreement with Col. Ward on the importance of Allen's first two books. A short review in *The Stage* gave Allen the chance to express further his thoughts on the historical knowledge and imaginative effort needed to understand the sensibilities of the Elizabethans.

> To deny, as my critic does by implication, the "inveterate tendency of Elizabethan writers towards subtlety and concealed second meaning," simply will not do. The fact has been proved, many times over, not merely in my own books but in those of Miss Lilian Winstanley and others; and the individual who refuses to accept that statement is merely proclaiming his failure to penetrate into Elizabethan mentality, and is judging the writers of that mysterious age by the wholly different psychological standards of today. The basically fallacious "assumption," therefore, is not mine but that of my critic; and until it has been exploded—a process that must take some time—no very widespread progress can, in my judgment, be made with the correct interpretation of Elizabethan drama and its needful correlation with the life and history of the time. Only through the mentality of their age can Shakespeare and his fellows be comprehended.[17]

G. B. Harrison's review in *The London Mercury* marked the second of at least five times that he and Allen would clash over the decade. The thrust of his review was that Allen must have been a secret Oxfordian when writing his first two books. The factual mistakes Harrison made in the following passage show how uninformed he was about the Oxfordian idea.

> Among the theories which Mr. Percy Allen puts forward in his second book are that both *Twelfth Night* and *Hamlet* are founded on incidents which took place in the 1570s during the negotiations for the Alençon marriage and in the career of Edward Vere [sic], 7th [sic] Earl of Oxford. He does not explain why Shakespeare, writing some twenty-five to thirty years later, should have had any interest in such musty scandal; nor does he show any proof that Shakespeare could have known about events which took place when he was still at school. I suspect that Mr. Allen, if not already an Oxfordite [sic] in disguise, will soon become one, when, in his next book but two, he finds as a logical conclusion of his "discoveries" that only one man could both have known the scandals and written the plays.[18]

Allen lost no time in responding.

> It is, I admit, on the face of it, somewhat strange that Shakespeare—assuming him to be the Stratford actor—should be so deeply concerned with events of the fifteen-seventies; but . . . I beg to remind [the reviewer] . . . that two principal events upon which I have shewn the plot of *Twelfth Night* to be partly based, namely the Massacre of St. Bartholomew (1570) and the Alençon courtship, remained sources of living interest in England up to the accession of James I, for the reason that Roman Catholic plots continued, beyond the turn of the century,

---

[17] Percy Allen, "Topical Dramatists," *The Stage*, May 30, 1929, p. 15.
[18] G. B. Harrison, "Shakespeare and Chapman as Topical Dramatists," *London Mercury*, vol. XX/118 (Aug. 1929).

deeply to disturb the nation; and secondly, that the question of the Queen's marriage necessarily linked, as it must be, with the vital issue of the succession to the crown, remained an open one, almost up to the day of Elizabeth's death.

If by an "Oxfordite" Dr. Harrison implies an upholder of the theory that the Seventeenth Earl of Oxford was the actual author of the Shakespearean plays, he is, in this instance, right, though, in supposing that I shall postpone my development of that theory to "my next book but two," he is, once more, wrong; since I intend to do so in my next book, upon which I am already at work. Should my distinguished critic do me the honour to take notice of that volume in print, I suggest that he should bring to his remarks a wider sense of fair-play, and a deeper sense of responsibility to truth, and to his readers, than are apparent in a review, which, not, I think, for the first time, compels me to call in question his authority.[19]

Their next exchange began with Harrison's combined review of Allen's first two books in *The Review of English Studies*. Harrison set Allen off by writing "Mr. Allen claims that 'imagination, and a knowledge of the period, are as imperatively needed for the reviewing as for the writing of such books as these'; he certainly possesses imagination."[20]

Allen addressed what he saw as the two principal flaws in Harrison's attack.

The fact that a case for borrowings and allusions, to be proved mainly by parallel passages, must necessarily rely much upon cumulative effect, is not modified by the further fact, that a hostile reviewer can select—in this instance, out of hundreds—two or three of the less convincing parallels: and thus, by removing them from their context, produce, deliberately, a false impression.[21]

Dr. Harrison . . . reveals, once more, complete failure, in my judgment, to understand the conditions of Shakespeare's age; since the question of a royal marriage—closely linked, as it must be, with that of succession to the Crown, as also with the anti-protestant intrigues, that continued deeply to trouble the country, right up to the Gunpowder Plot—necessarily continued to be of interest to the nation, almost to the day of Elizabeth's death. (197)

He then identified the core of the problem. "It is because Dr. Harrison cannot, or will not, bring that needful imaginative response to my books, or to their subject, that his repeated attacks—of which I believe this to be the third within a year—continue to be as shallow as they are obviously prejudiced."

Ivor Brown's review of *Shakespeare and Chapman as Topical Dramatists* in *The Saturday Review* launched another round of exchanges. It began with Brown commenting on how personal the back-and-forth had become. For that reason, he explained, "The review of this book must inevitably be written in the first person. In his preface Mr. Allen calls me out of the ranks of reviewers and proceeds to rebuke me for what I wrote in *The Saturday Review* about his last book."[22]

After praising "Mr. Allen's theories about Shakespeare's comments on topical matters and Chapman's relation to Shakespeare" as "very interesting," Brown made a curious statement that seemed to simultaneously accept and reject Allen's point:

It may be that Lord Oxford sat as an unwitting model for Lord Hamlet and that

---

[19] Percy Allen, "Shakespeare and Chapman," *London Mercury*, vol. XX/119 (Sept. 1929).

[20] G. B. Harrison, [reviews of *Shakespeare, Jonson, and Wilkins as Borrowers*, and of *Shakespeare and Chapman as Topical Dramatists*], *Review of English Studies*, vol. 6/21 (Jan. 1930): 100.

[21] Percy Allen, [letter], *Review of English Studies*, vol. 6/22 (April 1930): 196.

[22] Ivor Brown, "The Muse on Loan," *Saturday Review*, vol. 147 (Feb. 23, 1929): 251.

"just as Ophelia is Anne Cecil-cum-Anne Vavasour, so Laertes is Thomas Cecil with Thomas Knyvet and Thomas Vavasour contributing." If you think that is a likely way of writing such plays as Shakespeare wrote, you cannot be argued out of your opinion. But, before we settle down to agree with a builder of theory, it is important that we should agree on the nature of valuable or usable evidence. (252)

Having brought to the fore the question of methodology and of what types of evidence are legitimate, Brown retreated into an examination of a few of Allen's less valuable comparisons. In his response, Allen grasped the "methodology" angle and drove forward, stressing the importance of taking the evidence as a whole.

In setting out to prove deliberate, and systematic, imitations and plagiarisms of one playwright by another—in this case of *Hamlet* and *Macbeth* by Chapman, in his *Bussy* plays. . . . [T]here is only one way of doing so, namely, by a subtle, slow, laborious process of literal and other parallels and analogies—all cumulative in effect—by which, at last, the case is built up. To remove a couple of lines from their context, of page after page of closely-argued writing, and then to quote them as examples of my method is manifestly futile; and can enlighten no one concerning the purpose, argument, or implications of the book in question, or of its correlated predecessor. This, nevertheless, contrary to the elementary canons of literary criticism, my opponent again chooses to do, and I have, for a third time, to remind him of his fault.[23]

He again emphasized that "imaginative penetration" is an essential quality when attempting to understand a culture distant in time or place.

As many and great as are Mr. Brown's intellectual gifts—and he can have few more sincere admirers than myself—the faculty of imaginative penetration into the deeper meaning and implications of our mysterious and difficult Elizabethan drama is not among them. I appeal therefore to comprehending and open-minded readers, and—should he care to indite it—gladly leave to my distinguished adversary what I hope will be the last word in this somewhat strange discussion.

The discussion ended there until Allen's next book was published.

Muriel St. Clare Byrne also reviewed *Borrowers* for *The Times Literary Supplement*, igniting still another series of exchanges. She recognized that "Mr. Allen has chosen a subject that needs the investigation of modern scholarship. The topical nature of the Elizabethan drama has . . . with Miss Winstanley's work, taken an extreme ramification which demands serious attention."[24] She also recognized the critical point that by "current" allusions Allen meant those not recent but contemporaneous, to the minute. "His subject is not the topical, in the true sense, but the contemporaneous."

She claimed to be uncertain about whether Allen meant that the references in *Twelfth Night* alluding to the Alençon courtship of Queen Elizabeth (which lasted from about 1571 until 1583) resulted from "an original version of the play, written as propaganda for the Alençon match in the early eighties, . . . or whether he attributes it to the Shakespeare of the nineties who gave us the play in its present form," a feat made possible because of "Shakespeare's" "easy intercourse with Southampton, Oxford, and other great lords."

Allen's response addressed a familiar theme: that some reviewers address side issues

---

[23] Percy Allen, "Shakespeare and Chapman as Topical Dramatists," *Saturday Review*, March 2, 1929, p. 281.
[24] Muriel St. Clare Byrne, "Shakespeare and Chapman," *Times Literary Supplement*, March 21, 1929, p. 229.

while failing to present the major points of Allen's book and the evidence he massed in support of them.

> A hostile reviewer can ignore completely or can reject, with brief mention, any part of an author's case, making such play, instead, with secondary and relatively unimportant details, as quite to obscure the basic argument. This method your reviewer has made use of.
>
> My book, as a unity, is not dealt with. Excepting one sentence . . . your reviewer dismisses without comment the three concluding chapters, comprising 160 pages, in which I show, for the first time, and, I submit, beyond all shadow of doubt, that Chapman's *Bussey* plays are a running commentary upon *Twelfth Night*, *Macbeth* and especially *Hamlet*, and that, again conclusively, they identify Hamlet with the seventeenth Earl of Oxford.[25]

He turned again to the all-important necessity of possessing the "intuitive powers" needed to comprehend the works of the Elizabethan era in their full complexity—an ability he concluded Byrne did not possess.

> Shakespeare's plays . . . from *Love's Labour's Lost* onwards, comprise a running sequence of "manipulations' of historic fact, circumstance and of human character, to suit the exigencies and intentions of the dramatists' art. The measure of a scholar's ability to detect and bring to light those manipulations is the measure of his power imaginatively to comprehend the Shakespearian plays in their deeper historical, as well as dramatic, purport; and to link them intelligently with the events and personalities of the Elizabethan London that gave them birth.
>
> Your reviewer, for lack of that vision, as also of sympathetically intuitive powers, has missed the broader significance of my work; the real issue being not, as he [sic] supposes, one of method, nor of documentation, nor even of textual plagiarism, but of psychology—the question whether I have, or have not, penetrated imaginatively into the individual minds and into the subtle and complex mental inter-relations of the two rival Elizabethan poets.

Allen did acknowledge one area where Byrne perceptively called out his crafty presentation—perhaps tongue in cheek—of Shakespeare as incorporating "current" events from twenty years earlier as a serious idea.

> In one matter only does your reviewer hit me . . . and that is where he [sic] suggests, very justly, the extreme improbability of Shakespeare, in his plays, concerning himself so frequently, as he seems to do, with events of the early seventies, when the future actor was a boy of some ten years. That difficulty—of which I was fully conscious from the first—must be faced. That I failed to advance my own considered solution was simply due to reluctance to make more controversial a book which is already challenging enough.

That point would be addressed in his next book.

The Case for Edward de Vere as "Shakespeare" (1930)

With the publication of *The Case for Edward de Vere as "William Shakespeare,"* Allen added a new layer of controversial ideas on top of the startling ideas that Shakespeare's plays were topical and that the topicality was often to events and people prominent in the 1570s. Perhaps for many scholars and reviewers the situation had reached a point of

---

[25] Percy Allen, "Shakespeare and Chapman," *Times Literary Supplement*, March 28, 1929, p. 260.

brain overload.

Illustrative was the review in *The Saturday Review*. It's unsigned, but probably not by Ivor Brown. It must have been distressing for Oxfordians to see that even after fifty years of discussion of the authorship question and ten years of discussion of the Oxfordian claim reviewers continued to be so ill-informed.

> [T]here are those who, contemptuous of the nature of evidence, believe that Bacon or Oxford or another wrote the plays to which Shakespeare put his name. ... [These ideas are] amazing, gratuitous and impertinent.... Before we attempt to follow Mr. Percy Allen in his disclosure of a mare's-nest, let us ask why he or anyone should doubt for a moment that Shakespeare, the actor and successful manager of theatres, was the author of the plays that still bear his name. Actor is written all over them.

> Learning is not really in question. It is not questioned that the man could read as well as write, and there is nothing in the way of knowledge, save of the human heart and mind, to be discerned in the plays that [Shakspere] could not have acquired from books written in the tongue he spoke, or from travellers he must have met and conversed with.

So many misconceptions all in just a few short sentences! Here is Allen's response.

> I beg leave to reply that any person who, in this year 1930, supposes that arguments against the Stratford man, and for de Vere's intimate connexion with the Shakespearean plays and sonnets, can be disposed of by such airily contemptuous methods, is either so hide-bound by prejudice as to be impermeable to, or so little informed in the matter as to be ignorant of, the full case against Shakespeare, as it now stands. . . . Such epithets as 'amazing, gratuitous, impertinent' and the rest, are easily said, since they call for neither knowledge, intelligence nor thought.

> Our case for de Vere, which every month of further research powerfully strengthens, is fast gaining converts among the many thoughtful and open-minded people who are wholly dissatisfied with the Stratfordian case: and such progress can be hindered, if at all, only by an examination and exposure far more detached, judicial, just and searching than that concerning which I am now compelled to pen these few words of rebuke.[26]

The Christian Science Monitor reviewer saw more value in Allen's *Case*, writing that among the leading anti-Stratfordians is "Mr. Allen, whose erudition in Elizabethan literature and manners has been amply proved in several books." After examining the process through which Allen arrived at his conviction that Oxford was the real author of the Shakespeare works—"the series of remarkable correspondences, of language and idea, between them [Oxford's writings] and various of the Shakespearean writings," and "that the Elizabethan drama in general and the plays of Shakespeare and Chapman ... in particular are full of disguised allusions to contemporary affairs"—he concluded that even "if one prefers to suspend final judgment one cannot but admit that Mr. Allen has made a contribution to a difficult subject which cannot lightly be dismissed."[27]

Col. Bernard Ward wrote in the same vein, calling *Case* "the first comprehensive attempt—since the publication ten years ago of Mr. Looney's *"Shakespeare" Identified*"—to prove the justice of Mr. Looney's contention that the name 'William Shakespeare' was

---

[26] Percy Allen, "Fiddlesticks" [letter], *Saturday Review*, vol. 149 (May 17, 1930): 619.
[27] "De Vere as Shakespeare," *Christian Science Monitor*, July 19, 1930, p. 6.

first and foremost a pseudonym of the Earl of Oxford."[28] After noting that he himself had attacked the problem in connection with the publication of the *Sonnets*, that Admiral Holland had proved how topical allusions only become intelligible if looked at "through Oxford glasses," that Rendall had found in the *Sonnets* a "living personality, the soul of Hamlet shaped upon experiences of de Vere," Col. Ward showed that Allen "attempts to tackle the whole problem, [not just] . . . throw light on some particular aspect of it."

"It is not too much to say," he continued, that

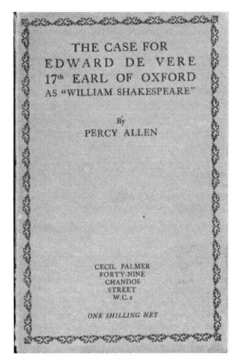

THE CASE FOR
EDWARD DE VERE
17ᵗʰ EARL OF OXFORD
AS "WILLIAM SHAKESPEARE"

By
PERCY ALLEN

CECIL PALMER
FORTY-NINE
CHANDOS
STREET
W.C. 2

ONE SHILLING NET

> [Allen's] combined historical and autobiographical interpretation . . . throws a more vivid and personal light upon these great dramas than they have received at the hands of any critic since they first appeared in print more than three hundred years ago.[29]

Although not expressing an opinion on the validity of the Oxfordian claim, *The Sunday Times* was direct in its praise of Allen. "That in his heroic endeavour to perform that task he proves his possession of a most complete and enviable knowledge of the Shakespearean dramas and of a vast mass of poetical and historical learning, a more than respectable critical faculty, and a really amazing if somewhat dangerous subtlety of intelligence, admits of no dispute. Whatever may be the ultimate fate of his theory, there can be no denial of the extraordinary cleverness of its presentation or of its charm of verbal style."[30]

Of a different opinion was Muriel St. Clare Byrne in *The Times Literary Supplement*. Her review filled two long columns, itself a tacit admission of the substantive nature of Allen's book and the Oxfordian claim. Col. Ward called her review "A landmark in the history of the Fellowship. . . . The repercussions that have resulted as a consequence of this review are remarkable, and may already be characterised without exaggeration as resounding."[31] He didn't explain the "remarkable" and "resounding" consequences to which he referred, but the review itself provides clues.

Byrne began well, showing a familiarity with the major works of the Oxfordians. But, in the same paragraph, she made two serious misstatements:

> The happy majority . . . neither know nor care to what obscure autobiographical recollections it is possible to ascribe certain features of the plays. They read Shakespeare because there is a timeless quality in his knowledge of human nature which is explained not by reference to the events of some largely conjectural "Life" but only by that unexplainable thing we call genius.

---

[28] Col. Bernard R. Ward, "The Case for Edward de Vere as 'Shakespeare,'" *Sh. Pictorial*, Sept. 1930, p. 16.

[29] Col. Bernard R. Ward, Review of *The Case for Edward de Vere*, *Sh. Pictorial*, Sept. 1930, p. 16.

[30] "The Shakespeare-de Vere Controversy," *Sunday Times*, May 4, 1930, p. 10.

[31] Col. Bernard R. Ward, "Henry Wriothesley and Henry de Vere," *Shakespeare Pictorial*, Nov. 1930, p. 16.

The first mistake was assuming that most people who enjoy Shakespeare's plays are uninterested in the life of the author. That is disproved by the scores of biographies of Shakespeare that have been written and the millions of people who have purchased them. The more important misunderstanding is of the nature of genius and literary creativity. In literature, free-floating genius means little without the life experiences of the author, from which are drawn the material that is transformed into literary works. Knowing about the most meaningful experiences in an author's life, and understanding the relationship between them and passages in the literary works they gave rise to, adds much to the depth of a reader's understanding and enjoyment of them.

Byrne continued with one misstatement after another; Allen handily disposed of them. In his short response immediately after the review was published, he stated that he would answer it in full in the introduction to his forthcoming book, *The Oxford-Shakespeare Case Corroborated*. Regarding his analysis of *As You Like It*, Allen wrote that,

> Your reviewer had the opportunity to demolish, if he [sic] could, a series of coincidences pointing so insistently in one direction as to damage the orthodox case as effectively as they supported my own; yet all he [sic] can do, by way of destruction, is to fasten upon a slip concerning the date of erection of the Globe Theatre, which . . . is, at bottom, irrelevant.
>
> In no single instance, as I shall show in due course, does your reviewer succeed in making any real impression upon my arguments for de Vere as Shakespeare.[32]

Byrne closed her review with an astounding statement: that she was ready to stake the entire Stratfordian claim on the similarities she believed exist between the signatures in William Shakspere's Will and "Hand D" in the manuscript of the play *Sir Thomas More*.[33] "Until the Oxfordians disprove all the evidence which has been steadily accumulating to show" similarities between the two handwritings, "to go on arguing the Oxford case along these lines is like flogging a dead horse."[34] Her challenge lasted all of two weeks, until Gerald H. Rendall's letter in *The Times Literary Supplement* definitively demolished the case for any such similarity. That challenge and its having been met only two weeks later must surely be what Col. Ward characterized as "remarkable" and as having "resounding" repercussions. (Rendall's letter will be discussed later in this chapter.)

The Oxford-Shakespeare Case Corroborated (1931)

Allen's next book began with a lengthy "Author's Foreword" in which he assessed the state of the Shakespeare authorship question and responded to criticism of his previous book, *The Case for Edward de Vere as "Shakespeare."* On the first subject he observed that in the autumn of 1930 the belief in the Stratford man had risen "in thousands of individual instances" almost to "the fervour of a religious cult fortified by the enormous prestige and power of ninety-nine out of every hundred universities and scholastic establishments throughout the English speaking world, and by an at least equal percentage of the world's press."[35] Those belonging to the cult he described as "slow-thinking, deficient in intellectual courage, and lacking in initiative." Nevertheless, even in England,

---

[32] Percy Allen, "Oxford as 'Shakespeare,'" *Times Literary Supplement*, Sept. 18, 1930, p. 735.
[33] Byrne drew her conclusions about handwriting from *Shakespeare's Hand in the Play of Sir Thomas More; Papers by Alfred W. Pollard, W. W. Greg, E. Maunde Thompson, J. Dover Wilson and R. W. Chambers*, edited by W. W. Greg (1923).
[34] Muriel St. Clare Byrne, "Oxford as 'Shakespeare,'" *Times Literary Supplement*, Sept. 11, 1930, p. 712.
[35] Percy Allen, *The Oxford Shakespeare Case Corroborated* (1931), pp. 2-3.

> The Stratfordian faith is crumbling, and . . . its continuing hold upon the mass of the nation is due, far more to the instinctive desire of our people, as a whole, to be left in peace with their chosen heroes and cherished beliefs, whether true or false, than to any conviction in favour of the Stratford man, based upon active intellectual process. Orthodoxy, saving when stirred by attack, is passive and timidly inert; the initiative in this controversy, the strategic position that permits of effective attack, having passed, and passed permanently, to us. (3)

Turning to his previous book, Allen noted that "some academic reviewers were so enraged by an outspoken preface . . . that a . . . reasonably just and impartial commentary was no longer to be expected from them. . . . They rushed blindly, and therefore fruitlessly, to the attack. Others deliberately ignored the book; yet there did appear a considerable number of favourable, and in some cases, charming reviews, for the most part, as was fitting in the circumstances, non-committal in tone, pending consolidation of opinion, and further corroborative or destructive research" (4). He characterized the review in *The Sunday Times* as "a guarded yet graceful and pleasing notice." Most, however, were neither.

> A majority of the notices, . . . including that of *The Times Literary Supplement*, with which I will deal later, were actively, and often unscrupulously—yet without exception, ineffectively—hostile; so much so that, from the negative view-point, I could ask for no greater encouragement than the gradual realization of my opponents' complete failure even to compromise, much less to destroy, our ever-strengthening case. No single critic has yet succeeded, honestly or dishonestly—and both methods have been tried—in so much as impugning one main line of my argument. (4)

> The position of a hostile reviewer, in cases of this sort, is admittedly difficult, since, consciously or subconsciously, he is aware that a single admission may, and often must, be logically followed by a second, and that second by a third; until the whole position is surrendered at last. Many of our opponents prefer therefore as, indeed, an eminent Stratfordian professor frankly admitted to me, not long ago—to fight, "not for truth, but for victory"; and, with that object in view, to adopt a system of utterly unintelligent, and sometimes disingenuous, denial, which, backed, it may be, by academic position, and by a well-known name, will serve to maintain authority upon the windy side of compromising acceptance! (4)[36]

Allen's description of "scholars" seeking to defend a position rather than to fulfill their duty to pursue the truth should be kept in mind when reading Chapters 11 and 12 of this book.

Turning to the Oxfordian claim, Allen observed that in spite of that "failure of academic scholarship really to come to grips with this matter,"

> The case for Edward de Vere as "Shakespeare"' is fast being established; and it was only a few months ago that a London lawyer of long experience, fully conversant with . . . the whole controversy, told me that, if the case for Oxford could be brought into court, and properly argued by trained counsel before an impartial judge, it would inevitably carry the day, as against Bacon, or the Stratford man; and I wholly agree, because in court the processes of subterfuge, and of evasion, which our opponents habitually employ against us, would be of no avail in the presence of a judge and advocates who can compel direct answers, and will ruthlessly turn either shiftiness or admission to instant and profitable

---

[36] Note the use of 22 commas in one paragraph.

account. (5)

After citing examples of the chains of evidence that Oxfordians were finding—"Let any open-minded person study carefully Chapter III of my *Case*, . . . and then he may deny, if he honestly can, the connection of the Earl with playwrights, with the Revels Office, and with theatrical companies of his day" (11)—he again expressed his incredulity that traditional scholars continued to deny what seemed so obvious to him. "How, I ask again, in the face of such facts, and their inescapable inference, is it possible to deny, unless in the most rigidly literal sense, that no documentary evidence exists, to connect Oxford with Elizabethan dramatic companies, or with Shakespearean plays in the same connection?" (12).

He next addressed Muriel St. Clare Byrne's review of *The Case for Edward de Vere as "Shakespeare"* in *The Times Literary Supplement* (March 21, 1929), which "had raised questions too numerous and too important for adequate discussion in *The Times Literary Supplement*. After describing academia's unrealistic understanding of the nature of genius and its "general failure . . . to correlate Elizabethan drama with the history of its own day", he concluded that "my main line of argument is neither challenged, nor even seriously called in question" (18) by Byrne's criticisms.

Regarding the challenge Byrne posed in the final paragraph of her review, Allen observed that her statement—"A thesis which aims at the complete overthrow of the general belief of scholars and laymen during the last three hundred years cannot afford to ignore, as Mr. Allen does, the positive results which have been steadily accumulating . . . . " (19-20)—had been backed up by only one example: the "similarity" between the only known examples of "Shakespeare's" writing—the six "cramped" signatures—and what is known as Hand D on a manuscript of the play *Sir Thomas More*.

Allen could scarcely restrain his "amused surprise" at her statement, writing that,

> Here are we building up, against the Stratford man, an ever-increasing mass of circumstantial evidence, which has never been answered, for the sufficient reason that it is unanswerable; and behold! I am informed, with pontifical assurance, and over-bearing authority, that no examination of texts or inferences can avail aught to injure the orthodox case, until we have concerned ourselves, "thoroughly and competently," with the question of hand-writing. (20-21)

> Concerning my opponent's attempt to transfer the whole of this argument, and for obvious reasons, to the charge of technical Stratfordian experts, I must remind my readers that such "expert evidence" is notoriously fallible and untrustworthy. . . . I have been personally concerned with law-cases in which "expert witnesses," engaged by the respective litigants, have sworn so steadfastly against each other, that there was no alternative but to reject the evidence of both, and to rely upon one's own intelligence and common-sense. (24)

The Times Literary Supplement did not run a full review of *Corroborated*, merely including it as one of six books in a joint review. The unnamed reviewer—clearly Muriel St. Clare Byrne—commented that

> It could reasonably be claimed that Mr. Percy Allen's is the most considerable of these books. It is a sequel to his work on the case for Edward de Vere, published in 1930. He recapitulates his arguments, reinforces them with others and replies to criticisms. . . . He replies that "no man, however highly endowed, ever can write, or ever did write, outside the basic experiences of his own life." He rejoins

robustly to other arguments put forward by the reviewer in these columns.[37]

Notes and Queries' short review made an assertion that, it thought, undercut the idea of Oxford as Shakespeare: "There is nothing in the plays that requires their author to have been a man of high station—while there is much that suggests such a work-a-day practical occupation with the theatre as a man of high station would hardly find possible or desirable."[38]

Here again a reviewer in a prestigious literary journal with limited knowledge of Edward de Vere showed no awareness of Oxford's extensive involvement with the theater. His father had owned a theater group that performed regularly when Oxford was a child. Oxford himself owned two theatrical companies, one of adults that performed at the Blackfriars Theater, the other, known as "Oxford's Boys," performed regularly at court and in the countryside. Nor did the reviewer seem to be aware that the shame expressed in sonnet 110 would fit Oxford, if he were "Shakespeare" and had been involved directly with the public theater, perhaps even acting on the public stage.

> Alas, 'tis true I have gone here and there,
> And made myself a motley to the view,
> Gor'd mine own thoughts, sold cheap what is most dear . . .

The Christian Science Monitor's reviewer also appeared to have grasped the wrong end of the stick—surprisingly so, since Percy Allen was the *Monitor's* drama critic and had written extensively on the Oxfordian idea in the paper. The reviewer made the odd comments that "Where Mr. Allen goes wrong is in the attempt to dethrone Shakespeare" and "he does not seem to disprove the genius of Shakespeare."[39] Never one to back away from a confrontation, Allen responded that the reviewer had made the faulty assumption that Shakspere and Shakespeare were the same person, which "wholly begs the question at issue." He added, "I seek to dethrone nobody. I seek the truth." After correcting several other "surprisingly loose and inaccurate" statements made by the reviewer, Allen reported on the status of the Oxfordian idea as of the middle of 1931.

> The irrefutable logic of our case—as my letter bag conclusively proves—is fast gaining converts from the four corners of the world; and it may interest your readers to know that even the portraits of "Shakespeare" are now yielding the inevitable secret. I assert, with full sense of responsibility, and hope soon to prove, that the "Grafton," "Ashbourne," and "Droeshout" portraits are all pictures of the Earl of Oxford.[40]

The Life Story of Edward de Vere as 'William Shakespeare" (1932)

Col. Montagu Douglas, President of the Shakespeare Fellowship, provided a succinct assessment of Allen's lengthy *Life Story."* "In this book Mr. Percy Allen follows step by step the eventful career of the Earl of Oxford, weaving into his story the Plays in their successive order, supported by topical illusions and explanatory incidents. Reviewers may submit that these are merely a series of conjectures. But conjectures cannot be multiplied indefinitely. When they revolve around one centre and their number is legion,

---

[37] [reviews of six books], *Times Literary Supplement*, Jan. 14, 1932, p. 29.
[38] "The Oxford-Shakespeare Case Corroborated," *Notes and Queries*, vol. 160/10 (March 7, 1931): 180.
[39] C.F.A., "The Oxford Theory," *Christian Science Monitor*, April 25, 1931, p. 12.
[40] Percy Allen, "The Oxford-Shakespeare Theory," *Christian Science Monitor*, June 5, 1931, p. 20.

they automatically pass into the less debatable land of evidence."[41]

Marjorie Bowen welcomed the book's complete examination of the personality concealed behind the name "William Shakespeare," a subject of "supreme importance" and a "delicate, intricate and highly specialised" task requiring "patient scholarship, an open mind and an unbiased viewpoint."[42] But therein lies a difficulty: "it is impossible for anyone who has not a [detailed] knowledge of Elizabethan letters . . . to judge the case;" others are apt to weary of it. Herein lay the value of Allen's book. "It is a book for all to read, for not only is it a lucid, judicious and almost incredibly erudite and painstaking setting forth of the case for Oxford, it is a vivid character study of a most remarkable man, whose erratic, lurid career, double love story, disgrace, imprisonment and blazing reputation among his contemporaries make him, in himself, a subject of the highest interest."

A widely admired author of several dozen novels who truly knew the art of writing, Bowen turned to a subject of the utmost importance.

> An author's life and circumstances, character and opinions, must make themselves felt, unconsciously perhaps, and perhaps reluctantly, but inevitably, in his work. He must, sooner or later, betray himself. . . . The greater the genius, the more passionately individual is the work likely to be. It is on this point, I think, that Mr. Allen's book attains the greatest success. He shows the brilliant, dazzling, tormented, sensitive, highly cultured, fantastic nature of Edward de Vere, brimming over into and colouring all he wrote; reveals how his own unhappy violent story, that nearly broke him, and then tempered him, is told again and again in the plays and poems where he many times repeated the tragic figures of the woman wrongly accused, the woman forsaken, the proud, wayward man, supremely gifted, supremely unhappy, touched perhaps by madness, or at least melancholia . . . appearing under this aspect, now under that, who is himself.

Gerald Rendall agreed, but sounded a note of caution.

> Much of [Allen's] argument is devoted to topical references in the Plays, for which research—biographical, historical and literary—is supplying new data every day. . . . [He] is admirably equipped by quickness of perception, wide range of reading . . . and a memory at once ready and retentive. But he too often falls a victim to his own gifts. That De Vere and Chapman are favoured vehicles for name-puns is unquestionable; but reiterated insistence on the pun in alien contexts and authors tends to provoke sceptical impatience and to prejudice the case.

> And in one particular direction, that of "dramatic identifications," his language is provokingly unguarded. . . . [T]raits of personal reminiscence, or manner, or experience, are at a far remove from dramatic embodiment. They are valuable as clues to authorship, but their value is discounted when stated in terms of dramatic identification, often of a precarious or untenable kind.[43]

Arthur Clutton-Brock, art critic of *The Times*, expressed a similar reservation in *The Times Literary Supplement*. "Mr. Allen would have improved his case if he had not overloaded his book with parallels, some of which are decidedly weak."[44] Beyond that,

---

[41] Col. M. W. Douglas, review of *The Life-Story of Edward de Vere as 'Shakespeare'* by Percy Allen, *Shakespeare Pictorial*, March 1932, p. 48.

[42] Marjorie Bowen, "The Identity of 'William Shakespeare,'" *Shakespeare Pictorial*, May 1932, p. 82.

[43] Gerald H. Rendall, "The Earl of Oxford as Shakespeare," *Everyman*, Aug. 25, 1932.

[44] Arthur Clutton-Brock, "Edward de Vere," *Times Literary Supplement*, June 23, 1932, p. 462.

Clutton-Brock largely ignored Allen's main points. Allen, as expected, was quick to respond.

> In justice to myself and to your readers, may I point out that not so much as a hint of my main line of argument is given and that your reviewer is strangely silent concerning the crucial pages of my book (Chapters VI and VII), wherein, at the very heart of my story, I show how Oxford's breach with his wife and also his quarrel with the Howard-Arundel group (1580-81), which sent the Earl to the Tower, are dramatised with extreme intimacy and exactness of detail in *Much Ado*, *Measure for Measure* and *Romeo and Juliet*? . . . Your readers are given, instead, the weakest parallel—when removed from its context—that your reviewer can select from a hundred or so. . . . The more open-minded among your readers will hardly fail to draw the obvious conclusions that my principal arguments were ignored because they could not be safely attacked and are mortally dangerous to the case for Shakespearean orthodoxy.[45]

The Saturday Review, in a surprisingly fair-minded review, commented that, "In his latest contribution to the Shakespeare Controversy [Mr. Allen] assumes the case as proved. Unless you remember that, many pages of this book will certainly infuriate you. . . . Those who may be termed the part-converted, those who find it hard to believe that Stratford's Shakespeare wrote the plays attributed to him, and are therefore prepared to consider the de Vere case without prejudice, will find Mr. Allen's book strongly suggestive, and, in places, very nearly cogent."[46]

Allen was quick to acknowledge what was perhaps the fairest review *The Saturday Review* had run of any of his books: "May I thank you for the just and impartial notice of *The Life Story of Edward de Vere as 'William Shakespeare'*—adjectives not always applicable to press comment upon work so unorthodox."[47] He reminded reviewers and readers of an important point to keep in mind when reading Elizabethan literature.

> The fact of Shakespeare's adherence, however close, to his literary sources, rarely or never precludes topical import; because, as even orthodox Professors will admit, it was a characteristic trick of Elizabethan dramatists, and especially of "Shakespeare"—a device known to contemporary audiences—to take some already well-known tale or legend, to which the circumstances of the projected play were analogous, and then most cunningly to weave into it their topical allusions.

The Plays of Shakespeare and Chapman in Relation to French History (1933)

So it was possible to encounter an increasingly polite and accepting tone in coverage of the topical idea and even of the Oxfordian claim. But the default mode was still hostile, if perhaps not quite as hostile. Or rather it's as though some reviewers' right hands did not know what their left hands were doing.

A case in point was Hugh R. Williamson's review of Percy Allen's *The Plays of Shakespeare and Chapman in Relation to French History* (1933). It appeared in *The Bookman*, which had run favorable and unfavorable reviews of *"Shakespeare" Identified*. Readers might at first have thought that Williamson had a favorable view of Allen's methods and of the Oxfordian claim, because he had quoted at length from Marjorie Bowen's criticism of traditionally-minded scholars in her "Foreword" to Allen's book:

---

[45] Percy Allen, "Edward de Vere," *Times Literary Supplement*, June 30, 1932, p. 480.
[46] "The Life Story of Edward de Vere as 'William Shakespeare,'" *Saturday Review*, June 4, 1932, p. 569.
[47] Percy Allen, "De Vere and Shakespeare," *Saturday Review*, vol. 153 (June 11, 1932): 591.

"The increasing weight of evidence in favour of Lord Oxford's claim as 'William Shakespeare,'" she writes, "the remarkable manner in which one discovery leads to another, until much of what was hopelessly puzzling becomes absolutely clear, has gradually become so extremely important that a sufficient number of people are being interested (and in many cases convinced) to ensure the movement is making headway, even without any official recognition whatever, and in face of regrettable, but perhaps inevitable, shallow criticism, baseless ridicule and the impatience of the conventional-minded, who are always ready to jeer at what they cannot or will not understand."[48]

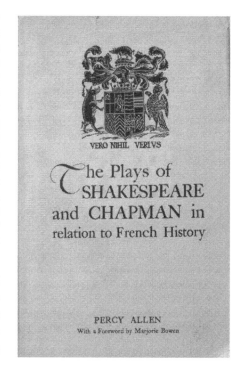

VERO NIHIL VERIVS

The Plays of SHAKESPEARE and CHAPMAN in relation to French History

PERCY ALLEN
With a Foreword by Marjorie Bowen

But Williamson then swerved, writing a review that is best characterized using language from Bowen's "Foreword": "shallow, baseless ridicule and the impatience of the conventional-minded, who are always ready to jeer at what they cannot or will not understand."

Harold H. Child's assessment of the same book in *The Times Literary Supplement* was surprisingly positive, given the earlier rejection of the Oxfordian claim in the same paper by Muriel St. Clare Byrne and others. Although Child was careful not to express an opinion about Allen's belief in Oxford's authorship, he appeared to have a great deal of respect for Allen's erudition.

> Throughout the book the reader cannot fail to be struck, in particular by the number of characters identifiable in whole or in part with Oxford, and in general by the complexity and variety of the allusions to French history, English history, Scottish history, literary squabbles, and much else, which lie in the most "innocent-looking" lines. The construction of such plays must have demanded more ingenuity, knowledge and memory than imagination. . . . [N]o reader but must be impressed by Mr. Allen's learning and by the ingenuity with which he uses it in his "fascinating game."[49]

Allen again responded promptly. "I thank you for the pleasingly impartial review of my *French History*," he began, before expressing his regret "that scholars and students of Elizabethan literature usually ignore the streams of allegories, and topical allusions, that run through nearly all Elizabethan plays and poems. Without a real comprehension of these basic facts, neither the Elizabethans, nor their writings, can be well understood; and critics who continue to neglect this fundamental characteristic of the period we are discussing will inevitably continue to be tripped up by that negligence."[50]

(Discussion of Percy Allen's extensive career as a public speaker and debater on behalf of the Oxfordian claim will be discussed in Chapter 14.)

---

[48] Hugh R. Williamson, "Poor Will," *Bookman*, vol. 84 (July 1933): 83-84. Quoting in part Marjorie Bowen's foreword to Percy Allen's *French History*.
[49] Harold H. Child, "History and Plays," *Times Literary Supplement*, Aug. 3, 1933, p. 522.
[50] Percy Allen, "History and Plays" [letter], *Times Literary Supplement*, Aug. 10, 1933, p. 537.

Gerald H. Rendall

Gerald Rendall was the most eminent British scholar to embrace the Oxfordian claim in the first twenty-five years after *"Shakespeare" Identified* was published. The prestige of his name and the two books he wrote on the personality of "Shakespeare" as revealed in his sonnets and other poems did much to raise the profile and acceptability of the Oxfordian case. His smaller books and pamphlets on sub-topics—including *Shake-speare Handwriting and Spelling* (1931), *Ben Jonson and the First Folio of "Shakespeare's" Plays* (1939), and *The "Ashbourne" Portrait of Shakespeare* (1940)—helped defend the legitimacy of Oxfordian ideas in these areas.

In its obituary early in 1945, *The New York Times* described Rendall as the "last of the great Victorian classical scholars and oldest retired headmaster in Great Britain."[51] He was one of the founders of the University of Liverpool in 1881, and had served as the Principal of its University College, until 1897. He later held the important educational positions of Vice Chancellor and professor of Greek at Victoria University in Manchester and Headmaster of Charterhouse School.

As one American wrote at the time of his death, "In addition to being Hon. Canon of Chelmsford, his degrees included those of Bachelor of Divinity, Doctor of Letters and Doctor of Laws. A highly accomplished Greek and Latin scholar, his translations were published in the Loeb Classical Library. That a man of his background should break with the orthodox Stratfordian dicta was something of a shock to the professional defenders of these hoary myths. But Dr. Rendall continued to put forward evidence of his high competence on behalf of Oxford until the last."[52]

Although *The New York Times* made no mention of Rendall's Oxfordian beliefs, other newspapers did. *The Birmingham Daily Post* noted that "In his later years much of his literary work was in the field of Shakespearean criticism. In his eightieth year [1930] he wrote a plea for Edward de Vere as the author of the *Sonnets*."[53] *The Essex Newsman* reported that "Dr. Rendall distinguished himself early in his career in mathematics, history, and Shakespearean studies. To the end his interest in Shakespeare was enthusiastic, for he was convinced that Edward de Vere, Earl of Oxford, was 'Shakespeare,' a theory he expounded in various books and articles."[54]

What drew such an accomplished scholar to the Oxfordian answer to the Shakespeare authorship question?

Rendall described how a look into Ignatius Donnelly's *Great Cryptogram* had produced in him a reaction of extreme revolt against the Baconian theory and indeed against all unorthodox authorship theories. Several decades later, though, his reaction to Looney's *"Shakespeare" Identified* was very different.

> In 1920, I naturally turned with averted eyes from a volume entitled *"Shakespeare" Identified*, till the representations of a friend[55] . . . induced me to try once more; and in Mr. J. T. Looney's pages I found a very different order of treatment and reasoning from that which I anticipated. Following up the various

---

[51] "Dr. Gerald H. Rendall," *New York Times*, Feb. 20, 1945, p. 19.
[52] "Death of Canon Rendall," *SF Quarterly*, vol. VI/2 (April 1945): 21.
[53] "Obituary: Canon G. H. Rendall," *Birmingham Daily Post*, Jan. 8, 1945, p. 4.
[54] "Canon Rendall Dies at the Age of 93," *Essex Newsman*, Jan. 9, 1945, p. 1.
[55] The friend was W. A. Ferguson, who later became a member of the Shakespeare Fellowship and who corresponded with J. Thomas Looney in 1925.

lines of evidence—biographical, personal, and literary—combining clues of poetic output and authoritative testimony, of historic sympathies and reminiscences, of personal and of dramatic episodes and allusions, and broad and striking chronological correspondences, he seemed to succeed in concentrating them upon a single objective, Edward de Vere, 17th Earl of Oxford. Startling and paradoxical as [it] sounded . . . here was a thesis, open to crucial and many-sided tests, whose walls could not fail to crumble, if built of lath or rubble.[56]

Rendall decided to test for himself the validity of the Oxfordian theory by bringing to bear on it the scholarly practices he had honed over a lifetime. He turned first to the *Sonnets*.

I decided to make the sonnets my test of the theory proposed, to approach them with an open mind, and see whether the proffered key helped to unlock the riddle, which the best critics perhaps have been most tempted to dismiss as insoluble. The actual life and personality of W. Shakspere are such a blank, that every critic can fill in the bare outlines, or leave them unfilled, almost at pleasure; but, on the other hand, the sonnets themselves are so full of indications, hints and data, direct or indirect, that it ought to be possible to give a clear idea of the background and the scenery, the social atmosphere and assumptions, the quality and characteristics of the culture and the personal relationships, which combined to produce them; and thence, if fortune favoured, to deduce, and even to identity, the personality of the writer, and the circumstances under which they were produced. (3)

Rendall's study of almost a decade culminated in the publication of *Shakespeare Sonnets and Edward de Vere*, in which he concluded that "When we subject the *Sonnets* to close personal scrutiny . . . we are met by coincidences so numerous, so circumstantial, so surprising and illuminating, that it becomes impossible to set them down to chance or to refuse to recognise in them the handiwork of Edward de Vere" (291-92).

That book brought Rendall into the public eye as the most prominent scholar yet who had accepted the validity of the Oxfordian claim. It was widely reviewed and elicited a range of reactions. *The Dundee Courier* was favorably impressed. "Dr. Gerald H. Rendall . . . propounds a very weighty argument displacing Shakespearean tradition. That tradition is not easily disturbed . . . Dr. Rendall almost persuades one into accepting the view that these sonnets were written by Edward de Vere, Earl of Oxford. . . . internal evidence [is] so elaborate that few students could be expected to examine it thoroughly. What they can do will be to absorb the explicit knowledge and the grateful atmosphere of scholarship disbursed in Dr. Rendall's account . . . the literary aspects of that morning splendour, and the men pre-eminent amongst the glory are treated with a freshness of learning and feeling that makes the larger part of the book a joy to read."[57]

---

[56] Gerald H. Rendall, *Shakespeare Sonnets and Edward de Vere* (1930), p. 2.
[57] "Tradition Disturbed," *Dundee Courier and Advertiser*, Feb. 27, 1930, p. 10.

The Manchester Guardian was more cautious. "Mr. Rendall . . . sets about his object in a plausible way, examining his material and laying out his facts in a conscientious and methodical fashion [and] . . . there is much that is eminently reasonable. What it amounts to is this—that one would not be surprised to find that the author of the sonnets was a man who in the flesh had been accustomed to the world of courtliness, culture, and affairs which we imagine to have constituted the environment of an Elizabethan nobleman. As far as such argument goes it is sound enough. But in fact it does not go very far. It does not carry us one inch towards the conclusion that the author of the sonnets *must* have been a nobleman."[58]

Gerald Henry Rendall, B.D., Litt.D., L.L.D.

Born: 1851. Died: January 4, 1945.
Age when *"Shakespeare" Identified* was published: 69

Born ten years before the American Civil War began, he nearly survived the Second World War.

Fellow, Lecturer, Tutor, Trinity College, Cambridge
Principal, University College, Liverpool, 1880-1897
Headmaster, Charterhouse School, 1897-1911
Canon, Chelmsford Cathedral, 1918-1945
Gladstone Professor of Greek and Vice Chancellor of Victoria University, Manchester
Educated at Harrow and Trinity College, Cambridge

Characterizations of Rendall: He brought to Charterhouse "high character, spiritual earnestness . . . great industry, wide scholarship, the gift of administration, charm of manner, and a strong belief in athletics." [*The Times*, January 6, 1945.] In the view of his life long friend W. F. Bushell, "It is the charm of manner, and power of conversation I should particularly like to stress in my dear friend of many years. His high standards of life and conduct and his powers of persuasion and conciliation stand out in memory." [*Liverpool Daily Post*, January 10, 1945.]

Oxfordian Books and Pamphlets
    1930   *Shakespeare's Sonnets and Edward de Vere* [Feb.]
    1931   *Shake-speare: Handwriting and Spelling*
    1934   *Personal Clues in Shakespeare Poems & Sonnets*
    1939   *Ben Jonson and the First Folio Edition of Shakespeare's Plays*
    1940   *The "Ashbourne" Portrait of Shakespeare* [Pamphlet]
    1941   *Arthur Golding, Translator – Personal and Literary – Shakespeare and Edward de Vere* [Pamphlet]
    1944   *Shakespeare in Essex and East Anglia* [Pamphlet]

Oxfordian Forwards, Articles, Published Letters (selected items)
    1930   "Shakespeare's Handwriting and Orthography" [letter: Response to Byrne], *Times Literary Supplement*, issue 1495 (Sept. 25): 757.
    1931   "Foreword" to *The Earl of Oxford as "Shakespeare:" An Outline of the Case* by Col. Montagu W. Douglas
    1932   "The Earl of Oxford as Shakespeare" [Review of *The Life-Story of Edward de Vere as Shakespeare* by Percy Allen], *Everyman*, Aug. 25.
    1937   "Shakespeare's Sonnets," *East Anglian Magazine*, vol. 3/2 (Nov.): 74-75.

Memorable Oxfordian Speech
    1930   Toast to Edward de Vere at the first Shakespeare Fellowship dinner (April).

Other Books
    1879   *Emperor Julian*
    1889   *Cradle of the Aryans*
    1892   *Marcus Aurelius, the Stoic*
    1926   *Marcus Aurelius Antoninus to Himself* (translator)

---

[58] H. B. C., "The Case Against Shakespeare," *Manchester Guardian*, May 5, 1930, p. 7.

If Rendall's book did not conclusively establish that Shakespeare "*must* have been a nobleman," it did establish that likelihood. The onus was now on proponents of candidates who were not noblemen to show how their candidate acquired the sensibilities and knowledge that a courtier would have had.

The Christian Science Monitor's review is important for the positive assessment it gave to Rendall's book and because it showed the status of the Oxfordian claim in the middle of 1930.

> Dr. Rendall, we believe, is the first accredited "scholar" to adopt the Oxford theory. He boldly claims both sonnets and plays for de Vere, basing his argument, for the poems, mainly upon the thesis that the sonnets contain indisputable internal evidence that they were written by a nobleman, and that de Vere was the only individual who, at all points, fits the case.

> It is, probably, no exaggeration to say that belief in the Stratfordian authorship of the Shakespearean poems and plays, though still accepted by the vast majority, is rapidly being discarded by inquiring and thoughtful scholars throughout the English-speaking world. . . . [E]ver since the publication in 1920 of J. T. Looney's *"Shakespeare" Identified*, the case for the seventeenth Earl of Oxford as "Shakespeare" has been coming gradually to the front.[59]

This was all too much for Muriel St. Clare Byrne. Her response to the mounting evidence of de Vere's authorship was to defy the common sensical interpretations and the baselines noted above. In her review in *The Times Literary Supplement* she disputed the application of the references to "lameness" in Sonnet 37 to Edward de Vere, writing that "there is no jot of positive proof" that he was lame, something she would not have written had she remembered (or perhaps actually read) Capt. Ward's *The Seventeenth Earl of Oxford*, which she had reviewed two years earlier. She also rejected the inapplicability of the references to "vulgar scandal" in Sonnet 112 to the man from Stratford, writing that "We cannot prove that there was no vulgar scandal ever attached to Shakespeare." A more open-minded approach would have acknowledged that although it is impossible to prove a negative, the extensive documentation of the life of William Shakspere compiled by J. O. Halliwell-Phillipps, Sir Sidney Lee and others comes close to doing so, as their work revealed no hint of lameness or vulgar scandal in his life.

Byrne also challenged the pun on de Vere's name in Sonnet 76, writing that,

Reviews of Gerald H. Rendall's		
Shakespeare's Sonnets and Edward de Vere (Feb. 1930)		
February 27, 1930	--	*Dundee Courier and Advertiser*, p. 10.
March 6, 1930	--	*Scotsman*, p. 2.
March 24, 1930	--	*Aberdeen Press and Journal*, p. 2.
April, 1930	--	*English Review*, pp. 520-21.
April 1930	Col. B. R. Ward	*Shakespeare Pictorial*, No. 26: 16.
April 20, 1930	H. I. Brock	*New York Times*, p. 56.
May 5, 1930	H. B. C.	*Manchester Guardian Weekly*, p. 7.
May 11, 1930	Stephan Gwynn	*Observer*, p. 7.
May 22, 1930	Muriel St. Clare Byrne	*Times Literary Supplement*, p. 430.
	Response by Rendall, May 29.	
July 19, 1930	--	*Christian Science Monitor*, p. 6.
Aug. 1930	Georges Connes	*Revue Anglo-Américaine*, vol. 7/6: 549-50.

---

[59] "De Vere as Shakespeare," *Christian Science Monitor*, July 19, 1930, p. 6.

It is equally the case with 76, which to the convinced Oxfordian provides positive proof in the shape of a punning signature:

> Why write I still all one, E.Ver the same,
> And keep invention in a noted weed,
> That EVERY word doth almost tell my name.

> The possibility of the pun upon E. Vere is patent; but as the lines fit perfectly into their context, in which the writer apologises for his old-fashioned writing, it is still only a possibility, not a proof.[60]

That was too much for Rendall, who wrote in response that,

> As regards the wordplay in

> EVERY word doth almost tell my name,

> your reviewer admits, I think, suggestive coincidence, though [s]he does not refer to the support I have adduced from De Vere's own poems, and other writers. And it is no small matter that it redeems the line, and even the sonnet, from apparent futility. My critics are bound to demur, because if accepted it is conclusive.[61]

He went on to show how convincingly the evidence being compiled by Oxfordian researchers made their case.

> The best critics have allowed and affirmed literary unity of authorship; but no previous writer has tried to trace and uphold personal unity of plot and development. On the background of William Shakespeare the attempt seems to be impossible, and one must fall back upon inexplicable dramatic fictions. But on the background of Edward de Vere things fit into their place with astonishing and almost unimaginable propriety. The links between the *Sonnets* and the poems assume a new significance, and I should have welcomed considered criticism of the interpretations I have put on them.

Shakespeare's Sonnets and Edward de Vere impressed Col. Ward so much that he invited Rendall to speak at the Shakespeare Fellowship's first annual dinner on April 12, 1930 (see Chapter 9). The book also impressed Sigmund Freud, founder of psychoanalysis, who recommended it in 1932 to Dr. Flatter, who had sent him a translation of the *Sonnets* (apparently into German).

> There are no doubts any longer about [the *Sonnets'*] serious nature and their value as self-confessions. The latter point is, I think, accounted for by the fact that they were published without the author's co-operation and handed on after his death to a public for whom they had not been meant.

> There lies in front of me a book—*Shakespeare's Sonnets and Edward de Vere*, by Gerald H. Rendall. . . . In it the thesis is put forward that those poems were addressed to the Earl of Southampton and were written by the Earl of Oxford. I am indeed almost convinced that none but this aristocrat was our Shakespeare. In the light of that conception the *Sonnets* become much more understandable.[62]

Freud had read *"Shakespeare" Identified* around 1923 and again in 1928, and had expressed his enthusiasm for the Oxfordian idea to his friend and colleague Ernest Jones

---

[60] Muriel St. Clare Byrne, 'De Vere and the Sonnets," *Times Literary Supplement*, May 22, 1930, p. 430.

[61] Gerald H. Rendall, "Shakespeare Sonnets and Edward de Vere," *Times Literary Supplement*, May 29, 1930, p. 457.

[62] Sigmund Freud, letter to Dr. Richard Flatter, Sept. 20, 1932, quoted from Richard Flatter, "Sigmund Freud on Shakespeare," *Shakespeare Quarterly*, vol. 2, No. 4 (Oct. 1951): 369.

as early as 1926.[63] He did not publicly express his doubts about William Shakspere's authorship until 1930, after Rendall's book was published. On March 23 he wrote to psychoanalyst Theodore Reik that "I have been troubled by a change in me . . . I no longer believe in the man from Stratford."[64] In his speech accepting the Goethe Prize on August 28, 1930, he stated that "It is undeniably painful to all of us that even now we do not know who was the author of the Comedies, Tragedies, and *Sonnets* of Shakespeare; whether it was in fact the untutored son of the provincial citizen of Stratford, who attained a modest position as an actor in London, or whether it was, rather, the nobly-born and highly cultivated, passionately wayward, to some extent *declassee* aristocrat Edward de Vere."[65] In the same year "he added a footnote to the new edition of *The Interpretation of Dreams* stating that he had 'ceased to believe that the author of Shakespeare's works was the man from Stratford.'"[66]

In a letter to James S. H. Bransom dated March 25, 1934, Freud, as recounted by Bransom, "related Lear's three daughters and the relative dates of their marriages to Oxford's three daughters and the dates of their marriages; he described *King Lear* as a play symbolically compensating for the fact that Oxford was a wretched father. If Oxford was Shakespeare, Freud said, he had suffered the miseries of Othello, too. Freud accepted the identification of Lord Derby, Oxford's first son-in-law, as Albany in *Lear*. . . . He went on to deduce from the discrepancy between dates of publication and performance on one hand and the date of Oxford's death (1604) on the other, that 'the poet did not finish one play after another,' but worked on several at once, so that when he died he left several unfinished. These, Freud concluded, were finished by friends" (58).

Freud publicly mentioned J. Thomas Looney again in 1935, in *An Autobiographical Study*:

> I no longer believe that . . . the actor from Stratford was the author of the works that have been ascribed to him. Since reading *"Shakespeare" Identified* by J. Thomas Looney, I am almost convinced that the assumed name conceals the personality of Edward de Vere, Earl of Oxford. . . . The man of Stratford seems to have nothing at all to justify his claim, whereas Oxford has almost everything.[67]

In 1938, Looney wrote to Freud to welcome him to England after his escape from Austria following the Nazi takeover of that country. Freud wrote back, expressing admiration for Looney's "remarkable book, to which I owe my conviction about Shakespeare's identity, as far as my judgment in this matter goes."[68]

Shakespeare's Handwriting

Gerald Rendall took up the challenge made by Muriel St. Clare Byrne that, in order to be taken seriously, Oxfordians were required to "disprove all the evidence which has been steadily accumulating" showing similarities between Shakespeare's signatures in his will with the handwritten passages by Hand D in the manuscript of the play *Sir Thomas More*.

---

[63] Norman N. Holland, *Psychoanalysis and Shakespeare* (1964), p. 56.

[64] Sigmund Freud, letter to Theodore Reik, March 23, 1930, quoted in Norman N. Holland, *Psychoanalysis and Shakespeare* (1964), pp. 56-57.

[65] Freud was ill and unable to attend the Goethe Prize ceremony; his remarks were read by his daughter.

[66] Norman N. Holland, *Psychoanalysis and Shakespeare* (1964), 57.

[67] Sigmund Freud, *An Autobiographical Study* (1935).

[68] Freud's letter is quoted in A. Bronson Feldman, "The Confessions of William Shakespeare," *American Imago*, vol. 10/2 (Summer 1953): 165.

In a letter published in *The Times Literary Supplement* only two weeks later, Rendall demolished "all the evidence."

> In your notice of Mr. P. Allen's volume on *The Case for Edward de Vere* your reviewer closes with a challenge on the question of handwriting. Oxfordians, he holds, are not entitled to so much as a hearing till they have disproved the inference drawn from "the thesis of Shakespeare's hand in *Sir Thomas More*." Till then they are "shirking a crux that is fundamental," and "flogging a dead horse." Hand D occupies a supplementary section (one of five) in a play by Anthony Munday. The attribution to Shakespeare is purely conjectural, and to myself far from convincing. For the handwriting of William Shakspere no data exist, except the six scrawled signatures, which bear a very distant resemblance to the features of Hand D, and so far as they go seem adverse to identification. I am amused at the assurance with which high authorities build upon foundations so shallow.[69]

After a careful study of handwriting, spelling and punctuation in Hand D, the *Sonnets* and Shakespeare's signatures, Rendall closed with,

> I have now touched all noticeable points in the autograph letter, and it is hardly too much to say that every turn and habit of writing characteristic of De Vere finds counterparts in Q [Hand D]; and that careful collation and comparison compels the conclusion that the autograph text of the *Sonnets*, in almost every particular of script and spelling, conformed to the pattern of Edward de Vere. In Sir E. M. Thompson's monograph no case comparable to this is even suggested.

As Col. Ward perceived, "It must have been a severe blow to [Byrne] to read in the issue of 25th September a long letter from one of our members, Canon G. H. Rendall, B.D., Litt.D., L.L.D., not only pouring scorn on the thesis of *Shakespeare's Hand in 'Sir Thomas More,'* but bringing forward tests from handwriting and orthography which completely justify the hypothesis that the manuscript supplied to the publisher of *Shake-speare's Sonnets* in 1609 was in the handwriting of Edward de Vere."[70]

After such a devastating response to her challenge—and after having reviewed the five most important Oxfordian books published in recent years—Byrne never addressed the authorship issue again. *Vanquished* is perhaps an apt word to use to describe her status after having tangled with two of the most extraordinary men carrying forward the Oxfordian banner.

The story didn't end there. Rendall expanded his findings and published them in book form as *Shake-speare: Handwriting and Spelling* the following year. "Accumulating evidence, direct and circumstantial, points to the de Vere authorship of the Shakespearean Plays and Poems."[71] Tradition has assigned authorship to William Shakspere, but "tradition, upon scrutiny, amounts to little more than passive acceptance of a title-name. Against it is arrayed an imposing body of *testimonia*, and behind them a throng of evidences—internal, literary, topical, and biographical—which converge with singular unanimity upon the person of Lord Edward de Vere, Seventeenth Earl of Oxford." He laid out in detail not only the steps in his careful examination of the relevant texts, but also the care with which he considered the reasoning and conclusions reached by other

---

[69] Gerald Rendall, "Shakespeare's Handwriting and Orthography," *Times Literary Supplement*, Sept. 25, 1930, p. 757.
[70] Col. Bernard R. Ward, "A Challenge and Its Acceptance," *Shakespeare Pictorial*, Dec. 1930, p. 16.
[71] Gerald H. Rendall, *Shake-speare: Handwriting and Spelling* (1931), p. 5.

scholars on these issues. He concluded that,

> Investigations of this kind are necessarily tedious in detail, yet they are not unimportant, if they establish [as they do] the conclusions:
>
> (1) That the autograph manuscript from which the Quarto text was built, possessed the determining characteristics, and many of the individual habits and peculiarities of the handwriting and spelling of Edward de Vere.
>
> (2) That in vocabulary, sentiment and turns of speech, the Earl's epistolary manner shows marked and arresting affinities with those of the *Sonnets*.
>
> Such implications take their place among the most crucial tests of origin and identification.

Col. Ward, in his review of the book, noted that "Dr. Rendall is to be heartily congratulated upon having made one of the most scholarly and convincing contributions ever put forward towards the solution of the Shakespeare Mystery."[72] The review in *The Times Literary Supplement* was very different, as should be expected; its author was W. W. Greg, the editor of the book that Rendall's work had countered.[73] Greg's review dealt almost entirely with whether spellings in the Hand D segments of *Sir Thomas More* were unique to Edward de Vere, and whether "misprints" in the *Sonnets* might have been a more logical explanation than attempts to understand de Vere's handwriting. Missing was any recognition of the absurdity of claiming similarity between William Shakspere's crabbed signatures on his will— which many scholars believe were written not by Shakspere, but by a scribe—and Hand D.[74]

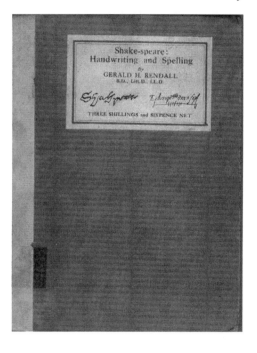

Personal Clues in Shakespeare Poems and Sonnets (1933)

In *Shakespeare Sonnets and Edward de Vere*, Rendall had restricted himself to consideration of the first 126 sonnets. In *Personal Clues in Shakespeare Poems and Sonnets*, he broadened his examination to include all the works mentioned in the title, as he "concentrates upon the personal clues in the poems and the *Sonnets . . .* which associate

---

[72] Col. Bernard R. Ward, "Oxford's Handwriting," *Shakespeare Pictorial*, April 1931, p. 63.

[73] W. W. Greg (editor), *Shakespeare's Hand in the Play of Sir Thomas More; Papers by Alfred W. Pollard, W. W. Greg, E. Maunde Thompson, J. Dover Wilson and R. W. Chambers* (1923).

[74] Sir Sidney Lee would have disagreed with Greg, et. al. He had written in *A Life of William Shakespeare* (1922) that "The extant authentic relics of Shakespeare's penmanship consist solely of six signatures, together with the two words, ' By me,' . . . This material is too scanty to offer positive marks of identification. Elizabethan handwriting—such as the native English script in which all parts of the Harleian manuscript are written—runs, moreover, in a common mould which lacks clearly discernible traces of the writer's individuality. In the absence of trustworthy external testimony, doubt attaches to any purely paleographical deduction" (xiii).

them conclusively with Edward de Vere, 17th Earl of Oxford."[75] The *Sonnets*, he believed, were "veiled or unconscious biography," and could tell us much about their author's life and personality, which in turn would provide a deeper understanding of the literary works.

The most interesting review of *Personal Clues* was by H. B. Simpson (the same H. B. Simpson who wrote the important article published in *The Nineteenth Century And After* back in 1917 discussed in Chapter 1), in which he stated his agreement with Rendall's conclusions. "Dr. Rendall shows in precise and scholarly language why it is impossible to believe that the *Sonnets* were written by the actor-manager from Stratford, and why the 17th Earl of Oxford is the most likely author."[76]

Simpson made a statement for which all Oxfordians should be grateful:

> Shakespeareans who believe that "Shake-speare" was the *nom de plume* not of the Stratfordian known as Shakspere who was living when *Shake-speare's Sonnets* were first published, but of Edward de Vere, "our *ever-living* poet," who died in 1604, find no difficulty in understanding. . . .

The reason for gratitude is that Simpson referred to Oxfordians not as a breed apart, but as *Shakespeareans*, persons just as fully "Shakespearean" as those who believe that William Shakspere was Shakespeare. Simpson recognized that Oxfordians' work is often more in line with evidence, less speculative, more tightly reasoned and their findings more correct than the work of those often referred to as orthodox scholars. He closed his piece by commenting that "The question of authorship is of supreme importance; and it is disappointing to find the editor [of a new edition of the *Sonnets*] not only ignoring the Oxford authorship, but also failing to provide the reader with any of the material necessary for forming an opinion thereon."

Reviewing Rendall's book for *The Times Literary Supplement*, Harold H. Child dedicated most of his space to suppositions and irrelevancies without giving readers much sense of what the book was about, let alone giving them any idea of the grandeur of Rendall's writing, the sweep of his knowledge of the Elizabethan era or the persuasiveness of his evidence and reasoning. Child noted that "one of his [Rendall's] arguments for the high birth and breeding of the author of the plays is that in the Histories 'the plots and dramatic interest centre about the persons of Kings and Queens, noblemen, dignitaries and officers of state.'" He asked, "What other sort of history could Halle or Holinshed offer to a dramatist in search of a plot?"[77] By citing only "one of his arguments," and by failing to mention the predominance of royalty and courtiers in the Comedies and Tragedies as well as the Histories, Child set up a straw man and successfully set it afire. But he had not touched the depth or persuasiveness of Rendall's book; he had only shown the bankruptcy of ideas of Stratfordian scholars such as himself.

---

[75] Gerald H. Rendall, *Personal Clues in Shakespeare Poems and Sonnets* (1934), p. 20.
[76] H. B. Simpson, "Shakespeare's Sonnets," *Shakespeare Pictorial*, February 1935, p. 32.
[77] Harold H. Child, "Oxford's Sonnets," *Times Literary Supplement*, March 28, 1935, p. 203.

9

The Oxfordians, 1929-1936, II: Activities and Publications

Eva Turner Clark

It was not only in England that giants walked the earth. Eva Turner Clark, an American Oxfordian, appeared seemingly out of nowhere with a book that established her overnight as a serious scholar of the Oxfordian claim. Her book was published first in London, by Cecil Palmer in 1930, under the title *Shakespeare's Plays in the Order of Their Writing*. It was released the following year in New York by W. F. Payson under the title by which it is better known today, *Hidden Allusions in Shakespeare's Plays*.

Clark would publish several other important books and more than forty articles during the 1930s and 1940s; she would be the driving force behind the founding of the American branch of the Shakespeare Fellowship at the end of 1939. Her book *The Man Who was Shakespeare*, published in 1937, brought the Oxfordian idea to the attention of many American readers at a time when *"Shakespeare" Identified* had been out of print in the United States for a decade and when Capt. Ward's *The Seventeenth Earl of Oxford* was not available for purchase. Her articles, published mostly in the *Shakespeare Fellowship News-Letter* (American branch), presented the results of original research into new topics or added important context to subjects others had already explored. She gave at least two important speeches: one introduced Percy Allen to members of the Colony Club in New York City in the fall of 1936; the other was given before the Browning Society of San Francisco in February 1942.

Hidden Allusions in Shakespeare's Plays

Eva Turner Clark's most important book, *Hidden Allusions in Shakespeare's Plays*, presents allusions to contemporary events and people found in each of the plays. She had begun by drawing on the records of the Court Revels—the record of theatrical performances in Queen Elizabeth's court. Matching titles and descriptions of plays found there with those of Shakespeare's, Clark developed a chronology for the plays that placed most of them about seventeen years earlier than traditional accounts: from the early 1570s to the early 1590s, rather than from about 1590 to 1610 as assumed by Stratfordian scholars. She then searched through the records and historical accounts of those earlier times, where she found so many personalities and events resembling characters and events in Shakespeare's plays that she needed 693 pages to describe them.

"Shakespeare's plays must be studied from this standpoint," that they are indeed the abstracts and brief chronicles of their time. "Lord Oxford filled them with contemporary references and from them the date of writing of the plays may be established. A study of them from this standpoint will throw a new light on the history of the Elizabethan period."[1] Clark's chronology directly supported the Oxfordian claim, as Oxford was the only authorship candidate for whom these earlier dates made sense. Born in 1550, he was thirty years old in 1580; Bacon and William Stanley, 6th Earl of Derby were only nineteen, and William Shakspere only sixteen.

Her findings, echoing to a large extent those of Adm. Hubert H. Holland though reached through a different process, laid the foundations for a new understanding of the Elizabethan era, the conditions in which the plays were written and the audiences for whom they were first performed.

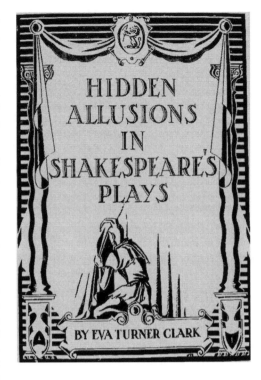

> In Queen Elizabeth's time, when London had a population under 200,000, the Court circle for which Lord Oxford wrote was composed of a few families more or less closely related. That circle, great and glorious as it then was and as it still appears in historical perspective, can be well visualized today if we think of it as a glorified country-house party, isolated from the rest of the world, among the members being an author who suggests theatricals as a means of passing the time, and in order to give zest to the plays, burlesques and satires the follies and foibles of many of those present, not even sparing himself. That this practice of alluding to contemporaries was sometimes carried surprisingly far seems to have been due to the fact that it amused the Queen.[2]

In his review Percy Allen made clear the revolutionary effect of this new understanding of the plays and their authorship. On the issue of why Shakespeare had never been arrested when so many other dramatists had been, Allen commented that "her retort might have run somewhat thus: 'Assume, instead, the Oxfordian authorship, and this mystery, in common with others, is solved; since the Earl, who again and again personifies himself in the Shakespearean characters, is referred to in *Twelfth Night* by Olivia (Elizabeth) as a privileged court jester (the clown, Feste), there being no slander in an 'allowed fool.' This 'allowed fool' is none other than Shakespeare (de Vere) himself, the audacity of whose allusions, in common with the immunity permitted to them, both arose from the fact that they amused the queen."[3]

Allen had no doubt that Clark's conclusions were correct: "The deeply significant fact is, that Colonel and Captain Ward, Mrs. Clark and I, working without collusion, and along wholly different lines of approach, have reached fundamentally identical conclusions." Reviewers at several smaller American papers tended to accept Clark's methods and

---

[1] Eva Turner Clark, *Shakespeare's Plays in the Order of Their Writing* (1930), p. 476.
[2] Eva Turner Clark, *Hidden Allusions in Shakespeare's Plays* (1930), preface [unnumbered page].
[3] Percy Allen, "The Oxford Theory Again" [review of *Hidden Allusions* by Eva Turner Clark], *Christian Science Monitor*, Feb. 28, 1931, p. 6.

findings. *The Evening Union* in Springfield, Massachusetts found that "The book is not only valuable in the theory it tracks to ground so unerringly, but as a textbook it belongs in every classical library of any importance. It is, in addition, a fascinating piece of reading."[4] In the opinion of *The News Leader* in Richmond, Virginia, "The book is free of sensationalism and is an honest and sincere study. . . . The merit of the thesis is a matter to be wrangled over by experts, but even if it is all wrong there are some uncanny parallels between the life of the man who wrote the plays and the life of Edward de Vere, seventeenth Earl of Oxford."[5] The reviewer for *The Philadelphia Public Ledger* noted that "If we are to believe Eva Turner Clark's *Hidden Allusions in Shakespeare's Plays*, there is hardly a line which has not some contemporary meaning, and hardly a character who cannot be identified with some personage of the day. It is from these allusions, which she interprets in fascinating manner, that she adds her contribution to the theory that the real author of Shakespeare's plays was Edward de Vere, seventeenth Earl of Oxford. . . . It is a surprisingly logical argument that Shakespeare never wrote the plays which bear his name."[6]

For some Shakespeare scholars it was, once again, too much to absorb. Hugh Kingsmill wrote that "one is surprised to learn that the plays of Shakespeare are merely a series of comments on such contemporary events as interested the Earl of Oxford." Note the word *merely*, which mischaracterized Clark's findings. He then ridiculed her work

---

Eva Turner Clark

Born: 1871. Died: April 1, 1947.
Age when *"Shakespeare" Identified* was published: 49

Founder and Vice President, American Branch of the Shakespeare Fellowship; served as editor of its *News-Letter* during the year that Charles Wisner Barrell served in the Army during the Second World War.

Corresponded extensively with J. Thomas Looney and organized the New York segment of Percy Allen's 1936 speaking tour of the east coast of North America.

Books
1926	*Axiophilus, or Oxford Alias Shakespeare*
1930	*Shakespeare's Plays in the Order of Their Writing* [Published in the United States as *Hidden Allusions in Shakespeare's Plays*]
1933	*The Satirical Comedy: Love's Labour's Lost*
1937	*The Man Who Was Shakespeare*

Articles and Letters (About 40 pieces, mostly in the *SF News-Letter* and *Quarterly*)
1939, Dec.	Introduction to the Shakespeare Fellowship, American Branch
1940, Feb.	Shakespeare Read Books Written in Greek
1940, Apr.	The Date of *Hamlet's* Composition
1940, Aug.	The Painting in Lucrece
1940, Oct.	Topicalities in the Plays
1942, April	Lord Oxford as Shakespeare [A paper read at the Browning Society]
1943, Oct.	Cryptic Passages by Davies of Hereford
1944, Jan.	Stolen and Surreptitious Copies
1945, Jan.	Lord Oxford's Shakespearean Travels on the European Continent
1945, Oct.	Lord Oxford's Letters Echoed in Shakespeare's Plays
1946, Oct.	Shakespeare's Strange Silence when James I Succeeded Elizabeth

---

[4] *Evening Union*, Springfield, Mass, quoted in *Shakespeare Pictorial* ad, Dec. 1931, unnumbered page.
[5] *News Leader*, Richmond, Va., quoted in *Shakespeare Pictorial* ad, Dec. 1931, unnumbered page.
[6] *Philadelphia Public Ledger*, quoted in *Shakespeare Pictorial* ad, Dec. 1931, unnumbered page.

without attempting to show where her evidence or reasoning was flawed. "Perhaps three hundred years from now, some American lady will discover that Joseph Chamberlain under the nom de plume of Thomas Hardy portrayed President Kruger as . . . Jude the Obscure."[7] The reviewer in *The New York Times*—Stanton Coblante, who wrote more than forty books of fiction and nonfiction—took a similar tack, writing that if Shakespeare were to return to earth "there would be few things to raise him to more ironic mirth than the labors of those who would identify him with the Earl of Oxford and who believe that the name of 'Shakespeare' was used merely as a smoke screen to protect this noble author."[8]

The reviewer for the *Philadelphia Inquirer*, after noting that "Oxford's activities as playwright and producer are unquestioned" and that "Mrs. Clark's inspection of each play, with copious quotation and an array of circumstantial evidence, makes interesting reading for Shakespeare students," expected that "[t]he great majority, will still think with reverence of a spot in Stratford-on-Avon. To overturn that feeling would be tantamount to uprooting a religion."[9] *The Northern Whig and Belfast Times* believed Clark's theory to be "built on the fallacy that the great tragedies are not what they seem—the dramatic representation of the great passions, love, hate, ambition and jealousy, where 'battle, murder and sudden death' are inevitable events, but a strange patchwork of concealed references to events in the life of the playwright or in the outside world of politics,"[10] without considering that they might be both.

In a long review for *The New York Herald Tribune*, Samuel C. Chew cited some of Clark's more questionable findings before concluding, "Not all Miss [sic] Turner's parallels are so silly as these, but all are forced and unconvincing. Her book is a labor of love, but love's labor is lost. Oxfordians will presumably go the way of Baconians, and nothing can more effectually hasten their departure than such a monument of misguided ingenuity as this."[11]

Reviewer D. Willoughby, however, believed that Edward de Vere, apart from Shakspere, "appears today to be the most formidable claimant. The Oxfordians have at least a fighting case" and "Mrs. Clark's new Shakespearean chronology should have attention. It is an arresting fact that publication of the plays ceased with Oxford's death, and was resumed exactly when his widow disposed of the house in which he had lived at Hackney." He accepted the validity of Clark's approach and called for more.

> Though too much can be made of them, allusions to contemporary events, as cited by the Oxonians, are a trail to be pursued without that loss of intellectual self-respect entailed in hunting ciphers with the Baconian pack.
>
> Oxford's life is a rich field to be exploited, and chapter after chapter of his biography can be paralleled in the plays. Assuming his authorship, half the most baffling Shakespearean riddles can be answered. . . . Mrs. Clark, Mr. Allen, and others have amassed a multitude of facts by patient research. What is now wanted is such a book upon the Earl as Mr. Frank Harris wrote upon the Stratford player."[12] [Allen's *Life-Story of Edward de Vere* would be published ten months

---

[7] Hugh Kingsmill, "Who Was Shakespeare?" *Yorkshire Post and Leeds Intelligencer*, Feb. 10, 1931, p. 6.

[8] Stanton A. Coblante, "Shakespeare as the Earl of Oxford," *New York Times*, May 31, 1931, p. BR17.

[9] S.W., "The Earl of Oxford Also a Candidate for Shakespeare's Crown," *Philadelphia Inquirer*, April 25, 1931, p. 14.

[10] "Anti-Shakespeare," *Northern Whig and Belfast Post*, Feb. 7, 1931, p. 11.

[11] Samuel C. Chew, "Who was W.S.?" *New York Herald Tribune*, March 15, 1931, p. J12.

[12] D. Willoughby, "Who Was Shakespeare?" *Saturday Review*, May 2, 1931, p. 53.

later]

The most amusing review of Clark's book was a short one in the *Chicago Daily Tribune*: "*Hidden Allusions in Shakespeare's Plays* by Eva Turner Clark is a lengthy volume, the result of four years' research which convinced the author that the plays attributed to William Shakespeare were really written by Edward de Vere, 17th Earl of Oxford. She shares with you all her findings. If you, after almost 700 pages, are still unconvinced that's just too bad."[13] Did the reviewer mean that it's "too bad for Clark, that she has not been persuasive enough in convincing you," or that it's "too bad for you if your own limited mental wattage prohibits you from accepting Clark's wealth of examples challenging traditional chronology and understanding"?

Esther Singleton

Eva Turner Clark had learned of Edward de Vere from Esther Singleton, a prominent American author, critic and editor who published more than seventy books on a variety of subjects including *The Shakespeare Garden*, an account of gardens and flowers mentioned in Shakespeare's plays. In 1921 she became one of the earliest American converts to the Oxfordian idea, though that was not widely known at the time. In a document not published until after her death, "Was Edward de Vere Shakespeare?" Singleton attributed her acceptance of his authorship to repeated readings of "*Shakespeare" Identified* and described just how difficult it had been even to consider that anyone other that William Shakspere could have been the author. Merely a mention of the idea had caused her to bristle up instantly, "like quills upon the fretful porcupine. . . . So intolerant was I of the barest hint of any other than the Stratford belief that to relinquish such a fixed idea with all the time-honoured atmosphere that has grown around the Warwickshire lore was not easy.'"[14]

But then, she explained, "a book fell into my hands: "*Shakespeare" Identified* by J. Thomas Looney, published in 1920."

> I opened it with prejudice and deep contempt and antagonism. I had no intention to surrender the William Shaksper of Stratford for any theory. . . . [I arose from my study of it it] amazed, fascinated, and elated. . . . Obscure passages in the plays, read with knowledge of de Vere's authorship and of the details of his life [had become] so clear, so plain, so reasonable, and so delightful. . . . I now pronounce myself a believer in the theory that Edward de Vere, Earl of Oxford, was the author of the great Shakespearean plays.

Singleton's first known "Oxfordian" work was a review of Capt. Ward's *The Seventeenth Earl of Oxford* in 1928. Though neither Ward nor Singleton had mentioned de Vere's use of the Shakespeare pseudonym, her review, in the widely read *Saturday Review of Literature*, helped to bring a new understanding of the Elizabethan era to the attention of American readers.

> On bringing down the curtain Mr. Ward concludes with an epitaph preserved among the Harleian Manuscripts: "Edward de Vere, only son of John, born the 12th day of April 1550, Earl of Oxenford, High Chamberlain, Lord Bolbec, Sandford and Badlesmere, Steward of the Forest in Essex, and of the Privy

---

[13] "Now It Seems de Vere Wrote Shakespeare Plays," *Chicago Daily Tribune*, March 14, 1931, p. 14.
[14] Esther Singleton, "Was Edward de Vere Shakespeare?" *SF News-Letter* (American), vol. 1/4 (June/July 1940): 9-10. This article, dated 1921, was found among Singleton's papers after her death in July 1930 by her sister, Shakespeare Fellowship member Mrs. Fitzroy Carrington.

Council to the King's Majesty that now is of whom I will only speak what all men's voices confirm: he was a man in mind and body absolutely accomplished with honorable endowment."

Happily the truth regarding this most distinguished member of a most distinguished race has at last triumphed over calumny and has been put forward in a book that will rank high both as a biography and as a picture of the Elizabethan period.[15]

Singleton was so enthralled by the Oxfordian idea that she put him into her only novel, written in the final year of her life. *Shakespearian Fantasias* is a delightful romp in which the narrator, a woman from the twentieth century, is magically transported back into the worlds of Shakespeare's plays where she is befriended by many of his most interesting characters. Several of them—Benedick from *Much Ado About Nothing*, Jacques from *As You Like It* and Berowne from *Love's Labour's Lost*—closely resemble Edward de Vere and even quote some of his early poems. Singleton was proud of this book, which she described to Col. Bernard R. Ward as "the best work that I have ever done, and the most original."[16]

The novel apparently charmed Henry Clay Folger, founder of the Folger Shakespeare Library, so much that he purchased at least twenty copies of it for his friends. He was negotiating for the purchase of the original manuscript of the book at the time of his death. She died only two weeks later, and her heirs presented the manuscript to the Folger Library, where it remains today.[17]

The second edition of Singleton's well-known *The Shakespeare Garden* was published the year after her death. It contained an introduction by Eva Turner Clark, her close friend, who described how she first learned from Singleton of *"Shakespeare" Identified* and of Edward de Vere's authorship.

About two years after *The Shakespeare Garden* was published, Miss Singleton said to me abruptly one day, "I don't know whether Shakespeare wrote Shakespeare!" "Bacon?" I queried. "No," she answered, "I've just read a book called *"Shakespeare" Identified as the Seventeenth Earl of Oxford*, and it has shaken my faith in the Stratford man. I don't know what to think." The result of this conversation, which was much longer than outlined, was that I secured a copy of that interesting book. Not only was my orthodox belief in the authorship of the Shakespeare plays shaken by it, but I became so interested in the new theory that

---

Esther Singleton

Born: 1865. Died: 1930.
Age when *"Shakespeare" Identified* was published: 55

Four Important Oxfordian Writings

1921	"Was Edward de Vere Shakespeare?" [Not published until *Shakespeare Fellowship News-Letter* (American), vol. 1, no. 4 (June/July 1940): 9-10.]	
1928	"A Great Courtier" [Review of *The Seventeenth Earl of Oxford* by Bernard M. Ward], *Saturday Review of Literature*, July 21, pp. 1049-51.	
1929	*Shakespearian Fantasias: Adventures in the Fourth Dimension* [New edition, 2019]	
1931	*The Shakespeare Garden* [Second edition] [First edition was 1922]	

---

[15] Esther Singleton, "A Great Courtier," *Saturday Review of Literature*, July 21, 1928, p. 1051.

[16] Esther Singleton, letter to Col. Bernard R. Ward, May 6, 1929.

[17] "The Oxford-Shakespeare Book that Charmed Mr. Folger: Esther Singleton's *Shakespearian Fantasias*," *SF Quarterly*, vol. VII/1 (Jan. 1946): 14.

I began a study of it on my own account. This study led me to the discovery of a key which has, to my satisfaction, more than confirmed the conclusions reached by the author of *"Shakespeare" identified*, the result of this study having been recently published under the title, *Hidden Allusions in Shakespeare's Plays, A Study of the Oxford Theory Based on the Records of Early Court Revels and Personalities of the Times.*[18]

William Kittle's *George Gascoigne or Edward de Vere* (1930)

Often overlooked is William Kittle's *George Gascoigne or Edward de Vere*. Professor of English Literature at the University of Wisconsin, Madison, Kittle was apparently interested in the connections between Gascoigne and de Vere even before Capt. Bernard M. Ward published his work on the subject in 1926. His findings, published in 1930, were the result of eight years of research in the United States and England, including nearly a year and a half in the British Museum Library and Public Record Office in London. His principal aim was to determine which, if any, of the three George Gascoignes known to have lived in or around London from 1542 to 1577 wrote the literary works attributed to a poet of that name. He stated that "no single piece of reliable record or evidence has ever been found to connect any one of the three or more Gascoignes with the Poet of 1562-1577, except Whetstone's *Jest* of October 7, 1577."[19] He concluded, citing many parallel passages in the works of Gascoigne and Oxford as well as thematic links between Gascoigne's poems and Oxford's life, that George Gascoigne was a pen name used by Edward de Vere.

In his review, J. R. Mez wrote that "This astounding book contains such an amount of documentary material about Edward de Vere that it ranks among the most important contributions to the problem of identifying 'Shakespeare.' . . . Mr. Kittle's book is one of the most important contributions to this ticklish problem."[20]

Kittle's second book, *Edward de Vere, 17th Earl of Oxford, 1550-1604*, was published in 1935 and revised in 1942. Copies of those two books (without their covers) were bound together with the manuscript of an unpublished third book in a single hardback volume. It is in the library at Brunel University, in the Uxbridge area of London. On the inside cover is a note by Oxfordian scholar R. Ridgill Trout:

> These three books of notes conform more closely to my own independent research than any other book yet published.
>
> Unfortunately Kittle died before he was able to bring these notes together in the form of a single publication.
>
> 1962 [signed] R. Ridgill Trout

Shakespeare Fellowship Events and Officers

The renewed public and scholarly attention to the Oxfordian claim as a result of the cascade of works by Col. Ward, Capt. Ward, Percy Allen, Gerald Rendall, Eva Turner Clark and others rejuvenated the Shakespeare Oxford Fellowship. One sign of renewed vigor was the first-ever Shakespeare Fellowship Dinner held April 12, 1930. From that time on

---

[18] Eva Turner Clark, "Foreword" to Esther Singleton's *The Shakespeare Garden*, 2nd ed. (1930). The timing stated doesn't quite match up. The first edition of *The Shakespeare Garden* was published in 1922, implying that their conversation, two years later, took place in 1924. Yet Singleton's statement about her new belief is dated 1921.

[19] William Kittle, *George Gascoigne or Edward de Vere* (1930), p. 3.

[20] J. R. Mez, "George Gascoigne," *SF News-Letter*, Sept. 1952, pp. 3-4.

the Fellowship would hold dinners every spring and general meetings every fall. A quick survey shows the issues of concern to Oxfordians at the time and how they changed over the first six years of the 1930s.

First Annual Fellowship Dinner, April 12, 1930

This dinner was the first formal occasion for members to get together socially. Among those attending were Col. Bernard R. Ward, Percy Allen, Ernest Allen, Marjorie Bowen and Gerald H. Rendall.

Colonel Ward, in his welcoming remarks, summarized some of the facts he and Capt. Ward had uncovered and already reported on, including the annual grant of £1,000 a year from Secret Service funds to the Earl of Oxford and the production of national patriotic plays from 1587 to 1600, some later attributed to Shakespeare. Percy Allen proposed a toast to the Fellowship. Gerald Rendall responded with a toast "To the Memory of Edward de Vere," in which he stated that "I believe it is true that heartfelt inspiration comes from autobiographical experience more than anything else, and I think it is true of the sonnets of Shakespeare that they present the soul of Hamlet shaped by the experiences of Edward de Vere."[21] He also expressed his belief that "de Vere stood at the very heart and center of the movements that combined to yield the output of the Elizabethan Age."

> His sympathies, catholic beyond those of other men, brought him into touch, close, personal and intimate, with every school and sect—with the Classical and Academic school of Golding, Chapman, Gabriel Harvey, and Bacon, with the Pastoral and Romantic group of Spenser, Sidney and his Areopagus, with the Euphuist clique of Lyly and Munday, with the exotic strains of the French, and still more the Italian Renascence, and above all with the great Dramatic outburst heralded by the meteoric splendors of Marlowe, and consummated in the dazzling constellations of the literature called Shakespearean. That literature, with growing confidence, we associate with Edward de Vere.[22]

Other guests expressed opinions at variance with the Oxfordian idea, showing how much work remained for the Fellowship and its members. Sir Denys Bray, who had proposed reordering the Sonnets according to his rhyming scheme, stated that he did not see "that it would add to or subtract from the artistic merit of *Macbeth* or *Hamlet* were it proved that Edward de Vere or anyone else wrote them." Mr. Ernest Shortt, Librarian of the Authors' Club, did not think there was any Oxfordian case to answer, and did not believe "that the writer of these plays was a man of extraordinary knowledge.'"[23]

A week later, Col. Ward commented on the dinner in a letter to Gerald Rendall. "Ernest Allen was witty, but some of it was undoubtedly due to champagne. P.A. [Percy Allen, Ernest's twin brother] was not quite happy about him and somewhat ineffectually tried to put on the sufflamen [brakes]. . . . It was [all] enough to make Marjorie Bowen somewhat 'wild and haggard' by the time she had to make her speech which I thought was not the least happy of the many speeches of the evening."[24] That letter caught the high spirits of the Fellowship's members, meeting in person at last after so many years of written communications. Their optimism would sustain the organization over the coming

---

[21] "Shakespeare's Plays: Edward de Vere and Their Authorship," *Morning Post*, April 14, 1930, p. 5. Also quoted in "Annual Dinner," *Shakespeare Pictorial*, May 1930, p. 16.

[22] Gerald H. Rendall, "1930 Toast to Edward de Vere," *Shakespearean Authorship Review*, No. 15 (Spring 1966), p. 3.

[23] "Shakespeare's Plays: Edward de Vere and Their Authorship," *Morning Post*, April 14, 1930, p. 5,

[24] Col. Bernard R. Ward, letter to Gerald Rendall, April 19, 1930.

decade and through storms not yet visible on the horizon.

Second Annual Fellowship Dinner, April 27, 1931

Col. Ward stated that "the main work of the society is research" and Percy Allen observed that "since last year our case had been very much strengthened, and there was not even a weak link in the ever increasing chain of evidence that bound into one individuality Edward de Vere and William Shakespeare as author of the plays."[25] He also alluded to "the boycott of our publications on the part of London reviewers, one however which he was convinced could not be permanently kept up, and which was in itself a sign of doubt and hesitancy rather than of confidence."

Ernest Allen thanked Cecil Palmer for his willingness to publish Oxfordian books, saying that "no practical progress would have been possible . . . [without] the services of a sympathetic publisher," and Palmer expressed his "determination . . . not to leave the work unfinished, but to see it through to the end."[26]

Third Annual Fellowship Dinner, May 11, 1932

Attendance was the largest ever even though several members, including Col. Ward and Capt. Ward, were kept away by illness. In his report on the meeting, Ernest Allen noted that Percy Allen's speech dealt mainly with Prof. J. Dover Wilson's book, *The Essential Shakespeare*, "published possibly as a counterblast to the recent numerous and important works of the members of the Fellowship, which books, however, and the arguments contained in them, Prof. Dover Wilson makes no attempt to answer."[27] Allen also noted that while Sir E. K. Chambers thought that Shakespeare's plays contain little that was topical, Dover Wilson held the opposite view. "This discrepancy in orthodox opinion naturally evokes critical comment," Allen noted, and he regretted "that there were no Stratfordian authors present. A little discussion . . . under circumstances which would admit of no evasion, might have been particularly interesting."

Gerald Rendall emphasized the aristocratic qualities of the *Sonnets* and "poured scorn upon the idea that a person of the humble origin of Will would have dared to tender impertinent advice to a cultured Earl like Southampton." He also showed "that the writer of at least one of the Shakespearean plays possessed an intimate acquaintance with obscure places and customs in Essex. There is no reason to suppose that such things would have been known to Will. Lord Oxford, on the other hand, had resided in the locality and all these matters would have been clearly within his ken."

Ernest Allen spoke last; he observed that, "The Baconians seem almost as shy as the Stratfordians of stating publicly, or indeed even privately, any definite arguments against the Oxford theory. This timidity in the expression of their opinions is not shared by the members of the Shakespeare Fellowship, whose aim is the discovery and circulation of the truth. The ultimate triumph of their views seems now positively assured." He concluded with an observation on recent reactions, or lack of them, to the Oxfordian claim.

> It would hardly be an exaggeration to say that the dominant note in the evening's discussion was the extraordinary reticence observed by the many opponents of the Oxford theory.

---

[25] "Shakespeare Fellowship," *The Stage*, April 30, 1931, p. 15.
[26] Col. B. R. Ward, "The Annual Dinner," *Shakespeare Pictorial*, June 1931, p. 96.
[27] Ernest Allen, "Annual Dinner," *Shakespeare Pictorial*, July 1932, p. 116.

During the last few years, book after book has appeared upon the subject, some of them written by men of high academic training, such as Dr. Rendall and Prof. Gilbert Slater. The cumulative weight of the arguments contained in these books is enormous, but, so far as he is aware, no single scholar or man of letters has ventured upon any criticism of the theories these books propound. A recent convert, Miss Marjorie Bowen, the famous historical novelist, who was present at the dinner but who did not speak, has latterly called attention to the subject, but so far has not succeeded in inducing anyone to break silence.[28]

Tenth Annual General Meeting, September 8, 1932

A resolution was passed "urging members to do their utmost to secure new recruits for the Fellowship during the ensuing year." It was decided that monthly meetings would be held on the second Tuesday of each month, October to March. Capt. Ward observed that the Oxfordian movement had become worldwide, with members outside the United Kingdom in the United States of America, Canada, Australia, New Zealand, the British West Indies, the Channel Islands, France, Switzerland and Korea.[29]

Illness and Death of Col. Bernard R. Ward

In a letter to Gilbert Standen in November 1932, Col. Ward related how he had been "carried off to a Nursing Home" ten months earlier and that "I am I hope really convalescent at last though able to do very little walking yet."[30] Even in his weakened state, Ward had continued to draft *Shakespeare Fellowship Circulars*. The *Circular* dated June 30, 1932, in which he announced the bankruptcy of Cecil Palmer's company (discussed below), was drafted in pencil (rather than having been professionally printed), giving the impression that he was doing all he could to summon up the strength needed to carry on the Fellowship's business from his bed.

In October 1932 he found the strength to write a lengthy letter to *The Review of English Studies*, which had run two articles making derogatory comments about the Earl of Oxford's character. The *Review* rejected the letter, which was printed in the January 1933 issue of *The Shakespeare Pictorial*, along with Ward's comment that,

> So now we know exactly where we are. It is another illustration of the old proverb: give a dog a bad name and hang him. . . . It is clear that there is still plenty of work to be done by the Shakespeare Fellowship in combating "the current view" as held by orthodox professors and their disciples, and in clearing up some of the many doubtful points still standing unknown in the tragic history of the Earl of Oxford.[31]

Col. Ward eventually returned home, but died on April 30, 1933. Col. Montagu W. Douglas, as president of the Fellowship, announced Col. Ward's death and expressed what an honor it had been to work with him.

> I regret to have to tell you that Col. B. R. Ward, our Secretary, died on April 30th.

---

[28] Ernest Allen, "Annual Dinner," *Shakespeare Pictorial*, July 1932, p. 116.

[29] Capt. Bernard M. Ward, "Annual General Meeting," *Shakespeare Pictorial*, Nov. 1932, p. 180.

[30] Col. Bernard R. Ward, letter to Gilbert Standen, Nov. 18, 1932.

[31] Col. Bernard R. Ward, "A Protest Addressed to the Editor of the *Review of English Studies*," *Shakespeare Pictorial*, Jan. 1933, p. 12-13. Eva Turner Clark expressed similar sentiments in a letter to J. Thomas Looney dated October 6, 1932: "The October number of *The Review of English Studies* came to me this morning and in it I find two gibes at Oxford . . . They are getting alarmed and are giving up ignoring his claims but are fighting by calling names. That means that sooner or later they will have to make a study of the case, getting his side of it instead of his enemies."

He was not only our very capable Secretary, but the Founder and "onlie begetter" of the Shakespeare Fellowship. Attracted by Mr. Looney's arguments in 1920, he collected his friends, myself included, and founded the Fellowship, with Sir George Greenwood as President. Since then, mainly owing to his exertions, it has grown from more to more. He and his son, Capt. B. M. Ward, have been tireless in research; and Col. Ward's literary contributions, notably his book, *The Mystery of "Mr. W. H.",* are second to none in importance. Col. Ward's intellectual powers covered a wide range of subjects. Besides writing many books on military matters, he was a competent poet, his songs included among others, the Regimental Song of the Rifle Brigade, "Colonel Coote Manningham." Poetry was his chief delight, and among the poets "Shakespeare," especially the *Sonnets*, took first place.[32]

Receivership of Cecil Palmer's Company

Cecil Palmer, the publisher of *"Shakespeare" Identified* and many other Oxfordian books, went into receivership in May 1932. From his sickbed Col. Ward sent a *Circular* on June 30 informing members of that development and noting that *"Shakespeare" Identified* was no longer available for purchase. It was not until almost three years later, in April 1935, that Capt. Ward sent out a *Circular* informing members that the book was again available.

With the demise of Palmer's company, Oxfordians no longer had a publisher ready, willing and able to publish works supporting the Oxfordian claim. Percy Allen moved to Dennis Archer, which published his next several books, as did Adm. Holland with his second book, *Shakespeare, Oxford and Elizabethan Times*, published in 1933. Col. Douglas moved to Rich and Cowan for the revised and enlarged second edition of his book, which appeared with a new title, *Lord Oxford was "Shakespeare,"* in 1934.

Palmer was one of many small publishers that went out of business during the Great Depression. He had made money on *"Shakespeare" Identified*, though. It had sold enough copies in England to recoup all expenses (including those connected with his extensive efforts to promote it).[33] Palmer, as Looney's agent, had received royalties for him from the American publisher of the book. Other Oxfordian books, though, did not sell as well and presumably lost money, as noted in a 1923 letter from Palmer to Looney.

> Very many thanks for your letter. I am very glad you like both Colonel Ward's book and Captain Holland's. Both I think should eventually help our case considerably, but it is wretchedly slow work and as difficult as ever to persuade folk to read books on the subject.[34]

The closing of Palmer's business affected Looney directly in two ways. Both resulted from unethical actions that Palmer had taken. The first was that Palmer never paid Looney any of the royalties due him from sales of the book in England, and he also pocketed the royalties received from the American publisher. Just before the closing of the company, Palmer dumped 500 copies of *"Shakespeare" Identified*—sold them off at a cheap price—and pocketed those proceeds, too, thereby defrauding both Looney and his own company.[35]

---

[32] Montagu W. Douglas, "Death of Colonel Ward," *Shakespeare Pictorial*, June 1933, p. 92

[33] That Cecil Palmer had indeed made a profit from *"Shakespeare" Identified* is confirmed in a letter from J. Thomas Looney to Messrs. Field Roscoe and Co., the firm representing the receivers in the Cecil Palmer case, dated Jan. 14, 1933.

[34] Cecil Palmer, letter to J. Thomas Looney, July 3, 1923.

[35] J. Thomas Looney letter to Messrs. Field Roscoe and Co., Jan. 14, 1933.

The second direct effect on Looney was a legal tangle that ensnared him. Cecil Palmer, at the time of the failure of his company, defrauded Looney and other authors—including Eva Turner Clark, who ended up losing all unsold copies in England of her book *Shakespeare's Plays in the Order of Their Writing*—by convincing them to approve what he presented as a financial restructuring of his company but was in reality the shifting of all legal responsibilities from Palmer and his company to a receiver. Looney and the others signed off on the transfer based on fraudulent financial statements presented by Palmer.

After the transfer of ownership to the receiver, the lawyers for the receiver told Looney that all inventory of *"Shakespeare" Identified* would be remaindered—destroyed or dumped—unless Looney himself paid the bills due Palmer's creditors. Looney responded, "First let me refer to the possible sale as remainders of the existing stocks of my books, and the possible legal action for damages which, according to the judgment in the James V. Grant Richard case, would be the normal consequence of such sale." In other words, Looney told the lawyers that they did not have the right to remainder the books, and if they did he would bring an action against them, citing a legal precedent in support of his position. (We know of these events today only because of the cache of Looney's papers found by his grandson early in 2019.)

The January 1934 issue of *Shakespeare Pictorial* had an advertisement for copies of *"Shakespeare" Identified* at "reduced prices." These were not the copies that the receiver possessed and threatened to remainder; they must have been from the 500 copies that Palmer surreptitiously sold off before transferring the company and its assets to the receiver.

The story of what happened to the bulk of Palmer's inventory will be recounted in Chapter 14.

Fourth Annual Fellowship Dinner, May 16, 1933

The event was attended by about thirty members and guests. As reported by Capt. Ward, "The President asked all present to stand in silent tribute to the memory of the late secretary and one of the founders of the Fellowship, Col. B. R. Ward, who died a few weeks ago, after a short illness."[36] Speakers at the dinner included Col. Douglas, Robert Atkins, Gerald Rendall, Ernest Allen and Percy Allen. Capt. Ward's report on Percy Allen's assessment of the spread of the Oxfordian thesis is worth noting.

> Percy Allen's speech was largely reminiscent of recent experiences in pursuit of the theme for which he stands. His enthusiasm for the

MR. LOONEY'S PIONEER BOOKS

Revealing the 17th Earl of Oxford as the true author of Shakespeare's works, are now offered at considerably

REDUCED PRICES.

"SHAKESPEARE IDENTIFIED"
(21/-)
Now 12/6 net.

"THE POEMS OF EDWARD DE VERE,"
(7/-)
Now 3s. net.

The English Copyright Editions are now on sale everywhere, including the United States of America, and may be obtained either through local Booksellers, or direct from the London Agent :—

FRANCIS CLARKE,
THE GOWER BOOKSHOP,
13, Duke's Road, Euston Road,
LONDON, W.C.1.

---

[36] Capt. Bernard M. Ward, "Annual Dinner," *Shakespeare Pictorial*, June 1933, p. 92.

cause, his wide knowledge of the subject and his long experience of public speaking, usually secure for him a ready hearing, and this occasion was no exception. He considers that the Oxford theory is spreading fairly rapidly over the English speaking world, particularly in the U.S.A.

Mr. Allen emphasized the rapidity with which orthodox scholars are shifting their ground on "Shakespeare," and adopting view points which have been hitherto regarded as the exclusive prerogative of their opponents—"stealing our thunder" was the speaker's comment. Amongst other instances he recalled a recent meeting of eminent men of letters, when a certain famous poet spoke on the Sonnets. "I might," said Mr. Allen, "have made the speech myself, the only difference being that I should have mentioned names, whereas no one was actually named by the poet."

Sir E. K. Chambers, who recently referred to the Oxfordians as "persons of small mind," came in for scathing comment. Sir Edmund, apparently, has not the patience to deal with us, but Mr. Percy Allen, no mincer of words when attacked, considered that under the circumstances "patience" or lack of it was hardly the true reason that held Sir Edmund back. (92-93)

Eleventh Annual General Meeting, September 27, 1933

The eleventh annual meeting, about which no details have survived, was followed by a debate on the topic "Whether there is sufficient evidence to show that Queen Elizabeth had a son by the Earl of Oxford." Percy Allen and Capt. Bernard Ward spoke in favor; Gerald H. Rendall and Gerald Phillips opposed. The background to the event and the fallout from it will be discussed in Chapter 10.

Capt. Ward was elected to the position of Hon. Secretary that his father had held, and formally took over the task of preparing the *Circulars* and editing the Fellowship's page in the *Shakespeare Pictorial* that he had been editing since the onset of his father's illness in 1932. A few months later he reported that the Oxfordian and historical interpretations of the plays of "Shakespeare" were beginning to win acceptance in America. He announced that Percy Allen was planning a lecture tour of the United States, and that the first branch of the Shakespeare Fellowship in England had recently been inaugurated, at Hampstead, with Mr. and Mrs. Hamlet Philpot as joint Hon. Secretaries.[37]

Fifth Annual Fellowship Dinner, May 16, 1934

Speakers included Col. Douglas, who reported on a lecture he gave on the Oxford-Shakespeare case in Marseilles, and Percy Allen, who "reported optimistically" that "many who had once scoffed now found it difficult to refute arguments."[38] Percy Allen's report on the year just passed, reprinted in a nearby text box, can serve as yet another marker as to the state of the Oxfordian idea.

Louis T. Golding, an American from Brookline, Massachusetts, attended. He had come to England to honor his distant ancestor, Arthur Golding, Edward de Vere's uncle and tutor, and the man to whom the Golding translation of Ovid's *Metamorphoses* is attributed. The ceremony, which Louis Golding organized, was held at Belchamp St. Paul in East Anglia on May 22, 1934, and included the unveiling of a heraldic family window with a memorial tablet to his ancestor. Among the speakers at that event was Percy Allen, who spoke on Golding's influence on Shakespeare. Several reports on the event in the local

---

[37] Capt. Bernard M. Ward, "The Other Side of the Atlantic," *Shakespeare Pictorial*, Jan. 1934, p. 4.
[38] Capt. Bernard M. Ward, "Shakespeare Fellowship Dinner," *Shakespeare Pictorial*, June 1934, p. 84.

media highlighted the Oxfordian claim.[39] Louis Golding would go on to write a biography of Arthur Golding that was published in 1937.

Sixth Annual Fellowship Dinner, May 13, 1935

Among the many recent developments noted by Col. Douglas in his opening remarks were that Prof. Clavel of Aix University had become an Honorary Member of the Fellowship, that Douglas's new book, *Lord Oxford was Shakespeare*, was being favorably reviewed by the press, and that the actor Lewis Casson had publicly mentioned his sympathy with the work of the Fellowship in a speech at the O.P. Club to some 300 theatrical people—a "sympathy" resulting from having read Douglas's book.

Percy Allen commented on the many speeches he had given and the reception to them.

> From October to January—when illness compelled me to abandon the course—I gave, also at the Club Room, a series of illustrated talks upon the plays of Shakespeare, interpreted as dramatizations of English, French, and Scottish history—a course which I propose to continue next autumn. Mr. Ernest Allen and myself have also given, during the past season, in London and the provinces, other talks upon the Oxford theory, and upon the historical interpretation of the

---

Percy Allen's Report on Oxfordian Developments in 1933-1934

Since our organization was founded, no single year has been so packed with encouragements as have the twelve months between the annual dinners of 1933 and 1934. Our membership, despite financial depressions, has been steadily increasing . . . A feature of our activities has been the series of successful monthly meetings . . . [at which] debates and discussions have been animated and well sustained. . . .

An important development, during the past year, has been the growth of offshoots from the parent tree, the first of these being the Hampstead Branch of our Fellowship. . . . [A second is] The Richmond Shakespeare Society, which is affiliated to the Shakespeare Fellowship. . . .

The published books, written by the Fellowship, during the period under discussion, include *Shakespeare, Oxford and Elizabethan Times*, by Admiral Holland; *A Reply to John Drinkwater* by Percy and Ernest Allen; *The Plays of Shakespeare and Chapman in Relation to French History*; and *Anne Cecil, Elizabeth & Oxford*, by Percy Allen—all published by Denis Archer. Also an edition of *Shakespeare's Sonnets* by G. W. Phillips, M.A., published by Basil Blackwell. . . .

During the past nine months I have given, in London, a large number of lectures, principally upon the historical interpretations of the plays, . . . An article, by myself, upon this topic, appeared, last April, in part 13 of *Theatre and Stage*.

Turning to the opposition, the verbal attacks which have been made, in my presence, by academic persons, upon the Oxford case in general, and upon myself in particular—together with the subsequent, and usually subdued, demeanour of the person making them—suggest grave doubts concerning the attacker's ability to cope with our arguments. In some instances our adversaries, having neglected to read our books, have shown themselves naively ignorant of the now unanswerable case they must answer.

The press, with certain notable exceptions, including *The Morning Post*, *The Revue Anglo-Américaine* (Prof. Georges Connes) and other newspapers, clings generally to traditional beliefs; but there are signs of a break-away. "Candidus," of *The Daily Sketch*, for example, recently advised all who were interested in the problem to read Mr. Looney's *"Shakespeare" Identified*, and *The Morning Post* quoted Mr. Shaw Desmond's opinion, that the Oxford hypothesis was "steadily undermining orthodoxy."

Percy Allen, "A Year's Results Epitomised," *Shakespeare Pictorial*, July 1934, p. 112.

---

[39] Louis T. Golding, *An Elizabethan Puritan: Arthur Golding* (1937), p. 270.

Shakespeare plays and Sonnets, including two meetings at Oxford, at the residence of our valued members, Mr. and Mrs. Hamlet Philpot. As proof of the growing interest which the Oxford movement is arousing, throughout the country, it is a noteworthy fact that, even when the subjects of my lectures have been non-Shakespearean, the Chairman has invariably made kindly, and courteous, if sometimes hostile, references to the controversy with which the name of the Shakespeare Fellowship is connected. Wherever I speak, I have now come to expect such references, as a matter of course. [40]

Thirteenth Annual Meeting, October 2, 1935

Although details of the meeting are not known, the year's events were summarized elsewhere by Percy Allen, who noted that monthly meetings were held throughout the 1934-1935 year and that speakers included Col. Douglas, Mr. G. F. Holland, Miss Katharine Eggar, and Mr. Ernest Allen. Taking a broad view of the Shakespearean situation, he wrote, "my general expression is, that the ideas for which the Fellowship is becoming known, though making no spectacular headway, are exercising an increasing influence upon the tone of the press, are making swift progress among the more thoughtful spirits, and are rapidly weakening orthodox prestige, throughout the English-speaking world. Another encouraging feature is the supine attitude of the most die-hard section of the academic authorities, faced by arguments which, however strongly they dislike them, they cannot effectively refute."

Annual Meeting, 1936

There is no record of an annual meeting in 1936. Percy Allen was on a speaking tour of North America from mid-September through early December. The crisis within the Shakespeare Fellowship, discussed in Chapter 10, which had been brewing since the summer, burst into the open in October.

Oxfordian Publications, 1930-1936

Members of the Shakespeare Fellowship published a large number of books and pamphlets supporting the Oxfordian cause in the first half of the 1930s. Half a dozen of those not already noted are highlighted here.

Gilbert Standen — *Shakespeare Authorship* (1930)

Although a Baconian at the time he joined the Fellowship in 1923, Gilbert Standen soon became a confirmed Oxfordian. He was an important contributor for three reasons. The first is his book—a thick pamphlet really—titled *Shakespeare Authorship: Summary of Evidence*, which made the case for Oxford and described the major developments in the Shakespeare Fellowship and the Oxfordian movement up to 1930. Describing his own experience in becoming a Baconian and then an Oxfordian, he wrote that "[i]nevitably, to most of us, there comes a period when we must question the authority in charge of the moulding of our minds and ideas, and frequently we find it to be personal and arbitrary in its opinions."[41] His second contribution was an extensive correspondence with Col. Bernard Ward from November 1923 until Ward's death in April 1933, with more than forty letters in each direction. Only two of Standen's letters to Ward survive, but he carefully preserved more than forty of Ward's letters, which provide a unique window into Col. Ward's activities and concerns.

---

[40] Percy Allen, "Our Year's Activities," *Shakespeare Pictorial*, June 1935, p. 93.
[41] Gilbert Standen, *Shakespeare Authorship: A Summary of Evidence* (1930), p. 5

Of greatest value for the Oxfordian community today are the two thick albums of Oxfordian ephemera that Standen compiled, one dated 1922-1929, the other 1930-1936. Their pages are filled with more than 500 Oxfordian items, including many clippings of published articles not available elsewhere. Among them are dozens of the Fellowship columns from *The Hackney Spectator* and the Fellowship page in *The Shakespeare Pictorial*, and dozens of issues of the *Shakespeare Fellowship Circular*—the most complete set known to exist. Also preserved are scores of letters, dinner cards from the Fellowship dinners, and other items of special interest.

Standen's library of Oxfordian books was donated to the Shakespeare Fellowship after his death in 1937. Those books and the two albums are now part of the Archives of the Shakespearean Authorship Trust housed in the Special Collections Room of the library at Brunel University in the Uxbridge area of London.

Gilbert Slater — *Seven Shakespeares* (1931)

The "group theory" of Shakespearean authorship was widely discussed in the 1930s and Gilbert Slater's name is often associated with it. As he explained in *Seven Shakespeares*, he did not mean that the works were written by a committee of seven, but rather that there were "seven out of all the claimants put forward whose claims seem most worthy of consideration. I call them 'claimants' here, though none of them, not even Shakspere, . . . ever made the claim for himself."[42] The "claimants," all closely connected with one another and with the Elizabethan court, are Francis Bacon; Edward de Vere, 17th Earl of Oxford; Sir Walter Raleigh; William Stanley, 6th Earl of Derby; Christopher Marlowe; Mary Sidney, Countess of Pembroke; and Robert Manners, 5th Earl of Rutland.

Slater was an economist and an acknowledged authority at the London School of Economics on the Elizabethan Poor Law and sixteenth century political economy; it was through his work on those subjects that he was drawn into the Shakespeare authorship question. In his view, "Neither the present nor the recent past of English social, political, and economic life can be understood without an understanding of the Elizabethan age; and that on that age the Works of Shakespeare throw a brilliant but also a confusing light. To make that illumination helpful, I find it necessary to form an opinion on the 'Shakespeare Mystery'" (vii).

It would be as wrong for professors of literature "to use a doubtful assumption" as to the author of Shakespeare's works, he wrote, "as it would be for an engineer to use girders which are suspected of flaws without first thoroughly examining them" (viii). To do so would result in a corruption within Shakespeare Studies itself. Of greatest importance to Slater was that a corruption of intellectual findings within Shakespeare Studies would inevitably seep into neighboring fields, corrupting them, which is why he spent so much time and effort examining the authorship question. He had to know whether findings within the Shakespeare field that affected his own fields of economic and social history could be relied on.

> If we can be sure that the "first master" really did belong to the provincial bourgeoisie, and that he did not even have the advantage of a University education, mingling at Oxford or Cambridge with the youth of the nobility, we have a fact of the first importance with regard to the social relations then existing between different classes. But if he did not, we are betrayed into false inferences if we assume that he was.

---

[42] Gilbert Slater, *Seven Shakespeares* (1931), p. xi.

Slater also showed how a misunderstanding of who Shakespeare was could corrupt study of the nature of genius and literary creativity.

> Inferences with regard to the nature of genius have been drawn freely from the case of Shakespeare, argued from the assumption that the traditional theory of his identity is undeniably true, and very little supported by evidence from other cases. The psychologist who works in this particular field cannot afford to ignore the contention that this assumption is unwarranted.

In his investigations into the Shakespeare authorship question, Slater wrote that "I have been privileged to play a part like that of Watson to two of the most unbiased and open-minded of the sleuths on the track of the Shakespeare Mystery, Col. B. R. Ward, the founder and Honorary Secretary of the Shakespeare Fellowship, and his son, Capt. B. M. Ward, the biographer of Edward de Vere" (xii). He also cited as "particularly notable" Looney's pioneering work on the Oxfordian claim and Rendall's on Oxford's handwriting. In examining the various theories of authorship and the evidence in support of them, he "endeavoured to avoid partisanship, and to think and feel as a conscientious judge should, and not as an advocate." "I have expressed my own opinions, but have tried not to press them unduly, but rather to put the reader in a position to form his own judgment" (xiii).

Although Slater, a vice president of the Shakespeare Fellowship for several years, was careful in his book not to express strong support for authorship by any of the seven claimants, he actually believed that the dominant pen was that of Edward de Vere. He made statements to that effect at least twice:

> <u>1931</u>: If I could, I would now present the case against this (Oxford) theory, but I cannot. To the best of my knowledge no reply to the Oxfordians has been

---

Gilbert Slater

Born: August 27, 1864. Died: March 8, 1938.

Age when *"Shakespeare" Identified* was published: 55.

British economist and scholar of economic and social history.

Principal, Ruskin College, Oxford 1909-1915.

Professor of Economics, University of Madras, 1915-1921.

Professor of Economics and Social History, London School of Economics.

Vice President of the Shakespeare Fellowship, 1930-1938.

He was the first to propose that Lady Pembroke (Sidney's sister and Pembroke's mother) must have had a role in the Shakespeare works.

<u>Oxfordian Books</u>

    1931   *Seven Shakespeares: A Discussion of the Evidence for Various Theories*
                    with Regard to Shakespeare's Identity

<u>Oxfordian Articles (selected)</u>

    1934, May   "Shakespeare's Literary Executor," *Shakespeare Pictorial*, no. 75: 80.
    1934, Aug.   "Can We Agree?" *Shakespeare Pictorial*, no. 78: 128.
    1938, March "The Rival Poet of the Sonnets," *Shakespeare Fellowship Newsletter*, no. 8: 1.

published.... [T]he positive evidence in favor of other Shakespeares is, so far as I can see, only sufficient to indicate that they should be included in the list of Oxford's collaborators.[43]

1938: I wish also to say in reply to Col. Douglas that I am not prepared to maintain "that the plays of the Folio were not, even in the main, the work of one man." I think they very likely were, and that Oxford was the man. But whether his contribution was more or less than that of all other contributors put together, cannot yet, I think, be estimated with any confidence.[44]

Seven Shakespeares was reviewed widely and favorably. *The Dundee Courier* stated that "No other book has compassed as much nor has any case for a particular claimant been presented in a form at once so satisfactory to scholars and clear to the average intelligence. Traditional belief must be disturbed by this precis and valuation of what is suggested or asserted on behalf of the Stratford actor-playwright, and Bacon, Edward de Vere, and other stars of magnitude in the intellectual galaxy in which he figured."[45]

The review in *The Manchester City News* could be cited as a model for how a serious, responsible review should be written by one with no special expertise on the authorship issue, just as Slater himself could be viewed as a model to be emulated by scholars in other fields writing on the subject. Noting how Slater found himself confronted with curious facts associated with the Shakespeare dramas, the reviewer judged the opening chapter, dealing with the practical matter of the historical background of the period in which the plays were written, to be "one of the most illuminating of its kind we have ever read."[46] He had the same opinion of the masterly way that Slater "demolishes utterly the case for 'the gentleman of Stratford" and how persuasively he made the case for each of the other claimants. "He simply leaves us overwhelmed," the reviewer wrote, concluding with the "fervent hope that some well-accredited scholar will arise either to prove once and for all that Dr. Slater's arraignment is a monstrous error and illusion, or to avow honestly that at last a definitive case has been established and we know who and what and wherefore 'Shakespeare' was."

In *The Saturday Review*, H. R. W. began with a surprising admission: "[Slater's] conclusion that the plays of 'Shakespeare' . . . were written by a cultured aristocrat, intimately familiar with Court life, who had travelled extensively in Northern Italy and was possessed of a remarkable knowledge of legal proceedings, must be accepted. In other words, he was *not* a tight-fisted, corrupt, small-town merchant."[47] What followed was just what would be expected in *The Saturday Review*: ridicule of every proposed candidate. However, H. R. W. returned to his seeming acceptance that the man from Stratford was not the author. "But who was that much-travelled aristocrat, with a vocabulary of 20,000 words and every recondite legal phrase at his finger-tips, the greatest poet who ever lived? A matchless mystery, and likely to remain so."

Percy Allen used his review to highlight the "Group-Theory of Shakespearean Authorship," which he saw as "gaining ground among the more open-minded scholars,"

---

[43] Gilbert Slater, *Seven Shakespeares* (1931), 205.

[44] Dr. Gilbert Slater, "Correspondence," *SF Newsletter*, no. 8 (March 1938): 12. The letter is undated, but was written after he read the January 1938 issue of the *SF News-Letter*. Slater died on March 8, 1938, which would make that letter one of the last he wrote.

[45] "For the Book-Lover," *Dundee Courier and Advertiser*, Dec. 3, 1931, p. 4.

[46] "The Shakespeare Maze: A Sevenfold Clue," *Manchester City News*, Nov. 28, 1931.

[47] "Seven Shakespeares," *Saturday Review*, vol. 152 (Oct. 31, 1931): 560.

orthodox Stratfordians and Oxfordians alike, "as the only satisfying solution of the otherwise baffling problems presented by the Folio of 1623, in which . . . the presence of many hands, among one master mind, are now indisputably visible. 'Shakespeare,' thus considered, becomes the pen-name of the Group's leader, and principal author, be he William of Stratford, Lord Oxford or Francis Bacon."[48] Capt. Ward was largely in agreement. "The general view seems to be that whereas Oxford was the 'Master Mind,' he collaborated with his cousin Bacon, and his son-in-law Lord Derby; and it may be that some of the unfinished plays by Oxford were completed by one or other of them and others. We do not know. Dr. Slater, and with good reason, would include Ralegh and Lady Pembroke in the group."[49] But, one might ask, how could Oxford have collaborated with his son-in-law, Derby, if the plays were written in the 1570s and 1580s, and William Stanley, 6th Earl of Derby, was only eighteen at the end of the 1580s and didn't become Oxford's his son-in-law until age thirty-three at the end of 1594?

Not to be overlooked is Slater's article "The Rival Poet of the *Sonnets*," in which he made the case for the playwright George Chapman as the Rival Poet—a view that Percy Allen also held briefly. What is most important is not the case made for Chapman but the reminder given of a larger point: "However great Oxford's contribution to the Shakespeare panel may have been, he was not merely—he wasn't even primarily—a playwright. He was also a great nobleman and a courtier."[50] That distinguished Oxford from all other playwrights, and poets, of the Elizabethan age, giving him a perspective shared by no other writer. And, Slater continued, "In that capacity also he had rivals, who probably exercised his mind much more." He went on to propose that Oxford was speaking in sonnet 86 as a courtier, not as a poet or dramatist. The sonnet, as he saw it, was about Oxford's rivalry with Raleigh—in his competition for the Queen's affection, an interpretation perhaps unique to Slater.

It is interesting to consider further how Slater was led into the authorship question. Unlike Looney, who was drawn in by the contrast between the carefree attitudes toward money and commerce expressed in *The Merchant of Venice* and the small-time grasping of the man from Stratford, and unlike Lefranc, who was struck by the naturalness of the presentation of courtly life and attitudes in *Love's Labour's Lost*, Slater's entry was through *Julius Caesar*. He was struck by the contrast between its stilted, stock presentation of characters from the lower classes and the realistic portrayal of working-class artisans in Thomas Dekker's *Shoemaker's Holiday*. The opposite was true of their portrayals of the higher classes; Shakespeare portrayed aristocratic characters with the naturalness of one at home among them, in contrast with Dekker's unconvincing efforts. Slater, like Looney and Lefranc reached the only conclusion toward which the evidence led: that Shakespeare had to have been "a cultured aristocrat intimately familiar with court life."

Col. Montagu W. Douglas — The *Earl of Oxford as "Shakespeare"* (1931) and *The Earl of Oxford Was "Shakespeare"* (1934)

In *The Earl of Oxford as "Shakespeare,"* Col. Montagu W. Douglas, president of the Shakespeare Fellowship, provided a succinct overview of the case for Oxford built on Looney's findings in *"Shakespeare" Identified* and incorporating subsequent discoveries

---

[48] Percy Allen, "As to Shakespearean Authorship," *Christian Science Monitor*, Jan. 9, 1932.

[49] Capt. Bernard M. Ward, response to Gilbert Slater's letter, *SF News-Letter*, no. 7 (Jan. 1938), p. 7.

[50] Gilbert Slater, "The Rival Poet of the Sonnets," *SF News-Letter*, no. 8 (March 1938): 1.

made by other Oxfordian researchers. Douglas issued a considerably amended second edition in 1934, with a slightly different title. It contained much new information on the "Welbeck" and "Ashbourne" portraits, and further evidence regarding the chronology of all the plays and the composition of the later ones. He also added his own hand-drawn illustrations of de Vere country.

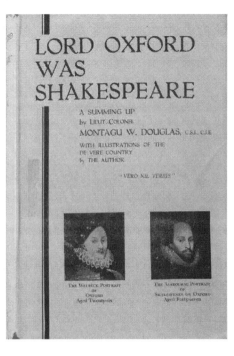

Douglas described *"Shakespeare" Identified* as "invaluable," remarking that Looney "presents the case with unanswerable logic. How conclusive his arguments are may be judged from the fact that no Stratfordian scholar has ever dared to try and refute them."[51]

Graham Sutton, reviewing the book for *The Bookman*, wrote that "Bigots must shun this book—a summary of all the arguments that Shakespeare's plays were written by the seventeenth Earl of Oxford. It is quite short; but it will give them sleepless nights."[52] He expressed doubts about five points—all based on his own misunderstandings—before stating that "on other points, too many to be even summarised here, I find Colonel Douglas unanswerable; and would direct the reader particularly to the following arguments: The cessation of authentic versions of the plays from Oxford's death in 1604 to the 1623 folio, . . . [i]nternal evidence pointing at autobiography [and] the circumstances surrounding the publication of the 1623 folio." He added that the ciphers Douglas included in support of the Oxfordian idea "very nearly shook my faith" in the validity of the rest of the evidence in the book "because they were so unnecessary and so shaky." All in all, this was a fair and favorable review of Douglas's book and of the Oxfordian claim.

A sketch of Castle Hedingham
by Col. Montagu W. Douglas

---

[51] Col. Montagu W. Douglas, *Lord Oxford Was Shakespeare* (1934), p. 190.
[52] Graham Sutton, "Another Theory About Shakespeare," *Bookman*, Nov. 1931, p. 132.

<u>Adm. Hubert Holland — *Shakespeare, Oxford and Elizabethan Times* (1933)</u>

Captain Hubert Holland, who had published one of the first Oxfordian books, *Shakespeare Through Oxford Glasses: Topical Allusions in Shakespeare's Plays,* in 1923, returned in 1933 (as Vice-Admiral Holland) with two more Oxfordian publications. The first, in June, was a review of Percy and Ernest Allen's *Lord Oxford and Shakespeare: A Reply to John Drinkwater*; the second, in October, was *Shakespeare, Oxford and Elizabethan Times.*

In the review, Holland observed that "Mr. Allen has made a considerable impression on the great body of independent opinion that holds no brief for either Oxford or Shakespeare. Whenever I personally meet people intimately connected with the production of the Shakespearean plays I invariably ask them their attitude toward the Oxford controversy. I have not yet met anyone in the professional world of the theater, as distinct from the academic world of the universities, who was not prepared to attach great weight to Mr. Allen's case."[53]

In his new book, Holland again tied allusions in Shakespeare's plays to real-life events, and used them as evidence in considering the authorship question and in establishing a new chronology for the plays. He found, for example, nearly fifty topical allusions in *Hamlet* to events occurring in and around 1583. The reviewer for *The Aberdeen Press and Journal* was thoroughly impressed: "This is definitely the best and most accessible book that has been written on the iconoclastic side of the Shakespearean problem."[54] The reviewer for the *New York Herald* generally agreed. Writing that Holland "presents an exhaustive list of what he terms 'topical allusions' [that] . . . bring the plays back to a time when Oxford was in the full bloom of creative effort and Shakespeare was still a boy. . . . He succeeds in building up an excellent case in favor of Oxford. . . . The book represents a vast amount of study and is certain to be of interest to every student of the problem."[55]

Holland presented some ideas that perhaps few Oxfordians would agree with; one was that Shakespeare's supposed final plays—*Pericles, The Winter's Tale, Cymbeline*, and *The Tempest*—were actually written by William Shakspere of Stratford. F. S. Boas, reviewing the book for *The Observer*, picked up on this idea of two dramatists writing at the same time—Will Shake-speare (alias Oxford) and William Shakspere—and was "curious to see how far the Admiral will be welcomed by the 'hard-shell' Oxfordians to their ranks."[56]

Percy Allen responded quickly. He first commented on points with which he agreed. The results of Holland's investigation are "pitilessly destructive to orthodoxy. . . . Holland reveals, for example, 18 contemporary allusions pointing to 1578 as the date of *Love's Labour's Lost.* . . . Most striking of all, however, is *Hamlet*, wherein our author detects more than 40 allusions of a most convincing kind, all showing with strong cumulative effect, that the tragedy, though afterward more than once revised, must have been drafted during, or close to, 1583."[57]

Turning to areas of disagreement, Allen observed that "[t]o Admiral Holland's thesis that William Shaksper of Stratford penned certain of the later Shakespearean plays, I demur for reasons which appear to me conclusive; but I do not hesitate to say that this

---

[53] Adm. Hubert H. Holland, "Oxfordian Rejoinder," *Christian Science Monitor*, June 17, 1933, p. 10.
[54] "A Plea for Oxford," *Aberdeen Press and Journal*, Nov. 21, 1933, p. 2.
[55] "Shakespeare? Oxford and Elizabethan Times," *New York Herald*, Nov. 1933 [exact date not known]
[56] F. S. Boas, "Shakespeare, Oxford and Elizabethan Times," *Observer*, Dec. 3, 1933, p. 3.
[57] Percy Allen, "Shakespearean Topicalities," *Christian Science Monitor*, Oct. 3, 1934, p. WM10.

book, written admittedly for the student, rather than for the general reader, is one of the most interesting, important and revealing that has appeared in recent years. Its quiet style adds to the effect; and it should be ignored by nobody who would keep abreast of modern Shakespeare research, or who cares really to understand the plays."

Holland became president of the Fellowship, in 1946 and wrote a third book that was never published. It exists only in manuscript, in a notebook marked in faded ink, *Shakespeare, Oxford and Elizabethan Times, II.* It is located in the Archives of the Shakespearean Authorship Trust at Brunel University.

Eva Turner Clark — *The Satirical Comedy: Love's Labour's Lost* (1933)

Eva Turner Clark returned to the fore in 1933 with this book, in which she provided a more detailed analysis of the many topical allusions found in *Love's Labour's Lost* than was possible to include in her earlier book *Hidden Allusions in Shakespeare's Plays.*

The reviewer for the *Cincinnati Enquirer* commented that "Mrs. Clark's analysis is informative, interesting, well written and easy to read," adding that "Mrs. Clark's text makes one want to read the play, *Love's Labour's Lost,* providing a large print edition is readily available and there is nothing more exciting to do."[58] There were no mixed messages from the reviewer for *The New York Herald Tribune,* who wrote that although Oxfordians "will doubtless endorse this new monograph as an important contribution . . . no recognized authority on Shakespeare has been impressed or convinced by the theory that Edward de Vere, Earl of Oxford, wrote the plays. . . . Any student not committed to one or another theory of non-Shakespearean authorship [will be] entirely skeptical of her method and its results."[59]

The reviewer for *The New York Times* accepted that "Miss Clark reveals herself as a past-master at matching actual events of 1578 and the imaginary action of the play," but avoided accepting her attribution of its authorship by speculating that "Shakespeare might very well have had these historical matters in mind when he wrote the play"[60] almost twenty years later. How the man from Stratford would have acquired such an in-depth knowledge of French political and social history—or why he would have bothered to include it in his play—are left unexplained.

Rev. Charles de Vere Beauclerk, S. J.

Oxfordians had done much to show that the prefatory materials in the First Folio and the supposed burial place of William Shakspere at Trinity Church in Stratford were deliberate attempts to present Shakspere as something he wasn't—the writer known as William Shakespeare. A third example of faked evidence were the so-called portraits of Shakespeare. Rev. Charles Sidney de Vere Beauclerk did much work to demonstrate that they had been altered.

OXFORD.   OXFORD. Covered.   "ASHBOURNE."

OXFORD.   "ASHBOURNE" Covered.   "ASHBOURNE."

---

[58] "Love's Labour's Lost," *Cincinnati Enquirer*, May 6, 1933, p. 10.
[59] "Love's Labour's Lost, A Study," *New York Herald Tribune*, May 21, 1933, p. H16.
[60] "Love's Labour's Lost," *New York Times*, May 28, 1933, p. BR15.

Percy Allen, referring to Beauclerk's work, wrote, "Oxfordians are now in a position to demonstrate . . . [that] some half dozen of the best-known portraits of 'Shakespeare' are actually pictures of Edward de Vere, with the dates, in some instances, apparently manipulated, to suit the Stratfordian hypothesis!"[61]

Beauclerk had acquired a number of reproductions of images of the Earl of Oxford and Shakespeare, including the "Ashbourne" portrait, believed to be a likeness of Shakespeare and the "Welbeck" portrait of the Earl of Oxford. By superimposing them, he demonstrated that they were so similar in all key aspects that they were, in fact, images of the same person.

Beauclerk produced similar comparisons between other portraits, copies of which he sent to J. Thomas Looney in the early 1930s. Among them are superimpositions of various combinations of the Ashbourne, Welbeck, Felton, Grafton, Loccaro and Lumley portraits and the Droeshout engraving. His work provided one base from which Charles Wisner Barrell carried the ball forward later in the decade.

Marjorie Bowen

Highly regarded novelist Marjorie Bowen, author of more than 150 books, became an Oxfordian by the end of the 1920s. She was one of the speech-givers at the first Shakespeare Fellowship dinner in April 1930, supplied an "Introduction" to Percy Allen's *The Plays of Shakespeare & Chapman in Relation to French History* in 1934, and wrote important reviews of several other Oxfordian books in the first half of the 1930s.

One of her most important articles, "April 23 Doesn't Impress Me: Why? Because I Don't Believe in Shakespeare," appeared in *Strand Magazine* in April 1946. It shows her understanding of the Oxfordian idea throughout the previous decade.

> I believe [William Shakespeare] was the pseudonym of Edward de Vere, seventeenth Earl of Oxford. . . . I write as the disciple of experts who have spent infinite talent and labour in solving the most remarkable puzzle in literary history. . . . The excuse of the Stratfordians for

---

Marjorie Bowen

Born: November 1, 1885. Died: December 23, 1952.
Age when *"Shakespeare" Identified* was published: 35

British writer whose real name was Gabrielle Margaret Long. Her most noted books were written under the pseudonym Marjorie Bowen, but she also wrote under many other names, including George R. Preedy, Robert Paye, John Winch, Joseph Shearing and Margaret Campbell.

Selected Oxfordian activities and publications

1930, April 12	Speech at first Shakespeare Fellowship Dinner
1932, May	"The Identity of 'William Shakespeare,' *Shakespeare Pictorial*
1933	"Introduction" to Percy Allen's *The Plays of Shakespeare & Chapman in Relation to French History*
1933, April	Review of *Shakespeare* by John Drinkwater, *Shakespeare Pictorial*
1934, March	Review of *Anne Cecil, Elizabeth and Oxford* by Percy Allen, *Sh. Pictorial*
1946, April	"April 23 Doesn't Impress Me: Why? Because I Don't Believe in Shakespeare," *Strand Magazine*, vol. 111: 26.

---

[61] Percy Allen, "As to Shakespearean Authorship," *Christian Science Monitor*, Jan. 9, 1932.

believing in the extreme erudition of an uneducated man of the sixteenth century is that "all is possible to genius." In the case of the Earl of Oxford, the character and the life exactly fit the literary output.... Oxford had the temperament and career of genius.... All his tumultuous longings, fantastical experiences, profound loves and scornful contempts, his shrewd opinions and beautiful visions, all his vast array of accomplishments and massed knowledge, he threw into the plays and sonnets ... in which his life can be followed.... [He was] a manifold genius whom social position could not be reconciled with his art.[62]

Bowen's introduction to Percy Allen's *The Plays of Shakespeare & Chapman in Relation to French History* summarized the status of the Oxfordian claim and academia's response to it up to the spring of 1933. It deserves today to be read in full by anyone interested in the Oxfordian thesis and scholarly reaction to it.

Ernest Allen

Ernest Allen, a barrister of Gray's Inn and twin brother of Percy Allen, was also an Oxfordian. In contrast to Percy, whose Oxfordian work was at the forefront of his activities, Ernest squeezed his Oxfordian activities in around his work as a distinguished lawyer. He was one of the speakers at the first Fellowship dinner in April 1930, and collaborated with his brother on the short book *Lord Oxford & Shakespeare: A Reply to John Drinkwater* (see Chapter 14).

His pamphlet *When Shakespeare Died* (1937) was written, in part, in response to critics who charged that it was fatal for the Oxfordians that their candidate had died in 1604, before many of Shakespeare's plays had been written. He considered relating to the death dates of the three principal candidates for authorship—Will Shakspere in 1616, Francis Bacon in 1626, and Edward de Vere in 1604—and showed that the evidence was heavily in favor of Shakespeare's death in 1604, with the cessation of the steady stream of publication of Shakespeare's plays in that year as one of the strongest indicators. He speculated that Francis Bacon must have had some role in preserving, editing or updating the plays between the death of Edward de Vere in 1604 and their publication in the First Folio in 1623.

The obituary of Ernest Allen in the Fellowship *News-Letter* in 1939 noted that "Like his brother, he became convinced of the soundness of the evidence connecting Lord Oxford with the creation of the plays and poems only after a long period of intensive study. During the past ten years, he had devoted more and more of his leisure to writing and speaking on this subject. A gentleman of energy and enthusiasm, he made many converts to the cause that was nearest his heart, sometimes in unexpected places."[63]

The obituary also described the context for a debate between Ernest Allen and a visiting American scholar on the proposition "Resolved: That William Shakspere of Stratford did not write the plays ordinarily attributed to him." Allen's American opponent later described what happened.

> I have never felt quite so foolish in public before or since.... I was supposed to be the Shakespearean authority with all the facts on my side. But the London barrister "by the name of Allen" with the amateur rating proceeded to riddle my side of the argument before I could get started. I thought I knew the plays, but he even had me there for he had acted in many of them. He quoted a man named

---

[62] Marjorie Bowen, "April 23 Doesn't Impress Me: Why? Because I Don't Believe in Shakespeare," *Strand Magazine*, vol. 111 (April 1946): 26.
[63] "Ernest Stirling Allen," *SF News-Letter* (American), vol. 1, No. 1 (Dec. 1939), p. 6.

Looney I had never heard of and a whole list of other works that I had to admit, put an entirely new light on questions I had been taught to accept as closed to argument. Allen won, hands down, though I've forgotten the official verdict. Anyway, I know when I've had the worst of it.

After the debate, we took supper together and I kept him talking until early morning about Edward de Vere, the literary Lord Chamberlain of England who had lost his good name and social prestige by turning public playwright. No, indeed, I'll never forget Ernest Allen! He gave me an entirely new point of view on the background of the Shakespearean age. And for that I shall always remember him with gratitude.[64]

A Roundup from the American and Australian Press

The following is a survey of articles on the Oxfordian thesis not mentioned elsewhere that appeared in the American and Australian press during the first half of the 1930s. As noted, they tended to be more favorable than those in England.

Oliver Herford, " A Great Peradventure," *San Francisco Examiner* (1933)

Oliver Herford, a writer and humorist based in San Francisco who saw through the fluff presented by traditional Shakespeare scholars, had written a favorable review of *"Shakespeare" Identified* in the summer of 1920. He next surfaced in August 1933, when he destroyed the Stratfordian position in one 190-word sentence in *The San Francisco Examiner*.

> To my mind it is one of the most amazing instances of human credulity that, after it has been, in the opinion of the most advanced 'Shakespeare specialists,' incontrovertibly proved that the plays and poems in question were most of them written by Edward de Vere, the seventeenth Earl of Oxford, so many grown-up people, who ought to know better still cling to the belief that these products of the finest learning, culture, experience and imagination of all time (all *English* time, anyway) are the work of a "Stratford villager" of whose education and culture nothing is known; whose signature was an illiterate scrawl; who knew no language or country but his own; who became an actor in a small way, but had other and more lucrative connections with the theater which in a few years enabled him to return to his "home town" and give his entire time to the buying of land and a coat-of-arms and the selling of malt, and never another thought to the creation [or] production of the plays he was supposed to have written.[65]

Herford continued (thankfully, in sentences somewhat shorter), explaining that "According to J. Thomas Looney, whose great work *"Shakespeare" Identified* set the Oxford ball rolling, the Stratford man had nothing to do with and took no interest in the publication of the *Plays*." In fact, he noted,

> The period of their appearance in [quarto] form corresponds exactly with William Shakespeare's busiest period in Stratford. . . . From that time on the life of the greatest genius in English letters was just one real estate deal and lawsuit after another.

> To the contention that this man of malt and tithes and petty lawsuits was the author and directing genius of the magnificent stream of dramatic literature which in those very years was bursting upon London, the business record just

---

[64] The name of this honorable American scholar was not mentioned. It may have been Dr. W. E. Peck, with whom Ernest Allen debated the authorship issue in Bath on November 7, 1930.
[65] Oliver Herford, "A Great Peradventure," *San Francisco Examiner*, Aug. 19, 1933.

presented would, in almost any court in the land, be deemed to have proved an alibi.

Herford concluded:

"What does it matter?" you ask.
It matters a lot to Edward de Vere's ghost—but peradventure you don't believe in ghosts.
I do.

Australia, 1930-1944

Coverage of the Oxfordian claim in the Australian media was sparse during the 1930s and 1940s.

In its review of Percy Allen's *Case*, *The Age* (Melbourne) wrote that "Mr. Allen . . . would make a much stronger case if he paid more attention to the quality than the quantity of evidence he puts forward."[66] This is a point worth considering. Allen, like Looney, stressed that his argument and his case was cumulative. When he started investigating the authorship question he had noticed the most obvious and most important correspondences between Oxford's personality and life and characters and events in the plays. Investigating further, he found other correspondences not as important, perhaps, but each adding its own particular weight and confirmation to the argument. As Looney had stated, confirming information found after a theory has been formed has a special significance that it would not have had it been discovered beforehand. The danger in presenting every correspondence is, as the reviewer noted, that the most important examples might be obscured. Looney had sidestepped that problem by presenting not just the correspondences, but also the step-by-step process of his search as it took place, noting where in that process each was discovered. Allen, laying out his data in a logical arrangement, was perhaps more likely to overwhelm reviewers than Looney had been.

Another Australian reviewer, reporting on Col. Douglas's book *Lord Oxford Was Shakespeare* in *Truth*, was impressed by the mass of correspondences. "Their ingenuity in hunting out every piece of circumstantial evidence that tells for their client, and making all the pieces fit into each other according to plan, excites my unbounded admiration."[67]

M. J. Carter, in a letter to *The Sydney Morning Herald* in June 1939, alerted readers to eight Oxfordian books of special importance published since *"Shakespeare" Identified* before noting that "one effect of the Bacon theory is to make a number of people unwilling to read anything on Shakespeare authorship. . . . Of those whom I know to have read *'Shakespeare' Identified,* the majority are convinced of the author's success, while all admit the strength of his claim."[68]

In a lengthy piece in *The Age* in April 1944, C. R.. B. gave a favorable view of Oxford and his poetry: "[Some of his poems] reveal a singular beauty, a deftness, a grace and cultivation, flowering in suspected cases in the depths of a dark and troubled soul, and registering a new note on the eternal theme of Love. . . . Here and there the author has penned a line that deserves to go singing down the centuries." Looney's *"Shakespeare" Identified*, he wrote, "was published twenty or more years ago, but it scarcely caused a ripple on the surface of the long-enduring controversy regarding the authorship of the

---

[66] "Shakespearian Problems," *Age* (Melbourne), March 15, 1930, p. 4.
[67] "In Vere Veritas," *Truth*, Feb. 6, 1935, p. 224.
[68] M. J. Carter, "Shakespeare" [letter], *Sydney Morning Herald*, June 17, 1939, p. 13.

works. Nevertheless, the volume is extremely interesting. It reveals extraordinary research, and . . . the cumulative effect of it all is distinctly arresting."[69]

V
J. Thomas Looney in the 1930s – Publications and Correspondence

Although J. Thomas Looney remained a vice president of the Shakespeare Fellowship from 1922 until his death in 1944, he did not attend any of its meetings or dinners. Following his final pieces in The *Hackney Spectator* early in 1924, he did not produce any further writings on the Oxfordian claim for more than a decade—with one exception. At the end of 1932 he wrote an article for *The Atlantic Monthly* in the United States, which quickly rejected it. That article was not known to anyone else at the time other than Eva Turner Clark, who had submitted it on Looney's behalf and who attempted to place it elsewhere afterward.

In 1935 Looney wrote three pieces for the *Shakespeare Pictorial* that brought to public attention puzzles casting doubt on the traditional story of Shakspere's authorship. The first, on Ben Jonson, ran in two parts in the April and May issues; the other two, addressing *The Taming of the Shrew*, appeared later.

In the Jonson piece, Looney highlighted an extraordinary puzzle. Jonson, who supposedly worked side by side with Shakespeare for a dozen years and who supposedly idolized him this side of idolatry, made no comment connecting the author Shakespeare with the man from Stratford in his free and open conversations with William Drummond of Hawthornden—conversations that touched on every other conceivable personality related to the theater. Nor did Jonson express a single thought about Shakespeare at the time of Shakspere's death in 1616, even though Jonson was a recognized master of obituary and complimentary verse. "Except in this connection Jonson was never a man of silence and reserve," Looney observed, before asking "Was the comradeship a reality or a much belated pretense?"[70] He concluded that "a strange mixture of secrecy and make-believe" hovers over Jonson's relationship with Shakespeare that casts doubt on the validity of his statements in the prefatory materials in the First Folio of 1623.

In the *Shrew* pieces, Looney identified passages that, when published in the First Folio, were altered from previous printings to remove references to the Earl of Oxford. He presented what he called "a carefully carried out scheme to conceal the author . . . [by] a deliberate exclusion from the authorized edition of . . . the one and only passage that might betray the Earl of Oxford's interest in [it]: a change so urgently demanded by the situation that an integral and characteristic element of the farce had to be sacrificed to it."[71] A similar change was made to *Richard II*, when "Salisbury" was substituted for "Oxford," completely wrecking the versification. These changes, Looney believed, help explain the mystery of why Edward de Vere "was the only first class dramatist the whole of whose plays are missing."

Throughout the 1930s, Looney engaged in considerable correspondence with other Oxfordians. Judging from the letters that have survived, most of it was with readers of his books. Among them was Prof. P. S. Porohovshikov, the most prominent promoter of the Earl of Rutland as Shakespeare. In his first letter, dated January 7, 1931, he stated that, "I

---

[69] C. R.. B., "Another Reputed Author: Edward de Vere," *Age*, April 15, 1944, p. 5.
[70] J. Thomas Looney, "Jonson v. Jonson, Part 1," *Shakespeare Pictorial*, April 1935, p. 64.
[71] J. Thomas Looney, "Lord Oxford and the Shrew Plays, Part 1," *Shakespeare Pictorial*, Nov. 1935, p. 176.

[spent] many delightful hours over your book. I read it again and again as soon as it was published. I was in London then on a military mission as Legal Advisor to a special mission from Russia to your Government. To think that this was more than twenty years ago. Sometime later, here in America I again not only read, but studied it and weighed your evidence comparing it with mine." However, he cautioned, "There is, I am afraid, not much hope of my ever turning into an Oxfordian, although some of your remarks are in a sense irrefutable."[72] He remained true to his belief in Rutland's authorship.

Eva Turner Clark and J. Thomas Looney carried on an extensive correspondence in 1932. In November she mentioned an article by Carolyn Wells, "another admirer of yours and a well-known writer, which testifies to her faith in your theory, so I enclose two cuttings of that article also. You are receiving belated attention in this country but it is good attention and I am very hopeful of the influence that these two writers [the other was Oliver Herford] may wield."[73]

On December 6 Looney wrote to Wells.[74]

> What I want to do now is simply to offer you my very warmest thanks for the delightful way in which you refer to my own work in your "Edward de Vere" article. To know that one's own words have been read and re-read, in the way you describe, ought to be very gratifying. In some ways it is; but my dominant feeling in reading your three concluding paragraphs has been one of personal unworthiness and heavy responsibility. They are words of appreciation for which any author might well be proud; particularly as I know that they express a conviction you proclaimed with just as much confidence over twelve years ago, before anyone else in the literary world had rallied to the cause: when in fact, the general attitude was that of skepticism and even ridicule. (Not that I take any credit to myself for having patiently borne with the latter; for I have felt singularly indifferent to it from the first; perhaps because that, feeling so confident that the truth was clear, I felt some pity for minds that could not see it.)
>
> The last few years, however, have made a marked change in the situation, and recognized scholars are coming round; but to myself, personally, the support that warms the heart is that which came in the early days from independent minds.[75]

Looney also stated that "immediately after reading" your article "I got to work upon an article for some American magazine. Owing to domestic sickness, however, the work has been very intermittent and was only finished a couple of days ago." This was the piece that was eventually submitted to *The Atlantic Monthly*, which rejected it with the comment that "We fear *The Atlantic* is too old to change its opinions regarding the authorship of Shakespeare's works."[76]

Clark, who received the article back from *The Atlantic*, wrote to Looney on January 7, 1933 to say that "From an experience of my own, I judge that the Editor of *The Atlantic* has a prejudice against our cause, so I am not surprised that he did not find your MS suitable. I have sent to you copies of three of our well known magazines, any one of which would be more likely to print your article.... I am told that *The FORUM*, a well-established magazine, is trying more than ever to live up to its name by publishing matters of a controversial nature. Since you were so good as to say in your letter that I might read your

---

[72] Prof. P. S. Porohovshikov, letter to J. Thomas Looney, Jan. 7, 1931.
[73] Eva Turner Clark, letter to J. Thomas Looney, Nov. 24, 1932.
[74] Looney and Wells had previously corresponded in 1920 and 1923.
[75] J. Thomas Looney, letter to Carolyn Wells, Dec. 6, 1932.
[76] *The Atlantic Monthly*, letter to J. Thomas Looney, Dec. 30, 1932.

manuscript, I have given myself that pleasure. The facts you mention are so incontrovertible that I simply cannot see anything to the other side of the argument."[77]

However, in a letter Clark had sent two days earlier, she explained that "The interest in literary matters has been so overwhelmed by the dangerous political trend that people can think of little else and this has given the Oxford theory a setback, along with a lot of other things, literary and artistic."[78] In the same letter she mentioned that she took a copy of a leaflet Looney had sent her to Mr. Payson, her American publisher, "who likes to keep up with what is going on in the Oxford theory . . . He believes firmly in it and frequently sets a discussion going among his literary friends and acquaintances."[79]

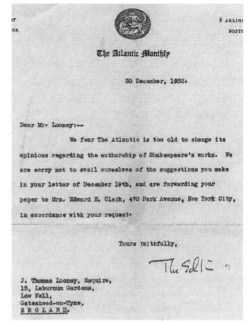

Gerald W. Phillips, author of several Oxfordian books, including *The Tragic Story of "Shakespeare,"* also wrote to Looney about "the great pleasure" he felt "to hear a letter from you read at yesterday's meeting of the Shakespeare Fellowship."[80] He explained that *"Shakespeare" Identified* "first roused my interest in this subject, and convinced me of the Oxfordian authorship. I have read it many times, and each time I am more astonished that it has not found its way at least into every library containing serious works, and that it seems to have received so much less recognition than was due." He added, "I am convinced that you put the case in truer perspective than any subsequent writer, especially in regard to the relations between Vere and Cecil. I regret that Ward did not follow your links in his biography and that Allen seems entirely to have lost sight of them."

Joan V. Robinson of Cambridge University, one of the nation's most respected economists, published a lengthy article, "Shakespeare and Mr. Looney," in *The Cambridge Review* in which she called on her academic colleagues to examine and respond to the Oxfordian claim (see Chapter 11). In August 1933 she wrote to Looney to tell him how convincing she had found *"Shakespeare" Identified*. He responded on September 3: "It was most gratifying on my return from holidays last week to receive your letter. . . . Such expressions of interest in the Earl of Oxford's claims, & of appreciation of my own efforts in bringing them to light are, I can assure you, no small reward for my labours."[81]

He expressed his confidence that the evidence in support of Oxford's authorship was so strong that "if the plays had come down to us anonymously, no reasonable person would now hesitate to attribute them to the Earl of Oxford." He then provided an astute analysis of the obstacles blocking the spread and acceptance of the Oxfordian claim and

---

[77] Eva Turner Clark, letter to J. Thomas Looney, Jan. 7, 1933.
[78] Eva Turner Clark, letter to J. Thomas Looney, Jan. 5, 1933.
[79] Neither the leaflet nor the article submitted to *The Atlantic* have surfaced; they may both be lost to history unless the Oxfordian papers of Eva Turner Clark can be located.
[80] Gerald M. Phillips, letter to J. Thomas Looney, Sept. 28, 1933.
[81] J. Thomas Looney, letter to Prof. Joan V. Robinson, Sept. 3, 1933.

laying out some of the actions most likely to result in its ultimate acceptance. Among them were the formation of small groups within universities that would push persistently for academia to examine the claim objectively, and for outreach to excite the interest of undergraduates in it. "It would certainly be a distinct gain if a nucleus for propaganda could be formed in Cambridge having the avowed object of forcing our case upon the attention of the literary authorities there. At any rate something might be done towards exciting the interest of the undergraduates—which is perhaps the best way of forcing the attention of the professors. The future is certainly with us, and, sooner or later, the authorities will have to succumb."

At the end of 1934 Looney sent copies of his two books to the library at St. John's College and to the public library of the Borough of Willesden. The public library was delighted to accept the books, but St. John's College was unable to find room for them, even though Oxford was a graduate of St. John's and the college's student newspaper, *The Eagle*, had run a long article, "Was Shakespeare a Johnian?" earlier in the year (see Chapter 14).

The Shakespeare Fellowship Page in *The Shakespeare Pictorial*

The Shakespeare Fellowship Page in each monthly issue of *The Shakespeare Pictorial* that had been launched in January 1929 ended in 1936 after a run of eight full years. The Page had given the Fellowship a unique platform in which to broadcast its findings and its views on publications by scholars Oxfordian and orthodox. In September 1934 Capt. Ward commented on the status of the Oxfordian case. "Oxfordians are now able to link up play after play in extreme intimacy, and perfect chronological exactitude, with all the important political events and which, as any trained lawyer would agree, is far more powerful than the slender 'direct' evidence of Ben Jonson that can be advanced against our case."[82]

In the final column in December 1936, Fellowship president Col. Douglas provided an update on recent encouraging developments, noting the important convergence of views that *Hamlet* had been written more than a decade earlier than the traditional dating of the late 1590s, making authorship by Shakspere, still in Stratford in the mid-1580s, impossible. "It is significant that Lord Sydenham, a Baconian, Admiral Holland a member of the Fellowship, and Doctor Cairncross, an orthodox scholar, should find themselves in agreement in conclusions which strike at the roots of orthodoxy."[83]

Yet all was not sweetness and light within the Fellowship.

---

[82] Capt. Bernard M. Ward, "A Companion to Shakespeare Studies," *Sh. Pictorial*, Sept. 1934, p. 144.
[83] Col. Montagu W. Douglas, "Last Words from the Shakespeare Fellowship," *Sh. Pict.*, Dec. 1936, p. 196.

10

The "Why and How" Questions and the Crisis of 1936

Two Issues Looney Didn't Address: Why and How

When reporting the news, journalists have traditionally sought to answer six questions—five "W" questions—who, what, when, where and why—and one "H" question—how. In *"Shakespeare" Identified*, J. Thomas Looney provided clear answers to the first four:

Who—Edward de Vere, 17th Earl of Oxford.

What—Authorship of the plays and poems traditionally attributed to William Shakespeare.

When—Written more than a decade earlier than had been thought, between the 1570s and 1604, not between 1592 and 1611.

Where—Written for performances at court and in private theaters; only later performed on the public stage.

But he did not provide fully convincing answers to the "why" and "how" questions: why Oxford hid his authorship and how the process of hiding it could have succeeded during his lifetime (and for centuries thereafter). He stated in *"Shakespeare" Identified* that he did not need to answer either question in order to prove his case. As to why Oxford hid his authorship, Looney stated that it was "clear that no obligation to furnish motives rests upon an investigator in such a case as this" (177).

> It is made as clear as anything can be that [de Vere] . . . had elected his own self-effacement, and that disrepute was one, if not the principal, motive. We may, if we wish, question the sufficiency or reasonableness of the motive. That, however, is his business, not ours. (174)

> When, therefore [de Vere] tells us, in so many words, that "vulgar scandal" had robbed him of his good name, and that although he believed his work would be immortal he wished his name to be forgotten, we are quite entitled to take his own word for it, and to demand no further motive for the adoption of a disguise. (175)

Looney had noted the prohibitions against a nobleman publishing his poems and acting on the public stage. Circulating manuscripts among friends was acceptable; publishing them was not. Acting in court masques with other courtiers was acceptable; acting in front of the masses was not.

These lines from sonnet 110 —

> Alas, 'tis true I have gone here and there,
> And made myself a motley to the view,
> Gor'd mine own thoughts, sold cheap what is most dear —

seem to express the shame that a high-ranking courtier would naturally have felt about having acted on the public stage—having made himself "a motley to the view."

Looney did not probe further to identify what might have brought about such feelings of shame. He ended his investigation into this subject with the comment that "however insufficient the motive may appear to us, it was evidently sufficient for him, and before we could fittingly discuss it we should have to see the matter from his point of view."[1]

As to how Oxford's authorship could have remained hidden, Looney stated, "We may wonder that the secret should have been so well kept, and be quite unable to offer a satisfactory explanation of the complete success of the 'blind,' just as we may stand puzzled before the other mysteries of history" (47). He noted that "Mystery and concerted secrecy were moreover characteristic not only of the literary life of the times, but even more so of the general social and political life" and that "when a superior intelligence is combined with what may be called a faculty for secrecy and a sound instinct in judging and choosing agents, secret purposes are carried through successfully in a way that is amazing and mystifying to simpler minds" (48). He speculated on who might have been involved.

> That such a work of secrecy could not have been done without the loyal cooperation of others goes without saying. In order to maintain our thesis, however, it is not necessary that we should solve the problem of who his associates were, or of how they went about their work. It is reasonable to suppose that Henry Wriothesley was one, and it is natural to conclude that the wife with whom he was living in evident comfort was another. We may venture a guess, too, that his cousin, Horatio de Vere, the eminent soldier, may have been a third. (362)

He also noted that "The social and political disturbances of the period immediately following Oxford's death would, moreover, assist in the preservation of the secret; and the political submergence of his own particular class would further facilitate matters."[2]

Looney went no further. He did not provide persuasive explanations for why the sizeable number of persons who would have known of Oxford's authorship continued to keep it secret even after Oxford and other key people had all passed from the scene.

His declining to address further the "why" and "how" questions in *"Shakespeare" Identified* and in his later writings weakened the effect of his other evidence, just as Greenwood's declining to propose an alternative candidate allowed Stratfordian defenders to maintain their belief in Shakspere's authorship. Without motive and means, the critics said, all other evidence could be dismissed as illusory or insubstantial.

So it fell to the first generations of Oxfordians to try to write "the rest of the story."

Two-Phase Process in Designing Theories

That Looney provided answers to the first questions but not the last two should not be surprising. In the sciences theories are seldom formulated or proved at one stroke; they often require two phases or waves of insight into the nature of the phenomena being studied. The first phase explains what happened or happens; the second, how and why. Charles Darwin's initial idea of evolution through natural selection wasn't widely accepted until the development in the 1920s—sixty years after *The Origin of Species*—of population genetics, which explained the mechanics of how traits were passed from one generation to the next. Alfred Wegener's initial theory of continental drift to explain the current position of the continents had to be supplemented, decades later, by the proof of

---

[1] J. Thomas Looney, "Is 'Shakespeare Identified'?" *Bookman's Journal*, vol. 1/24 (April 9, 1920): 452.
[2] J. Thomas Looney, April 9, 1920, p. 453.

sea floor spreading—plate tectonics—before the idea of continental movement was accepted.

Could it be that the Oxfordian theory was not immediately accepted by literary scholars because Looney's theory of what happened—Oxford's authorship—had not yet been supplemented with a second phase explaining why and how?

Two-Phase Introduction of Three Theories				
Issue under examination	**Initial Version of New Theory**		**Mechanics (how)/ motivating force (why) added later**	**Complete Theory**
Origin of species	Natural selection (Charles Darwin)	+	Population genetics (Th. Dobzhansky, G. Simpson, E. Mayr)	→	New Synthesis
Features of earth's crust	Continental drift (Alfred Wegener)	+	Sea floor spreading and movement of plates rather than continents per se (H. Hess, W. Menard)	→	Plate Tectonics
Authorship of works attributed to Shakespeare	Edward de Vere as author (J. Thomas Looney)	+	How de Vere's authorship was kept hidden and why not yet definitively answered.	→	Oxfordian Theory Remained Incomplete

Reasons for Looney's Reluctance

So far in this book I have focused on *"Shakespeare" Identified* and its effect on beliefs about Shakespearean authorship. I have largely refrained from addressing J. Thomas Looney's mind and character or the experiences and events in his life that influenced his approach to the authorship question. Those topics and much else will be discussed in the biography of him that I am now working on.

But one aspect of Looney's sensibilities must be discussed here because it directly affected his research into the Oxfordian thesis, which in turn influenced the development of the Oxfordian claim and the history of the movement. It goes directly to the heart of the why and how questions:

Looney's Clues

Reading between the lines we can see that Looney offered three clues, in three different publications, as to the nature of answers to the why and how questions. They reveal why he turned away from these questions even when challenged to address them.

Clue No. 1: Oxford's "Attitude Towards Woman." Looney suspected that the answer to those two questions had something to do with Oxford's attitude toward women. After discussing Oxford's poem "Women,"[3] he observed that,

> So far as his attitude towards woman [sic] is concerned, the poem already quoted in full is sufficient evidence of that deficiency of faith which we have pointed out as marking the Shakespeare sonnets; the very terms employed being as nearly identical as Shakespeare ever allowed himself in two separate utterances on one

---

[3] The poem is included in Palgrave's *Golden Treasury of English Songs and Lyrics*, a popular anthology of English poetry available in many editions.

topic. Then that capacity for intense affection combined with weakness of faith which is one of the peculiarities of Shakespeare's mind, has not, so far as we are aware, so close a parallel anywhere in literature as in the poems of Edward de Vere. It is not merely in an occasional line, but is the keynote of much of his poetry. Indeed we may say that it probably lies at the root of a great part of the misfortune and mystery in which his life was involved, and may indeed afford an explanation for the very existence of the Shakespeare mystery. (118)

Clue No. 2: Looney's treatment of the "bed trick" in *"Shakespeare" Identified*. He introduced what he called "the most remarkable piece of evidence met with in the whole course of our investigations," but added, apologetically, that "we would willingly be spared the penning of such matter: its importance as evidence does not, however, permit of this" (233). The "bed trick" is an essential plot element in *All's Well That Ends Well*, which Looney described as "the entrapping of Bertram into marital relationships with his own wife, in order that she might bear him a child unknown to himself" (233-34).

Looney duly reported that a similar event occurred in the life of Edward de Vere. The passage he discovered stated that "[Oxford] forsook his lady's bed, . . . [but] the father of Lady Anne by stratagem, contrived that her husband should unknowingly sleep with her, believing her to be another woman, and she bore a son to him in consequence of this meeting" (234). Elsewhere Looney twice referred to this incident in Oxford's life as "revolting":

> . . . incidents of his life present so amazing a parallel to the records of Oxford, even to the revolting crisis in the play . . . [4]

> . . . the records are brought into line with the revolting crisis in *All's Well*, and leave hardly any room for doubt respecting Oxford's identity with Bertram. (xxviii)

Why would Looney have preferred not to report the most remarkable piece of evidence he met with? Because he found it personally abhorrent.

Clue No. 3: Looney's comments about his 1922 article in *The Golden Hind*. *The Golden Hind* ran not only poems, stories and criticism, but also artistic drawings. In a letter to Eva Turner Clark in 1926, Looney said that his article contained his most important findings since *"Shakespeare" Identified* was published. But, he explained, "Unfortunately the art section of the magazine turned out to be such as I did not approve of, and so I have been prevented from broadcasting the article."[5] In other words, Looney was so offended by drawings of nudes in the publication—including on two pages on which his article was printed—that he couldn't bring himself to tell anyone about it.

Thus, we see that Looney was a real Victorian, unable to go down the path toward solving the mystery of why and how Oxford hid his authorship because he could not discuss sexual topics in a public forum. He was thirty years old when Queen Victoria died in 1901 and the Victorian Era ended. He apparently remained circumspect about public discussions of intimate matters throughout his life. Though he likely concluded that the full answer to the authorship question was somehow related to sex and to Oxford's relations with women, he couldn't address such matters in public.

A Fourth Clue

Looney later provided a fourth clue, in an article in the Shakespeare Fellowship's

---

[4] J. Thomas Looney, *The Poems of Edward de Vere* (1921), p. xxii.
[5] J. Thomas Looney, letter to Eva Turner Clark, June 26, 1926.

column in *The Hackney Spectator* on January 11, 1924. He connected the date of the birth of Oxford's son (by his second wife, Elizabeth Trentham), Henry de Vere, on February 24, 1593, to the publication date of *Venus and Adonis* in the spring of that year. He realized that "The preparation of *Venus and Adonis* for the press . . . [was] carried out under the influence of expected paternity, whilst the finishing touches were given under the influence of a realised paternity." He saw a link between the birth of his son and the dedication of the poem to the Earl of Southampton, who is spoken of as "god-father" to "the first heir of my invention." In this connection, Looney continued,

> it has to be emphasised that the dedication does not stand alone. Let anyone read, for example, the closing part of the poem itself, and judge candidly whether the following stanzas are not a later interpolation of the poet's and that they violate the sequence of his conceptions; suggested, as they seem to have been, by his personal circumstances:

> "Poor flower," quoth she, "this was my father's guise,

> > Sweet issue of a more sweet-smelling sire,
> > For every little grief to wet his eyes:
> > To grow unto himself was his desire,
> > And so 'tis thine; but know, it is as good,
> > To wither in my breast as in his blood.
> > Here was thy father's bed, here in my breast;
> > Thou art the next of blood and 'tis thy right.
> > Lo! in this hollow cradle take thy rest.
> > My throbbing heart shall rock thee day and night:
> > There shall not be one minute in an hour,
> > Wherein I will not kiss my sweet love's flower."

> Can there be the slightest doubt that these verses, actually forced into the poem, were written by a father, with his newly-born "heir" and its fond mother before his eyes? After having written them he passes immediately to the composition of the dedication, where, as we have just seen, everything turns upon the baptism of the same "heir."

> What I am specially concerned to point out is the tremendous force that evidence always gains by combination. The dedication by itself might have been an extraordinary coincidence. The closing of the poem might have been another extraordinary coincidence. But is it possible for anyone to dismiss the combination as a mere coincidence?[6]

Oxfordian Research After Looney

Oxfordian researchers approached the subject of de Vere's authorship from various angles. The first two, Col. Bernard R. Ward and Capt. Hubert Holland, sought, respectively, to extend knowledge of events related to Oxford's life in Hackney and what became of his works there after his death, and to identify linkages between the plays and real-life events to establish a more correct dating for them.

Early researchers sometimes went down false paths or accepted as facts things they later realized they had misinterpreted. Percy Allen, in particular, seems never to have met an idea he didn't like—on first acquaintance. But he was courageous enough to rethink his conclusions when confronted with new information.

---

[6] J. Thomas Looney, "Shakespearean Researches at Hackney and Southwark, VI," *Hackney Spectator*, Jan. 11, 1924, p. 9.

> I have not, nor have ever had "preconceived notions," concerning the Shakespeare mystery. . . . I have passed, during the last 30 years of my life, through Stratfordianism to agnosticism; thence to Baconianism; thence back to agnosticism; and, finally, to the Oxford creed; changing my views in a hundred and more points of detail, almost from day to day, as my tireless search among the evidences gradually forced me into opinions which, nevertheless, continually from time to time, I have been compelled inexorably to modify.

> No man can successfully investigate this problem, who is not always ready to modify his opinions, precisely as the detectives of the C.I.D. have to do, when unravelling complicated cases.[7]

This is, of course, the ideal approach to bring to scholarly work.

The issues about which Oxfordian researchers most often disagreed among themselves, and about which they most often changed their minds, were those related to the *Sonnets*. Among them were:

> ➢ The identity of "Mr. W. H.," the dedicatee;
> ➢ The correct order of the sonnets;
> ➢ The dates of composition;
> ➢ Authorship of *The Sonnets*;
> ➢ The identity of the Fair Youth;
> ➢ The identity of the Dark Lady;
> ➢ The identity of the Rival Poet.

Among other issues of intense disagreement were:

> ➢ The group theory of authorship;
> ➢ Bacon's role as author or editor;
> ➢ Authorship of *Venus and Adonis;*
> ➢ Southampton's role as go-between for Oxford with those staging his plays in the public theaters.

The first researchers did not consciously set out to answer the why and how questions, but they uncovered relevant information while investigating other issues. Later, at the very end of the 1920s, they and other Oxfordians began to formulate answers to those questions.

Col. Ward was the first to pick up on Looney's fourth clue, that Oxford's dedication of *Venus and Adonis* and a passage near the end of the poem related to the birth of his son and heir, Henry de Vere. In an article titled "Shakespeare and the *Sonnets*: A Suggested Interpretation,"[8] Ward recalled an older publication, *Shakespeare's Sonnets. To Whom Were They Addressed?* (1881), in which Mr. S. Smith Travers speculated that "the Fair Youth was an illegitimate son of the poet by a noble or high-born lady."[9]

Two years later, Col. Ward became the first to propose that the "noble or high-born lady" was Queen Elizabeth. He did so in "The Original *Venus and Adonis*," published on the Shakespeare Fellowship page in the *Shakespeare Pictorial* in October 1931.

---

[7] Percy Allen, "Mr. Percy Allen's Reply," *Supplement 1, SF Newsletter*, No. 14 (April 1939): 19.
[8] Col. Bernard R. Ward, "Shakespeare and the Sonnets: A Suggested Interpretation," *Poetry and the Play*, Winter 1929-1930, pp. 10-13. The article was later issued as a pamphlet.
[9] Same, p. 7. The reference is to S. Smith Travers, *Shakespeare's Sonnets* (1881).

> There is no reason to suppose that Shakespeare's poems were any less "ramm'ed with life"—to use Ben Jonson's phrase . . . than we know the plays to have been. . . . [W]e may feel pretty confident that the poem contains in its "straightforward narrative" a description of an actual love affair in which Oxford was one of the principals.

> Mr. Looney has pointed out that the last stanzas of *Venus and Adonis* draw a picture of a mother with her new-born child. Henry de Vere was born a few weeks before the publication of the poem. Can Venus therefore be in any sense a portrait of Oxford's second wife? Some of the sonnets addressed to the Dark Lady seem to support this hypothesis. On the other hand Venus is several times referred to . . . as being "immortal" and the "Queen of love." These expressions would be more applicable to Queen Elizabeth than to anyone else, and a love affair between Oxford and the Queen is by no means outside the bounds of possibility.[10]

Col. Ward was also the first to notice another important piece of evidence. In a 1927 letter to Katharine Eggar he noted that Oxford had changed his signature in 1603: "It is a curious thing that Oxford's signature changed after the Queen's death. The letter I sent you a day or two ago—that of the 25-27 April 1603—is the last one he signed in the old way. . . . His letters of the 7th May, 12th, 16th and 19th June [1603] are all signed [in the new way.] . . . I think he must have felt that he had become almost another personality after her death."[11]

Percy Allen's first attempt to answer the why and how questions along sexual lines appeared in Appendix A of *The Life-Story of Edward de Vere as "William Shakespeare,"* published in March 1932.

> It has been more and more insistently borne in upon me that, if we could fully understand them, Oxford's personal relations with Queen Elizabeth would provide the clue to a complete understanding of his life, and particularly to his mysterious withdrawal from court in 1589, the secret of which, as Lucio phrases it in *Measure for Measure*, must be "locked between teeth and lips."

> The references, in the plays and poems, to love affairs between de Vere and Elizabeth are many; but they are self-contradictory, and difficult wholly to reconcile with one another.[12]

Allen cited passages in the plays and poems that could be interpreted to support such a relationship and the birth of a son that resulted from it. He had formed these ideas while the book was already being printed, which is why they were inserted into an appendix. He closed with the promise to address the issue in depth and the hope that he had "set down enough here to justify my innate conviction, that de Vere's relations with Queen Elizabeth—could they be sufficiently known—would completely solve the mystery that still hangs about 'Shakespeare's' paradoxical and enigmatic career" (367).

---

[10] Col. B. R. Ward, "The Original *Venus and Adonis*," *Shakespeare Pictorial*, Oct. 1931, p. 164.
[11] Col. Bernard R. Ward, letter to Katharine E. Eggar, March 23, 1927.
[12] Percy Allen, "Appendix A," *The Life-Story of Edward de Vere as "William Shakespeare"* (1932), p. 361.

A few months later Gerald W. Phillips expressed agreement with Allen on some points and offered a few new theories in *The Tragic Story of "Shakespeare" Disclosed in the Sonnets*. He proposed that *Venus and Adonis* was written by Oxford's enemies to defame him and that Oxford addressed the *Sonnets* to an illegitimate son born before his marriage to Anne Cecil. He thought that the Dark Lady of the *Sonnets* was Oxford's second wife, Elizabeth Trentham.[13] Phillips believed that Shakespeare returned to the issue of a clandestine marriage and/or illicit love in at least nine plays. He argued that the child's mother must have been someone of high position, and, therefore that Oxford was required to use a pseudonym to provide "cover" for those involved.

Gerald W. Phillips

Born: 1884. Died: not known.
Age when *"Shakespeare" Identified* was published: 36

<u>Oxfordian Publications</u>

<u>Books</u>
1932   *The Tragic Story of "Shakespeare," Disclosed in the Sonnets*
1934   *Shakespeare's Sonnets*
1935   *Sunlight on Shakespeare's Sonnets*
1936   *Lord Burghley in Shakespeare*

<u>Articles and Published Letters</u>
1937, March   [letter: Response to K.C.T.'s review], *Shakespeare Pictorial*, No. 109: 36.
Additional articles and letters published in the *SF Newsletter*, 1948-1955.

H. K. Kennedy-Skipton, in his review of Phillips's *Tragic Story*, made a penetrating observation about what Shakespeare's plays might reveal about real-life events, and about the "historical foreground," as he termed it.

> If we accept the life of de Vere and his relation to the times as told in the plays, we may find they form a historical foreground, and will in fact be a criterion of the truth of the background. There can be no doubt that the plays and the life of Edward De Vere conceal facts of vital historical import, compared with which the mystery of the authorship is of minor consequence. How otherwise can one explain the erasure of the name of such an important person from the pages of our history?[14]

Kennedy-Skipton sensed that there was something to be uncovered in Shakespeare's works. He didn't quite know what it was but suspected it to be of such "vital historical import" that the authorship mystery is of only "minor consequence" in comparison. This was a compelling statement because it raised, first, the question of "literary evidence"—whether it is legitimate to cite events portrayed in works of literature as evidence of historical events—and, second, it brought to the fore the still unexplained fact that Edward de Vere had been virtually erased from "the pages of our history."

Walt Whitman, a most perceptive reader of Shakespeare's plays, had said something similar. "It is impossible to grasp the whole cluster of these plays . . . without thinking of them as . . . the result of an essentially controlling plan. What was that plan? Or, rather, what was veil'd behind it?—for to me there was certainly something so veiled."

---

[13] Gerald Phillips, *The Tragic Story of "Shakespeare"* (1932).
[14] H. K. Kennedy-Skipton, [review of *The Tragic Story of "Shakespeare"* by G. W. Phillips], *Shakespeare Pictorial*, Aug. 1932, p. 132.

Whitman's friend William O'Connor also had the impression of the plays having "a lurking sense of being in aid of some ulterior design, probably well enough understood in that age, which perhaps time and criticism will reveal."[15]

Despite some differences of opinion, in the summer of 1932 Col. Ward, Percy Allen and Gerald Phillips were all in essential agreement that Oxford, before his marriage to Anne Cecil, had a relationship with a noble or high-born woman that produced a child and that those events were somehow connected to his subsequent use of the William Shakespeare pseudonym.

Allen apparently talked up the issue, because it appeared in two newspaper accounts of Shakespeare Fellowship activities in 1933. One was Hugh Kingsmill's report on the Fellowship's Annual Dinner: "One speaker proclaimed 'it is now perfectly certain that the young man of the *Sonnets* was the illegitimate son of Oxford and Queen Elizabeth.[16] Is it not thrilling to think that the son of Shakespeare might have been King of England, had it not been for the bar sinister of illegitimacy?'"[17] This went beyond what Allen had mentioned in the Appendix to *The Life-Story of Edward de Vere as "Shakespeare"* and is the first published piece that brought together the connection between Oxford, Queen Elizabeth and a son resulting from that union on one hand, and the *Sonnets* on the other. Percy Allen first conjectured that the son was born in 1574, a point he stated in *Lord Oxford & "Shakespeare,"* issued in May 1933. He later moved the date to 1575 before returning firmly to 1574 in his 1943 pamphlet.

These ideas were highly controversial within Oxfordian circles. As can best be determined the majority were satisfied with the earlier explanations for why Oxford hid his authorship: that as a courtier, he couldn't acknowledge authorship of any published literary works; and that hiding his identity was necessary to make it less likely that anyone not already in the know would connect characters in the plays with real-life individuals. A minority believed that the earlier explanations did not adequately account for the shame that de Vere repeatedly expressed in the *Sonnets*. For them, the usual explanations were not emotionally weighty enough to explain why de Vere's authorship remained hidden after the deaths of de Vere and other key persons, or how the effort to hide his authorship could have succeeded.

Those disagreements led to an extraordinary event: a debate on "Whether there is sufficient evidence to show that Queen Elizabeth had a son by the Earl of Oxford" that took place after the Fellowship Annual General Meeting on September 27, 1933. Percy Allen and Capt. Bernard Ward spoke in favor, Canon Gerald Rendall and Gerald Phillips opposed.

The Morning Post reported on the event, highlighting the "new theory" presented by Capt. Ward and Percy Allen.

> Briefly stated, the theory is that Lord Oxford succeeded Leicester as the lover of the Queen; that the intimacy endured from 1573 to 1580; and that as a result of

---

[15] Walt Whitman and William O'Connor were both quoted in Col. Bernard R. Ward's "What Lurks Behind Shakespeare's History Plays," *Shakespeare Pictorial*, Sept. 1929, p. 16.

[16] In Chapter 2 I cited the similarity between Oberon and Titania in *A Midsummer Night's Dream* tussling over the changeling boy and what may have been the real life tussle between Elizabeth and Oxford over the illegitimate boy born to Anne Vavasour by Oxford. If, however, the goddess Diana is seen as the queen mentioned in the play and Elizabeth a votress of her, then the tussle resembles the scenario Allen was now proposing, with Elizabeth and Oxford tussling over their illegitimate son.

[17] Hugh Kingsmill, "Shakespeare Criticism," *English Review*, June 1933, p. 692.

it a son was born who, though never acknowledged, lived in his father's household, was a member of his company of players, and took part in the production of the Shakespeare drama.

Evidence in the records to sustain this theory was marshalled by Captain Ward with much cogency and plausibility, though, in the absence of any proof that the hypothetical son was ever born, the case was rather like that of an inquest without a body. Mr. Percy Allen dealt with the corroboration to be found in Shakespeare's works and in contemporary literature; and it was pointed out that on this hypothesis the mystery of the *Sonnets* became easily explicable—the youth being the son, and the Dark Lady being the Queen. It also explains the years of estrangement between Oxford and his wife, Anne Cecil—an estrangement enforced by the Queen's jealousy.

The case thus put forward, it should be understood, is by no means adopted as that of the Fellowship; and yesterday it was very strongly controverted by Dr. Rendall, himself the author of a well-known commentary on the *Sonnets*. It was also opposed by Mr. G. W. Phillips, who nevertheless sustains the theory that Oxford had a son before his marriage to Anne Cecil. A full statement of the case for the prosecution in this *cause célèbre* may be awaited with some eagerness.[18]

The day after the debate Gerald Phillips wrote to J. Thomas Looney that, although he was on the opposite side of the debate from Percy Allen and Capt. Ward, he agreed with much of what they believed; Phillips, however, did not accept that the well-born lady with whom Oxford had had a son prior to his first marriage was Queen Elizabeth.

I don't know if you will feel able to go with me in thinking that Vere was in love with some other lady before and at the time of his marriage with Anne Cecil: that he pre-contracted himself to her, and by her had a son who should have been his legitimate heir—thereby incurring Cecil's hostility, and finally disgrace: but I could make a stronger case for all this now than I did in the book I am sending you.[19]

How did Looney respond? He was concerned, to put it mildly, about the theory itself and the media attention given to it, just what we should expect given his Victorian sensibilities and his dedication to truth rather than speculation. Although his letters from 1933 on these points have not yet been found, two letters to him comment on the sentiments he had expressed.

The first, from Fellowship president Col. Montagu Douglas was sent two months after the debate.

Dear Mr. Looney,

Captain Ward has forwarded to me your comments on my *Circular,* in which I explained that the Fellowship was not responsible for the views of its "authors."[20]

We seem to have forestalled your wishes during the brief discussion on the suggested natural son of Oxford and the Queen; for Canon Rendall read out to the meeting your letter, and clearly explained your desire to be disassociated from the hypothesis under discussion.

The idea of an Oxford natural son is not uncommon. Phillips has written a book thereon; and a recent recruit to the Fellowship, and a scholar, H. B. Simpson CB

---

[18] "New Shakespeare Theory: Queen Elizabeth and Oxford; An Unacknowledged Son?" *Morning Post*, Sept. 28. 1933.

[19] Gerald M. Phillips, letter to J. Thomas Looney, Sept. 28, 1933.

[20] Col. Montagu W. Douglas, letter to J. Thomas Looney, Nov. 26, 1933.

JP Oxon, has sent me proofs of a book advocating this solution.[21] It seems to me that any kind of a son would be preferable to a stranger; but Allen and Ward go further and associate the Queen. So long as they proclaim that their views are personal, I see no danger to our cause; and the Secretary [Capt. Ward] would not submit for publication in *The Pictorial* any article that might disturb the Members. . . .

As the "onlie begetter" of the Oxford case, I can understand your solicitude for its safety; but you may rest assured that the Committee are always on the watch for the "red light."

I congratulate you on your practical conversion of "Candidus" of *The Daily Sketch*.

Yours sincerely,   [signed] M. Douglas[22]

The *Circular* to which Douglas referred, dated November 1, stated the "Object[ive]s of the Fellowship," unchanged since 1922, followed by a statement by him that read in part,

> The Fellowship is a social organisation providing Members with a common meeting ground for debates and lectures. . . . But the Fellowship, as such, is not committed either to the views of its Members, or to any opinion on the question of Shakespearean authorship.
>
> We have in our ranks followers of Oxford, Bacon, Derby, and Raleigh: and none of these groups can claim official support. This impartiality extends to differences of opinion within the Oxford group, a matter which assumed prominence at a debate held on the 27th September last.
>
> There are various schools of thought regarding the identity of the "Fair Youth" of the Sonnets: whether Southampton, Herbert, a natural son of Oxford, or of Oxford and Queen Elizabeth.
>
> The Fellowship is not committed to any one of these candidates; and should any particular view be published the author will no doubt make it clear that such view is adopted independently of the Fellowship. Further, it is obvious that if any issue is put to the vote at a meeting, the decision only reflects the views of those present.

The second letter to Looney (the first chronologically as it was sent before the debate) was from Capt. Bernard M. Ward. He attempted to ease Looney's mind about the event by laying out some of the evidence that had led him and Percy Allen to their conclusions. He showed that he entirely understood and even shared many of Looney's concerns.

> Although I identify myself entirely with what we may call Percy Allen's "Oxford-Elizabeth Son" theory, and intend to speak on his side at the meeting on 27th Sept., I am, paradoxically, largely in sympathy with the views you express in your letter. Believe me, the last thing in the world that either P.A. or I wanted was to have to conduct an argument of this sort. I am only too conscious that many members of the Fellowship are saying that P.A. and I are sliding down the slippery slope of Baconian insanity. And, frankly, I do not blame them. Unless people know the evidence that P.A. and I have collected they are bound to feel, as I felt for a long time, that anything would be better than to start a sort of rival to the Baconian cipher absurdities. But we must face facts—hence—the meeting on Sept. 27th. Let me assure you that the evidence that P.A. and I are going to produce at the meeting is genuine evidence—not cipher—and that it is absolutely

---

[21] This is the same H. B. Simpson who wrote the important article in *The Nineteenth Century and After* in December 1917. If the book referred to was ever published, Simpson was not the author.

[22] Col. Montagu W. Douglas, letter to J. Thomas Looney, Sept. 28, 1933.

incontrovertible as long as people are prepared to face up to the truth.[23]

Capt. Ward then related at length how the theory arose.

As I am, in a sense, the originator of this business I had better tell you how it arose. About 5 or 6 years ago my father and I made a study of the *Sonnets*, and we came to the conclusion that they were not addressed to the Earl of Southampton, i.e. that Southampton was not the "Fair Youth." We only reached this conclusion after considerable hesitation, because, as you pointed out in *"Shakespeare" identified*, the case for Southampton seems on the face of it very strong—the first 26 sonnets urging the Fair Youth to marry coinciding with S's engagement to Eliz. de Vere, the dedication of V & A, and the name Henry de Vere. But the trouble is this. While the first 26 Sonnets would fit S. in and about 1590-1594, the remainder, in my opinion, quite definitely do not. There are three main reasons for this:

1. Many of the Sonnets give one the impression of a father addressing his son, or

```
                                    3 Valley Green
                                    Welwyn Garden City
                                    Herts.

Dear Mr Looney

    Thank you very much for your letter.  Percy Allen is coming to
stay here next week when I will show him your letter, and when he
has read it I will send it on to Canon Rendall.

    I am very glad to have this opportunity of trying to explain the
position to you.  I say 'trying' because letters are poor sub-
stitutes for a talk.  I only wish it were possible for us to have
a talk together, because the subject is so vast that it is impos-
sible for me to do more than give you the briefest outline in a
letter.  All I would ask of you is this.  If you find my arguments
disjointed and unconvincing, please remember that I am trying to
tell you in a few pages what Percy Allen and I are going to express
in two books!

    Although I identify myself entirely with what we may call Percy
Allen's "Oxford-Elizabeth son" theory, and intend to speak on his
side at the meeting on 27th Sept, I am, paradoxically, largely in
sympathy with the views you express in your letter.  Believe me,
the last thing in the world that either P.A. or I wanted was to
have to conduct an argument of this sort.  I am only too conscious
that many members of the Fellowship are saying that P.A. and I
are sliding down the slippery slope of Baconian insanity.  And,
frankly, I do not blame them.  Unless people know the evidence
that P.A. and I have collected they are bound to feel, as I felt
for a long time, that anything would be better than to start a
sort of rival to the Baconian cipher absurdities.  But we must face
```

---

[23] Capt. Bernard M. Ward, letter to J. Thomas Looney, mid-Sept., 1933.

at any rate a boy of ten or less, rather than a middle aged man addressing a youth of twenty or so—especially when that youth, like S, was thinking only of war. (See my father's article in the *Poetry Journal* in 1929, when my father wrote that article we thought Oxford was addressing Henry de Vere; but we subsequently saw that Henry was much too young as he was only 11 when Oxford died, and the Fair Youth must have reached marriageable age during O's lifetime. (I assume, of course, that the order of the *Sonnets* is not the chronological order, and I think this is a fair assumption.)

2. Some of the sonnets seem obviously addressed to a boy-actor. This was first propounded by Oscar Wilde, and recently revived by Lord Alfred Douglas in his edition of the *Sonnets*. I am at a loss to understand why Dr. Rendall and Sir E. K. Chambers, *inter alia*, have persistently ignored this aspect of the *Sonnets*.

3. If we equate the Fair Youth with Southampton, it seems to me impossible to make any reasonable explanation of the Dark Lady Sonnets. The Stratfordians think that Shaksper handed over his mistress to Southampton—a most unpleasant if not impossible theory, which becomes quite incredible if we assume Oxford as the author.

The next step in the story is Phillips' *Tragic Story of Shakespeare*. I disagree with much of it, but I think he made two good points:

1. That the Fair Youth was an illegitimate son of Oxford, born about 1574, who was a boy actor (one of the "Oxford boys" in 1584).

2. That *V & A* was not written by Lord Oxford, but was the work of one of his enemies. I am not prepared to say definitely who wrote it. The evidence of Hall and Marston seems to point to Bacon.[24] But I believe that it was written in order to break off the engagement between Southampton and Eliz. de Vere. This would fit Bacon, an Essexian, who would naturally not wish to see the young Southampton married to Sir R. Cecil's niece.

But when Phillips postulates an unknown Maid of Honour as the mother of Oxford's illegitimate child, I disagree. The evidence that the Fair Youth was born about 1574 is exceedingly strong. And the evidence that Q.E. was O's mistress from 1573-1580, is also exceedingly strong.

I can only give you a bare outline of what I believe to be the story of this illegitimate son of Oxford's by Q.E. I grant you it is surmise. But you will see in a moment how it all fits in. I think the boy was born in or about 1574 (perhaps O's sudden flight to the Low Countries had something to do with this): that he was living in O's household in 1583/4 and was one of the "Oxford Boys" who were in that year amalgamated with the Paul's boys and, under the mastership of John Lyly, acted repeatedly at Court from 1584 to 1590. The Paul's Boys were undoubtedly the most popular Court company. In 1590 they were dissolved by order of Q.E. because they had infringed the law by bringing Martin Marprelate on to the stage as an Ape. (See Mrs. Clark's *Shakespeare Plays in the Order of Their Writing*.) In 1590 the boy would have been 15 or 16. Now, Mrs. Clark very pertinently suggests that the sudden appearance of Strange's company in 1591 as the most popular company at Court can be very easily explained. She suggests that the Paul's boys, who were growing up, having been dissolved, decided to form themselves into an adult company, and that they acquired Strange's patronage. It is, at any rate, certain that the new Strange company became the most popular company at Court. They acted repeatedly; and on Strange's death in 1594, they passed via Strange's widow to her sister's father in law Lord Hunsdon, the Lord Chamberlain. They now became the famous "Lord

---

[24] Percy Allen did not agree with that point.

Chamberlain's Men." In 1595 a certain "William Shakespeare" was payee of this company at Court; and I suggest that "William Shakespeare" was the Oxford-Elizabeth son. I believe that the boy died in 1601, but I am not certain.

Here, then, I suggest that we have the three characters in the *Sonnets*. The Fair Youth is the illegitimate Oxford/Elizabeth son: the Poet is Oxford: and the Dark Lady, Elizabeth. You will, perhaps, smile at my suggestion that Elizabeth is the "Dark" Lady. But have you ever read Hentzner's description of Q.E. (whom he saw in 1598)? It is quoted in Sidney Dark's *Life of Q.E.*, page 179. He said her eyes were small yet black and pleasing: her teeth black: and her hair red, and that false. Rosaline in L.L.L. is almost universally admitted to be the "Dark Lady" of the Sonnets; and if you look at a picture of Q.E. you will I think agree that Rosaline and Q.E. are one and the same:

> A whitely wanton with a velvet brow,
> With two pitch balls stuck in her face for eyes.

The interpretation that P.A. and I have worked out for the Sonnets is <u>allegorical</u> and not literal. Practically every Sonnet has a hidden meaning, which is disclosed directly [once] you know the four key words of the word-play:

> TRUE or TRUTH, which stands for Oxford.

> BEAUTY or FAIR, which stands for Elizabeth.

> ROSE, which stands for their son, the Tudor Rose — the repeated references to the "Canker-bloom" being his illegitimacy.

> TIME, when spelt with a capital in the 1609 Q., which stands for the Royal Succession.

So that the ostensible meaning of the first couplet of sonnet 1 is urging a young man to marry and not allow his beautiful stock to die out; the hidden meaning is Oxford urging his son not to allow Q.E.'s Tudor dynasty to perish. And so on.

It is rather interesting that in the preface to the second edition of the sonnets, John Benson declares that they are "of that purity which the author then living avouched them." Now, no <u>literal</u> interpretation of the *Sonnets* can possibly be pure, because you are always up against the problem of the poet handing over his mistress to the Fair Youth. But allegorically this simply means that the boy was cutting out his father with Q.E., probably about 1590, but not, of course, in a sexual sense.

You will find the Oxford-Elizabeth story in *A Lover's Complaint* and the death of the boy seems to be referred to in *The Phoenix and the Turtle*. There are many references in the plays which I cannot go into here.

Incidentally, the theory that Oxford was the father of Elizabeth's son would completely explain the £1,000 a year. It would also explain why Oxford's Will has never survived, that is, if we suppose that in his Will he mentioned this boy, and that it was destroyed for political reasons.

I am enclosing you a cutting sent me by Mrs. Clark which I am sure will interest you.

With best wishes.

Yours sincerely   [signed] BMWard

Ward's letter must have confirmed Looney's worst fears: that his theory of Oxfordian authorship was going to be tarnished by its association with matters that he believed were shameful and should not be openly discussed. Although Looney's response to Capt. Ward has not yet surfaced, he expressed his thoughts on the Allen-Ward theory and the potential harm it could cause in a letter to Cambridge economist Joan Robinson on

September 3, about two weeks before Ward's letter and three and a half weeks before the debate.

> P.S. re. Mr. Percy Allen. His personal loyalty to myself has been so staunch that I do not like to criticise him. I, of course, fully recognise the very great value of G. Rendall's support: by far the most valuable that has, as yet, been given to the cause.
>
> Mr. Allen, on the other hand, with the support of Captain Ward, is now advancing certain views respecting Oxford and Queen Eliz. which appear to me extravagant & improbable, in no way strengthen Oxford's Shakespeare claims, and are likely to bring the whole cause into ridicule.[25]

The dissension within the Fellowship in 1933 arising from the Southampton-as-Son-of-Oxford-and-Elizabeth theory was but a mere rumbling of what was to come in 1936 and 1939.

It is quoted in Sidney Dark's "Life of Q.E" page 179. He said her eyes were small yet <u>black</u> and pleasing: her teeth <u>black</u>: and her hair red, and that false. Rosaline in L.L.L. is almost univesally admiited to be the "Dark Lady" of the Sonnets; and if you look at a a picture of Q.E. you will I think ~~~~~~~ agree that Rosaline and Q.E. are one and the same:

 A whitely wanton with a velvet brow,
 With two pitch balls stuck in her face for eyes.

 The interprctation that P.A. and I have worked out for the Sonnets is <u>allegorical</u> and not literal. Practically every Sonnet has a hidden meaning, which is disclosed directly you know the four key words of the word-play:

TRUE or TRUTH, which stand for Oxford.

BEAUTY or FAIR, which stand for Elizabeth.

ROSE, which stands for their son, the Tudor Rose - the repeated references to the 'Canker-bloom' being to his illegimacy.

TIME, when spelt with a capital in the 1609 4to, which stands for the Royal Succession.

So that the ostensible meaning of the first couplet of Sonnet 1 is urging a young man to marry and not allow his beautiful stock to die out: the hidden meaning is Oxford urging his son not to allow Q.E's Tudor dynasty to perish. And so on.

 It is rather interesting that in the preface to the second edition

---

[25] J. Thomas Looney, letter to Joan V. Robinson, Sept. 3, 1933.

Percy Allen's *Anne Cecil, Elizabeth & Oxford* (1934)

The next development, six months later, was the publication of Percy Allen's *Anne Cecil, Elizabeth & Oxford*. This book addressed two big themes. The first was a further development of Kennedy-Skipton's rousing suggestion that hidden within the plays was information about historical events of far greater importance than the authorship question. Allen agreed: "in the historical interpretation of Shakespeare's plays, the vexed question of authorship—deeply important though it be—becomes almost secondary. . . . At what events, and at what contemporary personages, are the plays of 'Shakespeare' actually aimed?' With every year that passes, I incline to give less attention to the question of authorship as such, and more to the matter of historical interpretation."[26]

The second theme was that those historical events provided the answers to the vexing why and how questions. "The Shakespearean plays and poems, read together with other contemporary literature, [provide] . . . us, by internal interpretation, with clues which enable readers, for the first time since Elizabethan days, to find, in the complex relations between the Queen, Lord Oxford, and his Countess, Anne Cecil, the final solution of that Shakespearean mystery" (xi).[27] Allen's book is the promised development of the ideas he had introduced in the appendix to *The Life-Story of Edward de Vere as "William Shakespeare"* two years earlier.

Allen's thinking had shifted as new ideas occurred to him during his readings of "Shakespeare's" works. He had begun the book with the focus on the three people named in the title: "Oxford and Elizabeth, considered as lover and mistress, in conjunction with Anne Cecil . . . solved . . . almost every remaining difficulty with which we were confronted; . . . [W]hether one took up *Venus and Adonis*, the *Sonnets*, or *A Lover's Complaint* first published with them; or whether one turned to such early Shakespearean writings as *The Comedy of Errors*, the opening scenes of *Troilus and Cressida*, of *Two Gentlemen of Verona*, of *A Midsummer Night's Dream*, of *All's Well*, or of *Hamlet*—they all proved to be, in the main, concerned with the complex relations between the three above-named individuals" (xii).

But not too far into the book the emphasis shifted to a new trio: Oxford, Elizabeth and their son, the Fair Youth of the Sonnets.

> The love-affair . . . seems to have developed between Oxford and his queen, approximately, if my arguments are sound, during the early fifteen-seventies, and . . . culminated, probably during 1574, in the birth to Lord Oxford and Elizabeth of a son, who, but for the bar sinister of illegitimacy, would have become king of England, and, it may be, the founder of a new line of kings, to the exclusion of the Stuart dynasty. He will become the black changeling boy of *A Midsummer Night's Dream*, the "purple flower" of *Venus and Adonis* and of *The Dream*, and the Fair Youth of the *Sonnets*. As Lord Oxford's son and an actor at the Globe Theatre, he will also become, in part, "Will Shakespeare," traditionally jumbled in popular and professional minds with Will Shaksper of Stratford-upon-Avon. (22)

Allen found confirmation for his views in contemporary literature, citing especially "the strong corroboration afforded by Spenser's poems, *The Faerie Queene*, and *Muiopotmos*" (xiv-xv). He perceived "that Spenser—though he dared not, under his own name, treat very openly of matters so intimate in the life-stories of these highest in the

---

[26] Percy Allen, *Anne Cecil, Elizabeth & Oxford* (1934), p. ix.
[27] Here is a man who loved commas.

land—was, nevertheless, fully conversant with and deeply interested in the whole business," and regarded "the interpretations of Spenser contained in Chapters VII.-IX. (inclusive) of this book as of primary importance to the complete 'Oxford' case" (xv).

Allen recognized that he had "expose[d] myself, in certain quarters, to a charge of literary sensationalism or of deliberate exploitation of salaciousness" (3). Reviewers for the most part were respectful, though expressing concerns about the degree to which he had let his imagination run away with him. *The Aberdeen Press and Journal* observed that Allen "goes further in daring assumptions than the boldest of even the Baconians. For he asserts that there was a Shakespeare, indeed, a player who was the son of Oxford and Elizabeth," before concluding that "Ingenuity such as Mr. Allen's it would be difficult to match. . . . Mr. Allen tries to prove too much."[28]

The Times Literary Supplement, no friend to the Oxfordian idea, mocked Allen's findings without trying to refute them, writing that if he was correct, then Spenser and other great poets of the age were obsessed with court intrigues, which supplied "most of their metaphors and allusions" and that "all the vivid thinking that gives life to poetry" was "no more than a kind of crossword reference to Elizabeth's affair with Oxford and her jealousy of Anne Cecil, his wife."[29] Allen responded that "the fatal mistake, so persistently made by my opponents, is that they will endeavour to interpret those very matters by the standards, and from the viewpoint, not of the sixteenth century, but of academic scholarship of today. Therein is the basic reason for the complete failure of modern orthodoxy adequately to interpret these subtle Elizabethans."[30]

F.B., reviewing for *The Christian Science Monitor*, was more positive. "[T]he belief that the brilliant earl was the author of *Hamlet* has champions whose arguments cannot be lightly brushed aside. Among them Mr. Percy Allen is at once the most redoubtable and the most assiduous. Half a dozen substantial volumes are already to his credit, and more are promised. The present installment of what may be regarded as a single entity is among the most interesting."[31] Although not fully on board with all of Allen's claims, he concluded that "his premises granted, he works out his conclusions with extraordinary skill and ingenuity" even if "some of his analogies seem a little far-fetched." He also found that "some of the most interesting chapters are those in which Spenser, admittedly an allegorist, is called on for illumination."

Novelist and Oxfordian Marjorie Bowen, reviewing *Anne Cecil*, agreed. "In the writer's opinion the chapters devoted to the works of Edmund Spenser are the most important. It is the first time, I believe, that the writings of Spenser have been examined in this

---

[28] "Writings on Shakespeare," *Aberdeen Press and Journal*, April 3, 1934, p. 2.

[29] Philip Tomlinson, "Bottom's Dream," *Times Literary Supplement*, May 3, 1934, p. 2.

[30] Percy Allen, "Elizabeth, Anne Cecil and Oxford," *Times Literary Supplement*, May 10, 1934, p. 342.

[31] F. B, "Brief for the Oxfordians," *Christian Science Monitor*, June 13, 1934, p. WM11.

connection, and Mr. Allen's reading of the odd allegories, *Mother Hubbard's Tale* and *Miopotmas* are very striking and would be difficult to shake. Even more impressive is the evidence supplied by Books III and IV of *The Faerie Queen* which are dedicated to Lord Oxford in terms which reveal the poet's intention of portraying Edward de 'Vere under the guise of one of his allegorical figures."[32]

In her opinion Allen possessed the qualities needed to understand literary works from the Elizabethan era—qualities that the reviewer for *The Times Literary Supplement* lacked.

> In this book, Mr. Allen, by a combination, as uncommon as it is valuable, of keen specialised scholarship and well controlled imaginative insight, further expounds and clarifies the "story" that, more or less, disguised and distorted, he and other experts have found in the "Shakespearean" plays and poems. It is not a matter for wonder and incredulity that these famous works should contain such a "story" nor is it surprising that they should be full of topicalities though Mr. Allen is the first investigator to have made this discovery. Very few, in any, works of art, hang in the rarefied air of pure fantasy; great literature, painting, music, sculpture is usually full of portraits of the artist's contemporaries, autobiographical colouring, under and over tones echoing from the artist's own surroundings or experiences.

"The interested reader," Bowen concluded, "must consider the evidence and judge for himself. It is certainly obvious that the case which at first hearing seems extravagant, is much strengthened by the illusions in *The Faerie Queen*. As regards the possibility, or even the likelihood of such an intrigue, Mr. Allen is on sure ground. . . . It is not, therefore, far fetched to suppose that [Queen Elizabeth] may have had other lovers—platonic or otherwise—and there is much evidence to support the claim that Lord Oxford may have been one of them."

A year later Gerald Phillips returned with his second book, *Sunlight on Shakespeare's Sonnets* in which he endeavored to present "an adequately exact likeness of Shakespeare's thought, and to unfold some of the many compact meanings of his words and lines, without at any time twisting them to suit any preconceived hypothesis."[33] Among his most important conclusions were that "the principal series of sonnets was all concerned with one boy, or youth, for whom Shakespeare felt a very profound love, which most people agree was not of a sensual kind." The story told in the *Sonnets* is that Shakespeare, as a young man, had fathered a child by a woman to whom he was contracted to marry before being obliged, for weighty reasons, to marry another. The woman he married (or her father) had sufficient power to ensure that the contract with the first woman and their child were concealed. "The poet was not permitted to disclose that the boy was his son, still less to establish his legitimacy. The boy was brought up in his father's house as his page and became a stage player" (13, 14).

The purpose of the sonnets, according to Phillips, "was to leave a record for future ages of the son's existence . . . as well as to depict him in vivid likeness: to express the poet's deep love for him; to reveal the wrongs which were inflicted on them both, and who inflicted them; and to call upon future ages to render them the justice which their own refused."

In his review, Percy Allen, while not in agreement with every idea Phillips expressed,

---

[32] Marjorie Bowen, "Anne Cecil, Elizabeth and Oxford," *Shakespeare Pictorial*, March 1934, p. 48.
[33] Gerald W. Phillips, *Sunlight on Shakespeare's Sonnets* (1935), p. 9.

highlighted some of the most interesting ones:

> The words "Truth" and "Beauty," in these poems, seem often to stand for the boy's father (Vere), and his mother and that the frequent references to the "sun" almost invariably mean "son," and, in certain instances—as, for example, in XXIV—can be made sense of by no other interpretation. These ideas, of course, are not new. They have been "in the air" for several years past; and taking up my own annotated copy of the sonnets, I find the following entries, made in ink, beneath sonnet one, some two years ago, after a talk with Capt. Ward: 'True" and "Truth" are Lord Oxford; "Beauty" is Queen Elizabeth. "Time" is the Royal Succession, and "Rose" is the Tudor Rose.
>
> As for the interpretation of sonnet XXXIII —
>
> > Even so my sun (son) one early morn did shine
> > With all triumphant splendour on my brow —
>
> it was at a Shakespeare Fellowship dinner, two years ago, that I read aloud, and put that meaning upon, the 33rd sonnet. Questions of precedence are, however, unimportant and secondary. The important point is that, little by little, our common work, upon these poems, seems to be leading towards similar conclusions.[34]

Allen is right that these ideas were not original with Phillips even though he was the first to publish them in a book. Capt. Ward had expressed them in a letter to Looney in September 1933 (see images earlier in this chapter). In the same letter Capt. Ward had referred to "what we may call Percy Allen's 'Oxford-Elizabeth Son' theory," which seemed to imply that Allen had the major role in formulating it. But Ward's later reference to "the interpretation that P.A. and I worked out" suggests they jointly conceived it. It soon became known as Percy Allen's theory, probably because he wrote so many books, articles and letters propounding it while Capt. Ward wrote little.

Before continuing it would be useful to have a name by which to refer to the theory. Important factors to consider in selecting a name would be the identity of the three people most directly involved, that their relationships affected the succession to Queen Elizabeth (succession was the overarching political issue at the time the William Shakespeare name was launched in 1593), and that the hidden story was told in the *Sonnets*. "The Queen Elizabeth-Earl of Oxford-Earl of Southampton *Sonnets* Dynastic Succession Triangle Theory," which includes all these elements, is too unwieldly. I have shortened it to "The Dynastic Succession Theory," and will refer to it by that name from this point onward.[35]

An Enquiry and the Crisis of 1936

In the summer of 1936 a fifteen-page pamphlet was published; written by Percy Allen and Capt. Bernard Ward, it bore the lengthy title *An Enquiry Into the Relations Between Lord Oxford as "Shakespeare," Queen Elizabeth and the Fair Youth of Shakespeare's Sonnets*. The pamphlet's contents, and the belief that it had been published by the Shakespeare Fellowship, sparked the biggest crisis in the history of the Fellowship. The cover is reproduced nearby; its exact wording is important for understanding the course of events.

The pamphlet was exactly what its title promised: a presentation of Allen's and

---

[34] Percy Allen, "Sunlight on Shakespeare's Sonnets," *Shakespeare Pictorial*, July 1935, p. 112.
[35] In recent decades this theory has often been referred to as the Prince Tudor theory, sometimes shortened to PT, and the Tudor Heir theory.

Ward's latest thinking on the ideas introduced at the debate three years earlier.

> *Shakespeare's Sonnets* provide the only clues to the complete solution of the generally admitted Shakespeare mystery. . . . [W]e are now fully satisfied that the mysteriously "dynastic" quality of these sonnets can be accounted for only upon the supposition that they are historically linked with the English royal house reigning at the time when they were written—namely, the Tudor dynasty, with Queen Elizabeth as its crowned, and then living, head.
>
> Shakespeare, therefore, whoever he may have been, must, presumably, have experienced during his life, some close connection with the Queen of England in person.[36]

They reiterated their beliefs that Shakespeare, the Dark Lady, and the Fair Youth of the *Sonnets* were Lord Oxford, Queen Elizabeth, and their son. They also stated that the son was born early in 1575[37] and became an actor known as "Will Shakespeare," and that "the Fair Youth, who—because he was certainly an actor—cannot have been Southampton, nor any other English peer" (5). (Percy Allen would later conclude that Southampton was indeed the Fair Youth and the dedicatee of the *Sonnets*.)

Allen and Ward presented "a chronological epitome of the evidence in support of what, we submit, is a conclusive and unanswerable case" (4) and cited a long list of "mysteries" that became explicable if their theory was correct.

> Admit that . . . Oxford and Elizabeth were lover and mistress, and the whole story of Shakespeare's plays and sonnets howsoever strange and wonderful . . . becomes a coherent and easily comprehensible sequence of events. Deny our solution, and, as it seems to us, you are driven back, once again, into the old cloud-land of Shakespearean bewilderment, wherein all is seen, as through a glass, darkly, or in a distorting mirror.

There was more to the pamphlet, especially on the many allusions in the works of Shakespeare, Chapman, Jonson, Spenser and other writers, "which seem to hint at intimate relations existing between characters which, upon wholly different grounds, we have long since identified as representing, in the main, Oxford, as 'Shakespeare,' and his Queen." What is of concern here, however, are the reactions to it by other members of the Fellowship.

The most extreme reaction to the pamphlet and its Dynastic Succession ideas came from Fellowship Vice President Gerald Rendall. He left no doubt as to his opinion in a

---

AN ENQUIRY INTO THE RELATIONS BETWEEN
LORD OXFORD AS "SHAKESPEARE,"
QUEEN ELIZABETH and the FAIR YOUTH
OF
SHAKESPEARE'S SONNETS

BY

PERCY ALLEN and
CAPT. B. M. WARD

FROM WHOM COPIES
MAY BE OBTAINED

Price 6.

Also from The Hon. Sec.
THE SHAKESPEARE FELLOWSHIP
3 VALLEY GREEN, WELWYN GARDEN CITY
HERTS

---

[36] Percy Allen and Capt. Bernard M. Ward, *An Enquiry* (1936), p. 3.

[37] This is a change from their earlier writings, in which they had given the date as 1574. They would soon return to the earlier date.

letter to Katharine Eggar on November 23: "I deplore the pamphlet and still more its association with the Fellowship; in my judgment it is a disgrace to literary and historical scholarship."[38] Following several months of heated communications among many Fellowship members including J. Thomas Looney, Rendall and Executive Committee member Katharine E. Eggar resigned from their positions in November and canceled their memberships. It was believed for a time that Looney had also resigned, but that rumor proved to be untrue.

Apart from their beliefs that the Dynastic Succession idea was simply wrong and that in any event was mere speculation, not fact, and so should be avoided, Rendall, Eggar and others were concerned about two issues.

One was what to them was the unsavory nature of the theory. In a letter to Eggar on November 26, Looney used the word "revolting" to describe the relationship between Oxford and Queen Elizabeth that Allen and Ward believed to have occurred.[39] He had used the same adjective in the early 1920s to refer to the bed trick supposedly perpetrated on Oxford by Anne Cecil and her father. Looney clearly believed that extramarital sex and the producing of an illegitimate child were matters of the deepest shame—as did Rendall and Eggar. Because these matters are viewed differently today, effort is needed to appreciate their sensibilities, the same imaginative effort that Percy Allen believed was necessary to understand Elizabethan sensibilities.

The other concern was the negative effect they feared the theory would have on public opinion regarding the Oxfordian claim. In the same November 26 letter, Looney recounted Allen's and Ward's theory "just as I think it will read to the general public particularly the class of readers to which I desire specially to appeal," and asked, "Will it make for our recognition as respectable and competent investigators? Will it commend us for the ready respect of serious minds?" He feared the opposite.

> Whilst the case cannot be used for purposes of "conversion" (to the Oxford theory) it can and almost certainly will be used to turn possible converts aside, and to justify that conspiracy of silence which constitutes at present our most formidable difficulty.... In my personal opinion, only the most absolute certainty respecting the facts, combined with serving some really useful purpose, can justify us in affixing discreditable repute upon those who have served well their country or the world and who are no longer in a position to clear themselves.

Little would be known of all this were it not for recent discovery of the flurry of letters exchanged among J. Thomas Looney, Katharine Eggar, Gerald H. Rendall, Percy Allen, Capt. Ward and a few others.[40] They were written between October 1936 and early 1937. The first indication I found that something was amiss was Looney's letter to Katharine Eggar of October 29, 1936. It was also the first notice she had of the storm that had been brewing for some months.

> Are you aware that G. Rendall has resigned from the Fellowship because of the book by Capt. Ward and Percy Allen? I have not yet seen the offending volume, but, from what Dr. Rendall says of it, he has good reasons, as a scholar of repute,

---

[38] Gerald H. Rendall, letter to Katharine E. Eggar, Nov. 23, 1936.

[39] J. Thomas Looney, letter to Katharine E. Eggar, Nov. 26, 1936.

[40] The letters are housed in the Katharine E. Eggar Archives at the University of London's Senate House Library; in the Gerald H. Rendall Archives at the University of Liverpool; in the Archives of the Shakespeare Authorship Trust housed in the Special Collections Room in the library at Brunel University; and in the cache of J. Thomas Looney's papers found by his grandson early in 2019.

for not wishing to have his name associated with the publication. With so strong a case as ours is it is much to be regretted that valuable support should be lost by irrelevant theories.[41]

Eggar wrote to Looney in December (undated, but sent before the 14th), stating that Percy Allen had just sent her a bundle of correspondence discussing objections to the pamphlet, including three letters from Looney to Capt. Ward, two from Looney to Allen and two from Allen to Looney, with a note that he was sending them at Looney's request. Eggar stated that she was surprised by all this correspondence because she had heard nothing of the furor except Looney's brief mention of Rendall's resignation in an earlier letter.

She noted Allen's and Ward's "determination to stand by their deductions and their right of freedom of speech and pen to pursue the policy of aggression which has of late years been allowed to dominate the Fellowship," and then stated her intention to resign from the organization.

> As I have no use for the "fighting" methods so dear to Mr. Allen, and as he has been encouraged to assume the leading position in the affairs of the SF, I feel that at this point I must end my connection with that body, and am writing to give Pres. Douglas my resignation.
>
> I naturally much regret having to leave the society founded by Col. Ward to whom we owe so much for his research and exposition, but I feel that in doing so I am only being loyal to yourself to whom we owe the discovery of L. Oxford, and whose methods have been consistently of the type wh[ich] one can respect and support.[42]

Eggar ended her letter with a curious statement: "I will not enter into the matter more fully with you at the moment, as I am very anxious to slip quietly out of this unfortunate dispute and not to cause the kind of stir wh[ich] would draw attention to the things which we (you and I) most wish buried in oblivion." As I read it, Eggar means that she, and Looney by implication, were not challenging the validity of Allen's and Ward's beliefs that Oxford and Elizabeth had an affair and a child; rather, they wanted those facts to remain buried because they were "revolting" and because airing them would hinder efforts to promote the Oxfordian claim.

That the situation continued to heat up is shown by the first of two letters Percy Allen sent to Looney on December 14.[43]

> After a very busy weekend, on correspondence, articles, and a hundred other duties, I will now answer briefly the letters from you, which were handed to me by Capt. B. M. Ward. I do so reluctantly, because, in my judgment, much too much fuss has been made about this business; but the charges made against us by Dr. Rendall cry out for answer. Should he continue to make trouble, I, as a Vice-President, shall make official protest to the President. Were Dr. Rendall a younger man I should promptly request him to say what he has to say before a meeting of the Fellowship, in my presence.[44] He has preferred, without writing to me, to scatter attacks on Ward and myself (but principally on myself) among members of the Fellowship. I know that he has written to Col. Douglas and you. Probably

[41] J. Thomas Looney, letter to Katharine E. Eggar, October 29, 1936.

[42] Katharine E. Eggar, letter to J. Thomas Looney, undated, possibly mid December, 1936.

[43] Percy Allen had been on a speaking tour in North America while this crisis was brewing and erupting. He had departed in mid-September and returned home on or around December 10.

[44] Gerald Rendall, born in 1851, was 85 years old in 1936. Percy Allen, born in 1875, was 61.

others have been written to, but I do not know their names.[45]

Allen expressed "personal regret" that the words "Shakespeare Fellowship" had appeared upon the cover of the pamphlet, since Dr. Rendall had cited that fact as his reason for resigning. But, Allen continued,

> It is a very thin reason, because, as Ward, I think, has pointed out, we simply followed the ordinary practice of using our Secretary as agent for distribution of a work by two individual members, as in the case of a recent pamphlet by Miss Eggar. To suppose, however, that the Fellowship, as a whole, or its individual members are thereby made responsible for those opinions is about as sensible as to suggest that Ward and I are responsible for the opinions expressed by that lady therein. As a matter of fact I agreed with Miss Eggar. Had I disagreed would you expect me to resign? All our members have complete freedom of speech and pen, until that freedom is abused. Any suggestion that Ward and I have abused that freedom seems to me utterly absurd. Rendall is just looking for trouble.

Allen went on at length, drawing on *Venus and Adonis*, the *Sonnets* and plays by Shakespeare and Chapman, to justify the conclusions he and Capt. Ward had reached. Yes, he wrote, perhaps "the story of Elizabeth's relations with Oxford is one of 'wickedness in high places' . . . [but even so] the sixteenth century English were not so bad as the French, or the Italians." Perhaps, Allen suggested, we differ on the story told in the literary works because "our concept of Queen Elizabeth is wholly different from yours. I venture, very respectfully, to suggest—and I am sure that Ward would bear me out—that you have hardly fathomed the duplicities of the Elizabethan age, and of Elizabeth herself, which are hinted at in her very title of the Dark Lady, that 'mysterious centre of the circle (the court) which is her Majesty's mind' as a contemporary wrote. The age, I feel sure, was far more double-minded than you suppose; and its literature, correspondingly with its mind, far more secretly topical."

He confirmed the need to tailor to the level of his audiences the depth of information he provided in his lectures. He agreed that the primary purpose of the Fellowship is "conversion," and tried to reassure Looney that

> When I speak to new audiences, or write for new readers—e.g. when lecturing on *Hamlet* in New York, I naturally go to the fundamentals, and keep back the Elizabeth Oxford motive, until my hearers, or readers, are more sophisticated; so that I think you exaggerate a little the evil effect of such arguments upon our cause, while I wholly agree with you, in principle, that we must do as little as we can to alienate possible converts by promulgating views that are too extravagant, or, to the sensitive ones, too unpleasant. It is a question of policy, upon which there may easily be disagreement. My general principle, rightly or wrongly, is the whole truth, and nothing but the truth, which, with the aid of time, and of logical advocacy, must, in the end, prevail.

More letters flew between members in December 1936, some quite lengthy and all containing fascinating insights into the writers' thinking on the Dynastic Succession theory, the goals of the Fellowship and the nature of the methodology that Allen and Ward had used. Let's give the final word for 1936 to J. Thomas Looney, in his letter to Eggar of December 21.

> I have just received your letter, and copies of those you have sent to Mr. Percy

---

[45] Percy Allen, letter to J. Thomas Looney, December 14, 1936.

Allen and Colonel Douglas, and I hasten to say how very much I regret that you have felt compelled to resign your membership of the Shakespeare Fellowship. I quite realise, however, your position. My own special object, at present, is to prevent the Fellowship becoming irrevocably attached to the new ideas and methods. So far as personal contacts—which form a vital part of its London activities—are concerned, I am altogether an outsider, so cannot, of course, appreciate the immediate position as you can. It may be that I am doomed to disappointment. If the Fellowship cannot retain members like yourself and Dr. Rendall it seems unlikely that it will ever win others of equal value. Certainly any recognised connection between the Fellowship and the Oxford-Elizabeth-Actor son-theory, must alienate any serious student and scholar of repute; and it does seem as if the public linking together of Mr. Allen and Captain Ward in the advocacy of that theory will make it impossible to dissociate it from the Fellowship in the eyes of the public, particularly as Mr. Allen, in particular, seems disinclined to desist. For myself I shall continue to "wait and see"—a course only possible, naturally, to me not personally mixed in the society's social and administrative activities. But what a contrast is all this to the early years of the movement, especially when one thinks of the names which Colonel Ward was able to associate with his own!

Let me say how very much I appreciate your expressions of confidence in myself. I only wish I could be of more service than I am, to the cause I was fated to set going, and to those who have adopted it. Neither by circumstances nor by temperament am I, however, fitted for carrying on work like that begun by Colonel Ward. I do hope, however, that neither you nor Dr. Rendall, nor any others who may withdraw from the Fellowship, will lose interest in the object for which it stood—and may still stand—and that you may continue to enjoy amongst yourselves the pleasures of association under a common enthusiasm, in an atmosphere of mutual understanding.

Let me, in conclusion, thank you for all the trouble you have taken on my account. It is good to know that you have taken, quite spontaneously, the view that is mine.[46]

Developments 1937-1943

The why and how issues—or at least the Dynastic Succession answer to them—appeared to die away after the crisis of 1936 eased. But they had only gone underground; Percy Allen raised them again in 1938 in his examination of Herbert Lawrence's *The Life and Adventures of Common Sense*, first published in two volumes in 1769.[47]

Allen had been surprised to learn that doubt about authorship by the man from Stratford appeared in a publication as far back as 1769, the very year in which David Garrick inaugurated the Shakespeare Jubilee in Stratford-on-Avon. "I was thrilled by these two books," he wrote, "which to my thinking penetrate, in their own peculiarly symbolic way, far deeper into the actual facts of the Shakespearean mystery than do any other writings since the Restoration."[48]

Lawrence's story concerned characters with names such as Wit, Truth, Common Sense, Vanity and Wisdom, who, Allen believed, represented characters in the authorship

---

[46] J. Thomas Looney, letter to Katharine E. Eggar, December 21, 1936.

[47] In his letter to H.E. Wilson dated August 17, 1938, Allen thanked Wilson for alerting him to Lawrence's book. But in his articles in the *SF News-Letters* Allen said that he first learned of it from an article by Col. Douglas in the May *News-Letter*.

[48] Percy Allen, "The First Anti-Stratfordian," *SF News-Letter*, no. 11 (Sept. 1938): 1-5. The Restoration took place in 1660, when the English, Scottish and Irish monarchies were all restored under King Charles II.

story. The main storyline concerned plays written by Wit (whom Allen saw as Oxford in disguise) and acted in by his illegitimate son Humour (the Fair Youth of the *Sonnets*), whose mother was Vanity (Queen Elizabeth). The plays were stolen by an unnamed thief, and became known as written by Shakespeare. The few in the know, Humour explained, "agreed to maintain profound silence concerning this theft, being persuaded that my father and his friends would easily recover their loss. We feared, on the other hand, to put this man in the fetters of justice, which we could not have done without depriving the country of its greatest ornament" (4).

Allen provided an explanation for how Lawrence could have acquired the information on which he based his allegory. "Lawrence was an intimate of Lord Sandwich, and no doubt through him a friend of Lord de Vere Beauclerk, who was a collaborator with Lord Sandwich at the Admiralty. I read the above lines as a statement by Lawrence—made as openly as he dared—that he had first-hand authentic information from aristocrats, and members of the de Vere-Beauclerk family concerning Lord Oxford and the Shakespeare mystery; and also that he had access to written documents as well. . . . Lawrence tells us that he has been a 'faithful transcriber' of the secret information, written and oral, which has come down to him."[49]

Allen's purpose was to examine "the extent to which [Lawrence's work] corroborates, or disproves, the varying interpretations that members of the Fellowship have been putting hitherto upon this mystery of Shakespeare."[50] "The idea that Lawrence invented the allegory is, of course, utterly untenable, even [if] it were not, as it is, corroborated, in almost all the principal details, by the interpretation which, for years past, several members of the Shakespeare Fellowship have put upon the mystery. The fact that, in a matter so difficult, delicate, mysterious, and complicated, Herbert Lawrence and ourselves, working by wholly different methods, at a time-distance of a century and a half, should have arrived at substantially identical conclusions, seems to give authenticity to both interpretations. Each support the other."[51]

Allen explained how Lawrence's work cast light on the difficult position faced by academia and Shakespeare scholars in 1938.

> Another significant fact is that Herbert Lawrence's book, so far as I know, has been utterly ignored by Sir Edmund Chambers, and all other upholders of the traditional Shakespeare case. The reason is not far to seek. Shakespearean orthodoxy, these days, is having an unhappy time, when every passing year confronts its supporters with fresh and insuperable difficulties which they have long ago ceased to attempt to explain away; while almost every orthodox book that appears, instead of propping and a genuinely strengthening their tottering cause, only presents them with new problems.
>
> Our case gradually becomes more complete and unassailable. We have invited any opponent to meet us on the battlefield of facts. Thus far our challenge has not been accepted.[52]

Fellowship Board member T. M. Aitken, annoyed by Allen's raising the Dynastic Succession Theory yet again, sent a copy to Gerald Rendall, expecting, correctly, that he

---

[49] Percy Allen, "Commentary on *Life and Adventures of Common Sense* by Herbert Lawrence," *SF News-Letter*, no. 12 (Nov. 1938): 4.

[50] Percy Allen, "The First Anti-Stratfordian," *SF News-Letter*, no. 11 (Sept, 1938): 5.

[51] Percy Allen, "How Lawrence Acquired His Information," *SF News-Letter*, no. 12 (Nov. 1938): 17.

[52] Percy Allen, "The First Anti-Stratfordian," *SF News-Letter*, no. 11 (Sept, 1938): 5.

would also object to it. "I am enclosing the latest *News-Letter* from the Fellowship and hope it will not give you too much of a shock. . . . I can also assure you that Col. Douglas has no sympathy with P.A.'s methods or belief in his conclusions, and I have yet to find a single person whose opinion I value who thinks that the Fair Youth was a natural son of Q. E.'s."[53]

The Supplements to the *Newsletter*, No. 14 (April 1939)

Several members of the Fellowship were again angered by Percy Allen's presentations of the idea that the Shakespeare pseudonym was due to Oxford's having included in the plays and poems references to Southampton's true parentage as the son of Oxford and Elizabeth. In 1933 their disagreement with Allen's and Ward's ideas had led to the debate, and in 1936 to resignations by Rendall and Eggar. In 1939 their anger led to two extraordinary *Supplements* totaling twenty-eight pages published with the April 1939 issue of the *Shakespeare Fellowship News-Letter*.[54]

Although triggered in part by Allen's pieces on *Common Sense* in the *News-letter*, the *Supplements* were also a delayed reaction to Allen's and Ward's *Enquiry*. The first *Supplement* contained criticism of it by Gerald H. Rendall—"Notes and Comments on *An Enquiry*"—and by T. M. Aitken—"A Criticism of *An Enquiry*," with replies by Percy Allen and Capt. Ward. The second *Supplement* was Aitken's reply to them titled "Queen Elizabeth-Oxford-Son Theory."

The editor of the *News-Letter*, Capt. Ward, introduced the *Supplements* with a summary of the status of the Allen-Ward theory and the reactions to it.

> Two years ago Mr. Percy Allen and Capt. B. M. Ward published a pamphlet entitled *An Enquiry into the Relations Between Lord Oxford as "Shakespeare," Queen Elizabeth, and the Fair Youth of Shakespeare's Sonnets*. The purpose of the pamphlet was to show contemporary documentary evidence existing which pointed to the fact that in the mid-fifteen-seventies relations between Lord Oxford and Queen Elizabeth resulted in the birth of a son, who subsequently became the Fair Youth of Shakespeare's Sonnets. Since then Mr. Allen has amplified this theory from internal evidence of allegorical passages in 16th and 17th century books and plays.
>
> Some members, however, have disagreed with the evidence and the deductions advanced in the pamphlet and articles. This is all to the good, because we all feel that free and open discussion is the surest way to arrive at the truth. It was felt, however, that all members of the Fellowship are not particularly interested in this rather specialized and intricate aspect of the Shakespeare Problem, and that it would be unfair to many members to devote a whole *News-Letter* to it. Accordingly we are issuing a Supplement to the April 1939 *News-Letter*.

The *Supplements* contain much of interest on both sides. Two points warrant mention, one relating to external evidence such as documents and records, the other to internal evidence such as depictions in the plays of real-life people and events. On the first point Rendall charged that "no documentary evidence for the birth, existence, doings, or death

---

[53] T. M. Aitken, letter to Gerald H. Rendall, Nov. 29, 1938.
[54] The April 1939 *News-Letter* was issue no. 14. Issue no. 13, presumably issued in January or February, is lost. It would be fascinating to know what, if any, content in it was the direct trigger for the *Supplements* published with the April issue.

of this alleged bastard is produced."[55] Aitken made a similar point: "Every public and private library that offered hope of new material was searched. Not a paper . . . was left unseen."[56]

Percy Allen responded: "What does [Dr. Rendall] expect in a case such as this? I should have thought it unnecessary to remind him that the publication of 'documentary evidence,' of such matters, was mortally dangerous to those who might do so. Need I remind him that . . . among the things prohibited, on pain of death, [were] 'enquiry whether she (the queen) be still a virgin'?"[57]

On the second point, Aitken stated that "As regards what they call 'internal' evidence—I propose to ignore this altogether. Who can possibly decide what passages in the 37 plays and the poems have special reference to the personal experiences of the author?"[58] Allen's response was similar to his responses to Stratfordians on that point. "It is all very fine to tell us, as Mr. Aitken does, that all the internal evidence in this matter is 'absolutely valueless'; and to deny, as again he does, that we can anyway determine what particular passages in the plays, or in the poems, can refer to personal experiences of the author. That is a very easy escape from an unarguable position, and the indisputable fact is that the personalities and incidents of the Shakespeare plays of this period fit, with astonishing accuracy, the recorded facts of contemporary history, with such accuracy that the 'coincidence' solution becomes ludicrous."[59]

Commenting once again on the need for an informed imagination, Allen stated that "Neither of my opponents seem to have any understanding of the workings of the Elizabethan mind, or of their constant use of puns, double meanings, symbolic, and topical allusions, and elaborate word-play, sometimes in three languages, all methods which the Elizabethans looked upon as a legitimate form of art. . . . Until our opponents begin to understand these facts—for facts they certainly are—these gentlemen will never be able to agree with my interpretations. We think, and speak, in different languages" (15).

He also stated his view on the Elizabethans' clever use of classical stories as cover for topical references.

> Dr. Rendall's tendency to explain difficult passages, by pointing out that they are drawn from the classics, provides no escape from an, unwelcome to him, topical explanation. On the contrary, the ability of the Elizabethan writer, when challenged, to plead classical origin, or allusion, was the most convenient way of escape, when challenged by the censor, or other authority. Substantially, all Elizabethan literature was topical; and, as even orthodox professors, such as Dr. Harrison and Dr. Sisson, now admit, topicality was looked for both by readers and by audiences. Alike on the stage and in the study, it was the custom of a day which had no newspapers. (17)

In response to the charge that the examples Allen cited were mere coincidences,

> If you go before a judge with a series of coincidences which are sufficiently numerous, and hang sufficiently well together . . . that judge will give you judgement. Precisely in this manner are many of the most important criminal

---

[55] Gerald H. Rendall, "Notes and Comments on *An Enquiry*," *Supplement 1, SF News-Letter*, no. 14 (April 1939): 1.

[56] T. M. Aitken, "A Criticism of *An Enquiry*," *Supplement 1, SF News-Letter*, no. 14 (April 1939): 9.

[57] Percy Allen, "Mr. Percy Allen's Reply," *Supplement 1, SF News-Letter*, no. 14 (April 1939): 18.

[58] T. M. Aitken, "A Criticism of *An Enquiry*," *Supplement 1, SF News-Letter*, no. 14 (April 1939): 6.

[59] Percy Allen, "Mr. Percy Allen's Reply," *Supplement 1, SF News-Letter*, no. 14 (April 1939): 18.

trials solved; and the criminal is brought to justice. They do not leave behind them "documentary" evidence of their misdeeds. The truth must be sought, and is found, partly at least, in circumstantial evidence. (20)

We are, Allen reminded his readers, simply after the truth, whatever it is. "Capt. Ward and I have no axe to grind. We are endeavouring, single-mindedly, to ascertain the truth, in the most fascinating, mysterious, difficult, and important literary-historical problem with which students for hundreds of years past have been confronted."

In his rebuttal Capt. Ward similarly stated that their goal was simply to understand what happened. "I regard the two so-called 'Refutations' as lamentable failures. No attempt has been made to meet any of the external evidence except over Havering, which, as Allen has shown, is a pure mare's nest. It is true that you reject the evidence of the scandal letter as 'malicious gossip.' But that is neither here nor there. Of course it is 'malicious gossip'! The point is, is it true?"[60]

Ward then raised an interesting point needing further investigation:

> Why is there no will or administration in Somerset House of Oxford's estate? The officials there told me that they had never known a case of a nobleman, who left substantial property in London and Essex, leaving no will or administration. . . . I am not referring to the original will or administration, but to the copies which were scrupulously kept in the prerogative court of Canterbury. Without either a will or administration no property can pass. But . . . you may have noticed recently that when Prince Arthur of Connaught died his will was presented to the authorities and was sealed up and not transcribed into the records of Somerset House. Why? Because all wills of Royalty are sealed up and not made available to the public. (23)[61]

Allen took advantage of the opportunity to note a significant change in his thinking: "I am now coming round to the conclusion that the Fair Youth—though I have long denied it—may be Lord Southampton, because, during the last year or two, further evidence has come to light."[62]

The second *Supplement* concluded with a brief notice from the editor, Capt. Bernard M. Ward: "This controversy must now cease."

The dust settled for another two and a half years before Percy Allen again raised one aspect of the issue—whether Queen Elizabeth had borne any children—in an article in the *Fellowship News-Letter* in October 1941. Only one copy of that issue is known to have survived.[63] Allen wrote:

> An ex-member of the Fellowship . . . told the Editor [Percy Allen], some years ago, that a relative of hers, highly placed in the English Secret Service, told her that the Service possessed documentary evidence proving that Queen Elizabeth *did* bear a child, or children. That statement seems to be corroborated by a passage on p. 390 of a book published this year by John Murray, namely, *A Picture of Life*,

---

[60] Capt. Bernard M. Ward, "Reply to the 'Refutations,'" *Supplement 1, SF News-Letter*, No. 14 (April 1939): 23.

[61] That royal wills were "sealed up and not transcribed" is regarded as especially significant by some Oxfordian researchers, who proposed the idea that Edward de Vere himself was the oldest son of Elizabeth Tudor, born in 1548, a decade before she ascended the throne. That idea is not discussed here because it was not proposed until later, after the end of the first twenty-five years of the Oxfordian era. It is discussed in Chapter 21.

[62] Percy Allen, "Mr. Percy Allen's Reply," *Supplement 1, SF News-Letter*, No. 14 (April 1939): 19.

[63] The copy is in the Special Collections Room of the library at Brunel University in London.

1872-1940, by Viscount Mersey. The passage, which was kindly called to my attention by Mr. J. J. Dwyer, reads thus: "Jan. 19, 1936. Lady Wakehurst (Lady Louise Loder) told me of an account of a confinement of Queen Elizabeth being found among the archives at Windsor. It was given to Queen Victoria, who burnt it, saying that it was Queen Elizabeth's private affair."

I wrote to Lord Mersey, asking for further information upon the subject . . . he promptly replied as follows: "August 22, 1941. . . . As regards the tale about Queen Elizabeth . . . my only authority was Lady Wakefield (Wakehurst?), and I do not think she told me the date either of the birth of the child or of the find. Perhaps she might be able to give you some further information."

Concerning the natural tendency of persons compromised or embarrassed thereby, to destroy awkward evidence, the following passage from p. 236 of Lord Mersey's book is pertinent, and interesting. "Dec. 6, 1911. . . . On this being explained to the Duke, he said, 'That might cause a lot of trouble,' and put the document in the fire."[64]

With only the above exception, after the *Supplements* were published in April 1939 the *News-Letter* did not address the Dynastic Succession Theory again for more than a decade.

But Percy Allen did. Four years after the *Supplement*, during the Second World War, he wrote and printed for sale seventy copies of a pamphlet titled *Who Were the Dark Lady and Fair Youth of the Sonnets?* In it he drew together and updated all of his writings on the idea that references in the *Sonnets* and the plays to Southampton's true parentage and its dynastic considerations were the reason that Oxford's authorship was hidden. Drawing on more than forty literary works, he presented passages showing that the relationship between Oxford and the Queen was widely known and that Henry Wriothesley, Third Earl of Southampton, was widely regarded in theatrical circles as their illegitimate son. Allen was now fully convinced that he had answered the "why" question, if not the "how" question, of Oxford's having hidden the authorship of his literary works behind a pseudonym.

The most significant new development was Allen's unequivocal acceptance of the Earl of Southampton as the Fair Youth of the *Sonnets*.

The identification of the Fair Youth is to my mind, in the main, equally certain, though slightly more complex. . . . The Fair Youth's identity is not open to doubt, since no open-minded reader of Dr. G. H. Rendall's two valuable books on the sonnets can easily deny that the Fair Youth is the 3rd Earl of Southampton, an opinion also held by the only biographer of Southampton, Mrs. Charlotte Stopes, and accepted, I suppose, by a large majority even of orthodox Shakespeareans today.

This conclusion—when I reached it, about the middle of the nineteen-thirties—landed me in a dilemma, because I had satisfied myself not only that Oxford and his Queen had produced a son in 1575, but also that this son was no other than

---

[64] "Did Queen Elizabeth Bear a Child?" *Shakespeare Fellowship News-Letter*, October 1941, p. 3.
R. R. Trout told a similar story to Katharine Eggar in a letter dated September 28, 1951:

"I was told today a remarkable story. It appears to have been told direct to a member of a noted family, who herself told it to me. Sir John Fortescue, the military historian, was conversing with Queen Victoria and told her of an extraordinary document which he had recently discovered. She asked that she might read it and he handed it to her. After some weeks of waiting he at last took courage and asked her Majesty if she had read it and could he have it returned, as we wished to use it. She replied that she had burnt it. The document was the details of the birth of Queen Elizabeth's second son."

the Fair Youth of the *Sonnets*. But I was also satisfied that Southampton was the Fair Youth of the *Sonnets*. Therefore Southampton must be Elizabeth's son by Oxford![65]

It is interesting to note that Looney and Allen relied on a similar syllogism to make points of supreme importance:

Looney:

> The argument in favor of the Earl of Oxford may be summarised thus:
> 1. The Prince Hamlet is "Shakespeare" himself.
> 2. Hamlet is the Earl of Oxford.
> 3. Therefore the Earl of Oxford is "Shakespeare."[66]

Allen:

> Oxford and his Queen had produced a son.
> [The son was] the Fair Youth of the Sonnets.
> Southampton was the Fair Youth of the Sonnets.
> Therefore Southampton must be Elizabeth's son by Oxford.[67]

To understand most fully the events that occurred from 1937 until the end of the period covered by Part One of this book—1945 in England and 1948 in the United States—it is necessary to take a deeper look at how academia responded to the Oxfordian challenge.

---

[65] Percy Allen, *Who Were the Dark Lady and Fair Youth of Shakespeare's Sonnets?* (1943)
[66] J. Thomas Looney, "Who Wrote Hamlet?" *Hackney Spectator*, April 20, 1923, p. 4.
[67] Percy Allen, *Who Were the Dark Lady and Fair Youth of Shakespeare's Sonnets?* (1943)

11

Academia and the Oxfordian Challenge: Public Responses

Academia's Response to J. Thomas Looney and *"Shakespeare" Identified*

In July 1925, five years after J. Thomas Looney's *"Shakespeare" Identified* was published, the English Association issued a pamphlet titled *A Shakespeare Reference Library*. It listed books most useful for "the advanced study of Shakespeare and his relations to the contemporary drama and stage,"[1] arranged by sections such as Texts of the Works; Grammar, Phonetics, and Prosody; Sources of the Plots; Biography; Topography; Political and Social Environment; and Contemporary Drama. The pamphlet made no mention of an authorship question.

Its authors, Sir Sidney Lee and Sir Edmund Chambers, the most respected Shakespearean scholars of the day, were among the staunchest defenders of the traditional story of authorship by the man from Stratford.

<u>Sir Sidney Lee</u> (quoted 66 times in *"Shakespeare" Identified*), was regarded as England's greatest Shakespeare scholar of the first three decades of the twentieth century. His book, *A Life of William Shakespeare*, first published in 1898 and updated in several subsequent editions, provided the fullest account of the life of William Shakspere and the literary career of William Shakespeare, who Lee believed were the same person. In *"Shakespeare" Identified*, Looney called that book "invaluable" because Lee had "furnished more material in support of my constructive argument than any other single modern writer."[2]

Lee, who died in 1926, commented publicly on the Oxfordian claim only twice. One instance was in a footnote in the 1922 edition of *A Life of William Shakespeare*—in the section on the Baconian idea—he wrote: "Equally ludicrous endeavours have been made to transfer Shakespeare's responsibility to the shoulders of other contemporaries besides Bacon. . . . To the same category of futility belongs *"Shakespeare" Identified*—Edward de

---

[1] Sir Sidney Lee and Sir Edmund Chambers, *A Shakespeare Reference Library*, Pamphlet No. 61, English Association, July 1925, p. 1.
[2] J. Thomas Looney, *"Shakespeare" Identified* (2018), p. 111.

Vere, the Seventeenth Earl of Oxford, by J. Thomas Looney (London 1920)."[3]

The other was the brief letter in *The Bookman's Journal* already noted, in which he stated, "[Lefranc's] theory seems to me to present difficulties which are quite insuperable. . . . [M]uch of what I said of the French professor's theory applies equally well to Mr. Looney's."[4] It should not be forgotten, though, that before Looney introduced the Oxfordian claim, Lee had expressed a favorable opinion of Oxford's poetry in *The Dictionary of National Biography*.

Sir Edmund K. Chambers, author of several of the most authoritative books on William Shakespeare and the Elizabethan stage, paid almost no attention to the authorship question. His only reference to it was to the Derby theory—"I do not accept Mr. James Greenstreet's theory that W. Stanley was the real W. Shakespeare,"[5]—and even there he did not acknowledge the existence of Professor Abel Lefranc's massive two-volume *Sous le Masque de "William Shakespeare": William Stanley, Vle Comte de Derby*. His only mention of Looney's book was in the appendix to volume three of *The Elizabethan Stage*:

> J. T. Looney, *"Shakespeare" Identified* (1920), gives him (i.e. Lord Oxford) Shakespeare's plays, many of which were written after his death.[6]

Like Sir Sidney Lee, Chambers was fully aware of Edward de Vere's poetry, and expressed a favorable opinion of it. In *The Oxford Book of Sixteenth Century Verse* (1932), he stated that "The most hopeful of [the courtier poets] was Edward de Vere, Earl of Oxford, a real courtier, but an ill-conditioned youth, who also became mute in later life."[7] That collection included three of Oxford's poems, which were selected on their merits: "In the present [collection] an attempt has been made to apply a standard of absolute poetry, rather than one of merely historic interest" (vii). Chambers also made the interesting statement that "it is not easy to see why the first half of Elizabeth's reign . . . [in which] a settled and prosperous national life was shaping itself, should have proved so barren. Perhaps the simplest explanation is that no new genius happened to be born. Much verse, indeed, was written, and the habit of publication grew up among court hangers-on in search of patronage" (vi-vii). Chambers might have partially answered his own question by noting that much of the best poetry of the time was circulated in manuscript within court circles but not published—Oxford's own poetry being a prime example. He might also have noted that Oxford, as the primary patron of writers and musicians of the time other than the Queen herself, was responsible for the publication in 1573 of Bedingfield's translation of *Cardanus Comforte* and "George Gascoigne's" *A Hundreth Sundrie Flowers*.[8]

No Substantive Challenge to the Oxfordian Claim

Lee and Chambers had at least mentioned J. Thomas Looney and *"Shakespeare" Identified*. A review of the works of the fifty-two most prominent Shakespeare scholars of the day shows that thirty-four of them—listed in the nearby textbox—made no mention

---

[3] Sir Sidney Lee, *A Life of William Shakespeare* (1922), p. 651.

[4] Sir Sidney Lee, "The Identity of Shakespeare," *Bookman's Journal*, vol. 2/30 (May 21, 1920): 58.

[5] Sir Edmund Chambers, *The Elizabethan Stage*, vol. II (1923), p. 127.

[6] Sir Edmund Chambers, *The Elizabethan Stage*, vol. III (1923), p. 503.

[7] E. K. Chambers (editor), *The Oxford Book of Sixteenth Century Verse* (1932), p. vi-vii.

[8] Capt. Bernard M. Ward, in *The Seventeenth Earl of Oxford* (1928), made a persuasive case that Edward de Vere was the compiler, publisher, and primary author of *A Hundreth Sundrie Flowers* (see Chapter 7).

at all of Looney or the challenge the Oxfordian thesis presented to traditional Shakespearean beliefs. The failure by almost two-thirds of the leading Shakespeare scholars even to take notice of the Oxfordian claim—let alone respond to it—led many Oxfordians (beginning with Looney himself) to conclude that the thesis hadn't been disproved because it couldn't be. It wasn't that Oxfordians were hiding; on the contrary they directly and repeatedly challenged academia to examine their claim and to debate it.

Shakespeare Scholars Who Did **Not** Respond to Looney and *"Shakespeare" Identified*	
	Age in 1920
Joseph Quincy Adams, Jr. (1880-1946)	40
A. C. Bradley (1851-1935)	69
Andrew S. Cairncross (1901-1975)	19
Lily B. Campbell (1883-1967)	37
Harold Child (1869-1945)	59
Hardin Craig (1875-1968)	45
Albert Feuillerat (1874-1952)	46
Edgar I. Fripp (1861-1939)	59
Harold C. Goddard (1878-1950)	42
Israel Gollancz (1863-1930)	57
W. W. Greg (1875-1959)	45
Edward G. Harman (1862-1921)	58
Frank Harris (1856-1931)	64
G. B. Harrison (1894-1991)	26
Alfred Hart (1870-1950)	50
Leslie Hotson (1897-1992)	23
Hugh Kingsmill (1889-1949)	31
Abel Lefranc (1863-1952)	57
J. W. Mackail (1959-1945)	61
Arthur Quiller-Couch (1863-1944)	57
Sir Walter Raleigh (1861-1922)	59
Alfred L. Rowse (1903-1997)	17
George Saintsbury (1845-1933)	75
Felix E. Schelling (1858-1945)	62
Charles J. Sisson (1885-1966)	35
John Temple Smart (1868-1925)	52
G. Gregory Smith (1865-1932)	55
Caroline Spurgeon (1869-1942)	59
Charlotte Carmichael Stopes (1840-1929)	80
Samuel A. Tannenbaum (1874-1948)	46
E. M. W. Tillyard (1889-1962)	31
Mark Van Doren (1894-1972)	26
J. Dover Wilson (1881-1969)	39
Lilian Winstanley (1875-1960)	45

> ➤ J. Thomas Looney, 1920: "The ordeal has been passed through; I have watched anxiously every criticism and suggestion that has been made, and what is the result? . . . Not a single really formidable or destructive objection to the theory has yet put in an appearance."[9]

> ➤ Frederick Taber Cooper, 1920: "Every right-minded scholar who seriously cares for the welfare of letters in the bigger sense should face the problem that this book presents and argue it to a finish."[10]

> ➤ Col. Bernard R. Ward on Lord Sydenham and Mr. Crouch Batchelor, 1924: They "have issued a resounding challenge to the Shakespearean experts 'to descend from their pedestals, to abandon the pose of disdain, and, quitting vague generalities, to take up the challenges now thrown down by supplying—if they can—rational explanations of simple facts. . . . What is likely to be the effect of Lord Sydenham's challenge? Will it be seriously taken up, or will it be passed by as unworthy of serious notice?"[11]

> ➤ Ernest Allen, 1932: "The dominant note in the evening's discussion [at the Fellowship's annual dinner in April] was the extraordinary reticence observed by

---

[9] J. Thomas Looney, "The Identity of Shakespeare," *Bookman's Journal*, vol. 2/30 (May 21, 1920): 58.
[10] Frederick Taber Cooper, source not known.
[11] Col. Bernard R. Ward, "The 'Shakespeare' Myth," *Hackney Spectator*, August 15, 1924, p. 11.

the many opponents of the Oxford theory. . . . So far as the writer of this article is aware, no single scholar or man of letters has ventured upon any criticism of the theories these books propound. A recent convert, Miss Marjorie Bowen, the famous historical novelist, . . . has latterly called attention to the subject, but so far has not succeeded in inducing anyone to break silence."[12]

➤ Percy Allen, 1935: "The case for Lord Oxford as 'Shakespeare' may be accepted or rejected upon the evidence; but it can be successfully derided only by those who are ignorant of it—and then only when addressing the ignorant. Dr. Lawrence, however, as it appears, thinks otherwise; and I invite him, therefore, in the cause of Shakespearian truth, to demolish the "Oxford" case publicly, as soon as he pleases, by argument, either on the platform or in the Press. It will give me pleasure to meet him at any time."[13]

➤ Ernest Allen, 1937: "This evidence . . . has never been answered. It is now so strong that any adequate answer is impossible, and, so far as I am aware, not even a pamphlet has appeared from an orthodox pen containing any counter attack against ourselves. . . . On platform too, as well as on paper, our case stands untouched. It is difficult, almost impossible, to get any orthodox speaker to oppose our members in debate. I don't envy any aspirant to platform honours of this nature, if he or she supports the orthodox case. It is untenable."[14]

➤ William Kent, 1939: "My friend Mr. Percy Allen vainly challenges them. I also throw down the glove to anybody who chooses to debate on the issue: 'Is it now reasonable to believe that the Stratford actor wrote the Shakespeare plays?' I have little expectation of any response. The Stratfordians are so reluctant to enter the war they maintain they can so easily win; so mercifully reticent about publishing the book that must bomb us out of existence!"[15]

Were there, in fact, no efforts by respected Shakespeare scholars, within or outside of academia, to objectively consider the Oxfordian claim and pronounce their considered academic opinion of it and Looney's book? Of the fifty-two scholars whose works during the first twenty-five years of the Oxfordian era were examined, eighteen, including Lee and Chambers, did at least notice the existence of the Oxfordian claim. But their examinations were superficial.

Ivor Brown referred to the Oxfordian claim several times over more than a decade. Although he did not examine it in these comments from 1937, he did mention Oxford:

> Accordingly, it is possible that we are going to celebrate still further the memory of the wrong man, and that what we need is an Oxford or a Bacon Memorial Theatre. . . . To take that view is to be particular about the name. Chiefly we want to honour the author of the plays and poems, whatever his name. At the same time, we need not pretend that the name is unimportant. Here is the greatest master of the English language who ever lived. Is his identity a mere trifle? Not the most zealous Stratfordian can pretend that we know much about his hero.[16]

---

[12] Ernest Allen, "Annual Dinner," *Shakespeare Pictorial*, July 1932, p. 116.

[13] Percy Allen, "Lord Oxford as Shakespeare," *Times Literary Supplement*, Oct. 3, 1935, p. 612.

[14] Ernest Allen, "Correspondence," *East Anglian Magazine*, vol. 3/3 (Dec. 1937): 142.

[15] William Kent, "Mr. William Kent's New Book," *SF News-Letter*, no. 14 (April 1939), p. 8.

[16] Ivor Brown, "The World of the Theatre," *Illustrated London News*, October 9, 1937, p. 28. His assessments are considered more fully in Chapter 14.

<u>Muriel St. Clare Byrne</u>, who had reviewed several of Percy Allen's books for *The Times Literary Supplement* and other publications, mentioned J. Thomas Looney and his book only once, in her 1930 review of Percy Allen's *The Case for Edward de Vere as "Shakespeare."*

> Among the various candidates for Shakespearian honours. . . . Oxford is the favourite. Mr. Looney's *"Shakespeare" Identified* (1920) has been followed up by the work of Colonel and Captain Ward, Dr. Rendall and Mr. Allen, so that it may now fairly be said that the Oxford offensive is fully launched.[17]

<u>Professor Oscar James Campbell's</u> critique of Looney's book and the Oxfordian idea was so intellectually dishonest that Looney's response included this charge:

> I accuse him of a deliberate attempt, not to present the Oxford case fairly and squarely, as honest opponents of ideas do with the cases they controvert, but to set it forth so flimsily, and even grotesquely, that hardly anyone but an imbecile could very well believe in it if it rested on nothing more substantial. This is the kind of argumentation one associates with political maneuvering rather than a serious quest for the truth on great issues and it makes one suspect that he is not very easy in his own mind about the case.[18]

<u>John Drinkwater</u>, the popular playwright, challenged Percy Allen and the Oxfordian claim in his book, *Shakespeare* (1933). Among his many errors, he confused dates of publication with dates of composition: "Inconveniently for Mr. Allen's thesis, Edward de Vere the seventeenth earl of Oxford, died in 1604, after which date several of the Shakespearean plays were written."[19]

Shakespeare Scholars Who Responded to Looney and *"Shakespeare" Identified*, Even If Only Superficially		
	Age in 1920	**Mentions in**
Ivor Brown (1891-1974)	29	1927-29, 1937-39
Muriel St. Clare Byrne (1895-1983)	25	1930
Oscar James Campbell (1880-1970)	40	1940
Sir Edmund Chambers (1866-1954)	54	1923
John Drinkwater (1882-1937)	38	1933
Roderick L. Eagle (1887-1977)	33	1920, 1929
George Hookham (1851-1930)	69	1922
G. Wilson Knight (1897-1985)	23	1930
Basil Edwin Lawrence (1853-1929)	67	1925
Sir Sidney Lee (1859-1926)	40	1920, 1922
R. Macdonald Lucas (not known)	--	1921, 1924
Thomas O'Hagan (1855-1939)	65	1920
Alfred W. Pollard (1859-1944)	61	1920
J. M. Robertson (1856-1933)	64	1920
Hyder Edward Rollins (1889-1958)	31	1927, '31, '33, '35
Logan Pearsall Smith (1865-1946)	55	1933
John Collins Squire (Solomon Eagle) (1884-1958)	36	1921-23, 1928
Elmer E. Stoll (1874-1959)	46	1937

---

[17] Muriel St. Clare Byrne, "Oxford as 'Shakespeare,'" *Times Literary Supplement*, Sept. 11, 1930, p. 712.

[18] J. Thomas Looney, "The Author of "Shakespeare" Identified Comments on Professor Campbell's July 1940 *Harper's* Article," *SF News-Letter* (American), vol. 2, no. 1 (Dec. 1940): 2. Professor Campbell is discussed more fully in Chapter 16.

[19] John Drinkwater, *Shakespeare* (1933), p. 33.

Roderick L. Eagle, in his review of *"Shakespeare" Identified* in *Baconiana*, thanked Looney for "bringing into prominence the personality of this courtier-poet and the charming lyrics associated with his name," but went on to cite reasons why Bacon would be a more logical selection."[20]

George Hookham, a Baconian who had corresponded with Looney in 1922, relied on the same argument as Drinkwater: "Mr. J. T. Looney has lately advanced the claims of Edward de Vere, Earl of Oxford, to the authorship of the Plays, with, I think, greater assurance than can belong to such doubtful matter. Oxford died in 1604, nineteen years before the date of the First Folio: so that the difficulty in the case of Shakspere of Stratford arising from the facts of *Richard III* are magnified in the case of de Vere."[21]

G. Wilson Knight addressed the Oxfordian claim once, in a 1930 review of Percy Allen's *The Case for Edward de Vere as "Shakespeare."* Although he did not mention Looney or *"Shakespeare" Identified*, he made a remarkable admission. Responding to Percy Allen's statement that "Shakespeare's intimate familiarity with Oxford's poems is undeniable," Knight wrote, "Here is a sound deduction from a carefully correlated list of parallels." But, he continued, "those parallels prove nothing as to authorship;"[22] they merely suggest that Shakspere had read Oxford, a point that would have carried more weight if he had explained how Shakspere would have had access to Oxford's poems, which circulated in manuscript privately among his fellow courtiers.

Basil Edwin Lawrence, in *Notes on the Authorship of Shakespeare's Plays and Poems* (1925), addressed the Oxfordian claim directly. Of J. Thomas Looney and the case presented in *"Shakespeare" Identified*, he wrote, "I cannot see that the fact that Edward de Vere wrote a short poem in the same metre as that of *Venus and Adonis* is any proof that he wrote this latter poem."[23] Lawrence is right; the latter does not follow from the former. But Looney never said that it did. In citing that clue as the only piece of evidence upon which Looney based his theory, Lawrence misrepresented matters and did a disservice to his readers.

Lawrence then stated that "Every one must admit that Shakespeare made free use of the writings of others. . . . He took De Vere's thoughts and clothed them in more beautiful garbs. De Vere's verses were in existence in 1593, and I think it must be admitted that the ideas and thoughts, although they may be much the same as De Vere's, are much better expressed in *Venus and Adonis* than they are in De Vere's Echo verses" (105). His statement that Shakespeare "took de Vere's thoughts and clothed them in more beautiful garbs" is extraordinary. Did he realize that he had acknowledged a direct link between Oxford and Shakespeare? His statement that "Shakespeare" had "better expressed" the ideas than Oxford as a young man in the 1570s is beside the point. Such a statement is most likely true of every artist or writer—that their mature works were more accomplished than their youthful efforts.

R. Macdonald Lucas critiqued Looney and *"Shakespeare" Identified* in the *National Review* in 1921 (see Chapter 4). Of importance was his statement that "All lovers of literature must . . . be grateful to Mr. Looney for the scholarly care with which he has connected certain facts of Oxford's life . . . with 'Shakespeare's' Works, but must also regret

---

[20] Roderick L. Eagle, "Shakespeare and the Earl of Oxford," *Baconiana*, vol. XVI/63 (March 1921): 84-85.

[21] George Hookham, *Will o' the Wisp, or The Elusive Shakespeare* (1922), p. 60.

[22] G. Wilson Knight, "Shakespeare and the Earl of Oxford" [review of Allen's *Case*], *Nation & Athenaeum*, May 3, 1930, p. 150.

[23] Basil Edwin Lawrence, *Notes on the Authorship of Shakespeare's Plays and Poems* (1925), p. 103.

that he has passed beyond the true mark in an endeavor to set up a theory that is— *hopeless*. There is no other word for it."[24]

Thomas O'Hagan. Chapter II of his book *What Shakespeare is Not* (1920), which he titled "Shakespeare Identified," contained several brief passages touching on the Oxfordian idea. This one is the most substantive:

> J. Thomas Looney in his work, *"Shakespeare" Identified*, has been the last to train his guns on the citadel of Stratfordian claims; and has, in our opinion, made by far the best case for the guerilla literary band which he represents. The likeness, in style and phrase and poetic mannerism, found in the lyrics of Lord Oxford and the lyrics of Shakespeare is very striking indeed. Yet this we fear is not a satisfying solution of the Shakespeare problem.[25]

O'Hagan didn't mention that the title of his chapter was derived from the title of Looney's book, nor did he list Looney or Oxford in the index.

Alfred W. Pollard's carefully considered view of *"Shakespeare" Identified* in *The Times Literary Supplement*—"Fundamentally it is a sad waste of print and paper"[26]—has been noted. He never again mentioned in print Looney or his book.

J. M. Robertson. In *The Bookman's Journal*, Robertson wrote that "Mr. Looney . . . has not offered the faintest semblance of a 'proof' that the Stratford actor did not write [the plays]. . . . It is precisely because the data for the Stratford actor alone gives an intelligible biographical substratum for the plays that I hold to it."[27] Has a more nonsensical statement ever been made?

Hyder Edward Rollins dismissed Looney and *"Shakespeare" Identified* in harsh terms in his edition of *The Paradise of Dainty Devices*, one of the first Elizabethan era collections of poetry.

> It hardly seems worth while to pay much attention to Mr. J. Thomas Looney's *Poems of Edward de Vere Seventeenth Earl of Oxford* (1921), the sole purpose of which is to strengthen his theory, formally advanced in his *"Shakespeare" Identified* (1920), that Oxford and "Shakespeare" . . . were one and the same poet. . . . The verbal parallels . . . which Mr. Looney painstakingly amasses are, on the whole, mere commonplaces [that] prove nothing except that Shakespeare and Oxford, like all other Elizabethans, indulged in the use of fashionable commonplaces and figures.[28]

Given the harshness of his assessment, it is startling to see that, in the index to *England's Helicon,* the last of the four Elizabethan collections Rollins edited, the words "Alias Shakespeare" next to the entry for Edward de Vere.[29] It is not known whether Rollins himself inserted that phrase, and he never again mentioned Looney or *"Shakespeare" Identified* in his writings.

Logan Pearsall Smith, in *On Reading Shakespeare* (1933), mentioned Oxford (but not Looney) in his breezy dismissal of the entire authorship question.

> We hear . . . the war-cries of the Filiolaters and Disintegrators as they rush upon

---

[24] R. Macdonald Lucas, "Did Lord Derby Write Shakespeare?" *National Review*, vol. 78 (Nov. 1921): 69.

[25] Thomas O'Hagan, *What Shakespeare is Not* (1936), p. 20.

[26] Alfred W. Pollard, "Another 'Identification' of Shakespeare," *Times Literary Sup.*, March 4, 1920, p. 149.

[27] J. M. Robertson, "The Identity of Shakespeare," *Bookman's Journal*, vol. 2/30 (May 21, 1920): 58, 59. His review of *"Shakespeare" Identified* in *The Yorkshire Post* was discussed in Chapter 3.

[28] Hyder E. Rollins (editor), *The Paradise of Dainty Devices* (1927), p. lix, lx.

[29] Hyder E. Rollins (editor), *England's Helicon* (1935), vol. II, p. 239.

each other; and even wilder battle cries than these (for it is impossible to exaggerate their strangeness) will reach our ears. For listen! the fanatic followers of no less than five ghostly, resurrected Elizabethan Earls are shouting at each other, the two bands of Pembrokians and Southamptonites, each vociferating that their Lord was the inspirer of the *Sonnets*, while three other bands proclaim the more glorious boast (at least more glorious to some thinkers) that Lord Derby, or Lord Rutland, or Lord Oxford, was the author of them, and of Shakespeare's plays as well. And then, faint and far, as the wind shifts, we hear the ululations of those vaster herds of Baconian believers, as they plunge squeaking down the Gadarene slope of their delusion.[30]

John Collings Squire (using the pen name Solomon Eagle), who had engaged in a lengthy exchange of letters with J. Thomas Looney in *The Observer* in 1921 (see Chapter 4), returned to the Oxfordian thesis in *Essays at Large* (1922). After providing an accurate summation of the factors that led Looney into his investigations he dismissed the Oxfordian claim, largely because of Looney's unconvincing answers to the "why" and "how" questions. He found it easier to believe that Shakspere kept the secret of his genius hidden from the people of Stratford than that Oxford could have kept his authorship secret. "I can swallow the lawsuits, the acting, the will, the second-best bed . . . far more easily than I can this monstrous figment of a conspiracy, known to very many people and mentioned by none. . . . Does Mr. Looney seriously suppose that it would not have leaked out; that nobody would mention it in letter or diary; that nobody, after the masquerader's death, would pass it on by word of mouth?"[31]

Elmer E. Stoll, in his critique of Charles Barrell's presentation of the Oxfordian idea (see Chapter 16), mentioned "Oxonians" Percy Allen, Col. Bernard R. Ward and Eva Turner Clark, but, oddly, never referred to Looney or *"Shakespeare" Identified*. Sticking points for him were, like for so many others, the "why" and "how" questions. He wanted to know, if Oxford was Shakespeare, "why he robbed himself" of credit for his work and how his authorship could possibly have been kept hidden "without all of London knowing all about it."[32]

The sixteen Shakespeare scholars noted here, together with Lee and Chambers, are not just *representative* examples; they are the *only* instances in which the fifty-two most prominent Shakespearean scholars of the day responded to the Oxfordian claim and its first presentation in *"Shakespeare" Identified*. The list of scholars who did not respond to the Oxfordian challenge is almost twice as long as the list of those who did. Even within the latter group, most responded only in a cursory way.

Henry Clay Folger (1857-1930) belongs in a special category. He was not a Shakespeare scholar in the traditional sense but was prominent in the field of Shakespeare Studies because of his founding of the Folger Shakespeare Library. Although he never spoke or wrote publicly about the authorship question, he was reportedly a Baconian at some point. Near the end of his life he purchased and distributed to friends dozens of copies of Esther Singleton's novel *Shakespearian Fantasias*, which has an

---

[30] Logan Pearsall Smith, *On Reading Shakespeare* (1933), p. 31. A footnote at the end of that passage states: "I do not wish, however, to speak with any disrespect of that view of the authorship of Shakespeare's plays which is so firmly held by officers in the Navy and the Army, by one of his Majesty's judges, and the manager of more than one large drapery establishment, and is corroborated by the authority of Mark Twain, Mrs. Henry Pott, Prince Bismarck, John Bright, the late Mr. Crump, K.C., and several thoughtful baronets."
[31] John C. Squire, "Shakespeare and the Second Chamber," in *Essays at Large* (1922), pp. 133-34.
[32] Elmer Edgar Stoll, "The Detective Spirit in Criticism," *Saturday Review*, May 8, 1937, p. 12.

Oxfordian theme. It will be interesting to see what Folger's correspondence reveals about his thinking on the authorship question once it has been fully catalogued and published.

Academic Responses to the Oxfordian Challenge: Ideal

What was it exactly that Oxfordian scholars wanted from Stratfordian scholars? They wanted them to do what they were being paid to do: examine literary questions and issues in a scholarly way. They wanted the Shakespeare authorship question to be examined in the same manner in which all other literary matters were examined.

What did they mean by this? Stanley Fish, Dean Emeritus at the University of Illinois, Chicago, writing in 2008, provided guidance that would have been unquestioningly accepted by scholars in the 1920s and 1930s. "The evaluation, not the celebration, of interests, beliefs, and identities is what intellectual work is all about."[33] The goal of academic study isn't the promotion of any specific conclusions, but rather the study of a subject in a disinterested manner.

> [Subjects] should be discussed in academic terms; that is, they should be the objects of analysis, comparison, historical placement, etc.; the arguments put forward in relation to them should be dissected and assessed as arguments and not as preliminaries to action on the part of those doing the assessing. The action one takes (or should take) at the conclusion of an academic discussion is the action of tendering an academic verdict as in "that argument makes sense," "there's a hole in the reasoning here," "the author does (or does not) realize her intention," "in this debate, X has the better of Y," "the case is still not proven." These and similar judgments are judgments on craftsmanship and coherence— they respond to questions like "is it well made?" and "does it hang together?" (144)

Because the authorship question deals with events that took place in the past, methodologies appropriate to historical research are also relevant. Looney had noted that the authorship question was not a purely literary matter. The guidance most appropriate for historians—including literary historians considering the authorship question—was laid out by David Hackett Fischer in *Historians' Fallacies: Toward a Logic of Historical Thought* in 1970, and would have been accepted as uncontroversial half a century earlier. The most appropriate approach for historians consists of "adductive reasoning," which is sometimes called "abductive."

> History must begin with questions. Questions for historians are like hypotheses for scientists. . . . The logic of historical thought . . . is a process of adductive reasoning in the simple sense of adducing answers to specific questions, so that a satisfactory explanatory "fit" is obtained. . . . The questions and answers are fitted to each other by a complex process of mutual adjustment. . . . Always it is articulated in the form of a reasoned argument.[34]

An important step of the process of historical investigation is that of leaving behind modern ways of thinking. Historians must slough off current sensibilities in order to try to understand how people in the times and places they are studying understood developments as they occurred. Historian J. H. Elliott explained it best: they must "enter imaginatively into the life of a society remote in time or place, and produce a plausible

---

[33] Stanley Fish, *Save the World on Your Own Time* (2008), p. 11.
[34] David Hackett Fischer, *Historians' Fallacies: Toward a Logic of Historical Thought* (1970), pp. xx, 4.

explanation of why its inhabitants thought and behaved as they did."[35] This sounds very much like the "informed imagination" that Percy Allen repeatedly encouraged Shakespearean scholars to develop.

Several important academic scholars did, in fact, investigate the authorship question in a scholarly manner. Their names did not appear on the lists earlier in this chapter because none were literary scholars. All were from fields outside the study of literature who felt compelled, for one reason or another, to conduct the type of unbiased, academic investigation into the authorship issue that literary scholars should have conducted. Most prominent among them were three persons who have been discussed in previous chapters:

Gerald H. Rendall, classics scholar and professor of Greek, former Principal of Victoria College, University of Liverpool, and for fifteen years Headmaster of the Charterhouse School.

Dr. Gilbert Slater, Principal of Ruskin College, Oxford University, a prominent member of the British Royal Historical Society and a recognized authority on Elizabethan economics.

Dr. Joan V. Robinson, an economist at Cambridge University whose contributions to the development and furtherance of post-Keynesian economic theory earned her a national reputation.

Rendall explained that, "In my study of the *Sonnets* . . . I began with the single desire to get at the heart of the writer and his meaning, and so far as authorship was concerned to 'follow the argument, wherever it led.' . . . little by little I was led, nay driven, to conclusions for which I can hardly look for immediate or popular acceptance. They are too far-reaching and subversive; yet I hope to win the suffrages of fellow-students, not too much wedded or pledged to their own pronouncements, to entertain or reconsider new evidence, and that they will verify clues which I have only ventured to submit by way of suggestion or parenthesis."[36]

Slater said something similar: "In making this review of theories and of the evidence for them I have endeavoured to avoid partisanship, and to think and feel as a conscientious judge should, and not as an advocate. I have expressed my own opinions, but have tried not to press them unduly, but rather to put the reader in a position to form his own judgment."[37]

Robinson, in a lengthy article in *The Cambridge Review* in 1933, told readers of "the pleasure of reading Mr. Looney" and noted the contrast between Shakspere, "a person who, on all the external evidence, appears to have been a nonentity," and Oxford, "a very gifted, fascinating, and somewhat explosive character, claimed by his contemporaries to be the leading poet . . . of the court [and] the patron of a company of players."[38]

She went on to describe "successive historians, like sheep following each other through the gap in a hedge," who have left his life unexplored, in contrast with Capt. Ward's "meticulously impartial" *The Seventeenth Earl of Oxford*. In her judgment, among the "much unpublished material . . . brought to light by Mr. Ward no single fact emerges that is incompatible with Mr. Looney's hypothesis. . . . [E]very fresh touch which is added

---

[35] J. H. Elliott, *History in the Making* (2012), p. xi.
[36] Gerald H. Rendall, *Shakespeare Sonnets and Edward de Vere* (1930), p. 3.
[37] Gilbert Slater, *Seven Shakespeares* (1931), p. xiii.
[38] Joan V. Robinson, "Shakespeare and Mr. Looney," *Cambridge Review*, May 12, 1933, p. 389.

to the portrait of de Vere makes him resemble more closely, in character and in circumstance, the kind of man who might have written 'Shakespeare.'" She was as impressed by Gerald Rendall's analysis of the internal evidence in the *Sonnets* connecting Oxford's personality with "Shakespeare's" works as she was by the external evidence uncovered by Capt. Ward.

Robinson asked, and tried to answer, two questions: "If the case is as strong as I am affirming it to be, how does it happen that the orthodox scholars are content to meet it either by silence or by a few unkind jibes? Why do they not set seriously to work either to explode it or to establish it once and for all?" Given her prominent position within academia, her analysis is important.

> In the first place, the new theory is extremely disconcerting, the story which it unfolds is excessively queer, and, if it were established, the joke would be far too good. No one, particularly if he occupies a recognised position, wants to have his ideas so violently upset. Moreover the weight of vested interest, both of capital and of reputation, bound up with the Bard of Avon, is so great that the orthodox have naturally preferred to ignore the new hypothesis rather than to take the smallest risk of helping to establish it.

She rejected the Dynastic Succession Theory, and was in agreement with those who believed it was harmful to the Oxfordian movement.

> But secondly, there is some excuse for the scholars who refuse to put their natural scepticism to the test by trying to refute Mr. Looney. For Mr. Looney, as was to be expected, has been followed by a crowd of outrageous cranks. There are books in favour of de Vere which are full of ... fantastic identifications in the plays, and of such nonsensical theories as that the sonnets are addressed to an unknown bastard son of de Vere. To the academic critics they have been a god-send, for it is easy enough to protest that to refute such creatures is merely a waste of time, and lumping Mr. Looney and Dr. Rendall along with the rest, the academics dismiss the whole business with a shrug.

Drawing on her knowledge of economic history, she provided a framework for understanding interactions among Oxfordians, academics and the general public.

> My own subject provides instructive examples of the relationship between the academics and the cranks. To begin with, the cranks have the right intuitions, but they use the wrong arguments. They are coldly received by the academics, who have been taught how to argue. Then the cranks become embittered and begin to abuse the academics, at the same time strengthening the academic position by piling one absurdity upon another in defense of the crank theories. The academics try to teach the plain man to sneer at the cranks, but the plain man feels in his bones that there must be something in what the cranks are saying. The whole position is very unsatisfactory to all concerned.
>
> Then at last there arises someone who has the training of an academic, the insight of a crank, and the common sense of a plain man; and the whole muddle begins to be cleared up. The cranks, embittered by long oppression, attack him just as though he were orthodox, the academics look at him askance, and the plain man hails him as a prophet. It would be rash to press the analogy too far. But it seems to me that the Shakespeare controversy has reached the second stage, but not

the third.[39]

Robinson concluded by appealing "to Cambridge dons once more to come to the rescue."[40]

Looney's letter to Robinson, noting "the intellectual [in]competence of Shakespearean specialists," was sent four months after her article had appeared. He proposed that Robinson form a "working group" with colleagues open to consideration of the Oxfordian thesis and that such a group, working to "excite the interest of the undergraduates" could "perhaps [be] the best way of forcing the attention of the professors."[41]

Whether Robinson formed such a group or reached out to undergraduates is not known, but the following year a lengthy article appeared in *The Eagle*, the student-produced newspaper of St. John's College at Cambridge University—the college where Edward de Vere had studied along with other young men destined to play significant roles in their times. "Was Shakespeare a Johnian?" examined Oxford's poems and contemporary opinion of them, offered a detailed summary of the case made in *"Shakespeare" Identified*, and called for further examination of the Oxfordian thesis. "A *prima facie* case may be held to have been made out which at least merits further examination. The problem has a special interest for Johnians. Will not some member of the College explore further the history of one who was undoubtedly an outstanding poet, and may prove to have been the greatest poet of all?"[42] There is no evidence that *The Eagle's* call was answered. The chain of influence from Looney to Robinson to the undergraduates at St. John's College appeared to end there. It had made it into the body of the "cell" of Cambridge University but hadn't penetrated into the "nucleus" of the minds of its professors of literature.

Academic Responses to the Oxfordian Challenge: Actual

If academia's response did not rise to the level required by its duty to examine matters in an academic way, how did it respond? Scholars' reviews of Oxfordian books previously cited show that academia's public response, characterized by silence, ridicule and attack, was designed to suppress awareness and consideration of the Oxfordian idea. Several specific tactics are discussed here.

Continuing to present the Stratfordian story

Stratfordian scholars continued to present the Stratfordian story as though it were problem-free. Gaps between the man and the works were simply dismissed: the magic wand of genius explained everything. Whatever information Shakspere needed about Italy or the law or any other subject had been picked up through conversations at the Mermaid, or through diligent study at the Stratford grammar school. Such assuredness convinced many that there was little to the Oxfordian claim. Such blithe dismissals by senior scholars also helped keep younger scholars in line: there was no cause for concern, no need to examine the issue themselves.

---

[39] It perhaps reached that third stage with the publication of Charlton Ogburn, Jr.'s *The Mysterious William Shakespeare* in late 1984 (see Chapter 19).
[40] Joan V. Robinson, "Shakespeare and Mr. Looney," *Cambridge Review*, May 12, 1933, p. 389.
[41] J. Thomas Looney, letter to Joan V. Robinson, Sept. 3, 1933.
[42] "Was Shakespeare a Johnian?" *The Eagle* [St. John's College, Cambridge], vol. 48/213 (1934), pp. 86-87. The article came to light only in 2019, when J. Thomas Looney's surviving papers were first examined.

Ignoring and suppressing Oxfordian findings

Orthodox scholars' first line of defense was to ignore the Oxfordian challenge, hoping it would go away. As noted, almost two-thirds of the most prominent Shakespeare scholars of the day never mentioned J. Thomas Looney, *"Shakespeare" Identified* or the Oxfordian idea, and most of the others did so with only superficial glances.

The dust jacket for G. B. Harrison's *Shakespeare at Work* stated that the book was the first occasion upon which any writer "who knows anything about the period" had traced "the development of Shakespeare as man and dramatist alongside the events of the day."[43] Percy Allen, who had written several books on that very subject, wrote to the publisher and the author asking that the dust jacket "in the interests of truth and propriety, be immediately withdrawn."[44] It was not. As Allen later wrote, within the community of orthodox Shakespearean writers, "serious scholars" meant "conventional academic commentators—university men. No heterodox writer, especially if not a university man, can ever be 'a serious scholar.'"[45] They had perhaps forgotten that Edward Gibbon and Thomas Babington Macaulay, two of the most respected scholars and historians from years past, did not have university degrees in history, and that Sir Edmund Chambers, the most prominent historian of the Elizabethan stage and of William Shakespeare, was a government official who conducted research and wrote books in his spare time.

Some scholars disparaged Looney's qualifications by noting that he was from an isolated town far from London, implying that no rustic could possibly write anything worth reading about such an elevated topic. Such a tactic would work only with those readers dense enough not to remember that William Shakspere himself was from a town even smaller and more isolated than Looney's Newcastle. It would work only with those who did not know that many of the greatest writers of recent years—Hemingway, Faulkner, Steinbeck and Twain, for instance—did not have degrees in literature.

Related to silence was suppression. Major literary publications refused to run articles on the Oxfordian thesis. Percy Allen noted "the boycott of our publications on the part of London reviewers"[46] and Col. Douglas observed that the policy of the editors of *The Review of English Studies* was to "return to the publisher unopened any anti-Stratfordian book!"[47] *The Review of English Studies* had earlier rejected Capt. Bernard M. Ward's groundbreaking articles, "Shakespeare and the Anglo-Spanish War 1585-1604, Parts 1 and 2," which were then published by a French journal, *Revue Anglo-Américaine*, in 1929 and 1930.[48] The *Revue* was so honored to have them that it broke tradition and published them in English.

Those articles overturned the generally accepted idea that Shakespeare's works had been produced under normal conditions of peace and prosperity. They showed instead that many of the works had been "produced during the stress and strain of a great war: a war that is comparable in every respect to the war of 1914-1918, save that it lasted nearly a generation instead of four years;"[49] and that the Secret Service Department overseen by

---

[43] G. B. Harrison, *Shakespeare at Work* (1933), dust jacket.

[44] Percy Allen, "Shakespeare at Work," *Shakespeare Pictorial*, Nov. 1933, p. 176.

[45] Percy Allen, "Lord Oxford as Shakespeare," *East Anglian Magazine*, vol. 2/5 (May 1937): 343.

[46] Col. B. R. Ward, "The Annual Dinner," *Shakespeare Pictorial*, June 1931, p. 96.

[47] Col. Montagu W. Douglas, "Editorial," *SF News-Letter*, no. 1 (Jan. 1937): 2.

[48] Percy and Ernest Allen, *Lord Oxford & "Shakespeare:" A Reply to John Drinkwater* (1933), pp. 19-20.

[49] Capt. Bernard M. Ward, "Shakespeare and the Anglo-Spanish War 1585-1601, Part 1," *Revue Anglo-Américaine*, vol. 6/4 (April 1929): 298.

the Earl of Oxford "was responsible for producing war-propaganda," including many of "Shakespeare's" history plays, "in order to rouse the patriotism, loyalty, and war-spirit among the civil population of England."[50] Yet little of these ground-breaking discoveries made their way into academic publications.

Academics were even wary of allowing an authorship doubter to speak on an unrelated subject. "A leading English Stratfordian . . . actually tried to prevent Prof. Abel Lefranc from lecturing at London University, because of his heretical views on Shakespeare although his subject did not touch upon any Shakespearean problem!"[51]

Academic reluctance to tackle topics that might touch on the authorship question inhibited scholarly work. The puzzling unauthorized publication of the *Sonnets* in 1609 was glossed over. No mention was made of the absence of any known connection between the First Folio and Shakspere's family in Stratford. Nor was there any acknowledgment that the powerful men behind the publication of the First Folio were a son-in-law of Oxford and his brother, who had at one time been engaged to another of Oxford's daughters.

Suppression of Edward de Vere himself had become increasingly common since publication of Looney's book. In his discussion of *A Midsummer Night's Dream* in *Shakespeare at Work* (1933), G. B. Harrison acknowledged that the play had been written for and performed at the wedding of Elizabeth Vere in 1595, but identified her only as Lord Burghley's grand-daughter and avoided mentioning her father anywhere. J. M. Robertson did the same. In his *The Problems of the Shakespeare Sonnets* (1926), he could not bring himself to refer to Edward de Vere or the Oxfordian claim when it would have been appropriate for scholarly reasons to do so. He referred to Elizabeth Vere only as Lord Burghley's granddaughter. The chapter on "Fantastic Theories" refers only to the Baconian theory; the Oxfordian claim is ignored. Capt. Ward commented that "[i]t is evidently too dangerous to be alluded to."[52]

If for no other reason, the large number of works dedicated to Oxford during his lifetime should have made him a person of great interest to literary scholars and historians of the Elizabethan era, but he was rarely mentioned. The *Encyclopedia Britannica's* article on John Lyly, two full pages in length, did not mention the Earl of Oxford, even though Lyly was a servant of the earl's when all of his plays were written; he didn't write a single play afterwards, not even when he was desperately seeking employment and a new play could have brought in much-needed income.[53] When the Ashbourne portrait of Edward de Vere—altered to make it appear to be a portrait of Shakspere—was discussed, scholars never mentioned the chain of custody of the portrait—that it had remained in the possession of Oxford's descendants until it was offered for sale in 1910.

The great lengths to which literary scholars went to avoid mentioning Oxford's name is highlighted by Hardin Craig's article on *Cardanus Comforte*. In this lengthy article published in *The Huntington Library Bulletin* in 1934, Craig, a prominent literary scholar, used a footnote to inform readers that the two editions of Thomas Bedingfield's translation of Girolamo Cardano's *De Consolatione*, in 1573 and 1576, were "published by

---

[50] Capt. Bernard M. Ward, "Shakespeare and the Anglo-Spanish War 1585-1601, Part 2," *Revue Anglo-Américaine*, vol. 7/4 (April 1930): 298, 311.

[51] Percy & Ernest Allen, *Lord Oxford & Shakespeare: A Reply to John Drinkwater* (1933), pp. 19-20.

[52] Col. Bernard R. Ward, letter to Katharine E. Eggar, April 13, 1927.

[53] Capt. Bernard M. Ward, *The Seventeenth Earl of Oxford* (1928): 279

commaundement of the right honourable the Earle of Oxenford."[54] He did not mention Oxford in the body of the article, and didn't recount Oxford's critical role in introducing this important work to English readers. He said nothing about Oxford's lengthy and widely praised "Bedingfield Letter," written in Latin, or his verse written in English, which were prominent parts of the book. Although Craig discussed at great length the similarities in sentiment, tone and phrasing between *Cardanus Comforte* and *Hamlet*—which is why he called it "Hamlet's Book"—he made no mention of the many scholars who acknowledged that *Hamlet* appeared to have been modeled after the life of Edward de Vere.[55]

These omissions could not have been accidental. They can only serve as confirmation of a deliberate attempt by literary scholars to avoid mentioning the Earl of Oxford in any context that would tie him to authorship of Shakespeare's works—even at the cost of debasing their own work.

Changing the subject

When the Oxfordian challenge was unavoidably forced on them, literary scholars attempted to change the subject. The best way to do that was to shift readers' attention to the Oxfordians themselves. They could cast doubt on Oxfordians' qualifications and might even induce some of them to react angrily in inappropriate ways, further damaging their credibility. Sir E. K. Chambers, in a lecture before the British Academy, urged that the beliefs of "small-minded" doubters "should be refuted, that the people be not deceived, but the task must be left to someone with a better temper for the patient anatomizing of human follies.'"[56] This characterization slyly moved attention from doubt to doubters, who were then, along with their doubts, dismissed without having to address or refute their claims.

Stratfordians regularly cited the case of Delia Bacon, who had broached the idea of group authorship of Shakespeare's works back in the 1850s before suffering some kind of mental breakdown and dying in a Connecticut asylum. Emphasizing her later problems not only changed the subject from the implications of her Shakespeare work, but also implied that all doubters suffered from similar mental deficiencies. Scholars did not make the same argument about Friedrich Nietzsche—who, like Bacon, died in an asylum—nor did they disparage the music of Robert Schumann, who was institutionalized for the final five years of his life.

Repeating Outdated Charges

Throughout the period covered in Part One of this book (until 1945 in England and 1948 in the United States) academic scholars continued to make the same charges that had been made after the release of *"Shakespeare" Identified* in 1920. Some of the early critics had perhaps not examined Looney's book carefully enough to realize that he had anticipated and answered many of their criticisms. Scholars in the 1930s, however, would have had ample time to study the book and the hundreds of articles written by Oxfordians rebutting criticism, but they continued to bring up the same points.

The 1604 issue. The "fact" that many of Shakespeare's plays were written after

---

[54] Hardin Craig, "Hamlet's Book," *Huntington Library Bulletin*, no. 6 (Nov. 1934): 17.

[55] See discussion in Chapter 6.

[56] E. K. Chambers, *The Disintegration of Shakespeare*, [The Annual Shakespeare Lecture 1924], p. 3. Chambers's lecture was published as a pamphlet (1924) and was later included in a collection of Annual Shakespeare Lectures titled *Aspects of Shakespeare* in 1933.

Oxford's death in 1604 was often cited as conclusive proof against his authorship. Playwright John Drinkwater made that claim in his book *Shakespeare* in 1933, but he was a playwright, not a scholar. Scholars—experts in the field—who claimed that the dates of *composition* of Shakespeare's plays were known willfully misrepresented the extent of their knowledge; it was only dates of first performance or first publication that were often known. That they were unaware that some of the plays had been completed "by other pens" after Shakspere's "retirement"—something documented by one of their own respected voices, Sir Walter Raleigh—is simply not believable.

Hand D. Some orthodox scholars claimed that the handwriting by an unknown person and designated "Hand D" in a manuscript of *Sir Thomas More* was that of William Shakspere. Making the claim on the basis of the cramped and almost illegible signatures on Shakspere's Will was an abandonment of scholarly objectivity and common sense. Doing so in spite of the definitive refutation of that idea by Sir George Greenwood in *The Shakespeare Signatures and Sir Thomas More* (1924) and by Canon Gerald Rendall in *Shakespeare: Handwriting and Spelling* (1931) was a premeditated intellectual crime.

The Arundel-Howard slanders. Continuing to repeat the charges against the Earl of Oxford made by Charles Arundel and Henry Howard without explaining the context for them—that those two courtiers were traitors attempting to blacken the name of their primary accuser—is another intellectual crime. Captain Ward had set the record straight in *The Seventeenth Earl of Oxford* in 1928, and his explanation of that context had been accepted by many reviewers.

Dismissing the Claim: Rejecting, Distorting, Dissembling

Scholars who dismissed the Oxfordian claim as unworthy of serious examination in spite of the mountain of evidence presented in support of it failed in their academic duty to examine literary issues objectively.

Misstating the claim. On those rare occasions when the Oxfordian claim was "examined," it was misstated, with the misstatement then used to disparage the claim and those making it. The reviewer of six books by doubters in *The Times Literary Supplement* in January 1932 used this tactic. He commented that "If the reader accepts the assumption that the exercise of genius is impossible without high birth and high education, . . . then he can enjoy the ingenuity of these six demonstrations against the Stratford player, and even be half persuaded by the case for de Vere."[57] But none of the authors of those six books had claimed that "genius is impossible without high birth and high education." To state that false idea was to imply that the authors had rested their cases on nothing more substantial than class prejudice. Doing so was an intellectually invalid sleight of hand designed to enable the reviewer to dismiss rather than rebut the informed and well-reasoned judgments that each author had presented.

Changing assessments of Oxford's poetry. Before the 1920 publication of *"Shakespeare" Identified*, literary scholars had praised Edward de Vere's poetry; afterward they disparaged it.

---

[57] [reviews of six books], *Times Literary Supplement*, Jan. 14, 1932, p. 29. The six books are: *Exit Shakespeare* (1931) by Bertram Theobald; *The Earl of Oxford as "Shakespeare"* (1931) by Col. Montagu W. Douglas; *Seven Shakespeares* (1931) by Gilbert Slater; *Edward de Vere: A Great Elizabethan* (1931) by George Frisbee; *The Oxford-Shakespeare Case Corroborated* (1931) by Percy Allen; and *Shakespeare Authorship: A Summary of Evidence* by Gilbert Standen (1930).

Before *"Shakespeare" Identified*:

   ✓ Sir Sidney Lee: Oxford, "despite his violent and perverse temper, his eccentric taste in dress, and his reckless waste of substance, evinced a genuine taste in music and wrote verses of much lyric beauty. . . . A sufficient number of his poems is extant to corroborate Webbe's comment that he was the best of the courtier poets in the early days of Queen Elizabeth."[58]

   ✓ W. J. Courthope, Professor of Poetry at the University of Oxford, described Oxford's verses as "distinguished for their wit . . . and terse ingenuity. . . . His studied concinnity of style is remarkable . . . He was not only witty himself but the cause of wit in others."[59]

   ✓ Dr. Grosart gathered together all of Oxford's extant recognized poems and published them in the "Fuller Worthies Library" in 1872. Oxford's poems, he wrote, "are not without touches of the true Singer and there is an atmosphere of graciousness and culture about them that is grateful." Of Oxford himself, he commented that "an unlifted shadow lies across his memory."[60]

After *"Shakespeare" Identified*:

   ✓ R. H. C. [Alfred R. Orage]: "I [cannot accept that] the verse of Edward de Vere contains the promise of Shakespeare. I . . . marvel that Mr. Looney can have been so blind to literary values as to imagine that de Vere could have written Shakespeare. . . . Edward de Vere could not have possibly written a single true Shakespearian line."[61]

   ✓ Solomon Eagle [John C. Squire]: "I am still quite unshaken in my belief that Oxford did not write Shakespeare . . . What slight weakening there may have been on my part when I was reading the introduction soon disappeared when I was confronted with Oxford's intermittently convincing but often lame poems."[62]

Criticizing isolated allusions. As J. Thomas Looney, Percy Allen and other Oxfordian scholars had repeatedly explained, the Oxfordian case must be analyzed in its entirety to be judged fairly. They lamented that many reviewers dismissed their findings after citing only a few of the weaker topical allusions while ignoring the great mass of stronger ones, giving the readers the impression that the former were the only evidence on which the Oxfordian case rested. In doing so they encouraged lazy readers to make the WYSIATI mistake (the mistake of thinking that What You See Is All There Is). A responsible scholar would have stated the strongest evidence and then accepted or rebutted it.

Adm. Hubert Holland had documented fifty topical allusions that tie the original version of *Hamlet* to 1583, long before the traditional dates of 1599 to 1601. Holland hadn't noticed all fifty allusions at the same time. He was struck at first by a handful of the more obvious references; investigating further, he noted the others one by one. He, like Percy Allen, cited all of the examples he had found because the sheer number of them carried its own weight in support of the claim. Including the weaker examples gave an opening to reviewers interested in caricaturing his case rather than presenting an

---

[58] Sir Sidney Lee, "Vere, Edward," *Dictionary of National Biography*, vol. 58 (1898): 228.
[59] W. J. Courthope, *History of English Poetry*, vol. II, pp. 311-312.
[60] Alexander B. Grosart, *Fuller Worthies' Library*, vol. 4, p. 359.
[61] R. H. C. [Orage], "Readers and Writers," *New Age*, vol. 28/5 (Dec. 2, 1920): 55, 56.
[62] Solomon Eagle [John C. Squire], Mr. Looney and Lord Oxford," *Outlook*, March 12, 1921, p. 231.

accurate assessment of it. Perhaps staff reviewers not entirely familiar with the Shakespeare authorship question cited the lesser examples through ignorance; scholars had no such excuse.

Forming one-off explanations. Made-up explanations have been noted, the prime example being *ur-Hamlet*, an unknown play by an unknown author, concocted by traditional scholars to explain away references made as early as 1589 to a "Hamlet" play or character.

Forming convoluted explanations. Sometimes the explanations scholars offered were formed by twisting or contorting facts to mean something other than what a common sense reading of them would suggest. Donamy Dobree's article "Shakespeare and the Drama of His Time," in *A Companion to Shakespeare Studies* (1934) edited by G. B. Harrison, tried to explain the euphuistic style of *Love's Labour's Lost* not by sensibly recognizing that it originated in the late 1570s when that style was in vogue, but by maintaining that Shakespeare was "harkening back" to the period.[63] But Dobree provided no explanation why Shakespeare would have wanted to do that in what is often regarded as his first play, nor did he explain how a newly arrived immigrant from an unsophisticated part of the countryside could possibly have depicted, in such a dated style, the sophisticated, courtly manners of the crème of society so alien to his own experiences.

Portraying Edward de Vere as unworthy. Many scholars portrayed Edward de Vere as someone morally unworthy to have been Shakespeare, that his character was so flawed that he couldn't possibly have been the great playwright and poet. Col. Douglas observed that "Among disbelievers, both orthodox and Baconian, . . . there has shewn itself, of late, a marked tendency to prejudice, if they can, the Oxfordian case, by defaming Lord Oxford's personal character; the desired inference—openly avowed, in one instance—being that the Earl must have been too wicked and despicable a character to have conceived and written the noble Shakespearean plays."[64] He cited descriptions of Oxford by several scholars of the time: Professor E. Greenlaw: "the cowardly son-in-law of Burleigh;" Sir E. K. Chambers: "the ill-condition'd youth;" Professor J. W. Draper: "a notable case of aristocratic decadence;" Howard Bridgwater: "rascal, cad, trivial, poltroon, disgraceful companion of dreadful creatures." De Vere was presented as "ill-conditioned, decadent, fraudulent, grinder of the poor, coward, rascal, cad, frequenter of evil company." All these descriptions appeared several years after Capt. Ward, in *The Seventeenth Earl of Oxford*, had corrected the historical record and provided context for the Arundel-Howard slanders.

Col. Douglas also compiled a list of contemporary descriptions of Oxford that scholars could have cited but did not, including: (1) Talbot: "[Queen Elizabeth] delighteth more in his person, his dancing, and valiantness than any other;" (2) Chapman: "the most goodly fashioned man I ever saw; from head to foot in form most rare and absolute;" and (3) the Harleian MS: "Of whom I will only speak what all men's voices confirm, he was a man in mind and body absolutely accomplished with honourable endowments."

Gerald H. Rendall also noted the one-sided assessment of the Earl of Oxford. "Our

---

[63] Donamy Dobree, "Shakespeare and the Drama of His Time," in *A Companion to Shakespeare Studies*, edited by G. B. Harrison and H. Granville Barker (1934), p. 248.
[64] Lt. Col. W. M. Douglas, "Edward de Vere and Academic Scholarship," *Shakespeare Pictorial*, March 1933, p. 48.

erudite critics would be employed more consonantly with their authoritative positions in attempting honestly to answer our—as yet evaded—argument rather than in defaming Lord Oxford's character. Moreover, they have responsibilities towards their readers. Let certain of them look to it, before their losing case is irretrievably destroyed."[65]

Dismissing linkages and allusions as unreliable

Before the introduction of the Oxfordian claim in 1920, scholars had welcomed topical references in the plays that tied them to historical events or to William Shakspere. Afterwards, they rejected such linkages as invalid. Allusions to events in Edward de Vere's life were dismissed as coincidences or as evidence that Shakspere might have modeled some characters on de Vere. Allusions to real-life events and personages were dismissed as mere illusion, not allusion. Allusions to events occurring fifteen years before the traditional dates assigned to the plays were dismissed as Shakespeare's reaching into the past for reasons unknown, without explaining how Shakspere could have known of the historical events referred to. This tactic—this change in methodologies—is discussed further in Chapter 12.

A comprehensive example

Many of the above unscholarly practices were marshaled in one article that appeared in *The Shakespeare Association Bulletin* published by the Folger Shakespeare Library in 1941. The eighteen-page article purported to be a brief history of authorship doubts and theories. Its title, "The Shakspere-Bacon-Oxford Whoozis Mix-up," gives a sense of the ridicule to which the Oxfordian idea will be subjected.

The writer, Mark Holstein, attempted to dismiss the entire authorship question by presenting only the most inconsequential aspects of it. He began by stating that it made no difference who wrote the plays:

> It is perfectly true that if it were now definitely established, beyond all question or doubt, that no such person as Master Will Shakspere ever lived, it would make not the slightest difference to any living person anywhere in the world. We would still have the plays and, to baffle and beguile us, the miracle of their creation would still remain.[66]

He then discussed the work of traditional scholars who studied variants of the play texts—the "long line of editors [who] corrected, emended, collated, and quarreled violently"—during much of the eighteenth century. Holstein apparently believed that studying minor textual variations was more important than understanding the author, the nature of literary creativity, or the important place the theater held in the second half of the Elizabethan era. He devoted considerable space to doubts that surfaced in the eighteenth and nineteenth centuries. Only one page was given to the Oxfordian thesis, and no evidence in support of it was presented. Instead, Holstein alleged that the Oxfordian claim "in some measure, at least, rest[s] on ciphers," thus tying the thesis to the least persuasive aspects of the Baconian argument. Then, after studiously avoiding any presentation of the most persuasive evidence in support of Oxford's authorship, he implied that puns based on the word *Vere* were the strongest evidence that existed.

---

[65] Lt. Col. W. M. Douglas, "Edward de Vere and Academic Scholarship," *Shakespeare Pictorial*, March 1933, p. 48.
[66] Mark Holstein, "The Shakspere-Bacon-Oxford-Whoozis Mix-up," *The Shakespeare Association Bulletin*, vol. 16, no. 4 (Oct. 1941): 195-214.

His family name was "Vere," and so whenever he uses words like ever, never, disserver, persevere, forever, it appears that, by a slight manipulation of type, neVER, anyone will see that Oxford is intended. Since the letters VER are not uncommon in many English words, it is possible to cite numerous instances in support of the Oxonian theory.

In an article that was presented as a history of current authorship theories, Holstein provided not a word about the discoveries of Col. Bernard R. Ward, Capt. Bernard M. Ward, Percy Allen, Gerald H. Rendall, or Adm. Hubert Holland, or those of Americans Charles Wisner Barrell or Eva Turner Clark.

Holstein's article showed the depths of intellectual depravity to which many scholars in academia would descend to avoid having to address the Oxfordian thesis in the same responsible manner that they addressed all other literary issues. Having appeared in a publication of the Shakespeare Folger Library, Holstein's piece showed the limited effect of the Oxfordian movement's influence within academia even after two decades of spectatular findings. What little effect it had had on academia would soon be blown away by the winds of war.

12

Academia and the Oxfordian Challenge:
Internal Machinations

Institutions with Interests to Protect

Why did academia—Departments of Literature and especially the Shakespeare Studies Sections within them—not address the subject of Shakespearean authorship before *"Shakespeare" Identified* was published or the Oxfordian claim afterwards? Why was the topic not subjected to the same objective scholarly examination as all other literary matters?

One answer is that the belief by academics in Shakspere's authorship was so strong that any challenge to it had to be wrong and therefore not worth examining. That would explain academia's silence in response to the Oxfordian claim as well as to Sir George Greenwood's case against Shakspere's authorship a decade earlier.

Another answer is that Departments of Literature are institutions. They had been established to facilitate the study and teaching of literature; their leaders were tasked with creating environments supportive of that scholarly work. But once in existence, the Departments had interests and reputations of their own to be protected; their leaders now had a second duty, one that sometimes conflicted with their first duty to promote scholarly work. When conflicts arose, leaders had to seek the optimal balance between them; they could not fulfill either duty to the maximum extent possible.

This dual nature of their responsibilities explains why the founders of the newly established Departments of Literature went to such great lengths to ensure that their Departments were recognized as distinct from and equal in status to the Departments of History they had broken away from. Departments on both sides sought to distinguish themselves from the other. Departments of History, having shed their unwanted literary history programs, wanted nothing further to do with literature and withdrew into their core subjects of political, diplomatic and military studies. "The great majority of academic historians in the first half of the twentieth century maintained their defenses and protected their virtue,"[1] observed Stefan Collini, Professor of English and Intellectual History at Cambridge University.

Departments of Literature likewise, creating programs of study that had as little as possible to do with history. Among the new generation of literary scholars, "a striking one-sidedness developed in their subsequent relationship with their historical colleagues" (10). With both Departments de-emphasizing aspects of scholarly study common to both programs, an academic "no-man's land" existed between them, and it was there that literary history lay. It remained as much a stepchild within Departments of Literature as it had been within Departments of History.

Collini testified to the depth of that split.

---

[1] Stefan Collini, *The Nostalgic Imagination*, p. 10.

> In the first half of the twentieth century, as academic specialization developed and hardened, Literature ... came to be seen as a distinct mode of understanding, grounded in close attention to the formal properties of a canonical body of writing, principally poetry, drama, and eventually the novel, while History, centered on political history but with economic and social history increasingly prominent, strengthened its established position as another mode or discipline. Periodically, attempts were made at some kind of rapprochement or interdisciplinary cooperation, but indirectly such efforts confirmed the largely separate and autonomous existence of the two activities: Literary Criticism was one thing, History was another. (8)

The complete separation of the departments was noted by Col. Ward, who contrasted the situation in England by the end of the 1920s with France, where the two fields often cooperated.

> In England the system of water-tight compartments is practically universal so far as history and literature are concerned. *The Review of English Studies* is devoted to literature, branching off into philology, prosody, and textual criticism. *The Times Literary Supplement* equally avoids mixing history with literature. Very different are the principles that have actuated M. Lefranc in his historical teaching.... He is in fact the pioneer of the union of literary and historical studies. ... Literature and History are sister studies which mutually throw light on each other.
>
> Professor Lefranc's Shakespeare studies have shed a flood of light on the play *Love's Labour's Lost*. His knowledge of the history of the time and of the personalities at the Court of Henry of Navarre during the fifteen-eighties, formed the starting point for the discovery of a number of unmistakable topical allusions in the play. These discoveries [are] followed up as they have been by our own historical researches. ... The French Genius tends to take the general view, a common English fault being an inability to see the wood for the trees.[2]

Distinction between academia and outside

Just as Departments of Literature sought to raise their status by emphasizing the distinction between their activities and those of other Departments, so too academia sought to raise its status by emphasizing the distinction between the scholarly work carried out within its walls and the unscholarly efforts made outside.

Well into the nineteenth century the course of study in universities and colleges was based on the seven liberal arts that composed the Trivium and Quadrivium. Modern literature and history were among the fields studied outside institutions of higher education, and scholars wrote for the general public as well as for fellow scholars. Many great writers, historians and scientists of the time worked outside academia—something true of Charles Dickens, Henry James and Mark Twain in literature; Edward Gibbon and Thomas Babington Macaulay in history; and Sir Isaac Newton, Charles Darwin and (later) Albert Einstein in science; so did those who studied and critiqued literary works—something true of Edmund Malone, Sir Sidney Lee and Sir Edmund Chambers in Shakespeare Studies; T. S. Eliot and Edmund Wilson in literary criticism; and so on. To the list might be added Sir George Greenwood in Shakespearean criticism and even J. Thomas Looney, a member of the broad category of independent scholars whose time was fast coming to an end due to the rising institutionalization of the study of literature.

Once established, Departments of Literature provided protected environments in

---

[2] Col. Bernard R. Ward, "Presentation to Professor Lefranc," *Shakespeare Pictorial*, Aug. 1929, p. 14.

which scholars could conduct scholarly research and publish findings. They did that in part by maintaining high scholarly and methodological standards and in part by acting as gatekeepers, admitting into their realm only those deemed most highly qualified. If departments created walls to keep other departments out of "their" subject areas, the walls separating academia as a whole from the world outside were even higher. Because, by their definition, work done within the walls was scholarly and work done outside was not, scholars in academia saw no reason to examine outside work at all.[3]

The Oxfordian claim as the biggest challenge

Those in charge of Departments of Literature in the decades after *"Shakespeare" Identified* was published saw the Oxfordian thesis not as a "mere" scholarly issue, but as a serious threat to their institutions' status and prestige. What could be more damaging than having it widely believed that the foundational belief of Shakespeare Studies was false?

Those thinking further ahead might have realized that any such damage would be only temporary, that after an unsettled period the field of Shakespeare Studies could be reconstructed on firmer foundations and returned to its prior status as the pride and glory of Literature Departments. Shakespeare's works would not be harmed by attributing them to another author; insights might even be enhanced by the change. A new sense of excitement and energy might result as scholars and funding poured in to explore new lines of research and publishing.

At the same time, Departmental leaders must have sensed that they would probably not be players in any "New Golden Age" for Shakespeare Studies. The current generation of Stratfordian scholars would face an uncomfortable situation once the public, and scholars in other fields, realized that they had been misled about the identity of the greatest dramatist in the English language. They were too smart not to recognize the severity of the Oxfordian challenge, and too savvy to give in to it. Today's leaders would have to pay the price now for benefits to be received by others in the future. They were often at the height of their careers; better to stay the course and hope that the Oxfordian movement would burn out. If the change had to be made, better that it be made after they had left the scene.

Leading scholars, then, had nothing to gain and much to lose if Departments of Literature were to examine the Shakespeare authorship question and the Oxfordian claim in the same manner in which other literary questions were examined. Independent minded students were, as a consequence, less likely to be admitted to advanced study in Departments of Literature, and junior faculty interested in exploring authorship questions less likely to be granted tenure. Leaders' successors later made the same calculations, and so on it went.

Looney had recognized this situation and expressed his thoughts to Joan V. Robinson in 1933.

> If, of course, Oxford was the author of the Shakespeare plays the situation reflects no credit upon the intellectual competence of Shakespearean specialists. Naturally they are sensible of this and wish their exposure to be posthumous. We must look to the rising generation of students. It would be galling to a man whose

---

[3] It is ironic that the development of the scholarly practices that led to awareness of the gap between the mundane life of William Shakspere and the sophisticated, learned nature of Shakespeare's works also led to the creation of Departments of Literature that banished investigations into the Shakespeare authorship question.

position in literature rests wholly upon his reputation as a Shakespeare specialist, to have to admit that he had been befooled, that he had missed the significance of the biggest issue that could possibly have arisen in his peculiar domain, and that the most romantic discovery connected therewith had fallen to an entire outsider. These considerations affect in degree all the literature-specialists, who, without being Shakespeare-specialists, should have risen to the occasion. All alike have failed ignominiously upon a vital problem affecting their special province and can only find refuge now in a conspiracy of silence.[4]

Percy Allen expressed similar thoughts about what lay behind academia's resistance to the Oxfordian claim, and at about the same time.

We are indeed up against "vested interests," namely the vested interests of scholars and academics, who are mostly congregated at the universities. These gentlemen have arrogated to themselves, and to themselves alone, the right to lay down the law upon Shakespeare, and the Shakespeare plays. They say, in effect, "Our word is law. You must believe us, and nobody else;" and they maintain their doctrine by rigidly excluding from their class-rooms, and, in so far as they can, from the press (which is largely under their control), any anti-Stratfordian views whatsoever. They are the direct descendants of those pontifical inquisitors who hauled Galileo before them, and compelled him to recant: and—did they possess equal powers—Percy Allen would have been forced, long ago, to recant, or to perish at the stake.

Academia succeeds, Allen wrote, because the public, in its naiveté, did not recognize its perfidy.

The strength of the academic attitude is, in part, its very incredibility; since the average layman will not easily believe that professors, who have specialized in Shakespeare, could possibly be guilty of deliberately suppressing the truth.[5]

Protecting the Institution through Top-Down Control

Like many other institutions, academia has a hierarchical structure. At the top is a leadership that sets direction and makes decisions about beliefs, goals and operations. It also creates incentives for those lower in the structure to conform to them. If done correctly, this is a good thing. It enables institutions to accomplish far more than individuals could on their own. The whole becomes greater than the sum of the parts.

Beliefs selected by an institution's leadership are not a menu of ideas from which members may pick and choose, but a creed that must be accepted. Members must agree to subordinate their individual beliefs and preferences to the institution's. Sometimes additional persuasion is needed. Walter Bagehot noted the power of authority to "enforce a fixed rule" by "making it rational" to do so.[6] Controlling hiring and promotion as well as teaching assignments, leaders of academic institutions have many means for enforcing adherence to beliefs and practices they believe best.

Overt action by leaders such as weeding out those who would bring in contrary ideas or challenge the institution's beliefs and practices is not often necessary because peer pressure from colleagues at lower hierarchical level reinforces political pressure from the top. Most members are comfortable following the direction of the leaders, and believing and doing what others around them believe and do, and want others to do the same. They

---

[4] J. Thomas Looney, letter to Joan V. Robinson, Sept. 3, 1933.
[5] Percy & Ernest Allen, *Lord Oxford & Shakespeare: A Reply to John Drinkwater* (1933), pp. 18-19.
[6] Walter Bagehot, *Physics and Politics* (1999), p. 122.

see membership in the institution—especially an institution as prestigious as Shakespeare Studies—as an important source of self-identification, and don't want others to rock the boat.

Just as institutional leaders have the duty of enhancing the interests of their institutions and of promoting scholarly achievements within them, members farther down the hierarchy have the duties of remaining in good standing in their institutions and of producing scholarly work. Their two duties, like those of the leaders, sometimes conflict, and in such situations they must do what their leaders do: determine the optimal balance between them.

As human beings, literary scholars within academia have the same Human Resistance to changing strongly held beliefs that almost everyone else has (see Chapter 5). They are also subject to the same Cognitive Resistance that may arise when confronting the complexities of the Oxfordian theory. They are, in addition, subject to the pressures just described that flow from Institutional Resistance to the Oxfordian claim. George Bernard Shaw captured the power of these institutional pressures in a pithy aphorism: "You cannot convert a man whose living depends upon your not converting him." Upton Sinclair is reported to have said something similar: "It is difficult to get a man to understand something when his salary depends on his not understanding it."

In the first decades after *"Shakespeare" Identified* was published, some literature scholars might really have been unaware of much of the evidence that Oxfordian scholars had produced in support of Edward de Vere's authorship. This was due not only to the institutional factors already noted, but to the very nature of their own scholarly work. Such work often necessitates shutting out, at least temporarily, all other considerations. The Shakespeare authorship question was just another distraction. The irritation they felt in response to a potential disruption of their work could explain much of the anger directed at the thesis and those who propounded it.

Many Shakespeare scholars also had an emotional commitment to the story of a young man from the sticks who, through dint of his own genius and hard work, rose to the peak of artistic achievement. We have already seen this with Frank Harris. Albert Einstein once came up with a theory that he said was so beautiful that it simply had to be true; when the numbers didn't support it, he reluctantly abandoned it. He had no choice, because the tests theories must pass in the sciences are so rigorous. Theories in the Humanities face no such definitive tests.

Literature professors would not have been entirely without protection if they had bucked the party line. The practice of tenure was designed to protect professors from termination even if their investigations produced results opposed by the politically powerful—the politically powerful outside academia, that is. Within academia, institutional leaders and colleagues could find innumerable ways to make a wayward professor's professional life miserable without technically violating tenure protections.

Given the array of pressures and concerns literature professors faced, it could almost seem rational to ignore or suppress consideration of the Oxfordian claim. The three most prominent professors who came out in favor of the Oxfordian answer to the Shakespeare Mystery were, as noted, all from departments other than literature and therefore risked less harm to their careers: Gilbert Slater and Joan V. Robinson were both economists and Gerald Rendall was a professor of Greek and classical studies. They published their findings in books written for the general public, not in academic journals.[7]

All of the above factors support Walter Bagehot's observation that an organization's (or society's) difficulty was not in establishing beliefs or practices but in reversing or modifying them when conditions changed.

> The great difficulty which history records is not that of the first step, but that of the second step. What is most evident is not the difficulty of getting a fixed law, but of getting out of a fixed law; not of cementing . . . a cake of custom, but of breaking the cake of custom; not of making the first preservative habit, but of breaking through it, and reaching something better. (49)

Responding to the Oxfordian challenge. Oxfordians had been careful to call only for an academic examination of the Oxfordian claim, not for acceptance of it. They called only for critics to state Oxfordian arguments and evidence fairly before critiquing them. They called for academic journals to be open to scholarly examination of the case. In short, they wanted literary scholars to treat Oxfordian scholars as they themselves would want to be treated. These were not unreasonable requests, but academia failed to meet them.

Regarding the Oxfordian claim, academia faced difficulties no matter which way it turned. Percy Allen observed in 1934 that the Oxfordian thesis "is now winning ever wider acceptance the world over," but that it was a truth difficult for Stratfordian scholars to *publicly* acknowledge.

> Conventional orthodoxy throughout the English-speaking world is being abandoned, fast and everywhere; and I assert, without fear of honest contradiction, that many, though not all, scholars who still profess the Stratfordian faith do so no longer by conviction, but rather in fear of the consequences that must follow upon its repudiation. Nor may we too lightly blame them, since not every man possesses the courage or resolution necessary to blast, deliberately, a promising scholastic or university career, by renouncing traditional beliefs that have become, in countless minds, almost a national religion. That is a major reason why the work of the Oxfordian group had, necessarily, in general, to be done by amateurs, with no prospect of probably professional or academic loss, in position or in status, to counterbalance a certain intellectual and spiritual gain.[8]

Academia—Departments of Literature, Shakespeare Studies Sections and individual scholars within them—had a choice to make: launch an open, honest, objective, academic examination of the Oxfordian claim, or suppress it. It chose the latter.

There really was no middle ground. Even a small number of scholars calling for an open examination of the basic belief in Shakspere's authorship—and of Oxford's—might have been sufficient to trigger the avalanche that would have swept away the Stratfordian myth.

It became apparent, though, that merely suppressing the authorship issue would not

---

[7] The split between works written for academic colleagues and those written for the general public pervaded all academic disciplines. William H. McNeil's *The Rise of the West* (1963), a book I learned much from while in high school, had been a bestseller a decade earlier. A prominent historian, McNeil taught at the University of Chicago for four decades, and chaired its History Department for six years. But, as he wrote at the end of his career, some thirty years after *The Rise of the West* was published, not one of his colleagues ever mentioned the book to him. There is also the example of Isaac Asimov, tenured Professor of Biochemistry at Boston University, who faced an effort by a dean to oust him from his position because of the "unscientific" nature of his writing on science (and for his science fiction writing) for the general public.

[8] Percy Allen, *Anne Cecil, Elizabeth & Oxford* (1934), pp. ix-x.

be sufficient; further steps were needed to defend against the Oxfordian challenge beyond merely exerting tighter control over scholarly work and expression of opinion on the issue. The steps decided on were changes to the methodology—the set of rules, procedures or understandings that guided scholarly work within literary studies—so as to eliminate the Oxfordian threat. They set about changing—corrupting—the methodology of literary studies in two important ways.

The First Methodological Change: Allusions

The first (and smaller) of the methodological changes was that of declaring topical allusions to be illegitimate forms of evidence. This change arose within Shakespeare Studies and was largely confined to it.

Literary scholars seek to identify the factors that influence an author, either consciously or unconsciously. They often consider four types of influences:

- ✓ Literary sources;
- ✓ Cultural, political and social influences;
- ✓ Events in the author's life and persons important to the author;
- ✓ The author's personality, disposition, attitudes and interests.

Before the publication of *"Shakespeare" Identified* in 1920, Shakespeare scholars investigated all four areas. They had the greatest success in mining the vein of literary sources that Shakespeare drew on, identifying so many that Geoffrey Bullough's *Narrative and Dramatic Sources of Shakespeare* (1962) fills eight thick volumes. They had some success in matching characters in the plays to real-life people. In 1869 George Russell French identified, in *Hamlet*, the character of Polonius with Lord Burghley; Laertes with Thomas Cecil, Burghley's son; and Ophelia with Anne Cecil, Burghley's daughter. As Looney observed, French had "no axe to grind, no pet theories to support, and therefore offers an unbiased judgment upon the facts."[9] Regarding Italy, Horace Howard Furness, in his *Shakespeare Variorum*, wrote that "Shakespeare's knowledge of Venice and of Padua seems inconceivable, his fidelity in depicting them, marvellous; assuredly it may be said that *The Merchant of Venice* and the first act of *Othello* have not merely Venice for their background, but are actually placed in the very city."[10]

Scholars found rather few topical or personal allusions in the plays, though, and few if any representations of Shakspere's own personality. That was disappointing, but not unduly upsetting—until *"Shakespeare" Identified* was published.

Oxfordian scholars also investigated all four types of external influences. So successful were they that they showed, among other things, connections between Edward de Vere and those very same real-life people and events that orthodox scholars had already connected with Shakespeare. The characters from *Hamlet* certainly had direct connections to him: Lord Burghley, whom French believed was the model for Polonius, was Oxford's father-in-law; Thomas Cecil, on whom Laertes was modeled, was Oxford's brother-in-law; Anne Cecil, on whom Ophelia was modeled, was Oxford's first wife. Looney went a step further, identifying Hamlet as Oxford himself. Furness's comments about Italy also connected the plays with Oxford, who had spent more than a year there,

---

[9] J. Thomas Looney, "Was It Oxford, Bacon, or Derby, II," *Freethinker*, vol. 43/27 (July 8, 1923): 428.
[10] Horace Howard Furness, editor, *The Merchant of Venice* (1888) [New Variorum Edition of Shakespeare, 12th edition], p. 164.

living in the very same cities in which Shakespeare had set so many of his plays, including Venice, Padua and Verona.

Early Oxfordian scholars identified hundreds of allusions in the plays to other topical events, to Edward de Vere's personal experiences, to incidents and people important in his life, and to representations of his personality and disposition. The nearby text box compares linkages between William Shakspere and Edward de Vere with the works of William Shakespeare as they were known in the mid-1930s. Even the small number of examples shown in the text box reveals the multitudinous ties between Shakespeare and

Linkages/Allusions to . . .	Links to William Shakspere	Links to Edward de Vere, Earl of Oxford uncovered by J. Thomas Looney
Shakespeare's Literary Sources		
Ovid's *Metamorphoses*	None	Arthur Golding, the translator, was Oxford's uncle and tutor; they lived in the same house at the time the translation was made.
Geneva Bible	None	Oxford purchased a copy. The *Bible* and the receipt for its purchase still exist.
Cardanus Comforte ("Shakespeare's book")	None	Oxford had an English translation published (1573, 1576) and wrote a lengthy introduction to the publication.
Topical Allusions		
Queen Elizabeth (Gertrude in *Hamlet*, Olivia in *Twelfth Night*, etc.)	None	Oxford was Lord Great Chamberlain in her court, and reportedly her "favorite" in the early 1570s.
Lord Burghley (Polonius, in *Hamlet*)	None	Burghley was Oxford's guardian and later his father-in-law.
Robert Cecil (Richard III)	None	Oxford was his brother-in-law.
Third Earl of Southampton (dedicatee of *Venus and Adonis*, *Lucrece*, the *Sonnets*)	None	Both were wards raised by Burghley and later fellow courtiers in Queen Elizabeth's court.
Author's Life		
Gad's Hill Robbery (*1 Henry IV*)	None	Event actually perpetrated by the Earl of Oxford's Men.
Mother remarried soon after death of husband (*Hamlet*)	None	Oxford's mother remarried soon after the death of his father.
The "bed trick" (*All's Well, Measure for Measure*)	None	Two sources independently cite this as having happened to Oxford.
Othello believed wife to have been unfaithful (*Othello*)	None	Oxford notoriously believed his wife, Anne Cecil, had had a child fathered by someone else.
Author's Personality		
Hamlet: had "an antic disposition" (*Hamlet*)	None	Said of Oxford as a young courtier, "If it were not for his fickle head he would pass any of them shortly."
Jaques was a melancholy courtier who "sold [his] own lands to see other men's" (*As You Like It*)	None	Sold many estates to pay for his extravagant 16-month trip to the continent, 1575-76

Oxford in all four categories and the dearth of such ties between Shakespeare and Shakspere.

Because Stratfordian and Oxfordian scholars had the same historical records available to them, the difference in what they found came from knowing where to look and what to look for. Stratfordian scholars, guided by their basic beliefs and methodology, had found very few cultural references because they were looking in the wrong time period, fifteen years too late. They found very few personal references because they had identified the wrong man as author. Looney's Oxfordian thesis guided those who accepted it to the right person and the right time and place.

Scholars willing to tread the path Looney had blazed continued to mine all four veins of information. Stratfordian scholars, though, after 1920 largely limited themselves to the search for literary sources.

In response to this barrage of links tying the Earl of Oxford to the plays, Stratfordian scholars rejected

Post-1920 Scholarly Investigations		
Stratfordian Scholars	Types of Linkages	Oxfordian Scholars
✓	Literary Sources	✓
No	Topical Allusions	✓
No	Author's Life	✓
No	Author's Personality	✓

not merely the individual links, but also the validity of establishing biographical links between a work and real-life events and personages. They changed their methodology, making illegitimate all such findings, thereby eliminating as tainted an entire category of evidence supporting the Oxfordian claim.

This extreme step was necessary because it would not have been possible to accept some allusions but not others. Allowing any could bring down the entire structure of belief in Shakspere's authorship. If personal allusions were admissible evidence, they would have to be judged on the basis of their quantity and quality, tests that the Oxfordians would surely win. If topical allusions were admitted, the result would be a mass of allusions to events and personages prominent fifteen years too early for Shakspere to have been the author.

How severely this change in methodology corrupted Shakespeare Studies is shown by academia's failure to dig more deeply into the life of Edward de Vere, even apart from the authorship question after Looney had brought him to scholarly attention. Such numerous and direct connections between a previously little-known courtier and Queen Elizabeth's court—the Earl of Oxford was her Lord Great Chamberlain and was at one time her favorite—was surely a finding of great importance. If the connections had been to any other nobleman, their discovery would have been trumpeted far and wide.

From the perspective of the leaders of Departments of Literature seeking to protect their turf, disallowing the use of topical and personal allusions was the right move. Any harm to scholarly work was, in their view, more than outweighed by avoidance of major damage to the reputation and status of their institutions.

Yet even this corruption of the methodology was insufficient. It left Shakespeare Studies out of step with other fields within literary studies, in which knowledge of a writer's life and times contributed much to understanding his works. What to do about that?

The Second Methodological Change: "Death of the Author"

A second (and larger) methodological change began to be implemented in the 1920s, one that affected the entire study of literature, not just Shakespeare Studies. Before 1920 most literary scholars readily acknowledged that authors wrote from their own lives, and that understanding the conditions in which they lived and wrote provided greater insight into their works. That approach to literature began to change by the late 1920s, and to understand just how profound a change it was the context in which it occurred must be understood.

When independent Departments of Literature were established in the late nineteenth and early twentieth centuries, their founders were determined to create an environment conducive to the study of literature. They sought to establish programs in which literature would be studied "as the imaginative realization of human experience expressed in a unique sequence of words, and not as a piece of substandard documentary evidence."[11]

> When literature is approached as the most distilled or intense expression of life, it easily comes to serve as an index of human flourishing in whole societies.... If literature provided the most intense expression of lived experience, then the critic became the accredited assessor of the quality of life revealed by different moments in literary history. (186)

It was a heady moment for Literature Departments. They jump-started their new programs by adopting what had long been known as the Humanistic Tradition in literary criticism. That tradition had existed outside the universities for centuries. It stretched back to the earliest Western writings about the nature of literature, beginning with Aristotle and Horace, and continued through Alexander Pope, Samuel Johnson, Matthew Arnold and Henry James just prior to the time of Looney's investigations.

In that tradition the study of literature was conducted through two complementary approaches. One sought to enhance appreciation of literary works through knowledge of the lives and times of their authors. Practitioners of this approach, who could be called literary historians, examined authors' intentions and how they were influenced by the political, economic, social and literary currents of their times. Because most readers lived in societies very different from those of the authors whose works they read, they benefited from the knowledge of the author's life and times imparted by literary historians.

The second approach sought to explain the significance of works of literature by considering them as works of art important in themselves. Practitioners of this approach, who could be called literary connoisseurs, sought to understand and demonstrate the technical perfection or artistic unity of a work. They helped readers understand the genre, literary devices and rhetorical figures that authors used, and evaluated how successfully they did so.

These approaches were two sides of one methodological coin because both required close readings of literary works with the goal of teasing out the author's meanings. In that tradition, Professor Jonathan Culler explained,

> The task was the interpretation of literary works as the achievements of their authors, and the main justification for studying literature was the special value of great works: their complexity, their beauty, their insight, their universality, and their potential benefits to the reader.[12]

---

[11] Stefan Collini, *The Nostalgic Imagination: History in English Criticism* (2019): 187.
[12] Jonathan Culler, *Literary Theory: A Very Short Introduction* (2009), p. 7.

Applying this approach to the study of Shakespeare, J. Isaacs explained that the "true objects of Shakespeare criticism are (a) to give a picture of the author by tracing his treatment of material so far as it is conscious, or eliciting his unconscious processes without imposing an autobiography of the critic upon the victim of his inquiries; (b) to give the pattern of the man and dissect for admiration the beauties he produces, the complexity and explosive force of the poetry, and the deploying and juxtaposition of the characters."[13]

By the late 1920s literary scholars began to abandon the time-honored Humanistic approach to the study of literature that had only recently been brought within university walls. The move continued throughout the 1930s and 1940s, resulting in a methodology in which the intentions of an author were deemed largely irrelevant. By the end of the twentieth century, even that methodology had been superseded by one that didn't value close readings of literary works and in which the study of literature itself was subsumed within the larger field of Cultural Studies.

At the core of the change taking place over the middle decades of the twentieth century was a devaluation of the biographical approach to the study of literature. Scholars began to focus on the text itself, isolated from its relationship to the author, to the society in which it was created and to any other external factors. In Stefan Collini's description, it was a redirection of attention from "philological, historical, and biographical approaches" to "the words on the page." In the new approach, "the distinctive mode of English studies was literary-critical; . . . the chief capacity students needed to develop was that for close verbal analysis; . . . the standing and legitimacy of the discipline depended upon its emancipating itself from both the belletristic and the modes inherited from the nineteenth century."[14]

In part this change was brought about by literary scholars' desire to appear more "scientific." The practical effects or technological results of scientific study—the automobile, the electric light, the telephone, the refrigerator, etc.—gave tremendous cachet to science; any field of study that could bill itself as "scientific" did so. Even Humanities Departments felt the need to ape scientific practices. Literary scholars began to treat works of literature as mere texts, as lifeless objects that could be examined dispassionately through techniques designed to produce quantitative rather than qualitative results, such as word counts and rhyme patterns—whatever could be quantified began to outweigh whatever required seasoned judgment.

One of the first developments in this transformation was a change in emphasis from seeking to understand those aspects of an author's life and times that he consciously portrayed to seeking to understand those that he unconsciously revealed. Lionel Trilling, writing in *The Liberal Imagination*, described it as a change in focus from "the explicit statements that a people makes through its art" to what lies beneath them: the "culture's hum and buzz of implication . . . the whole evanescent context in which its explicit statements are made."[15]

This denigration of the conscious role of the author was reinforced by a second development: the complete separation of a work from its creator. The New Critics, still

---

[13] J. Isaacs, "Shakespeare Criticism from Coleridge to the Present Day," in G. B. Harrison & H. Granville-Barker, *A Companion to Shakespeare Studies* (1934), p. 302.

[14] Stefan Collini, *The Nostalgic Imagination: History in English Criticism* (2019), p. 11.

[15] Lionel Trilling, *The Liberal Imagination*, pp. 205, 206-07.

working within the Humanistic tradition, had made this separation in order to examine works of literature as works of art; others now did so to examine their political and social content unencumbered by any thoughts of the author.

The "flaw" in the older way of thinking, newer scholars believed, was summed up by W. K. Wimsatt and Monroe Beardsley as "the intentional fallacy." For them, "the design or intention of the author is neither available nor desirable as a standard for judging the success of a work of literary art."[16] What was important was what the author had embodied in the work, not what he or she might have intended at some point during its composition. The work of literary scholars was now, Culler explained, to "expose the unexamined assumptions on which a text may rely (political, sexual, philosophical, linguistic)."[17] With both new approaches focused on the text rather than the author's intentions, there was, some thought, no longer a need to consider the author at all. Literary criticism reached what Roland Barthes called "the death of the author." Although Wimsatt and Beardsley did not coin the phrase "the intentional fallacy" until 1946 and Barthes "the death of the author" until 1967, those movements began in the 1920s, within a decade of the publication of *"Shakespeare" Identified.*[18]

With an author's intentions—conscious or unconscious—now discarded as irrelevant, literature was stripped bare. Literary scholars had succeeded in banishing the creators of the literary works they studied—authors—just as surely as physical scientists had succeeded in banishing the creator of the matter they studied—God. The words on the page were to be studied as inanimate objects to be given meaning by the reader rather than as words imbued with the spirit of their creator. Analyzing works of literature as isolated objects was not an approach favorable to the authorship question, which is intimately bound up with consideration of the life of the author and his reasons for writing them. Neither factor is valued if works of literature are regarded as immaculately conceived and the result of virgin births.

The limitations of this new approach were noted at the time by T. S. Eliot. Too narrow a focus on literary criticism is a danger "which every honest literary critic, now and in the future will have to face.... You cannot treat literary criticism as a subject isolated from every other subject of study; you must take account of general history, of philosophy, theology, economics, psychology, into all of which literary criticism merges."[19] But even the weight of Eliot's great authority was not sufficient to stop the forces pushing toward the impersonal and ahistorical examination of literature. Collini observed of this time that "In the course of the twentieth century literary history in its scholarly forms has come to seem like the eternal poor relation ... [yet] it is not only a genre with a long lineage of its own, but one that has continued to be an essential part of, or concomitant to, all other forms of literary study" (13). "The very practice of literary criticism, in other words,

---

[16] W. K. Wimsatt and Monroe Beardsley, "The Intentional Fallacy" (1946/1954). [Details in Bibliography.]

[17] Jonathan Culler, *Literary Theory: A Very Short Introduction* (2009), p. 67.

[18] It is interesting to observe that in moving beyond a writer's intentions to discover what he had inadvertently revealed in his works, theorists were moving in the same direction that Looney had, but for very different reasons. Whereas Looney had sought to discover more about the author by seeking clues to his life and personality and, eventually, his identity, the new theorists had done so in order to escape from the author, at first, as Trilling pointed out, to discover more about the spirit of the times in which the author had lived, and later to discard the author altogether.

[19] T. S. Eliot, in *Varieties of Metaphysical Poetry* (1933), ed. Ronald Schuchard (1993), p. 74, quoted in Collini (2019), p. 24.

always already involves a wider intellectual history" (17).

Academia, increasingly bound by the new methodology over the rest of the twentieth century, remained actively hostile to the Oxfordian claim. Accepting it would require overthrowing several methodological practices: scholars would have to waive the distinction between history and literature, reverse their judgment that personal and topical allusions were invalid indicators of authorship, and restore the biographical approach to the study of literature.

The question arises as to what degree of responsibility Shakespeare scholars bore for these changes. In the early days of the transformation—in the 1920s and 1930s—they had already sought to cut off consideration of one type of support for the idea of de Vere's authorship by denying the validity of personal and topical allusions. The "death of the author" approach had the same effect: denying an author's importance further devalued the significance of any linkages between de Vere's life and Shakespeare's plays. Some Oxfordians have speculated that this new approach to literary theory may have arisen as a direct response to the mismatch between the mundane details known of Shakspere's life and the brilliance of Shakespeare's works.

What Shakespeare Scholars Were Doing

If Shakespeare scholars after 1920 were not using biographical information to increase understanding of his works, what were they doing?

As J. Isaacs explained in his study of Shakespearean scholarship, the eighteenth century "was the great age of pioneers working in a virgin forest of text, annotating it, and opening up fields of scholarly research under the direction of a growing idolatry and furor."[20] Scholars worked to establish a chronology of the plays, trace Shakespeare's selection of materials, and chronicle his "growth to maturity, his summits of achievement, and in general the pattern of his creative career."[21] Their work, Isaacs explained, resulted in clean texts easily readable by modern eyes, lists of *Dramatis Personae*, plays divided into acts and scenes, entrances and exits marked, and the first formal biography of the author. Much of that work was done by Louis Theobald, "the first giant of Shakespeare scholarship."[22]

Scholarly work in the following century was more narrowly focused. "The nineteenth century is so richly strewn with monographs and learned articles that the paths, when they can be seen, are found to be, in the main, the work of journeymen, often inspired journeymen it is true, contributing each his portion to the cleaning up of the text, the formation of a picture of Shakespeare the dramatist, and his relations with the age he lived in" (323).

During the late nineteenth and early twentieth century the focus was on more minute subjects: Shakespeare's grammar, linguistic practice, pronunciation, punctuation, vocabulary, and the preparation of glossaries and concordances. "During the last fifty years [prior to 1934]," Isaacs continued, "a growing realism of attack has produced a vast quantity of new . . . [work] revising the whole field, working at first hand on neglected or misunderstood documents, questioning old orthodoxies with the higher criticism of

---

[20] J. Isaacs, "Shakespearian Scholarship," in G. B. Harrison & H. Granville-Barker, *A Companion to Shakespeare Studies* (1934), pp. 322-23.

[21] J. Isaacs, "Shakespeare Criticism from Coleridge to the Present Day," in G. B. Harrison & H. Granville-Barker, *A Companion to Shakespeare Studies* (1934), p. 301.

[22] J. Isaacs, "Shakespearian Scholarship" (1934), p. 307.

intensive and minute bibliographical inquiry.... These minuter studies are in danger of obscuring the general picture of Shakespeare's achievement." (323).

With that overview, the trajectory of Shakespeare Studies snaps into focus. Five features stand out.

- ➢ The cutting off of literary studies from the study of history and the resulting impoverishment of the field of literary history;

- ➢ The rejection of the methodology of identifying personal or topical allusions in Shakespeare's works;

- ➢ The rejection of the biographical approach to literary studies, in which knowledge of an author's life and times was brought to bear on interpretation of his works (the so-called "death of the author");

- ➢ The narrowing of the scope of Shakespeare Studies, from the "pioneering days" of the eighteenth century, to the "journeyman days" of more narrowly focused work in the nineteenth century, to the "fractured" and highly specialized work on "minuter studies" beginning in the early part of the twentieth century;

- ➢ The suppression of study of the Shakespeare authorship question, supported by the above four factors.

<u>Effects of these developments on scholars</u>

By the 1920s the narrowing of the scope of Shakespeare Studies and the increasing specialization of research increased the danger that scholars would have a fractured view of their subject. Scholars often were concerned not with Shakespeare's literary works directly, but with analyzing and commenting on the work of previous generations of scholars. The necessary but mind-numbing tasks of comparing minor textual variations and studying Shakespeare's spelling and grammar had left many Stratfordian scholars with blinders on, even when they took the time to look up from their narrow fields of specialization. Many had become so mentally constricted that they were not capable of the wider understanding of the Elizabethan era needed to grasp the Oxfordian idea. Mired in small technical matters, they were vulnerable to missing the forest for the trees. And miss it they did.

This increasingly specialized work on relatively minor issues widened the split between scholars and creative writers. During the decades before *"Shakespeare" Identified* was published, when discussion of the authorship issue had already been quite intense, creative writers—persons who knew what literary creativity entailed—were largely on the side of the doubters: witness Walt Whitman, Ralph Waldo Emerson, Henry James and Mark Twain. Academics staunchly supported Shakspere's authorship. Some, like Sir Sidney Lee, denied any difficulties with the traditional story of Shakspere's authorship. Others attempted to narrow the gap between the man and the works by denying the learned nature of the plays and by fantasizing about the advanced nature of the education provided by the Stratford grammar school and the value of conversations about Italy, the law and other subjects that Shakspere supposedly engaged in at the Mermaid tavern.

Post-*"Shakespeare" Identified*, the same division existed. On the creative side were those with the qualities needed to enter imaginatively into the spirit of the Elizabethan age, including British novelists John Galsworthy and Marjorie Bowen, and American writers Carolyn Wells, Esther Singleton, Oliver Herford and, Gelett Burgess, to name only a few. Galsworthy had gone so far as to distribute dozens of copies of *"Shakespeare" Identified* to his friends, just as Henry Clay Folger, founder of the Folger Shakespeare Library later distributed copies of Esther Singleton's Oxford-themed novel *Shakespearian Fantasias* to his friends. On the academic side scholars again tried to explain the Oxfordian issue away by denying the use of legitimate forms of evidence, by denigrating Oxford's character and early poetry, and by deliberately misstating the Oxfordian claim in their attempts to demolish it..

An extreme example of the contrast between the creative and the scholarly modes of thought is shown by a comparison of statements by Walt Whitman and J. M. Robertson. Below is an example of informed historical imagination from Walt Whitman:

> Conceiv'd out of the fullest heat and pulse of European feudalism—personifying in unparallel'd ways the medieval aristocracy, its towering spirit of ruthless and gigantic caste, its own peculiar air and arrogance (no mere imitation)—only one of the "wolfish earls" so plenteous in the plays themselves, or some born descendent and knower, might seem to be the true author of those amazing works—works in some respects greater than anything else in recorded history.[23]

Contrast it with this example of narrow, inwardly-focused scholarly plodding from J. M. Robertson, who recommended that scholars speaking under the auspices of the British Council address such topics as "Shakespeare's Alleged Use of the Split Infinitive in *Julius Caesar* and in a Sonnet." "The audience probably would not be large," he recognized, "but what then? Scholarship would be vindicated."[24]

The methodology of Shakespeare Studies deprived scholars of the valuable insights that come from placing the works within the context of a writer's life and tracing allusions to it in his works. Cut off from history and scholarly work done outside academia, and denying the validity of allusions, scholars had no way of obtaining the knowledge needed to empower the imagination to act properly. Informed imagination could not exist; it remained uninformed, and uninformed imagination is also known as fantasy, which all scholars rightly decry. "The imagination needs not wings but weights," is how the English novelist Samuel Butler phrased it, the "weights" in this case being historical knowledge.

Unable to comprehend the context within which Shakespeare lived and wrote—focused only on the words on the page—orthodox scholars had no way of explaining how Shakspere, if he was Shakespeare, had come to write his plays and poems except through the magic wands of genius and imagination.

Just as Sir Sidney Lee before 1920 had seen the plays as either pure autobiography or pure fantasy because he did not recognize any middle ground, so too scholars in the 1920s and 1930s could see only the option of focusing on the small technical issues on one side and pure fantasy on the other. Caught up in that false dichotomy, they missed the middle ground of informed imagination.

The table nearby shows the extremes of the ideas just presented. It is not meant to include every scholar. By presenting extremes it makes clear the distinction between the approaches of the two sets of scholars regarding the use of the imagination, informed or otherwise, to understand a time and place very different from their own.

---

[23] Walt Whitman, *November Boughs*, quoted in *SF Quarterly*, vol. VII, No. 3 (July 1946), p. 46.
[24] J. M. Robertson, *The State of Shakespeare Study: A Critical Conspectus* (1931), p. 8.

	Stratfordian Scholars 1: Lack of imagination	*Oxfordian Scholars: Informed Imagination*	**Stratfordian Scholars 2:** Imagination uninformed by facts
Nature of understanding:	Literal, small-minded understanding	*Informed imagination: Middle ground recognized by Oxfordian scholars but unseen by Stratfordians*	Fantasy
Biographical content in plays:	Plays as pure biography of the author	*Plays as arising from the author's life, experiences and personality, imaginatively recreated*	Plays as fantasies with no biographical component
Contemporaneous political and social events portrayed in the plays:	Plays as representations of real events, as in historical fiction	*Plays as arising from the imaginative trans-formation of real-life cultural, historical and social developments and people involved in them*	Plays as pure fantasy unrelated to contemporary events and people
Nature of work to be done	Before Looney, dry-as-dust scholarly work to recover the texts and uncover other external historical facts	*Understanding of the spirit of the author and his works, through an informed imagination based on historical knowledge and inferences from the works themselves*	After Looney, dry-as-dust theoretical scholarly work focused on the text itself culminating in theoretical and statistical approaches such as Stylometrics

Percy Allen had repeatedly cited the lack of informed imagination or intuitive powers as the reason why traditional scholars had been unable to accept the topical allusions he identified or the Oxfordian thesis itself. He recognized that scholars, "while fully equipped with textual knowledge, learning, and classical attainment, have wholly failed, as yet, to bring to the interpretation of Elizabethan drama the two essential qualities, courage and imagination."[25] It was perhaps the same inward focus on scholarly minutiae that had led Looney, a decade earlier to state that he was "not optimistic about the future of British intellectual life." The attacks on the Oxfordian idea did not "reflect well on the intellectual credit of England. . . . The present-day handling by the 'intellectual classes' of all problems requiring *thought* rather than erudition and literary style gave [him] an uneasy feeling that the initiative which England held in the latter half of the nineteenth century is passing into other hands."[26]

Before Looney, two scholars had possessed the necessary informed imagination. They were Edward Dowden in his groundbreaking *Shakspere: A Critical Study of His Mind and Art* (1875), and Frank Harris in *The Man Shakespeare and his Tragic Life-Story*

---

[25] Percy Allen, *The Case for Edward de Vere as "Shakespeare"* [pamphlet] (1930), p. 40.
[26] J. Thomas Looney, "Stratford and Stony Stratford," *Bookman's Journal*, vol. 3/74 (March 25, 1921): 388.

(1909).[27] Both, though, remained hampered by Stratfordian beliefs. Like them, Looney had mined the works themselves for what they revealed about the characteristics and qualities, and the life and personality, of their author. Unlike them, he was able to carry the ball forward by seeking and finding an author who embodied those traits. Oxfordian scholars after Looney, having learned much from his use of an informed imagination, added further to understanding Shakespeare's works and the conditions in which Oxford wrote them.

Lytton Strachey was one of the few post-1920 Stratfordian scholars who recognized the value of that approach for understanding how greatly the Elizabethan mindset differed from the Victorian and Edwardian.

> The [Elizabethan] age . . . needs no description: everybody knows its outward appearances . . . but what is perhaps unattainable, would be some means by which the modern mind might reach to an imaginative comprehension of these beings of three centuries ago . . . might touch the very pulse of the machine. But the path seems closed to us. By what art are we to worm our way into these strange spirits?
>
> It is above all the contradictions of the age that baffle our imaginations and perplex our intelligence. . . . How is it possible to give a coherent account of their subtlety and their naïveté, their delicacy and their brutality, their piety and their lust? By what perverse magic were intellectual ingenuity and theological ingenuousness intertwined in John Donne? Who has ever explained Francis Bacon? How is it conceivable that the Puritans were the brothers of the dramatists?
>
> It is so hard to gauge, from the exuberance of their decoration, the subtle, secret lives of their inner nature.[28]

Four examples

Among the many aspects of the psychology of the Elizabethan mind and the conditions in which Shakespeare's works were written that many orthodox scholars were unable to penetrate, four are of special significance: the secretive and subtle nature of the Elizabethan mind; Edward de Vere's authorship of "Shakespeare's" works; his place at the center of the literary, intellectual and cultural life of the Elizabethan era; and Shakespeare's plays as telling the story of their times. Examples of the informed scholarship that Oxfordian scholars produced on those subjects—and that academia should have produced—are included in the following text boxes.

---

[27] Harris was not a scholar *per se*, but a man of letters—a journalist, novelist, biographer and autobiographer.
[28] Lytton Strachey, *Elizabeth and Essex* (1922), p. 89.

The nature of the Elizabethan mind.

Percy Allen:

> The cunning skill of Elizabethan writers, in at once concealing and revealing interesting facts and identities beneath an innocent-looking, yet usually penetrable disguise; and the corresponding cleverness of readers—and presumably of the elite among theatrical audiences also—at penetrating such disguises, and perceiving accordingly the inner purport of the text, made the game, though hazardous, an alluring and sometimes a profitable one, to the parties concerned. Even the dangers of these pursuits—dangers which, certainly, were not small—heightened enjoying to daring minds, in an age when great risks were willingly run, and "safety first" was a slogan much less honoured than now. [*Anne Cecil, Elizabeth & Oxford* (1934), p. 2.]

> In common with some of the historians, [literary scholars'] failure has been due, in the first place to neglect to corelate literature with history; secondly, to a strange inability to penetrate the subtleties of the Elizabethan mind, and to comprehend its inveterate tendency towards, and even its positive delight in, elaborate secrecies, and the use of double meanings, including puns, word-play, and ciphers numerical and verbal. Further, the scholars generally have overlooked the marked Elizabethan love for symbolic treatment of a historic theme—a characteristic equally evident in the painters, as in the dramatists of the day. [*The Case for Edward de Vere as "Shakespeare"* (1930), p. 39.]

> The secret of this general academic failure has been due, in my judgment, to . . . the widely prevalent idea that classical scholarship, rather than imaginative penetration, holds the key to Shakespeare's deeper meaning; and that classical quotations, detected in a speech, preclude the presence of simultaneous, contemporaneous, topical, and literary allusion. The subtleties of the Elizabethan mind, including its addiction to symbolism, as well as to secrecy, have largely escaped a scholarship which is often mentally too rigid to enter successfully upon such lines of investigation; and finds its academic dignity compromised—as it believes—by familiar contact with anagrams, puns, ciphers, and other philological trickery of three hundred years ago. Imagination, however, and due allowance for psychological change, are as essential to the interpretation as they are to the writing of an Elizabethan play. [*The Case for Edward de Vere as "Shakespeare"* (1930), p. 8.]

> It is undeniable that the commentators generally have examined the texts, not of Shakespeare only, but of his fellow-dramatists as well, with so complete a failure to comprehend the subterranean tendencies of Elizabethan thought and its subtle trick of weaving secret signs and patterns of hidden word meaning into its writings, that they have allowed to escape them many vitally important facts which, for three centuries, have been staring them in the face. ["The Rhyme-Linked Order of Shakespeare's Sonnets," *Christian Science Monitor*, Jan. 18, 1929, p. 4.]

Capt. Bernard M. Ward:

> [There is a] complete failure of scholars to comprehend the psychology of Elizabethan England. They impute to Shakespeare and his fellows a simple singleness of mind which was quite alien to an age more subtle and secret than any other in English history. Educated Elizabethans were a people who habitually expressed themselves through double meanings, puns, allegories, anagrams, and other forms of cryptic allusion, of which "serious scholarship" may take no cognizance. [A Companion to Shakespeare Studies," *Sh. Pictorial*, September 1934, p. 144.]

Edward de Vere was the principal author of "Shakespeare's" works.

Ernest Allen:

> The enormous strength of the case for Edward de Vere lies in the simple truth that the theory of his authorship agrees in every single date and detail, both as regards the interior evidence of the works and the exterior evidence of the facts, with all the circumstances surrounding Shakespeare over the full period of about fifty years. Under these circumstances it seems impossible that it can be untrue. It should be noted that the identity of Lord Oxford as Shakespeare was very carefully concealed. ["Claimants to 'Shakespeare' Authorship," *Shakespeare Pictorial*, July 1936, p. 116.]

Gerald H. Rendall:

> The Shakespearean Folio comprises a splendid output of dramatic invention, which lacks authentic origination; while in Edward de Vere, Earl of Oxford, there is a title author of surpassing merit, whose works have hitherto eluded the identification of posterity. Careful exploration of the trail discloses footprints that are unmistakable. Literary links make it impossible to dissociate the *Sonnets* from the *Venus and Adonis*, or *Venus and Adonis* and *Lucrece* from authentic productions of Edward de Vere. Rightly understood, both poems and *Sonnets* abound in convincing references to the Earl of Oxford's relations with other contemporary associates and episodes, and shed vivid lights upon his personal experiences and temperament. [*Personal Clues in Shakespeare Poems and Sonnets* (1934), pp. vi-vii.]

> The authors with whom in youth [Oxford] was most conversant—e.g., Ovid, *Metamorphoses*, and *Il Cortegiano*—and again those with whom later he collaborated or associated most intimately—Lyly and Munday, and from very different angles, Sidney and Chapman—are just those whose traces are clearest in Shakespearean handiwork. Just as the Plays, when scrutinised, reveal numerous and arresting coincidences with recorded incidents and traits in the career of Edward de Vere, so, too, in the Poems and *Sonnets*, the personal and literary relations, and the fugitive allusions to public events, find in his personality and doings a unifying centre of co-ordination; and for those in the secret he here and there inserts his cypher of identification. [*Shakespeare Sonnets and Edward de Vere* (1930), p. 292.

That Oxford stood at the center of the Elizabethan world.

Gerald Rendall:

> Only lately has it become plain how central a place belongs to Edward de Vere, 17th Earl of Oxford, at the confluence of the various currents of literary activity—poetic, dramatic, exotic, and academic—which combine to form the product known as "Elizabethan." Student, poet, playwright, and patron of the drama, he was in touch with the most versatile spirits of the age, and in the judgment of his best-informed contemporaries his own compositions were second to none in excellence. And when we subject the *Sonnets* to close personal scrutiny, or in the Plays analyse the incidents and characters and motives, which seem most to reflect the author's own experience, by the light of his career and personality, we are met by coincidences so numerous, so circumstantial, so surprising and illuminating, that it becomes impossible to set them down to chance or to refuse to recognise in them the handiwork of Edward de Vere. [*Shakespeare Sonnets and Edward de Vere* (1930), pp. 291-92.]

> He stood at the confluence of the rival and conflicting currents—Academic, Humanist, Romantic, Euphuist, Dramatic—which are the glory of the Elizabethan Renascence. He came into personal touch with the accepted leaders and representatives of every School, and without committing himself to any commanded the respect of all. [*Personal Clues in Shakespeare Poems and Sonnets* (1934), p. 7.]

> His return to England in 1576 coincided with a notable event in the history of English Drama, the opening of the Theater, the first licensed play-house in the metropolis, followed by that of the Curtain in 1577.... [After returning from the continent, Oxford] was a leading, and in some respects the foremost, figure. [*Shakespeare Sonnets and Edward de Vere* (1930), pp. 11, 40.]

That the plays told the story of the times.

Percy Allen:

It began, gradually, to dawn upon me, that Elizabethan poetry in general, including its drama, was far more closely inter-related than had hitherto been supposed, and that the poems, and plays, of the period teemed with topical allusions, personal, literary, and other, that modern scholarship, through timidity, and lack of penetrative imagination, had almost wholly, overlooked; and which carefully examined, and properly correlated with the history of its time, would, I felt certain, throw floods of light upon Elizabethan drama generally, and, in particular, upon the Shakespearean plays. [*The Case for Edward de Vere as "Shakespeare"* (1930), p. 3.]

The academic mind, by virtue of its official standing and responsibilities, and of the exalted trusts committed to it, is necessarily traditional, conservative, and slow to adopt new beliefs, especially such as must be drawn rather from intelligent inference, than from direct documentary proof. It has also its dignity to consider; and is, I think, apt to regard that dignity as being compromised by any serious concern with puns, ciphers, or anagrams, the interpretation of which must be, to some extent, conjectural; but which, nevertheless, were greatly used by the Elizabethans, including Shakespeare; and do, undoubtedly, supply essential clues to the most vital literary enigmas of that age. [*The Case for Edward de Vere as "Shakespeare"* (1930), p. 39 (pamphlet)]

The scholars, in fact, while fully equipped with textual knowledge, learning, and classical attainment, have . . . been unable to fathom the deeper meaning of the texts, and have been led to ignore the vital fact, that between the history of those days, and its literature, there exists an inseparable connection, even in so light and apparently fantastic and irresponsible a play as Shakespeare's comedy, *Twelfth Night*. (40)

For these reasons, most of the more important Shakespearean discoveries, of this century, have been, and are being, made, by amateurs; or it would be fairer to say, by non-professionals, who, unhampered by office or tradition, have dared to discard outworn traditional beliefs, and to bring fresh minds, and imaginative inference, to the difficult task of elucidating Shakespeare, and his fellows. I have reason to believe, however, that already a number of the more academic men, aware of their past mistakes, are changing their view-points, as swiftly as is consistent with their official status and dignity, and with the difficult circumstances of the case. (41)

Capt. Bernard M. Ward:

It is perfectly useless for anyone who is incapable of understanding symbolism or allegory to study the Elizabethan playwrights and poets. It is hardly too much to say that every stanza of poetry and every scene from a play has got a second meaning which is either symbolical or allegorical. To picture Shakespeare as Sir Edmund Chambers does, as a man entirely divorced from his surroundings, taking no interest whatsoever in current events, but merely engaged in churning out "box office successes," is laughable. The Shakespeare *Folio* and *The Fairy Queen* are two of the most valuable histories of England that we possess. Their vital importance lies in the fact that they tell us how Elizabethan history appeared to a *contemporary*. If our modern historians would study Shakespeare and Spenser they would not tumble into that universal pitfall—reading history backwards. ["Hamlet," *Shakespeare Pictorial*, March 1935, p. 48.]

13

Stratfordian Scholars Inadvertently
Make the Oxfordian Case

Academics Report Findings that Undermine Their Own Case

One of the strengths of J. Thomas Looney's *"Shakespeare" Identified* was that in making the Oxfordian case he drew largely on facts already uncovered by Stratfordian scholars. He brought their facts together, organized them in a new way and viewed the resulting combination from a new perspective. Although newly uncovered information about Edward de Vere strengthened the Oxfordian position, the basic case was made almost entirely from existing information. Looney used Stratfordians' own findings against them.

After 1920 orthodox scholars continued to make findings that when interpreted properly undercut the Stratfordian case and strengthened the Oxfordian. Col. Bernard R. Ward wrote in 1931 that the Shakespeare Fellowship "cordially welcome[s] . . . all new facts, whether found out by ourselves or by orthodox Shakespeareans. We prefer indeed that new facts should be unearthed by orthodox researchers on account of the wider publicity given to such finds. Discoveries are of no use unless public attention is drawn to them, and our own are simply not alluded to. Besides it is particularly good sport to see the enemy's engineer 'hoist with his own petard.'"[1]

This chapter recounts the most significant of those findings. Half are from the dozen years that ended in April 1933, when Col. Ward died. Half are from later years; surely they would have brought a smile to his face if only he had lived to see them.[2] In almost every instance the discoverers presented their findings without any overt recognition of their larger affects on the authorship question. They did not recognize that they were sawing off the limb on which they were sitting.

Charlotte Carmichael Stopes: *Life of Henry, Third Earl of Southampton, Shakespeare's Patron* (1922)

Stopes spent eight years of painstaking work in the Public Record Office and other manuscript repositories with the avowed intention of establishing a connection between William Shakspere and the Third Earl of Southampton other than the dedications to him in *Venus and Adonis* and *Lucrece*. But in the end, as she regretfully admitted, she found nothing—not a single document—connecting the two men. "I must confess that I did not start this work for the sake of the Earl of Southampton, but in the hope that I might find more about Shakespeare, which hope has not been satisfied."[3] She confessed to Percy

---

[1] Col. Bernard R. Ward, "A Great Shakespeare Discovery," *Shakespeare Pictorial*, Dec. 1931, p. 196.
[2] The final two examples were published in England after 1945, the cutoff point for this book, but the work reported in them had been reported on earlier in a different format and in the case of Feuillerat's work, was commented on by J. Thomas Looney.
[3] Charlotte Carmichael Stopes, *Life of Henry, Third Earl of Southampton* (1922), p. vi.

Allen shortly before her death that "My life has been a failure."[4] If she hadn't heard of the Oxfordian claim on her own, she surely learned of it from Allen, but she never accepted that she had searched for linkages to the wrong man. If she'd had the right author in mind she would have found what she sought: the Earl of Southampton had in 1593 been engaged to the Earl of Oxford's daughter, and both earls had been raised as wards of the Queen in Lord Burghley's house after the deaths of their fathers. Her failure to find any linkage between Southampton and Shakspere undercut an important element of the Stratfordian story, that of Southampton having been patron to the commoner playwright.

Sir Edmund Chambers: *The Elizabethan Stage* (1923)

Chambers's book, the most complete and detailed history of the Elizabethan stage yet written, had short sections in volume two about the actors in the troupes sponsored by the Earls of Oxford and Derby.[5] A section in volume one emphasized the importance of

---

**Works by Orthodox Scholars Published after 1920
that Undercut the Stratfordian Claim**

1922	Charlotte Carmichael Stopes — *Life of Henry, Third Earl of Southampton*
1923	Sir Edmund K. Chambers — *The Elizabethan Stage*
1924	Arthur Quiller-Couch — *Shakespeare's Workmanship*
1925	W. W. Greg (editor) — *English Literary Autographs, Part I. Dramatists*, 1550-1650
1925	Basil Edwin Lawrence — *Notes on the Authorship of Shakespeare's Plays and Poems*
1925	Edward G. Harman — *The Impersonality of Shakespeare*
1926	J. M. Robertson — *Problems of the Shakespeare Sonnets*
1927	Sir Henry Irving — *Works of Shakespeare*
1927	Felix E. Schelling — *Shakespeare and "Demi-Science:" Papers on Elizabethan Topics*
1928	Sir Walter Raleigh — *Shakespeare*
1928	John Temple Smart — *Shakespeare—Truth and Tradition*
1930	Sir Edmund K. Chambers — *William Shakespeare: A Study of Facts and Problems*
1930	G. B. Harrison — Review of Sidney Lee's *Elizabethan & Other Essays, London Mercury* (June)
1930	G. Wilson Knight — "Shakespeare and the Earl of Oxford," *Nation & Athenaeum* (May 3)
1931	Leslie Hotson — *Shakespeare Versus Shallow*
1931	J. M. Robertson — *The State of Shakespeare Study: A Critical Conspectus*
1932	J. Dover Wilson — *The Essential Shakespeare: A Biographical Adventure*
1933	G. B. Harrison — *Shakespeare at Work*
1934	G. B. Harrison & H. Granville Barker (editors) — *A Companion to Shakespeare Studies* J. W. Mackail: "The Life of Shakespeare," pp. 1-8 Muriel St. Clare Byrne, "The Social Background," pp. 187-218
1934	Alfred Hart — *Shakespeare and the Homilies*
1935	J. Dover Wilson — *Manuscript of Shakespeare's Hamlet and the Problems of Its Transmission*
1935	Caroline Spurgeon — *Shakespeare's Imagery, and What It Tells Us*
1936	Andrew S. Cairncross — *The Problem of Hamlet: A Solution*
1936	C. J. Sisson — *Lost Plays of Shakespeare's Age*
1937	Levin L. Schücking — *The Meaning of Hamlet*
1938	Edgar Fripp — *Shakespeare, Man and Artist*
1939	G. B. Harrison — *Introducing Shakespeare* (Revised 1954, 1966)
1942	Alfred Hart — *Stolne and Surreptitious Copies: A Comparative Study of Sh's Bad Quartos*
1944	E. M. W. Tillyard — *Shakespeare's History Plays*
1947	Lily B. Campbell — *Shakespeare's "Histories:" Mirrors of Elizabethan Policy*
1953	Albert Feuillerat — *The Composition of Shakespeare's Plays*

---

[4] Percy Allen, "Shakespeare Rediscovered," *SF News-Letter*, No. 9 (May 1938): 8.

[5] Sir Edmund Chambers, *The Elizabethan Stage*, vol. II, pp. 99-102. 118-27.

the queen and her court in connection with the drama: "The Palace was the point of vantage from which the stage won its way, against the linked opposition of an alienated pulpit and an alienated municipality."[6] This recognition of the key role of the Tudor court and "the conditions under which the presentation of plays formed a recurring interest in its bustling many-coloured life"[7] is an important shift from the earlier view that the Elizabethan drama arose primarily through the public stage. It supports the Oxfordian thesis because Oxford is known to have written plays and produced performances of them in the court, while the man from Stratford had no documented connection with it.[8]

Arthur Quiller-Couch: *Shakespeare's Workmanship* (1924)

"The longer we consider these later plays that fall to be dated between the great tragedies and *The Tempest*," Quiller-Couch wrote, "the more we are forced to feel that . . . *something had happened*." He was not referring to "the confusion of dates and places," but to "those laxities of construction [and] of workmanship," and "the *tours de force* mixed up with other men's botch work . . . with serious scamping of artistry."[9] After making that observation, Quiller-Couch didn't speculate as to what had happened; he simply moved on to an examination of the workmanship of *The Winter's Tale*.[10] What had happened, Oxfordian scholars said, was that the author of those works died in 1604, leaving unfinished works to be completed by others.

W. W. Greg (editor): *English Literary Autographs, Part I. Dramatists, 1550-1650* (1925)

Three oddities mar this collection of handwriting specimens of all English dramatists who lived between 1550 and 1650 for which holographs exist; all three weaken the Stratfordian case and strengthen the Oxfordian. The first is the omission of the signatures of William Shakspere "in order to avoid controversy." That omission allowed Greg to hide the facts that all six of Shakspere's known signatures differ from each other, that none are spelled "Shakespeare," that none appear to have been made by someone who was used to using a pen, and that except for those examples, Shakspere is not known to have signed his name to any of the documents related to his many lawsuits, land purchases or other commercial transactions.

The second oddity is Greg's inclusion of examples of the handwriting of the Earls of Oxford and Derby because of their "close connexion with the stage." Was this an admission that both men were recognized as dramatists writing for the public stage during their lifetimes even though none of their plays survive under their own names? Greg did not explain what he meant by their "close connexion with the stage."

The third oddity, as explained by Capt. Ward, is that "The second Oxford letter

---

[6] Sir Edmund Chambers, *The Elizabethan Stage*, vol. I, prefatory material, page not numbered.

[7] Capt. Bernard M. Ward, *The Seventeenth Earl of Oxford 1550-1604* (1928), pp. 390-91.

[8] The one exception is the record of a payment in 1595 to William Shakespeare, but it was entered long after the date on which the payment was supposedly made and is of suspect validity.

[9] Arthur Quiller-Couch, *Shakespeare's Workmanship* (1924), p. 296. The phrase "something had happened" is not italicized in the original, but is when quoted in *"Shakespeare" Identified*.

[10] "Where is Quiller-Couch's scholarly interest in understanding what happened?" readers might well ask. "Where is his normal human curiosity concerning the reason why '*tours de force* [are] mixed up with other men's botch work'"? Was it fear that he might find that he and his colleagues had identified the wrong man as the author that stopped him in his tracks? Whatever the reason, Quiller-Couch's failure to investigate the abrupt decline in the quality of Shakespeare's workmanship in a book dedicated to that very subject undermines the favorable impression that the rest of the book makes.

reproduced by Dr. Greg is dated July 7th, 1594, and is of interest on account of an allusion to an 'office' held by the writer, an allusion which naturally puzzled Dr. Greg. 'It does not appear,' [Greg] wrote, 'what was the "office" to which he alludes, but the affair may possibly have had to do with the import monopoly for which he was petitioning in 1592.'"[11] Since the letter noted interference with an 'office' that Oxford currently held, Greg's speculation that it might interfere with an office he did not yet hold (and never would hold) made no sense. The logical explanation is that it referred to Oxford's office as head of a propaganda department that organized the production of plays for the public stage (see Chapter 7).

Edward G. Harman: *The Impersonality of Shakespeare* (1925)

Harman unwittingly cast doubt on Shakspere as Shakespeare by noting the intensity with which a writer draws on his own experiences and personality in creating his works—something that was inapplicable to Shakspere, for whom the record showed much personal involvement with petty lawsuits but none with the creation or performance of dramatic works of literature. Harman was also astute in his recognition that investigations into the authorship question must "combine historical with literary criticism" and that works of literature can themselves be sources of historical information.

> The defect of our literary criticism is that it too often ignores history, and of our history that it seldom condescends to make use of literature. We hear a great deal in these days about original research, and the earth is raked over for "documents," when all the while there are the open documents of printed books, notably in the form of poetry, of which little or no use is made. The cause of this seems to lie in the misconceptions which prevail as to the origin of poetry, and in the belief that it springs in some mysterious fashion out of nothing.

He explained that literature, and especially poetry and drama, are by necessity sources of information about the author's life and times because of the processes through which they are produced. "For it is the most intellectual and definite of the arts and draws all its greatest effects out of reality. And its greatest effects are found in the poetry of action and characterization, that is to say in the epic and the drama. Genius must provide the combinations, but only reading, experience and observation can supply the knowledge."[12] The last point destroyed the Stratfordian argument. There is no documentary evidence that Shakspere had engaged in any of the "reading, experience and observation" that would have been necessary to write Shakespeare's works, whereas the Earl of Oxford's biography is one long description of those very things.

Basil Edwin Lawrence: *Notes on the Authorship of Shakespeare's Plays and Poems* (1925)

Although Lawrence was a Baconian, he acknowledged a direct connection between Edward de Vere and "Shakespeare:" "Shakespeare . . . took de Vere's thoughts and clothed them in more beautiful garbs. De Vere's verses were in existence in 1593, and I think it must be admitted that the ideas and thoughts, although they may be much the same as de Vere's, are much better expressed in *Venus and Adonis* than they are in de Vere's Echo verses."[13] Rather than make the obvious connection between Oxford and Shakespeare, Lawrence claimed that Sir Francis Bacon, Oxford's cousin by marriage, had used Oxford's

---

[11] Capt. Bernard M. Ward, *The Seventeenth Earl of Oxford 1550-1604* (1928), pp. 391-92.
[12] Edward G. Harman, *The "Impersonality" of Shakespeare* (1925), p. v.
[13] Basil Edwin Lawrence, *Notes on the Authorship of Shakespeare's Plays and Poems* (1925), p. 105.

poems as his starting point in writing *Venus and Adonis*.

J. M. Robertson: *The Problems of the Shakespeare Sonnets* (1926)

In April 1927 Col. Ward included in a letter to Katharine Eggar the comment that "J. M. Robertson's *Problems of the Shakespeare Sonnets* published last year is interesting from our point of view, as showing how genuinely frightened the orthodox are of the Oxford Theory."[14] Ward didn't explain further; perhaps he meant Robertson's statement that "For one reader who realises the multitude of difficulties as to the real authorship of much of the Folio, and grapples with these in a scientific fashion, there are three who are led aside, for awhile if not for life, by one or other of the 'anti-Stratfordian' solutions."[15] How interesting that three out of four readers seemed more interested in learning about alternative candidates than in considering Robertson's Stratfordian ideas. (This is another book in which Elizabeth Vere, Oxford's daughter, is referred to only as Lord Burghley's granddaughter with no mention made of Oxford, as though the highest ranking earl in the realm was a nonentity.)

Sir Henry Irving: *Works of Shakespeare* (1927)

Although he made no mention of the authorship question, J. Thomas Looney, *"Shakespeare" Identified* or the Earl of Oxford in his *Works of Shakespeare*, Irving did present findings that undercut the Stratfordian claim and supported the Oxfordian. In his depiction of events, 1604—the year of Oxford's death—was marked not only by the disbanding of the Lord Chamberlain's Men and their reformulation as the King's Men, and not only by "Shakespeare" ceasing to act, but also—and most significantly—by the loss of the leadership that had made the company such an effective organization.

> No sooner had our great dramatist ceased to take part in the public performances of the King's players, than the company appears to have thrown off the restraint by which it had been usually controlled ever since its formation and to have produced plays which were objectionable to the court, as well as offensive to private persons. Shakespeare, from his abilities, station and experience, must have possessed great influence with the body at large, and due deference, we may readily believe, was shown to his knowledge and judgment in the selection and acceptance of plays.[16]

Irving provided no explanation as to how Shakspere's ceasing to act while still remaining with the company could have had the effects he described. Nor did he provide any explanation as to how Shakspere, a man whose personality was so unremarkable that not a single account of it has survived, could have managed such an organization. His description of the man who had managed the company—someone whose "abilities, station and experience, must have possessed great influence" and engendered "due deference"—fits the Earl of Oxford, the Lord Great Chamberlain of the realm, like a tailor-made glove.

Felix E. Schelling: *Shakespeare and "Demi-Science:" Papers on Elizabethan Topics* (1927)

"Demi-Science," for Schelling, is the equivalent of pseudo-science, as opposed to "true science" for which Schelling has "a respect, and admiration and a veneration that will yield

---

[14] Col. Bernard R. Ward, letter to Katharine E. Eggar, April 13, 1927.
[15] J. M. Robertson, *The Problems of the Shakespeare Sonnets* (1926), p. 3.
[16] Sir Henry Irving, *The Complete Works of William Shakespeare* (1927), p. xxxixb, quoted in Charlton Ogburn, *The Mysterious William Shakespeare* (1992), p. 734.

to none."[17] Whose work did he term demi-science? Authorship doubters'.

Schelling also denounced "the psychological interpretation of dramatic works of art, especially those of the past," in which "the dramatic psycho-analyst . . . applies to these images of stage illusion the rigorous measurements that we habitually apply—and misapply—to actual men and women" (6). Among those most guilty of this "sin" are Professor Abel Lefranc, who "elaborated a theory whereby Shakespeare is once more deprived of authorship in his own plays" (19-20), and J. Thomas Looney, whom he described but didn't name: "When another writer, posing as a detective, scents fraud and deception in every unsuspected act of an author's life, and a malign and covert allusiveness in every other harmless passage of his poetry, we know just what to think of a nature so petty and prying. Depend upon it by their myths ye shall know them, for there is nothing so infallibly a man's own as the myth that he fashions" (24).

Schelling then showed that he had swallowed the Stratfordian myth hook, line and sinker: "Now if there is anything concerning Shakespeare about which we may be permitted to be certain, it is the circumstance that there is absolutely no mystery about the publication of his plays" (29-30). If ever a statement undermined the credibility of a professor of English at a major university—the University of Pennsylvania in this case—this is it. It rivals J. M. Robertson's ludicrous statement in 1920 that "It is precisely because the data for the Stratford actor alone gives an intelligible biographical substratum for the plays that I hold to it."[18]

Sir Walter Raleigh: *Shakespeare* (1907, reprinted 1928)

Two points made by Raleigh in this book, reprinted eight years after *"Shakespeare" Identified*, supported Looney's Oxfordian claim. The first explained how it came to be that "other pens" were found among the works categorized as Shakespeare's "final works": "At the beginning of his career Shakespeare made very free use of the work of other men. . . . Towards the end of his career his work is once more found mixed with the work of other men, but this time there is generally reason to suspect that it is these others that have laid him under contribution, altering his completed plays, or completing his unfinished work by additions of their own."[19]

The second point addressed a type of knowledge that would have been impossible for anyone not born and raised as a courtier to have acquired, thereby eliminating the man from Stratford as a candidate for authorship: "From the very first he has an unerringly sure touch with the character of high-born ladies; he knows all that can neither be learned by method nor taught in words—the unwritten code of delicate honour, the rapidity and confidence of decision, the absolute trust in instinct and the unhesitating freedom of speech" (31). How a commoner arrived from the sticks could have had that "unerringly sure touch" is not explained.

John Semple Smart: *Shakespeare: Truth and Tradition* (1928)

Writing eight years after the publication of *"Shakespeare" Identified*, Smart appeared never to have heard of the works of Greenwood or Looney. His formulation of the traditional authorship story is a classic example of circular reasoning: Stratford was a major center of learning in the sixteenth century, he asserted, because the joiners and

---

[17] Felix E. Schelling, *Shakespeare and "Demi-Science"* (1927), p. 1.
[18] J. M. Robertson, "The Identity of Shakespeare," *Bookman's Journal*, vol. 2/30 (May 21, 1920): 59.
[19] Sir Walter Raleigh, *Shakespeare* (1907/1928), p. 109.

tinkers in *A Midsummer Night's Dream* were able to read and write;[20] knowledge of Latin was widespread in Stratford because an inscription in that language was carved on Shakspere's monument in Trinity Church; the women of Stratford were literate because Maria, the maid in *Twelfth Night*, could write a script as beautiful as Olivia's (35); the young men of Stratford regularly traveled to other cities to broaden their horizons because the title characters in *Two Gentlemen of Verona* did so.

Smart's greatest blunder, one that directly supported the Oxfordian claim, was his insistence that Shakspere attended Oxford University, because of the erudite nature of the plays. He spent almost forty pages laying out the university learning apparent in the plays (125-162). Oxford, as is well known, had degrees from both Oxford and Cambridge Universities; Shakspere had no known education.

Sir Edmund Chambers: *William Shakespeare: A Study of Facts and Problems* (1930)

Here Chambers made the remarkable admission that Shakespeare's personality—the personality that created Hamlet and Macbeth and Romeo, and Ophelia and Cleopatra and Rosaline—was so unremarkable that not a single account of it from anyone in Stratford, where he lived more than half his fifty-two years, has survived. The people in his home town likewise made little impression on him. "Whatever imprint Shakespeare's Warwickshire contemporaries may have left upon his imagination inevitably eludes us. . . . It is no use guessing. As in so many other historical investigations, after all the careful scenting of clues and all the patient balancing of probabilities, the last word for a self-respecting scholarship, can only be that of nescience."[21]

Discussing the *Sonnets*, Chambers wrote with great insight of the glimpses they provide of

> a soul-side of Shakespeare imperfectly revealed by the plays. A perturbed spirit is behind the quiet mask. Here is a record of misplaced and thwarted affections, of imperfections and disabilities, inseparable perhaps from an undesired way of life, which clog a mind conscious enough of its own power. . . . He is tired of life before his time, conscious of "tann'd antiquity" in the full tide of years, brooding on the decay of beauty and the passing of friends, letting his imagination play freely with thoughts of death. (73-74)

These insights correlate exactly with known circumstances in the life of Edward de Vere. They have no relation to anything known about the life of William Shakspere.

G. B. Harrison: Review of Sir Sidney Lee's *Elizabethan and Other Essays*, in *The London Mercury*, June 1930

Although Harrison wrote a dozen books on Shakespeare and scores of articles, his only known reference to the Earl of Oxford came in a review of a book by Sir Sidney Lee in June 1930. Lee had portrayed Shakespeare as a man "[so] singularly industrious, [so] singularly level-headed," and so singularly focused on the pursuit of wealth that, Harrison wrote, "sensitive people . . . rejected Lee's Shakespeare" out of sheer boredom and turned instead to "Bacon or Derby or Oxford, or some other creature of their own creating."[22]

---

[20] John S. Smart, *Shakespeare: Truth & Tradition* (1928), p. 19.

[21] Sir Edmund Chambers, *William Shakespeare: Facts and Problems* (1930), vol. 1: 26.

[22] G. B. Harrison, review of Sir Sidney Lee's posthumous *Elizabethan and Other Essays*, in *London Mercury*, June 1930, quoted in Charles Wisner Barrell, "'Creature of Their Own Creating:' An Answer to the Present Day School of Shakespearean Biography," *SF Quarterly*, vol. VI/4 (Oct. 1945): 59.

G. Wilson Knight: "Shakespeare and the Earl of Oxford," *The Nation & Athenaeum* (May 3, 1930)

Knight's only known direct response to the Oxfordian claim appeared in his review of Percy Allen's *The Case for Edward de Vere as "William Shakespeare."* Although he did not mention Looney or *"Shakespeare Identified*, he made a singularly remarkable admission. Responding to Allen's statement that "Shakespeare's intimate familiarity with Oxford's poems is undeniable," Knight wrote "Here is a sound deduction from a carefully correlated list of parallels." "But," he continued, "those parallels prove nothing as to authorship;"[23] they merely suggest that Shakspere had read Oxford. Positing a direct connection between Oxford and Shakespeare was surprising; equally surprising was that Knight, a respected scholar, made no effort to follow up on it by considering how Shakspere could have acquired that "intimate familiarity." Some of Oxford's poems were published (under the initials "E.O.") in *Paradise of Dainty Devises* in 1576, but not all of the poems to which Allen had referred had been published. Knight provided no reasons for believing that Shakspere was ever at court or knew any courtiers. It was a blot on his scholarly competence (and a lack of ordinary human curiosity) not to have pursued the matter further.

Knight criticized the validity of topical allusions, and Allen for relying on them. Even if "no one of Mr. Allen's 'sources' is necessarily false," he wrote, "they are ever uncertain; and, once such an approach is adopted, the commentator quickly loses himself in a morass and welter of hypothetical deduction." Did Knight really intend to undermine the very activities that constitute historical and literary inquiry?

J. M. Robertson: *The State of Shakespeare Study: A Critical Conspectus* (1931)

In this book Robertson made no mention of the Oxfordian claim, J. Thomas Looney or *"Shakespeare" Identified*, and dismissed the Baconian idea as "ignorance parading as special knowledge."[24] He did, however, provide a short list of instructions as to how "lecturers on Shakespeare might establish a reasonable standard of scholarlike qualification." Among them is "Be careful not to commit yourself in an unduly bumptious manner to judgments on subjects which any student can see you have never studied" (10). It's almost laughable to see Robertson give that advice despite his own refusal to examine the Oxfordian claim.

At the same time, he acknowledged that "The Academy can hardly escape a sense of insecurity" (5) arising from "disintegrators," i.e., fellow orthodox scholars who had concluded that not every word in the First Folio was written by the man from Stratford; that Shakespeare had, on occasion, "collaborated" with other writers. Among those he attacked were Professor Dover Wilson, who "reveals himself as complacently ignorant of the theatre's normal practice; besides electing to proclaim a theatrical canon which he obliviously proceeded to destroy;" Mr. Peter Alexander, "who knows nothing of either . . . Greene or the taste of the Elizabethan theatre;" and Professor Alfred W. Pollard, "who distrusts all literary connoisseurship save his own and that of the deceased Dowden" (6).

The passage in Lee's book reads, "Evidence of his professional progress makes it clear that he was singularly industrious, singularly level-headed, and amply endowed with that practical common sense which enables a man to acquire and retain a moderate competence" (87).

[23] G. Wilson Knight, "Shakespeare and the Earl of Oxford" [review of Allen's *Case*], *Nation & Athenaeum*, May 3, 1930, p. 150.

[24] J. M. Robertson, *The State of Shakespeare Study: A Critical Conspectus* (1931), p. 14.

Robertson was worried about the "plain danger that they may make the Institution itself look ridiculous" (7). They have, he wrote, "already [provided] matter for rude ridicule to the more intelligent reader, [and] may become vaguely distasteful even to the non-academic audience" (8). It would, perhaps, be unrealistic to expect an academician so unwilling to tolerate a variety of opinion among his fellow orthodox scholars to give any credence to the heterodox views of doubters outside the closeted walls of academia.

Leslie Hotson: *Shakespeare Versus Shallow* (1931)

In *Shakespeare Versus Shallow*, Leslie Hotson presented evidence showing that Shakespeare and his company were acting at the Swan in 1596. Col. Ward observed that "This completely upsets the hitherto accepted belief that from 1594 to 1597 the Chamberlain's Men were occupying the Theatre in Shoreditch."[25] It also disrupted the accepted dating of the plays. Col. Ward attempted to sort it out.

> This would mean that we must ante-date *Twelfth Night* about four years, and place it at least as early as 1596. *Twelfth Night*, however, is not the only play that must now be pushed back in the Shakespeare chronology.
>
> The immediate effect of Dr. Hotson's discovery is to produce an accumulation of no fewer than seven plays in this one year [1596-97]. Nor is it possible, so long as we adhere to the orthodox theory, to reconstruct Chambers' table by successively antedating all the earlier plays back into the fifteen-eighties. Indeed, it is not too much to say that Dr. Hotson's discovery has given the coup-de-grace to the hitherto accepted theory of Shakespeare authorship.

Ward went on to note that "Dr. Hotson's discovery . . . lends very valuable support to Mrs. Clark's thesis" described in her book, *Hidden Allusions*.

How did orthodox scholars react to Hotson's discovery? G B. Harrison, in *Shakespeare at Work* (1933) (see below), didn't challenge Hotson's finding, but merely observed that it "creates more difficulties than it solves."[26] He was apparently so perplexed that he omitted Hotson from the book's index.

J. Dover Wilson: *The Essential Shakespeare: A Biographical Adventure* (1932)

In this important book, Wilson hardly seemed aware of the dangerous waters into which he had waded. Percy Allen observed that "Dr. Wilson makes admissions which—the question of authorship apart—constitute, in effect, an almost complete surrender of the orthodox position, and a presentation to the Oxfordians of a major part of the case for which they have been battling during the past five years."[27]

One of the most startling revelations was Wilson's break with orthodoxy on topicality in the plays. In Sir Edmund Chambers's orthodox views, "Shakespeare does not seem to have been greatly given to 'topical allusions,' and the hunt for them is dangerous."[28] Wilson, though, believed that,

> Shakespeare's plays reflect the passing intellectual and social fashions of his day as the plays of Bernard Shaw do of ours, and Shakespeare never minded in the least glancing at events or persons which were at the moment agitating the minds of his audience. . . . It is certain that Shakespeare did not deliberately avoid topical allusion, as those who worship the Olympian claim. And if so, may we not suspect

---

[25] Col. Bernard R. Ward, "A Great Shakespeare Discovery," *Shakespeare Pictorial*, Dec. 1931, p. 196.

[26] G. B. Harrison, *Shakespeare at Work* (1933), p. 312.

[27] J. Dover Wilson, *The Essential Shakespeare: A Biographical Adventure* (1932), p. 12.

[28] Sir Edmund Chambers, *William Shakespeare: A Study of Facts and Problems* (1930), p. 246.

allusion and reference in many passages where it has hitherto not been detected.

[W]e may look for him at the very heart of that life. Not "his tragic life-story," of which we know nothing, but the life at the courts of Elizabeth and James, the persons and doings of the great men of the land, the political and social events of the hour—these form the real background of his plays.[29]

Wilson had acknowledged only the existence of allusions to topical events, without accepting a change in author or the idea of allusions to events in the author's life. But his position was untenable. If events alluded to were truly contemporaneous, as he claimed, then they were allusions to people and events at the time the plays were first written. Because of the dating of the topical allusions documented by Oxfordian scholars such as Clark, Holland and Allen, the plays had to have been written fifteen years earlier than the traditional dates, far too early for William Shakspere to have been the author. No wonder Chambers had regarded topical allusions as "dangerous" and that he, Sir Sidney Lee and others remained adamant in their opposition to topicality.

These passages from Wilson also included another damaging admission: that Shakespeare participated in "the very heart of the life of his times," in "the life at the courts of Elizabeth and James, the persons and doings of the great men of the land, the political and social events of the hour." How could Shakspere, someone with no known linkages to any courtier and no documented attendance at any court function, possibly have been so involved? Allen's explanation for this "misstep" on Wilson's part was that, "one, at least, of the orthodox Professors has been reading our books, and—though without acknowledgment—has adopted some of our most important conclusions."[30]

Wilson also made a surprising statement about *Love's Labour's Lost*: "To credit that amazing piece of virtuosity to a butcher boy who left school at thirteen, or even to one whose education was nothing more than what a grammar school and residence in a little provincial borough could provide—is to invite one either to believe in miracles or to disbelieve in the man of Stratford."[31] How did Wilson square that circle? He simply insisted that Shakspere *must have had* the experiences necessary to have written the works, despite a complete lack of evidence for it.

G. B. Harrison: *Shakespeare at Work* (1933)

Attempting here to portray William Shakspere as Shakespeare, Harrison found that the best he could do was to create "an imaginary portrait, a conjectural reconstruction," which "is and must be sheer guesswork."[32] "Surely, it is an astonishing fact," Percy Allen observed, "that this latest Life of 'Shakespeare,' by one of the world's greatest living authorities upon the Elizabethan age, should be heralded by such words." By way of contrast, he noted, "The best books upon 'Shakespeare' by the Oxfordian writers, are not, at bottom, 'sheer guesswork,' but are built up, page by page, from a closely argued inter-relation of ascertained fact and legitimate inference."[33]

Harrison, like Dover Wilson in *The Essential Shakespeare* a year earlier, drew heavily on Stopes's recounting of the Southampton-Shakspere relationship in her *Life of Henry, Third Earl of Southampton* to explain how Shakspere became known to prominent

---

[29] J. Dover Wilson, *The Essential Shakespeare: A Biographical Adventure* (1932), p. 12.

[30] Percy Allen, *Shakespeare and Chapman in Relation to French History* (1933), pp. 3-4.

[31] J. Dover Wilson, *The Essential Shakespeare: A Biographical Adventure* (1932), pp. 41-42.

[32] G. B. Harrison, *Shakespeare at Work* (1933), preface. [unnumbered page]

[33] Percy Allen, "Shakespeare at Work," *Shakespeare Pictorial*, Nov. 1933, p. 176.

members of the court and familiarized himself with events there and in Europe. But Harrison, like Wilson, neglected to mention Stopes's admission she had never found a single document connecting Shakspere and Southampton. Harrison drew heavily on parts of Stopes's book that she had clearly indicated were products of her imagination without informing readers of Stopes's admission.[34] Instead, he went the other direction, stating that "I have chosen the form of plain narrative, unqualified by 'doubtless,' probably,' 'we may be sure that' and other phrases expressing scholarly diffidence."[35]

G. B. Harrison & H. Granville Barker (editors): *A Companion to Shakespeare Studies* (1934)

This collection of articles by eminent academic scholars revealed the difficulties they faced in writing on Shakespeare in 1934, after the barrage of Oxfordian books in the early 1930s. One tack was to ignore the authorship issue completely, and that is the course chosen by the editors. The reading lists includes no books that even hint at an authorship problem; the index contains no entries for authorship, the Earl of Oxford, J. Thomas Looney or *"Shakespeare" Identified*.

When it was necessary to address subjects touching on the authorship question, the contributors adopted such a contorted stance that the quality of their work could be called into question. To reduce such occurrences to a minimum, the editors declared in their preface that, "We are concerned with the poet-dramatist, apparent in the work he left us; nothing more."[36] That is practically an acknowledgement that nothing known of the man from Stratford suggests a literary or theatrical aspect to his life. To write about these things, therefore, scholars had to draw on what could be deduced from the literary works themselves, not from the biography of their man.

Two articles typify the approach taken in the book.

J. W. Mackail: "The Life of Shakespeare," pp. 1-8.

Mackail (at one time president of the British Academy), after reviewing numerous biographies of William Shakespeare concluded that,

> The portrait of Shakespeare thus produced remains substantially unchanged by the laborious research of two centuries. . . . Most modern Lives expand their contents partly by accumulation of details however minute and bearing however remotely on Shakespeare himself; and much more largely by inference and conjecture based on treatment of the plays and the sonnets as veiled or unconscious autobiography.

> The inverted pyramids of purely conjectural biography which have been and still are piled up on the slender basis of ascertained fact, and on the slight additions of legend which may be accepted as authentic or highly probable, may be dismissed here without notice. Many of them are of extreme ingenuity but they are exercises of fancy and do not belong to serious biography. Nor can any fabric woven of plausible guesses and precarious inferences be regarded as reconstituting either the outward incidents or the spiritual experiences of

---

[34] On page 8 in her *Life of Henry, Third Earl of Southampton*, Stopes explained in a note to readers that "My work strives to be accurate, above all things, but where, through long study and logical inference, I have used my imagination to fill up gaps, I always put such suggestions in large parentheses, to shew that I am aware that these passages contain an element of uncertainty, and are frequently controversial."

[35] G. B. Harrison, *Shakespeare at Work* (1933), preface (unnumbered page).

[36] G. B. Harrison & H. Granville-Barker, *A Companion to Shakespeare Studies* (1934), p. x.

Shakespeare's life.[37]

Despite the thinness of the biographical details, and despite the failure to establish "either the outward incidents or the spiritual experiences of Shakespeare's life," Mackail had no doubt that William Shakspere of Stratford-on-Avon, was the author of the works known as "Shakespeare's."

That anyone had ever doubted Shakspere's authorship is not mentioned.

Muriel St. Clare Byrne: "The Social Background," pp. 187-218.

Byrne, who had previously tangled with Percy Allen, Gerald Rendall and other Oxfordians, opened with what appeared to be an extraordinary admission: "Many of the Elizabethan writers . . . have given us so faithful a picture of the men and manners of the day that their value as artists is distinctly second to their value as social documents."[38] Was this an admission that Shakespeare's works had indeed been topical, that they were, as Oxfordians had insisted, "the abstract and brief chronicles of the time?"

No. This was apparently true for all writers except Shakespeare.

> For the detail that enables us to recreate the Elizabethan scene we go to a dozen other writers rather than Shakespeare. . . . [F]or the purposes of illustrative quotation Shakespeare figures hardly at all, in comparison to the minor writers. Where the ordinary Elizabethan writer is topical in the situation, characterisation and dialogue of an entire scene, Shakespeare is topical only out of his superfluity—in an aside, a simile, an image, a flourish jest.

> We are right to feel that he beyond all his fellows escaped more completely from that pressure of immediacy and the contemporaneous that mutes the poetry. . . . [W]e are right when we assert that the relation of Shakespeare to the manners and customs and topicalities of his age is matter for the editor of the annotated edition . . . [that it is] of interest to the antiquary. (188)

The obvious inference is that Shakespeare was not a "man of the people," that he was removed from the common life and differed from all other playwrights in some important way. Perhaps it was because Shakespeare was the Earl of Oxford, and the Earl of Oxford, as the Lord Great Chamberlain of the realm, did not have the experience of common life in Elizabethan society that all other playwrights had, a possibility Byrne never considered.

Alfred Hart: *Shakespeare and the Homilies* (1934)

Almost all of Shakespeare's plays have royal settings and portray kings, courtiers and statesmen absorbed in political activities and issues important during Queen Elizabeth's reign. Many of the plays portray the sensitive political issue that dominated all others during the last decade of Elizabeth's life: succession. As Hart noted,

> [Shakespeare's plays form] a series of simple lessons on the fundamental principles of Tudor politics.

> Shakespeare outdoes every dramatist of his time in the number and variety of the allusions made to those issues. References are scattered through at least twenty plays, including the comedies as well as the histories and tragedies. (27)

> What is peculiar to Shakespeare is that he treats the politico-theological

---

[37] J. W. Mackail, "The Life of Shakespeare," in G. B. Harrison & H. Granville-Barker, *A Companion to Shakespeare Studies* (1934), pp. 1, 8.

[38] Muriel St. Clare Byrne, "The Social Background," in G. B. Harrison & H. Granville-Barker, *A Companion to Shakespeare Studies* (1934), p. 186.

doctrines of divine right, non-resistance, passive obedience and the sin of rebellion, as the accepted and immutable law of almost every land in every age. He has adroitly woven into the fabric of his plays so many and varied references, direct and indirect, to these doctrines, that we may extract from them an excellent digest of the main articles of the . . . political creed of the Tudors concerning the constitution of the body politic in general and the relation of ruler to subject in particular. [39]

Hart's conclusions supported the Wards' findings that the Earl of Oxford was provided funding of £1,000 per year from 1586 on to direct a group of playwrights writing patriotic dramas for the public stage. Stratfordian scholars have yet to provide innocuous explanations for Shakespeare's wealth of allusions to "the fundamental principles of Tudor politics" or for the funding provided to Oxford.

J. Dover Wilson: *The Manuscript of Shakespeare's Hamlet and the Problems of Its Transmission* (1935)

This is the first of three books in which Wilson examined *Hamlet* from textual, exegetic and dramatic considerations. In this two-volume work, he presented much information supporting the Oxfordian idea that *Hamlet* had been written in 1583 rather than 1601.[40] He informed readers that Shakespeare's orthography (spelling and punctuation) in *Hamlet* was "archaic"[41] and gave examples of similar usages in *Love's Labour's Lost*, one of Shakespeare's first plays—a similarity that supported Admiral Holland's contention, itself supported by forty-four topical references, that the first draft of *Hamlet* was written in 1583. (Many Oxfordians date *Love's Labour's Lost* to 1578.)

Wilson concluded that the many mistakes and "omissions of these lengthy passages, together with most of the other omissions" in the second Quarto of *Hamlet* (published in 1604) were due "to undue haste on the part of the compositor" (98). Why such undue haste? Wilson had no answer, but Percy Allen did.

> To an Oxfordian the reason comes pat. Lord Oxford had died in 1604; and he or his representatives had been, or were, eager to remove the false impression caused by the publication of a spurious Q1. No doubt they hastened to tell to an interested world, with the least possible delay, "my story" (Oxford-Hamlet's story) with its vindication of a "wounded name."[42]

Wilson also argued that "In the production of *Hamlet* itself, Shakespeare exercised no supervision of any kind. On the contrary, we have seen his stage-directions altered or ignored, his text freely amended, and his punctuation revised from beginning to end . . . at the dictation of someone else."[43] He added that "a definite answer will never, can never, be granted to our questions. But one thing at least we may venture to suspect . . . *Hamlet* was not merely a turning-point in his career dramatically, but also marked some kind of crisis in his relations with his company" (98). Wilson was right about that second point. That was quite an admission, given that Edward de Vere died in June, 1604, several

---

[39] Alfred Hart, *Shakespeare and the Homilies* (1934), p. 29.

[40] My attention was drawn to this book by Percy Allen's review of it "More *Hamlet* Problems," *Shakespeare Pictorial*, Feb. 1936, p. 36.

[41] J. Dover Wilson, *The Manuscript of Shakespeare's Hamlet and the Problems of Its Transmission*, vol. 1 (1935). See, for instance, pp. 103-04.

[42] Percy Allen, "More *Hamlet* Problems," *Shakespeare Pictorial*, Feb. 1936, p. 36.

[43] J. Dover Wilson, *The Manuscript of Shakespeare's Hamlet and the Problems of its Transmission*, vol. 1 (1935), p. 172.

months before the second Quarto of *Hamlet* was published.

It is not hard to agree with Percy Allen's comment that this book provided "a further and striking example of the illuminating fact, that almost every honest Stratfordian book which comes nowadays from the press . . . strengthens automatically the ever-mounting Oxfordian case."[44]

Caroline Spurgeon: *Shakespeare's Imagery, and What It Tells Us* (1935)

After exhaustively studying Shakespeare's imagery, Spurgeon concluded that Shakespeare "gives himself away" through his images. He "unwittingly lays bare his own innermost likes and dislikes, observations and interests, associations of thought, attitudes of mind and beliefs, in and through the images, the verbal pictures he draws to illuminate something quite different in the speech and thought of his characters."[45]

His imagery, she documented, is drawn from many subjects—horticulture; animals, especially birds and horses; law; Italy; courtly pastimes such as hawking, riding, bird-snaring and falconry; classical Greek and Latin literature; modern languages such as French and Italian; and so on. The author of Shakespeare's works must have had a depth of knowledge of these subjects derived from sustained personal experience in them in order to have produced the imagery that permeates his works.

Orthodox Shakespeare scholars have been unable to demonstrate that Shakspere had any of those necessary experiences; Oxfordian scholars, though, have shown that Edward de Vere was educated by the foremost scholars of the day, that as a nobleman he would have participated in such activities as falconry, which Spurgeon specifically mentioned, and that as the highest ranking earl in Elizabeth's court he had direct and extended involvement with political developments at the highest levels. Building on that base, American scholar Louis P. Bénézet observed that "Miss Spurgeon comments on 'Shakespeare's love of humanity' and his 'sympathy' with 'the poor and broken bankrupt' and the underdog in general. . . . The lady does not realize that she is proving that the plays could never have been written by the man who sought to send the impoverished debtor to jail, knowing that the man's family were dependent on his labor. Far more probable, as their author, is the kind-hearted nobleman, who himself knew what it was to be 'lame, poor . . . despised' after he had lost his fortune and his standing at Court."[46]

Andrew S. Cairncross: *The Problem of Hamlet: A Solution* (1936)

In this book Cairncross concluded that *Hamlet* "was written by William Shakespeare not later than August 1589," more than a decade earlier than the usually accepted dates of 1599-1601. This change would not necessitate a change in the order of the plays; they need only be moved up in time *en masse*. "All the great tragedies seem to hang together in much the same order as before. The only change is that they come earlier, in Shakespeare's youth instead of in middle age." He concluded that *The Tempest*, which he still believed to be Shakespeare's last play, could have been written as early as 1603.[47] *The Times Literary Supplement* stated that "Dr. Cairncross thus makes alteration in accepted Shakespearian chronology, pushing everything back into Shakespeare's youth: *Hamlet, Othello, Macbeth*, and *King Lear* between 1589 and 1591, *Antony and Cleopatra*

---

[44] Percy Allen, "More *Hamlet* Problems," *Shakespeare Pictorial*, Feb. 1936, p. 36.

[45] Caroline Spurgeon, *Shakespeare's Imagery, and What It Tells Us* (1935), p. 4.

[46] Louis P. Bénézet, "The Stratford Defendant Compromised by His Own Advocates, Part One," *SF Quarterly*, vol. V/3 (July 1944), p. 45.

[47] A. S. Cairncross, *The Problem of Hamlet: A Solution* (1936), p. 183.

and *Coriolanus* to 1595, and *The Tempest* (the latest of all) to 1603."[48]

It is remarkable that Cairncross, a believer in the Stratfordian theory of authorship, had come to believe that all of Shakespeare's plays were written before Oxford died in 1604, thereby eliminating what academia had believed was one of the strongest reasons for discarding the Oxfordian claim. Cairncross said nothing about the authorship question in his book, and didn't give any indication that he realized how severely his findings undercut the Stratfordian claim and supported the Oxfordian. He even professed that there is nothing surprising about moving the tragedies up from Shakspere's later years to his youth. "This is natural. It is not your middle-aged men who write tragedies. World-weariness is a phase of heaviest incidence in youth. Older men generally succeed in putting it behind them."[49]

The absurdity of that statement, defying as it does all common human experience, is easily sidestepped by acceptance of the Oxfordian thesis in which the author of the tragedies was born in 1550, not 1564, and was thus a man of experience rather than youth when the great tragedies were written.

C. J. Sisson: *Lost Plays of Shakespeare's Age* (1936)

Sisson was the professor at the University of London with whom Capt. Bernard M. Ward studied the literature of the Elizabethan era after the First World War. In this book he pulled from obscurity four plays by Dekker, Webster, Rowley and Ford, and used them to show just how topical plays written for the Elizabethan stage actually were. Percy Allen was delighted: "To those who, in common with Captain Ward and myself, have been arguing for years past that substantially *all* drama of that age was topical, these . . . stage tales . . . possess the added interest of providing us, from first to last, with gratifying vindication of our case."[50]

> These dramatized scandals among the local citizenry of London confirm powerfully our Oxfordian conclusions. They show that "Shakespeare's" contemporary dramatists, including Chapman . . . drew their topical matter and characters directly from the "bourgeois" life of such districts as Clerkenwell and St. Paul's, with which they were intimately familiar. So also the courtier, "Shakespeare," dramatized the aristocratic world of lords and ladies, among whom he moved through the gardened palaces of Windsor and Whitehall.

> Will orthodox commentators, I wonder, including the author of this fascinating book, continue to deny that Shakespeare's plays, like Chapman's were topically propagandist?

Levin L. Schücking: *The Meaning of Hamlet* (1937)

It is not surprising that this insightful study came from Germany, far distant from the center of Stratfordian thought. The significance of the invisibility of William Shakespeare to which Schücking called attention should be obvious.

> The most surprising fact about Shakespeare is not, as is commonly supposed, the contrast between his education and his achievements, but rather that his personality left so slight an impression on the times in which he lived. It is difficult to understand how a playwright, who made a mark on theatrical history that has endured for centuries, and is almost comparable with that left by Julius Caesar on the political history of Europe, should have so little occupied the

---

[48] Review of *The Problem of Hamlet*, *Times Literary Supplement*, Dec. 19, 1936, p. 1053.

[49] A. S. Cairncross, *The Problem of Hamlet: A Solution* (1936), p. 178.

[50] Percy Allen, "Topical Events in Drama of Shakespeare's Age," *Shakespeare Pictorial*, Aug. 1936, p. 132.

attention of his contemporaries. . . . How is it that the incomparable intellectual and creative power of this man, the richness of his imagination, his liberating humour, his fascinating wit, did not keep his name continually on the lips and make him a familiar figure in the life of his time?[51]

Schücking speculated that there must have been some reason why we know so little about Shakespeare. The only possible explanation for him was that Shakespeare "lived in a particularly secluded way, took little part in social life, and came into contact with the public chiefly through his profession as an actor." That must have been the case because "not a single laudatory poem by him has been preserved, although it was a customary proof of friendship among writers of the time to dedicate such compositions to one another, and for the recipients to print them at the beginning of their works. . . . He must therefore have had no close friendship among the writers of a city in which he had spent almost a quarter of a century" (10).

Edgar Fripp: *Shakespeare, Man and Artist* (1938)

Fripp endeavored "to see Shakespeare in his context—to study and interpret him in the light of his environment, geographical, domestic, social, religious, dramatic, literary."[52] That sounds promising, but later in the same paragraph Fripp showed that his two-volume book would recount traditional fantasies: "We may see him emerge and develop, as a Latin school boy, as an attorney's clerk, as a poet and a dramatist, the rival of Marlowe, until he outrivals him and all others, and wins the favour and stimulating appreciation of the Queen."

But then came an interesting admission about the validity of topical and personal allusions, in violation of the Stratfordian party line: "Much information, too, is from the poems and plays. As they fall into their context they reveal allusions to men and things. . . . Certain of the dramas contain many topical allusions. It is short-sighted to speak of a dramatist's creations as 'impersonal'. . . . We may be sure that in innumerable instances Shakespeare has transferred and transformed the actual into the realms of art. But if we would recognize such obligations we must go warily, with open eyes" (x). He also expressed his belief that "The truest poetry . . . reveals the poet . . . He cannot hide himself, and the greater he is the more transparent is the disclosure. There must be sight, however, in those who would see the Poet, and see with him."

Fripp made no mention of the authorship controversy, Looney or *"Shakespeare" Identified*. He did mention Edward de Vere in connection with the bed trick portrayed in *All's Well*, stating that de Vere had fathered his daughter Elizabeth Vere, "so it is said, due to his wife's resort to Helena's deceit" (301). In another interesting passage he tied the Earl of Oxford to the *Sonnets*: "The late Earl of Oxford (he died in 1604) possessed, we may assume, a copy of at least Sonnets i-xxvi, wherein young Southampton was urged to accept the hand of his daughter, Elizabeth de Vere, and as a poet and patron of poets and players, he would value anything from Shakespeare's pen. The Countess, may have let the manuscript go [when King's Place was transferred from her ownership to that of Sir Fulke Greville], consisting of 154 sonnets and *A Lover's Complaint*, ignorant of its nature and literary worth (713-14). He also cited Col. Bernard R. Ward's article in *The National Review* in September 1922 for the manner in which the *Sonnets* reached William Hall, and through him, printer Thomas Thorpe.

---

[51] Levin L. Schücking, *The Meaning of Hamlet* (1937), p. 9.
[52] Edgar I. Fripp, *Shakespeare, Man and Artist* (1938), p. ix.

G. B. Harrison: *Introducing Shakespeare* (1939, revised 1954, 1966)

This book "is intended for the use of the general reader who needs some kind of aid in a first understanding of Shakespeare, and partly also as a general introduction to the Penguin Shakespeares."[53] It made no mention of Looney or *"Shakespeare" identified* and only one brief mention of Edward de Vere. The reading list has no books on Shakespearean biography. The first chapter, "Shakespeare's Fame," provides an overview of the changing nature of Shakespeare Studies over the past 200 years without hinting that doubts about authorship had arisen. The second chapter, "Materials for the Life of Shakespeare," briefly noted the authorship question and dismissed it. After stating that the issue "has long been so highly charged with emotion that even the driest of experts can hardly ignore the Anti-Stratfordians" (32), Harrison proceeded to do exactly that.

That pattern of making a provocative statement and providing no discussion of it is repeated throughout. Harrison's statement that "All great writers to some extent betray themselves. It is not difficult to guess that Jane Austen lived in a genteel circle or that the social background of Thackeray differed considerably from that of Dickens" (35-36), is followed by not a single example from the plays that relate to Shakspere's Stratford, nor by recognition that the social background reflected in the plays—the court—was the home ground of Edward de Vere. His statement that "Shakespeare has far more images drawn from sport than other dramatists" (24), is not followed by any examples or by recognition that the sports represented in the plays are all aristocratic sports. His comment that "There are many early references to Shakespeare collected in *The Shakespeare Allusions Book*, of which more than one hundred and fifty were made before Shakespeare's death," is followed by not a single example and without notice that the references are to the writer, not the man. His statement that title pages "are capable of rebuttal on sufficient external or internal grounds [has been] shown. Publishers are not always well informed or even honest," is followed by not a single example or by recognition of how the matter of incorrect title pages might play into the authorship question.

It's as though Harrison deliberately raised points that could be developed to challenge Shakspere's authorship but went no further. He remained staunchly committed to the Stratfordian story until his death in 1991 at the age of ninety-seven.

Alfred Hart: *Stolne and Surreptitious Copies: A Comparative Study of Shakespeare's Bad Quartos* (1942)

Almost lost to history, Hart's book was published in Australia during the Second World War. It was of exceptional importance for the Oxfordian claim because it independently confirmed the early dates of six Shakespeare plays. Hart stated that "All my work is directed to one end—to prove that the six bad quartos are derivative texts and take their origin from the corruption of the respective six plays written by Shakespeare"[54] and that "each bad quarto is a garbled abridgment of an acting version made officially by the play adapter of the company from Shakespeare's manuscript" (437).

Hart hit upon this idea after "study of Dr. Greg's book convinced me that all the problems arising from the interrelation of the first quarto and the second quarto of *Romeo*

---

[53] G. B. Harrison, *Introducing Shakespeare* (1939), p. 9.
[54] Alfred Hart, *Stolne and Surreptitious Copies* (1942), p. ix.

and Juliet or *Hamlet* could be completely solved by collecting and classifying all the relevant facts obtainable from each pair of parallel texts, and then deducing such inferences as the facts justified" (viii).[55] Applying the same reasoning in his examination of the other four "bad" quarto plays for which an authentic text was later printed in the First Folio or in a "good" quarto, he found the same results. In reaching this conclusion Hart reaffirmed Cairncross's findings about the early date of *Hamlet*.

The majority belief at the time was that the six bad quartos were plays by others that Shakespeare revised into the versions that we know today, an idea widely accepted since first proposed by Edmund Malone. The minority view was that the bad quartos were first drafts by Shakespeare himself. But neither was correct, Hart showed; they were mangled memorial reconstructions of the acting versions of the longer plays. Hart's work led to the important conclusion that those six plays must have been written and acted in something approaching their modern form before the corrupted memorial versions were assembled.

Advancing the dates for the plays raised the question of how early Shakspere could have written them. Not early enough for him, born in 1564, to have been Shakespeare is the only possible answer, which is why Hart's findings were such powerful support for the Oxfordian thesis. Hart remained a believer in the Stratfordian theory of authorship, however—there is no mention in his book of Looney, *"Shakespeare" Identified*, Edward de Vere or the Oxfordian claim—nor does he explain how the earlier dates could be reconciled with Shakspere's authorship.

As a side note, Hart offered the idea that perhaps the publication of the bad quartos spurred "Shakespeare" to begin publishing authorized editions of his plays beginning in 1597. Hart was the second scholar to propose this new idea, the first having been Dr. John Howard Dellinger in a lecture in Washington, D.C. the previous year (see Chapter 17).

In his introduction Hart offered a comment expressing his innate modesty, similar to one Looney had made in connection with *"Shakespeare" Identified*. Hart wrote:

> It may seem presumptuous for an unknown scholar living in Australia to compile a bulky volume on the bad quartos and omit mention of almost all the notable scholars who have written in the aggregate so many thousand pages on this still-vexed question; but what was the alternative? . . . I decided to pass over what had been written prior to 1912, begin afresh, treat the relation between the bad quartos and Shakespeare's plays as a problem in detection, and base my solution on a critical survey of all the facts.[56]

Two years later Eva Turner Clark would write that "Shakespeare students everywhere will feel indebted to Professor Hart of Melbourne for his independent research in a field which has attracted many before him and for a book which settles for all time the origin of the 'six bad quartos.' Such proof, scientifically arrived at, that these original plays of the real master were in existence and well known to professional thieves of the theatre and the print-shop years before Stratfordian authorities have been willing to admit their ascription (even in part) to the Bard, heralds a revolutionary change in Shakespearean chronology in general."[57] Clark found that three other Shakespeare plays had a similar publishing history, first appearing in mangled memorial versions too early to have been by William Shakspere before being published as Shakespeare's, as shown in

---

[55] Hart is referring to W. W. Greg's *Two Elizabethan Abridgments* (1923).

[56] Alfred Hart, *Stolne and Surreptitious Copies* (1942), p. x.

[57] Eva Turner Clark, "Stolne and Surreptitious Copies," *SF Quarterly*, vol. V/1 (Jan. 1944), p. 8.

the nearby text box.

Four years after Clark's article, Oxfordian Charles Wisner Barrell would write: "It is important to note in this connection that a whole modern school of Shakespearean bibliographers has adduced proof from study of the corrupt early quartos of the plays that masterpieces such as *Hamlet*, the historical cycle, and practically all of the comedies were written and staged years before the Stratford canon allows."[58]

Plays Compared by Alfred Hart (date of first publication)

The Bad Quartos (mangled memorized versions . . .	Later published in clean copies as Shakespeare's Plays)
The First Part of the Contention between the Two Famous Houses of Yorke and Lancaster (1594)	*2 Henry VI*
The True Tragedy of Richard Duke of Yorke (1594)	*3 Henry VI*
Romeo and Juliet, Q1 (1597)	*Romeo and Juliet*
The Famous Victories of Henry V (1598)	*Henry V*
The Merry Wives of Windsor Q1 (1602)	*The Merry Wives of Windsor*
Hamlet Q1 (early version by Sh.) (1602)	*Hamlet*
Three Other Plays Subjected to the Same Treatment (Added by Eva Turner Clark in 1944)	
Taming of a Shrew (1594, 1596)	*Taming of the Shrew*
Troublesome Raigne (1591)	*King John*
The True Chronicle of King Leir (1594)	*King Lear*

E. M. W. Tillyard: *Shakespeare's History Plays* (1944)

Tillyard provided inadvertent and unintentional support for the Oxfordian idea. In *Shakespeare's History Plays* he claimed that those plays embody not only what was implicit in Elizabethan cosmology but also a complete political philosophy. He discussed in detail the dozens of historical and literary works that influenced Shakespeare's religious, political and philosophical beliefs, and stated that understanding of the ideas in those works "was the possession only of the most learned part of society. It can be to the point only if Shakespeare too was learned."[59] But Tillyard provided no credible explanation for how William Shakspere of Stratford-on-Avon could have acquired such understanding. After showing how closely a passage in *Hamlet* followed a passage in Raymond de Sebonde's obscure *Natural Theology*, Tillyard stated, "How Shakespeare got hold of this material matters little" (15).

Tillyard also claimed that Shakspere enjoyed social access to the educated classes, but did not identify any courtiers to whom he had access. He claimed, rightly, that Shakespeare's "prose was founded on the normal speech cadence of the most intelligent and highly educated of the aristocracy'" (337), without explaining how such sophistication would have been possible for someone who spent the first quarter century of his life in a distant part of England where a dialect not easily understood outside of Warwickshire was spoken.

Still, Tillyard did bring some common sense to the fantastical Shakspere story by pointing out how absurd parts of it were.

---

[58] Charles Wisner Barrell, "Afterwords," in J. Thomas Looney, *"Shakespeare" Identified* (1948), p. 459.
[59] E. M. W. Tillyard, *Shakespeare's History Plays* (1944), p. 12.

> Generations of critics and readers [have accepted] a Shakespeare who offends against verisimilitude and common sense. They have made him an exception from the usual pattern of a great poet, denying him the attributes of learning and of originality in his early years. They have pictured him as a youth of poor education and one who began his dramatic career by mending the work of others. It is a picture so contrary to the usual order of things that one is confounded both by the ease and by the satisfaction with which men accepted it. (152)

Discussing several early plays, he wrote, "We find, not the brilliant apprentice and tinker of others' matter, but an original poet, educated, confident of himself, already dedicated to poetry; a man passing through the states common to any very great artist, akin to Dante and Milton not only through mature achievement but in the manner in which he began his life-work" (164).

Lily B. Campbell: *Shakespeare's "Histories:" Mirrors of Elizabethan Policy* (1947)

In this extraordinary work Campbell showed that "each of the Shakespeare histories serves a special purpose in elucidating a political problem of Elizabeth's day and in bringing to bear upon this problem the accepted political philosophy of the Tudors."[60] Her findings reaffirmed those of Alfred Hart in *Shakespeare and the Homilies* (1934), and contributed to the overthrow of the views of Alfred F. Pollard, who in 1919 had stated that

> No period of English literature has less to do with politics than that during which English letters reached their zenith; and no English writer's attitude towards the questions, with which alone political history is concerned, is more obscure or less important than Shakespeare. . . . Shakespeare himself, whose genius was less circumscribed than any other's, shuns the problems of contemporary politics.[61]

Although Campbell helped bring official Shakespearean scholarship into line with Oxfordian findings that had established the political nature of the history plays, she brought readers only half-way, by failing to explain how an illiterate butcher's apprentice who had spent almost all of the first half of his life in a small town far from London could have understood English political and diplomatic developments so deeply.

Albert Feuillerat: *The Composition of Shakespeare's Plays* (1953)

Although *The Composition of Shakespeare's Plays* was published after the cutoff date of this book, it is included because it is an outgrowth of Feuillerat's earlier work that Looney cited in his own writings.

Feuillerat's findings cast doubt on Shakspere's authorship and supported Oxford's in three ways. First is his challenge to the traditional belief that Shakespeare wrote quickly to meet the needs of the market and never revised them. Through a study of Shakespeare's versification and style, Feuillerat showed that the dramatist had repeatedly revised his works, and identified, at least to his own satisfaction, which passages had been revised and when. His basic conclusions were in line with the Oxfordian thesis that Oxford revised theatrical works originally written for court performance when they were later staged in public theaters, and revised them again during the last decade of his life as he prepared them for publication.

Second is Feuillerat's speculation that Shakespeare revised his work because "[h]e

---

[60] Lily B. Campbell, *Shakespeare's "Histories:" Mirrors of Elizabethan Policy* (1947), p. 125.
[61] A. F. Pollard, *The History of England, 1547-1603* (London, 1919), p. 440, quoted in Lily B. Campbell, *Shakespeare's "Histories:" Mirrors of Elizabethan Policy* (19447), p. 4-5.

wished to utilize the experiences he had acquired both as a man and as an actor-author. The development of his versification and style is but the shadow of the perfection which was being achieved in his mind. From imitation to mastery the journey for a man like Shakespeare must have been rich in adventures, and traces of them must be preserved in his works, where they may be discovered."[62] The significance of this passage is that the biographical information for Shakspere includes no experiences rising above the mundane, whereas Oxford spent a year in Italy and France, served on the tribunals judging Mary Queen of Scots and the Second Earl of Essex, and fulfilled other high-level functions within the court as the Lord Great Chamberlain of England, all of which would have broadened and deepened his views over the course of his life.

Third, Feuillerat found in *Romeo and Juliet* and five other plays the presence of someone he called Author A, "who more and more appears to have been the regular purveyor of plays to Shakespeare's company before Shakespeare himself . . . for all the characteristics of versification and style which distinguish this author are found in the play[s] from beginning to end" (288). Since no record exists of any such person, Oxfordians would identify the "regular provider" as the original author, Edward de Vere, Earl of Oxford, who wrote theatrical works for the court and private performances, revising them later for the public stage and eventual publication.

Lost in a Tangle of Errors

Surely some unease existed in Stratfordian minds as they conducted research and published findings after *"Shakespeare" Identified* had broadcast the Oxfordian claim to the world. "Whosoever ponders, speaks, writes about Shakespeare is, in his inmost soul, uneasy, not knowing to what extent the bases of his work are solid,"[63] commented Professor Georges Connes. And yet little sign of it comes through. Blatant inconsistencies abound; findings that undercut the Stratfordian narrative and support the Oxfordian appear repeatedly, all without the expressions of unease or exhilaration that would usually accompany findings that threatened to overturn one of the most foundational tenets of their field.

Two explanations might account for this strange behavior. One is that orthodox scholars were so focused on their research, and so convinced of its importance, that they had little time or inclination to gain a larger perspective on developments in related fields. Such intense concentration on intellectual or literary work is not uncommon. The other explanation is that Shakespeare scholars were aware of the Oxfordian claim and, not seeing a quick and easy way to refute it, turned away from it. Bothering to investigate it would have taken too much time; better to just ignore it, suppress awareness of it, and hope it goes away.

Early in 1934, Percy Allen expressed optimism about the inroads that the Oxfordian claim was making into academia, writing, "That the seventeenth Earl of Oxford wrote the greater part of some twenty or more of the plays published in the First Folio, is a thesis now winning ever wider acceptance the world over; . . . Conventional orthodoxy throughout the English-speaking world is being abandoned, fast and everywhere."[64]

---

[62] Albert Feuillerat, *The Composition of Shakespeare's Plays* (1953), pp. 81-82.
[63] Georges Connes, "Etat Present des Etudes Shakespeariennes," quoted in Percy Allen, "For the Stratfordians," *Christian Science Monitor*, May 21, 1932, p. 10.
[64] Percy Allen, *Anne Cecil, Elizabeth & Oxford* (1934), pp. ix-x.

He remained optimistic, writing a year later that "Almost every honest Stratfordian book which comes nowadays from the press . . . strengthens automatically the ever-mounting Oxfordian case."[65] In 1937 he observed that orthodox scholars were continuing to undermine their own Stratfordian story. "You, yourselves, are pushing the plays, one after another, to a date which is inconsistent with the work of a man who, on your own showing, did not come to London until 1588. Your own chronology is destroying your own case!"[66]

But by May 1945 he was forced to admit that traditional scholars continued to stand firmly behind the traditional narrative. "Academic scholars, in general, remain rigidly orthodox in their professed Shakespearean views, despite the fact that almost every book they publish, upon a Shakespearean subject, shatters their case, by the showing of their own arguments."[67]

Not much headway against academia had been made after almost two decades of furious Oxfordian activity. But what about public opinion? How widely was it affected by Oxfordian publications and public lectures? We'll examine that subject in the next five chapters.

---

[65] Percy Allen, "More *Hamlet* Problems," *Shakespeare Pictorial*, Feb. 1936, p. 36.
[66] Percy Allen, "Lord Oxford as Shakespeare," *East Anglian Magazine*, vol. 2/5 (May 1937): 344,
[67] Percy Allen, "The Group Theory and Some Modern Intellectuals," *SF News-Letter*, May 1945, p. 4.

14

The Oxfordians, Academia and Public Opinion in the British Isles, 1930-1940

Oxfordian Publications: *The Shakespeare Fellowship News-Letter*

For Oxfordians in England, 1937 opened with a bang: the launching of the *Shakespeare Fellowship News-Letter*, which reflected the high hopes of the Fellowship and expanded its ability to communicate with its members and others. Capt. Bernard M. Ward, who had edited the Fellowship's Page in *The Shakespeare Pictorial* for the last four years, took on the job of editing the new publication. Fellowship President Col. Montagu W. Douglas, in his welcome editorial in the first issue, explained the purpose of the bimonthly *News-Letter*.

> In addition to the Editorial, our *News-Letter* will consist of one or more Articles, Occasional Notes, and correspondence; and contributions from our members will be welcome under any of these heads.

> We anticipate many advantages therefrom. Apart from the unfettered freedom of opinion, hitherto unattainable in a public journal, and the circulation of interesting information constantly coming to our notice, we gain knowledge of the views of our members, hitherto, and regrettably so, an unknown quantity. As a result we may reasonably look forward to an increase in members.[1]

Douglas also noted the split between the public's interest in the authorship issue and academia's refusal even to consider it. He quoted an unnamed reviewer outside academia who wrote that, "The Oxford case indeed, whether we accept it or not, cannot be ignored" (2). He attributed that public interest in part to the Fellowship's earlier column in *The Hackney Spectator* and recent page in *The Shakespeare Pictorial*: "It is certain that our articles have been widely read and are in the main responsible for a tolerant and even sympathetic attitude towards the researches of the Fellowship." Academia's attitude was shown by the the editors of *The Review of English Studies* "who return to the publisher unopened any anti-Stratfordian book."

Among the most important early articles in the *News-Letter* was Admiral Holland's on the influence of Montaigne's essays on Shakespeare, "M.O.A.I. Doth Sway My Life: The

---

[1] Col. Montagu W. Douglas, "Editorial," *SF News-Letter*, no. 1 (Jan. 1937): 1

Influence of Montaigne's Essays on *Much Ado About Nothing*, *Romeo and Juliet* and *Twelfth Night*." In it he reported that "Stratfordian scholars have noted the influence of Montaigne on *Hamlet*, but not on these three plays. The reason is obvious. Florio's translation was not published until 1603. These three plays were all written before that date, and William Shakspere was not known to have been a French scholar. Consequently, the commentators never even thought of looking for Montaigne's influence on them. But it is there all the same."[2]

Percy Allen, in the next issue, agreed with Holland's contention, adding, "Lord Oxford, I am positively certain, entranced by the Frenchman's writings, said to himself in the year 1581: 'What he has done as an essayist, I will do as a dramatist;' and in 1583 he drafted *Hamlet*, the first and last purpose of which is, in Prince Hamlet's (Oxford's) own words, 'to tell my story' to succeeding generations. Almost every episode in *Hamlet*: the supernatural ghost-motive, the brooding over death, the political repentance without genuine will to repent, . . . the serene and poised character of Horatio, Hamlet's madness, the irresolute weakness of human will, the tyranny of custom, . . . and the decay of the human body after death, . . . were all dealt with, sometimes copiously, by Montaigne."[3]

In the same issue came news of Allen's discovery of a document by Percival Golding indicating that Edward de Vere had been buried in the Vere family tomb in Westminster Abbey in which Horatio Vere and Francis Vere were also interred. Golding had written:

> Edward de Vere . . . Of whom I will only speake, what all mens voices Confirme: he was a man in mind and body absolutely accomplished with honourable endowments: he died at his house at Hackney in the moneth of June Anno 1604 and lieth buried att Westminster.[4]

The *News-Letter* facilitated communication among Fellowship members. Admiral Holland's letter responding to Andrew S. Cairncross's criticism of his book, *Shakespeare, Oxford and Elizabethan Times* (1933), ran in the May 1937 issue: "I would therefore ask members of the Fellowship to read my book and see for themselves whether, with the single exception of *Love's Labour's Lost*, I do, as he states, use interpolation so universally."[5]

It was in the *News-Letter* that Gilbert Slater's final thoughts on the authorship appeared (see Chapter 9), providing the occasion for Capt. Ward to update readers on work by Oxfordian scholars to ferret out the true story of the plays' origins and how they came to be in the form in which we know them today.

> It seems to me that in estimating the contributions of the various authors of the plays of the Folio the foremost consideration should be chronology. . . . Is it not likely that the great majority of the plays were originally written by Oxford, as Court Masques, in the 1570s and early eighties; and that in the "nineties" and after Oxford's death, they were revised, re-written, added to, and amended? I suggest that this revision of his old Court Masques was, broadly speaking, undertaken by two groups (a) the aristocrats (his personal friends and relations, such as Bacon, Derby, Ralegh, and Lady Pembroke) and (b) the professional dramatists such as Marlowe, Greene, Chapman, and Fletcher, who adapted them

---

[2] Adm. Hubert Holland, "M.O.A.I. Doth Sway My Life," *SF News-Letter*, no. 2 (March 1937): 3.

[3] Percy Allen, "Shakespeare and Montaigne," *SF News-Letter*, no. 3 (May 1937): 6.

[4] Percival Golding, quoted in Bernard M. Ward, "Two New Oxford Discoveries," *SF News-Letter*, no. 3 (May 1937): 1.

[5] Adm. Hubert Holland, letter to *News-Letter* Readers," *SF News-Letter*, no. 3 (May 1937): 11.

for the public stage.[6]

The *News-Letter* also informed members of Oxfordian developments in other countries. In 1938 it reported that *Nieuwe Rotterdamsche Courant*, the most influential newspaper in The Netherlands, ran an editorial that compared Edward de Vere and his group of dramatic authors to Richelieu's "Bureau Politique," and quoted works by Looney, Rendall, Capt. Bernard M. Ward and Percy Allen.[7] It noted *La Tribune de Geneva's* February 1, 1938, report on a lecture by Fellowship member Charles Boissevain at the Lyceum de Suisse, Geneva. Col. Douglas reported on Prof. Abel Lefranc's article "La Question Shakespearienne au XVIII Siecle" in the February issue of *Revue Bleue* and gave the following summary of Lefranc's assessment of the worldwide reception given to the Oxfordian thesis.

> He finds that Shakespearian research, orthodox or other, is increasing in all countries, and the volume and variety of the problems is such as to compel the attention not only of scholars but even of the general public. Moreover, the growing number of representations of the plays bears testimony to their popularity, and tends to accentuate the contrast between these masterpieces and the life of their reputed author, an inexplicable feature of the orthodox case. Though tardily admitted by orthodox scholars, it is now certain that the plays "are the abstracts and brief chronicles of the time," and contain impersonations of prominent men.[8]

Douglas added that "These are spreading convictions, and traditional scholars are disquieted in consequence. But the day is at hand, nearer perhaps than is realized, when the eyes of the public will be opened and the real author of these works will emerge from obscurity, and be known. Nevertheless, in order that such a result may be achieved, additional workers must be recruited, and the research be continued" (3).

The Oxfordian Shakespearean Page in *The East Anglian Magazine*

Only a few months after the launch of its *News-letter*, the Fellowship found another publication willing to carry Oxfordian articles on a regular basis. In its April 1937 issue, *The East Anglian Magazine* ran a long article titled "Shakespeare Was an East Anglian" by Fellowship member F. Lingard Ranson. East Anglia, which includes Castle Hedingham and Earls Colne, was the Oxford family seat. Ranson's article presented the case for Edward de Vere as Shakespeare to readers who had probably not heard of it before, and focused on arguments likely to be of local interest: "Wherever one turns among the Shakespearean plays . . . connections are discernible between their author, or authors, and certain personalities, places or events in East Anglia."[9] He went on to describe how "the mass of topical allusions in the plays point conclusively to intimate knowledge by Shakespeare of events in the court circles of England, from about 1570 onward in unbroken sequence for the next thirty years until 1600 and after" (293).

In introducing the article, the magazine's editor had emphasized Shakespeare's connections with the area.

---

[6] Capt. Bernard M. Ward, "Correspondence" [response to Gilbert Slater's letter], *SF News-letter*, no. 8 (March 1938), p. 12.

[7] "News from Holland," *SF News-Letter*, no. 10 (July 1938): 2-3.

[8] Col. Montagu W. Douglas, "News from France," *SF News-Letter*, no. 9 (May 1938): 2.

[9] F. Lingard Ranson, "Shakespeare Was an East Anglian," *East Anglian Mag.*, vol. 2/7 (April 1937): 295.

The case of Oxford versus Shakespeare of Stratford, which Mr. Ranson expounds, will be of intimate interest to all East Anglians. In the article, it is suggested that fresh minds, if applied to the subject, would probably bring forth further supporting evidence not only that "Shakespeare" was an East Anglian, but that East Anglia, and particularly the Lavenham district, is the genuine "Shakespeare country."[10]

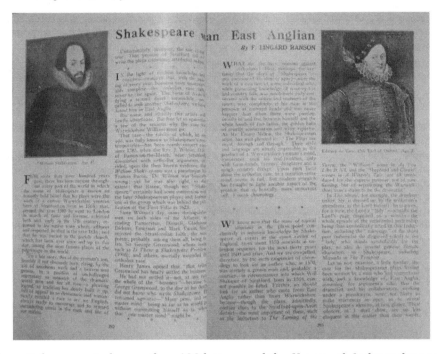

The article generated more than 400 letters and the *Yarmouth Independent* reported on it on April 10. On April 13 Fellowship President Col. Douglas traveled to Lavenham to give a lecture on "The Shakespeare Problem," which was covered by the *Bury Free Press*.

In May, *The East Anglian Magazine* ran a follow-up piece by Percy Allen. The editor's introduction highlighted the degree of public interest in the issue.

> Many letters in varying degrees of refutation or support have reached us. . . . It was only to be expected that no overwhelming agreement would be evoked; and, in fact, the majority of the letters expressed a scepticism if not an open disbelief on the Oxford theory. This again is only natural. After a period of rather more than three hundred years, it is obviously going to be very difficult to "change the identity" of this country's greatest playwright. Whether or not the Earl of Oxford's supporters will eventually succeed in doing so remains to be seen. That they have a "case" is not to be doubted; whether they will ever succeed in proving it is.[11]

If only the major literary publications in London had such a receptive attitude! Percy Allen, in his article, was more optimistic.

> It is an indisputable fact that the case for the 17th Earl of Oxford, as author of some twenty-two or so of the Shakespeare plays, grows stronger with every day, and is winning adherents throughout and beyond the English-speaking world. At the

---

[10] Editor, "Comments," *East Anglian Magazine*, vol. 2/7 (April 1937): 290.
[11] Editor, "Comments," *East Anglian Magazine*, vol. 2/8 (May 1937): 338.

present time—April, 1937—crucially important points of evidence … are coming to light with almost bewildering speed; and we may, I think, safely say that the case for Lord Oxford, already unanswerable, will be substantially complete within a year's time.[12]

He addressed the topicality of the plays and the reasons for secrecy in hiding Oxford's authorship, among them that the *Sonnets* were "dynastic through and through," a subject that "touches the personal relations between Lord Oxford and his Queen" (341). Allen concluded by urging readers to consider the issue for themselves.

> Do not jump to over-hasty conclusions; either for us, or against. Study the history of the time; and, above all seek to understand its complex mentality. . . . Do not forget that Shakespeare, in common with almost every other great romancer, wrote out of his own intimate personal experiences, seeking, and finding, his characters among the men and women of his own circle, whom, in his own lifetime, he had been interested in, or had hated, or had loved.

> Again, do not be in too great a hurry. Most of the wiser Oxfordians, I suppose, do not wish for too easy converts. For my own part, I sat "on the fence," for years, before coming down upon the Oxford side. Once down, however, you may probably find that, henceforth, the plays of our national poet are taking on, for you, an interest, dramatic, literary and historical, and an intimate significance, such as they have never contained nor conveyed before; and which will, with feeling, add immeasurably to their value, among the choicest of your intellectual possessions. (342)

The May issue contained many letters responding to Ranson's article. C. H. Lay wrote that "F. Lingard Ranson is heartily applauded by me, for he supports an old belief of mine, a belief that Shakespeare was a Suffolk man because his humour is of the Suffolk sort. That is quite proof enough for me."[13] In response to another letter Ranson provided his assessment of the current state of the authorship issue:

> The latest evidence in favour of Oxford is now overwhelmingly strong, and grows stronger every day. I would recommend a reading of Sir George Greenwood's pitiless destruction of the orthodox case and Theobald's *Exit Shakespeare!* . . . For years there have been deliberate suppressions of discussion in academic

---

F. Lingard Ranson

Born: 1880. Died: 1950.

Age when *"Shakespeare" Identified* was published: 40

Launched and edited the Shakespearean Page in *The East Anglian Magazine*, 1937-1940, which was mostly Oxfordian in content.

A third generation master tailor in Lavenham, Ranson is known for his efforts to preserve the cultural inheritance of Lavenham, the best preserved medieval town in England. Drawing on his keen instincts as an amateur historian and his skill as a photographer, he served as the first vice president of the Suffolk Preservation Society, helped form the Lavenham Preservation Society in 1944, and was an Honorary Life Member of the National Society for the Protection of Ancient Buildings.

He served as guide when members of the Shakespeare Fellowship visited Lavenham, including Eva Turner Clark who visited in 1928. His book, *Lavenham, Suffolk*, was dedicated to Col. Ward, and Col. Douglas wrote a Foreword to it.

---

[12] Percy Allen, "Lord Oxford as Shakespeare," *East Anglian Magazine*, vol. 2/8 (May, 1937): 340.
[13] C. H. Lay, "Shakespeare, a Suffolk Man" [letter], *East Anglian Magazine*, vol. 2/8 (May, 1937): 362.

circles—because, one can only assume, the professors know very well that they cannot answer our case, and dare not try.[14]

Reader interest remained strong, and *The East Anglian Magazine's* circulation soon doubled. In August the editor launched a monthly "Shakespearean Page," Oxfordian in content and edited by Ranson. He was unknowingly following the path of *The Hackney Spectator*—another periodical with a connection to a specific place associated with the 17th earl of Oxford—which had also responded to reader interest by making room for the Shakespeare Fellowship column that ran from 1922 to 1925.

The Shakespearean Page appeared in every issue of *The East Anglian Magazine* until it suspended publication in 1941 due to the Second World War. In all, the magazine ran more than 150 articles and letters on the authorship question, most from an Oxfordian perspective. Ranson recruited key members of the Shakespeare Fellowship, including Col. Douglas, Capt. Ward, Percy Allen and Charles Wisner Barrell, to write for it.

Throughout the run, Ranson provided introductions to the articles and guided readers through issues that posed particular difficulties. On dating the plays, for instance, he noted that "We have rejected the orthodox Stratfordian chronology because it has been constructed in order to fit into the supposed working life of William Shaksper of Stratford, and bears no relation at all to the internal evidence of the plays. . . . Admiral Holland

---

The East Anglian Magazine

First Oxfordian article: April 1937 — "Shakespeare Was an East Anglian" by F. Lingard Ranson

A "Shakespearean Page," mostly Oxfordian in content, ran from August 1937 until the magazine ceased publication because of the Second World War in April 1941.

<u>Selected Articles from the Page</u> (in addition to reader's letters and Ranson's replies):

April 1937	F. Lingard Ranson	Shakespeare Was an East Anglian*
May 1937	Percy Allen	Lord Oxford as Shakespeare*
Sept. 1937	Ernest Allen	Shakespeare's Sonnets*
Oct. 1937	Capt. Bernard Ward	The Dating of Shakespeare's Plays*
	Capt. Bernard Ward	Review of *When Shakespeare Died* by Ernest Allen*
Nov. 1937	Gerald H. Rendall	Reply to Ernest Allen's Sept. Article
	Col. Montagu Douglas	Letter from the President of the Sh. Fellowship.
Jan. 1938	Percy Allen	The Question of Locality
Feb. 1938	Charles W. Barrell	Review of *The Man Who Was Shakespeare* by Eva Turner Clark*
May 1938	F. Lingard Ranson	Chronology of the Oxfordian Theory
Sept. 1938	F. Lingard Ranson	The Trend of Shakespeare Thought Today
Sept.-Nov. 1939	Charles W. Barrell	*An Elizabethan Puritan*: Review of the Book by Louis T. Golding
Jan. 1940	Percy Allen	MOAI Doth Sway My Life
Feb. 1940	Col. Montagu Douglas	Ben Jonson and the First Folio*
	F. Lingard Ranson	Obituary of Mr. Ernest Allen*
April 1940	Col. Montagu Douglas	The American Branch of the Shakespeare Fellowship*
May 1940	Percy Allen	Shakespeare's *Cymbeline* and East Anglia
April 1941	Percy Allen	Review of *The "Ashbourne" Portrait* by Gerald H. Rendall

*These pieces have been reprinted in *Building the Case*, a ten-volume anthology of Oxfordian articles edited by Paul H. Altrocchi, the first five volumes co-edited by Hank Whittemore.

---

[14] F. Lingard Ranson, "Correspondence," *East Anglian Magazine*, vol. 2/9 (June 1937): 422.

pointed out that there are 45 topical allusions in *Hamlet* referring to the year 1583. There are no topical allusions to an earlier date. Oxfordians, therefore, maintain that *Hamlet* was first written in 1583, though it no doubt underwent several revisions, alterations, and additions, before it was published in 1604."[15]

These Oxfordian pieces were of general interest to residents of East Anglia, and *The Bury Free Press* ran reports on the May and June 1937 issues. A brief look at a few of the articles will show the depth of information to which readers in one location outside of London were being exposed in the final years of the 1930s.

Capt. Bernard M. Ward, "Shakespearean Page" (October 1937). This item was of special importance because Ward explained the Oxfordian process of establishing a date range for each of Shakespeare's plays based, in part, on topical allusions. Using *King Lear* as example, he wrote that,

> A "topical allusion"—as the name implies—is an allusion in the play to some outstanding event, the date of which is known. Let me take one example. In *King Lear* (I.ii) there is an allusion to "these late eclipses of the Sun and Moon." Now, a total eclipse of the Sun is a very rare event in England—it occurs about every 100 years or so. It is, moreover, an event which excites the interest of everybody—as, for instance, the famous eclipse visible in England in 1927. And all historians know that an eclipse is particularly valuable as a topical allusion, because its exact date is beyond all dispute.
>
> What eclipse, then, was Shakespeare referring to when he wrote: "these late eclipses of the Sun and Moon" in King Lear? *The Encyclopedia Britannica* gives a full list of all eclipses visible in England from the earliest times. Those which apply to our present investigation are: 17th June. 1433; 6th March, 1598; 8th April, 1652. It seems clear, therefore, that when Shakespeare wrote the words: "these late eclipses of the Sun and Moon," he must have been working on the manuscript of *King Lear* in 1598. The total eclipse of the Sun in 1598, moreover, was preceded a fortnight early by a nearly total eclipse of the Moon, also visible in England.[16]

The hundreds of topical allusions in other plays go to show, Ward observed, that Shakespeare plays, "almost without exception, were written *before* Lord Oxford's death in 1604," even though many of them were not published until years later.

Gerald H. Rendall, "Shakespearean Page" (November 1937). Rendall also addressed linkages between Shakespeare's works and real-life events. He explained that *Venus & Adonis* and the *Sonnets* "are connected by indissoluble links that are no mere parallels of word or phrase; certain stanzas incongruous with the setting of the poem are a resume of the theme which inspires the opening Sonnets."[17] He demonstrated that the only contemporary person "to which these terms could apply was . . . the Earl of Southampton," thus tying both works to the Earl of Oxford, to whose daughter Southampton had been betrothed in 1593. "Such correspondences exceed the bounds of any chance coincidence," Rendall concluded. The *Sonnets*, read as a journal in time, "give warmth and colour to trained poetic skills; the whole series shows a dramatic sequence and a coherent time-scheme in a framework of historical events that are the surest guarantee of actuality" (75).

---

[15] F. Lingard Ranson, "Lord Oxford and Shakespeare," *East Anglian Magazine*, vol. 2/12 (Sept. 1937): 551.

[16] Capt. Bernard M. Ward, "Shakespearean Page," *East Anglian Magazine*, vol. 3/1 (Oct. 1937): 40.

[17] Gerald H. Rendall, "Shakespearean Page," *East Anglian Magazine*, vol. 3/2 (Nov. 1937): 74.

<u>Capt. Bernard M. Ward, "Correspondence" (December 1937).</u> Responding to a reader who claimed that genius explained all, Capt. Ward cited the experiences that are necessary for genius to reach full flower. "The plain and indisputable fact is that it is impossible for 'genius' to supply unattainable information, or to show complete familiarity with matters of which it has never had actual cognisance. Genius alone has never provided a great vocabulary, a knowledge of foreign languages and cities, with geographical detail . . . or a close acquaintance with Courts and Kings, such as abound in the works of 'Shakespeare.' . . . Shaksper of Stratford had neither the education nor the knowledge of foreign countries and languages and aristocratic cultured life, to make it possible for him to have written the 'Shakespeare' plays and sonnets."[18]

<u>Ernest Allen, "Correspondence" (December 1937).</u> In the same issue Ernest Allen took issue with a reader who had written that the Oxfordian and Baconian theories had, by modern commentators, been "'blown sky-high." His response served as a marker for the state of academia at the end of 1937.

> The letter in your November issue from Miss E. Boileau should not be allowed to pass unchallenged. Miss Boileau leads off with an amazing assertion that the Baconian and Oxfordian theories have by modern commentators been "blown sky-high." It would be hard to conceive a statement more remote from the truth. I suspect that Miss Boileau knows little or nothing of the real position of this controversy. The facts are briefly these:
>
> (a) The Stratfordian case has been riddled with devastating criticism from every quarter.
>
> (b) No man of letters ever answers these criticisms, and no real attempt is ever made by those in literary authority to defend their own position.
>
> (c) There is a mass of evidence connecting both Bacon and Oxford with "Shakespeare." This evidence, so far from being "blown sky-high," has never been answered. It is now so strong that any adequate answer is impossible, and, so far as I am aware, not even a pamphlet has appeared from an orthodox pen containing any counter attack against ourselves. I can think of only one instance, the late John Drinkwater, with more daring than discretion, did leap "into the breach." The answer he got from my brother Percy and myself was so devastating that he retired at once, and for ever, from the field.
>
> On platform too, as well as on paper, our case stands untouched. It is difficult, almost impossible, to get any orthodox speaker to oppose our members in debate. I don't envy any aspirant to platform honours of this nature, if he or she supports the orthodox case. It is untenable.
>
> Would Miss Boileau be good enough to let me have a short list of books and their authors which, singly, or by their cumulative effect, have knocked out the Oxford-Bacon case![19]

In the same issue Ranson reported that "Readers will be interested to know that the E.A.M. is read and appreciated by many people in America."[20]

<u>F. Lingard Ranson, "Shakespearean Page" (May 1938).</u> Ranson described the circumstances in which "Shakespeare's" works had been written:

---

[18] Capt. Bernard M. Ward, Correspondence" [letter], *East Anglian Magazine*, vol. 3/3 (Dec. 1937): 141-42.

[19] Ernest Allen, "Correspondence," *East Anglian Magazine*, vol. 3/3 (Dec. 1937): 142.

[20] F Lingard Ranson, "Shakespearean Page," *East Anglian Magazine*, vol. 3/3 (Dec. 1937): 148.

Oxfordian believe that most of the plays passed through two distinct phases: (1) They were *originally written* during the fifteen-seventies and early eighties for *private* performance as Court Masques; (2) They were *adapted* during the late eighties and nineties for performance in the *public theatres*. Each play, therefore, has two dates—its first composition for performance at Court, and its revision and adaptation for performance in the public theatres. Moreover, certain plays— e.g., Hamlet—went through yet another revision before publication.[21]

F. Lingard Ranson, "The Trend of Shakespeare Thought Today" (September 1938).

Ranson continued to educate his readers about differences between Stratfordian and Oxfordian theories, this time through discussion of the concept of the unity of truth.

> From all these modern orthodox books, the significant and indisputable fact emerges after perusal—that the Stratfordian faith, howsoever honestly held by its upholders and based as it is in our view, upon a fundamental untruth, compels them, willy-nilly, to bolster up their arguments with unproven, and untenable, assumptions. There is unity, always, in truth; but in untruth there can be none; and that is why orthodox Stratfordians are inevitably thrown back upon a series of irreconcilable contradictions. Let me repeat that in European countries, as well as in England and America, these facts are fast being recognized, so that—to quote the words of Professor Abel Lefranc: "the day is at hand, nearer perhaps than is realised, when the eyes of the public will be opened and the real author of these works will emerge from obscurity and be known."[22]

Percy Allen, "Shakespeare's *Cymbeline* and East Anglia" (May 1940).

Through his study of *Cymbeline*, Allen came to see that certain places mentioned in the play actually referred to places in East Anglia: "Milford and Cambria really mean Melford and Cambridge, [and] that the play is set in that district, and dramatizes, or at least points at, events which actually took place in that part of Suffolk and Essex."[23] These ties help date parts of the theme of the play, though not necessarily its composition, to the 1570s, "after Lord Oxford's return from Europe in 1576, at a time when we know that he was not living with his wife, and during which he was, at least once, at Long Melford, while the Queen was on progress through East Anglia to Audley End and Cambridge in 1578."

From the February 1938 issue:

"In view of the interest aroused by articles in the *East Anglian Magazine* on the authorship of the Shakespearean plays the Shakespeare Fellowship have recently presented the following books to the Ipswich Public Library:

"Shakespeare" Identified by J. Thomas Looney
Seven Shakespeares by Gilbert Slater
The Poems of Edward de Vere by J. Thomas Looney
Lord Oxford as Shakespeare by Col. Montagu W. Douglas
The Life-story of Edward de Vere as "William Shakespeare" by Percy Allen
The Seventeenth Earl of Oxford by Capt. Bernard M. Ward

(None of the books were on the library's shelf list in 2020.)

---

[21] F. Lingard Ranson, "Shakespearean Page," *East Anglian Magazine*, vol. 3/7 (May 1938): 351.
[22] F. Lingard Ranson, "The Trend of Shakespearean Thought Today," *East Anglian Magazine*, vol. 3/11 (Sept. 1938): 521.
[23] Percy Allen, "Shakespeare's *Cymbeline* and East Anglia," *East Anglian Mag.*, vol. 5/4 (May 1940): 153.

Shakespeare Fellowship Events, 1937 to mid-1939

The Shakespeare Fellowship did not hold an Annual General Meeting in 1936 because of the crisis within the Fellowship described in Chapter 10. Although the regular schedule of a spring dinner and a fall meeting resumed in 1937, an undercurrent of tension lingered between those who found the *Sonnets* Dynastic Succession Theory credible and those who did not.

Annual Dinner, June 6, 1937

Forty-five people attended. Ernest Allen took the chair, as Col. Douglas, Percy Allen and Captain Ward were unable to attend. D. F. Allen's[24] report noted the many developments over the past year, the most important of which were the discovery of a report that Oxford was buried in Westminster Abbey, Percy Allen's speaking tour of North America, the end of the Fellowship Page in *The Shakespeare Pictorial*, the launching of the *Shakespeare Fellowship News-letter*, the launching of the Oxfordian Shakespearean Page in *The East Anglian Magazine*, and the publicity given to Cairncross's finding that *Hamlet* had been performed by the end of the 1580s, which strengthened the Oxfordian case. In his remarks, D. F. Allen emphasized that "the protagonists of the Oxford theory had nothing to hide and nothing to fear. He threw out a universal challenge to the learned world to refute their discoveries."[25] No mention was made of the events of 1936 that had caused such turmoil within the organization.

Annual General Meeting, October 17, 1937

Col. Douglas and Capt. Ward were re-elected as president and secretary. A vote of thanks was made to F. Lingard Ranson for creating the Oxfordian Shakespearean Page in *The East Anglian Magazine*. Percy Allen made the surprising announcement that "for the first time, editors of responsible periodicals both in this country and America were asking us to send them articles. This was quite a new departure, because hitherto the anti-Stratfordian and Oxfordian cases had been almost entirely tabooed by the press."[26] He also noted two pieces that generated much reader response in the United States: Charles Wisner Barrell's lengthy "Elizabethan Mystery Man" in *The Saturday Review of Literature* and George Frisbee's "The Shame of the Professors" in *Reading and Collecting* (see Chapter 16). The meeting was followed by a discussion on "The Present State of the Shakespeare Controversy."

Annual Dinner, May 11, 1938

Fifty-one members and guests attended, including Marjorie Bowen and Hermon Ould, Secretary of the PEN Club. Col. Douglas chaired. Percy Allen noted that there is no longer a Stratfordian case to answer; he also read a skit on the Oxford Theory by someone who cloaked his anonymity behind the name "Lewis Carroll."

Annual General Meeting, October 19, 1938

Fifteen attended, including Col. Douglas, Percy and Ernest Allen, and T. M. Aitken. The meeting concluded with a general discussion on the present position of the Shakespeare controversy and the status of the Shakespeare Fellowship."[27]

---

[24] It's not known who D. F Allen was.
[25] D. F. Allen, "The Annual Dinner," *SF News-Letter*, no. 4 (July 1937): 6.
[26] "Annual General Meeting," *SF News-Letter*, no. 6 (Nov. 1937): 1.
[27] "Annual General Meeting," *SF News-Letter*, no. 12 (Nov. 1938): 1.

Annual Dinner, May 10, 1939

Percy Allen spoke on Ivor Brown's new book, *Amazing Monument* and Marjorie Bowen "delivered a graceful and generous eulogy of the work of our more active members, and expressed appreciation of the keen intellectual interest their labours had afforded her." Ernest Allen touched on the topic of Shakespeare as an aristocrat, and J. Foster Forbes "outlined some of his own experiences in archaeological investigation. He too had found how difficult it was to get new ideas taken up and treated seriously." Shaw Desmond "spoke in his characteristically brilliant and elusive style. His chief point was that few writers are really responsible beings. They are usually controlled by spirits outside themselves, urging them almost unconsciously to write. He thought this joint control might finally solve the difficult problem 'who was Shakespeare.'"[28]

In the second half of 1939 the outbreak of the Second World War disrupted almost all Oxfordian work (see Chapter 15).

Public Lectures and Media Coverage of Them

Sixty-eight public lectures by Oxfordians are known to have been presented in England from 1928 to 1941, sixty-four of them either by Percy Allen or including him. He gave an additional twenty talks in the United States and Canada in the fall of 1936. He addressed a wide range of topics, some of which are listed in a nearby text box.

By all accounts Allen was a mesmerizing speaker. In one reviewer's description, "With his austere appearance, topped by a large-brimmed black hat, he was a striking figure. In argument on theatre matters, particularly where Shakespeare and Stratford-upon-Avon were concerned, he was a formidable but courteous opponent."[29] Another wrote that Allen "was a very pleasant person and a pleasant lecturer who held his audience tightly in his mesh of literary fascination. He would lead the audience gradually up to his final point, repeat it, and pause. Then with a triumphant smile or chuckle would come: 'You can't possibly escape from it!' That final 'no escape clause' became quite a popular trademark and the audience loved it."[30]

Allen's lectures were often reported on in local media. His talk on October 9, 1928, before the British Empire Shakespeare Society, Haymarket Branch, generated a report in *The Stage* that characterized his lecture as "obviously controversial," and noted that "in Mr. Allen's view any real knowledge of Shakespeare must be founded on an acquaintance with the historical events and personages about which and whom he wrote. . . . Mr. Allen's pet theories . . . were warmly contested by Mr. Littlewood."[31] Allen's talk on "The Case for Oxford as Shakespeare" on October 24, 1929, was the first known occasion in which he publicly stated his belief that Oxford wrote Shakespeare. Col. Ward observed that "It is safe to say that no one who heard the two lectures on the above subject . . . will ever forget the experience. From a trained lecturer professional technique is to be expected, but when to professional skill is added intense interest and enthusiasm it is difficult to exaggerate the impression produced. . . . [S]o disarming was the effect produced by the personality of the lecturer that nothing could have exceeded the general friendliness displayed all round."[32]

---

[28] Percy Allen, "Annual Dinner," *SF News-Letter*, no. 15 (July 1939): 1.
[29] "Percy Allen," *The Stage*, Feb. 12, 1959, p. 17.
[30] T. L. Adamson, "Obituary: Percy Allen," *Shakespearean Authorship Review*, no. 1, Spring 1959, p. 22.
[31] B.E.S.S., "Shakespeare and Chapman," *Stage*, Oct. 11, 1928, p. 17.
[32] Col. Bernard R. Ward, "The Case for Oxford as Shakespeare," *Shakespeare Pictorial*, Dec. 1929, p. 20.

Allen's lecture at the Gallery First-Nighters' Club on December 13, 1931, was reported in *The Manchester Guardian*, *The Leeds Mercury* and *The Birmingham Gazette*. *The Mercury* well as the dates of the various works, alone shatter the Stratfordian theory."[33] It must have been quite a night at the British Drama League on March 9, 1932, when the audience was addressed by Gerald H. Rendall, Adm. Hubert H. Holland, Col. Montagu W. Douglas, Marjorie Bowen, Mr. G. F. Holland, President of the O. O. Club, and Percy Allen, who spoke on "The Three Williams in Shakespeare." wrote that "the intimacy with details of Court life expressed in the *Sonnets* and plays, as A media report noted that "Allen argued that the three 'Williams' were deliberately introduced by Oxford into the plays for the express purpose of affirming his own claim and of repudiating the spurious claim of William Shakspere of Stratford to the authorship."[34]

Capt. Ward's report on Allen's December 9, 1933, lecture at The International Fellowship of Literature captured the impact of the experience on what he described as "a large and responsive audience" that included several well known writers.

> Mr. Allen's subject was "The Elizabethan Drama," a method of play-writing which—the speaker con-

---

Percy Allen's Talks in England, 1928-1941:
A Sampling of Subjects Addressed

As You Like It as Autobiographical Drama
Ben Jonson, Shaksper and Shakespeare
The Case for Oxford as Shakespeare: Oxford in Some Comedies
The Case for Oxford as Shakespeare: Oxford in the Great Tragedies
The Case for Oxford as Shakespeare: Oxford in the *Sonnets*
The Case for Oxford as Shakespeare: Late Spurious Plays and Burlesques of Oxford as Shakespeare in the Plays of Chapman and Johnson
Chapman's Skit on *Love's Labour's Lost*: An Humour's Day's Mirth
Cymbeline and *Pericles*
David Garrick
Did the Earl of Oxford Write *Hamlet*?
Edward de Vere, Earl of Oxford, as Shakespeare
The Elizabethan Drama
The Fair Youth of Shakespeare's *Sonnets* as Portrayed in Elizabethan Drama
Hamlet and Edward de Vere
Hamlet and the *Sonnets* from an Oxfordian Viewpoint
Hamlet and *Twelfth Night*
Lord Burghley in Shakespeare's Plays and Spenser's Poems
Lord Oxford as Author of Shakespeare's *Sonnets*
Lord Oxford Wrote the Plays and *Sonnets* of Shakespeare
The Man Behind the Name
The Man Behind the Playwright
Measure for Measure as Autobiographical Drama
The Mystery of the First Shakespeare Folio
Oxford as Shakespeare
The Oxford Theory and Historical Interpretations of the Plays and *Sonnets*
Present State of the Shakespeare Controversy
The Present Trend in Shakespearian Studies
Shakespeare and Chapman
Shakespeare and French History
Shakespeare and Montaigne
Shakespeare: The Man Behind the Mask
Shakespeare's Influence
Shakespeare's Plays as Dramatizations of English, French and Scottish History
The Stratfordian Tradition
The Three Williams in Shakespeare
Topicalities in Shakespeare's Plays
Twelfth Night as a Topical Play
Twelfth Night as Autobiographical Drama
The Winter's Tale
The Wonder-Motive in *The Winter's Tale* and Other Late Shakespearean Plays

---

[33] "Who Wrote Plays of Shakespeare?" *Leeds Mercury*, Dec. 14, 1931, p. 1.
[34] Capt. Bernard M. Ward, "The Three Williams in Shakespeare," *Shakespeare Pictorial*, April 1932, p. 68.

tended—has never yet been properly understood, principally because the academic authorities have never yet perceived the full significance of its topicalities, nor fathomed the complex, and subtle, mentalities that produced it. The question of Shakespearean authorship was incidentally raised; thus leading up to a long and animated discussion, at the close of which the lecturer was generally considered to have held his own. Mr. Allen obviously enjoys being heckled.[35]

At Allen's February 7, 1937 lecture on "Shakespeare: The Man Behind the Mask" at the York Repertory Theatre, "the discussion which followed, and which was kept up till a late hour, was one of the best for quality and animation, that Mr. Allen's lectures have so far aroused."[36] His talk on "The Mystery of the First Shakespeare Folio" drew about fifty persons, the most of any lecture in the series. It was followed by a debate and animated discussion chaired by Fellowship President Douglas which included Ernest Allen, William Kent, J. J. Dwyer and the Hon. Mark Pakington. As reported by Capt. Ward, "The lecturer and the debaters, between them, seemed to make out an unanswerable case for the Folio being due to the collaboration of a number of aristocrats and writers, with Lord Oxford as principal pen, and including his son-in-law, Lord Derby, Francis Bacon, Sir Walter Raleigh, Lady Pembroke, the Earls of Montgomery and Pembroke (sons of Lady Pembroke), Benjamin Jonson, and, probably, George Chapman—Heminge, Condell, and William Shaksper of Stratford all being 'masks' for the concealed aristocrats."[37]

At Allen's lecture on *The Winter's Tale* at the Bath Branch of the British Empire Shakespeare Society on February 7, 1941, however, the *Bath Chronicle and Weekly Gazette* reported that "many left the hall thoroughly angry. Or dismayed."[38] The newspaper's report was titled "Don't Marry a Genius," in response to Allen's description of how "Oxford's disgraceful treatment of his wife was depicted, in a disguised way, in *The Winter's Tale*," an interpretation of the play new to most attendees. A similar reaction occurred back in 1936, at the lecture on "Shakespeare Authorship" by Col. F. E. G. Skey on February 22, about which *The Dover Express* reported "those who hold to the commonly accepted theories on the identity of the author had their orthodox views thoroughly upset."[39]

Col. Douglas, in his lecture in Lavenham in April 1937, presented "the Group Theory," which he called "the only alternative if the orthodox view is rejected." In that theory, the Earl of Oxford was the "master mind" working in collaboration with his son-in-law Lord Derby and his cousin Francis Bacon. A reviewer in *The Times Literary Supplement* summed up the group theory, "which holds the field at the moment," this way: "'Shakespeare's' works are a syndicated orchestration, with the Earl of Oxford as conductor."[40]

Oxfordian Pamphlets

British Oxfordian scholars did not publish books between 1937 and 1945. (Books by American scholars will be discussed in Chapter 16.) They did, however, publish a number

[35] Capt. Bernard M. Ward, "Lecture on The Elizabethan Drama," *Shakespeare Pictorial*, Jan. 1934, p. 4.
[36] "Occasional Notes," *SF News-Letter*, no. 2 (March 1937), p. 10.
[37] "Occasional Notes," *SF News-Letter*, no. 15 (July 1939), p. 8.
[38] "Don't Marry a Genius," *Bath Chronicle and Weekly Gazette*, Feb. 8, 1941, p. 18.
[39] "Shakespeare Authorship," *Dover Express*, Feb. 28, 1936, p. 4.
[40] [reviews of six books], *Times Literary Supplement*, Jan. 14, 1932, p. 29.

of pamphlets, building on their earlier practice of reprinting important articles in pamphlet form. The nearby text box lists Oxfordian pamphlets issued from 1920 to 1945.

Oxfordian Pamphlets Published in England, 1920-1945

1925
Capt. Bernard M. Ward — *The Authorship of The Arte of English Poesie, A Suggestion*
[Reprinted from *Review of English Studies*, vol. 1/3 (July 1925)]

1926
Capt. Bernard M. Ward — *George Gascoigne and His Circle*
[Reprinted from *Review of English Studies*, vol. 2/5 (Jan. 1926)]

1928
Percy Allen — *Shakespeare as a Topical Dramatist*
[Published by The Poetry League]

Capt. Bernard M. Ward — *The Famous Victories of Henry V*
[Reprinted from *Review of English Studies*, vol. 4/15 (July 1928)]

1929
Percy Allen — *Manifesto of Conversion*
Gerald H. Rendall — *Ben Jonson and the First Folio of Shakespeare's Plays*
[expanded version reissued in 1939]

1930
Col. Bernard R. Ward — *The Elizabethan Chronicle Play as War Propaganda*
[Reprinted from *Royal Engineers Journal*, v. 44/1 (March 1930)]

Col. Bernard R. Ward — *Shakespeare's Sonnets: A Suggested Interpretation*
[Reprinted from Poetry and the Play (Winter 1929-1930)]

Col. Bernard R. Ward — *Shakespeare and Elizabethan War Propaganda*
[Reprinted from *Royal Engineers Journal*, vol. 43/4 (Dec. 1928)]

1935
Katharine E. Eggar — *The Seventeenth Earl of Oxford as Musician, Poet and Controller of the Queen's Revels* [Reprinted from *The Proceedings of the British Musical Association*, vol. lxi (Jan. 17, 1935)]

1936
Percy Allen &
  Capt. Bernard M. Ward — *An Enquiry into the Relations Between Lord Oxford as "Shakespeare," Queen Elizabeth and the Fair Youth*

1937
Ernest Allen — *When Shakespeare Died*
F. Lingard Ranson — *Lavenham, Suffolk*

1938
C. Y. C. Dawbarn — *Oxford and the Folio Plays: A Supplement*
[Reprinted from *Baconiana* (Oct.)]

1939
Gerald H. Rendall — *Ben Jonson and the First Folio*

1940
Gerald Rendall — *"Ashbourne" Portrait of Shakespeare*

1941
Gerald Rendall — *Arthur Golding, Translator – Personal and Literary – Shakespeare and Edward de Vere* [Reprinted from *Essex Review* (April 1941)]

Gerald Rendall — *Autograph – Edward de Vere Signatures*

1943
Percy Allen — *Who Were the Dark Lady and Fair Youth of the Sonnets?*

1944
Gerald Rendall — *Shakespeare in Essex and East Anglia*

Among those of special interest not already mentioned were:

F. Lingard Ranson's *Lavenham, Suffolk* (1937). In this seventy-eight page pamphlet Ranson outlined the history of Lavenham, nestled in the heart of de Vere country and one of the best preserved medieval towns of England. He described hundreds of historic buildings still standing, including Lavenham Church, one of the finest existing structures of its kind, which was built by the 13th earl of Oxford. Ranson included a brief recounting of the life of Edward de Vere and dedicated the pamphlet to Capt. Ward. In his Foreword, Col. Montagu Douglas, while remaining a proponent of the "group authorship" theory, wrote that "should it in the fullness of time be accepted that the seventeenth Earl of Oxford was 'Shakespeare,' in collaboration to some extent with Lord Bacon, his cousin, and the Earl of Derby, his son-in-law, Lavenham—the home of his ancestors—its Lords of the Manor, will be entitled to its full share of distinction."[41]

Gerald Rendall's *Ben Jonson and the First Folio* (1939). Sir George Greenwood had reached the conclusion that the prefatory matter in the First Folio by Ben Jonson must be understood as duplicitous and misleading. Rendall reached a similar conclusion. He shows that Ben Jonson was in close touch with those most concerned with the production of the Folio, and that, as Col. Douglas noted in his review, "the dedicatory epistle and address as well as the tributary odes, were the work of Ben Jonson, and form part of a definite scheme to mislead the interested public. . . . We have in this pamphlet a formidable attack on the citadel of orthodoxy, 'the evidence of Ben Jonson.' Coming from a scholar of Dr. Rendall's judgment and standing it deserves consideration."[42]

Gerald Rendall's *"Ashbourne" Portrait of Shakespeare* (1940). Rendall provided much background information about the Ashbourne portrait of Edward de Vere that Charles Wisner Barrell had had to omit from his article about the portrait in the January 1940 issue of *Scientific American* (see Chapter 16). Especially important was Rendall's documenting of the chain of custody of the portrait by Oxford's descendants from the time of the death of Oxford's widow, Elizabeth Trentham, until it was sold in 1910.

Gerald Rendall's *Arthur Golding, Translator—Personal and Literary—Shakespeare and Edward de Vere* (1941). In this short pamphlet, a review of Louis T. Golding's biography of his distant ancestor Arthur Golding, Rendall discussed three translations prepared by Golding, uncle and tutor to the adolescent Edward de Vere, that "left their lasting impress on the genius of his pupil:"[43] Ovid's *Metamorphoses* (1565), Justin's *Abridgement of Tragus Pompeius* (1564) and Caesar's *Commentaries* (1565). He showed that these three works and the imaginative nature of the translations in them were completed before Golding fell under the dominating influence of Calvin and "produced a continuous stream of Puritan expositions and homilies in ever growing volume." And he documented just how closely passages in Shakespeare's plays "point irresistibly to the handiwork of Edward de Vere, and are helpful in determining date, and even authenticity of the plays or passages concerned" (8).

In his letter to Rendall thanking him for a copy of the pamphlet, Looney observed that "Like everything else about the Oxford case the Golding argument becomes stronger the more closely it is examined: the surest evidence that we hold the true key to the

---

[41] Col. Montagu W. Douglas, "Foreword," *Lavenham, Suffolk* by F. Lingard Ranson (1937).

[42] Col. Montagu W. Douglas, "Review of *Ben Jonson and the First Folio* by Gerald Rendall," *SF News-Letter* (American), vol. 1/2 (Feb. 1940), p. 8.

[43] Gerald H. Rendall, "*Arthur Golding, Translator—Personal and Literary—Shakespeare and Edward de Vere*" [review of Louis T. Golding's *An Elizabethan Partisan*] (1937), p. 3.

Shakespeare 'mystery' and I must congratulate you on having made the Golding-Shakespeare case unanswerable. If only people would listen! But then, this is just the difficulty which Truth has always had to face."[44]

Gerald Rendall's *Shakespeare in Essex and East Anglia* (1944). In this preliminary look into the subject, Rendall sought to establish the chronology of Shakespeare's plays through topical references in them to Essex and East Anglia, "with passing attention called to allusions connecting the plays with Edward de Vere, 17th Earl of Oxford."[45]

The Oxfordian Movement in the Media

What was the effect on public opinion of Oxfordian research and publications so far? One way to answer this question is through the number of pieces on the Oxfordian answer to the authorship question in the media over the period 1920 through 1940, and how it changed over time.

The total number of books, articles, reviews and letters to editors in periodicals by Oxfordians each year from 1920 to 1940 is shown in the nearby chart. For items in periodicals, only periodicals in general circulation are included, including newspapers and magazines read by the public and publications available to general readers but read mostly by scholars, such as *The Review of English Studies*. Not included are the *Shakespeare Fellowship News-Letters* or *Circulars*, which were available only to Fellowship members.

The highest column, in 1920, was due to the number of reviews of *"Shakespeare" Identified*. The jump in 1923 and 1924 is due to the Fellowship page in *The Hackney Spectator*. After a precipitous drop, the sudden rise in 1928 is due to publication of Capt.

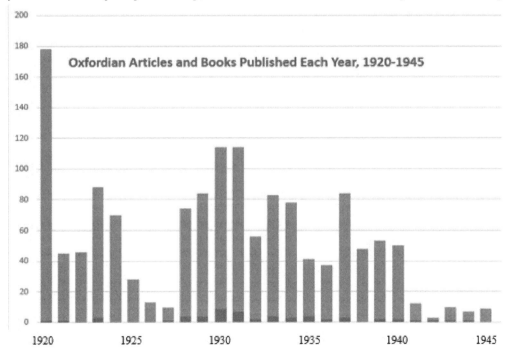

Oxfordian Articles and Books Published Each Year, 1920-1945

---

[44] J. Thomas Looney, letter to Gerald H. Rendall, May 2, 1941.

[45] Gerald H. Rendall, *Shakespeare in Essex and East Anglia* (1944), p. 4. [Born in 1851, Rendall was ninety-three when this pamphlet was published.]

Ward's *The Seventeenth Earl of Oxford* and the beginning of Percy Allen's tsunami of books, articles and letters. The significant drop starting in 1941 was due to the Second World War, during which many periodicals suspended publication.

The publications in the British Isles with the most items addressing the Oxfordian claim between 1920 and 1945 were those that had run Oxfordian pages or columns: *The Hackney Spectator* (1922-1925) and *The Shakespeare Pictorial* (1929-1936). *The Times Literary Supplement* ran a surprisingly large number of pieces, 104, given that its coverage ranged from hostile to skeptical. *The Christian Science Monitor*,

Periodicals with the Most Items Mentioning the Oxfordian Idea in the UK, 1920-1940	
Shakespeare Pictorial (1929-1939)	167
Hackney Spectator (1922-1925)	145
Times Literary Supplement (1920-1939)	104
East Anglian Magazine (1937-1941)	78
Christian Science Monitor (1920-1939)	38
Saturday Review (London) (1920-1933)	33
Morning Post (1920-1934)	30
Western Morning News and Mercury (1928-1939)	28
Bookman's Journal (1920-1921)	20
Observer (1921-1937)	17
Review of English Studies (1925-1933)	17
Yorkshire Post and Leeds Intelligencer (1920-1938)	16
Manchester Guardian (1920-1933)	14
Scotsman (1920-1932)	14
Bookman (1920-1933)	12
Aberdeen Press and Journal (1920-1935)	10
Spectator (1920-1932)	10
Sunday Times (1920-1938)	10
Notes and Queries (1920-1939)	9
Telegraph (1920-1939)	9
Times (1928-1939)	7

whose Drama Critic was Percy Allen, unsurprisingly had the most positive coverage and among the most pieces, with thirty-eight.

The Oxfordian Movement and Public Opinion: Three Interesting Stories

Percy Allen's exchanges with reviewers of his books have been noted, among them Muriel St. Clare Byrne in *The Times Literary Supplement*, and G. B. Harrison and Ivor Brown in other publications. Percy Allen's further engagement with Brown is considered here, as are his exchanges with John Drinkwater and A. S. Cairncross.

The Tantalizing Case of Ivor Brown

In October 1937, a few years after he had reviewed three of Percy Allen's books, Brown commented in passing in the *Illustrated London News* that "It is possible that we are going to celebrate still further the mystery of the wrong man."[46] Two years later, in his book *The Shakespeare Industry: Amazing Monument*, he examined the effect that discrediting Shakspere as the author would have on his home town, Stratford-on-Avon. He traced open attributions of Shakespeare's works to someone other than Shakspere as far back as 1597 (*Hall's Satires*), before examining the Baconian theory. Then, noting that "the cause of Oxford was first taken up by a Mr. Looney," he asked, "Is it credible that debate between supposed scholars should be interspersed with jests on that gentleman's name?"[47] and showed unusual familiarity with the Oxfordian cause.

> The Oxford Movement, which allots the authorship to Edward de Vere, 17th Earl of Oxford, is much more recent. It seems to have a particular appeal for the Naval and Military mind. After Mr. Looney had led off in 1920 with *"Shakespeare" Identified*, he was followed into print by an Admiral, a Colonel, a Major and a

---

[46] Ivor Brown, "The World of Theatre," *Illustrated London News*, Oct. 9, 1937, p. 28.
[47] Ivor Brown and George Fearon, *This Shakespeare Industry*, p. 201.

> Captain. But the most industrious and ingenious supporter of Oxford has been Mr. Percy Allen, a mere civilian, but as tough for his man, de Vere, as any who ever swore allegiance to their Verulam. (201-02)

> Those who wish to pursue the Oxford claim can do so in the works of Mr. Looney, Admiral Holland, Major Montagu Douglas, Colonel B. R. Ward, Captain B. M. Ward, Dr. Gerald Rendall, and Mr. Percy Allen.... What they will not find [there] is the tenable suggestion in the literary remains of de Vere that he was capable of writing in the least like the supposedly illiterate, rustic actor, drunkard, miser, and general Stratford "bum," William Shakespeare or, if they prefer it, Shagsper. (202)

Though Brown opined that Oxford's poetry could have been written by "any ingenious Tudor graduate of the arts," he concluded that "The identity of the Bard flickers hauntingly before the public eye and incites a genuine curiosity. It is idle to pretend there is no riddle when so many, remaining Stratfordian, have confessed their difficulty in equating the poet's life with his work" (207). It is refreshing to find Brown, in 1943, recommending that "All the Shakespeareans ought honestly to read the best anti-Stratfordians, Greenwood, Eagle, and others. They'll find much they will think silly—and much that takes a deal of answering.... I remain a moderate Stratfordian, but I find the way of an Eagle a bracing Challenge to the faith and good fun to pursue."[48]

In 1944 Brown went even further. "It is an astounding thing as well as an appalling nuisance that, concerning the greatest of the English, possibly of the world's, writers, we should know for certain so very little.... It isn't impossible that the man [making] small loans and investments in Stratford, was also hobnobbing with the grand courtiers and their Dark Ladies and creating with astonishing speed the imperishable poetry 'for all time.' Nothing is beyond the scope and range of human oddity. But quite a number of intelligent people cannot make sense of the Shakespeare story as it stands."[49]

Was Brown, while publicly a Stratfordian, on the brink of accepting Edward de Vere as "Shakespeare?" It seemed so to Oxfordians. Marjorie Bowen wrote to Percy Allen that "Ivor Brown as good as admits that he does not accept the Stratford legend, and the serious reference to the Oxfordian theory is most gratifying."[50]

A year later, in May 1945, assessing the imperviousness of academia to its own findings, Percy Allen found that it stood firmly behind the traditional authorship story. But, he observed, it seems "certain that several well known writers and journalists today are wavering from orthodoxy, and are tending to accept, in one form or another, the group-theory of Shakespearean authorship."[51] He identified Ivor Brown as one of them. [Brown] comments upon the extraordinary amount of contemporary knowledge, literary, historic and philosophic, possessed by Shakespeare, and pertinently asks how the dramatist acquired all this learning, while actively engaged in theatrical and mercantile pursuits." Allen wondered where Brown's questions were leading: "To Baconianism or Oxfordianism? Not necessarily; but the questions, 'How did Shakespeare spend his time?' 'How did he fit it all in?' have to be faced." Allen then offered his own answer: "This Editor's opinion, now shared by many others, is, that Ivor Brown, at bottom, is today more

---

[48] Ivor Brown, "Theatre and Life," *Observer*, July 11, 1943, p. 2. Brown was referring especially to Roderick L. Eagle's *Shakespeare: New Views for Old* 1930/1943.

[49] Ivor Brown, "Theatre and Life," Observer, April 30, 1944, p. 2.

[50] Marjorie Bowen, letter to Percy Allen, May 1, 1944, quoted in *SF News-Letter* (Oct. 1944): 1.

[51] Percy Allen, "The Group Theory and Some Modern Intellectuals," *SF News-Letter*, May 1945, p. 4.

than dubious concerning the validity of the orthodox case."

But it was not to be. Once pressure from the Oxfordian side eased during the Second World War (see Chapter 15), Brown swung back into the Stratfordian groove. He later wrote six books on Shakespeare, all in line with traditional Stratfordian views.[52] One of them, *How Shakespeare Spent the Day* (1963), seemed almost to have been written in direct response to Percy Allen's questions. It was an expanded version of an article Brown published in 1945 in which he provided answers to the same questions. In that article (a review of Tillyard's *Shakespeare's History Plays*), Brown agreed with Tillyard that Shakespeare's works do indeed "show a profound knowledge of the Tudor philosophy of history, considerable reading, and a determined resolve to transmit through the medium of the stage certain principles of politics, the divine office of the King or Prince, the abominable nature of schism and civil war, the natural rightness of social 'degree' and of the harmony prevailing when 'degree' is accepted and the nation is free of civil 'jars.'"[53] He also recognized that Shakspere as a working actor would not have had the time for study of those issues and that such in-depth knowledge could not have been picked up through casual conversations in the Mermaid or other taverns on the Bankside. So how did he come by it?

Brown's solution was that "certain of the leading political men of the time," recognizing the importance of the theater and "wanting to 'put across' the ideas of social stability," but socially barred from the theatre and lacking the craft for it, hired Shakspere to put their ideas into dramatic form. "They took to the rising dramatist their notions, their view of English history, possibly even their texts and told him to work on them. He did so. The plays . . . were handed to him, either for 'propaganda' purposes in the case of the histories or for fun, in the case of the comedies." In Brown's eyes, "a theory of this kind saves us from the difficulty of believing that "[Shakspere found time to become] learned in the finer details of Platonic scholarship and Pauline theology as well as of English history and political philosophy. The great learning was all part of what was handed on by his social superiors, who were naturally fascinated to discover that their protégé could turn their silver, even their lead, into imperishable gold by the redrafting and rewriting which he could so speedily and brilliantly achieve. That, in my opinion, is how Shakespeare spent his time."

The Perplexing Case of John Drinkwater

Drinkwater's plays were among the most successful on the British stage in the 1930s. To the degree his popularity reflected his understanding of public opinion, it is significant that he was willing to rush in where angels feared to tread; he publicly expressed doubts about some aspects of the traditional authorship story even in Stratford-on-Avon, as in his toast at the annual Stratford Town Hall luncheon in April, 1931.

> Did that energy, that stupendous energy, suddenly cease, five years before Shakespeare died, still a young man? I have never been able to believe it. The nonsense about his having made a fortune, being a little ashamed of his stage associations, wishing to indulge great ambitions in the retirement of his native town, and setting his art aside, as being of no further use to him, defies all reason.

---

[52] *Shakespeare* (1949), *Shakespeare in His Time* (1960), *How Shakespeare Spent the Day* (1963), *Shakespeare and His World* (1964), *The Women in Shakespeare's Life* (1969), and *Shakespeare and the Actors* (1970).

[53] Ivor Brown, "Had Shakespeare Leisure?" *John O'London's Weekly*, Jan. 26, 1945, p. 175.

... To suggest that the creator of *Lear* ... decided in a day that he would never again employ the instrument of which so unapproachably he was the master, is entirely to disregard experience.

If Shakespeare wrote *The Tempest* in 1611, if he then returned to Stratford in health, and if he lived a further five years in his prime, then it can be surmised with a confidence approaching certainty that his last years produced masterpieces that have been lost. Not, we may suppose, since he had left the theatre, plays; lyric poetry, perhaps, the songs and sonnets of Shakespeare's serene maturity. If the cypherers could but find a clue to that treasure.[54]

The report on his remarks in *The Stage* notes that "The toast was honoured in silence."

Two years later Drinkwater again demonstrated his fearlessness or foolhardiness by publishing a book on Shakespeare with a chapter attacking Percy Allen's views on the authorship question. Given Drinkwater's prominence as a dramatist, the book, *Shakespeare*, was reviewed in *The New York Herald Tribune* by Logan Clendening, who wrote that "I like Mr. Drinkwater's forthright demolition of the authorship claims of Edward de Vere."[55]

After noting that it is difficult to write about Shakespeare without addressing "the question of disputed authorship" because "everybody knows that it has been raised and silence might be mistaken for evasion," Drinkwater acknowledged that Oxford had replaced Bacon as the strongest of the alternative candidates. He identified Percy Allen as "the Oxonians' 'major prophet'"[56] and "the ablest advocate of what I take to be the most up-to-date heresy" (13). He critiqued Allen's ideas as expressed in *The Oxford-Shakespeare Case Corroborated* (1931), in part by raising the why and how questions. On the why question he "saw no plausible reason why whoever it was who wrote the plays wrote them secretly ... [and] used Shakespeare's name to cover the deception" (31-32). He believed that "no nobleman, during a long period of years, could have succeeded in putting something over thirty plays into Shakespeare's pocket without the whole of London society, which was then a small and assiduously cultivated hot-bed of gossip where nobody's business was his own, knowing all about it" (32).

Following the Stratfordian playbook, Drinkwater presented and attacked a distorted versions of Allen's work. He stated that "whenever [Shakespeare] uses words like EVER, NEVER, DISSEVER, PERSEVERE, FOREVER, ... [Allen] is able to proclaim Oxford calling from the page,"[57] whereas Allen had only stated that in certain instances, such as in sonnet 76— "That EVERY word doth almost tell my name,"—Oxford was signaling his true name.

Drinkwater also challenged Allen's statement—"I hold it to be an unanswerable fact, that no man, however highly endowed, ever can write, or ever did write, outside the basic experiences of his own life" (38)—with the unconvincing claim that, "There is not a scene in the plays that shows a social knowledge beyond the opportunities that Shakespeare of the playhouses must have enjoyed" (39). Drinkwater then confidently dismissed Allen's case without having studied it. "If we could allow his case any basic probability, we might find much satisfaction in his exhaustive, not to say exhausting presentation of it. As it is, we do not feel it necessary to examine the body of his evidence in detail" (36).

Percy Allen—Looney's Bulldog—did not take this attack lying down. He and his twin

---

[54] John Drinkwater, "The Immortal Memory," *Stage*, April 30, 1931, p. 15.
[55] Logan Clendening, "Good Reading," *New York Herald Tribune*, Nov. 22, 1933, p. 15.
[56] John Drinkwater, *Shakespeare* (1933), pp. 30-31.
[57] John Drinkwater, *Shakespeare* (1933), p. 33.

brother Ernest did not mince words in their response, as the subtitle of their book indicates: *Lord Oxford & "Shakespeare:" A Reply to John Drinkwater: A Ruthless Exposure of Faulty Reasoning*: "Since the matter is deeply serious, and vitally important, [our] retorts may be occasionally ruthless; they will not, I hope, be rude."[58] The Allens responded at length because Drinkwater's book was "the first occasion upon which any individual, known or obscure, has ventured, in a book, seriously to challenge the Oxfordian case. We honestly wish that the attack had been a more formidable one; but, such as it is, we answer."[59]

Responding to Drinkwater's demand that "[Allen] really must prove his case," Allen responded with "My answer—concurred in by my collaborator in this book, who is a practising lawyer—must be, that our case, as it stands, is unanswerably proved, as regards a majority of the plays, by a mass of circumstantial evidence, which, if capably presented by trained counsel, must, by its cumulative effect, convince any competent and open-minded judge."[60]

The Allens' response to the "how" question was that,

> The courtiers and principal writers of Queen Elizabeth's day did know the truth of the whole matter, and refer to it many times, though, of course, guardedly, and under disguises that are not always easy to penetrate; for the sufficient reasons that some of the persons principally concerned, including Lord Oxford himself, seem to have been under oath of secrecy; and that the whole mysterious business—by far the strangest and most enthralling in the wide range of the world's literary problems—was mortally dangerous, because of its intimate connection with great persons, and great affairs of state and also with certain sexual intimacies, that seem to have taken place—with a child born, in consequence—about the year 1574, between Elizabeth and Lord Oxford.[61]

Percy Allen closed their book with this courteous personal comment:

> May I, Percy Allen, personally, at parting, assure [Drinkwater] that I have much enjoyed this little controversy, of which he was the "only begetter;" and have, and shall continue to have, for the author of *Abraham Lincoln*, warm admiration and regard. Nothing would give me greater pleasure than to accompany him, one evening, to a play of "Shakespeare's" and to enjoy, by his side, the matchless word-music of him, who, from our respective angles, we both love "this side idolatry." (69)

Drinkwater responded to Percy Allen's rebuttal in a letter a few months later. It shows the courtesy with which prominent literary figures could and did engage each other in spite of their differences of opinion on professional matters.

> I am sure you will not attribute my delay in thanking you for your book either to discourtesy or indifference. I have been desperately busy, and it was only this last week that I have had a chance to read it, which I have now done, with respect for your erudition and gratitude for your good humour. Obviously it would be futile for me in a note of acknowledgement to attempt any discussion of your arguments but in brief I still feel that the evidence in favour of the traditional

---

[58] Percy and Ernest Allen, *Lord Oxford and "Shakespeare:" A Reply to John Drinkwater: A Ruthless Exposure of Faulty Reasoning* (1933), pp. 9, 7.
[59] Percy Allen, "Mr. John Drinkwater's *Shakespeare*," *Shakespeare Pictorial*, March 1933, p. 37.
[60] Percy & Ernest Allen, *Lord Oxford & Shakespeare: A Reply to John Drinkwater* (1933), pp. 20-21. Another interesting sentence by a man who loved comments.
[61] Percy & Ernest Allen, *Lord Oxford & Shakespeare: A Reply to John Drinkwater* (1933), pp. 24-25.

authorship is so convincing in its simplicity that, until it has been manifestly discredited, your own very ingenious evidence does not really come before the court. This I know you will take to be a very unsatisfactory view, but there it is. In the meantime let me repeat that I do respect the skill and enthusiasm that you bring to your case in spite of my obstinacy.[62]

Novelist and Oxfordian Marjorie Bowen also found Drinkwater ill-informed on the matter he chose to address. Contrasting Drinkwater's ignorance of the authorship issue with Allen's expertise, she wrote,

The chapters in which Mr. Drinkwater, with ingenuous courage, takes up the cudgels in a dispute on a subject exceedingly complex, difficult and obscure, are astonishing; for he rushes into the fight while frankly acknowledging that he knows next to nothing of the case.[63]

Probably there never was a mystery of greater historical and literary importance, nor one that required more patience, learning, sensitive skill, balanced taste and exhaustive labour to investigate. The scholars who have for years examined this problem cannot be lightly dismissed as cranks, fanatics, or sufferers from delusions. To attempt to do so is merely childish. It is, also, obviously useless for Mr. Drinkwater, or any one else, to write a line on this matter without the fullest equipment of relative knowledge available. To declare "I think so" or "I want to think so," and to flick with ridicule some easy point in the proffered evidence simply will not do. It must be clear to any fair-minded person that if "the case for Oxford'" is to be faced and answered, this must be done by some impartial person who has studied all the material that has been collected.

Mr. Drinkwater has not made this study and, therefore, should not have pronounced on the matter at all. I can find no sign that he has read more than one of Mr. Percy Allen's books, that he is familiar with that by Mr. Thomas Looney which so deeply impressed many cultured and highly intelligent people, that he has studied Dr. Rendall's exhaustive work on the *Sonnets* or this same author's pamphlet on the handwriting . . . or that he has faced the question of the Ashbourne and Welbeck portraits or that of the Shakespeare signatures.

Drinkwater's book, she concluded, "is not a life of William Shakespeare of Stratford, because no one could write that, and it is not a contribution of any value towards the question 'Who was Shakespeare?' because Mr. Drinkwater has not troubled to study that subject."

The Puzzling Case of Andrew S. Cairncross

In *The Problem of Hamlet: A Solution* (1936), Cairncross concluded that *Hamlet* had been written by William Shakespeare not later than August 1589, and that as a consequence the whole sequence of Shakespeare plays could have been written as early as 1603—the year before Edward de Vere died (see Chapter 13).[64]

Percy Allen recognized the book's revolutionary implications immediately. In his review, "Another Bombshell," he commented on "how frequently during the present year books by orthodox writers have unconsciously aided the Oxfordian cause." Cairncross's book was "more revolutionary by far than any that has ever yet come from the pen of a learned Stratfordian Professor—a work almost certainly destined to arouse wrath and controversy, and to provide a new landmark for students of Shakespeare's life and

---

[62] John Drinkwater, letter to Percy Allen, Aug. 3, 1933.
[63] Marjorie Bowen, "*Shakespeare* by John Drinkwater," *Shakespeare Pictorial*, April 1933, p. 64.
[64] A. S. Cairncross, *The Problem of Hamlet: A Solution* (1936), p. 183.

work."[65] He thought that Cairncross might have read books by Oxfordian scholars.

> The implications of this shrewd, courageous, and quietly confident book are sensational; . . . and strike at the deepest roots of traditional and orthodox belief. To Oxfordians, the thesis here propounded merely corroborates what we already know; to Stratfordians it teems with insuperable difficulties and contradictions. Dr. Cairncross, I surmise, has been reading our books. If that be so, shall we, one day, have the pleasure of welcoming him among the Oxfordians?

Allen continued in this vein in his response to a review of Cairncross's book that had appeared in *The Times Literary Supplement*, in which he directed attention to the work of members of the Shakespeare Fellowship.

> May I, in fairness to members of the Shakespeare Fellowship, remind, through your columns, all who may be interested or concerned, of the fact that Dr. Cairncross's discovery—if such it be—has long been forestalled. In 1930 Mrs. E. T. Clark published her *Shakespeare's Plays in the Order of Their Writing* and in 1933 Admiral H. H. Holland followed, with his *Shakespeare, Oxford, and Elizabethan Times*—both writers ascribing the first draft of Hamlet to 1583, for the reason that the play teems with clues to topical events occurring on, or near, that date.
>
> Dr. Cairncross, no doubt, was unfamiliar with our work, when he published his cleverly reasoned book, which, let me add, in addition to *Hamlet*, confirms closely, though unwittingly, other unorthodox dates put forward, years ago, by our group, including *Othello* (ca. 1588), and a revision of *Twelfth Night* in 1590.[66]

Cairncross responded by distancing himself from the Oxfordians, though not from their conclusions about dates. He rejected their methodologies even as their findings confirmed his:

> I should like to dissociate my investigations from his work and methods and from those of Mrs. Clark and Admiral Holland. The topical allusions, on which they rely, are notoriously unsure ground in Shakespearian chronology; and their use of interpolation and revision is so universal that it loses all value. The "memorial" theory, however, which I have followed, is now well established, thanks to the work of Dr. Greg, Mr. Crompton Rhodes, the late Dr. Smart, and Professor Peter Alexander; and, if properly applied, can be trusted to give results of scientific value.[67]

Cairncross rejected the methodology of dating the plays through topical allusions even though J. Dover Wilson had accepted it as valid two years earlier in *The Essential Shakespeare*. It is hard to avoid the supposition that it was not the methodology of citing topical allusions that so many scholars had objected to, but rather that so few of them supported the Stratfordian claim and so many supported the Oxfordian.

Allen responded, but the *Supplement* declined to publish his letter, saying that "it would lead to controversy." Allen then printed his response in the *Shakespeare Fellowship News-Letter*.

> The Oxford hypothesis, and the conclusions that follow thereupon, are not grounded, any more upon those of Dr. Cairncross himself, solely upon topical allusions; but are built up upon a mass of evidence, documentary and circumstantial, into which topicalities are rightly fitted. Admiral Holland's notes

---

[65] Percy Allen, "Another Bombshell for the Orthodox," *Shakespeare Pictorial*, Oct. 1936, p. 164.

[66] Percy Allen, "The Date of *Hamlet*" [letter], *Times Literary Supplement*, Jan. 2, 1937, p. 12.

[67] A. S. Cairncross, "*Hamlet* Problems" [letter], *Times Literary Supplement*, issue 1823 (Jan. 9, 1937): 28.

on *Hamlet*, in his *Shakespeare, Oxford, and Elizabethan Times*, provide forty-five topical clues to about 1583. Among these clues is the "impress of shipwrights" (for defense against Spain), which is used by Dr. Cairncross himself, and with the same implication! If, therefore, such topicalities are "notoriously unsure ground", may I ask why Dr. Cairncross uses a stream of them in his book (pp. 81, 82, 101-115)? And why he has entitled Chapter 8, "The Topical References"? and why he concludes this chapter thus:

In short, it seems impossible to account for the topical allusions . . . in *Hamlet* (Q.1), unless by referring the play and the piracy to a date not later than 1593.

It would, indeed, be more accurate to say "a date not later than 1589", because he argues that the so-called *Ur-Hamlet*, mentioned by Nashe in that year, was simply a "memory" version of Shakespeare's *Hamlet*.

Has Dr. Cairncross forgotten what he wrote?

May I ask all open-minded readers to consider which of our two conflicting hypotheses is the more rationally probable, granted that the date of *Hamlet* must now be put somewhere in the fifteen-eighties:

1) That the Shakespeare plays, including *Hamlet*, were the work of an English nobleman born in 1550, incidents from whose life-story (identity of 'Shakespeare" apart) are dramatized many times over in the plays.

2) That the plays are the work of a Stratford burgess, born in 1564, who came to London about 1588 at the age of 24 with such plays as *The Taming of the Shrew*, *The Merchant of Venice*, *Romeo and Juliet*, *Twelfth Night*, and others, in his pocket; and with *Othello* and *Hamlet* either already written or seething in his brain.

In conclusion, I would respectfully remind Dr. Cairncross that there is unity in truth; which explains why we have both arrived at approximately the same date for the writing of *Hamlet*.[68]

Four Lengthy Letter Exchanges in the Public Media

Public interest in the authorship question was keen enough to generate many letters to editors. Four lengthy exchanges are noted here.

1929 — *The Morning Post* — "Shakespeare and Richard III"

A letter to the editor of *The Morning Post* by Marjorie Bowen printed on August 30, 1929 sparked an exchange of sixteen others from more than a dozen senders stretching over three weeks. In a letter responding to a reader's interest in a recent book of hers, she noted that "A great deal of interest and controversy has arisen on the matter of the character of Richard III as I have portrayed it in my book *Dickson*"[69] After stating that her book was fiction and that she made no charges against Richard III for the murder of the two princes in the Tower, she asked *The Morning Post*'s readers what they thought about the charges. Though Bowen had broached a subject unrelated to the authorship issue, responders quickly swung it in the Oxfordian direction.

First to respond was Col. Ward, on September 3, who wrote that "recent searches of the Shakespeare Fellowship confirm the view that the charges against Richard III are

---

[68] Percy Allen, "Dr. Cairncross and *Hamlet*," *SF News-Letter*, no. 8 (March 1937): 9-10.
[69] Marjorie Bowen, "Shakespeare and Richard III: Little Evidence and 'A Mass of Legend and Calumny,'" *Morning Post*, Aug. 30, 1929, p. 7.

based on Tudor Government propaganda, and have no relation to actual fact."[70] He stated that *Richard III*—and indeed, all of Shakespeare's historical plays—were Tudor Government propaganda intended to infuse a warlike spirit into the people at a time when England was at war with Spain, a war that was "a Great War in precisely the same sense as the Napoleonic War and the recent World War deserve to be classed as Great Wars."[71] The same day *The Morning Post* ran an editorial, "The Way of History" highlighting Col. Ward's points and suggesting that "It may have been so: there was certainly never a better propagandist than William Shakespeare."[72]

Sir Charles Oman declared it "a delusion" that *Richard III* was "a piece of government propaganda designed to influence the mentality of the nation with reference to the great Spanish War,"[73] and Sir Mark Hunter cited reasons "to show that Shakespeare was not a political propagandist, directly or indirectly, in the pay of the Government."[74] Marjorie Bowen replied that "the most important point is not whether Shakespeare deliberately blackened Richard III or not, but the fact that his play set the seal of genius on a version of history that passed, for hundreds of years, for truth."[75] The editors then declared the correspondence closed, but did print a letter from Shakespeare Fellowship President Montagu W. Douglas a week later confirming the ruinous cost of the War with Spain"[76]

These letters showed the level of resistance to the first mention in the general media of the existence of a propaganda department headed by the earl of Oxford, of the use of the history plays for propaganda purposes and of the ruinous cost of the Anglo-Spanish War. (The first published notice of these facts had been in specialized literary and military journals.)

1933-1934 — *The Times Literary Supplement* — "These Late Eclipses"

This series of letters concerned Gloucester's reference to "these late eclipses" in *King Lear*. It was fought over so tenaciously because Oxfordians used it to establish such an early date for the play that it could not have been written by the man from Stratford. The series of letters began with one by G. B. Harrison on November 30, 1933, in which he claimed that the reference was to an eclipse on February 11, 1606, and thus helped date the play "after February and before Christmas, 1606, when it was performed at Court."[77] That date would be in line with Stratfordian authorship.

Capt. Ward responded a week later noting that "It would appear that the eclipses of 1606 were only visible in Central Europe, so they obviously cannot be the ones referred to by Gloucester. Total or annular eclipses of the sun—which are, of course, invariably preceded or followed a fortnight before or afterwards by a total or nearly total eclipse of the moon—are usually only visible in England about once a century."[78] He then noted that

---

[70] Col. Bernard R. Ward, "Shakespeare and Richard III: A Tudor Government Propaganda Department," *Morning Post*, Sept. 3, 1929, p. 5.

[71] See Chapter 7 for a discussion of how the Wards (father and son) uncovered the propagandistic nature of Shakespeare's history plays, the existence of a government propaganda department and the financial effect of the War with Spain.

[72] "The Way of History" [Editorial], *Morning Post*, Sept. 3, 1929, p. 10.

[73] Charles Oman, "Shakespeare and Richard III," *Morning Post*, Sept. 6, 1929, p. 6.

[74] Mark Hunter, "Shakespeare and Richard III: A Modern Parallel," *Morning Post*, Sept. 12, 1929, p. 9.

[75] Marjorie Bowen, "Shakespeare and Richard III," *Morning Post*, Sept. 14, 1929, p. 7.

[76] Col. Montagu W. Douglas, "First of England's Three Fights Against Famine," *Morning Post*, Sept. 19, 1929, p. 9.

[77] G. B. Harrison, "These Late Eclipses" [letter], *Times Literary Supplement*, Nov. 30, 1933, p. 856.

[78] Capt. Bernard M. Ward, "These Late Eclipses" [letter], *Times Literary Supplement*, Dec. 7, 1933, p. 878.

a complete eclipse of the sun visible in Scotland occurred March 6, 1598, which had led Adm. Holland, in *Shakespeare through Oxford Glasses*, to assign *Lear* to that year.

Harrison replied, claiming that Shakespeare wasn't referring to any specific eclipses. Ward then nailed him: "Dr. Harrison makes another extraordinary statement in his latest letter. He says 'Nowhere did I suggest that Shakespeare was referring to any particular eclipse.' And yet in his original letter he wrote: 'Even the most hardened believers in a Shakespeare aloof from his own times usually accept Gloucester's remark on "these late eclipses" as topical.' Now, Dr. Harrison cannot have it both ways. If Gloucester's remark is *topical*, then he must obviously be referring to some *particular* eclipses; but if there is no reference to any *particular* eclipse, then obviously the remark is not *topical*. I suggest that Dr. Harrison should decide what he really means."[79] He continued, "By all means, let us play the game of hunting for topical allusions in Shakespeare, but let us play it fairly. If we agree that Gloucester's allusion to 'these late eclipses of the sun and moon' is *topical*, let us try to find the most probable eclipses to which it refers."

Harrison countered, "I suspect that our fundamental difference lies in the notions that we severally associate with the word 'topical.'"[80] The editor then jumped in: "We cannot continue this correspondence."

This public exchange showed an Oxfordian scholar using common sense to establish the date of *King Lear*, while one of the most prominent Shakespearean scholars was unable to rise to the occasion by responding in a convincing manner.

1934 — *The Times Literary Supplement* — "The Mortal Moon Sonnet"

The exchange of letters over "these late eclipses" had hardly ended when another exchange erupted in the same publication, this one focused on the dating of Sonnet 107 and whether it referred to Queen Elizabeth's passing. Some of the biggest names in Shakespeare Studies wrote letters, including E. K. Chambers and G. B. Harrison. Oxfordians who entered the fray included Capt. Bernard Ward (thrice), Gerald Rendall (twice), and Percy Allen (once), all of whom showed how the date of 1603 supported the Oxfordian claim.

The series began with Chambers, who challenged Harrison's assertion that Sonnet 107 referred to an illness affecting Queen Elizabeth in 1596, finding "Dr. Harrison's evidence for any such illness quite illusory."[81]

Capt. Ward then jumped in with an additional reason for the 1603 date: Another line in the sonnet—"And peace proclaims olives of endless age"—coincides with the ending of England's War with Spain by the signing of a peace treaty later in 1603, after King James succeeded Queen Elizabeth. Percy Allen cited yet another reason for 1603: the use of the words "mortal," "moon," "peace", "olive" and "eclipse in both the sonnet and in similar ways in *Antony and Cleopatra*, which he also dated to around 1603:

Ant.	Alack, our terrene *moon*
	Is now *eclipsed* (III.xiii)
Caes.	The time of universal *peace* is near . . . the three nook'd world
	Shall bear the *olive* freely (IV.vi)
Cleo:	I have im*mortal* longing on me. (V.ii)

---

[79] Capt. Bernard M. Ward, "These Late Eclipses" [letter], *Times Literary Supplement*, Dec. 21, 1933, p. 909.

[80] G. B. Harrison, "These Late Eclipses" [letter], *Times Literary Supplement*, Jan. 4, 1934, p. 12.

[81] E. K. Chambers, "The 'Mortal Moon' Sonnet," *Times Literary Supplement*, Jan. 25, 1934, p. 60.

He explained further that "Cleopatra standing, topically, for Queen Elizabeth.... Cleopatra and the Dark Lady are identical ... In my judgment, both women are Elizabeth."[82]

Then, with the date of 1603 established for Sonnet 107, and "the one practically certain reference of 'The Mortal Moon' is to the death of Queen Elizabeth," Gerald H. Rendall connected all this to the subject of authorship. "So far the argument . . . is independent of considerations of authorship or destination. But its practical result is to rule out conjectural claims of William Herbert, Earl of Pembroke.... [O]n the other hand it falls into striking accord with the career of the Earl of Southampton . . . [who] in February, 1601, was committed to the Tower, under sentence of death, for participation in the treasonable plots of Essex. 'Forfeit to a confined doom' perfectly describes the situation, and read as a sonnet of welcome on his release, the references to Queen Elizabeth and to King James assume exactly the complexion we should expect."[83]

1938 — *The Northern Whig and Belfast Post*

This exchange, in a regional paper, took place between readers with track records of writing letters on related subjects. Debate centered around who wrote Shakespeare: Bacon, Oxford, or a group of writers. It is worth noting because of the depth of Oxfordian knowledge presented by one of the correspondents, W. R. R. It was kicked off by an article by Felix Holt giving four reasons for believing that Shakespeare was the man from Stratford. The first respondent, J. A. Hogg, who had been a master at Winchester College for thirty-two years, wrote in agreement, arguing that the plays and poems contain "lots of topical allusions and personal touches which stamp [them] as incontrovertibly the work of the incomparable Bard of Stratford."[84] He didn't cite any passages, though.

In his first letter, W. R. R. (actually a member of the Shakespeare Fellowship named W. Ringland Robinson), debunked Holt's statement that "no Shakespeare scholar" doubts Shakspere's authorship by reminding readers that they should not "ignore such great scholars as Greenwood, Allen, Slater, Douglas, Chambers, Harrison, Rendall, and Cairncross, who have all appeared inside the last quarter of a century" and had much to say about "this fascinating controversy."[85] Hogg responded with an attack on the Baconian idea.

Then came W.R.R.'s second letter. He turned quickly to J. Thomas Looney, who, he wrote, "is more than a scholar."

> His wonderful and original work, *"Shakespeare" Identified*, is the product of a man of learning, insight and originality. Since Mr. Looney wrote the name of Bacon has necessarily been removed from the front place in this "theory" and others have now taken his place.[86]

After discussing the group theory of authorship he came down on the side of authorship by a small set of aristocratic authors led by a supreme genius. He identified Edward de Vere, Earl of Oxford, as that genius, in part because "his life and behaviour had so many parallels with that of the Prince of Denmark that *Hamlet* might partly be taken as his autobiography," and in part because the publication of Shakespeare's plays stopped in 1604, the year of Oxford's death. He concluded by quoting several passages from

---

[82] Percy Allen, "The 'Mortal Moon' Sonnet" [letter], *Times Literary Supplement*, March 8, 1934, p. 162.

[83] Gerald Rendall, "The 'Mortal Moon' Sonnet" [letter], *Times Literary Supplement*, March 15, 1934, p. 194.

[84] J. A. Hogg, "The Bard of Stratford" [letter], *Northern Whig and Belfast Post*, Jan. 13, 1938, p. 3.

[85] W. R. R., "Bacon-Shakespeare Theory" [letter], *Northern Whig and Belfast Post*, Jan. 13, 1938, p. 3.

[86] W. R. R., "A Group of Authors?" [letter], *Northern Whig and Belfast Post*, Jan. 27, 1938, p. 9.

Gilbert Slater's *Seven Shakespeares*, including, "If I could, I would now present the case against the Oxfordian theory, but I cannot. To the best of my knowledge no reply to the Oxfordians has been published. Nor can I make out any substantial adverse case myself."[87]

Another Exchange: *John O'London's Weekly*, 1939

An interesting series of articles about Shakespearean authorship ran in *John O'London's Weekly* between January and March 1939. The number of letters in response to the articles showed that interest in the authorship issue remained high even as tensions between England and Germany increased.

The editors introduced the discussion by noting the key questions that had generated the authorship mystery:

> Who was William Shakespeare?
>
> In all literary history no other problem has attracted so much controversy, or given rise to so many rival theories. Was he, as most people believe, the commoner of Stratford? If so, how did he acquire his vast knowledge of the arts, of statecraft, of history, of foreign lands, of court life, of sport? Was he, on the other hand, a man of noble birth, of university training, widely travelled, and naturally experienced in many walks of life? If so, how are we to reconcile these things with a mass of documentary evidence and a stubborn tradition that supports the Stratford case?[88]

They turned first to Professor P. S. Porohovshikov, a former High Court Judge in Russia, now Professor of History at Oglethorpe University in Georgia in the United States. In the first of two articles, Porohovshikov demonstrated the weakness of the case for William Shakspere and in the second he made the claim for authorship by the Earl of Rutland. Early in his first article he described a situation Oxfordians knew all too well.

> The attitude of orthodox writers towards heretics and sceptics is as firm as a rock. They do not examine heretic arguments; as a rule they simply brand them as arrogance, ignorance and mid-summer madness.

After echoing the editor's recognition of the vast gulf between the facts known of Shakspere's life and the sophisticated and learned impression of the author inferred from the plays and poems, Porohovshikov brought an interesting piece of information to light for the first time.

> In 1595 and 1596, four anonymous Latin comedies, *Laelia*, *Silvanus*, *Hispanus* and *Machiavellus*, were performed by undergraduate students at Cambridge University. These four comedies contain characters, images, and whole scenes which in later years reappeared in *The Comedy of Errors*, *Richard III*, *Two Gentlemen of Verona*, *Midsummer Night's Dream*, *The Merchant of Venice*, *Twelfth Night*, *As You Like It*, *Hamlet*, and *Macbeth*. (661)

Porohovshikov explained this discovery by noting that the Earl of Rutland was a student at Cambridge at the time, and proposed that he wrote these plays originally in Latin and later turned them into the plays we know as Shakespeare's. He also noted that the lists of students attending the university at the same time as Rutland included two named Rosencrantz and Guildenstern.

---

[87] Gilbert Slater, quoted in W. R. R., "A Group of Authors?" [letter], *Northern Whig and Belfast Post*, Jan. 27, 1938, p. 9.

[88] P. S. Porohovshikov, "Who Was Shakespeare?" *John O'London's Weekly*, Jan. 27, 1939, p. 657.

JOHN O'LONDON'S WEEKLY

Vol. XL   No. 1,033   FRIDAY, JANUARY 27, 1939   Two Pence
[Registered at G.P.O. as a Newspaper and for the Canadian Post.   Entered as Second-class Matter at the Post Office at New York, N.Y., under the Act of March 3rd, 1879.]

The following week Professor W. P. Barrett provided the traditional view of Shakespearean authorship, in part by making a statement that he must have known was false: that there is "direct personal evidence" that the man from Stratford was the author from "the testimony of responsible witnesses who knew him and lived with him."[89]

Percy Allen then entered the fray (why are we not surprised?) with a response to Porohov-shikov and Barrett. After pointing out holes in the traditional case, he assessed the status of the Stratfordian and Oxfordian theories.

Who Was Shakespeare?
A NEW EXAMINATION OF THE PROBLEM OF THE PLAYS
By P. S. POROHOVSHIKOV

WHO was William Shakespeare? In all literary history no other problem has attracted so much controversy, or given rise to so many rival theories. Was he, as most people believe, the commoner of Stratford? If so, how did he acquire his vast knowledge of the arts, of statecraft, of history, of foreign lands, of court life, of sport? Was he, on the other hand, a man of noble birth, of university training, widely travelled and naturally experienced in many walks of life? If so, how are we to reconcile these things with a mass of documentary evidence and a stubborn oral tradition that support the Stratford case?

The riddle may never be solved, but it will never lose its fascination on that account. We have therefore undertaken to publish a new examination of the problem by one who has devoted many years of study to it. Mr. Porohovshikov, formerly a High Court Judge in Russia, is now Professor of History in Oglethorpe University, Georgia, U.S.A. In developing his theory that the author of the plays was Roger Manners, Earl of Rutland,

he has studied all the available evidence in the British Museum and in the Library of Congress, Washington, and has consulted many documents preserved at Belvoir Castle (the home of the Duke of Rutland), Lambeth Palace, the Bodleian Library at Oxford, and the archives of Padua University.

In fairness to Professor Porohovshikov it should be stated that we have asked him to compress his case, which runs to 100,000 words, into two short articles. The first appears below and the second will appear next week. To enable our readers to judge for themselves the validity of his arguments we have arranged, with his consent, to publish a third article examining his conclusions from the orthodox point of view. This will be written by Dr. W. P. Barrett, Lecturer in English at the University of London, who is an authority on Elizabethan dramatic literature. This third article, besides being an answer to Professor Porohovshikov, may be regarded also as a general answer to all those who support the claims of Bacon, the Earl of Oxford, and others.—ED.

THE tradition that William Shakspere of Stratford was the author of Shakespeare's plays has not to-day the sacrosanct inviolability it had a century ago. Scholarly researches have discovered no fewer than nine possible contributors to the First Folio of 1623.

The following notes will place before the reader the evidence for one of these possible Shakespeares. It happens to concern the least known of the heresies, yet it covers the case so simply and so completely that it seems to me to be the final solution of "the greatest literary problem of our time." Readers of JOHN O' LONDON'S WEEKLY, however, must judge that for themselves.

*   *   *

IT must be understood from the outset that the two poems, *Venus and Adonis* and *Lucrece*, and the comedy *Love's Labour's Lost*, are outside this discussion. Whoever wrote them, I

maintain that it was not the author of *Hamlet*. As to the *Sonnets*, some of them were probably written by the poet, others probably not. This is all that can be said about them.

THE more we study the works of a great philosopher or a great poet, the better we understand the man and his writings. And the more Shakespeare is read, the less he is understood.

"Shakespeare's life is a fine mystery," wrote Dickens. "I cannot reconcile his life with his works," said Emerson. "The whole matter is a great Perhaps," asserted George Saintsbury. Every new commentator discovers new problems and new enigmas. Other great poets are the torch-bearers of humanity. Why should Shakespeare, the greatest of all, confuse us with mist and mysteries?

The orthodox, traditional, "Stratfordian" case is finished. It will no longer bear examination, whether from chronological, topical, or other view-points. It no longer fits either the known facts, or the obvious inferences to be drawn therefrom. It is fast being rejected throughout the English-speaking world.

The case for Oxford, as we can now present it, is substantially complete. It has never been answered, and is, in my judgment, unanswerable.[90]

In his view,

---

[89] W. P. Barrett, "Who Was Shakespeare? III: The Traditional View," *John O'London's Weekly*, Feb. 10, 1939, p. 733.

[90] Percy Allen, "Who Was Shakespeare?" *John O'London's Weekly*, Feb. 10, 1939, p. 821.

Many of the plays—e.g. *Hamlet* and *Twelfth Night*, in which we can now identify most of the characters—are intimate dramatizations of episodes in the lives of Oxford and his circle at court; and contain so long a stream of unmistakable allusions to events of the fifteen-seventies and 'eighties, that the orthodox case falls on chronology and topicality, alone. . . . The *Sonnets*, equally, "shout" Lord Oxford.

After a half-dozen readers provided their thoughts, Barrett responded to Allen, dismissing the Oxfordian argument by saying that if it had never been answered by academia, "it must surely be because no one has found it worth answering."[91]

Enter William Kent

William Kent, a future vice-president of the Shakespeare Fellowship, responded to Barrett's statement, showing himself to be a man of rare courage. Five years earlier, in 1934, he had published a book, *London for Shakespeare Lovers*, intended to serve as a guide for those wanting to visit places in London associated with Shakespeare, who he thought was the man from Stratford. Later he was exposed to the Oxfordian claim. His response to Barrett explained what happened next. "Having written a book entitled *London for Shakespeare Lovers* on orthodox assumptions, I was unwilling to be convinced of my errors, but eventually I had to yield. I could hold out no more."[92] He rewrote his book from the Oxfordian point of view and reissued it, with other material, as *London Worthies*. He congratulated Barrett on having shown "more courage than many other professors [by] entering the lists against the sceptics." But he feared "that he has only exposed the weakness of the Stratfordian faith," and suggested that perhaps Barrett should follow his example.

London Worthies was published about the same time that Kent's letter appeared in *John O'London's Weekly*. A month later he commented elsewhere that,

It is significant too, that so popular a periodical as *John O'London's Weekly* should arrange a literary duel between a Stratfordian believer and a denier of the faith. . . . My friend Mr. Percy Allen vainly challenges them. I also throw down the glove to anybody who chooses to debate on the issue: "Is it now reasonable to believe that the Stratford actor wrote the Shakespeare plays?" I have little expectation of

John O'London's Weekly, 1939		
Jan. 27, 1939	Porohovshikov, P.S.,	"Who Was Shakespeare? I: A New Examination"
Feb. 3, 1939	Porohovshikov, P. S.,	"Who Was Shakespeare? II: The Case for the Earl of Rutland"
Feb. 10, 1939	Barrett, W. P.	"Who Was Shakespeare? III: The Traditional View"
Feb. 10, 1939	Habgood, Francis E. C.	"Who Was Shakespeare?" [letter]
Feb. 24, 1939	Allen, Percy	"Who Was Shakespeare?" [letter]
	Johnson, Edward D.	"The Notes in the First Folio [letter]
	Theobald, Bertram G.	"Unreliable Witness" [letter]
	Habgood, Francis E. C.	"Shakespeare's Signature" [letter]
	Hauger, E. G.	"Shakespeare and Italy" [letter]
	Megroz, R. L.	"Loosely Spelt Proper Names" [letter]
	Barrett, W. P.	"Who Was Shakespeare?" [Reply to letters]
Mar. 10, 1939	Kent, William	"Who Was Shakespeare?" [letter]
	Barrett, W. P.	"Who Was Shakespeare?" [Reply to Kent]

[91] W. P. Barrett, "Who Was Shakespeare?" [letter], *John O'London's Weekly*, Feb. 21, 1939, p. 822.
[92] William Kent, "Who Was Shakespeare?" [letter], *John O'London's Weekly*, March 10, 1939, p. 888.

any response. The Stratfordians are so reluctant to enter the war they maintain they can so easily win; so mercifully reticent about publishing the book that must bomb us out of existence![93]

Kent's first foray into the authorship mine field had been in April 1935, in the *Freethinker,* responding to two recent articles that contained derisive references to authorship doubters. "Why should a journal, redhot in leftwing religious heterodoxy, in so facile a manner, dispose of heretics in another department? . . . It is surprising in contributors to the *Freethinker* whom, one would have thought, had learned long ago that it is the heretic who digs most deeply into a subject."[94]

In July 1939, a few months after his letter in *John O'London's Weekly,* Kent responded to G. B. Harrison's dismissal of authorship skeptics with an open letter printed in the *Shakespeare Fellowship News-Letter.* After expressing his "amazement at your lack of frankness on the authorship question," he took Harrison to task for repeatedly changing the spelling of the name of the man from Stratford. "Why, sir, do you alter it? You give 'William Shakespeare' again at the end, whereas Chambers has 'Shakspeare.' You are not very

---

William Kent

Born: 1884. Died: 1963.

Age when *"Shakespeare" Identified* was published: 36

Vice President, Shakespeare Fellowship, 1946-1953

Editor, *Shakespeare Fellowship News-Letter,* 1947-1953

Began adult life with only an elementary school education; worked in the law department of the London County Council for many years. Serving as a guide for parties visiting famous streets in London in his spare time led eventually to his many books about London, including *London for Everyone,* which became a best-seller.

Kent's magnificent library of more than 5,000 volumes, many of them irreplaceable, was destroyed by German bombing during the Second World War.

Books
1931/1938   *London for Everyman*
1934   *London for Shakespeare Lovers*
1937   *Encyclopedia of London*
1938   *Testament of a Victorian Youth*
1939   *London Worthies*
1947/1957   *Edward de Vere, the Seventeenth Earl of Oxford: The Real Shakespeare*

Articles
1935   "A Plea for Shakespearean Freethinking," *Freethinke*r, vol. 55/17: 268-69
1939   "Who Was Shakespeare?" [letter], *John O'London's Weekly,* Mar. 10, p. 888.
1939   "An Open Letter to Dr. G. B. Harrison," *Sh. Fellowship News-Letter,* No. 15 (July): 4-7.
1945   "An American Myth Maker," *Shakespeare Fellowship Newsletter,* Nov., pp. 5-6.
1949   "My War With the Professors" [unpublished; the MSS is in the Shakespearean
             Authorship Trust archives at Brunel University]
. . . and a dozen other Oxfordian publications.

---

[93] William Kent, "Mr. William Kent's New Book," *SF News-Letter,* no. 14 (April 1939), p. 8.
[94] William Kent, "A Plea for Shakespearean Freethinking," *Freethinker,* vol. 55/17 (April 28, 1935): 268.

candid with your readers."[95] He continued with, "I am glad, however, you tell us that the allusions to Shakespeare 'give no indication of what the man himself was like.' This may give some readers to pause and think. It is mighty strange that the great writer was so unimpressive a personality that nobody seems to have kept a letter he wrote, nor penned a literary sketch of him,"

Harrison replied with a letter to Kent that did not address any of the points he had raised, stating only that "If you are not convinced that William Shakespeare of Stratford wrote the plays attributed to him, I do not think there is much point in starting a controversy" (7).

A Roundup from the English Press

The following selection of articles and other pieces reflect public interest in the Shakespeare authorship question, usually the Oxfordian claim, in the British press from 1930 through 1945. Most are from rather unusual publications.

Grudging Acceptance of Topical Allusions by G. B. Harrison, 1930

Harrison had repeatedly clashed with Percy Allen over a number of issues, including the topicality of Shakespeare's plays. Allen, of course, found topical allusions throughout the plays and Harrison mostly denied their existence. Then, at the end of 1930, Harrison wrote two articles for *The Times Literary Supplement* addressing "Shakespeare's Topical Significances," the first dealing with those in *King John* and the second with those alluding to the Earl of Essex. In them Harrison tried to have it both ways. Although he mostly denied "topical allusions" he accepted what he called "topical significances," which, he argued, were obvious to Shakespeare's audiences but whose meaning was hidden from modern readers.

> There is such constant contention among Shakespearian critics between those who "see things" and those who do not that anyone who ventures on an exposition of contemporary allusions in the plays takes great risks. . . . Yet Shakespeare was interested in his fellow creatures; he can scarcely have avoided all comment upon the events of his time; and indeed as soon as one sees the plays against the background of their own times it becomes clear at once that they were full of special meaning to their original audiences. When the story gave him a chance of creating a situation or a speech full of significance to his audience, Shakespeare seldom neglected it; but because his sense of dramatic fitness was so acute the speech remains apt long after the significance has been lost. Direct topical allusions are not very common in Shakespeare, but topical significances abound.[96]

It appeared that Harrison was responding to the interest in topical allusions generated by Percy Allen's many books and articles on the subject by grudgingly and tacitly accepting, to a limited degree, Allen's case. In the first article Harrison's examples are very general. "At all times those plays are most popular which have some special meaning for their first audiences. . . . Shakespeare also lived through a great war, and for those who will make the effort to hear he has recorded, perhaps unconsciously, its phases and its moods."

---

[95] William Kent, "Open Letter to Harrison," *SF News-Letter*, no. 15 (July 1939): 4.
[96] G. B. Harrison, "Shakespeare's Topical Significances I: *King John*," *Times Literary Supplement*, Nov. 13, 1930, p. 939.

In the second article Harrison provided a specific and important example, that of the 1596 Cadiz voyage, after which "Essex had claimed the ransoms of his prisoners for himself when the Queen demanded them. The Queen appealed to old Lord Burghley; but when he suggested that Essex should be heard she lost her temper with the old man, called him a miscreant and a coward, and accused him of regarding the Earl for fear or favour more than herself. Essex was equally angry." Harrison then cited the scene in *1 Henry IV*, in which Henry and Hotspur argue over prisoners, a scene that may have "reminded the audience of the similar dispute between Essex and Queen Elizabeth a year before."[97]

In a second example Harrison noted similarities between Achilles sulking in his tent in *Troilus and Cressida* and Essex absenting himself from Court and Parliament, a withdrawal "that was causing so much comment that men came almost to be divided into parties pro- and anti-Essex." He concluded that "The reasonable inference is that *Troilus and Cressida*, in its present form, was performed privately before an anti-Essex audience, either in the summer of 1598, or else about two years later when Essex and his followers were brewing treason."

Although Harrison would continue to clash with Oxfordians, he would no longer dismiss topical references as mere imaginings.

Percy Allen Defends the Oxfordian Claim, 1931

In a review of a biography of Thomas Heywood, A. P. Nicholson deviated from the main purpose of the piece to attack the Oxfordian idea.

> There would be an easier case to be made out in favour of somebody else writing [Heywood's] plays than there ever was in the case of Shakespeare. . . . [W]hy should there not have been lurking in Elizabeth's Court a master craftsman, some Edgar Wallace of his day, who dictated to nimble scribes not only Shakespeare's plays but most of the dramatic literature of the period? . . . Perhaps it is not too late to commend this wholesale treatment to the amusing people who are now concentrating on Edward de Vere, 17th Earl of Oxford, as the real Shakespeare.[98]

Nicholson apparently hadn't learned that one mocks the Oxfordian claim at one's peril if Percy Allen is around. Sure enough, Allen noticed and responded a week later. "If . . . after duly reading and pondering that evidence, [Nicholson] still finds it merely amusing, in the sense of ridiculous, the fault, I suggest to him, must lie with his own want of penetration, and his complete failure to perceive the cogency of innumerable inferences, which, argued in a Court of Justice, would, as we believe, speedily convince any competent judge or intelligent jury."[99]

Percy Allen Writes for Theater Professionals in *Theatre and Stage*, 1934

Here Allen showed how understanding who the author really was could help directors, actors, costume designers, and other theater professionals in their work. He explained that Shakespeare's works

> teem throughout with topical allusions, [which] are, in most instances, clearly recognizable dramatization of events and personalities well known at the courts

---

[97] G. B. Harrison, "Shakespeare's Topical Significances II: The Earl of Essex," *Times Literary Supplement*, Nov. 20, 1930, p. 974.
[98] A. P. Nicholson, "A Good Playwright," *Saturday Review*, Sept. 5, 1931, pp. 303-04.
[99] Percy Allen, "The Shakespeare-Oxford Problem," *Saturday Review*, Sept. 12, 1931, p. 327.

of Western Europe.... An age that did not know lecture-halls, newspapers, or any well-protected right of free speech, turned naturally to that mirror of its time, the stage, as the one available public debating platform of the day. Dangerous topicalities of course, had to be cunningly introduced; and the Elizabethan dramatists, Shakespeare among them, developed great skill at weaving contemporary allusions into a framework provided by well-known older plays, stories, sagas, or folk-tales, which were selected because their outlines, or plots, fitted conveniently in with the Elizabethan story that the playwright desires secretly to tell.[100]

All this matters to producers and actors, he continued, "since it may greatly assist all concerned in the stage-production of a Shakespearean play to know the actual historic incidents that a particular piece records, together with the historic identities of its principal characters. Mr. Tyrone Guthrie, for example, would not, I presume, have dressed his production of *Twelfth Night* in costumes of Charles I's time had he understood that the comedy of Illyria dramatizes the marriage negotiations between Queen Elizabeth (Olivia) and the Duke of Alençon (Orsino), along with other incidents that took place at the Court of Whitehall, *circa* 1579-80—some years before Charles I was born! *Twelfth Night*, set in the Stuart period, becomes, ipso facto, almost meaningless."

After citing other examples, Allen closed: "Surely a comprehension of some of these deeply meaningful topicalities in Shakespearean drama, would greatly enlighten producers and actors alike, besides adding enormously to their potential interest in our national poet."

Hugh Kingsmill on Other Shakespeare Scholars, 1933

It's satisfying to see Stratfordian scholars criticize each other for a change. Here is Hugh Kingsmill criticizing Professor Stoll, who was to write the article in *The Saturday Review* critical of Charles Wisner Barrell and J. Thomas Looney in 1940 (see Chapter 16).

> Professor Stoll . . . has no understanding at all of the relation between an imaginative writer and his work, in general, and the relation between Shakespeare and his work, in particular. He does not, like the body-snatchers, say that some one else wrote Shakespeare, but he argues the equally foolish, though more complex, theory that Shakespeare wrote without any appreciation of the interest and value of his own work.

> Being unable to grasp the elementary truth that a great poet alternates between imaginative detachment and intense personal experience, Professor Stoll is left with a lyrical robot on his hands.[101]

Queen Elizabeth giving audience to Shakespeare

The View from Westminster, December 1934

The Christmas card depicting Queen Elizabeth giving audience to Shakespeare on her Royal Barge, sent by H.R.H., The Prince of Wales, shows just how little traction the Oxfordian claim had made in official circles

---

[100] Percy Allen, "Topicalities in Shakespeare," *Theatre and Stage*, April 1934, p. 585.
[101] Hugh Kingsmill, "Shakespeare Criticism," *English Review*, June 1933, pp. 692-94.

after fourteen years.[102]

Ernest Allen Makes the Case and Takes on Critics, 1936

Ernest Allen reviewed the case for the three major claimants for Shakespeare's crown—Shakspere, Bacon and Oxford—in *The Shakespeare Pictorial*, highlighting the weaknesses in the case for the first two before turning to reasons supporting the Oxfordian claim.

> I note again in passing that neither orthodox or Baconians will admit for a moment any validity in our claim. We have examined and answered theirs, but they have never examined or answered ours and I think the simple reason in both cases is that they dare not. It seems to be just a case of fear, the facts are awkward and too many reputations might go by the board. No doubt they are wise, for so strong is the case for Lord Oxford that any attempt even to shake it must inevitably fail.
>
> The enormous strength of the case for Edward de Vere lies in the simple truth that the theory of his authorship agrees in every single date and detail, both as regards the interior evidence of the works and the exterior evidence of the facts, with all the circumstances surrounding Shakespeare over the full period of about fifty years. Under these circumstances it seems impossible that it can be untrue.[103]

T. M. Aitken Responds to *The British Weekly*, 1938

Fellowship member T. M. Aitken presented aspects of the Oxfordian case and the idea of group authorship to readers of *The British Weekly* in response to its review of R. Macdonald Lucas's book making the case for the Earl of Derby, *Shakespeare's Vital Secret*.

> You are to be congratulated on publishing a favourable review of Mr. Lucas's book, *Shakespeare's Vital Secret*, as it is an unfortunate fact that many of the best-known journals have been boycotting anti-Stratfordian writers of any kind for quite a long time, with the result that several scholarly books on one of the most interesting and important subjects in all literature have passed almost unnoticed.
>
> There is . . . a growing body of opinion that the works are not by any one individual but by a group of aristocratic authors of whom one at least was a supreme genius. . . . Lord Oxford was the true genius of the group, an older man and one whose life and behaviour have so many parallels with that of the Prince of Denmark, that *Hamlet* might partly be taken as his autobiography?[104]

Oxford as Shakespeare in *The News Chronicle*, 1939.

Robert Lynd's "Saturday Essay" is accompanied by a picture in which Longfellow looks like Longfellow, Dickens looks like Dickens, but Shakespeare looks suspiciously like the Ashbourne portrait of Edward de Vere.[105]

---

[102] A. D. McCormick, "The Prince of Wales Christmas Card," *Shakespeare Pictorial*, Dec. 1934, p. 190.

[103] Ernest Allen, "Claimants to 'Shakespeare' Authorship," *Shakespeare Pictorial*, July 1936, p. 116.

[104] T. M. Aitken, "A New Shakespeare Candidate" [letter], *British Weekly*, Jan. 20, 1938, p. 314.

[105] Robert Lynd, "Saturday Essay," *News Chronicle*, Jan. 14, 1939, p. 7. Technical analysis of the image showed that the picture of Edward de Vere's head had been cut and pasted over the original image.

E. Kellett and Public Opinion, *The News Chronicle*, 1939

This letter to *The News Chronicle* protested against the paper's blithe dismissal of the Oxfordian thesis. "It is too late in the day to ignore the 'anti-Stratfordian theories.' Right or wrong, they are not unreasonable, and are supported by very plausible arguments, if also by some very reckless ones. . . . They might at least be mentioned and even the most extravagant of their advocates have at least drawn attention to facts which have been too often neglected."[106]

Common-sensical View in the *Blackheath Local Guide and District Advertiser*, 1940

Even with the War underway, the local newspaper in Blackheath, a neighborhood in southeast London, called for an objective examination of the authorship question in an editorial titled "A Humble Petition."

> It is supposed to be a British habit to give a fair hearing to every case. Unfortunately, this is not always so: and a notable exception is to be seen in the treatment accorded to those who doubt the "Stratfordian" authorship of the Shakespeare plays. Rarely, indeed, are they argued with; it is considered sufficient to dismiss them as maniacs, whom it is a kindness to allow to live at large.
>
> The fact is that, apart from the "cranks," always to be found in a large company of people, they are eminently reasonable. They may be right or wrong, but they have much to say for themselves, and they are not to be thrust aside with a sneer.[107]

The Oxfordian Movement and the *Christian Science Monitor*

Special note must be made of *The Christian Science Monitor*, which ran more substantive coverage of the Oxfordian idea than any other publication from 1928 through the end of the 1930s—interest almost certainly due to Percy Allen's serving as its drama critic. Although the *Monitor's* thirty-three articles over the twelve-year period never exceeded five in a year, they kept the issue before readers without overwhelming them. Its coverage can serve as a barometer of interest in the issue.

One important article was Percy Allen's "The de Vere-Shakespeare Controversy Today" on October 18, 1930. Allen noted that *"Shakespeare" Identified* "met with the fate usual to pioneer works. It was ignored, or derided, by the orthodox school; but it has never yet been *answered*; and its ruthless logic has won for it, from that day to this, an increasing flow of approval and support."[108] After a brief review of the most important findings of the Oxfordian movement, he concluded:

> [Oxfordian scholars] have brought . . . the authentic man to light.
>
> [We] have arrived by wholly different processes, at identical conclusions; for Mr. Looney worked upon a general survey of evidence, the Wards by documentary research, Captain Holland by topical allusion, Canon Rendall "by communion with a living personality, the soul of Hamlet shaped upon experiences of de Vere," and myself by the comparative methods of literary parallel and analysis.

---

[106] E. E. Kellett, "Shakespeare" [letter], *News Chronicle*, Jan. 18, 1939, p. 4.

[107] *Blackheath Local Guide and District Advertiser*, "A Humble Petition," April 6, 1940, p. 14. This newspaper has never been indexed or included in databases. I learned of it only because a copy of the page with the editorial was among J. Thomas Looney's papers discovered in 2019.

[108] Percy Allen, "The de Vere-Shakespeare Controversy Today," *Christian Science Monitor*, Oct. 18, 1930, p. 18.

"And how," he asked, "do the academic authorities greet this momentous discovery, which involves re-editing afresh the whole of 'Shakespeare'?" "Their position was difficult and delicate, because, while as accredited trustees of the Shakespearean tradition, it is their duty searchingly to examine every new interpretation, at the same time they are almost bound to support reputations that have been built upon Stratfordian orthodoxy— a fundamental position which, by its very nature, has precluded them from admitting even the existence of any 'Shakespeare mystery.'" There is the core of the problem: those with the sworn academic duty to examine literary matters in an academic—an objective— manner, have the most to lose by doing so. The defendants are also the judges, a setup not conducive to unbiased examinations and judgments.

> Modern scholarship . . . almost without exception unimaginative, has consistently neglected to correlate Shakespeare with the history of his time, has *burked* most of his topical allusions, and has wholly failed to realize that this mighty drama is largely symbolic: nor have scholars, in general, envisaged the innate tendency of Elizabethans to work underground, and to take delight in concealing meaning within meaning, and play within play.
>
> Naturally enough, then, academic Shakespeareans, confronted with what we assert to be discoveries of first-rate literary import and importance, have, for the most part, utterly rejected our conclusions, meeting them not with argument but with silence, or evasion, or ridicule, or comprehensive denial—attitudes which, though serviceable to themselves, it may be, for awhile, can only make their position more difficult when what we believe, of course, must be the inevitable admissions that are, at last, to be made. This is because it is evident that one admission must, logically demand the next; and so on, until by unescapable sequence, the complete surrender is brought about.
>
> The orthodox position, however, though, as we maintain, intellectually untenable, remains still immensely strong. With all the prestige of the great universities, and the enormous power of the press almost solidly behind them, many believe that the strongholds of orthodoxy are impregnable. Personally, I dissent from that view, feeling sure that every confirmatory inference, and every individual convert—and both these are appearing very fast—hasten the day when the truth of this most strange and arresting literary discovery will be more and more widely admitted.

Shortly afterward, on October 18, 1930, the paper ran a long letter from Reuben Pogson offering the thought that perhaps academia had not examined the Oxfordian claim because it had examined other claims in the past and found them flawed. Percy Allen, glad perhaps for another opportunity to address the Oxfordian claim, replied, "While the Stratfordians continue thus to attack us with uninformed complacencies and airy generalities of this irrelevant sort, we are quietly amassing and piecing together into an ordered whole a thousand facts and inferences which already are fast gaining converts and, as we firmly believe, will finally determine this difficult, though intensely interesting, problem. Already the circumstantial evidence is unanswerable."[109]

Allen may have been right, that the day was fast approaching when academia could no longer sweep the authorship issue under the rug. Even stronger evidence in favor of the Oxfordian claim was to come from Oxfordian scholars in the United States in the first half of the 1940s. But for Allen and the Oxfordian movement in England, it would be too

---

[109] Percy Allen, "The de Vere-Shakespeare Controversy" [letter], *Christian Science Monitor*, Feb. 9, 1931, p. 14.

little too late, as the Second World War swept aside the momentum of the Oxfordian movement and so much else in British intellectual life. England had no choice but to devote its entire energies into protecting itself and combatting the Nazi menace and the threat from imperial Japan for almost six years (see Chapter 15).

The Christian Science Monitor
Coverage of the Authorship Question, 1920-1939

1920, May 18	-----.	"Is Shakespeare Identified?
1923, May 19	Percy Allen	"Hamlet's Identity with an Elizabethan" [review of *"Shakespeare" Identified*]
1928, June 15	Percy Allen	"With Hamlet in Hackney" [review of Ward's *Seventeenth Earl*]
1928, July 3	Percy Allen	"Versatile Elizabethan" [review of Ward's *Seventeenth Earl*]
1928, Aug. 18	Percy Allen	"Musings Over the Shakespearean First Folio"
1928, Aug. 23	C. F. A.	"Elizabethan Borrowers" [review of Allen's *Borrowers*]
1929, May 19	-----.	"Shakespeare and Chapman as Popular Dramatists" [review of Allen's *Topical*]
1929, Dec. 27	Percy Allen	"How Shakespeare Wrote *King Lear*"
1930, July 19	-----.	"De Vere as Shakespeare" [reviews of Rendall's *Shakespeare's Sonnets* and Allen's *Case*]
1930, Oct. 18	Percy Allen	"The de Vere-Shakespeare Controversy Today"
1931, Feb. 28	Percy Allen	"The Oxford Theory Again" [review of Clark's *Hidden Allusions*]
1931, April 25	C. F. A.	"The Oxford Theory" [review of Allen's *Case Corroborated*]
1932, June 9	Percy Allen	"As to Shakespearean Authorship" [reviews of Slater's *Seven Shakespeares* and Douglas's *Earl of Oxford as "Shakespeare"*]
1932, May 17	J. B. D.	"Why There is a Shakespeare Problem?"
1932, May 21	Percy Allen	"For the Stratfordians"
1932, Oct. 1	Percy Allen	"Shakespeare in the East"
1933, April 22	Percy Allen	"New Shakespearean Books" [review of Clark's *Satirical Comedy*]
1933, June 17	Hubert Holland	"Oxfordian Rejoinder" [review of the Allens' *Lord Oxford and Shakespeare: A Reply to John Drinkwater*]
1933, Aug. 19	-----.	"Shakespeare and Politics" [review of Allen's *French History*]
1934, June 13	F. B.	"Brief for the Oxfordians" [review of Allen's *Anne Cecil, Elizabeth & Oxford*]
1934, Oct. 3	Percy Allen	"Shakespearean Topicalities" [review of Holland's *Elizabethan Times*]
1935, Dec. 4	Percy Allen	"Hamlet, Topically" [review of Wilson's *What Happens in Hamlet*]
1939, Dec. 21	Herbert Nichols	"Wonders of Research: Three Portraits of Shakespeare X-rayed Seeing Through Paint"

The Oxfordian Movement in the British Isles During the Second World War

All Major Developments in Place by the End of the 1930s

By mid-1939, all major aspects of the Oxfordian claim and reactions to it were in place. The main lines of evidence on which it was based—the personal and topical allusions in the plays, and the close correspondences of theme and phrasing between Edward de Vere's early poems and Shakespeare's mature works—had been documented. Oxfordian scholars had shown that de Vere had had the experiences that Shakespeare would have needed to acquire the knowledge of literature, Italy and the law, politics and diplomacy and courtly pursuits exhibited in the plays. That many of them had originated as court entertainments as early as the 1570s (organized by de Vere), and that he had been at the that center of the intellectual and literary life of his time, with known connections to virtually all important writers of the Elizabethan age, had been established.

Stratfordians had solidified their practice of ignoring or dismissing Oxfordian findings whenever possible, and, when cornered, of attacking Oxfordians, often in intellectually dishonest ways. The media had largely followed the lead of academia, and only occasionally ran items presenting the Oxfordian point of view. Many of those items were reviews of Oxfordian books and the letters written in response to them. As the output of Oxfordian books decrease during the later 1930s, so too did media coverage of the Oxfordian claim.

Effects of the Second World War on Oxfordian Activities

By the summer of 1939 it was widely recognized in England that war with Germany was inevitable. A notice enclosed with the July 1939 issue of the Fellowship's *News-Letter* indicated that its editor, Capt. Bernard M. Ward (Reserve Officer, K. D. Gds), who was forty-six at the time, would soon be called up for active duties. He went on to serve with the Royal Observer Corps for five and a half years, and was present at the D-Day invasion of Normandy, before mustering out early in 1945. The notice also said that Percy Allen would take on the duties of Hon. Secretary until the next annual general meeting.[1] However, as Eva Turner Clark later related, events "moved with great rapidity since the July *News-Letter* was issued and all of England's men and women have been mobilized for war emergencies. In view of this stern fact, Mr. Allen has issued the following statement: 'With the concurrence of our President, it has been decided, regretfully, that the activities of the Shakespeare Fellowship be suspended until further notice. . . . It is intended to

---

[1] The notice was not in the body of the July *News-Letter*, but was on an insert, no copy of which has survived. It is known because Eva Turner Clark referred to it in the first issue of the *News-Letter* of the American branch of the Shakespeare Fellowship.

continue publication of the *News-Letter*, delivery of lectures, etc., as soon as international circumstances permit.'"[2]

Shakespeare Fellowship Activities

The Shakespeare Fellowship's annual general meetings and dinners were suspended. The only event known to have been held after the annual dinner in May 1939 was a meeting on March 2, 1940. At that event the Fellowship issued a hearty welcome to the newly-formed American branch (see Chapter 17) and acknowledged, "with sincere thanks," the launching of the American branch's *News-Letter* by Eva Turner Clark, Charles W. Barrell and Professor Louis Bénézet.[3] The next known Fellowship gathering was the general meeting on August 22, 1945, more than five years later. The Fellowship's officers remained essentially unchanged during those years.

The Fellowship *News-Letter*, suspended after the July 1939 issue, did not resume regular publication until November 1945, when it began to appear semiannually (before the War it had been bimonthly). However, Percy Allen asked for and received authorization to prepare issues on an *ad hoc* basis during the War. These much shorter issues were not numbered (the final regular issue, in July 1939, was no. 15), which has generated uncertainty about whether all of them have been identified. Having examined internal clues and Oxfordian correspondence, I am confident that the list in the nearby text box is accurate and complete.

Shakespeare Fellowship News-Letters
Issued on an Ad Hoc Basis During the Second World War, 1939-1945

July 1939   No. 15, final issue edited by Capt. Bernard M. Ward before publication was suspended.

Ad hoc issues edited by Percy Allen

1940 – April	1943 – May, October
1941 – April, October	1944 – May, October
1942 – April, October	1945 – May

November 1945   The *News-Letter* re-established as a semi-annual publication. Percy Allen remained as editor.

General Media

Many general interest periodicals also suspended publication, reducing the number of venues where the limited Oxfordian research that continued could be reported. *The Shakespeare Pictorial*, which had run occasional features on Oxfordian developments even after the run of the dedicated Shakespeare Fellowship Page ended in December 1936, ceased publication in 1939. *The Christian Science Monitor*, which had run more than thirty articles on the Oxfordian claim from 1928 to 1939, ran none on the issue for more than ten years thereafter.

The East Anglian Magazine, with its regular (and mostly Oxfordian) Shakespearean Page appeared only intermittently starting in late 1939 because of paper and fuel shortages. There was no issue in December of that year, only five in 1940, and only one in

---

[2] Eva Turner Clark, "To Members of The Shakespeare Fellowship," *SF News-Letter* (American), vol. 1/1 (Dec. 1939): 1.

[3] "Minutes of the General Meeting," *SF News-Letter*, April 1940, p. 2.

1941, in April, after which it stopped publication. When it returned in 1946, it had new management, a new format, and no Shakespearean Page.

In January 1940 the editor described the dire situation. He then addressed the larger question of the place of cultural activities or intellectual work during a time of great national crisis.

> Although the war's effect on East Anglia will not, we suppose, be greater or less than on other parts of the country, we in these four counties have already been denied much of the cultural activity that we should have enjoyed in peace time. . . . Many of our local societies, and the activities which they were in the midst of organising, have been peremptorily disbanded and curtailed. Such eruptions in the tenor of our ways are to some extent a necessity because the first essential of the moment and of the immediate future is to win the war.
>
> But it is to be hoped that it will not be necessary to exclude entirely from our lives those interests and pursuits which, in peace time, make life worth living. To deny archeology to the archaeologist, architecture to the student of it, beauty to the country-lover and knowledge to all those in search of it, may not be too big a price to pay for the establishment of freedom and security, but it is a price which has

---

J. Thomas Looney, Letter to Eva Turner Clark, early 1940 (excerpts)

It comes quite as a "pick-me-up" to learn that you intend to go straight ahead, and indeed to add new initiative in the cause of Shakespeare authorship. In these days when the mind of the world is engrossed with war interests, with all my heart I wish you success. You of course have an advantage in not being so directly implicated in the international trouble as we are; but even in this country I feel that it would be all to the good if people kept constantly in mind the things of the 'spirit' that are destined to endure, and refused to be absorbed by the forces and movements of rebarbarisation which today hold European civilization in their grip.

I cannot help recalling the circumstances under which I wrote, at the close of the last great war, in the conclusion of *"Shakespeare" Identified*, a protest against the materialistic aims then in vogue. . . . [T]hose materialistic aims pursued in Europe during the intervening twenty-one years have borne their natural fruit. . . . [T]e consummation of that materialism harnessed to a stupendous national egoism . . . has afflicted other nations besides Germany.

To me, however, it does not appear to be a struggle between democracy and dictatorship so much as between material force and spiritual interests; between a brutal national egoism and the claims of Humanity; and as an Englishman I am proud to feel that my country stands on the side of Humanity and spiritual liberty, and alongside of France is destined to lead the way towards a recovery in Europe of a true sense of spiritual values.

This is where our interest in Shakespeare and all the greatest of the poets come in.

Amidst the darkness of the present times we shall do well therefore to make a special effort to keep alive every spark of interest in their work. More even than in normal times we need them today, however incompatible they may seem with the tragedy that overshadows us. My own work, *"Shakespeare" Identified*, was largely the result of an attempt to do this during the last war: a refusal to be engulfed by an untoward environment even when suffering most poignantly from the loss of many who were dear to me.

This then is part of our share in the present day struggle: to insist even in the slaughter and distress of battle fields and bombardments by sea and air on the supremacy of the things of the human soul.

From J. Thomas Looney, letter to Eva Turner Clark, early 1940, excerpts in "Dean of Literary Detectives on the War," *Shakespeare Fellowship News-Letter* (American), vol. 1/2 (Feb. 1940): 5.

For more of Looney's thoughts on the subject, see J. Thomas Looney, Letter to Flodden W. Heron, July 5, 1941, reprinted in "A Great Pioneer's Ideas on Intellectual Freedom," *Shakespeare Fellowship Quarterly*, vol. VI, no. 3 (July 1945): 33-34.

---

not been demanded and is not yet required. It may or may not be necessary to demand it. If it is, there are few people who will refuse the sacrifice. Until then, we should do well to live our lives sanely and simply, while at the same time taking any opportunity there may be to help the common cause. Avoidance of intellectual interests will in no way help this cause. War is a most unintellectual business at any time, but there is no need to make it more so.[4]

The editor's judgment about the importance of continuing with artistic and intellectual activities even in a time of war—that the unnecessary sacrifice of these things would be, indeed, unnecessary—was shared by C. S. Lewis, who made a similar defense of humanistic learning during difficult times in his "Learning in Wartime" speech at Oxford University on October 22, 1939. It was also a constant focus of J. Thomas Looney's life. He addressed that theme several times in relation to his Oxfordian work, once in a letter to Eva Turner Clark early in 1940, from which a lengthy excerpt is reprinted in the text box below. Another was in a letter to Flodden W. Heron in July 1941.

Public Lectures

Only two lectures are known to have been given in 1940, and two in 1941. In 1942 Percy Allen gave several talks at Welwyn Garden City, where he lived as a houseguest of Capt. Ward during the summer. Seven new members joined the Fellowship at that time, all but one residents of Welwyn Garden City.

Destruction of Unsold Copies of *"Shakespeare" Identified*

It's long been known that the plates for Cecil Palmer's edition of *"Shakespeare" Identified* and all unsold copies of the book were destroyed in 1940 in a bombing raid during the Blitz. It was assumed that the books were in Cecil Palmer's warehouse but they weren't. After Looney obtained possession of the unsold copies in the late 1930s, he found a company willing to market them. But almost immediately after he transferred all the copies, the bookseller, who was German, was deported from England.

Looney then found another bookseller, Leonard Hyman, to market the books. But soon after they were transferred to Hyman's warehouse on Fleet Street in London, the building was destroyed by German bombing.[5] Looney later filed an insurance claim, only to find out that Hyman hadn't purchased insurance. Given Palmer's previous misappropriation of funds (see Chapter 9) and the destruction of all unsold copies of the book in 1940, Looney received nothing, not a penny, from the 1920 English and American editions of *"Shakespeare" Identified*.

Other destruction

Many sites of importance for the Oxfordian story were destroyed.

> ➤ Brooke House (King's Place), where Oxford lived during the final years of his life and where he died, was seriously damaged during a German air raid. The Elizabethan portion of the house was almost wholly destroyed.[6]

---

[4] Editor, "Comments by the Editor," *East Anglian Magazine*, vol. 4/11 (Oct. 1939): 610.

[5] "Books and Flames," *SF News-Letter* (American), vol. 2/3 (April 1941): 30. The fires ignited by bombing during that attack raged so fiercely that Simpkin Marshall, the book wholesaler located on Paternoster Row, a quarter-mile from Fleet Street, lost more than three million books.

[6] "Oxfordian News, "*SF News-Letter*, May 1943, p. 3. For more on Brooke House, see "Hackney Mansion to be Destroyed," *Sphere*, March 6, 1954, p. 327. See also "Review of *The Lost Treasures of London* by William Kent," *SF Quarterly*, vol. VIII/2 (Summer 1947): 26. See also the ten articles on Brooke House in *The Hackney Spectator* in the first four months of 1909.

> The Elizabethan wing of Melford Hall was destroyed on February 14, 1942. The Hall, and other places in Long Melford, were closely connected "with 'Shakespeare' and with the plays *Twelfth Night, Romeo and Juliet* and *Cymbeline*. . . . Queen Elizabeth, during her progress into East Anglia, in 1578, was overtaken at Melford Hall by the French Ambassadors, come to negotiate the Alençon marriage, which is the principal theme of *Twelfth Night* . . . [and in] *Cymbeline*, Milford Haven . . . is certainly Long Melford."[7]

Effects of the War on Members of the Fellowship

Members of the Shakespeare Fellowship were uprooted in different ways, spreading out all over England to escape the bombing in London and other sites targeted during the Blitz.

J. Thomas Looney was forced to relocate from Gateshead, just south of Newcastle, a major port city subject to heavy bombing, to Swadlincote, Staffordshire, near Burton-on-Trent, where he lived with his daughter and her son.

Capt. Bernard M. Ward was called into active service at the outbreak of the War. He was initially placed on the inactive list due to a physical disability dating from the Great War, but he expected to be available for "light service" in the first months of 1940. The American Fellowship reported that "Captain Ward's many friends in this part of the world would like to see him assigned to a study of the military tactics of Shakespeare or some similar duty at the Folger Library in Washington or the Huntington Library in San Marino, California."[8]

Percy Allen was forced to leave his house in London in 1941. A report in the *Bath Weekly Chronicle* provided some details of his movements. "Mr. Percy Allen, the distinguished Shakespearean critic, . . . expects to stay [in Bath] until the middle of March. He will then return to Huntspill, near Bridgwater, where he spent last summer. Mr. Allen has a house in London, but does not expect to return to the metropolis until the end of the war."[9] He is known to have stayed with Capt. Ward during the summer of 1942.

William Kent lost his priceless library of 5,000 books in 1941 due to bombing during the Blitz, and was again bombed in his new residence. He wrote to the American branch of the Fellowship with an update in late 1944. "Last July we went through a third enemy attack. All our furniture went, and our flat was a heap of ruins. This was the work of a pilotless plane. Fortunately, injuries were slight. I have recovered some of my books this time, but many in a torn, filthy condition. I have also lost two valuable Shakespeare notebooks, containing material for a volume I contemplated. However, I have started new ones and, indeed, filled one already. But the loss is grievous . . . I wonder if you could manage to send me duplicates of the *News-Letters* and *Quarterlies* you send me?"[10]

Other members were also affected.

> E. Morgan was bombed out of his house at Bromley early in 1941.

---

[7] Percy Allen, "Melford Hall and Shakespeare," *SF News-Letter*, April 1942, p. 4.
[8] "Best Wishes from Abroad," *SF News-Letter* (American), vol. 1/2 (Feb. 1940): 10. Capt. Ward's replacement as Hon. Secretary, Mr. T. L. Adamson, had for fourteen years been Vice President of the Shakespeare Reading Society. Adamson had been converted to the Oxfordian idea three years earlier by reading *"Shakespeare" Identified*, whereupon he resigned his office in the Reading Society. The London County Council retained his services as a lecturer in spite of his Oxfordian views.
[9] "A Literary Visitor," *Bath Weekly Chronicle and Herald*, Feb. 8, 1941, p. 18.
[10] "A London Worthy's Letters," *SF Quarterly*, vol. VI/2 (April 1945), p. 26.

> ➤ In 1941 T. M. Aitken was forced to leave London for the countryside.

> ➤ Rev. A. H. Lee, Vicar of St. Martin's who had been a constant attendant at Fellowship meetings, died in an air raid.

> ➤ Rev. W. Pennington-Bickford, Rector, St. Clement Danes, which became a charred ruin after being bombed three times, died. In September his widow, heart-broken, died by her own act.

Oxfordians' Reports on their Experiences During the War

Oxfordians in England kept their American counterparts apprised of their conditions in England (to the extent that censors allowed). Many expressed relief that an American branch of the Shakespeare Fellowship had been established and was able to continue support for Oxfordian work, and gratitude for having received letters and the American Fellowship's *News-Letters* from across the Atlantic. The following excerpts from their reports give some sense of things.

1940

F. Lingard Ranson wrote to Charles Barrell in October about the determined spirit of the English people.

> It would interest you to be in England today; there is a different feeling spreading all over the country which augurs well for the future; I have seen it in the towns and in the countryside. A common danger has made an united nation. Never for a moment have the people doubted the ultimate success of their efforts, and we all recognise and appreciate the tremendous help the U. S. A. is giving to England in just the way that is most needed. We do not need men; we have them ready, keen and trained, but just waiting for equipment; and when all is ready, then we shall strike.

He also commented on the stir Barrell's discoveries about the Ashbourne portrait had made in England.

> Your history-making discoveries regarding the portraits of "Shakespeare" created quite a sensation in England. If it had not been for other more serious events occupying all our minds, it would have made "front-page" news. As it was, the Stratfordians received a nasty jolt. . . . To all and sundry, your wonderful discovery was a great revelation, even the many biased Stratfordians and other Oxfordian critics who have approached me on this subject—and who, whilst arguing that, allowing your discovery to be correct, this did not prove that Oxford was the author of the works of Shakespeare have been completely stumped for an answer as to why proved portraits of Edward de Vere were chosen to represent and were passed on to the world as portraits of Shakespeare.[11]

1941

In the spring came letters from J. Thomas Looney, Percy Allen, J. J. Dwyer and Mrs. Fitzroy Carrington, conveying, in the *News-Letter's* summary, that "All are full of courage and hope, in spite of the devastation surrounding them."[12] Allen reported that "Your June *News-Letter* did not come through to any of us, so far as I know, so that I was double glad to have the August number, with its interesting contents. I enjoyed most the articles on

---

[11] F. Lingard Ranson, letter to Charles Barrell dated Oct. 31, 1940. Excerpts in "A Letter from Lavenham," *SF News-Letter* (American), vol. 2/2 (Feb. 1941): 21.

[12] "News from England," *SF News-Letter* (American), vol. 2/4 (June 1941): 52.

"Sebastian of Messaline" and "Fluellen." It is wonderful how, little by little, it is becoming clear that even the apparently trifling episodes in Shakespeare are actually topical and symbolical. . . . I am getting out here a short *News-Letter*, which will probably be out by mid-October. . . . I shall be wintering with Captain Ward, at Welwyn Garden City. . . . [W]hat is in store for us all here, in England, nobody knows, but we are not despondent. This much is certain—we will never bow the knee to Hitler; upon whom, as also upon the German nation, sooner or later, the judgments of the Most High will inevitably descend. America will be one of the instruments of that doom."[13]

1942

Marjorie Bowen: "I have just received the December and February numbers of your invaluable *News-Letter* and I want to thank you most sincerely for your great kindness and courtesy in sending me these copies. We are rather starved in England just now of this kind of thing and you can perhaps hardly realise the pleasure it is to receive your extraordinarily interesting publication. I hope that this letter reaches you, with my profound acknowledgments for your great kindness."[14]

Later that year Bowen wrote to Charles Barrell. "I am in complete agreement with all your surmises and feel a great admiration for the industry and enthusiasm behind your discoveries. . . . It is most heartening to know that it [the Oxfordian cause] has been taken up in America with such zeal, skill and enthusiasm and it is undoubtedly from your side of the Atlantic that Edward de Vere will finally receive his due recognition. . . . I might mention, apropos of an author being able to conceal his identity during his lifetime, that I have myself been in *Who's Who* under three different pen names without the editor discovering the fact until I pointed it out myself."[15]

1943

T. L. Adamson, who replaced Capt. Ward as Hon. Secretary in 1939, provided this update on academia's response to the Oxfordian challenge in England.

> It's all to the good that we "heretics" continually come out into the open with our different ideas, argue stoutly about them, and so gradually widen the common ground of understanding of all that the word "Oxford" implies. What must the poor orthodox professors think about it all? Do they honestly weigh the wealth of material we of the united Fellowship have for years been digging up to the damnation of their orthodoxy? They are men of intelligence, and I cannot believe that they do not admit to themselves in their cloistered seclusion that there's something rotten in the State of Stratford. I imagine that the combined assault of England and America will never drive them to unconditional surrender: they would rather suffocate in the odour of their orthodoxy.
>
> I once asked one of the most learned orthodox men I know to tell me what was in the mind of the dramatist when he wasted some 80 lines in Act II, sc. I, of his finest play describing in meticulous detail the unholy art of espionage. . . . Do the lines carry on the dramatic action of the play? They tediously retard it, with the result that most of them are ruthlessly cut in production. Then, I asked, is not the only explanation that there was some bee in the dramatist's bonnet so powerful

---

[13] "Our Third Year," *SF News-Letter* (American), vol. 3/1 (Dec. 1941): 8.

[14] Marjorie Bowen, letter to Editors, April 18, 1942, excerpts in *SF News-Letter* (American), vol. 3/4 (June 1942): 53-54.

[15] Marjorie Bowen, letter to Charles Barrell. Reprinted in "From Letters Received," *SF News-Letter* (American), vol. 3/6 (Oct. 1942), p. 78.

that he must send it aimlessly buzzing round the head of the scorned Polonius? Surely the dramatist had himself been stung to the quick by such loathed spying or his artistic soul would have resisted the temptation of 80 such lines. And then I told him of Oxford's well-known bitter protest to Burghley. A tolerant shake of the head was his only comment, and he changed the subject. So few of the orthodox will shake a spear in their own defense.[16]

Important Oxfordian Work Accomplished During the War

The work of Oxfordian scholars in Great Britain continued to a limited extent. The following are publications or productions not noted elsewhere.

Percy Allen manuscripts

Early in 1941 Allen reported to Eva Turner Clark that in the six months he had been in Somerset (where he had gone to escape the Blitz), he had compiled "voluminous notes on the Shakespeare plays."[17] "I have got through much of this annotation work . . . and have now almost complete Oxfordian notes . . . not only of the Shakespeare plays, but of many of those of Jonson, Chapman, and Lyly, as well as many other notes on the Folio verses, and other allusions to Shakespeare by contemporaries and others, as quoted in Sir Edmund Chambers' two-volume work on Shakespeare. From these notes one could annotate and edit at any time an 'Oxford' edition of the plays—a work that must be done one of these days." This work was of inestimable importance, drawing on Allen's extraordinary knowledge of the subject acquired through a decade and a half of nonstop study, writing and lecturing. His notes are presumably in the archives of his papers, which have not yet been located.

Leslie Howard's feature film (1941)

Leslie Howard's *Mister V*, also known as *Pimpernel Smith*, gave unexpected publicity to the Oxfordian claim. In what was essentially an anti-Nazi thriller, Howard played Professor Horatio Smith, an undercover agent masquerading as an English archaeologist excavating "Aryan" remains in Germany just before the outbreak of the Second World War. During the course of conversations with German authorities who had begun to suspect his real identity and who claimed that "Shakespeare" was German, Professor Smith on two occasions held up a copy of *"Shakespeare" Identified* and stated that "Shakespeare" could not be German because that book proved that his works had been written by the Earl of Oxford. Because

Leslie Howard holding a copy of J. Thomas Looney's *"Shakespeare" Identified* in *Pimpernel Smith* (Mister V).

---

[16] T. L. Adamson, letter to Charles Barrell, no date given, excerpts in "Letters from England," *SF News-Letter* (American), vol. 4/5 (Aug. 1943), p. 68.

[17] Percy Allen, letter to Charles Barrell, March 1941, excerpt in *SF News-Letter* (American), vol. 2/3 (April 1941): 36.

Howard produced and directed the film, it seems likely that the inclusion of the Shakespeare-Oxford connection was his own idea. Howard was killed in an air crash in June 1943; German fighter planes shot down the BOAC passenger plane, on a flight from Lisbon to England, over the Bay of Biscay.[18] In 1936 Percy Allen had met with Howard in his dressing room in New York after a performance of *Hamlet* in which Howard played the title role; perhaps that occasion sparked Howard's interest in the Oxfordian thesis.

Roderick L. Eagle cites Stratfordian fraud (February 1942)

Eagle, the staunch Baconian who corresponded with Looney in 1920, published an article charging the so-called Birthplace of Shakespeare with fraud in connection with the relics displayed there. Evidence shows that John Shakespeare "did not buy the house called the 'Birthplace' until 1575—eleven years *after* the birth of William—yet visitors are shown a room on the first floor in which the poet was born! The house itself was, with the exception of the cellar, completely rebuilt and enlarged between 1858 and 1860, and has no resemblance to the old tumbledown place as shown in old prints and photographs.'"[19] He concluded with a call for "the rejection of all the spurious 'relics' and 'portraits' of Shakespeare. . . . They have little value in themselves and would not be missed. It is discreditable that 'relics' unsupported by evidence should be displayed. In no other industry would such a state of things be tolerated."

Adm. Hubert Holland's work on topical allusions (April 1942)

After writing two books on topical and personal allusions in Shakespeare's plays in 1923 and 1933, Holland had continued his investigations of those subjects. He published his latest findings, in summary form, in the April 1942 *News-Letter*. The number of allusions he documented had reached 433, with an average of twenty-five per play.[20] He also found more than thirty references in Shakespeare's plays to works by other dramatists. "They are mostly the plays of Lyly (9), Greene (6), Peele (5), Marlowe (4), Kyd (2), and Munday (1)." He found references to Edward de Vere and to many of Shakespeare's plays in works by other dramatists.

William Kent cites Stratfordian absurdities (October 1942)

Kent pointed out examples of the wild speculations that Hesketh Pearson engaged in in the "Biography" section of the prefatory material in each of the plays issued in the Penguin series. As

Number of Topical Allusions in Shakespeare's Plays Found by Adm. Holland (April 1942)			
Hamlet	50	*Othello*	23
Twelfth Night	41	*All's Well that Ends Well*	22
Much Ado About Nothing	40	*Love's Labour's Lost*	22
Merry Wives of Windsor	34	*King John*	19
Romeo and Juliet	31	*Winter's Tale*	18
As You Like It	30	*Midsummer Night's Dream*	16
Measure for Measure	30	*1 Henry IV*	12
Merchant of Venice	28	*Richard II*	10

---

[18] For more information on the film and its Oxfordian content, including transcriptions of key Oxfordian scenes, see "Editorial Notes," *SF News-Letter*, April 1942, p. 1, and "Mister V," *SF News-Letter* (American), vol. 3/4 (June 1942): 52. Also important is Charles Boyle, *Another Hamlet: The Mystery of Leslie Howard*, second edition (2013).

[19] Roderick L. Eagle, "El-Dorado-on-Avon,*"Everybody's*, Feb. 28, 1942, reviewed in "Stratford Relics," *SF News-Letter* (American), vol. 4/3 (April 1943): 38.

[20] Adm. Hubert. H. Holland, "Shake-Spear 1573-1593: A Short Report on Latest Research into Internal Evidence by Topical Allusions," *SF News-Letter*, April 1942, p. 2.

one example, he quoted Pearson's statement that "The 'domestic and rustic nature' of *The Winter's Tale* showed that the author had 'put in a fair amount of time at Stratford in 1610.'"[21]

> How does he know all this? is a question always in the reader's mind. We are told, for example, that Shakespeare's mother was "helpful and docile." "Exceptional men use their mothers as material for their art, unless, like Dickens, they dislike them; so we may infer from the fact that William left no recognizable portrait of his that he was fond of her." This is a priceless specimen of Mr. Pearson's deductions. Shakespeare's wife was "Of a religious and charitable disposition. She imparted a thorough knowledge of the Scriptures to her eldest child, but Shakespeare could not have shared the religious convictions of his wife and father."
>
> He could not have been inferior in character, for he was "friendly, gentle, obliging, kindly, unassuming, engaging, good-natured, and sweet-mannered." He had too a constitutional infirmity that prevented him out-Falstaffing Falstaff in liquor, as in his Shoreditch days he "often excused himself from what threatened to be a drunken debauch on the ground that he did not feel well."

After citing many other examples of Pearson's "pure and puerile speculation," and others that are "not speculation but mis-representation," Kent concluded that "The book is an asset to us sceptics."

Percy Allen on Francis Bacon's share in the Shakespeare Folio of 1623 (May 1944)

Allen produced several major pieces of work during the War years. One was his thirty-five-page pamphlet *Who Were the Dark Lady and Fair Youth of the Sonnets?* (see Chapter 10), itself only a summary of a much longer work that was never published. Allen also produced a pamphlet on another complicated issue, *Bacon's Share in the Shakespeare Folio of 1623*, also never published, though a summary of its conclusions appeared in the *News-Letter*. Allen cited Ben Jonson's topical comedy *The Staple of News* (1625) as "the most important conclusive single piece of evidence" for his conclusions. "The bulk of the Shakespearean output, including nearly all the greater tragedies and comedies, and the *Sonnets*, is from the pen of Lord Oxford, excepting *The Tempest*, which is by Walter Raleigh. Bacon inserted, or caused to be inserted, into several of the plays, episodes and signature-acrostics which, in most cases, seem to have been added shortly before the appearance of the Folio. . . . Baconian signatures are usually on the first and last Folio pages of the plays, and on the first and last pages of the poems."[22]

Percy Allen on "The Group Theory and Some Modern Intellectuals" (May 1945)

Allen noted that although "Academic scholars, in general, remain rigidly orthodox in their professed Shakespearean views despite the fact that almost every book they publish upon a Shakespearean subject shatters their case by the showing of their own arguments . . . it seems certain that several well known writers and journalists today are wavering from orthodoxy, and are tending to accept, in one form or another, the group-theory of Shakespearean authorship."[23] He cited Ivor Brown, but also H. G. Wells, someone not usually regarded as a doubter. "In his recent Pelican book, Mr. H. G. Wells admits his conversion to the group hypothesis when he alludes to *The Merchant of Venice* as 'the

---

[21] "The Life of William Shakespeare," *SF News-Letter*, Oct. 1942, p. 2.

[22] Percy Allen, "Francis Bacon's Share in the Shakespeare Folio of 1623," *SF News-Letter*, May 1944, p. 8.

[23] Percy Allen, "The Group-Theory and Some Modern Intellectuals," *SF News-Letter*, May 1945, p. 4.

dullest play perhaps produced by the Shakespeare group.' Mr. Wells writes further . . . [of] the obvious probability of a mixed origin for Shakespeare's plays. . . . You cannot tell whether that composite person Shakespeare was a Catholic or Protestant.'" In a related article J. W. Tierney observed that "H. G. Wells, Ivor Brown, and James Agate, are said to be among the recent adherents to the belief that 'Shakespeare' was written by a group which did not include the Stratford-on-Avon actor, but did include Bacon, the master-mind being Edward de Vere, seventeenth Earl of Oxford, hereditary Lord Great Chamberlain. . . . You will find all this in a literature to which Lieut.-Col. Montagu W. Douglas, C.S.I., Sir Clement Markham, and Col. Ward have contributed."[24]

Deaths and Illnesses, 1939-1946

Beyond the hardships imposed by the War, those years coincided with the illness and death of many leaders of the Oxfordian movement, thinning the ranks.

Of the most active Oxfordians in the 1930s, only Percy Allen, Adm. Holland and Marjorie Bowen were still living and active in 1947. Katharine E. Eggar was living, but not active during the War years. Gilbert Standen died in 1937, Gilbert Slater in 1938. In 1939 came deaths of Hamlet Philpot, founding member of the Fellowship, and Ernest Allen, twin brother of Percy Allen. J. Thomas Looney died in January 1944.

There were several deaths in 1945. Gerald H. Rendall, the oldest of the most prominent Oxfordians of the first quarter-century of the Oxfordian era, died in January at age ninety-three. Capt. Bernard M. Ward died on October 2 at fifty-two. Col. Montagu W. Douglas, who had been president since 1928, resigned from the position at the general meeting in August, 1945, at the age of eighty-two and in poor health.

Capt. B. M. Ward remembered

Although Capt. Ward lived until October 2, 1945, his active involvement in the Oxfordian movement had ended early in 1939, before he was called to duty. His final published piece was his rebuttal in the *Supplement* to the April 1939 *News-Letter*. Percy Allen penned an obituary of his friend and colleague in the November 1945 *News-Letter*.

> Capt. Bernard Ward—formerly of the King's Royal Dragoons—possessed a first-rate intellect, and a perseverance, and historical sense and knowledge, which peculiarly fitted him for successful Shakespearean research. His inferences were cautious, and his judgment sound. His main purpose, from first to last, was the establishment of truth by means of documentary, and therefore indisputable, evidence. The Editor—who was Ward's close personal friend, as also of his father before him—found him a most generous and inspiring collaborator.
>
> Unfortunately, however, Bernard Ward had a strain of eccentricity in his character and was lured, during the late war, into intense enthusiasm for Communism; with the result that he shed nearly all his interest in matters Elizabethan, and no longer sought the society of those of his own social class. That fact explains his almost complete, and much regretted, disappearances from the later activities of the Fellowship. Yet the names of the two Wards, father and son, will be permanently associated with the early history of the Oxfordian movement.[25]

---

[24] J. W. Tierney, "In the Country and Out of It," *The Countryman*, Spring 1945, p. 46, quoted in *SF News-Letter*, May 1945, p. 4.

[25] Percy Allen, "Editorial Notes," *SF News-Letter*, Nov. 1945, p. 1.

Percy Allen

Percy Allen had had bouts of severe illness throughout the second half of the 1930s and suffered other setbacks during those years, including large financial losses. He felt deeply the death of his twin brother Ernest in October 1939. The dislocations caused by the War also took their toll, and yet his Oxfordian activities continued at a pace that outdistanced all other British Oxfordians of the time.[26]

Allen had published eleven Oxfordian books and pamphlets from 1928 to 1934. Over the next decade he published more than forty articles and several pamphlets, edited the Fellowship *News-Letter* for five years, gave scores of talks in England and North America and wrote several unpublished books. The American *News-Letter* reported on his "desire to get out a new edition of his *Life Story of Edward de Vere*."[27] As noted, by 1941 he had almost completed Oxfordian notes or annotations not only to all of Shakespeare's plays but also to many of those of Jonson, Chapman and Lyly.[28]

J. Thomas Looney

Looney was seriously ill during the summer of 1942. In October his daughter wrote to Percy Allen with an update. "I am glad to be able to report considerable progress, and my father is now almost where he was before the relapse. He is having the best medical attention (suffers very little and is quite cheerful), and there is every hope of an adequate recovery. He hopes that your efforts in the Oxford cause are meeting with the best success."[29]

Looney was again ill in the middle of 1943, and Allen reported on another update: "Looney, who had been making a good recovery from his recent illness, has had a relapse, and has been very ill; as his daughter, Mrs. Bodell, kindly tells me, in a letter dated September 13 1943 last: 'He has turned the corner and although very weak is certainly showing signs of recovery.' Good wishes will go to him from both sides of the Atlantic."[30]

Ultimately Looney's illnesses proved too much for him. He died on January 17, 1944, at age seventy-three years and five months. Two memorial services were held, one at the Temple of Humanity in Liverpool in February 1944 organized by Rev. Otto Baier, the other at St. Paul's Cathedral in London in April 1946. The second service was attended by his widow, Elizabeth Looney, his two daughters, Evelyn Bodell and Gladys Looney, and other family and friends. Rev. Canon V. A. Demant (a former student of Looney's)

---

[26] Illness had compelled Allen to cancel his series of talks at the Club room in late 1934. He was seriously ill again in spring 1941 and spring 1943. He had been blind in one eye for several months in 1937. On June 26 he told Looney, "I have been very ill, operation, nursing-home . . . I have lost (temporary they tell me) all use of my right eye, so that I can read and write very little, perhaps for some months to come." (Percy Allen, letter to J. Thomas Looney, June 26, 1937.) In 1940 he was again "entirely deprived of sight in one eye" and living "on a farm in Somerset, collating his voluminous notes on Oxford-Shakespeare matters." ("Under the Stukas' Shadow," *SF News-Letter* (American), vol. 1/5 (Aug.-Sept. 1940): 6.)

[27] "Best Wishes from Abroad," *SF News-Letter* (American), vol. 1/2 (Feb. 1940): 10.

[28] Percy Allen, letter to Charles Wisner Barrell, March 1941. Excerpt in "Letters from England," *SF News-Letter* (American), vol. 2/3 (April 1941), p. 36. Allen's son, John, was an Oxfordian, which increases the likelihood that his papers have survived. If so, they will be a treasure trove of correspondence, notes and manuscripts that could greatly deepen understanding of the first forty years of the Oxfordian era.

[29] Evelyn Bodell, letter to Percy Allen, Oct. 14, 1942, excerpts in "Editorial Notes," *SF News-Letter*, May 1943, p. 1.

[30] "Editorial Notes," *SF News-Letter*, Oct. 1943, p. 1.

presided.[31]

News of his passing was reported in several Oxfordian publications.[32] the obituary in *The New York Times*, which briefly summed up Looney's Oxfordian accomplishments, is reprinted in a nearby text box.

Obituary in *The New York Times*

JOHN T. LOONEY:

Shakespearean Scholar Held that Edward de Vere Wrote Plays:

News of the death early this month of John Thomas Looney, British Shakespearean scholar, at his temporary home in Swadlincote, Staffordshire, has reached this country, the American Branch of the Shakespeare Fellowship, 17 East Forty-eighth Street, announced yesterday. Mr. Looney, who spent most of his life as a teacher of English at Newcastle and Gateshead-on-Tyne, was the author of *"Shakespeare" Identified in Edward de Vere*, published in 1920. The purpose of the book was to identify Shakespeare with Edward de Vere, seventeenth Earl of Oxford. Part of the evidence Mr. Looney adduced in an effort to substantiate his thesis consisted of indications that certain portraits of the Earl had been altered, and that the Earl's personality, tastes and known activities were reflected in Shakespeare's writings. During the last five years, the announcement of the death stated, a group in this country has issued the *Shakespeare Fellowship Quarterly* to carry on the research started by Mr. Looney.

A Look Ahead to the Fall of 1945 and Beyond

The loss of so many prominent members of the Shakespeare Fellowship in the first half of the 1940s spelled the end of an era for the Oxfordian movement in England. It would have to reconstitute itself after the War ended.

New signs of life began almost immediately after the War officially ended on V-J Day, August 15, 1945. On August 22 the Shakespeare Fellowship held a general meeting, its first gathering since May 1940. The event was attended by twenty-three members, most of whom had not seen each other for five years. Before the meeting Col. Douglas, who had served as president for seventeen years, since 1928, submitted his resignation due to ill health (he was 82 years old). Percy Allen was unanimously elected as his successor. In its report, the *News-Letter* noted that "The Secretary was asked to convey to Col. Douglas the meeting's sense of the great loss of judicious and scholarly leadership the Fellowship had sustained in his resignation, their sympathy, and their earnest hopes that the years to come will be restful and happy." The report also noted that "Mr. Percy Allen was pre-eminently marked out by his twenty-one devoted years of investigations, writings, and lectures, as successor to the Presidential chair; and he was elected with acclamation and unanimity."[33]

A feeling of optimism had returned to the organization. Percy Allen wrote of the change in conditions and sentiment apparent at the August meeting in the November *News-Letter*.

---

[31] For further details, see Rev. V. A. Demant, "Personal Recollections of the Late J. T. Looney," *SF News-Letter*, Sept. 1946, p. 3; and "Obituary of John Thomas Looney (1870-1944)," *Shakespearean Authorship Review*, issue 8 (Autumn 1962): 8-9.

[32] "Discoverer of the True Shakespeare Passes," *Shakespeare Fellowship Quarterly*, vol. V, no. 2 (April 1944): 17-23; and Percy Allen, "John Thomas Looney (1870-1944): A Biographical Sketch," *SF News-Letter*, May 1944, pp. 2-4.

[33] "The General Meeting," *SF News-Letter*, Nov. 1945, p. 2.

The general meeting was a pleasantly *live* one. We have, perforce, to some extent, slumbered and slept during these years of battle; but we are wide awake again now. To see, once more, some of the familiar faces, invisible for years past, was a real and great pleasure to us all and soon we shall be meeting again for debates and lectures. But the Fellowship needs some younger blood! Let us hope that the early future will supply it.[34]

With Allen serving as president of the Fellowship and editor of the *News-Letter* it appeared that the organization had both continuity and stability. It was not so. Allen was forced to resign as president at an Extraordinary General Meeting held on January 12, 1946 after other officers learned that he was about to publish a book in which he claimed to have had conversations with William Shakspere and Edward de Vere through a series of seances.

The seances had been led by Mrs. Hester Dowden, who, decades earlier, had held seances at which Sir Arthur Conan Doyle was convinced he had communicated with his recently deceased and much loved son. Allen had sought her assistance in communicating with his twin brother, Ernest, who had died on their birthday in 1939. The seances had apparently been held as early as 1942, judging from a letter that Allen sent to the BBC. In it he presented "Bacon's own message," in which Bacon revealed "My true identify, and what I did as statesman, as philosopher, educationalist and teacher. A selfless patriotism was the consuming fire from which I produced those 'Histories' I wrote under the pen-name of Shake-speare."[35] Allen's book, *Talks with Elizabethans: Revealing the Mystery of William Shakespeare*, was published in 1947.[36]

The presidency remained vacant until the next general meeting on September 14, 1946, when new leadership was established. Most officers remained in their positions for more than five years, giving a degree of stability to the Fellowship. Adm. Holland, who had expressed his desire to serve as president for only one year, served for nine.

Oxfordian Accomplishments and Realizations

Over the course of twenty-five years after the publication of J. Thomas Looney's *"Shakespeare" Identified*, British Oxfordian scholars substantiated Looney's initial findings, and established the case on an ever firmer foundation. They and Looney accomplished much in overcoming two of the three types of resistance to the Oxfordian idea described in Chapter 5: the Human Resistance to new ideas, and the Cognitive Resistance due to the complexities of the Oxfordian claim.

They were not successful in overcoming the Institutional Resistance within academia. The War interrupted their efforts. The progress that had been made was largely reversed as Oxfordian pressure on academia lessened, allowing Stratfordian scholars to maintain their adherence to the Stratfordian myth unchallenged.

But another story should also be noted: the path Oxfordians traveled from their initial expectations that simply presenting the facts supporting Oxford's authorship would cause traditional scholars to abandon their Stratfordian beliefs and move to the Oxfordian camp. Those expectations proved to be illusory, even naïve.

It took the bitter experiences of the 1930s to show Oxfordians just how adamantly

---

[34] Percy Allen, "Editorial Notes," *SF News-Letter*, Nov. 1945, p. 1.
[35] Percy Allen, "Shake-speare Speaks Again?" *SF News-Letter*, October 1942, p. 4.
[36] Although the book is commonly attributed to Percy Allen, the Library of Congress lists Hester Dowden as author.

academia would reject the Oxfordian claim, how completely scholars would reject it without examining it objectively. Whether Oxfordian pressure would have succeeded in generating acceptance of Oxford's authorship of "Shakespeare's" works if the War had not intervened is an open question. What is not open to question is that the Stratfordians won the battle against the Oxfordian challenge in the 1920s and 1930s. Whether they would win the war remained to be seen.

Would there indeed be further battles?

The Second World War left England so exhausted that the initiative in Oxfordian matters, as in so much else, passed to the United States. The American branch of the Shakespeare Fellowship, founded in December 1939, flourished through the War years with an amazing stream of articles reporting on original research that undermined the Stratfordian claim and strengthened the Oxfordian, and, increasingly, a series of public lectures and other forms of engagement designed to ensure a growing public awareness of, and support for, the Oxfordian idea. It all seemed to justify a high level of optimism about the prospects for the Oxfordian claim in the postwar era. That that American optimism was also inflated or even naïve was not apparent until American Oxfordians had gone through the same bitter experiences in the 1940s that their British colleagues had endured in the 1930s.

16

The Rise of the Oxfordian Movement
in North America, 1936-1940

Percy Allen's North American Tour, September-December, 1936

While the crisis within the Shakespeare Fellowship was developing in England (see Chapter 10), Percy Allen was on a speaking tour of the East coast of the United States and Canada. The tour was made "with the hope, and intention, of planting, in both those countries, some fresh seeds of the Oxfordian faith, and the new interpretations of Shakespeare which must necessarily arise therefrom."[1] The seeds would soon bear fruit.

His trip began auspiciously. Allen later related that during his passage, "after much questioning of my views about Shakespeare . . . one of the judges of the Court of Quebec, the Hon. Justice Gibsone, shewed himself much interested." Allen reported that "Both in Canada and the States my experience was that the legal minds took a keen, though always cautious, interest in my arguments and points of view."[2]

He docked in Canada, where he gave public talks in Montreal, Ottawa and Toronto, before crossing the border and speaking in Concord, Hanover and Manchester, New Hampshire, Boston and New York City. At many talks people were so fascinated by his presentation that they invited him to speak at other events they quickly set up. At one such follow-up event at the Colony Club in Ottawa, he presented the Oxfordian case to the principal correspondent of the *London Times* in Canada, two judges of the High Court of Ottawa and the Chief Justice of the Supreme Court of Canada.

Of his presentations at the Elmwood School in Ottawa, Allen wrote, "The interest aroused by the second of these talks was very keen, among mistresses and pupils alike—an encouraging fact, seeing that Elmwood is one of the most prominent schools in the City" (3). His talk at the Montreal Repertory Theatre generated prominent newspaper coverage, and "many of those present expressed interest in the Shakespeare question, and to those who gave me their addresses, leaflets concerning the Fellowship, and our books,

---

[1] Percy Allen, "Shakespearean Adventures in Canada and the United States," *SF News-Letter*, no. 1 (Jan. 1937): 2. Allen left England on Sept. 26, 1936 and arrived in Quebec on Oct. 4. He departed from New York in early December.
[2] Percy Allen, "Shakespearean Adventures," *SF News-Letter*, no. 1 (Jan. 1937): 2.

have already been sent out."

Allen addressed the Toronto Shakespeare Society on *The Winter's Tale*, which was being performed locally. "I took the opportunity to tell the diners something of the historical events which are dramatized in the play," he wrote, "a viewpoint which, I think, greatly surprised most of those present who had not the remotest idea that *The Winter's Tale* was anything else than a work of fantastic imagination."

In Hanover, New Hampshire, Allen spoke to several professors from Dartmouth College at one event, and to professors and undergraduates at another. "I spoke, from the Oxfordian viewpoint, upon *Hamlet* and the *Sonnets*, with an animated discussion following. Subsequently, some half dozen of the Professors invited Mr. O'Connor [Allen's "unofficial agent in the U.S.A."] and myself to dine with them at the local hotel, where the Shakespearean discussion was continued until a late hour" (4). He later described the evening as "historic," and commented that "never before, so far as I know, had any University, in any English-speaking country, opened its academic gates to an Oxfordian!"

Among those present at his talk at St. Paul's School in Concord, on "*Twelfth Night* as a Topical Play," was Prof. W. B. Draygon Henderon, whose introductory notes to Castiglione's *The Book of the Courtier* Allen knew well. Allen later heard from O'Connor that "ever since our Oxfordian incursion upon them, St. Paul's School has been in something of a turmoil over this Shakespeare business, and is staging an Oxford-Shakespeare debate. We fluttered some dove-coat in Corioli; and the boys are eagerly seeking further information" (5).

On November 16 in New York City Allen spoke at the Colony Club on "A New Interpretation of *Hamlet*," a topic chosen in part because two of Allen's favorite actors, John Gielgud and Leslie Howard, were then starring in productions of the play in New York. Allen was introduced by Eva Turner Clark, a member of the Club, who organized the event.[3] Allen "tried to show that the *Hamlet* play, and Shakespeare's *Sonnets* were both, unmistakably, the autobiographical work of Lord Oxford, the original Hamlet-Shakespeare, as surely as Lord Burleigh was the original of Polonius, ... the subject being further thrashed out during the tea and cocktail party that followed. If all enjoyed the afternoon as much as I did, the function was certainly a success."[4] Several of the actors from Leslie Howard's production of *Hamlet* attended the talk and later introduced Allen to Howard after a performance of the play.

At the very end of his tour, Allen "was interviewed by a representative of the *New York Sun*, which . . . published nearly a column of matter, which, I thought, was very cleverly and accurately put together, in view of the complexity of the subject, by a young journalist who was being introduced to the Oxford case for the first time. The reporter told me that this was the first occasion on which Shakespeare unorthodoxy had been made convincing, and intelligible, to him" (7).

Allen was full of praise for those who had helped organize his trip; he singled out three as of special importance. "Mrs. W. S. Waugh, of Toronto; Mrs. Edward Hardy Clark [Eva Turner Clark], of New York; and that indefatigable toil of my unofficial agent in the U.S.A.—Mr. Thomas O'Connor, of Concord, to whom much of my gratitude is due." Eva Turner Clark was the author of *Hidden Allusions in Shakespeare's Plays*; she would go on to play an indispensable role in promoting the Oxfordian cause in the United States over

[3] A copy of Clark's speech exists in the Gerald H. Rendall Archives at the University of Liverpool.
[4] Percy Allen, "Shakespearean Adventures," *SF News-Letter*, no. 1 (Jan. 1937): 6.

the next decade.[5]

Allen's general impression of his trip was that "audiences, both in Canada and the States, are more open-minded concerning Shakespeare than are corresponding audiences over here; and that the Oxford case is destined to make much progress there during the next few years." He also wrote that "Personal contact with our members abroad was one of the great pleasures of this trip," and that he hoped "to repeat the tour, or a part of it, during the autumn of 1938."

Professor Louis P. Bénézet

Percy Allen's 1936 speaking tour was perhaps the catalyst for the rise of the Oxfordian movement in the United States and Canada. One of the most immediate and far-reaching effects was that it galvanized Professor Louis P. Bénézet, who would write two books and dozens of articles, and give scores of lectures promoting the Oxfordian thesis, over the following decade. With the other two most important American Oxfordian scholars of the time—Eva Turner Clark and Charles Wisner Barrell—he founded the American branch of the Shakespeare Fellowship and served as president throughout its existence, from 1939 to 1948.

Bénézet had hosted Percy Allen's talk at the Manchester (New Hampshire) Public Library in early November 1936, when he served as head of the city's public school system. He joined the faculty of Dartmouth College soon after, eventually serving as Chairman of its Department of English and the Humanities from 1944 to 1948. Allen later wrote that Bénézet "has interested himself deeply in the Oxford-Shakespeare subject, which, he confesses, has eclipsed his other hobbies. He is already a member of the Fellowship, and is contemplating the preparation of a text book upon the subject, for use in schools. Mr. Bénézet's interest was first aroused by our indefatigable member, Mr. O'Connor" (5).

In March 1937—only five months after Percy Allen's visit and lectures—Bénézet published a short book, *Shakspere, Shakespeare and de Vere*, to make the Oxfordian case better known to American readers. However, it mentioned J. Thomas Looney only once and *"Shakespeare" Identified* not at all. It was dedicated "To Percy Allen, Esq. and Capt. B. M. Ward, whose research into matters Shakespearean is constantly revealing new and surprising facts."[6]

Col. Montagu Douglas, reviewing the book in the *Shakespeare Fellowship News-Letter*, wrote that "this brief and eloquent appreciation of the Earl of Oxford in thirty-four pages is unanswerable. Dr. Bénézet might not have solved the problem of the Fair Youth, . . . but he leaves no doubt in the mind of an impartial reader that Oxford was the author of the *Sonnets*, and thus 'the Master Mind' responsible for most of the Shakespearean works."[7]

Most Oxfordians would agree with many of Bénézet's conclusions, including these:

---

[5] I have not yet found further information on Mrs. Waugh or Thomas O'Connor.

[6] Louis P. Bénézet, *Shakspere, Shakespeare and de Vere* (1937).

[7] Col. Montagu W. Douglas, [review of *Bénézet's Shakspere, Shakespeare and De Vere*], *SF News-Letter*, no. 8 (March 1938): 8.

The Stratfordians tell us that the reason why [Shakspere] ceased writing plays after 1605 (the year after Oxford had died), contenting himself with allowing inferior dramatists to finish off some uncompleted plots, was that, frankly, he had made his "pile" and was not interested in exercising his brain any further. This, in the first place, is false to every tradition of literature. Imagine Goethe or Wagner, at the age of forty-one, retiring to a small village to brew beer and sue debtors. It is as natural for a genius of this sort to produce beautiful literature as it is for the ordinary man to breathe or eat. His restless, powerful mind could no more have been content with inglorious rustication with an illiterate daughter in a bookless house than Edison, Burbank or Steinmetz would have been under

---

Louis P. Bénézet

Born: 1878. Died: 1961.

Age when *"Shakespeare" Identified* was published: 42

One of the three founders of the American Branch of the Shakespeare Fellowship, the others being Eva Turner Clark and Charles Wisner Barrell. Served as president of the American branch, 1939-1948. He gave scores of lectures on the Oxfordian claim at colleges and other fora all over the United States.

He was a high school principal and city superintendent in Lacrosse, Wisconsin, Evansville, Indiana, and Manchester, Hew Hampshire, for 31 years before becoming a member of the faculty at Dartmouth College, where he served as Chairman of the Department of English and the Humanities (1944-1948). From 1925 to 1937 he was a League of Nations lecturer. After retiring from Dartmouth he served as a professor at Bradley University in Illinois (1948-1950), Evansville College (1950-1952) and Jackson College in Honolulu (1952-1960).

Bénézet was the most active—and most dynamic and effective—public speaker on behalf of the Oxfordian cause in the United States and Canada, giving more than half the 100 or so known public talks to promote awareness of the idea between 1937 and 1948.

Oxfordian Publications

> Books
> 1937   *Shakspere, Shakespeare and de Vere*
> 1958   *The Six Loves of Shakespeare*
>
> 30+ Articles in the *Shakespeare Fellowship (American) News-Letter* and *Quarterly*, including:
> 1939, Dec.   Organization of the Shakespeare Fellowship, American Branch*
> 1939, Dec.   President Louis Bénézet's Message*
> 1941, Aug.   Nineteenth Century Revolt Against the Stratford Theory, Part I*
> 1941, Oct.   The Great Debate of 1892-1893: Bacon vs. Shakespeare*
> 1942, Aug.   Every Word Doth Almost Tell My Name
> 1943, Apr.-Oct. Look at the Chronicles, Part 1, 2, 3*
> 1944, Jan.   Frauds and Stealths of Injurious Imposters*
> 1944-1946   Stratford Defendant Compromised by His Own Advocates* [Six articles published on this theme over two years.]
>
> Other articles
> 1938, April 21   [title not known], *The Dartmouth* [student-run college newspaper]
> 1947, Nov.   "The Shakespeare Hoax: An Improbable Narrative," *Dartmouth Alumni Quarterly"**
> 1947   "Veres, Earls of Oxford," a 2,400-word piece in *Grolier's Encyclopedia*

Other Interesting Publications

> 1904   *Three Years of Football at Dartmouth: Being the Story of the Seasons of '01, '02 and '03.*
> 1918   *The World War and What was Behind It, Or, The Story of the Map of Europe*
> 1922   *Young People's History of the World War* [This book was translated into Czech and used in all secondary schools in Czechoslovakia.]

* These articles are reprinted in Paul Altrocchi's ten-volume anthology of Oxfordian articles, *Building the Case* (the first five volumes co-edited by Hank Whittemore).

similar circumstances.[8]

Most of Bénézet's book consisted of an examination of the *Sonnets*, in which he reached conclusions that not all Oxfordians would have agreed with. Some of his views were similar to those of Percy Allen, Capt. Ward and G. W. Phillips noted in Chapter 10. He believed that the Fair Youth of the *Sonnets* was the author's illegitimate son, that he was an actor in his father's company of players, that he was not the result of a union between Oxford and Queen Elizabeth, that most of the *Sonnets* were addressed to him, and that he was not the Earl of Southampton.

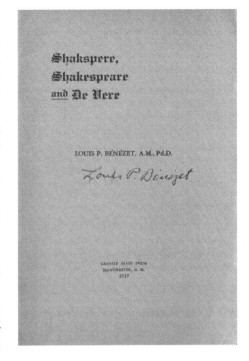

> The existence of this young man, who was seventeen years old in 1592, throws a flood of light upon the Shakespeare *Sonnets*, for, in the opinion of Allen and Ward, he is the beautiful youth to whom the greater part of these verses are addressed. J. Thomas Looney, the man who first proclaimed Oxford as the real Shakespeare, has felt that the youth was Henry Wriothesley, Earl of Southampton, to whom *Venus and Adonis* and *Lucrece* are both dedicated and who, about this time, was affianced to marry Oxford's daughter. However, it seems very strange for any man to give such affection to one who merely was related to him through the tie of approaching marriage. I hold with Ward and Allen that the fair youth is the son of Oxford. (12)

The final paragraphs of Bénézet's book, posing two questions, almost appeared to give credit for the Oxfordian idea to Capt. Ward rather than J. Thomas Looney.

> First, why should the name William Shakespeare have been selected as the nom de plume of the real author if the author was not the Stratford man, and, second, what would be anyone's motive in attributing the works to the almost illiterate man of Stratford?
>
> Captain Ward has given us the answer to the first question. He points out that the son of the Earl of Oxford bore the title of Viscount Bulbec, and that the crest of the Bulbec arms was a lion brandishing a spear. Here is at least strong hint as to why the name "Shakespeare" should have been given to the boy. As for the second question, the answer is more evident. The legitimate offspring of the Earl, knowing of the Stratford man, who may have been connected in some business or executive capacity with the Oxford players, seized upon the similarity of names to throw the public off the trail which would lead to the family scandal. If the illegitimate son was the young actor named William Shakespeare in the Earl of Oxford's company, then the last piece slips into the puzzle to make a complete picture. (31)

The book contained two appendices. The first was a poem of eighty lines compiled by Bénézet, which mixed forty lines from Edward de Vere's early poems with forty from

---

[8] Louis P. Bénézet, *Shakspere, Shakespeare and de Vere* (1937), p. 13.

Shakespeare's. Bénézet challenged readers to identify which lines were from which poet. The second appendix was a chart matching eight candidates for Shakespearean authorship with fourteen characteristics. Edward de Vere is the only candidate with all fourteen; the next highest are William Stanley with eight or nine and Mary Sidney with seven. William Shakspere has zero or one.

Bénézet sent a copy of his book to J. Thomas Looney, who wrote back noting Bénézet's failure to acknowledge his intellectual debts to Looney and *"Shakespeare" Identified*. Bénézet's reply included a sincere apology and an explanation.

> I have such a profound admiration for yourself and for what you have done that I had a sinking feeling as I read your letter and realized that it was true, that I should have given you credit for much that I used.

> In explanation, let me say that this was a hastily published pamphlet, gotten out rather hurriedly to anticipate the possible publication of the same thing by another writer. I had heard of *Will Shakspere, Factotum and Agent* by Alden Brooks, a book in which the author proves that Shakespeare could not have been the poet and playwright. He promised, in the review that I saw of the book, to publish shortly another volume revealing the author of the sonnets as he understands the case, and I was afraid that he would steal my thunder.[9]

> I am at work now on another book which I hope to have used as a textbook in high schools and colleges, and in this you may be sure, I shall give you full credit for the wonderful bit of work that you have done.[10]

Bénézet then explained his position on the issues that had caused such consternation within the Shakespeare Fellowship a year earlier.

> Regarding the question of the identity of the Fair Youth of the *Sonnets*, you are right in saying that the essential thing, after all, is that the Earl of Oxford wrote them. Since I sent my manuscript to the printer, I have come across new evidence which induces me to think that there is more than one young man who is addressed in the *Sonnets*. I feel just as positive as ever that some of the sonnets are addressed to an illegitimate son, but it may well be that others are addressed to such a man as the young Earl of Southampton. I do not know. The theory that the "dark lady" was Elizabeth, I cannot accept, nor would I say that the illegitimate boy was the son of Queen Elizabeth. This would be very difficult of proof.

> I am sorry to hear that the Shakespeare Fellowship is divided over this question. You echo my feelings exactly in saying that there is danger that each theorist may pursue his own particular hobby. The trouble is that the Stratfordians seize upon every little flight into the spectacular or the fanciful as an excuse to discredit the whole Oxford theory. I shall attempt, in my new book, to stick to statements that can be documented or to those which are supported by very strong internal evidence.

He concluded by noting the cautious nature of publishers. "My main trouble is going to be to find a publishing house that is not afraid to print it. These people are very cautious, as a rule, and very much afraid of leading the procession. They follow only after the great majority of the people have gone ahead of them."[11]

Bénézet was the most active public speaker on the Oxfordian claim in the United

---

[9] Alden Brooks's book, *Will Shakspere and the Dyer's Hand*, did not appear until 1943.

[10] Louis P. Bénézet, letter to J. Thomas Looney, Jan. 29, 1938.

[11] The book Bénézet referred to was never published. It is one of several Oxfordian books known to exist in manuscript at one time that are presumed lost.

States and Canada. His report titled "Youthful Minds are Open," printed in the first issue of the *Shakespeare Fellowship News-Letter* of the American branch, gave a sense of the receptivity of audiences. "After many attempts to convert friends of mine who are professors of English to at least a position of open mindedness on the question of the authorship of the Shakespeare plays, I have come to the conclusion that such efforts pay small dividends." However, "The group of people who are willing to listen, to give the matter the benefit of a doubt, to investigate and think for themselves are the students in our high schools, colleges and universities. In the past two years I have lectured before student audiences at State Teachers Colleges in four different states, and I never fail to find an eager and excited group among them." As one student told Bénézet after a lecture, "If anyone had told me that this whole student body would sit with their mouths open, on the edge of their seats for a full hour listening to a lecture on Shakespeare, I would have said he was crazy."[12] Another, a college senior, stated "I'm thoroughly convinced" before asking "if I go out next year and teach a group of high school seniors that Shakespeare did not write Shakespeare, what is my school board going to say to me?'" Bénézet's reply ("'You'll have to send for me to come over and convert your school board") might address long term concerns but the student was surely right to be apprehensive.

Bénézet's most enthusiastic recent audience "was at the Ball State Teachers College at Muncie, Indiana. Here the fourteen hundred young people, soon to be grammar and high school teachers, listened attentively for a full hour, and kept me afterwards in an adjourned meeting, answering questions for another forty-five minutes. This was on September 19th, and followed an informal talk to members of the faculty the night before. Professor Van Cleve of the English Department was the man responsible for the lecture, and he tells me that he still hears echoes of the talk." Bénézet also recalled that "[A]fter a lecture to the Hathaway Shakespeare Society of Philadelphia, I had a most interesting event . . . with a group composed of members of the faculties of that college [Bryn Mawr] and Haverford. Again it was the members of the English Department who clung tenaciously to the old faith. The teachers of other subjects were keenly alive to the possibility that the ancient story, after all, might be a fable. Thus the process of 'selling' the idea goes on, gaining impetus as it goes." He noted elsewhere of that November 1938 talk, that "The only two who refused to open their minds were the teachers of English."[13]

Charles Wisner Barrell and *The Saturday Review of Literature*

Charles Wisner Barrell's article, "Elizabethan Mystery Man," in the May 1, 1937 issue of *The Saturday Review of Literature*, did much to bring the Oxfordian claim to public attention in the United States. In his prefatory note, the editor explained that,

> The theory that the Earl of Oxford wrote the plays usually attributed to William Shakespeare has for some years had an increasing vogue. *The Saturday Review* believes that the movement has gained enough momentum to interest its subscribers, and publishes Mr. Barrell's summary of the theory for the literary record. It has asked Professor Elmer Edgar Stoll of the University of Minnesota to reply to Mr. Barrell's article in a discussion of the Oxford theory and similar

---

[12] Louis P. Bénézet, "Youthful Minds are Open," *SF News-Letter* (American), vol. 1/1 (Dec. 1939): 4.

[13] "News from America" includes excerpts from Benezet's letter to Percy Allen of February 13, 1939. *SF News-Letter*, No. 14 (April 1939), p. 9.

hypotheses. Mr. Stoll's article will be published next week.[14]

Barrell began by introducing J. Thomas Looney as "the greatest of literary detectives" and noting that novelist John Galsworthy was so captivated by the idea of Oxford's authorship that he bought dozens of copies of *"Shakespeare" Identified* for his friends.[15] He cited many facts well known to readers of Looney's book but perhaps not to readers of *The Saturday Review*. Among them were weaknesses in the case for the man from Stratford: "There is no record of his having had any formal education whatever or any of the broadening influence of foreign travel. He left no books, letters, or manuscripts, not a scrap of paper to prove that he was personally able to construct one grammatical sentence. The entire extent of his manuscript bequest to humanity consists of six wretchedly scrawled signatures, spelled in four different ways." Barrell also detailed the many ways that de Vere's experiences had given him the knowledge of languages and literature, of Italy and of the law, and of the Elizabethan court and its entertainments and styles of social interaction that the author of Shakespeare's works must have had, as well as many instances of events in the life of Edward de Vere portrayed in the plays.

"Ultimately," Barrell wrote in a 141-word sentence,

> The trail led to the previously disregarded and half-obliterated footprints of Edward de Vere, Queen Elizabeth's wayward and unhappy Lord Great Chamberlain and one-time lover—a poet, Court dramatist, and patron of players of outstanding contemporary fame, but a man whose consuming passion for art and scholarship made him a prey to the designing machinations of politicians and courtiers, to escape whose blighting influences he turned to the companionship of common poets, dramatists, musicians, and actors; one who fell afoul of the taboos of his own caste and "lost his good name" as a result; a nobleman, bearing the second oldest title in the realm, who "wasted his substance" and "squandered his patrimony" on men of letters whose bohemian mode of life seems to have attracted him. (11)

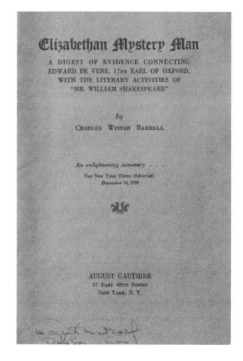

Barrell had read Looney's *"Shakespeare" Identified*, with its "masterful presentation of the claims of Edward de Vere to the pen-name of 'William Shakespeare,'"[16] in 1934. Over the following decade and a half he devoted much of his time, and considerable resources, to researching the Oxfordian claim, and produced more than eighty articles, including many that drew on his expertise in photographic science. "Elizabethan Mystery Man" was the first. In 1940 an expanded version of it and a previously unpublished paper, "Shakespearean Detective Story: Throwing New Light on

[14] Editor's Prefatory Note to Charles Wisner Barrell, "Elizabethan Mystery Man," *Saturday Review*, May 1, 1937, p. 11.

[15] Charles Wisner Barrell, "Elizabethan Mystery Man," *Saturday Review*, May 1, 1937, p. 11.

[16] Charles Wisner Barrell, *Elizabethan Mystery Man* [pamphlet] (1940), inside front cover.

the Creation of *Hamlet*," were published together as a pamphlet titled *Elizabethan Mystery Man: A Digest of Evidence Connecting Edward de Vere and the Literary Activities of "Mr. William Shakespeare"* in order to fill the need for cheaply priced works connecting Edward de Vere with the Shakespearean works.

Looney was highly pleased with Barrell's piece and its appearance in such a prominent magazine.

> May I take the liberty of congratulating you on a very admirable paper—one of the best on the subject that I have been privileged to receive. I have already read it several times, each time with increased admiration, and I cannot conceive how anyone seriously interested in the great things of literature could possibly read it without being moved to go more deeply into the question.[17]

The article by University of Minnesota professor Elmer Stoll in the next issue of *The Saturday Review*, "The Detective Spirit in Criticism," was billed as a response to Barrell's "Elizabethan Mystery Man." Stoll turned first to the why and how questions. He wanted to know, if Oxford was Shakespeare, "why he robbed himself" of credit for his work and how his authorship could possibly have been kept hidden, "without all of London knowing all about it." Stoll showed himself to be familiar with Oxfordians and their research. He noted in passing Percy Allen's idea that Queen Elizabeth had a child by the Earl of Oxford

---

Charles Wisner Barrell

Born: 1885. Died: 1974.
Age when *"Shakespeare" Identified* was published: 35

One of the major figures in the Oxfordian movement during the later 1930s and throughout the 1940s. Cofounder of the American branch of the Shakespeare Fellowship (with Eva Turner Clark and Louis P. Bénézet). Editor of the *Shakespeare Fellowship News-Letter* (American) and the *Shakespeare Fellowship Quarterly* through their entire nine-year run, except for one year when he served in the U.S. Army during the Second World War.

Published more than 80 articles detailing the findings of his Oxfordian research, many of them of the greatest importance in supporting the Oxfordian claim.

Began his career as a magazine and newspaper writer at the age of sixteen before becoming a photographic contact man for The Rotograph Company. Later served as a publicity writer for the Triangle Film Corporation and other motion picture companies. In January 1919 joined the public relations staff of the Western Electric Company as Director of the Motion Picture bureau, where he worked for fifteen years as a photographic expert, writer and picture director, positions requiring close association with many of the foremost physicists and engineers in the fields of sound transmission and photographic research.

After reading *"Shakespeare" Identified* in 1934, decided that Looney had carried the evidence to a point where photographic science and subsidiary research might clinch the argument. Undertook at his own expense the now famous investigation into three ancient paintings of Shakespeare that have turned out to be slightly disguised originals of Lord Oxford.*

Selected Articles and Pamphlets
1937, May 1   "Elizabethan Mystery Man," *Saturday Review of Literature*, v. 12: 11-15.
1940, Jan.   "Identifying Shakespeare," *Scientific American*, vol. 162/1: 4-8, 43-45.
1940   *Elizabethan Mystery Man* [pamphlet]

For a complete list of Barrell's 80+ articles, see Mark Alexander's Shakespeare Authorship Sourcebook at www.sourcetext.com

Shakespeare Fellowship News-Letter (American), vol. 1/2 (Feb. 1940).

---

[17] J. Thomas Looney, letter to Charles Barrell, June 6, 1937.

and that this delicate situation, obliquely referred to in the plays, was the reason for hiding Oxford's authorship.[18]

But Stoll simply dismissed Oxfordians as amateurs not worthy of serious attention and their findings as not worthy of refutation.

> A little more of a case for Oxford was made out by Mr. Percy Allen, who has been laboring "almost without respite, day and night, for not less than ten years. . . . [Their work] has borne the earmarks of a mania or a hobby. Some, like Mr. Allen and Delia Bacon, have given their lives to it; some, like Mr. Allen's brother, their leisure; but the largest number, made up of retired lawyers, physicians, officers of the army and navy, only their idle years. Women, favored with more of these, have found it a solace or distraction—Miss Bacon, Mrs. Pott, Mrs. Gallup, Miss Eva Clark. It takes the place of bridge or backgammon. It is an historical literary crossword puzzle. (14)

In his reply, Charles Barrell raised the critical distinction between arguing backwards—from the works to a supposed author—and arguing forward—from a supposed author to the works. Anybody could do the former merely by claiming that the supposed author had read the sources or had the experience that gave him the knowledge needed to write the works. Stratfordians, Barrell noted, did that all the time. But only the Oxfordians could argue forward, and he provided an important example. Knowing that the phrase "I am that I am" appears in Sonnet 121 and in the Geneva Bible of 1560, Stoll had assumed (arguing backward) that Shakspere must have read it in the Geneva Bible. "But there is not one scintilla of personal evidence to show that Will Shakespeare of Stratford ever owned or read a Geneva Bible," Barrell observed, before noting (arguing forward) that records document de Vere's purchase of a copy of the Geneva Bible, along with a Chaucer and Plutarch's works (in French) in 1569.

> Here in one entry we have three books mentioned as the personal property of the literary Earl, each one of which is known by Stratfordians to have been read by Shakespeare. Yet no record exists to show that any book of any type was ever owned by the Stratford man.[19]

Furthermore, de Vere had used the phrase "I am that I am" in a letter to his father-in-law in 1584—a fact that Barrell had mentioned in his article but Stoll had conveniently ignored. Continuing his critique, Barrell wrote,

> Parallels in word imagery between Oxford's writings and Shakespeare's mean little or nothing, says Professor Stoll. By the same token, I suppose, similarities in design, color-treatment, or brush strokes count for nothing in identifying a painter's works. Textual affinities are certainly of paramount importance in tracing questionable literary identities. What, may I ask, is literature if not text? Lord Oxford's letters and other writings are studded with Shakespearean ideas expressed in the distinctive phraseology that sets Shakespeare's work apart. . . . Oxford was using the Shakespearean imagery and word-patterns years before any [other] . . . men came to the fore.
>
> If the proponents of orthodoxy could show us one—only one—letter or other personal document from the hand of the rustic Will containing a single Shakespearean phrase, no question of his responsibility for the creation of the

---

[18] Elmer Edgar Stoll, "The Detective Spirit in Criticism," *Saturday Review*, May 8, 1937, p. 12. Note also Barrell's reference to Oxford having been the Queen's lover in the 141-word sentence already cited.
[19] Charles Wisner Barrell," The Oxford Theory," *Saturday Review*, May 22, 1937, p. 9.

poems and plays would ever have been raised.

"Elizabethan Mystery Man" had a far-reaching influence on many people. Some, such as Dorothy and Charlton Ogburn and their son, Charlton Ogburn, Jr., would play leading roles in the Oxfordian movement. Charlton Ogburn, Jr., later described its impact: "The article . . . made my parents and me immediately aware of our profound, if heretofore mostly unconscious, dissatisfaction with the conventional Shakespeare. We were no less quickly stirred by the force and persuasiveness in the alternative Mr. Barrell offered. At last and Of Course expressed our reaction."[20] Others such as author and statesman Louis J. Halle, Senator Paul H. Douglas, *New York Herald Tribune* publisher Philip S. Weld, Chicago Bar Association president and *American Bar Association Journal* editor Richard Bentley, President of Fairleigh Dickinson University Peter Sammartino, philanthropist David Lloyd Kreeger, businessman Sol Feinstone and *Boston Globe* drama critic Cyrus Durgin would play significant roles in promoting the Oxfordian claim (166).

American author Carolyn Wells[21] wrote an effusive letter in response to Barrell and Stoll that was published in the June 5 issue. It appears in full nearby. One of the most interesting lines in it is, "anyone who has read Mr. Looney's book with an open mind, has an open mind no longer; he is a disciple of Mr. Looney."

In her autobiography, *The Rest of My Life*, also published in 1937, Wells never openly stated her conclusions about Shakespearean authorship, though she provided hints. She described her first visit to Stratford as "absolutely unforgettable," but added that it took

---

Carolyn Wells, Letter to *The Saturday Review of Literature*, June 5, 1937

Sir: I don't know when I have had a more joyous thrill than when I opened your paper of May first, and found Mr. Barrell's paper on Edward de Vere.

I have been a constant student of the Oxford-Shakespeare question since 1920, and have much literature on the subject, following upon Mr. Looney's book. *"Shakespeare" Identified* is not only a fascinating book, it is clear and convincing argument that cannot be ignored or disbelieved by a thinking reader.

Of those who don't care who wrote Shakespeare, Mr. Looney calmly states, "Indifference to the personality of the author is usually but the counterpart of an indifference to the writings themselves." So of these people and of those who persist in believing in the Stratford Shakespeare, we can but say, as was said of Ephraim, "he is joined to his idols, let him alone."

But remember, when the sneering and jeering takes place, to inquire if the dissenters have read and studied the subject exhaustively. A negative reply will automatically disqualify them for participation in the argument. And a negative reply you will surely get, for anyone who has read Mr. Looney's book with an open mind, has an open mind no longer: he is a disciple of Mr. Looney and the Shakespeare Fellowship, which now has branches in every civilized country.

When I read Mr. Barrell's paper in the S.R.L. of May first, I was moved to write to the editor, asking him to beware of articles by contributors who had not read *"Shakespeare" Identified*. Then I thought it would be an unnecessary warning. Then the next issue appeared with a paper written in the well-known vein of the Stratfordian adherents, and I decided it would be more help for our Oxford side than if it had not been printed! And I feel justified in my decision by the delightful page in a recent issue, whereon Mr. Barrell agrees that Mr. Stoll gives no evidence of having read the two basic books on the controversy. The great literary question of the ages has been opened up by *The Saturday Review of Literature*, and for that no gesture, no praise is too high.

---

[20] Charlton Ogburn (Jr.), *The Mysterious William Shakespeare* (1992), p. 165.
[21] She had corresponded with Looney in the early 1920s and again in 1932.

place "before I had ever heard of Mr. Looney's book,"[22] a statement not clarified by an explanation of who "Mr. Looney" was or the title or significance of his book. A return visit some years later, though, "had no more thrill in it than a bat of cotton [because] by that time I had put my belief in the Stratford Shakespeare into the discard, with my faith in Santa Claus. . . . I had learned beyond all doubt that the ignorant yokel, who could not write his own name legibly, who had never been to Italy, who had no schooling, no experience in court life, and no aristocratic friends, could never have given the world the glory of the immortal plays" (155). Elsewhere in her book Wells attributed "assume a virtue if you have it not"—a line from *Hamlet* (III.4.160)—to Oxford rather than William Shakespeare (228), but that is the extent of her references to the Oxfordian thesis.

Carolyn Wells (sometimes referred to as Miss Wells, though she had been married to publisher Hadwin Houghton until his death in 1919) had become a "fervent believer in the theory of Shakespeare authorship . . . set forth"[23] in *"Shakespeare" Identified* after reading it soon after it was published. She was great friends with two other writers who were also noted early American Oxfordians, Gelett Burgess and Oliver Herford. It would be interesting to learn if they knew Margaret L. Knapp and Esther Singleton, two other noted Oxfordians and writers of their generation. Knapp, Wells and Burgess had all corresponded with Looney soon after *"Shakespeare" Identified* had been published, and again in the 1930s.

A few months before her death in 1942 Wells wrote to Eva Turner Clark concerning efforts to make the Oxfordian idea more widely known.

> Our mission should be—must be—to teach that the Earl of Oxford wrote the plays and that he used the name William Shakespeare as a pen name, with the full knowledge and willingness of the Stratford man who bore that name. . . . So I ask when members of our Fellowship explain our beliefs to novices, that they dwell on the fact that the name of William Shakespeare is not thrown into the discard, but is the acknowledged pseudonym of Edward de Vere, and instance

---

Carolyn Wells

Born: June 18, 1862. Died: March 26, 1942.

Age when *"Shakespeare" Identified* was published: 58

An American author who wrote more than 170 books beginning in the early 1890s, she was best known for her dozens of mystery novels, children's books and humorous verse.

She bequeathed her collection of Oxfordian materials to Harriet C. Sprague, a friend who also had a great interest in the Oxfordian thesis.

She corresponded with J. Thomas Looney in 1920, 1923 and 1932.

Oxfordian publications

1937, June 5 "The Oxford Theory" [letter], *Saturday Review of Literature*.
At least three other articles not yet located.

---

[22] Carolyn Wells, *The Rest of My Life* (1937), p. 152.
[23] "Carolyn Wells," *SF News-Letter* (American), vol. 3/4 (June 1942): 56.

the case of Lewis Carroll. (56)

Wells bequeathed her collection of Oxfordian materials to Harriet Chapman Jones Sprague, widow of Frank J. Sprague, who was also deeply interested in the Oxford theory and among the first Oxfordians in the United States."[24] Sprague was also the collector and holder of the famous Walt Whitman Collection, which she bequeathed to the Library of Congress.

An interesting account of interactions between noted American Oxfordians is reprinted nearby.

Interactions Among American Oxfordians

Mrs. [Harriet] Sprague, the well-known authority on the works of Walt Whitman . . . said that Carolyn Wells, the writer, spent several weeks with her about twenty years ago and at that time asked her to read *"Shakespeare" Identified*, by J. Thomas Looney, and to read it through before discussing it at all; Miss Wells added that it was completely skillful, very convincing, and one of the best detective stories ever written.

Later, Mrs. Sprague talked the book over with Miss Wells, Gelett Burgess, and Oliver Herford, all of whom had been convinced by Mr. Looney's arguments. One day Oliver Herford asked Mrs. Sprague to dine with him, saying he had something very interesting to show her. On arrival, she found him pacing the floor in a state of excitement and before she could take off her coat, he handed her what looked like a very common-place book, saying, "Look at it, look at it carefully!" On the outside was printed "The Works of Edward de Vere." On the title-page she found *Complete Works of Edward de Vere, Seventeenth Earl of Oxford, First Edition, 1922*." "Go on," he said, turn to the Contents," and there she found a list of thirty-seven plays beginning with—*The Tempest*! After Oliver Herford's death, Mrs. Sprague was able to purchase the book from the executors of his estate and, having brought it to the meeting, members were privileged to handle and examine this unique volume.*

*"The Annual Meeting," *Shakespeare Fellowship News-Letter* (American), vol. 2/1 (Feb. 1941).

Eva Turner Clark's *The Man Who Was Shakespeare* (1937)

1937 was a banner year for Oxfordian publications in the United States, as all three American Oxfordians who would go on to found the American branch of the Shakespeare Fellowship in December 1939—Barrell, Bénézet and Clark—published significant works within a year of Percy Allen's speaking tour.

In *The Man Who Was Shakespeare*, Clark correlated events in Oxford's life with the plays, and showed just how tight were the connections between Oxford, theatrical entertainments in the Court and the development of the Elizabethan stage. She also documented his relationships with other dramatists, in contrast with the Stratford claimant who had no such relationships. As she explained to Looney,

> [The book is] my most recent effort at contributing something to your wonderful discovery of the seventeenth Earl of Oxford as the true author of the Shakespeare plays. . . . You will note that I have had to make much use of Captain Ward's biography but I had his kind permission to do so. Without your *"Shakespeare" Identified* and his *Seventeenth Earl*, no one can write on the subject. They are the basic works on which all later writers must depend. Please know that I am always grateful to you for the knowledge you first gave me of this fascinating mystery. If I try to add some little contribution to your story, it is only for unbelievers, in the

---

[24] "Whitman Collection," *SF News-Letter* (American), vol. 3/5 (Aug. 1942): 68.

hope of bringing them more quickly to our ranks.[25]

In a follow-up letter, she described the "great pleasure" that his reply had given her, and added, "The theory is taking hold slowly in the country but is beginning to gain recognition and possibly my book may achieve its purpose of arousing further interest."[26] Her book, she noted, "is the only one now generally available to American readers which details recovered facts in the life of the mysterious Elizabethan Court poet and dramatist, Edward de Vere."[27] *"Shakespeare" Identified* had been out of print in the United States for more than a decade and Ward's biography had never had an American edition.

In his review Barrell had also credited Clark with the startling discovery of the illustration on the title page of Henry Peacham's *Minerva Britanna* (1612) depicting a hand reaching out from behind a curtain to write the Latin phrase "Mente Videbori," which translates as "By the mind I shall be seen."[28]

Clark speculated that the lack of surviving documentary evidence for Oxford's authorship of the plays might have been due to John Payne Collier, who was known to have forged many documents "proving" Shakspere's authorship. "As Collier worked at will among many collections of manuscripts," Clark wrote, "it is a natural presumption that he destroyed those documents which did not fit in with his ideas." The reviewer for *The New York Herald Tribune* was skeptical. "This [speculation] does not give us confidence in Mrs. Clark's mode of handling evidence. In the chapters that follow this unpromising beginning there is much learning and much ingenuity... . [but] open the book at random and the most far-fetched arguments leap to the eye." He noted, however, that Mr. Looney's Oxford theory "has driven the 'Baconian Theory' from the field."[29]

John Waldron, reviewing in *The Washington Post*, noted that "Mrs. Clark sets 'aristocratic feeling' down as an essential qualification of 'Shakespeare' ... that, I think, is a fair demand." He immediately followed that acknowledgment with his conviction that "the Shakespeare of the 'academic' biographies meets it,"[30] without providing evidence of even a single connection between Shakspere and the nobility or the court. He finished

---

[25] Eva Turner Clark, letter to J. Thomas Looney, Nov. 20, 1937.

[26] Eva Turner Clark, letter to J. Thomas Looney, Dec. 17, 1937.

[27] Charles Barrell, "Alias William Shakespeare? The Man Behind the Plays," *New York Sun*, Dec. 11, 1937.

[28] Peacham, *Minerva Brittania* (1612), quoted in Capt. Bernard M. Ward, [review of *The Man Who was Shakespeare* by Eva Turner Clark], *SF News-Letter*, no. 7 (Jan. 1938): 2-3.

[29] "The Mantle of Shakespeare," *New York Herald Tribune*, Feb. 13, 1938, p. G11.

[30] John Waldron, "Flying Trapeze: 'Shakspere' vs. 'Shakespeare,'" *Washington Post*, Dec. 10, 1937, p. 13.

with the recommendation that readers should peruse the Barrell and Stoll pieces in *The Saturday Review of Literature*.

In his review of *The Man Who Was Shakespeare*, Capt. Ward observed that Clark "has correlated Lord Oxford's life with the plays. The latter, one by one, are fitted into the pattern of the many and varied events of his career, and the result is a perfect harmony."[31] He reminded readers that in her earlier book, *Hidden Allusions in Shakespeare's Plays* (1930), Clark had cited a wealth of topical allusions and evidence from the records of the Court Revels to show that "the plays were originally written some twenty years earlier than is commonly supposed—i.e., from 1576 to 1590, and not from 1590 to 1610." Recalling also "the pioneer chronological work of Admiral Holland," he noted how significant it was that "Mrs. Clark and Admiral Holland, working independently, more often than not arrived at approximately the same date for the original composition of the plays" (1). He also recognized that,

> The importance of the chronology of the Shakespeare plays cannot be over-emphasized. The Oxford theory alone makes it possible to understand the many topical allusions to the fifteen-seventies that are to be found in the majority of the comedies. In 1580 Oxford was thirty; Bacon and Derby nineteen; and Shakspere of Stratford sixteen. No more need be said—at least so far as the original composition of the comedies is concerned, though there must have been many revisions.

A Roundup of Oxfordian Items in the North American Press, 1937-1940

Back and Forth in *Reading and Collecting*, 1937

George Frisbee's "Shame of the Professors" in the July 1937 issue of *Reading and Collecting* is one of the most reprinted Oxfordian articles of all time. Written in response to an article by a Mr. Gekle, it generated a storm of response over several months to which Frisbee replied in the January 1938 issue. He launched his piece with a grabber:

> The circus has its clowns; the drama its comedians; while for their humorous fellows the universities have the professors of English literature who teach innocent youngsters that the plays and poems of William Shake-speare were written by a man born in Stratford-upon-Avon. They are a comical crew and their antics in evading discussion of the truth regarding Shakespeare authorship afford real students of Elizabethan literature a big laugh.[32]

Frisbee divided professors into three classes: the "tricksters," or bigshots "who garble data to bolster the Stratford myth;" the "cowards," "the many timid souls who know better;" and the "gulls," "who never gave birth to an idea; who swallow everything peddled by the big shots; and whose greatest ambition is to cadge a junket from some Foundation, to waste time and money on alleged research." Frisbee clearly hadn't yet read *How to Win Friends and Influence People*, Dale Carnegie's new book.

Frisbee drew on Sir George Greenwood's big books, *The Shakespeare Problem Restated* (1908) and *Is There a Shakespeare Problem?* (1916), to show that professors, in the absence of even "the tiniest scrap of proof . . . that Shakespur of Stratford wrote *Hamlet*, or the *Sonnets*," had offered only "guesswork, imagination, conjecture." He

---

[31] Capt. Bernard M. Ward, [review of Clark's *The Man Who Was Shakespeare*], *SF News-Letter*, no. 7 (Jan. 1938), p. 2.

[32] George Frisbee, "Shame of the Professors," *Reading and Collecting*, July 1937, vol. 1/8: 6.

observed that, "Greenwood . . . showed so clearly that the Stratford man could not have written the 'Shake-speare' work that no professor has dared reply. George Greenwood simply mopped up with them. And the professors shun his work as if it were the plague. Perhaps it does plague their consciences; perhaps."

He then asked the questions that had plagued traditional scholars for so long: "Where and how did the Stratford man acquire his profound learning, culture, knowledge of mankind, and all the rest of 'Shakespeare's' equipment?'" Academia had no answer to such questions or to the Oxfordian answers. "In his magnificent work, *"Shakespeare" Identified*, J. T. Looney shows so clearly that none but Edward de Vere could have written them that no professor has dared question his findings. Dr. Gilbert Slater, in *Seven Shakespeares* writes that Mr. Looney has never been answered."

J. V. McAree, *Globe and Mail*, Toronto

On August 2, 1937, John Verner McAree launched a storm of reader responses to his regular column by writing of the man from Stratford that "Not a great deal seems actually to be known about him, but what is known suggests that there must have been hundreds, if not indeed, thousands, of Englishmen in his time likelier to have responded to the kiss of the divine fire."[33] After expressing doubt that a butcher's apprentice from "one of the dirtiest, most wretched towns in England," could have, within three years, written *Love's Labour's Lost* and *Venus and Adonis*, and after remarking that "It is hard indeed to believe that these were not the works of a ripe scholar, a man familiar with the literatures of several lands, with the usages of court," he asked, "Where did Shakspere get that polish, that erudition?"

Addressing the issue in a later column, McAree stated that "Many a student of Shakespeare has, in the words of Emerson, been unable to 'marry the man's vulgar and profane life to his verses,' and, concluding that Will of Stratford was not the author of the immortal plays, has searched among his contemporaries for a more probable source."[34] He then presented evidence from *"Shakespeare" Identified*, and observed that "Undoubtedly Oxford was a remarkable character," before mentioning in passing that "He is supposed to have been a lover of Elizabeth." McAree noted that "Flippant reviewers fastened upon his name rather than upon the contents of his book" before concluding that Looney "had amassed an array of facts not so easily to be laughed off." Readers might

---

J. V. McAree, *Globe and Mail* (Toronto), 1937, 1940, 1955

Seemingly positive assessment of the Oxfordian Claim

1937, Aug. 2	"Makes Shakespeare Look Dubious," *Globe and Mail*, p. 6.
1937, Aug. 7	"Shakespeare Fans Read the Column," *Globe and Mail*, p. 6.
1937, Sept. 8	"Another Claimant for Poet's Crown," *Globe and Mail*, p. 6.
	Response in the *SF News-Letter*, no. 6 (Nov. 1937): 2-5.

Neutral column, presentation of news only

1940, Jan. 5	"Barrell Rolls Out Some Rich Stuff," *Globe and Mail*, p. 6.

Adamant rejection of the Oxfordian claim without explanation for the change

1940, Jan. 13	"Not a Controversy But a Good Imitation," *Globe and Mail*, p. 6.

A partial explanation

1955, June 27	"It's Shakespeare, After All," *Globe and Mail*, p. 6.

---

[33] J. V. McAree," Makes Shakespeare Look Dubious," *Globe and Mail*, August 2, 1937, p. 6.
[34] J. V. McAree, "Another Claimant for Poet's Crown," *Globe and Mail*, Sept. 8, 1937, p. 6.

easily assume that McAree was largely in sympathy with the Oxfordian claim.

Then, nothing; McAree made no mention of the issue for twenty-eight months, until a column in January 1940 highlighted Charles Wisner Barrell's investigative work on the Ashbourne portrait as reported in *Scientific American*. He reported Barrell's findings that all three portraits he examined had been tampered with, with the evidence suggesting that the same artist made all the changes and that the alterations had been made at some point in the seventeenth century not long after the portraits had been painted. He included no discussion of the authorship question, instead stating that "we do not desire to open our column to a further discussion of the various points at issue, but merely to record what purports to be a new discovery bearing on the problem."[35]

A week later he returned to the topic, this time to highlight readers' letters on the authorship question, including one claiming that there exists "no Shakespearean authority . . . who would give his opinion that what we call Shakespeare's plays were written by any one other than William Shakespeare of Stratford." McAree didn't mention the evidence in support of the Oxfordian thesis he had presented earlier. He backed away from any sympathy with the Oxfordian idea without a word of explanation.

What happened? McAree provided a clue fifteen years later, in his June 27, 1955, column that appeared near the end of its fifty-five year run. It opened with the startling statement that "So far as this column and its adherents are concerned the mystery of who wrote the William Shakespeare plays is solved. It has been solved by the discovery that there never was any honest doubt. Claims put forward for other authors were simply fakes."[36]

McAree reported that he reached this conclusion after reading a book review by Alfred Harbage in *The New York Times*. He apparently found convincing Harbage's statement that "If we look, then, for the basis of doubt about Shakespeare's authorship, some small bit of evidence, however exaggerated, some tiny point of departure, we find no basis, no evidence, no point of departure whatever. His claim to his works is of the same nature and validity as Hemingway's claim to his."[37] This was not a refutation, but a rejection without explanation.

There was more. McAree provided a further clue in a seemingly unrelated section of the same column subtitled "Nearly Cost Us Rise."

> And so as we dismiss all past and future claims we are reminded of another piece we wrote about the Baconian theory. It was many years ago, and the article was commonplace, inspired no doubt by some recent claimant or some alleged discovery by a Baconian. We suppose it was read by some people but we had no evidence of this until one day several weeks or months later when we waited upon Mr. J. S. Douglas, then general manager of *The Mail and Empire*, to stammer out our request for a small rise in pay. He regarded us silently for a minute or two, then opening his desk and briefly rummaging in it he confronted us with a letter. It was from somebody or other who had disliked our article. Mr. Douglas seemed to think that this was a sufficient reason for refusing our request. However, we think, we were able to convince him otherwise, for while we never received an increase without asking for it, we do not remember that we were

---

[35] J. V. McAree, "Barrell Rolls Out Some Rich Stuff," *Globe and Mail*, Jan. 5, 1940, p. 6.

[36] J. V. McAree, "It's Shakespeare, After All," *Globe and Mail*, June 27, 1955, p. 6.

[37] McAree was quoting from Alfred Harbage, *Theatre for Shakespeare*, published by the University of Toronto Press. *The Globe and Mail* for whom McAree wrote was also based in Toronto.

ever refused.

So there we have the answer. Too many readers had complained about his presentation of evidence challenging Shakspere's authorship. He had to cool it to stay in good graces with the powers that ran the paper.

The Angell-Baldwin Exchanges in *PMLA*, 1937 and 1940

Pauline K. Angell wrote a lengthy article on *Willobie his Avisa*, a verse of seventy-two cantos published in 1594. *Avisa* included a character named "W.S.", which many scholars believe was the first printed allusion to William Shakespeare after the publication of *Venus and Adonis* and *Lucrece*. She posed a key question: "Why should a [story about a] charge of loose conduct with an innkeeper's wife arouse the censors and hold public interest for two generations? The answer is that it would not, and that Avisa was not an innkeeper's wife."[38]

She asked whether it is correct to believe, as some scholars did, that *Avisa* "was designed to make a public scandal out of the illicit love of Shakespeare and Southampton for the Dark Lady (of the *Sonnets*)." She found that if the key reference was not to the city of Oxford, but to the Earl of Oxford, "the whole story unfolds easily and with conviction in every detail.... Since *Willobie his Avisa* was written not to conceal but to spread a scandal, the ease with which persons and places may be identified once the reader is on the right track, is a point in favor of the interpretation" (653).

With "W. S." established as the Earl of Oxford, Angell went on to identify "H. W." as Henry Wriothesley, Third Earl of Southampton. The stanzas in which H. W. woos Avisa comprise about a third of the book. Not only is a disproportionate amount of space given to his wooing, but two prose passages describe the personal idiosyncrasies of H. W. with a thoroughness not found in the treatment of the other suitors. This indicates, Angell believed, "that the presentation of the suit of H. W. was of paramount importance and that readers' recognition of him was particularly desired by the author of the libel" (665-66). With these two characters established, Angell noted that the only part played by W. S. in the story was giving advice to H. W. on how to win Avisa.

Angell then put all the pieces together as she saw them: Avisa was Lady Oxford—Elizabeth Trentham, the second wife of the Earl of Oxford. The hidden scandal was that Oxford and Trentham's son, born in February 1593, was fathered by Southampton. Angell did not explain why the almost-thirty-year-old wife of the Earl of Oxford would have had an affair with the twenty-year-old Southampton, or why Oxford would have advised him on how to convince her to do so.[39]

Almost three years later, in June 1940, T. W. Baldwin, professor at the University of Illinois, wrote to the PMLA to challenge one of Angell's reasons for concluding that W. S. represented the Earl of Oxford. She replied, noting "In this evidence . . . there is no keystone. The force of the evidence lies in the fact that all the items point in the same direction. The removal of one or two or even three of them does not negate the

---

[38] Pauline K. Angell, "Light on the Dark Lady," *PMLA*, vol. 52/3 (Sept. 1937): 674.

[39] Here is an alternative interpretation. If Percy Allen's and Capt. Ward's Dynastic Succession idea is correct, then what W.S. and H.W. wanted from Avisa (the Queen) was not to possess her sexually or to marry her, but to get her to recognize Southampton's claim, as her son, to the throne of England. Elizabeth was sixty years old for most of 1594, and the country's attention had turned from the issue of her marriage to that of succession. Oxford and Southampton wanted what Percy Allen had speculated Elizabeth had given privately to be given publicly. See Chapter 10.

conclusion."[40] These exchanges, though not addressing the authorship question directly, show that the Earl of Oxford, having been brought to light by J. Thomas Looney and kept in the public eye by proponents of the Oxfordian claim, remained in scholars' minds as they examined other literature of the Elizabethan age.

Vincent Towns, "Human Riddles That Have Vexed the World," *Boston Globe*, 1937

Towns turned to the Shakespeare authorship riddle in December 1937. He was receptive to the idea of alternate candidates, writing that "the author of Shakespeare's plays displayed the most profound classical learning and a deep knowledge of law, as well as an intimate acquaintance with the details of royal etiquette and of court life. He must also have been an ardent reader of history who had mastered Latin, French, Italian and Spanish, and who devoured the world's literature, ancient and modern. To some who have sought the man Shakespeare in the chronicles of his time it seems inconceivable that a country lad of his parenthood and rearing could have acquired all of this knowledge."[41]

Uncle Dudley, *Boston Globe*, 1938

A year later "Uncle Dudley," in his weekly column in the same paper, wondered why Shakespeare gave up the theater business at age forty-one to live with his illiterate daughter and sell malt. The author of Shakespeare's works "is at home in aristocratic life, he seems to understand war like a trained soldier, he knows law, he is familiar with music, his education suggests wide reading in Greek and Latin, he appears to have traveled in France and Northern Italy and to have read Danish and Spanish books in their originals."[42] It is a reasonable question, he implied, why such a man would be content to live in a small town engaged in small-time commercial activities.

Uncle Dudley had acquired his information from Bénézet's *Shakspere, Shakespeare and De Vere*. He mentioned Bénézet's belief in the existence of a nine-year-old boy who acted as Oxford's page in 1584 and who is thought to have been his unacknowledged son. He further noted Bénézet's belief that "It is supposed that Oxford's illegitimate son, the fair youth of the *Sonnets*, was an actor in his father's company of players, and that he passed under the name of William Shakespeare." Eventually, though "the plays were published under the name of the actor Shakespeare [the Earl's illegitimate son], and the earl's legitimate heirs squashed the scandal by fathering them, in 1623, on the Stratford man of the same name who was known to have had a long connection with the theatre."

He concluded by addressing the nature of literary creativity.

> One useful effect of such controversy is to dissipate the nimbus of miracle which hovers over a collection of amazing masterpieces attributed to the hand of an obscure person. You would think such works were produced like rabbits out of a hat. Biographies of other men of equal genius—Michelangelo, Goethe, Beethoven, Wagner—tell quite a different story. They are chronicles of patient apprenticeship, painful struggle and long labor. If the identity of the man who wrote the plays which we traditionally call Shakespeare's is ever established beyond question, and the facts of his career are authenticated, the story will be one not of miracle, but of industry plus an extraordinary talent. (C4)

---

[40] Pauline K. Angell, "Light on the Dark Lady," *PMLA*, vol. 55/2 (June 1940): 599.

[41] Vincent Towns, "Human Riddles that have Vexed the World: The Mystery of Shakespeare," *Boston Globe*, Dec. 30, 1937, p. 14.

[42] Uncle Dudley, "A Mystery Tale of Shakespeare," *Boston Globe*, July 10, 1938, p. C4.

The Argonaut, San Francisco, 1939

In April 1939, Flodden W. Heron, President of the Literary Anniversary Club in San Francisco, wrote about the fabrication of Shakespeare anecdotes and relics in the Stratford Museum. After noting that "all schools, universities, and colleges have endorsed" the deceptions begun 170 years earlier (at Garrick's Stratford Jubliee in 1769), he issued a challenge to individual readers to free themselves from inculcated beliefs.

> All we believers ask is that [you] . . . select those of the so-called Shakespeare plays you like best . . . Then try to impute the "miracle of genius" to William Shakespeare, a butcher's apprentice and later in life a maltster and land-speculator, who resided in a village with a population of less than one thousand people.
>
> Read two books, the one[s] written by Looney . . . and Clark. . . . With each year bringing additional information from researchers it would seem that it is only a question of time when all serious students of the great myth will join the growing army of believers who are convinced that Edward de Vere was the genius who should be crowned king of poetry and the Muses.[43]

In a letter to J. Thomas Looney, Lois Adelaide Book provided background on how this article came into being. Heron, a prominent book collector, was introduced to the Oxfordian thesis in 1937 by George Frisbee, the author of "Shame of the Professors" noted above. Heron's article originated as an address before the Shakespeare Society in the Shakespeare Garden in Golden Gate Park. It created an uproar because "everyone went expecting to hear the Stratford man praised and instead listened to a talk on Edward de Vere."[44] Mowry Saben, editor of *The Argonaut,* heard about it and asked Heron to write it up as an article, which he published. Saben also borrowed a copy of *"Shakespeare" Identified* from Frisbee, to whom he wrote,

> I am surprised to report that it has virtually converted me to his point of view, which is also your own. I did not expect to be converted, though my faith in the man from Stratford has been growing less for some time. Furthermore I did not wish to be converted, and the only genuine satisfaction that I find in my conversion is that it reveals that a man who lacks only a few weeks of being seventy years of age has still a brain sufficiently supple to weigh evidence, and to change when a change is logically imperative. As a literary sleuth Mr. Looney has no superior in my reading, and few equals. . . . I intend to go into the matter more deeply as soon as I have a little more time, for it is an extremely fascinating subject.[45]

Saben would write an important editorial on the subject in January 1940. Heron would go on to play an important role in the Oxfordian movement and serve as a vice president of the American branch of the Shakespeare Fellowship (see Chapter 17).

Barrell's 1940 *Scientific American* Article

In this article Barrell presented the most important Oxfordian discoveries he had made so far. His principal finding was that, when subjected to X-rays and infrared rays, the so-called Ashbourne portrait and two other paintings that purported to be images of William Shakespeare revealed images beneath the surface level showing they were

---

[43] Flodden W. Heron, "The Shakespeare Anniversary—Literature's Greatest Mystery," *Argonaut,* April 21.
[44] Lois Adelaide Book, letter to J. Thomas Looney, May 10, 1939.
[45] Mowry Saben, letter to George Frisbee, December 21, 1939.

Figure 1: Left: Edward de Vere 17th Earl of Oxford and Lord Chamberlain of England. Born April 12, 1550, died June 24, 1604. Painted in 1575 when this mysterious poet-peer was 25 years of age. From the original owned by the Duke of Portland

Figure 2: Right: A heretofore unpublished portrait of Lord Oxford, identifiable as the work of Marcus Gheeraedts. "It has frequently been reported," says A. Wivell (1827), "that Marcus Gheeraedts had painted Shakespeare, but nobody knows whence it originated." Painting owned by the Duke of St. Albans

IDENTIFYING 'SHAKESPEARE'

Science in the Shape of Infra-red Photography and the X ray Brings to Light at Last the Real Man Beneath the Surface of a Series of Paintings of the Bard

By CHARLES WISNER BARRELL

A SENSE of mystery has always surrounded the personality of Shakespeare, the prince of dramatists, as compared with the citizen of Stratford-on-Avon who signed himself—evidently with painful difficulty—Willm Shakspere. The latter left no letters, manuscripts, books or other relics of creative endeavor. Both of his parents, as well as his own 26-year-old daughter, were so illiterate that they could not write their own names, as the village records testify. Will himself is stated by two 17th Century investigators to have been working as a butcher's apprentice up to the time he left his wife and three small children to seek his fortune in London. There is no contemporary citation of his ever having attended school a day in his life or of having received any training whatever in any of the liberal arts with which Shakespeare, the dramatist, shows such intimate familiarity. Finally, during the heyday of the playwright's creative career, the Stratford citizen appears in the annals of his native town as malt dealer, money lender, and land speculator.

While it is entirely possible that this jack-of-all-trades may have had some

Figure 3: Lord Oxford's head, enlarged from the Portland portrait

Figure 4: Shakespeare's head. To be compared with those of Oxford

Figure 5: Lord Oxford's head enlarged from the St. Albans painting

5

actually portraits of Edward de Vere, Earl of Oxford.

> In each instance, my technical associates and I have uncovered clear-cut evidence to show that details of the original portraiture have been changed and that certain areas which previously displayed symbols of personal identification have been completely painted over. The manner in which this work of concealment and disguise was carried out, the character of the brush strokes employed, and the present condition of the surfaces of all three pictures, make it apparent that the changes were made at some remote period. It also seems evident that the hand of the same furtive craftsman was utilized throughout.
>
> Comparative research on recovered details of the original compositions and on all personal symbols of both the sitter and the artists who painted him, now for the first time brought to light, show beyond reasonable doubt that the Shakespeare who appears in these works must have been the mysterious Elizabethan court poet, Edward de Vere, 17th Earl of Oxford, and not the member of the illiterate Shakespeare family who was buried at Stratford-on-Avon, April 25th, 1616.[46]

The imaging techniques showed that alterations to the Ashbourne portrait had raised the forehead, retouched the hair, greatly reduced the size of the neck ruff, and scraped out the original inscription date. They also revealed two insignia that identified the subject as Edward de Vere: the image on the thumb ring and the crest of the Trentham family. They further revealed the monogram "C.K." of the original artist, Cornelius Ketel, who was known to have painted a portrait of the Earl of Oxford that had been lost.

Scientific American thoroughly vetted Barrell's findings before running the article. Bénézet provided background information on that effort in a 1938 letter to Looney.

> Have you had some correspondence with Mr. Charles Wisner Barrell, 6 Grove Street, New York City? He tells me that he is about to publish a book in which there will be new and startling documentary proof of the Oxford theory. I am not at liberty to tell some of the facts that he has put in his letters to me, but I learned through the editor of the *Atlantic Monthly* that Mr. Barrell had been at work with X-ray and infra-red examinations of the early Shakespeare portraits, betraying that the dates, etc. had been tampered with. He is sure that the Earl sat for the earliest portraits of the Bard. I am looking forward to his book with great eagerness.[47]

Bénézet's letter indicated that Barrell had approached the *Atlantic Monthly*—the periodical that had rejected Looney's article in 1932—before approaching *Scientific American*; it also suggested that Barrell's efforts took at least two years, as the article did not appear until the January 1940 issue. That timing is in line with a letter that Barrell wrote to Looney in March 1940 describing how thoroughly the magazine double-checked his findings with outside experts before agreeing to publish them.

> I wish to thank you most heartily for your words of commendation on the *Scientific American* article. As I think you know, this was a digest of work covering only the Ashbourne portrait although my investigation included the Hampton Court palace and the so-called "Janssen" Shakespeare also. The editors of the *Scientific American* studied my material for some three months before accepting it. All members of the staff are now thorough-going Oxfordians and your book

---

[46] Charles Wisner Barrell, "Identifying 'Shakespeare,'" *Scientific American*, Jan. 1940, p. 6.
[47] Louis P. Bénézet, letter to J. Thomas Looney, Jan. 29, 1938.

has an honored place in the editor's library.

There will be an editorial summing-up of the general reactions to the portrait article in the May issue of the magazine, a copy of which I will send you. The new material will include an X-ray photograph of the Ashbourne head, which was crowded out in the first publication. This picture is especially valuable in that it shows Lord Oxford's characteristically large ear very clearly defined under the synthetic Shakespearean hair. The infra-red picture used in the magazine did not include this particularity inasmuch as the hair contains a portion of lamp black which cannot be penetrated by the infra-red ray. I hope to have all of this pictorial evidence together with the complete narrative and documentation published in book form during the present year although it will be an expensive undertaking.[48]

Barrell's follow-up piece in the May issue mentioned J. Thomas Looney's "scholarly volume," *"Shakespeare" Identified*, and noted that his work had

won the endorsement of such scholars, historians and students of the Elizabethan period as Dr. Gilbert Slater of Oxford University; Dr. Gerald H. Rendall, former Headmaster of the Charterhouse School; Alan Gordon Smith, author of *William Cecil, the Power Behind Elizabeth*; Sir Geoffrey Callender, historian of the Tudor Navy and knighted for his writings on the Elizabethan Age; Dr. Sigmund Freud, the psycho-analyst, whose studies of the Shakespearean plays had a profound influence upon his professional theories; and John Galsworthy, the novelist, who helped distribute the book by Looney.[49]

The editors reported that *Scientific American* sold 5,000 extra copies of the January issue because of Barrell's article.[50] They also noted that the magazine had received more reader responses to it than to any other article in its history. They quoted from representative letters, and noted that responses fell into three classes:

those whose writers objected to doubt being cast upon the identity of the "officially approved" Bard of Avon, those whose writers demanded more proof of Lord Oxford's identity before drawing any conclusions, and those—evidently already possessing some acquaintance with subsidiary evidence connecting Oxford with the Shakespearean authorship—whose writers greeted the publication of the X-ray and infra-red investigation as an event, charged with important historical and biographical implications. We quote a paragraph from one of these latter, written by Fred H. Colvin, editorial veteran of the McGraw-Hill Publishing Company:

The disclosures made by modern photographic methods show clearly that the old paintings had been altered. The resemblance of the faces and features, as shown, together with the careful study of the hands, ring and wild boar device, should convince the most skeptical. It has long been a mystery to me why so many cling with a sort of blind loyalty to the idea that an illiterate butcher boy could have written of life and places of which he could have known nothing whatever.[51]

The Associated Press distributed Barrell's article as a special wire feature, which resulted in versions printed in some 2,000 outlets in the United States and Canada. Many

---

[48] Charles Wisner Barrell, letter to J. Thomas Looney, March 16, 1940.
[49] Editors, "Who Was Shakespeare?" *Scientific American*, May 1940, vol. 162/5, p. 299.
[50] "Oxfordian News," *SF News-Letter* (American), vol. 1/5 (Aug.-Sept. 1940): 6.
[51] Editors, "Who Was Shakespeare?" *Scientific American*, May 1940, vol. 162/5, p. 299.

were given front page-space and several well-known columnists wrote about it. "From Maine to California and from Winnipeg to San Antonio, millions of newspaper readers had their attention called to the first discoveries of their kind ever announced in the field of Shakespearean research. Nearly a hundred prominent journals devoted editorials to the ensuing controversy" (264). Furthermore, "Newspapers in France, Switzerland and Holland have also played up the story. Charles Boissevain, a well-known journalist of Geneva, is translating the complete *Scientific American* article into Dutch for publication

---

Reporting and Commentary on Charles Wisner Barrell's "Identifying Shakespeare"
in *Scientific American*, vol. 162 (Jan. 1940): 4-8, 43+

Dec. 13, 1939
St. Louis Post-Dispatch	-----. "X-Ray Expert Says Shakespeare Portraits Are of Earl of Oxford"

Dec. 14, 1939
Los Angeles Times	-----. "X-Ray Tests Called Proof Shakespeare Earl of Oxford"
Baltimore Sun	-----. "Fuel for a Fresh Shakespearean Squabble"
Newsweek	-----. "Was Shakespeare Oxford? Old Row Brought Up to Date by X-Rays of Portraits"

Dec. 16, 1939
New York Sun	-----. "The Roentgen Shakespeare"
New York Times	-----. "Alias Shakespeare" [Editorial] Reply by Charles Barrell, "Shakespeare's Portraits" [Dec. 18]

Dec. 21, 22, 23, 1939
Christian Science Monitor	Herbert B. Nichols. "Wonders of Research: Three Portraits of Shakespeare X-Rayed—Seeing Through Paint"

Dec. 24, 1939
San Francisco Examiner	Ada Hanifin. "Forceful Clew on Real Shakespeare"

Dec. 25, 1939
Newsweek	-----. [On book page]

Dec. 29, 1939
San Francisco Chronicle	Joseph Henry Jackson. "Science Takes a Hand in the Shakespearean Controversy"

Jan. 26, 1940
Argonaut	-----. "Who Was Shakespeare?"

January 1940 [Dates not known]
Baltimore Sun	-----. "X-Rays Find Hamlet's Ghost"
Boston Globe	-----. "Bard was Noble, Researcher Says"
Brunswick Daily News	-----. "Shakespeare Paintings Really Earl of Oxford, Says Student"
Chicago Tribune	-----. "X-Rays Reveal Real Shakespeare"
Daily Herald [Biloxi, MS]	-----. [Front page story]
Des Moines Register	-----. "Tis This the Poet I See Before Me?"
New York Post	-----. [Commentary]
New York Times	-----. "To Be or Not To Be: A New Shakespeare?"
Kansas City Star	-----. "X-Rays Reveal True Shakespeare"
Los Angeles Times	-----. "Shakespeare Fraud, Critic Says"
North Peoria Journal-Star	-----. "Painting Proves Bard Switched"
Rapid City Journal	-----. "Researcher Proves Bard Fake"
Spokesman Review	-----. "Painting Hints at Shake-Fraud"
Villager	-----. [Greenwich Village, New York]
Warwick Weekly Dispatch	-----. [Front page story]
Cleveland Plain Dealer	Herlow R. Hoty [Commentary]
San Francisco Chronicle	Joseph Henry Jackson. "Shakespeare: Who Was He?"
New York Times	Walter Winchell. [column]

in the Lowlands" (264, 299).

A list of some of the most important publications to run editorials or commentary on Barrell's findings is in a nearby text box. Anna Hanifin, drama critic for *The San Francisco Examiner*, announced that she had been convinced for some years that Oxford was the real author of the Shakespeare plays and was now glad that the portrait evidence confirmed her belief. *The San Francisco Chronicle's* erudite Joseph Henry Jackson also addressed the subject in his column, with the title "Science Takes a Hand in the Shakespearean Controversy."

The *Shakespeare Fellowship Newsletter* (American), reporting on the coverage in *The New York Times*, noted that,

> Walter Winchell also broke the news in his typically breezy style in the column that now enjoys the widest syndicated coverage. "William Shakespeare's real name was Edward de Vere" . . . Walter whispered. . . . "Charles Wisner Barrell, American secretary of the Shakespeare Fellowship, will so allege in the Jan. *Sci Am.* Bill, it appears, was the 17th Earl of Oxford and Lord Chamberlain of England under Queen Liz. For the first time in history scientific tools—infra-red photography and the X-ray—were employed by Barrell to probe the true personality of the Bard."

> The lengthy news article carried by *The New York Times* and later amplified in editorial treatment and correspondence provided an interesting contrast to Mr. Winchell's staccato telegraphese. And from all of these many sources millions of readers of the news have heard that Edward de Vere, 17th Earl of Oxford, not only devoted himself to the writing of plays and poems in the Shakespearean age but actually posed for three of the best known "life" portraits of Mr. William Shakespeare.[52]

Among the high points of the coverage was the editorial that appeared in *The New*

The New York Sun Editorial, December 16, 1939

The Roentgen Shakespeare

Who was the model for three paintings generally accepted as portraits of Shakespeare? ("O England! model to thy inward greatness . . .") The American secretary of the Shakespeare Fellowship, Charles W. Barrell, has been taking X-ray photographs of the Hampton Court Palace portrait of the poet, and of the two possessed by the Folger Shakespeare Library in Washington. ("Titan's rays on earth!") Mr. Barrell presents the evidence of his photographs to support his belief that the Earl of Oxford wrote the works of Shakespeare, and that the paintings were made of the Earl, Edward de Vere, and later altered to remove all identifying signs. ("What, have you got the picture of old Adam new-appareled?") He declares that the hand of the same craftsman is to be discerned in the alterations in all three portraits. ("Who was he / That, otherwise than noble nature did, / Hath alter'd that good picture?") He reports that details of the original paintings were carefully changed. ("He wrought better than made the painter.") He implies that the result of these revisions of the portraits has therefore concealed for posterity the name of the true author of the plays and poems published as Shakespeare's. ("'Twere concealment / Worse than a theft, no less than a traducement, / To hide your doings.")

It is known that some thirty years ago a British authority on art charged that the Ashbourne portrait of Shakespeare had been tampered with. ("To spurn at your most royal image / And mock your workings in a second body.") The advocates of the Oxford authorship of Shakespeare's works have frequently cited evidence in the language and historical incidents of the plays and will naturally make much of X-ray evidence uncovered by Mr. Barrell. ("I cannot hide what I am.")

---

[52] "Scientific Proof Given that Lord Oxford Posed for Ancient Portraits of the Bard," *SF News-Letter* (American), vol. 1/2 (Feb. 1940): 4.

York Sun, reprinted in the text box.

As a result of the massive publicity given to the Oxfordian thesis by Barrell's *Scientific American* article, the *Shakespeare Fellowship News-Letter* announced that "The Oxford theory is definitely on the map at last!" (4) The coverage "marked a culminating point in the history of Shakespearean research, detailing the high lights of the first scientifically conceived and illustrated revelation of the hidden personality behind the painted camouflage of the so-called 'Bard of Avon'" (2). The article also noted that "arrangements are now being made to publish the complete narrative of the pictorial discoveries in book form during the coming months" (3). The book would include about seventy-five "comparative photographs taken by Mr. Barrell and his technical associates. These cover the three ancient Shakespeare portraits and the only two inscribed paintings of the 17th Earl of Oxford known to exist today, one dated 1575 and owned by the Duke of Portland at Welbeck Abbey, the other ascribed to Marcus Gheeraerts the Younger and owned by the Duke of St. Albans at Bestwood Lodge."[53]

Barrell's article in the January 1940 issue and his follow-up in the May issue (which was available by the middle of April), marked the high point for the first quarter century of the Oxfordian movement. On May 10 the Germans attacked France and the Low Countries and the "phony war" became real. The English-speaking world, like much of the rest of the world, faced matters far more urgent than questions about Shakespearean authorship.

Nevertheless, Oxfordians in North America remained optimistic about what to expect. The Fellowship's *News-Letter* had declared that "[t]he work of [the] American Secretary of the Shakespeare Fellowship [Barrell] represents a landmark in Elizabethan research and may cause immediate revaluation of the commonly accepted theory of the authorship of the plays" (1). And again, "The Ashbourne portrait, owned by the Folger Shakespeare Library, and two other famous paintings of the poet have been dissected scientifically for the first time in history—with results likely to change the whole course of Shakespearean research. Solution of authorship mystery [is] at hand."

Oscar James Campbell and *Harper's* — Academia's Response to Barrell's Article

In February 1940 the *Shakespeare Fellowship News-Letter* (American) observed that "Although six weeks have passed since the first news story was released, no Stratfordian expert has come forward as yet to offer any reasonable refutation of Mr. Barrell's pictorial conclusions."[54] Associated Press representatives had asked Stratfordian authorities at leading American universities for their reactions, but none offered a coherent explanation for the alterations to the Ashbourne portrait. The most common responses were along the lines of "'Absurd!' or 'I don't believe it!' or 'There must be some mistake—I never heard of the Earl of Oxford!'" showing "emotional reaction[s] of high authority rather than rational consideration of the evidence." As late as March 16—more than three months after the AP report—Barrell wrote to Looney that "[n]o Stratfordian authority has ventured as yet to dispute the pictorial evidence featured by the *Scientific American*." He continued, "You probably will be pleased to hear that one of the very last letters written

---

[53] The book was never published and the manuscript is presumably lost unless it can be located in the papers that Barrell left behind at the time of his death in 1974.

[54] "Scientific Proof Given that Lord Oxford Posed for Ancient Portraits of the Bard," *SF News-Letter (American), vol. 1/2 (Feb. 1940): 3.*

by the late Lord Tweedsmuir, Governor General of Canada,[55] expressed his deep interest in the *Scientific American* article and thanks for the manner in which it had been presented."[56]

Finally a response appeared. Oscar James Campbell's fourteen-page article, "Shakespeare Himself," ran in the June issue of *Harper's Magazine*. As Campbell was a professor of literature at Columbia University, his piece is indicative of the thinking of Shakespeare scholars on the authorship issue. It began on a positive note:

> Mr. Barrell's evidence is so clear and so cogent that it is impossible to question seriously the truth of his main contention. It seems probable that at some time before the middle of the nineteenth century an unknown painter altered a number of details in a portrait of the Earl of Oxford in order to pass it off as a likeness of William Shakespeare.[57]

"Positive," that is, if one overlooked how compromised it is by Campbell's claim that the alterations had occurred in only one portrait of Oxford, even though Barrell had made it clear that his team had examined three portraits supposedly of Shakespeare—the Ashbourne, the Hampton Court and the so-called Janssen—and found similar alterations in all three. It was downhill from there, as Campbell relied on one whopper after another to prop up the Stratfordian story. He claimed that Stratford was "the business metropolis of a large and fertile area," when it was really an isolated village of fewer than 1,500 people. He claimed that "the grammar school there was one of the best in England," when nothing is actually known of its curriculum or reputation. He denied the learned nature of the plays, writing that "Shakespeare's knowledge was not exceptional . . . [his] 'learning' can be shown to be no more than the knowledge in the possession of all intelligent persons of his day." That view was so contrary to the findings of so many respected scholars that it is hard to believe Campbell held it as late as 1940.

He went on to quote an authority—historian and U.S. Senator Albert J. Beveridge—whose testimony undermined his position and supported the Oxfordian.

> "A genius wrote the plays, but genius does not supply learning, facts, experience. These plays were the great repository of his time. They abound in accurate legal learning then current. They are full of rabbinical lore. They bristle with the kind of martial facts which are to be learned only on the field of battle. They are saturated with personal experiences upon the high seas. . . . [O]nly a linguist could have written most of the plays, since most of them were taken from works in foreign languages, then untranslated. But Shakespeare knew no French, no Italian, no German, no Danish . . . He took no sea voyage. He was never at court."[58]

How had Shakspere managed to write the plays without these formative experiences? Campbell's answer was "imagination" and "genius."

Turning to Barrell's specific claims, Campbell speculated that "the Ashbourne portrait is almost certainly one of those spurious . . . portraits [that] art dealers in London hired hacks to doctor . . . into some resemblance to the Stratford bust" in order to make a quick pound. But he ignored Barrell's documentation that the Ashbourne had remained in the possession of descendants of the Earl of Oxford until 1910.

---

[55] Lord Tweedsmuir was John Buchan, the famous author of more than a dozen adventure novels and half a dozen biographies and personal memoirs.

[56] Charles Wisner Barrell, letter to J. Thomas Looney, March 16, 1940.

[57] Oscar James Campbell, "Shakespeare Himself," *Harper's Magazine*, June, 1940, p. 181.

[58] Quoted in Campbell (1940), p. 179. The source of Senator Beveridge's statement is not given.

And so it goes, for fourteen pages. Rather than rebut Campbell point by point, it's better to turn to J. Thomas Looney's response to the article. When asked about it by Lois Adelaide Book, an American Oxfordian, Looney wrote her a lengthy letter that was published in the December 1940 issue of the American branch's *News-Letter*.

Looney observed that Campbell proceeded in the manner of "counsel for the defense of a criminal faced with a mass of mutually corroborating evidence against his client" by engaging in the common legal trick of pointing to isolated pieces of evidence in order "to divert attention from the manner in which the different elements in the evidence all fit in with one another."[59] Looney noted that "Professor Campbell recognized that the appearance of the Oxford theory is rapidly ousting all competitors," and suggested that "had he known something of the mental caliber of many of the men who now support it, it should have made him realize that it rests upon a body of evidence vastly stronger than anything he represents in his article." Then came an attack on Campbell's honesty.

> I accuse him of a deliberate attempt, not to present the Oxford case fairly and squarely, as honest opponents of ideas do with the cases they controvert, but to set it forth so flimsily, and even grotesquely, that hardly anyone but an imbecile could very well believe in it if it rested on nothing more substantial. This is the kind of argumentation one associates with political maneuvering rather than a serious quest for the truth on great issues and it makes one suspect that he is not very easy in his own mind about the case. (2)

The editors of the *News-Letter* noted in a separate criticism of Campbell's article that "Academic conjectures are boldly exaggerated throughout Prof. Campbell's critique to make them appear as attested truth, while independent research in the Shakespearean authorship field, as represented by leading Oxfordian scholars, is arrogantly dismissed as the pitiable stumblings of 'the mentally unemployed.'"[60]

The editors also commented on *Harper's* failure to run any letters from readers. "Although the editors of *Harper's Magazine* admit that they have received many letters objecting to the tenor of Prof. Campbell's article, and asking for the presentation of adequate evidence for Oxford as 'Shakespeare,' they have up to date steadfastly refused to give any Oxfordian writer opportunity to reply in their columns." In March 1941 Fellowship President Louis Bénézet submitted to *Harper's* a lengthy rebuttal to Campbell. It was rejected and appeared instead in the July 1941 issue of the *News-Letter*. The editor of *Harper's* did send the letter to Campbell, and forwarded to Bénézet Campbell's brief reply that ignored all the major issues. The *Harper's* editor also stated "that there was such a crisis in Greece and Yugoslavia that there was no space in *Harper's* to devote at present to Shakespeare and such subjects." The *News-Letter* concluded its report with the comment that, "So ended the attempt to induce *Harper's* to give some space to the other side of the debate. It is the same story: until some 'recognized Shakespeare authority' comes out for the theory, orthodox-minded editors and publishers shy away from it. There was a still greater war crisis last June, but yet there was room for a Shakespeare article at that time. This is why we are forced to print our own *News-Letter*."[61]

---

[59] J. Thomas Looney, "The Author of *"Shakespeare" Identified* Comments on Professor Campbell's July 1940 *Harper's* Article," *SF News-Letter* (American), vol. 2/1 (Dec. 1940): 1.
[60] "... Let No Dog Bark," *SF News-Letter* (American), vol. 1/5 (Aug.-Sept, 1940): 6.
[61] "Bénézet versus Campbell," *SF News-Letter* (American) vol. 2/4 (June 1941): 44.

The American Branch of the Shakespeare Fellowship, 1939-1948, I

Founding of the American Branch

An American branch of the Shakespeare Fellowship was founded at the end of 1939, in response to the suspension of activities by the mother branch in England due to the onset of the Second World War. Eva Turner Clark played the leading role; her energy and determination brought individuals in the United States together, preventing the splintering of the Oxfordian movement. The new branch's *News-Letter* served as a lifeline for British scholars isolated in the countryside during the war, as well as for those scattered throughout North America and elsewhere.

Attending the organizational meeting held on November 10 at Clark's New York residence were Clark, Charles Wisner Barrell, Prof. Louis P. Bénézet, James Stewart Cushman, Dr. Will Howe (a literary advisor to Charles Scribner's Sons), Mary B. Herridge of Ottawa, Paul Munter, and several friends concerned about the deterioration of conditions supportive of the study of the Oxfordian claim in England. Executives were chosen, practical working plans outlined, and the decision made to launch a bimonthly *News-Letter*. Bénézet was selected as president, Clark and Cushman as vice presidents, and Barrell as secretary, treasurer and editor of the *News-Letter*.

Col. Montagu Douglas, in announcing these developments to readers of *The East Anglian Magazine*, wrote "We accord a hearty welcome to the American branch of the Fellowship, and wish the members all success in their resolve to organise research and literary enterprise towards the elucidation of the problem of Shakespearean authorship." Moreover, he continued, "there is in America an impartial Press, and a spacious receptive literary world, which will give full attention to, and consideration of, any arguments and evidence which the Fellowship may publish."[1] Although Douglas may have let his hopes color his views, he gave voice to the relief that so many active Oxfordian scholars in England felt at the formation of an organization in the United States.

Clark echoed their sentiments in an announcement in the first issue of the American branch's *News-Letter*:

> The interest that has been aroused in the question of the authorship of the Shakespeare Plays must not be allowed to sleep—it will not die—for lack of a publication to keep members of the Fellowship informed of what is transpiring in the way of research in the field.

> The example of the officers of the Shakespeare Fellowship, whose untiring devotion to the literary problem for the solution of which the society was organized, has been an inspiration to members on this side of the Atlantic. As a tribute to these officers and to the cause for which they stand, it is the desire of

---

[1] Col. Montagu W. Douglas, "The American Branch of the Shakespeare Fellowship," *East Anglian Magazine*," vol. 5/3 (April 1940): 121.

the American members of the Fellowship to "carry on."[2]

The chief objects of the American branch "will be research in the field of Shakespearean literature and history, with special attention to the claims made for the Seventeenth Earl of Oxford as author of the Plays, and the publication of the bi-monthly *News-Letter*, by means of which members may be kept informed of what is going on in the field." She also urged members in England to keep the American branch informed of developments on their side of the Atlantic.

President Bénézet addressed wider concerns and laid out his hopes and expectations for the American branch. His message is reproduced in a nearby text box.[3]

Within two months the American branch had more than sixty members—people Charles Barrell identified as "writers, scholars, and Shakespearean students who had developed a permanent interest in the Oxford-Shakespeare evidence." Among them were writers Gelett Burgess and Carolyn Wells, as well as "numerous members of the legal, medical and scientific professions, including publicists, bibliophiles and speakers such as Mrs. Mallet-Prevost, diplomatist and international attorney; Mrs. [Harriet] Sprague;

American Branch President Prof. Louis P. Bénézet's Message

To the Members of the American Branch of the Shakespeare Fellowship, and to open-minded students of Shakespeare everywhere:

As war raises its ghastly figure among the most enlightened and cultured people of the earth, art and literature flee into hiding places. The pages of European magazines are full of pictures of men burying priceless stained glass in the earth, hiding rare statues and paintings in underground vaults, and covering the delicate stone carvings of historic cathedrals with shapeless bags of sand.

Education must yield to the need for building up morale, and the thoughts of all citizens must be devoted to nothing but defeating the enemy.

So only is victory to be achieved in modern conflicts.

Thus it is not surprising that our parent organization, the Shakespeare Fellowship of Great Britain has suspended operations for the duration of the war.

However, it becomes all the more incumbent upon the American members to carry on the torch which Mr. Looney, Professor Lefranc, Captain Ward, Admiral Holland, Professor Slater, Col. Douglas, Canon Rendall, the Brothers Allen and others have kept alive in England and France, but are now compelled to drop.

Much has been gained already. Anti-Stratfordian articles and letters are appearing in increasing numbers in magazines and newspapers.

If we all put forth our best efforts now, while people are beginning to ask questions and to express their doubts regarding the Stratford story, we shall not only consolidate our gains but push on into new territory. It is surprising how many people become keenly interested as soon as the theory that only a scholarly aristocrat could have written the Shakespeare works is broached to them.

Startling new testimony will soon be in print. The advocates of the orthodox version of the Bard's identity are due to find themselves distinctly on the defensive. They will be unable any longer loftily to ignore the accumulated evidence against them. Papers will be eager to print letters that contain reasonable arguments, to pose questions that our Stratfordian friends can not answer satisfactorily. United effort is needed. Let each of us do his bit. It is time that this "Greatest of Literary Problems" as James Phinney Baxter called it, should be moving toward a solution.

---

[2] Eva Turner Clark, "To the Members of the Shakespeare Fellowship," *SF News-Letter* (American), vol. 1/1 (Dec. 1939): 1.

[3] Louis P. Bénézet, "President Bénézet's Message," *SF News-Letter* (American), vol. 1/1 (Dec. 1939): 1.

Charlton Ogburn of Washington and New York; T. Henry Foster of Iowa; Flodden W. Heron of San Francisco; Forrest S. Rutherford of Washington, and J. L. Astley-Cock of *The Chicago Tribune*. " All, he wrote, "have taken active parts in developing American public interest in the Oxford evidence."[4]

In two letters to Looney in March 1940,[5] Barrell identified early members of the American branch as including: [6]

- The library of one of the most progressive colleges in the United States.
- The oldest college library in the United States.
- The librarian of one of the ancient chartered companies of London.
- One of the world's foremost rare book experts who has owned at various times more copies of Shakespeare's First Folio than any other living person.
- The business manager of one of America's finest theaters.
- Two playwrights.
- Two popular novelists.
- A distinguished motion picture producer.
- The senior member of a famous and highly successful firm of book publishers.
- Five college professors, one of them formerly a Shakespearean editor and now literary adviser to a great publishing house.
- A typographical expert.
- Three American attorneys of international reputation.
- One prominent barrister of British Columbia.
- Two well-known musicians.
- The foremost American engraver of armorial devices.
- A famous American physician and Shakespeare scholar.
- A well-known New York advertising man.
- An executive officer of the United States Forest Service.
- One of the most widely read dramatic critics on the Pacific Coast.

For a brief time American universities were also open to the Oxfordian idea—at least in comparison with universities in England. By the spring of 1940 at least seven American universities were members of the Fellowship, compared with none in England, as shown in the nearby text box.

Notable Members, Shakespeare Fellowship (American), Spring 1940

Individuals	Faculty at	University Libraries
Editor, Chicago Tribune	Ball State University	Ball State University (Indiana)
Drama Critic, SF Examiner	Boston University	Harvard University
Literary Advisor, Scribner's	Dartmouth	Mt. Holyoke College
Secretary, American Museum	Penn State University	Lehigh University
of Natural History	Yale	Rollins College (Florida)
Three American novelists		University of Michigan
Three playwrights		University of Pennsylvania

---

[4] Charles Wisner Barrell, "Afterwords," in J. Thomas Looney, *"Shakespeare" Identified* (1948), p. 460.

[5] The second letter, dated March 22, specifically mentioned Charlton Ogburn, General Counsel for the American Federation of Labor, thereby linking the past (Looney), the present (Barrell), and the future (Ogburn).

[6] "Rapid Growth of Research Fellowship Means End of Pompous Obstructionists," *SF News-Letter* (American), vol. 1/2 (Feb. 1940): 7.

Barrell stated his expectation that the press would henceforth cover the Oxfordian idea in an impartial, if not outrightly favorable, manner. During that brief window in 1940 between the publication of Barrell's *Scientific American* article in January and Professor James Campbell's piece in the June issue of *Harper's Magazine*, media coverage had indeed become more even-handed and positive. Reflecting the optimism of the moment, he titled his piece "Rapid Growth of Research Fellowship Means End of Pompous Obstructionists."

> Contacts made with leading American newspaper and magazine editors, art directors and writers assure the Shakespeare Fellowship on this side of the Atlantic full and fair consideration of all its aims and accomplishments. We are definitely "on the map" and henceforth our point of view cannot be ignored by anyone who undertakes seriously to evaluate the evidence relating to the personality behind the creations of "Mr. William Shakespeare."

> Editorial barricades that have heretofore been guarded by dyed-in-the-wool Stratfordians have been breached if not entirely removed. Anyone with a thorough grounding in Oxfordian research who can write an interesting article or give voice to a stimulating talk can now secure a hearing.

> For years it has been the practice of many . . . "authorities" to condemn all Oxfordian literature out of hand without bothering to read it. Their stock phrases "absurd" and "quite impossible" have now lost weight.

> The 1940 editor, publisher and producer is going to demand a bill of particulars from those who seek to demolish Oxfordian research with a pompous pursing of oracular lips.

The American branch established an endowment fund to ensure the continuance of research. The call for contributions recognized the sacrifices that individual researchers had made on behalf of the cause during the Great Depression.

> All major discoveries in this field have been accomplished to date by individuals working on their own time and at their own expense—a situation that has entailed considerable self-sacrifice. These enthusiasts have fought an uphill battle against entrenched prejudice and the powerful vested interests of professional Stratfordia. To date not one penny has come their way from any of the numerous research foundations that during the same period have lavished thousands upon proponents of ineffective "orthodoxy." But despite all handicaps, needlessly imposed delays and misrepresentations, the Oxfordian explorers have finally succeeded in excavating the richest vein of biographical and historical ore ever opened before the eyes of living men.

> At the same time, these pioneers realize only too well that time and tools of high precision are needed to bring the new-found treasures to the surface intact. Therefore—individuals or foundations with funds to allot for the advancement of knowledge are respectfully urged to investigate the Oxfordian discoveries with the idea of insuring the permanence of the facts which they represent. Oxfordian projects already mapped out along scientific lines must also be assured of completion. Monetary aid rendered for such purposes can be made to return the same substantial dividends of prestige that inevitably accrue to backers of successful expeditions.[7]

---

[7] "Funds Needed for Exploration," *SF News-Letter* (American), vol. 1/2 (Feb. 1940): 6.

The *News-Letter* of the American Branch

The American branch's *News-Letter* was launched in December 1939. In the first issue, editor Charles Barrell wrote that it was primarily dedicated "to the task of solving the most unusual mystery in the whole realm of English literature, to wit: Identification of the personality of the one unique creative genius that our race has produced, whose works appear to have been published under the pen-name of 'William Shakespeare.'"[8] In contrast with traditional Shakespearean authorities who often behave "like members of certain medieval cults," the scholars comprising the Shakespeare Fellowship "prefer truth to fundamental conjecture." He was confident that "Our inquiry, already successfully developed, . . . [will] bring into the light of day at last the true answers to the long-acknowledged mystery behind the creation of the outstanding masterpieces of our language" (2).

The first issue "was distributed to all persons here and abroad who were known to have some interest in the Oxfordian answer to the issue of the Shakespeare Mystery." Barrell would later report that within a month, "The American Branch of The Fellowship had coalesced into a vigorous and enthusiastic group, determined to carry on the work of enlightenment so ably inaugurated in the year 1920 by Mr. J. Thomas Looney with the publication of his unique masterpiece of research, *"Shakespeare" Identified*."[9]

Reports on original research and discoveries by Barrell, Clark and Bénézet, and occasionally by

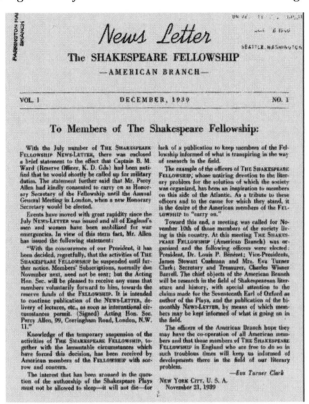

other members, began with the inaugural issue and continued over the next nine years. J. Thomas Looney, after a long absence from publication, was among the contributors. The rest of this section summarizes some of the articles that strengthened support for the Oxfordian claim in especially direct and persuasive ways. The summaries do not do justice to the depth of information presented in the articles, or to the often sparkling quality of the writing. Interested readers can now easily access all issues of the *News-Letter* on the website of the Shakespeare Oxford Fellowship. The most important articles have been collected and reprinted in full in *Building the Case for Edward de Vere as Shakespeare*, the ten-volume anthology of early Oxfordian articles prepared by Paul Altrocchi, with Hank

---

[8] Charles Wisner Barrell, "To Pluck the Heart of the Mystery," *SF News-Letter* (American), vol. 1/1 (Dec. 1939): 1.

[9] "Introducing the *Quarterly*," *SF Quarterly*, vol. V/1 (Jan. 1944): 1.

Whittemore serving as co-editor of the first five volumes.

Charles Wisner Barrell, "Scientific Proof that Lord Oxford Posed for Ancient Portraits of the Bard" (February 1940): Barrell summarized his discoveries, described in the *Scientific American* article and elsewhere, that X-ray and infra-red photographic dissections carried out under his direction on the Ashbourne, Janssen and Hampton Court portraits of "Shakespeare" revealed that all three were portraits of Edward de Vere, Earl of Oxford that had been altered. These findings "marked a culminating point in the history of Shakespearean research, . . . [They are] the first scientifically conceived and illustrated revelation of the hidden personality behind the painted camouflage of the so-called 'Bard of Avon.'"[10]

Eva Turner Clark, "Shakespeare's Birthday" (April 1941): Clark established that Edward de Vere was born on the very day that is widely celebrated as William Shakespeare's birthday. "According to the old calendar in force at the time of his birth, Edward de Vere was born on April 12, 1550, but the change of eleven days in the calendar which took place on the Continent in 1582 and sometime later in England, makes his anniversary fall on April 23rd."[11] "That these two birthdates should fall together is a remarkable coincidence," Clark commented. "Or is it a coincidence? The more we study the lives of these two men, the more inclined we are to believe that details of the Stratford man's life were made to conform to a plan which would make him appear with some realism as the poet-dramatist, just as portraits of Edward de Vere were altered to reappear as 'Shakespeare.'"

Charles Wisner Barrell, "Shakespeare's 'Fluellen' Identified as a Retainer of the Earl of Oxford" (August 1941): Barrell established yet another link between Edward de Vere and Shakespeare. "One of the most picturesque real-life notables of Elizabethan times, the doughty Sir Roger Williams, the Welsh soldier of fortune, who is said by all modern editors of *King Henry the Fifth* to have been the prototype of Shakespeare's characterization of Captain Fluellen,"[12] is described in a letter from Sir Francis Vere, Oxford's favorite cousin and intimate friend, as "a follower of my Lord of Oxford's, to whom he sometimes resorted." "Here we have," Barrell continued, "unquestionable contemporary proof that the playwriting Earl of Oxford knew the living prototype of Shakespeare's Fluellen from personal contact. . . . Oxford is the one man who can be proven to have possessed the poetical genius, plus the particular knowledge and essential *opportunity* to meet the definite requirements of 'Mr. William Shakespeare's' role in this all-important matter of creative background." (61).

Charles Wisner Barrell, "Shake-speare's Unknown Home on the River Avon Discovered" (December 1942): The discovery that Edward de Vere "had an estate in eastern Warwickshire, overlooking the valley of the Avon, which can be proved to have been retained by him after most of his other properties and known residences had been

---

[10] Charles Wisner Barrell, "The Secret Personality of 'Shakespeare' Brought to Light After Three Centuries," *SF News-Letter* (American), vol. 1/2 (Feb. 1940): 2.
[11] Eva Turner Clark, "Shakespeare's Birthday," *SF News-Letter* (American), vol. 2/3 (April 1941): 31.
[12] Charles Wisner Barrell, "Shakespeare's 'Fluellen' Identified as a Retainer of the Earl of Oxford," *SF News-Letter* (American), vol. 2/5 (Aug. 1941): 60.

sold"[13] undercuts the Stratfordians claim that the phrase "Sweet Swan of Avon" unequivocally linked William Shakspere with Shakespeare's plays, and reinforced what Oxfordians saw as the deliberate ambiguity of Ben Jonson's prefatory materials in the First Folio.

Charles Wisner Barrell, "Lord Oxford as Supervising Patron of Shakespeare's Theatrical Company" (July 1944): Two Lord Chamberlains existed in Queen Elizabeth's England: the Lord Great Chamberlain, who was Edward de Vere throughout the final forty years of her reign, and the lesser position of Lord Chamberlain, who oversaw the management of the royal household, a position occupied by several people over the same period of time. Barrell documented that the title held by Edward de Vere was often referred to by the first and last words only—Lord Chamberlain. Drawing on further evidence, he concluded that references to the Lord Chamberlain's Company—the so-called "Shakespeare's" company—were in fact references to Edward de Vere, not to the holders of the lower position."[14]

Charles Wisner Barrell, "New Milestone in Shakespearean Research: 'Gentle Master William'" (October 1944): In one of his most important discoveries, Barrell found contemporary evidence "that the 17th Earl of Oxford, whose 'countenance shakes a spear' bore the nickname of 'Gentle Master William' among his literary intimates of the early 1590s.'"[15] Traditional scholars had long believed that in using that nickname Thomas Nashe was referring to "William Shakespeare." This discovery also provided a response to those "critics of the Oxford-Shakespeare case who have claimed that the literary Earl could not have been the real 'Shakespeare' without the matter being known to his contemporaries." They did know, and with Barrell's new findings, "Edward de Vere here stands out clearly enough for even the myopic to see [him] as the living personage behind the mask of 'Gentle Master William.'"

Louis P. Bénézet, "Another Stratfordian Aids the Oxford Cause (April 1946): "It is strange that commentators have not pointed out that there are just three persons at Elizabeth's court who are named in properly sponsored Shakespeare publications, Southampton, to whom the two great poems are dedicated, and the Herbert brothers, to whom the First Folio is dedicated; and that *the only person in all England who was closely connected with all three was Edward de Vere.*"[16] [emphasis in original]

Louis P. Bénézet, "The Frauds and Stealths of Injurious Imposters" (January 1944): Bénézet showed that the "case for William Shakspere rests solely on the statements written by Ben Jonson for those who published the First Folio, and signed by him and by Heminge and Condell, the aged, retired actors." Their statements claim that the Folio was

---

[13] Charles Wisner Barrell, "Shakespeare's Unknown Home on the River Avon Discovered," *SF News-Letter* (American), vol. 4/1 (Dec. 1942): 2.

[14] Charles Wisner Barrell, "Lord Oxford as Supervising Patron of Shakespeare's Theatrical Company," *SF Quarterly*, vol. V/3 (July 1944): 34.

[15] Charles Wisner Barrell, "New Milestone in Shakespearean Research: 'Gentle Master William,'" *SF Quarterly*, vol. V/4 (Oct. 1944): 66.

[16] Louis P. Bénézet, "Another Stratfordian Aids the Oxford Cause," *SF Quarterly*, vol. VII/2 (April 1946): 18. [This article was the fifth in a series in which Bénézet presented findings by Stratfordian scholars that, although providing some insight into Shakespeare's works, undercut the case for authorship by the man from Stratford. The first four articles were titled, appropriately enough, "The Stratford Defendant Compromised by His Own Advocates, Parts, I-IV." See also Chapter 13.

printed from "True Originall Copies," "absolute in their numbers, as he conceived them," written out by the author "with scarce a blot," and then, "handed over by him to his friends the actors to be published, but not until he had been dead several years!"[17]

But, Bénézet continued, "There is not a 'responsible Shakespeare scholar' who believes it. What is more, they take no pains to conceal their skepticism." He cited three respected scholars who "admit that it [the prefatory material in the Folio] cannot be taken literally. In other words, *it is not the truth.*" Then came the crux of his argument. "After a man is caught in one lie he is never believed again. . . . If we admit one lie, then what becomes of the authority for the rest of the story? . . . Not one of the 'recognized Shakespeare authorities' defends the Jonson-Heminge-Condell fiction. Yet, in the last analysis, this is the foundation stone of the whole Stratford edifice" (5). In other words, if those statements were deliberately false, why would anyone believe their other statements pointing toward William Shakspere as the author? Where does that leave the story of Stratfordian authorship? Without any foundation whatsoever, says Bénézet.

Charles Wisner Barrell, "Shakespeare's Own Secret Drama, Parts 1-6" (December 1941-October 1942):

In this series, Barrell, observing that J. Thomas Looney did not have space or time in *"Shakespeare" Identified* "to develop the autobiographical leads of the *Sonnets* beyond a general surface outline . . . decided to take up the problem where Mr. Looney had been obliged to leave it."[18] "That was the beginning of a seven years' search," he explained, "which has led through the dusty files of the Public Record Office and Somerset House . . . [and] among the yellowing pages of many thousands of volumes of genealogical records, State Papers, personal letters, diaries, armorial devices, biographic commentaries, histories—and finally to privately-owned collections of Elizabethan and Jacobean portraits."

Barrell believed he had emerged from the paper chase with "documentation that appears to play a vital part in the permanent identification of Edward de Vere, Earl of Oxford, with the creative life of 'Mr. William Shakespeare.' Complete corroboration of Mr. Looney's pioneer discoveries is now available. And the secrets which the author of the *Sonnets* set down in his amazing diary more than three centuries ago can be interpreted in realistic detail. The creation of many of the poems can even be accurately dated."

Barrell's findings deserve far more attention than can be given here. He established first that the illegitimate son born to Edward de Vere and Anne Vavasour, a Gentlewoman of the Queen's Bedchamber was Sir Edward Vere, who went on to achieve considerable fame as a military hero. That birth had landed all three of them in the Tower in June of 1581. The son had been known of before, as had Sir Edward Vere; what was new was Barrell's showing that they were the same person—a fact missed by Capt. Bernard M. Ward in his 1928 biography of Edward de Vere.[19] With Edward Vere's identity now established, Barrell found similarities between real-life events involving Oxford, Anne Vavasour and their son and events obliquely described in the *Sonnets*.

---

[17] Louis P. Bénézet, "The Frauds and Stealths of Injurious Imposters," *SF Quarterly*, vol. V/1 (Jan. 1944): 2.

[18] Charles Wisner Barrell, "'Shake-speare's' Own Secret Drama, Part 2," *SF Letter* (American), vol. 3/2 (Feb. 1942): 15, 16.

[19] It was also missed by E. K. Chambers in his biography of Sir Henry Lee (1936). Lee and Vavasour had lived together from 1590 until his death in 1611 even though she was married to someone else. Lee willed several household items to Vere.

Regarding the real-life persons portrayed in the *Sonnets*, Barrell concluded that Anne Vavasour "filled the same place in the life of Edward de Vere ... that the 'Dark Lady of the Sonnets' occupied in the career of 'Shake-speare.'"[20] And, he concluded, "*Two* handsome young men are clearly discernible" in the *Sonnets*. One of these was "fair, kind and true, dependable and heroic, but the victim of a crooked eclipse."[21] This was his illegitimate son Edward Vere, for whom certain sonnets express "a heart-broken father's renunciation of the open pride of parenthood in a charming and worthy son born out of wedlock! ... It is plain that the writer of these lines was primarily interested in dissociating the scandals and mistakes of his own career, as far as possible, from the boy's future" (23).

The other was "a noble of impeccable birth, brilliant and given to impulsive generosity, but essentially undependable" (17). "All circumstances considered, there can, I think, be little question that Henry Wriothesley, Earl of Southampton, was the real-life original of the [second] young nobleman in this highly personal drama."[22]

Then came the critical development in Barrell's thinking: the second youth "meets and seduces or is seduced by the Bard's dark-eyed and insatiable mistress."[23] In other words, Southampton, seduced (or was seduced by) Anne Vavasour. It was to protect Edward Vere from any taint of that scandalous affair that "Lord Oxford and his survivors so effectually concealed" their blood relationship that it "has remained a mystery to British historians and genealogists up to this present writing."[24] It was in 1593, "when Oxford's new Countess, Elizabeth Trentham, gave the peer a male heir, legally qualified to inherit the Earldom of Oxford ... [that] the name 'William Shakespeare' first appeared in English literature. ... It thus becomes obvious," Barrell believed, "that the playwriting nobleman took a pen-name to cover the works that were so essentially autobiographical in structure that they could not help but revive old scandals and cause pain to his growing children and to his new wife" (30).

"Mr. C. Wisner Barrell is to be warmly congratulated upon his discovery," Percy Allen was quick to write. But, he cautioned, "Identifications of the Dark Lady, the Fair Youth, and so forth, are and must remain matters of personal interpretation."[25] Barrell's conclusions differed markedly from those of Percy Allen and Capt. Ward. Although Allen agreed with Barrell that an illegitimate son of Oxford's was involved in the story told in the *Sonnets*, he believed him to be Southampton and his mother, the Dark Lady of the *Sonnets*, to be Queen Elizabeth.[26]

Allen reminded readers that "the theory of the Fair Youth of the *Sonnets* as Oxford's son was first promulgated among our members about 1927," citing books by himself, Gerald Phillips and Dr. Gerald Rendall. Allen had also recognized Anne Vavasour as a

---

[20] Charles Wisner Barrell, "'Shakespeare's' Own Secret Drama, Part 3," *SF News-Letter* (American), vol. 3/3 (April 1942): 28.

[21] Charles Wisner Barrell, "'Shake-speare's' Own Secret Drama, Part 2," p. 17.

[22] Charles Wisner Barrell, "'Shakespeare's' Own Secret Drama, Part 3," p. 28.

[23] Charles Wisner Barrell, "'Shake-speare's' Own Secret Drama, Part 2," p. 17.

[24] Charles Wisner Barrell, "'Shakespeare's' Own Secret Drama, Part 3," p. 32.

[25] Percy Allen, "Sir Edward Vere and Mr. Barrell's Discovery," *SF News-Letter*, Oct. 1942, p. 2.

[26] In his May 1, 1937, article in *The Saturday Review*, Barrell had described Edward de Vere as "Queen Elizabeth's wayward and unhappy Lord Great Chamberlain and one-time lover" (p. 11). But his views changed upon the discovery of Sir Edward Vere's parentage. In August 1942 he wrote that "I do not hold with those Oxfordian writers who have boldly claimed that the literary peer at one time involved himself in a serious love affair with the Virgin Monarch." ["Shakespeare's Own Secret Drama, Part 5," *Shakespeare Fellowship News-Letter*, vol. 3/5 (August 1942): 64).]

possible model for Ophelia in 1928, even before Oxford's affair with her became known.[27]

Looney, however, latched on to Barrell's findings and wrote on May 15, 1942, to congratulate him after the third article. "I have read the critical chapter of your Sonnet researches with a more absorbing interest than I have read anything else for quite a long time. You have certainly fulfilled every promise and expectation suggested in the preliminary articles, and I congratulate you most heartily on a very notable elucidation of the age-long *Sonnets* mystery. This, and your unique work on the Shakespeare portraits will, I am confident, give your name an enduring and prominent place in the history of Shakespearean research."[28]

Looney continued, "It is unpleasant that our Shakespeare researches should compel us to stir up so much Elizabethan mud, but when we have settled down to the new viewpoint, we shall be able to enjoy the literature just as we are able to read the poems of Burns, Byron and Shelley without an undue consciousness of their irregularities. In the Oxford-Shakespeare case there is at any rate the satisfaction, in bringing forward one set of irregularities, that suspicion of worse irregularities seem to be conclusively disposed of." Ever the good Victorian, Looney expressed relief that he need only accept the lesser sin of Oxford's having fathered a child out of wedlock and could reject any idea that he might have fathered a child by Queen Elizabeth. Barrell's findings also enabled him to reject what at that time was regarded as an even more unsavory transgression, homosexual relations, that some readers of the *Sonnets* see chronicled in them.

Born in 1885, Barrell too may have had the same Victorian reluctance to discuss sexual matters, as shown by his use of a quaint word, "enceinte," in the following passage, where "pregnant" or "with child" or "eating for two" would have made the meaning clearer to readers not having a dictionary handy: "Finally, at about the same time that Anne Cecil de Vere passed away, Anne Vavasour found herself again enceinte, this time evidently by the veteran soldier and Queen's Champion, Sir Henry Lee of Woodstock."[29] Oxfordian scholar Mike A'Dair also noted that Barrell's writings are "almost Victorian in

---

[27] Percy Allen, "The Historic Originals of Ophelia," *Shakespeare Review*, July 1928: "Though it has long been reasonably probable to me that Burleigh's daughter, Oxford's first wife, was, to some extent, the Ophelia of the Hamlet story, I always felt, nevertheless, unable to trace, in the relations of Anne Cecil and Oxford, as historical characters—so far as we know them—any of that wistfully, tragically romantic quality, that is apparent in the duologue between Hamlet and Ophelia; and, feeling sure also that Shakespeare, quite frequently, drew upon two or more originals for one character, I opined that, could we discover her, there existed, quite possibly, somewhere in the precincts of Elizabeth's court, another lady who stood for Ophelia more nearly than did Anne Cecil. I was, therefore, intensely interested to read, upon page 228 of Mr. Ward's book, the following verses, written by Oxford himself, to one of Elizabeth's Maids of Honour, Anne Vavasour; and preserved in a manuscript in the Bodleian Library" (168). "That this tenderly scornful lyric by Oxford, upon Anne Vavasour's love-affairs with him, expresses, with surprising accuracy, in turn of phrase, idea, image, and incident, the psychology of the Ophelia scenes of Hamlet, seems to me to be an unescapable conclusion; and if the Prince of Denmark's identity with Oxford be also accepted, then his furious outburst to Ophelia: . . . To a nunnery, go!—reflects the bitter disillusionment of a young man already married, unhappily, to Anne Cecil; and, at that moment indignant against matrimony in general. It seems to follow that Shakespeare, when he wrote the Ophelia scenes, either had that poem before him, or in memory; or was fully acquainted with the man by whom it was written, and the circumstances with which it is concerned" (169-70). And, "I have, I hope, set down enough to show that, in all probability, both Anne Cecil and Anne Vavasour were present to Shakespeare's mind, when creating the character and part of Ophelia" (171).
[28] J. Thomas Looney, letter to Charles Barrell, May 15, 1942. Excerpts reprinted in "Discoverer of the True Shakespeare Passes," *SF Quarterly*, vol. V/2 (April 1944): 23.
[29] Charles Wisner Barrell, "Secret Drama, Part 3," p. 30.

their propriety and tone."[30]

Barrell's final articles in the "Shakespeare's Own Secret Drama" series sometimes resemble traditional biographies of William Shakespeare in their use of such phrases as "there can be no doubt," "it thus becomes obvious," "seems to have been," "may have wished," and "there is every reason to believe." At one point he wrote that "Oxford <u>may have wished</u> to marry Anne Vavasor after his first wife died in 1588 . . . <u>There is every reason to believe</u>, also, that Oxford retained a deep and abiding interest in Anne Vavasor and that he spent much time in her company, even after his 1591 marriage to Elizabeth Trentham" (underscoring added).[31] Yet Barrell provided no evidence in support of those suppositions.

Upon closer examination, other problems with his description of events can be seen.

- ✓ Barrell stated that "Oxford may have wished to marry Anne Vavasor after his first wife died in 1588," but he already noted that "Vavasour found herself again enceinte" by Sir Henry Lee "at about the same time that Anne Cecil de Vere passed away." Did he really mean to imply that Oxford wanted to marry a woman who was carrying another man's child?

- ✓ He believed that Oxford cut all connections between himself and his beloved illegitimate son Edward Vere to "conceal from the general public his paternal relationship to Edward Vere," and to protect him from the stain of illegitimacy. But his illegitimacy would already have been widely known: That Oxford and Anne Vavasour had been thrown into the Tower in 1581, immediately after Vavasour gave birth to a child, was one of the most talked about scandals of the year. Oxford could do nothing to change that.

- ✓ Barrell stated that Oxford adopted the William Shakespeare pen name in 1593 in part to separate his newly-born son, Henry Vere, from any taint of the scandalous Vavasour-Southampton affair. But if so, why did he dedicate *Venus and Adonis* and *Lucrece*, his first uses of the pen name, to Southampton? Why would a supposed liaison between Anne Vavasour and Southampton have anything to do with Oxford? His own affair with her had ended more than a decade before. Why would Oxford have cared any more about that affair, if it ever happened, than any of Vavasour's many other affairs?[32] There isn't even a hint of a Vavasour-Southampton affair in the official records even though her affairs with many other men are well documented.

- ✓ If the Vavasour-Southampton liaison took place in 1591 (before the first use of the Shakespeare pen name and at least nine months before the birth of Henry Vere), she was thirty-two years old, and he was eighteen. It would be quite unusual for a woman who had been described as the most beautiful of all of Queen Elizabeth's ladies and who had already had affairs with several rich and powerful men (and children by two of them) to begin an affair with a minor fourteen years her junior who had no wealth of his own and would not obtain his inheritance for

---

[30] Mike A'Dair, "Charles Wisner Barrell: A Biographical Sketch," *Sh. Matters*, vol. 9/1 (Winter 2010): 20.
[31] Charles Wisner Barrell, "Secret Drama, Part 3," p. 30.
[32] Holders of the Dynastic Succession Theory have an answer: Southampton was Oxford's son.

several more years?[33]

Barrell reached other conclusions not widely accepted by Oxfordians:

- That Oxford sold his published plays for personal profit, that "he was already commercializing his talents through the book-stalls and the public stages. He could, however, take all necessary pains to protect his already sadly damaged social position by employing a living mask or business agent to represent the pseudonym under which these works were issued. This would account for William Shakspere's role in the proceedings."[34]

- That "all evidence indicates that Oxford's alliance with Anne Cecil began as a mutual love-match. In the early summer of 1571 when their engagement was formally announced by Lord Burghley in a letter to the Earl of Rutland. . . . The literary Earl and his 'sweet little Countess' seem to have been a happy and loving couple for some years following their marriage."[35] A private letter to a junior earl is not a "formal announcement." More importantly, the evidence that this marriage was not happy or successful is overwhelming.

- That the *Sonnets* as published in 1609 are in an arbitrary order, that "at least 41 and perhaps 45 of the sonnets feature Anne Vavasor . . . [and that] a second group of 51 of the sonnets can be identified with Oxford's interest in his illegitimate son,"[36] that "Anne Cecil, Oxford's first wife, can be shown to have inspired the writing of [four] sonnets . . . [and that] ten . . . poems appear to comment upon Oxford's personal relationship to Queen Elizabeth" (64).

J. Thomas Looney in *The Shakespeare Fellowship Newsletter* (American)

Looney's stream of Oxfordian articles and letters to editors stopped in February 1924. He published nothing Oxfordian until 1935, when five items appeared on the Fellowship page of *The Shakespeare Pictorial*. He was silent again for another five years, until two pieces were published in the *News-Letter* of the American branch in 1940 and 1941. The first was his response to James Campbell's article in *Harper's Magazine* in December 1940, the other was a two-part article, "Shakespeare: A Missing Author," in the February and April, 1941 issues. These were his last known Oxfordian publications.

At that time Looney was living with his daughter in Swadincote, Straffordshire, having moved there to escape the bombing in the Newcastle area during the Blitz. The "Missing Author" two-parter was a fitting close to Looney's Oxfordian career. His description of the tight correspondences that must exist between great literature and the personalities of its creators was an effective statement on an important aspect of literary creativity. Perhaps even more important were his final thoughts on the enduring place that Shakespeare's works and their relationship to the man who wrote them will have for future generations.

> Although mankind has certainly to face in these days graver and more pressing problems than that of the authorship of the Shakespeare plays, this question has a claim, if only a secondary one, amongst the serious interests of life, and deals

---

[33] It was only upon reaching his majority, his twenty-first birthday, that Southampton could sue to retain his paternity, thus launching a complicated and lengthy process.

[34] Charles Wisner Barrell, "'Shakespeare's' Own Secret Drama, Part 5," *SF News-Letter*, Aug. 1942, p. 60.

[35] Charles Wisner Barrell, "'Shakespeare's' Own Secret Drama, Part 6," *SF News-Letter*, Oct. 1942, p. 77.

[36] Charles Wisner Barrell, "Secret Drama, Part 5," p. 57.

with matters that are destined to endure when the special problems of today will have passed out of mind. Centuries hence, when the entire world will have changed, socially, politically and religiously, the works will be read with wonder, and the personality behind them command the admiration and even the affections of readers.[37]

Fellowship External Events and Public Opinion

With the establishment of the American branch of the Shakespeare Fellowship, Oxfordian speakers could present themselves as representatives of an official body. The *News-Letter* also provided a venue through which to report on the receptiveness of their audiences.

Prof. Louis Bénézet, president of the American branch, was the most active—and most captivating—American speaker. Of the eighty public talks known to have been given by American Oxfordians between 1937 and 1948, he gave almost half. His lectures were described as "uniformly brilliant, poetic, convincing. It was routine for listeners to go away saying the lecture ended all too soon, also that they had been persuaded of something they had not wanted to believe."[38]

Lois Adelaide Book, who had sent James Campbell's *Harper's* article to Looney, was also an active speaker. The *News-Letter* reported that by the spring of 1940 it had members in twenty states and that Indiana "leads all others in proportion to population. . . . This is very largely due to the efforts of Miss Lois Adelaide Book of Columbus in that state, an Oxfordian who knows the art of translating conviction into action. . . . Miss Book is one who takes active part in building the only kind of dues-paying membership for the Fellowship that will guarantee our ability to 'do something about it.'"[39] Book explained to Looney

> It was just five years ago last November that I read your book and from that time on I have been trying to "convert" others to the cause. I have a friend who tells me that that is my missionary spirit cropping up. Perhaps she's right. My father is a minister. I always tell her, though, that I'm glad it took a literary instead of a Biblical turn. I have never been as interested in anything else. It is all so fascinating. And your book, *"Shakespeare" Identified*, is the most fascinating of all that has been written upon the subject. I have four copies—three for lending.[40]

A list of talks given to promote awareness of the Oxfordian claim by Fellowship members from 1937 to 1948 is at the end of this chapter. Here are some highlights.

Shakespeare "Birthday Party" (April 23, 1940)

The Shakespeare Fellowship held a "birthday party" for Shakespeare in New York City on April 23, 1940, organized by Eva Turner Clark and attended by eighty persons. In his opening remarks, Bénézet, chair of the event, reviewed the growth of the Oxfordian movement and contrasted the creative psychologies of Shakespeare and Ben Jonson. Severo Mallet-Prevost of the New York Bar followed with an analysis of Oxfordian theory from the view of a legal expert. Fellowship officers James Cushman and Eva Turner Clark also spoke, Clark on the work of the Fellowship and the need for a strong organization

---

[37] J. Thomas Looney, "Shakespeare: A Missing Author, Part 1," *SF News-Letter* (American), vol. 2/2 (Feb. 1941): 13.

[38] "Notice of Death of Bénézet," *Shakespearean Authorship Review*, no. 6 (Autumn 1961): 23.

[39] "Miss Book of Indiana," *SF News-Letter* (American), vol. 1/3 (April-May 1940): 13.

[40] Lois Adelaide Book, letter to J. Thomas Looney, April 15, 1940.

with an adequate endowment to support research projects already underway.[41] Charles Barrell gave a lecture on the images of Edward de Vere that X-ray and infra-red revealed beneath the surface coats of the Ashbourne portrait."

Most of those attending were teachers of English, librarians and "personalities prominent in literary, stage and legal circles." One attendee commented that "the next meeting of the Fellowship should bring out hundreds of interested auditors, as the Oxford evidence can no longer be ignored by anyone with an interest in the actual personality of the Bard." Several of those attending joined the Fellowship.

Charles Wisner Barrell Lecture, University Club, Baltimore (May 8, 1940)

Barrell's talk on his examination of the "Shakespeare" portraits, five months after his findings had been published in *Scientific American*, drew "a distinguished and critical audience" that included members of the faculties of Johns Hopkins University, St. John's College, Annapolis, Temple University and executives of the Baltimore public schools. It lasted more than three hours and drew more than twenty questions from the audience. The *News-Letter* reported that "Orthodox proponents of the Stratfordian point of view were frankly astounded to find how vulnerable their own case appeared when subjected to the searchlight of scientific media—plus Oxfordian research. Many of the academicians who had come to scoff remained until nearly midnight, seeking additional information. More than fifty members of the University Club made requests for copies of the *News-Letter* and other literature. Shakespeare had suddenly become one of the liveliest topics of conversation among the molders of thought in the free city of Baltimore."[42]

Elizabeth R. Davidson Lecture (December 12, 1940)

In this important speech given before the Columbia Delphian Chapter, Davidson, a long-time Assistant Librarian at the Library of Congress, provided an independent assessment of the Oxfordian thesis. Her talk, "Unbelief in the Belief," focused on the Folger Shakespeare Library and on what Henry Clay Folger's views on the authorship question might been if he had lived beyond 1930. "To have stated out loud twenty years ago that the Wrong Man had been identified," she said, "would have brought down scorn, contempt, derision . . . upon one's helpless pate." But now, doubters are daring "to express their unbelief . . . and are daring unhesitatingly, for good and valid reasons." The beautiful, unique Folger memorial "may have [to have] a re-dedication in a time to come!"[43] Soon after her speech Davidson joined the Shakespeare Fellowship.

Dr. John Howard Dellinger Lecture (February 10, 1941)

Physicist John Dellinger, who had played a critical role in the development of radar, spoke early in 1941 in Washington, D.C., on "Who Wrote Shakespeare?" Citing Looney's *"Shakespeare" Identified* and Barrell's work on the portraits, he concluded that "the Oxford hypothesis bids fair to clear up much of the mystery about Shakespeare."[44] He went on to propose that seeing the badly mutilated versions of his plays being published by "pirates" spurred Oxford to "insist on his true manuscripts being preserved in print, though, being bound by the convention already mentioned, it was necessary that they be published under a pseudonym." Alfred Hart, half a world away, in Australia, would present the same

---

[41] "Oxfordian News," *SF News-Letter* (American), vol. 1/4 (June-July 1940): 4.

[42] "Baltimore Discovers Oxford," *SF News-Letter* (American), vol. 1/4 (June-July 1940): 8.

[43] Elizabeth R. Davidson, "Unbelief in the Belief," *SF News-Letter* (American), vol. 2/4 (June 1941): 45-47.

[44] Eva Turner Clark, "Washington Physicist Speaks," *SF News-Letter* (American), vol. 2/4 (June 1941): 41.

idea in *Stolne and Surreptitious Copies* a year later.

Bénézet's Talks at Universities (Spring 1941)

The *News-Letter* reported that "interest in the Oxford theory of Shakespeare authorship is increasing steadily [as] shown by the demand for lectures on the subject."[45] It cited as examples James Cushman's lecture at the Kent School in Connecticut in February and Bénézet's talk on "The Real Author of Shakespeare's Plays," arranged by the Boston University School of Education. In Introducing Bénézet, Professor Everett L. Getchell, head of the English Department "confessed that after a two hour conversation with him some two years ago, he had begun a serious study of the Oxford case, with the result that he had been completely converted. . . . Among the auditors was Sir Thomas Beecham, the well known musical composer and conductor of the London Philharmonic Orchestra, who remarked after the lecture to Professor Getchell that at last he had heard a satisfying solution of the 'Shakespeare mystery.'"[46] The lecture received favorable comment in three Boston newspapers and a sympathetic editorial in *The Boston Post*.

Flodden W. Heron's Lectures in San Francisco (April 1941, early 1942)

Heron's lectures were of special importance in creating an Oxfordian community in the San Francisco Bay area in the late 1930s and 1940s. The effect of his talks on the editor of *The Argonaut* was noted in Chapter 16. In February 1940 the *News-Letter* was to comment that "Flodden W. Heron, who with Ada Hanifin of *The San Francisco Examiner* and George Frisbee, the Elizabethan rancher of Sonoma County, keeps the new Oxfordian lamps burning brightly on the Pacific Coast."[47]

In 1941 he gave talks at literary clubs in San Francisco—the Browning Society, the Novo Club, the Pi Chapter Study Group, the Literary Anniversary Club and the San Francisco Club[48]—and several more in 1942—including the Speech Arts Association of

---

Flodden W. Heron

Born: not known. Died: not known.

Vice president of the Shakespeare Fellowship, 1945-1948
Gave many talks on the Oxfordian thesis in the San Francisco Bay area.

Created an image resembling a postage stamp with the picture of Edward de Vere on it. He was one of the earliest advocates for what became the popular Famous American series of U.S. commemorative postage stamps issued in 1940-1941. He was also a noted collector of Lewis Carroll memorabilia.

Books and pamphlets

1942, April	*Who Wrote Shakespeare?* [Compilation of Heron's lectures published by the Literary Anniversary Club of San Francisco.]
1945, April 23	*April 23, Birthday of a Genius*

Articles

1939, April 21	"The Shakespeare Anniversary: Literature's Greatest Mystery," *The Argonaut*
1941, October	"Shakspere-Shakespeare," *SF News-Letter* (Am.), vol. 2/6.
1941, December	"Folger Shakespeare Library: A Suggestion," *SF News-Letter* (Am.), vol. 3/1.
1942, April	"Bacon was Not Shakespeare," *SF News-Letter* (Am.), vol. 3/3.

---

[45] "Growing Interest," *SF News-Letter* (American), vol. 2/3 (April 1941): 30.
[46] "Oxfordian News," *SF News-Letter* (American), vol. 2/4 (June 1941): 42.
[47] "An Oxfordian's Happy Thought," *SF News-Letter* (American), vol. 1/2 (Feb. 1940): 12.
[48] Eva Turner Clark, "De Vere Theory Growing in California," *SF News-Letter* (American), vol. 2/4 (June 1941): 43.

California, the Literary Section of the California Club and at the Philetheia Club, where his talk was later recalled as "one of the highlights of the Club year."[49]

In his April 1942 article, "Bacon Was Not Shakespeare," Heron wrote that in spite of the publicity the de Vere theory had received so far, "the greatest weakness . . . in connection with [it] is the ignorance of people regarding it. . . . [Only] a fraction of the number who know the Bacon story are aware that Edward de Vere is the true author of the Shakespeare productions." As of late, however, "Baconians are now flocking to the Edward de Vere standard because here they find concrete evidence and the necessary proofs to back it up."[50]

Edward de Vere "stamp" designed by Flodden W. Heron

James Cushman Lecture (Early 1943)

James Cushman's lecture in Florida drew an audience of about one hundred. A lawyer who was present commented to Cushman, "I had never heard this theory before. I do not know if you are a lawyer or not, but you built your case up like a lawyer, and it is unanswerable."[51]

T. Henry Foster Lectures (Early 1945, October 1946)

Foster, chief executive of the John Morrell Co. of Ottumwa, Iowa, lectured on "A Business Man Looks at Literature" before the School of Journalism at the University of Iowa. He described how "very difficult" it is "for an informed and unprejudiced person to accept the Stratford view of the authorship. There is ample evidence, irrefutable historical evidence, that William Shakspere was not the author of the so-called 'Shakespeare' plays, poems and sonnets."[52] Another lecture, "Shakespeare: Man of Mystery," delivered before the McCormick Theological Seminary in Chicago, "aroused so much favorable interest" that he published it as a pamphlet. "A special edition was run off for members of the Shakespeare Fellowship. . . . [F]or private friends of his family, a de luxe edition, on handmade paper, and embellished with a special frontispiece of the Duke of Portland's portrait of Oxford, was printed in board covers."[53]

Bénézet Lecture Tour(s) (February-March 1945)

During one tour, Bénézet brought the Oxfordian story to more than 2,200 persons. At Connecticut State Teachers College, Danbury, he spoke to 260 senior and junior high school students and eight teachers. "After the talk, Prof. Harold Bohn conceded that 'This theory is just too good. I can't get through your armor."[54] Three talks at Montclair State Teacher's College followed. In Charleston, South Carolina, he spoke to the entire English Department of The Citadel and many writers, artists and editors. One English professor admitted that "so many of the facts of Lord Oxford's private life . . . are clearly and unmistakably referred to in 'Shake-speare's' otherwise enigmatic *Sonnets*" (19). Bénézet

---

[49] "De Vere in San Francisco," *SF News-Letter* (American), vol. 3/4 (June 1942): 33.

[50] Flodden Heron, "Bacon was Not Shakespeare," *SF News-Letter* (American), vol. 3/3 (April 1942): 36.

[51] "What Members Are Doing," *SF News-Letter* (American), vol. 4/4 (June 1943): 46. Cushman is the least known of those who served on the Fellowship Board throughout its nine-year existence.

[52] "Foster of Iowa Speaks Out," *SF Quarterly*, vol. VI/2 (April 1945): 32.

[53] "Shakespeare: Man of Mystery," *SF Quarterly*, vol. VIII/1 (Spring, 1947): 3.

[54] "President Bénézet's Lecture Tour," *SF Quarterly*, vol. VI/2 (April 1945): 18.

said of Black Mountain College in North Carolina that "more than at any college he has visited, the English teachers displayed an open-minded eagerness to hear the facts about the authorship question and reacted without hostility or hysteria to logical arguments—no matter how devastating they may be to the cut-and-dried dogma of the Shakespeare text books." In Philadelphia the president of the Board of Education noted that "We must expect reprisals from the book concerns who at present have the monopoly of supplying the text-books featuring the outworn myths and whole-cloth conjectures regarding the greatest name in English literature. The threat to this monopoly becomes apparent when the foremost educational leaders of a great English-speaking city seek first-hand information on the Oxford discoveries" (20).

Bénézet also gave lectures in Florida, Georgia and California. Percy Allen reported Barrell's assessment that "We are making a strong impression on the big public university and college libraries over here. Some fifty of them have now purchased complete files of our publication.'"[55]

Bénézet's Lectures in Philadelphia (June 5, 1945)

At the invitation of school officials, Bénézet returned to Philadelphia for lectures at the city's two elite high schools. At Philadelphia High School for Girls, he addressed the entire student body. The event opened with 1,800 girls singing a Shakespeare lyric set to music from Tchaikovsky's *Fifth Symphony* followed by his fifty-minute lecture on the life of Edward de Vere as related in the plays and poems of Shakespeare. "The girls listened with keen interest . . . and the applause was spontaneous and prolonged." He then visited three senior Shakespeare classes, and attended a luncheon with the principal and several English teachers.[56]

At William Penn High School, Bénézet spoke for ninety minutes with high school principals and English teachers, followed by questions for another half-hour. In the evening he gave a talk at the home of the president of the Philadelphia Board of Education before an audience of judges, lawyers and English teachers. The following morning he addressed an assembly of some 800 boys at Central High School, followed by a class discussion on *Macbeth*. As the *News-Letter*'s report concluded, "It is safe to say that many of Philadelphia's keenest adolescents who listened to President Bénézet's lectures are going to keep their English teachers busy defending the Stratford story for a long while to come, while some ten or twelve teachers, keenly interested in the evidence for Lord Oxford, will find new meanings in what they teach from the works of the greatest of the heretofore unknown great" (36).

Bénézet Gives Four Talks (October 23-31, 1945)

At the Holderness School in New Hampshire, Bénézet spoke at the invitation of the Rector, separately addressing the student body and the faculty. At his talk at the English Department of the Massachusetts State College in Amherst (now the University of Massachusetts), the audience included Frank Willco of the Holyoke Public Library, the first American librarian to become a member of the Shakespeare Fellowship. His talk at Stanstead College, Quebec, was given extensive coverage by *Newport* [Vermont] *Daily Express*. The *News-Letter* reported that by concentrating on the authorship of the plays and poems, Bénézet "brings to life the creative personality behind them in a way that

---

[55] Percy Allen, "The Group Theory and Some Modern Intellectuals," *SF News-Letter*, May 1945, p. 4.
[56] "President Bénézet Lectures in Philadelphia," *SF Quarterly*, vol. VI/3 (July 1945): 35.

fascinates audiences of all ages and conditions. Instead of repeating the prosy and fabulous conjectures of the usual professional Shakespearean 'authority,' who is almost invariably guaranteed to act as a sleeping potion on his hearers, Bénézet opens new and exciting vistas on his subject and stimulates vital interest in the immortal works. If the Fellowship only had about a dozen such speakers, constantly employed, the Oxford-Shakespeare case would soon be a live topic in every English class in the country."[57]

Bénézet Talk at The Clark School (February 22, 1946)

The Clark Clarion, published by students at The Clark School in Hanover, New Hampshire, ran a report on Bénézet's talk. Because it captures the essence of his "platform presence," a lengthy excerpt is reprinted nearby.[58]

Report on Professor Louis P. Bénézet's Talk on Feb. 22, 1946
at the Clark School, Hanover, New Hampshire
(from *The Clark Clarion*)

Having pondered for many hours on the fate of "Willie the Shake" after the lecture on William Shakespeare by Professor Bénézet on Friday, February 22, it seems I find my thoughts wandering again and again to the almost too conclusive proof of the lecturer.

The informal lecture gained momentum and interest from the first line of "I always feel at home with boys like you" to the final line of, "I know how anxious you are to get back to your studies." Although the first statement made us feel more at ease, I doubt the veracity of the latter, for the lecture which I and many more were prepared to dislike and proclaim boring, ended all too soon for most of us.

While taking notes for this article, although I really haven't the aspects of an intellectual, I found myself absorbing point after point of why Edward de Vere, Earl of Oxford, was supposed to have written the Shakespearean plays and sonnets, and not a poor country boy called Bill Shackspur, who was proclaimed the great writer of England. Much to mine and all romanticists' disappointment, the lecturer made us believe, practically against our will, that the Earl of Oxford definitely wrote the Shakespearean stories....

During the lecture the professor continually stressed the fact that "the man who wrote Shakespeare" was a man of great intelligence, a man who knew the languages of many foreign countries and had a wide knowledge of Latin. Reciting case after case from the plays and sonnets where the writer used his knowledge of law, music, soldiery, the aristocracy's way of living, terms of the sea and battlefield, and knew the theatre and stage well, he proved that definitely the writer was a man of great education, travel, and had a great amount of *savoir faire*. He then compared the lives of Bill Shackspur and Edward de Vere, pointing out the poor country town and little education that Bill was born into, while Edward had all the advantages of education and travel and graduated from Cambridge with a degree at the great age of fifteen. You are then asked the self-explanatory question of which of these two had the ability to write stories such as the Shakespearean plays and sonnets. (And if your answer wasn't the same as mine, I'll eat my hat.) This is the professor's main point although the episode of the X-rayed pictures is also an interesting factor in the final clinching conclusion.

Professor Bénézet . . . is from the Department of Education at Dartmouth College here in Hanover. His hobby is this same theme which his lecture covered, and he states that he read many volumes of Shakespeare before the age of twelve and then when older kept on reading, finally finishing up with twelve years of Latin at Dartmouth, where he also went to college. In my opinion the professor himself would make a marvelous Shakespearean actor. A sweeping cloak would be the only necessary addition to his countenance to make him a convincing and certainly earnest trouper of John Barrymore's caliber.

---

[57] "Our President Rings the Bell Again," *SF Quarterly*, vol. VI/4 (Oct. 1945): 57.
[58] "Shakespeare Authorship Fraudulent," *SF Quarterly*, vol. VII/3 (July 1946): 44-45.

Charles Wisner Barrell's Articles in *Tomorrow* (February, March 1946)

A magazine of high literary quality and national circulation, *Tomorrow* brought the Oxfordian claim to the attention of readers nationwide. In the *News-Letter's* summary, "Mr. Barrell effectually disposes of certain pernicious fallacies regarding the persons to whom many of the sonnets are addressed, and at the same time presents the strongest arguments in his armory for Edward de Vere as their author. Without sacrificing essential scholarship, he has turned out an exciting and persuasive narrative that seems certain to arouse wide interest."[59] In the article itself, Barrell quoted a sentence from Alfred W. Pollard's *Shakespeare's Fight with the Pirates* (1917) concerning the activities of literary pirates that had direct relevance to Edward de Vere: "the appropriation of literary rights without permission or payment which we call piracy, in so far as it can be proved, was largely concerned with the works of *dead authors, or of men whose rank would have forbidden them to receive payment for their books.*"[60] In 1609, the year the *Sonnets* were published, Edward de Vere was, of course, both: deceased and a nobleman.

Burgess-Barrell Radio Broadcast (July 22, 1946)

Charter member of the Fellowship and versatile author Gelett Burgess was behind the thirty-five-minute presentation by himself and Charles Barrell making the case for Edward de Vere as the real "Swan of Avon" broadcast on WEAF, the flagship station of the NBC radio network, in July 1946. It was described as "a delightfully effective dialogue and the most stimulating Shakespearean authorship discussion . . . ever listed to on the air."[61] Comments were "emphatically favorable" and several people joined the Fellowship as a result of the broadcast. Unfortunately, following standard practice at the time, no recording was made.

September 27, 1946 — Burgess-Barrell Roundtable Discussion

Burgess and Barrell were the principal speakers in a round-table discussion by the Wednesday Culture Club in New York. The event introduced influential writers, editors and publicity experts to the Oxfordian idea, including the editor of the *Grolier Encyclopedia*, who would soon invite Louis Bénézet to write the article on Oxford for the new edition.

Other Indicators of Public Opinion, 1940-1946

The Argonaut (January 26, 1940)

The editorial "Who Was Shakespeare?" in the San Francisco-based magazine generated this comment in the Fellowship *News-Letter*: "This sixty-four-year-old weekly has been staunchly Stratfordian in its editorial point of view up to recent years. But as the Oxfordian evidence of the authorship of the plays has increased in weight and graphic clarity, the foremost weekly journal of the Pacific Coast has become frankly hospitable to the new order of Shakespearean research."[62]

Warren P. Munsell, Jr.'s Play (July 1940)

Munsell's play, *By Any Other Name*, premiered July 29, 1940, at the McCarter Theater

---

[59] "National Circulation for Oxford-Shakespeare Story," *SF Quarterly*, vol. VI/4 (Oct. 1945): 64.

[60] Charles Barrell, "Verifying the Secret History of *Shake-speare's Sonnets*," *Tomorrow*, February 1946.

[61] "Radio Presentation of Oxford-Shakespeare Case," *SF Quarterly*, vol. VII/3 (July 1946): 33.

[62] "Who Was Shakespeare?" *SF News-Letter* (American), vol. 1/3 (April-May 1940): 4.

in Princeton.[63] Covering the period 1581 to 1601, it began with Oxford's activities as collaborator with John Lyly writing comedies for Court audiences and ended with the Essex Rebellion. The item in the *News-Letter* did not provide any information about Munsell, so presumably he was not a Fellowship member.

Progress in the *PMLA* (1942)

Josephine Waters Bennett, a historian knowledgeable about Elizabethan times though not a card-carrying Shakespeare scholar, published an article that largely supported the Oxfordian position on topical allusions. She opened it with an important observation about the topical nature of Elizabethan drama performed in the court.

> [T]he evidence is too extensive to be ignored that a good deal of the entertainment especially prepared for the Queen was topical, that she thoroughly enjoyed interpreting that kind of enigma, and that personal pleas for her favour often took that form.[64]

She then connected that interest in topical drama to Edward de Vere and to what she called "perhaps the most crucial episode in his life" (354). *Endymion*, the play by John Lyly, Oxford's secretary, was, she suggested, written as an apology to the queen for Oxford's transgressions with Anne Vavasour. "It was well known that Lyly was in Oxford's service and therefore under obligation (or suspicion) to promote his interests. Therefore, as soon as *Endymion* appeared on the stage and began to protest his devotion to Cynthia, as he does in the opening scene, would not the Queen and her court begin to look for parallels between Endymion and Oxford?" (361)[65]

After pointing out that the parallels or puzzles to be figured out "must have had some reasonably intelligible meaning" based on real-life events—for "the Elizabethans were not given to inventing merely senseless enigmas" (368)—she concluded that

> Interpretation of *Endimion* as an apology for the Earl of Oxford has at least the merit of meeting, more fully than any previous explanation, the three requirements which have been laid down for this kind of interpretation. It is timely as commemoration of a recent very great favor which the Queen had showed Oxford. Lyly's motive for writing such a play is direct and obvious. And the data of the play correspond with the data of history to a surprising extent if no topical references were intended (359).

Friend W. Richardson's Editorial (1943)

Richardson, former governor of California and president of the Publishers Association of California, wrote an op-ed titled "Fighting a Man of Straw" for the *Hemet News* in March 1943 advising professors at UCLA to tell their students about Edward de Vere if they really want to enlighten them.

Alden Brooks and *Will Shakspere and the Dyer's Hand* (1943)

Although Brooks made no mention of J. Thomas Looney or *"Shakespeare" Identified* in *Will Shakspere and the Dyer's Hand*, he was clearly inspired by them. He followed Looney's process of identifying characteristics or qualities that the author of Shakespeare's works must have had, but outdid him by identifying fifty-four characteristics, to Looney's mere

---

[63] "First Play Presenting Oxford as 'Shakespeare,'" *SF News-Letter* (Am.), vol. 1/5 (Aug.-Sept. 1940): 12.

[64] Josephine Waters Bennett, "Oxford and *Endimion*," PMLA, vol. 57/2 (June 1942): 359.

[65] This point would have been seen even more clearly if Oxford himself acted the part of Endymion, which may have been the case.

eighteen. His study revealed "the outline not of one man, but of two, a man of Stratford and a man of the plays."[66] The former "showman, man of business, agent, was a vital factor in the production of the Shakespearean plays. He made choice of plays and writers, offered advice, acted as general supervisor" (402). Brooks also found that "The man of the plays, creator of the Shakespearean thought and style, was an impoverished courtier, who, while need held him to revising and rewriting plays, earnestly sought and obtained for himself anonymity" (xix). After considering Oxford and other candidates, Brooks concluded that Sir Edward Dyer, a member of the Countess of Pembroke's circle, "turned to revising, rewriting plays for Pembroke's men then led by Will Shakspere" (416).

Brooks's book was published by Charles Scribner's Sons after being championed by Max Perkins, the editor who first recognized the talents of F. Scott Fitzgerald, Ernest Hemingway and Thomas Wolfe. As a biographer explained, the book was published only because of Perkins's "obstinacy." "For some time the book had been a mania with him. At every editorial conference Perkins brought it up and the board unanimously voted it down. 'So, being a man of infinite patience,' one Scribner's employee recalled,' 'he would reintroduce his suggestion at the next conference, with the same result.' . . . Eventually the board gave in, to please Perkins."[67]

Interestingly, Will Howe, a literary reader for Scribner's and a founding member of the American branch, wrote to Looney in 1938 inquiring about the possibility of a new American edition of *"Shakespeare" Identified*. Looney responded at length, but nothing came of the idea.

Oxfordian Radio Broadcast (April 23, 1945)

Rod Hendrickson dedicated the entire April 23, 1945, episode of his program, "This Business of Living," broadcast on WEAF, to the presentation of evidence in the case for Lord Oxford as Shakespeare. His material was drawn from *April 23—Birthday of a Genius* by Fellowship Vice President Flodden Heron. Among the interesting arguments advanced was one first offered by Eva Turner Clark in the Fellowship *News-Letter* of April 1940, that as a result of the eleven-day adjustment required by adoption of the Gregorian calendar, "Edward de Vere was really born on the day that is now generally accepted as 'Shakespeare's' Birthday."[68]

Burton Rascoe on the Battle Over Shakespeare (July 31, 1945)

In his Theater column in the *New York World-Telegram*, Rascoe wrote that nowadays the scholarly publication "I find most agreeable to my palate is the *Shakespeare Fellowship Quarterly*." He went on to explain that "The writers for this *Quarterly* are ingenious, bright and entertaining. Their spade work is indefatigable and they have dug up the darndest things. But there is no scholar's dust on them; they are crusaders full of joy and devilment. They delight in tripping up the Shakespearean bigwigs with new discoveries; they love to shy rocks at the high hats of Dr. J. Q. Adams and Dover Wilson, but they will annoy any Stratfordian, big or little, if the spirit so moves them. They seem to have fun."[69]

Nathan S. Olds, "Revisions May Have to be Made" (January 1946)

---

[66] Alden Brooks, *Will Shakspere and the Dyer's Hand* (1943), p. xix.
[67] A. Scott Berg, *Max Perkins: Editor of Genius* (1978, 2016), p. 398.
[68] "Oxford's Birthday Signalized," *SF Quarterly*, vol. VI/3 (July 1945): 36.
[69] Burton Rascoe, "The Battle Still Rages Over Who Was Shakespeare," *New York World-Telegram*, July 31, 1945, reprinted in *SF Quarterly*, vol. VI/4 (Oct. 1945): 57.

In a commentary for *The Villager*, Olds wrote that "Anne Vavasour . . . has now been identified as the 'Dark Lady' of Shakespeare's sonnets [and] at the same time, and with the same impressive documentation to prove it, the author of Shakespeare's sonnets is declared to be . . . Edward de Vere, seventeenth Earl of Oxford."[70] After citing Barrell's work on the portraits and his recent articles in *Tomorrow*, Olds raised the conundrum facing traditional scholars: "What the Stratfordians will find to answer this higher criticism with is rather difficult to forecast. Mr. Barrell has the faculty of nailing his points down with dates, pages and paragraphs." Noting that Barrell will soon publish a book with his latest findings, he commented that "Curious disclosures are expected. Some critics even prophesy that revisions may have to be made in the English literature textbooks."

Warwick Valley [New York] *Dispatch* (January 30, 1946)

Lewis Hammond Webster's article ran in a newspaper in the town where Charles Wisner Barrell was born and to which he would retire. In January 1946, Webster described his efforts to get information on Oxfordian theory from professors of English who dismissed the issue even though they had never read *"Shakespeare" Identified*. Webster posed many questions of obvious importance and made relevant observations about the supposed knowledge, competence and expertise of so-called experts.

> What are we to think of authorities in a field who do not know some of the most obvious literature in the field? What are we to think of the Departments of English at Yale and Columbia when Ph.D. degrees are granted for work in the Elizabethan period and the men taking the degrees are so obviously ignorant of developments in their field? Unfortunately many other universities sit in similar placid ignorance.

> All the authorities form a consensus for establishing truth in any given field, but when each authority depends on the scholarship of the next man or some antiquated predecessor, then collectively they become authorities of ignorance only. That is what happens in many schools, often prominent ones, all over the world and in all periods. The *authorities* condemned Socrates. The *authorities* condemned Jesus Christ. The *authorities* condemned Galileo. The *authorities* mocked Pasteur.

> In field after field the authorities have been wrong, especially when dealing with an entirely new point of view. In time each heresy may become a new orthodoxy. . . . Those holding to an antiquated view fail to see how weak it is. In the Shakespearean question anyone reading a sample "Life of Shakespeare" identified with the Stratford-on-Avon individual, can see the weakness of the case provided the reader is not a member of an English department in a leading university with a reputation for scholarship, mostly pedantry.[71]

This recounting of public events and their effect on public awareness of the Oxfordian claim will continue in the next chapter after consideration of important developments within the Shakespeare Fellowship.

---

[70] Nathaniel S. Olds, "Revisions May Have to be Made in English Literature Textbooks," *The Villager*, reprinted in *SF Quarterly*, vol. VII/1 (Jan. 1946): 13.

[71] Lewis Hammond Webster, "Those Authorities," *Warwick Valley Dispatch*, Jan. 30, 1946.

Public Talks by American Oxfordians, 1937-1943

<u>Percy Allen's North American Speaking Tour, Fall 1936</u>

1938, April	James Cushman	Lecture, Princeton, "Edward de Vere as Shakespeare"
1938, Nov. 25	Prof. Louis Bénézet	Lecture, Hathaway Shakespeare Club, Philadelphia
	Prof. Louis Bénézet	Talks, home of Prof. Herbert Miles, Byrn Mawr College, for a dozen faculty from Byrn Mawr and Haverford
1938, Dec.	Prof. Louis Bénézet	2 lectures, Connecticut State Teachers' College
1939, April	Flodden W. Heron	Lecture on Oxford/Shakespeare, Shakespeare Gardens, Golden Gate Park, San Francisco
1939	James Cushman	Lectures, Rockford College, Wesleyan on the Oxford-Shakespeare question
1939	Prof. Louis Bénézet	Lectures, state teachers colleges in four states
1939	Prof. Louis Bénézet	Talk, at the Hathaway Shakespeare Society, Philadelphia
1939-1940	Lois Adelaide Book	Talks (many) in Indiana

<u>Founding of the American Branch of the Shakespeare Fellowship, Nov. 1939</u>

1940, Feb. 2	Charles Barrell	Lecture, Hathaway Shakespeare Society, Philadelphia
1940, April 23	Sh. Fellowship	Talks, "Shakespeare "Birthday Party" in New York City, by Bénézet, Barrell, Clark, Cushman, others.
1940, May 8	Charles Barrell	Lecture, University Club, Baltimore, "X-rays and the Shakespeare Portraits"
1940, Fall		People who were convinced of Oxford's authorship by Prof. Bénézet and who went on to give talks of their own:
		--Prof. R. L. Morrow, University of Maine
		--Prof. Everett Getchell, Boston University
		--Prof. F. Allen Burt, Boston University. Talks at two Rotary clubs
		--Louise Kroeger, St. Louis
1940, Dec. 12	Elizabeth R. Davidson	Lecture, Columbia University Delphian Chapter, "Unbelief in the Belief," re Folger Library
1941, Feb. 10	Dr. John H. Dellinger	Lecture, All Souls Unitarian Church, Washington, DC, "Who Wrote Shakespeare?"
1941, Feb. 26	James Cushman	Lecture, Kent School, Connecticut
1941, April 5	Prof. Louis Bénézet	Lecture, Boston University, "The Real Author of Shakespeare's Plays"
1941, April	Flodden W. Heron	Talks, four literary clubs in San Francisco

<u>Attack on Pearl Harbor, The United States enters the Second World War, December 1941</u>

1942, Jan. 28	Flodden Heron	Lecture, Philetheia Club, San Francisco
1942, early Feb.	James Cushman	Lecture, University of Michigan, "The Oxford-Shakespeare Problem"
1942, Feb. 7	Flodden Heron	Lecture, Speech Arts Association of California
1942, Feb. 13	Eva Turner Clark	Lecture, Browning Society, San Francisco, "Lord Oxford as Shakespeare"
1942, March 10	Flodden Heron	Lecture, Literary Section of the California Club
1942, March 12	James Cushman	Lecture, Rutgers College
1942, May	James Cushman	Lecture, Bryn Mawr College
1943, Jan.?	James Cushman	Lecture, Harder Hall, Sebring, Florida
1945, end of Feb.	Prof. Louis Bénézet	Lecture, Connecticut State Teachers College, Danbury
	Prof. Louis Bénézet	Three lectures, Montclair State Teachers College
	Prof. Louis Bénézet	Lecture, English Dept., The Citadel, Charleston, SC
1945, March 8	Prof. Louis Bénézet	Lecture, Black Mountain College, NC
	Prof. Louis Bénézet	Lecture, All Souls Unitarian Church, Washington, DC
1945, March 13	Prof. Louis Bénézet	Lecture, Philadelphia Board of Education

Public Talks by American Oxfordians, 1945-1948

1945, Spring	T. Henry Foster	Talk, School of Journalism, U. of Iowa, "A Business Man Looks at Literature"
1945, April 23	Flodden W. Heron	Broadcast, WEAF radio, on Heron's pamphlet
1945, Spring	Prof. Louis Bénézet	Lecture tour to Florida, Georgia, California
1945, June 5, 6	Prof. Louis Bénézet	Lectures, Philadelphia
1945, June 5	Prof. Louis Bénézet	Lectures, events at girls school, faculty luncheon
1945, June 5	Prof. Louis Bénézet	Talk, William Penn High School, principals and teachers
1945, June 5	Prof. Louis Bénézet	Talk, evening event, home of Leon Obermayer, President, Philadelphia Board of Education
1945, June 6	Prof. Louis Bénézet	Lecture and classroom discussions, Central High School

End of the Second World War

1945, Oct. 23	Prof. Louis Bénézet	Two lectures, Holderness School, New Hampshire
1945, Oct. 25	Prof. Louis Bénézet	Lecture, Massachusetts State College, Amherst
1945, Oct. 31	Prof. Louis Bénézet	Lecture, Stanstead College, Quebec
1946, Feb. 22	Prof. Louis Bénézet	Annual lecture, Clark School, "Edward de Vere as the Real Shakespeare"
1946, July 22	Gelett Burgess &l Charles Barrell	Broadcast, WEAF radio program
1946, Sept. 27	Burgess & Barrell	Principal speakers, Lamb's Club, Wednesday Culture Club, New York
1946, October	T. Henry Foster	Address at McCormick Theological Seminary, Chicago
1947, Jan. 13	Mrs. De Witt Owen	Lecture, Alumnae Assoc., School of Expression, Dallas
1947, March 21	Charles Barrell	Inaugural meeting of the New Shakespeare Society of Philadelphia, presentation by Barrell
1947, April 25	Dr. Bronson Feldman	Lecture, The New Shakespeare Society, "The War of Loves in *King Lear*"
1947, May 4	Glendon Allvine	Lecture, Young Adults Club
1947, May 16	Glendon Allvine	Lecture, Worcester Better Films Committee, "Did William of Stratford Write 'Shakespeare'?"
1947, May 24	Prof. Louis Bénézet	Lecture, The New Shakespeare Society of Philadelphia, "The Case for Shakspere"
1947, May	Prof. Louis Bénézet	Tufts College, Annual lecture
1947, June	Prof. Louis Bénézet	Wedgwood Club, Boston
1948, Jan. 5	Prof. Louis Bénézet	Debate on Oxford vs. William of Stratford, English Dept. Skidmore College, Saratoga, New York; broadcast over radio WGY of Schenectady
1948, Jan. 9	Charles Barrell	Lecture, Philomathean Society, U. of Pennsylvania, on X-rays and portraits
1948, Sept. 6	Gelett Burgess	Lecture, Puzzlers League, "The Oxfordian Case"

18

The American Branch of the Shakespeare Fellowship, 1939-1948, II

Internal Operations of the American Branch and Expectations of Its Officers

The Shakespeare Fellowship continued to punch above its weight throughout the nine years of its existence. In part that was due to continuity; its principal officers remained in office from its founding in late 1939 until its sudden cessation of activity at the end of 1948: President Prof. Louis P. Bénézet, Vice Presidents Eva Turner Clark and James Cushman, and Secretary, Treasurer and editor of the *News-Letter* Charles Barrell.[1] The Fellowship's outsized effectiveness was also due to the energy, spirit and optimism of the leadership.

Charles Barrell in the Army (September 3, 1940)

The first change in the Fellowship's operations was a temporary one. Charles Barrell, who served in the Army reserves, was called for duty on September 3, 1940. He served as Editor and Director for Training Film Field Unit No. 1, headquartered at Fort Monmouth, New Jersey. The unit produced training films for use in all branches of military tactics.[2] Eva Turner Clark took over editing and publishing the *News-Letter* until he returned.

In July 1941 Barrell was called back to his former job with Western Electric Company to produce films on the fabrication of war materials. He reported to Percy Allen in December that he had been "working long hours, weekends and holidays. In the few hours of leisure I have tried to do my bit in contributing to the *News-Letter*, . . . [but] with civilization girding for the greatest battles in all history, our success in keeping the Oxford movement alive in this country has been about all we could hope for. Once the Axis powers have shot their bolt, and the sound of the guns has died down into something like righteous normality again, we shall go forward by leaps and bounds."[3]

First Annual Meeting (November 30, 1940)

The meeting took place at the home of James Cushman in New York City. Charles Barrell spoke on the founding of the American branch and its growth over the past year, and noted that every college and library had renewed its membership for the coming year. Eva Turner Clark announced that a thousand copies were printed of each issue of the *News-Letter*, with many sent to English teachers (a different list for each issue). She also stressed the amount of work that had to be done to re-evaluate the great mass of literary and historical matter connected with the Elizabethan and Jacobean drama and stage from the angle of Oxfordian authorship. President Bénézet spoke on James Campbell's recent

---

[1] The one exception was Eva Turner Clark, who died on April 1, 1947.

[2] "In the Army Now," *SF News-Letter* (American), vol. 1/6 (Oct.-Nov. 1940): 6.

[3] Charles Wisner Barrell, letter to Percy Allen, December 21, 1941 [Excerpt reprinted in "Charles Wisner Barrell and Our American Branch," *SF News-Letter*, April 1942, p. 3.]

article in *Harper's Magazine*, citing facts refuting it. Dr. Howe, literary advisor to Charles Scribner's Sons, spoke on "The Publisher's Attitude Toward the Oxford-Shakespeare Question."[4]

Second Annual Meeting (November 29, 1942)

About forty members attended. Also present was Ada Comstock, President of Radcliffe College. The report on the past year's activities described the challenges of publishing the *News-Letter* during wartime conditions.

> By that one fell stroke [the attack on Pearl Harbor, which occurred just after the December 1941 issue went out], our people were united by the thought that the war must be won. Our young men flocked to the colors and now, in less than a year, are to be found fighting on every front. At home, the factories are turning out immense quantities of equipment for our soldiers and sailors and for our Allies. Of equal importance is the impetus given to transportation—ship, train, and plane. It is a major effort....
>
> No person, no organization has escaped the impact of the war. Even our American Branch of the Shakespeare Fellowship, bent only on solving the problem of Shakespeare authorship, is beginning to feel the pressure of the advancing cost of printing the *News-Letter*. But your editors feel that the little magazine must be continued, if possible.
>
> There comes an end to war, and we begin to see glimmerings of a righteous end to this one. Art endures, and the study of Shakespeare's plays and poems belongs in that category. The threads of our study should not be lost and, by the help of those of us who are older or otherwise unfitted for war activities, need not be lost. As long as we can continue our research and publish the results of our findings, we shall do so. We hope our members will agree with our decision. We count on your support. Let us make our fourth year the best of all.[5]

Despite the difficulties, the tone of the reporting throughout the nine years of the American branch's existence was consistently positive and upbeat, as shown by this report from Eva Turner Clark in the August 1942 *News-Letter*:

> Our membership has held up, even increased during times so difficult that it would not have been surprising if it had dwindled. This fact indicates that our society will go forward with leaps and bounds when the war comes to an end. Most of the larger college libraries have become subscribers to our small periodical, of which each one now has a complete file. This is a recognition of the value of the *News-Letter* and of the theory it supports.
>
> The cordial reception given our speakers at colleges and clubs is evidence of a growing interest in the cause of the Earl of Oxford and the consistency which marks our Shakespeare authorship theory appeals to the listeners. Instead of a lay figure, they find the poet-dramatist a breathing, pulsing man of his times, of all times, a person they can understand.[6]

Membership Increasing

Within two months of its founding, the American branch had more than sixty members (see Chapter 17). At the end of 1941 Charles Barrell reported that headway had been made even during wartime conditions. "We have as regular members of the

---

[4] "The Annual Meeting," *SF News-Letter* (American), vol. 2/1 (Feb. 1941): 19-20.
[5] "Our Fourth Year," *SF News-Letter* (American), vol. 4/1 (Dec. 1942): 10.
[6] "Encouragement," *SF News-Letter* (American), vol. 3/5 (Aug. 1942): 66.

Fellowship such collegiate bigwigs as Harvard College, Yale, the Universities of Chicago, Pennsylvania, and Michigan, Ball State College of Indiana, Pennsylvania State College, Rollins College of Florida, Mills College for Women in California, etc.: The New York Public Library, Holyoke, Mass. Public Library, and a number of distinguished scholars, bibliophiles and jurists."[7] Some notable members and comments from them are noted here.

The famous actor <u>John Barrymore</u> joined the American branch in 1940. Percy Allen recounted his earlier meeting with Barrymore after a performance of his in the title role in *Hamlet* on the stage in London, before commenting that "We did not, then, suppose that the distinguished American actor would, one day, be, as he is, a member of The American Branch of the Shakespeare Fellowship."[8]

<u>Paul McAllister</u>, who joined the Fellowship in 1940, was a well known stage and screen actor of New York and Hollywood, and who had been one of the foremost Shakespearean players on Broadway. He read *"Shakespeare" Identified* soon after it was published and had been a fervent admirer of Looney and his work ever since.[9]

<u>Canon Gerald Rendall</u>, who had resigned his membership in the Shakespeare Fellowship in London in 1936, joined the American branch in 1940.

<u>Prof. Everett L. Getchell</u>, Boston University: "We had Dr. Bénézet speak in our 'Contemporary Writers' Course. His zeal and enthusiasm carried all before him. I think he won every hearer to his cause. So there are some seventy new adherents to spread the gospel of the seventeenth Earl of Oxford."[10]

<u>John L. Astley-Cock</u>, *Chicago Tribune*: "I became an Oxfordian immediately after reading Looney's book, the original edition soon after publication. . . . So far as I know there is but one other member of the Fellowship in these parts, at the University of Chicago, whom I have not yet met. . . . I wish we had a chapter here from a missionary point of view!"

<u>Professor Pierre S. Porohovshikov</u>, Atlanta, Georgia: "it is a distressing fact that it is now more than a hundred years since Lord Palmerston in England and Delia Bacon in America first showed to the public that the legend of Stratford is only good for infantile minds. It is a shame for our civilization that that silly story has lasted as long as several decades and that school children are still brought up with a firm belief in the lie. . . . But we, the heretics, may confidently say that the old structure of ignorance and willful blindness has been shaken to the foundations and cannot survive much longer."

<u>A. C. Gifford Heretaunga</u>, the famous astronomer from Wellington, New Zealand, wrote twice to express his appreciation for the research being published in the *News-Letter*. In 1941 he wrote, "I had for many years been convinced that the Stratford theory was absolutely untenable. But I didn't know who was the real author until 1922, when I got *"Shakespeare" Identified*. . . . I now have about thirty books on the problem. . . . Every number of the *News-Letter* is full of discoveries."[11] A year later he wrote, "The April number of the *News-Letter*, which I have read through with the greatest interest, carries

---

[7] Charles Wisner Barrell, letter to Percy Allen, Dec. 21, 1941. Excerpt in "Charles Wisner Barrell and Our American Branch," *SF News-Letter*, April 1942, p. 3.

[8] "Mr. John Barrymore," *SF News-Letter*, April 1940, p. 7.

[9] "The Honor of Authorship," *SF News-Letter* (American), vol. 1/4 (June-July 1940): 12.

[10] "Letters from Members: Brief Excerpts," *SF News-Letter* (American), vol. 2/6 (Oct. 1941): 71.

[11] A. C. Gifford, letter to the Fellowship, excerpts printed in "Our Third Year," *SF News-Letter* (American), vol. 3/1 (Dec. 1941): 8.

the thrilling story a stage further. We are very much indebted to you for carrying on the research with such enthusiasm and success."[12]

Phyllis Carrington, a niece of the late Esther Singleton, in her first article reported on the death of the Sixth Duke of Portland, owner of the portrait of Edward de Vere in his collection at Welbeck Abbey.[13] That portrait was pictured as the frontispiece in *"Shakespeare" Identified*, and on the acknowledgements page Looney thanked the Duke for providing the image.[14]

Glendon Allvine, former Story Editor, Paramount Pictures, currently executive staff of Mr. Eric Johnson's Motion Picture Association, was the organizer of the September 27 Wednesday Culture Club meeting at which Gelett Burgess and Charles Wisner Barrell were the principal speakers. He went on to become a vice president of the Fellowship.[15]

Dr. Josiah Combs, Head of the Department of French and German Languages, Texas Christian University. He explained that "It is high time that the Stratford myth be thoroughly and completely debunked. . . . I have discovered that college professors of English literature refuse even to discuss the matter—since the claim is not backed by 'authority.' Almost without exception, these academic gentlemen refuse to read and study research in the disputed field since 1910."[16]

Libraries With Complete Sets of the *News-Letter*

By mid-1943, some forty leading public, university and college libraries had not only subscribed to the *News-Letter*, but had placed orders for all copies printed.[17] A year later, the number was upped to fifty libraries.[18] By early 1944, "our membership and the readers of our publication have increased to a degree that has made the Oxford-Shakespeare evidence a live issue in most sections of North America, from Florida and Texas to the Dominion of Canada, and from the Atlantic to the Pacific seaboards."[19] "It is gratifying to know that our research is thus being filed permanently where it will meet the attention of many thousands of present and future students."[20]

Around the same time Eva Turner Clark noted that since 1920 "some fifty books, pamphlets and

---

Among the Forty Libraries with Full Sets of the *News-Letters* as of early 1943:

University of Chicago
University of Colorado
Dartmouth College
Folger Shakespeare Library
Harvard College
Holyoke [Mass.] Public Library
State University of Iowa
University of Michigan
University of Minnesota
New York Public Library
New York University
Ohio State University
University of Pennsylvania
Pennsylvania State College
Princeton University
Rollins College
Stanford University
Swarthmore College
University of Tennessee
Wells College
University of Wisconsin
Yale University

---

[12] A. C. Gifford, letter to the Fellowship, excerpts printed in "From Letters Received," *SF News-Letter* (American), vol. 3/6 (Oct. 1942): 77.

[13] Phyllis Carrington, "Was Lord Oxford Buried in Westminster Abbey," *SF News-Letter* (American), vol. 4/4 (June 1943): 41.

[14] Looney sent an inscribed copy of *"Shakespeare" Identified* to the Duke of Portland in gratitude for his support. I was fortunate enough to be able to purchase that copy in 2019.

[15] "Lord Oxford Among the Lambs," *SF Quarterly*, vol. VII/4 (Oct. 1946): 54, 60.

[16] "Truth from Texas," *SF Quarterly*, vol. VII/3 (July 1946): 34.

[17] "Reference Files," *SF News-Letter* (American), vol. 4/3 (April 1943): 40.

[18] "Recognition of Merit," *SF Quarterly*, vol. VI/2 (April 1945): 21.

[19] "Introducing the *Quarterly*," *SF Quarterly*, vol. V/1 (Jan. 1944): 1.

[20] "Progress and a Handicap," *SF Quarterly*, vol. V/3 (July 1944): 48.

widely publicized magazine articles have been issued, amplifying and corroborating Mr. Looney's original discoveries."[21] She stated that "During the four years that have passed, we have printed various papers that we believe to be of permanent value in arriving at a true identification of the creator of the greatest works in English literature."[22] Among those not already cited were:

- Bénézet's commentaries on the wealth of anti-Stratford evidence contained in Philip Henslowe's Diary of Elizabethan theatrical affairs; the forgeries of John Payne Collier; and his keen expose of the glaring inconsistencies and misreadings in the accepted chronology of Shakespearean creations.

- J. J. Dwyer's proof that the real Shakespeare—far from being an unschooled rustic genius—was a cosmopolitan scholar with an intimate knowledge of the untranslated works of the Italian master, Dante.

- Clark's own studies of the topical and historical references in the Shakespeare plays, together with her identification of anonymous poems by Oxford's friend Thomas Watson.

- Barrell's papers on Arthur Golding, Oxford's "traditionally Shakespearean uncle."

In January 1945 the *News-Letter*, after surveying the research presented in its first twenty-nine issues, commented that even if a "comprehensive brief, embodying all valid evidence that has been submitted from various sources to date, were drawn up . . . it would by no means cover the whole story . . . [because] new facts in the dual career of the nobleman who was Shakespeare are continually coming to light. He was obviously too great and dynamic a personality not to have cut a wide swath in the creative life of his era, and not to have made lasting impressions upon many persons with whom he had intimate contact."[23] The report cited recent expressions of appreciation for the *News-Letter* and *Quarterly* from new members and others, including:

- Joseph T. Shipley, encyclopedist and editor of *The American Bookman*: "It becomes increasingly clear that no one concerned with such problems can properly omit consideration of the evidence advanced for the Earl of Oxford as 'William Shakespeare'" (2).

- James J. Dwyer, from Wales: "Your July (1944) *Quarterly* is excellent. You have proved cumulatively (the only way possible) that all those references to the 'Lord Chamberlain' (patron of Shakespeare's acting group) really mean the 'Lord Great Chamberlain' who was Oxford. There was no fixed and accurate use of titles and official designations in that age, or for long afterwards; it is a thing that grew up slowly. . . . It all depends upon the context."

- Dorothy Ogburn, novelist, in her first appearance in print as an Oxfordian: "My admiration for the brilliance and scholarship with which you have assembled and presented this new evidence is profound. It is an example of one of the most fascinating exercises of the mind—literary sleuthing of the highest order. I am amazed by the scope of your references, as well as by the keenness of your perception and of the rapport you have established with the Elizabethan literary scene. On page

---

[21] "'Shakespeare' Identified," *SF Quarterly*, vol. VI/1 (Jan. 1945): 10.
[22] "Introducing the *Quarterly*," *SF Quarterly*, vol. V/1 (Jan. 1944): 1.
[23] "Beginning Our Sixth Year," *SF Quarterly*, vol. VI/1 (Jan. 1945): 1.

63 (October *Quarterly*) you say, 'From this point of view, the pert and irreverent *Epistle Dedicatorie* must be considered one of the great documents of literary history.' I should like to add that your exposition is surely one of the great documents of literary deduction. Mrs. Eva Turner Clark's contribution to the October number is also of outstanding merit. She is very astute, marvelously alert for every nuance, applying her wide knowledge with imagination and precision."[24]

Stratfordian Responses

In response to a letter from T. L. Adamson in England, the *News-Letter* commented "Whatever the 'orthodox' may be thinking about the Oxford evidence, we learn from Mr. Adamson and others that many young people are finding it most acceptable. With their youthful enthusiasm, they are the ones who will carry on until the theory is accepted as a fact. It will then be 'orthodox.'"[25] That openness to new ideas could be contrasted with the hostility of Stratfordian professors who, Adamson stated, "would rather suffocate in the odour of their orthodoxy."[26] That assessment was confirmed by Prof. Bergen Evans of the English Department of Northwestern University: "I must confess that such is the levity of my mind, that I never could bring myself to read a book written by a person with a name like Looney."[27]

Elsewhere the Fellowship observed that

> Professional Stratfordians try to ignore us as studiously as possible. But if it happens that a representative of the accepted brotherhood is exposed to a particular strong example of the Oxford-Shakespeare documentation under circumstances that oblige him to recognize its veracity, he will sometimes say:
>
> *This* may be true enough, but it does not prove conclusively that Oxford was Shakespeare.
>
> In other words, advocates of the Stratford claimant will admit much piecemeal evidence for Oxford under pressure, while denying the full effect of testimony they have been careful to avoid considering. (1)

It also observed that "[o]f the proof offered in our last issue that Oxford bore the magic nickname of 'Gentle Master William' among his literary intimates, not a paragraph in rebuttal has been so far expressed by any Stratford authority—although the material has been brought to the personal attention of twenty of them. Their combined silence bears striking witness to the overwhelming truth of our documentation!"[28]

The Fellowship "has been obliged to issue its own publication to ensure the permanency of its research" because "we have found [mainstream academic] publications so consistently inhospitable to the presentation of evidence connecting Edward de Vere, Earl of Oxford, with the Shakespearean creative background."[29] Citing the case of the Oxfordians vs. *Harper's Magazine*, they wrote, "although Professor Campbell's treatment of this evidence was superficial, containing several notable misstatements of fact, with generous suppression of essential documentary records, and although we know of at least

---

[24] Dorothy Ogburn, [letter, no date given], reprinted in "Beginning Our Sixth Year," *SF Quarterly*, vol. VI/1 (Jan. 1945): 2.

[25] "Letters from England," *SF News-Letter* (American), vol. 4/5 (Aug. 1943): 68-69.

[26] T. L. Adamson, letter to Charles Barrell (no date given), *SF News-Letter*, vol. 4/5 (Aug. 1943), p. 67-68.

[27] Louis P. Bénézet, "Dr. Smart's Man of Stratford Outsmarts Credulity," *SF Quarterly*, vol. VIII/2 (Summer 1947), p. 32.

[28] "Beginning Our Sixth Year," *SF Quarterly*, vol. VI/1 (Jan. 1945): 2.

[29] "Editorial Policy," *SF Quarterly*, vol. V/1 (Jan. 1944): 16.

fifty well-informed Oxfordians who wrote to the Editor of *Harper's* asking for the right to correct some of these errors—not a line, not a word would be accepted. Sir Oracle had spoken, and there the case must rest!"

The Shakespeare Fellowship Quarterly (January 1944)

As the publication entered its fifth year, the Fellowship changed its title from the *Shakespeare Fellowship News-Letter* to the *Shakespeare Fellowship Quarterly*. The change to quarterly publication was due to wartime conditions;[30] the "general format and editorial policies will remain the same."[31] The *Quarterly* described itself as the "Official organ of the Shakespeare Fellowship—American Branch" and observed that it "is the only publication now printed which is devoted chiefly to the perpetuation of documentary evidence that Edward de Vere, 17th Earl of Oxford (1550-1604) was the real creative personality behind the plays and poems of 'Mr. William Shakespeare.'" (2).

Incorporation (February 1945)

On February 20, 1945, the Fellowship filed papers to incorporate itself as a literary and educational association under the laws of the District of Columbia as part of its effort to raise funds. It had become an independent charitable organization registered in the United States.[32]

Certificate of Incorporation

The business and purposes of the corporation for which it is formed are to stimulate and conduct research in the field of Elizabethan literature and history; to promote study of the plays and poems published under the name of 'William Shakespeare'; to publish a periodical, entitled *The Shakespeare Fellowship Quarterly*, in which the results of such study and research shall be presented to its members and to the general public; to print, publish and circulate pamphlets and books devoted to a better understanding of the Shakespearean works and of the personalities prominent in the Elizabethan and Jacobean eras, with special attention to the claims made for Edward de Vere, the 17th Earl of Oxford, as the creative personality responsible for the Shakespearean works; to promote public lectures and discussions and the presentation of radio programs, stage plays, illustrated talks and motion picture productions, designed to entertain and educate its members as well as the general public in all matters relating to the Shakespearean plays and poems and the creative background in which they originated.

---

[30] "To Our Readers," *SF News-Letter*, vol. 4/6 (Oct. 1943): 80.

[31] "Introducing the *Quarterly*," *SF Quarterly*, vol. V/1 (Jan. 1944): 1.

[32] The application for incorporation was signed by Secretary-Treasurer Charles Wisner Barrell, and by Mr. Burton Rice and Miss Margaret Sterbutzel, both of Washington, D.C. The Fellowship's Legal Adviser, Mr. Charlton Ogburn of Washington and New York, handled all legal details. ["Incorporation of the Fellowship to Stimulate Oxford Research," *SF Quarterly*, vol. VI/2 (April 1945): 17.]

The first executive meeting after incorporation was held on March 12, 1945, "at our Washington headquarters," though the location was not stated. Nine trustees were elected to manage the affairs of the corporation for the first year.

Publication of a Second American Edition of *"Shakespeare" Identified*

One of the difficulties Americans faced was that few copies of any Oxfordian books were available. The American edition of *"Shakespeare" Identified* had gone out of print by 1927. Many important books by English Oxfordians had no American editions; they could be found, if at all, in only a few of the largest American libraries.

The American Fellowship did what it could to import books from England, but limited supplies and wartime conditions made things difficult. In the spring of 1940, Looney and Barrell arranged for fifty copies of the Cecil Palmer edition to be shipped to New York (these were from the copies Looney had obtained from Palmer's receiver).[33] In early 1941 the Fellowship was able to offer for purchase a few copies of some eleven core Oxfordian books and pamphlets. In June six copies of Capt. Ward's *The Seventeenth Earl of Oxford* were available, as were a few more copies of *"Shakespeare" Identified*. In January 1946 the Fellowship offered copies of Eva Turner Clark's *The Man Who Was Shakespeare* (1937), *The Satirical Comedy* (1933) and *Hidden Allusions* (1931), as well as Percy Allen's *The Life-story of Edward de Vere as "William Shakespeare"* (1932) and Barrell's pamphlet, *Elizabethan Mystery Man* (1940). In October 1945 the *News-Letter* reported that Capt. Ward had transferred all unsold copies of his *The Seventeenth Earl of Oxford* to the American branch's New York office.

Carolyn Wells weighed in about a new edition of *"Shakespeare" Identified* in 1941. "If every United States citizen could be made by law to read Mr. Looney's book, there would be no need to reiterate its message. It is all so indubitably true, that he who reads it must believe. I have never known an intelligent reader of the book who did not believe it implicitly."[34] "When missionaries go to heathen countries to spread the gospel, they take Bibles with them," she noted, but "[w]e cannot spread our discoveries except by Mr. Looney's book, and—the book is unobtainable! Misfortune followed that blessed volume. Its first publication was held back by one war, its present progress is impeded by another. Even the few copies left in London have been destroyed and we have but a handful of copies over here. What is wanted is a very large and very inexpensive edition, and at present that does not look at all probable."

Discussions between Barrell and Looney about a new American edition of *"Shakespeare" Identified* had been underway since the end of the 1930s. In February 1940 Barrell wrote that

> I am having a conference with the general manager of F.A. Stokes & Co., the firm that published your book here in 1920. He is very sympathetic to the idea of getting out a new edition of *"Shakespeare" Identified*. If you will forward me power of attorney to inspect your 1920 contract with Stokes & Co., I will see that you get the best "deal" possible in the event of a re-issue.

A month later he reported that

> About a week ago I had a long talk with Mr. Horace Stokes, the new president of Stokes and Company. He spoke highly of your book and asked me to submit a

---

[33] Charles Wisner Barrell, "Mountainous Error," *SF News-Letter* (American), vol. 1/3 (April-May 1940): 11. And, Charles Wisner Barrell, letter to J. Thomas Looney, February 16, 1940.

[34] Carolyn Wells, "Oxford's Pseudonym," *SF News-Letter* (American), vol. 2/6 (Oct. 1941): 71.

plan for republishing it, together with the complete manuscript of the portrait studies. I had told him that the two works naturally complemented one another, as I had taken up where you left off. He seemed very sympathetic to the idea. I offered to project the X-ray and infra-red pictures with a stereopticon (having had a set made) so that he and his editors could all see the pictures at the same time. But he only wanted to see the manuscript.

Only a day or two later, however, Stokes sent back the manuscript, saying that they "did not see their way clear to publishing my material or re-issuing yours. Of course neither he nor his editors really saw the . . . pictures—except those reproduced in the *Scientific American*—nor did any of his staff except he himself know your book. So are decisions made in the publishing field!"[35]

Barrell suggested another option.

> There are other newer and more progressive houses than Stokes that are interested in the Oxford evidence. I have come to an agreement with one of these on a book to be written on my evidence relating to Oxford's private life and the *Sonnets*. They have also asked me to hold up further dickerings on the portrait material until the full outline of the life-story material has been approved. They have an idea that it may fit into the single volume they have asked me to write. I know that the combination would be unwieldy, but am saying nothing until my outline on the new script is completed. If this full outline lives up to the preliminary material I have already handed in, I have their written agreement to advance me $1,000 against completion of the book and subsequent royalties.

> The president of the concern is an enthusiastic member of the Fellowship. He has taken the trouble to read all the Oxford evidence available and knows what it is all about. He is also interested in the idea of reissuing *"Shakespeare" Identified* and will be your best bet, if I continue to satisfy him with the late corroborative material, now in hand. I find it best not to push too many things at one time with this publisher, but to suggest casually and let him believe that he has developed the plan himself. He says if things work out the way they are going, he will back a whole new edition of Shakespeare, edited and annotated from the Oxfordian point of view. And there is no doubt that he will do this, if we can live up to his expectations! There would be a grand job in such an undertaking for one J. Thomas Looney. So, altogether, the future looks promising. I have had too many disappointments to go into the poultry business before the eggs have hatched, but we are now definitely in the market place.

Fellowship Developments, 1947-1948

Death of Eva Turner Clark (April 1, 1947)

The obituary in the spring 1947 issue of the *Quarterly* got it right: "The Shakespeare Fellowship of the United States has sustained an irreparable loss in the passing of its gifted founder and senior Vice-President, Mrs. Eva Turner Clark."[36] She had been in the United States what Col. Bernard R. Ward had been in England: the indispensable personality and force behind the creation of the Shakespeare Fellowship. The obituary mentioned her three books and her string of important articles before identifying the qualities that made her writing so effective: "With a natural gift for clear and concise expression, Mrs. Clark combined good judgment, remarkable executive energy and

---

[35] Charles Wisner Barrell, letter to J. Thomas Looney, March 22, 1940.
[36] "Mrs. Eva Turner Clark: Founder of the Shakespeare Fellowship, U.S.A.," *SF Quarterly*, vol. VIII/1 (Spring 1947): 1.

meticulous care in the preparation of her materials, with great personal modesty." It went on to note that "Many of her discoveries and conclusions have already modified the orthodox approach to the Shakespeare authorship problem to a considerable extent. And it can be said with full assurance that her best books and essays will be read so long as the world retains interest in Shakespeare as a man of human reality. Yet she was always the first to give other workers in the same field more credit than herself."

Clark had corresponded with J. Thomas Looney, and was one of the few Americans who had met practically all of the first generation of British Oxfordians (except Looney). She was selfless in her dedication to the Oxfordian cause: in early 1940 when the War was heating up in Europe, she sent, at her own expense, copies of Barrell's *Scientific American* article to every known Oxfordian in England and Europe.[37] When Barrell was called up for military duty later that year, she took on the job of editing the *Shakespeare Fellowship News-Letter*.

One of Clark's most important contributions was sustaining the morale of Fellowship members through several pieces commenting on the meaningful place that Oxfordian work could have in their lives as they struggled to deal with the hardships of daily life during wartime. One of them, "If We Have Leisure," is reprinted nearby.

She returned to the theme in "War and the Fellowship" in February 1942, also reprinted.

She returned to it again in April 1945. "Efforts to strengthen our membership must not be relaxed at this time despite the inescapable exigency of world events. For, as the

---

Eva Turner Clark, "If We Have Leisure!"

We do not need to be reminded that the days we live in are full of problems and anxiety, both foreign and domestic. That is a self-evident fact! What we must consider in such times of stress is how to keep our minds steady. We must not allow ourselves to become 'jittery.' We all need a certain amount of idle amusement—that is good for the human animal—but there are times when the lighter things do not satisfy. The question arises, can we use our leisure to better advantage?

Members of the Shakespeare Fellowship have found an answer to that query. They have found it in the study of the plays and poems of Shakespeare in the light of new discoveries which show them to have been written by Edward de Vere, Earl of Oxford, scholar and courtier, a knowledge of whose life makes the writings more comprehensible. Reading of the plays, with the background now given to them, will be found stimulating to an unusual degree and will help us to retain our sanity in a world given over to insanity.

Shortly after the outbreak of the present European War, an English newspaper printed some lines that should make an indelible impression on all our minds. We quote: 'Literature is the brooding human spirit of today, of yesterday and of tomorrow. It can bind hearts that are broken by evil. The task of politics has its day and ends: the task of art is eternal."

In pursuing our investigations as to the authorship of the Shakespeare plays, we are following an art that is eternal, for the superb plays are as nearly eternal as anything in the literary field of this transitory world can be. Research into the mystery of authorship often brings results which thrill the student as few things can.

Members of the Fellowship who have been active in research are happy to find an increasing interest in the problem of authorship. While we are no longer uncertain as to the identity of the author, there are innumerable details yet to be cleared up which should occupy the minds of hundreds of students, even thousands, and give them great satisfaction in the doing.

From *The Shakespeare Fellowship News-Letter* (American), vol. 1, no. 6 (Oct.-Nov, 1940): 12.

---

[37] Charles Wisner Barrell, letter to J. Thomas Looney, February 16, 1940.

shattering tides of war subside, all civilized persons are bound to turn with freshened interest to those goodly intellectual pursuits which lift the mind of man above the level of the sub-human savages whose mad career is ending. This is our apology for trying to keep the Oxford-Shakespeare case alive in a devastated world."[38]

Eva Turner Clark, "War and the Fellowship"

The entrance of the United States into the war, brought into sharp focus by the dastardly attack on Pearl Harbor by the Japanese, has forced new and greater problems on our Government. In a very small way, the Shakespeare Fellowship—and each and every member—shares in the problems of the difficult days ahead. We shall all do our part, in whatever way necessary, to win through to victory, for only such an outcome can bring peace and freedom to a distraught world.

In the meantime, whatever contribution can be made to our cultural life should be continued. The experience of England, apparently completely preoccupied with war duties, gives us a pattern to follow. One of her librarians recently asserted that the nation is reading today as it has never troubled to read before, and with much more discrimination.

English members of the Fellowship have assured us of the American Branch that each issue of our *News-Letter* has given them a short respite from their troubles and anxieties. With rapidly increasing troubles and anxieties among American members, and in spite of them, we believe the same welcome will be accorded our small periodical here. Unless there come restrictions over which we can have no control, we shall try to carry on!

From *The Shakespeare Fellowship News-Letter* (American), vol. 3, no. 2 (Feb. 1942): 18.

Establishment of the New Shakespeare Society of Philadelphia (March 21, 1947)

This society was founded to promote the study and presentation of the Shakespeare works "with a truer understanding of the dramatist as man and artist." At the inaugural meeting Fellowship member Gelett Burgess was elected Honorary President and Charles Barrell gave a presentation on "Shakespeare's" portraits. The *News-Letter* reported that "As Mr. Barrell's scientifically grounded and carefully documented evidence was unfolded, many skeptics who had come prepared to scoff, remained to pay the tribute of silent attentiveness to the mass of Oxfordian identifications disclosed. . . . The conclusion must be, Mr. Barrell went on to argue, that the Oxford portraits were slightly disguised to provide a pictorial mask for this same nobleman's commonly known pen-name, the latter purposely confused with the approximately similar patronymic of"[39] the man from Stratford.

Bénézet Returns to Philadelphia (May 24, 1947)

Bénézet's lecture for The New Shakespeare Society of Philadelphia, "The Case for Shakspere," had been widely publicized in orthodox Stratfordian circles "for the purpose of securing some advocate of the generally accepted authorship theory to share the platform with Dr. Bénézet and give the public an opportunity to hear an effective answer to the Oxford arguments." Not a single one of the "twenty or more well known Stratfordian professors who reside in the vicinity of Philadelphia" responded or attended. Professors of Mathematics, history and physics, on the other hand, were present and participated in the discussion that followed. "Two of them openly denounced the artful dodger tactics of their English teaching colleagues in refusing to face up to the challenge

---

[38] Eva Turner Clark, "Keep the Light Burning," *SF Quarterly*, vol. VI/2 (April 1945): 29.
[39] "Philadelphia's New Shakespeare Society Points Way to Truer Understanding of the Dramatist," *SF Quarterly*, vol. III/1 (Spring 1947): 15-16.

of the Oxford authorship case."[40]

University Professor Sends Letter (Spring 1947)

A letter from an unnamed college instructor showed the effectiveness the research published in the *Quarterly* could have on those with open minds.

> I marvel at the quality of historical accuracy, literary pungency and astounding variety of your Oxford-Shakespeare research. So far as real news is concerned, logical deduction from heretofore unknown or disregarded evidence for the mysterious literary nobleman and his all-revealing associations in the Shakespearean creative circle, one issue of the *Quarterly* is worth more than a whole year's supply of any publication in the so-called "orthodox" field. Every teacher of Shakespeare in the land should be required to study the *Quarterly* regularly.
>
> I wonder whether your readers generally appreciate the truly epoch-making potentials of your mighty atom amid the flood of conjectural bosh that passes for Shakespearean "research"? Your work deserves the most generous and whole-hearted support financially, and otherwise.[41]

1947 General Meeting and Its Aftermath

Held on May 29, almost two months after Eva Turner Clark's death, the meeting at the home of Vice President James Cushman in New York City, was attended by seventy-five members and guests, including five from the British Isles. The press also attended, including two representatives of the British Broadcasting Corporation, John Astley-Cock from the editorial staff of *The Chicago Tribune*, and a reporter from *The New York Herald Tribune*.

Following a tribute to Clark, President Bénézet presented an overview of the development of the Oxfordian movement, the success of its members' research and the need to create an endowment fund for the Fellowship to support additional research. Gelett Burgess, honorary president of The New Shakespeare Society of Philadelphia, announced the topics of the six lectures on the Shakespeare authorship

The Shakespeare Fellowship Officers for 1947-1948
Dr. Louis P. Bénézet (Hanover, New Hampshire), President and Chairman, Board of Trustees
James Stewart Cushman (New York), Vice-President
Flodden Heron (San Francisco), Vice-President
Elsie G. Holden (Denver), Vice-President
T. Henry Foster (Ottumwa, Iowa), Vice-President
Charles Wisner Barrell (New York), Secretary-Treasurer and Trustee
Charlton Ogburn (New York and Washington, D. C.), Counsel and Trustee
S. Mallet-Prevost (New York), Trustee
Frank C. Doble (Cambridge, MA), Trustee
John Howard Dellinger (Washington, D. C), Trustee
Burton Rice (Paris), Trustee
Glendon Allvine (New York) , Trustee

question scheduled for the next season. Speakers would include Dr. Abraham Feldman, who would go on to become a noted Oxfordian scholar. The final talk was by Barrell on "New X-ray and Infra-red Oxford Evidence in Famous Paintings of 'Shakespeare' in which he presented the results of his examination of the Hampton Court Palace portrait of

---

[40] "Oxford-Shakespeare Talks," *SF Quarterly*, vol. VIII/2 (Summer 1947), p. 20.
[41] "What Do You Think?" *SF Quarterly*, vol. VIII/2 (Summer 1947): 32.

Edward de Vere."[42]

Astley-Cock wrote a thoughtful piece on the gathering for *The Chicago Daily Tribune*, "Infra-Red Peers into Mystery of Shakespeare," highlighting Barrell's finding that the Hampton Court portrait, like the Ashbourne and Janssen portraits, was an image of Edward de Vere that had been over-painted to hide the sitter's identity. The reporter for *The Herald Tribune*, however, ran snooty and misleading coverage. As the *News-Letter* reported,

> Members and guests of The Fellowship were pictured as a choice collection of crackpots "sighing" over their "hero" and exerting misapplied energy in attacking the memory of Sir Francis Bacon. . . . A final paragraph of his report is typical of the way in which the Oxford case as a whole was misrepresented.
>
> > The evidence on which is based the belief that he was the author— under the name "Shakespeare"—of the plays can best be described as tenuous. For example, on a screen was flashed a picture of De Vere, which showed he had long fingers. A portrait of Shakespeare also was shown, in which he also had long fingers. Therefore, De Vere was Shakespeare.
>
> The adroit use of a mere fraction of the portrait evidence to mislead readers generally and belittle the vast accumulation of the Oxford-Shakespeare case as a whole indicates a distinguished career for this reporter in the field of orthodox Shakespeare criticism. With two or three more articles of this type to his credit, he should even be in line for a chair in Stratfordian biography![43]

That hit piece caught Fellowship officers by surprise, given that *The Herald Tribune* had run reviews of all four of Eva Turner Clark's books and had run an obituary respectful of her Oxfordian activities only a few weeks earlier.

Gelett Burgess wrote a 1,000-word response that was published on June 8, 1947, as "Modern Research Sheds New Light on Bard of Avon." His piece was such a convincing brief on behalf of the Oxfordian claim that the Fellowship distributed copies as a special insert in the *News-Letter*.[44] It generated a large number of responses from *Herald Tribune* readers, twelve of which were run in the following seven Sunday issues. The Fellowship couldn't have asked for better publicity. Almost all the responses were emphatic in their endorsement of the Oxfordian claim; even those that weren't were respectful in tone. Of special note was Joseph Carter's 2,500-word article, "The Shakespeare Controversy: Now It Is a Case for the 17th Earl of Oxford," which concluded that "The Stratfordian theory may still be the accepted one in the twenty-first century; but it will have to defeat the strongest

---

[42] "The Fellowship's General Meeting Highly Successful," *SF Quarterly*, vol. VIII/2 (Summer 1947), p. 17. Prior to the General Meeting the Board of Trustees met with officers elected for the coming year. Present at the meeting were voting members Dr. L. P. Bénézet, S. Mallet-Prevost, J. S. Cushman, Charlton Ogburn and C. W. Barrell, and other non-voting Oxfordians, including Elsie G. Holden, Gelett Burgess, Mrs. [Harriet] Sprague, Taber Sears, Miss Clara Van Benthuysen, Lewis H. Webster and Glendon Allvine. Allvine was unanimously chosen to succeed Eva Turner Clark as Trustee, and T. Henry Foster of Ottumwa, Iowa, was unanimously voted to succeed Clark as Vice-President. Officials for the coming year were also elected.

[43] "The Fellowship's General Meeting Highly Successful," *SF Quarterly*, vol. VIII/2 (Summer 1947), p. 18, quoting "Bacon Has a Rival in Shakespeare" De Vere Supporters Make Post-War Appearance," *New York Herald Tribune*, May 30, 1947, p. 17.

[44] Burgess's article has been reprinted in *Avalanche of Falsity* (2014), vol. 7 of Paul H. Altrocchi's *Building the Case*, a ten-volume anthology of pieces important in Shakespeare authorship research.

contender in almost 100 years."[45]

Burgess's piece in the *Herald Tribune* played a key role in a lawsuit that Charles Barrell was to become involved in.[46] It also signaled Burgess's rise to prominence as the most effective spokesman for the Oxfordian movement. That lengthy exchange of views in the *Tribune* was only the first of three in which he would play the leading role.

The New York Herald Tribune — Selected Coverage of the Oxfordian Claim, 1947		
May 30	--	"Bacon Has a Rival as Shakespeare: De Vere Supporters Make Post-War Appearance"
June 8	Gelett Burgess	"Modern Research Sheds New Light on Bard of Avon: Recent Discoveries Concerning Authorship"
June 15	Charlton Ogburn	"Oxford, Poet and Playwright?" [letter: response to Burgess]
	Harriet Peasley	"Oxford, Poet and Playwright?" [letter: response to Burgess]
	Mrs. H. C. Sprague	"Oxford, Poet and Playwright?" [letter: response to Burgess]
June 22	Gelett Burgess	"The Modern Challenge of Shakespearean Authorship" [letter: reply to recent letters]
	Edmund Collins	"Genius and Lowly Origins" [letter: response to Burgess]
	Peter G. Earle	"De Vere's Poetry" [letter: response to Burgess]
July 19	Gordon Allvine	"Oxford's Literary Genius" [letter]
	Dorothy Ogburn	"Oxford's Literary Genius: Shakespeare's Background" [letter: responses to Collins and Earle]
July 20	Joseph Carter	"The Shakespeare Controversy: Now It Is a Case for the 17th Earl of Oxford" [2,500-word examination of the issue]
July 29	Sydney Thompson	"Asks Photographic Proof" [letter]
Sept. 7	Florence W. Sears	"Acclaimed as a Poet" [letter: response to Burgess]

Progress Continues

In its summary of progress made during 1947, the *News-Letter* noted that nearly 150 new members had joined, and that more than a thousand others had attended lectures or gatherings. "Spokesmen for our cause have not only broken new ground. In every openly conducted argument Oxfordian speakers and writers have won popular approval—to the surprise and sometimes discomfiture of their orthodox Shakespearean opponents."[47] Stratfordians "are finding that it will not suffice any more to discount the playwright Earl's documentation with cheap ridicule, to silence skepticism with some labored wisecrack, nor to wave aside recorded fact with stuffed shirt complacency. As our reading circles in schools, colleges and universities widen, more and more embarrassing questions are being asked by undergraduates of Shakespearean teachers and professors regarding the flimsy biographical data upon which the greatest literary reputation of historical times has been arbitrarily assigned to a person so significantly lacking in contemporary certification as William of Stratford."

Progress seemed almost palpable. "In certain instances which have come to our attention, the professors thus annoyed by their heckling students have been men of some

---

[45] Joseph Carter, "The Shakespeare Controversy: Now It Is a Case for the 17th Earl of Oxford," *New York Herald Tribune*, July 20, 1947, p. A2.

[46] The "Three B's" carrying the Oxfordian banner forward in the later 1940s were not Bach, Beethoven and Brahms, but Barrell, Bénézet and Burgess.

[47] "Progress During the Passing Year," *SF Quarterly*, vol. VIII/4 (Winter 1947-48): 49.

reputation as Stratfordian authorities. One of these blandly retorted that doubts regarding the accepted authorship of the plays and poems must reflect seriously upon the intelligence of all those expressing such distrust. As for the 17th Earl of Oxford, this Elizabethan 'authority' solemnly averred that he himself had 'never even heard of him as a poet or playwright' of the Shakespearean Age!"

The report also cited the following developments:

Publication of Dorothy and Charlton Ogburn's *The Renaissance Man of England*

In 1945 Dorothy Ogburn had written for the *Quarterly* "The Wounded Name of Truth," "a moving plea for better understanding of the personality of Oxford, as revealed in his Shakespearean roles." That psychologically penetrating study deserves to be better known even apart from its startling suggestion that Oxford's theatrical activities had played a significant role in triggering the Spanish Armada:

> Lord Oxford had served the state, and they knew it; but nothing must be said of that, for he had sworn to keep secret his authorship of the plays, which are full of topical political allusions, personalities, and caricatures.

> She paid him 1,000 pounds a year for this secret service to the state, on the pain of anonymity. (In July 1586 the Venetian ambassador in Spain wrote, apropos of the King of Spain: "but what enraged him [most] ... is the account of masquerades and comedies which the Queen of England orders to be acted at his expense.")

> Moreover, he [Oxford] had saved the state from its traducers—the Howard-Arundel faction—at a tremendous risk and with supreme courage and patriotism. It is the recorded slurs of these cornered traitors, still accessible in the Record Office in London, which have lived after Oxford, wounding his name, setting down much in malice against this noble genius whose very name—the honor of which, at the cost of oblivion, he never betrayed—meant *truth*.[48]

Then in 1947 came *The Renaissance Man of England* by Dorothy and Charlton Ogburn (her husband), a book that served almost as a short biography of Edward de Vere. The *Quarterly* described it as "an introductory handbook to the study of Edward de Vere's many-sided personality and a brief but illuminating discussion of his leading role in the authorship mystery. . . . [A book] of unusual value."[49] They, together with their son Charlton Ogburn, Jr., would go on to play roles of crucial importance in the Oxfordian movement over the following half-century.

A Tale of Two Encyclopedias

S. Edgar Farquhar, chief editor of *Grolier's Encyclopedia*, had been impressed by what he'd heard about the Oxfordian idea at the Burgess-Barrell roundtable discussion in New York in September 1946. After investigating further, he invited Prof. Bénézet to write an article on "Shakespeare Authorship Theories" for the new edition of the *Encyclopedia* even in the face of opposition "vigorously expressed" by professional Stratfordians. His response to their "high-pressure intimidation" was to commission Bénézet also to write the piece on Oxfordian authorship [in vol. 10, p. 301]. After Farquhar's death the *News-Letter* wrote of the pleasure of paying tribute "to the courage and independent fairness of

---

[48] Dorothy Ogburn, "The Wounded Name of Truth," *SF Quarterly*, vol.VI/4 (Oct. 1945): 62.
[49] "Convincing Brief by Charlton Ogburn," *SF Quarterly*, vol. VIII/4 (Winter 1947-48): 49. The original manuscript, circulated in 1947 was listed as by Charlton Ogburn. The published 1947 and 1955 revised editions are listed as by Dorothy and Charlton Ogburn.

our late friend."[50]

In contrast, *The Encyclopedia Britannica* had run for the past thirty-five years an entry for "Oxford, Edward de Vere, 17th Earl of" that was "so faulty in detail, prejudiced in tone, and notably lacking in easily ascertainable information attested by twentieth century research, as to bring into question the general reliability of this famous work of reference." The editors of the *News-Letter* "can find no excuse whatever for the perpetuation in the current (1943) edition of such questionable gossip and outright misstatement of historical fact—compounded in effect by the omission of every constructive element that might help readers to a balanced judgment of the foremost poet at Elizabeth's Court." The editors posed the key question, "What are the several thousands of intelligent, truth-seeking persons who know the facts of the Oxford documentation going to do about it?"[51]

Bénézet at Tufts College (May and June 1947)

One of Bénézet's two lectures in May and June 1947 was marred by a Stratfordian professor who took the floor at the start of the question period and talked for an hour to block anyone else from speaking. The report in the *News-Letter* described the boorish behavior "not to criticize any individual Shakespearean professor's manners in debate, but to indicate the intolerance, misrepresentation and medieval thinking which still characterizes the reactions of certain collegiate representatives of the orthodox persuasion when confronted with perfectly legitimate Oxfordian arguments. Facts which they cannot answer, they seek to drown out with distortion, prevarication and vocal vehemence. Is it any wonder, then, that educational surveys now stress the sad estate into which the teaching of English has fallen in this country?"[52]

Bénézet in Boston (June 1947)

Boston, the *News-Letter* noted, "was once a center of dissatisfaction with the Stratford authorship interpretation, the outspoken skepticism of such writers as Emerson, Hawthorne, Lowell, Dr. Holmes and Whittier being echoed in many quarters." Later the Baconian ideas held sway, but then "the late Professor [George Lyman] Kittredge of Harvard not only helped discredit the Baconians, but preached the 'back to Stratford' doctrine with such assurance that he literally . . . browbeat dissidents into line with his own interpretations. . . . Kittredge refused to meet or converse with any advocate of the playwright Earl's credentials." That situation is now changing with talks by Bénézet, Prof. Allen Burt, Thomas O'Connor and others. "Dr. Bénézet's cordial reception by the members and guests of the Wedgwood Club also proves . . . that a fertile field for the extension of Oxford-Shakespeare intelligence awaits cultivation in the old Bay Colony."[53]

Bénézet's "The Shakespeare Hoax: An Improbable Narrative" (1947)

Bénézet wrote "The Shakespeare Hoax" in the summer of 1947 during an engagement as Visiting Professor of Education at Bradley University in Peoria, Illinois. It was published in the November issue of *The Dartmouth Quarterly*, much to the consternation of the college's English professors. Drawing heavily on research published by the Shakespeare

---

[50] "Oxford in *Grolier Encyclopedia*," *SF Quarterly*, vol. VIII/4 (Winter 1947-48): 50-51.
[51] "Thou Shalt Not Bear False Witness," *SF Quarterly*, vol. VII/4 (Oct. 1946): 70-71.
[52] "Tufts College," *SF Quarterly*, vol. VIII/4 (Winter 1947-48): 54-55. The speaker was Prof. Myrick, a Tufts Shakespeare specialist.
[53] "Bénézet at Wedgewood Club in Boston," *SF Quarterly*, vol. VIII/4 (Winter 1947-48): 54-55.

Fellowship, he poked holes in the Stratfordian case and presented the latest evidence in support of the Oxfordian.

The *Quarterly* described "The Shakespeare Hoax" as "a bold and breezy attack on the Stratford claims and presents the Bénézet view of the new Shakespeare evidence with characteristic enthusiasm. Quite a sensation was caused in both undergraduate and faculty circles at Dartmouth by its appearance. Some of the English professors who have long resented Dr. Bénézet's Shakespearean activities, took it as another example of the deplorably disruptive influence he exerts in the field they regard as closed to iconoclastic profanation. The student body, however, greeted 'The Shakespeare Hoax' with much the same joy that the undergraduates in 'The Propagation of Knowledge' welcomed the anti-Stratfordian arguments to which they were introduced in Rudyard Kipling's diverting tale. ["Debits and Credits"]"[54] Demand for copies was so high that Bénézet later issued it as a pamphlet.

"The Shakespeare Hoax" noted several linkages between Edward de Vere and Shakespeare that had not yet appeared in print:

- It was known that the Strachey letter, which many scholars believe was used as a source of information for the storm scene that opens *The Tempest*, was addressed to "an excellent Lady of the London Company." What is new is that Oxford's daughter Elizabeth, the Earl of Derby's wife, was a member of the Company's Council.
- It was known that no member of Shakspere's family had anything to do with the First Folio and that the two earls behind its publication were a son-in-law of Edward de Vere and his brother who had once been engaged to another of Oxford's daughters. What is new is that two dozen copies of the Folio have been traced to Oxford's family and connections.
- That Shakspere's supposed ownership of shares in the Blackfriars Theater is based on one of Collier's forgeries, but is quoted still as genuine "evidence" in support of Shakspere's authorship.
- That attendance records for the grammar school in Stratford exist for every decade except the 1570s, the years during which William Shakspere would have attended.

Funding to Keep the Work Going

Charles Barrell issued a call for funding in the fall of 1947. I suspect that Eva Turner Clark had funded much of the Fellowship research, but with her recent passing that source of funds was no longer available. The effort to capitalize on the discoveries made over the past eight years had to move forward, Barrell explained, because of strengthened Stratfordian resistance.

> We have rallied to our standard a goodly force of men and women of open-minded vision, logic and common sense. We have at the same time irritated so many of the self-appointed "authorities" in the field of Stratfordian research and biography that no orthodox version of a Shakespearean book or commentary is now considered complete unless it contains a warning to its readers to beware of Oxfordian "heresies." . . . Instead of facing up to the advocates of the Oxford-Shakespeare evidence and besting them in fair and logically founded argument, it is now considered most effective form for the spokesmen of Stratfordia to smother all opposition in ridicule.

> An organized effort to misrepresent Oxfordian aims and accomplishments has

---

[54] "Dr. Bénézet's 'Shakespeare Hoax,'" *SF Quarterly*, vol. VIII/4 (Winter 1947-48): 56.

become apparent. Wherever the accepted "authorities" can exert pressure upon editors or publishers to prevent publication of the Oxford discoveries, they do so with alacrity. Several examples of this type of underground activity have been brought to our attention during the past year. Fear is, of course, the basis of all such misrepresentation. Every Stratford "expert" is vitally concerned in protecting his personal stake in the very large vested interest which standardized Shakespearean biography now represents. What, indeed, would be the value of the copyright to Professor Dustin Mildoo's charming dream-life of William of Stratford if the reading public should suddenly learn that the playwright Earl of Oxford was the authentic "Gentle Master William"?

Bénézet-Bolton Debate and Radio Broadcast (January 5, 1948)

As a direct result of "The Shakespeare Hoax" in *The Dartmouth Quarterly*, Bénézet was invited by Joseph Bolton, Chairman of the English Department at Skidmore College, Saratoga, New York, to debate him on "Oxford versus William of Stratford," an event that would also be broadcast over radio station WGY of Schenectady.[55] The audience of 225 was so engaged that debate continued for an extra hour. Skidmore's president came to the stage to express his keen enjoyment of the program, and informal discussion continued at Bénézet's hotel until past midnight. *The Daily Saratogian* published a full account of the discussion, which was voted the most interesting of the local season.

Barrell Lecture at the University of Pennsylvania (January 9, 1948)

Barrell spoke on Oxfordian discoveries over the past twenty-eight years, including how his use of X-ray and infra-red techniques revealed three paintings of "Shakespeare" to be over-paintings of portraits of Edward de Vere. He emphasized "the scientifically sound methods" pursued by Looney and the foremost of his followers, and "the pains, expense and thought which have been given to the task of uncovering and verifying" their evidence. But, Barrell continued, their "work has been accompanied by much ill-conceived ridicule and misrepresentation on the part of entrenched obscurantists who seem to feel that their monopoly of Shakespearean biographical interpretation is endangered by any new facts proving Oxford a serious candidate for high creative honors." Barrell "warned those addicted to [such practices] that they cannot continue to ignore and misrepresent honest documentation indefinitely without stultifying their own reputations. . . . [Y]ounger, more alert and less prejudiced minds demand the truth and refuse to be intimidated by such 'authority.'" His remarks elicited hearty applause, and "some of the English instructors present were observed making notes of all the Oxford documentation specified."[56]

1948 Annual Meeting and Its Aftermath

More than 200 members and guests attended this momentous meeting on April 30, organized by Mrs. Arthur F. Schermerhorn and held in the auditorium of the New York Genealogical Society. The four main speakers were President Bénézet; Siegfried Hartman; prominent member of the New York Bar and an Oxford advocate; Charlton Ogburn, the Fellowship's attorney; and Charles Barrell.

During Hartman's talk, the *News-Letter* reported, an incident occurred that "started a chain of events which has resulted in the filing of a libel suit by our secretary [Barrell]

---

[55] "The Bolton-Bénézet Debate," *SF Quarterly*, vol. VIII/4 (Winter 1947-48): 57
[56] "Our Secretary at Pennsylvania," *SF Quarterly*, vol. VIII/4 (Winter 1947-48): 57

against an executive of the Folger Shakespeare Library in Washington, D. C."[57] Meredith Underhill, a teacher of Shakespeare, interrupted Hartman to declare that the Oxfordian arguments were unworthy of credence because of a letter he had received from a real authority. The letter had been written by Dr. Giles E. Dawson, Curator of Books and Manuscripts at the Folger Shakespeare Library, on July 25, 1947. Dawson's letter was in response to a letter that Underhill had written after seeing Joseph Carter's July 20 article in *The New York Herald Tribune*. As noted, the *Herald Tribune* ran several items in the wake of the Fellowship's 1947 Annual Meeting.

In his letter, Dawson stated that Barrell's X-ray and infra-red negatives—on which he had based his 1940 *Scientific American* article—had been manipulated: "As to Mr. Barrell and the portraits, they can be dismissed at once. Two of those portraits are here [in the Folger Shakespeare Library]—the Janssen and the Ashbourne. And Mr. Barrell made his X-ray photographs here. The plain fact is that we were entirely unable to see any of the things he saw in the negatives. They just weren't there. If he can produce pictures of these things they must have been doctored up."[58]

Dawson also took the occasion to slight Oxfordian scholars: "All of them approach the subject fully convinced of this or that 'truth' and close their minds to any evidence on the other side. Indeed they are quite incapable of weighing evidence." Dawson did not attempt to refute the Oxfordian thesis by challenging specific points of evidence or reasoning. His intent was to convince Underhill that Oxfordians were members of a "cult" who suffer from "an attitude of mind compounded of a love for the mysterious and sensational and a dislike for the established and orthodox."

On July 1, 1948, Charlton Ogburn "entered suit against Dr. Dawson on behalf of Mr. Barrell, claiming malicious libel, and asking damages in the sum of $50,000."[59] That was the extent of the report in the Summer issue of the *News-Letter*. The Autumn issue contained no update. The lawsuit generated considerable media attention, most extensively in *The Washington Post*, which ran several editorials and printed a dozen or so letters over the following two months. As with his defense in *The New York Herald Tribune* in 1946, Gelett Burgess provided the most insistent and persuasive pieces in response to the ill-informed and snide editorials and letters in the *Post*.

The *Post*'s own reportage gave prominence to Dawson's charges as expressed in his letter to Underhill rather than to the evidence and reasoning in support of the Oxfordian claim. Dawson was presented as a prestigious expert, while Barrell's work on the portraits was presented mostly as the work of a single individual, with no mention of Looney or other Oxfordian scholars, and only a short mention that Barrell's findings had been prominently published by *Scientific American*. No mention was made of how carefully that magazine's editors had vetted Barrell's findings before publishing them.

In its July 10 editorial, the *Post* attributed to Oxfordians a claim that not a single Oxfordian had ever made, that they "insist on replacing the barefoot country boy from Stratford with some elegant, court-bred nobleman, on the premises that the Shakespeare plays are just too damn good to have been written by anybody below the rank of a

---

[57] "Libel Suit Grows Out of Fellowship's Annual Meeting," *SF Quarterly*, vol. IX/2 (Summer 1948): 16.

[58] Giles E. Dawson, letter to Meredith Underhill, reprinted in "Charles Wisner Barrell, Plaintiff v. Giles E. Dawson, Defendant: Action for Damages for Libel," Civil Action No. 2698-48, United States District Court for the District of Columbia, filed July 1, 1948.

[59] "Libel Suit Grows Out of Fellowship's Annual Meeting," *SF Quarterly*, vol. IX/2 (Summer 1948): 16.

baronet."[60]

The *Post* went on, "It is also the sort of controversy which is eminently suited to democratic methods of discussion, since no particular qualifications of scholarship are required to entitle one to an opinion and each disputant is at liberty to devise his own rules of evidence." The *Post* then offered its own solution: "not only the Shakespeare plays and poems, but the *Novum Organum*, the *Apologie for Poetry* and all the other famous works of the period [should] be declared the products of multiple authorship. In other words, we can assume a sort of general production and editorial board, assisted by an extensive research department, prepared on short notice to knock out a masterpiece in almost any field, including drama and philosophy."[61]

The Washington Post — Selected Coverage of the Barrell-Dawson Lawsuit, 1948		
July 2	--	"Authorship of Shakespeare Plays Basis of Court Action"
July 3	Lee Grove	"'Shakespeare' Just Pen Name of Oxford Earl, Barrell Says"
July 10	--	"Who Wrote What?" [editorial]
July 14	Harrison Tilghman	"Who Wrote What?" [letter]
July 15	Robert W. Wooley	"Who Wrote What?" [letter]
July 25	PUCK	"Who Was Shakespeare? A Communication" [letter]
July 31	Gelett Burgess	"Oxford Is Shakespeare: A Communication"
Aug. 4	I. P. Skovar	"Shakespeareski" [letter]
Aug. 8	MUMPSIMUM	"Who Was Shakespeare?" [letter]
Aug. 9	E. V. Wilcox	"Who Was Shakespeare?" [letter]
	T. M. Kerr, Jr.	"Who Was Shakespeare?" [letter]
Aug. 10	Antonio Spiggonio	"Shakespeare Solved" [letter]

In a lengthy response, someone using the name "PUCK" made a strong justification for doubts about Shakspere's authorship before citing the case for Edward de Vere. Then came Gelett Burgess's forceful rejoinder. After noting important findings by Oxfordian researchers supporting the Oxfordian thesis, and after noting that more than one hundred American colleges subscribe to the *Shakespeare Fellowship Quarterly* in which these new discoveries are reported, he observed that "not one English professor has ever disproved any of the evidence or even commented on it. Their only reaction has been, 'The question is settled. There is nothing to discuss.'"[62]

The learned Shakespeare scholars interviewed by *The Washington Post*, Burgess observed, "pussyfooted the subject. Not one showed that he had ever read the Oxford evidence, not one mentioned the Folger photographs." The explanation for their "ostrich-like refusal" to examine the evidence "is simple":

> They are no fools, these Ph.Ds. They know enough to come in when it rains. And boy, is it going to pour! They are frightened out of their logical wits. Afraid of stultifying themselves, afraid of losing their jobs, afraid of the fast approaching band wagon. They are haunted by the dread that modern scholarship based on historic research instead of fanciful dreams, which is making more progress

---

[60] In the five years I have spent researching this book I have not come across a single instance of an Oxfordian making that claim. I have often, though, come across statements expressing doubt that that one particular individual from Stratford could have written those particular works without leaving behind even a single trace of how he did it.

[61] "Who Wrote What?" [Editorial], *Washington Post*, July 10, 1948, p. 4.

[62] Gelett Burgess, "Oxford is Shakespeare: A Communication," *Washington Post*, July 31, p. 5.

towards Oxford every day, will soon supersede their legendary Shakespearean mythology so insecurely rooted in seventeenth century gossip.

So still dodge, shuffle, while you may. . . . Suppress, ignore, ridicule, obscure. . . . Your time is short, brother.

"Mumpsimum" raised an interesting question in his August 8 letter: "If the aim was to conceal that Oxford was Shakespeare, by 'changing the head and obliterating all identifying details,' why should anyone start with a portrait of Oxford as basis for a Shakespeare forgery in the first place?"[63] That is an interesting question. Another interesting question is why at least three of the portraits altered to resemble "Shakespeare," were originally of the same sitter, Edward de Vere.

Gelett Burgess Takes the Lead

Burgess had, essentially, taken over the debate, recentering it from the libel suit to the case he made on behalf of the Oxfordian answer to the Shakespeare Mystery and Stratfordians' inability to respond to it effectively.

Later that year he was at the center of a third extended exchange of views, this time in *The Saturday Review*. The series was launched on October 2 with Burgess's long letter critical of G. B. Harrison's new edition of Shakespeare's plays, in which he noted that Edward de Vere "had every possible qualification for authorship while the dummy of Stratford had not one."[64] He cited several prominent British scholars who had publicly declared their belief that Edward de Vere had written "Shakespeare's" works, in contrast with the United States, in which "hardly a single important professor of English literature has been willing even to consider the new historical evidence that has changed the whole Elizabethan picture." Many Shakespeare scholars had been invited to refute the new evidence that has accumulated over the past thirty years, he noted, but all had refused.

More than thirty letters were printed in response, most showing not even the most basic understanding of the Oxfordian claim and, in some cases, a poor understanding even of the Stratfordian claim. The most important rebuttal to Burgess, a long cover story by Bergen Evans, Professor of English at Northwestern University, was published on May 7, 1949, to which *The Saturday Review* gave Burgess space for a lengthy reply on June 4. Noting that "not a single one of my traditional opponents has shown any knowledge of

Saturday Review of Literature — **Selected Coverage the Oxfordian Claim, 1948-1949**		
June 5	Ben Ray Redman	Review of G. B. Harrison's new edition of Shakespeare's Plays
Oct. 2	Gelett Burgess	"Pseudonym, Shakespeare"
Nov. 6	T. C. Hoepfner & others	"The Shakespeare Confusion" [6 letters: response to Burgess]
Nov. 20	G. R. Garrett	"Nobody Named Shakespeare" [letter]
May 7	Bergen Evans	"Good Friend for Jesys Sake Forbeare; Was Shakespeare Really Shakespeare?"
June 4	John L. Aycock & others	"Was Shakespeare, Shakespeare?" [4 letters}
June 4	Gelett Burgess	"The Oxford Primer" [reply to responses to his October 2 article]
June 25	Clara de Chambrun	"Was Shakespeare Really Shakespeare?" [letter]

---

[63] Mumpsimum, "Who Was Shakespeare?" [letter], *Washington Post*, Aug. 8, p. B4.
[64] Gelett Burgess, "Pseudonym, Shakespeare," *Saturday Review*, Oct. 2, 1948, p. 22.

the recently discovered historical facts indicating the Oxford authorship of the Shakespeare plays," he presented "an Oxfordian primer"—a fourteen-point listing of the reasons that led Oxfordians to their belief that Edward de Vere wrote "Shakespeare's" works.[65]

Burgess's concluding summary can also serve as ours for the findings of the American Oxfordians over the nine-year existence of the American branch of the Shakespeare Fellowship.

> If we compare these facts with the complete lack of any similar contemporary certification of the Stratford [Shakspere's] association with any literary activity, the logical conclusion is evident, *i.e.*, that Oxford used the name "Shakespeare" as a pseudonym. Not only did [Shakspere] have *none* of these qualifications for authorship, but Oxford was the *only* Elizabethan writer who possessed them all.

> One of the happiest results of the scholarship and research that have been given to Oxford's life is the fact that a new and authentic chronology of the plays has proved that the so-called "crude" plays which Shakespeare has been supposed to rewrite and improve were actually pirated publications of memory versions of his own works, which rescues the author's name from the traditional charge of plagiarism.

> Thus, in bringing to light the life, environment, and activities of Edward De Vere, a consummate genius who, though neglected and maligned heretofore by history, was the true leader of the British Renaissance, there has been revealed the man who, by all scientific standards, is the most logical and believable candidate for the authorship of the Shakespeare plays and sonnets. (25)

Gelett Burgess

Born: January 30, 1866. Died: September 17, 1951.
Age when *"Shakespeare" Identified* was published: 56

Humorist, novelist, short story writer, essayist. Author of more than forty books.
Graduate of the Massachusetts Institute of Technology.
Coined several new words in common use today, including "blurb."

Corresponded with Looney beginning in May, 1920.
Honorary president of the newly-formed New Shakespeare Society of Philadelphia, 1947

Important Oxfordian Publications

1947, June 8	"Modern Research Sheds New Light on Bard of Avon [a 1,000-word letter to the editor]. *New York Herald Tribune*
1947, June 22	"The Modern Challenge of Shakespearean Authorship [reply to recent letters], *New York Herald Tribune*
1948, July 31	"Oxford is Shakespeare: A Communication" [long rebuttal to critics of the Oxfordian idea], *Washington Post*
1948, Oct. 2	"Pseudonym, Shakespeare," *Saturday Review*
1949, June 4	"Was Shakspere Shakespeare? An Oxfordian Primer" [letter] *Saturday Review*
1949, Dec. 11	"Shakespeare a Pen Name" [letter], *New York Herald Tribune*
1950, May 12	The Three Centuries-Old Mystery of Shakespeare Solved," *Argonaut*

---

[65] Gelett Burgess, "An Oxford Primer," *Saturday Review*, June 4, 1949, p. 24.

And Then It Ended

By the end of 1948 it was all over. Eva Turner Clark had died in April 1947. Prof. Louis Bénézet retired from Dartmouth College in 1948 and moved to Illinois. Charles Barrell withdrew from active involvement in the Oxfordian movement and at some point left New York City to live on his farm in Warwick Valley, New York. The Autumn 1948 issue of the *Quarterly* was to be the last, though it contained no indication that anything was amiss. As far as can be determined, no explanation or notice was given to members, and no other trustee stepped in to lead the organization after the departures of Bénézet and Barrell.

The publication of Barrell's *Scientific American* piece in January 1940 had raised public awareness and media receptivity to the Oxfordian claim in the United States to heights never before imagined. The Fellowship had built on that high base through a steady stream of substantive research findings and publications over the following nine years. The nearly one hundred public talks to promote awareness of the Oxfordian thesis had continued all through the war years. As 1948 opened, the Shakespeare Fellowship appeared to be moving full speed ahead, with the first issues of the *Quarterly* describing the enthusiastic responses to recent lectures. But then it all vanished.

What happened? No definitive explanation has surfaced. The English Shakespeare Fellowship, which published its *News-Letter* semi-annually until 1958, never reported that the American organization had become inactive. In 1959, in the first issue of *The Shakespearean Authorship Review*, the publication of the Shakespearean Authorship Society that succeeded the Shakespeare Fellowship in England, there was a short note that "soon after the death of Mrs. Clark in 1947 the American Branch ceased to exist as an organized body, though its members retained their interest and many of them joined, or rejoined, the original society with its headquarters in London." [66] A decade later, then, had come a brief note, but not a word of explanation.

Wrapping up

Charles Barrell: Barrell lived until 1974. He continued to research the Oxfordian claim privately after 1948, but published very little. His only known publications after 1948 were a piece he had contracted to write for *Grolier's Encyclopedia*[67] and a piece he wrote twenty-four years later, in 1972, for Ruth Loyd Miller.[68] The two books Barrell had repeatedly said were almost ready for publication never appeared. One detailed his examinations of all three portraits said to be of Shakespeare that Barrell had shown were over-paintings of Edward de Vere. It included seventy-five color photos and was said to be nearing completion in the middle of 1940. The other, for which Barrell had a contract with Creative Age Press, described the story told in Shakespeare's *Sonnets* involving Edward de Vere, Anne Vavasour and Edward Vere, their illegitimate son. A prospectus had appeared as the two articles in *Tomorrow* early in 1946.

Barrell's papers are reported to be in secure hands but have not yet been systematically inspected and inventoried. It is possible that the manuscripts for both books exist, as well as much correspondence with Looney, Clark, Bénézet and others.

---

[66] Gwynneth M. Bowen, "Ave Atque Vale," *Shakespearean Authorship Review*, no. 1 (Spring 1959): 3.

[67] Mike Adair reported that Barrell had contracted to write an article for *The Story of Our Time*, the *Grolier's Encyclopedia Yearbook*. ["Charles Wisner Barrell: A Biographical Sketch," *Shakespeare Matters*, vol. 9/1 (Winter 2010): 20.]

[68] "The Strange Silence of William Shakespeare's Son-in-Law, Dr. John Hall of Stratford-on-Avon," written in 1972 specifically for *Oxfordian Vistas* (1975), edited by Ruth Loyd Miller.

Those papers could shed much light on the first decades of the Oxfordian movement. Further correspondence and documents might also come to light if the archives or papers of other noted Oxfordian scholars are located.[69]

The lawsuit: Barrell's libel case did not go to trial. Depositions were taken in September and October of 1949.[70] During Dawson's deposition, when asked by Charlton Ogburn, "Did anyone in Stratford in his lifetime ever refer to him as an author?" Dawson, being under oath, had to answer, "Not that I know of" (11). Questions about whether Shakspere had been an actor and a writer solicited similar responses. Ogburn: "Those references are all to the author, and not to the Stratford man, unless they be the same person?" Dawson: "This is right." Then came an interesting moment when Dawson was questioned by his attorney. After questions about Barrell's X-rays, the attorney asked, "Did you yourself have X-rays made of the Ashbourne portrait?" Dawson responded, "Yes." The attorney followed up: "In those X-Rays were you able to see any of the three things you have mentioned?" Dawson answered, "No" (23-24). In his redirect examination, Ogburn established that Dawson's X-rays had been taken within the past year (26), after the action had been filed.. That the Folger had made its own X-rays and that Dawson did not introduce them as evidence in his defense suggest that the results either confirmed Barrell's findings or were ambiguous.

The case was dropped on November 7, 1950, without judgment or financial compensation going to either party. The Stipulation for Dismissal stated in full that "The within action having been settled, it is hereby stipulated that said action may be dismissed with prejudice, each party to bear his own costs." Mike A'Dair later reported that

> In September 1948, no doubt at his lawyer's insistence, Dawson did write a corrective letter to Underhill, in which he softened some of the things he had said about Barrell and his work. While Dawson said that he "unqualifiedly" retracted any slur he may have made against Barrell's character in his earlier letter, the retraction was couched in so many qualifications that this second letter to Underhill was more of an equivocation than an apology. . . . The conventional Oxfordian assertion that Dawson made a public apology to Barrell should be revised, because [that letter] was not public and was not published in any newspaper or magazine, nor was it even written to or addressed to Barrell. (20)

Financial considerations may have played a role in Barrell's decision not to pursue the case. Perhaps he realized that if the case went to trial and he lost he could be liable for payment of Dawson's attorney's fees and perhaps even the Folger Shakespeare's Library's legal costs, expenses that would have bankrupted him.

Prof. Louis Bénézet: He retired from Dartmouth College in 1948. As far as is known, he published no articles on the Oxfordian thesis after that and gave no more public talks. He did write a letter on the subject to the editor of *The American Bar Association Journal*, which was printed in 1960. He also published a small Oxfordian book, *The Six Loves of Shakespeare*, in 1958. The book, drawing partly on Barrell's ideas, proposed that Oxford

---

[69] Conflicting accounts of where Barrell lived after 1948 exist. Some state that he moved to his farm in Warwick Valley, others that he was still living on Grove Street in Greenwich Village in the early 1970s and that his papers and books were still there. Some accounts state that he became almost a recluse, others that he remained in frequent contact with Ruth Loyd Miller and had occasional contact with others, including Craig Huston, A. Bronson Feldman and Warren Hope.

[70] Deposition of Giles E. Dawson, Oct. 6, 1949, p. 1. I am grateful to Mike A'Dair for providing me with a full set of all legal documents related to the lawsuit. See also his "Charles Wisner Barrell: A Biographical Sketch," *Shakespeare Matters*, vol. 9/1 (Winter 2010): 1, 14-21.

wrote his sonnets to six persons: Queen Elizabeth, his prospective son-in-law the Earl of Southampton, his two wives (Anne Cecil and Elizabeth Trentham), and his mistress Anne Vavasour and their son Edward. In the opening chapter, "Shakspere of Stratford Is Not 'Shakespeare'—A Background," he presented twenty-seven characteristics of Shakespeare's background and experiences drawn from the works of traditional Shakespeare scholars together with his finding that "not one fits into the life of the Stratford man," while "there was only one man in Elizabethan England whose many-sided life shows a facet for every accomplishment or experience in the list:" Edward de Vere.[71]

Bénézet had written "The Shakespeare Hoax"—the article in the November 1947 issue of *The Dartmouth Quarterly*—during a summer engagement as Visiting Professor of Education at Bradley University in Peoria, Illinois, in 1947. It was there that he moved in 1948. After teaching at Bradley for two years, he taught at Evansville College (Indiana) for two years, then at Jackson College in Honolulu for eight years (1952-1960).[72]

Explanations: Nothing has surfaced to explain why Barrell and Bénézet turned their backs so completely on the Oxfordian movement at about the same time, after having made it the center of their life's work for so long. Perhaps it was frustration from the growing realization, after eight years of stunning research findings supporting the Oxfordian claim, that the accumulation of facts did not matter a whit to academia. Stratfordian professors would continue to believe what they wanted to, no matter how much circumstantial evidence Oxfordian researchers piled up and no matter how weak the foundation for their own Stratfordian beliefs became. Perhaps they had learned the lessons that British Oxfordians had learned earlier. Perhaps, too, they had a growing realization that the general public was inclined to stick with the traditional story.

In Barrell's case, the situation could have been complicated by the need to earn a living. During his years as an Oxfordian researcher, he had given "about half of his time to the work of the Fellowship, spending the rest largely in free-lance writing."[73] Perhaps the costs of raising a family required a full-time commitment.

Fellowship trustees perhaps initially regarded the difficulties, whatever they were, as only temporary, initially expecting that the next issue of the *Quarterly* would only be delayed and that replacement officers would be found. The absence of any notice in the English *News-Letter* about the difficulties, however, suggests that there were more unpleasant aspects to the situation.

There is another intriguing possibility: that the lack of consensus among Oxfordians on the why and how questions—why Oxford hid his authorship and how such a far-reaching effort could have been successful—was the principal cause of the demise of the Shakespeare Fellowship in the United States. Barrell had been a strong proponent of the idea that Oxford was forced to hide his authorship of the works because of the illegitimate child he fathered by Anne Vavasour, the son who Barrell had discovered was named Edward Vere. Charlton Ogburn believed that Barrell was mistaken, that what lay behind the use of the pseudonym was related to Oxford's son by Queen Elizabeth. He and his wife, Dorothy, had formulated that idea independently before learning of the work of Percy Allen and Capt. Ward. By the end of 1948 they were already engaged in the research on

---

[71] Louis P. Bénézet, *The Six Loves of Shakespeare* (1958), pp. 33, 35.
[72] J. H. D., "Professor Louis P. Bénézet," *Shakespearean Authorship Review*, no. 6 (Autumn 1961): 23.
[73] Lee Grove, "'Shakespeare' Just Pen Name of Oxford Earl, Barrell Says," *New York Herald Tribune*," July 3, 1948, p. B1.

their massive 1,300-page biography of Edward de Vere which would be published in 1952 as *This Star of England: "William Shakespeare" Man of the Renaissance*.

By some accounts, disagreements between Barrell and Ogburn led to such a cooling of relations that Ogburn withdrew as counsel for Barrell in the lawsuit against Dawson. One long-time Oxfordian commented that "The old Fellowship to a large extent dissolved because of the split between the senior Ogburns and Barrell over the issue. Barrell had to settle his court case against Giles Dawson out-of-court because that split left him without legal representation or the financial backing to pursue it. Charlton Ogburn Sr. had brought the case on Barrell's behalf but then backed off as a result of the split." If that account is correct, then the disagreements over the why and how questions that had led to the crisis in the English Shakespeare Fellowship in 1936 had also played a role in the demise of the Shakespeare Fellowship in the United States. Similar disagreements would arise again early in the twenty-first century (see Chapter 21).

The new edition of *"Shakespeare" Identified*: The second American edition, published by Duell, Sloan and Pearce, bore a publication date of 1948/1949. The first reviews did not appear until October 15 and 30, 1949, with two more on November 6. The new edition included an introduction, "The Master Mystery," by American novelist William McFee and an "Afterwords" by Charles Wisner Barrell. Oddly, the final issues of the *News-Letter* made no mention of the forthcoming new edition.

The Shakespeare Fellowship: No record of what happened to the legal entity that had been incorporated in 1945 has been found. In the late 1950s a new American Oxfordian organization, the Ereved Foundation, was formed that continues in existence today as the Shakespeare Oxford Fellowship.[74] It launched a *News-Letter* in 1965, but for many years it was a mere shadow of the dynamic and robust *News-Letter* and *Quarterly* of the 1940s. It took the Oxfordian movement in the United States nearly forty years to regain the momentum that had been lost.

Up to a New Generation to Rise up and Carry On the Work

Only a few Americans joined the British Shakespeare Fellowship after it reconstituted itself following the end of the Second World War. American research and publishing took place on an individual basis, with practically none of it appearing in the British *News-Letter*. Among those who had proceeded on their own were:

The Ogburns—Dorothy and Charlton, and their son, Charlton, Jr., became the biggest assets of the American Oxfordian movement over the following half-century. Their story is a fascinating one, but their many contributions to the movement will have to be told elsewhere.

Gelett Burgess would continue to carry the Oxfordian banner forward until his death in 1951.

A. Bronson Feldman's article "Shakespeare's Jester—Oxford's Servant," which ran in the Spring 1947 issue of the *Quarterly*, had established yet another linkage between Oxford and Shakespeare: Robert Armin. It had been rejected by a prominent British scholarly journal "because of lack of paper" and by a prominent university quarterly in the United States "on the advice of our drama editor" before appearing in the *Quarterly*. He would go on to publish many important Oxfordian pieces over the following decades.

---

[74] "Ereved" being De Vere backwards.

PART TWO:
THE CONTINUING INFLUENCE
OF *"SHAKESPEARE" IDENTIFIED*

19

The Second Wave of the Oxfordian Movement

The Forty-Year Lull and the Second Wave

The history of the Oxfordian claim in the British Isles after 1945 and in North America after 1948 can be divided into two distinct periods: a forty-year period of intermittent activity by individuals followed by a second wave sparked by the publication of Charlton Ogburn, Jr.'s *The Mysterious William Shakespeare* near the end of 1984.

The following two chapters offer a brief overview of the re-energizing of the movement and a snapshot of some aspects of the movement today.

To gauge the effectiveness of the Oxfordian movement in the early 2020s—a century after publication of J. Thomas Looney's *"Shakespeare" Identified*—let's begin with a look at three discrete groups—scholars supporting the Oxfordian claim, orthodox scholars and public opinion—at three points in time: early spring 1920, early spring 1940 and early spring 2020.

Early spring 1920 is easy to describe. Just before the publication of *"Shakespeare" Identified*, almost no one had heard of Edward de Vere. The only people who knew of the Oxfordian claim were J. Thomas Looney, his publisher Cecil Palmer, and a few persons who had seen advance copies of the book.

By early spring 1940, an active community of Oxfordian scholars had been engaged in research, publishing and public outreach for almost twenty years. Public awareness of the Oxfordian idea reached a new high with the publication in *Scientific American* of Charles Barrell's research on the Ashbourne portrait. The article also created a new receptiveness to the idea in the media. Academia, unsettled by the new findings, had yet to determine how best to respond. It recovered quickly, though; by the early summer of 1940 it had returned to ignoring the idea whenever possible, changing the subject whenever it could, and belittling the claim and its adherents whenever it couldn't. The media, after having given much attention to Barrell's findings, also returned largely to taking its cue from academia.

On the surface, the situation in early spring 2020, one hundred years after publication of *"Shakespeare" Identified* and eighty years after the high point of the first wave of Oxfordian activity, appeared similar to what it had been in mid-1940. Oxfordian scholars were researching the claim and publishing their findings, traditional scholars within academia continued to support the Stratfordian story and to disparage the Oxfordians, and, although millions of people had heard of the idea of Edward de Vere as Shakespeare, the media for the most part continued to take its lead from academia. From another perspective, however, everything was different, as will become apparent.

The collapse of the Shakespeare Fellowship in 1948 had resulted in a disappearance of the Oxfordian claim from sustained public awareness for close to forty years. Some Oxfordian activity continued during that time, but it was sporadic and seldom came to the attention of the public. The Oxfordian organizations, once they had reestablished themselves in England at the end of 1945 and in the United States in the late 1950s, functioned primarily to facilitate communication among Oxfordians rather than to promote the Oxfordian claim elsewhere. The *Newsletter* of the American Shakespeare Oxford Society (SOS), launched in 1965, seventeen years after the demise of *The Shakespeare Fellowship Quarterly*, was prepared on a typewriter by one person, and was distributed only to members. No university library subscribed to it, in contrast with the hundred or more libraries that had subscribed to the *Quarterly* in the mid-1940s. In England, the Shakespeare Fellowship morphed into the Shakespearean Authorship Society (SAS) and finally into the Shakespearean Authorship Trust (SAT), an organization that regards itself as a big tent in which all authorship candidates are given equal billing.

Many of the most important contributions during that period were made by members of the Ogburn family—Dorothy and Charlton Ogburn and their son, Charlton Ogburn, Jr. A number of essential Oxfordian texts were reprinted by Ruth Loyd Miller in the mid-1970s. In 1975 she edited and published the third American edition of *"Shakespeare" Identified*, making Looney's book once again available to the public. With it she published a companion volume, *Oxfordian Vistas*, with dozens of important articles. She also edited and issued new editions of Eva Turner Clark's *Hidden Allusions in Shakespeare's Plays* and Capt. Bernard M. Ward's edition of *A Hundreth Sundrie Flowers*. And she made Capt. Ward's *The Seventeenth Earl of Oxford* available to American readers for the first time, in the form of an authorized photocopy of the original 1928 edition. It is impossible to overestimate the importance of the availability of these essential texts then or now.

During those years Gordon and Helen Cyr did much to rescue the moribund Shakespeare Oxford Society by calling members to a pivotal meeting in Baltimore in 1976 that turned what had been a one-man operation into a base for the launch of Charlton Ogburn, Jr.'s book. Also of special note during those lean years were the dozen articles by A. Bronson Feldman in psychoanalytic journals from the 1950s through the 1970s that kept awareness of Freud's Oxfordian beliefs alive. These events and publications, and the history of the Oxfordian movement from the mid-1940s through 1984, will be recounted in a separate volume.

That half-century lull in public attention to the Oxfordian claim ended in late 1984, with the publication of Charlton Ogburn, Jr.'s 892-page book, *The Mysterious William Shakespeare*. Ogburn's sophisticated, cogent and comprehensive presentation of the mass of evidence and reasoning produced by Oxfordian scholars over the previous sixty-four years, along with a recounting of academia's unscholarly response to it, was a game changer. It presented a challenge that neither academia nor the media could ignore.

The book was reviewed in more than forty newspapers and magazines. Especially important was William F. Buckley's inviting Ogburn to appear as a guest on his popular television show *Firing Line* on December 11, 1984. More than surprising was the receptive attitude to the book in *The Shakespeare Quarterly*, a publication of the Folger

Shakespeare Library. "New Perspectives on the Authorship Question" by Richmond Crinkley, former Director of Programs at the Folger, was as notable for its praise of Ogburn as for its criticism of the Folger's previous administration. Crinkley confirmed that Ogburn's scholarship was of the highest quality, noting that E. A. J. Honigman's "sympathetic review" of Ogburn's book "is the first time in my memory that a Stratfordian has made laudatory (or even courteous!) acknowledgment of an anti-Stratfordian work. That the most resourceful Shakespeare biographer has something to learn from the most distinguished anti-Stratfordian may signal a salutary change in the tenor of the discussion."[1] Especially satisfying for Ogburn must have been Crinkley's final statement that "Shakespeare scholarship owes an enormous debt to Charlton Ogburn" (522).

Crinkley severely criticized Louis B. Wright, the Folger's former director and Crinkley's former boss.[2] He wrote that Wright had "adhered to the orthodox view of the authorship question and displayed its orthodoxy with a contempt for dissenters that was as mean-spirited as it was loudly trumpeted" (515). He also commented that "The work of Ogburn's parents and anti-Stratfordian sentiment in general had been treated with vitriolic contempt by the Library's previous administration." Of his former colleagues he wrote that he "was enormously surprised at what can only be described as the viciousness toward anti-Stratfordian sentiments expressed by so many otherwise rational and courteous scholars. In its extreme forms the hatred of unorthodoxy was like some bizarre mutant racism. . . . This baffled me. One did not, after all, have to agree with heterodoxy to accord it intellectual courtesy, or, for that

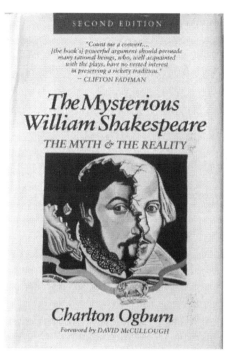

matter, to present it accurately." He described Ogburn as "among the most congenial of men," who felt "rightly, in my opinion, that such treatment [by the Folger and others] violated the benign neutrality with which libraries should properly regard intellectual controversy."

The Mysterious William Shakespeare, together with Ogburn's presentation of the case on *Firing Line* and reviews such as Crinkley's, altered the media landscape. It created a more receptive environment for stand-alone articles on the Oxfordian claim in leading journals, such as James Lardner's "Onward and Upwards with the Arts: The Authorship Question," in *The New Yorker* in May 1988, and the lengthy cover stories on the issue in *The Atlantic Monthly* in October 1991 and in *Harper's Magazine* in April 1999. It also set the stage for several major public events in the final years of the 1980s that brought the

---

[1] Richmond Crinkley, "New Perspectives on the Authorship Question," *Shakespeare Quarterly*, vol. 36/4 (Winter 1985): 520. He referred to E. A. J. Honigman, "Sweet Swan of Oxford?" *New York Review of Books*, Jan. 17, 1985, pp. 23-26.

[2] Ogburn's book was published in November 1984. Wright died December. 26, 1984. Crinkley's article was published in the Winter 1985 issue, which came out at the end of that year.

Oxfordian case to public attention in the most prominent way since Barrell's article in *Scientific American* in 1940.

The first major public event was a moot court held at the National Law School of American University in Washington, DC, on September 25, 1987. There a panel of three U.S. Supreme Court Justices—William Brennan, Harry Blackmun and John Paul Stevens—considered the Shakespeare Authorship Question. A second moot court was held at the Inns of Court in London fourteen months later, presided over by three of England's most senior appellate judges. Charlton Ogburn played a key role in organizing both events, and both were supported by Washington philanthropist and entrepreneur David Lloyd Kreeger. Even though the justices in both events ruled in favor of Shakspere, by focusing on the Shakspere-Oxford duality the events effectively raised Oxford's status and lowered that of other alternate candidates. Both events were widely covered by the media. The participation by esteemed justices signified to the public that the Oxfordian claim was one worthy of serious consideration, just as Crinkley's article had among academics.

The third major public event was the broadcast of "The Shakespeare Mystery"," written, directed and produced by Al Austin and hosted by Judy Woodruff, on PBS's *Frontline* on April 18, 1989. Featuring interviews with many prominent Shakespeare scholars, both Stratfordian and Oxfordian, it made a strong case that William Shakspere was not—could not have been—the author of Shakespeare's plays and poems and that Edward de Vere probably was. It generated not only widespread coverage of the Oxfordian claim in newspapers across the United States but also inspired editorials in more than a dozen papers the day after the broadcast. Many of the Oxfordian scholars most active today cite watching that program as the event that launched their interest in the authorship issue.

To gauge the effectiveness of these four events (including Ogburn's book), compare the number of articles mentioning the Oxfordian claim in newspapers and literary journals read by the general public in Great Britain and the United States in the decade prior to the publication of Ogburn's book and the decade following it. From mid-1974 to mid-1984, ninety-eight articles mentioned the Oxfordian idea, fewer than ten per year on average. From mid-1984 to mid-1994, the number jumped to 498, or almost fifty per year.[3]

Let us look at the momentum that the Oxfordian movement has today. To get a sense of its strength, consider the number of articles about the Oxfordian thesis in non-Oxfordian publications—newspapers and periodicals read by the public—at various points in time. The greater the number of points considered, the stronger and more recent the momentum appears. First, let's examine the number of articles at just two points, 1919 and 2019, as in the first of the three nearby charts. With only two points shown, it indicates a steady rise in the number of articles and hence in public awareness of the Oxfordian issue. This chart

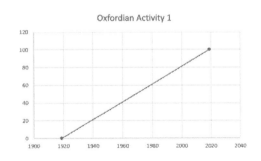

---

[3] These numbers come from counting the listings for those years from the forthcoming fifth edition of *An Index to Oxfordian Publications*. A similar percentage increase can be calculated by counting the listings for the same time periods in the fourth edition of the *Index* (2017), pp. 635-714.

is quite misleading.

Adding a third point, 1939, near the high point of the first wave of the Oxfordian movement, shows a steady rise from 1919 to 1939, but a leveling off over the following eighty years. This chart is also misleading. It obscures the true dynamic aspects of the Oxfordian movement and public awareness of the Oxfordian idea during the latter eighty years.

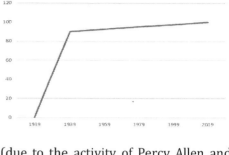

As more data points are added we see a steep decline into a half-century lull, followed by the resurgence of the Oxfordian claim. The third chart, with many data points, shows the rise in 1928 (the year of Capt. Ward's biography), the further rise in the mid-1930s (due to the activity of Percy Allen and others), and the rise again in 1939-1940 (following publication of Barrell's piece in *Scientific American*), all followed by the steep decline due to the Second World War. Especially important is the suddenness of the beginning of the second wave of the Oxfordian movement shown by the rise in 1984-1989 generated by the four events mentioned above: the publication of Ogburn's book, the two moot courts and the broadcast of "The Shakespeare Mystery." After 1989 is a continued rise to new heights of public awareness.

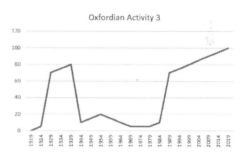

The point of the three charts is to emphasize the existence and critical importance of the momentum of the second wave of the Oxfordian movement.

The Media and Public Opinion Today

Many events were organized independently from the activities of those active in the movement. One example was a debate on the authorship issue organized by the Smithsonian Institution in Washington, DC, in 1987, which soon after published a lengthy piece in its monthly *Smithsonian Magazine*. The events, publications and broadcasts that happened without direct Oxfordian initiatives are themselves a healthy sign of increased public interest in the Oxfordian claim.

Print publications

The Oxfordian idea has been mentioned in many places. Expected places include newspapers and magazines, which have run thousands of items over the past several decades. News-magazines such as *The Atlantic*, *Harper's* and *U.S. News and World Report* ran cover stories on the authorship mystery, with an emphasis on the Oxfordian answer. Specialized magazines also ran stories, including *Skeptic Magazine*, *Skeptical Inquirer*, *Mathematics Teacher* and *Cryptologia Magazine*, which ran articles in three issues. The editors all knew that their readers were interested, a point made apparent when 1,700 comments were posted to *Newsweek's* blog within a month after its online edition ran a lengthy piece on doubts about Shakspere's authorship at the end of 2013.

Especially noteworthy were writers who had no vested interest in the issue but concluded after examining it that Edward de Vere wrote Shakespeare's works. In the first edition of *The 100: A Ranking of the Most Influential Persons in History*, Michael Hart listed "William Shakespeare" at position number 31, believing him to be Shakspere of Stratford. In the second edition in 1992, Hart wrote that while preparing it he had carefully examined the arguments and concluded that "the skeptics have much the better of the argument and have reasonably established their case." He accordingly revised the entry and retitled it "Edward de Vere better known as 'William Shakespeare.'"

James F. Broderick, coauthor of *Web of Conspiracy: A Guide to Conspiracy Theory Sites on the Internet* (2008), had a similar experience. "What I discovered is that most [conspiracy theories] do not hold up under scrutiny. The more one digs, the shakier and less credible they become. The Authorship Question was different. The more I dug, the more credible it seemed, until I became fully convinced of its validity. What I had set out

---

William S. Niederkorn on the Oxfordian Claim (selected articles), 2002-2013

New York Times

2002, Feb. 10	"A Historic Whodunit: If Shakespeare Didn't, Who Did?"
2002, June 20	"A Scholar Recants His 'Shakespeare' Discovery"
2002, June 26	"Beyond the Briefly Inflated Canon: Legacy of the Mysterious 'W.S."
2003, Aug. 19	"All Is True?" Naye, Not If Thy Name Be Shakespeare"
2003, Sept. 2	"Seeing the Fingerprints of Other Hands in Shakespeare"
2003, Nov. 16	"Where There's a Will, or Two, or Maybe Quite a Few"
2004, Aug. 21	"To Be or Not to Be . . . "Shakespeare"
2004, Fall	"Jumping o'er Times: The Importance of Lawyers and Judges in the Controversy Over the Identity of Shakespeare, as Reflected in the Pages of *The New York Times*" [*Times Higher Education Supplement*]
2005, Aug. 30	"The Shakespeare Code, and Other Fanciful Ideas from the Traditional Camp" [Reviews of *1599: A Year in the Life of William Shakespeare* by James Shapiro; *Will in the World* by Stephen Greenblatt; *Shadowplay: The Hidden Beliefs and Coded Politics of William Shakespeare* by Clare Asquith; and *"Shakespeare" by Another Name* by Mark Anderson]
2007, April 22	"Shakespeare Reaffirmed"

Brooklyn Rail

2010, April	"Absolute Will" [Review of *Contested Will: Who Wrote Shakespeare?* by James Shapiro]
2011, March	"The Bard's Evangelist" [Review of *Shakespeare's Freedom* by Stephen Greenblatt]
2011, April	"The Shakespeare Chronology Recalibrated" [Review of *Dating Shakespeare's Plays* edited by Kevin Gilvary]
2011, July	"Canonizer's Feast" [Review of *The Anatomy of Influence: Literature as a Way of Life* by Harold Bloom]
2011, Oct.	"A Binary Star with Anonymous" [Review of *Shakespeare's Lost Kingdom* by Charles Beauclerk]
2011, Dec.	"Beyond the Previously Known Bard" [Review of *The Shakespeare Guide to Italy* by Richard Paul Roe]
2012, Feb.	"Occupying W. S." [Review of *Nine Lives of William Shakespeare* by Graham Holderness]
2013, Feb.	"Shake-Speare Fission"

Edmonton Journal (Alberta)

2002, Feb. 24	"Much Ado About the Bard: What's In a Name? One Theory is Gaining Ground – That the Real Bard Was Edward de Vere, Earl of Oxford"

expecting to debunk turned out to be the most compelling, fact-based 'conspiracy' I had ever researched."[4]

A third and highly visible example was William Niederkorn, who as a cultural editor for *The New York Times* wrote eight high-profile articles on the authorship question for the paper between 2002 and 2007; after leaving the *Times* he wrote another dozen that appeared in *The Brooklyn Rail* and elsewhere between 2010 and 2013. These addressed topics ranging from the views on the authorship issue of Justices of the U.S. Supreme Court to reviews of books dealing with the issue. His first piece for the *Times*, on February 10, 2002, in addition to bringing readers up to speed on many important Oxfordian developments, broke the news that all of the U.S. Supreme Court Justices who had judged the 1987 moot court had since modified their views: Justice Blackmun had written that "If I had to rule on the evidence presented, it would be in favor of the Oxfordians," and Justice Stevens had told Niederkorn that "If I had to pick a candidate today, I'd say it definitely was Oxford."[5]

The welcoming tone of these items was surprising to many readers, given the paper's longstanding hostility to the Oxfordian idea beginning with its review of *"Shakespeare" Identified* in 1920 and its refusal to print Looney's response to it. Yet, Niederkorn later explained, "the thinking at the *Times* is not monolithic. Articles appear all the time depicting the different sides of various issues. Every writer brings an individual

---

Scholarly Writings on Other Subjects Drawing on the Oxfordian Claim, 1984-2020

➤ Linda Bridges and William F. Richenbacker, *The Art of Persuasion: A National Review Rhetoric for Writers* (1991)
>> The authors note that they were "persuaded by the Ogburn arguments that the works attributed to the bumpkin 'Shakspere' were from the hand of Edward de Vere."

➤ Douglas Hunt, *The Riverside Guide to Writing* (1991)
>> The author uses Edward de Vere's authorship of the works of Shakespeare as the principal example in Chapter 6, "Arguing When the Facts are Disputed."

➤ Jonathan Furner, "Conceptual Analysis: A Method for Understanding Information as Evidence and Evidence as Information," *Archival Science* (2004)
>> In his effort to develop a conceptual framework for "evidentiariness" in archival science, the author cites the appropriateness of a comparison of the stylistic means for resolving the question of who wrote Shakespeare's works.

➤ Jiexun Li, et. al., "From Fingerprint to Writeprint," *Communications of the ACH*, vol. 49, No. 4 (April, 2006)
>> In their discussion of how crime investigators can identify and track those committing crimes online, the authors note the validity of comparing the poems of Shakespeare with those of Edward de Vere, "the leading candidate as the true author of the works credited to Shakespeare."

➤ Jens-Christian Bjerring, "Problems in Epistemic Space," *Journal of Philosophic Logic*. (Feb. 2014)
>> The author discusses the usefulness of the concept of "epistemic space" in resolving several questions, one of which is whether Edward de Vere was the author of "Shakespeare's" works.

---

[4] James Broderick, quoted in "Doubter Response to Question 55," in *Shakespeare Beyond Doubt? Exposing an Industry in Denial* (2013), edited by John M. Shahan and Alexander Waugh, pp. 212-13.
[5] William S. Niederkorn, "A Historic Whodunit: If Shakespeare Didn't, Who Did?" *New York Times*, Feb. 10, 2002.

perspective to every piece, and editors bring individual perspectives as well."[6] However, after Niederkorn's departure the paper again resumed its hostile approach to the authorship question.

The subject of de Vere's authorship had become so well recognized that even writers on unrelated subjects have cited the Oxfordian claim, as shown in the nearby text box.

Legal Profession

Judges and lawyers have been particularly fascinated by the authorship issue. Several law journals have examined the issue, including *The American Bar Association Journal*, *The Tennessee Law Review* and *The American University Law Review*. At one point (early in the twenty-first century) five sitting U.S. Supreme Court justices had publicly expressed doubt about Shakspere's authorship; three—Blackmun, Scalia and Stevens—had publicly stated their belief that Edward de Vere was the real author.[7] Justice Powell had recently joined the public doubters, writing, "I have never thought that the man of Stratford-on-Avon wrote the plays of Shakespeare. I know of no admissible evidence that he ever left England or was educated in the normal sense of the term. One must wonder, for example, how he could have written the *Merchant of Venice*."[8] The fifth was Justice Sandra Day O'Connor. Yet there has been little apparent effort by academia to come to terms with the opinions of these learned justices, whose profession involves weighing evidence and evaluating arguments made by opposing sides.

Broadcasts

"The Shakespeare Mystery" was only the first of many television and film documentaries to examine the Oxfordian claim (see nearby text box). Many of them generated their own reviews, further bringing the Oxfordian claim to public attention. Three recent documentaries that have received worldwide distribution are of special note.

Last Will. & Testament (2012) is an 84-minute film documenting the life of Edward de Vere, directed by Laura Wilson Matthias and Lisa Wilson (Roland Emmerich served as executive producer). "It's the greatest literary mystery of all time: who actually wrote the works of Shakespeare? Derek Jacobi leads an impressive cast featuring Vanessa Redgrave and Mark Rylance on a quest to uncover the truth behind the world's most elusive author."

Nothing is Truer than Truth (2019), a film produced and directed by Cheryl Eagan-Donovan, tracks the travels of Edward de Vere, who journeyed to Venice and throughout Italy and Europe in 1575-76, where he discovered commedia dell'arte, and collected many of the experiences that would become known as the works of Shakespeare. It was filmed on location in Venice, Verona, Mantua and Padua, sites visited by de Vere and the settings for *The Merchant of Venice*, *Othello*, and *Romeo and Juliet*, and in England, at Castle

---

[6] William S. Niederkorn, "Letter to the Editors," *Shakespeare Matters*, vol. 1/4 (Summer 2002): 2.

[7] Bryan H. Wildenthal, "End of an Oxfordian Era on the Supreme Court?" *Shakespeare Oxford Newsletter*, vol. 52/3 (Summer 2016): 9-13.

[8] Quoted in Charlton Ogburn, *The Mysterious William Shakespeare* (1992), p. vi.

Hedingham, the ancestral home of the de Vere family, and Poets Corner in Westminster Abbey. It features interviews with Sir Derek Jacobi, Mark Rylance, Tina Packer and other notable Shakespeare scholars.

SHAKESPEARE: The Truth Behind the Name (2020), written and produced by Robin Phillips, is "a delightful and meticulously-research documentary [that] reveals why 'Shakspere from Stratford' isn't the author of 'Shakespeare.'" Phillips brings charm and excitement to this theatrically-conceived presentation of facts showing

the implausibility of an illiterate tradesman being the greatest writer in the English language and the near certainty that Shakespeare was no other than Edward de Vere, a poet and Lord Great Chamberlain of the realm.

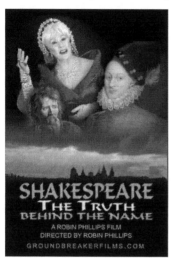

Discussion programs, too, increased public awareness of the issue; the *Firing Line* episode with Charlton Ogburn was the first of many. National Public Radio's *Morning Edition* prominently hosted discussions of the authorship question on half a dozen occasions, most notably on July 3 and 4, 2008, when host Renee Montagne, picking up on information from William Niederkorn's first article, announced on the most listened-to radio program in America that all three of the Supreme Court Justices who participated in the 1987 moot court later "came to doubt

---

Documentaries Addressing the Oxfordian Claim, 1984-2020

1986	"The Shakespeare Mystery" (first broadcast on *Frontline* on April 18, 1989), produced by Al Austin with Yorkshire Television in conjunction with American public television station WGBH and broadcast on PBS.
1994	*The Trial of William Shakespeare* [Coverage of the American Inns of Court Conference Moot Court. Scenario is that Shakspere has filed suit against Edward de Vere because of his claims of authorship].
2002	"Much Ado About Something: Marlowe's Case for Shakespeare." This PBS *Frontline* documentary, produced by Mike Rubbio, has much to say about Edward de Vere.
2011	*The Shakespeare Conspiracy* [Directed by Michael Peer]
2012	*Last Will. & Testament*, an 84-minute film documenting the life of Edward de Vere. Directed by Laura Wilson Matthias and Lisa Wilson. Roland Emmerich served as Executive Producer.*
2012	*The Naked Shakespeare.* English language version of *Der Nackte Shakespeare*, a German language documentary film by Claus Bredenbrock
2016	"Shakespeare's Tomb" [A BBC documentary]
2019	*Nothing is Truer than Truth*, a film produced and directed by Cheryl Eagan-Donovan.*
2020	*SHAKESPEARE: The Truth Behind the Name*, written and produced by Robin Phillips,* GroundbreakerFilms.

*Indicates that this production was initiated by Oxfordians active in the Oxfordian movement.

their [earlier] decisions" in favor of Shakspere. The title of the July 4 program, "The Real Shakespeare Points to Earl," explicitly gives the nod to Oxford. Montagne later explained that she had been intrigued by the possibility that the author was someone other than William Shakespeare of Stratford-on-Avon ever since reading the *Harper's* article.[9] She tried, she later explained, to go into any situation with as much knowledge as she could and "entertains all possible realities."[10]

What most persuasively demonstrates the extent to which the Oxfordian idea has

---

TV and Radio Discussion Programs Addressing the Oxfordian Claim (and other broadcasts mentioning it), 1984-2020

1984	*Firing Line*: "The Mysterious William Shakespeare" hosted by William F. Buckley, with guests Charlton Ogburn and Rutgers Professor Maurice Charney. (Dec, 11)
1984	Call-in program: Interview with Charlton Ogburn, Jr., WJNO Radio (Palm Beach). (Dec. 18)
1985	Voice of America Broadcast, pro-Ogburn comments by Gordon C Cyr, anti-Ogburn comments by David Kastan. Rebroadcast four times. (Jan. 7)
	Midday with Sondra Gair, NPR, Chicago interview with Charlton Ogburn, Jr. (Jan. 17, 1985)
1989	"In Search of the Bard" on *First Tuesday* TV program, UK. [Enoch Powell presented the case for doubters.]
1992	*Uncovering Shakespeare: An Update* (September 1992), An interactive videoconference hosted by William F. Buckley, Jr., with 15 guests, including Charles Boyle, Warren Hope, Felicia Londre, Roger Stritmatter and Charles Vere. (Produced by Gary Goldstein and John Mucci.)
1994	NPR Call-in program featuring Charles Vere. (October)
1994	"Battle of Wills," an episode of the BBC2 TV's *Bard on the Box* (1994), Charles Vere defends Oxford against claims for Bacon, Marlowe, and the man from Stratford.
	Talk of the Nation [Charles Vere debates Stratfordian scholars in this two-hour NPR program on KCMO in Kansas City, Missouri. (June 1)
2001	710 AM Talk Radio Professor Felicia Londre discusses the authorship question in this 45-minute program. (late June)
2003	NPR interview with Diana Price. (April 27)
2004	"Looking for the Real Shake-Speare," an episode of *The Breakfast Show* on WDR TV. (Germany)
2004	*The Shakespeare Enigma* [Stanley Wells argues for Shakspere, Francis Carr and Mark Rylance for Francis Bacon, A. D. Wright for Christopher Marlowe, and Elizabeth Imlay for Edward de Vere.]
2008	"Who Wrote Shakespeare's Plays? The Debate Goes On," NPR's *Morning Edition*. Renee Montagne, host, talks with guests Daniel Wright, Diana Price and Steven Greenblatt. (July 3)
2008	"The Real Shakespeare Points to Earl," NPR's *Morning Edition*. Renee Montagne, host, talks with James Shapiro, Mark Rylance, Charles Beauclerk, Mark Anderson, Daniel Wright and Kenneth Branagh.
2011	"For Anonymous Scribe, a Shakespeare Speculation," NPR's *Morning Edition*. Ari Shapiro, host, talks with John Orloff, Derek Jacobi, and Rhys Ifans. (Oct. 28)
2016	"Two Shakespearean Actors Revive Debate Over the Bard's Identity," NPR's *Morning Edition* host Ari Shapiro talks with Mark Rylance and Derek Jacobi. (April 25)
2016	"Listener Responses," to the April 25 program, *Morning Edition*. (April 29)

---

[9] Lewis H. Lapham, "The Ghost of Shakespeare," *Harper's Magazine*, vol. 298 (April 1999): 10-21. Lapham's article was followed by twenty-eight pages of articles by ten Shakespeare scholars, five on each side of the Shakspere-Oxford divide.

[10] Howard Schumann, "Concordia Authorship Research Center Set to Open," *Shakespeare Matters*, vol. 8/2 (Spring 2009): 10.

sunk into the public mind is its appearance in the most unusual places. Among these are U.S. television sitcom *Granite Flats* (2014), which had a regular character (portrayed by Christopher Lloyd) who was an Oxfordian. At the 1995 Academy Awards ceremony, Anthony Hopkins brought up the issue. The Oxfordian claim was also mentioned on several episodes of the popular U.S. television game show *Jeopardy!*[11] Actors, also, have expressed anti-Stratfordian and even pro-Oxfordian beliefs, including Derek Jacobi, Mark Rylance, Michael York , Jeremy Irons, and Keanu Reeves. Sir Derek Jacobi stated he was "99.9 per cent certain 'that the actual author of the plays and *Sonnets* was Edward de Vere, the Earl of Oxford.'"[12]

Other Broadcasts that Mentioned the Oxfordian Claim, 1984-2020

1986	*Head of the Class* (U.S. TV sitcom, one episode had an Oxfordian character.)
1991	*Seinfeld*, "The Nose Job," Season 3, Episode 9. (Nov. 20) [One character contends that Shakespeare was an imposter.]
1995	Academy Awards: Actor Anthony Hopkins, in presenting the award for best screenplay, noted that scholars have argued about whether or not Shakespeare wrote the plays. (March)
	Jeopardy: Contestant Alex McNeil mentioned Edward de Vere and described activities of the Shakespeare Oxford Society and won the round. (Spring)
2000	*Sabrina the Teenage Witch* [On one episode Sabrina confronts Shakespeare for not having written his own works.]
2002	*Malcolm in the Middle* [U.S. TV sitcom; in one episode Malcolm said something like "Everybody knows it was the Earl of Oxford."]
2011	*Anonymous*, Roland Emmerich, director; John Orloff, writer
2012	*Jeopardy!*: The "answer" was "The 2011 film *Anonymous* claimed it was this man, not Shakespeare, who actually wrote the works of Shakespeare." (March 22)
2012	*Jeopardy*: Final Jeopardy category was "Shakespeare's Plays." Introducing it, host Alex Trebek said something like "Shakespeare's plays, whether he wrote them or not . . ." The "answer" was "*Measure for Measure* contains one word twice. The title of which other Shakespeare play also contains the same word twice, not counting small words like 'and' and 'the'?" (April 12)
2014	*The Gambler* [A movie in which the Oxfordian theory is mentioned briefly]
	Granite Flats [U.S. TV sitcom with a regular character who was an Oxfordian character played by Christopher Lloyd.]

Fictional and Theatrical Works

Many creative writers have been inspired by Edward de Vere's life story. Since 1984, at least sixty-two books of fiction have portrayed the authorship mystery and the Oxfordian answer to it. Among them were several novels for children or young adults, including Lynne Kositsky's *A Question of Will* (2000), Norma Howe's *Blue Avenger Cracks the Code* (2000) and Elise Broach's *Shakespeare's Secret* (2005). The nearby text boxes show the extent to which more than forty novelists have been inspired by the Oxfordian

---

[11] Host Alex Trebek may have learned of the Oxfordian idea from Alex McNeil, long time Oxfordian and editor of *The Shakespeare Oxford Newsletter*, who had been a contestant in spring, 1995. (He won the round.) Trebek mentioned Edward de Vere and the authorship issue in extemporaneous remarks on at least two episodes with a Shakespeare category. A question directly about Edward de Vere was "asked" on March 22, 2012. See Richard F. Whalen "Shakespeare/Oxford in 'Jeopardy,'" *Sh. Oxford Fellowship Newsletter*, vol. 31/2A (Spring 1995): 12; and "What's the News?" *Sh. Oxford Newsletter*, vol. 50/2 (Spring 2014): 7.

[12] Sir Derek Jacobi, quoted in Mark Blunden, "Shakespeare Did Not Write His Own Plays, Claims Jacobi," *Evening Standard*, April 23. 2009, p. 19.

idea in recent decades.

	Fictional Portrayals of Shakespeare Doubts/the Oxfordian Thesis, 1984-2017	
1990	Andrew Field	*The Lost Chronicle of Edward de Vere*
1993	Sue E. Bridgers	*Keeping Christina*
1995	Robert D'Artagnan	*Against this Rage*
1998	Muriel Spark	*A Far Cry from Kensington*
1999	Nicholas Hagger	*Prince Tudor: A Verse Drama*
2000	Paul H. Altrocchi*	*Most Greatly Lived: A Biographical Novel of Edward de Vere, Seventeenth Earl of Oxford, Whose Pen Name was William Shakespeare*
	Norma Howe*	*Blue Avenger Cracks the Code*
	Lynne Kositsky*	*A Question of Will*
2001	Robert D'Artagnan	*Oxford Summer: Shakespeare's Dark Lady Tells All*
	Eric Flint	*1632*
2002	Eliot Baker	*Delia*
	Robin Matchett	*The Lion Bats the Butterfly, or, The True and Tragicke Historie of Shake-speare*
	James Sherwood*	*Shakespeare's Ghost: An Historical Mystery Novel*
	Alan Wall	*School of Night*
2003	Sarah Smith*	*Chasing Shakespeares*
2005	Elise Broach	*Shakespeare's Secret*
2007	Jennifer Lee Carrell	*Interred With Their Bones/The Shakespeare Secret*
2008	Simon Fry	*Paper Trail*
	Emanuel E. Garcia	"Sherlock Holmes and the Mystery of *Hamlet*"
	Michael Langford	*The de Vere Papers*
2009	George Dillon	*The Man Who Was Hamlet*
	Lisa L. Dorward	*Whose Worth's Unknown: The Life of Edward de Vere: The Man who Was Shakespeare: A Novel*
2010	Ted Bacino	*The Shakespeare Controversy: A Novel About the Greatest Literary Deception of All Time*
	Jennifer Lee Carrell	*Haunt Me Still*
	Scott Evans	*First Folio: A Literary Mystery*
	Barry Grant	*Sherlock Holmes and the Shakespeare Letter*
2011	Al Austin	*The Cottage*
	Simon Fry	*The Shakespeare File: A Novel*
	Brünhilde Jouannic	*Shakespeare, c'est moi: La confession d'Edward de Vere*
2012	Ros Barber	*The Marlowe Papers: A Novel in Verse*
	Sky Gilbert*	*Come Back*
	Peter Hildebrandt	*The Rest is Silence: A Novel*
	Lynda Taylor	*Or Not to Be*
2013	Bruce Hutchison	*Love's Labour's Lost: The Man who Was Shakespeare*
	Syril Levin Kline	*Shakespeare's Changeling: A Fault Against the Dead*
2014	Newton Frohlich*	*The Shakespeare Mask*
	Paul Streitz*	*Shakespeare and the Courtesan*
2015	Jon Benson*	*The Death of Shakespeare As It Was Accomplisht in 1616 & the Causes Thereof, Part One*
2016	James A. Warren*	*Summer Storm: A Novel of Ideas*
2017	Mike A'Dair*	*The Ashbourne Saga: A Cinematic Epic in Fourteen Episodes*
	Eliza Todd	*Bethy*

*Oxfordians active in the Oxfordian movement at the time the pieces were written.

Dramatists and musicians, too, have found inspiration in the life of Edward de Vere, writing more than three dozen plays and musicals since 1984. Musicians have written several song cycles, including Joseph Summer's *The Oxford Songs*, which consists of songs from the Shakespeare canon, and Daniel Steven Crafts's *The Real Shakespeare*, which consists of songs from poems by Edward de Vere.

Plays and Musicals with an Oxfordian Theme, 1984-2016		
1988	Ernest Ferlita	*The Truth Will Out: S Play in Two Acts*
	John Nassivera	*All the Queen's Men* [A two-act play]
	O. M. Ironside Wood	*Proud Passionate Boy*
	Winifred L. Frazer	*Truth is Stranger* [A play/musical about a grad student who is an Oxfordian trying to get a Ph.D. in English literature. Songs by David Stryker]
1992	Richard Desper"	*Star-Crossed Lovers: A Play in Three Acts*
	Jerry Fey	*Oxford's Will: A Play*
1997	Alan J. Hovey	*Aye, Shakespeare: The Dramatist Unmasked* [A one-man play]
	Elizabeth Imlay*	*Edward de Vere, Part I*
2001	George Contes	*The Crazy Wisdom Sho* [A musical based on the life of Ed. de Vere]
	Bill Dorian	*A Rose By Any Other Name: A Play*
	Graham Jones & Jepke Goudsmit	*Shake-speare* [A play about the life of Edward de Vere]
2002	Patricia C. Brown	*Edward de Vere, aka William Shakespeare: A Life in Two Acts*
	Marion Buckley	*By Any Other Name* [A humorous dramatization of the life and times of Edward de Vere]
	Norma Howe"	*Blue Avenger Cracks the Code* [A play based on her novel]
2004	Amy Freed	*The Beard of Avon*
	Gary Graves	*The Mysterious Mr. Looney* [A dramatic presentation of a fictional confrontation between J. Thomas Looney and "Sir Sidney Chambers"]
	Sally H. Llewellyn*	*Edward's Presents: An Oxfordian Play on London's Bankside*
	Louise Young	A play about Oxford. [Title not known]
2007	Sarah Smith"	*Chasing Shakespeares: The Play*
2009	Ryan Gladstone	*The Shakespeare Show or How an Illiterate Son of a Glover Became the Greatest Playwright in the World*
	Aubrey Hampton	*Elizabeth and Edward*
	Alan Navarre	*The Crown Signature* [A three-act play on the life of Edward de Vere]
2011	Michael Kositsky*	*Detective Superintendent Blattshap Gets His Man* [A play in one act]
2012	Mark Rylance	*The Big Secret Live "I am Shakespeare" Webcam Daytime Classroom Show!: A Comedy of the Shakespearean Identity Crisis*
2013	Margaret Becker"	*Snatches From History: A Play in Five Acts*
2014	Christopher Plummer	*Nothing Truer than Truth* [MA thesis: Oxfordian story in the form of a drama]
2016	Phil Hoke	*Truth; will Out. A Play*
?	Stephanie Caruana*	*Edward Oxenford: Spear-shaker*
?	K. C. Ligon*	*Isle of Dogs* [a play about Edward de Vere]

*Oxfordians active in the Oxfordian movement at the time the pieces were written.

Musical Compositions with an Oxfordian Theme, 1984-2020		
?	Daniel Steven Crafts	*Bury My Name* [A theatrical presentation of songs by Shakespeare and Edward de Vere]
?	Daniel Steven Crafts	*The Real Shakespeare* [A song cycle from poems by Edward de Vere]
2013	Melora Creager	*Fa La La – The Bastardy of Shakespeare's Madrigals* (a song cycle for four cellos, three voices, percussion and digital looping)

Even cartoonists have been confident that readers would recognize the name Edward de Vere and get the connection with the authorship controversy, as was Tom Batiuk, creator of the Funky Winkerbean comic strip, in 1997.

The Modern Wave: An Overview

The Oxfordian events of the late 1980s and the public attention given to them re-energized the movement, sparking renewed Oxfordian research, publications and outreach. In the mid-1990s the largest and most active Oxfordian organization, the Shakespeare Oxford Society (SOS), based in the United States, launched two extensive efforts that would pay dividends in greater public awareness of the Oxfordian claim and increased membership for decades thereafter.

The first effort—the most ambitious project ever undertaken by the SOS—was a series of speaking tours by Charles Burford (also known as Lord Burford, Charles Vere and Charles Beauclerk) that included talks at more than 200 schools, colleges, universities, libraries and other venues for audiences totaling more than 20,000 people. The series was the brainchild of John Louther, who was impressed by the success of Beauclerk's lectures at the Folger Shakespeare Library and the Harvard Faculty Club in 1991. The first tour, in the fall of 1991, included thirteen talks in Connecticut, Florida, Massachusetts, New York and Pennsylvania,[13] reaching thousands. SOS President Betty Sears described the first tour as a "smashing success," and noted that the event at the Loomis-Chaffee School was so successful that a special colloquium was arranged the next day for faculty from all private schools in Connecticut.[14] More tours were organized over the next six years.

A report in early 1993 by John Louther noted that Beauclerk had made more than 125 appearances since the Folger event, and that these events had resulted in a doubling of

---

[13] A list of many of the venues at which Charles Beauclerk spoke, along with a partial list of media coverage of them, is in *An Index to Oxfordian Publications, Fourth Edition* (2017), pp. 418-24.
[14] Elisabeth Sears, "Letter," *Shakespeare Oxford Newsletter*, vol. 28/1 (Winter 1992): 12.

SOS membership. "Lord Burford has carried the Oxford banner with persuasive force, high style and easy humor. He's proven himself to be a dynamic and authoritative advocate, uses no notes in his lectures, [and] enjoys the give and take with audiences."[15] In another report, President Sears described her thrill at seeing Beauclerk's audiences being transformed.

> At the outset, there might be snickering and snide whispering to neighbors, but within less than a minute, his listeners would be stunned to silence. With mouths literally agape and eyes riveted on Charles, there would be a sudden mass conversion. Always, during the question period at the end of his talks, people would ask why they had never heard all these facts before. They seemed to feel outraged that they had been duped and misled by teachers and professors they had trusted to teach them true knowledge.[16]

And yet the excitement might all have evaporated as completely as had interest in the Oxfordian claim after the collapse of the Shakespeare Fellowship at the end of 1948. Charles Beauclerk had returned to London by the end of 1997, active SOS board member Charles Boyle had suffered a stroke in late 1996, and Charlton Ogburn's Oxfordian activities had ceased by the end of that year (he was eighty-six). He died in 1998, which left the Oxfordian movement without three of its most active leaders.

That the Shakespeare Oxford Society and the Oxfordian movement more generally did not suffer the eclipse that had occurred fifty years earlier was due in large part to the extraordinary efforts of William E. (Bill) Boyle. Following the departures of Charles Beauclerk and Charles Boyle (Bill's brother), he filled the roles of SOS treasurer and newsletter editor, and created its first website. He played the leading role in launching these and other projects that in sum constitute the SOS's second big initiative, one that set the organization and the Oxfordian movement on the course it follows to this day.

Boyle had been appointed by the SOS board in 1995 to serve as editor of the newsletter and manage its production and publication. After extensive discussions with others, he expanded its content and modernized it. What had been a simple typewritten newsletter distributed only within the society became a professionally prepared product suitable for presentation to outsiders. The old newsletter name, *The Shakespeare Oxford Society Newsletter*, was retired and *The Shakespeare Oxford Newsletter* was born.

Boyle launched the SOS's website in September 1995, which made a wealth of information about the Oxfordian claim instantly available to anyone interested in seeing it. The SOS was one of the first Shakespeare-related organizations to establish a presence on the web; a search for "Shakespeare" at that time—using one of the most popular search engines, Alta Vista—would bring up only around one hundred hits. This accomplishment ensured that the work of Oxfordian researchers, past and present, would not be lost or forgotten.

Boyle also launched an online magazine, *The Ever Reader*, which offered a wealth of important and timely articles, mostly reprints. Its success—along with the success of *The Elizabethan Review* founded and edited by Gary Goldstein—prompted the SOS to publish an annual journal in addition to its *Newsletter*. In 1998 *The Oxfordian*, was launched, a

---

[15] "Burford Reaches 15,000 With the Case for Oxford," *Shakespeare Oxford Newsletter*, vol. 29/2 (Spring 1993), pp. 14-15.
[16] "Information and Commentaries from Betty Sears, Our Past President," *Shakespeare Oxford Newsletter*, vol. 30/1 (Winter 1994): 19-20.

ewed academic journal devoted to study of the Oxfordian claim under the p of Stephanie Hopkins Hughes. Boyle was also a founder of the Oxfordian blog e, which he and Marty Hyatt began after discussion of the authorship question was banned from another blog, SHAKSPER. In 1996 Nina Green took over the job of moderating Evermore and renamed it Phaeton.

In 2005 Boyle established the New England Shakespeare Oxford Library (NESOL), dedicated to the study of Shakespearean literature and the authorship question. It is comprised of a permanent collection of books and journals and an online database, Shakespeare Online Authorship Resources (SOAR) (www.shakespeareoxfordlibrary.org). SOAR now consists of an index of more than 10,000 articles of special interest published in Oxfordian periodicals, the general media and scholarly journals over the past century. It also includes brief summaries of hundreds of the most important articles, and hyperlinks to searchable full-text versions of all articles for which copyright restrictions do not apply.

The momentum of the Oxfordian movement took another upward swing in the first decade of the 2000s, with the awarding of a Ph.D. in Comparative Literature to Roger Stritmatter by the University of Massachusetts, Amherst, in 2001; the publication of the first full biography of Edward de Vere, Mark Anderson's *"Shakespeare" By Another Name* in 2005; the publication of Hank Whittemore's *The Monument*; and the launching of master's degree programs in authorship studies at Brunel University in London (set up by Dr. William Leahy) and at Concordia University in Portland, Oregon (set up by Dr. Daniel Wright). Wright also established in 2008 the Edward de Vere Research Centre at Concordia, whose mission was to support scholarly inquiry into the authorship of Shakespeare's plays and poems. Wright had earlier established an annual Shakespeare Authorship Studies Conference held at Concordia every April since 1997.

This brief sketch of the rise of the modern Oxfordian movement—which I regard as its second wave—provides an account of what William Niederkorn described in 2005 as its transformation "from a handful to a thriving community with its own publications, organizations, lively online discussion groups and annual conferences."[17] Observing the dramatic increase in Oxfordian activity, James Shapiro wrote that "The resurrection of the Oxfordian movement has been little short of miraculous—one of the most remarkable and least remarked episodes in the history of Shakespeare studies."[18]

A list of some of the most significant developments in the rise of the second wave of the Oxfordian movement 1984-2020 is in the text boxes at the end of the chapter.

An Extraordinary Oxfordian "Event" in 2005

The publication of Mark Anderson's *"Shakespeare" by Another Name: The Life of Edward de Vere, Earl of Oxford, the Man Who Was Shakespeare* was more than the release of another new title; it was an event. Brought out in a print run of 40,000 by a recognized publisher (Gotham Books, a unit of the Penguin Group) that put considerable marketing effort behind it, the book was unique among Oxfordian publications. It brought more converts to the Oxfordian thesis than any book since Ogburn's *The Mysterious William Shakespeare* twenty years earlier, and is still the Oxfordian book most likely to be found on bookstore shelves.

---

[17] William S. Niederkorn, "The Shakespeare Code . . .," *New York Times*, Aug. 30, 2005, p. E3.
[18] James Shapiro, *Contested Will* (2010), pp. 203-04.

Anderson, a journalist who spent more than a decade researching the life of Edward de Vere, drew a 400-page portrait of Edward de Vere as a courtier, scholar, poet and dramatist whose life events are convincingly mirrored in, and inspired themes in, Shakespeare's plays. Promotional materials accurately describe how Anderson, "weaving together a wealth of evidence . . . [brought] to life this ingenious and sometimes reckless figure who, when cast out from Elizabeth I's court in disgrace, pled his case to his queen through her favorite art form—the theater."

In his "Foreword" to the book, Sir Derek Jacobi wrote that *"Shakespeare" by Another Name* "presents the logical, valid, and excitingly precise arguments for recognizing that de Vere, like all writers, drew from his own experiences, interests, accomplishments, education, position, and talents, and that he invested his writing with universal truths, emotional reality, and recognizable humanity drawn from his own unique life. The great excitement of this seminal work is the precise relationship between de Vere's life and his art, unveiling many thrilling revelations of how much of himself de Vere put into his characters. . . . Innumerable instances of de Vere's experiences, his relationships, his travels, and his unusual circumstances find expression in his plays and poems."[19]

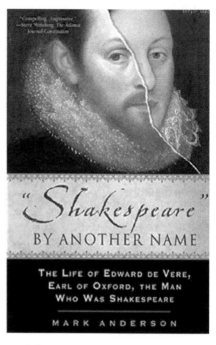

Anderson, like Capt. Ward in his 1928 biography of Edward de Vere, chose not to mention J. Thomas Looney or *"Shakespeare" Identified* in any substantive way. There is only one passing reference to them; there is only one passing reference to Capt. Ward, too, and no mention of the title of his book. Anderson did not make any reference to other early Oxfordians such as Col. Ward, Percy Allen or Gerald Rendall in spite of their seminal contributions to understanding the topical and personal nature of the plays (in Allen's case) and representations of Oxford's personality in the poems and sonnets (in Rendall's).

Even so, as Oxfordian Gary Goldstein observed, "Anderson's literary biography should serve as an effective antidote to the misrepresentations of those . . . hostile to the very idea of a Shakespeare authorship issue."[20] Writer Sarah Smith's assessment was that "without exaggeration, this is the most important Shakespeare biography of the past 400 years. . . . Anyone who claims to have a serious interest in Shakespeare must read Mark Anderson."[21] Stephanie Hopkins Hughes speculated that "at some point in the future, the summer of 2005 may be seen as a watershed in Shakespeare studies, due to the publication of Mark Anderson's biography of Edward de Vere, which makes the case for him as author of the Shakespeare canon more thoroughly and succinctly than anything

---

[19] Sir Derek Jacobi, "Foreword," in Mark Anderson, *"Shakespeare" by Another Name: The Life of Edward de Vere, Earl of Oxford, the Man Who Was Shakespeare* (2005), p. xxiv.
[20] Gary Goldstein, [Review of *"Shakespeare" by Another Name* by Mark Anderson], *The Oxfordian*, vol. 8 (2005): p. 128.
[21] Sarah Smith, Comment from back of the book's dust jacket.

that has gone before."[22]

The following text boxes are a list of important events, publications and broadcasts in the second wave of the Oxfordian movement.

Selected Developments in the Oxfordian Movement, 1984-2001		
1984, Nov.	Publication	Charlton Ogburn's *The Mysterious William Shakespeare*
1987, Sept. 25	Event	Moot Court with three U.S. Supreme Court justices
1988, Nov. 26	Event	Moot Court in London's Inner Temple
1989, April	Broadcast	"The Shakespeare Mystery" produced by *Frontline*, on PBS
1986, Fall	Publication	William P. Fowler, *Shakespeare Revealed in Oxford's Letters*
1988	Event	De Vere Society (London) founded
1991, April	Event	Charles Beauclerk lectures at the Folger Shakespeare Library and the Harvard University Faculty Club
1991-1997	Event	Charles Beauclerk (Lord Burford) lectures at 200 schools, libraries and other public venues in the United States and Canada
1991, Oct.	Publication	*Atlantic Magazine* cover story "Looking for Shakespeare"
1992	Publication	*The Shakespeare Controversy: An Analysis of the Authorship Theories, 1st ed.* by Warren Hope & Kim Holston
1992, Sept.	Broadcast	"Uncovering Shakespeare: An Update" moderated by William F. Buckley, produced by John Mucci and Gary Goldstein
1993, Spring	Publication	*The Elizabethan Review* launched by editor Gary Goldstein
1994, Oct.	Publication	*Shakespeare: Who Was He? The Oxfordian Challenge to the Bard of Avon* by Richard F. Whalen
1995	Event	Shakespeare Oxford Society Website launched, created by Bill Boyle
1996, Jan.	Publication	*Shakespeare Oxford Newsletter* launched in modern format by Bill Boyle
1997	Event	Annual Edward de Vere Studies Conference at Concordia University launched by Daniel Wright
1997, March	Publication	*Alias Shakespeare: Solving the Greatest Literary Mystery of All Time* by Joseph Sobran
1997, Summer	Publication	*Neues Shakespeare Journal* launched, Uwe Laugwitz, editor (Germany)
1998, Oct.	Publication	*The Oxfordian*, the SOS's peer-reviewed scholarly journal launched and edited by Stephanie Hopkins Hughes
1999, April	Publication	*Harper's Magazine* cover story "The Ghost of Shakespeare," Lewis Lapham, editor
2001, Spring	Event	Roger Stritmatter awarded Ph.D. in Comparative Literature by the University of Massachusetts, Amherst
2001	Publication	*The Marginalia of Edward de Vere's Geneva Bible: Providential Discovery, Literary Reasoning and Historical Consequence*, Dr. Roger Stritmatter's Ph.D. Dissertation
2001, Spring	Publication	*Shakespeare's Unorthodox Biography: New Evidence of an Authorship Problem* by Diana Price [Not Oxfordian, but widely quoted]
2001, Summer	Event/Pub.	Founding of the Shakespeare Fellowship (see Chapter 21)
2001, Fall	Event/Pub.	Launching of the Shakespeare Fellowship's new publication, *Shakespeare Matters* (see Chapter 21)

---

[22] Stephanie Hopkins Hughes, [Review of *"Shakespeare" by Another Name* by Mark Anderson], *Shakespeare Oxford Newsletter*, vol. 41/3 (Summer 2005): 2.

Selected Developments in the Oxfordian Movement, 2002-2012

2002, Feb. 10	Publication	First of William Niederkorn's pieces in *The New York Times*
2002, Spring	Event	Opening of the Shakespeare Authorship Research Centre at Concordia University, Portland, Oregon
2002, Fall	Publication	*Shakespeare's Fingerprints* by Michael Brame & Galina Popova
2002, 2003	Publication	*The Dark Side of Shakespeare, vol. 1: An Iron-fisted Romantic in England's Most Perilous Times; vol. 2: An Elizabethan Courtier, Diplomat, Spymaster & Epic Hero* by W. Ron Hess
2003, Jan.	Event	Smithsonian hosts Authorship Debate (Richard F. Whalen vs. Gail Kern Paster)
2003, June	Event	Shakespearean Authorship Trust First Annual Event at Shakespeare's Globe (organized by Mark Rylance)
2004/2005	Event/Pub.	The University of Tennessee College of Law symposium "Who Wrote Shakespeare?" An Evidentiary Puzzle" (June 2004), followed by publication of papers in the *Tennessee Law Review* in 2005.
2005	Publication	*"Shakespeare" By Another Name: The Life of Edward de Vere, Earl of Oxford, the Man Who Was Shakespeare* by Mark Anderson
2005	Publication	*The Monument* by Hank Whittemore
2006	Event	Master's Degree Program in Authorship Studies launched at Brunel University near London by Dr. William Leahy
2007	Event	Masters Degree Program in Authorship Studies launched at Concordia University in Portland, Oregon
2007, Sept.	Event	Declaration of Reasonable Doubt, created by John Shahan, launched at ceremony at Shakespeare's Globe Theatre. Derek Jacobi and Mark Rylance sign. the Shakespeare Authorship Coalition launched
2008, July 3/4	Broadcast	NPR's "Morning Edition" programs: "The Real Shakespeare: Evidence Points to Earl"
2008	Event	Shakespeare Authorship Studies Centre established at Concordia University
2009	Publication	*The Shakespeare Controversy: An Analysis of the Authorship Theories, 2nd ed.* by Warren Hope & Kim Holston
2009	Publication	*Building the Case for Edward de Vere as Shakespeare*, Paul H. Altrocchi & Hank Whittemore (editors) [vol. 1-5]
2009, Fall	Publication	*Brief Chronicles* launched by the Shakespeare Fellowship
2009, Fall	Event	Oxfordian of the Year awarded to U.S. Supreme Court Associate Justice John Paul Stevens
2010, Spring	Publication	*Shakespeare's Lost Kingdom: The True History of Shakespeare and Elizabeth* by Charles Beauclerk
2011, Spring	Publication	*Dating Shakespeare's Plays: A Critical Review of the Evidence*, Kevin Gilvary, editor
	Publication	*Bardgate: Shake-speare and the Royalists Who Stole the Bard* by Peter W. Dickson
2011, Fall	Publication	*Shakespeare Suppressed: The Uncensored Truth about Shakespeare and His Works* by Katherine Chiljan
	Publication	*The Shakespeare Guide to Italy: Retracing the Bard's Unknown Travels* by Richard P. Roe
2012, Fall	Event	Formation of the Shakespeare Oxford Fellowship through merger of the Shakespeare Oxford Society and the Shakespeare Fellowship
	Publication	*The Earl of Oxford and the Making of "Shakespeare* by Richard Malim

Selected Developments in the Oxfordian Movement, 2013-2020

2013, Summer	Publication	*Shakespeare Beyond Doubt? Exposing an Industry in Denial,* edited by John M. Shahan and Alexander Waugh
2013, Fall	Publication	*A Poet's Rage: Understanding Shakespeare Through Authorship Studies*, William Boyle, editor
	Publication	*On the Date, Sources and Design of Shakespeare's The Tempest* by Roger Stritmatter & Lynne Kositsky
2016, Fall	Publication	*100 Reasons Shake-speare was the Earl of Oxford* by Hank Whittemore
2018, Fall	Publication	Centenary Edition of J. Thomas Looney's *"Shakespeare" Identified*
2018	Publication	*Necessary Mischief: Exploring the Shakespeare Authorship Question* by Bonner Miller Cutting
	Publication	*Shakespeare's Apprenticeship: Identifying the Real Playwright's Earliest Works* by Ramon Jiménez
2019, Feb.	Publication	*"Shakespeare" Revealed: The Collected Articles and Published Letters of J. Thomas Looney*, James A. Warren, editor
2019, Summer	Publication	*Early Shakespeare Authorship Doubts* by Bryan H. Wildenthal
2020	Event	100th Anniversary of Publication of *"Shakespeare" Identified* Celebration held at the National Press Club, Washington, DC (March 4)
2020	Publication	*Who Wrote That? Authorship Controversies from Moses to Sholokhov* by Donald Ostrowski

20

The Oxfordian Movement Today

The rise of the current wave of the Oxfordian movement having been briefly recounted, this chapter examines some aspects—*some* aspects only—of the movement as it exists today, and some of the most important Oxfordian events that have occurred in recent decades.

Greater Depth

The unprecedented amount of activity and media attention to the authorship issue over the past several decades is due in part to the greater depth of the Oxfordian movement.[1]

Depth in Number of Oxfordian Organizations

In 1940 only two formal Oxfordian organizations existed: the Shakespeare Fellowship in England, which had suspended its operations for the duration of the War, and the newly-formed American branch based in New York. Today there are still two principal Oxfordian institutions—the Shakespeare Oxford Fellowship (SOF) in the United States and the De Vere Society in England—but they are informally associated with more than a dozen other organizations, including:

> The Shakespeare Authorship Coalition established by John M. Shahan, with Alexander Waugh serving as Honorary Chairman. Although it is not an Oxfordian organization, its work is critical to legitimizing the authorship issue in academia by promoting awareness of the weakness of the Stratfordian claim. Of special importance is its Declaration of Reasonable Doubt, available at www.DoubtAboutWill.org, which has been signed by nearly 5,000 persons.

> The Shakespeare Authorship Roundtable, founded by Carole Sue Lipman in the Los Angeles area thirty years ago. It is a forum for the study of the Shakespeare canon, the Elizabethan theater, and the social and political life of the Elizabethan period, with emphasis on an open-minded exploration of the Shakespeare authorship debate.

> In England, the Shakespearean Authorship Trust traces its roots to the original Shakespeare Fellowship founded in 1922. It is dedicated to discovering the truth about the authorship of the works known as William Shakespeare's, and takes a big-tent approach in which supporters of all candidates for authorship can meet and discuss the issue. Its annual lecture is held at Shakespeare's Globe Theatre in London.

---

[1] I have undoubtedly overlooked important organizations, individuals and activities that are contributing to the effectiveness of the Oxfordian movement. I apologize to those I have overlooked in my effort to keep this overview as compact as possible.

Depth in Range of Activities

In 1940 the Shakespeare Fellowship in England had suspended its activities after the onset of the Second World War. The newly formed American branch, though, was dynamic, publishing a steady stream of important Oxfordian research in its *News-Letter* and conducting occasional public events. But even its range of activities pales in comparison with activities undertaken by successor organizations today.

The Shakespeare Oxford Fellowship (SOF) has numerous ongoing activities.

- ✓ It publishes the *Shakespeare Oxford Newsletter*, a quarterly publication that keeps members informed of developments, reviews books related to the authorship question, and features a wide range of articles on related topics. Most issues are 32 or 36 pages.

- ✓ It publishes *The Oxfordian*, a peer-reviewed annual journal that features lengthier articles on authorship-related topics as well as book reviews. *The Oxfordian* is now included in several academic databases, making its articles readily available to scholars and students.

- ✓ Its website (www.shakespeareoxfordfellowship.org) serves as a gateway to information about the Oxfordian thesis, with a wealth of information on the site itself available to all, as well as links to many other sites. Recently added are links to older newsletters and journals that contain important research findings and information. Among them are the *News-Letters* issued by the Shakespeare Fellowships in England (1937-1958) and the United States (1939-1948) and *The Elizabethan Review* (1993-1999) founded and edited by Gary Goldstein. All are indexed and searchable in SOAR.

- ✓ It holds an annual three or four day conference filled with interesting presentations.

- ✓ It sponsors a Research Grant Program to support Oxfordian scholars in conducting primary research at the world's leading archives and libraries.

- ✓ It now has a professional Public Relations Director to publicize the Fellowship's activities and the Oxfordian claim. Among the most successful endeavors is the "Don't Quill the Messenger" podcasts, hosted by Steven Sabel and broadcast on Dragon Wagon Radio, launched in 2019. New episodes are produced biweekly on a wide range of topics; most are sixty minutes in length.

- ✓ The SOF channel on YouTube includes dozens of informative videos on the Oxfordian claim, including presentations from recent annual conferences.

- ✓ The annual Video Contest gives film makers the chance to compete in making three-minute videos about the Oxfordian position. Cash prizes are awarded.

- ✓ The "How I Became an Oxfordian" series of articles on the SOF website, created by Robert Meyers, chronicles how individual Oxfordians became interested in the Shakespeare Authorship question.

The De Vere Society, founded by Charles Beauclerk in 1986, is the most prominent and active Oxfordian organization in England. Its quarterly *Newsletter* reports on new Oxfordian research and provides reviews of new books and videos of interest. Its website contains a goldmine of information and links to other sites and publications.

Special note must be made of an active Oxfordian organization in Germany. Verlag

Uwe Laugwitz, in Buchholz, Germany, established an annual Oxfordian journal, *Neue Shakespeare Journal*, in 1997. It publishes articles by Oxfordian researchers and scholars, mostly in German. Among the many interesting articles that have appeared was one by Charlton Ogburn, "The Collapse of Shakespeare Orthodoxy," in volume 2 (1998). It is in German (Ogburn was fluent in the language) and has never been translated into English. Laugwitz also publishes collections of articles by prominent Oxfordian scholars whose works had never before been collected. Five collections have been produced so far, with several others planned.

Special Issues of *Neue Shake-speare Journal* (pub. by Verlag Uwe Laugwitz, Buchholz, Germany)		
2009	Peter R. Moore	*The Lame Storyteller, Poor and Despised: Studies in Shakespeare.* Edited by Gary Goldstein.
2012	Robin Fox	*Shakespeare's Education: Schools, Lawsuits, Theater and the Tudor Miracle.* Edited by Gary Goldstein.
2014	Noemi Magri	*Such Fruits Out of Italy: The Italian Renaissance in Shakespeare's Plays and Poems.* Edited by Gary Goldstein.
2016	Gary Goldstein	*Reflections on the True Shakespeare.* Edited by Gary Goldstein.
2019	A. Bronson Feldman	*Early Shakespeare.* Edited by Warren Hope.

Depth in Number of Active Oxfordians

In 1940 only three persons—Charles Wisner Barrell, Louis P. Bénézet and Eva Turner Clark—played an active role in the operations of the American branch of the Shakespeare Fellowship. When they died or retired, the organization and the movement collapsed, showing just how fragile things were at that time. The SOF now has well over 400 members. No longer can the withdrawal from active involvement by a few persons lead to organizational demise. The wealth of information available through the website ensures the permanent survival of its research findings.

Oxfordian Research and Publications

A list of subjects investigated in *The Oxfordian* over the past three years shows how varied are the approaches to the Oxfordian thesis by scholars at work today:

- ✓ Edward de Vere and the translation of Ovid's *Metamorphoses*
- ✓ Edward de Vere in Italian Archives
- ✓ A Spanish connection to the First Folio
- ✓ An examination of Ben Jonson's "Small Latin and Less Greeke"
- ✓ Edward Webbe and *Troublesome Travailes* and the authorship question
- ✓ J. Thomas Looney's forgotten writings uncovered
- ✓ Shakespeare's dramatic juvenilia
- ✓ Ancient Greece in Shakespeare's plays
- ✓ Shakespearean biographies
- ✓ The Shakespeare author debate and six authorship candidates
- ✓ Edward de Vere defamed on stage
- ✓ Role the Herbert family played in the authorship cover-up
- ✓ Shakespeare's references to river navigation in Italy
- ✓ French influence in Shakespeare
- ✓ The politics of Edward de Vere

- ✓ The model of the butcher in *2 Henry VI*
- ✓ Transformations in productions of Shakespeare's plays
- ✓ Edward de Vere and the psychology of creativity
- ✓ Nicholas Hilliard's portraits of the Elizabethan court
- ✓ The poems of Edward de Vere
- ✓ Recovery of the Oxfordian writings of A. Bronson Feldman

Below is a small sample of other interesting articles on important topics from the current wave of the movement not mentioned elsewhere in Part 2 of this book:

- ✓ "Ten Eyewitnesses Who Saw Nothing" by Ramon Jiménez,[2] identifies ten persons who had known Shakspere or one of his daughters but never mentioned him as having had any literary connections, or who wrote about Stratford-on-Avon without ever mentioning that it was the home of a famous writer. One of them was Dr. John Hall, Shakspere's son-in-law, whose diary mentioned another writer, Michael Drayton, but not his father-in-law.

- ✓ "Was *The Famous Victories of Henry the Fifth* Shakespeare's First Play?" by Ramon Jiménez,[3] establishes that "there is substantial historical, theatrical and literary evidence that [the anonymous play *The Famous Victories of Henry the Fifth*] was written by the author of the Shakespeare canon"—an important finding for all Shakespeare scholars—and that "he wrote it in the early 1560s, while still in his teens" (15).

- ✓ Several articles by Dr. Earl Showerman establish beyond doubt that Shakespeare drew on ancient Greek works, including many not yet translated into English.[4] Stratfordians have no convincing explanation for how someone like Shakspere, with no known educational attainments, could possibly have been familiar with such works.

- ✓ Dr. Richard Waugaman has documented that Shakespeare, in drawing on the Psalms, relied not on the translation in the Geneva Bible—his main Biblical source—but on the now-obscure translation known as *The Whole Book of Psalms*.[5] A copy of that work is bound together with de Vere's copy of the Geneva Bible, now in the Folger Shakespeare Library, thus providing another strong link between Edward de Vere and the work known as "Shakespeare's."

- ✓ "Sweet Swan of Avon" by Alexander Waugh[6] documents that Hampton Court, the royal palace at which dramatic entertainment was presented before the courts of Queen Elizabeth and King James, was commonly known at the time as "Avon,"

---

[2] Ramon Jiménez, "Shakespeare in Stratford and London: Ten Eyewitnesses Who Saw Nothing," in *"Report My Cause Aright"* Shakespeare Oxford Society (2007), pp. 74-86.

[3] Ramon Jiménez, "Was *The Famous Victories of Henry the Fifth* Shakespeare's First Play?" *The Oxfordian*, vol. 22 (Sept. 2020): 15-47.

[4] They include "The Rediscovery of Shakespeare's Greater Greek," *The Oxfordian*, vol. 17 (2015): 163-91; and *"A Midsummer Night's Dream*: Shakespeare's Aristophanic Comedy, *Brief Chronicles*, vol. 6 (2015): 107-36.

[5] See especially "Maniculed Psalms in the de Vere Bible: A New Literary Source for Shakespeare," *Brief Chronicles*, vol. 2 (2010): 109-20; and "The Sternhold and Hopkins' Whole Book of Psalms is a Major Source for the Works of Shakespeare," *Notes and Queries*, vol. 56/4 (Dec. 2009): 595-604. Having written close to a hundred articles, Waugaman is one of the most productive Oxfordians at work today.

[6] Alexander Waugh, "Sweet Swan of Avon," *The Oxfordian*, vol. 16 (2014): 97-103.

undercutting the interpretation of Ben Jonson's encomium "the Sweet Swan of Avon" as referring to William Shakspere from Stratford-on-Avon.

✓ "Vere-y Interesting: Shakespeare's Treatment of the Earls of Oxford in the History Plays" by Professor Daniel Wright[7] shows how Shakespeare departed from the sources of his history plays in ways that exaggerated the prominence of some of the prior Earls of Oxford and asks what explanation could account for those changes other than a subsequent Earl of Oxford having been Shakespeare.

A number of recently published books (not mentioned elsewhere) persuasively undermine the pillars of support for the Stratfordian claim or buttress the Oxfordian:

✓ *Shakespeare Suppressed: The Uncensored Truth about Shakespeare and his Works*, in which Katherine Chiljan[8] uncovered "93 instances of 'too early' allusions to 32 different Shakespeare plays"—"too early" meaning that the allusions had been made in the 1580s or earlier, when Shakspere, born in 1564, was still a boy. "They were made by 30 different writers . . . and occurred in 53 different sources." This evidence meant that "either the great author was a serial plagiarist [if he had only updated existing plays] and therefore was not a creative genius, or his works were written far earlier than supposed" (343). The earlier timing placed the plays perfectly into the prime of Edward de Vere's life.

✓ *Bardgate: Shake-speare and the Royalists Who Stole the Bard*, Peter Dickson's 2013 book, makes the case that the historical setting in which the First Folio was issued was deliberately erased from history. Rather than being a mere collection of plays, the First Folio was an intensely political statement. "The sudden rush in 1621-1623 to collect and preserve for posterity the Shakespearean dramas . . . was energized by paranoia among Anglican-minded courtiers and like-minded actors and publishers that there might be a top-down restoration of Roman Catholicism if King James succeeded in his effort to arrange a dynastic union with Catholic Spain via a marriage of Prince Charles to a sister of King Filipe IV."[9]

✓ *Shakespeare Revealed in Oxford's Letters*, by William Plumer Fowler,[10] provides documentary evidence linking Edward de Vere with the works known as "Shakespeare's." Fowler provides the full transcriptions of thirty-seven of de Vere's letters, together with a detailed study of their remarkable parallels, in both thought and phraseology, to the writings ascribed to Shakespeare.

✓ *Dating Shakespeare's Plays: A Critical Review of the Evidence*, edited by Kevin Gilvary,[11] brings together the fragmentary evidence uncovered by scholars over the past 200 years to establish earliest, latest and most probable dates of composition of each of Shakespeare's plays. Approaching the task from both Stratfordian and Oxfordian perspectives, Gilvary renders obsolete the efforts by previous scholars such as Malone and Chambers to assign dates to the plays by

---

[7] Daniel L. Wright, "Vere-y Interesting: Shakespeare's Treatment of the Earls of Oxford in the History Plays," *Shakespeare Oxford Newsletter*, vol. 36/1 (Spring 2000): 1, 14-21.

[8] Katharine Chiljan, *Shakespeare Suppressed: The Uncensored Truth About Shakespeare and His Works* (2011).

[9] Peter W. Dickson, *Bardgate: Shake-speare and the Royalists Who Stole the Bard* (2013), p. 21.

[10] William Plumer Fowler, *Shakespeare Revealed in Oxford's Letters* (1986).

[11] Kevin Gilvary (editor), *Dating Shakespeare's Plays: A Critical Review of the Evidence* (2010).

placing them within the supposed theater career of William Shakspere.

✓ *The Shakespeare Guide to Italy: Retracing the Bard's Unknown Travels*, by Richard Paul Roe.[12] Through many trips to Italy, Roe determined the exact locations of nearly every scene in *Romeo and Juliet*, *The Two Gentlemen of Verona*, *The Merchant of Venice*, *Much Ado about Nothing*, *The Tempest* and the other Shakespearean dramas set in Italy. His detailed descriptions, complete with maps and drawings, show that Shakespeare must have visited those spots.

✓ *Early Shakespeare Authorship Doubts*, by Bryan H. Wildenthal,[13] undermines the claim that no one had any doubts about William of Stratford's authorship until hundreds of years later by examining dozens of expressions of such doubt during his lifetime, including five indications that the real author died years before Shakspere's death in 1616.

✓ *Reflections on the True Shakespeare* by Gary Goldstein provides a summary of how findings by Oxfordian scholars have radically transformed our understanding of Shakespeare's works and Elizabethan society.

> The Oxfordian argument . . . may be summed up by stating that a Shakespeare different from the one we know provides us with an entirely different understanding of the development and history of English literature and theater, and revises our knowledge of the cultural politics of Elizabethan England.
>
> Should the Earl of Oxford be accepted as Shakespeare, the entire canon of plays will be transformed, from a series of brilliant yet superficial public entertainments to ambitious dramas on the crises facing the Elizabethan state: the English and Scottish royal successions, the 19-year war with Spain, the French civil war, internal dissension by English Puritans and more. In addition, the ten plays set in Italy and France will finally be perceived as the dramatist's lifelong effort to transplant the Renaissance culture of Europe into England through the public stage. Instead of imaginative displays of wit by a provincial genius to amuse a variety of publics, Shakespeare's dramatic efforts will be seen originating in the personal experiences and observations of a highly educated aristocrat who lived at the apex of Elizabethan society.[14]

I should also note the Oxfordian Shakespeare Series edited by Richard F. Whalen. This series of Shakespeare's plays does not present new research *per se*, but instead draws on

The Oxfordian Shakespeare Series, Richard F. Whalen, General Editor		
Published		
2010	*Othello*	Edited by Ren Draya and Richard F. Whalen
2013	*Macbeth*	Edited by Richard F. Whalen
2015	*Anthony and Cleopatra*	Edited by Michael Delahoyde
2018	*Hamlet*	Edited by Richard F. Whalen
In progress		
--	*The Tempest*	Roger Stritmatter & Lynne Kositsky
--	*Love's Labour's Lost*	Felicia Londré
--	*Much Ado About Nothing*	Anne Pluto

---

[12] Richard Paul Roe, *The Shakespeare Guide to Italy* (2011).
[13] Bryan H. Wildenthal, *Early Shakespeare Authorship Doubts* (2019).
[14] Gary Goldstein, *Reflections on the True Shakespeare*, 2016, p. 9-10.

all Oxfordian research to give readers the fullest possible understanding of Oxford's great plays.

Many individuals operate independent websites, blogs and list-servs with more specialized information. Links to them can be found on the SOF website. Of special importance is Mark Andre Alexander's Shakespeare Authorship Sourcebook (sourcetext.com), which provides access to the full texts of several hundred publications of special interest. Most of the most important books from the first wave of the Oxfordian movement are available there, as well as thirty-two of Charles Barrell's articles. Also available are publications from the 16th century dedicated to Edward de Vere. The site also includes links to the complete works of many Elizabethan dramatists and poets.

Nina Green's Oxford Authorship Site (oxford-shakespeare.com) is indispensable. It contains transcripts of thousands of documents related to Oxford's life and authorship of Shakespeare's works.

Six scholars of the greatest importance

Six scholars are mentioned many times throughout Part Two of this book. Their research is too varied to categorize and their publications too numerous to summarize; each is represented here by a publication or two not mentioned elsewhere that shows the depth of their research and the persuasiveness of their presentations.

Roger Stritmatter is the holder of the first (and still the only) Ph.D. awarded in literary studies that openly postulates Edward de Vere as the literary mind behind the *nom de plume* "William Shakespeare." His dissertation, *The Marginalia of Edward de Vere's Geneva Bible: Providential Discovery, Literary Reasoning, and Historical Consequence* (2001), presents the results of his decade-long examination of the 1568-70 Geneva Bible originally owned and annotated by Edward de Vere and now owned by the Folger Shakespeare Library. It documents that the Bible "contains over a thousand marked and underlined Bible passages in the fine italic handwriting of Edward de Vere" (48). Correspondences between the markings and passages in Shakespeare's works are so numerous that U.S. Supreme Court Justice John Paul Stevens called Stritmatter's dissertation "an impressive piece of work . . . [which] demonstrates that the owner of the de Vere Bible had the same familiarity with its text as the author of the Shakespeare canon."

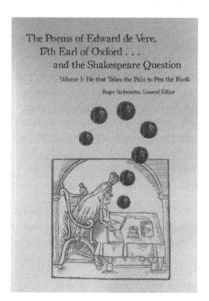

In the two decades since, Stritmatter brought his scholarly skills to bear on innumerable subjects related to the authorship question. Most recently he has built on Looney's pioneering work on Edward de Vere's poems. The first volume of Stritmatter's study examines the twenty-one poems generally accepted as by de Vere. In addition to examining and explicating them, it provides the historical context for their rediscovery by scholars beginning in the 1800s and the evolution of scholarly opinion of them. The volume includes articles by Bryan H. Wildenthal, Gary Goldstein and Robert R. Prechter.

One hundred of the many hundreds of postings on <u>Hank Whittemore's</u> blog (hankwhittemore.com) explain why Looney got it right. Each reason, masterfully combining logical thought and solid historical support, is powerful in itself. Combined into a book, *100 Reasons Shake-speare was the Earl of Oxford*, and read one after another, their effect is overwhelming. It led Mark Anderson to comment that "If Stratfordians could assemble even a handful of arguments this powerful and this persuasive for Will Shakspere of Stratford as the author of the Bard's plays and poems, they'd say 'Game over.' We've proved our case."

Each reason focuses on one aspect of the circumstantial evidence connecting Oxford with Shakespeare. The topics include Oxford and the theater, events in Oxford's life depicted in *Hamlet*; Oxford in northern Italy, the setting for many of Shakespeare's plays; Marlowe and the University Wits; Elizabeth and other nobles portrayed in the plays; and many specialized subjects such as the law, music and horsemanship depicted in Shakespeare's works.

Whittemore suggests that one reason high schools, colleges and universities are choosing to phase out or drop Shakespeare courses is "that there has been no way to inspire students by linking the creation of those works with the personal experience and intentions of their creator; without that dynamic connection to an author's lived life, it is difficult for students to see how the poems and plays relate to their own lives. The entranceway to fully comprehending and appreciating Shakespeare has been blocked" (viii). Whittemore unblocks it; his book is an entertaining journey into the heart of the Shakespeare mystery and shows why Oxford's authorship is the key that unravels it.

Since serving as the founding editor of *The Oxfordian* for its first decade (1997-2007), <u>Stephanie Hopkins Hughes</u> has published dozens of articles and posted hundreds more to her blog at politicworm.com. They bring the Shakespearean story, or rather the Oxfordian story, to life in ways that textbooks, "drained of much of the color," cannot.

Her pamphlet, *The Relevance of Robert Greene to the Oxfordian Thesis* (1998), is an extended examination of whether Greene, "either as a real stand-in or as an entirely fictional being, was a pseudonym used off and on from 1580 to 1592 by the Earl of Oxford as a cover for publication"[15] of his works. She asked, "Doesn't it make a great deal more sense in terms of what is actually humanly possible, to consider the very similar and sometimes identical styles, plots, and characters of the Euphues books, the pamphlets,

---

[15] Stephanie Hopkins Hughes, *The Relevance of Robert Greene to the Oxfordian Thesis*, second edition (1998), p. 23.

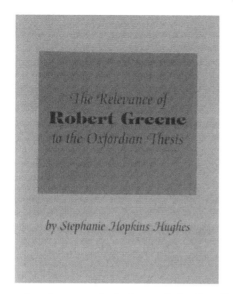

poetry and plays of Robert Greene, and the plays and poetry of Shakespeare, as the work of one evolving writer, particularly a writer with such cogent reasons for hiding his identity? Doesn't it seem much easier to swallow a few fake names on title pages, requiring a simple substitution on the part of the compositor, and the complicity of the printer and perhaps the clerk at the Stationer's Registry, than an entire style faked, not just once, but over and over, by two, three, four, or even five different writers?" (25)

It was wanting to know what others thought of Hughes's ideas—and also the ideas of Michael Brame, Galina Popova and Joseph Sobran[16]—about what other literary works might have been written by Edward de Vere that led me to prepare what became *An Index to Oxfordian Publications*.

Alexander Waugh has contributed to the Oxfordian cause through many media: books, articles, a newspaper column, and audio and video broadcasts. Many of his pieces, always original and insightful, are posted on his YouTube channel. One piece, *Shakespeare in Court*, presents a dramatic courtroom cross-examination of "a typical orthodox Shakespeare pundit." It is, the product description at amazon.com states, an exposé of the Shakespeare Birthplace Trust, a registered charity from Stratford-upon-Avon, which is "a prime source of misinformation and subversion concerning the life and times of the world's greatest playwright. . . . Waugh provocatively accuses the Trust of 'making false statements' about its tourist museums, of concealing information about Shakespeare authorship, of abusing those who challenge or contradict its 'expert authority' and of having 'a clear and obvious conflict of interest concerning its revenues and its representation of Shakespearean history.' . . . It clearly reveals why the case for Shakespeare of Stratford, if submitted to the judicial scrutiny of any court of law, would be instantly dismissed."[17]

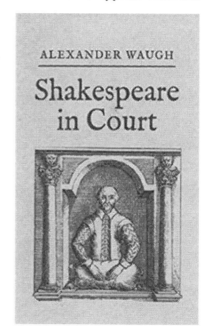

Of Richard Malim's many writings on a variety of subjects, two were especially important in helping me

---

[16] See, for instance, Michael Brame & Galina Popova, *Shakespeare's Fingerprints* (2002), and Joseph Sobran, "Before He was Shakespeare, Parts 1 and 2," *Shakespeare Oxford Newsletter*, vol. 41/1 (Winter 2005): 1, 13-16 and vol. 41/2 (Spring 2005): 1, 12-14). See also Hughes's "Hide Fox and All After: The Search for Shakespeare," *Shakespeare Oxford Newsletter*, vol. 43/1 (Winter 2007): 1, 5-11.

[17] *Shakespeare in Court* at amazon.com: https://www.amazon.com/Shakespeare-Court-Kindle-Single-Alexander-ebook/dp/B00O4V4V9W/ref=sr_1_2?dchild=1&keywords=shakespeare+in+court&qid=1622434103&sr=8-2.

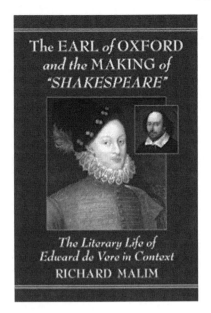

understand the context in which Oxford worked and how extensively he influenced his times, and how probable it was that William Shakspere was neither a playwright nor an actor. His book *The Earl of Oxford and the Making of "Shakespeare:" The Literary Life of Edward de Vere in Context* made clear that a revolution in English literature had indeed occurred—as opposed to the mere evolution of literary styles—and that it had taken off at exactly that moment that de Vere returned from his sixteen-month travels in Italy and France and elsewhere in Europe. From the dramatic enrichment of the language itself, to the startling new sophistication of the dramas and poetry produced from the mid-1570s onward, to the establishment of the first public theater in 1576 and on to the so-called "pamphlet wars," Oxford's influence could be felt wherever one looked. In sum, "the primary leader of the English literary revolution was Oxford writing as 'Shakespeare'."[18]

Malim provided another of those "Oh, of course!" moments with the title of his article "Shaksper the Nonentity." After seeing every orthodox scholar and many Oxfordian scholars monotonously refer to "the actor from Stratford" or "Shakespeare the player," it was a a pleasure to see it stated so succinctly that Shakspere "was no sort of actor or impresario, and indeed was seldom in London after 1599."[19]

Shakespeare: Who Was He? The Oxford Challenge to the Bard of Avon by then-Shakespeare Oxford Society president <u>Richard F. Whalen</u>, was the first Oxfordian book I read, and it largely transformed me into an Oxfordian. With a clear presentation of almost all major issues relating to Oxford's authorship—and Shakspere's non-authorship—laid out so clearly, and accompanied by an annotated bibliography for further reading, it remains, even a quarter-century after its appearance, the single best shorter introduction for those new to the Oxfordian claim.

That reading list, and Whalen's many scores of reviews of important books I would not otherwise have known about, published in the *Shakespeare Oxford Newsletter* and *Shakespeare Matters*, served as my initial point of entry into the wider world of authorship studies.

---

[18] Richard Malim, *The Earl of Oxford and the Making of "Shakespeare"* (2012, pp. 1-2).
[19] Richard Malim, "Shaksper the Nonentity," *De Vere Society Newsletter*, vol. 22/1 (Jan. 2015): 14.

Other work

The following works were of special importance in helping me understand various aspects of the Oxfordian story.

- ✓ Barbara Burris's investigative reporting on the Ashbourne portrait in *Shakespeare Matters* in the early years of this century.[20]

- ✓ Robert Prechter's and John Rollett's work to decipher the dedication to the *Sonnets.*[21]

- ✓ Bonner Cutting's work on Shakspere's Will, Oxford's wardship and how the coverup of his authorship took place in the decades after his death.[22]

- ✓ Christopher H. Dams's work on the dating of Shakespeare's plays laid the foundation for Kevin Gilvary's *Dating Shakespeare's Plays* a decade later.[23] Ron Hess's work on the same subject was one of the first Oxfordian pieces I read.[24]

- ✓ Noemi Magri's research showing that the allusions to Italy and its culture in the ten plays by "Shakespeare" set in that country could have been written only by someone with personal experience in the country and who knew first-hand its culture, painting and geography. Her many articles have been collected and published in *Such Fruits Out of Italy: The Italian Renaissance in Shakespeare's Plays and Poems.* (2014).

- ✓ On the subject of what awareness of Oxford as Shakespeare existed before *"Shakespeare" Identified,* I learned much from Richard Whalen, Peter Dickson and Charles Berney.[25]

- ✓ Tom Regnier's articles on how deeply Shakespeare/Oxford's understanding of legal issues colored his thinking and his works are required reading.[26] Regnier's outsized contribution to the movement included leading the Shakespeare Oxford

---

[20] The first of Burris's ten articles was "A Golden Book, Bound Richly Up: Comparing Chapman's Words with the Ashbourne Portrait," *Shakespeare Matters*, vol. 1/1 (Fall): 1, 12-17.

[21] See, for instance, Robert R. Prechter, Jr., "The *Sonnets* Dedication Puzzle, Parts I and 2," *Shakespeare Matters*, vol. 4/3 (Spring 2005): 1, 12-19 and vol. 4/4 (Summer 2005): 1, 18-27; and *John Rollett*, "The Dedication to Shakespeare's *Sonnets*," *Elizabethan Review*, vol. 5/2 (Autumn 1997): 93-122, and "Secrets of the Dedication to Shakespeare's *Sonnets*," *The Oxfordian*, vol. 2 (1999): 60-75.

[22] Cutting's research in these and other important areas has been collected and published in her book, *Necessary Mischief: Exploring the Shakespeare Authorship Question* (2018).

[23] See, for instance, Christopher H. Dams, "The Dates of Composition of 'The Plays of William Shake-Speare' by Edward de Vere, 17ᵗʰ Earl of Oxford," *De Vere Society Newsletter*, vol. 3/4a (Aug. 1999): 1-44.

[24] W. Ron Hess, "Shakespeare's Dates: Their Effects on Stylistic Analysis," *The Oxfordian*, vol. 2 (1999): 25-59.

[25] See, for instance, Richard F. Whalen, "Before Looney, Did Anyone Know Oxford was Shakespeare? A Novel, a Song and a Portrait Inventory Suggest So," *Shakespeare Oxford Newsletter*, vol. 31/4 (Autumn 1995): 12-16 and [Letter], *Shakespeare Oxford Newsletter*, vol. 36/3 (Fall 2000): 23-24. Charles V. Berney, "Sir Walter Scott as Paleo-Oxfordian, Part 1," *Shakespeare Oxford Newsletter*, vol. 36/3 (Fall 2000): 17, and Part 2, *Shakespeare Matters*, vol. 3/1 (Fall 2003): 30-32. Peter Dickson, "Oxford's Literary Reputation in the 17ᵗʰ and 18ᵗʰ Centuries," *Shakespeare Oxford Newsletter*, vol. 34/3 (Fall 1998): 14-15.

[26] See, for instance, Thomas Regnier, "Could Shakespeare Think Like a Lawyer," *University of Miami Law Review*, vol. 57/2 (Jan. 2003); "Teaching Shakespeare and the Law," *Shakespeare Matters*, vol. 6/1 (Fall 2006): 1, 11-13; "The Law in *Hamlet*: Death, Property, and the Pursuit of Justice," *Brief Chronicles*, vol. III (Fall 2011): 109-34;

Fellowship during the first years after its formation, and giving many talks, in law schools and universities and elsewhere, to increase public awareness of the Oxfordian claim. He died unexpectedly in 2020.

Morse Johnson's contributions to the movement—by editing the *Shakespeare Oxford Society Newsletter* for a decade and by the many pieces he wrote for it—is a story waiting to be told. So too are the contributions of Tom Bethell, Robert Brazil, Derran K. Charlton, Russell Des Cognets, Richard Desper, Warren Dickinson, W. Ron Hess, Edward Holmes and Peter Moore, and, in Germany, Robert Detobel. The ongoing work of Stephanie Caruana, Keir Cutler, Frank Davis, Michael Delahoyde, Ren Draya, Michael Dudley, Robin Fox, Tom Goff, Steven Steinberg and Peter A. Sturrock in the United States; Sky Gilbert in Canada; Jan Cole, Sally Hazelton, Elizabeth Imlay, Philip Johnson, Eddi Jolly, David Roper and Heward Wilkinson in England; Walter Klier in Austria; Kurt Kreiler in Germany; and Jan Scheffer in the Netherlands—and that of so many others—will be examined when the full story of the second wave of the Oxfordian movement is told in a future volume.

Quick Response to Stratfordian Publications

During the first wave of the movement, individuals responded quickly to inaccuracies in Stratfordian articles and reviews—Looney's twenty letters and articles in 1920 and Percy Allen's scores of letters beginning in 1928, for instance. Today, individuals also respond quickly. Two examples are prominent doubter Diana Price's response[27] to an attack on the Oxfordian idea in *Skeptic Magazine* in 2003,[28] and Oxfordian Bryan H. Wildenthal's[29] to an attack in *Skeptical Inquirer* in 2012.[30]

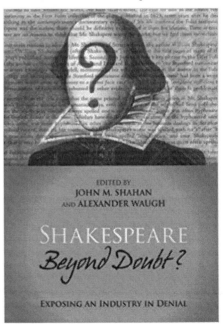

The depth of the Oxfordian movement now makes it possible to respond not just to individual articles but to Stratfordian books with Oxfordian books of superior scholarship.

Exposing an Industry in Denial: Authorship doubters respond to "60 Minutes with Shakespeare," issued by the Shakespeare Birthplace Trust on September 1, 2011 (November 21, 2011). Organized and edited by John M. Shahan on behalf of The Shakespeare Authorship Coalition, this publication was a response by authorship doubters to "60 Minutes with Shakespeare," a video in which sixty questions were posed and answered by "experts" recruited by the Shakespeare Birthplace Trust (SBT). This

---

[27] Diana Price, Letter to Editor, *Skeptic Magazine*, vol. 10/1 (Spring 2003): 22. See also her lengthy piece, "Shakespeare's Authorship and Questions of Evidence," *Skeptic Magazine*, vol. 11/3 (Fall 2005): 10-15.

[28] Scott McCrea, "Two Shakespeares" A Skeptical Analysis of Shakespeare and His Works Reveals the Real Author, *Skeptic Magazine*, vol. 9/4 (Winter 2002).

[29] Bryan H. Wildenthal, letter to Editor, *Skeptical Inquirer*, March-April 2012, p. 62. Wildenthal was the sole defender of the Oxfordian claim against Nickell's sneering ad hominem ridicule of doubters. All the other published letters supported Nickell.

[30] Joe Nickell, "Did Shakespeare Write Shakespeare? Much Ado About Nothing," *Skeptical Inquirer*, Nov.-Dec. 2011.

quick turnaround—only eighty days after the Trust's presentation—was a masterly presentation of evidence and well-reasoned arguments that showed many of the SBT responders to be ill-informed about the issues they had addressed.

Shakespeare Beyond Doubt? Exposing an Industry in Denial (2013). Edited by John M. Shahan and Alexander Waugh, this publication of The Shakespeare Authorship Coalition was a quick and withering reply to the book *Shakespeare Beyond Doubt: Evidence, Argument, Controversy* edited by Paul Edmondson and Stanley Wells. See Chapter 24.

Contested Year: An Anthology of Critical Reviews and Corrections to Each Chapter of James Shapiro's The Year of Lear: Shakespeare in 1606, edited by Mark Anderson, Alexander Waugh & Alex McNeil (2016). This response to Shapiro's book was organized quickly as a corrective to it. The editors recruited twenty international Shakespearean scholars, who responded to every chapter of Shapiro's book, showing how he repeatedly presented speculations as though they were proven facts, failed to acknowledge evidence that was contrary or detrimental to his thesis and repeatedly made false assertions and unsupported statements.

The 1623 Shakespeare First Folio: A Minority Report (2016). A special issue of *Brief Chronicles* edited by Roger Stritmatter in response to the Folger Shakespeare Library's First Folio Tour, it pointed out the absurdity of commemorating the 400th anniversary of the death of William Shakspere with exhibitions on the First Folio, the collection of Shakespeare's works published seven years after Shakspere's death, that provided very little information about the man himself. See Chapter 24.

Inroads Into Academia

Beyond the two major efforts to establish master's degree programs in authorship studies at Brunel University (by Dr. William Leahy) and at Concordia University (by Dr. Daniel Wright) already noted, a number of professors and teachers have taught courses on the subject or brought significant information about it into courses on related subjects.

Don Rubin taught courses on the authorship question for several years while Chair of the Department of Theatre at York University in Toronto. In an article in *The Oxfordian*, he provided an outline of what subjects were addressed, the course reading list and a description of the papers and presentations required of students—information useful for others wanting to teach similar courses.[31]

Especially interesting was his recounting of the difficulties—often career-ending for young professors—encountered when one's Oxfordian beliefs, or even mere doubts about Shakspere's authorship, become known. He described how he was able to overcome departmental opposition to the course by framing it not as an attack on William of Stratford or as a study of Oxford as Shakespeare, but "as a course looking into arguments generally around the Shakespearean Authorship Question, a question that was becoming of wider and wider interest" (72). That line of argument was persuasive because the university "like[s] to feel it is *au courant*, that it is relevant and cutting edge. . . . [G]iven the number of books coming out every year on the issue, how can any university English or Theatre Department continue to ignore it? . . . [They do so] at their intellectual risk today." This approach was an effective way "to get the authorship question taken seriously in both the academic world and the wider sphere" (65), Rubin explained, because it present[ed] the authorship question "in a way that [was] both accessible and

---

[31] Don Rubin, "Spinning Shakespeare," *The Oxfordian*, vol. 17 (2015): 63-77.

[didn't] threaten the modest knowledge someone might already have" (71).

James Norwood, who taught humanities and the performing arts for twenty-six years at the University of Minnesota, offered a semester course on the Shake-speare authorship question for more than a decade.

Felicia Londré, Curators' Distinguished Professor Emerita of Theater, University of Missouri-Kansas City, actively promoted awareness of the authorship question for thirty years. In addition to lectures on the subject in theater classes, since 1991 she has given an annual lecture, "The Questionable Identity of Shake-speare," open to the entire student body. The 70-minute lecture (with PowerPoint slides) is designed to

The Questionable Identity of Shakespeare

Felicia Londré's annual lecture at UMKC on the Shakespeare authorship question will be presented at

3:30 - 4:45 p.m.
Monday 4 November 2019
UMKC campus: Miller Nichols Learning Center 451

This 65-minute slide presentation surveys the evidence relating to the authorship of the plays and sonnets of the author known as William Shake-speare. **Whodunnit???** Was it William Shaksper of Stratford-upon-Avon or was it Edward De Vere, 17th Earl of Oxford?

Felicia Londré has presented this lecture to open-minded intellectuals (and others) in the capitals of Europe and Asia as well as in Chicago and Kalamazoo. YOU are now invited to attend—**admission FREE**—the same lecture that has often elicited big bucks, not to mention the tears and laughter of freshly tapped hearts and minds!

There will be handouts and time for questions afterward. **This is your chance** to get the basic information that will allow you to weigh the evidence and **form your own opinion!**

introduce the issue to those not familiar with it. Most of the talk focuses on biographical and textual evidence for Oxford. A flier for one of the talks is reprinted nearby. Londré has given similar talks at dozens of universities and Shakespeare conferences around the United States, and in London, Budapest, Tokyo and Beijing.

Greater Self-Awareness

The Oxfordian movement has become more aware of its own history. One sign of that awareness is the creation of a Data Preservation Committee by the Shakespeare Oxford Fellowship. A brainchild of Kathryn Sharpe, its original mission was to make arrangements with owners of websites and blogs so that the Oxfordian content on them would not be lost. In several cases owners had spent decades ferreting out documents and posting the results of their research, resulting in irreplaceable troves of important materials. The Committee soon widened its mandate to preserve important print materials (books, letters, pamphlets, organizational records) as well; work is underway to determine what Oxfordian documents from the past century are worth preserving, and then to collect, store and share them. This preservation effort gives the SOF a third core undertaking alongside its research and public engagement activities.[32]

The forty-year hiatus in the Oxfordian movement was unfortunate, as it allowed the large bulk of papers from the first generations to slip away. Officers of the Shakespeare Fellowship in the 1950s did not know the history of their own organization's publications or have copies of them. Fellowship Secretary Gwynneth M. Bowen wrote in 1959 that "The

---

[32] The new Committee is working closely with the Shakespeare Online Authorship Resources (SOAR) online database noted in Chapter 19. It's founder, Bill Boyle, is a member of the Committee.

first *News-Letter* must have appeared towards the end of 1936, or early in 1937—No. 4 was dated July—but no copies of pre-war *News-Letters* can be traced. If any still exist we should be very glad to have them for the archives."[33]

The following is a list of items from the first quarter-century of the Oxfordian movement worth preserving, and their current status:

> ➤ J. Thomas Looney's *"Shakespeare" Identified* (1920) and *The Poems of Edward de Vere* (1921). Looney's first book was out of print in the United States by 1927 and in England by 1940. The second U.S. edition, published in 1949, was soon out of print. The third U.S. edition, published in 1975, omitted important parts of the book and was no longer marketed by the publisher by the end of the twentieth century. The Centenary edition, with fully restored text, was published in 2018. *The Poems of Edward de Vere* went out of print soon after it was published in 1921. It was reprinted in 1975, but much of Looney's prefatory material was omitted and the rest edited without notice to the reader. The full prefatory materials became available again in 2019 with the publication of *"Shakespeare" Revealed: The Collected Articles and Published Letters of J. Thomas Looney*. In addition, Looney's personal copy of the book, with his many handwritten notes penciled into the margins, was found in 2019.

> ➤ J. Thomas Looney's forty-eight articles and letters to editors, 1920-1924. Oxfordians who became active in the Shakespeare Fellowship in 1922 or later—including Col. Ward—were apparently unaware of the twenty or more letters and articles that Looney sent to publications in 1920 and 1921. Of the twenty-five or so additional articles he wrote after 1922, memory of only five survived and later Oxfordians were largely unaware even of them.[34] American Oxfordian Gordon Cyr was to write in 1976 that "once having announced his candidate, Looney did little to advance the cause other than a subsequent publication of all of the known poetry of Edward de Vere."[35] My work to rediscover, collect and publish Looney's fifty-three shorter pieces—in *"Shakespeare" Revealed: The Collected Articles and Published Letters of J. Thomas Looney* (2019)—resulted in a sea change in assessments of him.

> ➤ J. Thomas Looney's library of books, and his papers, correspondence and media clippings. These were largely discarded after the death of Looney's widow, Elizabeth, in 1950 and the sale of their house in 1952. A small number of items— 386 pieces totaling 1,940 pages—inadvertently survived and were discovered early in 2019, but they were just a fraction of what must have been in Looney's possession at the time of his death (see Preface).

> ➤ The Shakespeare Fellowship's *Circulars* and *Notices to Members* (1922-1936). These were completely forgotten until 2018. Several dozen of them have survived in the Archives of the Shakespearean Authorship Trust in the library at Brunel

---

[33] Gwynneth W. Bowen, "Ave Atque Vale," *Shakespearean Authorship Review*, no. 1 (Spring 1959): 5.

[34] The five of Looney's articles of which memory survived were his lengthy pieces in *The National Review* (February 1922) and in *The Golden Hind* (October 1922), and the three pieces in the American *News-Letter* in 1940 and 1941.. The three pieces that appeared in *The Freethinker* in 1923 were known of in 1952, when excerpts were published in the September issue of the *News-Letter* but then forgotten again.

[35] Gordon C. Cyr, "Book Review," *Shakespeare Oxford Society Newsletter*, Spring 1976, p. 5.

University; a few others are in the Katharine E. Eggar Archives in the University of London's Senate House Library.

➤ Underline: The Shakespeare Fellowship's columns in *The Hackney Spectator* (1922), its page in *The Shakespeare Pictorial* (1929-1936) and articles and letters by Shakespeare Fellowship officers on *The East Anglian Magazine's* "Shakespearean Page" (1937-1941). I tracked down all 300 of these pieces and am preparing them, along with all known *Shakespeare Fellowship Circulars* and *Notices*, for publication.

➤ The Shakespeare Fellowship *News-Letter* (1937-1958) of the English branch and of the American branch (1939-1943) and *The Shakespeare Fellowship Quarterly* (1944-1948) which succeeded the American *News-Letter.* Complete sets of these publications (except for one missing issue of the English *News-Letter*) have been collected and preserved by Bill Boyle and are now available on the SOF website and through SOAR. Paper copies of many issues exist in the Oxfordian archives at Brunel University.

➤ Oxfordian correspondence (1920-1945). More than 500 letters are known of, and more than 400 have been collected and transcribed. An annotated collection of them is being prepared, which will give insights into the thinking of the first generations of Oxfordians. It is possible that many more letters will come to light.

➤ The papers or archives of prominent early Oxfordians. The papers of Col. Ward and Capt. Ward were not secured when Capt. Ward died at the end of 1945. Surely they had kept extensive files about the activities of the Shakespeare Fellowship, and Col. Ward's correspondence was voluminous. No collection of papers would be more important to locate than these.

➤ The papers of Percy Allen, who died in 1959, would also be invaluable. Did no one at the time realize the value of preserving the papers of the Oxfordian scholar who had been its most prolific author and public speaker? He, like Col. Ward, was an inveterate letter writer and kept carbon copies of the letters he sent, so both directions of his correspondence would have been among his papers. He also subscribed to a clipping service that monitored the press for pieces on the Oxfordian idea; his files would presumably have contained the most comprehensive record of Oxfordian publications over a period of several decades.

➤ The papers of other early Oxfordians would also be of great value in providing further information on the early years, especially those of Adm. Hubert Holland, Col. Montagu Douglas, Eva Turner Clark and Prof. Louis P. Bénézet. As would those of persons who wrote articles and were in correspondence with Looney, including Gelett Burgess, Carolyn Wells and Margaret L. Knapp. The papers of Charles Wisner Barrell (or at least a large quantity of them) have survived, but haven't yet been examined.

➤ Archives of notable Shakespeare scholars, Stratfordian and Baconian. Looney was in correspondence with dozens of people, including Sir George Greenwood, Sir Sidney Lee and others who were not Oxfordians. Copies of many of their letters to him have survived; what about his letters to them? Their archives should be located and searched so that the entire correspondence can be examined.

> ➢ The eighty or so books of special importance to Oxfordians published between 1920 and 1945. Copies of most exist in the Oxfordian archives at Brunel University, and in the Archives of Gerald H. Rendall and Katharine E. Eggar. A list of them is in *An Index to Oxfordian Publications*. Occasionally copies are offered for sale by online booksellers.

> ➢ The forty or more pamphlets published by Oxfordian scholars 1920-1945. Copies of them exist in one archive or another in London and Liverpool.

> ➢ The 4,000 other articles and letters to editors published about the Oxfordian claim 1920-1948. These appeared in newspapers, literary magazines and academic journals. Several hundred were by Oxfordian scholars such as Percy Allen; the rest were reviews of Oxfordian's books, reports on Oxfordian activities, examinations of the Oxfordian claim and letters to editors. I have obtained copies of almost all known items; they were of great value in preparing this book.

> ➢ Other Oxfordian ephemera 1920-1945. These include the menu cards from early Oxfordian dinners, advertising cards for Fellowship lectures and related items. Those that have survived are in the archives.

Archives of Oxfordian Materials

The most notable collections of Oxfordian materials from the 1920-1945 period in England are located at Brunel University, the University of London and the University of Liverpool. Collectively they hold nearly 2,400 items—letters, media clippings, notes and manuscripts—of special interest to Oxfordians.

Archive	Oxfordian Ephemera	Books
Shakespearean Authorship Trust Archives, Brunel U.	1,070	249
De Vere Society Archives, Brunel University	398	192
Brunel University and not yet identified	53	925
Brunel University Subtotal	*1,521*	*1,366*
Katharine E. Eggar Archives, U. of London	545	251
Gerald H. Rendall Archives, U. of Liverpool	309	126
Totals	**2,375**	**1,743**

The Oxfordian Archives in the Special Collections Room of the library at Brunel University located in Uxbridge, just outside London. This is the largest collection of Oxfordian materials known to exist. Among its holdings are the papers of the Shakespearean Authorship Trust (SAT), a successor to the Shakespeare Fellowship founded by Col. Bernard R. Ward, and the archives of the De Vere Society founded in 1986. Of prime importance are two large red albums of more than one hundred pages each, holding more than 500 irreplaceable Oxfordian items from the periods 1922 to 1929 and 1930 to 1936. Other items of special importance are a notebook containing twenty or so reviews of Capt. Bernard M. Ward's biography *The Seventeenth Earl of Oxford*, and the unpublished manuscript of a book by Adm. Hubert H. Holland.

The Gerald H. Rendall Archives in the Special Collections Section of the Sydney Jones Library at the University of Liverpool. Rendall, one of the founders of the university, had made arrangements for it to house his papers after his death. This archive consists of six boxes of materials, mostly Oxfordian. They include several hundred pages of notes that Rendall made while writing his books and pamphlets, and several hundred other items, including correspondence, articles and pamphlets, many unavailable elsewhere. Rendall's collection of 126 books on the authorship question are located in another part of the Special Collections area. All materials are available for examination by appointment.

The Katharine E. Eggar Archives in the Special Collections Section of the Senate House Library at the University of London. The archive consists of twenty-eight boxes of manuscripts, notes, letters, and other documents from the 1910s through the late 1950s. Among hundreds of pieces of Oxfordian ephemera are thirty letters from J. Thomas Looney addressing important developments in the Oxfordian movement during the 1920s and 1930s—the largest collection of his Oxfordian letters known to exist. It also contains the manuscripts of dozens of talks Eggar gave on Oxfordian subjects but didn't publish, and the manuscript of her unpublished book, *The Life of Edward de Vere*.

The British Library. Though not an Oxfordian archive *per se*, the British Library holds a vast number of Oxfordian items not available elsewhere. Among them is the only known complete collection of *The Hackney Spectator*, which ran a column by the Shakespeare Fellowship from 1922 to 1925. It also houses a complete collection of *The East Anglian Magazine*, which ran many Oxfordian articles from 1937 to 1941, and a complete set of *The Freethinker*, with articles by J. Thomas Looney and other Oxfordians. Thousands of other important articles exist in its newspaper and periodical files.

Efforts to Recover Early Oxfordian Materials

In addition to SOAR (mentioned above), the most important efforts to recover and make available older Oxfordian articles not yet mentioned include the following:

- ✓ *The Shakespeare Controversy: An Analysis of the Authorship Theories* (1991, second edition 2009) by Warren Hope and Kim Holston. This book documents and critically assesses the leading theories on the Shakespeare authorship question since modern doubts were first expressed by Delia Bacon in the 1850s. Its historical overview and analysis, combined with the annotated bibliography of more than 300 articles and books make it the best place to begin for anyone interested in acquiring an overview of the subject.

- ✓ *Building the Case for Edward de Vere as Shakespeare* (2009, 2014) is a ten-volume anthology compiled and edited by Paul H. Altrocchi, with Hank Whittemore as co-editor of the first five volumes. This collection of some 550 important articles from the earliest days of the movement through the early years of the twenty-first century is an invaluable resource. See nearby textbox.

- ✓ *An Index to Oxfordian Publications*, 4th Edition (2017), edited by me. This index lists more than 9,000 articles and books of special interest to Oxfordians. It has listings sorted by author's name as well as by publication, including every newspaper and journal that ran pieces on the Oxfordian thesis. Another section lists reviews for every Oxfordian book. The *Index* serves as a complement to SOAR, which also includes all items in it. The forthcoming edition will include several thousand more listings of items uncovered while researching this book.

Collections of more recent Oxfordian items

- ✓ *Great Oxford: Essays on the Life and Work of Edward de Vere* (2004), General

Editor: Richard C. W. Malim. This collection of thirty-nine 39 essays from the *De Vere Society Newsletter* was prepared on the occasion of the 250th anniversary of Oxford's death. A second edition is underway.

✓ *"Report my Cause Aright:" The Shakespeare Oxford Society Fiftieth Anniversary Anthology* (2007). This collection contains key articles from the first decades of *The Shakespeare Oxford Newsletter*, revised and updated. As its editors explained, "In our fiftieth anniversary year, it is appropriate for us to look back and pay tribute to those who came before us. The small band of intrepid souls who first founded and then conscientiously nurtured our society for the past five decades, often through periods of great difficulty, deserve our undying respect and gratitude" (5).

✓ The "How I Became an Oxfordian" series of articles on the SOF website, edited by Robert Meyers, shows how valuable it would be to conduct more extensive interviews with long-time Oxfordians.

Building the Case for Edward de Vere as Shakespeare: A Series of Volumes Devoted to Shakespeare Authorship Research

Edited by Paul H. Altrocchi (vol. 1-5 co-edited by Hank Whittemore)

Through the end of the first wave of the Oxfordian movement (to 1945/48) (190 pieces)

Volume 1: The Great Shakespeare Hoax (2009)
> [Articles concerning the growing disbelief in the Stratford man as Shakespeare]

Volume 2: Nothing Truer Than Truth (2009)
> [Authorship articles from England in the 1930s and from *The Shakespeare Fellowship News-Letters* from the American Branch, 1939-1943]

Volume 3: Shine Forth (2009)
> [Articles from *The Shakespeare Fellowship Quarterly*, 1943-1947]

Volume 4: My Name Be Buried (2009)
> [Articles from *The Shakespeare Fellowship Quarterly*, 1947-1948 and from the English *Shakespeare Fellowship News-Letters* after the Second World War]

During the lull (mid-1940s to mid-1984) (140 pieces)

Volume 5: So Richly Spun (2009)
> [From *The Shakespearean Authorship Review*, 1959-1973]

Volume 6: Wonder of Our Stage (2014) [First Half]
> [Articles from *The Shakespeare Oxford Newsletter*, 1965-1984]

After publication of *The Mysterious William Shakespeare* (mid-1984 onwards) (300 pieces)

Volume 6: Wonder of Our Stage (2014) [Second Half]
> [Articles from *The Shakespeare Oxford Newsletter*, 1984-1990]

Volume 7: Avalanche of Falsity (2014)
> [Articles from *The Shakespeare Oxford Newsletter*, 1990-1997]

Volume 8: To All the World Must Die (2014)
> [Articles from *The Shakespeare Oxford Newsletter*, *The Elizabethan Review* and *The Pennsylvania Law Review* and *The Tennessee Law Review*, 1993-2004]

Volume 9: Soul of the Age (2014)
> [Articles from *The Shakespeare Oxford Newsletter*, *Shakespeare Matters*, *The Oxfordian* and *Brief Chronicles*, 1995-2013]

Volume 10: Moniment (2014)
> [Articles from *The Shakespeare Oxford Newsletter*, *Shakespeare Matters*, *Brief Chronicles* and *The Tennessee Law Review*, 2002-2011]

Looney Pronunciation

Oxfordians had been misled by statements made by Charles Wisner Barrell, which implied that the name Looney should be pronounced to rhyme with "Tony" or "bony." It is understandable that Barrell and others wanted to direct attention away from pronouncing it "looney" and the expected jokes that would be made by those who wanted to disparage the movement.

The correct pronunciation of the surname rhymes with names like Rooney and Clooney. This was discovered by Kathryn Sharpe of the Shakespeare Oxford Fellowship, after conversations with Looney's grandson. I have verified it as well. That pronunciation was confirmed by another descendant of the family who grew up in the Low Fell district of Gateshead where Looney lived the last thirty years of his life. She further noted that the Looney children were often ridiculed by school mates because of their family name.

It is to the credit of the Oxfordian movement that it moved quickly to correct this historic error once it was discovered.

Observations

Since the founding of the Shakespeare Fellowship in November 1922, every Oxfordian researcher and scholar has had the option of interacting with an Oxfordian organization; they were not completely on their own as Looney had been. Yet most scholars have worked in only loose affiliation with those organizations even when they have been members—even officers—of them. That was true of Capt. Ward, whose investigations into the public records resulted in *The Seventeenth Earl of Oxford 1550-1604* in 1928. It was true of Mark Anderson, whose investigations resulted in *"Shakespeare" By Another Name: The Life of Edward de Vere, Earl of Oxford, the Man Who was Shakespeare* in 2005. And it was true of Charlton Ogburn. As historian David McCullough explained in his foreword to *The Mysterious William Shakespeare*, "that Charlton Ogburn persisted and succeeded in so monumental a task, all alone, without institutional backing, without the support or blessing of academia, makes the accomplishment all the more extraordinary."[36] (The Oxfordian community that existed at that time, before the rise of the second wave, was very small; only twelve people attended the SOS annual conference in 1980.)

The founders of the Shakespeare Fellowship worked as individuals, both before and after the organization was established. None of them were paid employees of the Fellowship or acted on instructions from it. That was true of Col. Ward, Percy Allen and Gerald Rendall in England, and of Eva Turner Clark, Charles Wisner Barrell and Louis Bénézet in the United States. Those who set up branches of the Fellowship in several cities in England during the 1930s acted on their own initiative.

Individuals and institutions bring different qualities to the movement, and the movement has been most productive when they have worked effectively together.

Individuals bring initiative and inspiration to their work; they make the discoveries and take the actions that move the Oxfordian ball forward. They do that in part by bringing unique mixes of knowledge, expertise, perspectives and approaches to their work. Looney brought an approach colored by Positivist intellectual training. Col. Ward brought not only the sensitivities of a poet but also the capabilities of a military commander. Both he and Capt. Ward brought extensive knowledge of the Elizabethan era.

---

[36] Charlton Ogburn, *The Mysterious William Shakespeare* (1992), p. x.

Percy Allen approached the issue with the insight of a drama critic gained through decades of reviewing live performances of Shakespeare's plays. Gerald Rendall, one of the most respected scholarly minds in England, brought skills honed through a lifetime of scholarly achievements. Charles Wisner Barrell brought photographic expertise acquired through decades of experience, and literary connections developed as a freelance writer that enabled him to place his pieces in *The Saturday Review of Literature* in 1937 and *Scientific American* in 1940.

This variety of experiences and expertise gave the Oxfordian movement advantages over the Stratfordians. As Looney had recognized, the authorship question "is not . . . strictly speaking a literary problem."[37] The French scholar Georges Lambin similarly concluded that "the Shakespeare mystery" will "be definitely resolved" only when the issue "escape[s] the somewhat narrow and jealous competence of the exclusive specialist in literary studies."[38]

Oxfordian organizations bring complementary qualities. They facilitate the sharing of information, discoveries and views of individual scholars through newsletters, journals and websites. Their conferences, which provide the venues at which individual scholars can get together in collegial surroundings, are invaluable. Through interactions in such settings, weaker ideas fall by the wayside and stronger ones gain adherents. That is how knowledge grows and spreads.

Institutions also coordinate efforts to address new targets of opportunity that arise from individual initiative but are too big for individuals to handle effectively. Coordinating Charles Beauclerk's speaking tours in the 1990s is one example. John Louther conceived the idea after observing Beauclerk's effective talks at the Folger Shakespeare Library and Harvard University. Leaping into action, he convinced Beauclerk to reorganize his life for several years, convinced the SOS to engage in the fundraising needed to support the tours and convinced Oxfordian Trudy Atkins in Greensboro, North Carolina, to provide logistical support and handle much of the correspondence with local sponsors. Largely forgotten today, Louther was the source of the entrepreneurial energy that made the tours a reality. Charles Beauclerk described him this way: "His energy, without which the tour would never have happened, had something elemental about it, and prompted Charlton Ogburn to exclaim, 'Are you a man or a storm at sea?'"[39] But the tours would not have happened without institutional support.

This informal arrangement of individuals working independently within a context that Oxfordian organizations help frame works when organizations are not top-down, but bottom up. Ideas rise up from individuals, who retain freedom of action, deciding for themselves which aspects of the Oxfordian claim merit study and how best to engage the public and academia. This style contrasts significantly with the more formal Stratfordian institutions in and outside of academia. Symbiosis in the Oxfordian world exists because individuals are not forced to adopt a party line or defend institutional interests as in academia.

Without individuals' initiative and energy, organizations become moribund. Without the organization, individuals become isolated. To understand how their activities dovetail

---

[37] J. Thomas Looney, *"Shakespeare" Identified* (2018), p. 71.
[38] Georges Lambin, quoted in Gary Goldstein, *Reflections on the True Shakespeare* (2016), p. 44.
[39] Charles Beauclerk, "John Louther: A Recollection," *Shakespeare Oxford Newsletter*, vol. 39/2 (Spring 2003): 20.

and reinforce each other, consider this military analogy. The initiative displayed by individual Oxfordians is similar to that shown by General George Patton when he drove the U.S. Third Army deep into Germany in 1945, surprising not only the Germans but also his own central command with his boldness. Yet even Patton had to stop at some point to wait for others to resupply him. The Oxfordian organizations are like the larger allied forces, bringing up the rear, managing logistics and supply chains. They support the innovative work of individuals, who, like the bit of the drill, are most effective with the power of the machinery behind them. Again, the movement has been most effective when individuals and organizations have worked in loose affiliation.

Oxfordian organizations can, but rarely have, engaged in strategic thinking. Doing so would be a two-edged sword. Strategic thinking is valuable when it gets the organization and movement aimed in the right direction. But too much top-down direction can inhibit scholars from pursuing individual interests and dampen members' enthusiasm.

But this freedom also can be a double-edged sword. The lack of a single set of beliefs on some matters within the Oxfordian community is confusing for outsiders seeking to understand the Oxfordian claim. That they get different answers from different Oxfordians is one of the problems with the persuasiveness of the Oxfordian message. In contrast, Stratfordians have both a top-down organization and a largely unified message because they ignore facts they don't want to acknowledge. Oxfordians, being truth seekers, can't do that. It would be beneficial to have brainstorming sessions at Oxfordian conferences to sort through the most difficult questions and determine just where specifically the points of disagreement are, and why. Similar sessions could thrash out differences over how best to engage academia and the public.

It is tempting to think that with more central control the Oxfordian movement would be more effective. But that is not necessarily true. The movement has always been more of a loose collection of individuals working on their own than a coordinated movement. I believe it should remain this way. Individuals can think boldly and take bold actions. Institutions by their very nature are timid, watching their flanks, and the larger they become the more extensively that mindset prevails. If an Oxfordian organization or the movement as a whole ever becomes monolithic on important issues, either the issues will have been resolved and the work of the movement finished, or the organization will have succumbed to tunnel vision and group-think, with institutional death imminent.

Because the Oxfordian movement draws its strength from the initiative and efforts of individuals, the key to its future is drawing into it individuals with those key qualities. The way forward is not for organizations themselves to become more proactive in a big way, but to continue to support individuals in the movement who are, just as it supported the Beauclerk tour twenty-five years ago. It must limit itself chiefly to herding cats or risk stultification. Oxfordians are indeed cats, not sheep.

Has the Oxfordian Movement Peaked? Institutional Resistance Remains Strong

The first wave of the Oxfordian movement peaked in 1940, twenty years after the publication of *"Shakespeare" Identified*, at least as far as public recognition of the Oxfordian claim was concerned. It didn't hit that level of public interest again until the end of the 1980s, a gap of nearly fifty years. The current wave, which began in 1984-85, has lasted more than thirty-five years, far longer than the first wave. It is not out of bounds to ask if the second wave has peaked or is showing signs of peaking.

The movement might have crested in the mid- to late 1990s if not for the new technology of the Internet. Websites, blogs and list servs all gave a boost to the movement that kept momentum high. A cresting might also have occurred just after 2012—after the closing of the Shakespeare Authorship Studies Centre at Concordia University and the suspension of the master's degree programs in authorship studies there and at Brunel University—but again technology provided a boost, in the form of self-publishing. New user-friendly platforms created opportunities for getting the Oxfordian word out by those without much technical expertise or funding. The Centenary edition of *"Shakespeare" Identified* that brought Looney's book back into print in 2018 is one example of how effective this platform can be.

Nevertheless there are signs that a peak might be approaching. One is that the major events that launched the second wave of the Oxfordian movement occurred *more than thirty years ago*:

- Charlton Ogburn's *The Mysterious William Shakespeare* was published in 1984—thirty-seven years ago.

- The Supreme Court Justices' moot court was held in 1987—thirty-four years ago.

- "The Shakespeare Mystery" was broadcast on *Frontline* in 1989—thirty-two years ago.

Many Oxfordians who first learned of Edward de Vere's authorship from those events are now thirty years older. Actuarial tables tell us to expect a reduction in their numbers over the coming decade.

Of course since then many important books have been published and video programs broadcast, but none captured the public imagination the way those earlier events did.

Consider also that there has been a move away from teaching Shakespeare in schools and colleges. Most university English departments no longer require even English majors to take a course on Shakespeare. That move, together with the closing of the Shakespeare Authorship Studies Centre and the discontinuance of the two master's degree programs are signs that academia has not become significantly more receptive to the authorship question.

Despite the apparently widespread public awareness of the Oxfordian claim, not everybody has heard of it. On a 2012 episode of the TV game show *Jeopardy!* one of the "answers" was: "The 2011 film *Anonymous* claimed it was this man, not Shakespeare, who actually wrote the works of Shakespeare." The correct response was, of course, "Who was Edward de Vere, 17th Earl of Oxford?" However, none of the three contestants even ventured a guess. This from *Jeopardy!* contestants, who often appear to know everything about everything![40]

Consider how completely academia shoughs off new findings that challenge the Stratfordian paradigm. Alexander Waugh recently discovered that "Avon" was the nickname used by the nobility in Oxford's day for Hampton Palace, the venue for many royal theatrical performances, which gives a new connotation to the phrase "Sweet Swan of Avon" in the First Folio. Michael Delahoyde and Coleen Moriarty recently uncovered a document in Venice giving the Earl of Oxford access to the Doge's private quarters in order to see the works of art displayed there. At that time (1575) Titian's portrait of Venus

---

[40] Even if the contestants hadn't seen *Anonymous*, one would have thought they would be aware of one of the most heavily reviewed "Shakespeare' events of the year, with many newspapers and literary journals running reviews and editorials.

and Adonis, newly painted, was on public display in Venice; that particular copy was the only one showing Adonis wearing a cap or bonnet, just as Shakespeare would later describe him. All this strengthens ties between Oxford and Shakespeare's works.

What was academia's response to these two sensational discoveries? It had no response. This should be a further wake-up call, if one is needed, about academia's refusal to see what it doesn't want to see.

Unlike eighty years ago, the danger today is not that the Oxfordian movement will wither away, but rather that it will drift along without storming academia. The movement has made great progress in overcoming the Human Resistance, the normal resistance to new ideas that decreases over time as people become more familiar with them. The same is true of the Cognitive Resistance; progress has been made as people have had time to understand more deeply the full impact of the Oxfordian claim.

But, as at the peak of the first wave, the movement has not made much progress in overcoming Institutional Resistance. Academia remains adamant that the authorship question is not worthy of serious examination. Teachers and professors continue to teach their students that Shakespeare's works were written by the man from Stratford, and the media largely continues to take its lead from them. Until the Oxfordian idea conquers academia, the danger exists that the movement's momentum could be stalled.

In sum, the Oxfordian movement today is far stronger than it was at the peak of the first wave in 1940. It is still on the upward swing that began at the end of 1984. The depth in the number of Oxfordian organizations, scholars and researchers is at an all-time high, as is the number of people aware of the Oxfordian thesis. The work under way to uncover, recover and preserve early Oxfordian materials is, I believe, a sign that the movement has come of age. It is now aware of itself as a movement with a history stretching back a full century that must be preserved and is making great strides in doing so.

All these are healthy signs indicating that the Oxfordian movement is not only not going away but is rising to new heights of purposefulness and determination. No crest or peak is yet in sight, although there are always reasons for concern.

One of those reasons arises from within the movement itself: disagreements between Oxfordians over answers to the "why" and "how" questions that so wracked the movement in its first wave. That topic is addressed in the following chapter.

21

The Why and How Questions and the Crisis of 2001

The Oxfordian Movement Today: The Why and How Questions

The questions of why Oxford hid his authorship and how such an extensive effort to keep it hidden could have succeeded—and the answers to them proposed by Percy Allen and Capt. Bernard M. Ward that caused a severe crisis within the Shakespeare Fellowship in the 1930s—did not go away. Or rather, they did go away but then returned—twice.[1]

After Allen's final writings on the subject in his 1943 pamphlet *Who Were the Dark Lady and Fair Youth of the Sonnets?*, the Dynastic Succession Theory—the idea that the third Earl of Southampton was the illegitimate son of Queen Elizabeth and Edward de Vere and that his parentage was somehow related to the necessity of hiding Oxford's authorship of the works now known as Shakespeare's—disappeared for nine years.[2] It returned after having been independently formulated by Dorothy and Charlton Ogburn (Sr.), who published their account of it in their 1,300-page book *This Star of England* in October 1952. After the final reviews of that book appeared in the English *Shakespeare Fellowship News-Letter* in 1954, with only two exceptions,[3] no mention was made of the idea in Oxfordian publications for more than thirty years, until it resurfaced in Charlton Ogburn, Jr.'s *The Mysterious William Shakespeare* in late 1984.[4]

Ogburn had wanted to avoid presenting the Dynastic Succession idea in his book, but found that "it could not be avoided," that he "had to confront it squarely." He did so, summarizing "the evidence from Shakespeare's writing that Henry Wriothesley was the son of Elizbeth and Oxford."[5] In the 1984 edition Ogburn took a neutral stance:

> The emotional apogee between Oxford and Elizabeth probably was reached sometime in 1572 or 1573. During this period a boy was conceived who would be given the name of Henry Wriothesley and later the title of 3rd Earl of

---

[1] This theory did not have a name during the first wave of the Oxfordian movement that ended in the mid-1940s. Capt. Ward sometimes referred to it as "Percy Allen's theory," and he and others sometimes called it "the Southampton theory." I call it the Dynastic Succession theory for reasons explained in Chapter 10. Since the 1990s the idea has often been referred to as the "Prince Tudor theory," "PT," and the "Tudor Heir theory."

[2] It might have resurfaced in the middle of that nine-year period. Disagreements over answers to the why question between Charles Wisner Barrell and Charlton Ogburn, Sr., were rumored to have been a significant cause of the demise of the Shakespeare Fellowship in the United States, as noted in Chapter 18.

[3] The only known exceptions are 1) a short except in *The Shakespeare Oxford Newsletter* from *The New York Times's* Nov. 29, 1971 (p. 57), review of Gertrude Gale's play *Masquerade*, based on the Dynastic Succession thesis, which had recently been performed in New York. I suspect that Gertrude Gale was really Gertrude Ford and *Masquerade* was her musical *Shakespeare and Elizabeth Unmasked*, published in 1968, under new names; and 2) William Plumer Fowler, "Shake-speare's Heart Unlocked," *Shakespeare Oxford Society Newsletter*, vol. 18/4 (Fall 1982): 1-7.

[4] Born Charlton Ogburn, Jr., he later dropped the "Jr." In this book I use "Jr." only when necessary to distinguish him from his father.

[5] Charlton Ogburn, *The Mysterious William Shakespeare* (1984), p. 519.

Southampton. Was there a causal relationship? Some have been led to believe so as the only way of accounting for the tenor of the *Sonnets*. My inability to think of any other is balanced by my inability to regard such a theory of Southampton's parentage as other than far-fetched—which is not, however, to say impossible. As I stipulated in bringing up the theory before, I take no position on it. (519)

By the time of the second edition in 1992, Ogburn had encountered new information that led him, reluctantly, to come out in support of the theory.

> Having learned that on the day Oxford died, 24 June 1604, King James had Southampton imprisoned, only to release him the next day, I can think of but one explanation: the King's fear that with Oxford's restraining hand removed, the young Earl might claim the throne, an intention he must have immediately disavowed.
>
> In her *Shakespeare and the Tudor Rose* (1991), Elisabeth Sears, of Boxford, Massachusetts, explores the subject to further arresting affect.[6]

Since then the idea has been addressed in more than a dozen Oxfordian books and in more than 200 articles and letters in Oxfordian periodicals.

Discussion heated up during the late 1990s and caused such divisions within the Shakespeare Oxford Society (SOS) that it was one of the principal reasons why a second American Oxfordian organization was formed in the summer of 2001. The havoc resembled that of 1936, described in Chapter 10, when two of the Shakespeare Fellowship's Board members—Gerald H. Rendall and Katharine E. Eggar—resigned from the organization. Rendall never rejoined, though he did become a member of the American branch in the early 1940s. Eggar rejoined the English organization in the late 1940s and led its Edward de Vere Study Group in the 1950s.

Following the 2001 crisis the Shakespeare Oxford Society retained its name, while the new organization adopted the name used by the first two Oxfordian organizations, the Shakespeare Fellowship. The two organizations operated independently, each producing its own newsletter and peer-reviewed journal and holding separate annual conferences for several years before agreeing to hold joint conferences beginning in 2005. The two groups reunited in 2013, merging to form a new organization called the Shakespeare Oxford Fellowship (SOF). But disagreements over the answers to the why and how questions have not subsided; every issue of the SOF *Newsletter* in 2020 had considerable back and forth on how best to deal with those questions.

It is helpful to have in mind the principal responses to the why and how questions made by Oxfordians today. As to "why," a minority hold that the two motives presented by J. Thomas Looney are sufficient to answer the question: 1) as the most senior earl in the court and the Lord Great Chamberlain of the realm in a society with a strictly hierarchical social structure, Oxford could not take any action that would weaken that structure without bringing disgrace to himself, his family and the entire nobility; allowing his name to be associated with published literary works—the so-called "stigma of print"—or with the public theater, were just such socially-forbidden actions; and 2) Oxford had ridiculed and satirized powerful members of the court and government in the theatrical works he originally devised to entertain the queen and her court. Having fellow courtiers laughing at them—all in good fun—was barely tolerable for some powerful courtiers; for the public to laugh at them, however, would have been intolerable. Cutting

---

[6] Charlton Ogburn, *The Mysterious William Shakespeare* (1992), p. 349.

the connection between Oxford and the plays, by making it appear that a commoner from a distant town was the author, would make it less likely that the public would make any adverse connections.

Most Oxfordians, though, believe that those justifications do not fully explain why Oxford's authorship was hidden, and offer one of two additional answers.

➢ There was a need to protect the reign of King James from any potential challenge by Southampton. Under the Dynastic Succession Theory, Henry Wriothesley, the third Earl of Southampton, was the illegitimate son of Queen Elizabeth and Edward de Vere and a potential heir to the throne. Because Oxford had alluded to Southampton's true parentage in many of his plays and poems, especially the *Sonnets*, the connection between him and the works had to be cut to make it less likely that anyone not already in the know would understand what was hinted at. Cutting the connection first arose after Queen Elizabeth decided around 1594 not to publicly recognize Southampton as her heir. It became an absolute necessity after the accession of James in 1603.

    A variant of this theory adds the idea that Oxford himself was also a son of Queen Elizabeth, born in 1548 when she was still the teenaged Elizabeth Tudor (and, as third in line to the throne, not considered likely ever to become queen). Inherent in this theory is the idea of incest, which was brought out in the 2011 feature film *Anonymous* that portrayed Edward de Vere as "Shakespeare," as the Queen's son, and, with her, as the father of the third Earl of Southampton.

➢ The Bisexual Theory, the core of which stresses the need to protect the interests of Oxford's family. In this theory, in his plays and poems, especially the *Sonnets*, Oxford had alluded to his sexual relationship with the Earl of Southampton, a relationship regarded as shameful and sinful (as well as a capital crime). The family undertook measures to separate Oxford from the works to make it less likely that such allusions would be recognized and harm the family's good name.

Both theories involve Southampton, both are sexual in nature, both rely on literary evidence in Shakespeare's works, principally in the *Sonnets*, and supporters of each claim that their theory adds additional support to the Oxfordian claim. Some proponents accept that the two motives identified by Looney were sufficient to justify the use of the Shakespeare pseudonym in 1593 on the publication of *Venus and Adonis*. But, they would say, those motives did not explain the extraordinary steps taken later to hide Oxford's authorship from future generations: the ambiguous prefatory material in the First Folio, the oddities of the monument in Trinity Church in Stratford and the alterations to at least three portraits of Edward de Vere to make them resemble more closely the Droeshout engraving in the Folio, all apparently undertaken around the time it was published in 1623. That the *Sonnets* appear to have been suppressed immediately after publication in 1609 tends to confirm the idea that something in them needed to be kept under wraps.

Turning to the how question—how it was possible to hide de Vere's authorship—evidence would have to have been eradicated not only of Oxford's authorship, but also of William Shakspere's non-authorship. As Ogburn explained, "all testimony as to the actual authorship and all testimony as to the surrogate's ineligibility would have to be forestalled and where it was committed to paper the incriminating documents would have to be gathered up and destroyed."[7] Ogburn characterized such a far-reaching effort as "highly implausible" and believed that "its implausibility is what has chiefly blocked a more general acceptance of 'Shakespeare' as having been a pseudonym."

Nevertheless, he concluded, "a nearly clean sweep was made of contemporary documentation touching on the authorship. . . . The fact is that every contemporary document that might have related authorship of Shakespeare's plays and poems to an identifiable human being subsequently disappeared. Every last scrap of paper that would have told who Shakespeare was—whether the Stratford man or any other—simply vanished. . . . To me there can be but one explanation for the empty-handedness of generations of scholars after lifelong quests. Someone saw to it that those quests would be fruitless" (198, 183).

The effort to destroy evidence that would interfere with the cover story of Shakspere's authorship was, as noted, supplemented by the creation of misleading evidence in the form of the prefatory material in the First Folio, the oddities in Trinity Church, and the alterations to the portraits.

Those who hold to the Dynastic Succession Theory believe that the campaign to destroy evidence must have been orchestrated by those who controlled State power. Only they would have had access to documents such as the records of the Privy Council and the Office of the Revels, which are missing for just those years likely to have mentioned the Earl of Oxford's theatrical activities. State officers would have had the power to seize private papers of important officials and letters in private hands, as well as other items such as attendance records of the Stratford grammar school, which are complete except for the decade during which William Shakspere would have been of age to attend. Only Robert Cecil, they claim, had sufficient control over the reins of State power to have accomplished all this. The greater the use of State power, they also claim, the greater the chances that it was used for reasons of State. And no use of such power would been more legitimate in their eyes than protecting the reign of the Stuart dynasty from challenges to its legitimacy.

Those who hold the Bisexual Theory presumably believe that Oxford's relatives carried out the destruction of evidence, though I haven't come across an explanation for how they would have had the same access to the range of documents that Robert Cecil did. Nor have I come across justification for why they would have felt the need to hide Oxford's relationship with Southampton from future generations by taking the additional steps with the Folio, at Trinity Church, and with the portraits two decades after Oxford's death.

The Course of Events, Part 1

The first book published after *The Mysterious William Shakespeare* to propose answers to the why and how questions was Elisabeth Sears's *Shakespeare and the Tudor Rose* (1991), which presented the Dynastic Succession Theory in a more developed form. She presented almost a biography of those parts of Oxford's life that she saw as emotionally portrayed in the sonnets, supplemented by historical facts that she cited in support of her reading of them. Ogburn, as noted, had been so affected by one little-known historical fact cited in Sears's book—that Southampton was imprisoned on the day Oxford died—that he came out, reluctantly, in support of the Dynastic Succession thesis in the

---

[7] Charlton Ogburn, *The Mysterious William Shakespeare* (1992), p. 198.

second edition of *The Mysterious William Shakespeare*, published in 1992.

Diana Price weighed in with a fierce criticism of Sears's book and the Dynastic Succession idea (which she called the "Tudor Rose" theory) in "Rough Winds Do Shake: A Fresh Look at the Tudor Rose Theory," in the Fall 1996 issue of *The Elizabethan Review*. Price was adamant that the theory could not be correct because Queen Elizabeth could not have gone through a full pregnancy without anyone noticing. Price acknowledged that the theory, arising from literary evidence, "appears to have some factual underpinnings," and examined the historical evidence. She concluded that "[a]s attractive as the Tudor Rose theory may be on interpretive grounds, the historical facts plainly refute it." The events of state known to have occurred at the time when a royal son was supposedly born (May-June 1974) "preclude any royal pregnancy, confinement, or clandestine delivery." In her view, Sears's errors "are so numerous as to undermine the legitimacy of the theory." Adherents "have not constructed their case with a single piece of documentary evidence, and the inaccurate arguments advanced to support the theory serve only to discredit it. Since ample documentation contradicts it, the Tudor Rose theory cannot be viewed as having any substance."[8]

Among the first to respond to Price were "The Editors" of the *Shakespeare Oxford Newsletter*. Their piece, "Writing History: Facts are Facts, But Interpretation is All," sought to establish the legitimacy of literary evidence and the often suspect nature of documentary evidence, which was susceptible to being "deliberately sanitized."[9] The article was much discussed at the time.

The Elizabethan Review published seven letters responding to Price under the title "Plucking the Tudor Rose" in its Spring 1997 issue. Five persons supported her findings, including noted Oxfordians Verily Anderson and Father Francis Edwards. The two taking issue with Price's findings were Sears and Ogburn. As Ogburn explained,

> That [Southampton was the son of Queen Elizabeth and Oxford] is a proposition I resisted for years for obvious reasons and have come to accept only because I have felt I had no choice. No other scenario of which I have heard accommodates the facts in the case.
>
> Ms. Price, it seems to me, has scored a success in nearly all the challenges she has mounted.... The trouble is that these are all focused on subordinate issues while the central considerations are overlooked until at the end she touches on one and then only to shy away from it. Her argument, unless I mistake her, comes down to denying the possibility of Elizabeth's concealing a pregnancy during the crucial period and of her being able to bear a child in secret. My response to that is: let her think again. Plenty of women, I do not doubt, have succeeded in carrying out what Ms. Price maintains the Queen could not have.... I find no difficulty in believing that the Queen could have borne a child with only a few persons in on it.[10]

He identified the key political stakes involved in the cover-up of Oxford's authorship.

> If, as I am constrained to believe—much against my will, I may repeat—that the identification of Shakespeare as Oxford must lead to that of the young friend of

---

[8] Diana Price, "Rough Winds Do Shake: A Fresh Look at the Tudor Rose Theory," *Elizabethan Review*, vol. 4/2 (Fall 1996): 19.

[9] William E. Boyle, Charles Burford [Beauclerk], Charles Boyle, "Writing History: Facts are Facts, But Interpretation is All," *Shakespeare Oxford Newsletter*, vol. 33/1 (Winter 1997): 7.

[10] Charlton Ogburn, letter in "Plucking the Tudor Rose," *Elizabethan Review*, vol. 5/1 (Spring 1997): 7-8.

the *Sonnets* as the son of Oxford and Elizabeth, then the need for dissimulation of Oxford's authorship of Shakespeare's works was absolutely imperative. It was not simply a matter of preserving the reputations of the Queen and those around her, which would be recognized in the plays were these attributed to an insider at Court, though given the unsparing treatment of some of them this would be reason enough. What was at stake in the identity of the poet-dramatist was the succession to the throne of the United Kingdom. For all I know, this may be dynamite even today. (8)

He also reiterated the importance of the key fact he had learned from Sears's book: "Surely the facts are that James had Oxford's assurance in 1603 that Southampton would not claim the throne and could be safely freed, but that when Oxford died James feared that with his restraining hand withdrawn, Southampton might indeed make a bid for the throne" (9). "The only explanation I can find is that, as Elizabeth's son, Southampton would indeed, certainly in his own view, have had a rightful claim to the Crown, upon which he might be expected to act, while to me this explanation accords with what we may deduce of the relations of Oxford, Elizabeth and Southampton from Shakespeare's works. I do not know how otherwise the circumstances known to us may be accounted for" (9).

The Bisexual Theory was also undergoing development and refinement by Joseph Sobran, who would publish the fullest expression of his ideas in 1997 in his book, *Alias Shakespeare: Solving the Greatest Literary Mystery of All Time*, and an article in *The Shakespeare Oxford Newsletter*, "Shakespeare's Disgrace: Is This the Key to Identifying and Understanding the Poet?" In the article Sobran came down on the side of "the *Sonnets* refer[ing] to real people, events, experiences, and emotions," rather than being "mere 'literary exercises' about fictional characters, in which even the narrator is not to be literally identified with the author. . . . On their face, the *Sonnets* bespeak real and often painful emotions the Youth and the Mistress cause the poet."[11] Turning to "the homosexual view" of the *Sonnets*. he explained that "Since no Elizabethan poet would be likely to feign homosexual love— sodomy being a capital crime—we can presume that if correct, the poet is hinting at biographical information of startling implication" (4). The "homosexual view is essentially sound and, I would say, undeniable," and is a key piece of evidence in support of authorship by Edward de Vere: "If the Youth was the Earl of Southampton,

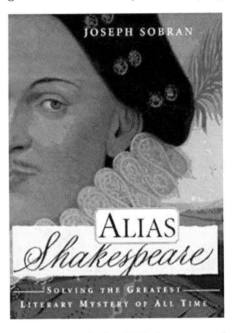

it follows that the poet could not have been the mainstream scholars' 'Shakespeare of Stratford'" because "Shakespeare could not have addressed a nobleman in such amorous terms." But, "[i]t could well have been Edward de Vere, Earl of Oxford."

Sobran believed that "a long, sometimes turbulent affair ensued between the poet and

---

[11] Joseph Sobran, "Shakespeare's Disgrace," *Shakespeare Oxford Newsletter*, vol. 33/2 (Spring 1997): 1.

Southampton. The poet is clearly in love with the Youth in an erotic sense. He is fascinated by his physical beauty. He is obsessed with him. He idealizes him. He is jealous of him. He suffers during his absence" (5). The poet, he continued, "fears that his unnamed disgrace will also rub off on the Youth. . . . [W]hat kind of disgrace is so contagious? A reputation for sodomy certainly would have been."

In his review, Charles Boyle declared *Alias Shakespeare* to be "probably the most important publication since Charlton Ogburn's *The Mysterious William Shakespeare*," because "[i]t gathers together in one simple volume all one needs to know to be convinced that Shakespeare is not some poor person from Stratford-on-Avon, but rather a major figure in the English aristocracy, writing about his world because he cannot do what he wants to do in real life."[12] However, as to the why and how questions, Boyle thought that Sobran offered tantalizing hints at several explanations but didn't deliver a full explanation for any of them. The odd omission of Shakespeare's poems from the First Folio (which also omitted any mention of the Earl of Southampton to whom the two major poems had been dedicated) was due, according to Sobran, to "the controversial nature of the poetry itself and the relationship between the poet and the Fair Youth (Southampton)—i.e., homosexuality and disgrace." Yet, Boyle observed, "when it comes to delivering on the promise to [explain] how the *Sonnets* reveal the homosexual relationship between the poet and the Fair Youth, Sobran seems to pull his punches. Chapter 9 [the chapter dedicated to that purpose], is only six and one-half pages long, barely a third of the average length of all the other chapters in the book." The book didn't, in Boyle's view, live up to the promise made in its subtitle to "solve the greatest literary mystery of all time."

Elliott Stone's response to Sobran's article was similar to Boyle's to his book: "Those of us who had been thoroughly primed by Mr. Sobran at the Minnesota Conference were still waiting for the startling new discoveries and controversial, fascinating and rewarding details which were to be revealed in the author's examination of the *Sonnets* as the autobiography of the Earl of Oxford as a sexual deviant personality."[13] Sobran's article did not deliver what he had promised. The literary evidence in support of this interpretation is scanty, hardly more than an isolated word here and there, Stone observed; it did not seem substantive enough to justify "the homosexual view" itself, let alone its use as evidence in support of Oxford's authorship. Nor did Sobran explain how the deception could have been carried out, or why Oxford's relatives, almost two decades after his death, would have countenanced the fraudulent prefatory material in the First Folio, the creation of the monument in Trinity Church and the over-painting of the portraits.

Ogburn also responded to Sobran's article, lamenting that "he has put us to the necessity of rescuing Oxford from the charge of conducting a homosexual relationship with the young friend, certainly the Earl of Southampton. The charge is one that must fail upon examination."[14] The real cause of Oxford's disgrace is not sodomy, but, as Oxford himself explained in sonnet 110, "Alas, 'tis true I have gone here and there and made myself a motley to the view." The shame and disgrace came from the Lord Great Chamberlain's theatrical activities, including appearances on the public stage. "Oxford has

---

[12] Charles Boyle, Review of *Alias Shakespeare: Solving the Greatest Literary Mystery of All Time* by Joseph Sobran, *Shakespeare Oxford Newsletter*, vol. 33/3 (Summer 1997): 16.

[13] Elliott Stone, letter to the editor, "*Shakespeare Oxford Newsletter*, vol. 33/3 (Summer 1997): 21.

[14] Charlton Ogburn, "Shakespeare and the Fair Youth," *Shakespeare Oxford Newsletter*, vol. vol. 33/3 (Summer 1997): 4.

disgraced a family name as noble as any in England by writing for the stage, by playing 'kingly parts in sport' himself under his pseudonym 'Shakespeare' when otherwise he might have 'been a companion for a king,' and doubtless worst of all, by associating with actors on their own level as Prince Hall with the patrons of the Boar's Head Tavern."

Although Price's article and Sobran's book and article were all published after the 1996 SOS Conference held in Minneapolis, the ideas in them were debated there in a panel discussion, "Shakespeare and the Fair Youth." Sears, Sobran and Charles Boyle were among the six panelists. This was "perhaps the first time that Oxfordians have presented and discussed their own major differences of interpretation in a formal, public setting,"[15] Bill Boyle wrote, adding that "It was during these exchanges that the depth of the disagreements between the panelists began to emerge."[16] Much of the discussion focused on the *Sonnets*, with both sides citing them to justify their respective positions. During the concluding remarks by the moderator, a letter from Charlton Ogburn was read which stated in part,

> Honesty finally compelled me to concede that the crucial elements of the case, especially the tenor of the *Sonnets*, could be accounted for only in terms of Southampton's having been in fact the son of Oxford and Elizabeth. The poet of the *Sonnets* addresses the Fair Youth in terms that only a father admonishing an erring son would employ while also acknowledging him as his sovereign, whose "vassal" he is.... [I]f there is any other postulation to which the facts in the case can be accommodated, I have yet to hear of it.[17]

Ogburn went on to express further opposition to the Bisexual Theory. "There is not the slightest indication that Oxford ever had a homosexual impulse in his life." Commenting on the point in Sears's book that had prompted him to address the issue in the second edition of *The Mysterious William Shakespeare*, Ogburn added, "Mr. Sobran's theory cannot explain why Southampton should have been imprisoned on the day of Oxford's death by a reportedly panic-stricken king who had forbidden the prince his heir to appear out of doors. Clearly he feared that the young Earl would exercise a claim to the throne, one that would have been his as Elizabeth's son."

Roger Parisious responded to Ogburn with a with a lengthy article that contained many interesting and little known facts about the development of the Dynastic Succession theory. His account also included assertions unsupported by any references that conflict with the facts presented in Chapter 10 of this book.[18]

Christopher Paul also entered the discussion on the "why" question. "We find sufficient evidence that it was the repressive politics of the period, Oxford's rank and social standing, and the concern of his family that their reputations would be damaged if the world knew who wrote the plays, that explains why he chose to publish under a

---

[15] Unknown to the participants in the debate in 1996 was the debate sixty-three years earlier, on September 27, 1933, "Whether there is sufficient evidence to show that Queen Elizabeth had a son by the Earl of Oxford," in which Percy Allen and Capt. Ward spoke in favor and Gerald Rendall and Gerald Phillips opposed. It was rediscovered only in 2019 during research for this book.

[16] William E. Boyle, "Shakespeare and the Fair Youth," *Shakespeare Oxford Newsletter*, vol. 32/4 (Fall 1996): 6-7.

[17] Charlton Ogburn, "Excerpts from Charlton Ogburn's Letter," *Shakespeare Oxford Newsletter*, vol. 32/4 (Fall 1996): 7.

[18] See his "Occultist Influence on the Authorship Controversy," in *The Elizabethan Review*, vol. 6, no. 1 (Spring 1998): 9-43, and his "Postscript to the Tudor Rose Theory, same publication, vol. 6, no. 2 (Autumn 1998): 90-93.

pseudonym."[19] Paul, then, had presented the minority view that social standing and the ire of courtiers enraged at being skewered in the plays were the motives for Oxford's use of a pseudonym. This view, though, does not address why Oxford's descendants would have felt the great need twenty years later to take the steps designed to mislead future generations. The courtiers ridiculed in the plays were all long gone by that time; even Robert Cecil, the most powerful of them all, had died in 1612, a decade before the First Folio was published. Paul did not address the "how" question.

In England, John Rollett, though not a supporter of the Dynastic Succession Theory, weighed in with important evidence that supported it. He presented "new evidence which shows, or appears to show, that in the 1590s Southampton was indeed thought by many people to be the Queen's son."[20]

> Thus what for fifty years in this century remained "almost unbelievable" turns out to have been "widely believed" in the early 1590s.
>
> The insight of those early pioneers [Percy Allen, Capt. Bernard M. Ward] now seems to be vindicated, and since the theory predicted what appears to be a fact, it follows almost inevitably that Oxford must be both the father of Southampton and the author of the *Sonnets*.

He summed up additional findings in a second article: "From purely literary evidence, the dynastic sonnets, it was deduced fifty years ago that Southampton was the son of Oxford and the Queen. However unlikely that deduction may have seemed, it is now apparently confirmed by documentary evidence from 1592 and '93, where one publication actually styles him 'Dynasta,' a Prince, one of a line of hereditary princes or rulers. It seems that the dynastic sonnets were written in an attempt to urge the queen to legitimize Southampton by marrying Oxford, and although the attempt (almost inevitably) failed, we are as a consequence left with what appears to be conclusive evidence that it was Oxford who wrote them under the pen-name 'Shakespeare.'"[21]

Prominent British Oxfordian Christopher H. Dams acknowledged that Rollett "shows some sound evidence that Southampton was regarded by at least some contemporaries . . . as the son of queen Elizabeth." But the "simple and credible hypothetical explanation" was that although "Oxford may have believed that Southampton was his son by the Queen,"[22] he really wasn't.

Dams urged the De Vere Society to steer clear of the Dynastic Succession Theory[23] for three reasons:

---

[19] Christopher Paul, "The Prince Tudor Dilemma: Hip Thesis, Hypothesis, or Old Wives' Tale?" *Oxfordian*, vol. 5 (2002): 66.

[20] John M. Rollett, "Was Southampton Regarded as the Son of the Queen?, 1" *De Vere Society Newsletter*, Jan. 2000, p. 8.

[21] John M. Rollett, "Was Southampton Regarded as the Son of the Queen?, 2" *De Vere Society Newsletter*, July 2000, p. 26. October 6, 1594, the date on which Southampton reached his majority, coincided roughly with the peak of the attention paid to him. It would have been an apt moment for Queen Elizabeth, age sixty-one, to have declared him her heir—if he had indeed been her son and she had been inclined to do so. Could it be that the attention paid to him aroused her jealousy? Her refusal to share power with or cede power to a husband had perhaps been a motive for her never marrying; perhaps her refusal to name a heir was due in part to the same fears of being replaced or sidelined.

[22] Christopher H. Dams, "Was Southampton Regarded as the Son of the Queen?" *De Vere Society Newsletter*, Oct. 2000, p. 20.

[23] Dams referred to the theory as "the PT Theory," a short version of "The Prince Tudor Theory," a term attributed to Oxfordian W. Ron Hess in the 1990s.

1. "It is not relevant to the broader Authorship Question: if it were proved incontrovertibly tomorrow, it would not advance the Oxfordian case in any significant way;

2. It is distracting and divisive, as I think events in the SOS are showing;

3. It involves Oxfordians in the classic strategic blunder—war on two fronts; we are already battling with the academics of English Literature, espousing the PT [Dynastic Succession] theory would also bring us into conflict with historians, some of whom are presently sympathetic to our case."

This was a rollback to Looney's view that it was not necessary to answer the why and how questions to prove Oxford's authorship and that the issue was so controversial that it gave others more reason to dismiss the entire Oxfordian claim. Several persons responded, arguing that the answers to the why and how questions were the most persuasive evidence in support of the claim. Oxford's hidden authorship and the reasons for it are not two separate issues, they argued. Just as it is difficult to convict someone of a crime without also establishing a motive, so too here motive is a paramount consideration. Rollett responded on that very point while disagreeing with Dams's first point.

> If letters, or DNA tests, or some other technique proved incontrovertibly that Southampton was the son of the Queen and Oxford, the case for Oxford as the author of the Sonnets would be virtually proven, and the case for his authorship of the poems and plays would follow almost automatically. The logical inevitability of this outcome, if the PT [Sonnets Dynastic Succession] theory were to be proved, is one of the considerations that motivates those who incline towards it. It has been remarked on many occasions that the *Sonnets* are the key to the real Shakespeare, and to place a moratorium on research into their meaning (as Christopher suggests) can only delay the solving of the Authorship Question. At the same time, there are good reasons, which I need not go into, for containing discussion on the PT theory within the circle of Oxfordian supporters.[24]

The Monument

Then came something startlingly original and of inestimable importance. Hank Whittemore—author, actor and playwright—introduced a new interpretation of *Shakespeares Sonnets* grounded on the insight that the publication was a "masterwork" with a deliberate design and structure. It was not a collection of individual poems in random order, but a complete work in which each sonnet played a part. His view was that the *Sonnets* told the story of the most important real-life events taking place at the end of Elizabeth's reign. One long time Oxfordian scholar described Whittemore's investigations as "the most significant research in the history of the Oxfordian movement." His book, *The Monument*, was published in 2005.

Whittemore first presented his ideas in a 75-page paper distributed in May 1999 and in a presentation before the Shakespeare Authorship Roundtable in Los Angeles in June. As explained in *The Monument*, he approached the *Sonnets* with the assumptions shared by many other scholars that they were autobiographical and chronological; he then sought to see to what degree they alluded to events in the historical record. He found not

---

[24] John M. Rollett, letter to the Editor, *De Vere Society Newsletter*, Jan. 2001, p. 18.

only that the sonnets did indeed refer to actual events, but also that the very structure of the publication had been organized around those events and Oxford's reactions to them.

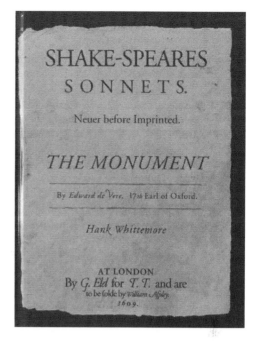

> What then emerged was a very different result involving the structure and time frame as much as the actual content of the poems. Suddenly the pieces of the puzzle began to move into place to form a clear picture; and once the verses were placed as "stencils" over the contemporary events and their dates on the calendar, what unfolded was a flesh and blood story that challenged the standard or "official" versions of the history and the traditional or "orthodox" interpretations of the literature.[25]
>
> The most startling aspect of the new picture was the emergence of exactly eighty chronological sonnets . . . addressed to Henry Wriothesley, third Earl of Southampton during the more than two years (1601-1603) he spent imprisoned in the Tower of London as a traitor to the Crown, after which, following the death of Queen Elizabeth, he was inexplicably released by the new monarch, James I of England. Then it became clear that the next twenty sonnets match the twenty days from Southampton's liberation to the day immediately following the Queen's funeral, when she was "officially" dead and the Tudor dynasty was no more. And I finally realized that this string of precisely 100 emotion-laden sonnets—recording Southampton's crime, disgrace, treason trial, death sentence, reprieve, continued imprisonment and liberation, leading to a new phase of his life in the next reign—is positioned at the exact center of an elegantly structured monument.

The *Sonnets* thus had a logical and elegant structure.

- ➢ A 100-sonnet center (27-126), with 80 sonnets (27-106) detailing Southampton's arrest, trial and incarceration in the Tower of London after the failure of the so-called Essex Rebellion in February 1601, followed by 20 sonnets (107-126) chronicling the final days of the Tudor dynasty (which officially ended with Elizabeth's funeral on April 28, 1603).

- ➢ The central series was preceded by a 26-sonnet sequence (1-26), one for each year of Southampton's life before the Essex Rebellion.

- ➢ The central series was followed by another 26-sonnet sequence (127-152), the so-called Dark Lady sonnets.

- ➢ The final two sonnets (153-154) concern the Elizabeth-Oxford rendezvous at Bath in 1573 (perhaps early October) during which Southampton was conceived.

According to Whittemore, "The real-life context of the 100-sonnet center has been

---

[25] Hank Whittemore, *The Monument* (2005), p. xi.

hiding in plain sight within the monument. The key to seeing it is our own perception. Now the verses shed light on the history and the history, in turn, illuminates the verses. Neither the official record of events on the calendar nor the consecutive numbering of the verses needs to be rearranged; these two fixed documents, brought into alignment, produce the record that 'Shakespeare' left behind for readers in the future."[26]

He weighed in again in the Summer 1999 SOS *Newsletter*:

> The structure provides an overall view of the *Sonnets* as a "dynastic diary" within the context of the inevitable succession to the throne and Oxford's attempt to preserve "the living record" (55) of Southampton's royal existence.
>
> This proposed solution goes beyond personal interpretation to provide a consistent conceptual framework within which existing but long-neglected evidence can be seen. It includes both an internal dynamic and an external context for the entire collection of 154 verses. In doing so, it brings together all the puzzle pieces to form a clear picture of who wrote the *Sonnets* and what they were about, along with a coherent story of why, how, when and under what circumstances they were written.[27]

Whittemore's *Monument* theory supported the answers to the why and how questions offered by the Dynastic Succession Theory. Under the cover of traditional love poetry the *Sonnets* report Southampton and his royal status, the political event known as the Essex Rebellion, Southampton's confinement in the Tower and the end of the Tudor dynasty. Whittemore thus found it easy to identify the three main persons referred to in the *Sonnets*: Henry Wriothesley, the Third Earl of Southampton, was the Fair Youth (and the dedicatee); Queen Elizabeth was the Dark Lady; and Oxford was the speaker. Whittemore also argued that the "Rival Poet" mentioned in some sonnets was not another poet, but was Oxford himself in the guise of his pen name, William Shakespeare.

The first notice of Whittemore's interpretation in the SOS *Newsletter* was taken by editor Bill Boyle, who noted the extraordinary nature of the events that gave rise to the sonnets. "It is, in Whittemore's estimation, the love-hate relationship between the author and his Queen—compounded by the fate of their unacknowledged son Southampton—that is the driving force that begat these brilliant poems. His unique contribution to the scholarship of the *Sonnets* is the thesis that the sonnets' greatness was forged in the brief, intense heat of the Essex Rebellion crisis, with Southampton's life on the line, and when both the author and his Queen were themselves close to death."[28]

Other Oxfordians who believed that Whittemore had solved the mystery of the *Sonnets* were Charles Berney, the first president of the newly-formed Shakespeare Fellowship, who wrote that "Hank Whittemore has written the most important book on Shakespeare's *Sonnets* in 400 years," and Dr. Paul H. Altrocchi, who stated that "Hank Whittemore clearly details the powerful evidence which proves beyond reasonable doubt that only de Vere could have written Shakespeare's *Sonnets* as a poetic monument to his son, Henry Wriothesley, 3rd Earl of Southampton." Charles Beauclerk agreed: "Whittemore's *Monument* is a monumental work in every sense of the word. Finally, after 400 years, the *Sonnets* of Shake-speare have found a worthy interpreter, one who has

---

[26] Hank Whittemore, *The Monument: An Abridged Introduction to the 918-page First Reference Edition* (2005): 40.

[27] Hank Whittemore, "Abstract & Brief Chronicles," *Sh. Oxford Newsletter*, vol. 35/2 (Summer 1999): 1.

[28] William E. Boyle, "Shakespeare's Invention: The Royal Story of the *Sonnets*," *Shakespeare Oxford Newsletter*, vol. 35/1 (Spring 1999), p. 2.

been able to discover their original historical and political context and so reveal their true meaning."

The first critical response came from Stephanie Hopkins Hughes, founding editor of *The Oxfordian*, who vehemently disagreed with Whittemore's interpretations and the Dynastic Succession Theory. In her view, the Sonnets are "among the greatest love poems ever written, [and] it is almost insulting to suggest that this monarch of language would stoop to using this classic verse form, traditional for poems of love, for anything but what he openly declares, over and over, right from the beginning, is his sole purpose, to relieve his heart of its burden of love and to give his beloved immortality through his verse."[29]

In the same issue (Summer 1999) editor Boyle noted that Whittemore's thesis "raises, in one fell swoop, all the foremost issues of contention within the Oxfordian movement today: evidence vs. interpretation, literary vs. non-literary documents as evidence, conspiracy vs. coincidence, and last but not least—the 3rd Earl of Southampton as the son of the Virgin Queen and Oxford/Shakespeare vs., well, apparently anything else in all the world except that."[30] He hoped that presenters at the upcoming SOS conference would take on these issues.

That they did. The 1999 conference in suburban Boston featured a session with three presentations: John Rollett, Stephanie Hopkins and Hank Whittemore all addressed the topic of Southampton, his relationship to the Sonnets' author and the Queen, and how these relationships were portrayed in the *Sonnets*. Rollett presented evidence that in his view established beyond a reasonable doubt that Southampton's contemporaries regarded him as having a status equivalent to a son of a Queen. Hughes stated her view that "It is evident to any adult reader with any experience of life that these poems of passionate love, poems suffused with sexual imagery, were written about a member of Shakespeare's own sex."[31] Whittemore argued that the *Sonnets* told the story of the final years of the Tudor Dynasty and that the main love story in them is that of paternal love, not sexual passion. Afterward one prominent Oxfordian commented that "No minds were changed. And none ever will be." "While that prediction might not have been literally true," Boyle commented, "it accurately assessed the commitment to their views of those on both sides of the 'Southampton' issue."

The Dynastic Succession/*Monument* Answers Since 2001

Surprisingly, after the report on the 1999 conference the Dynastic Succession Theory was not directly addressed in the *SOS Newsletter* over the next year and a half. But the issue had not disappeared, merely gone underground; it erupted in the late spring of 2001, not in the *Newsletter* but in developments within the organization. At that time certain members of the SOS Board of Trustees took actions that others found to be so egregious that a sizable minority of the members left to form a separate organization (many also remained members of the SOS). At the heart of the hornets' nest was the Dynastic Succession Theory's answers to the why and how questions, with certain Board members attempting to "save" the Society by ousting those holding such views from any positions or role within it.

---

[29] Stephanie Hopkins Hughes, letter to the Editor, *Shakespeare Oxford Newsletter*, vol. 35/2 (Sum. 1999): 26.
[30] William E. Boyle, "From the Editor: Shakespeare, Southampton and the *Sonnets*," *Shakespeare Oxford Newsletter*, vol. 35/2 (Summer 1999): 24.
[31] Stephanie Hopkins Hughes, quoted in William E. Boyle, "Shakespeare, Southampton and the *Sonnets*," *Shakespeare Oxford Newsletter*, vol. 35/3 (Fall 1999): 7.

To be sure, there were other factors that precipitated the founding of a second American Oxfordian organization.[32] Here, though, we are concerned only with status of the Dynastic Succession/*Monument* Theory answers to the why and how questions after the split. The *Newsletter* of the Shakespeare Oxford Society did not address the theory for more than four years. *Shakespeare Matters*, the newsletter of the newly-formed Shakespeare Fellowship, was open to it. In the first issue, ready for distribution at the SOS's fall conference in 2001, its editors, Roger Stritmatter and Bill Boyle, announced in one of the first issues that, "We think that the 'Tudor Heir' theory[33]—which argues that the Shakespeare question is inextricably linked to issues of the dynastic succession of the Tudor government under Queen Elizabeth I—merits open-minded consideration and very close examination."[34] *Shakespeare Matters* "will evaluate submissions . . . on the basis of the quality of argument and analysis, not on whether we happen to agree with the conclusions of a given writer. We will deploy our editorial prerogatives to combat the unfortunate tendency of Oxfordians to replicate the censorious values which have produced the present intellectual cul-de-sac of Shakespearean orthodoxy. Banning discussion of 'offensive' topics which can't harm anyone, and might open up new avenues for inquiry and investigation, is bad ethics, bad strategy, and bad thinking." They expected and hoped "to publish articles which will challenge the presuppositions of our readers, and of ourselves. We vow to go out of our way to find articles which offer controversial interpretations, to print them, and then to facilitate as much dialogue, debate, and discussion as possible. We regard this as our editorial responsibility."

The editors addressed several topics connected to the Dynastic Succession theory, including the nature of evidence. Bill Boyle addressed the issue in a short piece, "Can Literature Be Evidence?" that raised questions of the utmost importance about the nature of literary evidence. Rarely had this critical issue been stated so succinctly. He distinguished between two types of literary evidence: one impersonal, as in the plays, and the other personal, as in the *Sonnets*. The first type of literary evidence supports Oxford's authorship; the second (together with the first) addresses the questions behind the decision to hide his authorship. The article is reprinted in full nearby.

The editors also addressed the issue of "speculation," which must necessarily be part of any historical account of events for which knowledge is less than perfect. This is the same point that Percy Allen had frequently made—that an "informed imagination" was necessary to understand people who lived in times and conditions very different from our known.

> [S]ome of us have been disturbed for many months by the prevailing tendency in certain Oxfordian circles to turn 'speculation' into a dirty word. Sometimes there seems to be a visceral need to categorize every sentence, lecture or essay into the philosophically naïve categories, 'speculative' and 'factual.' Such a trend, we think, deserves to be resisted: all significant inquiry in the humanities involves the creative interdependence of the factual and the speculative. Rigorous

---

[32] Bill Boyle later explained to me that "The Prince Tudor [Sonnets Dynastic Succession] rift was a key factor in the split, but not the only one. My own conclusion is that, without the Prince Tudor rift, the split might not have happened, and a way to deal with the political, power sharing, and money problems might have been found. EXCEPT THAT . . . the Prince Tudor issue was at the center of the power sharing fights." [Private communication, March 2021]

[33] Another phrase sometimes used to refer to the Sonnets Dynastic Succession Theory.

[34] Roger Stritmatter and William E. Boyle [Editors], "Tender Airs, Tudor Heirs," *Shakespeare Matters*, vol. 1/2 (Winter 2002): 3.

scholarship employs the factual to bolster and establish what often originated as pure speculation. That was the method employed by Oxfordian pioneers such as J. Thomas Looney, and we see no reason to abandon it now."

In our mailbox is a letter from Toronto journalist Sky Gilbert which illustrates the commitment to responsible speculation which, we hope, will characterize the content of these pages:

> "I think it's terribly important to make it clear that the Shakespeare Fellowship is not setting up another orthodoxy. What's appalling and revealing to me, is how the Shakespeare-the-actor-of-Stratford defenders get hysterical when defending their views. My answer back is another question: 'Aren't people allowed to question? Isn't questioning, in fact, important, and the very province and duty of scholars?'"[35]

In the same issue, Shakespeare Fellowship president Alex McNeil weighed in with thoughts on the importance of investigating the Dynastic Succession ideas in their *Monument* formulation.

> Hank Whittemore has made what may be a real breakthrough in analyzing Shakespeare's *Sonnets*, arguing powerfully that they were published in correct order, that they have a sequential structure, and—perhaps most importantly—that they relate directly to very real events in the lives of Edward de Vere and Henry Wriothesley. . . . Is Hank Whittemore's interpretation the only plausible one? Of course not. Does it deserve careful scrutiny and thoughtful criticism? Of

---

Bill Boyle, "Can Literature Be Evidence?"

Our two articles in this issue really lead right to the heart of the single most important question in the Shakespeare authorship debate: can literature—plays and poems in this instance—be used as evidence? Hotly debated when it comes to PT, but otherwise accepted by Oxfordians as self-evidently true. Without the evidence of the plays and poems of Shakespeare, there would be no authorship debate. The works themselves are the *primary* evidence in the whole matter. Everyone who has ever become interested in this issue did so because they had that familiar moment when they said to themselves: *these works* could not have been written by *that man.*

Where the debate gets interesting is in considering just what kind of evidence the works are. We are all familiar with the debate over the education and station in life of the probable author, with the works forming the basis of theories pointing to someone 1) highly educated, and 2) in or connected to the Elizabethan Court.

However, beyond these broad general categories things get more complicated. If a character in a play says something, is that the same thing as the author saying it? And if the "I" in a poem says something, is that the same thing as the author saying it? This is where there is indeed legitimate concern about where to draw the line between fact and fiction.

With a new theory of the *Sonnets* being published and promoted in these pages, we are undoubtedly journeying into new territory. A core principle of the "*Monument* theory" is that the sonnets were designed to be "testimony:" a "living record" of the lives of the Poet and the Fair Youth. The sonnets are cited in this issue as if they were personal letters, with all the evidentiary value that personal letters have in writing history.

We fully understand that this is controversial—and risky. So we invite our readers to let us know what they think of the "*Monument* theory," and what they think of the proposition of using the *Sonnets* as historical testimony.

Shakespeare Matters, vol. 3/4 (Summer 2004): 3.

---

[35] Bill Boyle and Roger Stritmatter, "From the Editors: Oxford is Shakespeare: Any Questions?" *Shakespeare Matters*, vol. 1/1 (Fall 2001): 20.

course it does. Will it prove to be the "correct" interpretation? Only time will tell. In the meantime, we welcome your comments—pro-and-con—on this topic.[36]

Hank Whittemore's *The Monument* was apparently ready to be published in the summer of 2004 but publishing issues delayed it for six months. A piece enthusiastically supportive of the ideas in it, by Bill Boyle (writing as an individual, not as editor), ran in the Summer issue of *Shakespeare Matters*.

> The Whittemore solution has made crystal clear what was once mysterious and opaque.
>
> In short, once one has 1) the correct author (Oxfordians do), 2) the correct Fair Youth and Dark Lady (Southampton and Queen Elizabeth), and, finally, 3) the all-important correct historical context, then reading the *Sonnets* becomes as clear and uncomplicated as reading a signed, dated letter to a known addressee about the events of the day. In this case, of course, the "events of the day" are "your crime, your trial, your death sentence, my anguish, my attempts to save you, I have saved you!, she has betrayed us both, and now we both must live in this new post-crime world, and here's my advice on how you should now live your second life." It's that easy.[37]

That the Shakespeare Fellowship and *Shakespeare Matters* were open to arguments on all sides of the Dynastic Succession/*Monument* thesis was shown by the lengthy critique by Roger Stritmatter and Lynne Kositsky in the following issue. One challenge they posed was to the existence of the 100-sonnet sequence that Whittemore had found at the center of the *Sonnets*, which they described as a "superficially attractive schema [that] suffers from a number of obvious defects."[38] One defect, they maintained, was the lack of a marked change of theme and tone beginning with sonnet 27 if that sonnet had indeed marked the beginning of a 100-sonnet sequence. The other end of the sequence was not a problem, however, given the break between sonnets 126 and 127 already "acknowledged by many commentators, including Stephen Booth."

Stritmatter and Kositsky were also troubled by an apparent lack of consistency in the time period covered by each sonnet within the 100-sonnet sequence. In Whittemore's accounting, the 100-sonnet center was broken into three segments that covered time periods of different lengths: 1) the first sixty (27-86) covered the first two months of Southampton's imprisonment (February to April 1601) at the rate of one sonnet per day; 2) the next twenty (87-106) spanned the next twenty-four months, culminating with Southampton's release on April 10, 1603; and 3) the final twenty (107-126) covered the twenty-day period from his release until Queen Elizabeth's funeral on April 28, 1603, reverting to the rate of one sonnet per day. On this inconsistency of periods, they write, "It is unfortunate that the rules governing the sequence change. Why, for instance, may one poem in the second segment cover many days or even months, while each poem in the first and third segments describes only one day? The inconsistency is troubling and Whittemore provides no coherent justification for it. . . . If Shakespeare set out to write a 100-sonnet 'center' to the 'monument,' surely the rules would remain the same throughout? Anything else appears arbitrary."

---

[36] Alex McNeil, "From the President: 'Who will believe my verse?,'" *Shakespeare Matters*, vol. 3/4 (Summer 2004): 3.

[37] William E. Boyle, "With the Sonnets Now Solved . . .," *Shakespeare Matters*, vol. 3/4 (Summer 2004): 11.

[38] Roger Stritmatter & Lynne Kositsky, "A Critique of *The Monument* Theory," *Shakespeare Matters*, vol. 4/1 (Fall 2004): 10.

Washington State University (Pullman) English professor Michael Delahoyde addressed that point in his review of *The Monument*, observing that "Shakespeare was more poet than architect or mathematician," and "compromises to the elegance of the structure of the 'monument' do not, for me, close the case"[39] against it.

In a more substantive criticism of Whittemore's application of a "stencil of time" prepared from the historical record, Stritmatter and Kositsky stated that "with the possible exception of 107, 112, and 124, a close reading of sonnets 27-126 reveals no evident connection to the events of the rebellion and Southampton's imprisonment, and some of the sonnets manifestly cannot be about either."[40] They are correct that not every sonnet appears to be directly about the Essex Rebellion and Southampton's imprisonment, but, as I see it, Shakespeare/Oxford had not intended them to be; the sonnets are in part a journal of the author's own emotional journey during the period in which those events took place.

Stritmatter and Kositsky were also critical of Whittemore's interpretation based on "the adroit selection of certain words and phrases with no regard for their immediate or larger context as parts of sonnets or sonnet sequences" (11). These and other criticisms led them to conclude that "the Whittemore-Boyle 'monument' theory is flawed both in its method and its conclusions" (14). In his response, Whittemore acknowledged that it takes time to absorb and understand a theory as complicated as this one, and invited readers to examine the full case as laid out in his book.

In 2005 two important Oxfordians voiced support of the *Monument* theory. In the spring, Daniel Wright endorsed it at the Edward de Vere Studies Conference at Concordia University, reportedly calling *The Monument* "the most important Oxfordian book since *"Shakespeare" Identified.*" A few months later, Paul H. Altrocchi wrote an article supportive of it for *Shakespeare Matters*. He urged all Oxfordians "to give careful study and thought to Whittemore's inspired and powerful book, *The Monument*, which this writer firmly believes will come to be regarded as one of the most significant books of the twenty-first century. Perhaps with time, *The Monument* will end the disharmonious Oxfordian debate over the Prince Tudor theory, terminate their age of discord, and initiate a pattern of celestial peace as we all work together to bring about the long-delayed, now inevitable Shakespeare authorship paradigm shift."[41]

More recently, Peter Rush has weighed in with books, articles and letters in support of Whittemore's *Monument* thesis. In *Hidden in Plain Sight: The True History Revealed in Shake-speare's Sonnets*, he showed how *The Monument* filled the hole that existed at the core of the Oxfordian theory ever since Looney pointedly refused to speculate about Oxford's motives for hiding his authorship.

Discussion would continue, with interest in the Dynastic Succession theory showing no signs of ending even today. More than a dozen articles and letters addressed it in the four issues of *The Shakespeare Oxford Newsletter* in 2020. But we must turn to other answers to the why and how questions in the years after the crisis in the movement erupted in 2001.

---

[39] Michael Delahoyde, "Recent Publications in Oxfordian Studies," *Rocky Mountain Review of Literature and Languages*, vol. 60/2 (Fall 2006): 58.
[40] Roger Stritmatter & Lynne Kositsky, "A Critique of *The Monument* Theory," *Shakespeare Matters*, vol. 4/1 (Fall 2004): 10-11.
[41] Paul H. Altrocchi, A Royal Shame: The Origins and History of the Prince Tudor Theory," *Shakespeare Matters*, vol. 4/1 (Summer 2005): 17.

Non-Dynastic Succession/*Monument* Answers Since 2001

The first non-Dynastic Succession/*Monument* answer to the why and how questions to be raised in any Oxfordian publication after the crisis of 2001 was Hank Whittemore's reintroduction of Col. and Capt. Ward's idea that the Earl of Oxford had been the head of an informal government department charged with using the public theater to increase public support for the government and raise morale during the War with Spain. The plays had been produced anonymously, with some later revised and published as by "Shakespeare" (see Chapter 7). The Bisexual theory returned in 2004. A year later John Hamill introduced a new idea, one involving Oxford's second wife, Elizabeth Trentham.

The Bisexual Theory

The Bisexual Theory that Joseph Sobran had done so much to promote in the late 1990s returned in the Summer 2004 issue of *Shakespeare Matters*. In "Was Shakespeare Gay?" Michael Brame and Galina Popova concluded that the *Sonnets* and other works by Oxford "give incontrovertible evidence . . . that Shakespeare's love for the fair youth was not homosexual in nature, but rather parental."[42] Given that "the orthodox candidate relates to no noble son or potential son-in-law that could by any remote stretch of the imagination exemplify the fair youth of the sonnets," and that "such a son or potential son-in-law is immediately available to the 17th Earl of Oxford," they concluded that the parental references are evidence in support of Oxford's authorship of the *Sonnets*.

Former president of the Shakespeare Oxford Society (and later president of the Shakespeare Oxford Fellowship) John Hamill, on the other hand, revived Sobran's conclusion that Oxford was bisexual, that he and Southampton had a sexual relationship that was described in veiled terms in the *Sonnets*. Sobran, he wrote, "was not the first to point out Shakespeare's homoeroticism, but he was the first to connect it to apparent homosexual behavior in the biography of the Earl of Oxford."[43] Hamill argued that Oxford, if bisexual, would have had a strong reason for hiding his authorship of the *Sonnets*: "If it can be shown that they are autobiographical, it would reveal much about the author's sexual orientation" (39). "If the Master Storyteller chose to hide his characters and plot behind a veil of mystery it must have been for a reason. The most likely explanation is that the characters and events are too real to reveal to any readers but those most intimately involved. Understanding how sexual the *Sonnets* are, the need for anonymity should be clear. This anonymity and subtlety are necessary for the author's own protection as much as for his loved ones, for if any of the protagonists could be identified, not only embarrassment but potentially dishonor and ruin would befall all involved" (40).

Hamill's presentation, like Sobran's, would have been stronger if additional literary evidence had been cited in support of it; neither cited more than a few general passages in the works that have been interpreted in a variety of ways. The theory also suffered from insufficient motivation for the actions taken in 1623 in the Folio, in Trinity Church and with the portraits to hide Oxford's authorship. The pseudonym already in place was sufficient cover, especially twenty years after Oxford's death and fourteen years after the *Sonnets* had been published before being quickly suppressed.

---

[42] Michael Brame & Galina Popova, "Was Shakespeare Gay?" *Shakespeare Matters*, vol. 3/4 (Summer 2004): 34.

[43] John Hamill, "Shakespeare's Sexuality and How It Affects the Authorship Issue," *The Oxfordian*, vol. 8 (2005): 25.

Elizabeth Trentham

Following up on an idea suggested by Mark Anderson, Hamill proposed another answer to the why and how questions a few months later, one complementary to the Bisexual Theory. Drawing on interpretations of *Willobie His Avisa* (1594) and the *Sonnets* (1609), he proposed that Henry Vere, the son born in 1593 to Edward de Vere and his second wife, Elizabeth Trentham, had actually been fathered by Henry Wriothesley, the Third Earl of Southampton.[44] He further asserted that Oxford had described these events in a veiled way in the *Sonnets*, as had the writer of *Avisa*, thus generating the need to cover up this scandal through use of a pseudonym. In his reading, "the hypothesis that Elizabeth Trentham was the Dark Lady and Henry Wriothesley the father of Henry de Vere reveals the extraordinary bisexual triangle that finally explains the conflicted and abiding anguish expressed in *Shake-speare's Sonnets*." The purpose of the First Folio "would have been to officially preserve the pseudonym, and thus bury any association of it with Edward de Vere or Henry Wriothesley."

> The Folio created the impression that William Shakespeare was solely a dramatist. . . . Henry de Vere, Henry Wriothesley, Elizabeth Trentham, and their families, a strong closely-knit group allied by blood, marriage and politics, had the most to lose should Oxford be exposed as the author "Shakespeare." But they were in a unique position to safeguard the pseudonym, and prevent the scandal that could have destroyed the de Veres, Wriothesleys and Herberts. The pseudonym also protected the legitimacy of Henry de Vere as the 18th Earl and the Lord Great Chamberlain.[45]

Hamill refined this theory in two articles in 2009 and 2012, writing that, "I argued that *Willobie His Avisa* was a cleverly disguised exposé of a bisexual, triangular love affair involving Edward de Vere (i.e., 'Shakespeare'), his wife Elizabeth Trentham, and Henry Wriothesley. This arrangement is also reflected in *Shakespeare's Sonnets*. In addition, by subtly identifying the main characters in the *Sonnets*, something which of course they take great care to conceal, *Willobie His Avisa* provides powerful support for the overall Oxfordian thesis. If de Vere's second wife was indeed the subject of the piece, then why in 1594, in a poem naming 'Shakespeare' and *The Rape of Lucrece*, would he be satirized under the initials 'W.S.'"? Does *Willobie His Avisa* provide the key to the Shakespeare authorship issue?"[46]

Assessments by Leading Oxfordians

At the conclusion of the moot court in 1987, U.S. Supreme Court Justice John Paul Stevens commented that "the Oxfordians really have not yet put together a concise, coherent theory that they are prepared to defend in all respects."[47] He went on to state that the "strongest theory of the case requires an assumption": that for "some reason we don't understand . . . the Queen and her Prime Minister decided, 'We want this man to be writing under a pseudonym.'" Stevens's statement implicitly assumed that reasons of

---

[44] Pauline K. Angell had proposed this idea in *PMLA* back in 1937, and it may have reached Hamill through Mark Anderson (see Chapter 16).

[45] John Hamill, "The Dark Lady and Her Bastard: An Alternative Scenario," *Shakespeare Oxford Newsletter*, vol. 41/3 (Summer 2005), pp. 8-9.

[46] John Hamill, "New Light on *Willobie His Avisa* and the Authorship Question," *The Oxfordian*, vol. 14 (2012): 130.

[47] Associate Justice John Paul Stevens, quoted in William E. Boyle (editor) *A Poet's Rage* (2013), p. 119.

state must have been behind the decision to separate Oxford from the plays and poems, and, further, that the Queen and her "Prime Minister" were involved in it.

Richard Whalen, past president of the Shakespeare Oxford Society and author of *Shakespeare: Who Was He? The Oxford Challenge to the Bard of Avon* (1994), was cautiously receptive to the Dynastic Succession Theory, writing that "solving the riddle of the *Sonnets* would be one of the most sensational discoveries in English literature. Their meaning has been debated for many decades by both Stratfordians and Oxfordians. Now, Hank Whittemore's book, *The Monument*, provides by far the most comprehensive interpretations supporting the hypothesis. . . . [T]he questions at this point in time are whether the hypothesis is valid and whether skeptics and outright opponents have raised effective counter-arguments."[48] Although they "can find a number of quite plausible arguments against the Prince Tudor [Dynastic Succession] hypothesis, they are still at a disadvantage in the debate. They have not yet coalesced around an alternative, convincing scenario that would solve the riddle of the *Sonnets*, explain the silence in the surviving records about Oxford's authorship of Shakespeare and thus displace the Prince Tudor hypothesis. Whether they ever will is an open question" (17). "For their part," he added, "establishment Stratfordian scholars have all but given up trying to find a story-line and a clear meaning for *Shake-speares Sonnets*" (18).

Bill Boyle agreed, writing in effect that answers to the why and how questions must be considered an integral part of the Oxfordian claim.

> With a theory in hand that would seem to solve the *Sonnets* mystery, and also solve the "how and why of the authorship problem," I would now submit that it is now up to others to refute—if they can—rather than reactionarily reject what Whittemore has accomplished.

> It is time to build on what [he] has discovered and defined in his "monumental" study and complete our work in gaining the world's acceptance of Edward de Vere as Shakespeare with attendant appreciation for the reasons this writer wrote what he did and allowed his name to be buried these many centuries, in expectation of a time when 'eyes to be' could behold his work and 'tongues to be' could salute his noble purpose.[49]

Charles Beauclerk, who had offered early support for *The Monument* and how it explained the context for Oxford's authorship, went on to write *Shakespeare's Lost Kingdom: The True Story of Shakespeare and Elizabeth* (2010), which chronicled more acutely than elsewhere Shakespeare's obsessive focus on the matter of identity: "mistaken identity, concealed identity, loss of identity, and enforced anonymity." The theme colors all Shakespeare's/Oxford's works, most especially *Hamlet*. "Hamlet is one of a host of characters who must feign madness or assume a new identity in order to survive the rigors of the state. A prince by blood, he is prevented not only from inheriting the throne but from exercising any form of political power, turning instead to the theater as a means of influencing the ruling class."[50]

Richard Malim revived the argument that Looney had earlier advanced of playing down any controversial aspects of the Oxfordian claim until it had been accepted by

---

[48] Richard F. Whalen, "The 'Prince Tudor' Hypothesis: A Brief Survey of the Pros and Cons," *Shakespeare Oxford Newsletter*, vol. 42/2 (Spring 2006): 10.
[49] William E. Boyle, "Unveiling the Sonnets," in William E. Boyle, *A Poet's Rage* (2013), p. 120.
[50] Charles Beauclerk, *Shakespeare's Lost Kingdom: The True History of Shakespeare and Elizabeth* (2010), p. 4.

academia. "PT theorists seek to gain academic respect in Oxfordian circles by suggesting that Oxfordians should give house room to them to present a united front of Oxfordianism to the world, believing this would make the strongest possible impact; but it is the inclusion of PT that reduces our case to an object of derision. . . . ditch it, and be able to point out the clear idiocy of 'orthodoxy' Shakespeare theory without attracting fairly enough the derision that all or any versions of PT arouse."[51]

Others pointed out that Stratfordian scholars have ridiculed the Oxfordian idea for close to a century and would continue to do so regardless of Oxfordians' positions on the Dynastic Succession theory. Beauclerk expressed the view that "this debate will not be won on the Stratfordians terms, i.e., on their standards of scholarship, but on ours. Moreover, it will only be won by asserting the whole truth, and nothing but the truth, however shocking to the sensibilities of our culture. Intuition and imagination are vital components in understanding works of art which transcend the rational mind. . . . So, perhaps we should not try too hard to be Oxfordians, but dig deeply into the works to become true Shakespeareans."[52]

Anonymous (2011)

The film *Anonymous*, which depicted Edward de Vere as the author of "Shakespeare's" works and William Shakspere as a front for him, was, like Mark Anderson's *"Shakespeare" by Another Name*, not a mere film or book but an event that affected the Oxfordian movement in many ways. One was the attention the film drew to the Oxfordian claim. It was reviewed more widely than any other Oxfordian event or publication or broadcast since the moot courts of 1987 and 1989. The reviews, numbering more than a hundred, included many by prominent scholars and film critics in widely-read publications, among them James Shapiro in *The New York Times*, Alexandra Alter in *The Wall Street Journal*, David Denby in *The New Yorker* and Oliver Kamm in *The Times* in London. Most of the reviews were hostile to the Oxfordian claim, but if it's true that "there's no such thing as bad publicity," the movie was a godsend for the movement.

Audiences were often puzzled by the film, perhaps expecting a blockbuster along the lines of *The Patriot* and *Independence Day* that its director, Roland Emmerich, was known for. This was a different kind of film for him, but one that he felt so strongly about that he reportedly invested $20 million of his own money in it.[53]

---

[51] Richard Malim, letter to the editor, *Shakespeare Matters*, vol. 12/2 (Spring 2013): 2.

[52] Charles Beauclerk, letter to the editor, *Shakespeare Matters*, vol. 4/3 (Spring 2005): 2.

[53] I saw the movie twice in public theaters; both times audience reactions were different from any I had ever seen. After the first, the audience applauded as if at a live performance. After the second, the entire audience sat silently through all of the final credits as though they were completely caught up in the profundity of the experience and didn't want it to end. Not a single person left.

Adding to the critical hostility and audiences' puzzlement was that *Anonymous* presented, in addition to the Dynastic Succession idea that Edward de Vere and Queen Elizabeth had been lovers and the Earl of Southampton their son, the even more controversial idea that de Vere himself was Elizabeth's eldest son. Emmerich presented the authorship issue as intimately related to succession to the throne. Supporters of various candidates seeking to succeed the aging Elizabeth clashed throughout the film, with de Vere attempting to use his plays to influence developments in support of his candidate, the Earl of Essex. His actions backfired and contributed to the triumph of James VI of Scotland, the candidate supported by Robert Cecil, the Queen's most powerful minister. James became James I of England; Essex ended up beheaded and Southampton locked in the Tower.

The antagonisms within the Oxfordian movement over the Dynastic Succession theory had largely been papered over since the Shakespeare Fellowship had broken off from the Shakespeare Oxford Society a decade earlier. *Anonymous* brought them again to the fore, and all three Oxfordian organizations—including the De Vere Society in England—felt compelled to issue editorials about the film and the Dynastic Succession ideas presented in it.

Emmerich also funded *Last Will. & Testament*, the documentary directed by Laura Wilson Matthias and Lisa Wilson, and allowed them to use scenes from the film in it (see Chapter 19). The film also galvanized the Shakespeare Birthplace Trust to prepare its "60 Minutes with Shakespeare" video (see Chapter 20).

Assessments by Conference Attendees

What was the status of the ideas presented in this chapter within the larger Oxfordian community early in the twenty-first century? Data on this question exists because former Shakespeare Fellowship president Alex McNeil conducted surveys of members' views on these and other topics at the Shakespeare Oxford Fellowship's annual conferences in 2008, 2011, 2014 and 2017.[54] Of the thirty or so questions he asked, I have assembled information on the responses to those that directly relate to the why and how questions. Thirty surveys were completed at the conference in 2008, fifty in 2011, thirty-six in 2014 and forty-two in 2017, though not every respondent answered every question. In reporting the 2011 results, McNeil explained that "I believe that the respondents represent a good cross-section of American Oxfordians for several reasons.... [A]most all of the conference attendees were from the United States.... To the extent that conference attendees are a self-selecting group, they are persons who are very interested in and knowledgeable about the Shakespeare authorship question . . . the responses are generally consistent with those from the 2008 survey."[55]

The surveys, then, probably give a fairly accurate sense of where the Oxfordian community stood on the subjects of greatest disagreement.[56]

---

[54] Alex McNeil, "What Do 'the Oxfordians' Think?" *Shakespeare Matters*, vol. 8/3 (Summer 2009): 19; "Survey Says (2011)," *Shakespeare Matters*, vol. 11/1 (Winter 2012): 29; Alex McNeil, "Survey Says," *Shakespeare Oxford Newsletter*, vol. 50/4 (Fall 2014): 19; "2017 SOF Conference Survey Results, *Shakespeare Oxford Newsletter*, vol. 54/1 (Winter 2018): 14.

[55] Alex McNeil, "Survey Says (2011)," *Shakespeare Matters*, vol. 11/1 (Winter 2012): 29.

[56] Regarding the "median" column in the text boxes, the surveys used a 9-point scale, with "9" indicating the greatest agreement with the statement, and "1" indicating the strongest disagreement.

**Surveys of Oxfordians Attending SOF Conferences,
2008, 2011, 2014, 2017
(Conducted by Alex McNeil)**

	Agreed	Uncertain	Disagreed	Median

That Oxford's literary anonymity was state-imposed:

	Agreed	Uncertain	Disagreed	Median
2008	18/28 (64.3%)	10 (35.7%)	2 (7.1%)	7.2
2011	29/49 (59.2%)	11 (22.5%)	9 (18.1%)	7.0
2014	20/35 (85.7%)	10 (28.6%)	5 (14.3%)	7.0
2017	30/39 (76.9%)	7 (17.9%)	2 (5.1%)	7.1

That de Vere played a key role in sparing Southampton's life after the Essex Rebellion conviction:

	Agreed	Uncertain	Disagreed	Median
2008	16/28 (57.1%)	10 (35.7%)	2 (7.1%)	7.3
2011	35/49 (71.4%)	12 (24.5%)	2 (4.1%)	7.7
2014	25/36 (64.4%)	8 (22.2%)	3 (8.3%)	7.6
2017	26/36 (72.2%)	8 (22.2%)	2 (5.6%)	7.4

That de Vere had a sexual relationship with Queen Elizabeth:

	Agreed	Uncertain	Disagreed	Median
2008	16/30 (53.3%)	7 (23.3%)	7 (23.3%)	6.8
2011	30/37 (81.1%)	14 (37.8%)	4 (10.8 %)	7.5
2014	13/36 (36.1%)	12 (33.3%)	11 (30.6%)	5.0
2017	16/39 (41.0%)	17 (43.6%)	6 (15.4%)	5.9

That Henry Wriothesley, the 3rd Earl of Southampton, was the object of a homosexual infatuation by de Vere:

	Agreed	Uncertain	Disagreed	Median
2011	10/50 (20.0%)	10 (20.0%)	30 (60.0%)	1.8
2014	7/32 (21.9%)	10 (31.2%)	15 (46.9%)	4.0
2017	11/36 (30.6%)	8 (22.2%)	17 (47.2%)	4.4

That the principal story of the *Sonnets* is love and romance, heterosexual or homosexual, among real persons:

	Agreed	Uncertain	Disagreed	Median
2008	17/27 (74.1%)	6 (22.2%)	4 (14.8%)	7.8
2011	17/47 (36.2%)	13 (27.7%)	17 (36.2%)	5.0
2014	16/35 (45.7%)	8 (22.9%)	11 (31.4%)	6.0
2017	16/42 (38.1%)	10 (23.8%)	16 (38.1%)	5.7

That the principal story of the *Sonnets* is homosexual love and romance among real persons:

	Agreed	Uncertain	Disagreed	Median
2011	13/48 (27.1%)	13 (27.1%)	22 (45.8%)	4.5
2014	9/33 (27.3%)	10 (30.3%)	14 (42.4%)	4.0
2017	8/37 (21.6%)	9 (24.3%)	20 (54.1%)	3.4

That the principal story of the *Sonnets* is one of politics and succession:

	Agreed	Uncertain	Disagreed	Median
2008	7/26 (26.9%)	10 (38.5%)	9 (34.6%)	5.7
2011	21/49 (42.9%)	20 (40.8%)	8 (16.3%)	6.2
2014	16/32 (50.0%)	7 (21.9%)	9 (28.1%)	6.5
2017	18/38 (47.4%)	7 (18.4%)	13 (34.2%)	5.9

That Henry Wriothesley, 3rd Earl of Southampton, is the Fair Youth of the *Sonnets*:

	Agreed	Uncertain	Disagreed	Median
2008	20/28 (71.4%)	6 (21.4%)	2 (7.1%)	7.3
2011	40/49 (81.6%)	6 (12.2%)	3 (6.1%)	8.6
2014	26/35 (74.3%)	8 (22.9%)	1 (2.9%)	8.1
2017	30/36 (83.3%)	2 (5.6%)	4 (11.1%)	8.5

McNeil's assessment after the first survey was that "these results suggest that the strongest issues that Oxfordians need to address—among themselves and with outsiders—is whether, at its core, the Shakespeare Authorship issue is primarily a literary mystery or is primarily a political and historical mystery."[57]

As to the areas of greatest agreement, most respondents believed that Oxford's

---

**Surveys of Oxfordians Attending SOF Conferences,
2008, 2011, 2014, 2017
(Conducted by Alex McNeil)**

	Agreed	Uncertain	Disagreed	Median
That Henry Wriothesley, the 3rd Earl of Southampton, was . . .				
the natural son of the 2nd earl and his wife:				
2008	11/25 (44.0%)	7 (28.0%)	7 (28.0%)	5.2
2011	18/50 (36.0%)	14 (28.0%)	18 (36.0%)	5.8
2014	12/35 (34.3%)	11 (31.4%)	11 (31.4%)	5.0
2017	10/37 (27.0%)	14 (37.8%)	13 (35.1%)	4.8
the son of Queen Elizabeth:				
2008	7/25 (28.0%)	6 (24.0%)	12 (48.0%)	4.5
2011	20/48 (41.7%)	8 (16.7%)	20 (41.7%)	6.2
2014	11/35 (31.4%)	7 (20.0%)	17 (48.6%)	4.0
2017	13/37 (35.1%)	9 (24.3%)	15 (40.5%)	5.0

	Agreed	Uncertain	Disagreed	Median
That the Dark Lady of the *Sonnets* is . . .				
Elizabeth Trentham:				
2008	3/24 (12.5%)	9 (37.5%)	12 (50.0%)	3.5
2011	9/47 (19.1%)	15 (31.9%)	23 (48.9%)	2.8
2014	5/34 (14.7%)	11 (32.3%)	18 (52.9%)	2.5
2017	1/36 (27.8%)	8 (22.2%)	27 (75.0%)	2.4
Emilia Bassanio:				
2008	3/22 (13.6%)	8 (36.4%)	11 (50.0%)	4.0
2011	2/47 (4.3%)	17 (36.2%)	28 (59.6%)	2.0
2014	1/33 (3.0%)	13 (39.4%)	19 (57.6%)	3.5
2017	3/36 (8.3%)	7 (19.4%)	26 (72.2%)	2.4
Queen Elizabeth:				
2008	11/26 (42.3%)	6 (23.1%)	9 (34.6%)	4.5
2011	14/47 (29.8%)	17 (36.2%)	16 (34.0%)	6.2
2014	12/34 (35.3%)	11 (32.4%)	11 (32.4%)	6.0
2017	11/33 (33.3%)	8 (24.2%)	14 (42.4%)	4.8
Penelope Rich:				
2017	11/35 (31.4%)	7 (20.0%)	17 (48.6%)	4.9

The results of a vote held after a panel on "The Dark Lady of the *Sonnets*" at the 2018 conference were:

Queen Elizabeth	41 (45.0%)
Anne Vavasor	30 (33.0%)
Emilia Bassanio	10 (11.0%)
Penelope Rich	10 (11.0%)

---

[57] Alex McNeil, "What Do 'the Oxfordians' Think?" *Shakespeare Matters*, vol. 8/3 (Summer 2009): 19.

literary anonymity was state-imposed and that de Vere had played a key role in sparing Southampton's life after the Essex Rebellion conviction. Solid majorities agreed with these points in the earliest survey and increased over time.

Turning to the relationships between Edward de Vere and Queen Elizabeth and between de Vere and Southampton, opinions changed over time. Belief that de Vere had had a sexual relationship with the Queen swung from a high of eighty-one percent in 2011 to only forty-one percent in 2017. Belief that he had had a homosexual relationship with the Earl of Southampton rose during those years, from twenty to thirty percent, but still remained below that of belief in Oxford's sexual relationship with the Queen. The percentages disagreeing tell the same story; only fifteen percent disagreed with the idea of Oxford's sexual relationship with the Queen whereas forty-seven percent disagreed that he'd had such a relationship with Southampton.

Belief in the idea that Henry Wriothesley was the natural son of the Second Earl of Southampton and his wife dropped from forty-four percent to twenty-seven percent, while belief that he was the son of Queen Elizabeth and the Earl of Oxford rose from twenty-eight percent to thirty-five percent. These findings tend to give credence to the idea of growing support for the Dynastic Succession theory.

Turning to the *Sonnets*, the belief that the principal story told in them was one of love and romance dropped, from seventy-four percent to thirty-eight percent, while belief that it is one of politics and succession rose from twenty-seven percent to forty-seven percent, again suggesting growing support for the Dynastic Succession theory and the ideas in *The Monument*. Belief that Southampton is the Fair Youth of the *Sonnets* grew during this time, with eighty-three percent supporting it in 2017.

The question that most directly reveals beliefs about the Dynastic Succession theory versus other theories is that of the identity of the Dark Lady. Queen Elizabeth received the highest percentages in each survey. Elizabeth Trentham received the second highest percentages in the first three surveys. But in 2017 Penelope Rich, proposed in a new theory recently introduced by Alexander Waugh, edged Trentham out for second place, thirty-one percent to twenty-eight. However, a great deal of uncertainty remains, as the number of those who disagreed with all these candidates for the Dark Lady outweighed the number of those who agreed, as shown in the nearby tables.

In sum, although uncertainty remains about the answers proposed to the why and how questions, the Dynastic Succession/*Monument* idea holds a plurality.

<u>My assessments</u>

The following is a summary of the most prominent answers to the why and how questions proposed by Oxfordians in the first and second waves of the movement and my assessments of them. I recognize that all Oxfordians have made good-faith examinations of the theories proposed and that some hold views different from mine.

> Oxford's status as a courtier and that the plays satirize fellow courtiers might have been sufficient reason for the use of a pseudonym early in his adulthood, but they do not, in themselves, justify the extraordinary efforts designed to hide his authorship from future generations undertaken in the 1620s, twenty years after his death: the ambiguous and misleading prefatory materials in the First Folio, the oddities of the monument in Trinity Church in Stratford, and the over-painting of at least three portraits of Oxford to make them resemble more closely the Droeshout engraving in the Folio.

➤ The Bisexual Theory—that Oxford had to cut the connections between himself and his literary works because they, especially the *Sonnets*, contained veiled references to a sexual relationship between himself and the Earl of Southampton—suffers, I believe, from several limitations. One is the scanty literary evidence; I have gone through Sobran's and Hamill's articles several times, searching for exactly what sonnets or words or phrases led them to their conclusions, each time coming up empty. They did not identify them. The few passages cited are general in nature, capable of multiple interpretations. Hamill mentioned other scholars who reached conclusions in line with his, but did not cite specific sonnets or phrases that led them to their conclusions.

➤ The theory that veiled references in the *Sonnets* indicate that the Earl of Southampton had fathered the 18th Earl of Oxford by a liaison with Oxford's second wife, Elizabeth Trentham, seems fanciful in the extreme. It relies on tortured interpretations of a few phrases in the *Sonnets* and has no evidence of real-life events to buttress it. Unlike Whittemore's use of informed imagination to connect the sonnets to real-life events at the end of Elizabeth's reign, Trentham theory supporters' reading of the sonnets seems both too literal and too fantastical. It is too literal because the Dark Lady of the *Sonnets* is dark in spirit only, yet supporters cite Trentham's dark hair and eyes as evidence. It is too fantastical because there is no independent documentation that the supposed affair between Trentham and Southampton ever took place.

➤ For both the Bisexual Theory and the Trentham Theory, the use of the pseudonym would have been sufficient; neither explain why Oxford's family would have undertaken a new effort to hide his authorship in 1623, almost twenty years after his death. Why take such extraordinary measures to hide veiled references in the *Sonnets*, which had apparently been suppressed immediately after publication in 1609, fourteen years before the Folio was published, and wouldn't be republished for decades, and which, therefore, almost nobody at the time had read, remembered or was even aware of?

➤ The Dynastic Succession Theory is the only theory I know of that justifies the extraordinary effort taken in the 1620s to hide Oxford's authorship from future generations, which was the intent of the misleading prefatory material in the First Folio, the odd aspects of the monument in Trinity Church and the over-paintings of at least three portraits of the Earl of Oxford to make them closer in appearance to the Droeshout engraving in the Folio. It is the only explanation that justifies the use of State power that would have been necessary for the extensive effort to seek out and destroy government and private papers related to Oxford's authorship and William Shakspere's non-authorship.

➤ The explanation provided by Hank Whittemore in *The Monument* complements and strengthens the Dynastic Succession idea. The existence of a 100-sonnet core to the *Sonnets*, and the idea of a stencil of real-life events—including the Essex Rebellion, Southampton's imprisonment and release and the end of the Tudor Dynasty—adds to the literary evidence and documentary evidence.

22

Academia's Public Response:
Defensive and Offensive

Defense Through Offense

During the first decades after *"Shakespeare" Identified* was published, academia responded to the Oxfordian challenge with two complementary strategies—ignoring it whenever possible and attacking it when it wasn't. Most modern Stratfordian scholars use the same strategies, but the mix has tilted toward attacking.

Those who follow the strategy of ignoring the Oxfordian idea often strain to avoid mentioning Edward de Vere in any context, perhaps taking a perverse pride in demonstrating how little they know of him or the Oxfordian claim. In *Anonymity in Early Modern England: "What's in a Name?"* (2011) edited by Janet Wright Starner and Barbara Howard Traister, only one of its seven chapters even mentions him even though contemporaries had praised him as a skilled poet who wrote anonymously.[1] The editors managed to get his name wrong in the index, listing him as "Edmund de Vere."[2] Cyndia Susan Clegg made a similar "mistake," listing him as "Robert de Vere" in the index to her book, *Press Censorship in Elizabethan England*. Penny McCarthy, in *Pseudonymous Shakespeare* (2006), mentioned Oxford four times in the text but omitted him from the index altogether. Others didn't bother to mention him at all, including Janet Clare in *'Art Made Tongue-tied by Authority:' Elizabethan and Jacobean Dramatic Censorship* (1990), Marcy L. North in *The Anonymous Renaissance* (2003), and John Mullan in *Anonymity: A Secret History of English Literature* (2007). John Guy, in *Elizabeth: The Forgotten Years*, forgot to mention Oxford though he mentioned one of his daughters four times.

Many other scholars, aware of the widespread public awareness of the Oxfordian idea, realized that it could no longer be ignored. In 1995, Thomas Pendleton, editor of *The*

---

[1] *The Arte of English Poesie* (1589), dedicated to Queen Elizabeth and Lord Treasurer Burghley, for instance, stated that "in Her Majesty's time that now is are sprung up another crew of Courtly makers (poets). Noblemen and Gentlemen of Her Majesty's own servants, who have written excellently well as it would appear if their doings could be found out and made public with the rest, of which number is first that noble gentleman Edward Earl of Oxford."

[2] Janet Wright Starner and Barbara Howard Traister, editors, *Anonymity in Early Modern England: "What's In a Name?"* (2011), p. 182.

Shakespeare Newsletter, expressed his dismay at the level of interest in the Oxfordian claim.

> It is surprising, if not disheartening, to learn that while [Oxfordian] Charles Burford has lectured at 56 colleges and universities [and the Folger Library], Irvin Matus has been invited to two. . . . Burford is fluent and entertaining, his appearances are energetically promoted, and the iconoclastic obviously has an attraction that the orthodox lacks; but still—Burford 56, Matus 2.[3]

Alan Nelson, Professor of English at UC Berkeley (now emeritus), expressed similar unease in a 1999 review of Joseph Sobran's *Alias Shakespeare: Solving the Greatest Literary Mystery of All Time*. After recounting how he discovered that one "highly cultured and superbly educated couple" believed that the earl of Oxford was really Shakespeare, and that around the same time he met two others, a lawyer and a software engineer, who held the same view, Nelson concluded that "Establishment Shakespeareans . . . are losing the public debate over the 'authorship question.'"[4] Nelson would soon try to rebalance the scales with his highly unflattering biography of Oxford, *Monstrous Adversary* (2003).

Several scholars took the initiative to respond directly to the Oxfordian claim—or at least give the appearance of responding to it. This move from ignoring the thesis to addressing it directly is the most significant change in academia's approach between the first and second waves of the Oxfordian challenge. It would have been even more significant if academia had conducted its examinations in the scholarly and academic manner called for by Professor Stanley Fish and historian David Hackett Fischer (see Chapter 11).[5] Their guidance could be supplemented by that from Stratfordian scholar Giles E. Dawson (the same Giles E. Dawson that Charles Wisner Barrell had sued) who presented this idealized account of scholarly work:

> The scholar has no axes to grind. He is not eager to prove his own hypotheses correct, but rather to find out whether they are correct or not. He is ever ready

---

[3] Thomas Pendleton, "From the Editors," *Shakespeare Newsletter*, vol. 45/2 (Summer 1995): 26.

[4] Alan Nelson, [review of *Alias Shakespeare: Solving the Greatest Literary Mystery of All Time* by Joseph Sobran], *Shakespeare Quarterly*, vol. 50/3 (Autumn 1999): 376. The reference to Charles Burford is to Charles Beauclerk's speaking tours on behalf of the Oxfordian claim noted in Chapter 19.

[5] Their thoughts are reprinted here. In academic study, Stanley Fish noted,

> "[Subjects] should be discussed in academic terms; that is, they should be the objects of analysis, comparison, historical placement, etc.; the arguments put forward in relation to them should be dissected and assessed as arguments and not as preliminaries to action on the part of those doing the assessing. The action one takes (or should take) at the conclusion of an academic discussion is the action of tendering an academic verdict as in 'that argument makes sense,' 'there's a hole in the reasoning here,' 'the author does (or does not) realize her intention,' 'in this debate, X has the better of Y,' 'the case is still not proven.' These and similar judgments are judgments on craftsmanship and coherence—they respond to questions like 'is it well made?' and 'does it hang together?'" [*Save the World On Your Own Time* (2008), p. 144.]

Because the authorship question deals with events that took place in the past, methodologies appropriate to historical research are relevant. David Hackett Fischer. In his book *Historians' Fallacies: Toward a Logic of Historical Thought* he described the approach most appropriate for historians as consisting of "adductive reasoning."

> "History must begin with questions. Questions for historians are like hypotheses for scientists. . . . The logic of historical thought . . . is a process of adductive reasoning in the simple sense of adducing answers to specific questions, so that a satisfactory explanatory 'fit' is obtained. . . . The questions and answers are fitted to each other by a complex process of mutual adjustment. . . . Always it is articulated in the form of a reasoned argument." [*Historians' Fallacies* (1970), pp. xx, 4.]

to reevaluate and reinterpret his evidence and to discard one hypothesis in favor of a better. When he uncovers a fact that does not square with his hypothesis he neither shuts his eyes to it nor tries to explain it away nor trims it to fit the facts.[6]

Unfortunately, the Stratfordian scholars who examined the Oxfordian claim in their books did not conduct their examinations in line with these scholarly practices. Mostly they used only a veneer of seemingly academic study as a cover for attacks. The most prominent scholars who "examined" the Oxfordian thesis in this manner are listed in the nearby text box.

Stratfordian Attacks on the Oxfordian Claim After 1984

1987	Marjorie Garber	*Shakespeare's Ghost Writers: Literature as Uncanny Causality*
1988	Leah S. Marcus	*Puzzling Shakespeare: Local Reading and Its Discontents*
1989	Gary Taylor	*Reinventing Shakespeare: A Cultural History from the Restoration to the Present*
1990	Peter Gay	*Reading Freud: Explorations and Entertainments*
1991	S. Schoenbaum	*Shakespeare's Lives* [1970]
1994	Irvin Matus	*Shakespeare, in Fact*
1996	John Michell	*Who Wrote Shakespeare?*
1997	Jonathan Bate	*The Genius of Shakespeare*
2002	Harold Love	*Attributing Shakespeare*
2003	Alan Nelson	*Monstrous Adversary: The Life of Edward de Vere, 17th Earl of Oxford*
2004	Stephen Greenblatt	*Will in the World: How Shakespeare Became Shakespeare*
2005	Scott McCrea	*The Case for Shakespeare*
2009	Helen Hackett	*Shakespeare and Elizabeth: The Meeting of Two Myths*
2010	James Shapiro	*Contested Will: Who Wrote Shakespeare?*
2012	David Ellis	*The Truth About Shakespeare: Fact, Fiction and Modern Biographies*

Stratfordian scholars continue to use the same methods of attacking the Oxfordian claim that their predecessors resorted to in the 1920s and 1930s:

- Changing the subject to focus on Oxfordian scholars themselves rather than on the specifics of the Oxfordian thesis;

- Stating the thesis and dismissing rather than disproving it;

- Presenting distorted versions of the thesis, then showing the ridiculousness of them;

- Repeating old criticisms of the thesis without mentioning the substantive rebuttals Oxfordians had already made to them;

- Highlighting Oxford's personal failings to imply that no one with his character flaws could have written Shakespeare's works;

- Rejecting the Oxfordians' methodology of citing allusions in the works to Edward de Vere and people and events important to him, even though literature scholars have long recognized the value of using such linkages when interpreting the works of other writers;

- Continuing to present the Stratfordian story with suppositions stated as fact.

---

[6] Giles E. Dawson, "Review of *This Star of England* by Dorothy and Charlton Ogburn," *Shakespeare Quarterly,* vol. 4/2 (1953): 165.

James Shapiro's *Contested Will* (2010)

I have selected this book, by a professor of English at Columbia University, as representative of works by academics which purport to deal with the Oxfordian claim. It was widely reviewed and highly praised. Terry Teachout, drama critic for *The Wall Street Journal*, who believes that there exists "no credible evidence whatsoever to support" the claims of doubters, lauded *Contested Will* as a "no-nonsense study of the zanies whose theory-mongering has blighted the world of legitimate Shakespeare studies."[7] Among orthodox scholars, Shapiro is regarded as having refuted the Oxfordian thesis in *Contested Will*, consigning it to the oblivion it deserves. Did he?

Shapiro began well enough: "This is a book about when and why many people began to question whether William Shakespeare wrote the plays long attributed to him, and, if he didn't write them, who did" (3). Shapiro reassured readers about his intentions, writing that his interest "is not in what people think . . . so much as why they think it. . . . I think it's possible to get at why people have come to believe what they believe about Shakespeare's authorship, and it is partly in the hope of doing so that I have written this book" (8). Readers are led to expect an examination of the substantive reasons why doubters reached the conclusions they did.

Another hopeful sign was that Shapiro acknowledged doubts by "some brilliant writers and thinkers," including Sigmund Freud, Henry James, and Mark Twain. He observed that "the biographers of Freud, Twain, and James weren't keen on looking too deeply into these authors' doubts" (9). He candidly admitted that "there yet remains one subject walled off from serious study by Shakespeare scholars: the authorship question. . . . [T]his subject remains virtually taboo in academic circles" (5). He acknowledged "the decision by professors to all but ignore the authorship question" (5) and that "[t]hose who would deny Shakespeare's authorship" have been "long excluded from publishing their work in academic journals or through university presses" (8). Surely, the reader is led to believe, Shapiro will attempt to rectify this acknowledged failure of academia to examine the authorship issue.

But red flags soon appear, indicating that Shapiro isn't going to engage in a scholarly examination after all. One is that the name of the man from Stratford is consistently given as "William Shakespeare," even though he was baptized as "Gulielmus Shakspere" and neither he nor any member of his family spelled their surname as "Shakespeare" at any time during his life. Intentionally using the "Shakespeare" spelling immediately prejudices the issue. A second error was that Shapiro regarded every mention of the name "Shakespeare" during Shakspere's lifetime as a reference to the man from Stratford rather than to the person who wrote the plays and poems (whoever he may have been). These conflations suggest that Shapiro's methodology is suspect almost from the start.

Shapiro's real intent, it becomes clear, was to investigate not the substantive reasons why doubters doubted, but a side issue: the psychological makeup that predisposed them toward doubts. Based on his assumption that the Stratfordian story is correct and that doubters of it are wrong, he examines what he determined were the psychological reasons why Delia Bacon, J. Thomas Looney, Sigmund Freud and others were drawn to the authorship question. "For a debate that largely turns on how one understands the relationship of Shakespeare's life and works, there has been disappointingly little attention devoted to considering how Bacon's and Looney's experiences and worldviews

---

[7] Terry Teachout, "Denying Shakespeare," *Wall Street Journal*, April 17, 2010, p. W14.

determined the trajectory of their theories of authorship. Scholars on both sides of the debate have overlooked a great deal by taking these two polemicists at their word" (10).

Shapiro is right to emphasize the relationship between a writer's life and his or her works; the many points of correspondence between Oxford's life and personality on one hand, and developments and characters in *Hamlet*, *King Lear* and the *Sonnets* on the other, are one of the strongest types of evidence in support of his authorship of them, just as the lack of such correspondences between Shakspere's life and the works is one of the strongest reasons for doubt about his. But Shapiro's focus is not on such substantive linkages.

Regarding Sigmund Freud's belief in Edward de Vere's authorship, Shapiro asks "why one of the great modern minds turned against Shakespeare," and found the answer not in Freud's examination of the weakness of the Stratfordian claim and the strength of the Oxfordian, but that "[t]he answer might well lie elsewhere: Freud's devotion to Oxford's cause was no psychic riddle but a response to a threat to his Oedipal theory, the cornerstone of psychoanalysis—which in turn rested in no small way upon a biographical reading of Shakespeare's life and work. From this perspective, Freud's rejection of Shakespeare of Stratford seems both inevitable and necessary—though, like the claims of many others, it reveals more about the skeptic than it does about the authorship of Shakespeare's plays" (156).

Despite a pretense of objectivity, Shapiro mischaracterized Freud's thinking by saying that he had "turned against Shakespeare." Neither Freud nor any other Oxfordian turned against Shakespeare; they all loved Shakespeare's works. That is why they wanted to see the author who wrote under that pen name get credit for them.

Turning to Charlton Ogburn, Jr., Shapiro explained the resurrection of the Oxfordian movement in 1984 as due not to the strength of the case in *The Mysterious William Shakespeare*, but instead to the tenor of the times. "The resurrection of the Oxfordian movement has been little short of miraculous—one of the most remarkable and least remarked episodes in the history of Shakespeare studies. What brought it about? Oxfordians usually point to the publication in 1984 of Charlton Ogburn's *The Mysterious William Shakespeare*. It would be more accurate to say that Ogburn's timely book rode the wave of some sweeping cultural changes" (203-04). Shapiro, of course, did not delve into any of Ogburn's arguments.

The following are examples of Shapiro's odd and unscholarly approach to the authorship question.

<u>Dismissal, not refutation, of the views of doubters or Oxfordian scholars</u>. Shapiro seems to pursue two contradictory lines of thought. On one hand, he sometimes presents reasons cited by doubters fairly and objectively, almost in terms that they themselves might have used. He seems to understand the substantive reasons for those doubts and beliefs. On the other hand, he simply dismisses them, without bothering to refute the substantive reasons he has just cited in support of them. Here are two examples:

✓ Shapiro wrote of Henry James that

> But this for James was the most troubling thing about *The Tempest*: how could the genius who wrote it renounce his art at the age of forty-eight and retire to rural Stratford to "spend what remained to him of life in walking about a small, squalid country-town with his hand in his pockets and ear for no music but the chink of the coin they might turn over there"? (147)

This rift between the received biography [of William Shakspere] and the poetic genius James had encountered over the course of a lifetime of reading the works attributed to Shakespeare was clearly unbridgeable, the most "insoluble mystery that ever was." Either something was terribly wrong about the biography of the author of *The Tempest* or James misunderstood something fundamental about literary genius. The stakes here couldn't be higher. (148)

o How did Shapiro address this enigma? He didn't. After stating James's puzzlement he changed the subject, leaving the mystery unexplained. This odd posing of a problem and then turning away from it happens frequently in *Contested Will*.

✓ Shapiro argues throughout the book against what he calls the autobiographical approach to understanding literary works. But in the section on Mark Twain and his doubts about Shakspere's authorship he writes that "Time and again Twain reaffirms the intrinsic link between powerful writing and an author's life experience" (137). "For Twain, the notion that great writing had to be drawn from life—rather than from what an author heard, read, or simply imagined—was an article of faith, at the heart of his conception of how serious writers worked" (114). Shapiro follows that up with additional testimony from other writers reinforcing Twain's beliefs.

o How did Shapiro square that testimony with his own insistence on an anti-autobiographical approach to understanding literature? He didn't. Again he changed the subject, perhaps counting on readers not to notice his gliding over the distinction between "drawn from life" and "autobiographical." There is a world of difference, with "drawn from life" being the wide middle ground between the extremes of autobiographical writing and pure imagination. Conflating the two is an intellectually dishonest attempt to steer readers into accepting the Stratfordian story.

Posing extremes and ignoring the middle. Shapiro often poses two extremes as the only possibilities, ignoring the middle ground as in the Mark Twain example just cited. He distorts doubters' views by placing them at one extreme. After establishing the ridiculousness of that extreme, he reasons that the opposite extreme must therefore be true, a logically fallible assumption.

✓ "Some suppose that only Shakespeare and the real author were in the know. At the other extreme are those who believe that it was an open secret, so widely shared that it wasn't worth mentioning" (225).

o Shapiro left out the middle ground: that Oxford's authorship of Shakespeare's works was known by those who needed to know it (including some persons in Elizabeth's court and some in the theater world), but not by others.

✓ "Looney also found it 'impossible' to believe that Shakespeare could have quit the stage and 'retired to Stratford to devote himself to houses, lands, orchards, money and malt, leaving no traces of a single intellectual or literary interest.' No writer of this stature could have cared that much about money. Shakespeare of Stratford was either a hypocrite or an imposter. . . . His logic is unassailable—but only if you believe that great authors don't write for money and that the plays are transparently autobiographical. Looney believed both unquestioningly" (171).

- o There are numerous distortions and deliberate misstatements in this passage. There is the implication that only Looney and other Oxfordians found it "'impossible' to believe that Shakespeare could have quit the stage," when in fact many found it odd that the great dramatist retired at the height of his creative power to engage in small-time commercial activities "leaving no trace of a single intellectual or literary interest." Yet Shapiro makes no effort to explain it.

    There are also the false extremes of caring about money and caring about literary activities. Of course it is possible to be concerned about both. Furthermore, according to Shapiro, it was his literary activities that had made Shakspere wealthy, so claiming now that he abandoned them to pursue wealth in his hometown makes no sense.

Misrepresentation of Stratfordian findings as Oxfordian. Shapiro often portrays as crackpot ideas scholarly findings by noted Shakespearean scholars that support the Oxfordian claim. To undercut their credibility he attributes them to Oxfordian scholars.

- ✓ "Oxfordians claim" that others touched up or finished Shakespeare's work after his death or retirement, implying that the claim is a desperate invention by Oxfordians to justify their belief. Yet Shapiro, as a Shakespeare expert, knew full well that that claim was proposed and established by the respected Stratfordian scholar Sir Walter Raleigh before J. Thomas Looney proposed de Vere's authorship, and was reaffirmed by Raleigh after *"Shakespeare" Identified* was published.

- ✓ Shapiro implied that Looney created out of thin air the eighteen qualities he believed the author of Shakespeare's plays had to have had. But he had given *"Shakespeare" Identified* such a careful reading that he was surely aware that Looney adopted virtually all of the eighteen qualities from the works of Stratfordian scholars. Looney's second list might indeed have been "more controversial," than his first, but it was still drawn from the work of orthodox scholars.

- ✓ Shapiro noted that the dedication to *Venus and Adonis* was signed William Shake-speare, "the first time the notorious hyphen appeared in the printed version of his name, a telling sign, for skeptics, of pseudonymous publication" (224). Setting aside Shapiro's glaring error—the name is not hyphenated on the *Venus and Adonis* dedication page[8]—it is traditional scholars, not sceptics alone, who hold that hyphens often indicated pseudonyms during the Elizabethan Era.

Selective use of Oxfordian claims. Shapiro mischaracterized aspects of the Oxfordian claim in ways that he surely knew Oxfordians had already repeatedly refuted.

- ✓ "The greatest challenge Looney had to meet was the problem of Oxford's death in 1604, since so many of Shakespeare's great Jacobean plays were not yet written, including *Macbeth*, *King Lear*, *Coriolanus*, *Antony and Cleopatra*, *Timon of Athens*, *Pericles*, *The Winter's Tale*, *Cymbeline*, and *Henry the Eighth*. Looney concluded that these plays were either written before Oxford died (and posthumously

---

[8] The error was corrected in the paperback edition of *Contested Will* (2010).

released one by one to the playgoing public) or left incomplete and touched up by lesser writers (which explains why they contain allusions to sources or events that took place after Oxford had died)" (178-79).

- o Here again is the statement of a sensible position held by many respected Stratfordian scholars presented with the implication that Looney alone held them, a practice deliberately misleading and not scholarship worthy of respect. Shapiro ignores findings by other Stratfordian scholars such as A. S. Cairncross that all the plays could have been written by 1604.

  Shapiro is aware that scholars have not determined the dates of composition for any of Shakespeare's plays; that it is only dates of performances and printings that are known. By Shapiro's logic, those Shakespeare plays not printed until the First Folio in 1623, seven years after Shakspere's death, couldn't have been written by him. As a Shakespeare expert, he knew that the dates traditionally assigned to the plays were selected in order to space them out in a logical way within Shakspere's lifetime—a process with no validity if Shakspere was not the author.

  Also interesting was Shapiro's use of the term "Jacobean" to describe Shakespeare's plays, which in years past were always described as Elizabethan. He even goes so far as to note Edmond Malone's observation that "topical correspondences" in the plays were "centered on the court, mostly from the reign of Elizabeth" (39), before airily dismissing it.

One illustrative section (on pages 176-177)

- ✓ "Enough incidents in Oxford's life uncannily corresponded to events in the plays to support Looney's claims that the plays were barely veiled autobiography" (176).
  - o This unexpected admission is partly true—"incidents in Oxford's life . . . corresponded to events in the plays"—and partly false—"Looney's claims that the plays were barely veiled autobiography." Looney never made that claim. Rather, he maintained that the plays were inspired in part by Oxford's personality and experiences; they were not the products of pure fantasy or imagination.

    If it is true that events in the plays correspond "uncannily" to events in Oxford's life, that would seem to be strong evidence of Oxford's association with the plays, perhaps even his authorship of them. How did Shapiro deal with that? He didn't. He simply moved on, leaving the issue hanging.

- ✓ "Looney matched [*Hamlet's*] cast of characters with those of Oxford's courtly circle: Polonius is Lord Burleigh, Laertes is his son Thomas Cecil, Hamlet is Oxford himself, and Ophelia is Oxford's wife, Anne," who was also Burleigh's daughter (177).
  - o Shapiro implied only Looney and other Oxfordians held that crazy idea, leaving the reader unaware that many other traditional scholars had made most of those identifications as far back as 1869, decades before Looney. That omission is intellectually dishonest. Shapiro himself had noted those identifications on page 39 of his book; had he expected that

readers would have forgotten it by page 177?

✓ "But such claims about representing on the public stage some of the most powerful figures in the realm betray a shallow grasp of Elizabethan dramatic censorship. . . . Looney didn't understand that Edmund Tilney, the master of the Revels, whose job it was to read and approve all dramatic scripts before they were publicly performed, would have lost his job—and most likely his nose and ears, if not his head—had he approved a play that so transparently ridiculed privy councillors past and present" (177).

    o In acknowledging strong linkages between events in the plays and events in Oxford's life, and in raising the issue of allusions to prominent members of the court in the plays that, if true, would have resulted in Shakspere being questioned, Shapiro has touched on another mystery that the Stratfordian story is unable to explain: why wasn't Shakspere arrested for passages in his plays that others would have been arrested for? Thomas Kyd was thought to have been tortured for what he wrote and died less than a year later. Ben Jonson was jailed on several occasions, and branded, for his writings. How did Shapiro explain that Shakespeare, and only Shakespeare, avoided being arrested or questioned? He didn't. He never considered the common-sense solution to it, that the author was someone to whom the ordinary rules did not apply.

✓ "Oxford's authorship, Looney was convinced, made everything clear" (177).

    o This is another false statement. Looney did not say that Oxford's authorship made everything clear; his position was that Oxford's authorship was the key that enabled scholars to *begin* the work of understanding the plays, and that, "the real study of 'Shakespeare,' as distinct from the merely literary and academic, is only now in its early stages."[9]

✓ "Looney's scheme also defies common sense, for Lord Burleigh was dead by the time *Hamlet* was written, and nothing could have been in poorer taste, or more dangerous, than mocking Elizabeth's most beloved councillor soon after his death, onstage or in print" (177).

    o Here Shapiro has loaded several false statements into one sentence. Burleigh was not "Elizabeth's most beloved councillor;" he was the most powerful and most feared man in England. Many were glad to see him gone. As to the claim about mocking him so soon after his death, Shapiro ignored evidence that *Hamlet* could have been written as early as 1583, when Burghley, who died in 1598, was very much alive. Even traditional Shakespeare scholars such as A. S. Cairncross believed that *Hamlet* had been well known to the public by the end of the 1580s.

Shapiro on Shakspere

Shapiro devoted the final sections of *Contested Will* to a defense of the case for William Shakspere's authorship characterized in large part by glossing over its weaknesses and

---

[9] J. Thomas Looney, "'Shakespeare's' Identity" [letter], *Sydney Morning Herald*, July 15, 1921, p. 12.

by stating suppositions as fact. He began by noting that doubts had arisen as early as the 1850s.

> By 1857 . . . an unbearable tension had developed between Shakespeare the poet and Shakespeare the businessman; between the London playwright and the Stratford haggler; between Shakespeare as Prospero and Shakespeare as Shylock; between the kind of man revealed in the "autobiographical" poems and plays, and the one revealed in tax, court, and real estate records; between a deified Shakespeare and a depressingly mundane one. Surely he was either one or the other. (69)

Logically, the next step should have been to alleviate those concerns by presenting evidence uncovered since the 1850s connecting the man from Stratford with the plays and poems. Shapiro did the opposite, citing further doubts expressed early in the twentieth century in what he described as the most influential biography of the age, Halliwell-Phillipps's *Outlines of the Life of Shakespeare* (first published in 1881): "It must be admitted that nothing whatever has yet presented itself which discloses those finer traits of thought and action we are sure must have pervaded the author of *Lear* and *Hamlet* in his communication with the more cultivated of his contemporaries" (65). Shapiro simply moved on, leaving that testimony against Shakspere's authorship unanswered.

He then cited three types of evidence that for him were definitive in proving Shakspere's authorship beyond reasonable doubt. "The first is what early printed texts reveal . . . the second, what writers who knew Shakespeare said about him. Either of them, to my mind, suffices to confirm his authorship—and the stories they tell corroborate each other. . . . All this is reinforced by additional evidence from the closing years of his career, when he began writing for a new kind of playhouse, in a different style, in active collaboration with other writers" (223). All three types of evidence are flawed.

<u>"What early printed texts reveal"</u>: Shapiro wrote that "Then, as now, writers gossiped about one another. Fortunately, a surprising amount of what his fellow writers thought about Shakespeare has survived" (235). But, as noted, Shapiro equates all references to the writer Shakespeare as references to the man from Stratford.

✓ "In 1592, [Robert] Green (or possibly his fellow playwright Henry Chettle) . . . warned established dramatists that . . . there is an upstart crow, beautified with our feathers'" (234) who was a threat to them. This famous passage, often cited as confirmation that Shakspere had become a well-known dramatist by 1592, does not mention Shakespeare or Shakspere by name, but paraphrases a line from one of Shakespeare's plays that did not appear in print until later. Many Oxfordians believe that the reference is not to the writer of the play but to Edward Alleyn, believed to have been the actor who spoke that line and who was notorious for inserting lines into his parts.[10] It's like the actor Clint Eastwood, not the writer, becoming famous for a line in *Dirty Harry*: "Go ahead. Make my day." Yet Shapiro (and most other Stratfordian scholars) ignore this possibility.

✓ Shapiro cited references in *Willobie His Avisa* (1594) as evidence of Shakspere's authorship. Those references are to "W.S.," but even if it is correct that they refer to the writer William Shakespeare, there is nothing to connect them to the man

---

[10] For the definitive examination of this subject, see Bryan H. Wildenthal's *Early Shakespeare Authorship Doubts* (2019), pp. 71-112.

from Stratford.

✓ Shapiro cited references to Shakespeare in Richard Barnfield's "A Remembrance of Some English Poets" in 1598 (235). Again this is a reference to the writer, not to the man from Stratford. The same is true for Francis Meres's mention of Shakespeare in *Palladis Tamia* in 1598.

<u>"What writers who knew Shakespeare said about him:"</u> These, again, are either references to the author or are figments of Shapiro's imagination.

✓ Shakespeare, "as an actor, playwright, and shareholder in the most popular playing company in the land [was] . . . also one of the most familiar faces in town and at court" (224). Really? No record connects him with anyone at court. No record mentions him as performing in London or in the provinces, and only two obscure references to the name occur in court records, both of suspect validity. No personal reminiscence about him exists from his lifetime. Sir Sidney Lee had written that "He never obtained much reputation as an actor."[11]

✓ Shapiro writes that "One of those who recognized Shakespeare and knew him by name was George Buc," who "knew Shakespeare well enough to stop and ask him about the authorship of an old and anonymous play published in 1599" (224). "Buc's flesh-and-blood encounter [was] with a man he knew as both actor and playwright." (224). But there is no evidence that the two men knew each other. Shapiro acknowledged, however, that Buc was "a familiar acquaintance of the Earl of Oxford." Given that acquaintance, it could have been to the Earl that Buc asked the question. Readers are left wondering why Shapiro introduced the Buc-Oxford connection that undercut his own supposed Buc-Shakspere explanation without addressing it further.

<u>"Active collaboration with other writers:"</u> There is no evidence that Shakespeare ever actively collaborated with anybody else. This point is discussed in Chapter 23.

<u>Other Contradictions and Dubious Statements</u>

The following examples of Shapiro's errors and distortions are included here because they are typical of those of many other Stratfordian scholars.

✓ Shapiro stated that Shakespeare's "two great narrative poems, *Venus and Adonis* and *Lucrece*," published in 1593 and 1594, were "bestsellers that went through many editions" (225). Two pages later he stated that "1598 turned out to be the very year that two publishers independently decided that Shakespeare's popularity had reached the point where it was profitable to put his name on the title page of his plays" (227).

  o If Shakespeare's name had been associated with two bestsellers published in 1593 and 1594, why did publishers wait another four years to put his name on dramatic works? That delay is particularly puzzling given that there is no record of any mention of Shakespeare the writer during those four years. Shapiro provides no explanation.

✓ "If there really was a conspiracy and 'Shake-speare' a pseudonym, a score of publishers who at various times over a quarter-century owned and published

---

[11] Sir Sidney Lee, *Elizabethan and Other Essays* (1929), p. 87.

Shakespeare's works, and then their various printers and compositors, and then those to whom they sold their rights, would each in turn have had to be let in on the secret" (227).

    o   What is the logic in assuming that all those publishers and printers "would have had to be let in on the secret?" "B" does not follow from "A." In any event, the hoax was posthumous. The First Folio, with its ambiguous prefatory material and the ambiguous monument in Trinity Church in Stratford were both created in the 1620s, seven years or so after Shakspere's death and nineteen after Oxford's. They weren't designed to fool contemporaries of either man as much as to mislead future generations.

✓ "Spelling simply wasn't uniform at the time. Shakespeare himself didn't even spell his own name the same way. On his will alone (which bears his signature on each page), he spelled it 'Shakspere' on the first two pages and 'Shakespeare' on the last one" (227-28).

    o   None of the six signatures that exist are spelled "Shakespeare" and four are spelled differently. Additionally, Shapiro left out relevant information and important context. He failed to mention that there is no evidence that any of those signatures were written by Shakspere himself rather than a scribe. Or that Shakspere left behind only six signatures—five on the will and one on another legal document—while no evidence exists that he signed any of the many documents arising from his lawsuits, property purchases and commercial transactions, lending credibility to the idea that he was illiterate.

✓ "For most of his professional life, Shakespeare [worked] for an unusually stable and prosperous company, named the Chamberlain's Men from their formation in 1594, and after King James came to the throne in 1603, rechristened the King's Men. . . . The evidence is of a piece: the surviving texts confirm that whoever wrote the plays had to have been a long-term partner in an all-absorbing theatrical venture" (229, 230).

    o   Charles Barrell had shown that "the Lord Great Chamberlain" was sometimes referred to as "Lord Chamberlain," and that Oxford, as the Lord Great Chamberlain, was director of the Lord Chamberlain's Men throughout its existence, which accounts for its "unusually stable" condition.

✓ "There were times when Shakespeare was thinking so intently about the part he was writing for a particular actor that in jotting down the speech headings he mistakenly wrote the actor's name rather than his characters" (229).

    o   There is no reason to believe that the author himself wrote those names. Plays were often printed from prompters' copies, which likely would deliberately have used the actors' names.

✓ "How could anyone but a shareholder in the company know to stop writing comic parts for Will Kemp the moment he quit the company in 1599—and start writing parts in advance of the arrival of his replacement, Robert Armin, whose comic gifts couldn't have been more different?" (230).

- o Why would a writer have to be shareholder to know about the departure and upcoming arrival of two of the most famous actors of the day? In any event, Armin was a servant of the Earl of Oxford (a fact uncovered by A. Bronson Feldman), so of course he would have known in advance that Armin was soon to join the company.[12]

✓ "Jonson left the most personal and extensive tributes to Shakespeare. For many, his testimony alone resolves any doubts about Shakespeare's authorship of the plays." He also claimed that "Their relationship dates at least as far back as 1598, when Jonson's breakthrough play—*Every Man in His Humour*—was purchased and staged by the Chamberlain's Men. Jonson proudly lists Shakespeare among those who performed in it" (239).

- o Jonson's reminiscences, made decades later, were about the writer Shakespeare. There is nothing in them to indicate that Jonson was talking about William Shakspere from Stratford. On the second point Shapiro failed to point out key facts that undermine his claim. When *Every Man in His Humour* was first published in 1601 (while the play was still new), Shakespeare was not mentioned in the cast list. It was only later, in 1616, after Shakspere's death, that Jonson included "Shakespeare" in the list of actors in that play. Curiously, Shakespeare is the only actor not matched with any specific part. His name has merely been added to the list in a way different from the others.

✓ "A curious Shakespeare could have learned everything he needed to know about the Italian settings of his plays from a few choice conversations.... This obsession with hands-on experience extends to the playwright's familiarity with hawking, hunting, tennis, and other aristocratic pursuits. It would be surprising if, during his years as a traveling player performing at various aristocratic households around England, Shakespeare hadn't frequently observed the rich at play. As for the ways of the court, Shakespeare visited royal palaces scores of times and was ideally placed to observe the ways of monarchs and courtiers" (275).

- o There is no evidence that Shakspere ever was a traveling player performing at aristocratic households or that he "visited royal palaces" even once. Scholars with decades of involvement in the subjects about which Shakespeare demonstrated deep knowledge state unequivocally that no one without substantive experience in those fields could possibly have written Shakespeare's works.

✓ "One of the most habitual charges against Shakespeare is that he didn't have enough formal education to have written the plays—and, some have argued, there's no record that he received *any* formal education. What they fail to add is that no evidence survives that anybody in Shakespeare's day was educated in Stratford, since the records for all pupils at that time have been lost" (276).

- o It is not that "some have argued," that there's no record of Shakspere receiving any formal education, as though the real facts have been misconstrued by Oxfordians. No documents exist showing that Shakspere

---

[12] A. Bronson Feldman, "Shakespeare's Jester—Oxford's Servant," *SF Quarterly*, vol. VIII/3 (Autumn 1947): 39-43.

had any education, in Stratford or elsewhere. Moreover, records for the grammar school in Stratford do exist; they are missing for only one decade—the decade in which Shakspere would have been the right age to have attended the school.

✓ Shapiro insisted that William Shakespeare personally delivered this epilogue from *2 Henry IV* on the public stage: "If you look for a good speech now, you undo me. For what I have to say is of my own making."

   o Shapiro could not possibly know whether Shakespeare, whoever he was, personally delivered the epilogue. Even if Shakspere had made the statement, does that not appear to be an admission that he had not written what came before it? Shapiro has raised another mystery that Stratfordians have no explanation for.

✓ Shapiro decries the false assumption that "what makes people who they are now made people who they were back in Shakespeare's day. . . . Elizabethans didn't think of motivation, individuality, or behavior in the ways we do now" (270, 272).

   o Of course there were differences, which is why an informed imagination is necessary to recapture the spirit of the times. But on the big aspects of human life people then and now are so similar that Shakespeare's works continue to capture our attention even after 400 years, and it is the human interactions in the plays that are of greatest interest. Shakespeare's works would not have inspired so many other works of art—painting, operas, music, books—if that wasn't the case.

✓ "In pursuing this idea [that the history plays were written in part to serve political purposes], Looney had to argue that the plays Oxford wrote were sophisticated political allegories" (176).

   o Shapiro implies that only Looney held that view, when in fact it was held by respected Stratfordian scholars from the 1930s onwards, Alfred Hart and Lilian Winstanley among them. Shapiro also had to ignore how widespread such views had become at the time he was writing *Contested Will*, as expressed more recently by scholars such as John Alvis, Thomas G. West, David Bevington and, more recently, Peter Lake.[13]

✓ "Underlying such claims are far-fetched assumptions about how and why the playwright went about creating his characters. For Looney, these *dramatis personae* weren't creations of the writer's fertile imagination; they were rather 'living men and women, artistically modified and adjusted to fit them for the part they had to perform.' And many of them turn out to be well-known courtiers or privy councillors in the dramatist's immediate orbit."

   o Here again Shapiro presented Looney's views mockingly. But he did not challenge them; he merely stated them, mocked them, and moved on.

✓ "Looney also concluded that *The Tempest*—a play that scholars confidently date to well after 1604—didn't belong in the canon and was entirely the work of

---

[13] See, for instance, John Alvis & Thomas G. West, *Shakespeare as Political Thinker* (1981), David Bevington, *Tudor Drama and Politics: A Critical Approach to Topical Meaning* (1968) and Peter Lake, *How Shakespeare Put Politics on the Stage: Power and Succession in the History Plays* (2016).

another hand" (179).

- o Shapiro failed to mention that several Stratfordian scholars—Looney identified four of them in *"Shakespeare" Identified*—dated *The Tempest* no later than 1604. Shapiro failed to mention that Looney's reasons for rejecting the play as Shakespeare's were stylistic, and had nothing to do with the date.

✓ Regarding Looney's article in *The Golden Hind*, Shapiro wrote, "He shared a new reading of *The Merry Wives of Windsor*. Once again, characters were understood to be barely concealed historical figures: the play's dashing young lover, Fenton, was another of Oxford's self-portraits, while the woman he woos, Anne Page, was an obvious stand-in for the young woman Oxford married, Anne Cecil. The doltish Slender, whom Fenton outmaneuvers, is Oxford's rival Sir Philip Sidney, who had unsuccessfully sought Anne Cecil's hand in marriage. Even the setting in Windsor corresponded exactly with where the events on which the play was based had taken place three decades earlier. The stories matched so perfectly that Looney doubted 'whether another case could be cited in which a dramatist so closely followed facts of this nature and placed an identification so entirely outside the range of reasonable dispute'" (191).

- o How did Shapiro respond to this accurate description of how closely developments in the play matched real life events? He didn't. He simply moved on.

Shapiro wrote his book in such a manner that casual readers, ill-informed about the authorship question and Shakespeare's works, could easily be deceived. Scholars who know the subject matter, though, cannot help but regard the book as intentionally deceptive.

Did Shapiro's Libel J. Thomas Looney?

In his comments on *"Shakespeare" Identified* in *The Bookman's Journal* in May 1920, J. M. Robertson, a member of Parliament and a self-styled Shakespeare scholar, had challenged the veracity of Looney's presentation of his method of investigation, charging him with "prepossession;" i.e., having had the idea of Edward de Vere's authorship in mind from the very beginning and then setting out to find evidence to support it.[14] In short, Robertson had called Looney a liar. In 2010 James Shapiro did something similar. He took a penetrating insight by Looney—that World War II was less a struggle between political systems than a struggle "between the human soul and elemental brute force"—and twisted it to imply that Looney's criticism of certain tendencies in democracy meant that he favored the politics of the Allies' enemies, that he was some kind of crypto-Nazi. He averred that Looney's open-ended search for the author of Shakespeare's works actually had a secret "agenda" at its core: to find an author who shared Looney's own supposed anti-democratic attitudes. Shapiro further implied that anyone who accepted Looney's conclusions must also accept the same reactionary political beliefs.

Shapiro began by conceding that "Looney certainly sounds open-minded at the beginning of *"Shakespeare" Identified*, where he explained [why] he became interested in the authorship question" (171) and how he formed his list of eighteen qualities that the

---

[14] J. M. Robertson, "The Identity of Shakespeare," *Bookman's Journal*, vol. 2/30 (May 21, 1920): 59.

author must have had. "Looney's approach was a tour de force. Rhetorically, it was the most compelling book on the authorship controversy to have appeared, and in this respect it has yet to be surpassed" (173).

But Shapiro set all that aside and declared that Looney had really been motivated by previously held convictions that had nothing to do with literature. With a magician's sleight of hand, Shapiro had changed the definition of an open mind: from not having a pre-conceived determination of what one's scholarly investigations would find to not having pre-conceived ideas about any subject. He accused Looney of engaging in a sleight of hand because "insisting that he began with no particular candidate in mind [he] distracts us from what he did start with: questionable assumptions about the nature of authorship and a deeply held conviction that whoever wrote the plays shared his Positivist worldview."

This is another moment in *Contested Will* when careful readers have to ask themselves if they have understood correctly what they had just read. By changing the definition of what an open mind on an academic question means, Shapiro invalidated all scholarly work by imposing a definition that no human being could ever meet. He then applied his new definition to only one man, J. Thomas Looney. He certainly did not apply it to himself. His focus from that point on was only on Looney's supposed hidden or unconscious motivations, not on the validity of his findings.

Shapiro did not actually claim that Looney possessed the Positivist view he described; he said that some Positivists held that view, and inferred that Looney also held it. Nor did he provide any justification for his statement that Looney "held questionable assumptions about the nature of authorship," whatever that means, or that he had "a deeply held conviction that whoever wrote the plays shared his Positivist worldview." Shapiro went on to develop the idea that Looney held deep-seated anti-democratic ideas that consciously or unconsciously prejudiced him against the traditional author and in favor of a medievalist like Edward de Vere—an irrelevancy even if true, as the Oxfordian conclusions stand or fall based on the evidence, not the motivations of scholars who examine them.

In fact, Shapiro's charges are not correct. He grossly mischaracterized Looney's description of contemporary developments, writing that *"Shakespeare" Identified* was also a product of Looney's profound distaste for modernity; 'I have for very many years,' [Looney] explained, 'had a settled sense of our own age as one of increasing social and moral disruption tending towards complete anarchy" (170). It is odd to regard statements critical of horrific developments—the First World War, the Great Depression, and the beginnings of the Second World War—as a "distaste for modernity," as though Looney had rejected the whole of the modern era since the Renaissance, and as though he had been the only person at the time to have the sense that the world was veering "towards complete anarchy." A less biased observer might have attributed great insight and perceptiveness to Looney's observations.

Shapiro also distorted Looney's thoughts on Shakespeare's views as shown in the plays, characterizing them as "feudal, antidemocratic and deeply authoritarian" (182). Compare Looney's actual words: the author of the plays was someone "whose sympathies, and probably his antecedents, linked him more closely to the old order than to the new . . . [he was] not the kind of man we should expect to rise from the lower middle-class population of the towns."[15] This is another astute analysis by Looney, a view shared by Walt Whitman and other highly perceptive writers and critics. Shapiro continued, stating that "Looney insists, time and again, that the author of the plays stood firmly against the forces of individualism and materialism, which threatened 'the complete submergence of the soul of civilized man" (174). This is a fair characterization of Looney's thinking about his own time, given his concern with spiritual matters throughout his life;[16] it is not correct to say that it is Looney's characterization of Shakespeare's thought.

Note the subtlety of Shapiro's efforts:

❖ He attributes to Looney characteristics more applicable to the author of Shakespeare's works: "a distaste for modernity," and "feudal, antidemocratic and deeply authoritarian."

❖ He further attributes to Looney a characterization of Shakespeare more applicable to Looney himself regarding his own time: he "stood firmly against the forces of individualism and materialism."

Through these two distortions, Shapiro has attempted to equate Looney's attitudes toward his own time with Looney's supposed beliefs about Shakespeare's attitude toward his time. Shapiro used these distortions to justify his statement that Looney had set out (perhaps not consciously) to find a candidate who shared his own views.

Shapiro then attempted to tie it all together by claiming that anyone who accepted Oxford as Shakespeare also accepted Looney's supposed anti-democratic attitude.

> Looney's Oxfordianism was a package deal. . . . Looney had concluded that the story of the plays' authorship and the feudal, antidemocratic and deeply authoritarian values of those plays were inseparable; to accept his solution to the authorship controversy meant subscribing to this troubling assumption as well. (182)

Shapiro's sometimes clever sleights of hand, when revealed, actually serve to support Oxford's authorship of Shakespeare's works. His characterization of Shakespeare as expressed in the plays as "feudal, anti-democratic and deeply authoritarian" isn't inaccurate; it was Shapiro's attributing that characterization to Looney that was incorrect. The "feudal, antidemocratic and deeply authoritarian values" do in fact come far closer to the values of Edward de Vere, Seventeenth Earl of Oxford and the Lord Great Chamberlain of the realm, than those of a small-time commercial trader of no great accomplishment or

---

[15] J. Thomas Looney (2018), pp. 93-94.

[16] As an example of Looney's spiritual approach even to public events, consider this passage addressing the spiritual values that underlie civilization at a deeper level than its political systems, written in July 1941, as the Second World War raged around him.

> I often regret therefore that the war is represented as a struggle between dictatorship and democracy. At the bottom it is one between the human soul and elemental brute force; it just happens that the present dictatorships stand for brutal domination and spiritual tyranny, and that to the democracies has fallen the defence of the soul's freedom. The opposite is, however, quite conceivable. "Majority rule" might be as tyrannically repressive of spiritual liberty as any other form of government. I prefer to think of our two nations as being united in a struggle for the preservation of spiritual liberty rather than the maintenance of what is called "democratic government." [J. Thomas Looney, letter to Flodden W. Heron, July 5, 1941, from "A Great Pioneer's Ideas on Intellectual Freedom," *SF Quarterly*, vol. VI/3 (July 1945): 33-34. Reprinted in *Contested Will*, pp. 181-82.]

position such as William Shakspere. To impute those values to the plays and their author is almost to state that Oxford was the author.

Shapiro provided a more detailed chronicling of the Oxfordian movement, especially in its early decades and in the decades just prior to 2010, than had any other scholars except Warren Hope and Kim Holston in their *The Shakespeare Controversy* (1991, 2009). He noted that "The first twenty years of the movement were so successful and Oxfordians so prolific that the circumstantial case was fairly complete" (193) by the end of the 1930s.[17]

Yet his account was incomplete. He made no mention of the indispensable Col. Bernard R. Ward. In the place where Ward should have figured prominently, Shapiro wrote: "Recognizing the need for a central organization to promote 'research and propaganda,' a Shakespeare Fellowship was founded in 1922" (192). Not only is the sentence grammatically flawed, with the subject—the person who did the recognizing—omitted, but Col. Ward's central role in building an Oxfordian organization, community and movement is slighted. With the grammar corrected and and historical content added, the sentence would, and should, read:

> Recognizing the need for a central organization to promote "research and propaganda," Col. Bernard R. Ward founded the Shakespeare Fellowship in 1922.

Shapiro noted that Percy Allen had privately printed an open letter describing his conversion to belief in Oxford's authorship, yet had nothing to say about Allen's substantive work documenting hundreds of linkages between Shakespeare's plays and Oxford's life and the works of other dramatists. Instead, he spent three full pages reporting on a development in the 1940s that had nothing to do with J. Thomas Looney, the first two decades of the Oxfordian movement, or the Oxfordian claim.[18]

In sum, Shapiro's *Contested Will* was little more than a sustained *ad hominem* attack on the personalities and motives of doubters in general and Oxfordian scholars in particular. Shapiro did just what Carl Sagan urged scholars to avoid doing in this wise passage quoted by Stratfordian scholar Bruce Danner:

> The reasoned criticism of a prevailing belief is a service to the proponents of that belief; if they are incapable of defending it, they are well advised to abandon it. This self-questioning and error-correcting aspect of the scientific method is its most striking property, and sets it off from many other areas of human endeavor where credulity is the rule. . . . Any substantive objection is permissible and encouraged; the only exception being that ad hominem attacks on the personality or motives of the author are excluded. It does not matter what reason the proponent has for advancing his ideas or what prompts his opponents to criticize

---

[17] Percy Allen had said something similar back in 1939. "The case for Oxford, as we can now present it, is substantially complete. It has never been answered, and is, in my judgment, unanswerable." ["Who Was Shakespeare?" *John O'London's Weekly*, Feb. 10, 1939, p. 821.]

[18] After the death of his twin brother in 1939, Percy Allen began consulting Hester Dowden, a spiritualist medium seemingly able to communicate with the dead. In the sessions or seances with her, Allen came to believe that he was able to communicate with Edward de Vere, William Shakspere and Sir Francis Bacon. These sessions did not arise until the 1940s, after Allen's many ground-breaking books and articles—on the topical, personal and literary linkages between Oxford's/Shakespeare's works, the life of Edward de Vere and the works of other playwrights of the times—had been published. That Shapiro devoted three full pages of *Contested Will* to Allen's spiritualist activities while hardly mentioning his Oxfordian work provides yet another example of how his focus was on the idiosyncratic lives and beliefs of doubters rather than on the substantive reasons for their doubts.

them; all that matters is whether the ideas are right or wrong, promising or retrogressive.[19]

We now turn to the methodological maneuvers that academia uses to try to avoid examining the validity of the Oxfordian claim.

---

[19] Carl Sagan, from *Broca's Brain: Reflections on the Romance of Science* (1979), quoted in Bruce Danner (2011), p. 143.

23

Academia's Internal Response:
An Institution in Crisis

A Methodological Error and Adler's Solution

When American geologists set out to explore the geology of North America in the nineteenth century, they deliberately employed a strictly inductive methodology. They believed it was good scientific practice to conduct their investigations of rock formations, outcroppings and other geological features without preconceived explanations for what they might find. One historian noted that "With a vast, largely undefiled geological laboratory stretching before them, American geologists devoted themselves to exploration and observation rather than to speculation and to theory building."[1] Another observer described their insistence of keeping "explanations for what they observed . . . clearly separate from the facts. Only after such appraisal did one know what was in need of explication" (145).

The geologists believed that their approach was necessary to defend against the natural human tendency to seek support for theories already held, and to reject evidence that contradicts them. Geologist T. C. Chamberlin justified it this way:

> Once any theory is held in a preferred position . . . There is the imminent danger of an unconscious selection and a magnifying of phenomena that fall into harmony with the theory and support it, and an unconscious neglect of phenomena that fail of coincidence. . . . Instinctively, there is a special searching-out of phenomena that support it. . . . [T]he mind rapidly degenerates into the partiality of paternalism. The search for facts, the observation of phenomena and their interpretation, are all dominated by affection for the favored theory until it appears to its author or its advocate to have been overwhelmingly established. . . . [A] premature explanation passes first into a tentative theory, then into an adopted theory, and lastly into a ruling theory. (139)

When Shakespeare scholars such as Edmond Malone set out in the eighteenth century to investigate the life of the man who wrote Shakespeare's plays and poems and the conditions in which they had been written, performed and published, they believed they already knew who the author was. They were not exploring mostly unknown territory, but rather, in their minds, filling in blanks in a structure of knowledge that already existed. Speculations about or allusions to who the author "Shakespeare" really was—made during Shakspere's lifetime—were either not known to them or were not appreciated until the nineteenth and twentieth centuries.[2] Doubts about Shakspere's authorship based on the gap between the mundane details known of his life and the

---

[1] Naomi Oreskes, *The Rejection of Continental Drift* (1999): 126.

[2] These early speculations and allusions, arising during the lifetime of William Shakspere of Stratford-on-Avon, have been collected and analyzed by Bryan H. Wildenthal in *Early Shakespeare Authorship Doubts* (2019).

learned and sophisticated nature of the literary works had not yet arisen because the scholarly investigative practices that would reveal it were still in their infancy.

Shakespeare scholars in the eighteenth and nineteenth centuries, then, saw no need to draw a distinct line between findings and theory as there would be a century later for the geologists. For them, Shakespeare's professional career could be—indeed, it had to be—constructed within the framework of what was already known about his life. His career was assumed to have begun around 1589, when he was thought to have moved to London, and ended sometime between 1604 and 1611, when he moved back to Stratford. The works had to have been written within that period of about fourteen to twenty-two years. Scholars such as E. K. Chambers worked out dates of composition for the plays within those boundaries. Each new piece of information was placed within the Stratfordian story following logical rules inherent in a deductive methodology. That the Earl of Southampton was Shakespeare's patron, for instance, was deduced from the dedications of *Venus and Adonis* and *Lucrece* to him.

When the mismatch between the details of the life of the businessman from Stratford and the highly sophisticated nature of the literary works began to be noticed in the middle of the nineteenth century, it was noticed by scholars already holding one theory of authorship in a preferred position—exactly the position that the geologists sought to avoid for the reasons explained by Chamberlin. By the time the weaknesses in the Stratfordian claim became too obvious to ignore, it was too late. The Stratfordian claim had already passed from "a premature explanation . . . into a tentative theory, then into an adopted theory, and lastly into a ruling theory."

In his book *Ten Philosophical Mistakes*, Mortimer J. Adler cited Aristotle's observation that "The least initial deviation from the truth is multiplied later a thousandfold."[3] He showed how ten modern philosophical errors arose from ten small mistakes made by philosophers starting in the seventeenth century that led, after many steps and through long trains of thought, to false conclusions and paradoxes that were hard to unravel. The proper solution, Adler explained, was "to retrace our steps to find out where we went wrong. Only then is the erroneous premise that at first appeared innocent revealed as the culprit—a wolf in sheep's clothing" (xv). But that is not what modern philosophers did.

> Instead of retracing the steps that led back to their sources in little errors at the beginning, modern thinkers have tried in other ways to circumvent the result of the initial errors, often compounding the difficulties instead of overcoming them.
>
> The advances that have been made in modern thought do not mitigate the disasters produced by conclusions that were not abandoned by discovering the initial mistakes from which they sprang.

It has been the same in Shakespeare Studies. Scholars have not returned to the source of their error, the misidentification of the author, to correct the problem. The bureaucratic supports for the idea of Shakspere's authorship and for deductive methodology were too strong. If the philosophers had returned to the source of their error, Adler explained, "Making new starts by substituting true premises for false would have radically changed the picture that modern philosophy presents." Imagine what the field of Shakespeare Studies would look like today if the correction—the substitution of Edward de Vere for William Shakspere—had been made in 1920 or anytime thereafter.

---

[3] Aristotle, quoted in Mortimer J. Adler, *Ten Philosophical Mistakes* (1985), p. xiii.

Scholars would now be devoting their considerable energies and expertise to ferreting out the context in which the works had really been written, in understanding the life and mind of the true author, and in presenting deeper and more comprehensive understandings of the works.

Instead, most Shakespeare scholars remain intransigent, refusing to acknowledge even the possibility that an error has been made. They devote themselves to trying to explain away paradoxes and anomalies that cannot be explained away.

An Institution in Crisis

The problems that Shakespeare Studies faces today are similar to those it confronted in the late 1930s and early 1940s at the height of the first wave of the Oxfordian movement. Faced with the often conflicting tasks of promoting scholarly work while also promoting the interests and status of their institution, leaders of Departments of Literature and the Shakespeare Studies Sections within them often give priority to the latter. In doing so they continue the practice of isolating their fields from other academic fields and from scholarly work done outside academia, and they maintain a stricter top-down hierarchical structure than is ideal for scholarly work. They maintain these practices to ward off the Oxfordian challenge, and in doing so deepen the state of crisis Shakespeare Studies suffers from. They recognize the threat posed by the Oxfordian thesis; they see how severely the reputations of scholars such as themselves would be hit if it were correct. They dare not even consider whether the most fundamental belief underlying their field could be wrong. Better to follow the lead of their predecessors and avoid examining it.

Looney's observation is as valid today as it was in 1923: "To admit now that the Shakespeare problem is a reality would convict their class of incompetency, and entail personal retractions to which average human nature is unequal."[4] More recently, Gary Goldstein nailed it with this assessment:

> Should a public consensus proclaim Oxford to be Shakespeare, the resulting damage to the reputation of professional scholars—with their students, academic peers and the general public—would be so significant it is unlikely that English professors will admit the question to research, debate or instruction.[5]

And so protecting the institution by isolating it from outside pressures remains the default position. Roger Stritmatter, an American academic, observed that "The absence of curiosity [about scholarly work outside academia] is most revealing. As Richard Waugaman has said, we [Oxfordians] are in trouble not because we don't know how to notice evidence, but because we routinely notice evidence that Stratfordians have agreed to completely ignore."[6] Following that Stratfordian logic, would the work of the greatest Shakespeare scholars of the past—Malone and Chambers, for instance—even receive a hearing if conducted outside the walls of academia today? Academia has recreated the world of the guilds of the Middle Ages in which, in effect, only members are allowed to practice their profession.

It's hard not to feel a degree of sympathy for Stratfordian scholars, stuck as they are between a rock and a hard place. There is no way to ease into the change to Oxford. It is

---

[4] J. Thomas Looney, "*The Church Times* and a Rejected Letter, II," *Hackney Spectator*, Sept. 14, 1923, p. 4.
[5] Gary Goldstein, *Reflections on the True Shakespeare*, 2016, p. 244.
[6] Roger Stritmatter, private communication, June 3, 2018.

either/or. They face a dilemma far different from what physicists faced when Albert Einstein introduced the idea of relativity. They could accept relativity while still maintaining belief in Newtonian physics, which remained useful for everyday purposes. Not so for Shakespeare scholars. With no easy way to transition from Shakspere to Oxford, it's best, they conclude, not even to examine the Oxfordian claim.

And so institutional leaders continue to keep the Oxfordian claim outside; they circle the wagons and raise the walls to protect their Departments from infiltration by the Oxfordian bacillus. Oxfordian scholars—even tenured professors with Ph.D.'s in literature—are routinely rejected as speakers at academic conferences. Their papers are rejected by academic publications. Discussion is banned from blogs and online discussions and even from many university classrooms. In *Contested Will*, as noted, James Shapiro confirmed that academia has raised barriers against consideration of Oxfordian ideas: "there remains one subject walled off from serious study by Shakespeare scholars: the authorship question. . . . [T]his subject remains virtually taboo in academic circles, as well as in the consequences of this collective silence" (5). Shapiro even confirmed his own role in suppressing discussion of the authorship question, admitting that he told students in his classrooms, "That's rubbish and I'll fail you if you ask that question again."[7]

Recent examples of Oxfordians being banned from academic publications and events include:

On the Date, Sources and Design of Shakespeare's *The Tempest*

Roger A. Stritmatter and Lynne Kositsky
Foreword by William S. Niederkorn

➢ Roger Stritmatter and Lynne Kositsky were denied the opportunity to respond to articles in several academic publications that were critical of their article in *The Review of English Studies* challenging traditional beliefs about Shakespeare's sources for *The Tempest*. Because of the article, "their acceptances as speakers at two major academic conferences were rescinded."[8] They later published their findings in the book *On the Date, Sources and Design of Shakespeare's The Tempest* (2013).

➢ Richard Waugaman's article "The Psychology of Shakespearean Biography" was accepted by the editor of the Italian journal *Memoria di Shakespeare* for a 2015 issue on Shakespeare's biography. He called it "absolutely pertinent," but the new editor withdrew it because of its Oxfordian content and later compared Waugaman and Oxfordians to Holocaust

---

[7] James Shapiro, "On the Media" [Shapiro Interview with Brooke Gladstone], WNYC broadcast, April 22, 2016. Quoted in Donald Ostrowski, *Who Wrote That?* (2020), p. 126.
[8] William S. Niederkorn, "Forward," in Roger A. Stritmatter and Lynne Kositsky, *On the Date, Sources and Design of Shakespeare's The Tempest* (2013), p. 1. The article referred to was "Shakespeare and the Voyagers Revisited," *Review of English Studies*, Sept. 2007, pp. 447-72.

deniers.[9]

> ➤ William Niederkorn called *The Oxfordian* "the best American journal covering the authorship question" and noted that although it "published papers by Stratfordians," "there is no tolerance for anti-Stratfordian scholarship at the conferences and journals Stratfordians control."[10]

> ➤ The Shakespeare Oxford Fellowship, seeking a suitable venue for its event to commemorate the 100th anniversary of the publication of *"Shakespeare" Identified* in March 2020, found the gates in academia closed. Requests for space were summarily rejected by the Folger Shakespeare Library in Washington, D.C., the Huntington Library in San Marino, California and the Harry Ransom Center at the University of Texas, Austin.

> ➤ Authorship books are hard to find in many university libraries. As one example, the Jones Library at the University of Liverpool has almost every Oxfordian book published during the first wave of the Oxfordian movement, but they're all in the Rendall Archives and aren't listed in the main catalogue. No Oxfordian books, and very few on the general subject of Shakespearean authorship are on the main shelves or in the regular catalogue. There is nothing to alert students to an issue that Gerald Rendall, one of the University's founders and one of the most respected scholars in England at the time, considered so important that he wrote four books and several pamphlets on it.

Internal harm caused by isolation and suppression

The effort to protect the status and reputation of Literature Departments and Shakespeare Studies Sections comes at the expense of the scholarly work conducted within them.

Higher levels of political pressure. Institutions that feel threatened enforce greater top-down direction and control of members than those that don't, a practice inherently harmful because it conflicts with bottom-up practices conducive to scholarly work.

Paralyzed by fear, I. Fear becomes pervasive. Fear of losing prestige, status and authority if the Stratfordian story is shown to be false; fear of damage to careers by not adhering to political pressure to suppress the authorship question; fear of having to junk thousands of books in libraries' collections. Those most farsighted in imagining the extent of the damage are likely to be the most active in repressing the Oxfordian claim. Looney remarked in *"Shakespeare" Identified* that "Orthodox faiths . . . are usually intrinsically weakest when most vehemently asserted."[11] In gauging the rising levels of fear in academia, Alexander Waugh commented: "The Stratfordians have been trying to pretend we don't exist for a long time, but now they're running scared. As Mahatma Gandhi said,

---

[9] Matthew Reisz, "Much Taboo, But Not About Nothing," *Times Higher Education* [a weekly supplement to *The Times*], issue 2169 (Sept. 11, 2014): 10.

[10] William S. Niederkorn, *"Absolute Will," Brooklyn Rail*, April 2010.

[11] J. Thomas Looney, *"Shakespeare" Identified* (2018), p. 15. Someone once remarked that "Deny a fact, and that fact will be your master." Agatha Christie, in *The Murder of Roger Ackroyd*, observed that "It is odd how, when you have a secret belief of your own which you do not wish to acknowledge, the voicing of it by someone else will rouse you to a fury of denial." Irving Stone presented just such a situation in *Passions of the Mind*, his historical novel of Sigmund Freud. When the young Freud is dumfounded after one of his early supporters turns his back on him, an older colleague explained that "Always remember, Sigmund, the adversary who fights you the hardest is the one who is the most convinced you are right." Irving Stone, *Passions of the Mind* (1971), p. 423.

'First they ignore you, then they ridicule you, then they fight you, and then you win.' We've got to the fight bit."[12]

Fear of the Oxfordian idea keeps academia tied in knots, unable to move forward even in areas in which everybody agrees change is needed. It is widely accepted, for instance, that the dates traditionally assigned to Shakespeare's plays are incorrect, but every step taken to correct them leads inevitably down the Oxfordian path. As Peter Moore noted, "nearly every scholarly authority of the dating issue agrees that Chambers' dates are too late, yet those dates still stand."[13]

<u>Paralyzed by fear, II</u>. Junior faculty are especially vulnerable to political pressure. Charlton Ogburn, arguably the most important Oxfordian of the second half of the twentieth century, observed that

> There would seem . . . to be no mystery in the maintenance of academic uniformity. No young instructor in a Department of English, even if his early educational conditioning does not preclude his examining objectively that which he has been taught to scoff at as the badge of his professionalism, will find his career advanced if he threatens to expose the tenets of his elders as nonsense.[14]

And, Ogburn noted, once a faculty member "has his professorship he is hardly likely to repudiate the steps by which he attained it and certainly he is not going to read himself out of his profession and bring down on his head the obloquy of his fellows, vicious as we have seen such can be." Professor Roger Stritmatter also described the pressures that exist within academia for adherence to the "party line":

> There is, of course, a price to be paid [for admission into academia]. . . . [T]he initiate must solemnly promise not only to forgo dalliance in the field of unauthorized ideas, but to zealously defend, as a matter of honor and sanity, the jurisdiction of the paradigm into which he has been initiated. A reluctance to do so marks him, at best, as an outsider or a misfit: unqualified for employment, tenure, or professional respect.[15]

<u>Groupthink</u>. Elisabeth Waugaman recently observed that groupthink—the term coined by William H. Whyte, Jr., in 1962 for "a rationalized conformity . . . guided almost totally by the whims and prejudices of the group"—has become quite common in American intellectual life, with scholars "increasingly subservient" and predisposed to "embrace groupthink as the road to security.'"[16] She cited a 2009 study, "Groupthink in Academia: Majoritarian Departmental Politics and the Professional Pyramid," in which its authors

> observe that scholars are less likely to engage with colleagues whose work threatens their own, . . . gradually producing ideological uniformity. Since disagreement with accepted academic thought threatens the entire academic hierarchy, scholarly thinking becomes circular. The authors then provide a shocking list of discoveries that were discounted for years in the sciences, from

---

[12] Alexander Waugh, quoted in Robert Gore-Langton, "The Campaign to Prove Shakespeare Didn't Exist," *Newsweek* online edition, Dec. 29, 2014.

[13] Gary Goldstein, "From the Editor: Expanding the Canon," *The Oxfordian 21* (2019), p. 11.

[14] Charlton Ogburn, *The Mysterious William Shakespeare* (1992), p. 162.

[15] Roger Stritmatter, "What's in a Name? Everything, Apparently . . .," *Rocky Mountain Review of Languages and Literature*, vol. 60/2 (Fall, 2006): 38.

[16] Elisabeth Waugaman, "A Reassessment of the French Influence in Shakespeare," *The Oxfordian*, vol. 21 (2019): 158.

genetics and the vital transmission of cancer to continental drift and DNA research. Shakespeare studies could easily be added to this list.

This attitude is reminiscent of the mindset of the priests who refused to look through Galileo's telescope 400 years ago when he was being tried by the Roman Inquisition for his heliocentric views. There is no point in looking, they told him. They would not see the moons orbiting other planets that Galileo insisted he'd seen (and whose existence would justify the heliocentric view of the solar system), because they weren't there. Even if they did see them, they said, that would only be because the Devil had placed the images there to mislead them. There is no point in examining the work of authorship doubters, Shakespeare scholars say, following similar reasoning; the Oxfordian claim can't be true because we already know who the author was, so why waste time on it? Their attitude also brings to mind Herbert Spencer's dictum that "There is a principle which is a bar to all information, which is proof against all argument and which cannot fail to keep a man in everlasting ignorance: this principle is contempt prior to investigation."

<u>Harm to Stratfordian scholars' own work</u>

It should be of concern to all scholars that Shakespeareans have refused to investigate an issue of great importance to their field. Longtime Oxfordian Richard Malim recognized that "if you shut off an avenue of investigation, the rest of your investigations are likely to be adversely affected and may well be rendered valueless: a point which applies . . . to the whole of Shakespeare biographical scholarship, where presentation of the academic legitimacy of the authorship question is generally denied."[17]

The Tempest provides an example of how the inward focus and groupthink is harming scholarly work within the Shakespeare Studies walls. Although Oxfordian scholars outside have shown that the play contains thirteen references to places in the Mediterranean Sea, most Stratfordian scholars insist that the locale of the play is the island of Bermuda. They find support for this claim based on the use of the word "Bermoothes" in a conversation between Ariel and Prospero:

> Safely in harbour
> Is the king's ship; in the deep nook, where once
> Thou call'dst me up at midnight to fetch dew
> From the still-vex'd **Bermoothes**, there she's hid.
> (*The Tempest*, II.1)

But "Bermoothes" had nothing to do with Bermuda. Oxfordian scholar Paul H. Altrocchi has shown that the Bermoothes was a neighborhood in London where alcohol was distilled and available for purchase—hence Ariel talks of being summoned "at midnight to fetch dew [alcohol]" from the stills there.[18]

In support of the Bermuda setting Stratfordian scholars cite a letter describing a 1609 shipwreck there that bears similarities to the description of the shipwreck in the opening scene of the play. The letter is dated 1611, thus providing a reason to conclude that the play was written no earlier than that year, long after Edward de Vere had died. Stratfordians have been unable to satisfactorily explain how Shakspere could have seen the letter, as it wasn't published until after his death. In any event, many similar descriptions of storms at sea and shipwrecks existed, so there was no need for

---

[17] Richard Malim, "Shaksper the Nonentity," *De Vere Society Newsletter*, vol. 22/1 (Jan. 2015): 13.
[18] Paul H. Altrocchi, "Bermoothes: An Intriguing Enigma," *Sh. Matters*, vol. 5/3 (Spring 2006): 10-15.

Shakespeare (whoever he was) to have drawn on that letter for inspiration. Oxford himself had been to sea many times. Yet Stratfordians continue to ignore and suppress this information. What are Oxfordians to do in the face of such unacademic wooden-headedness? I'll propose a way forward in Chapter 26.

Stratfordian scholars are capable of clear thinking on subjects not involving authorship, but then resort to unscholarly thinking once the authorship question is introduced. Consider the topic of the order and dates of Shakespeare's plays. To determine the order in which they were written, scholars examined internal stylistic evidence and external records of performances and publication. As for the order of composition, Oxfordians are in general agreement with Stratfordians; i.e., that plays such as *The Comedy of Errors* and *The Two Gentlemen of Verona* are early works, while plays such as *Hamlet* and *King Lear* (as published in the First Folio) are works of the mature playwright. But when considering the actual dates, Stratfordian scholars remain constrained by their insistence that Shakspere wrote them; the plays had to be shoehorned into a fairly narrow period of fifteen to twenty-two years, from 1589-1590 to 1604-1611.

Further harm comes from burying past Oxfordian discoveries. Academia shows little interest in Edward de Vere. Alone among the major courtiers of the Elizabethan era, he is ignored by historians, and his literary works, to the extent they were published under his own name, are little studied. Exceptions such as Steven W. May's scholarly examination of Oxford's poetry are few and far between. Oxford has become a potato too hot to touch.

The work of the great scholars of the first generations of Oxfordians in the 1920s, 1930s and 1940s, which brought great insights into Shakespeare's works and the literary life of the Elizabethan era even apart from the authorship question, is ignored. Capt. Ward's biography of de Vere has been out of print since the early 1930s. Many recent histories of the Elizabethan era continue to give short shrift to the dreadful effects on England of the long war with Spain. Of the few that do recognize the difficult conditions, not one acknowledges Col. Ward's and Capt. Ward's contributions to bringing that information to light.

Stephanie Hopkins Hughes has written on "the attempts by a whole generation of English historians to eliminate Sir Thomas Smith [Oxford's first tutor] from the history of the reign of Edward VI. . . . an egregious effort by the Academy to remove what it rightly sees as a threat to the Stratford myth."[19] She has also written on the disappearance from scholarly work of historian Mary Dewar for similar reasons. The silence surrounding the circumstances in which the First Folio was published in 1623, uncovered by Oxfordian scholar Peter W. Dickson (see Chapter 24) is deafening.

Most Stratfordian scholars are amateurs when it comes to the authorship question. Their expertise is in other areas of literary scholarship. Because the authorship question has been an important part of the story of Shakespearean scholarship over the past 170 years, they are ignorant of an important part of the history of their own field. On this point they might benefit by advice from Plato. In *The Republic* he identified three types of men who love three types of pleasures: "lovers of wisdom, lovers of honor, and lovers of gain." Which of these men, he asked, could give us the best advice about which pleasures are best? After noting that each one would claim his own type as best, Plato concluded that

---

[19] Private communication from Stephanie Hopkins Hughes.

the philosopher is best suited to answer the question because he had had the widest experience.

> The philosopher . . . has greatly the advantage; for he has of necessity always known the taste of the other pleasures from his childhood upwards: but the lover of gain in all his experience has not of necessity tasted—or, hardly have tasted— the sweetness of learning and knowing truth.[20]

Following that line of reasoning, Oxfordians are best able to answer the question of Shakespearean authorship because nearly all of them were once Stratfordians. They have seen both sides of the question, while most Stratfordians have seen only one.

Training for future literary scholars is also misguided and leaves them ignorant of large parts of the field in which they will be presumed to have expert knowledge. Consider the Ph.D. course in English Literature at UC Berkeley. At a glance, the description of the program in English Literature looks great: "The Berkeley English Department offers a wide-ranging Ph.D. program, engaging in all historical periods of British and American literature, Anglophone literature, and critical and cultural theory. The program aims to assure that students gain a broad knowledge of literature in English as well as the highly-developed skills in scholarship and criticism necessary to do solid and innovative work in their chosen specialized fields."[21] Yet on closer examination, the directives are narrowly focused; the requirement for a course on "17th and 18th Century Literature" can be met by taking this course: "Research Seminar: Representing Non-Human Life in Seventeenth- and Eighteenth-Century Britain." Required reading includes Erasmus Darwin's *The Botanic Garden* and other obscure works on flora and fauna. Missing from the reading list are Shakespeare (even though he wrote extensively about plants and animals), Jonson and the other Johns: Milton, Dryden, Donne and Bunyan. Also missing are the King James Bible and Alexander Pope, and Fielding, Richardson, Defoe, Addison and Steele, and Sheridan and Sterne. It's hard to believe that a student taking this course would acquire any true expertise in English literature of those two important centuries.

The mental contortions that Stratfordians must engage in to defend their ideology is shown by their response to the illiteracy of members of Shakspere's family. It is accepted that most of his relations signed their name with an "X", the logical implication being that they were illiterate.[22] Stratfordians needed to explain this away. One proffered explanation is that Shakspere's relatives actually were literate, but that literate people of the time often used an "X" rather than affixing their signature. Another somewhat contradictory explanation is that even literate people weren't actually taught to write their own names. That excuse was offered on the website of the Folger Shakespeare Library in 2019 by Karen Lyon, quoting historian David Chessy:

> Children would begin by imitating written letters, syllables, and words they had learned orally until they could reproduce them without following a copy. Oddly (to us, at least), one thing Ben [Jonson] and his peers would not have been encouraged to write was their names. In fact, according to Cressy, "none of the educators of pre-industrial England recommended children to learn to write

---

[20] Plato, *Republic* (1990), pp. 421-22

[21] This description is from the Handbook for Graduate Study in English, a document given to all Ph.D. students in 2016, which contains the Department's policies and procedures for graduate study.

[22] As Sir Derek Jacobi put it in a 2016 interview, it's odd that "Shakespeare's" genealogy is "illiterate, illiterate, illiterate, illiterate, World's Greatest Writer, illiterate." Quoted in Alex McNeil, "Jacobi and Rylance Go Public," *Shakespeare Oxford Newsletter*, vol. 52/2 (Spring 2016): 1, 28.

their own names . . . since [personal names] did not conform to the rules of spelling that the teachers were trying to instill." So when Renaissance people were unable to produce a signature, it did not necessarily mean that they were illiterate.[23]

The convoluted (and hilarious) efforts some Stratfordian scholars have made as they attempt to evade the authorship question was commented on by professor, writer and actor Dr. Luke Prodromou: "Traditional Shakespeare scholars, in rejecting even a possible case for reasonable doubt, often engage in extremely tortuous arguments, evasions and distortions to keep a wall of such taboos in place, thus betraying their supposed professional *raison d'être*: scholarly impartiality and the pursuit of truth."[24] After noting the harm that Departments of Literature suffer from their inward focus and suppression of the authorship question, he asked his academic colleagues to consider this question,

> What is lost when we avoid and even demonize research on any topic, especially one as significant as the Shakespeare authorship? Much important research has already been done by a surprising number of fine scholars—including historians and lawyers, professions interested in actually turning up facts. . . . Yet this scholarly research is considered somehow taboo by academia. Perhaps we prefer to preserve our scholarly innocence or even our vested professional interests, but at the same time, we must acknowledge that we are failing to follow trails that may be relevant to the origin and meaning of the works we love.

Orthodox scholars, like the philosophers cited by Adler, have not taken the logical step of returning to the source of the error, the misidentification of the author. They have "tried in other ways to circumvent the result of the initial error," with the result that they, like the philosophers, have "compounded the difficulties instead of overcoming them."

Continuing Corruption of Methodology: Allusions and Death of the Author

In every crime story there is a perpetrator. The perpetrator's identity is hidden; the process of uncovering it is the story told.[25] Usually the perpetrator is discovered by finding and analyzing clues to his identity. Sometimes those clues are writings. In one actual case, the letters that the Unabomber sent to *The New York Times* and *The Washington Post* in 1995 enabled police to prepare a psychological profile of him that led to his identification and capture.

The same techniques are valid in investigating the authorship of Shakespeare's works. Analyzing the writings to prepare a psychological profile of the author was the method that Looney followed. Investigations into the topical and personal allusions in the works then followed, and the first generations of Oxfordian scholars had great success in identifying them and tying them to the life, experiences and personality of Edward de

---

[23] Karen Lyon, "Elizabethan Education and Ben Jonson's School Days, Folger Shakespeare Library website, Sept. 3, 2019. The article was still there a year and a half later when it was accessed on Jan. 27, 2021. https://shakespeareandbeyond.folger.edu/2019/09/03/ben-jonson-school-elizabethan-education/?utm_source=wordfly&utm_medium=email&utm_campaign=ShakespearePlus4Sep2019&utm_content=version_A&promo=.

[24] Luke Prodromou, "The Shakespeare Authorship Debate Continued: Uncertainties and Mysteries," *The Oxfordian 21*, p. 16.

[25] There was even a perpetrator in Agatha Christie's *And Then There Were None*, in which everyone on an inaccessible island was murdered, and even in Edgar Allen Poe's *The Murders in the Rue Morgue*, though it turned out to be an orangutan.

Vere.

Orthodox scholars at the time recognized the danger of this approach to the Stratfordian story. They could see that accepting even one point of Oxfordian theory would lead to accepting a second and then a third, until the entire Stratfordian story was swept away. Accepting the validity of topical allusions would lead to questions about why they were to events fifteen years earlier than the plays were supposedly written, which would in turn lead to further questions about when they were really written, and by whom.

Their efforts to respond to the Oxfordian challenge by declaring topical and personal allusions to be illegitimate forms of evidence, and then by making the methodological changes summed up in the phrase "the death of the author," was recounted in Chapter 12. We now turn to efforts by the current generation of orthodox scholars to engage in the same two lines of defense.

<u>Literature as autobiography or fantasy; no middle ground</u>

In his attempts to delegitimize topical and personal allusions as valid forms of evidence in support of Oxford's—or anyone's—authorship, James Shapiro returned to ideas espoused by Sir Sidney Lee before 1920. Shapiro, like Lee, believed that "a few— surprisingly few—lines in Shakespeare's plays refer explicitly to contemporary events... . They were so few in number that their absence seems to have been a deliberate choice on Shakespeare's part" (38). Oxfordians, of course, regard the plays as intensely topical. Many of them began as entertainments in the court, where witty half-veiled references to contemporaneous events were understood by the Queen and her courtiers.

Although he denied the widespread existence of allusions in the plays, Shapiro cited several pre-Looney scholars who got it right: George Russell French, for example, who "assures us that 'nearly all Shakespeare's *dramatis personae* are intended to have some resemblance to characters in his own day.' Such readings turned the plays into something other than comedies, histories, and tragedies: they were now coded works, full of in-jokes and veiled political intrigue for those in the know" (39). Shapiro also cited another of the greatest Shakespeare scholars of all time, Edmond Malone, who saw that "the topical correspondences" were "centered on the court, mostly from the reign of Elizabeth."

Wedded to the idea that many of the plays were written in the Jacobean era—after 1603—Shapiro was unable to recognize how astute French and Malone had been in their conclusions about the origins of the plays in the world of Queen Elizabeth's court. He dismissed Malone's conclusions without disproving them, writing that he "badly skews the plays, turning them into court allegories, in which a Jacobean Shakespeare seems stuck in an Elizabethan past, unable to get out of his mind a slap administered by his queen, in a very different context, many years earlier."

Shapiro took even greater exception to the idea of personal allusions. "The problems with Malone's topical assumptions pale in comparison with those precipitated by his biographical ones," Shapiro charged. "Malone's argument presupposed that in writing his plays Shakespeare mined his own emotional life in transparent ways and, for that matter, that Shakespeare responded to life's surprises [by] finding an outlet for his grief in his work" (41, 40). He went on to quote Margreta de Grazia's observation in support of Malone's: "'Malone's pursuit from the externally observed to the inwardly felt or experienced marked more than a new type of consideration: it signaled an important shift in how Shakespeare was read. Shakespeare was cast not as the detached dramatist who observed human nature but as the engaged poet who observed himself'" (41).

How did Shapiro respond to French, Malone and De Grazia? He didn't. He simply disparaged and dismissed their insights, without attempting to explain why he thought they were misguided. He again left readers puzzled about why he would introduce such persuasive testimony against his own position and then leave it unchallenged.

Like Sir Sidney Lee, Shapiro framed the issue by using the extremes of completely autobiographical writing on one hand and complete fantasy or imagination on the other. He excluded the vast middle ground in which literary works arise from or were influenced by an author's personality, disposition and experiences, which were, as Looney phrased it, "imaginatively recreated."

Shapiro made clear that the reason he opposed topical and personal allusions was not because they weren't there but because they support the doubter's position.

> The more that Shakespeare scholars encourage autobiographical readings of the plays and poems, the more they legitimate assumptions that underlie the claims of all those who dismiss the idea that Shakespeare wrote the plays. and every step scholars have taken toward embracing such readings has encouraged their adversaries to make even more speculative claims. (267)

In that passage Shapiro revealed his hand. He showed that his goal was not to get to the truth of the matter—of determining whether the allusions were real or not—but to avoid examining the matter at all because doing so legitimized the adversary's position. This is a political approach, not a scholarly one.

The following are additional examples of Shapiro's trivializing the issue of allusion.

✓ Once Edmond Malone had proposed the idea of topical and personal allusions, "writing the life of the author of Shakespeare's works is a game that anyone with enough ingenuity and conviction could play.... The impulse to interpret the plays and poems as autobiographical was a direct result of the failure to recover enough facts to allow anyone to write a satisfying cradle-to-grave life of Shakespeare [by whom he means Shakspere]" (45).

  o Notice the sleights of hand. The issue is not whether the plays are autobiographical or that a cradle-to-grave autobiography of the author could be constructed from them; it's that allusions to events in de Vere's life really do exist in the plays. Shapiro had to set up a straw man and then demolish it to distract attention away from the real issue: the validity of the allusions.

✓ "It is hard to avoid concluding that autobiographical details Shakespeare is alleged to have embedded in the plays are a lot like Baconian ciphers: something hidden there for posterity, about which contemporaries were oblivious, but that hundreds of years later brilliant detective work can uncover and decode" (269).

  o The allusions were not ciphers—coded messages—written for future generations, but overt references to topical events written for the queen and fellow courtiers to recognize and appreciate. They had been "hidden" for centuries only because scholars had misplaced the plays in time and place.

✓ "What I find most disheartening about the claim that Shakespeare of Stratford lacked the life experience to have written the plays.... [is that it] diminishes the very thing that makes him so exceptional: his imagination" (277).

- o Shapiro presupposes the subject that is at issue. Were the plays the result of pure imagination, or were they imaginatively recreated from real-life events? No documented experiences in Shakspere's life relate to the events portrayed in the plays he supposedly wrote, but many of Oxford's are.

✓ "Even if Shakespeare occasionally drew in his poems and plays on personal experiences, and I don't doubt that he did, I don't see how anyone can know with any confidence if or when or where he does so" (269).

- o Finally, after 269 pages of denying it, Shapiro admits that the author did indeed draw on personal experiences. But the reason scholars like Shapiro can't "know with any confidence if or when or where he does so" is because they have the wrong author and the wrong time frame. That is why the idea that the plays were written fifteen years earlier, and for the court and educated audiences, is so supportive of the Oxfordian thesis. There is a true match between the plays and the life of the man who wrote them.

✓ "Surely he was too accomplished a writer to recycle [his experiences] in the often clumsy and undigested way that critics in search of autobiographical traces— advocates and skeptics of his authorship alike—would have us believe. Because of that, and because we know almost nothing about his personal experiences, those moments in his work which build upon what he may have felt remain invisible to us, and were probably only slightly more visible to those who knew him well." And, "It's wiser to accept that these experiences can no longer be recovered. We don't know what to look for in any case, and even if we did, I'm not at all sure we would know how to interpret it correctly. In the end, attempts to identify personal experiences will only result in acts of projection, revealing more about the biographer than about Shakespeare himself" (269-70).

- o What if we did know of the author's personal experiences? We do know of much of the details of Edward de Vere's life and they match events and personages in the plays to an astonishing degree, as even many orthodox scholars have acknowledged. But Shapiro won't examine the issue.

✓ "You would think that the endless alternatives proposed by those reading his life out of the works—good husband or bad, crypto-Catholic or committed Protestant, gay or straight, misogynist or feminist, or, for that matter, that the works were really written by Bacon, Oxford, Marlowe, and so on—would cancel each other out and lead to the conclusions that the plays and poems are not transparently autobiographical" (270).

- o Shapiro is arguing that because so many theories have been proposed about who the author was, they all must be wrong. Was Einstein's theory of relativity wrong because others had proposed other solutions? Surely a serious scholar would have confidence that scholarly methods would, eventually, determine which facts are correct and which theories come closest to describing the reality of the situation.

✓ "Perhaps it's time to shift our attention from debating who wrote Shakespeare's works to whether it's possible to discover the author's emotional, sexual, and religious life through them" (268).

- o Finally, twelve pages from the end of the book, Shapiro ventures to ask whether the biographical approach might be worth pursuing after all. Yet even here he skirts the issue of whether biographical details from Oxford's life appeared in the plays. He turns only to the most obscure passages; then, having failed to understand their meaning, concludes that it would be impossible to identify any events alluded to. This is another instance of the intellectual dishonesty that pervades so much of the book.

✓ "The evidence strongly suggests that imaginative literature in general and plays in particular in Shakespeare's day were rarely if ever a vehicle for self-revelation. . . . autobiography as a genre and as an impulse was extremely unusual" (269).

- o Shapiro again misstates the issue. It wasn't that literature in general or plays in Shakespeare's day served as a vehicle for self-revelation, but whether they were inspired by events in the lives of their authors. Oxfordians would say that that was just what Oxford did when, shortly after he was banished from court in 1580, he wrote *Romeo and Juliet*, a play in which Romeo is so shocked by his banishment from Verona that he uses the words "banished" or "banishment" fourteen times in forty-two lines. The plays were autobiographical in the sense that the settings, plots, characters and situations portrayed give rise to emotions important in the life of the author, not in the sense that they portray his life or serve as personal confessions.

Change in methodology of literary studies to invalidate allusions

The more extensive methodological change launched in the 1920s and recounted in Chapter 12—that of separating all works of literature from their authors' intentions, lives and experiences—continued through the rest of the twentieth century. Recent developments are sketched out in this section.[26]

Although eliminating the author when considering literary works—the so-called "death of the author" mentality—might have seemed like intellectual suicide by Literature Departments, worse was to come. Devaluing the author was only the first in a series of steps whose cumulative effect was to transform the study of literature from studying works of literature through the history of their times, to studying societies and cultures through works of literature. In the new methodology, literary criticism lost its status as an independent field of study that it had fought so hard to achieve decades earlier in breaking away from History. The study of literature became largely subsumed within the larger subject of Cultural Studies. From being the ends to be examined, literary works had become merely one means through which non-literary subjects were studied. Cultural theorists regarded literary works as mere artifacts to be mined for data about the political, economic, social or sexual practices in the society from which they arose in the same manner that advertising or other anonymously written documents could be

---

[26] I have told the story of these methodological changes in more detail elsewhere. See, for instance, "Oxfordian Theory, Continental Drift and the Importance of Methodology," *The Oxfordian*, vol. 17 (2015): 193-221; "Literary Criticism and the Authorship Question," *Brief Chronicles*, Special Issue (2016): 117-32.

examined. One standard book in the field, *The Norton Anthology of Theory and Criticism*, declared that "Literary texts, like other artworks, are neither more nor less important than any other cultural artifact or practice. Keeping the emphasis on how cultural meanings are produced, circulated and consumed, the investigator will focus on art or literature insofar as such works connect with broader social factors, not because they possess some intrinsic interest or special aesthetic value."[27]

To state it clearly, when the so-called "death of the author" is discussed, the death of literary criticism itself is necessarily implied. Consideration of works of literature as works of art important in themselves—the approach of literary connoisseurs—has little place in this methodology, and has largely ended within academia. Gone is any sense that literature has something meaningful to say about the deeper aspects of life.

The Humanistic tradition in literary criticism has come close to vanishing from English literature programs and journals. The editors of *The Norton Anthology* couldn't find much space in their 2,785-page volume for the giants of traditional humanistic literary criticism in the twentieth century. Lionel Trilling isn't represented at all, and only one unrepresentative essay by Edmund Wilson was included, even though the book claims to "present a staggeringly varied collection of the most influential critical statements from the classical era to the present day."

The introduction to the widely used text *Cultural Studies* advises that "although there is no prohibition against close textual readings in Cultural Studies, they are also not required."[28] Thus, as literary critic Jonathan Culler observed, "In theory Cultural Studies is all-encompassing: Shakespeare and rap music, high culture and low, culture of the past and culture of the present" (47) are all equally worthy of study.

> Interpreting *Hamlet* is, among other things, a matter of deciding whether it should be read as talking about, say, the problems of Danish princes, or the dilemmas of men of the Renaissance experiencing changes in the conception of the self, or relations between men and their mothers in general, or the question of how representations (including literary ones) affect the problem of making sense of our experiences. (33)

Inevitably, as Seaton observed, "in some of the most influential academic centers literary criticism has been replaced by Cultural Studies."[29] The situation isn't that Cultural Studies courses are taught alongside literature courses. It's not even that the methodology of literary studies has been expanded to include new factors. It's that a takeover has occurred in which there appears to be little room left for the traditional Humanistic approach to literary studies.

In sum, the Humanistic tradition, in place for centuries before Looney identified Edward de Vere as Shakespeare, was supplanted twice. It was first replaced by a method in which an author was regarded as an outmoded "construct" to be bypassed in favor of cultural forces that determine the content of literary works. That entire field of literary studies itself was then subsumed under the field of Cultural Studies. The Cultural Studies approach to the study of literature that dominates "Departments of Literature" today is not one in which academic study of the Shakespeare authorship question can easily take place.

---

[27] James Seaton, *Literary Criticism from Plato to Postmodernism* (2014), p. 20.
[28] Jonathan Culler, *Literary Theory: A Very Short Introduction* (2009), p. 50.
[29] James Seaton, *Literary Criticism from Plato to Postmodernism* (2014), p. 1.

I speculated earlier (see Chapter 12) as to the degree to which Shakespeare Studies was not just a beneficiary of these changes but an important force behind them. It is still an open question. It would indeed be ironic if it was the case that the study of literature itself was blown away by misguided attempts by orthodox scholars to protect the Stratfordian myth. The ultimate corruption of literature studies may well have resulted from scholars' unwillingness to deal with the Oxfordian challenge head-on.

The Humanistic tradition remains as valid an approach to understanding and appreciating literature as ever. Because works of literature are unique, understanding their authors—their motivations and the conditions under which they wrote—enhances understanding of them. For scholars to toss out this path into the inner nature of a work in order to focus solely on the sterile words on the paper taken completely out of context was an astonishing betrayal of their duty to study and teach literature. But they felt they had no choice if they were to protect the Stratfordian story. The historical context and personal connections between Shakespeare's works and Edward de Vere were so strong—and the lack of connections between William Shakspere and the works so apparent—that to protect the Stratfordian myth the Humanistic tradition had to be destroyed.

The decline in teaching Shakespeare in American universities might be yet another example of academia destroying the village in order to save it, or at least save the Stratfordian paradigm. Shakespeare has long been taught "as an indispensable foundation for the understanding of English language and literature,"[30] the American Council of Trustees and Alumni recalls, yet its recent survey reveals that "[t]oday, a mere 4 of the [top] 52 colleges and universities require English majors to take a course focused on Shakespeare. . . . It is a sad irony that not even Amherst College, which administers the Folger Shakespeare Library, requires its English majors to take a course that focuses on Shakespeare" (3). The editors of *Shakespeare Matters* found that "those advocating this elimination [of required courses on Shakespeare] are also, predictably, often the most vehement defenders of the orthodox view of Shakespearean authorship. One way to avoid uncomfortable discussions about who Shakespeare was—and therefore what his works might say to a 21st century readership—is simply to eliminate the course offerings in which such a discussion might naturally become a part of the curriculum. This is called orthodoxy with a vengeance."[31]

Corruption of Methodology: Stylometrics

Journalists used to adhere to what they called the "two witness rule." Newspapers wouldn't report on an event unless and until two independent witnesses had confirmed what had happened. Given the importance of the Shakespeare authorship question, as many reliable witnesses as possible are needed. Many traditional scholars, though, seem content with one witness, that witness being the process known as Stylometrics. Yet Stylometrics itself can be seen as another methodological process designed to avoid direct examination of the Oxfordian claim.

Stylometrics is a computer-assisted statistical method for analyzing the text of literary works without consideration of other factors beyond the words (including

---

[30] American Council of Trustees and Alumni, *The Unkindest Cut: Shakespeare in Exile 2015*, p. 2.
[31] Bill Boyle and Roger Stritmatter, "From the Editors: Oxford is Shakespeare: Any Questions?" *Shakespeare Matters*, vol. 1/1 (Fall 2001): 3.

spelling and punctuation) on the page. In certain circumstances it is a useful technique in trying to determine who might have written a work published anonymously, or in trying to determine which parts of a work a particular author may have contributed to.

Through Stylometrics, scholars determine the "footprint" of an author by examining such factors as the frequency of certain words or phrases, types of punctuation, line endings, and other easily quantifiable aspects of style. Once a footprint has been

		Commentary on Stylometrics, 1998-2016
1990	Peter R. Moore	"Claremont McKenna College's Shakespeare Clinic: Who Really Wrote Shakespeare," *Shakespeare Oxford Newsletter*, vol. 26/3 (Summer): 7-10.
1998	W. Ron Hess	"Hotwiring the Bard into Cyberspace," *The Oxfordian*, vol. 1, pp. 88-101.
1999	Hess	"Shakespeare's Dates: Their Effects on Stylistic Analysis," *The Oxfordian*, vol. 2, pp. 25-59.
2000	Ward E. Y. Elliott & Robert J. Valenza	"Can the Oxford Candidacy Be Saved?" *The Oxfordian*, vol. 3, pp. 71-97.
2001	John Shahan	Letter [Flawed Reasoning in Elliott and Valenza], *The Oxfordian*, vol., pp. 154-165.
2003	George Warren	"The Proof is in the Pembroke: A Stylometric Comparison of the Works of Shakespeare with 12 Works by 8 Elizabethan Authors," *The Oxfordian*, vol. 6, pp. 133-149.
	Elliott & Valenza	Letter [Reply to letters by John Shahan and W. Ron Hess], *The Oxfordian*, vol. 6 pp. 154-163.
2004	Elliott & Valenza	"Oxford By the Numbers: What Are the Odds that the Earl of Oxford Could Have Written Shakespeare's Poems and Plays?" *Tennessee Law Review*, vol. 72/1: 323-453.
	Richard F. Whalen	"A Response to 'Oxford By the Numbers,'" pp. 275-76.
2006	John M. Shahan & Richard F. Whalen	"Apples to Oranges in Bard Stylometrics: Elliott & Valenza Fail to Eliminate Oxford," *The Oxfordian*, vol. 9: 113-25.
2007	Elliott & Valenza	"My Other Car is a Shakespeare: Response to Shahan and Whalen," *The Oxfordian*, vol. 10, pp. 142-53.
2007	Sally Mosher	Letter: The Shahan-Elliott Debate at the Shakespeare Authorship Roundtable, *The Oxfordian*, vol. 10.
2008	Mosher	"Dueling Stylometricians: Shahan vs. Elliott," *Shakespeare Matters*, vol. 7/3 (Spring): 5, 14, 32.
2009	David Kathman	Shakespeare Wrote Shakespeare, *Oxfordian*, vol. 11, pp. 13-28.
	Shahan & Whalen	"Auditing the Stylometricians: Elliott, Valenza and the Claremont Shakespeare Authorship Clinic," *The Oxfordian*, vol. 11: 235-65.
	Whalen & Shahan	"Elliott and Valenza's Stylometrics Fail to Eliminate Oxford as Shakespeare," *Discovering Shakespeare*, edited by Daniel L. Wright, pp. 137-42.
	Ramon Jiménez	"Stylometrics: How Reliable is It Really?" in *Shakespeare Beyond Doubt?* edited by John M. Shahan & Alexander Waugh, pp. 228-36.
2010	Shahan & Whalen	"Reply to Elliott and Valenza," *The Oxfordian*, vol. 12, pp. 167-81.
2011	Jiménez	"How Reliable is Stylometrics? Two Orthodox Scholars Investigate," *Shakespeare Oxford Newsletter*, vol. 47/1 (Jan): 11-16.
2016	Richard Malim & Gary Goldstein	"Stylometrics: The Imperial Computer Takes Center Stage," *Sh. Oxford Newsletter*, vol. 52/4 (Fall): 14-15.

established, it can be compared with those of other authors.

In the later 1980s Ward E. Y. Elliott and Robert J. Valenza, both associated with the Claremont Authorship Clinic at Claremont McKenna College, began applying Stylometric techniques to the issue of Shakespearean authorship. They compared the footprints of three dozen other writers (including Edward de Vere) with the footprint formed from samples of Shakespeare's plays; they found that none of them had written Shakespeare's works. Therefore, they concluded, William Shakspere should continue to be regarded as their author.

Two prominent Oxfordian scholars, Richard F. Whalen and John M. Shahan, analyzed Elliott's and Ward's findings and found several problems that warranted invalidating their findings when it came to Edward de Vere. The two pairs of scholars engaged in an exchange that lasted more than a decade, as shown in the nearby text box.

One critical flaw identified by Whalen and Shahan was that the Claremont team had nothing to say about whether the plays were written by either William Shakspere or Edward de Vere because neither left behind plays under their own names from which footprints could be prepared and compared with "Shakespeare's." In Shakspere's case, he left behind no writings of any kind—no plays, poems, letters, or other documents—except for six wobbly signatures (and perhaps, the short doggerel poem on what is traditionally regarded as his tomb).

It was the same with Edward de Vere. Although he was regarded as "best for comedy" during his lifetime, none of his plays have survived under his own name. Elliott and Valenza prepared his footprint by examining sixteen of his poems; half of them were really song lyrics, yet the de Vere footprint was compared with the texts of Shakespeare's plays, not his poems or lyrics. Cross-genre comparisons are less likely to match than intra-genre comparisons, but the Claremont team ignored this point. Whalen and Shahan did examine it, and concluded that "This mishandling of genres, . . . by neglecting to compare songs to songs and poems to poems, casts serious doubt on the validity of their findings." Further, "Even if a re-analysis of the inputs changed the outputs . . . other input problems are so serious that the results of re-analysis would not suffice to salvage their conclusion regarding Oxford."[32]

One of the other "input problems" was that Oxford's youthful poems and lyrics were compared with Shakespeare's mature works. Most of Oxford's surviving poems were published when he was twenty-six years old, but they were almost certainly composed at least a decade earlier (the editor of the compilation in which they appeared died in 1566, though the work was not published until 1576). Back in 1920-1921 Looney had examined the ways that early works should be expected to differ from mature works (see Chapter 4).[33] Using similar reasoning, Whalen and Shahan concluded that "Elliott and Valenza's research design cannot rule out the possibility that any stylistic differences between Oxford's youthful verse and Shakespeare's mature verse, first published two decades later, could be entirely due to Oxford's stage of development as a writer. The correct response to such a design issue would have been to discount stylistic differences

---

[32] Richard F. Whalen and John M. Shahan, "Elliott and Valenza's Stylometrics Fail to Eliminate Oxford as Shakespeare," *Discovering Shakespeare* (2009), edited by Daniel L. Wright, p. 138.

[33] See also James A. Warren "Comparisons of Oxford's Poetry with Shakespeare's: Five Letters from J. Thomas Looney to *The New Age* (1920-1921) and *The Outlook* (1921)," in *The Oxfordian*, vol. 22 (Sept. 2020): 103-20.

as possibly due to developmental factors, and focus on similarities. Elliott and Valenza did the opposite."[34]

After identifying other problems that invalidated the Claremont project's findings, Whalen and Shahan summarized theirs:

> The inputs that Elliott and Valenza used in their study do not warrant the unqualified conclusion they reached for Oxford. Their Shakespeare baseline was not representative and was biased because it excluded nine plays and two poems. They did not compare Oxford's songs to Shakespeare's songs, nor did they compare a clean, "unconfounded" sample of Oxford's poems to Shakespeare's poems. They incorrectly assumed that publication dates during Elizabethan times were always close to dates of composition, and they consequently assumed that Oxford's youthful verse was representative of his mature poetry.
>
> They ignored consistent praise by Oxford's contemporaries that he was among the greatest of Elizabethan poet-playwrights. The contrast with the works in their sample ought to have alerted them to the likelihood that they were working with an incomplete, invalid sample, and that any differences between Oxford's and Shakespeare's verse could be developmental. They ought to have concluded that although they found little stylometric support for Oxford, he was not a fully testable claimant, and so could not be eliminated. The study, therefore, lacks validity and cannot be said to possess meaningful authority; its conclusions, assessed by scientific standards, must, accordingly, be rejected. (142)

Oxfordian Peter R. Moore noted another flaw: "The Clinic feels that one of its best tests is its exclamation mark count; Shakespeare's works show some exclamation marks, and May's edition of Oxford's poems show none. But according to Partridge (pp. 124-126), the exclamation mark was not used in England until the 1590s, that is, after Oxford's poetry was written!"[35]

Curiously, Elliott and Valenza noted that "For the first two years the tests were favorable to Oxford. . . . But in 1989 we discovered what looked like serious flaws in our then-best test . . . and turned to six other tests that showed mismatch after mismatch between Shakespeare and twenty-seven testable poet claimants, including the front runners Oxford, Bacon and Marlowe. Oxford's poems flunked five of the six new tests and seemed particularly different from those of Shakespeare."[36] Not having detailed the nature of the flaw or the changes made in the tests, one wonders whether Elliott and Valenza, not happy with the outcome of their tests, reconfigured their criteria to obtain a desired result. In line with that idea, Moore stated that "Serious bias is seen in setting up the scoring system . . . but even if they were redone properly, they would only have the status of evidence, data, or tendencies subject to interpretation rather than decisive tests. At any rate, and for what they're worth, they support the Oxford Theory."[37]

<u>Stylometrics and authorship of selected passages</u>

Elliott and Valenza also used Stylometric techniques to try to identify passages or entire scenes in Shakespeare's plays that didn't quite seem to fit his usual footprint. This

---

[34] Richard F. Whalen and John M. Shahan, "Elliott and Valenza's Stylometrics," p. 141.

[35] Peter R. Moore, "Claremont McKenna College's Shakespeare Clinic," *Shakespeare Oxford Newsletter*, vol. 26A/3 (Summer 1990): 8.

[36] Ward E. Y. Elliott and Robert J. Valenza, "Can the Oxford Candidacy Be Saved?" *The Oxfordian*, vol. 3 (2000): 71.

[37] Peter R. Moore, "Claremont McKenna College's Shakespeare Clinic," *Shakespeare Oxford Newsletter*, vol. 26A/3 (Summer 1990): 8

work was extended by Brian Vickers and, most extensively, by Gary Taylor and the team of scholars who prepared *The New Oxford Shakespeare* published in 2018. Their effort revealed, to their own satisfaction, that various passages in several plays had been written by eleven other playwrights, including Thomas Middleton (who wrote parts of *All's Well that Ends Well*, *Timon of Athens* and *Measure for Measure*), and Christopher Marlowe and others (who co-authored all three parts of *Henry VI* with Shakespeare). They also concluded that Shakespeare co-authored with an unknown author another seven plays not usually attributed to him, including *Edward III* and *Arden of Faversham.*, raising the number of plays in the Shakespeare canon from thirty-seven to forty-four. What is especially interesting about the latter claim is that *Edward III* and *Arden* are among those anonymous works that some Oxfordian scholars believe were written by Edward de Vere.

Oxfordian scholars have long accepted that some passages or scenes in Shakespeare's plays were likely written by someone other than Oxford. They see two scenarios in which such work may have taken place. The first, proposed by Col. Ward and Capt. Ward in the late 1920s, was that many history plays, including the three parts of *Henry VI*, were written by playwrights who worked under Oxford's supervision in drafting a large number of plays (perhaps as many as ninety) with patriotic themes designed to increase support for Elizabeth's reign and to increase morale during the War with Spain. That work was funded, many Oxfordians believe, by the grant of £1,000 that was paid to Oxford annually from Secret Service funds beginning in June 1586, though the work may have begun earlier.

The other scenario involves work left incomplete at the time of Oxford's death in 1604, including plays from early in his career. These plays include many of those in which Taylor and others detected contributions by other writers, including *Pericles*, *Henry VIII*, *Cymbeline* and *The Winter's Tale*. That such plays came from multiple pens, including "Shakespeare's" was most prominently acknowledged by respected Shakespeare scholar Sir Walter Raleigh before Looney wrote *"Shakespeare" Identified*. In his view, many of the plays were finished by other hands after 1604 (the year of Oxford's death, and the year that some Stratfordians believe marked Shakespeare's retirement), which could easily account for references to events taking place after that date.

Regarding the idea of revisions or multiple authors contributing to Shakespeare's plays resulting in the texts that exist today, the wheel has turned round. E. K. Chambers, in his "The Disintegration of Shakespeare" lecture in 1924 concluded that a limited number of revisions of the plays by Shakespeare himself and by others likely took place. J. M. Robertson went further in identifying passages he believed had been authored by others, not just revised, but decried the work of yet other scholars who reached similar conclusions about other passages.[38]

---

[38] J. M. Robertson, *The State of Shakespeare Study: A Critical Conspectus* (1931), p. 5. In 1931 Robertson lamented that "The Academy can hardly escape a sense of insecurity" arising from "disintegrators," from fellow orthodox scholars who had concluded that Shakespeare had, on occasion, "collaborated" with other writers. He wrote of the "plain danger that they may make the Institution itself look ridiculous" (7). They have, he wrote, "already [provided] matter for rude ridicule to the more intelligent reader, [and] may become vaguely distasteful even to the non-academic audience" (8). What might Robertson have said of Gary Taylor and the new generation of "disintegrators" who have moved far beyond the findings of scholars in his day, identifying as much as one third of the text of the First Folio as not by the man whose name was supposedly on it?

Collaboration

Taylor and his co-editors on *The New Oxford Shakespeare* did not accept the explanation cited by Raleigh and Looney that other pens had merely completed unfinished drafts. They concluded that the other writers had not merely added passages to Shakespeare's plays, but had actively collaborated with him. Yet the editors had jumped from A to B, from their initial findings that more than one author contributed to the text of a play as we know it today to the conclusion of co-authorship without providing any evidence besides Stylometrics that such collaboration ever took place. Even if Stylometrics itself is considered as one witness, they violated the two-witness rule.

Three Oxfordian scholars—Michael Dudley, Gary Goldstein and Shelly Maycock—reviewed *The New Oxford Shakespeare Authorship Companion*, in which Taylor and the co-editors had reported their conclusions. The editors, they noted, overlooked the absence of any connection between Shakspere and his supposed collaborators. "Even though Francis Meres in *Palladis Tamia* named twenty-two contemporary authors, including William Shakespeare, none of the other twenty-one had any contact, in writing or reported, with Shakespeare."[39] Lacking independent corroborative evidence, the collaboration idea resembles the *Ur-Hamlet* fantasy made up in the 1930s to explain how references could have been made to a character named Hamlet at a date far too early for the play to have been written by Shakspere.

The reviewers also noted that the Stylometricians provided no explanation for why Shakespeare, at the peak of his powers, would have wanted to collaborate with other playwrights, especially with those whose powers were so far below his. "The editors cannot explain why the first two acts of *Pericles* had to be co-authored by pamphlet writer George Wilkins in 1608—while Shakspere was still alive" or why "three other plays, *Cardenio*, *Henry VIII* and *The Two Noble Kinsmen*, had to be co-authored by John Fletcher—also while Shakspere was alive" (200). The editors, they noted, had rejected this question as "unscholarly." They (Gabriel Egan and Gary Taylor) "cannot bring themselves to consider that for a master playwright in the maturity of his craft to leave four plays unfinished might mean that he was no longer alive. Such alternatives are instead excluded from the consideration of both the authors and the readers of this expensive book."

Dudley, Goldstein and Maycock also noted that Stylometric scholars followed different methodologies and reached different conclusions, which tends to undermine the validity of all results. Referring to *1 Henry VI* as they summed up what was being presented by the editors, "we have four different scholars assigning the play to five or six authors, and Act 1 alone to three of them. Who are we supposed to believe? And doesn't a failure to agree on a coherent methodology, coupled with the disparate and sometimes contradictory results of the practitioners invalidate, or at least call into question, the premises of the enquiry—at least to the extent of suggesting the value of scholarly humility about the results of the findings?" (201)

Given the uncertainty of the results, why would these scholars make this leap from different pens to collaboration? Here I offer a speculation of my own. Stratfordian scholars know full well that the dates of composition have not been established for any of Shakespeare's plays, which makes the Raleigh-Looney idea of plays being finished by

---

[39] Michael Dudley, Gary Goldstein, and Shelly Maycock, "All That Is Shakespeare Melt into Air," *The Oxfordian*, vol. 19 (2017): 202.

other pens after Shakspere's retirement or Oxford's death reasonable and hard to refute. But if, Stylometricians think, it could be claimed that the plays resulted from active collaboration, then—*Voila!*—Shakespeare had to have been alive after 1604 and could not have been Edward de Vere. At one stroke Oxford is eliminated as Shakespeare, the authorship question is vanquished, and dates are established for some of the later plays. A triple win!

That this proposed motive for the editors' choices is more than mere speculation is shown by another methodological choice. Taylor & Co. cannot identify the most important of Shakespeare's collaborators, simply calling him "Anonymous." He is not any of the authors whose work they have examined. Yet Edward de Vere was not among the poets whose work was tested. He was excluded from consideration. It doesn't take a genius to consider that the reason "Anonymous" wasn't identified is because he was intentionally not tested.

The three reviewers reached a similar conclusion, writing that "one has to wonder at the motivations behind this monumental effort. At 741 pages, the *Authorship Companion* represents an astonishing amount of energy directed at delegitimizing and dethroning Shakespeare. . . . [I]t seems intended instead to be a deliberate attempt to pre-empt the actual debate over authorship."[40] *The New Oxford Shakespeare* shows yet again the convoluted lengths that Stratfordian scholars will go to, to avoid having to confront the Oxfordian challenge head-on.

It is no surprise that James Shapiro weighed in on the side of active collaboration. Although *Contested Will* was written six years before publication of the *New Oxford Shakespeare*, he swallowed the Stylometrics "revolution" hook, line and sinker, writing that "attribution studies have transformed our understanding of how Shakespeare worked" (258). "A revolution has since occurred in how Shakespeare professors think about collaboration, largely as a result of the investigations of a new and creative generation of scholars interested in attribution" (254).

The passages on collaboration in *Contested Will* employ the same sleights of hand that affect so many other parts of the book. After noting the indications in Henslowe's Diary that it was not uncommon for more than one playwright to work on a play, Shapiro leaped to the conclusion that collaboration must have been a common practice with Shakespeare as well. 'To alter, new-model, and improve the unsuccessful dramas of preceding writers, was I believe, much more common in the time of Shakespeare than is generally supposed.' It followed, then, that *Pericles* was 'new modeled by our poet' rather than jointly composed" (30). That conclusion doesn't follow. It is only a possibility, one not supported by any evidence in the record. There are no mentions of any payments to Shakespeare in Henslowe's Diary even though the other playwrights who collaborated on other plays are all mentioned as payees—indeed, it is those mentions that established their joint work on a play. Shapiro deceived his readers by failing to mention that Henslowe makes no mention of Shakespeare in any capacity.

Among other sleights of hand he engaged in in relation to collaboration are:

✓ "The conviction that Shakespeare was a solitary writer whose life can therefore be found in his works cannot comfortably accommodate the overwhelming

---

[40] Michael Dudley, Gary Goldstein, and Shelly Maycock, "All That Is Shakespeare Melt into Air," *The Oxfordian*, vol. 19 (2017): 205.

evidence of co-authorship" (62).

- o Shapiro never showed any evidence of Shakespeare as co-author. The "overwhelming evidence" is that co-authorship was not infrequent, not that it was the manner in which plays were usually written or that Shakespeare ever did so.

✓ "Shakespeare . . . co-wrote plays with several dramatists, acted in the plays of many others, and would have heard still others pitch their plays to his company's sharers" (234).

- o There is no evidence that any of this took place.

✓ "Even as a lyric poet he didn't work in isolation, sharing his *Sonnets*, we are told, with his 'private friends.'"

- o Shapiro is confusing the act of writing with the act of sharing pieces already written.

✓ Based on Stylometrical evidence, "we now have a pretty clear sense of which scenes were first drafted by Shakespeare and which by his coauthors" (255). But "we are still in the dark about some of the most pressing questions about the nature of each collaborative effort. Did Shakespeare invite others to work together on a play, or did they approach him? Who worked out the plot? Why do these collaborations seem inferior to Shakespeare's solo-authored plays?" (256).

- o This is all speculation; stating an assertion does not make it a fact. There is no independent evidence that Shakespeare ever collaborated with any other playwrights in the manner Shapiro implies.

✓ "One of the great challenges, then, to anyone interested in the subject is that we know so little about how dramatists at the time worked together. We just know— primarily from Philip Henslowe's accounts of theatrical transactions from 1591 to 1604—that they did, and that in the companies that performed in his playhouses it was the norm, not the exception" (256).

- o It is refreshing to see Shapiro admit that we know so little about how dramatists at the time worked together, but it is incorrect to state that collaboration "was the norm, not the exception." "Not uncommon" is the best way to phrase it. And again, there is no mention of Shakespeare in Henslowe's Diary, as there is for all other playwrights presumed to have engaged in collaboration.

✓ "It's impossible to picture any of their aristocrats or courtiers working as more or less equals with a string of lowly playwrights" (258).

- o Oxford's involvement in producing works for the public stage explains one source of the shame that he felt, as the Lord Great Chamberlain of the realm, as expressed in sonnet 110: "Alas! 'tis true, I have gone here and there, / And made myself a motley to the view." Note also Shapiro's misleading "more or less equals" phrase: a courtier working with non-courtier playwrights or theater people would not necessarily have worked with them as equals. Shapiro has once again gone to extremes— either courtiers did not work with playwrights at all or they worked with them as equals—leaving out the wide middle ground of working with them as someone of a higher social status.

✓ "For Oxfordians in particular, attribution studies are a nightmare. Their strategy has long been to argue that after de Vere's death in 1604, any unfinished works were touched up or completed by other playwrights. Orthodox Shakespeareans deride this as a 'jumble sale' scenario. You'd have to imagine something along the lines of Middleton, Wilkins, and Fletcher coming upon Oxford's estate sale in 1604, finding these unfinished plays for the having, and each making a grab for them, with the dexterous Fletcher making off with three, the others with one each" (258).

   o Shapiro again ignores the idea proposed by Sir Walter Raleigh and other respected Stratfordian scholars that other pens finished Shakespeare's unfinished plays after his death or retirement. The "jumble sale" nonsense is not a serious scholarly attempt to understand what really happened to the unfinished drafts.

Group authorship

Some Stylometric scholars go beyond the idea of collaboration to that of group authorship. For them, plays were written by a group of writers who agreed to put the name "William Shakespeare" on them regardless of who in the group worked on them.

Early Oxfordian scholars had also proposed the idea of two forms of group authorship. In one, as described by Gilbert Slater in *Seven Shakespeares* (1931), William Shakespeare was the name given to works produced by any member of the group. In the other, writers engaged in true collaboration with each other, the contributions varying from work to work, with the resulting play presented as by "William Shakespeare."

J. Thomas Looney himself had speculated on the group idea in *The Hackney Spectator* in 1923. He described how "the suddenness and brilliancy of the great literary outburst of the latter half of Queen Elizabeth's reign, which had puzzled students of literature," resulted from "the active association of representatives of the intellectual movement with people educated by the refinements of the court." It was only through such "group activity," led by "the soul of the [great Elizabethan] age," Edward de Vere, that "the Shakespeare dramas could have been made to embody, as they do, the whole culture of the age."[41] Looney was miles ahead of today's academics who merely document, through computer methods such as Stylometrics, that more than one writer had a hand in a play without providing the context for their claims.

---

[41] J. Thomas Looney, "An Elizabethan Literary Group," published in three parts in *The Hackney Spectator* in 1923, on Aug. 3 (p. 4), Aug. 14 (p. 9) and Aug. 24 (p. 4).

24

Stratfordian Scholars Embarrass Themselves

Poor Scholarship

In 1908 an English paleoanthropologist set out to embarrass his colleagues through what became known as the Piltdown Man Hoax. He planted, where he knew they would be found, an apparently apelike jaw together with cranial fragments from an apparently modern human, all carefully altered to resemble fossils with structural features midway between pre-hominid species and modern homo sapiens—the so-called missing link.

The hoax succeeded in part because paleoanthropologists' desire to find the missing link was so strong that anomalies about the fossils were waved away in the excitement. It succeeded also because the perpetrator had known just what faked evidence his colleagues would accept because of their false beliefs, their unrealistic expectations and the faulty methodology that guided their work. It was, in fact, frustration over his colleagues' beliefs, expectations and methodology that prompted the perpetrator to launch the hoax.

Unfortunately it succeeded all too well. The findings were announced with great fanfare and accepted by most paleoanthropologists throughout the world. Although some had doubts at the time, the hoax was not definitely exposed until chemical tests became available decades later. By that time the deception had corrupted work and findings in the field for close to half a century. The exposure resulted in great embarrassment for the entire field of paleoanthropology, not just because a mistake had been made, but because the "experts" had been fooled by one of their own.

The lesson to be drawn from the Piltdown Man hoax is that fields that are inwardly focused and that ignore findings from related fields are vulnerable to false beliefs.[1]

In the large gray areas where ideas cannot be directly tested by experiment or observation, scholars are led toward conclusions by the methodologies that guide their work. A particular methodology, deemed appropriate at the time it was developed, might become inappropriate as fields of investigation and technological capabilities change. The problem is that the longer a given methodology is officially sanctioned, the stronger the supports for it becomes. Bureaucratic pressures begin rewarding adherence to it over substantive accomplishments. Sooner or later a point is reached when those following the

---

[1] The Piltdown Man case is discussed by Ian Tattersall in *The Strange Case of the Rickety Cossack* (2015). Tattersall went on to show that the closed nature of paleoanthropology that gave rise to the hoax remains in place a century later. His account of how the field has been dominated by authorities who insist that the hominid species evolved in a step-by-step process from older species directly to modern human beings with few side branches—a development at variance with the wide-branching evolutionary process through which all other species evolved—makes for fascinating reading. The story of how a field of intellectual investigation had latched onto a theory before all the relevant facts were known shows the harm from moving too soon from an inductive to a deductive methodology—exactly the danger that the geologists mentioned in Chapter 23 were so intent on avoiding.

methodology look down and realize that there is no ground under their feet. At that point it is too late. Like Wile E. Coyote in pursuit of the Roadrunner, they have already run off the cliff.

This unpleasant end can be avoided, Tattersall showed, by re-evaluating methodologies and inherited beliefs from time to time.

> The Piltdown debacle reminds us with unusual force that, when, we look at any paleoanthropological—or other—question, we need always to examine our preconceived beliefs. But more than that, we need also to be aware of where those beliefs come from. Particularly if they were formed early enough in our experience, we may be unaware that they *are* preconceptions, rather than truths, about the world that we are justified in taking for granted. . . . [I]t turns out that what we are initially taught about such things has an enormous influence on how we will view them in the light of future evidence. . . . [as] practitioners try to fit new facts into existing frameworks. (44-45)

Shakespeare Studies has been in Wile E. Coyote's position several times. Scholars were fooled twice by forgers who created documents supposedly owned or written by William Shakespeare: by William Henry Ireland in the 1790s and again by John Paine Collier in the 1830s.[2] They were predisposed to accept the forged documents as legitimate for the same reason that the paleoanthropologists had been deceived: by their flawed beliefs and inappropriate methodology. Shakespeare Studies today seems to be unaware that a third hoax had been perpetrated on it.

The field is protected from the criticisms that all others would face if they produced findings that contradicted those in related fields. Like the field of human evolution, which enjoys immense prestige within the larger field of biology, Shakespeare Studies enjoys high prestige within the larger field of literary studies, which largely shields it from outside criticism. But its high status externally cannot protect it from internal intellectual dishonesty.

This chapter provides examples of how recent work done in the closed field of Shakespeare Studies embarrasses the field—or would do so if its leaders recognized their failures. The methodological follies regarding topical allusions, the "death of the author" and Stylometrics have already been discussed. Five more will be considered here.

- ✓ Biographies of William Shakespeare
- ✓ *Monstrous Adversary* by Alan Nelson (2003)
- ✓ *Shakespeare Beyond Doubt* edited by Paul Edmondson and Stanley Wells (2013)
- ✓ The First Folio Tour organized by the Folger Shakespeare Library (2016)
- ✓ Stratfordian scholarly praise for James Shapiro's *Contested Will* (2010-2011)

Shakespearean Biographies Today

The earliest accounts of the life of William Shakspere, prepared before the rise of modern scholarly practices, were mainly collections of anecdotes uncritically strung together around the few facts known of his life. A century and a quarter ago, to flesh out a full biography, scholars relied largely on weasel words such as "undoubtedly," "no doubt," "may be said to have," "assumed to have," "seems to have been," "is generally accepted as," "is possible that" and "may have been" (see Chapter 1). As Kevin Gilvary

---

[2] See James Shapiro, *Contested Will* at pp. 32-36, 47-48, 64-66.

observed in his study of Shakespearean biographies, the few historical records that exist "do not reveal his personality or describe his 'life trajectory.'"

> What passes for Shakespearean biography offer extensive description of the historical, developed by the dubious practices of speculation, using uncorroborated posthumous anecdotes, and making biographical inferences from the works.[3]

In attempting to portray William Shakspere as Shakespeare in *Shakespeare at Work* in the 1930s, G. B. Harrison found that the best he could do was to create "an imaginary portrait, a conjectural reconstruction," which "is and must be sheer guesswork."[4] "Surely, it is an astonishing fact," Percy Allen observed, "that this latest Life of 'Shakespeare,' by one of the world's greatest living authorities upon the Elizabethan age, should be heralded by such words."[5] In contrast, he noted, "The best books upon 'Shakespeare' by the Oxfordian writers, are not, at bottom, 'sheer guesswork,' but are built up, page by page, from a closely argued inter-relation of ascertained fact and legitimate inference."

It's not much different today. New biographies continue to be written almost yearly even though no new facts about Shakspere's life have been uncovered since 1931, and before then, 1910. (1). With documents existing for only the most mundane details in his life, writers found imagination and speculation essential tools in writing about what would be, if Shakspere were indeed the author, the most interesting parts of his life. "The small number of historical documents which reference William Shakespeare," Gilvary continued, "offers no insight into the poet's thoughts and motives, but consist mainly of legal documents.... As a result, the biographies of Shakespeare only offer historical fact in their treatment of the context and in dealing with a few external events of his life. For the inner man, these narrative accounts are entirely conjectural" (4, 6). Even S. Schoenbaum, one of the most noted of Shakespeare's biographers, concluded that "Perhaps we should despair of ever bridging the vertiginous expanse between the sublimity of the subject and the mundane inconsequence of the documentary record."[6] More recently David Ellis observed that "Because so little is known about Shakespeare, and all authors of his 'life' are obliged to speculate, one of their problems is how to acknowledge the uncomfortable fact without giving their readers the impression that they might just as well have opened an historical novel."[7]

Over the last few decades scholars have become increasingly open in their acknowledgment of the degree to which they rely on imagination and speculation to tell the story of Shakspere's life. Dropping any pretense that they are presenting a factual story, they nevertheless expect readers to accept the tale they tell as fact. Perhaps the biography that most openly flouts scholarly standards in this regard is Stephen Greenblatt's *Will in the World: How Shakespeare Became Shakespeare* (2004), which opens with the words "Let us imagine,"[8] followed by a hundred-page fantasy. As he explained in a note to the reader, "There are huge gaps in knowledge that make any biographical study of Shakespeare an exercise in speculation" (18). The runner-up prize

---

[3] Kevin Gilvary, *The Fictional Lives of Shakespeare* (2018), p. 2, 130.

[4] G. B. Harrison, *Shakespeare at Work* (1933), preface. [unnumbered page.]

[5] Percy Allen, "Shakespeare at Work," *Shakespeare Pictorial*, Nov. 1933, p. 176.

[6] S. Schoenbaum, *Shakespeare's Lives* (1991), p. 568.

[7] David Ellis, *The Truth About William Shakespeare* (2013), p. 12.

[8] Stephen Greenblatt, *Will in the World: How Shakespeare Became Shakespeare* (2004), p. 23.

might go to René Weis for *Shakespeare Unbound: Decoding a Hidden Life* (2007), with the bronze medal awarded to Jonathan Bate for *The Soul of the Age* (2008).

A case could be made that the stream of recent biographies noted in the nearby text box was triggered by the Oxfordian challenge to the Stratfordian narrative. The increase in public interest in the authorship question, and public receptivity to the Oxfordian explanation, gave rise not just to efforts to counter that interest by attacking authorship doubters (e.g., Shapiro's *Contested Will*), but also to efforts to create biographies that would reassure the public that Shakspere did write Shakespeare. The latter effort could be accomplished only through extensive use of the faculty that Shapiro so admired in Shakspere: imagination.

Such biographies served a scholarly need, helping scholars out of the tight corner they had painted themselves into. Having proclaimed the "death of the author" in their extreme efforts to develop a methodology that banished consideration of the author, his motivations for writing and the conditions in which he wrote—as absurd an approach to understanding literature as I have ever heard (and one perhaps developed to avoid dealing with the abundant evidence connecting Edward de Vere to the plays)—scholars suddenly found they had succeeded all too well. The flimsy William Shakspere story now seemed too inconsequential when compared to that of a rival candidate for whom strong biographical linkages could be documented. A believable life for their guy had to be constructed, at least for the public.

In imagining these fanciful biographies, Stratfordian scholars, finding no connections in the historical records between Shakspere and the plays, have attempted to find events in the plays that could be drawn from his life. But in doing so, as Oxfordian scholar Richard F. Whalen observed, they have misused the literary evidence. There are two ways of researching and writing biography, he explained, one legitimate and the other not, and Shakspere's biographers have relied on the wrong one.

> The first method, which is fundamental to biographies of writers, is to take the documented facts of a writer's biography and then determine how a writer, such as Shakespeare, drew on his documented life experience and his times to write his plays. This might be called reading forwards from the writer's known biography to the imaginative works.[9]

> The second, more dubious method is to *discover* in writer's works supposed biographical details about his life and emotions that are not supported by his documented biography. This method has been called reading backwards from the works to write biography. Fiction becomes a source for biography but a conjectural and unreliable source. (10-11)

Mainstream Shakespeare scholar Bruce Danner recognized the absurdity of the situation:

> In their engagement with alternative constructions of Shakespeare, contemporary critics struggle to fix a coherent portrait of the dramatist in the absence of Humanist tropes of the artist as a stable, creative origin. Having largely exchanged these ideals for a destabilized, Foucauldian model of the author—as a locus of concern for the interests of power, ownership, and the suppression of dissent—current scholars find themselves in the uncomfortable

---

[9] Richard F. Whalen, "Stratfordian Professor Takes Authorship Question Seriously," *Shakespeare Oxford Newsletter*, vol. 46/1 (May 2010): 7.

Selected Biographies of William Shakespeare, 1984-2020, and Selected Reviews of Them

1985	E. Honigmann	*Shakespeare: The "Lost Years"*
1988	P. Levi	*The Life and Times of William Shakespeare*
1991	D. Kay	*Shakespeare: His Life, Work and Era*
1992	P Thompson	*Shakespeare's Professional Career*
1993	S. Schoenbaum	*Shakespeare's Lives*
	M. Skura	*Shakespeare the Actor and the Purposes of Playing*
	I. Wilson	*Shakespeare: The Evidence*
1994	Stanley Wells	*Shakespeare: A Dramatic Life*
1995	Stanley Wells	*Shakespeare: A Life in Drama*
1998	Jonathan Bate	*The Genius of Shakespeare*
	Park Honan	*Shakespeare: A Life*
	D. Shelland	*William Shakespeare*
1999	Anthony Holden	*William Shakespeare: His Life and Work*
2000	Garry O'Connor	*William Shakespeare: A Popular Life*
	J. Southworth	*Shakespeare, the Player: A Life in the Theatre*
2001	Katherine Duncan-Jones	*Ungentle Shakespeare – Scenes from His Life* (editor)
2003	Stanley Wells	*Shakespeare: For All Time*
	Michael Wood	*In Search of Shakespeare*

2004	**Steven Greenblatt**	***Will in the World: How Shakespeare Became Shakespeare***

  <u>Reviews</u>
  -----, *Shakespeare Matters*, vol. 4/1 (Fall 2004): 3.
  William E. Boyle, *Shakespeare Matters*, vol. 4/2 (Winter 2005): 6-7.
  Kevin Gilvary, *De Vere Society Newsletter*, Jan. 2005, p. 22.
  Richard Malim, *De Vere Society Newsletter*, Jan. 2005, pp. 21-22.
  Richard F. Whalen, *Shakespeare Oxford Newsletter*, vol. 40/2 (Spring 2004): 18.
  Daniel L. Wright, *Shakespeare Matters*, vol. 4/1 (Fall 2004): 4, 32.

2005	Peter Ackroyd	*Shakespeare, The Biography*
	James Shapiro	*1599: A Year in the Life of William Shakespeare*
2007	Bill Bryson	*Shakespeare: The World as Stage*

2007	**René Weis**	***Shakespeare Unbound: Decoding a Hidden Life***

  <u>Reviews</u>
  Richard Malim, *De Vere Society Newsletter*, vol. 15/1 (March 2008): 30-31.

2008	Marjorie Garber	*Profiling Shakespeare*
	J. Pearce	*The Quest for Shakespeare*

2009	**Jonathan Bate**	***The Soul of the Age***

  <u>Reviews</u>
  Richard Malim, *De Vere Society Newsletter*, vol. 16/1 (Feb. 2009): 24-26.
  Richard F. Whalen, *Shakespeare Oxford Newsletter*, vol. 45/2 (Sept. 2009): 28-29.
  Richard F. Whalen, *Shakespeare Oxford Newsletter*, vol. 45/3 (Dec. 2009): 25-26.

2011	Graham Holderness	*Nine Lives of William Shakespeare*
2012	N. Fogg	*Hidden Shakespeare: A Biography*
	Potter, Lois	*Life of William Shakespeare: A Critical Biography*
2013	D. Callaghan	*Who Was William Shakespeare?*
2015	Paul Edmondson &	*Shakespeare Circle: An Alternative Biography*
	Stanley Wells (editors)	
	James Shapiro	*1606: William Shakespeare and the Year of Lear*
2016	Richard Dutton	*Shakespeare, Court Dramatist*

> position of serving just such interests as gatekeepers of orthodoxy.[10]

> If the naïve belief in a retrievable authorial presence must be relinquished, what remains to prevent the wholesale rejection of Shakespeare altogether? (148)

In other words, once scholars have dismissed the idea of the author, how are they to put up a candidate to compete with Edward de Vere? They have attempted to do so, Danner observed, by following the illegitimate biographical method identified by Whalen and using imagination and fantasy. "In their efforts to discover a Shakespearean presence in resistant or inconclusive evidence, orthodox scholars have fashioned theories that resemble their own worst caricatures of anti-Stratfordianism" (156). "The more orthodox scholars attempt to differentiate their vision of Shakespeare from the irrational fictions of anti-Stratfordianism, the more similar their views appear to become" (145). Shapiro had expressed a similar concern in *Contested Will* (267).

Stratfordian scholars face multiple problems. They cannot create a convincing portrait of Shakespeare without violating their "death of the author" methodology. But having taken that step, they find that they still cannot do it without engaging in imagination and speculation. The larger problem is the outright deception they must engage in: presenting assertions as facts, engaging in intellectual sleights of hand, and omitting facts that contradict their story. If relying on imagination and speculation will come to be seen as embarrassing, deception and sleights of hand will come to be seen as shameful.

Monstrous Adversary: Alan Nelson's Biography of Edward de Vere

In the 1920s Looney and Capt. Ward brought new attention to Edward de Vere, 17th Earl of Oxford, Queen Elizabeth's Lord Great Chamberlain. One might have expected scholars to rush to investigate the life of one of the most brilliant, colorful and overlooked courtiers of the age. Yet the opposite happened: there was an antipathy toward anything having to do with de Vere. Although his reputation as a poet and dramatist had been recognized before Looney claimed he was Shakespeare, afterwards scholars depreciated his poetry and ignored him. With very few exceptions, research into his life and personality and literary works was left to scholars outside academia, principally those interested in the issue of Shakespearean authorship.

So it was big news in 2003 that, after eighty years of academic silence, Alan Nelson, a professor of English at U.C. Berkeley, would publish a biography of Edward de Vere. Here, hopefully, would be the great work by a professional scholar at a renowned institution that Oxfordians had expected would one day be written. But it was not what they had hoped for. William Niederkorn, writing for *The Brooklyn Rail*, described Nelson's book, *Monstrous Adversary*, as "one of the most bilious biographies ever written."

> Riddled with errors, which Oxfordians have pointed out since its publication in 2003, Nelson's book is an embarrassment to scholarship. *Contested Will*, whose title is cast in the same syntactical form as Nelson's and which revels in the same spirit, is almost as bad. Though both books assemble a great deal of interesting information, they are patently biased and need to be read skeptically. While it is hard to find one page of Nelson's book that is free of unfair statement, though,

---

[10] Bruce Danner, "The Anonymous Shakespeare: Heresy, Authorship, and the Anxiety of Orthodoxy," in *Anonymity in Early Modern England*, edited by Janet W. Starner and Barbara H. Traister (2011), p. 144.

Shapiro can occasionally sound seductively considerate.[11]

In Warren Hope's assessment, the book "is a piece of propaganda posing as scholarship.... It is typical of Nelson's method that he dwells on this murder to connect Oxford with violence without justification while ignoring or slighting the clear and justifiable connections of Oxford with literature."[12] Roger Stritmatter concluded that "For all its window-dressing of scholarship, the book is neither plausible nor believable. In place of a judicious scholarly critique of the Oxfordian case it substitutes a sustained *ad hominem* attack on Oxford's character which bends or breaks every canon of fairness which might impede its single-minded pursuit of ideological conformity to orthodox belief."[13] And in Thomas Hunter's assessment, "Dr. Nelson employs practically every kind of propaganda technique known to man, including but certainly not limited to innuendo, smear, hearsay, omission, misrepresentation, guilt by association, and *non sequitur*. The book is a virtual textbook of propaganda technique.... *Monstrous* ... is itself a personal attack upon Oxford from first page to last."[14]

Nelson claimed to be objectively reporting what he found as he investigated the life of Edward de Vere. But that is disingenuous. Nobody spends a decade engaged in a project unless he expects it to be something more than an academic study. Stritmatter, noting Nelson's "thorough hostility towards the subject of his own biography," rightly expected readers to "wonder why a man would devote ten years of his life to writing a book about a man whom he so obviously despises."[15]

The answer is that we must often engage in unpleasant tasks in order to reach greater goals. For Nelson, the greater goal was tarnishing Edward de Vere's reputation so thoroughly that he would be forever disqualified from having written the great works of literature known as "Shakespeare's." This is shown by the title of his book: "monstrous adversary" is a phrase that Arundel and Howard used in their attempts to deflect attention away from their treason to England and the Queen by blackening the name of the person who revealed it. It is also demonstrated by Nelson's selective presentation of facts and documents. He included and exaggerated the significance and reliability of every negative fact or rumor about Oxford, while excluding practically all the documents and incidents that do him credit. Joseph Sobran saw clearly that,

> Nelson seldom misses a chance to disparage Oxford. Apparently his years of research have failed to turn up a single fact to Oxford's credit. The reader's respect for his impressive scholarship soon gives way to weariness at his obsessive denigration, which shows him no less biased than those who adulate Oxford. He is always ready to believe Oxford's most scurrilous foes ... but he largely omits the many contemporary tributes to Oxford's genius (unless he can ascribe them to base motives). About the only thing Nelson is willing to credit Oxford with is elegant penmanship.[16]

Nelson largely omitted mention of the Shakespeare authorship question, thereby making it possible to ignore the reasons why so many others outside academia had

---

[11] William S. Niederkorn, "Absolute Will," *Brooklyn Rail*, April 2010.
[12] Warren Hope & Kim Holston, *The Shakespeare Controversy* (2009), p. 118.
[13] Roger Stritmatter, "'Monstrous Animosity:' How Nelson's Oxford Bio Distorts Both Oxford and Oxfordians," *Shakespeare Matters*, vol. 3/1 (Fall 2003): 9
[14] Thomas Hunter, "The Nelson Dilemma," *Shakespeare Matters*, vol. 3/4 (Summer 2004): 5
[15] Roger Stritmatter, "'Monstrous Animosity," *Shakespeare Matters*, vol. 3/1 (Fall 2003): 8.
[16] Joseph Sobran, "Nelson's Flawed Life of Oxford," *Sh. Oxford Newsletter*, vol. 39/4 (Autumn 2003): 9.

concluded that Oxford was Shakespeare.

> Because Nelson ostensibly excludes the "authorship controversy" from consideration, he doesn't feel he must confront the seeming links between Oxford and "Shakespeare;" . . . In fact, the earl of Southampton, Pembroke, and Montgomery—the three dedicatees of the Shakespeare works—were all, at various times, candidates for the hands of Oxford's three daughters. An interesting coincidence, at least, but Nelson's biographical strategy allows him to avoid mentioning it. The same strategy allows him to deal only glancingly, if at all, with other interesting coincidences. (9)

Although Nelson did mention that "'true believers' think Oxford was Shakespeare, . . . he leaves the impression that he has no idea *why* they think so, just as he has no idea why Edmund Spenser, George Puttenham, Francis Meres, and many other Elizabethan writers called Oxford a poet and playwright of great distinction" (11). Stritmatter observed that "Nelson somehow fails to offer any reference to their contents. This is not, it must be emphasized, because Nelson is unaware of the relevance of these arguments; it is clear from the shape of his own 'refutation' that he is often formulating his own narrative with these very arguments in mind."[17] Sobran agreed. "The only reason Nelson wrote this book—and the only reason anyone will read it—is the 'authorship controversy' Nelson both deprecates and dodges. Though *Monstrous Adversary* is beyond question an important addition to that debate, readers can draw their own conclusions from the fact that Oxford's detractors continue to find it necessary to deal with the evidence so disingenuously."[18]

Nelson's effort to tarnish Oxford failed. Citing Oxford's failings only made him sound more like a genius writer, as Richard F. Whalen noted. "Oxford did lead an eccentric,

Selected Reviews of Prof. Alan Nelson's *Monstrous Adversary* (2003)		
Oxfordian		
2003	K. C. Ligon	*Shakespeare Matters*, vol. 3/1 (Fall): 21.
	Joseph Sobran	*Shakespeare Oxford Newsletter*, vol. 39/4 (Autumn): 1, 9-10, 16.
	Roger Stritmatter	*Shakespeare Matters*, vol. 3/1 (Fall): 8-9.
	Richard F. Whalen	*Shakespeare Matters*, vol. 3/1 (Fall): 1, 20-21.
2004	William E. Boyle	*Shakespeare Matters*, vol. 3/4 (Summer): 7.
	Kevin Gilvary, Kevin Johnson & Eddi Jolly	*De Vere Society Newsletter* (Jan): 6-7.
	Thomas Hunter	*Shakespeare Matters*, vol. 3/4 (Summer): 5-6.
	Stephanie H. Hughes	*Shakespeare Oxford Newsletter*, vol. 40/2 (Spring): 19-23.
	Peter R. Moore	*Shakespeare Oxford Newsletter*, vol. 40/1 (Winter): 1, 15-22.
	Richard F. Whalen	*Shakespeare Matters*, vol. 3/2 (Winter): 22-23.
		Shakespeare Matters, vol. 3/4 (Summer): 7-8.
2006	Christopher Paul	*Shakespeare Matters*, vol. 6/1 (Fall): 22-27.
Other		
2003	Thomas Pendleton	*Shakespeare Newsletter*, vol. 53/3 (Fall): 65, 69. Response by Richard F. Whalen, vol. 53/4: 104.
2004	Andrew Barnaby	*Renaissance Quarterly*, vol. 57/4 (Winter): 1,529.
2005	Catherine G. Camino	*Sixteenth Century Journal*, vol. 36/3 (Fall): 908.
	Steven W. May	*Shakespeare Quarterly*, vol. 53/2 (Summer): 214-26.

[17] Roger Stritmatter, "'Monstrous Animosity,' *Shakespeare Matters*, vol. 3/1 (Fall 2003): 8.
[18] Joseph Sobran, "Nelson's Flawed Life of Oxford," p. 16.

tumultuous, sometimes scandalous life, but that does not preclude him from having written the great plays and poems. To the contrary, it argues that like many other writers of genius who were guilty of similar erratic behavior he was just the kind of writer who would have produced the works of Shakespeare."[19] Nelson "misunderstands the typical personality of a great genius. The life that he finds 'so privately scandalous' (publicly, too) sounds just like the life of most artists and writers of genius. Indeed, it is their complex and sometimes outrageous personalities that are richly reflected in the works of great writers" (21).

Despite its flaws, *Monstrous Adversary* did contain new information. Nelson located many previously unknown documents from Oxford's life and provided full or nearly full transcriptions of them. Elsewhere, however, Nelson made little or no effort to assess the credibility of witnesses or statements critical of Oxford, such as the Arundel-Howard slanders made against him after he exposed their treasonous plans.

But as Peter R. Moore noted, assessing credibility was the last thing Nelson wanted to do. With "the application to historical documents of such fashionable lit-crit inanities as 'the author is dead' and 'all reading is misreading,' Nelson wrenches his documents from their backgrounds, which he then replaces with his own commentary to support his thesis that Oxford was a monster. Nelson no more acknowledges an obligation to the normal rules of historical scholarship than a deconstructionist recognizes rules of literary scholarship. And just as the poststructuralist believes that texts are infinitely malleable, so Nelson feels entitled to recreate the past to suit his fancies."[20]

Thomas Hunter wrote that "One would think that any academic would immediately see *Monstrous* for what it is, a flagrantly biased presentation which contorts logic and fact to make a point. Not so in today's academic publishing world. Liverpool University Press accepted it without a quibble, according to Nelson."[21] And Thomas Pendleton, editor of *The Shakespeare Newsletter*, approached the book with the same see-no-evil attitude, praising it as "an extremely thorough and ferociously well-documented biography. . . . a work so assiduously researched and documented that it is hard to imagine that there ever will be a more authoritative or reliable life of Edward de Vere."[22] Observing academia's unwillingness to acknowledge the book's unscholarly nature, Hunter asks, "What should Oxfordians do about Prof. Alan Nelson's *Monstrous Adversary*?"[23] "It would seem to me that the only true and honest answer for Oxfordians must be to continue to disassemble *Monstrous* point by point, to demonstrate its errors fully for the record, and to make this record available for public reference. . . . In terms of honesty, duty, and our own integrity, we have no choice" (6).

Christopher Paul, like William Niederkorn, recognized just how thoroughly Nelson had embarrassed himself and his profession. "Encumbered under the ponderous weight of his own biases, Nelson has proved himself incapable of impartially interpreting the piles of material heaped before him. In the end, his transparent agenda is an

---

[19] Richard F. Whalen, "Nelson's New Oxford Biography," *Shakespeare Matters*, vol. 3/1 (Fall 2003): 1, 20.

[20] Peter R. Moore, "Demonography 101: Alan Nelson's *Monstrous Adversary,*" *Shakespeare Oxford Newsletter*, vol. 40/1 (Winter 2004): 22.

[21] Thomas Hunter, "The Nelson Dilemma," *Shakespeare Matters*, vol. 3/4 (Summer 2004): 5.

[22] Thomas A. Pendleton, "Alan H. Nelson's *Monstrous Adversary: The Life of Edward De Vere, 17th Earl of Oxford,*" *The Shakespeare Newsletter*, vol. 53/3, no. 258 (Fall 2003): 65, 69.

[23] Thomas Hunter, "The Nelson Dilemma," *Shakespeare Matters*, vol. 3/4 (Summer 2004): 5.

embarrassment, not only for himself, but also for the whole of academia."[24]

Readers will probably not be surprised to learn that *Monstrous Adversary* has largely been accepted as the standard "life of Oxford." Nelson has been invited to write for reference works such as *The Dictionary of National Biography* as the authority on Oxford's life.[25]

Shakespeare Beyond Doubt Absurdities

In 2013, the Shakespeare Birthplace Trust in Stratford-on-Avon, unsettled by growing public interest in the Shakespeare authorship question and the movie *Anonymous* that portrayed Edward de Vere as "Shakespeare" and Shakspere as a front for him, published *Shakespeare Beyond Doubt: Evidence, Argument, Controversy (SBD)*, which aimed to establish authorship by William Shakspere as "beyond doubt." Edited by the Trust's Head of Research and Knowledge Paul Edmondson and its Honorary President Stanley Wells, it contained articles by twenty-two "distinguished scholars" who "explore the issues in the light of biographical, textual and bibliographical evidence to bring fresh perspectives to an intriguing cultural phenomenon."[26]

Was this, finally, a substantive response to doubters? Sadly, no. In his trenchant assessment of *SBD*, Oxfordian scholar Tom Regnier commented that,

> One might have thought that, given the chance to put the authorship controversy to rest once and for all, the authors and editors of *SBD* would have laid out their evidence in all its glory, with clear, cogent explanations of its significance and coolly reasoned rebuttals to any arguments questioning its authenticity. That they have chosen instead to assert authority, disparage open-mindedness, and belittle adversaries says a great deal about the mindset and the state of scholarship as it regards the authorship question, of the Shakespeare establishment.[27]

John Shahan, founder of the Shakespeare Authorship Coalition that promulgated *The Declaration of Reasonable Doubt*, soon realized that *SBD* contained many misrepresentations that readers new to the authorship question might not catch. He organized a point-by-point response to it that was published only a few weeks later. Titled *Shakespeare Beyond Doubt? Exposing an Industry in Denial* (*SBD?*) and edited by himself and Alexander Waugh, it presented responses by thirteen scholars to each of the pieces in *SBD* and also provided much additional information that documented the many holes in the Stratfordian narrative. The editors asked readers to read both *SBD* and *SBD?* before reaching a conclusion about the authorship question.

Among the scores of misrepresentations in *SBD* are these, each of which is followed by *SBD?'s* response:

✓ Stanley Wells's reference to "the mass of evidence that the works were written by

---

[24] Christopher Paul, "A First Blast of the Trumpet Against the *Monstrous Adversary*," *Sh. Matters*, vol. 6/1 (Fall 2006): 27.

[25] I am indebted to Warren Hope for this important point.

[26] Paul Edmondson & Stanley Wells (editors), *Shakespeare Beyond Doubt: Evidence, Argument, Controversy* (2013), back cover.

[27] Thomas Regnier, [review of *Shakespeare Beyond Doubt: Evidence, Argument, Controversy*], *Brief Chronicles*, vol. V (2014): 204.

a man named William Shakespeare."[28]

- o *SBD?* pointed out that such evidence did not show that the works had been *written* by someone named William Shakespeare, only that they'd been *published* under that name.[29] The references are to the name of the author; not one statement connected the writer William Shakespeare to William Shakspere of Stratford-on-Avon during his lifetime.

✓ Wells's statement that "No one expressed doubt that 'William Shakspere of Stratford' wrote the works attributed to him . . . until the middle of the nineteenth century."[30]

- o *SBD?* responded: "No one expressed doubt that Shakspere wrote the works during his lifetime because no one ever suggested he did in the first place. Wells never shows that anyone ever said he did. One does not bother to deny something unless there is reason to think it in the first place. Does the fact that no one has expressed doubt that I am a king mean that I am one?"[31]

✓ Charles Nicholl stated that "The true author of the plays, asserted the leading Oxfordian, J. Thomas Looney, was not 'the kind of man we should expect to rise from the lower middle-class population of the towns.' As well as being objectionable, this is inaccurate in terms of literary history. Many Elizabethan and Jacobean playwrights sprang precisely from this industrious, aspiring artisan class."[32]

- o Nicholl quoted Looney correctly but twisted his statement. Looney said nothing about playwrights in general. He did not say that it was impossible for playwrights to come from the lower middle class. His statement was about one playwright, William Shakespeare, and was based on his writings, which habitually presented society and human interactions "from the standpoint of Feudal relationships," a fact that distinguished him from all other playwrights.

✓ Daniel Kathman criticized Looney for having written of Stratford that "dirt and ignorance . . . were outstanding features of the social life of Stratford in those days and had stamped themselves very definitely upon the family life under which William Shakspere was reared."[33] Kathman added that "More recent anti-Shakespearians are usually not quite so blunt, but they typically present a bleak picture of sixteenth-century Stratford."

- o Kathman attributed the unpleasant description of Stratford to "anti-Shakespearians," implying that it arose out of bias on their part. But he omitted four important words from Looney's quotation—"according to

---

[28] Stanley Wells, "Allusions to Shakespeare to 1642," in *Sh. Beyond Doubt: Evidence, Argument, Controversy* (2013), p. 81.

[29] John M. Shahan, "General Introduction and Challenge to the Shakespeare Birthplace Trust," in *Shakespeare Beyond Doubt? Exposing an Industry in Denial* (2013), p. ii.

[30] Stanley Wells, "Allusions to Shakespeare to 1642," p. 87.

[31] John M. Shahan, "General Introduction and Challenge to the Shakespeare Birthplace Trust," in *Shakespeare Beyond Doubt? Exposing an Industry in Denial* (2013), p. iii.

[32] Charles Nicholl, "The Case for Marlowe," in *Shakespeare Beyond Doubt* (2013), p. 30.

[33] David Kathman, "Shakespeare and Warwickshire," in *Shakespeare Beyond Doubt* (2013), p. 121

this authority"—that made it clear that the source of Looney's information was the respected Stratfordian scholar J. Halliwell-Phillipps.[34] If anything, Looney was being kind in his use of the phrase "dirt and ignorance." Halliwell-Phillips's descriptions are much more graphic.[35]

How is it that the respected publisher Cambridge University Press would publish such a book? Not only did Edmondson and Wells *not* put the authorship issue to rest, they increased doubts among readers who read *SBD* carefully. After Prince Philip mentioned his doubts about Shakspere's authorship to his eldest son, Prince Charles put him in touch with Stanley Wells. When Wells asked if he was a heretic, Philip replied, "all the more so after reading your book!"[36]

John Shahan co-editor of *SBD?*, later commented that "Stratfordians must be in shock that we responded to *Shakespeare Beyond Doubt* so quickly, and with a book that is clearly superior to theirs in addressing the evidence. Here they thought they were putting a stake

Commentary on	
Shakespeare Beyond Doubt **(2013) and** ***Shakespeare Beyond Doubt?*** **(2013)**	
Oxfordian	
-----	*Shakespeare Matters*, vol. 12/3 (Summer 2013): 1, 19, 36.
Michael Egan	*Shakespeare Oxford Newsletter*, vol. 49/3 (Fall 2013): 25-32.
Kevin Gilvary	*De Vere Society Newsletter*, vol. 20/2 (July 2013): 18.
Gary Goldstein	*The Oxfordian*, vol. 15 (2013): 92-99.
Richard Malim	*De Vere Society Newsletter*, vol. 20/2 (July 2013): 11-15.
	Heythorp Journal, vol. 53/2 (March 2015): 321-22.
Tom Regnier	*Shakespeare Matters*, vol. 12/3 (Summer 2013): 28-33.
	Brief Chronicles, vol. V (2014): 193-204.
Don Rubin	*Brief Chronicles*, vol. V (2014): 189-92.
Michael St. Clair	*Shakespeare Matters*, vol. 12/4 (Fall 2013): 26, 35.
Richard Waugaman	*Journal of the American Psychoanalytic Association*, March 7, 2014.
Other	
-----	*Shakespeare Newsletter*, vol. 63/1 (Summer 2013): 25.
-----	*Times Literary Supplement*, issue 5754 (July 12, 2013): 24.
Dalva Alberge	*Observer*, March 31, 2013, p. 23.
Jonathan Bate	*New Statesman*, vol. 142 (April 26, 2013): 44.
Paul Dean	*The New Criterion*, vol. 32/3 (Nov. 2013): 66.
Jack Malvern	*The Times*, April 19, 2013, p. 22.
Micah Matrix	*Weekly Standard*, March 17, 2014, pp. 38-39.

[34] The full sentence from which Kathman extracts his phrase is, "Dirt and ignorance, according to this authority [Halliwell-Phillipps], were outstanding features of the social life of Stratford in those days and had stamped themselves very definitely upon the family life under the influence of which William Shakspere was reared. Father and mother alike were illiterate . . ." [*"Shakespeare" Identified* (2018), p. 16].

[35] The passage in Halliwell-Phillipps reads: "At this period, and for many generations afterwards, the sanitary condition of the thoroughfares of Stratford-on-Avon was, to our present notions, simply terrible, Under-surface drainage of every kind was then an unknown art in the district. . . . House-slops were recklessly thrown into ill-kept channels that lined the sides of unmetalled roads. . . . In April, 1552, John Shakespeare was amerced in the sum of twelve-pence for having amassed what was no doubt a conspicuous *sterquinarium* [sewage] before his house in Henley Street, and under these unsavoury circumstances does the history of the poet's father commence in the records of England." [J. Halliwell-Phillipps, *Outlines* (1887), pp. 23, 25.]

[36] Chris Hastings, "Bard Blood at the Palace as Princes Split Over Shakespeare," *The Mail Online*, April 2, 2014.

in the heart of the authorship controversy, when actually they were giving it a whole new life. There's no way we could have gained this much attention unless they attacked us first, giving us an opportunity to respond on something close to a level playing field."[37]

The Failed First Folio Tour (2016)

April 2016 marked the 400th anniversary of the death of "William Shakespeare." To commemorate the occasion, the Folger Shakespeare Library and its co-sponsoring institutions organized a First Folio Caravan Tour in which original copies of the First Folio were displayed at libraries, universities and museums in all fifty states. Accompanying the Folios were display panels and publicity materials.

The Tour would have been an ideal opportunity for the Folger Library to have put the authorship question to rest forever. It could have used public interest and media contacts to explain why it believed William Shakspere wrote the works. Instead, it hid William Shakspere, making little mention of him at a major event purportedly held to commemorate his passing.

The exhibition provided very little information about the subjects that would seem to have been most relevant on this particular anniversary.

The author. Of greatest interest would have been information about the supposed author of the works in the publication on display, but the exhibition provided little about who he was and how and when he came to write each of the plays.

The historical setting at the time of publication. Why was the Folio published in 1623? Who organized it, and why? Was the publication a purely literary event, or was it related to larger historical and political events at the time? Again, little context.

The content of the Folio. Scholars have disagreed, at times vehemently, about the oddities in the Folio's prefatory material and the veracity of the statements in it by Ben Jonson and others. Why is there no mention of this important controversy?

Instead, the exhibition provided information on the general cultural environment at the time the Folio was published and on general publishing and printing practices. Such information would perhaps be more relevant for an exhibition organized in 2023, the anniversary of the Folio itself; they have little relevance at an exhibition marking the passing of the author.

An obvious reason for these omissions is that subjects that touch on the authorship question were buried. Viewers' attention was steered toward the book rather than the author, and even then only to inconsequential aspects of it.

An honest and informative exhibition would have brought the following fascinating information to viewers' attention:

On the author and his family: An honest exhibition would have noted that there was no known connection between the Folio and Shakspere's family. No member of his family was involved in the production of it and no indication exists that any member of the family ever owned a copy. An informative exhibition would have included information about the two patrons who sponsored and financed the publication—the "Incomparable Pair of Brethren" mentioned prominently in the prefatory materials—including the fact that one, the Earl of Montgomery, was a son-in-law of Edward de Vere, and that the other, his brother, the Earl of Pembroke, had been engaged to another of de Vere's daughters.

---

[37] John Shahan, quoted in "*Shakespeare Beyond Doubt* or *Shakespeare Beyond Doubt?* You Decide," *Shakespeare Matters*, vol. 12/3 (Summer 2013): 36.

"These patrons," wrote Shelly Maycock in a publication organized by Roger Stritmatter to provide a more comprehensive assessment of the Folio's publication, "named and celebrated on the next page after the Folio's Droeshout image, . . . were among the most directly living relatives of the 17th Earl of Oxford in 1623. . . . They were Oxford's family members, closely associated with the Folio, and . . . these facts have long been central to the case for Oxford's authorship of the plays."[38] Surely, she continued, "a museum-worthy display about an 'iconic' literary artifact should consider the actual historical circumstances under which the book appeared in print, which prominently and undeniably include the patronage of the two brothers with such close ties to the de Vere family" (14-15).

On the historical and political events surrounding publication: Viewers would have benefited from knowing that the two dedicatees were also, as Maycock explained, "close political allies of Oxford's son, the 18th Earl, Henry de Vere, who throughout the printing of the Folio, was imprisoned in the Tower of London for too vigorously contradicting the King's plan to marry his son to the Spanish infanta" (8). Viewers would have been interested to know that "the striking political and cultural reality that the book was being published partly in response to a bitter three-year long parliamentary controversy (1621-1624) over King James's design to marry Prince Charles to a Catholic Spanish princess" (15).

As noted elsewhere in this book, independent scholar Peter W. Dickson was the first to show that rather than being a mere collection of plays, the First Folio was an intensely political statement. "The sudden rush in 1621-1623 to collect and preserve for posterity the Shakespearean dramas . . . was energized by paranoia among Anglican-minded courtiers and like-minded actors and publishers that there might be a top-down restoration of Roman Catholicism if King James succeeded in his effort to arrange a dynastic union with Catholic Spain via a marriage of Prince Charles to a sister of King Filipe IV."[39] Six of Dickson's writing on this subject are listed in a nearby text box.

On the controversies about the prefatory materials: Viewers would have been interested in learning that many Stratfordian scholars believe that the statements by Ben Jonson and others in the Folio's prefatory materials are ambiguous and even deceptive. Maycock explained that "[t]he Folger also appears poised to sweep under the rug the long-standing scholarly dispute, dating back to the late eighteenth century, questioning the attribution of the Heminges and Condell prefaces, with many scholars suggesting that the real author of at least one of them was actually Folio editor Jonson—a finding which, if true, automatically calls into question almost every other aspect of the Folio's genesis, design and intent. It is also ignoring contemporary scholarly inquiry into the striking and enormous ambiguities of Jonson's prefatory contributions" (15).

Stratfordians reluctantly acknowledge that no document during William Shakspere's lifetime directly connected him with the literary works. Stanley Wells admitted that "among the allusions [to the writer Shakespeare by his contemporaries] that I have cited so far . . . there is none that explicitly and incontrovertibly identifies him with Stratford-

---

[38] Shelly Maycock, "Branding the Author: Feigned Authorship Neutrality and the Folger Folio Tour," in *The 1623 Shakespeare First Folio: A Minority Report* edited by Roger Stritmatter (2016), p. 8.
[39] Peter W. Dickson, *Bardgate: Shake-speare and the Royalists Who Stole the Bard* (2013), p. 21.

upon-Avon."[40] The prefatory material in the First Folio, published seven years after Shakspere's death is, therefore, of critical importance to the authorship issue. It is of great significance, then, that Stratfordian scholars such as Bruce Danner readily speak of "the text of the First Folio [prefatory material], whose omissions, errors, and outright lies have long been common knowledge."[41]

But for those scholars actively involved in defending the Stratfordian claim, no such admissions can be made. They must adamantly defend the literal truth of the prefatory materials because without them their entire case for Shakspere's authorship folds. They suffer from what John Shahan and others have called "First Folio Fundamentalism."

> Stratfordianism resembles a quasi-religious cult in its reliance on a single revered text, treated as infallible despite being in conflict with other evidence. The Stratfordian case depends almost entirely on the prefatory material in the First Folio. Without it, they would be hard pressed to make a convincing case for the Stratford man. In this they resemble other fundamentalists, committed to a sacred text treated as gospel.

> Stratfordians view themselves as the defenders of rigorous academic standards, but they are no such thing. Rather, they are defenders of orthodoxy, and enforcers of conformity. Rather than "Stratfordians," they might more aptly be called First Folio Fundamentalists.[42]

The Folger Shakespeare Library, as a library and member of the American Library Association (ALA), is bound to neutrality in all matters of academic controversy. Maycock informed readers that "According to the ALA, libraries are decidedly not supposed to take definitive positions of this sort on controversial scholarly matters. . . . Invited speakers at an exhibit sponsored in part by the ALA . . . should be actively neutral, practicing an academic freedom that encourages broad inquiry and allows scholars to acknowledge doubts and diversity of opinion in an atmosphere of civil discussion and debate."[43]

Yet, through its organization of the Tour, the Folger Shakespeare Library, Maycock explained, "promot[ed] a view of the Folio that ignores questions about its authorship and origins. . . . Nothing in the pre-tour documents or the original application packet . . . indicates that Folger-approved experts will be informed about, or prepared to respond neutrally to, questions about Shakespeare's authorship that often arise in relation to any study of the Folio's historical and cultural context, creation and design" (15). In her summation,

> Collectively these omissions confirm the impression . . . that the Folger has no plan to explore any aspects of the Folio that don't readily conform to its pre-established Stratfordian narrative. . . . The Folio tour seems more intended to deflect attention from the book's disputed authorship than to educate tour attendees about the Folio as a cultural artifact. . . . [It] offer[s] little opportunity for the kind of intellectual engagement that the Folio tour purports to supply. . . . [It] evades, rather than encounters, questions about authenticity and authorship.

---

[40] Stanley Wells, "Allusions to Shakespeare to 1642," in *Sh. Beyond Doubt: Evidence, Argument, Controversy* (2013), p. 81.

[41] Bruce Danner, "The Anonymous Shakespeare: Heresy, Authorship, and the Anxiety of Orthodoxy," in *Anonymity in Early Modern England*, edited by Janet W. Starner and Barbara H. Traister (2011), p. 147.

[42] John Shahan, "Is There a Shakespeare Authorship Issue?" *Shakespeare Oxford Newsletter*, vol. 43/3 (Summer 2007): 18-19.

[43] Shelly Maycock, "Branding the Author: Feigned Authorship Neutrality and the Folger Folio Tour, in *The 1623 Shakespeare First Folio: A Minority Report* (2016), pp. 10, 9.

[The Folger] ignore[s] a long history of controversy that a publicly funded tour should embrace and invite. Instead we are treated to another version of the clichéd circular reasoning that "Shakespeare is Shakespeare," a paper chase that fails to counter authorship questioning with evidence and arguably obscures the true historical meaning of the document it purports to illuminate for the public. If the engraving is so "authentic," why does editor Jonson tell us to look not on it, but on the book itself, to discover the author? (14)

The Folio Tour, however, is only one project in "the Folger's consistently unimpressive track record of false neutrality in dealing with topics closely related to the authorship controversy. As much as Stratfordians need the Folio to divert attention from the flawed nature of their biographical tradition, they are also—and not without good reason—afraid of it and somehow understand its destabilizing potential. This contradiction lies behind the library's careful effort to closely control the exhibit's messaging" (9).

In her indictment of the Folger Library's faux neutrality, Maycock condemned

its unofficial tradition, since the 1980s, of allowing research privileges to nonconformists, while actively suppressing the results of their research because it does not meet some unexamined standard of "decisive" proof—as if anything approaching "decisive proof" existed on the orthodox side! The entirely

Selected Oxfordian Commentary on the First Folio, 1984-2020		
1998	Peter W. Dickson	"Henry Peacham and the 1923 First Folio," *Elizabethan Review*, vol. 6/2 (Autumn): 55-76.
1999	Peter W. Dickson	"The Jaggard-Herbert-De Vere Connections (1619-1623)," *Sh. Oxford Newsletter*, vol. 34/4 (Winter): 14-15+.
	Peter W. Dickson	"Are British Scholars Erasing Two Heroic Earls From Jacobean History to Protect the Shakespeare Industry?" *Sh. Oxford Newsletter*, vol. 35/1 (Spring): 8-9, 24.
	Peter W. Dickon	"Bacon Begs the Two Henries as First Folio Appears," *Sh. Oxford Newsletter*, vol. 35/2 (Summer): 7, 28.
	James Fitzgerald	"Know Ye Not This Parable? The Oxford-du Bartas Connection," *The Oxfordian*, vol. 2: 76-116.
2000	Mark K. Anderson	"Nero Caesar: The First Folio's Straight-Man," *Shakespeare Oxford Newsletter*, vol. 36/2 (Summer): 5, 24.
2001	John Rollett	"Oxford Blue, or Possible Clues in Ben Jonson's Eulogy in the First Folio," *De Vere Society Newsletter*, Jan. 2001, pp. 43-48.
2006	Bonner Miller Cutting	"The Case of the Missing First Folio," *Shakespeare Matters*, vol. 5/4 (Summer): 6-11.
2009	Stephanie Hopkins Hughes	"Jonson's Ode to Shakespeare: What was Ben Jonson Actually Saying in His Dedicatory Ode in the 1623 First Folio?" *De Vere Society Newsletter*, vol. 16/1 (Feb.): 21-24.
2011	Peter W. Dickson	*Bardgate: Shake-speare and the Royalists Who Stole the Bard.*
2013	John Shahan	"The First Folio and the Stratford Monument," and "Appendix D: Heminge and Condell Letters in the First Folio," *Shakespeare Beyond Doubt?*, pp. 112, 249-50.
	Richard F. Whalen	"The Ambiguous Ben Jonson: Implications for Assessing the Validity of the First Folio Testimony," in *Shakespeare Beyond Doubt?* edited by John M. Shahan and Alexander Waugh, pp. 126-135.
2016	Peter W. Dickson	*Bardgate II: Shakespeare, Catholicism and the Politics of the First Folio of 1623.*

oxymoronic implication is that the standard for academic inference is that one side in a debate should possess 'decisive proof' before evidence on either side can be considered or debated. It does not take an advanced degree in Shakespeare Studies to recognize that this is not neutrality. It is also not progress. (17)

As stewards of the Shakespeare and the Folger legacies, as representatives of a powerful academic institution accepting public funding, Folger librarians and publicists should perform this service with courageous conscience, avoiding both the errors of censorship and the legacy of misinformation that have for so long plagued traditional Shakespeare scholarship and created so much basis for legitimate doubt. (22)

The Folger has, therefore, not lived up to its duty to maintain neutrality in matters of academic disagreement by its "rigid adherence to the orthodox theory of authorship, and therefore, to continually disregard the library's fiduciary responsibility to maintain authentic neutrality and acknowledge the diversity of informed opinion" (6).

The publication providing the most comprehensive Oxfordian assessment of the First Folio and the Tour is Roger Stritmatter's compilation of new and reprinted pieces, *The 1623 Shakespeare First Folio: A Minority Report* (a special issue of *Brief Chronicles*), published in 2016 while the Tour was in progress. Its contents are listed nearby.

The 1623 Shakespeare First Folio: A Minority Report, edited by Roger Stritmatter
[A special issue of *Brief Chronicles*, 2016]

Roger Stritmatter	"What's Past is Prologue," pp. 1-3.
Shelly Maycock	"Branding the Author: Feigned Neutrality and the Folger Folio Tour," pp. 5-29.
John M. Rollett	"Shakespeare's Impossible Doublet," pp. 31-46.
Richard F. Whalen	"'Look Not on this Picture': Ambiguity in the First Folio," pp. 47-59.
George Greenwood	From *Ben Jonson and Shakespeare* (1921), pp. 61-68.
Katherine Chiljan	"First Folio Fraud," pp. 69-87.
Roger Stritmatter	"'Bestow, when and How You List'" The de Veres and the 1623 Folio," pp. 89-93.
William E. Boyle	"Shakespeare's Son on Death Row," pp. 95-102.
Roger Stritmatter	"Puzzling Shakesperotics," pp. 103-109.
Roger Stritmatter	"'Publish We This Peace': A Note on the Design of the Shakespeare First Folio and the Spanish Marriage Crisis," pp. 111-115.
James A. Warren	"Literary Criticism and the Authorship Question," pp. 117-132.
Michael Dudley	"Look Not on His Picture, but His Books," pp. 133-138.

Stratfordian and Oxfordian Scholars' Reviews of *Contested Will*

The critical response to James Shapiro's *Contested Will* was almost uniformly highly positive. Even publications that did not usually carry reviews of books on literature ran laudatory notices. Reviewers seemed to sigh with relief that here at last was a book to save the world from the Oxfordian menace. The fulsome praise by scholars who surely recognized but ignored the book's many scholarly defects will come to be seen as a particularly embarrassing moment in the story of Shakespearean scholarship.

The forty reviews of *Contested Will* by Stratfordian scholars listed in the nearby text box are too numerous to describe individually. Respected critic John Gross's[44] review is representative of the vast majority. In his view, "The idea that William Shakespeare was not the man who wrote the works of Shakespeare flies in the face of both evidence and common sense. It is not even an interesting theory, but rather quite simply a delusion."[45] He went on to repeat several of Shapiro's most egregious misstatements. On Shapiro's presentation of the Stratfordian claim, he stated that "Shapiro's measured approach . . . makes his concluding explanation of why he is so confident that Shakespeare wrote Shakespeare particularly impressive" (43). Regarding the Oxfordian claim, he was of the belief "[t]hat Looney's writing—which combined implausibility with bizarre judgment—could have made so many converts to his belief that the Earl of Oxford was the author of the plays is testimony to the power of the will to believe" (42).[46]

Given the prominence of the Oxfordian claim and the unsettling feeling it had generated in academia, Stratfordian scholars must have sighed with relief after seeing the positive reviews. Here was a work by a noted scholar they could cite in support of their belief in Shakspere's authorship: "There's now no need to examine the Oxfordian claim ourselves; we can simply cite Shapiro and be done with it."

That a book so chock full of intellectually dishonest sleights of hand could generate so many enthusiastic reviews is not a good sign about the intellectual health of American letters. It brings to mind Looney's statement that as a result of reactions to *"Shakespeare" Identified* in England, he "was not optimistic about the future of British intellectual life," that "The attacks on the Oxfordian idea did not reflect well on the intellectual credit of England." "The present-day handling by the 'intellectual classes' of all problems requiring *thought* rather than erudition and literary style," gave him, "an uneasy feeling that the initiative which England held in the latter half of the nineteenth century is passing into other hands."[47] If writing today, he might have applied that assessment to countries on both sides of the Atlantic.

Looney's spirits might have been lifted by the reviews of *Contested Will* from Oxfordian scholars, who, more astute and more honest, saw through Shapiro's distortions. William Ray noted that "Like the defense lawyer to the jury, [Shapiro] wishes only to cast doubt on questioners' credibility and to minimize their standing to speak," resulting in "a book of profound pretension and patronization."[48] On Shapiro's belief that Shakespeare's deep and enduring knowledge of human nature was due not to a lifetime of bitter experience in the actual world of men and women but only to "imagination," Ray responded, "This is as stunted a reduction of creativity to dreamy-time scribbling as I have ever read" (25). On Shapiro's conjectures stated as facts—that "Shakspere's was one of the most familiar faces in London or at court" being just one of the score already cited—

---

[44] I have for many years been a follower of John Gross's writings on literature and have learned much from him. It was distressing, therefore, to see that he remained committed to the Stratfordian tradition and gave such fulsome praise to such a flawed book. It is disappointing that he had apparently not yet investigated the issue for himself.

[45] John Gross, "Denying Shakespeare," *Commentary*, March 2010, p. 38.

[46] Oxfordians could easily turn Gross's statement around: "That [Shapiro's] writing—which combined selective and misleading and outright false statements to justify his belief that [William Shakspere] was the author of the plays is testimony to the power of the will to believe."

[47] J. Thomas Looney, "Stratford and Stony Stratford," *Bookman's Journal*, March 25, 1921, p. 388.

[48] William J. Ray, "Two Years after Contested Will or, How are the Stratfordians Doing?" *Sh. Matters*, vol. 10/4 (Fall 2011): 24.

Ray nailed it: "No evidence exists to support this drivel. It is weak self-serving speculation. Selective, factually loose, sloppy, morally shabby, slyly coercive uses of language by any writer regrettably tells [us] that he has profaned his native tongue's sanctity as an instrument of truth" (30). Ray concluded that "Shapiro's patronizing manner and self-lamed reactionary book are symptomatic of the Stratfordians' increasingly malignant doctrine" (30).

Bonner Miller Cutting asked a question that many Oxfordians must have wondered about after reading Shapiro's attribution of Shakespeare's knowledge to "imagination:" "One might ask what goes through the minds of these reviewers when they pull off the

Selected Non-Oxfordian Reviews of James Shapiro's *Contested Will* (2010)		
2009	Thomas A. Pendleton	*Shakespeare Newsletter*, vol. 58/3 (Winter): 81, 103.
2010	-----	*Economist*, March 27, p. 93.
	-----	*Folger Magazine*, vol. 4/1: 16-23.
	-----	*Times*, April 5, p. 2.
	-----	*Wall Street Journal*, April 1.
	Alexandra Alter	*Wall Street Journal*, April 2, p. W12.
	Jonathan Bate	*Sunday Telegraph*, April 4, p. 25.
	Ralph Berry	*Contemporary Review*, issue 292 (Winter): 518-19.
	Brian Bethune	*MacLean's* (Toronto), April, p. 60.
	Craig Brown	*Mail on Sunday*, April 11, p. 11.
	Peter Conrad	*Observer*, April 4, p. 46. [See also Jan. 9, 2011, p. 41.]
	T. L. Cooksey	*Library Journal*, vol. 135/3 (Feb. 15): 95-96.
	Ben Crystal	*Independent*, March 28, p. 34.
	Michael Dobson	*Financial Times*, March 20, p. 16.
	John Cary	*Sunday Times*, March 21. p. 44.
	Ward Elliott	*Los Angeles Times*, May 9, p. E8.
	David Ellis	*Cambridge Quarterly*, vol. 39/3: 297-302.
	John Gross	*Commentary*, vol. 129/3 (March): 38-44. [Responses and reply by Gross in the June issue.]
	Helen Hackett	*London Review of Books*, March 11, pp. 21-22.
	Daniel Hannan	*Telegraph*, March 16.
	Philip Hensher	*Spectator*, April 3 [Response by Richard Malim, April 10]
	Jennifer Howard	*Chronicle of Higher Education*, vol. 56/29 (Mar. 28): B11+.
	Hilary Mantel	*Guardian*, March 20, p. 6.
	Jenny McCarter	*New York Times Book Review*, May 2, pp. 10-11.
	Robert McCrum	*Observer*, March 14, p. 18.
	Robert Miola	*First Things*, Aug./Sept., pp. 63-64.
	Charles Nicholl	*Times Literary Supplement*, issue 5583 (April 23): 3-4. [Response by Ren Draya, May 7, p. 6.]
	Jeremy Noel-Tod	*Telegraph*, March 20, p. 20.
	Ray Olson	*Booklist* (Chicago), vol. 106/15 (April): 12.
	Lloyd Rose	*Washington Post*, June 6, p. B6.
	Saul Rosenberg	*Wall Street Journal*, April 8, p. A19.
	David Sexton	*Evening Standard*, March 18, p. 36.
	Will Sharpe	*Shakespeare Bookshop Newsletter*, vol. 16: 1-2.
	John Simon	*Weekly Standard*, Aug. 23, pp. 30-32.
	Terry Teachout	*Wall Street Journal*, April 17, p. W14.
	John Timpane	*Philadelphia Inquirer*, June 30.
	Stanley Wells	*New York Review of Books*, vol. 57/9 (June 30): 31-33.
	Hans Werner	*Toronto Star*, May 9, p. 6.
2012	Rebecca Chapman	*Shakespeare International Yearbook*, vol. 12: 169-94.
	Oliver Kamm	*Times*, April 20, p. 4.
	Leah Marcus	*Shakespeare Johrbuch*, vol. 148: 215-20.

shelf any one of the eight volumes of Geoffrey Bullough's *Narrative and Dramatic Sources of Shakespeare*. . . . Are they unable to see that the Shakespeare Canon is among other things, an encyclopedia of classical and Renaissance literary reference? . . . Plucking all this information from [the] air is a lot to ask of imagination. It suggests that the imagination is all their own."[49] She concluded that "The academic establishment would be well advised to open up its intellectual borders and join in the quest for truth and justice, rather than circling the wagons in a steely effort to maintain the official story. But, sadly, the purpose of *Contested Will* is to preserve the status quo" (31).

Tom Hunter, noting Shapiro's tactic of questioning doubters' motives, turned the tables: "What motivation drives Shapiro to find the reasons for questioning Shakespeare's authorship in those questioning authorship, and not in the evidence against the Stratfordian view?"[50] The answer, Hunter suggested, is that "the offenses to logic and scholarship [that] go on and on in this book . . . are—in a perverted way—a compliment to what laborers in the authorship vineyard have accomplished. For, if their work has received such attention from one of the establishment's anointed, perhaps it is a measure of how the establishment might be running scared after all" (13).

Richard Whalen raised the same point. "Although Shapiro uses the predispositions of the early skeptics to disparage their heretical skepticism, he is hardly in a position to do so. As a career Stratfordian, he is naturally predisposed to believe in Shakspere of Stratford as the poet-dramatist."[51] Whalen identified many scholarly lapses, "including material omissions, unbalanced emphases, unsupported opinions, faulty judgments, the usual straw-man arguments, contradictory stances and some other clever rhetorical tactics. At times, his handling of evidence is so devious as to deftly conceal his errors of interpretation." Whalen ultimately found a silver lining in the *Contested Will* cloud:

> Shapiro shows a fair measure of appreciation for the Oxfordian proposition, and he freely acknowledges Oxfordian successes. . . . In addition, the book's title and

	Selected Oxfordian Responses to James Shapiro's *Contested Will* (2010)	
2009	Thomas Hunter	*Shakespeare Matters*, vol. 8/4 (Winter): 2, 26.
2010	Bonner Miller Cutting	*Shakespeare Matters*, vol. 9/3 (Fall): 16.
	Michael Dudley	*Winnipeg Free Press*, May 15, p. E8.
	Warren Hope	*Brief Chronicles*, vol. 2: 212-223.
	Thomas Hunter	*Shakespeare Oxford Newsletter*, vol. 46/1 (May): 12-13.
	Richard Malim	*De Vere Society Newsletter*, vol. 17/2 (Aug.): 22-26.
	Richard Malim	*De Vere Society Newsletter*, vol. 17/3 (Nov.): 28-29.
	William S. Niederkorn	*Brooklyn Rail*, April.
	Richard F. Whalen	*Shakespeare Oxford Newsletter*, vol. 46/1 (May): 7-11.
2011	William Ray	*Shakespeare Matters*, vol. 10/4 (Fall): 24-30.
	Roger Stritmatter	*Shakespeare Matters*, vol. 10/2 (Spring): 1, 17-23.
	Richard Waugaman	*Psychoanalytic Quarterly*, vol. 80: 225-231.
	Richard F. Whalen	*Shakespeare Oxford Newsletter*, vol. 47/2 (Spring): 9-11.
	Heward Wilkinson	*Shakespeare Matters*, vol. 10/2 (Spring): 1, 24-26.

---

[49] Bonner Miller Cutting, "A Contest of Wills: Reviewing Shapiro's Reviewers," *Shakespeare Matters*, vol. 9/3 (Fall 2010): 31.

[50] Thomas Hunter, "Shapiro and Why Authorship Doubters Don't Believe," *Sh. Oxford Newsletter*, 46/1 (May 2010): 12.

[51] Richard F. Whalen, "Stratfordian Professor Takes Authorship Question Seriously," *Shakespeare Oxford Newsletter*, vol. 46/1 (May 2010): 7.

cover deliver a strong message of legitimacy for the authorship question. . . . [A]nd he observes that the long-standing taboo against authorship studies in most of academia has not made the question go away, and acknowledges that the case for Oxford has achieved some legitimacy in academia.

In sum, the very fact that a tenured professor of English and comparative literature at Columbia University, a leading Shakespeare scholar, and the author of two other books on Shakespeare, would devote three or four years to researching and writing a book on the authorship controversy will give greater prominence to the Shakespeare authorship issue. (11)

"On balance," Whalen concluded, "Shapiro's book might be considered good news for Oxfordians."

The most provocative review was by Oxfordian scholar Warren Hope, who was puzzled by the lack of scholarly standards in *Contested Will* and Alan Nelson's *Monstrous Adversary*. He began with the observation that "They are both grotesque books . . . but they are grotesque for a reason. The authors treat evidence as if they were preparing show trials or cooking up disinformation for some nightmarish dictatorship not because they are demonic or dumb, but because they are expressions of the painful change that must take place if the study of Shakespeare is to be put on a rational footing."[52]

Hope at first wondered whether "Professors Shapiro and Nelson might be crypto-Oxfordians, determined to demonstrate to their colleagues that the price of continuing to maintain the Stratford cult is the utter abandonment of not only all scholarly standards but also common decency—and that the price is just too high to pay."[53]

I also had similar thoughts: Had Shapiro smuggled pro-Oxfordian ideas into his work and left them unrefuted because that was the only way to get his fellow scholars to consider the possibility that the Oxfordians might be right? How else to explain passages such as these:

Enough incidents in Oxford's life uncannily corresponded to events in the plays to support Looney's claims that the plays were barely veiled autobiography.

Yet there were things in favor of Oxford's candidacy. He had been praised in his lifetime as both poet and playwright, and his verse was widely anthologized. (176, 177)

Hope eventually concluded that Shapiro and Nelson were not crypto-Oxfordians. "But then I came to my senses, realizing that would be too far-fetched. Although they perform that function, they do so unintentionally and unconsciously." I, too, came to that conclusion. Ultimately, Hope wrote, "Shapiro distorts not only Looney's arguments but also Shakespeare's work because of his faith in the Stratford cult. . . . It is Shapiro's self-identification with his Shakespeare that causes him to misrepresent Looney to such an extent that it almost constitutes character assassination" (210, 215).

Academia Today vs. 1940: Has Much Changed?

Academia finds itself in a strange position regarding the Shakespeare authorship

---

[52] Warren Hope, "'Is that True?' A Review of James Shapiro's *Contested Will*," *Brief Chronicles*, vol. 2 (2010): 209.

[53] Warren Hope, "'Is that True?' A Review of James Shapiro's *Contested Will*," *Brief Chronicles*, vol. 2 (2010). This passage is in the version of the review accessed on the Shakespeare Fellowship website on April 20, 2010, but is omitted from the version on the Shakespeare Oxford Fellowship website accessed on December 18, 2020.

question. Externally it continues to prop up the Stratfordian story and to attack the Oxfordian claim, which represents a change from ignoring it whenever possible during the first wave of the movement. Internally the mess is more apparent. Although the Oxfordian claim is rarely spoken of, it is apparently on everybody's mind. Even when Stratfordians don't mention it directly, they appear to be desperately searching for alternatives to it. Some of the extraordinary steps being taken are:

- ➢ Efforts to destroy perceptions of the character of Edward de Vere—Alan Nelson's unscholarly and vituperative *Monstrous Adversary.*

- ➢ Efforts to destroy the reputations of Looney and other Oxfordians—James Shapiro in *Contested Will* attempting to tie Looney and others to the Nazis.

- ➢ Efforts to create a believable Shakspere story line through two dozen recent biographies even though no new facts about William Shakspere have been discovered since 1931. These books have shown that it cannot be done without resorting to fantasy and fiction, the presentation of supposition as fact and the selective omission of material facts.

- ➢ Corruption of the methodology of literary studies by denying the validity of topical and personal allusions and through a "death of the author" mentality that rules out any context that might provide insight into the words on the page.

- ➢ Manipulation of criteria used in Stylometric studies to rule out Oxford as Shakespeare, combined with the introduction of the supposition of collaboration in order to establish that Shakespeare was alive and writing after Oxford's death in 1604.

- ➢ Direct efforts in *Shakespeare Beyond Doubt* and elsewhere to buttress the Stratfordian story and undermine the Oxfordian.

Academia Today vs. 1940: Breakthrough With Academic Presses?

Very recently a crack appeared in the Stratfordian dike: the first-ever publication by academic presses of books presenting Edward de Vere as Shakespeare: Donald Ostrowski's *Who Wrote That? Authorship Controversies from Moses to Sholokhov*, published by Northern Illinois University Press (2020); Michael Wainwright's *The Rational Shakespeare: Peter Ramus, Edward de Vere, and the Question of Authorship*, published by Palgrave Macmillan (2018); and Sky Gilbert's *Shakespeare Beyond Science: When Poetry Was the World*, published by Guernica Editions (2020).

Ostrowski's reasoned, objective, academic examination of the Oxfordian claim came

Authorship Books Published by Independent Publisher McFarland & Company		
2006	William Farina	*De Vere as Shakespeare: An Oxfordian Reading of the Canon*
2009	Warren Hope & Kim Holston	*The Shakespeare Controversy: An Analysis of the Authorship Theories, Second Edition* [1992]
2012	Richard Malim	*The Earl of Oxford and the Making of "Shakespeare"*
2013	Roger Stritmatter & Lynne Kositsky	*On the Date, Sources and Design of Shakespeare's The Tempest*
2015	John M. Rollett	*William Stanley as Shakespeare: Evidence of Authorship by the Sixth Earl of Derby*
2018	Ramon Jiménez	*Shakespeare's Apprenticeship: Identifying the "Real Playwright's" Earliest Works*

out in spring 2020, exactly one hundred years after Looney's *"Shakespeare" Identified.* Its thirty-two-page chapter analyzing the Stratfordian and Oxfordian claims was so even-handed that one reviewer described it as "all but a legal brief for the Oxfordian argument in that it raises question after question about the methods and conclusions of orthodox Shakespeare scholars, and supplies fact after fact that support Oxford's authorship of the Shakespeare canon."[54] Wainwright's and Gilbert's books also show how accepting Edward de Vere as Shakespeare transforms understandings of Shakespeare's plays and the conditions in which they were created.[55]

Another promising sign is that the December 2018 issue of *Critical Stages*, a web-based journal for the professional theater community, contained an eighty-seven-page section devoted to the Shakespeare Authorship Question. Prepared by managing editor Don Rubin, Professor Emeritus at Toronto's York University, it included theater-focused pieces by actors Sir Mark Rylance, Sir Derek Jacobi and actor Keir Cutler, and by scholars Hank Whittemore, Gary Goldstein, Diana Price and Tom Regnier, among others, all of which brought the Oxfordian perspective to theater professionals. Of particular importance was the article by Prof. Luke Prodromou, "The Shakespeare Authorship Debate Continued: Uncertainties and Mysteries," noted earlier, which was reprinted in the 2020 issue of *The Oxfordian.*

The three academic presses followed the lead of McFarland & Company, which has published half a dozen books on the authorship question, most of them from an Oxfordian perspective. Although it is an independent publisher, McFarland specializes in academic and reference titles.

Is this a sign that academia is on the verge of major change? Or are these rare and isolated examples of courageous scholars following a lonely path?

It is possible to think that the triumph of the Oxfordian claim is only a matter of time. Copernicus's theory of the heliocentric solar system in astronomy, Darwin's theory of natural selection in biology, Einstein's theory of relativity in physics, the idea of continental movement in geology—all replaced older theories even though professional opinion had been heavily against them when they were introduced. Might the same be possible for the Oxfordian theory?

Or is it possible for two contradictory bodies of knowledge to exist side by side indefinitely without either being vanquished? Examples of this situation exist now in other fields. Within anthropology, various subfields continue to hold beliefs contradicted by findings in neighboring sub fields, as Ian Tattersall has shown.

Contradictions also exist across fields. Many anthropologists and historians marvel at how certain civilizations—those in the Indus River Valley in what is now Pakistan and the one that built the pyramids in what is now Egypt, for instance—seem to have arisen suddenly, possessing a great deal of sophistication in language and culture without having developed slowly as all other civilizations had. At the same time, geographers and climatologists have established that sea levels rose more than 400 feet quite suddenly, sometime after 12,000 years ago—so quickly that the runoff from the glaciers that had covered much of North America two miles thick cut the Grand Canyon. These latter findings solve the mystery of the sudden rise of those civilizations. They hadn't sprung

---

[54] Ramon Jiménez, review of *Who Wrote That?* by Donald Ostrowski, *The Oxfordian*, vol. 22 (Sept. 2020): 153.

[55] Early in 2021 Ostrowski's book is in 168 libraries worldwide, Wainewright's in 163 and Gilbert's in 22.

from nothing after all. Having been founded near the sea, they had retreated inland over several thousand years as sea levels rose. Their previous habitations are now underwater. Yet, incredibly, many anthropologists and historians continue their scholarly investigations as though the seas had always been at their current level.

As one example of this blinkered thinking—which also shows how scholars can modify their view—consider Jared Diamond. In the first edition of his book *Guns, Germs and Steel* in 1997, he described how the original settlers on the island of Tasmania, 130 miles south of Australia, lost their knowledge of sea travel and fishing after having arrived there by boat more than 10,000 years ago. That a scholar as accomplished as Diamond was able to claim that the settlers had traveled by boat rather than by walking when sea levels were much lower—and to make that claim long after the rise in sea levels had been established by geographers—shows that it is possible for two bodies of scholarly knowledge that contradict each other to co-exist for lengthy periods of time.

In the 2017 edition of *Guns, Germs and Steel* Diamond corrected himself: "At Pleistocene times of low sea level, the shallow Bass Strait now separating Tasmania from Australia was dry land . . . When the strait was at last flooded around 10,000 years ago, Tasmanians and mainland Australians became cut off from each other because neither group possessed watercraft capable of negotiating Bass Strait. Thereafter, Tasmania's population of 4,000 hunter-gatherers remained out of contact with all other humans on earth."[56]

Misunderstanding the Challenges Faced

Many Oxfordians continue to believe that the challenge the Oxfordian movement faces is that of trying to convince Shakespeare scholars to examine the evidence. If only the professors could be convinced to do that, their thinking goes, the paradigm shift to acceptance of Oxford's authorship would occur quickly. They assume that Shakespeare scholars are scientists, in the sense that they are interested in the pursuit of truth and that facts will convince them. But those Oxfordian optimists fail to recognize that orthodox scholars are also members of institutions and are subject to the institutional pressures found in any large organization.

It is the same naïve belief that most Oxfordians had during the 1920s and early 1930s. It took a decade or more of bitter experience for them to realize that acceptance of Oxford's authorship was not going to happen merely because the evidence supported it. They eventually came to realize that professors who are members of Departments of Literature were not going to shift to supporting the Oxfordian claim unless a dramatic event were to occur to spark such a shift and give them a face-saving way forward. That attitude persists today.

Oxfordians must recognize that their task is not to convince individual scholars in academia, but to overturn the institutional pressures that block consideration of the Oxfordian claim within academia and outside. Looney succeeded in his first task, that of solving the Shakespeare authorship mystery. But neither he nor his successors were able to breech the walls of academia.

As a closed institution, academia continues its time-tested practices of ignoring and/or attacking the Oxfordian claim. It cannot admit even the possibility that the authorship question is worthy of academic examination without starting down the

---

[56] Jared Diamond, *Guns, Germs and Steel* (2017) [The 20th Anniversary Edition], p. 312.

slippery slope leading to acceptance of Edward de Vere's authorship. What are Oxfordians to do? How are they, as outsiders, ever going to be successful in effecting change within the closed circle of academia whose members listen only to each other? That is the subject addressed, two chapters hence, in Chapter 26.

PART THREE:
PROSPECTS FOR THE OXFORDIAN IDEA

25

Looney, Oxford and Why It Matters

Should It Have Been Done?

Now that we have a picture of what happened during the first quarter-century of the Oxfordian movement and an overview of recent decades, other questions come to the fore. One of them is whether it was right for Looney to reveal Oxford's authorship of "Shakespeare's" works.

That Oxford made efforts to conceal his authorship of those works is beyond question. Neither his name nor his initials appeared on any of his works after the age of twenty-six. He made no effort to collect and publish his youthful poems under his own name. He wrote, produced and acted in theatrical entertainments for the court, yet none of those productions exist in manuscript or in published form under his own name. Hiding his authorship of "Shakespeare's" works—if he was indeed Shakespeare—would not have been something new for him.

There are indications in the literary works themselves that Shakespeare (whoever he was) expected his name to be forgotten. In sonnet 72 he wrote,

> My name be buried where my body is,
> And live no more to shame nor me nor you.
>> For I am shamed by that which I bring forth,
>> And so should you, to love things nothing worth.

And in sonnet 81 he wrote,

> From hence your memory death cannot take,
> Although in me each part will be forgotten.
> Your name from hence immortal life shall have,
> Though I, once gone, to all the world must die:

This sonnet implies that the author expected his works to live forever; it is only his name what will be buried. Whether Oxford, as the author, voluntarily undertook this effort to conceal his name is an open question, and his desires on this point may have changed over time. There are passages in the plays suggesting that a deal of some sort had been struck and that secrecy regarding his authorship was one part of that deal. In *The Winter's Tale*, Antigonus is forced by Leontes to swear he will uphold his end of a bargain.

> *Leontes*
>   Swear by this sword
>   Thou wilt perform my bidding.
> *Antigonus*
>   I will, my lord.
> *Leontes*
>   Mark and perform it, see'st thou! for the fail
>   Of any point in't shall not only be
>   Death to thyself but to thy lewd-tongued wife,
>   Whom for this time we pardon. . . .
> *Antigonus*
>   I swear to do this, though a present death
>   Had been more merciful. (II.iii)

That the deal involving Oxford was not initiated by him is suggested by that famous line in sonnet 66:

> And art made tongue-tied by authority.

If there was a deal, whom it was struck with, and what its exact terms were, are not made clear in the historical record.

There are literary passages suggesting that Oxford himself broached the deal and brought others on board, that he himself enforced it, perhaps with the same intensity with which Hamlet swears his companions to secrecy near the beginning of the play that is widely regarded as Oxford's most personal portrayal of himself.

> *Hamlet*
>   Never make known what you have seen tonight.
> *Horatio, Marcellus*
>   My lord, we will not.
> *Hamlet*
>   Nay, but swear't. . . .
>   Upon my sword. . . .
> *Horatio*
>   Propose the oath, my lord.
> *Hamlet*
>   Come hither, gentlemen,
>   And lay your hands upon my sword:
>   Never to speak of this that you have heard,
>   Swear by my sword. . . .
>   And therefore as a stranger give it welcome. . . .
>   As I perchance hereafter shall think meet
>   To put an antic disposition on,
>   That you, at such times seeing me, never shall,
>   With arms encumber'd thus, or this headshake,
>   Or by pronouncing of some doubtful phrase,
>   As 'Well, well, we know,' or 'We could, an if we would,'
>   Or 'If we list to speak,' or 'There be, an if they might,'
>   Or such ambiguous giving out, to note
>   That you know aught of me: this not to do,
>   So grace and mercy at your most need help you, Swear. (I.v)

Yet there are other indications in *Hamlet* suggesting that permanent secrecy might not have been Oxford's final thoughts on the matter. Consider Hamlet's dying demand of Horatio that he "report me and my cause aright . . . to tell my story:"

> Horatio, I am dead;
> Thou livest; report me and my cause aright
> To the unsatisfied.
> . . .
> O good Horatio, what a wounded name,
> Things standing thus unknown, shall live behind me!
> If thou didst ever hold me in thy heart
> Absent thee from felicity awhile,
> And in this harsh world draw thy breath in pain,
> To tell my story. (V.ii)

As Oxford had probably worked on revisions to *Hamlet* right up until his death in June 1604, and as the play was published with great fanfare that December, these instructions give every appearance of his having put his dying wish into his most personal dramatic work, which was then made public. That was Looney's view.

> The introduction into the play of Oxford's own cousin, Sir Horace de Vere . . . seems only explicable upon the assumption that the dramatist was then meditating—just before his death—coming forward to claim in his own name the honours which he had won by his work; or, at any rate, that he had decided that these honours should be claimed on his behalf immediately after his death, and that Horatio de Vere had been entrusted with the responsibility. Such an assumption has full warrant in the last words which Hamlet addresses to Horatio. Certainly the agreement is of a most surprising character and must not be neglected. (407)

Othello makes a similar plea to Lodovico and Cassio near the end of his play, urging them to "speak of me as I am . . . when you shall these unlucky deeds relate:"

> Soft, you; a word or two before you go,
> I have done the state some service, and they know it;
> No more of that. I pray you, in your letters,
> When you shall these unlucky deeds relate,
> Speak of me as I am; nothing extenuate,
> Nor set down aught in malice; then must you speak
> Of one that lov'd not wisely but too well;
> Of one not easily jealous, but, being wrought,
> Perplex'd in the extreme; of one whose hand
> Like the base Indian, threw a pearl away
> Richer than all his tribe; of one whose subdu'd eyes
> Albeit unused to the melting mood,
> Drop tears as fast as the Arabian trees
> Their med'cinable gum. (V.ii)

These indications that Oxford cared deeply about his name and reputation in his mature years are in line with the thoughts expressed decades earlier in his letter to his father-in-law on April 27, 1576, shortly after returning from his travels on the continent:

> My Lord . . .
> This might have been done through private conference before, and had not needed to have been the fable of the world if you would have had the patience to have understood me; but I do not know by what or whose

advice it was to run that course so contrary to my will or meaning, which made her so disgraced to the world, raised suspicion openly, that with more private conference might have been more silently handled, and hath given me more greater cause to mislike.[1]

It would appear that Oxford would not have opposed, and might have welcomed, having the circumstances of his life, including the events that led to the tarnishing of his name, revealed after his death, if the story were accurately told. But would that telling of his story go only so far as explaining the circumstances in which the Arundel and Howard slanders had arisen, or would it also include revealing his authorship of his literary works? If the latter, the contradiction in the *Sonnets* would be resolved.

In the *Sonnets* Oxford had stated his expectation that the name of the Fair Youth "hence immortal life shall have," but not his own name ("Though I, once gone, to all the world must die'"). Because the identity of the Fair Youth is not revealed in the *Sonnets*, it can be recovered only by knowing the identity of the author. Both names will have to be remembered or both would be forgotten. That inconsistency would be resolved if the desires expressed in *Hamlet* and *Othello* that his story be told included revealing his authorship.

Even if Oxford wanted his authorship known after his death, the question of whether Looney would have been right to reveal it if he hadn't remains of interest. I believe Looney would have been right to reveal it.

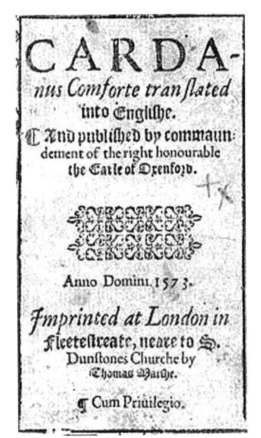

One reason is that Edward de Vere himself, as a young man, published a work that a friend had shared with him and had asked him not to publish (or at least that's the story that de Vere has told us). The friend was Thomas Bedingfield; the work was his translation from Latin into English of Jerome Cardan's work known as *Cardanus Comforte*. The key point is not that Oxford published the work over his friend's objection, but that he also published Bedingfield's name as the translator. He revealed his literary accomplishments by naming him publicly.

Bedingfield's translation was published in 1573 "by commaundement of the right honourable the Earle of Oxenford" when Oxford was twenty-three years old. In deciding to disregard his friend's wishes, he explained that the work was of such great merit that not to publish it would be a disservice to the world. "At length," he wrote in a letter that prefaced the work, "I determined it were better to deny your unlawful request, than to grant or condescend

---

[1] Edward de Vere, letter to Lord Burghley, April 27, 1956, quoted in William Plumer Fowler, editor, *Shakespeare Revealed in Oxford's Letters* (1986), p. 248.

to the concealment of so worthy a work."[2]

Oxford could have published it without mentioning his friend's name, but he didn't, he explained, because the publication would "erect you such a monument that in your lifetime you shall see how noble a shadow of your virtuous life shall remain when you are dead and gone" (133). This is just the point at issue with Oxford: whether to reveal his authorship of "Shakespeare's" works. Doing so brings to light the "virtuous life" that had been hidden for more than 300 years until Looney discovered it. That, to me, is the most important reason it was right for Looney to make public Oxford's authorship.

Looney recognized the injustice wrought by the slanders to Oxford's name; he cited the restoration of Oxford's reputation as one of the most important results of "Shakespeare" Identified.

> A long overdue act of justice and reparation to an unappreciated genius who, we believe, ought now to be put in possession of his rightful honours; and to whose memory should be accorded a gratitude proportionate to the benefits he has conferred upon mankind in general, and the lustre he has shed upon England in particular. (3)

Restoring Oxford's reputation required, in large part, transferring to him the honors already bestowed upon the author of "Shakespeare's" works.

> These generous estimates of "Shakespeare," being almost wholly inferred from the plays he has left us, must in all honesty be passed on to Edward de Vere when he is accepted as the author. They are his by right. We cannot go back upon the judgments that have been so passed upon "Shakespeare," simply because it transpires that the Stratford man is not he.... What the world has written in this connection it has written, and must be prepared to stand by. (343-44)

Beyond that, there is the additional honor due him for having written them during the often difficult circumstances that we now know he endured. There is also the honor due him for the central role he played in the English Renaissance. He was, Looney found, "the personal embodiment of the great literary transition by which the lyric poetry of the earlier days of queen Elizabeth's reign merged into the drama of her later years. Thus we get a sense both of the literary unity of the times, and of the great and consistent unity of his own career" (292).

Three accomplishments, then, tower above all others in "Shakespeare" Identified: establishing Edward de Vere's rights to the Shakespeare laurels, clearing his name of the Arundel and Howard libels that had come down in the historical record, and establishing the central role he played in the literary and intellectual and cultural life of his country.

Why It Matters

I have come across many instances of Shakespeare scholars and reviewers of "Shakespeare" Identified rhetorically asking "What does it matter who wrote the plays; the important thing is that we have them." One such statement was made by an unnamed reviewer in The Bookman's Journal in 1921:

> For myself, I may be wrong, but I cannot see that the question whether Shakespeare's works were written by Shakespeare, or Bacon, or the Earl of

---

[2] J. Thomas Looney, "Shakespeare" Identified (2018), p. 132.

Oxford, or by any other man of the period, is of the least importance.[3]

Another was by Mark Holstein in *The Shakespeare Association Bulletin*, published by the Folger Shakespeare Library in 1941:

> It is perfectly true that if it were now definitely established, beyond all question or doubt, that no such person as Master Will Shakspere ever lived, it would make not the slightest difference to any living person anywhere in the world. We would still have the plays and, to baffle and beguile us, the miracle of their creation would still remain.[4]

The Wall Street Journal editorialized in 1953 that,

> We think it really doesn't matter if de Vere or Shakespeare wrote those works. The short and the long of it is that someone wrote them and they are here, chronicles in immortal language to ease the winter of our discontent, to make more pleasant this existence swift as a shadow, short as any dream though it may be.[5]

Such statements appear to be yet another tactic to squelch doubts about Shakspere's authorship. Looney certainly thought so.

> The indifference to the issue professed by some of the critics seldom rings true; for everybody interested in literature knows that the general adoption of any of the solutions offered to this problem would be one of the biggest events in literary history.[6]

> The transference of the honour of writing the immortal Shakespeare dramas from one man to another, if definitely effected, becomes not merely a national or contemporary event, but a world event of permanent importance, destined to leave a mark as enduring as human literature and the human race itself.[7]

It matters tremendously who wrote "Shakespeare's" works. One set of reasons, as stated above, relates to restoring the reputation of the man who has given so much pleasure and enjoyment, and taught so much, to thinking men and women over the past 400 years, and to understanding the wider role he played in the English Renaissance.

Another set of reasons relates to better understanding Shakespeare's plays and poems by laying bare the personal nature of them. The change in author was not a matter of merely plucking one man out and putting another in his place. As Looney had recognized, "the adoption of the de Vere solution, particularly, would revolutionise Shakespeare study, by converting the great dramas into the most directly personal literature."[8] The Oxfordian thesis includes the claim that Oxford was the actual prototype for "outstanding characters like Hamlet, Othello, Romeo, Berowne, Bertram, Prince Hal, Timon, and King Lear." Once that insight is accepted, the study of Shakespeare's plays "undergoes a profound revolution. . . . Furnished for the first time with the principle of interpretation, the real study of 'Shakespeare,' as distinct from the purely literary and

---

[3] S. "Stratford and Stony Stratford," *Bookman's Journal*, March 4, 1921.

[4] Mark Holstein, "The Shakspere-Bacon-Oxford-Whoozis Mixup," *The Shakespeare Association Bulletin*, vol. 16, No. 4 (Oct., 1941): 195-214.

[5] "Tis Neither Here Nor There," *Wall Street Journal*, Feb. 11, 1953, p. 12.

[6] J. Thomas Looney, "Shakespeare, Lord Oxford, Solomon Eagle and Mr. Looney" [letter], *Outlook*, June 25, 1921, p. 543.

[7] J. Thomas Looney, *"Shakespeare" Identified* (2018), p. 1.

[8] Looney, *Outlook*, June 25, 1921, p. 543.

academic, is only now in its early stages."[9]

Yet another set of reasons relates to how Shakespeare's works can be understood better once it is recognized just how topical they were. Scholars had long suspected that many obscure passages in the plays were references to topical events long forgotten; recognizing that Edward de Vere wrote the plays for performances in the Court and for educated audiences in private theaters, and did so long before they appeared on the public stage or were published, opens a new door to the search for those contemporaneous events and people. As Eva Turner Clark saw,

> By placing the plays some fourteen or fifteen years earlier than the Stratfordian chronology would have them written, I have, in *Hidden Allusions in Shakespeare's Plays*, pointed out many topicalities, references to contemporary events of importance or to trifling incidents. These are obvious when the plays are placed in that earlier period. Great events are often referred to many years after they occur, but this is not true of small matters, which are soon forgotten. For them to mean anything to an audience, they must be included in a play soon after they happen. For this reason, in arranging a chronology by allusions, more stress should be laid on insignificant happenings than upon the important ones.[10]

Having the correct context for such references brings the plays alive, and also helps modern audiences appreciate the effects that these allusions would have had on their original audiences. The reference to magnetism in *Hamlet* is one small example. When Gertrude tells Hamlet, "Sit here," and he replies, "No, Mother, here is metal more attractive," and then sits down next to Ophelia, Oxford is making a topical reference to a new book on magnetism that was the subject of discussion in court circles in the early 1580s.[11] There would have been no reason for Shakspere, writing for illiterate public audiences fifteen years later, to have made such a reference. Queen Elizabeth particularly enjoyed entertainments that commented on contemporary events in an entertaining way. There is nothing unusual about that; even today, revues and stand up comedians derive their popularity from the contemporaneousness of the subjects they address.

The larger point is not that the literary works contain references to contemporary events and people, but that the connections work both ways. We can understand the plays better by knowing Elizabethan history at the time the plays were actually written. But perhaps even more importantly, scholars can learn much about the historical foreground—about the Elizabethan era at the time the plays were originally written—once it is fully recognized just how extensively they comment on current events. They really were the "abstracts and brief chronicles" of their times.

Still other reasons why it matters relate to understanding why and how Shakespeare's works were written. Beyond the personal and topical references, and beyond changes in audience and venue from the general public and the public theaters to royalty and courtiers and private theaters, inspiration for the works is seen to come not exclusively from literary sources and imagination or fantasy, as Stratfordian scholars

---

[9] J. Thomas Looney, "To the Editor of *The Herald*," *Sydney Morning Herald*, July 15, 1921, p. 12.

[10] Eva Turner Clark, "Some Character Names in Shakespeare's Plays," *SF Quarterly*, vol. V/2 (April 1944), p. 31.

[11] As noted in Chapter 5, this allusion was discovered by Julia Cooley Altrocchi, "From Mrs. Julia Cooley Altrocchi," *Shakespeare Oxford Society Newsletter*, vol. 7/1 (March 30, 1971): 3. See also Paul Altrocchi and Hank Whittemore (editors), *My Name Be Buried* (2009), pp. 419-20.

would have it, but from Oxford's actual experiences and personality.

Recognition of Oxford's authorship restores not only Oxford's reputation, but also "Shakespeare's." No longer is he seen as a patcher-upper of second-rate plays early in his career. Instead, he is an innovator: the influencer, not the influencee, of Lyly, Munday, Marlowe and others. The works he revised later in life for the public stage and for publication were his own works first drafted decades earlier for private performances. It has become clear that the "bad quartos" were pirated, memorial versions of Oxford's own early plays performed on the public stage. It becomes clear that their publication was a significant factor leading Oxford to publish accurate versions of them. It becomes clear that the reason so many plays produced in the 1580s were lost to history is that they resurfaced later as Shakespeare's. There would have been no need to retain the 1580s versions, the thinking of the time might have been, once revised versions had been published in the second half of the 1590s.

Nor is the notion of Shakespeare collaborating with second-rate playwrights in the final years of his career—when he was still in his mid-forties—needed to explain passages of distinctly inferior workmanship. The common sense Oxfordian view is that many of the so-called late plays were unfinished drafts from earlier in Oxford's career that were finished by others after his death. The idea that other writers completed unfinished drafts did not arise from Oxfordian scholars; it was presented by prominent Shakespeare scholars long before Looney proposed Edward de Vere as Shakespeare.

Oddly enough, the Oxfordian claim rescues William Shakspere's reputation as well, raising him from a grain hoarder and loan shark who sued his neighbors for non-payment of small debts, to one who played an honorable, if minor, role in the Shakespeare story. In Looney's view,

> Whatever opinions may be formed of William Shakspere on other grounds, we do not wish to suggest any reproach for the part he took in assisting Oxford to hide his identification with the authorship of the plays. The former's role in life was indeed a humble one from the standpoint of literature, and, in view of the glory he has enjoyed for so long, becomes now somewhat ignominious. Nevertheless, whatever inducements may have been held out to him he fulfilled his part loyally. His task was to assist a remarkable but unfortunate man in the performance of a work, the value of which he himself could probably not have estimated; and though it will be the duty of Englishmen to see that the master is ultimately put in possession of the honours that have for so long been enjoyed by the man, it will be impossible ever totally to dissociate from the work and personality of the great one, the figure and name of his helper. Such, at any rate, would be the desire of Oxford, if we may interpret it in the light of the principle of *noblesse oblige* that shines through the great Shakespearean dramas. (361-62)

These revolutions in understanding of the plays and the conditions in which they were produced are still limited to those outside the universities. They will sweep like wildfire through academia, too, once literature professors accept Oxford's authorship. Brushed aside will be much of the work done over the last century or two interpreting the plays with the man from Stratford in mind as the author. Author, dates, venue, audience, sources, personal and topical references—the plays will have to be reconsidered with all these and many other matters in mind. It will indeed be a Brave New World for those scholars and readers courageous enough to enter it.

Because normal human curiosity leads us to want to know more about the lives of those extraordinary people who have produced the works of literature, art and music that touched our hearts and souls, to state that "it doesn't matter who wrote Shakespeare's works" is to disrespect an essential part of human nature. Those who fail to honor the greatest human achievements and the mere mortals responsible for them dishonor themselves.

Misidentifying Shakespeare provides false models to emulate. Perhaps, we tell ourselves, by living as these great men and women lived, we too can achieve something worthwhile—but that becomes possible only when we identify the right persons and understand the conditions under which their works were created.

Oxfordian scholars too must be careful to place the facts they have uncovered in the proper context in order to understand how literary activity grows out of the life of the author. Edward de Vere was first and foremost a courtier—the 17th Earl of Oxford and the Lord Great Chamberlain of the realm. He did not introduce the pen name William Shakespeare until his forty-third year. His literary activities must be seen in this context, as Gilbert Slater pointed out in 1938 (see Chapter 9): "However great Oxford's contributions to the Shakespeare panel may have been, he was not merely—he wasn't even primarily—a playwright. He was also a great nobleman and a courtier. . . . In that capacity he had rivals, who probably exercised his mind much more."[12] His contemporaries would have seen him first as a courtier of high rank and his literary activities second. The issue of greatest concern to them in 1593—the year Queen Elizabeth turned sixty—was who would replace her, not the publication of *Venus and Adonis*.

Oxfordians must be careful also to give proper weight to several other factors. They recognize the distinction between literary evidence and documentary evidence—literary evidence being the foundation of the Oxfordian claim. Yet they often overlook the historical evidence that supports and confirms the literary evidence. Col. Ward commented on this point in two letters to Katharine Eggar in 1929 (see Chapter 7):

> The historical approach to the problem is quite as important as the literary approach. Our historical discoveries have—in my judgment—made our final victory over public opinion certain. Without these historical discoveries—which as you may have noticed I keep rubbing all the time in *The Shakespeare Pictorial*—I am not so sure that Looney with his *"Shakespeare" Identified*, Holland with his *Shakespeare Through Oxford Glasses* and I with my *"Mr. W. H."* would have carried the enemy's position. . . . Percy Allen with the historical discoveries in addition to his own literary discoveries . . . will, I believe, carry the 'mullet agent' to victory next year.[13]

> Like most people [Looney] looks upon our problem as a purely literary one. As a matter of fact our discoveries in general history are far more important than any literary discoveries which people in general simply won't look out.[14]

The importance of understanding the historical setting that lay behind the works was also recognized by others. Walt Whitman saw that the history plays could only have come from the pen of one of "the wolfish earls" in Elizabeth's court. Whitman's friend William O'Connor stated that plays "carry to me a lurking sense of being in aid of some ulterior design, probably well enough understood in that age, which perhaps time and criticism

---

[12] Gilbert Slater, "The Rival Poet of the Sonnets," *SF News-Letter*, no. 8 (March 1938): 1.
[13] Col. Bernard R. Ward, letter to Katharine E. Eggar, July 2, 1929.
[14] Col. Bernard R. Ward, letter to Katharine E. Eggar, Sept. 4, 1929.

will reveal." The Irish scholar H. K. Kennedy-Skipton also intuited that "something of 'vital historical import' lay behind the authorship mystery," something so important that the authorship mystery itself "is of only minor importance in comparison"—something of such great importance that it required Oxford to be virtually "erased from the pages of our history."

In my view, the most comprehensive answers to the "why" and "how" questions that address these historical factors are those provided by the Dynastic Succession theory— the idea that the Earl of Southampton was the son of Queen Elizabeth and Edward de Vere and that this has something to do with the creation of the pen name. It ties the Oxfordian claim to larger historical events, as Hank Whittemore showed in *The Monument* by overlaying a "historical stencil" on the sonnets. It answers the "how" question that is often overlooked by Oxfordians by showing that State power was the only power capable of finding and destroying documentary evidence supporting Oxford's authorship and undermining Shakspere's, and that those efforts must have been undertaken for reasons of greatest importance to the state.

Identifying the right man as the author and the correct historical setting in which the plays were written also matters to scholars who work in related fields such as history or psychology, or the theater. Their professional interest in the authorship question is discussed later in this chapter; their important role in garnering full acceptance of the true author is explained in Chapter 26.

Why It Matters: The Unity of Truth

Approaching the question from a different angle reveals a new facet of the answer. That different angle is a concept that J. Thomas Looney referred to in *"Shakespeare" Identified* as "the universal harmony of truth."

> "Every fact in the universe," says one writer, "fits in with every other." To suppose that all the above considerations are merely fortuitous is to suggest that the very gods had conspired to make the death of "Shakespeare" seem to synchronize with the death of the Earl of Oxford in 1604. In other words our theory seems to be supported by nothing less than the principle of the universal harmony of truth. (366)

The concept was considered under a slightly different name, "the unity of truth," by philosopher Mortimer J. Adler, who observed that "In the history of Western thought there are only two major theories of truth."[15] One is the Correspondence Theory, which states that there is a reality independent of the mind, and that truth or knowledge exists in the mind when an idea agrees with, conforms or corresponds to,

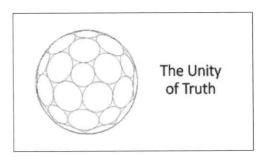

The Unity of Truth

that independent reality. The other is the Coherence Theory, which states that assertions about an external reality must be consistent with each other.

Applying this concept to fields of intellectual investigation, scholarly findings produced within each field must be consistent with one another and with those produced

---

[15] Mortimer J. Adler, *Intellect: Mind Over Matter* (1990), pp. 98-99.

in all other fields. Conflicts between knowledge from one field of intellectual investigation and another are a sure sign that findings in at least one of those fields are incorrect.

Furthermore, if knowledge exists in any given field and if it must align with knowledge in all other fields, then knowledge in one field *limits* the range of knowledge possible in all other fields. For the authorship question, findings in psychology *limit* the range of knowledge possible in the field of history of the Elizabethan era, and both of these *limit* findings in the field of literature.

One way to visualize this idea of limits is to compare knowledge in a given field of intellectual investigation to a magician's box. The full range and scope of all possible knowledge in the field is limited by the size and dimensions of the box. The actual knowledge in the field, represented by the person in the box, is limited further by findings in related fields, represented by the swords the magician sticks into the box.

The swords do not absolutely determine the size and position of the person inside, but do limit the range of possibilities. An expert in one field does not have free reign to determine solutions to problems within that field. The task is to apply expert knowledge

in the field being studied, but within the allowable limits imposed by findings already existing in surrounding fields. Solutions that might initially seem possible or correct will have to be ruled out if they contradict knowledge existing in other fields—or that knowledge will have to be shown to be incorrect.

On the question of Shakespearean authorship, the range of answers is limited by the concept of the unity of knowledge, especially the knowledge existing in other closely related fields. Those fields would include the study of literature outside the subfield of Shakespeare Studies, the history of the Elizabethan era, and (from psychology) the study of genius and literary creativity. Other fields are shown in the nearby chart.

Shakespeare Studies, sadly, has cut itself off from all these neighboring bodies of knowledge. It has become not just independent of them, but insular and inward-focused.

One reason for this is that Shakespeare Studies regards itself as superior to other fields. Shakespeare scholars tend to confuse themselves and their field with the subject they study. That this prestige is real and pervasive was testified to by Richmond Crinkley, former Director of Programs at the Folger Shakespeare Library, in 1985.

> To be an authority on Shakespeare has long conferred a special intellectual standing that has set many defenders of the orthodox citadel apart from their opponents and invested them with a special status. Is there any more fantastic zealot than the priest-like defender of a challenged creed? Orthodox scholarship defends its inherited wisdom from the exalted position of a clerisy somehow

attuned to special knowledge.[16]

David Ellis expressed a similar view in 2012: "Of all the various claims which make up the tribe of 'academic English,' the one devoted to Shakespeare Studies is the most numerous and powerful. Often riven by internal disputes, nothing is more likely to unite it than criticism from outside."[17] Its leaders have indeed moved to protect it in the time-honored ways—circling the wagons, strengthening the borders between the institution and outsiders, and enforcing stricter discipline within the institution.

This perceived special status has resulted in two problems.

One is the corruption of the field of Shakespeare Studies itself by its self-imposed isolation, which blocks the inflow of knowledge from other fields. The normal interactions between fields would have allowed into Shakespeare Studies much knowledge that would have undercut the Stratfordian story long ago: knowledge about the nature and development of genius and literary creativity; knowledge about class structure and social conditions in the Elizabethan era; and so on.

This isolation has turned Shakespeare Studies from science into "demi-science," in

---

[16] Richmond Crinkley, "New Perspectives on the Authorship Question," *Shakespeare Quarterly*, vol. 36/4 (Winter 1985): 518.
[17] David Ellis, *The Truth About Shakespeare* (2012), p. viii.

Felix E. Schelling's phrase.[18] As T. S. Eliot noted (see Chapter 12), too narrow a focus in literary criticism is a danger "which every honest literary critic, now and in the future will have to face. . . . You cannot treat literary criticism as a subject isolated from every other subject of study; you must take account of general history, of philosophy, theology, economics, psychology, into all of which literary criticism merges."[19]

Corruption of neighboring fields

The second problem is equally damaging. It has been an unfortunate fact that other fields of intellectual study also regard Shakespeare Studies as having a special status. Its prestige has made other fields reluctant to challenge flawed findings flowing outward from Shakespeare Studies, even when they conflict with theirs. The fields into which this corrupted knowledge flowed most severely were those very fields most important for Shakespeare scholars to have learned from.

The following sections contrast the findings of scholars in several intellectual fields of study with beliefs emanating from Shakespeare Studies. In the instances cited, Stratfordian beliefs are inconsistent with, if not directly opposed to, those from the other branches of knowledge, which are themselves largely in line with each other and with the views put forth by J. Thomas Looney one hundred years ago and that form the twelve Mental Revolutions discussed in Chapter 5. In other words, Oxfordian views are in line with the findings of scholars in the fields of psychology, history and philosophy, and are consistent with the principle of unity of knowledge; those of Stratfordian scholars are not.

Corruption of the Field of Psychology

Development of genius: Psychologists tell us that genius must be developed through hard work and years of apprenticeship, that it flowers best under certain well-established conditions. One common experience of those with exceptional achievements later in life was "family provision for, and encouragement of, mental stimulation,"[20] often combined with adversity or traumatic events in childhood that stimulated the development of independent thought and action. Psychologists tell us that "a person needs 50,000 chunks of discipline-germane expertise to become an original problem solver" (94); that it takes ten years of intense effort with the subject matter of any complex field to acquire a foundation for expertise in it. During that time, the developing genius will spin off some works of genius, but also ones of inferior quality.

Stratfordians, though, tell us that genius arises fully formed. They acknowledge that Shakspere was raised in an illiterate household and overcame a youth spent in an isolated town with few books and a mostly illiterate population, yet they claim that he created his great works despite having no known education, engaging in no known apprenticeship studies and having produced no known juvenile works. They tell us he did so without leaving any trace of involvement with the subjects so intimately portrayed in the plays.

Are we to suppose that psychologists' findings apply to all writers except Shakespeare? Because of the high status in which Shakespeare Studies is held, these

---

[18] Felix E. Schelling, *Shakespeare and "Demi-Science"* (1927), p. 1. Schelling used the term "demi-science" in reference to authorship doubters. How ironic that the phrase is more aptly applied to defenders of the Stratfordian claim.

[19] T. S. Eliot, quoted from *Varieties of Metaphysical Poetry* (1933), ed. Ronald Schuchard (1993), p. 74, quoted in Stefan Collini, *The Nostalgic Imagination: History in English Criticism* (2019), p. 24.

[20] Dean Keith Simonton, *Greatness: Who Makes History and Why* (1994), p. 144.

fantasies about Shakspere's accomplishments have corrupted public understanding of the nature of genius and have even tainted study of the subject within the field of psychology. Gilbert Slater expressed concerned about this as far back as 1931.

> Inferences with regard to the nature of genius have been drawn freely from the case of Shakespeare, argued from the assumption that the traditional theory of his identity is undeniably true, and very little supported by evidence from other cases. The psychologist who works in this particular field cannot afford to ignore the contention that this assumption is unwarranted.[21]

More recently, psychiatrist Richard Waugaman and medieval French scholar Elisabeth Waugaman have commented on this corruption: "Our profession has been remarkably submissive to 'authority' in accepting the traditional author, despite the glaring inconsistencies between his documented life and the Shakespeare canon."[22]

Scholars of Sigmund Freud have even gone so far as to censor his expressions of belief that Edward de Vere was Shakespeare, as documented by Mark Anderson: "Practically all of Freud's Oxfordian endorsements . . . have been expurgated by disciples eager to paper over Father Freud's heretical beliefs vis à vis Shakespeare."[23] Freud's famous statement in the 1935 edition of his *Autobiographical Study*—

> I no longer believe that . . . the actor from Stratford was the author of the works that have been ascribed to him. Since reading *Shakespeare Identified* by J. Thomas Looney, I am almost convinced that the assumed name conceals the personality of Edward deVere Earl of Oxford. . . . The man of Stratford seems to have nothing at all to justify his claim, whereas Oxford has almost everything.[24]

—was excised from more recent editions, such as the 1952 edition edited by James Strachey; it was reissued in 1989 with prefatory material by Peter Gay. That edition merely states, "(Additional note, 1935.) I have particular reasons for no longer wishing to lay any emphasis upon this point."[25] At least the editors had the decency to note that material had been excised.

<u>Dedication to their work.</u> Psychologists tell us that one doesn't give birth to creative works at the highest levels merely by chance. One doesn't accidentally acquire the depth of knowledge in so many areas needed to create them. One doesn't engage in ten years of intense involvement with a subject merely to fill the time. These things happen *only because of an intense determination to do them.* Creative people are obsessed with their work and can barely stand to be away from it. Dean Keith Simonton's observations are especially revealing: "They deeply love what they do, showing uncommon enthusiasm, energy, and commitment, usually appearing to friends and family as 'workaholics.' They are persistent in the face of obstacles and disappointments, but at the same time they are flexible enough to alter strategies and tactics when repeated failure so dictates."[26] Their works are hard-won creations that they go to great lengths to get just right. "Behind the attainment of greatness in any domain is a common cluster of attributes essential for success. To be successful at any demanding profession requires intelligence, enthusiasm,

---

[21] Gilbert Slater, *Seven Shakespeares* (1931), p. vii.

[22] Richard and Elisabeth Waugaman, "Review of *Early Shakespeare* by Bronson Feldman and edited by Warren Hope," *The Oxfordian*, vol. 21 (Sept. 2019): 269.

[23] Mark Anderson, *"Shakespeare" By Another Name* (2005), p. 21.

[24] Sigmund Freud, *An Autobiographical Study* (1935).

[25] Sigmund Freud, *An Autobiographical Study* (1989), p. 72.

[26] Dean Keith Simonton, *Origins of Genius: Darwinian Perspectives on Creativity* (1999), pp. 87-88.

drive, persistence, commitment, and plain hard work" (89).

Writers have testified to the accuracy of those findings:

✓ George Bernard Shaw: "The true artist will let his wife starve, his children go barefoot, his mother drudge for his living at seventy, sooner than work at anything but his art."

✓ William Faulkner: "An artist is a creature driven by demons. He is completely amoral in that he will rob, beg, borrow or steal from anybody and everybody to get the work done. . . . He has no peace till then. Everything goes by the board: honor, pride, decency, security, happiness, all, to get the book written."

Stratfordian scholars, though, tell us that geniuses turn out works of art as easily as cooks turn out pancakes. They tell us that Shakspere traveled back and forth between London and Stratford, alternating between acting and writing plays and poems in London and brewing malt, speculating in grain and suing his neighbors for small amounts of money back home. They tell us that he wrote only for money, and that once he had accumulated a pile, he abandoned his literary career in his mid-forties to return to Stratford to engage in small-time commercial activities for the rest of his life, with nary a trace of any intellectual or literary activities during those years.

Again, are we to suppose that psychologists' findings apply to all writers except the man from Stratford?

Valuing of Their Works. Psychologists tell us that artists care greatly about the works of art they produce and go to great lengths to ensure that purchasers will care for them. Scientists likewise have great personal attachment to their discoveries and seek priority in publication of them.

Stratfordians, though, give us the example of a genius not caring any more about what happens to his works after they leave his hands than cooks do about the baskets of fried chicken they serve up. Shakespeare had, they tell us, no interest in the fate of his plays after having been paid for them, that he did not so much as raise a finger when they were published surreptitiously in corrupted form in the so-called bad quartos. James Shapiro acknowledged that "he showed little interest in when or even whether his plays were published and even less in the quality or accuracy of their printing."[27]

These fantasies demean the true author and the work of psychologists, yet they have seeped into public consciousness through the innumerable and fantastic "biographies" of Shakespeare that continue to be published.

Scholars of Literary Creativity – Corruption of Their Field

Works grow out of a writer's life. Those who study literary creativity tell us that works of literature grow out of a writer's experiences and personality. They tell us that the greater the work the more personal the inspiration for it, that writers' greatest works originate in the depths of their souls. In *Creating Literature Out of Life*, Doris Alexander effectively showed that writers are impelled to write particular works by the urgent life problems they face. "They were able to resolve the problem [in their life] through the resolution they found for the problems of their characters in their story."[28] "The creative impulse can live only as long as the stress of unresolved problems propels it, and as long

---

[27] James Shapiro, *Contested Will* (2010), p. 225.
[28] Doris Alexander, *Creating Literature Out of Life* (1996), p. 2.

as it is nourished by blended memories" (84).

This personal source of creative energy has been attested to by many writers.

✓ Samuel Butler: "Every man's work whether it be literature or music or pictures or architecture or anything else is always a portrait of himself, and the more he tries to conceal himself, the more clearly will his character appear."

✓ William Faulkner: In his speech upon receiving the Nobel Prize for Literature, Faulkner spoke of "the problems of the human heart in conflict with itself which alone can make good writing because only that is worth writing about, worth the agony and the sweat."

✓ Virginia Woolf: "Every secret of a writer's soul, every experience of his life, every quality of his mind, is written large in his works, yet we require critics to explain the one and biographers to expound the other."

✓ Edward Albee: "Your source material is the people you know, not those you don't know. . . . Every character is an extension of the author's own personality."

✓ Flannery O'Connor: "The writer can choose what he writes about but he cannot choose what he is able to make live."

✓ Georges Lambin: "No literary work can be rightly and fully appreciated unless the greatest attention be paid to its human surroundings: social, political, geographical. These create indissoluble links between a writer and his production. No literary work can be deemed independent of the living man, no inspiration of his drawn from book-lore only. Between the works of William Shakespeare, the dramatist, and the life of William Shakspere, the actor, no such links could be detected."[29]

Yet Stratfordian scholars tell us that literary works are impersonal, the results of fantasy and imagination, lacking in all but the most inconsequential aspects of the writer's life. That Shakspere wrote purely from imagination had to have been the case because he had no known education and no known experience in the subjects and settings of his plays. But, having got Shakespeare wrong, Stratfordians misunderstand the entire process of literary creativity. They have been reduced to arguing that Shakespeare was an idiot savant who "knew" all these things—Italy, the law, courtly pursuits, diplomatic and political matters, as well as deep insights into human nature—not because of his experiences in his life and his learning, but because he was a genius who imagined it all. That's not the way the human mind works.

Are these findings by scholars of literary creativity and the testimonies of great writers to be set aside in favor of scholars within Shakespeare Studies merely because they profess to study the greatest literary masterpieces written in English while ignoring those with real expertise in the matter?

Three steps in creativity. Scholars of the creative process in literature, as in the other arts and sciences, tell us that creativity results from a three-step process. Simonton has shown that an initial phase of intense conscious focus on issues and subjects of interest is followed by a second phase in which the subconscious brain rearranges pieces of information into new combinations, followed by a third phase in which the more successful of those combinations break through into consciousness, where the mind

---

[29] Georges Lambin, "Professor Abel Lefranc," *Shakespearean Authorship Review*, no. 8 (Autumn 1962): 11.

winnows and shapes them into finished products such as artistic creations and scientific theories.[30] Critical in forming those new combinations is having an associative richness, a wealth of knowledge to draw on, and a wealth of images to employ. Only in a mind already filled with such riches could surprising new combinations be formed and put into creative works.[31] Because "this combinatory work takes place mostly below the threshold of consciousness," (94) "the creator must suspend conscious ego control to dip down deep into 'primary-process' thinking—the process of fantasy, daydreaming, wishes, and irrationality" (95).

Shakespeare scholar Caroline Spurgeon said something similar in *Shakespeare's Imagery* in 1935—that Shakespeare "gives himself away" through his images. He "unwittingly lays bare his own innermost likes and dislikes, observations and interests, associations of thought, attitudes of mind and beliefs, in and through the images, the verbal pictures he draws to illuminate something quite different in the speech and thought of his characters."[32] His imagery is drawn from many subjects—horticulture; animals, especially birds and horses; law; Italy; courtly pastimes such as hawking; classical Greek and Latin literature; modern languages such as French and Italian; and so on. In other words, Shakespeare's knowledge in all these areas must have been deep and penetrating for his unconscious brain to have generated the flow of imagery that permeates his works.

Today's academic scholars haven't yet explained how their candidate for authorship acquired the deep knowledge of the many subjects reflected in Shakespeare's imagery. Instead, they tell us, Shakspere didn't need to go through the usual process. He managed to create the wealth of images in his works without in-depth knowledge of the subjects he wrote about because he picked up exactly what he needed through casual conversations with fellow drinkers in the Mermaid.[33]

Corruption of the Field of History

Social history. Historians of the era tell us that Elizabethan society was one of strict hierarchical organization and separation of the social classes. Paul Johnson noted that

> [Elizabeth's] second principle was that government should express itself through, and seek always to maintain, the natural hierarchy of society. Thus, in 1580, when rebuking Sir Philip Sidney for failing to apologize after a quarrel with the Earl of Oxford . . . [she] enunciated a harsh but clear doctrine:
>
> > She laid before him the difference in degree between earls and gentlemen; the respect inferiors owed to their superiors; . . . and how the gentleman's neglect of the nobility taught the peasant to insult both.[34]

Yet Stratfordian scholars would have us believe that Shakspere, born a commoner in a small town a three-day ride by horse from London—a status so low as hardly even to be acknowledged by the nobility—was so intimate with courtiers and their lives that he

---

[30] See, for instance, Dean Keith Simonton, *Origins of Genius: Darwinian Perspectives on Creativity*, Chapter 2, "Cognition," pp. 25-74.

[31] For a fuller discussion, see Dean Keith Simonton, *Greatness: Who Makes History and Why* (1994), Chapter 4 "The Creative Quest," pp. 84-122.

[32] Caroline Spurgeon, *Shakespeare's Imagery, and What It Tells Us* (1935), p. 4.

[33] Oxfordians sometimes call it the Tavern of Universal Knowledge.

[34] Paul Johnson, *Elizabeth: A Study in Power & Intellect* (1974), p. 73.

could portray courtly pursuits in his plays with the sure touch of one to the manner born. Shapiro made the remarkable statement that Shakspere was "one of the most familiar faces in town and at court."[35] Yet not a single document connects Shakspere to any courtier; none supports his ever having been at court, not even during the winters of 1594-95 or 1604-05, when many of Shakespeare's plays were performed.

Are we to suppose that the fantasies of Shakespeare scholars are more accurate than the findings of historians? Economic historian Gilbert Slater had warned of this corruption of history back in 1931 (see Chapter 9).[36]

Law Professionals

Legal knowledge. Legal scholars and practitioners tell us that Shakespeare demonstrated such a deep understanding of the law that it would have been impossible for someone without legal training and experience to have written the plays. His legal knowledge was so extensive that it attracted the attention to the authorship issue of five U.S. Supreme Court justices, all of whom doubted Shakspere's authorship, and the attention of several important law journals that ran full issues on the controversy.

Yet Stratfordian scholars tell us that Shakespeare's legal knowledge was scanty, hardly sufficient to write the scenes portraying legal situations, and even then he often got the legal details wrong. His knowledge was acquired through casual conversations with buddies in the Mermaid. Are we to take their word?

Italian Experts

Knowledge of Italy. Italian scholars, especially those born and raised in Italy, routinely tell us that Shakespeare captured the distinct atmosphere of the specific Italian cities that serve as settings for many of his plays. They assure us that he must have spent time there.

Yet Stratfordian scholars tell us that Shakespeare never traveled outside England and hadn't needed to. The few details he picked up about Italy he got from conversations with those who had traveled there. It should bother us, like it does these Italian experts, that pronouncements by Shakespeare scholars go unchallenged even by many who know better.

Art Historians

Charles Barrell documented the extent to which three portraits of Edward de Vere had been altered to resemble more closely the Droeshout engraving supposedly of William Shakspere in the prefatory material of the First Folio. Surely those portraits and their provenance would be of great interest to art historians, yet they have shown minimal interest in them.

Art historians are wiping away previous findings concerning van Dyke's magnificent triptych portraying the Earl of Pembroke and his family that might draw attention to the Oxfordian claim. Modern historians have misidentified the wife in the painting as Pembroke's second wife, Lady Anne Clifford, even though earlier historians had correctly identified her as his first wife, Countess Susan Vere, daughter of Edward de Vere. As Bonner Miller Cutting has noted, "If one examines the time line of this error, Countess Susan Vere was correctly identified prior to Charles Wisner Barrell's landmark study of

---

[35] James Shapiro, *Contested Will* (2010), p. 224.

[36] On corruption of the work of historians, see Peter W. Dickson, "Are British Scholars Erasing Two Heroic Ears?," *Shakespeare Oxford News-Letter*, vol. 35/1 (Spring 1999), p. 8.

the Ashbourne Portrait published in *Scientific American* in January of 1940. Thereafter, the 'powers that be' removed the correct information from public view, perhaps as it might trigger the obvious connection that the celebrated patrons of Shakespeare's First Folio were part of Oxford's extended family."[37]

Departments of Literature

The humanistic tradition in the study of literature in place when Looney investigated the authorship question, a tradition not opposed to study of the authorship question, was replaced by methodologies hostile to it. Banishing consideration of topical and personal allusions when attempting to determine authorship was a corruption limited mostly to Shakespeare Studies. But the move away from considering an author's life, personality, intentions and times when interpreting a work of literature—in effect banishing all information outside the text—corrupted all of literary studies. Proclaiming intentional ignorance as a goal is hardly a scholarly way to proceed when examining personal creations such as works of literature.

Theater Professionals

<u>Acting and directing</u>. Actors aim to give convincing performances of the characters they portray. Some even go so far as to say their intention is to bring the author's works to life. For the works of Shakespeare, would that mean bringing to life works written by William Shakspere directly for the public stage? Or would it mean bringing to life the works of Edward de Vere, written for courtiers and other educated audiences in private theaters before later being performed in public theaters? It should be obvious that recognition of the true author would materially affect how the plays should be performed.

For directors, too, it matters. Directors often try to reimagine Shakespeare's plays in exotic settings. Think how revolutionary it would be to set the plays in English court life of the 1570s, showing how they arose out of masques and other entertainments in the court, with characters imaginatively modeled after people in the very audience for which they are being performed, and with their author playing to the vanity of the queen who is also in the audience, portraying her in all her splendor and glory in one guise after another, from Olivia to Gertrude to Cleopatra.[38] And with the author himself perhaps playing leading roles such as Romeo, Othello, Brutus and Hamlet.

Philosophers – and Everybody Else: The Importance of the Pursuit of Truth

For philosophers, the pursuit of truth is important in itself. Understanding what is true, seeking to understand what is true, wanting to know what is true—these ideals are valued above and beyond whatever practical benefits they may have. One of the ways philosophers determine whether an idea is true is by comparing it with other ideas already regarded as true. Underlying this effort is the concept of the unity of truth. If two ideas conflict, at least one must be false. That knowledge generated within Shakespeare Studies conflicts so often with findings arising within other fields of intellectual

---

[37] Bonner Miller Cutting, "The Case of the Missing First Folio," *Shakespeare Matters*, vol. 5/4 (Summer 2006), p. 8.

[38] For an important discussion of this subject, see Gary Goldstein's paper, "Transforming Productions of Shakespeare's Plays," in *The Oxfordian*, vol. 21 (2019), the crux of which is "how does the authorship debate change the way in which the plays can be produced for modern audiences if the true Shakespeare was Edward de Vere, 17th Earl of Oxford, and if the plays were written twenty years earlier and then revised?" (199).

investigation is a sure sign that problems exist within it. The onus is, or should be, on Shakespeare Studies to show why its findings are indeed correct and the others aren't.

For all people, philosophers included, the pursuit of truth matters for practical reasons. The pursuit of truth cannot be turned on and off at will without harmful effects for all aspects of life. Truth must always be pursued or corruption of the truth-seeking ability seeps in. This is perhaps the most important reason why the truth of Shakespearean authorship matters. This idea, which comes to us from Aristotle by way of Adler,[39] will be briefly explained.

Aristotle argued that many forces—internal emotional pressures and external social pressures—push us toward acting in ways not in our own best interest. We can best resist those wayward pressures by developing the habit of acting correctly—the habit of acting in ways that are in our own best interest. Once this habit is formed and nurtured through repetition, it can become strong enough to carry us through difficult times when internal emotional pressures and external social pressures are high.

Actually, two habits must be formed and strengthened. One is that of thinking well, of being able to determine which actions or goals are indeed best. This is the habit that concerns us here. The other is that of acting well once we know which actions are best, which requires both temperance and courage.

If we turn off the effort to think carefully about the issue of Shakespeare authorship, we weaken the habit of thinking carefully in all other aspects of our lives. If our lives are more important to us than the Shakespeare authorship question, then to ignore the contradictions in order to protect the Stratfordian narrative is to place something of lower importance over the habit of thinking well that is essential to living the best possible life. It is an inversion of values.

This conclusion is as valid for society as a whole as it is for individuals. For society to tolerate unendingly the conflicts between findings in Shakespeare Studies and those in other fields of intellectual study—to accept evasion of the truth by scholars with a professed duty to objectively pursue it—is to weaken the habit of truth-seeking in society as a whole. Even those with no interest in the authorship question cannot be indifferent to scholars abandoning their duty as scientists of literature. Col. Ward had made a similar point in 1924: "If it be true that civilization and make-believe cannot indefinitely co-exist, . . . intellectual degradation must be the inevitable consequence of juggling with historical evidence." But, he added with his usual optimistic outlook, "in the end—unless civilization is destroyed in the meanwhile—truth is bound to prevail."[40]

Honoring J. Thomas Looney and the Oxfordians

J. Thomas Looney and the other early Oxfordians restored Edward de Vere's reputation. They cleansed it of the libels hurled against it by traitors attempting to blacken the name of their chief accuser. Oxfordian scholars brought to de Vere's name the glory and honor due to the author of Shakespeare's works. They deserve to be honored for their work.

Looney was one of the greatest Shakespeare scholars of all time. Modern Shakespeare Studies should begin with *"Shakespeare" Identified* and the introduction of the Oxfordian

---

[39] See, for instance, Mortimer J. Adler, *Aristotle for Everybody* (1978), *The Time of Our Lives* ((1970/1976), and *Desires Right & Wrong: The Ethics of Enough* (1991).
[40] Col. Bernard R. Ward, "The 'Shakespeare' Myth," *Hackney Spectator*, August 15, 1924, p. 11.

claim. That book was as revolutionary in its field in 1920 as Darwin's *The Origin of Species* was in biology in 1859. The American novelist and essayist William McFee agreed. "In my own opinion, after several readings, *"Shakespeare" Identified* is destined to occupy, in modern Shakespearean controversy, the place Darwin's great work occupies in evolutionary theory. It may be superseded, but all modern discussion of the authorship of the plays and poems stems from it, and owes the author an inestimable debt."[41] McFee's statement suggests how easily and accurately a comment by the great geneticist Theodosius Dobzhansky—"Nothing in biology makes sense except in the light of evolution"[42]—could be modified to read "Nothing in Shakespeare Studies makes sense except in the light of authorship by Edward de Vere."

The importance of *"Shakespeare" Identified* was perhaps best expressed by Looney himself when he wrote that his book "raised the problem to a level which will not permit of its being airily dismissed without thereby reflecting adversely on the capacity and judgment of the controversialists who would thus persist in giving artifice instead of argument" (11-12).

If part of the attraction of the Shakspere story is its showing that genius can arise anywhere, and if it is right to honor those who raise themselves up from difficult beginnings by dint of sheer effort and perseverance, then J. Thomas Looney is eminently deserving of the fullest honor and gratitude that readers can give. Already noted (in Chapter 2) was the early disappointment of having his educational hopes dashed by the bankruptcy of his father's and uncle's real estate project. Another difficulty faced and overcome was the constraints imposed by working as Deputy Headmaster at a nearby school and raising a family during the years when he researched and wrote *"Shakespeare" Identified*. Much more remains to be said about J. Thomas Looney and the personal and intellectual qualities he brought to bear on the authorship question, and I am in the process of writing a biography of him that will address them.

Gratitude is surely due also to the founder of the Shakespeare Fellowship, Col. Bernard R. Ward. He brought readers convinced of Oxford's authorship together to form an Oxfordian community and movement that continue to this day. Eva Turner Clark played a similar role in the United States. Her quick and determined action resulted in the formation of the American Branch of the Fellowship at a moment of crisis when the onset of the Second World War forced the English branch to suspend its operations indefinitely.

Capt. Ward, Percy Allen and Gerald H. Rendall in England and Charles Wisner Barrell, Eva Turner Clark and Louis P. Bénézet in the United States were the great Oxfordian scholars of the first quarter-century of the Oxfordian movement. Allen and Bénézet were its most prominent spokesmen. Rendall was the most highly regarded scholar to become a publicly avowed Oxfordian; his books established on an even firmer foundation the psychological links between Edward de Vere and Shakespeare. There were many others—including Adm. Hubert H. Holland, Gilbert Slater, Col. Montagu Douglas and Katharine E. Eggar—whose work helped flush out the Oxfordian claim and make it better known. There was also Sir George G. Greenwood, who, though not an Oxfordian, did much to establish the validity of the anti-Stratfordian position and the *bona fides* of the

---

[41] William McFee, "The Master Mystery," in J. Thomas Looney, *"Shakespeare" Identified* (1948), p. xix.
[42] Theodosius Dobzhansky, "Nothing in Biology Makes Sense Except in the Light of Evolution," *American Biology Teacher*, vol. 35 (1973): 125-29.

Shakespeare Fellowship. Few of them were wealthy, and their Oxfordian work required great sacrifices of effort, time and income.

Would Anybody Else Have Discovered Oxford if Looney Hadn't?

This chapter opened with a question—whether it was right for J. Thomas Looney to have revealed Edward de Vere's authorship—and it will end with one. But before addressing that question directly the context for it must be set and two other questions answered.

Psychologists have identified two types of creativity, one personal, one impersonal. An example of personal creativity is Beethoven and his Third Symphony, the "Eroica." It's a work of art that no one other than Beethoven could possibly have created. An example of impersonal creativity is Einstein and his theory of relativity. That theory is also unique, but unlike the symphony it was not created but discovered. If Einstein hadn't discovered it, others would have. He was only half a generation ahead of Max Planck and Konrad Lorentz.

Adding Looney to the mix, we can ask whether *"Shakespeare" Identified* is more like a work of art or a scientific theory. My answer is that it is more like the former. It is unique; no one else could have written the book the way Looney did. Is And we can ask whether the idea of Oxford's authorship was created or discovered. Those who believe that Oxford was indeed Shakespeare will say that Looney discovered it, not that he created it.

And now the final question: If Looney hadn't discovered Oxford's authorship, would anyone else have? Before jumping to an answer, recall how effectively his authorship had been hidden. Consider how effectively Oxford had been erased from history. But also consider the signs that his literary accomplishments had not been completely forgotten. Delia Bacon, in *The Philosophy of Shakespeare's Plays Unfolded* (1857) included him in the group of courtiers that she believed had written Shakespeare's works under the overall direction of Francis Bacon. Oxford's poems, too, Looney noted, "had been examined by men of recognized competency, like Courthope [1910], before [Oxford's] name had been connected with Shakespeare's; and just those distinctive qualities of the great dramas— terseness, epigram, ingenuity, concinnity—had been noticed."[43] The young scholar Joseph Quincy Adams, who later became the first regularly appointed director of the Folger Shakespeare Library, had also mentioned Edward de Vere in 1917, noting that "The young Earl of Oxford, himself a playwright and the patron of a troupe of boy-actors, came to the rescue of the theatre [Blackfriars]. He bought the lease from Evans, and undertook to reorganize its affairs. . . . Shortly after the purchase . . . he made a free gift of the lease to his private secretary,"[44] John Lyly.

Other scholars had begun to connect real-life persons related to Oxford with characters in Shakespeare's plays. Looney found that "The conviction that Elizabethan personalities would . . . be found in the play led first to the identification of 'Polonius' with Burghley [Oxford's father-in-law], and in 1869 George Russell French was to identify 'Laertes' with [Thomas] Cecil [Oxford's brother-in-law] and 'Ophelia' with Anne Cecil [Oxford's wife]."[45] But the fact that French had not taken the next logical step suggests how hard it would have been for scholars to make the mental leap to identifying Hamlet,

---

[43] J. Thomas Looney, "'' Was it Oxford, Bacon, or Derby, II," *Freethinker*, vol. 43/27 (July 8, 1923): 428.

[44] Joseph Quincy Adams, *Shakespearean Playhouse* (1917), pp. 108-09.

[45] J. Thomas Looney, "''Was it Oxford, Bacon, or Derby, II," *Freethinker*, vol. 43/27 (July 8, 1923): 428.

and hence the author of the play, with Edward de Vere.

These two developments—slight but increasing awareness of Oxford as a poet, dramatist and patron of a theater troupe and slight but growing recognition of the topicality of the plays—"if continued had in them the possibility of the discovery; though how long that discovery might have had been deferred, no one can say."[46] Would anyone else have brought Looney's wealth of knowledge of historical matters and literary insight together? Would anyone else have brought together the findings of innumerable Stratfordian scholars, combined them in a new way and viewed them from just the right perspective to see just how firmly they aligned to point toward Edward de Vere?

I don't know whether anyone else would have discovered Oxford's authorship if Looney hadn't. To me it is an open question.

---

[46] J. Thomas Looney, *"Shakespeare" Identified* (2018), p. 8.

26

Completing the Oxfordian Revolution

Progress so Far: The Human Resistance and the Cognitive Resistance

Over the last several decades the Oxfordian movement has made great progress in increasing public awareness of the Oxfordian claim. It has made much progress in overcoming the public's Human Resistance (the normal human resistance to new ideas that conflict with long-held beliefs) and its Cognitive Resistance (the resistance arising because of the complexity of the Oxfordian claim). This progress is in part the result of exposure to the Oxfordian idea over a lengthy period of time.

Ultimately the general public, not Oxfordian or Stratfordian scholars, will determine the fate of the Oxfordian claim. J. Thomas Looney had clearly recognized this, writing near the end of *"Shakespeare" Identified* that,

> The matter must now pass out of our hands, and the case must be tried in public by means of a discussion . . . Whether such discussion be immediate or deferred, we have no doubt that it must come at some time or other, and that, when it does come, the ultimate verdict will be to proclaim Edward de Vere, Seventeenth Earl of Oxford, as the real author of the greatest masterpieces in English literature.

> We venture, therefore, to make an earnest appeal first of all to the thoughtful sections of all classes of the . . . public, and not merely of the literary classes, to examine, and even to insist upon an authoritative examination, of the evidence adduced.[1]

Looney showed how such a reasoned discussion could be conducted by the forty or so articles and letters in which he responded to reviews of his book. Invariably measured in content and reasonable in tone, they provide a model of how to engage in what has been called "the great conversation," through which people of good will seek to discover the truth of a subject. Throughout that difficult first year after publication of *"Shakespeare" Identified* he responded to criticism and hostility with courage, steadfastness, perseverance and grace—qualities required of all sides to the discussion today.

But the Oxfordian gains are not secure. It takes great effort to keep the Oxfordian idea before the public and to introduce new people to it. Constant effort is necessary because of the constant pressure against the idea from orthodox scholars wedded to the idea of Shakspere's authorship.

Stratfordian scholars do not judge the Oxfordian idea as individuals as the public does, but as members of institutions with interests to protect and a party line to adhere to. That is why the third type of resistance to the Oxfordian idea—Institutional Resistance—is distinctly different from Human Resistance and Cognitive Resistance, and far harder to overcome.

---

[1] J. Thomas Looney, *"Shakespeare" Identified* (2018), pp. 423-24.

The Oxfordian movement has, indeed, made only limited progress in overcoming Institutional Resistance. Unequal funding is part of the problem. Another is that the stature and prestige of Shakespeare Studies remains so great that the media almost unthinkingly takes its lead on the authorship question from academia. The Oxfordian idea, supported by the work and findings of Oxfordian scholars, must contest in the public mind with the Stratfordian idea, supported by far more numerous Stratfordian scholars backed by the funding and prestige of Shakespeare Studies. The result of this unequal contest is that the gains made against the Human Resistance and Cognitive Resistance are vulnerable to reversal.

The situation resembles the board game Othello, in which two opponents attempt to flip the color of each other's pieces. The side that appears to dominate the game at one point can have its pieces flipped over permanently by a few strategic moves by the other side. The Oxfordian movement's apparent advances are vulnerable to just such quick and extensive reversals, given academia's influence and the intellectually dishonest lengths to which some Stratfordian scholars will go to avoid acknowledging the validity of the Oxfordian claim and the weakness of their own.

Two such reversals have already happened, The Oxfordian claim almost vanished from public consciousness a year or two after *"Shakespeare" Identified* was published because Looney was almost alone in defending it until the Shakespeare Fellowship was founded in late 1922. Public awareness of the Oxfordian idea almost vanished again during the Second World War in England and after the collapse of the Shakespeare Fellowship in the United States in 1948, reaching near-invisibility during the 1970s and early 1980s.

Looney recognized the nature of this problem. The passage above quoted from *"Shakespeare" Identified* was incomplete; the full text shows his understanding of how critical academia's support would be for shaping public opinion.

> The matter must now pass out of our hands, and the case must be tried in public by means of a discussion in which expert opinion must play a large part in the formation of a definitive judgment. (423)

> We are bound, however, to make a special appeal to those, whose intellectual equipment and opportunities fit them for the examination of the argument, to approach the problem in an impartial spirit. It will not be an easy thing for Stratfordians or Baconians of many years' standing to admit that they were wrong, and that the problem has at last solved itself in a way contrary to all their former views. To sincere admirers of "Shakespeare," however, those who have caught something of his largeness of intellectual vision and fidelity to fact, the difficulty of recognizing and admitting an error will not prove insuperable, whilst their power of thus aiding in a great act of justice will be immense. (424)

Given that Oxfordian scholars have not been successful in overcoming Institutional Resistance and that Shakespeare Studies continues to push against the progress they have made, Oxfordians have no choice but to continue the battle to win over academia.

Some members of the first generation of Oxfordians recognized that a tougher approach would be needed in engaging academia than was appropriate for engaging individuals, though not all agreed. Katharine Eggar, for instance, wrote to Looney of her disapproval of "the policy of aggression which has of late years been allowed to dominate the Fellowship," and cited "the 'fighting' methods so dear to Mr. [Percy] Allen"[2] as her reason for resigning from the Shakespeare Fellowship. In a letter to Looney the same month, Percy Allen wrote, "You speak of the primary purpose of the Fellowship as 'conversion.' I agree, and when I speak to new audiences, or write for new readers . . . I naturally go to the fundamentals." But, he continued, sometimes it is necessary to take a different tack. "I am, as you know, a fighter, by temperament. I thoroughly enjoy intellectual battles; and I revel in controversy; . . . You are equally for the truth, in a sense; but you are a much more politic and cautious individual than we [Allen and Capt. Bernard M. Ward] are."

Allen believed that the combination of strategies could be effective. "In this business, as I have said, a hundred times, we have got to think in decades. Thus considered, our progress is swift, and it is my belief—who am more in the thick of it than you are—that we are making, both underground and above, much more progress than you, probably, suppose. The orthodox people are becoming terrified of us, as they realize more and more fully the unanswerable nature of our arguments."[3]

If Percy Allen were around today he might call for a more aggressive stance: if academia can't be reasoned with, it must be conquered. Its wall blocking the Oxfordian idea must be breached. It is the height of wishful thinking, he might say, to believe that academia or the Folger Shakespeare Library will spontaneously shift to belief in Edward de Vere as Shakespeare, or even to openly acknowledge the weakness of the case for William Shakspere.

Two Approaches

Two approaches to the problem of how to overcome Institutional Resistance need to be considered before I offer my own solution.

The Two-Step Strategy

A strategy of two sequential steps has been proposed by some prominent anti-Stratfordians. In the first step, the aim is only to demonstrate the weakness of the Stratfordian claim without considering the case for any other candidate. In the second step, Oxford would be introduced into what would presumably be a more receptive environment than exists now. I believe such a strategy, while perhaps having some benefits for engaging individuals, would not be successful in engaging academia. In explaining why, the components of the strategy I believe has the best chance of succeeding will become apparent.

Leading proponents of the two-step strategy include John Shahan, founder and former Chairman of the Shakespeare Authorship Coalition, and Dr. William Leahy, currently Vice Provost for Students, Staff and Civic Engagement at Brunel University in

---

[2] Katharine E. Eggar, undated letter to J. Thomas Looney, December 1936.

[3] The letters from Percy Allen to J. Thomas Looney quoted in these two paragraphs are both dated December 14, 1936. The second was written immediately upon completion of the first, in response to a letter from Looney that had just arrived. (Allen had returned from his speaking tour in North America on or about December 10.)

London. They argue that this strategy is necessary to overcome resistance to consideration of the Oxfordian claim.

In support of this idea, Shahan quoted Charlton Ogburn, who wrote "You can't get anywhere with Oxford unless you first dispose of the Stratford man."[4] "Oxford is the answer to a question people are not asking," Shahan explained further. "First, we must get them to ask. Educating the public requires a two-step strategy: first, raise doubts about Mr. Shakspere, then get people to ask who 'Shakespeare' really was, and demand an answer of scholars."[5] Doubters "are becoming increasingly organized around a strategy of focusing first on the weakness of the case for Shakspere in order to legitimize the authorship issue, rather than trying to solve it outright by advancing another candidate."[6] Leahy expressed similar views, observing that "the conversion of academics is not going to happen in current circumstances. . . . Only when . . . academia begins to accept that the case for Shakespeare of Stratford is weak, or at least weaker

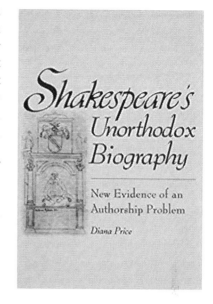

than they realised, will the field open up to other, wider possibilities. That, it seems to me, is what those involved in the Authorship Question need to do before anything else: alter the rules before starting to play a new game."[7]

Both men cited the importance of Diana Price's book, *Shakespeare's Unorthodox Biography: New Evidence of an Authorship Problem* (2001/2012), which documented weaknesses in the Stratfordian thesis without complicating the matter by making the case for an alternative candidate. Leahy wrote that it "crystallised the poverty of [Shakspere's] case superbly."[8] Shahan called it a *tour de force*, and stated that "Diana Price did us an enormous service when she published *Shakespeare's Unorthodox Biography*."

> She put the focus squarely on the documentary record, and pointed out that the life Mr. Shakspere lived was that of a successful businessman, theatre entrepreneur and minor actor, but not a dramatist. She also debunked the orthodox claim that there is nothing unusual about the lack of documentary evidence for Shakspere's literary career. He is unique in that regard. So we now have a book that provides a comprehensive, scholarly presentation of the case against Shakspere that we can point to for anyone who is interested in that level of detail.[9]

Both called for similar books to be written. A list of books doing just that is in a nearby text box.

---

[4] Charlton Ogburn, quoted in John Shahan, "Is There a Shakespeare Authorship Issue?" *Shakespeare Oxford Newsletter*, vol. 43/3 (Summer 2007): 19.
[5] John Shahan, "Is There a Shakespeare Authorship Issue?," p. 19.
[6] John M. Shahan and Alexander Waugh (editors), *Shakespeare Beyond Doubt?* (2013), p. v.
[7] William Leahy, "'Two Households, both alike in dignity,'" *De Vere Society Newsletter*, Feb. 2007, pp. 7, 9.
[8] William Leahy, "'Two Households, both alike in dignity,'" p. 8.
[9] John Shahan, "Is There a Shakespeare Authorship Issue?" p. 19.

Recent Books Documenting the Weakness of the Stratfordian Claim without Making the Case for Alternative Candidates		
2001	Diana Price	*Shakespeare's Unorthodox Biography: New Evidence of an Authorship Problem* [Revised edition, 2012] [Documents just how unusual William Shakespeare's literary trail, or rather lack of a literary trail, was.]
2011	Richard Paul Roe	*The Shakespeare Guide to Italy: Retracing the Bard's Unknown Travels* [Documents that Shakespeare had detailed knowledge of the specific cities in which Shakespeare's plays are set, undercutting the Stratfordian claim that his knowledge was superficial.]
	Anthony J. Pointon	*The Man Who was Never Shakespeare* [Examines the life of the businessman from Stratford-on-Avon.]
2013	John Shahan & Alexander Waugh (editors)	*Shakespeare Beyond Doubt? Exposing an Industry in Denial* [A withering reply to the Shakespeare Birthplace Trust's claim that Shakspere's authorship is "Beyond Doubt."]
2019	Bryan H. Wildenthal	*Early Shakespeare Doubts* [Documents dozens of publicly expressed speculations about Shakespearean authorship during William Shakspere's lifetime.]

Observing that "Orthodox scholars have power to suppress heretical authorship books [including Price's] because they write most of the book reviews," Shahan realized that, "Something else is needed—something that takes up the idea of focusing on the weakness of the case for the Stratford man, but that makes it more accessible to a general audience, and that bypasses orthodox authorities and focuses on highly credible authorship skeptics." Shahan devised the *Declaration of Reasonable Doubt About the Identity of William Shakespeare*, a 3,000-word statement that called attention to the many highly credible doubters of the past, and provided a way for present-day doubters (especially prominent ones), to put themselves on the record [www.doubtaboutwill.ord/declaration].

He founded the Shakespeare Authorship Coalition (SAC) to promote the *Declaration* and to hold public signing events. One of its most important publications was *Shakespeare Beyond Doubt?*, a book that provided a withering reply to those denying the existence of any reasons for doubt (see Chapter 24).

Professor Leahy, too, recognized that more was needed beyond books such as Price's. He observed that,

> Academics very often reject the Authorship Question, despite the fact that many independent researchers in the field use the same methodology as them and produce research as scholarly as their own. . . . This suggests that the research undertaken under the rubric of the Authorship Question is often rejected by academics not because of its methodology or even its conclusions. It is rejected because it is, simply put, produced by non-academics. It is outside of the discourse, outside of the game.[10]

If academia rejects consideration of the authorship question in part because it originated elsewhere, the solution, Leahy reasoned, might lie in bringing the issue inside the walls. He sought to do just that. To persuade his colleagues that the authorship question was indeed substantive enough to merit academic scrutiny and to create conditions in which that scrutiny would be supported, Leahy undertook to establish a Master's Degree in Authorship Studies at Brunel University. With great effort, courage and determination, he overcame the innumerable bureaucratic obstacles thrown in his way. "The life of Shakespeare the author and the whole ideology and concept of authorship is so central to literary studies and to these texts that it is crucial for the health of the institution of Literature that space be given for such investigation," he explained. "Refusing to allow space for the study of the important literary and cultural phenomenon that is the Shakespeare Authorship Question is equally an argument for ignorance and anti-intellectualism. . . . [It is] unscholarly and un-academic" (8). "The resistance that such a programme will generate within academia is a part of the very process that I wish to investigate. Paradoxically, this academic resistance to giving space to the authorship question should make it clear to academia that it is a legitimate academic subject" (4).

But even with the best of intentions and a decade of hard work, neither project sparked the change Shahan and Leahy had hoped for.

Shahan's *Declaration*, launched in 2007, had less than 5,000 signatories by mid-2021 and the media has been mostly indifferent to it. Perhaps it was not more successful because of the contradictions inherent in the two-step strategy that lay behind it. Shahan realized that the orthodox think they "have much to lose, and little to gain by seriously considering alternative candidates."[11] But it is also true—and this points to a possible flaw in his strategy—that the orthodox have as much to lose, and as little to gain, from consideration of the strength or weakness of the Stratfordian thesis as they do from consideration of alternative candidates. There isn't a lot of difference between the two; both start the ball rolling in what academia sees as the wrong direction.

Similar contradictions underlay Leahy's approach. One is the opposition of what he called "the militant minority." Many of them "are very well versed in the issues and still resist any talk of Shakespeare not being the author of all of the works attributed to him. Such academics are set in their ways, convinced of their case and can for the most part, counter fact with fact and evidence with evidence. They are often very aggressive and dismissive in their views and seek not only to win the argument but to humiliate the opponent."[12] Although a minority within Departments of Literature, some of them "are very powerful within the institution and have access to a number of media outlets. . . . The positions of these academics is the dominant one, at least for the foreseeable future."

---

[10] William Leahy, "'Two Households, both alike in dignity,'" *De Vere Society Newsletter,* Feb. 2007, p, 10, 11.

[11] John Shahan, "Is There a Shakespeare Authorship Issue?," p. 19.

[12] William Leahy, "'Two Households, both alike in dignity,'" p. 7.

When Leahy was promoted to a higher position and no longer had direct responsibility for the Authorship Studies program, no one stepped up to run it, and it died. It was a grand experiment, one well worth trying, and it set a precedent for other such programs in the future. That the experiment did not derail Leahy's career at Brunel University is in itself a positive development.

The reality today, Leahy wrote, remains that "The academic institution does not have to accept or even listen to the positing of possibilities because it knows the truth. . . . Shakespeare of Stratford wrote the plays attributed to him and nobody else did. The end. . . . [I]t is academia which determines if there is uncertainty in a field or not and in this area it has determined that there is no uncertainty. Such is how the discourse works" (9). The attitude of the Stratfordians carried the day.

Shahan and Leahy are surely right that it's easier to persuade someone to examine the Oxfordian claim if they already have doubts about Shakspere's authorship. But I believe that their strategy is not the best one. It doesn't work from a human standpoint. People won't be captured by a purely negative argument; they need a positive story to draw them in. They must have something to replace the old theory with. Doubts about Will and interest in Edward go together. Either can be the entry point into the authorship question. Although Shahan cited Charlton Ogburn's statement that "You can't get anywhere with Oxford unless you first dispose of the Stratford man,"[13] Ogburn also said that, "In order to establish the case against the Stratford man, the great need, to begin with, has been to do more than expose the foundations of the Stratford case as unconvincing. A believable alternative had to be found."[14]

No example exists of a scientific theory being proposed only after doubts about the reigning theory were proved or widely accepted. Darwin did not wait until the Lamarckian theory of how species change was disproved before proposing the theory of evolution through natural selection. Einstein did not hold back the theory of relativity until all other attempts to explain radioactivity and other anomalies had been shown to be false. The new ideas themselves were the most powerful arguments for the weaknesses or incorrectness of the older.

Ideational Change

Dr. Paul H. Altrocchi has thought deeply about the obstacles that block acceptance of Edward de Vere as Shakespeare and the steps Oxfordians might take to overcome them. In one of his thought pieces, "Ideational Change: Why Is It So Difficult?" subtitles such as "The Power of Conventional Wisdom," "Guild Dogma" and "Universities: Safe Harbors for Conventional Wisdom?" introduced discussions of important points. Another, "The Latency Concept," recognized that it takes time to become familiar with and comfortable with new ideas. His observation that "A wrong idea, e.g., the earth is flat, or bloodletting is the cure for disease, may persist for centuries but the latency clock does not start ticking until new ideas are easily accessible,"[15] which is another reason why the two-step strategy is not effective within academia.

Most important of all was Altrocchi's discussion on "How Might We Hasten the

---

[13] Charlton Ogburn, quoted in John Shahan, "Is There a Shakespeare Authorship Issue?" *Shakespeare Oxford Newsletter*, vol. 43/3 (Summer 2007): 19.

[14] Charlton Ogburn, *The Mysterious William Shakespeare* (1992), p. xvi.

[15] Dr. Paul H. Altrocchi," Ideational Change: Why Is It So Difficult?" *Sh. Oxford Newsletter*, vol. 42/4 (Fall redux 2006): 24.

Paradigm Shift?" "It is now clear to [Altrocchi] that [the de Verean paradigm shift] must begin within the Stratfordian guild itself, not amongst the general public. Oxfordians have concentrated too long on 'spreading the word' to the uninitiated and have generally steered clear of Stratfordians" (28). He believes "it is now essential to plant the seed of change within Stratfordian soil, give it time to germinate, and then fertilize the concept during its inevitable growth towards Truth."

But how will it be possible to plant the seed within the closed circle of academia when its members—most of them, most of the time, listen only to others within the closed circle?

An Oxfordian Game Plan for Overcoming Institutional Resistance

What are Oxfordians to do? They will need to seek out allies. They will need to seek out funding. But most of all they will need to devise a well thought out Game Plan detailing how best to organize, motivate and coordinate their own actions and those of their allies.

What follows is the beginning of an Oxfordian Game Plan. Even if every idea in this draft gets tossed out as Oxfordians debate among themselves how best to proceed, the draft plan will have served its purpose if it gets the movement to engage in the serious thought and coordinated effort needed to complete the Oxfordian Revolution.

Before considering the components of the Plan, two general considerations should be noted. The first concerns funding. Because Oxfordians are trying to create something new, not merely maintain what already exists, they must think like entrepreneurs, not bureaucrats. They are the challengers, and challengers must be aggressive. This mindset must be reflected in matters of funding. In many organizations, internal units, when informed of funding levels for the coming year, set to work to determine how best to use the funds allocated to them to support the organization's goals. For Oxfordians, as outsiders and challengers, that procedure is backwards. Instead, thinking like entrepreneurs, they must first determine their goals, then determine what activities are necessary to reach them, calculate their cost, and finally go out and get the needed funds.

The second general consideration is that the goal is not to do the best they can with the funds available. It is not to make a good effort or to be able to say that they tried hard. It is to achieve widespread recognition within academia of Edward de Vere's authorship of Shakespeare's works. Toward that end it will be helpful for Oxfordians to keep in mind James Q. Wilson's distinction between inputs, outputs and outcomes. *Inputs* are resources such as dollars or staff time invested in carrying out the game plan. *Outputs* are what has actually been done with those resources: the number of speeches given, the number of comments posted on blogs, and so on. Outputs are often regarded as accomplishments in themselves, but *outcomes* are what's most important. Outcomes—what has changed as a result of the inputs and outputs—are such things as the number of people who have changed their views about Edward de Vere's authorship or the legitimacy of the authorship question.

Goals

The first step in considering how best to complete the Oxfordian Revolution is determining the goal line, the point at which it will be generally recognized that the revolution has been completed. For present purposes, the goal is that Departments of Literature accept and teach that William Shakespeare was a pseudonym used by Edward de Vere, Seventeenth Earl of Oxford, just as they accept and teach that Mark Twain was a pseudonym used by Samuel Langhorne Clemens, Lewis Carroll a pseudonym used by Charles Dodgson, and Joseph Conrad a pseudonym used by Józef Teodor Konrad Korzeniowski.

With the acceptance of Edward de Vere as Shakespeare will come the use of academia's vast resources to encourage, rather than block, the study of Oxford's authorship and the conditions in which the plays were written and first performed. It will ensure that future generations have a deeper and more correct understanding of the great works and appreciation of the man who wrote them.

Although Oxfordians want literature professors to accept Edward de Vere as Shakespeare, they cannot demand it. Academia is a "scientific" body in that its responsibility—beyond that of educating students—is to examine issues in an academic manner; that is, to subject them to objective study without preconceived conclusions about what will be found as a result of that examination. Stanley Fish's guidance on this point has been noted.

Limiting the call to an academic examination of the Oxfordian claim is not a problem for Oxfordians; that is just what Oxfordians have repeatedly called for since 1920. It is sufficient, many would say, to call not for an examination of the Oxfordian claim *per se* but for a more general examination of the issue of Shakespearean authorship that also includes consideration of the Oxfordian idea and that would test the claim for William Shakspere as rigorously as the claims for alternative candidates. Such an objective examination of the broader issue is really all that is needed because of the overwhelming strength of the case for Oxford.

The key point in an effective strategy comes from Thomas Kuhn. Although he had intended his analysis to be merely descriptive, and although he wrote about the physical sciences, not the humanities, his ideas on paradigm shifts contain information crucial for developing an effective Oxfordian Game Plan.

Thomas Kuhn and Paradigm Shifts

In *The Structure of Scientific Revolutions*, his *descriptive* study of the process through which scientific knowledge grows as scientific bodies change their beliefs over time, Thomas Kuhn provided what is, in effect, important *prescriptive* guidance on how Oxfordians might seek to move Departments of Literature toward acceptance of the Oxfordian thesis.[16] In Kuhn's model, scientific communities operate within an existing set of beliefs and practices—a paradigm—a set of "universally recognized scientific achievements that for a time provide model problems and solutions to a community of practitioners."[17] Paradigms are effective in "defin[ing] the legitimate problems and methods of a research field for succeeding generations of practitioners" (10) because their core idea has two complementary characteristics. It is "sufficiently unprecedented to attract an enduring group of adherents away from competing modes of scientific activity," while "[s]imultaneously . . . sufficiently open-ended to leave all sorts of problems

---

[16] Other Oxfordian scholars have commented on how Kuhn's work illuminates the history of the authorship controversy, most notably Mark Anderson in "A Little More than Kuhn, And Less than Kind," *Shakespeare Oxford Newsletter*, vol. 32/1 (Winter 1996): 12-14. However, their work drew on Kuhn's to provide a *descriptive* analysis of how change occurs. The analysis I present in this chapter is *prescriptive*, aimed at determining how to trigger the moment of crisis within academia that is necessary for acceptance of Edward de Vere as Shakespeare to occur.

[17] Thomas Kuhn, *The Structure of Scientific Revolutions*, Fourth Edition (2012), p. xliii.

for the redefined group of practitioners to resolve" (10-11). Scientists work within the paradigm to solve problems and in doing so are challenged by "the conviction that, if only [they are] skillful enough, [they] will succeed in solving a puzzle that no one before has solved or solved so well" (38). "Failure to achieve a solution discredits only the scientist and not the theory" (80).

But sometimes, Kuhn explained, problems or puzzles arise that resist solution. They can be set aside while other problems are dealt with, but eventually further attempts must be made to solve them. If the problems continue to resist explanation, they come to be regarded as anomalies, which begin to discredit not the scientist unable to solve them but the paradigm itself. Scientists tend to resist recognizing that a puzzle has become an anomaly because anomalies are unsettling. They are a sign "that an existing paradigm has ceased to function adequately in the exploration of an aspect of nature to which that paradigm itself had previously led the way" (xliii). Because such a realization would be disruptive of the community's work, defenders "will devise numerous articulations and *ad hoc* modifications of their theory in order to eliminate any apparent conflict" (78).

Eventually, if the anomalies are severe enough, they result in a growing-sense-of-crisis phase that is greatly disconcerting to its members because the community itself is defined by its commitment to the existing paradigm. If that paradigm falls, the community falls with it. It is for that reason that this phase can last indefinitely; it explains why members won't abandon the paradigm even as evidence in support of it weakens.

Eventually a moment of crisis arrives when a rival paradigm that explains the anomalies is introduced—and is not just introduced, but is practically forced on the community by those few who see its value. That moment of crisis triggered by the demonstrated superiority of the new paradigm is the key moment of change. Scientific communities *never* move from one paradigm to another, Kuhn found, simply because of weaknesses in the original paradigm. They do so *only* when a point of crisis is reached, and that point of crisis is *always* generated by a confrontation with a new paradigm that explains anomalies that the old one couldn't. "Competition between segments of the scientific community is the only historical process that ever actually results in the rejection of one previously accepted theory or in the adoption of another. . . . No process yet disclosed by the historical study of scientific development at all resembles the methodological stereotype of falsification by direct comparison with nature" (77). Again, "Once it has achieved the status of a paradigm, a scientific theory is declared invalid only if an alternate candidate is available to take its place." The key point for Oxfordians is that,

> The act of judgment that leads scientists to reject a previously accepted theory is always based upon more than a comparison of that theory with the world. The decision to reject one paradigm is always simultaneously the decision to accept another, and the judgment leading to that decision involves the comparison of both paradigms with nature and with each other (78).

Historians such as Walter Bagehot, Frederick Teggart and Sir Henry Maine reached similar conclusions: moments of crisis are necessary to break the cake of custom.

Applying this idea to Shakespeare Studies within academia, its core belief of authorship by William Shakspere of Stratford-upon-Avon is a paradigm in trouble. Even in an environment in which the reigning methodology is colored by the "death of the author" idea that papers over the anomalies, scholarly work is hampered by the paucity of connections that can be drawn between the works and the man the paradigm says wrote them. The two most important anomalies that cannot be explained within the Stratfordian paradigm are: (1) the contrast between the wealth of information about Shakspere's business activities and the dearth of information about his education and literary activities, coupled with the absence of any reasonable explanation for how he had acquired the depth of knowledge of so many subjects that the author of the works had to have had; and (2) the frequency of allusions in the works to events that occurred fifteen years earlier than when the plays were supposedly written, coupled with the fact that many of the allusions are to events in the life of Edward de Vere. These anomalies have become too obvious for many Stratfordians to ignore, and the field is now in the growing-sense-of-crisis phase. Other Stratfordians, though, by refusing to focus too closely on these issues, engage in the pretense that the Stratfordian paradigm, though perhaps frayed here and there, is fundamentally sound.

Following Kuhn's model, we should expect Stratfordians to avoid acknowledging the seriousness of the anomalies of their paradigm for as long as possible. As uncomfortable as the growing-sense-of-crisis phase might be for orthodox scholars, the moment of crisis would be far more disruptive, even disastrous.

The task for Oxfordians is clear: they must continually highlight the weakness of the evidence supporting Shakspere's authorship so that problems are seen for what they are: anomalies so severe that the inability to explain them challenges the entire Stratfordian paradigm. They must seek to ratchet up the emotional pressure on Stratfordians, to increase their nagging feeling that something is not right. Intellectual recognition that anomalies exist must be accompanied by emotional discomfort to heighten the sense of crisis.

But if Kuhn's model is correct, Oxfordians cannot stop there. They must also bring the growing-sense-of-crisis phase to a head. The move to a new paradigm requires a crisis, and if crises are always generated by awareness of a new paradigm that explains anomalies the old one couldn't, then Oxfordians have no choice but to push the Oxfordian paradigm. They cannot allow Stratfordians to muddle through; they must push them to acknowledge the failure of the older paradigm and the benefits of the new. They must bring the situation to a boil because they are the ones who want a paradigm shift to occur.

Again, if Kuhn's findings are correct, Shahan's and Leahy's two-step strategy can't be the best way to proceed. Oxfordians cannot push only for recognition of the weakness of the Stratfordian claim, deferring consideration of the Oxfordian idea to some unknown point in the future. They must generate the crisis needed to break the institutional hold that keeps the failed Stratfordian paradigm in place. Academia, serving as defense, judge and jury on the issue, won't change on its own.

Stratfordians, in fact, would not be able to stop at the point of a neutral academic consideration of the authorship question. The emotional energy—the vexation—that had been bottling up inside them would not let them stop at the halfway point. That emotional pressure will continue to build until the shock of the realization that the new Oxfordian paradigm explains the vexing anomalies pushes them into a paradigm shift. The new paradigm will be fiercely resisted until the moment when it is accepted. There can be no middle ground.

Shakespearean authorship is winner-take-all. The shift from Shakspere to Oxford is similar to the shift from the Ptolemaic geo-centric system to that of the Copernican heliocentric system. Both cannot be right. The Stratfordian and Oxfordian paradigms are in a head-to-head contest. The more intensely the pressure builds through the growing-sense-of-crisis phase, the greater the resulting force will be at the moment of crisis. It is the emotional energy of that crisis that Oxfordians must harness to move Stratfordians across the divide, safely into the Oxfordian paradigm.

Target Audiences

The key institutions that must become persuaded of Oxford's authorship are university Departments of Literature and a few independent organizations such as the Folger Shakespeare Library. Ultimately literature professors, particularly those who specialize in researching and teaching Shakespeare's works, must become convinced. If the scholarly community accedes to the new paradigm, all others will follow as a matter of course.

The academic community of literary scholars will be the toughest nut to crack; it is the group least open to consideration of the Oxfordian idea. But Departments of Literature are not monolithic. Some scholars are more receptive than others to consideration of the authorship question. Literature professors' commitment to the Stratfordian story ranges from those who strongly defend Shakspere's authorship—they could be called Militant Stratfordians—to those who don't have strong feelings about the authorship issue but go along with traditional beliefs—Ordinary Stratfordians—to those who secretly have doubts strong enough to consider the authorship question worthy of academic study—Secret Doubters. Literature professors could also be categorized by the stage they are at in their careers: Senior Professors, Rank and File Professors, or Assistant Professors. Combining these two ways of distinguishing between literary scholars results in the nine types shown in the following chart.

	Militant Stratfordians	Ordinary Stratfordians	Secret Doubters
Senior Professors	A	D	G
Rank and File Professors	B	E	H
Assistant professors	C	F	I

Militant Stratfordians—Leahy's "Militant Minority"—should not be the primary target for engagement because they are fierce defenders of Shakspere's authorship and are hostile to any attempt even to discuss the authorship issue.

Most Stratfordians in academia either believe that the man from Stratford was the author or have not investigated the issue. As Leahy saw, they are not adamantly opposed to consideration of the authorship question; it simply isn't on their radar. Absorbed in work focused "upon the texts and their contexts rather than on the life of the author" (6), they "are not fully aware of the problem of tying Shakespeare the man to Shakespeare the texts. . . . The majority just do not concern themselves with the problems of attribution. . . . They are currently dismissive of the Question, but not necessarily for all time." Most of them "simply do not know the facts . . . but go about their business as though the matter has been more or less settled and that enough evidence exists to clearly tie Shakespeare to the plays and poems" (6).

Should Oxfordians try to convince this group? Perhaps, but they would not be the primary target because people must convince themselves, as Mark Twain knew. Asked if he was trying to persuade others that Shakspere did not write the works, he responded with, "Ah, now, what do you take me for? Would I be so soft as that, after having known the human race familiarly for nearly seventy-four years? It would grieve me to know that any one could think so injuriously of me, so uncomplimentarily, so unadmiringly of me."[18]

Lastly there are the Secret Doubters, those who already have doubts about Shakspere's authorship but who keep their beliefs to themselves. They are more numerous than it might appear. A *New York Times* survey in April 2007 showed that seventeen percent of literature professors saw reason to doubt Shakspere's authorship.[19] That percentage might actually have been higher, given the reluctance of Secret Doubters to make their views known, even anonymously; it could be much higher now.

Few actions could be as beneficial and far-reaching as persuading Secret Doubters to become Public Doubters. Once out of the closet, so to speak, they could alert their students to the importance of the authorship issue, and perhaps even organize courses on that topic. They could engage their colleagues on the issue, and perhaps even organize conferences on it. Because they are already in academia, they would be well placed to push academic publications to accept papers on the issue.

Oxfordians face two related challenges when it comes to Secret Doubters. The first is identifying who they are. Assistant Professors are a good place to look. As is widely recognized, younger members of any community are more open to alternative views simply because they do not have as extensive a history of support for a community's views as their more senior colleagues.

The second challenge is persuading Secret Doubters to go public with their beliefs, to act on their desire to see academia conduct honest, objective, academic investigations into the subject. The challenge here is motivating this group of scholars strategically placed within Departments of Literature to act in ways contrary to institutional pressures to adhere to the party line.

Young professors, eager to promote their careers, will be under the greatest pressure, so the subgroup within academia most open to consideration of the Oxfordian claim is also the group most subject to institutional pressure to adhere to Stratfordian beliefs. Oxfordians, then, must seek to create conditions in which Secret Doubters would be able to get out from under that pressure.

Bringing Pressure to Bear: Diplomacy

If Secret Doubters do not feel free to act on the basis of their beliefs because of pressure from one side, then perhaps an effective strategy would be for Oxfordians to bring pressure to bear from the opposite.

What sort of pressure could be brought? How could it be applied? Considering the second question first, a model comes from the field of diplomacy—not the feel-good diplomacy associated with photos of smiling diplomats shaking hands, but the tough diplomacy Teddy Roosevelt had in mind when he talked of speaking softly and carrying a big stick. The key to this type of diplomacy is (1) explaining the reality of the situation to those with whom we are engaged, (2) highlighting the benefits that will flow to them if they act in accordance with it and the harm they will suffer if they don't; and (3) getting out of the way so they can make their own decision based on their new understanding of the situation.

An example of this diplomacy comes from none other than Edward de Vere, speaking

---

[18] Mark Twain, *Is Shakespeare Dead* (1909), p. 127.
[19] William Niederkorn, "Shakespeare Reaffirmed," *New York Times*, April 22, 2007, p. A4.

as the title character in *Henry V*. He wanted the leaders of the town of Harfleur to open the town's gates so that his army could enter, just as Oxfordians want literature departments to open their curricula and publications to discussion of the authorship question.

How did Henry proceed? By the steps just outlined. After the town leaders rebuffed his request, Henry explained to them aspects of the situation they had not fully realized. He then highlighted the benefits of acting in accordance with those realities and the harm the town would suffer if it didn't. Then he sat back to wait for the town leaders to discuss the situation among themselves. In the end, they decided to open the gates.

The reality, Henry had explained, is that the English are implacable. One way or another we're coming in. It's up to you whether to let us in peacefully or have the town destroyed as we force our way in. Henry did not just convey that reality in pleasant terms, but used vivid and forceful language to drive home the harm that the town would suffer if he unleashed his forces:

> ... the fleshed soldier, rough and hard of heart,
> In liberty of bloody hand shall range
> With conscience wide as hell, mowing like grass
> Your fresh fair virgins and your flow'ring infants. . . .
> What is't to me, when you yourselves are cause,
> If your pure maidens fall into the hand
> Of hot and forcing violation?
> What rein can hold licentious wickedness
> When down the hill he holds his fierce career?
> We may as bootless spend our vain command
> Upon th' enragèd soldiers in their spoil
> As send precepts to the leviathan
> To come ashore.
>   Therefore, you men of Harfleur,
> Take pity of your town and of your people
> Whiles yet my soldiers are in my command,
> Whiles yet the cool and temperate wind of grace
> O'erblows the filthy and contagious clouds
> Of heady murder, spoil, and villainy.
> . . .
> What say you? Will you yield, and this avoid?
> Or, guilty in defense, be thus destroyed?
> (*Henry V*, III.iii)

In modern English, Henry informed the town leaders that we can do this the easy way or the hard way. The easy way is for you to open the gates. If not, I'll be forced to unleash my soldiers, and we all know what soldiers are like during and just after the heat of battle. They will be out of my control, just as they will be out of yours. They will take the spoils of war, and we all know what that means. As Henry plainly said, what is it to me if your pure maidens are violated and your flow'ring infants cut down, when you yourselves are the cause because you did not open the gates?

Bringing Pressure to Bear: Talking Points

Oxfordians cannot threaten to sack Departments of Literature if they don't open their curricula and publications. So what form of pressure can they bring to bear on Secret Doubters to convince them to come out of the closet?

Beyond pushing for greater awareness of how extensively the anomalies undermine the Stratfordian claim and how strongly the evidence and reasoning support the Oxfordian, there is one other factor that many have overlooked: the strength of the interest in the Oxfordian claim outside of academia (see Chapter 19). Sudden awareness of it could trigger Secret Doubters into going public with their true beliefs, which could trigger the moment of crisis that is necessary for change in academia's beliefs. The following talking points might bring that home to them:

> ➤ The groundswell of opinion in support of the legitimacy of the authorship question—and even of de Vere's authorship—has been building for decades outside of academia.

> ➤ Many major publications have recognized the legitimacy and importance of the authorship question, including *The Atlantic, Harper's, The Smithsonian, The Wall Street Journal, The New York Times,* and *The Washington Post.*

> ➤ A December 2014 *Newsweek* article favorable to Edward de Vere's authorship sparked more than 1,700 comments on its blog in less than one month, most of them supportive.

> ➤ Five U.S. Supreme Court Justices have expressed their conviction that William Shakspere did not write the works attributed to him; three have publicly stated their belief that Oxford wrote "Shakespeare's" works.

> ➤ Many of the greatest literary minds in American and English letters in the past 150 years have doubted Shakspere's authorship, including Walt Whitman, Mark Twain, Henry James, John Greenleaf Whittier, John Galsworthy, Marjorie Bowen, John Buchan, and Anne Rice.

> ➤ Many of the greatest actors of the past hundred years have doubted Shakspere's authorship, including Leslie Howard, Charlie Chaplin, Orson Welles, Sir John Gielgud, Michael York, Sir Derek Jacobi, Mark Rylance, Jeremy Irons, and Keanu Reeves.

> ➤ Scores of diplomats, politicians and other public figures have publicly doubted Shakspere's authorship, including Frederick Nietzsche, Benjamin Disraeli, Otto von Bismarck, Charles de Gaulle, Sigmund Freud, Clifton Fadiman, Mortimer J. Adler, David McCullough, Paul Nitze, Helen Keller, Malcolm X and Clare Boothe Luce.

> ➤ The reality is that academia has already lost the public debate, with Professor Alan Nelson concluding in 1999, "Establishment Shakespeareans . . . are losing the public debate over the 'authorship question.'"

Oxfordians should seek to increase the intensity of the sense of crisis that many Shakespeare scholars already feel and that others will feel as they become more aware of the anomalies, the Oxfordian case and the extent of public interest in them. They must work to vex Stratfordians: to increase the stress and tension they feel, to heighten their agitation and anxiety. They must generate the emotional pressure that will push Stratfordians forward through the growing sense of crisis stage to the moment of crisis and beyond, to acceptance of the Oxfordian paradigm. They can do that by making their remarks up front and personal (psychologists tell us that losses are two and one-half times as painful as gains are pleasurable) by asking questions like these:

- ➤ How do you feel about Departments of Literature being left behind as others outside academia investigate a subject of great importance to literature?

- ➤ Why have you, a professional in this field, failed to do your scholarly duty to examine the authorship issue in an objective manner?

- ➤ Don't you have normal human curiosity about why so many prominent and accomplished people today and over the past century have had doubts about Shakspere?

- ➤ Do you believe in the Unity of Truth? If so, how do you feel about scholars in Shakespeare Studies producing work that conflicts with findings in related fields such as psychology, history and other subfields within the study of literature?

- ➤ Are we to believe that psychologists' findings about the nature of genius and literary creativity are valid for all writers except Shakespeare?

- ➤ Are we to believe that hierarchical social practices in the Elizabethan era were valid for everyone in the society except Shakspere?

- ➤ Edward de Vere's authorship has already been proved beyond a reasonable doubt. Public recognition is coming. Why not join the vanguard and be recognized as a leader?

- ➤ If you don't—if you abdicate your responsibility to examine an important literary question in an academic manner—how will you explain your failure to those outside academia? How will you respond to charges that academia tried to block progress on this important issue?

- ➤ Aren't you embarrassed by the shoddy scholarship and vituperative attacks on other scholars in Stratfordian publications such as *Shakespeare Beyond Doubt*, *Contested Will*, and *Monstrous Adversary*?

- ➤ A posting on the website of the Royal Shakespeare Company described those who doubt Shakspere's authorship as suffering from "a psychological aberration" attributable to "snobbery . . . ignorance; poor sense of logic; refusal . . . to accept evidence; folly, the desire for publicity; and even . . . certifiable madness."[20] Do you think such comments accurately describe five Justices of the U.S. Supreme Court? If not, why do you remain part of a group that honors people who make such comments?

- ➤ Suppose the plays had recently been found with no author's name on them. Would anyone think to inquire as to whether a man from Stratford was the author? Or would the logical choice be someone whose works were highly praised by his contemporaries but are missing under his own name, someone who was one of the biggest patrons of literature in the Elizabethan era and whose life story

---

[20] From the website of the Royal Shakespeare Company, quoted in "Royal Shakespeare Company's Psychological Aberration?" *De Vere Society Newsletter*, October, 2013, p. 27.

is told in many of the plays?

➢ Suppose the Shakespeare works had been ascribed to Oxford in the First Folio in 1623, and that his authorship had been accepted for four centuries. What in these works would have led you to break with the herd and challenge Oxford's authorship? What in those works would have led you to believe that the real author was William of Stratford?[21]

Bringing Pressure to Bear: Allies

Oxfordians can't do this alone; their numbers are too small. But potential allies can be recruited in the effort to generate stress and friction with academia. They include students, other academic departments, the theater community and the general public.

Indirect engagement through allies will be especially useful in approaching professors who are already wary of the Oxfordian movement and want to have as little to do with it as possible. The nearby chart shows some of the many avenues through which academia can be approached.

Students can raise the issue in their classes by asking questions, a most effective way of drawing professors' and teachers' attention to the Oxfordian idea. Looney had recognized this in a letter to Cambridge University professor Joan V. Robinson in 1933: "Something might be done towards exciting the interest of the undergraduates—which is perhaps the best way of forcing the attention of the professors."[22] Even someone as gentlemanly as Looney recognized that "forcing" was the right verb to use in such attempts.

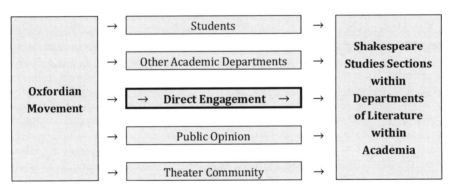

In "Youthful Minds Are Open" in 1939, Prof. Louis Bénézet contrasted the unreceptiveness of English professors with the receptiveness of students and professors in other subjects. He described how his many "attempts to convert friends of mine who are professors of English to at least a position of open mindedness on the question of the authorship of the Shakespeare plays" had paid "small dividends," but that "students in our high schools, colleges and universities . . . . are willing to listen, to give the matter the

---

[21] This is from an actual conversation between Joseph Sobran and Stylometrician and Stratfordian scholar David Kathman, as reported by Joseph Sobran, in "The End of Stratfordianism," *Shakespeare Oxford Newsletter*, vol. 36/1 (Spring 2000): 31.

[22] J. Thomas Looney, letter to Prof. Joan V. Robinson, Sept. 3, 1933. See Christopher Paul, "A New Letter by J. T. Looney Brought to Light," *Shakespeare Oxford Newsletter*, vol. 43/3 (Summer 2007): 8.

benefit of a doubt, to investigate and think for themselves."[23] "In the past two years," he added, "I have lectured before student audiences . . . in four different states, and I never fail to find an eager and excited group among them."

Beyond serving as a means of "forcing" the issue, students in English classes are the pool from which future generations of English professors and teachers will come. They need to be exposed to the Oxfordian case before the Stratfordian thesis has become fixed in their heads. Based on his years of effort to convince colleagues of the value of his quantum hypothesis, physicist Max Planck concluded that "A new scientific truth does not triumph by convincing its opponents and making them see the light, but rather because its opponents eventually die, and a new generation grows up that is familiar with it."[24]

Planck's belief is in line with Charles Darwin's findings in *The Origin of Species*. Darwin explained that one species can evolve into another even though the genetic makeup of each individual does not change over its lifetime. What changes is the gene pool, the sum of all genes in all individual members of the species alive at any given point in time and the frequency with which each gene exists within the pool. The relevance of this process for Oxfordians is that prevalence of belief in the validity of the Oxfordian claim can change within academia even if no one teaching in Shakespeare Studies today ever changes his views. All that is necessary is that each succeeding generation of scholars has a more favorable opinion of the Oxfordian claim, or at least a less hostile reaction to it.

Other Academic Departments within academia could express their unhappiness at seeing flawed findings from within Shakespeare Studies infiltrating and corrupting the scholarly work being done within their own departments. Feedback from within academia would carry more weight than that from independent scholars outside the walls, and could, if frequent enough and insistent enough, induce Shakespeare scholars to re-examine their beliefs and methodologies.

Historians could express dissatisfaction with how severely Shakespeare scholars have twisted the history of the Elizabethan era to fit the Stratfordian narrative.

Psychologists could express dismay at the way their understandings of genius and literary creativity are traduced by Shakespeare scholars eager to support Shakspere's authorship. So could professional organizations such as the American Psychoanalytic Association and the International Psychoanalytic Association.

Literature professors in other subfields could weigh in on the inappropriateness of banishing consideration of topical and personal allusions from authorship questions. They could even challenge the "death of the author" mentality and push for a more common-sensical methodology of literary analysis in which knowledge about authors' lives, personalities and intentions contributes to understanding their works.

Theater directors and actors could express anger at how the false story of William Shakspere's authorship corrupted their efforts to bring the true author's intentions to life.

Librarians in professional academic libraries could express irritation at how misinformation from Shakespeare Studies has led them to ignore a subject of real historical and intellectual importance.

Law professors could express irritation at seeing Shakespeare's vast knowledge of legal issues and concepts dismissed as mere tidbits acquired casually. They could express

---

[23] Louis P. Bénézet, "Youthful Minds are Open," *SF News-Letter* (American), vol. 1/1 (Dec. 1939): 4.
[24] Max Planck, *Scientific Autobiography*, quoted in Dean Keith Simonton, *Greatness: Who Makes History and Why* (1994), p. 201.

their dismay at the disparagement of circumstantial evidence emanating from Shakespeare Studies.

And then there is the general public. John Shahan recognized the effectiveness of bringing public pressure on academia in 2007, writing that Oxfordians must "get people to ask who 'Shakespeare' really was, and demand an answer of scholars."[25] Through broad engagement they can alert readers to the fantastic nature of the biographies of Shakespeare that have been palmed off on them. The public could then express its anger by asking Departments of Literature about the authorship question and the Oxfordian claim. This already happens on occasion. In 2014 a secretary at an English Department wrote to Miss Manners to say that she had been "besieged" by mail from people asking if the Department was part of a conspiracy to cover up the fact that Edward de Vere was Shakespeare and asking if she had to be polite to them. Miss Manners advised her that there was no need to respond to those letters, but merely add them to a "crank" file.[26] Perhaps Miss Manners herself could be urged to educate herself on subjects before speaking out publicly on them.

Legal pressure. John Shahan had recognized the power of bringing legal pressure to bear on Stratfordian entities that make statements that are not true. "My view," he wrote, "is that we need to engage in more advocacy through the legal system and undermine Stratfordians' credibility in the media." The Shakespeare Authorship Coalition (SAC) issued a challenge to the Shakespeare Birthplace Trust—the entity controlling the tourist sites in Shakspere's hometown of Stratford-upon-Avon—by offering to donate £40,000 to a charity of the Trust's choosing if it could establish, in open debate, beyond reasonable doubt, that Shakspere was the author of Shakespeare's works. In an interview, SAC Honorary President Waugh said, "I am publicly accusing them of [taking money under false pretenses]."[27] The Trust declined the offer, and took no legal action against Waugh for his accusations.

Local support. Regional newspapers gave more favorable coverage to *"Shakespeare" Identified* in 1920 than did those in London, perhaps because of the same factor that contributed to Looney's success: being farther from the center of intellectual power, they had weaker institutional commitments to the traditional idea of authorship. Beyond that consideration, regions with connections to Edward de Vere and the preceding sixteen earls of Oxford would naturally have greater interest in the Oxfordian claim and be natural allies for the movement today. The paper with the most coverage of Looney's book in 1920 was *The Yorkshire Post*, the largest newspaper in northern England, where Looney lived. Two other regional publications ran extensive coverage of the Oxfordian idea because of Edward de Vere's connection to those places: *The Hackney Spectator*— Edward de Vere lived in Hackney during the last decade or so of his life—and *The East Anglian Magazine*—East Anglia was the center of the Earls of Oxford's vast estates and the site of Castle Hedingham where Edward de Vere was born. Ward had hoped that recognition of Edward de Vere as Shakespeare could "turn the footsteps of many eager worshippers of the Immortal Bard in the direction of Hackney in the near future."[28] The beautiful church in the town of Long Melford in the heart of Oxford country, with its

---

[25] John Shahan, "Is There a Shakespeare Authorship Issue?," p. 19.

[26] Miss Manners, "Crank Letters Need No Response, *The Times*, March 15, 2014, p. E7.

[27] Quoted in Robert Gore-Langton, "The Campaign to Prove Shakespeare Didn't Exist," *Newsweek Blog*, Dec. 29, 2014. Accessed early in 2015.

[28] "Problems of Past and Present," *Hackney Spectator*, Sept. 8, 1922, p. 6.

stained glass picture memorializing the de Vere family by depicting an ox crossing a ford is only one of many sites that tourists might be interested in.

The media is a tool Oxfordians can use to reach its allies, the public and academia all at once. Because the media focuses on what is new, Oxfordians can aim for media attention in three ways: 1) writing articles and letters, as Charles Barrell did with his pieces in *The Saturday Review* and *Scientific American*; 2) writing books that can generate reviews, as Charlton Ogburn's *The Mysterious William Shakespeare* and Mark Anderson's *"Shakespeare" By Another Name* did; and 3) organizing events designed to generate media coverage, such as the moot court on the authorship question participated in by three justices of the U.S. Supreme Court. Local newspapers are just as good as those with national circulation for local audiences, and they will be far more likely to cover local events.

When talking to the public, Oxfordians can declare victory, and use the term "post-Stratfordian" to make clear their belief that a new phase in Shakespeare Studies has begun. In some cases, when talking with a particular media outlet, Oxfordians can cite its past coverage of the Oxfordian idea.

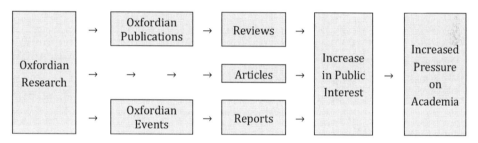

Cumulative effect

Pressure from multiple sources on Shakespeare Studies Sections within Departments of Literature is the core of the strategy outlined here. The task is to generate or enhance dissatisfaction with the distortions resulting from the Stratfordian story and direct it toward Shakespeare Studies with the goal of forcing it to do its academic duty to examine the authorship in an objective manner.

Secret Doubters becoming Public Doubters as a result of this pressure could be the step that triggers the war over who really wrote Shakespeare's works that must take place within academia. That war could result from a single scholar of established reputation daring to come out publicly, a possibility Looney recognized: "What we now need is one man of letters, sufficiently well established to be independent of the literary press, clear in judgment, strong in courage, willing, for truth's sake, to face the derision of smaller men and help to redress a wronged memory."[29]

Today's Oxfordians will not be principal players in that civil war; their role is to serve as the A-bomb that triggers the much larger H-bomb inside academia.

Bringing It Home

When the moment of crisis comes, Oxfordians will need to guide Stratfordians across the abyss. They can do that by emphasizing two points: (1) the psychic and emotional benefits of the move to the Oxfordian paradigm, and (2) the practical benefits of the move.

---

[29] J. Thomas Looney, "*The Church Times* and a Rejected Letter, II," *Hackney Spectator*, Sept. 14, 1923, p. 4.

On the psychic benefits, Oxfordians can show that accepting the new paradigm will provide relief to orthodox scholars from the emotional tension they have experienced throughout the increasing-sense-of-crisis phase and during the moment of crisis itself. They can emphasize these points:

➤ You can lay down the burden of trying to defend a creed that is indefensible.

➤ The hit to your good name during the transition phase would not be as severe as you might imagine. On the contrary, many of your colleagues already secretly have doubts about Shakspere's authorship—many more than you might imagine—who would admire your courage in taking a stand.

➤ You would not be venturing out on your own, isolated and alone, but instead joining a real community of scholars dedicated to the same scholarly work.

➤ Oxfordians value the works of Shakespeare just as you do. They are dedicated to understanding them and how they came to be written just as you are. Oxfordians have pushed for the shift to the Oxfordian belief for that very reason.

➤ Even if you are more comfortable being orthodox and working within an institution instead of being a pioneer, you will still be able to do that within the Oxfordian paradigm. You will be orthodox within it and the newly reconstructed Shakespeare Studies Sections. The disruption during the transition from the old to the new will be less than you fear. You will be leaving an institution that is crumbling and joining one that is rising.

➤ Oxfordians understand how difficult it is to jettison lifelong beliefs. After all, nearly all Oxfordians were once Stratfordians. We have gone through the transition that Esther Singleton described so movingly in her article. You too, will experience the elation she described on discovering that obscure passages in the plays, reread with knowledge of de Vere's authorship, became "so clear, so plain, so reasonable, and so delightful."[30]

➤ You are losing the inspiring story of a common man rising to the greatest heights through dint of his own genius and hard work, but you are gaining the even more inspiring tale of how Edward de Vere, through great personal integrity and endurance, triumphed over the strife in his own life and times to create the greatest literary works in the English language.

On the practical benefits of the move to the Oxfordian paradigm:

➤ You will be joining a new and exciting and growing community of scholars exploring the works of Shakespeare almost as a whole new world. You can recapture some of the pioneering spirit of the days of Malone and others of 200 years ago.

➤ The Oxfordian community, strong and growing, would welcome you with open arms. Your scholarly training would be given full scope for meaningful work as the effort to understand the works, the author and the conditions of the Elizabethan era is re-established on a much firmer basis.

➤ The new paradigm offers you many professional advantages. There will be

---

[30] Esther Singleton, "Was Edward de Vere Shakespeare? *SF News-Letter* (American) vol. 1/4 (June/July 1940) pp. 9-10.

significant new opportunities for research and publishing. The intellectual challenge of opening up a new literary field for academic study is a once in a lifetime opportunity. Aren't such challenges and the opportunities for meaningful work in the field of literature the reasons you entered the field in the first place?

Oxfordians must keep the pressure on until the paradigm shift has occurred. Orthodox scholars must understand that Oxfordians aren't going away.

Even if Oxfordians use all of these tactics, they cannot "convince" Stratfordians of the validity of de Vere's authorship; paradoxically, Stratfordians cannot "convince" themselves, either. Paradigm shifts do not occur within individual minds through logic or reasoning, but instead through insight—and insights cannot be commanded to occur. Kuhn saw that "the issue of paradigm choice can never be unequivocally settled by logic and experiment alone . . . It cannot be made logically or even probabilistically compelling for those who refuse to step into the circle."[31] Rather, "because it is a transition between incommensurables, the transition between competing paradigms cannot be made a step at a time, forced by logic and neutral experience. Like the gestalt switch, it must occur all at once (though not necessarily in an instant) or not at all" (149).

Oxfordians' most important task is that of creating the conditions in which Stratfordians can transform their own beliefs. They will become convinced of the validity of the new paradigm at different rates, in response to different types of evidence. Some will never be convinced. That's okay. Oxfordians will have reached their goal if a predominant number of scholars accept his authorship.

As more in academia recognize de Vere's authorship—as battles break out within literature departments—neither side will entirely understand how the other thinks. Stratfordians, of course, will not understand the new converts to the Oxfordian paradigm. What is surprising is that the new Oxfordians will not understand how any of their colleagues could fail to see what they now see.

Those who move to the new paradigm will have experienced a true revolution in how they see their own field. Shakespeare's literary works that they know so intimately will become new territory, requiring them to become explorers as in the days of Edmond Malone. The shift is not that of merely replacing one author with another, but of changing the central fact through which all other facts are interpreted. As Kuhn found,

> The transition from a paradigm in crisis to a new one . . . is a reconstruction of the field from new fundamentals, a reconstruction that changes some of the field's most elementary theoretical generalizations as well as many of its paradigm methods and applications. . . . [W]hen the transition is complete, the profession will have changed its view of the field, its methods, and its goals. (85)

Once academia shifts to the Oxfordian paradigm we can anticipate a period of extraordinary discovery as its vast resources are brought to bear on the authorship question, just as astronomers discovered more than twenty new planets and asteroids in the fifty years after Herschel's modification of Copernicus's paradigm told them what to look for and where to look.

Oxfordians' goal, then, is to make themselves history: first by making history in the sense of accomplishing something of historic importance, and second by making themselves part of history, part of the past. Their work will be finished.

---

[31] Thomas Kuhn, *The Structure of Scientific Revolutions*, Fourth Edition (2012), p. 94, 95.

Prospects

Will all that be enough? Will the Oxfordian movement succeed in completing the revolution? I have great confidence that academia will eventually accept Edward de Vere as Shakespeare. I believe the Oxfordian claim Looney presented in *"Shakespeare" Identified* is correct and that the evidence in support of it grows stronger all the time. Being correct, it will surely prevail. Indeed, even after a full century the claim has never been substantially undermined. What Looney wrote on May 21, 1920, after reviewing ten weeks of responses to *"Shakespeare" Identified* is still true today.

> The ordeal has been passed through; I have watched anxiously every criticism and suggestion that has been made, and what is the result? . . . not a single really formidable or destructive objection to the theory has yet put in an appearance. To the contrary, those critics and reviewers who have made themselves most intimate with the many-sidedness of the evidence, have confessed themselves most impressed and "almost persuaded," sometimes apparently against their evident wish.[32]

Progress is to be measured in decades, not months, Percy Allen said. By that standard, the Oxfordian movement has made large strides and there is little sign of it stopping. It is easy, though, to let that progress lead to thinking that success is just around the corner. That mistake has been made many times.

Here's Abel Lefranc writing in 1918:

> It is clear for all that that a new era of Shakespearian studies is about to open. The scepticism about the man of Stratford is spreading in spite of the resistance of the defense-quarters of the tradition. . . . Beliefs long accepted as dogma are on their way out: the block is cracking. . . . The contradictions which several years ago struck nobody, cannot fail in the near future to attract general attention.[33]

J. Thomas Looney (1920):

> The future, I am confident, is ours. Only let us have the matter properly examined by men who are more anxious for truth than for the defense of their own over-confident past dogmatism.[34]

The Christian Science Monitor (1930):

> It is, probably, no exaggeration to say that belief in the Stratfordian authorship of the Shakespearean poems and plays, though still accepted by the vast majority, is rapidly being discarded by inquiring and thoughtful scholars throughout the English-speaking world.[35]

Col. Montagu Douglas (1938):

> These are spreading convictions, and traditional scholars are disquieted in consequence. But the day is at hand, nearer perhaps than is realized, when the eyes of the public will be opened and the real author of these works will emerge from obscurity, and be known. Nevertheless, in order that such a result may be

---

[32] J. Thomas Looney, "The Identity of Shakespeare," *Bookman's Journal*, May 21, 1920, p. 17.

[33] Abel Lefranc, *Under the Mask of William Shakespeare*, tr. by Cecil Cragg, 1988, pp. 34-35.

[34] J. Thomas Looney, "Shakespeare Identified: A Reply to Critics and Some New Facts," *Yorkshire Post and Leeds Intelligencer*, April 1, 1920, p. 8.

[35] "De Vere as Shakespeare," *Christian Science Monitor*, July 19, 1930, p. 6.

achieved, additional workers must be recruited, and the research be continued.[36]

Percy Allen (1939):

> The orthodox, traditional, "Stratfordian" case is finished. It will no longer bear examination, whether from chronological, topical, or other view-points. It no longer fits either the known facts, or the obvious inferences to be drawn therefrom. It is fast being rejected throughout the English-speaking world.... The case for Oxford, as we can now present it, is substantially complete. It has never been answered, and is, in my judgment, unanswerable.[37]

Against these overly optimistic expectations one can frame overly pessimistic assessments by noting that a century after publication of *"Shakespeare" Identified* academia seems as intransigent as ever. Patience and determination will continue to be necessary. But it is not necessary to win every battle to triumph in the end. At the Paris Peace Talks in 1973 at the close of what Americans call the Vietnam War, Henry Kissinger, representing the United States, commented to Lê Đức Thọ, representing Vietnam, that the United States had won every battle. Lê thought for a moment, then replied that that was true, but irrelevant; Vietnam had won the war and the Americans were leaving. Perhaps the Oxfordians are following the same path as the Vietnamese, losing many battles so far, but eventually winning the war.

Over the past century, no more than a few thousand persons have been members of an Oxfordian organization. At any given time only a few dozen Oxfordians are actively involved in research or in publicizing the thesis. Yet they are enough. The great German poet Johann Wolfgang von Goethe recognized that "In the realm of ideas everything depends on enthusiasm. . . . [I]n the real world all rests on perseverance." The anthropologist Margaret Mead once observed that, "A small number of committed individuals can change the world; indeed, it is the only thing that ever has."

Like Hotspur, Oxfordians should take pride in what they will achieve. The smaller our numbers, Hotspur said after some of his forces failed to appear before the big battle, the greater the glory for each of us when we succeed.

> I rather of his absence make this use:
> It lends a luster and more great opinion,
> A larger date to our great enterprise,
> Than if the earl were here; for men must think,
> If we, without his help, can make a head
> To push against a kingdom, with his help
> We shall o'errun it topsy-turvy down.
>
> (*1 Henry IV*, IV.1)

Oxfordians need only outlast their Stratfordian opponents. With dedication and perseverance they will, and the revolution that J. Thomas Looney launched one hundred years ago will, finally, be completed.

---

[36] Col. Montagu W. Douglas, "News from France," *SF News-Letter*, no. 9 (May 1938): 3.
[37] Percy Allen, "Who Was Shakespeare?" *John O'London's Weekly*, Feb. 10, 1939, p. 821.

APPENDICES

BIBLIOGRAPHY

INDEX

Appendix 1

J. Thomas Looney's Oxfordian Writings

<u>Books</u>

"Shakespeare" Identified in Edward de Vere, the Seventeenth Earl of Oxford.
1920	London: Cecil Palmer.
1920	First U.S. Edition. New York: Frederick A. Stokes.
1948	Second U.S. Edition. Introduction by William McFee; Afterword by Charles Wisner Barrell. New York: Duell, Sloan and Pearce.
1975	Third U.S. Edition. Ruth Loyd Miller, Editor. Port Washington, NY: Kennikat Press for Minos Pub. Co.
2018	Centenary Edition. James A. Warren, Editor. Somerville, MA: Forever Press. [Reprinted by Veritas Publications, Cary, NC (2019)]

The Poems of Edward de Vere, Seventeenth Earl of Oxford.
1921	London: Cecil Palmer.
1975	Ruth Loyd Miller, Editor. Port Washington, NY: Kennikat Press for Minos Pub. Co. [Included with *"Shakespeare" Identified*]

<u>Published Articles and Letters to Editors</u>

1920, March 11	"Shakespeare Identified," *Yorkshire Post and Leeds Intelligencer*, p. 4. [letter: response to the March 4 and March 6 reviews]
1920, March 20	"Shakespeare Identified," *Scotsman*, p. 11. [letter: response to the March 4 review]
1920, March 25	"Shakespeare Identified," *Times Literary Supplement*, issue 949: 201. [letter: response to Alfred Pollard's March 4 review]
1920, April 1	"Shakespeare Identified: A Reply to Critics and Some New Facts," *Yorkshire Post and Leeds Intelligencer*, p. 8. "Shakespeare Identified," *The Daily Telegraph*. [letter: response to the March 19 review]
1920, April 9	"Is 'Shakespeare Identified'?" *Bookman's Journal*, vol. 1/24: 252-53. [letter: response to the March 19 review]
1920, April 10	"Edward de Vere and Shakespeare," *Spectator*, p. 487. [letter: response to the March 27 review]
1920, April 17	"Edward de Vere and Shakespeare," *Saturday Review*, vol. 129: 370. [letter: response to the March 27 review]
1920, April 23	"The Shakespeare Controversy," *Bookman's Journal*, vol. 1/26: 484. [letter: response to the March 19 and April 9 reviews]
1920, April 30	"Edward de Vere and Shakespeare," *Athenaeum*, issue 4696: 595. [letter: response to M's April 2 review]
1920, May 6	"Shakespeare's Identity: Case for Lord Oxford," *Western Mail*, p. 7. [letter: response to the April 23 review]
1920, May 8	"Query: Edward de Vere's Mother," *Notes and Queries*, issue 208: 190.
1920, May 8	"Query: Henry de Vere's Sponsors," *Notes and Queries*, issue 208: 190.
1920, May 21	"The Identity of Shakespeare," *Bookman's Journal*, vol. 2/30: 58-59. [letter: response to the March 19 review]
1920, May 28	"The Identity of Shakespeare," *Bookman's Journal*, vol. 2/31: 68. [letter: response to Robertson's May 21 letter]
1920, Dec. 23	"Readers and Writers," *New Age*, vol. 28/2: 91.

	[letter: response to R. H. C.'s Dec. 2 review]
1921, Jan. 20	"Readers and Writers," *New Age*, vol. 28/12: 138-39.
	[letter: response to R.H.C.]
1921, Feb. 17	"Shakespeare Identified," *New Age*, vol. 28/16: 192.
	[letter: response to R.H.C.]
1921, March 25	"Stratford and Stony Stratford," *Bookman's Journal*, vol. 3/74: 388.
	[letter: response to the March 4 review]
1921, June 25	"Shakespeare, Lord Oxford, Solomon Eagle and Mr. Looney," *Outlook*, pp. 543-44.
	[letter: response to Solomon Eagle's March 12 review]
1921, July 15	"'Shakespeare's' Identity," *Sydney Morning Herald*, p. 12.
	[letter: response to the April 23 article]
1921, July 16	"Rejected Contributions," *Outlook*, pp. 58-59.
	[letter: response to Eagle's July 2 reply]
1922, February	"'Shakespeare': Lord Oxford or Lord Derby?" *National Review*, vol. 78: 801-09. [response to R. Macdonald Lucas's Nov. 1921 article]
1922, October	"The Earl of Oxford as 'Shakespeare': New Evidence," *Golden Hind*, vol. 1/1: 23-30.
1922, Nov. 24	"Shakespeare at Hackney," *Hackney Spectator*, p. 14. [letter accepting position of Shakespeare Fellowship vice-president]
1923, April 13	"The Oxford Movement," *Hackney Spectator*, p. 8.
1923, April 20	"Who Wrote Hamlet?" *Hackney Spectator*, p. 4.
1923, May 11	"How the *Observer* Observes," *Hackney Spectator*, p. 2.
1923, May 25	"The Tracking of Margery Gryffyn" *Hackney Spectator*, p. 2.
	[includes excerpts from three letters to Col. B. R. Ward]
1923, June 10	"The Shakespeare Problem," *Freethinker*, vol. 43/23: 364-65.
1923, July 1	"Shakespeare": Was it Oxford, Bacon, or Derby, Part 1," *Freethinker*, vol. 43/26: 412-13.
1923, July 8	"Shakespeare": Was it Oxford, Bacon, or Derby, Part 2," *Freethinker*, vol. 43/26: 428-29.
1923, Aug. 3	"An Elizabethan Literary Group, I," *Hackney Spectator*, p. 4.
1923, Aug. 14	"An Elizabethan Literary Group, II," *Hackney Spectator*, p. 9.
1923, Aug. 24	"An Elizabethan Literary Group, III," *Hackney Spectator*, p. 4.
1923, Aug. 31	"A *Daily News* Critic," *Hackney Spectator*, p. 4.
1923, Sept. 7	"The *Church Times* Critic and a Rejected Letter, I," *Hackney Spec.*, p. 2.
1923, Sept. 14	"The *Church Times* Critic and a Rejected Letter, II," *Hackney Spec.*, p. 4.
1923, Nov. 9	"Annual General Meeting," *Hackney Spectator*, p. 2.
	[letter to Col. Ward to be read at the Annual General Meeting]
1923, Nov. 30	"Shakespeare Research at Hackney and Southwark, I," *Hackney Spectator*, p. 4.
1923, Dec. 7	"Shakespeare Research at Hackney and Southwark, II," *Hackney Spectator*, p. 2.
1923, Dec. 21	"Shakespeare Research at Hackney and Southwark, III," *Hackney Spectator*, p. 4.
1923, Dec. 28	"Shakespeare Research at Hackney and Southwark, IV," *Hackney Spectator*, p. 7.
1924, Jan. 4	"Shakespeare Research at Hackney and Southwark, V," *Hackney Spectator*, p. 4.
1924, Jan. 11	"Shakespeare Research at Hackney and Southwark, VI," *Hackney Spectator*, p. 9.
1924, Jan. 25	"Shakespeare Research at Hackney and Southwark, VII," *Hackney Spectator*, p. 9.
1924, Feb. 1	"Shakespeare Research at Hackney and Southwark, VIII," *Hackney Spectator*, p. 9.

1924, Feb. 15	"Shakespeare Research at Hackney and Southwark, IX," *Hackney Spectator*, p. 5.
1929, Feb.	"Death of George Greenwood" [letter], *Sh. Pictorial*, No. 12: 16.
1935, April	"Jonson v. Jonson, Part 1," *Shakespeare Pictorial*, no. 86: 64.
1935, May	"Jonson v. Jonson, Part 2," *Shakespeare Pictorial*, no. 87: 80.
1935, Aug.	"A More Important Christopher Sly," *Shakespeare Pictorial*, no. 90: 120.
1935, Nov.	"Lord Oxford and the Shrew Plays, Part 1," *Sh. Pictorial*, no. 93: 176.
1935, Dec.	"Lord Oxford and the Shrew Plays, Part 2," *Sh. Pictorial*, no. 94: 190-91.
1940, Dec.	"Author of *'Shakespeare' Identified* Comments on Professor Campbell's Article 'Shakespeare Himself' in *Harpers* (June 1940, pp. 172-85)," *Shakespeare Fellowship Newsletter* (American), vol. 2/1: 1-3.
1941, Feb.	"Shakespeare: A Missing Author, Part 1," *Shakespeare Fellowship Newsletter* (American), vol. 2/2: 13-17
1941, April	"Shakespeare: A Missing Author, Part 2," *Shakespeare Fellowship Newsletter* (American), vol. 2/3: 26-30.

Misc. Published Pieces

| 1918, December 14 | *"Shakespeare" Identified: A Preliminary Notice*
 A two-page leaflet, printed privately by J. Thomas Looney. The only copies known to exist are one in the library at Cambridge University and several inserted into the British Library's copy of the 1920 Cecil Palmer edition of *"Shakespeare" Identified.* |

Pieces Apparently Lost

1920, March	"The Solving of the Shakespeare Problem" [Mentioned in Cecil Palmer's April 8, 1920 letter to J. Thomas Looney]
1920, April 1	Letter to *The Daily Telegraph* [Cecil Palmer's April 8, 1920 letter to J. Thomas Looney notes that *The Telegraph* printed only a short excerpt from Looney's lengthy letter]
1920, October	Letter to *The New York Times* [William Morrow's October 29, 1920 letter from the Frederick A. Stokes Company to J. Thomas Looney discusses the letter]
1932, December	Article submitted to *The Atlantic Monthly* [Discussed in several letters between J. Thomas Looney and Eva Turner Clark in December 1932 and January 1933]

Unpublished Materials

| Various dates | Drafts of several unpublished articles and dozens of shorter fragments are in the cache of Looney's papers found in 2019. |

Personal Correspondence Addressing the Oxfordian Claim

| 1920-1942 | More than 250 letters that Looney sent from 1920 to his death early in 1944 are known of. Of those, sixty are in hand, and of those half are housed in the Katharine E. Eggar Archives, Senate House Library, University of London. |

Appendix 2

Short Excerpts from Reviews of *"Shakespeare" Identified*

Gelett Burgess (1920)

"I have been fascinated beyond measure by *"Shakespeare" Identified*. It has all the charm, all the excitement of the most thrilling detective story. Indeed, it is a detective story; and, if the author's conclusions are accepted by posterity, it chronicles the most important literary pursuit and discovery ever given to the world.

"No one, whatever his conventional prejudices in favor of the Man of Stratford, can read it without being impressed by the fairness of view, the logical pursuance of the inquiry, and the elegance of clarity of **Mr. Looney's** style.

"One cannot help being moved and inspired by this extraordinary and sincere attempt to solve the greatest literary mystery of modern times. Once having read the book, I doubt if anyone, friend or foe, will ever forget it."[1]

John Galsworthy (1920)

"The best detective story I've ever read."[2]

Frederick Taber Cooper (1920)

J. Thomas Looney's *"Shakespeare" Identified* is a sane, dignified, arresting contribution to the abused and sadly discredited Shakespeare controversy. It is one of the most ingenious pieces of minute, circumstantial evidence extant in literary criticism.... Every right-minded scholar who seriously cares for the welfare of letters in the bigger sense should face the problem that this book presents and argue it to a finish.[3]

Edwin Björkman (1920)

"It is impossible in an article like this to do justice to the wealth of evidence collected by **Mr. Looney**, or to the ingenuity displayed by him in its coordination. Perhaps the most remarkable aspect of his labors is that they affect not only the central problem of William Shakespeare's relation to the work named after him, but a whole series of literary enigmas that have puzzled every painstaking student of this period for nearly two hundred years.... The peculiar thing is that all these problems seem to fall into place and form a consistent picture the moment you accept the theory of Oxford's connection with the Shakespeare plays."[4]

---

[1] Gelett Burgess, letter to Frederick A. Stokes, May 19, 1920. [Excerpts quoted in a Stokes advertisement, *New York Times*, June 6, 1920. Stokes forwarded the letter to J. Thomas Looney.]

[2] The source of Galsworthy's oft-quoted statement is unknown. One of the earliest mentions of it was on the back cover of Charles Wisner Barrell's pamphlet *Elizabethan Mystery Man* (1940): "John Galsworthy hailed this work as 'the best detective story I've ever read.' He purchased many copies and distributed them among his friends."

[3] Frederick Taylor Cooper, source unknown, though rumored to be from the Spring 1920 issue of *Forum*.

[4] Edwin Björkman, "Shakespeare?" *Bookman*, August 1920, vol. 51/6: 681-82.

Esther Singleton (1921)

"A week ago I still believed that William Shaksper of Stratford-upon-Avon was the author of the great plays that have borne his name for three hundred years. . . . However, a book fell into my hands, *"Shakespeare" Identified*, by **J. Thomas Looney**, published in 1920. I opened it with prejudice and deep contempt and antagonism. I had no intention to surrender the William Shaksper of Stratford for any theory. Long ago I had rejected Bacon and every other new candidate brought forward. But I read on and on, much impressed with the modesty of the discoverer of the new author, much enthralled by his careful and original process of discovery, the fine marshaling of facts and logical deductions, the painstaking examination of the evidence, and the skill, honesty, and charm of the presentation of the theory.

"Amazed, fascinated, and with mind clarified, I rose from a study of the book. I read it again, then I read it for the third time (a big book, 458 pages). And I now pronounce myself a believer in the theory that Edward de Vere, Earl of Oxford, was the author of the great Shakespearean plays. . . . At last, thanks to **Mr. Looney**, we can find our Shakespeare, the dramatist, in such characters as Hamlet (biographical throughout), Biron in *Love's Labour's Lost*, and Bertram in *All's Well* (another biography)."[5]

Col. Bernard R. Ward (1922)

"It is not too much to say that [**Mr. Looney's *"Shakespeare" Identified***] is the most remarkable and convincing book on the Shakespearean question which has been published since doubts concerning the authorship of the famous dramas first arose in the minds of a few Shakespeare students about 75 years ago."[6]

Clement Wood (1925)

"We turned to this book [*"Shakespeare" Identified*] . . . with a bias against it. But that mood could not continue; for here, for the first time, we have a study of the authorship of the 'Shakespeare' literature that is written by a man of compelling intellect, skillful in the marshalling of his facts, and fair in stating evidence even when it mitigates against his theory. The book is practically conclusive, to any fair-minded reader. . . . As a presentation of a legal case, as a masterly marshalling of evidence, I have encountered few books in my life that can compete with this."[7]

Percy Allen (1930)

"**Mr. Looney's** book—as was inevitable, in the case of so daring a pioneer work— aroused more opposition than consent; yet it contained an admirably honest, courageous, and highly intelligent, presentation of its subject, including much matter that could not possibly be ignored, and posing, again and again, with remorseless logic, a number of pertinent questions, which had been clamouring, long and insistently, for an answer, in many a doubtful and enquiring mind."[8]

Margaret Blanton (1930)

"Shakespeare" Identified "is a thoroughly sound work, based on solid scholarship, and its subject was approached with exemplary scientific objectivity. It is obviously a

---

[5] Esther Singleton, from the unpublished paper "Was Edward de Vere Shakespeare?" found among her belongings after her death in 1930. It was dated 1921. [Printed in *Shakespeare Fellowship News-letter* (American), vol. 1/4 (June/July 1940): 9-10.
[6] Col. Bernard R. Ward, "'Shakespeare' in Hackney," *Hackney Spectator*, Nov. 3, 1922, p. 11.
[7] Clement Wood, "The Shakespeare Riddle: Has It at Last Been Solved?" *New Leader*, Sept. 26, 1925, p. 9.
[8] Percy Allen, *The Case for Edward de Vere as "Shakespeare"* (1930), p. 2.

book to command respectful attention."[9]

Gerald H. Rendall (1930)

"In **Mr. J. T. Looney's** pages I found a very different order of treatment and reasoning from that which I anticipated. Following up the various lines of evidence—biographical, personal, and literary—combining clues of poetic output and authoritative testimony, of historic sympathies and reminiscences, of personal and of dramatic episodes and allusions, and broad and striking chronological correspondences, he seemed to succeed in concentrating them upon a single objective, Edward de Vere, 17th Earl of Oxford."[10]

Percy Allen (1930)

"I close upon a parting word of appreciative remembrance to **Mr. J. T. Looney**, whose *"Shakespeare" Identified*—and rightly identified too, as every year more unanswerably shows—will ever be the principal pioneer work in this increasingly fruitful branch of Shakespearean study."[11]

Percy Allen (1932)

"It is significant that although **Mr. Looney** has been attacked on matters of minor detail, his main thesis and arguments have never been challenged or refuted. And, indeed, it is safe to say that they never will be, for the simple reason that they are unanswerable. . . . It is a remarkable tribute to **Mr. Looney's** great work that it stands today as unshaken and unshakable as ever, although, of course, in matters of detail—e.g., the chronology of the plays—it has been necessary to make some slight modifications."[12]

Carolyn Wells (1937)

"Shakespeare" Identified is not only a fascinating book, it is clear and convincing argument that cannot be ignored or disbelieved by a thinking reader. . . . Any one who has read **Mr. Looney's** book with an open mind, has an open mind no longer; he is a disciple of **Mr. Looney**."[13]

W. R. Robinson (1938)

"**J. Thomas** Looney is more than a scholar. His wonderful and original work, *"Shakespeare" Identified*, is the product of a man of learning, insight and originality."[14]

Sigmund Freud (1935)

"I no longer believe that . . . the actor from Stratford was the author of the works that have been ascribed to him. Since reading *"Shakespeare" Identified* by **J. Thomas Looney**, I am almost convinced that the assumed name conceals the personality of Edward de Vere, Earl of Oxford. . . . The man of Stratford seems to have nothing at all

---

[9] Margaret Blanton, quoted by her husband, Smiley Blanton, in *Diary of My Analysis with Sigmund Freud* (1971), pp. 36-37, in *Peter Gay, Reading Freud: Explorations & Entertainments* (1990), p. 13.
[10] Gerald H. Rendall, *Shakespeare's Sonnets and Edward de Vere* (1930), p. 2.
[11] Percy Allen, *The Oxford Shakespeare Case Corroborated* (1931), p. vi.
[12] Percy Allen, *The Life-Story of Edward de Vere as "William Shakespeare"* (1932), p. xi.
[13] Carolyn Wells, "The Oxford Theory," *Saturday Review*, June 5, 1937, pp. 9, 16.
[14] W. R. R., "A Group of Authors?" [letter], *Northern Whig and Belfast Post*, Jan. 27, 1938, p. 9.

to justify his claim, whereas Oxford has almost everything."[15]

John L. Astley-Cock (1941)

"I became an Oxfordian immediately after reading **Looney's** book, the original edition soon after publication; up till then . . . I was completely agnostic, neither Baconian nor Stratfordian."[16]

William McFee (1948)

"*'Shakespeare' Identified* is the sober, careful, conservative record of what [**Mr. Looney**] found. On the surface it is as deceptively undramatic as the evidence of a policeman in court who is reporting that he has found the murderer.

"There is nothing sensational in **Looney's** methods of presentation, nothing smacking of the Sunday supplement. It resembles in its general tenor *The Origin of Species*. In my opinion, after several readings, *"Shakespeare" Identified* is destined to occupy in modern Shakespearean studies the place Darwin's great work occupies in evolutionary theory . . . [A]ll modern discussion of the plays and poems will stem from it, and owe the author an inestimable debt."[17]

Hamilton Basso (1950)

"[**Mr. Looney's**] contention, put forward in nearly five hundred sober, modest, heavily documented pages is . . . that Shakespeare was not the Shakespeare that . . . [we] take for granted. . . . **Mr. Looney** is no crank. He is an earnest level-headed man who has spent years trying to solve the world's most baffling literary mystery. . . . If the case were brought to court, it is hard to see how Mr. Looney could lose. . . . The various mysteries that surround Shakespeare . . . are mysteries no longer if the man we know as Shakespeare was really Edward de Vere."[18]

T. L. Adamson (1955)

"Somerset Maugham has recently reminded us that in the long run an author can only write out of himself. I came to the conclusion that nothing of Shakespeare was written out of Shakspere of Stratford, and that the writer of the plays was veiled in mystery. Then in 1937 I came by chance to read **J. T. Looney's** *"Shakespeare" Identified*. Three weeks of fascinated absorption in this book of revelation brought me the sure knowledge that Edward de Vere the 17th Earl of Oxford was the real Shakespeare. Here was the perfect accord between a man and his work. **Mr. Looney** had given me the greatest literary thrill of a lifetime. . . . The plays and poems at last came fully to life with the personality of Oxford as their inspiration and explanation. . . . My understanding, appreciation and enjoyment of "Shakespeare" increased . . . thanks to **Mr. Looney**."[19]

Charlton Ogburn, Jr. (1992)

"We were no less quickly stirred by the force and persuasiveness in the alternative Mr. Barrell offered. At last and Of Course expressed our reaction. Even so we were

---

[15] Sigmund Freud, *An Autobiographical Study* (1935). [This statement was removed from later editions by Freud's editors after his death.]

[16] John Astley-Cock, [letter], excerpt reprinted in "Letters from Members: Brief Excerpts," *Shakespeare Fellowship News-letter* (American), vol. 2/6 (Oct. 1941): 71.

[17] William McFee, "Introduction" to the 1948 edition of *"Shakespeare" Identified* (1948), pp. xvii, xix.

[18] Hamilton Basso, "The Big Who-Done-It," *New Yorker*, April 8, 1950, p. 118.

[19] T. L. Adamson, "Shakespeare and Oxford in the Lecture Room," *SF News-Letter*, Spring 1955, p. 7.

hardly prepared for the excitement with which we would read **J. Thomas Looney's** book itself.... It was this way with ***"Shakespeare" Identified***, except that, gripped by the unfolding parallels between Oxford and Shakespeare, I did not put it down, at least for long. That this thrilling work of ratiocination, this landmark in English literary history, as many view it, has largely disappeared from ken, smothered by the hostility or silence of our literary mentors, is to me as reprehensible an act of bibliocide as any public book-burning."[20]

Mortimer J. Adler (1997)

"I myself have become sufficiently convinced that Lord Oxford is the author of Prince Hamlet's tragedy, and highly recommend a reading of **J. Thomas Looney's** treatise, ***"Shakespeare" Identified in the 17th Earl of Oxford, Edward de Vere***. It is one of the 20th Century classics."[21]

---

[20] Charlton Ogburn, *The Mysterious William Shakespeare* (1992), p. 165.
[21] Mortimer J. Adler, letter to Max Weisman, November 7, 1997. [Reprinted in "The Great Shakespeare Hoax," The Great Ideas Online, No. 203 (November 2002).

Appendix 3

Comparison of the Five Editions of *"Shakespeare" Identified*

J. Thomas Looney's *"Shakespeare" Identified* has been published five times, once in England and four times in the United States.

The most recent edition, known as the Centenary Edition, was edited by the author of this book and published by Veritas Publications. This edition has two advantages over the original edition published by Cecil Palmer in London in 1920. One is that it is in print and can be readily purchased through amazon.com for a reasonable price; Palmer's edition is available only as rare and expensive second hand books. The other is that it is the only edition that provides the full citation—author, title, edition and page number—for more than 230 passages that Looney quoted from other books and articles, thereby showing the source of the information on which he based his arguments for Edward de Vere's authorship.

The Centenary Edition also has two advantages over all other editions. One is that it is in the first new typesetting since the original 1920 editions. The text is laid out in a modern setting with those aspects of older punctuation that grate most on today's eyes modernized and inconsistencies in formatting standardized. The second is that it is the only edition since the Cecil Palmer edition in London in 1920 to include the full text. All previous American editions omitted important parts of the book. The first U.S. edition, in 1920, omitted half a dozen of the section headers, probably accidentally. The second U.S. Edition, in 1948/1949, omitted those same section headers and Appendix 2: Supplementary Evidence.

Omissions were more extensive in the third U.S. Edition, in 1975. It omitted those things and also Looney's Preliminary Note, Preface, the final paragraph of Chapter XVI: Dramatic Self-Revelation: *Hamlet*, and the entire final chapter titled "Conclusion." In addition, Appendix II is omitted and Chapter XVII: *The Tempest* is heavily edited, with material omitted and other material added with no notice given to the reader.

The 1975 edition was published with Looney's *The Poems of Edward de Vere* in the same volume. Important parts of that book were also dropped. The important "Biographical Outline," which summarized Looney's most important findings in the year since *"Shakespeare" Identified* had been published was omitted. The first third of Looney's "Introduction to the Poems" was also omitted and the part that was included was heavily edited, with material omitted or rewritten and new material added, again with no notice to the reader of these changes.

The following six-page chart compares the five editions and shows where differences occur.

Appendix 3: Comparison of Five Editions of "Shakespeare" Identified

First English Edition	First American Edition	Second American Edition	Third American Edition	Centenary Edition
"Shakespeare" Identified in Edward de Vere the Seventeenth Earl of Oxford by **J. Thomas Looney** **Cecil Palmer** **London (1920)**	*"Shakespeare" Identified in Edward de Vere the Seventeenth Earl of Oxford* by **J. Thomas Looney** **Frederick A. Stokes Company** **New York (1920)**	*"Shakespeare" Identified in Edward de Vere the Seventeenth Earl of Oxford* by **J. Thomas Looney** **Introduction by William McFee** **Afterwords by Charles Wisner Barrell** **Duell, Sloan and Pearce** **New York (1949)**	*"Shakespeare" Identified in Edward de Vere the Seventeenth Earl of Oxford* *and* *The Poems of Edward de Vere* by **J. Thomas Looney** **Third Edition** **Ruth Loyd Miller, Editor** **Published by Kennikat Press for Minos Publishing Company, Jennings, Louisiana: Port Washington (1975)**	*"Shakespeare" Identified in Edward de Vere the Seventeenth Earl of Oxford* by **J. Thomas Looney** **Centenary Edition** **James A. Warren, Editor** **Forever Press** **Somerville MA (2018) /** **Veritas Publication** **Cary, NC (2019)**
Title Page — 3	Title Page — iii	Title Page — iii	Title Page — iii	Title Page — i Editor's Note — i
Preface (December 15, 1919) — 5	Preface (December 15, 1919) — v	Preface (December 15, 1919) — v	[Preface omitted] Dedication to Minos D. Miller, Sr. — v	Preface (December 15, 1919) — v
Contents — 7	Contents — vii	Contents — vii	Contents — vii	Contents — vii List of Illustrations — xii
Preliminary Note — 12	Preliminary Note — xi	Preliminary Note — xi Illustrations — xii The Master Mystery: Introducing J. Thomas Looney's *"Shakespeare" Identified*, by William McFee — xiii-xxi	[Preliminary Noted omitted] Illustrations and Facsimiles — xv Foreword (by Minos D. D. Miller, Jr.: from an address delivered at the Shakespeare Authorship Society Conference to Celebrate the Society's 50th Anniversary, Cambridge, England, July 7-9, 1972) — xix-xliii	Preliminary Note — xiii
Introduction — 13 Chapter I: The Stratfordian View — 23 Chapter II: Character of the Problem and Method of Solution — 90	Introduction — 1 Chapter I: The Stratfordian View — 11 Chapter II: Character of the Problem and Method of Solution — 68	Introduction — 1 Chapter I: The Stratfordian View — 11 Chapter II: Character of the Problem and Method of Solution — 68	Introduction — 1 Chapter I: The Stratfordian View — 11 Chapter II: Character of the Problem and Method of Solution — 68	Introduction — 1 Chapter I: The Stratfordian View — 11 Chapter II: Character of the Problem and Method of Solution — 68

Appendix 3: Comparison of Five Editions of *"Shakespeare" Identified*

Appendix 3: Comparison of Five Editions of *"Shakespeare" Identified*

Edition 1	Edition 2	Edition 3	Edition 4	Edition 5
Index 537	Index 459	Index 467	Index 471	Index 471
Illustrations	**Illustrations**	**Illustrations**	**Illustrations**	**Illustrations**
Edward de Vere, Earl of Oxford — frontispiece	Edward de Vere, Earl of Oxford — frontispiece	Edward de Vere, Earl of Oxford — frontispiece	Edward de Vere, Earl of Oxford — ii, iii	Edward de Vere, Earl of Oxford — frontispiece
			Europa — xxxvii	
			Shaksper's Will — 30A-F	
			Oxford's Prefatory letter to Bedingfield's *Cardanus Comforte* — 133	
			Title Page, *Venus and Adonis* — 162	
William Cecil, Lord Burghley — 252	William Cecil, Lord Burghley — 210	William Cecil, Lord Burghley — 210	William Cecil, Lord Burghley — 210, 246	William Cecil, Lord Burghley — 210
Sir Philip Sidney — 294	Sir Philip Sidney — 246	Sir Philip Sidney — 246	Sir Philip Sidney — 246	Sir Philip Sidney — 246
			Henry de Vere, 18th Earl of Oxford — 375	

Appendix 1: Sources of *The Tempest*, by Ruth Loyd Miller — 438

Appendix II: Chronological Summary of Edward de Vere and Shakespeare [expanded from 6 to 66 pages by Ruth Loyd Miller] — 471

Appendix III: *The Poems of Edward de Vere* by John Thomas Looney [see below for more detail] — 537

Appendix IV: A "Just for Fun" Test for the Lynx-Eyed Scholar in Shakespearology, by Dr. Louis P. Bénézet — 645

Appendix V: John Thomas Looney (1870-1944). Biographical Notes, by Ruth Loyd Miller — 647

Appendix VI: "Mr Looney's Book is Off in a Corner by Itself," from a review of *"Shakespeare" Identified* by Hamilton Basso — 658

[Index is at end of Volume II]

Appendix 3: Comparison of Five Editions of *"Shakespeare" Identified*

Item	Ed. 1	Ed. 2	Ed. 3	Ed. 4	Ed. 5
Henry Wriothesley, Third Earl of Southampton	388	328	328	375	328
Horace, Lord Vere of Tilbury	476	408	408	408	408
Frobisher's unicorn				445	
Martinus Frobisherus, Eques Auratus				446	
Best's Map of Frobisher's Discoveries in 1576-78				447	
Title Page of *The Third and Last Volume of the Voyages, Navigations, Traffiques, and Discoveries of The English Nation,* collected by Richard Hakluyt, 1600				451	
Pages from *The English Voyages*				453-55	
Map of 1582, showing Bermuda				455	
Dedication to the Earle of Oxenforde of *Zelauto* by Anthony Munday, his Servaunt				460	
Title Page, *Dionyse Settler's Report of Frobisher Voyage of 1577*				470	
Great Bronze "cloven pine Cone," Court of the Belverdere, Rome				470	
Vere Arms				471	
Hereditary Crest of Edward de Vere as Lord Bolebec				471	
Vere Cecil Arms				474	
Earl of Oxford bearing the Sword of State, 1572				476	
Tiltyard at Whitehall				479-80	
Dutch visitor's sketch of a London theatre stage, 1596				482	
Pallas Athena, Goddess of the Drama and Useful Arts				495	
Events in Lord Oxford's Life				504	
Lady Mary Vere				508	
Burghley Monument,				515	

[Note: Appendix II: Supplementary Evidence from the 1920 editions is not included in the 1949 edition. Also excluded are references in the Index relating to materials covered in the Supplement, including:
–Droushout engraving
–Grafton, portrait
–Motto of the De Veres
–Oxford's Crest (second reference)
–Posthumous argument and Prof. Sir Walter Raleigh
–Portland, Duke of, and Oxford's Portrait
–Portrait, of Oxford]

Appendix 3: Comparison of Five Editions of *"Shakespeare" Identified*

Westminster	
Vere Trentham Arms	519
Pallas Athena, Goddess of wisdom and the useful arts, patron of the drama	520
The Earl of Oxford's Tomb, 1604	528
Site of Lord Oxford's burial place, 1604	529
Sir Francis Vere	535
Tomb of Sir Francis Vere	535
Title page, 1576 edition of *Paradise of Dainty Devises*	558
John Thomas Looney, 1570-1944	647

[Volume 2: *Oxfordian Vistas*; a collection of articles edited by Ruth Loyd Miller, is not included here.]

The Poems of Edward de Vere, Seventeenth Earl of Oxford

With Biographical Notice, Introduction to the Poems and Notes

By Thomas Looney

Ruth Loyd Miller, Editor

2nd edition
[Note: not published separately; included as Appendix III, pp 537-644, in

"Shakespeare" Identified in Edward de Vere the Seventeenth Earl of Oxford

The Poems of Edward de Vere, Seventeenth Earl of Oxford

With Biographical Notice, Introduction to the Poems and Notes

By J. Thomas Looney

Cecil Palmer, London (1921)

Appendix 3: Comparison of Five Editions of "Shakespeare" Identified

			and *The Poems of Edward de Vere* *by* *J. Thomas Looney* **Third Edition** **Ruth Loyd Miller, Editor**	
Title Page	v		Title Page	537
Foreword	vii			
Contents	ix		Contents	539
Biographical Outline	xiii		[Biographical outline omitted]	
Extract from Puttenham's *Arte of Poesie* (1589)	xxxviii			
Introduction to the Poems	xxxix-lxxvii		Introduction [Looney's	543-558
			"Introduction to the Poems" [Excerpted, edited, and Supplemented by Ruth Loyd Miller]	
			Editor's Note	558-559
Section I: Poems accepted as authentic by Dr. Alexander B. Grosart and published in *The Miscellanies of the Fuller Worthies' Library, Volume IV* (1872), along with a letter written by the poet	1		Section I: Poems accepted as Authentic by Dr. Alexander B. Grosart and published in *The Miscellanies of the Fuller Worthies' Library, Volume IV* (1872), along with a letter written by the poet.	560
First Group. Probably written prior to the crisis of 1576 (age 26)	2		First Group. Probably Written prior to the crisis of 1576 (age 26)	560
			Oxford's Statement of Creative Principles Dominate Shakespeare's Thought and Imagery: Oxford's Prefatory Letter to Thomas Bedingfield's *Cardanus Comforte* and Shakespeare's Works Compared, by Ruth Loyd Miller [continued in next column]	582
Second Group. Poems of the 1576 crisis and after.	22		Second Group. Poems Of the 1576 crisis and after.	580
Section II: Songs written for Lyly's plays whilst he was in the service of the Earl of Oxford (1580-1587)	46		Section II. Songs written for Lyly's plays whilst he was in the service of the Earl of Oxford (1580-1587)	603
Section III. Selected Poems Signed "Ignoto" in *England's Helicon.*	61		Section III. Selected Poems Signed "Ignoto" in *England's Helicon.*	

Appendix 4

Shakespeare Fellowship Officers and Events

Inaugural Meeting – November 6, 1922

Present: Mr. Francis Clarke, Lieutenant R. Dubau, Sir George Greenwood, Rev. and Mrs. Hobart-Hampden, Colonel B. R. Ward, T. Aldred (Chief Librarian, Central Library, Hackney), Mr. A. Hester (St. Kilda's Studio, Clapton), Mr. C. W. Slade (representing *The Hackney Spectator*), A. Walrond Clarke, Mr. Thurkill Cooke, Col. M. W. Douglas, C.S.I., C.I.E.

Officers for 1923: President: Sir George Greenwood. Vice-Presidents: The Hon. Sir John Cockburn, K.C.M.G., M.D.; Professor Abel Lefranc; Mr. J. Thomas Looney; Mr. L. J. Maxse; Mr. William T. Smedley, Executive Committee: Sir George Greenwood; Mr. Francis Clarke; Colonel M. W. Douglas, C.S.I., C.I.E.; Colonel B. R. Ward, C.M.G. (Hon. Sec. and Hon. Treasurer).

First Annual Meeting – October 30, 1923

Present: Canon and Mrs. A. K. Hobart-Hampden and others.

Second Annual Meeting – October 24, 1924

Present: Sir George Greenwood, Katharine Eggar, Mrs. Hunter, Miss Ursula Smithers, Col. Montagu W. Douglas, Col. Bernard R. Ward.

Third Annual Meeting – October 14, 1925

Present: Sir George Greenwood (in the chair), Mrs. Atkinson, Miss Eggar, Miss Smithers, Miss Wend, the Rev. and Mrs. Hobart-Hampden and the Hon. Secretary. Non-members: Mrs. Thurkill Cooke, Rev. Dr. Moor, Mr. Cecil Palmer, Mr. John White.

Officers for 1926: President: Sir George Greenwood. Executive Committee: Mr. Francis Clarke, Col. M. W. Douglas, Miss Ursula Smithers, Col. Ward.

Fourth Annual Meeting – September 18, 1926

Present: Mr. and Mrs. Barley, C. W. Hooper, Col. Montagu W. Douglas, Mrs. Helson, Brig. Gen. E. M. Paul, Miss Ward, Capt. Ward, Col. Ward.

Fifth Annual Meeting – October 7, 1927

Present: Katharine Eggar, Rev. W. Aldworth Ferguson, Rev. Canon and Mrs. Hobart-Hampden, Brig. Gen. E. M. Paul, C.B., C.B.E., Gerald H. Rendall, F. A. Richards, Col. Bernard R. Ward.

Officers for 1928: President: Sir George Greenwood; Executive Committee: Col. Douglas, C.S.I., C.I.E., Mrs. Jackson, Col. Bernard R. Ward, C.M.G.

Sixth Annual Meeting – October 3, 1928

Present: Katharine Eggar, Cecil Palmer, Frank Richards, Gilbert Standen, Capt. Bernard M. Ward, Col. Bernard R. Ward.

Seventh Annual Meeting – September 11, 1929

Present: Canon and Mrs. Hobart-Hampden, Percy Allen and others.

Officers for 1930: President: Lt. Col. Montagu W. Douglas. Vice Presidents: Percy Allen, Prof. Abel Lefranc, J. T. Looney, L. J. Maxse, Cecil Palmer. Executive Committee: Katharine Eggar, Col. Bernard R. Ward, C.M.G., Hon. Secretary, Hon. Treasurer.

First Annual Dinner – April 12, 1930

Present: Col. Bernard R. Ward, Percy Allen, Ernest Allen, Marjorie Bowen, Gerald H. Rendall. Guests: Sir Denys Bray, Ernest Shortt and others.

Eighth Annual Meeting – September 30, 1930 – no report has been found.

Second Annual Dinner – April 27, 1931

Present: Col. Douglas, Percy Allen, Dame May Whitty, Ernest Allen, Cecil Palmer, Col. Bernard R. Ward, Gerald Rendall.

Ninth Annual Meeting – September 30, 1931 – no report has been found.

Officers for 1932: Gerald Rendall and Eva Turner Clark were added as Vice Presidents.**

Third Annual Dinner – May 11, 1932 – no report has been found.

Tenth Annual Meeting – September 8, 1932

Officers for 1933*: President: Lt. Col. W. M. Douglas; Vice Presidents: Percy Allen, Marjorie Bowen, Eva Turner Clark, Adm. H. H. Holland, Prof. Abel Lefranc, Mr. J. T. Looney, Prof. Gilbert Slater. Hon. Sec. and Treasurer: Col. Bernard R. Ward. [The *Circular* dated Nov. 1, 1933 lists as vice presidents only Allen, Clark, Lefranc, Looney and Rendall.]

Fourth Annual Dinner – May 16, 1933

Present: Col. Douglas, Robert and Mrs. Atkins, Dame Adelaide Anderson, Capt. Ward, Robert Atkins, Gerald Rendall, Percy Allen, Ernest Allen.

Eleventh Annual Meeting – September 27, 1933

Present: Col. Douglas, Percy Allen, Capt. Bernard M. Ward, Gerald Rendall, Gerald M. Phillips, many others.

Meeting was followed by debate: "Whether there is sufficient evidence to show that Queen Elizabeth had a son by the Earl of Oxford."

Fifth Annual Dinner – May 16, 1934

Present: Col. Douglas, Percy Allen, Shaw Desmond, Bernard Hall (from Australia), Louis Golding, Mrs. Eriksen.

Twelfth Annual Meeting – September 28, 1934 – no report has been found.

Sixth Annual Dinner – May 13, 1935

Present: Col. Douglas, Mrs. Hobart-Hampden. Guests: Rev. William Paxton, the Hon. Mark Pakington, dramatist, Mr. G. F. Holland, President of the O.P. Club, Driffiled Hawkin, Mrs. Sverre Eriksen.

Thirteenth Annual Meeting – October 2, 1935 – no report has been found.

Officers for 1936***: President Lt. Col. Montagu W. Douglas. Vice Presidents: Sir John Cockburn, Admiral Hubert H. Holland, J. Thomas Looney, Percy Allen, Rev. Dr. Canon Gerald Rendall, Prof. Abel Lefranc, Prof. Georges Connes. Hon Secretary: Capt. Bernard M. Ward.

Seventh Annual Dinner – April 12, 1936 – no report has been found.

1937 Annual Dinner – June 6, 1937

Present: Ernest Allen, D. F. Allen and 44 others.

1937 Annual Meeting – October 17, 1937

Present: Col. Douglas, Capt. Ward, Percy Allen, F. Lingard Ranson, forty others.

Officers for 1938: President: Col. Douglas; Secretary: Capt. Ward; and others.

1938 Annual Dinner – May 11, 1938

Present: 51 members and guests, including Marjorie Bowen, Hermon Ould, Col. Douglas, Percy Allen and T. L. Adamson.

1938 Annual Meeting – October 19, 1938

Present: 15 people attended, including Col. Douglas, Percy and Ernest Allen and T. M. Aitken.

1939 Annual Dinner – May 10, 1939

Present: Percy Allen, Ernest Allen, Marjorie Bowen, J. Foster Forbes, Shaw Desmond, others.

1939 Annual Meeting – Not held, due to the launching of the Second World War

*From Col. Montagu W. Douglas, *Lord Oxford Was "Shakespeare,"* (1934), p. 184.

**From Col. Bernard R. Ward, Letter to Gerald Rendall, October 18, 1931.

***From Eva Turner Clark, Speech at The Colony Club, New York, November 16, 1936.

Shakespeare Fellowship Officers 1940, 1944

	1940 Officers	**1944 Officers**
President	Col. Montagu W. Douglas	Col. Montagu W. Douglas
Hon. Sec.	T. L. Adamson	T. L. Adamson
News-letter editor	Percy Allen	Percy Allen
Hon. Treasurer	J. J. Dwyer	J. J. Dwyer
Hon. Asst. Sec.	Phyllis Carrington	Phyllis Carrington
Executive Committee	Douglas, Adamson, Allen, Dwyer, Atkinson	Not known

Elected at the August 22, 1945 General Meeting

President: Percy Allen

Vice Presidents: Mrs. Arthur Long (Marjorie Bowen), Mrs. Eva Turner Clark, Adm. H. H. Holland, C.B., Professor Abel Lefranc, Capt. Bernard M. Ward.

News-Letter Editor: Percy Allen and J. J. Dwyer, Joint Editors

Hon. Treasurer: J. J. Dwyer

Hon. Secretary: T. L. Adamson

Committee: President, Treasurer, Secretary, and J. Shera Atkinson and William Kent

Elected at the Fall 1946 General Meeting

President: Adm. H. H. Holland, C.B. (until end of 1955)

Vice Presidents: Canon Demant (through 1951), T. L. Adamson (at least through 1958), William Kent (through 1953), Mrs. Arthur Long (Marjorie Bowen), Eva Turner Clark (until 1947)

Secretary-Treasurer: H. Cutner (through 1949)

Secretary: Mrs. Robbins (1950-1953)

Treasurer: J. Shera Atkinson (1950-1958)

Editor of the *News-Letter*: William Kent (through 1953)

Appendix 5

Chronological Timeline of Oxfordian Events and Publications –
❖ In England, 1920-1945
❖ In North America, 1920-1948

[Due to the maximum number of pages allowed by the printer, only a short excerpt of the Timeline can be included. The full Timeline is available at the website of Veritas Publications, at veritaspublications.net.]

EVENTS, LETTERS & SF CIRCULARS	PUBLICATIONS
	1930, September 25 Rendall, Gerald. "Shakespeare's Handwriting and Orthography" [response to Byrne's review of Allen's *Case*], *Times Literary Supplement*, issue 1495: 757.
	1930, September 27 Aitcheff. "Week After Week," *The Graphic*, p. 486.
1930, September 30 SF Annual General Meeting	
	1930, October Connes, Georges. [review of Standen's *Shakespeare Authorship*], *Revue Anglo-Américaine*, vol. 8: 253-54. [in French] Connes, Georges. [review of Clark's *Shakespeare's Plays in the Order of Their Writing*], *Revue Anglo-Américaine*, vol. 8: 439-40. Connes, Georges. [review of Rendall's *Shake-speare's Handwriting and Spelling*], *Revue Anglo-Américaine*, vol. 8: 544. [in French] Pruvost, Rene. [review of Allen's *Topical*], *Revue Anglo-Américaine*, vol. 8: 149-50. Ward, Colonel B. R. "Which Was the Earliest Propaganda Play?" *Shakespeare Pictorial*, no. 32: 16. Ward, Colonel B. R. [review of Standen's *Sh. Authorship*], *Shakespeare Pictorial*, no. 32: 16. Ward, Colonel B. R. "Mr. Allen's Lectures," *Sh. Pictorial*, no. 32: 16.
1930, October 5 SF *Circular*: Annual Meeting held Sept. 30	
	1930, October 8 -----. "Playgoers' Circle Plymouth" [report on Allen's lecture], *Western Morning News*, p. 4.
	1930, October 18 Allen, Percy. "The de Vere-Shakespeare Controversy Today," *Christian Science Monitor*, p. 18. [reprinted in *China Press* (Shanghai), Dec. 4, 1930, p. 14.
1930, October 23 Percy Allen lecture at the British Drama League: "The Case for Oxford as Shakespeare I: Oxford in the Sonnets"	
	1930, October 28 Pogson, Reugen "Shakespeare Was Not an Earl," *New York Sun*.
1930, October 30 Percy Allen lecture at the British Drama League: "The Case for Oxford as Shakespeare II: Oxford in Some Comedies"	

1930, November
 Ward, Colonel B. R. "Henry Wriothesley and Henry De Vere,"
  Shakespeare Pictorial, no. 33: 16.
 Boissevan, K. D. W. "The Farnese Library," *Sh. Pictorial*, no. 33: 16.
1930, November 1
 Thurston, Herbert. "'Mr. W. H.' of Shakespeare's Sonnets," *The Month*,
  vol. 156/797: 425-437.
1930, November 4
 PA [Percy Allen]. "Shakespearean Research" [review of Standen's
  Shakespearean Authorship], *Christian Science Monitor*, p. 6.

1930, November 6
 Percy Allen lecture at the British Drama League:
  "The Case for Oxford as Shakespeare III: Oxford in the Great Tragedies"

1930, November 7
 Ernest Allen debates Dr. W. E. Peck: "The Case for the
  17th Earl of Oxford as the Author of the Shakespeare Plays"
1930, November 8
 -----. "Shakespeare Discussion in Bath," *Bath Chronicle and
  Weekly Gazette*, p. 12.

1930, November 13
 Percy Allen lecture at the British Drama League:
  "The Case for Oxford as Shakespeare IV: "Late Spurious
  Plays; and Burlesques of Oxford as Shakespeare in the
  Plays of Chapman and Jonson"
1930, November 13
 Harrison, G. B. "Shakespeare's Topical Significances I: *King John*,"
  Times Literary Supplement, issue 1502: 939.
1930, November 15
 -----. "Surprise at Bath Meeting," *Bath Chronicle and Weekly Gazette*, p.
  15.
1930, November 20
 Harrison, G. B. "Shakespeare's Topical Significances II: The Earl of
  Essex," *Times Literary Supplement*, issue 1502: 939.

1930, November 21
 SF Circular: Percy's Allen's "The de Vere-Shakespeare
  Controversy Today" in *The Christian Science Monitor*
1930, November around the 23rd
 Percy Allen lecture at the Playgoers' Club
1930, November 22
 -----. "Shakespeariana," *The Age* [Melbourne, Australia], p. 6.

1930, November 24
 -----. [report on Percy Allen's lecture], *Nottingham Journal*, p. 4.

1930, November 25
 Dixon-Scott, J. "A Suffolk Tudor Village—Lavenham's Wattle Walls &
  Lovely Tudor Lavenham," *The Telegraph*, p. 14.

1930, November 26
 Steed, Wickham. "Protecting the Old Church" [letter], *Telegraph*.

1930, December
 Ward, Col. Bernard R. "A Challenge and Its Acceptance," *Sh. Pictorial*,
  no. 34: 16.

1930, December 4
 Allen, Percy. "The De Vere-Shakespeare Controversy Today," *China
  Press* (Shanghai).

1930, December 24
 Pogson, Reuben. [letter: Percy Allen's Oct. 18 article], *Christian
  Science Monitor*.

Bibliography

A. Sr. J. A.
  1920   "Shakespeare and the Lilliputians," *The Bookman*, May, p. 84.
  1923   "Shakespeare's Ghosts," *The Bookman,* April, pp. 34-35.
A. W.
  1828   "A Forgotten Elizabethan," *The Daily Telegraph*, May 4, p. 6.
Aberdeen Daily Journal
  1920   "Shakespeare," April 5, p. 5.
Aberdeen Press and Journal
  1922   "Bacon-Shakespeare Controversy," October 23, p. 2.
  1923   "Yet Another 'Shakespeare,'" March 26, p. 2.
  1923   "Shakespeare and Oxford," June 5, p. 5.
  1933   "A Plea for Oxford," November 21, p. 2.
  1934   "Writings on Shakespeare," April 3, p. 2.
A'Dair, Mike
  Screenplays
  2017   *The Ashbourne Saga: A Cinematic Epic in Fourteen Episodes*. Lulu.
  Articles
  2010   "Charles Wisner Barrell: A Biographical Sketch," *Shakespeare Matters*, vol. 9, no. 1
          (Winter): 1, 14-21.
Adams, Joseph Quincey
  1917   *Shakespearean Playhouses: A History of English Theatres from the Beginnings to the
          Restoration* (Gloucester, MA: P. Smith).
Adamson, T. L.
  Articles
  1955   "Shakespeare and Oxford in the Lecture Room," *Shakespeare Fellowship News-Letter*,
          Spring, p. 7.
  1959   "Percy Allen" [obituary], *Shakespearean Authorship Review*, no. 1 (Spring): 22-23.
  Personal letters
  1943   Letter to Charles Barrell [date not stated] [excerpts reprinted in "Letters from England,"
          Shakespeare Fellowship News-Letter (American), vol. 4, no. 5 (August): 67-68.]
Adler, Mortimer J.
  Books
  1978   *Aristotle for Everybody: Difficult Thought Made Easy* (New York: Touchstone).
  1985   *Ten Philosophical Mistakes: Basic Errors in Modern Thought—How They Came About,
          Their Consequences, and How to Avoid Them* (New York: Macmillan).
  1990   *Intellect: Mind Over Matter* (New York: Macmillan).
  1991   *Desires Right & Wrong: The Ethics of Enough* (New York: Macmillan).
  1996   *The Time of Our Lives: The Ethics of Common Sense* (New York: Fordam University Press).
          [1970]
  Personal Letters
  1997   Letter to Max Weismann , November 7. [Reprinted in *The Great Ideas Online*, no. 203
          (November 2002): 7-8]
Advocate, The (Melbourne, Australia)
  1920   "Who Wrote Shakespeare?" May 20, p. 3.
Age, The (Melbourne, Australia)
  1930   "Shakespearian Problems," March 15, p. 4.
Aitken, T. M.
  Articles
  1938   "A New Shakespeare Candidate" [letter], *British Weekly*, January 20, p. 314.
  1938   "A Criticism of *An Enquiry*," *Shakespeare Fellowship News-Letter*, no. 14, Supplement 1

(April): 5-9.

1957   "Lieut.-Col. Montagu W. Douglas" [obituary], *Sh. Fellowship News-Letter*, Spring, p. 11.

Personal letters

1938   Letter to Gerald H. Rendall, November 29. [Gerald H. Rendall Archives, University of Liverpool]

Alexander, Doris

1996   *Creating Literature Out of Life: The Making of Four Masterpieces* (University Park: Pennsylvania State University Press).

Allen, D. F.

1937   "The Annual Dinner," *Shakespeare Fellowship News-Letter*, no. 4 (July): 6.

1938   "The Annual Dinner," *Shakespeare Fellowship News-Letter*, no. 10 (July): 2.

Allen, Ernest

Books

1933   *Lord Oxford & "Shakespeare:" A Reply to John Drinkwater: A Ruthless Exposure of Faulty Thinking* (London: Denis Archer). [with Percy Allen]

Articles and reviews

1932   "Annual Dinner," *The Shakespeare Pictorial*, no. 53 (July): 116.

1936   "Claimants to 'Shakespeare' Authorship," *The Shakespeare Pictorial*, no. 101 (July): 116.

1936   "In Reply," *The Shakespeare Pictorial*, no. 106 (September): 136.

1937   "Correspondence," *East Anglian Magazine*, vol. 3, no. 3 (December): 142.

1938   "Correspondence," *Shakespeare Fellowship News-Letter*, no. 8 (March): 12-13.

Allen, Percy

Books and pamphlets

1928   *Shakespeare, Jonson, and Wilkins as Borrowers* (London: Cecil Palmer).

1928   *Shakespeare as a Topical Dramatist* (London: The Poetry League). [pamphlet]

1929   *Shakespeare and Chapman as Topical Dramatists* (London: Cecil Palmer).

1929   *Declaration of Faith/Manifesto of Conversion* [Shakespeare Fellowship *Circular*]

1930   *The Case for Edward de Vere, 17th Earl of Oxford, as "Shakespeare"* [pamphlet]

1930   *The Case for Edward de Vere, 17th Earl of Oxford, as "Shakespeare"* (London: Cecil Palmer).

1931   *The Oxford-Shakespeare Case Corroborated* (London: Cecil Palmer).

1932   *The Life-Story of Edward de Vere as "William Shakespeare"* (London: Cecil Palmer).

1933   *Lord Oxford & "Shakespeare:" A Reply to John Drinkwater: A Ruthless Exposure of Faulty Thinking* (London: Denis Archer). [with Ernest Allen]

1933   *The Plays of Shakespeare & Chapman in Relation to French History* (London: Denis Archer).

1934   *Anne Cecil, Elizabeth & Oxford* (London: (Denis Archer).

1936   *An Enquiry into the Relations Between Lord Oxford as "Shakespeare," Queen Elizabeth and the Fair Youth* [London: Percy Allen] [pamphlet, with Capt. Bernard M. Ward]

1943   *Who Were the Dark Lady and the Fair Youth of Shakespeare's Sonnets?* (printed privately)

1946   *Talks with Elizabethans: Revealing the Mystery of William Shakespeare* (London, New York: Rider). [Also attributed to Hester Dowden]

Articles, reviews and published letters

1923   "Hamlet's Identity With an Elizabethan," *The Christian Science Monitor*, May 19, p. D7.

1928   "Shakespeare, Jonson and Wilkins" [letter], *Saturday Review*, issue 145 (March 31): 388.

1928   "Shakespeare, Jonson and Wilkins as Borrowers" [letter], *The Manchester Guardian*, April 4, p. 5.

1928   "Shakespeare, Jonson and Wilkins" [letter], *Saturday Review*, April 14, pp. 462-463.

1928   "The Historic Originals of Ophelia," *The Shakespeare Review*, July, pp. 166-171.

1928   "Versatile Elizabethan: Willful Young Earl," *The Christian Science Monitor*, July 3, p. 12.

1929   "Rhyme-Linked Order of Shakespeare's Sonnets," *The Christian Science Monitor*, January 18, p. 4.

1929   "Elizabeth and Essex" [letter], *The Times Literary Sup.*, issue 1410 (February 7): 98.

1929   "Shakespeare and Chapman as Topical Dramatist" [letter], *Saturday Review*, March 2, p. 281.

1929   "Shakespeare and Chapman," *The Times Literary Sup.*, issue 1417 (March 28): 260.

1929   "Topical Dramatists" [letter], *The Stage*, May 30, p. 15.

1929   "Authorship of the Sonnets" [letter], *Daily Telegraph*, June 5.

1929   "Shakespeare and Chapman," *London Mercury*, vol. XX, no. 119 (September).

1929   "Shakespeare and Chapman," *The Times Literary Sup.*, issue 1443 (September 29): 747.

1930   [untitled letter], *Review of English Studies*, vol. 6, no. 22 (April): 196-198.

1930   "Fiddlesticks" [letter], *Saturday Review*, vol. 149 (May 17): 619.

1930   "Oxford as 'Shakespeare,'" *The Times Literary Sup.*, issue 1494 (September 18): 735.

1930   "The de Vere-Shakespeare Controversy Today," *Christian Sci. Monitor*, October 18, p. 18.

1931   "The de Vere-Shakespeare Controversy" [letter], *Christian Sci. Monitor*, February 9, p. 14.

1931   "The Oxford Theory Again," *Christian Science Monitor*, February 28, p. 6.

1931   "The Oxford-Shakespeare Theory" [letter], *Christian Science Monitor*, June 5, p. 20.

1931   "The Shakespeare-Oxford Problem" [letter], *Saturday Review*, vol. 152 (September 12): 327.

1932   "As to Shakespearean Authorship," *Christian Science Monitor*, January 9, p. 7.

1932   "For the Stratfordians," *Christian Science Monitor*, May 21, 1932, p. 10.

1932   "The Essential Shakespeare," *The Shakespeare Pictorial*, no. 52 (June): 100.

1932   "De Vere and Shakespeare," *Saturday Review*, vol. 153 (June 11): 591.

1932   "Edward de Vere," *Times Literary Supplement*, issue 1597 (June 30): 480.

1932   "The Inner Story of *Twelfth Night*," *The Shakespeare Pictorial*, no. 56 (October): 164.

1932   "Shakespeare in the East," *Christian Science Monitor*, October 1, p. 6.

1932   "As You Like It," *Christian Science Monitor*, December 3, p. 10.

1933   "King Lear—The Castle and the Storm: An Adventure in Burgundy," *The Shakespeare Pictorial*, no. 60 (February): 22-23.

1933   "Mr. John Drinkwater," *The Shakespeare Pictorial*, no. 61 (March): 37.

1933   "New Shakespearean Books," *Christian Science Monitor*, April 22, p. 10.

1933   "Sir Edmund Chambers and Shakespeare Orthodoxy," *The Shakespeare Pictorial*, no. 63 (May): 80.

1933   "History and Plays" [letter], *The Times Literary Supplement*, issue 1645 (August 10): 537.

1933   "Shakespeare at Work," *The Shakespeare Pictorial*, no. 69 (November): 176.

1934   "The 'Mortal Moon' Sonnet" [letter], *The Times Literary Supplement*, issue 1675 (March 8): 162.

1934   "Topicalities in Shakespeare," *Theatre and Stage*, vol. 13 (April): 585-86.

1934   "Elizabeth, Anne Cecil and Oxford" [letter], *The Times Literary Supplement*, issue 1684 (May 10): 342.

1934   "A Year's Results Epitomised," *The Shakespeare Pictorial*," no. 77 (July): 112.

1934   "Shakespearean Topicalities," *Christian Science Monitor*, October 3, p. WM10.

1935   "Our Year's Activities," *The Shakespeare Pictorial*, no. 88 (June): 93.

1935   "Sunlight on Shakespeare's Sonnets," *The Shakespeare Pictorial*, no. 89 (July): 112.

1935   "Lord Oxford as Shakespeare" [letter], *The Times Literary Supplement*, issue 1757 (October 3): 612.

1935   "Hamlet, Topically," *Christian Science Monitor*," December 4, p. WM12.

1936   "More *Hamlet* Problems," *The Shakespeare Pictorial*, no. 96 (February): 36.

1936   "Stage or Study?" [letter], *The Times Literary Supplement*, issue 1788 (May 9): 400.

1936   "Names in *The Winter's Tale*" [letter], *The Times Literary Supplement*, issue 1798 (July 18): 600.

1936   "Topical Events in Drama of Shakespeare's Age," *The Shakespeare Pictorial*, no. 102 (August): 132.

1936   "Another Bombshell for the Orthodox," *The Shakespeare Pictorial*, no. 104 (October): 164.

1937   "Shakespearean Adventures in Canada and the United States, *Shakespeare Fellowship News-Letter*, no. 1 (January): 2-7.

1937   "The Date of *Hamlet*" [letter], *Times Literary Supplement*, issue 1827 (January 2): 12.

1937   "Dr. Cairncross and *Hamlet*," *Shakespeare Fellowship News-Letter*, no. 8 (March): 9-10.

1937   "Was Oxford Shakespeare?" [letter], *Western Morning News*, April 28, p. 11.

1937   "Shakespeare and Montaigne," *Shakespeare Fellowship News-Letter*, no. 3 (May): 6.

1937   "Lord Oxford as Shakespeare," *East Anglian Magazine*, vol. 2, no. 8 (May): 340-43.

1938   "[review of *I, William Shakespeare* by Leslie Hotson], *Shakespeare Fellowship News-letter*, no. 7 (January): 3-5.

1938   "Shakespeare Rediscovered," *Shakespeare Fellowship News-Letter*, no. 9 (May): 6-7.

1938   "Recent Books on the Sonnets," *Shakespeare Fellowship News-Letter*, no. 9 (May): 7-9.

1938   "The First Anti-Stratfordian," *Sh. Fellowship News-Letter*, no. 11 (September): 1-5.

1938   "Commentary on *Life and Adventures of Common Sense* by Herbert Lawrence," *Shakespeare Fellowship News-Letter*, no. 12 (November): 2-16.

1938   "How Lawrence Acquired His Information," *Shakespeare Fellowship News-Letter*, no. 12 (November): 17-18.

1939   "Who Was Shakespeare?" *John O'London's Weekly*, February 10, p. 821.

1939   "Mr. Percy Allen's Reply," *Supplement 1, Shakespeare Fellowship News-Letter*, no. 14 (April): 18-19.

1939   "Annual Dinner," *Shakespeare Fellowship News-Letter*, no. 15 (July): 1.

1939   "The Other View-Point," *East Anglian Magazine*, vol. 4, no. 9 (August): 534-435.

1940   "Shakespeare's *Cymbeline* and East Anglia," *East Anglian Magazine*, vol. 5, no. 4 (May): 153-154.

1942   "Melford Hall and Shakespeare," *Shakespeare Fellowship News-Letter*, April, p. 3-4.

1942   "Sir Edward Vere and Mr. Barrell's Discovery," *Shakespeare Fellowship News-Letter*, Oct. 1942, p. 2.

1942   "Shake-speare Speaks Again?" [letter], *Shakespeare Fellowship News-Letter*, October, p. 4.

1944   "John Thomas Looney (1870-1944): A Biographical Sketch," *Shakespeare Fellowship News-Letter*, May, pp. 2-4.

1944   "The Elizabethan Mind," *Shakespeare Fellowship News-Letter*, May, p. 6.

1944   "Francis Bacon's Share in the Shakespeare Folio of 1623," *Shakespeare Fellowship News-Letter*, May, p. 8.

1945   "The Group Theory and Some Modern Intellectuals," *Shakespeare Fellowship News-Letter*, May, p. 4.

1945   "Editorial Notes: The General Meeting," *Sh. Fellowship News-Letter*, November, pp. 1-2.

Personal Letters

1936   Letter to J. Thomas Looney, Dec. 14. [1] [JTL papers]

1936   Letter to J. Thomas Looney, Dec. 14. [2] [JTL papers]

1937   Letter to J. Thomas Looney, June 26. [JTL papers]

1938   Letter to H. E. Wilson, August 17. [JW]

1939   Letter to J. Thomas Looney, June 26. [JTL papers]

1941   Letter to Charles Wisner Barrell, March. (Excerpt reprinted in *Shakespeare Fellowship News-Letter* (American), vol. 2, no. 3 (April 1941): 36.

Altrocchi, Julia Cooley

1971   "From Mrs. Julia Cooley Altrocchi," *Shakespeare Oxford Society Newsletter*, vol. 7/1 (March): 3.

Altrocchi, Paul H.

Books

2010   *Malice Aforethought: The Killing of a Unique Genius* (Xlibris Corporation).

2009   *Building the Case for Edward de Vere as Shakespeare* [Ten-volume anthology of Oxfordian articles; Hank Whittemore served as co-editor of the first five volumes]

2009   *vol. 1: The Great Shakespeare Hoax* (iUniverse.com).

2009   *vol. 2: Nothing Truer Than Truth* (iUniverse.com).

2009   *vol. 3: Shine Forth* (iUniverse.com).

2009   *vol. 4: My Name Be Buried* (iUniverse.com).

2009   *vol. 5: So Richly Spun* (iUniverse.com).

2014   *vol. 6: Wonder of Our Stage* (iUniverse.com).

2014   *vol. 7: Avalanche of Falsity* (iUniverse.com).

2014   *vol. 8: To All the World Must Die* (iUniverse.com).

2014   *vol. 9: Soul of the Age* (iUniverse.com).

2014   *vol. 10: Moniment* (iUniverse.com).

Articles

2005   "A Royal Shame: The Origins and History of the Prince Tudor Theory," *Shakespeare Matters*, vol. 4, no. 4 (Summer): 1, 12-17.

2006   "Bermoothes: An Intriguing Enigma," *Shakespeare Matters*, vol. 5, no. 3 (Spring): 10-15.

2006   "Ideational Change: Why Is It So Difficult?" *Shakespeare Oxford Newsletter* , vol. 42, no. 4 (Fall redux): 24-29.

Alvis, John and Thomas G. West

1981   *Shakespeare as Political Thinker* (Durham, North Carolina: Carolina Academic Press)

American Council of Trustees and Alumni (ACTA)
    2007   *The Vanishing Shakespeare* (Washington, D.C.: ACTA).
    2015   *The Unkindest Cut: Shakespeare in Exile 2015* (Washington, D.C.: ACTA).

Anderson, Mark
    Books
    2005   *"Shakespeare" By Another Name: The Life of Edward de Vere, Earl of Oxford, the Man Who was Shakespeare* (New York: Gotham Books)
    Books edited with Alexander Waugh and Alex McNeil
    2016   *Contested Year: An Anthology of Critical Reviews and Corrections to Each Chapter of James Shapiro's The Year of Lear: Shakespeare in 1606.*
    Articles
    1996   "A Little More than Kuhn, And Less than Kind," *Shakespeare Oxford Newsletter*, vol. 32/1 (Winter): 12-14.

Angell, Pauline K.
    1937   "Light on the Dark Lady," *PMLA*, vol. 52, no. 3 (September): 652-74.
    1940   "Light on the Dark Lady," *PMLA*, vol. 55, no. 2 (June): 599.

Argonaut, The
    1940   "Who Was Shakespeare?" January 26.

Athenaeum, The
    1920   "Another Shakespeare," April 2, p. 450.
    1920   "Correspondence: *'Shakespeare' Identified*," April 16, p. 521.

Athos
    1921   "The Real Shakespeare," *The Bulletin* [Australia], October 27, p. 25.

Atlantic Monthly, The
    1932   Letter to J. Thomas Looney, December 30.

Avon Gazette and York Times [Australia]
    1920   "Out and About," May 22, p. 2.

B. E. S. S.
    1928   "Shakespeare and Chapman," *The Stage*, October 11, p. 17.

B. H. N. [see B. H. Newdigate]

Bacon, Delia
    1856   "William Shakespeare and His Play; An Inquiry Concerning Them," *Putnam's Monthly*, January, pp. 3-21.

Bagehot, Walter
    1999   *Physics and Politics* (Chicago: Ivan R. Dee). [1872]

Barker, H. Granville & G. B. Harrison
    1934   *A Companion to Shakespeare Studies* (Cambridge: The University Press).

Barrell, Charles Wisner
    Books and booklets
    1940   *Elizabethan Mystery Man* (New York: August Gauthier). [booklet]
    Articles
    1937   "Elizabethan Mystery Man," *Saturday Review of Literature*, vol. 12 (May 1): 11-15.
    1937   "The Oxford Theory," *Saturday Review of Literature*," vol. 16 (May 22): 9.
    1937   "Alias William Shakespeare? The Man Behind the Plays," *New York Sun*, December 11.
    1939   "To Pluck the Heart of the Mystery," *Shakespeare Fellowship News-Letter* (American), vol. 1, no. 1 (December): 1-2.
    1940   "Identifying 'Shakespeare,'" *Scientific American*, vol. 162 (January): 4-8, 43+.
    1940   "The Secret Personality of 'Shakespeare' Brought to Light After Three Centuries," *Shakespeare Fellowship News-Letter* (American), vol. 1, no. 2 (February): 1-4.
    1940   "Mountainous Error," *Shakespeare Fellowship News-Letter* (American), vol. 1, no. 3 (April-May): 7-8.
    1941   "Shakespeare's 'Fluellen' Identified as a Retainer of the Earl of Oxford," *Shakespeare Fellowship News-Letter* (American), vol. 2, no. 5 (August): 59-62.
    1942   "'Shake-speare's' Own Secret Drama, Part 2," *Shakespeare Fellowship News-Letter* (American), vol. 3, no. 2 (February): 13-17, 23.
    1942   "'Shake-speare's' Own Secret Drama, Part 3," *Shakespeare Fellowship News-Letter*

(American), vol. 3, no. 3 (April): 25-33.

1942   "'Shake-speare's' Own Secret Drama, Part 5," *Shakespeare Fellowship Newsletter* (American), vol. 3, no. 5): 57-65.

1942   "'Shake-speare's' Own Secret Drama, Part 6," *Shakespeare Fellowship Newsletter* (American), vol. 3, no. 6): 69-77.

1942   "Shakespeare's Unknown Home on the River Avon Discovered," *Shakespeare Fellowship News-Letter* (American), vol. 4, no. 1 (December): 1-8.

1944   "Lord Oxford as Supervising Patron of Shakespeare's Theatrical Company," *Shakespeare Fellowship Quarterly*, vol. V, no. 3 (July): 33-40.

1944   "New Milestone in Shakespearean Research: 'Gentle Master William,'" *Shakespeare Fellowship Quarterly*, vol. V, no. 4 (October): 49-66.

1945   "'Creature of Their Own Creating:' An Answer to the Present Day School of Shakespearean Biography," *Shakespeare Fellowship Quarterly*, vol. VI, no. 4 (October): 59-60.

1946   "Verifying the Secret History of Shake-speare's Sonnets," *Tomorrow*, February.

1948   "Afterwords," in J. Thomas Looney, *"Shakespeare" Identified* (1948), pp. 454-466.

1975   "The Strange Silence of William Shakespeare's Son-in-Law, Dr. John Hall of Stratford-on-Avon," *Oxfordian Vistas*, edited by Ruth Loyd Miller, pp. 286-289.

Personal letters

1940   Letter to J. Thomas Looney, February 16. [JTL papers]

1940   Letter to J. Thomas Looney, March 16. [JTL papers]

1940   Letter to J. Thomas Looney, March 22. [JTL papers]

1940   Letter to Gerald H. Rendall, May 6. [Rendall Archives]

1941   Letter to Percy Allen, December 21, 1941 [Excerpt reprinted in "Charles Wisner Barrell and Our American Branch," *Shakespeare Fellowship Newsletter*, April 1942, p. 3.]

1945   Letter to Percy Allen, March 8, 1945 [Excerpt reprinted in "The Group Theory and Some Modern Intellectuals," *Shakespeare Fellowship News-Letter*, May 1945, p. 4.]

Barrett, W. P.

1939   "Who Was Shakespeare? III: The Traditional View," *John O'London's Weekly*, Feb. 10, p. 733.

1939   "Who Was Shakespeare?" [letter], *John O'London's Weekly*, February 21, p. 822.

Basso, Hamilton

1950   "The Big Who-Done-It," *The New Yorker*, pp. 113-114, 117-119.

Bath Weekly Chronicle and Herald

1941   "Shakespeare Under the Microscope: A Literary Visitor," February 8, p. 18.

1941   "Don't Marry a Genius," February 8, p. 18.

Baxter, James Phinney

1915   *The Greatest of All Literary Problems* (New York: AMS Press).

Bayne, Rev. Ronald

1907   "Lesser Elizabethan Dramatists," in *Cambridge History of English Literature*, vol. 5, Chapter 13, pp. 309-355 (Cambridge, England: University Press).

Beauclerk, Charles

Books

2010   *Shakespeare's Lost Kingdom: The True History of Shakespeare and Elizabeth* (New York: Grove Press).

Articles

2003   "John Louther: A Recollection," *Shakespeare Oxford Newsletter*, vol. 39, no. 2 (Spring): 20.

2005   [letter], *Shakespeare Matters*, vol. 4, no. 3 (Spring): 2.

Bénézet, Louis P.

Books

1937   *Shakspere, Shakespeare and de Vere* (Manchester, NH: Granite State Press).

1958   *The Six Loves of Shakespeare* (New York: Pageant Press, Inc.).

Articles

1939   "President Bénézet's Message," *Shakespeare Fellowship Newsletter* (American), vol. 1, no. 1 (December): 1.

1939   "Youthful Minds are Open," *Shakespeare Fellowship News-Letter* (American), vol. 1, no. 1 (December): 4.

1944   "The Frauds and Stealths of Injurious Imposters," *Shakespeare Fellowship Quarterly*, vol. V, no. 1 (January): 2-6.

1944   "The Stratford Defendant Compromised by His Own Advocates, Part One," *Shakespeare Fellowship Quarterly*, vol. v, no. 3 (July): 44-46.

1946   "Another Stratfordian Aids the Oxford Cause," *Shakespeare Fellowship Quarterly*, vol. VII, no. 2 (April): 17-19.

1947   "Dr. Smart's Man of Stratford Outsmarts Credulity," *Shakespeare Fellowship Quarterly*, vol. VIII, no. 2 (Summer): 27-31.

Personal letters

1938   Letter to J. Thomas Looney, January 29. [JTL papers]

Benham, Sir W. Gurney

1920   "Edward de Vere, Earl of Oxford, 'Identified' as Shakespeare," *The Essex Review*, vol. 29 (April 1): 95-100.

Bennett, Josephine Waters

1942   "Oxford and *Endimion*," *PMLA*, vol. 57, no. 2 (June): 354-369.

Benson, Jon

2016   *The Death of Shakespeare As It Was Accomplisht in 1616 & The Causes Thereof, Part One* (Annapolis, MD: Nedward, LLC).

2016   *The Reader's Companion to The Death of Shakespeare, Part One* (Annapolis, MD: Nedward, LLC).

Berg, A. Scott

2016   *Max Perkins: Editor of Genius* (New York: New American Library). [1978]

Berney, Charles V.

Books

2017   *Shakespeare Confidential* (Somerville, MA: Forever Press).

Articles and reviews

2000   "Sir Walter Scott as Paleo-Oxfordian, Part 1," *Shakespeare Oxford Newsletter*, vol. 36, no. 3 (Fall): 17.

2003   "Sir Walter Scott as Paleo-Oxfordian, Part 2," *Sh. Matters*, vol. 3, no. 1 (Fall): 30-32.

Bethell, Tom

1991   "The Case for Oxford" [part of the cover story "Looking for Shakespeare: Two Partisans Explain and Debate the Authorship Question"], *Atlantic Monthly*, vol. 268, no. 4 (October): 44-61.

Birmingham Daily Post

1945   "Canon G. H. Rendall" [obituary], January 8, p. 4.

Birmingham Daily Gazette

1931   "Old Controversy. Who Wrote Shakespeare's Plays?" December 14, p. 7.

Björkman, Edwin

1920   "Shakespeare?" *The Bookman*, vol. 51, no. 6 (August): 677-682.

Blackheath Local Guide and District Advertiser

1940   "A Humble Petition," April 6, pp. 14-15.

Blunden, Mark

2009   "Shakespeare Did Not Write His Own Plays, Claims Jacobi," *The Evening Standard* (April 23): 19.

Boas, F. S

1933   "Shakespeare, Oxford and Elizabethan Times," *The Observer*, December 3, p. 3.

Bodell, Evelyn

1942   Letter to Percy Allen, October 14, 1942. [reprinted in "Editorial Notes," *Shakespeare Fellowship News-Letter*, May 1943, p. 1.]

Bone, Capt. F. D.

Personal letters

1941   Letter to Charles Barrell, date not stated. [excerpt reprinted in "Letters from England," *Shakespeare Fellowship News-Letter* (American), vol. 2, no. 3 (April): 36.]

Book, Lois Adelaide

Personal letters

1939   Letter to J. Thomas Looney, May 10. [JTL papers]

1940   Letter to J. Thomas Looney, April 15. [JTL papers]

Book Bulletin of the Chicago Public Library Book Bulletin, The
1920   "Literature," vol. 11, no. 10 (December): 157.

Bookman The: A Review of Literature and Life
1920   "Looking Ahead with the Publishers," vol. 51, no. 4 (June): 499.
1921   "Notes on New Books," vol. 60, no. 356 (May): 78.

Bookman's Journal & Print Collector, The
1920   "A New Mask for Shakespeare," vol. 1, no. 21 (March 19): 408.
1920   "Is Shakespeare Identified?" vol. 1, no. 24 (April 9): 452-453.
1921   "Stratford and Stony Stratford," vol. 3, no. 71 (March 4): 335.

Boston Globe, The
1931   "Claims Earl of Oxford was Really Shakespeare," February 7, p. 17.

Bowen, Gwynneth M.
1959   "Ave Atque Vale," *Shakespearean Authorship Review*, no. 1 (Spring): 3-5.

Bowen, Marjorie
Articles and reviews
1929   "Shakespeare and Richard III: Little Evidence and 'A Mass of Legend and Calumny'"
        [letter], *The Morning Post*, August 30, p. 7.
1929   "Shakespeare and Richard III" [letter], *The Morning Post*, September 14, p. 7.
1932   "The Identity of 'William Shakespeare,'" *The Shakespeare Pictorial*, no. 51 (May): 82.
1933   "Introduction" to Percy Allen's *The Plays of Shakespeare & Chapman in Relation to French
        History*.
1933   "*Shakespeare* by John Drinkwater," *The Shakespeare Pictorial*, no. 62 (April): 64.
1934   "Anne Cecil, Elizabeth and Oxford," *The Shakespeare Pictorial*, no. 73 (March): 48.
1946   "April 23 Doesn't Impress Me: Why? Because I Don't Believe in Shakespeare," *Strand
        Magazine*, vol. 111 (March): 26.

Personal letters
1942   Letter to Charles Barrell, April 18, 1942. [Excerpt reprinted in "London Letter,"
        Shakespeare Fellowship News-Letter (American), vol. 3, no. 4 (June): 53-54.]
1942   Letter to Charles Barrell, undated. [Excerpt reprinted in "From Letters Received,"
        Shakespeare Fellowship News-Letter (American), vol. 3, no. 6 (October): 78.]
1944   Letter to Percy Allen, May 1. [Excerpt reprinted in "Editorial Notes," *Shakespeare
        Fellowship News-Letter*, October 1944, p. 1.]

Boyle, Charles
Books
2013   *Another Hamlet: The Mystery of Leslie Howard*, second edition (Somerville, MA: Forever
        Press).
Articles and reviews
1997   [Review of *Alias Shakespeare* by Joseph Sobran], *Shakespeare Oxford Newsletter*, vol. 33,
        no. 3 (Summer): 16.

Boyle, William E.
Books
2013   *A Poet's Rage: Understanding Shakespeare Through Authorship Studies* (Somerville, MA:
        Forever Press).

Articles
1996   "Shakespeare and the Fair Youth," *Sh. Oxford Newsletter*, vol. 33, no. 4 (Fall): 6-7.
1997   "Writing History: Facts are Facts, but Interpretation is All," *Shakespeare Oxford
        Newsletter*, vol. 33, no. 1 (Winter): 1, 6-7, 15. [With co-authors Charles Boyle and
        Charles Beauclerk]
1999   "Shakespeare's Invention: The Royal Story of the *Sonnets*," *Shakespeare Oxford
        Newsletter*, vol. 35, no. 1 (Spring): 2.
1999   "From the Editor: Shakespeare, Southampton and the *Sonnets*," *Shakespeare Oxford
        Newsletter*, vol. 35, no. 2 (Summer): 24.
1999   "Shakespeare, Southampton and the *Sonnets*," *Shakespeare Oxford Newsletter*, vol. 35, no.
        3 (Fall): 6-7.
2001   "From the Editors: Oxford is Shakespeare: Any Questions?" *Shakespeare Matters*, vol. 1,
        no. 1 (Fall): 1, 3, 20. [as editor, with co-editor Roger Stritmatter]

2002 "Tender Airs, Tudor Heirs," *Shakespeare Matters*, vol. 1, no. 2 (Winter): 3. [as editor, with co-editor Roger Stritmatter]

2004 "With the Sonnets Now Solved . . . ," *Shakespeare Matters*, vol. 3, no. 4 (Summer): 1, 11-15.

2004 "From the Editor: Can Literature Be Evidence?" *Shakespeare Matters*, vol. 3, no. 4 (Summer): 3.

2013 "Unveiling the Sonnets," in *Discovering Shakespeare*, ed. by Daniel L. Wright, pp. 63-85.

2013 "Appendix A: The Prince Tudor Theory," in *A Poet's Rage*, pp. 235-249.

Bragdon, Claude

1920 Letter to William Morrow, September 24.

Brame, Michael & Galina Popova

Books

Shakespeare's Fingerprints (Adonis Editions).

Articles and reviews

2004 "Was Shakespeare Gay?" *Shakespeare Matters*, vol. 3, no. 4 (Summer): 34-36.

Broderick, James F. & Darren W. Miller

2011 *Web of Conspiracy: A Guide to Conspiracy Theory Sites on the Internet* (Medford, NJ: Information Today).

Brooks, Alden

1943 *Will Shakspere and the Dyer's Hand* (New York: Charles Scribner's Sons).

Brown, Ivor

Books written with George Fearon

1939 *The Shakespeare Industry: Amazing Monument* (New York: Harper & Row).

Articles, reviews and published letters

1928 "The Theatre: Merchandise Marks," *The Saturday Review*, vol. 145 (March 24): 215-216.

1928 [reply to Percy Allen], *The Saturday Review*, vol. 145 (April 14): 462-463.

1929 "The Muse on Loan," *The Saturday Review*, vol. 147 (February 23): 251-252.

1937 "The World of the Theatre," *The Illustrated London News*, October 9, p. 28.

1938 "The World of the Theatre," *The Illustrated London News*, April 23, pp. 29-30

1943 "Theatre and Life," *The Observer*, July 11, p. 2.

1944 "Theatre and Life," *The Observer*, April 30, p. 2.

1945 "Had Shakespeare Leisure?" *John O'London's Weekly*, January 26, p. 175.

Buckley, Marion

2004 "The Shakespeare Authorship Debate and the Proper Standard of Proof," *The Tennessee Law Review*, vol. 72, no. 1: 295-307.

Burgess, Gelett

Articles and published letters

1947 "Modern Research Sheds New Light on Bard of Avon: Recent Discoveries Concerning Authorship," *New York Herald Tribune*, May 8, p. A7.

1948 "Oxford is Shakespeare: A Communication," *Washington Post*, July 31, p. 5.

1948 "Pseudonym, Shakespeare," *Saturday Review*, October 2, p. 22.

1949 "An Oxford Tutorial," June 4, 1949, p. 24-25.

Personal letters

1920 Letter to Frederick Stokes [publisher of the 1920 American edition], May 19. [Reprinted in "Gelett Burgess' Tribute to *"Shakespeare" Identified*," *Shakespeare Fellowship Quarterly*, vol. VI, no. 3 (July 1945): 34.

Burris, Barbara

2001 "A Golden Book, Bound Richly Up: Comparing Chapman's Words with the Ashbourne Portrait," *Shakespeare Matters*, vol. 1, no. 1 (Fall): 1, 12-17.

Bushell, W. F.

1945 "Canon Rendall" [letter], *The Liverpool Daily Post*, January 10, p. 2.

Butcher, Fanny

1920 "Tabloid Reviews," *The Chicago Daily Tribune*, June 13, p. 9.

Byrne, Muriel St. Clare

1928 "Reviews and Notices," *The Library*, vol. 9, no. 2 (September): 211-214.

1929 "Shakespeare and Chapman," *The Times Literary Sup.*, issue 1416 (March 21): 229.

1929 "Stuart Politics in Chapman," *The Times Literary Sup.*, issue 1443 (September 26): 741.

1930   "De Vere and the Sonnets," *The Times Literary Supplement*, issue 1477 (May 22): 430.
1930   "Oxford as 'Shakespeare,'" *The Times Literary Sup.*, issue 1493 (September 11): 712.
1934   "The Social Background," in *A Companion to Shakespeare Studies* edited by G. B. Harrison & Granville Barker, pp. 187-218 (Cambridge: The University Press).

C. B.
1920   "Shakespeare's Identity," *The Western Mail*, April 23, p. 7.

C. F. A.
1931   "The Oxford Theory," *Christian Science Monitor*, April 25, p. 12.

C. H. H. [See Charles H. Herford]

C. R..
1920   "Shakespeare: Was He Edward de Vere, Lord Oxford?" *Nottingham Journal and Express*, April 22, p. 4.

C. R.. B.
1944   "Another Reputed Author: Edward de Vere," *The Age*, April 15, p. 5.

Cairncross, Andrew S.
   Books
1936   *The Problem of Hamlet: A Solution* (London: Macmillan).
   Articles, reviews and published letters
1937   "*Hamlet* Problems" [letter], *Times Literary Supplement*, issue 1823 (January 9): 28.

Campbell, Lily B.
1947   *Shakespeare's "Histories:" Mirrors of Elizabethan Policy* (San Marino, CA: The Huntington Library).

Campbell, Oscar James
1940   "Shakespeare Himself," *Harper's Magazine*, vol. 181 (June): 172-185.

Carrington, Phyllis
1943   "Was Lord Oxford Buried in Westminster Abbey," *Shakespeare Fellowship News-letter* (American), vol. 4, no. 4 (June): 41-44.
1962   "Col. Ward," *Shakespearean Authorship Review*, no. 8 (Autumn): 5.

Carter, Joseph
1947   "The Shakespeare Controversy: Now It Is a Case for the 17th Earl of Oxford," *New York Herald Tribune*, July 20, p. A2.

Carter, M. J.
1939   "Shakespeare" [letter], *The Sydney Morning Herald*, June 17, p. 13.

Cecil Palmer, Publishers
1920   [advertisement], *Publishers' Circular*, August 14, p. 160.

Chambers, Sir Edmund K.
   Books
1923   *The Elizabethan Stage*, vol. I-III (Oxford: The Clarendon Press).
1924   *The Disintegration of Shakespeare* [The Annual Shakespeare Lecture 1924] (London: Oxford University Press for The British Academy).
1930   *William Shakespeare: A Study of Facts and Problems* (Oxford: Clarendon Press).
   Books edited
1932   *The Oxford Book of Sixteenth Century Verse* (London: Oxford University Press).
   Articles and published letters
1934   "The 'Mortal Moon' Sonnet," *The Times Literary Supplement*, issue 1669 (Jan. 25): 60.

Chandler, David
2000   "Historicizing Difference: Anti-Stratfordians and the Academy," *The Elizabethan Review*, Internet edition (Spring).

Chelmsford Chronicle, The
1922   "Shakespeare: An Essex Claim," December 1, p. 3.

Chew, Samuel
1931   "Who was W. S.?" *The New York Herald Tribune*, March 15, p. J12.

Chicago Daily Tribune, The
1920   "A Line o' Type or Two," March 24, p. 8.
1920   "Tabloid Book Reviews," June 13, p. 9.
1920   "A Line o' Type or Two," August 8, p. 8.

1931   "Now It Seems De Vere Wrote Shakespeare's Plays," March 14, p. 14.

Chicago Public Library Book Bulletin

1920   "Literature," December, p. 157.

Child, Harold H.

1926   [review of *A Hundreth Sundrie Flowers by George Gascoigne*, edited by Capt. Bernard M. Ward], *The Times Literary Supplement*, issue 1271 (June 10): 391.

1933   "History and Plays," *The Times Literary Supplement*, issue 1644 (August 3): 522.

1935   "Oxford's Sonnets," *The Times Literary Supplement*, issue 1730 (March 28): 203.

Chiljan, Katherine

2011   *Shakespeare Suppressed: The Uncensored Truth about Shakespeare and His Works* (San Francisco: Faire Editions)

Christian Science Monitor, The

1920   "Shakespeare and Bacon Again," May 7, p. 3.

1930   "De Vere as Shakespeare," July 19, p. 6.

1933   "Shakespeare and Politics," August 19, p. 8.

Cincinnati Enquirer, The

1933   "Love's Labour's Lost," May 6, p. 10.

Clare, Janet

1990   *'Art Made Tongue-tied by Authority:' Elizabethan and Jacobean Dramatic Censorship* (Manchester: Manchester University Press).

Clark, Eva Turner

Books

1930   *Shakespeare's Plays in the Order of Their Writing* (London: Cecil Palmer).

1931   *Hidden Allusions in Shakespeare's Plays* (New York: W. F. Payson). [American edition of *Shakespeare's Plays in the Order of Their Writing*]

1937   *The Man Who Was Shakespeare* (New York: R. R. Smith).

Articles, reviews and introductions

1930   "Introduction" to *The Shakespeare Garden*, second edition, by Esther Singleton (New York: W. F. Payson).

1939   "To Members of the Shakespeare Fellowship," *Shakespeare Fellowship News-Letter* (American), vol. 1, no. 1 (Dec. 1939): 1.

1940   "If We Have Leisure!" *Shakespeare Fellowship News-Letter* (American), vol. 1, no. 5 (August-September 1940): 12.

1941   "Shakespeare's Birthday," *Shakespeare Fellowship News-Letter* (American), vol. 2, no. 3 (April): 31.

1941   "De Vere Theory Growing in California," *Shakespeare Fellowship News-Letter* (American), vol. 2, no. 4 (June): 43.

1941   "Washington Physicist Speaks," *Shakespeare Fellowship News-Letter* (American), vol. 2, no. 4 (June): 41.

1942   "War and the Fellowship," *Shakespeare Fellowship News-Letter* (American), vol. 3, no. 2 (February 1942): 18.

1944   "Stolne and Surreptitious Copies." *Shakespeare Fellowship Quarterly*, vol. V, no. 1 (Jan.): 8.

1944   "Some Character Names in Shakespeare's Plays," *Shakespeare Fellowship Quarterly*, vol. V, no. 2 (April): 31.

1945   "Keep the Light Burning," *Shakespeare Fellowship Quarterly*, vol. VI, no. 2 (April): 29.

Personal letters

1932   Letter to J. Thomas Looney, October 6. [JTL papers]

1932   Letter to J. Thomas Looney, November 24. [JTL papers]

1932   Letter to J. Thomas Looney, December 28. [JTL papers]

1933   Letter to J. Thomas Looney, January 5. [JTL papers]

1933   Letter to J. Thomas Looney, January 7. [JTL papers]

1937   Letter to J. Thomas Looney, November 20. [JTL papers]

1937   Letter to J. Thomas Looney, December 17. [JTL papers]

Clarke, Francis

1920   "Correspondence: 'Shakespeare' Identified" [letter], *The Athenaeum*, April 16, p. 521.

1921   "Stratford and Stony Stratford" [letter], *The Bookman's Journal*, March 25, p. 388.

1923   [letter], *Hackney Spectator*, January 19, p. 2.

Clendening, Logan
    1933   "Good Reading," *The New York Herald Tribune*, November 22, p. 15.

Clutton-Brock, Arthur
    1932   "Edward de Vere," *The Times Literary Supplement*, issue 1586 (June): 462.

Coblante, Stanton A.
    1931   "Shakespeare as the Earl of Oxford," *The New York Times*, May 31, p. BR17.

Collini, Stephan
    2019   *The Nostalgic Imagination: History in English Criticism* (Oxford: Oxford University Press).

Connes, Georges
    1927   *The Shakespeare Mystery: Abridged and Translated into English by a Member of the Shakespeare Fellowship* (London: Cecil Palmer) [From Connes's *Le Shakespearian Mystere* (Paris: Bovin & Cie.)]
    1964   "I Have Changed My Mind: Some Afterthoughts by Georges Connes," *Shakespearean Authorship Review*, Autumn 1964, p. 4 (Article in French media translated by R. M. D. Wainewright).

Corbin, John
    1920   "Who is 'Baconian' Now?" *The New York Times*, June 27, p. 58.

Courthope, W. J.
    1910   *History of English Poetry*, vol. II. (New York/London: Macmillan and Co.).

Courtney, W. L.
    1920   "Shakespeare Identified," *The Daily Telegraph*, March 19, p. 16.

Craig, Hardin
    1934   "Hamlet's Book," *The Huntington Library Bulletin*, no. 6 (November): 17-37.

Crinkley, Richmond
    1985   "New Perspectives on the Authorship Question," *Shakespeare Quarterly*, vol. 36, no. 4 (Winter, 1985): 515-522.

Crosse, Gordon
    1917   "The Real Shakespeare Problem," *The Nineteenth Century and After*, vol. 81 (April): 883-894.
    1920   "Yet Another Shakespeare," *Commonwealth*, October, p. 290.

Culler, Jonathan
    2009   *Literary Theory: A Very Short Introduction* (New York: Oxford University Press).

Cutting, Bonner Miller
    Books
    2018   *Necessary Mischief: Exploring the Shakespeare Authorship Question* (Jennings, LA: Minos Publishing Company).
    Articles and reviews
    2006   "The Case of the Missing First Folio," *Shakespeare Matters*, vol. 5, no. 4 (Summer): 6-11.
    2010   "A Contest of Wills: Reviewing Shapiro's Reviewers," *Shakespeare Matters*, vol. 9, no. 3 (Fall): 125-14, 31.

Cyr, Gordon C.
    1976   "Book Review," *Shakespeare Oxford Society Newsletter*, vol. 12, no. 1 (Spring): 5.

Daily Sketch, The
    1936   "Judge Meets Witness After Forty Years," April 13, p. 10.

Dams, Christopher H.
    1999   "The Dates of Composition of 'The Plays of William Shakespeare' by Edward de Vere, 17th Earl of Oxford," *De Vere Society Newsletter*, vol. 3, no. 4a (August): 1-44.
    2000   "Was Southampton Regarded as the Son of the Queen?" [letter], *De Vere Society Newsletter*, October, p. 20.

Danner, Bruce
    2011   "The Anonymous Shakespeare: Heresy, Authorship, and the Anxiety of Orthodoxy," in *Anonymity in Early Modern England* edited by Janet W. Starner and Barbara H. Traister, pp. 143-158.

Davidson, Elizabeth R.
    1941   "Unbelief in the Belief," *Shakespeare Fellowship News-Letter* (American), vol. 2, no. 4

(June): 45-47.

Dawson, Giles E.
1953   [Review of *This Star of England* by Dorothy and Charlton Ogburn], *Shakespeare Quarterly*,
        vol. 4, no. 2: 165.

Delahoyde, Michael
2006   "Recent Publications in Oxfordian Studies," *Rocky Mountain Review of Literature and
        Languages*, vol. 60, no. 2 (Fall): 52-59.

Dellinger, John Howard [J. H. D.]
1961   "Professor Louis P. Bénézet," *Shakespearean Authorship Review*, no. 6 (Autumn): 23.

De Vere Society Newsletter, The
2013   "Royal Shakespeare Company's Psychological Aberration?" vol. 20, no. 3 (October, 2013):
        27.

Demant, Rev. V. A.
1946   "Personal Recollections of the Late J. T. Looney," *Shakespeare Fellowship News-Letter*,
        September, p. 3.
1962   "John Thomas Looney," *Shakespearean Authorship Review*, no. 8 (Autumn) 8-9.

Diamond, Jared
1997   *Guns, Germs and Steel* (New York: W. W. Norton & Co.) [First edition]
2017   *Guns, Germs and Steel* (New York: W. W. Norton & Co.). [20th anniversary edition]

Dickson, Peter W.
    Books
2011   *Bardgate: Shake-speare and the Royalists Who Stole the Bard* (Mount Vernon, OH:
        Printing Arts Press).
2016   *Bardgate II: Shakespeare, Catholicism and the Politics of the First Folio of 1623*. (Mount
        Vernon, OH: Printing Arts Press).
    Articles and reviews
1998   "Oxford's Literary Reputation in the 17th and 18th Centuries," *Shakespeare Oxford
        Newsletter*, vol. 34, no. 3 (Fall): 14-15.
1999   "Are British Scholars Erasing Two Heroic Earls from Jacobean History to Protect the
        Shakespeare Industry?" *Sh. Oxford Newsletter*, vol. 35, no. 1 (Spring): 8-9, 24.

District Court of the United States for the District of Columbia
1948   Charles Wisner Barrell, Plaintiff v. Giles E. Dawson, Defendant: Action for Damages for
        Libel. [Civil Action No. 2698-48, filed July 1]

Dobree, Donamy
1934   "Shakespeare and the Drama of His Time," in *A Companion to Shakespeare Studies*, edited
        by G. B. Harrison and H. Granville Barker, pp. 243-262.

Dobzhansky, Theodosius
1973   "Nothing in Biology Makes Sense Except in the Light of Evolution," *American Biology
        Teacher*, vol. 24: 125-129.

Douglas, Col. Montagu W.
    Books and Circulars
1931   *The Earl of Oxford as "Shakespeare"* (London: Cecil Palmer).
1933   *Shakespeare Fellowship Circular*, November 1, 1933 [Object[ive]s of the Fellowship]
1934   *Lord Oxford Was Shakespeare* (London: Rich & Cowan, Ltd.).
1952   *Lord Oxford and the Shakespeare Group* (Oxford: Alden Press, Ltd.).
    Articles, reviews, forewords and published letters
1924   "Recent Research," *The Hackney Spectator*, June 27, p. 2.
1929   "First of England's Three Fights Against Famine," *The Morning Post*, September 19, p. 9.
1932   [review of *The Life-Story of Edward de Vere as "Shakespeare,"* by Percy Allen], *The
        Shakespeare Pictorial*, no. 49 (March): 48.
1932   "Ben Jonson and Shakespeare," *The Shakespeare Pictorial*, no. 58 (December): 196.
1933   "Edward de Vere and Academic Scholarship," *The Sh. Pictorial*, no. 61 (March): 48.
1933   "Death of Colonel Ward" [letter], *The Shakespeare Pictorial*, no, 64 (June): 92.
1933   "The Plays of Shakespeare & Chapman in Relation to French History," *The Shakespeare
        Pictorial*, no. 67 (September): 144.
1935   "Shakespeare, the Great Unknown," *The Freethinker*, vol. 55, no. 33 (August 18): 522-523.

1935   "The Shakespearean Group," *The Shakespeare Pictorial*, no. 93 (October): 160.

1936   "Last Words from the Shakespeare Fellowship," *The Shakespeare Pictorial*, no. 106 (December): 196.

1937   "Foreword" to *Lavenham, Suffolk* by F. Lingard Ranson (1937).

1937   "Editorial," *The Shakespeare Fellowship News-Letter*, no. 1 (January): 1-2.

1937   "Book Reviews," *Shakespeare Fellowship News-Letter*, no. 3 (May): 8.

1938   "News from France," *Shakespeare Fellowship News-Letter*, no. 9 (May): 2-4.

1938   [review of *Shakspere, Shakespeare and de Vere* by Louis P. Bénézet], *Shakespeare Fellowship News-Letter*, no. 8 (March): 6-8.

1940   [review of *Ben Jonson and the First Folio* by Gerald Rendall], *Shakespeare Fellowship News-Letter* (American), vol. 1, no. 2 (February): 8.

1940   "The American Branch of the Shakespeare Fellowship," *East Anglian Magazine*, vol. 5, no. 3 (April): 121-122.

Personal letters

1933   Letter to J. Thomas Looney, November 26. [JTL papers]

Dover Express, The

1936   "Shakespeare Authorship: Col. F. E. G. Skey's Lecture," February 28, p. 4.

Dowden, Edward

1875   *Shakspere: A Critical Study of His Mind and Art* (Elibron Classics Replica Edition, 2005).

Drinkwater, John

Books

1933   *Shakespeare* (London: Duckworth).

Articles

1931   "The Immortal Memory," *The Stage*, April 30, p. 15.

Personal letters

1933   Letter to Percy Allen, August 3. [Brunel]

Dudley, Michael

2017   "All That is Shakespeare Melts into Air" [with Gary Goldstein and Shelly Maycock], [review of *The New Oxford Shakespeare Authorship Companion*, ed. by Gary Taylor, et. al.], *The Oxfordian*, vol. 19: 195-208.

Dundee Courier and Advertiser, The

1930   "Tradition Disturbed," February 27, p. 10.

1931   "For the Book-Lover," December 3, p. 4.

Durning-Lawrence, Sir Edwin

1910   *Bacon is Shakespeare* (London: Gay & Hancock, Ltd.)

1914   *The Shakespeare Myth* (London: Gay & Hancock, Ltd.).

Dwyer, J. J.

1942   Letter to Charles Barrell, August 25. [excerpts in "From England," *Shakespeare Fellowship News-Letter* (American), vol. 4, no. 1 (December): 11.]

Eagan-Donovan, Cheryl

2019   *Nothing is Truer than Truth*. [film]

Eagle, The [St. John's College, Cambridge]

1934   "Was Shakespeare a Johnian?" vol. 48, no. 213: 83-87.

Eagle, Roderick L.

Books

1930   *Shakespeare: New Views for Old* (London: Cecil Palmer).

Articles

1920   "Correspondence: 'Shakespeare' Identified," *The Athenaeum*, April 16, p. 521.

1921   "Shakespeare and the Earl of Oxford," *Baconiana*, vol. XVI, no. 63 (March): 84-85.

1943   "El-Dorado-on-Avon," *Everybody's*, February 28.

Personal letters

1920   Letter to J. Thomas Looney, April 9. [JTL papers]

1920   Letter to J. Thomas Looney, April 14. [JTL papers]

Eagle, Solomon [SEE John C. Squire]

East Anglian Magazine, The

1937   "Comments" [editor], vol. 2, no. 7 (April): 290.

1937   "Comments" [editor], vol. 2, no. 8 (May): 338.
1937   "Lord Oxford and 'Shakespeare'" [editor], vol. 2, no. 11 (August): 518.
1939   "Comments by the Editor," vol. 4, no. 11 (October): 610.
1939   "Important Announcement," vol. 4, no. 11 (October): 610.
1940   "Comments by the Editor," vol. 5, no. 1 (January): 2.

Eastbourne Gazette, The
1930   "Edward de Vere and Shakespeare," March 12, p. 27.

Edinburgh Evening News, The
1932   "Down with Shakespeare!" May 17, p. 8.

Edmonson, Paul and Stanley Wells (editors)
2013   *Shakespeare Beyond Doubt: Evidence, Argument, Controversy* (Cambridge: Cambridge University Press).

Eggar, Katharine E.
1936   Letter to J. Thomas Looney, mid-December [not dated] [Eggar Archives]

Eliot, T. S. (Thomas Stearns)
Books
1933   *The Varieties of Metaphysical Poetry*, edited and introduced by Ronald Schuchard (New York: Harcourt, Brace and Company).
Articles and reviews
1928   "Poet's Borrowings," *The Times Literary Supplement*, issue 1366 (April 5): 255.
1934   "Shakespearian Criticism from Dryden to Coleridge," in *A Companion to Shakespeare Studies* edited by G. B. Harrison & Granville Barker. pp. 287-299.

Elliott, Ward E. Y. & Robert J. Valenza
2000   "Can the Oxford Candidacy Be Saved?" *The Oxfordian*, vol. 3: 71-97.

Elliott, H. J.
2012   *History in the Making* (New Haven: Yale University Press).

Ellis, David
2012   *The Truth about William Shakespeare: Fact, Fiction and Modern Biographies* (Edinburgh: Edinburgh University Press).

Emerson, Ralph Waldo
1906   "Representative Men," in *Works*, vol. IV (Philadelphia: J. D. Morris and Co.).

Encyclopedia Britannica
1910-11 "Vere," pp. 1019-1020.
2020   "Elizabeth I and England's Golden Age." [Accessed June 26, 2020.] [https://web.archive.org/web/20061112031836/http://www.britannica.com/ebi/article-200261]

Era, The
1935   "Talking Shop," May 22, pp. 1-2.

Essex Newsman, The
1945   "Canon Rendall Dies at the Age of 93," January 9, p. 1.

Evans, C. S. [William Heinemann Co.]
1919   Letter to J. Thomas Looney, May 1. [JTL papers]

Evening Standard, The
1922   "The Shakespeare Fellowship," November 23.
1923   "Under the Greenwood Tree," November 25.

Evening Union, The (Springfield, Mass.)
1931   [review of Clark's *Hidden Allusions in Shakespeare's Plays*]. [Excerpt quoted in Cecil Palmer ad, *Shakespeare Pictorial*, December 1931.]

Ewing, Quincy
1924   Letter to Col. Bernard R. Ward, date not known. [excerpts published in *The Hackney Spectator*, July 25, 1924, p. 9.]

F. B.
1934   "Brief for the Oxfordians," *Christian Science Monitor*, June 13, p. WM11.

Feldman, A. Bronson
1947   "Shakespeare's Jester—Oxford's Servant," *Shakespeare Fellowship Quarterly*, vol. VIII, no. 3 (Autumn 1947): 39-43.

1953   "The Confessions of William Shakespeare," *American Imago*, vol. 10, no. 2 (Summer): 165.

1984   "Amendments to Bernard M. Ward's *The Seventeenth Earl of Oxford*," *The Bard*, vol. 4. No. 2: 53-67.

Feuillerat, Albert

1953   *The Composition of Shakespeare's Plays* (Freeport, NY: Books for Libraries Press). [Original edition: same year, Yale University Press]

Fischer, David Hackett

1970   *Historians' Fallacies: Toward a Logic of Historical Thought* (New York: HarperCollins).

Fish, Stanley

2008   *Save the World On Your Own Time* (New York: Oxford University Press).

Flatter, Richard

1951   "Sigmund Freud on Shakespeare," *Shakespeare Quarterly*, vol. 2, no. 4 (October): 368-369.

Fowler, William P.

Books

1986   *Shakespeare Revealed in Oxford's Letters* (Portsmouth, NH: Peter E. Randall).

Articles

1982   "Shake-speare's Heart Unlocked," *Shakespeare Oxford Society Newsletter*, vol. 18, no. 4 (Fall): 1-7.

Frederick A. Stokes Company

1920   [advertisement], *The Review*, May 22, p. 551. [Same ad was also in *The New York Times*, May 30, 1920, p. 281; *The Atlantic Monthly*, June 1920; and *Library Journal*, June 1, 1920, p. 519]

1920   Letter to J. Thomas Looney, October 29. [JTL papers]

Freeman's Journal

1920   "Shakespeare Identified," November 11, p. 11.

Freud, Sigmund

Books

1935   *An Autobiographical Study* (New York: W. W. Norton and Company).

1989   *An Autobiographical Study*, translated and edited by James Strachey, with a biographical introduction by Peter Gay (New York: W. W. Norton and Company).

Articles and speeches

1930   "Address Delivered in the Goethe House, Frankfurt," reprinted as Ansprache im Frankfurter Goethe-Haus," *Neues Shake-speare Journal*, edited by Uwe Laugwitz, New Series, vol. 1: 6-10 (Nov. 2010).

Letters

1930   Letter to Theodore Reik, March 23. [quoted in Norman N. Holland, *Psychoanalysis and Shakespeare* (1964), pp. 56-57.]

1932   Letter to Dr. Richard Flatter, Sept. 20. [quoted in Richard Flatter, "Sigmund Freud on Shakespeare," *Shakespeare Quarterly*, vol. 2, no. 4 (Oct. 1951): 368-369.]

Fripp, Edgar

1938   *Shakespeare, Man and Artist* (London: Oxford University Press).

Frisbee, George

1937   "Shame of the Professors," *Reading and Collecting*, vol. 1, no. 8 (July): 6-7.

Furness, Horace Howard (editor)

1888   *The Merchant of Venice* [A New Variorum Edition of Shakespeare, twelfth edition] (J. B. Lippincott Company).

Garber, Marjorie

2004   *Shakespeare After All* (New York: Anchor Books).

Garvin, J. L.

1923   "Who Shakespeare Was: The Comedy of Doubt," *The Observer*, April 22, p. 12.

Gay, Peter

1990   *Reading Freud: Explorations & Entertainments* (New Haven: Yale University Press).

Gifford, A. C.

1941   Letter to the Shakespeare Fellowship, not dated. [Excerpt quoted in "Our Third Year," *Shakespeare Fellowship News-Letter* (American), vol. 3, no. 1 (December): 8.

1942   Letter to the Shakespeare Fellowship, not dated. [Excerpt quoted in "From Letters Received," *Sh. Fellowship News-Letter* (American), vol. 3, no. 6 (October): 77.

Gilvary, Kevin
2010   *Dating Shakespeare's Plays: A Critical Review of the Evidence* (Turnbridge Wells: Parapress). [Editor]
2018   *The Fictional Lives of Shakespeare* (New York: Routledge).

Globe and Mail, The
1920   "Life and Letters" [Review of *"Shakespeare" Identified*], May 1, p. 13.

Golding, Louis Thorn
1937   *An Elizabethan Puritan: Arthur Golding the Translator of Ovid's Metamorphoses and also of John Calvin's Sermons* (New York: Richard R. Smith).

Goldstein, Gary B.
<u>Books</u>
2016   *Reflections on the True Shakespeare* (Buchholz, Germany: Verlag Uwe Laugwitz).
<u>Articles and reviews</u>
2005   [Review of *"Shakespeare" by Another Name* by Mark Anderson], *The Oxfordian*, vol. 8 (September): 124-128.
2017   "All That is Shakespeare Melts into Air" [with Michael Dudley and Shelly Maycock], [review of *The New Oxford Shakespeare Authorship Companion*, ed. by Gary Taylor, et. al.], *The Oxfordian*, vol. 19: 195-208.
2019   "From the Editor: Expanding the Canon," *The Oxfordian*, vol. 21: 11.
2019   "Transforming Productions of Shakespeare's Plays," *The Oxfordian*, vol. 21: 199-213.
2020   "From the Editor: The Oxfordian Hypothesis Gains Academic Acceptance," *The Oxfordian*, vol. 22 (September): 13.

Gore-Langton, Robert
2014   "Could the Real Mr. Shakespeare Please Stand Up?" *The Daily Express*, October 27, p. 13.
2014   "The Campaign to Prove Shakespeare Didn't Exist," *Newsweek* blog, December 29, accessed at http://www.newsweek.com/2014/12/26/campaign-prove-shakespeare-didn't-exist-293243.htm.

Greenblatt, Stephen
2016   *Will in the World: How Shakespeare Became Shakespeare* (New York: W. W. Norton). [2004]

Greenwood, Sir George G.
<u>Books</u>
1908   *The Shakespeare Problem Restated* (London: John Lane).
1909   *In re Shakespeare: Beeching v. Greenwood: Rejoinder on Behalf of the Defendant* (London: John Lane).
1911   *The Vindicators of Shakespeare: A Reply to Critics* (London: John Lane).
1916   *Is There a Shakespeare Problem?* (London: John Lane).
1916   *Sir Sidney Lee's New Edition of A Life of William Shakespeare: Some Words of Criticism* (London: John Lane).
1920   *Shakespeare's Handwriting* (London: John Lane).
1920   *Shakespeare's Law* (London: Cecil Palmer).
1921   *Ben Jonson and Shakespeare* (London: Cecil Palmer).
1922   *Baconian Essays (by E. W. Smithson, with an Introduction and two essays by Greenwood)* (London: Cecil Palmer).
1923   *Lee, Shakespeare and a Tertium Quid* (London: Cecil Palmer).
1924   *Shakespeare's Signatures and Sir Thomas More* (London: Cecil Palmer).
1925   *The Stratford Bust and the Droeshout Engraving* (London: Cecil Palmer).
<u>Articles and reviews</u>
1917   "The Real Shakespeare Problem: A Reply to Mr. Gordon Crosse," *The Nineteenth Century and After*, vol. 81 (June): 1340-1354.
1923   "The Shakespeare Fellowship," *The Hackney Spectator*, January 5, p. 11.
1926   "A Cambridge Scholar on Shakespeare," *The National Review*, vol. 87 (March): 900.
<u>Letters</u>
1921   Letter to J. Thomas Looney, April 3. [JTL papers]
1922   Letter to J. Thomas Looney, February 19. [JTL papers]

1928   Letter to Col. Bernard R. Ward, October 20. [Repr. in the November 6, 1928 *Circular.*]

Greg, W. W.

   <u>Books</u>

   1923   *Shakespeare's Hand in the Play of Sir Thomas More; Papers by Alfred W. Pollard, W. W. Greg, E. Maunde Thompson, J. Dover Wilson and R. W. Chambers* [edited by Greg] (Cambridge: The University Press).

   1925   *English Literary Autographs, Part I. Dramatists, 1550-1650* (London: Oxford University Press).

   <u>Articles and reviews</u>

   1926   "A Hundreth Sundry Flowers," *The Library*, vol. VII, no. 3 (December): 281.

   1929   "*The Seventeenth Earl of Oxford, 1550-1604,*" *Modern Language Review*, vol. 24, no. 2 (January): 216-221.

   1931   "Tudor Handwriting [Review of Rendall's *Shake-spear: Handwriting and Spelling*] *Times Literary Supplement*, issue 1531 (June 4): 446.

Grosart, Alexander B.

   1872   *Fuller Worthies' Library*, vol. 4 (London).

Gross, John M.

   2010   "Denying Shakespeare," *Commentary*, March, pp. 38-44.

Grossberg, Lawrence, Cary Nelson & Paula Treichler (editors)

   1992   *Cultural Studies* (New York: Routledge).

Grove, Lee

   1948   "'Shakespeare' Just Pen Name of Oxford Earl, Barrell Says," *New York Herald Tribune*, July 3, p. B1.

Guardian, The

   1928   "The Seventeenth Earl of Oxford," April 27, p. 258.

Guy, John

   1988   *Tudor England* (Oxford: Oxford University Press).

H. B. C.

   1930   "The Case Against Shakespeare," *The Manchester Guardian*, May 5, p. 7.

H. D. S.

   1920   [review of *"Shakespeare" Identified*], *The Bookseller*, March, pp. 147-48.

H. H.

   1933   "Oxfordian Rejoinder," *Christian Science Monitor*, June 17, p. 10.

H. T.

   1932   "The Shakespeare Authorship Controversy," *The British Museum Quarterly*, vol. 7, no. 2 (October): 40-41.

Hackney Spectator, The

   1922   "Problems of Past and Present," September 8, p. 6-7.

Halifax Evening Courier

   1920   "The Real Shakespeare," March 4, p. 4.

Halliwell-Phillipps, J. O.

   1883   *Outlines of the Life of William Shakespeare*, 3rd edition (London: Longmans, Green & Co.).

   1907   *Outlines of the Life of William Shakespeare*. 7th edition (London: Longmans, Green & Co.).

Hamill, John

   2005   "Shakespeare's Sexuality and How It Affects the Authorship issue," *The Oxfordian*, vol. 8: 25-59.

   2005   "The Dark Lady and Her Bastard: An Alternative Scenario," *Shakespeare Oxford Newsletter*, vol. 41, no. 3 (Summer): 1, 4-9, 11.

   2009   "Bisexuality and Bastardy: The Reasons for the Shakespeare Cover-up," *Discovering Shakespeare*, edited by Daniel L. Wright, pp. 29-39.

   2012   "New Light on *Willobie His Avisa* and the Authorship Question," *The Oxfordian*, vol. 14: 130-147.

Hansen, Harry

   1944   "Who's Looney Now?" *The Chicago Tribune*, March 5, p. D9.

Harman, Edwin G.

   1925   *The Impersonality of Shakespeare* (London: Cecil Palmer)

Harris, Frank
    1909   *The Man Shakespeare and His Tragic Life-story* (New York: Mitchell Kennerley).
Harrison, G. B.
    Books
    1933   *Shakespeare at Work* (London: Routledge).
    1934   *A Companion to Shakespeare Studies* [co-editor, with Granville Barker] (Cambridge: The
            University Press).
    1939   *Introducing Shakespeare's Plays* (Harmondsworth, Middlesex, Eng.: Penguin Books, Ltd.)
    Articles and reviews and published letters
    1929   "Shakespeare and Chapman as Topical Dramatists," *The London Mercury*, vol. XX, no. 118
            (August).
    1930   [reviews of *Shakespeare, Jonson and Wilkins as Borrowers* and of *Shakespeare and
            Chapman as Topical Dramatists*, both by Percy Allen], *The Review of English Studies*,
            vol. 6, no. 21 (January): 100.
    1930   [review of Sir Sidney Lee's *Elizabethan and Other Essays*], *The London Mercury*, vol. XXI,
            no. 128 (June 1930).
    1930   "Shakespeare's Topical Significances I: *King John*," *The Times Literary Supplement*, issue
            1502 (November 13): 939.
    1930   "Shakespeare's Topical Significances II: The Earl of Essex," *The Times Literary
            Supplement*, issue 1503 (November 20): 974.
    1933   "These Late Eclipses" [letter], *The Times Literary Supplement*, issue 1661 (November 30):
            856.
    1934   "These Late Eclipses" [letter], *The Times Literary Supplement*, issue 1666 (January 4): 12.
Hart, Alfred
    1934   *Shakespeare and the Homilies* (New York: Octagon Books).
    1942   *Stolne and Surreptitious Copies: A Comparative Study of Shakespeare's Bad Quartos*
            (Melbourne: Melbourne University Press).
Hart, Michael H.
    1992   *The 100: A Ranking of the Most Influential Persons in History, Revised and Updated for the
            Nineties* (New York: Citadel Press)
Hastings, Chris
    2014   "Bard Blood at the Palace as Princes Split Over Shakespeare," *The Mail Online* (April 2).
Herford, Charles H. [C. H. H.]
    1920   "Shakespeare Deposed Again," *The Manchester Guardian*, March 7, p. 7.
    1923   "New Books: Mr. W. H.." *The Manchester Guardian*, June 5, p. 7.
Herford, Oliver
    Books
    1899   *An Alphabet of Celebrities* (Boston: Small, Maynard).
    Articles and reviews
    1920   "'Shakespeare' Identified Again," *Leslie's Weekly*, June.
    1933   "A Great Peradventure," *The San Francisco Chronicle*, Aug. 19.
Heron, Flodden W.
    1939   "The Shakespeare Anniversary—Literature's Greatest Mystery," *The Argonaut*, April 21.
    1942   "Bacon was Not Shakespeare," *Shakespeare Fellowship News-Letter* (American), vol. 3, no.
            3 (April): 36-38.
Hess, W. Ron
    1999   "Shakespeare's Dates: Their Effects on Stylistic Analysis," *The Oxfordian*, vol. 2: 25-59.
Hogg, J. A.
    1938   "The Bard of Stratford" [letter], *The Northern Whig and Belfast Post*, January 13, p. 3.
Holland, Capt. Hubert H., C.B.
    Books
    1923   *Shakespeare Through Oxford Glasses* (London: Cecil Palmer).
    1933   *Shakespeare, Oxford and Elizabethan Times* (London: Denis Archer).
    Articles, reviews and published letters
    1933   "Oxfordian Rejoinder," *Christian Science Monitor*, June 17, p. 10.

1937   "M.O.A.I. Doth Sway My Life," *Shakespeare Fellowship News-Letter*, no. 2 (March): 3.

1937   "Letter to *News-Letter* Readers," *Shakespeare Fellowship News-Letter*, no. 3 (May): 11.

1942   "Shake-Speare 1573-1593: A Short Report on Latest Research into Internal Evidence by Topical Allusions," *Shakespeare Fellowship News-Letter*, April, p. 2.

Holland, Norman N.

Books

1964   *Psychoanalysis and Shakespeare* (New York: McGraw-Hill).

Articles and reviews

1960   "Freud on Shakespeare," *PMLA: Publication of the Modern Language Association*, vol. 75, no. 3 (June): 169-173.

Holstein, Mark

1941   "The Shakspere-Bacon-Oxford-Whoozis Mixup," *The Shakespeare Association Bulletin*, vol. 16, no. 4 (October): 195-214.

Honigman, E. A. J.

1985   "Sweet Swan of Oxford?" *New York Review of Books* (Jan. 17): 23-26.

Hony, T. H. L.

1939   "Oxford or Bacon?" *The Western Morning News*, July 15, p. 13.

Hookham, George

Books

1922   *Will o' the Wisp, or The Elusive Shakespeare* (Oxford: B. Blackwell).

Articles

1922   "Edward de Vere and Shakespeare Plays," *National Review*, vol. 79 (March): 94-96.

Personal Letters

1922   Letter to J. Thomas Looney, November 26.

Hope, Warren

Books co-authored with Kim Holston

2009   *The Shakespeare Controversy: An Analysis of the Authorship Theories*, Second Edition (Jefferson, North Carolina: McFarland & Company, Inc., Publishers). [1992]

Articles and reviews

2010   "'Is that True?' A Review of James Shapiro's *Contested Will*," *Brief Chronicles*, vol. 2: 212-233. [Also cited is the version accessed on the Shakespeare Fellowship website on April 20, 2010.]

Hotson, Leslie

1931   *Shakespeare Versus Shallow* (Boston: Little, Brown and Co.).

Howard, Keble

1920   "Mr. Looney on Shakespeare," *The Sketch*, March 17, p. 4.

Howard, Shafter

1920   "Scholarship and the Baconian Controversy," *The San Francisco Chronicle*, Aug. 21, p. 16.

Hughes, Stephanie Hopkins

Books and pamphlets

1998   *The Relevance of Robert Greene to the Oxfordian Thesis*, 2nd edition (pamphlet) (Portland, OR: Paradigm Press).

Articles and reviews

1999   Letter to Editor, *Shakespeare Oxford Newsletter*, vol. 35, no. 2 (Summer): 26.

1999   "Shakespeare, Southampton and the *Sonnets*," *Shakespeare Oxford Newsletter*, vol. 35, no. 3 (Fall): 7.

2005   [review of *"Shakespeare" by Another Name* by Mark Anderson], *Shakespeare Oxford Newsletter*, vol. 41, no. 3 (Summer): 2, 12-14.

2007   "Hide Fox and All After: The Search for Shakespeare," *Shakespeare Oxford News-Letter*, vol. 43, no. 1 (Winter, 2007): 1, 5-11.

Hull Daily Mail, The

1920   "Mr. J. Thomas Cooney [sic] Almost Proves that Shakespeare's Works Were Written by Edward de Vere," March 4, p. 4.

Hunter, Mark

1929   "Shakespeare and Richard III: A Modern Parallel" [letter], *The Morning Post*, Sept. 12, 1929, p. 9.

Hunter, Thomas
    2003   "The Nelson Dilemma," *Shakespeare Matters*, vol. 3, no. 4 (Summer): 5-6.
    2010   "Shapiro and Why Authorship Doubters Don't Believe," *Shakespeare Oxford Newsletter*, vol. 46, no. 1 (May): 12-13, 23.

Irish Times, The
    1920   "Books of the Week," May 7, p. 7.
    1921   "Elizabethan Poems," April 1, p. 2.

Irving, Sir Henry
    1927   *The Complete Works of Shakespeare* (New York: Funk & Wagnalls).

Isaacs, J.
    1934a   "Shakespearian Criticism from Coleridge to the Present Day," in *A Companion to Shakespeare Studies* edited by G. B. Harrison & Granville Barker, pp. 300-304.
    1934b   "Shakespearian Scholarship," in *A Companion to Shakespeare Studies* edited by G. B. Harrison & Granville Barker, pp. 305-324.

J. B. D.
    1932   "Why There Is a Shakespeare Problem," *Christian Science Monitor*, May 17, p. 16.

J. H. D. [J. Howard Dellinger]
    1931   "Professor Louis P. Bénézet," *Shakespearean Authorship Review*, no. 6 (Autumn): 23.

Jacobi, Sir Derek
    2005   "Foreword," in *"Shakespeare" by Another Name: The Life of Edward de Vere, Earl of Oxford, the Man Who Was Shakespeare* by Mark Anderson, pp. xxiii-xxiv (New York: Gotham).

James, Henry
    1948   [Letter to Miss Violet Hunt, Aug. 26, 1903], in *The Letters of Henry James*, selected and edited by Percy Lubbock (New York: Charles Scribner's Sons, 1920; reissued by Octagon Books, 1970).

Jiménez, Ramon
    Books
    2018   *Shakespeare's Apprenticeship: Identifying the Real Playwright's Earliest Works* (Jefferson, NC: McFarland & Company).

    Articles
    2007   "Shakespeare in Stratford and London: Ten Eyewitnesses Who Saw Nothing," in *Report My Cause Aright: The Shakespeare Oxford Society Fiftieth Anniversary Anthology, 1957-2007*, (The Shakespeare Oxford Society), pp. 74-86; and in *Shakespeare Beyond Doubt?* edited by John M. Shahan and Alexander Waugh (2013), pp. 47-57.]
    2020   "Was *The Famous Victories of Henry the Fifth* Shakespeare's First Play?" *The Oxfordian*, vol. 22 (September): 38.
    2020   [Review of *Who Wrote That?* by Donald Ostrowski], *The Oxfordian*, vol. 22: 145-153.

Johnson, Paul
    1974   *Elizabeth: A Study in Intellect & Power* (London: Weidenfeld and Nicolson).

Kathman, David
    2013   "Shakespeare and Warwickshire," in *Shakespeare Beyond Doubt*, edited by Paul Edmondson and Stanley Wells (2013), pp. 121-132.

Keller, Helen
    1909   "The Question Now Remains: Who Was William Shakespeare?" *Matilda Ziegler Magazine* (January). [quoted at https://www.perkins.org/stories/helen-keller-shakespeare-skeptic.]

Kellett, E. E.
    1939   "Shakespeare" [letter], *News Chronicle*, January 18, p. 4.

Kennedy-Skipton, H. K.
    1932   [review of *The Tragic Story of "Shakespeare"* by G. W. Phillips], *The Shakespeare Pictorial*, no. 54 (August): 132.

Kent, William
    Books and pamphlets
    1939   *London Worthies* (London: Heath Cranton, Ltd.).
    1947   *The Lost Treasures of London* (London: Phoenix House).

1947   *Edward de Vere, the Seventeenth Earl of Oxford: The Real Shakespeare* (The Shakespeare Fellowship). [pamphlet; two chapters by Kent, a third by "Another;" revised edition, 1957]

Articles, reviews and published letters

1935   "A Plea for Shakespearean Freethinking," *The Freethinker*, vol. 55, no. 17 (April 28): 268-69.

1939   "Who Was Shakespeare?" [letter], *John O'London's Weekly*, March 10, pp. 888-889.

1939   "Mr. William Kent's New Book," *Shakespeare Fellowship News-Letter*, no. 14 (April): 8.

1939   "Open Letter to Harrison," *Shakespeare Fellowship News-Letter*, no. 15 (July): 4-7.

Kingsmill, Hugh

1931   "Who Was Shakespeare?" *The Yorkshire Post and Leeds Intelligencer*, February 10, p. 6.

1933   "Shakespeare Criticism," *The English Review*, June, pp. 692-94.

1944   *The Poisoned Crown* (London: Eyre & Spottiswoode).

Kittle, William

1930   *George Gascoigne or Edward de Vere Seventeenth Earl of Oxford* (Washington, D. C.: W. F. Roberts Company).

Knapp, Margaret L.

1924   "Oxford Theory Coincidences," *The Hackney Spectator*, June 13, p. 10.

Personal Letters

1920   Letter to J. Thomas Looney, November 11.

1921   Letter to J. Thomas Looney, January 10.

Knight, G. Wilson

1930   "Shakespeare and the Earl of Oxford," *The Nation and Athenaeum*, vol. 46, no. 4 (May 3): 150.

Kositsky, Lynne [with Roger Stritmatter]

Books

2013   *On the Date, Sources and Design of Shakespeare's The Tempest* (Jefferson, NC: McFarland & Co.)

Articles and reviews

2004   "A Critique of *The Monument* Theory," *Shakespeare Matters*, vol. 4, no. 1 (Fall): 1, 10-14.

Kuhn, Thomas S.

2012   *The Structure of Scientific Revolutions, Fourth Edition* (Chicago: University of Chicago Press). [1962]

Lambin, Georges

1962   "Professor Abel Lefranc," *Shakespearean Authorship Review*, no. 8 (Autumn): 11.

Lancashire Evening Post, The

1934   "And a Claim," November 29, p. 5.

Lapham, Lewis H.

1999   "The Ghost of Shakespeare," *Harper's Magazine*, vol. 298 (April): 10-21.

Lawrence, Basil Edwin

1925   *Notes on the Authorship of Shakespeare's Plays and Poems* (London: Gay and Hancock).

Lawrence, Herbert

1769   *The Life and Adventures of Common Sense*. Two volumes. (Dublin: R. Moncrieffe).

Lay, C. H.

1937   "Shakespeare, a Suffolk Man" [letter], *East Anglian Magazine*, vol. 2, no. 8 (May): 362.

Leahy, William

Books

2010   *Shakespeare and His Authors: Critical Perspectives on the Authorship Question* (London: Continuum).

2018   *My Shakespeare: The Authorship Controversy: Experts Examine the Arguments for Bacon, Neville, Oxford, Marlowe, Mary Sidney, Shakspere, and Shakespeare* (Edward Everett Root, Publishers).

Articles and reviews

2007   "'Two Households, Both Alike in Dignity:' The Authorship Question and Academia," *The De Vere Society Newsletter*, February 2007, pp. 4-11.

2009   "The Shakespeare Question: A Suitable Subject for Academia*?*" *Discovering Shakespeare*, edited by Daniel Wright, pp. 5-11.

Lee, Sir Sidney
> Books
> 1915   *A Life of William Shakespeare* (London: Smith, Elder & Co.).
> 1922   *A Life of William Shakespeare* (London: J. Murray).
> 1929   *Elizabethan and Other Essays*, selected and edited by Frederick S. Boas (Oxford: The Clarendon Press).
>
> As Editor
> 1910   *Dictionary of National Biography*, 11th edition. (London: Smith, Elder & Co.).
>
> Articles
> 1910   "Shakespeare, William," *Dictionary of National Biography*, 11th edition, vol. 51: 348-397 (London: Smith, Elder & Co.).
> 1910   "Vere, Edward," *Dictionary of National Biography* , 11th edition, vol. 58: 225-228 (London: Smith, Elder & Co.).
> 1919   "More Doubts About Shakespeare," *Quarterly Review*, vol. 231 (July): 194-206.
> 1920   "The Identity of Shakespeare," *The Bookman's Journal*, vol. 2, no. 30 (May 21): 58.
>
> Personal letters
> 1921   Letter to Cecil Palmer, June 13. [British Library Archives, RP 9086, PC 320, Box 250]

Lee, Sir Sidney & Sir Edmund Chambers
> 1925   *A Shakespeare Reference Library* (English Association, July). [pamphlet no. 61]

Leeds Mercury, The
> 1931   "Who Wrote Plays of Shakespeare?" December 14, 1931, p. 1.

Lefranc, Abel
> 1988   *Under the Mask of William Shakespeare*, translated by Cecil Cragg (Braunton: Merlin Books, Ltd.). [*Sous le Masque de William Shakespeare*. 1918/1919]

Leitch, Vincent B. and William E. Cain (General Editors)
> 2010   *The Norton Anthology of Theory and Criticism, 2nd Edition* (New York: Norton).

Literary Digest, The
> 1920   "'Shakespeare' Identified Again," August 14, p. 32-33.

Londonderry Sentinel, The
> 1932   "Lord Sydenham on Authorship Dispute," May 3. p. 3.

Londré, Felicia
> 1997   *Love's Labour's Lost: Critical Essays* (New York: Garland Pub.).

Looney, J. Thomas
> Books and pamphlets
> 1918   *"Shakespeare" Identified: A Preliminary Notice*, December 14 (Printed privately).
> 1920   *"Shakespeare" Identified* (London: Cecil Palmer).
> 1920   *"Shakespeare" Identified* (New York: Frederick A. Stokes).
> 1921   *The Poems of Edward de Vere* (London: Cecil Palmer).
> 1948   *"Shakespeare" Identified* (New York: Duell, Sloan & Pearce). [second U.S. edition]
> 1975   *"Shakespeare" Identified*, Ruth Loyd Miller, editor (Port Washington, NY: Kennikat Press for Minos Pub. Co.). [third U.S. edition]
> 2018   *"Shakespeare" Identified*, James A. Warren, editor (Somerville, MA: Forever Press; reprinted in 2019 by Veritas Publications, Cary, NC.) [centenary edition]
> 2019   *"Shakespeare" Revealed: The Collected Articles and Published Letters of J. Thomas Looney*, edited by James A. Warren (Cary, NC: Veritas Publications).
>
> Articles, reviews and published letters
> 1920   "Shakespeare Identified" [letter], *The Scotsman*, March 4, p. 2.
> 1920   "Shakespeare Identified" [letter], *Yorkshire Post and Leets Intelligencer*, March 11, p. 4.
> 1920   "Shakespeare Identified" [letter], *The Scotsman*, March 20, p. 11.
> 1920   "'Shakespeare' Identified" [letter], *The Times Literary Supplement*, issue 949 (March 25): 201.
> 1920   "Shakespeare Identified: A Reply to Critics and Some New Facts," *The Yorkshire Post and Leeds Intelligencer*, April 1, p. 8.
> 1920   "Is Shakespeare Identified?" [letter], *The Bookman's Journal*, vol. 1, no. 24 (April 9): 452-53.
> 1920   "Edward de Vere and Shakespeare" [letter], *The Saturday Review*, vol. 129: (April 17)

370.

1920   "The Shakespeare Controversy" [letter], *The Bookman's Journal*, vol. 1, no. 26 (April 23): 484.

1920   "Shakespeare's Identity: The Case for Lord Oxford" [letter], *Western Mail*, May 6, p. 7.

1920   "The Identity of Shakespeare" [letter], *The Bookman's Journal*, vol. 2, no. 30 (May 21): 58-59.

1920   "The Identity of Shakespeare" [letter], *The Bookman's Journal*, vol. 2, no. 31 (May 28): 68.

1920   "Readers and Writers" [letter], *The New Age*, vol. 28, no. 8 (December 23): 91.

1921   "Readers and Writers" [letter], *The New Age*, vol. 28, no. 12 (January 20): 138-139.

1921   "Readers and Writers" [additional response to reviewer], *The New Age*, vol. 28, no. 16 (February 17): 192.

1921   "Stratford and Stony Stratford" [letter], *The Bookman's Journal*, vol. 3, no. 74 (March 25): 388.

1921   "Shakespeare, Lord Oxford, Solomon Eagle and Mr. Looney" [letter], *The Outlook*, June 25, p. 543-45.

1921   "'Shakespeare's' Identity" [letter], *The Sydney Morning Herald*, July 15, p. 12.

1921   "Mr. Looney Replies" [letter], *The Outlook*, July 16, pp. 58-59.

1922   "'Shakespeare'—Lord Oxford or Lord Derby?" *The National Review*, vol. 78 (February 1922): 801-809.

1922   "The Earl of Oxford as Shakespeare: New Evidence," *The Golden Hind*, vol. 1, no. 1 (October): 23-30.

1923   "The Oxford Movement," *The Hackney Spectator*, April 13, p. 8.

1923   "Who Wrote *Hamlet*?" *The Hackney Spectator*, April 20, p. 4.

1923   "How the *Observer* Observes," *The Hackney Spectator*, May 11, p. 2.

1923   "The Shakespeare Problem," *The Freethinker*, vol. 42, no. 33 (June 10): 364-365.

1923   "'Shakespeare:' Was it Oxford, Bacon, or Derby? Part I," *The Freethinker*, vol. 43, no. 26 (July 1): 412-13.

1923   "'Shakespeare:' Was it Oxford, Bacon, or Derby? Part II," *The Freethinker*, vol. 43, no. 27 (July 8): 428-429.

1923   "An Elizabethan Literary Group," *The Hackney Spectator*, August 3, p. 4.

1923   "An Elizabethan Literary Group, II," *The Hackney Spectator*, August 14, p. 9.

1923   "An Elizabethan Literary Group, III," *The Hackney Spectator*, August 24, p. 4.

1923   "A *Daily News* Critic," *The Hackney Spectator*, August 31, p. 4.

1923   "The *Church Times* and a Rejected Letter, I," *The Hackney Spectator*, September 7, p. 4.

1923   "The *Church Times* and a Rejected Letter, II," *The Hackney Spectator*, September 14, p. 4.

1923   "The Shakespeare Problem," *The Freethinker*, vol. 42, no. 33 (June 10): 364-65.

1923   "Shakespearean Research at Hackney and Southwark, I," *The Hackney Spectator*, November 30, p. 4.

1924   "Shakespearean Researches at Hackney and Southwark, VI," *The Hackney Spectator*, January 11, p. 9.

1935   "Jonson v. Jonson, Part 1," *The Shakespeare Pictorial*, no. 86 (April): 64.

1935   "Lord Oxford and the Shrew Plays, Part 1," *The Sh. Pictorial*, no. 93 (November), 176.

1940   "The Author of *"Shakespeare" Identified* Comments on Professor Campbell's July 1940 *Harper's* Article," *Sh. Fellowship News-Letter* (American), vol. 2, no. 1 (Dec.): 1-3.

1941   "Shakespeare: A Missing Author, Part 1," *Shakespeare Fellowship News-Letter* (American), vol. 2, no. 2 (February): 13-17.

Personal letters

1922   Letter to Katharine E. Eggar, March 4. [Eggar Archives]

1922   Letter to Sir George Greenwood, March 14. [Folger Shakespeare Library]

1922   Letter to Sir George Greenwood, November 3. [excerpts reprinted in *Hackney Spectator*, November 24, 1922]

1926   Letter to Eva Turner Clark, June 26. [reprinted in "Discoverer of the True Shakespeare Passes," *Shakespeare Fellowship Quarterly*, vol. V, no. 2 (April 1944): 17-23.]

1929   Letter to Katharine E. Eggar, August 25. [Eggar Archives]

1930   Letter to Katharine E. Eggar, January 12. [Eggar Archives]

1932   Letter to Carolyn Wells, December 6. [reprinted in *Shakespeare Fellowship Quarterly*, vol. V, no. 2 (April 1944): 17-23.]

1933   Letter to Messrs. Field Roscoe and Co., January 14, 1933. [JTL papers]

1933   Letter to Prof. Joan V. Robinson, September 3. [Reprinted in *Shakespeare Oxford Newsletter*, vol. 43, no. 3 (Summer 2007): 8-9.]

1935   Letter to Katharine E. Eggar, September 19. [Eggar Archives]

1936   Letter to Katharine E. Eggar, February 21. [continuation of the letter begun February 19.] [Eggar Archives]

1936   Letter to Katharine E. Eggar, October 29. [Eggar Archives]

1936   Letter to Katharine E. Eggar, November 26. [Eggar Archives]

1936   Letter to Katharine E. Eggar, December 21. [Eggar Archives]

1937   Letter to Charles Wisner Barrell, June 6. (excerpts reprinted in *Shakespeare Fellowship Quarterly*, vol. V, no. 2 (April 1944): 22-23)

1937   Letter to Charles Wisner Barrell, June 6. [reprinted in *Shakespeare Fellowship Quarterly*, vol. V, no. 2 (April 1944): 22-23.]

1938   Letter to Katharine E. Eggar, January 22. [Eggar Archives]

1940   Letter to Eva Turner Clark, early in year. [excerpt reprinted in *Shakespeare Fellowship News-Letter* (American), vol. 1, no. 2 (February 1940): 5.]

1941   Letter to Gerald H. Rendall, May 2, 1941. [Rendall archives]

1941   Letter to Flodden W. Heron, July 5. [excerpts reprinted in *Shakespeare Fellowship Quarterly*, vol. VI, no. 3 (July 1945): 33-34.]

1942   Letter to Charles Barrell, May 15. [excerpts reprinted in Charles Wisner Barrell, "Afterwords," in J. Thomas Looney, *"Shakespeare" Identified* (1948), p. 464; and in "Discoverer of the True Shakespeare Passes, *Shakespeare Fellowship Quarterly*, vol. V, no. 2 (April): 23.]

Lucas, R. Macdonald

    Articles and reviews

1921   "Did Lord Derby Write Shakespeare?" *The National Review*, vol. 78 (November): 359-369.

    Personal Letters

1922   Letter to J. Thomas Looney, February 14. [JTL papers]

1922   Letter to J. Thomas Looney, April 15. [JTL papers]

Lynd, Robert

1939   "Saturday Essay," *News Chronicle*, January 14, p. 7.

Lyon, Karen

2019   "Elizabethan Education and Ben Jonson's School Days," Folger Shakespeare Library Website, Sept. 3. [Accessed Jan. 27, 2021. https://shakespeareandbeyond.folger.edu/2019/09/03/ben-jonson-school-elizabethan-education/?utm_source=wordfly&utm_medium=email&utm_campaign=ShakespearePlus4Sep2019&utm_content=version_A&promo=]

Mackail, J. W.

1934   "The Life of Shakespeare," in *A Companion to Shakespeare Studies* edited by G. B. Harrison & Granville Barker, pp. 1-8 (Cambridge: The University Press).

Magri, Noemi

2014   *Such Fruits Out of Italy: The Italian Renaissance in Shakespeare's Plays and Poems*, edited by Gary Goldstein (Buchholz, Germany: Laugwitz Verlag).

Malim, Richard

    Books

2012   *The Earl of Oxford and the Making of "Shakespeare:" The Literary Life of Edward de Vere in Context* (London: McFarland and Co.).

    Articles, reviews and published letters

2013   [letter], *Shakespeare Matters*, vol. 12, no. 2 (Spring): 2.

2015   "Shaksper the Nonentity," *The De Vere Society Newsletter*, vol. 22, no. 1 (January): 13-18.

2017   "Southwell and Oxford," *The De Vere Society Newsletter*, January, p. 20, pp. 17-21.

Manchester City News, The

1931   "The Shakespeare Maze: A Sevenfold Clue," November 25.

Manchester Guardian, The

1928   "The Seventeenth Earl of Oxford," April 27, p. 258.

1932   "Miscellany: This Bacon Business," March 24, p. 7.

Marcus, Leah S.

1888   *Puzzling Shakespeare* (Berkeley: University of California Press).

Mattias, Laura Wilson
    2012   *Last Will. & Testament.* [film]

Matus, Irvin Leigh
    1994   *Shakespeare, in Fact* (New York: Continuum).

Maycock, Shelly
    2016   "Branding the Author: Feigned Authorship Neutrality and the Folger Folio Tour," in *The 1623 Shakespeare First Folio: A Minority Report*, pp. 5-29 [A special issue of *Brief Chronicles*] (Baltimore: Shakespeare Oxford Fellowship).
    2017   "All That is Shakespeare Melts into Air" [with Michael Dudley and Gary Goldstein], [review of *The New Oxford Shakespeare Authorship Companion*, ed. by Gary Taylor, et. al.], *The Oxfordian*, vol. 19: 195-208.

McAree, J. V.
    1937   "Makes Shakespeare Look Dubious," *The Globe and Mail*, August 2, p. 6.
    1937   "Shakespeare Fans Read This Column," *The Globe and Mail*, August 7, p. 6.
    1937   "Another Claimant for Poet's Crown," *The Globe and Mail*, September 8, p. 6.
    1940   "Barrell Rolls Out Some Rich Stuff," *The Globe and Mail*, January 5, p. 6.
    1940   "Not a Controversy But Good Imitation," *The Globe and Mail*, January 13, p. 6.
    1955   "It's Shakespeare, After All," *The Globe and Mail*, June 27, p. 6.

McCarthy, Penny
    2006   *Pseudonymous Shakespeare* (Burlington, VT: Ashgate Publishing Company).

McCormick, A. D.
    1934   "The Prince of Wales Christmas Card," *The Sh. Pictorial*, no. 82 (December): 190.

McCrea, Scott
    2002   "Two Shakespeares: A Skeptical Analysis of Shakespeare and His Works Reveals the Real Author," *Skeptic Magazine*, vol. 9, no. 4 (Winter): 70.

McFee, William
    1948   "The Master Mystery," in J. Thomas Looney, *"Shakespeare" Identified*, pp. xiii-xxi.

McNeil, Alex
    <u>Books edited with Mark Anderson and Alexander Waugh</u>
    2016   *Contested Year: An Anthology of Critical Reviews and Corrections to Each Chapter of James Shapiro's The Year of Lear: Shakespeare in 1606.*
    <u>Articles and reviews</u>
    2004   "From the President: 'Who will believe my verse?,'" *Shakespeare Matters*, vol. 3, no. 4 (Summer): 3.
    2009   "What Do 'the Oxfordians' Think?" *Shakespeare Matters*, vol. 8, no. 3 (Summer): 6, 15, 18-19.
    2012   "Survey Says (2011)," *Shakespeare Matters*, vol. 11, no. 1 (Winter): 29-34.
    2014   "Survey Says," *Shakespeare Oxford Newsletter*, vol. 50, no. 4 (Fall): 17-19.
    2016   "Jacobi and Rylance Go Public," *Sh. Oxford Newsletter*, vol. 52, no. 2 (Spring): 1, 28.
    2018   "2017 SOF Conference Survey Results," *Shakespeare Oxford Newsletter* (Winter): 13-15.

McQuilland, Louis J.
    1920   "The Mystery of William Shakespeare," *Oamaru Mail*.

Metcalf, W. Day
    1938   "Shakespeare Plays: Several People Had Hand in Composition," *The Yorkshire Post*, October 31, p. 3.

Mez, J. R.
    1952   "George Gascoigne," *Shakespeare Fellowship News-Letter*, September 1952, pp. 3-4.

Miller, Ruth Loyd (editor)
    1975   *"Shakespeare" Identified*, 2 vols. Second vol. is titled *Oxfordian Vistas*. Ruth Loyd Miller, editor. [Third U.S. edition] (Port Washington, N.Y.: Kennikat Press and Jennings, LA: Minos Publishing).

Minchin, H. C.
    1920   "Who Was Shakespeare?" *The Sunday Times*, April 4, p. 5.

Miss Manners
    2014   "Crank Letters Need No Response," *The Times*, March 15, p. E7.

Moore, Peter R.
  1990   "Claremont McKenna College's Shakespeare Clinic," *Shakespeare Oxford Newsletter*, vol. 26, no. 3A (Summer): 7-10.
  2004   "Demonography 101: Alan Nelson's *Monstrous Adversary*," *Shakespeare Oxford Newsletter*, vol. 40, no. 1 (Winter): 1, 15-22.

Morning Post, The
  1920   "A New Round Game," April 1, p. 5.
  1929   "The Way of History" [editorial], September 3, 1929, p. 10.
  1930   "Shakespeare's Plays: Edward de Vere and Their Authorship," April 14, p. 5.
  1933   "New Shakespeare Theory: Queen Elizabeth and Oxford; An Unacknowledged Son?" September 28.
  1934   "One Shakespeare or Two?" April 27.

Morrow, William [Frederick A. Stokes, Publisher]
  1920   Letter to J. Thomas Looney, Oct. 29. [JTL papers]

Mumpsimum
  1948   "Who Was Shakespeare?" [letter], *The Washington Post*, August 8, p. B4.

Nelson, Alan H.
  Books
  2003   *Monstrous Adversity: The Life of Edward de Vere, 17th Earl of Oxford* (Liverpool: Liverpool University Press).
  Articles and reviews
  1999   [review of *Alias Shakespeare: Solving the Greatest Literary Mystery of All Time* by Joseph Sobran], *Shakespeare Quarterly*, vol. 50, no. 3 (Autumn): 376-382.

Newdigate. B. H. [B. H. N.]
  1929   [review of *Shakespeare and Chapman as Topical Dramatists* by Percy Allen], *The Shakespeare Pictorial*, no. 13 (March): 8.

New Statesman, The
  1920   "The Latest Shakespeare," March 20, p. 713.
  1921   "New Poems of Shakespeare," June 4, p. 252.
  1928   "The Seventeenth Earl of Oxford," June 2, pp. 268-69.

New York Herald Tribune, The
  1933   "*Love's Labour's Lost*: A Study," May 21, p. H16.
  1933   "Shakespeare? Oxford and Elizabethan Times," November. [date not known]
  1938   "The Mantle of Shakespeare," February 13, p. G11.
  1947   "Bacon Has a Rival as Shakespeare: De Vere Supporters Make Post-War Appearance," May 30, p. 17.

New York Sun, The
  1942   "Shakespeare's Day" (April) [excerpts reprinted in *Shakespeare Fellowship News-Letter* (American), vol. 3, no. 4 (June): 54]

New York Times, The
  1933   "Love's Labour's Lost," May 28, p. BR15.
  1944   "John T. Looney," February 21, p. 15.
  1945   "Dr. Gerald H. Rendall," February 20, p. 19.
  2007   "Did He or Didn't He? That Is the Question," 22 April.

News Leader, The (Richmond, VA)
  1931   [review quoted in *Shakespeare Pictorial* ad], December.

Nicholl, Charles
  2013   "The Case for Marlowe," in *Shakespeare Beyond Doubt* edited by Paul Edmondson and Stanley Wells, pp. 29-38.

Nicholson, A. P.
  1931   "A Good Playwright," *Saturday Review*, September 5, pp. 303-304.

Nickell, John
  2011   "Did Shakespeare Write Shakespeare? Much Ado About Nothing," *Skeptical Inquirer*, November-December, p. 38.

Niederkorn, William
  2002   "A Historic Whodunit: If Shakespeare Didn't, Who Did?" *New York Times*, February 10.

2002   "Letter to the Editors," *Shakespeare Matters*, vol. 1, no. 4 (Summer 2002): 2.

2005   "The Shakespeare Code, and Other Fanciful Ideas from the Traditional Camp," *New York Times*, August 30.

2007   "Shakespeare Reaffirmed," *New York Times*, April 22, p. A4.

2010   "Absolute Will," *The Brooklyn Rail: Critical Perspectives on Arts, Politics, and Culture*, April.

2013   "Foreword," in *On the Date, Sources and Design of Shakespeare's The Tempest* by Roger A. Stritmatter and Lynne Kositsky, pp. 1-6.

Northern Whig and Belfast Post, The

1931   "Anti-Shakespeare," February 7, p. 11.

Notes and Queries

1928   "Shakespeare, Jonson and Wilkins as Borrowers," vol. 154 (March 24): p. 215.

1931   "The Oxford-Shakespeare Case Corroborated," vol. 160, no. 10 (March 7): 180.

1939   "De Vere, Earl of Oxford, Author of Shakespeare's Plays," vol. 177, no. 21 (November 18): 368.

Nottingham Journal

1920   "Interesting Half Hour Talk at Carrington," March 19, p. 5.

O'Connor, Rt. Hon. T. P.

1928   "Sir George Greenwood" [letter], *The Sunday Times*, November 4, p. 14.

Ogburn, Charlton, Jr.

   Books

1984   *The Mysterious William Shakespeare: The Myth & the Reality* (McLean, VA: EPM Publications, Inc.).

1992   *The Mysterious William Shakespeare: The Myth & the Reality*, second edition (McLean, VA: EPM Publications, Inc.).

1995   *The Man Who Was Shakespeare: A Summary of the Case Unfolded in The Mysterious William Shakespeare: The Myth and the Reality* (Delaplane, VA: EPM Publications).

   Articles, reviews, prefaces and published letters

1952   "Preface" to *This Star of England* by Dorothy and Charlton Ogburn (New York: Coward-McCann, Inc.).

1970   "Shakespeare, Who He?" [letter], *The Washington Post*, Sept. 6, p. 9.

1996   "Excerpts from Charlton Ogburn's Letter," *Sh. Oxford Newsletter*, vol. 32, no. 4 (Fall): 7.

1997   [letter reprinted in "Plucking the Tudor Rose"], *The Elizabethan Review*, vol. 5, no. 1 (Spring): 7-17.

1997   "Shakespeare and the Fair Youth" [letter: response to Sobran], *Shakespeare Oxford Newsletter*, vol. 33, no. 3 (Summer): 4, 12.

Ogburn, Charlton, Sr.

1947   "Oxford, Poet and Playwright?" [letter], *New York Herald Tribune*, June 15, p. A7.

Ogburn, Dorothy

1945   [letter], reprinted in "Beginning Our Sixth Year," *Shakespeare Fellowship Quarterly*, vol. VI, no. 1 (January): 2.

1945   "The Wounded Name of Truth," *Sh. Fellowship Quarterly*, vol. VI, no. 4 (October): 61-62.

1947   "Oxford's Literary Genius" [letter], *New York Herald Tribune*, July 29, p. A7.

Ogburn, Dorothy & Charlton

1952   *This Star of England: "William Shakespeare" Man of the Renaissance* (New York: Coward-McCann, Inc.).

1955   *The Renaissance Man of England,* newly corrected and augmented by the authors (New York: Coward-McCann, Inc.). [1947]

O'Hagan, Thomas

1936   *What Shakespeare is Not* (Toronto: The Hunter-Rose Co., Ltd.).

Olds, Nathaniel S.

1946   "Revisions May Have to be Made in English Literature Textbooks" *The Villager*. [excerpts reprinted in *Shakespeare Fellowship Quarterly*, vol. VII, no. 1 (January): 13.]

Oman, Charles

1929   "Shakespeare and Richard III" [letter], *Morning Post*, Sept. 6, p. 6.

Orage, Alfred R. [R. H. C.]

1920   "Readers and Writers," *The New Age*, vol. 28, no. 5 (Dec. 2): 55.

1920   "Readers and Writers" [reply to Looney], *The New Age*, vol. 28, no. 8 (Dec. 23): 92.

1921   "Readers and Writers" [second reply to Looney], *The New Age*, vol. 28, no. 12 (January 20): 139.

1921   "Readers and Writers" [additional reply], *The New Age*, vol. 28, no. 13 (January 27): 155-156.

Oreskes, Naomi

1999   *The Rejection of Continental Drift: Theory and Method in American Earth Science* (Oxford: Oxford University Press).

Ostrowski, Donald

2020   *Who Wrote That? Authorship Controversies from Moses to Sholokhov* (Ithaca: Northern Illinois University Press).

Palmer, Cecil (See also Cecil Palmer, Publisher)

<u>Articles, reviews and letters for publication</u>

1920   Letter to trade publications. [reprinted in *"'Shakespeare' Identified in Edward de Vere,"* *The Publishers' Circular*, March 6, p. 237.]

<u>Personal Letters</u>

1920   Letter to J. Thomas Looney, February 23. [JTL papers]

1920   Letter to J. Thomas Looney, April 8. [JTL papers]

1923   Letter to J. Thomas Looney, July 3. [JTL papers]

1930   Letter to Col. Bernard R. Ward. [reprinted in "John Lyly and the Office of the Revels," *Shakespeare Pictorial*, August, p. 16.]

Parisious, Roger

1998   "Occultist Influence on the Authorship Controversy," *The Elizabethan Review*, vol. 6, no. 1 (Spring): 9-43.

1998   "Postscript to the Tudor Rose Theory," *The Elizabethan Review*, vol. 6, no. 2 (Autumn): 90-93.

Parsons, J. M.

1932   "Shakespeare's Ghost," *The Spectator*, vol. 148 (January 30): 149.

Paul, Christopher

2002   "The Prince Tudor Dilemma: Hip Thesis, Hypothesis or Old Wives' Tale?" *The Oxfordian*, vol. 5: 47-69.

2002   [review of *Oxford, Son of Queen Elizabeth I* by Paul Streitz], *Shakespeare Matters*, vol. 1, no. 4 (Summer): 17-18.

2006   "A First Blast of the Trumpet Against the *Monstrous Adversary*," *Shakespeare Matters*, vol. 6, no. 1 (Fall): 22-27.

2007   "A New Letter by J. T. Looney Brought to Light," *Shakespeare Oxford Newsletter*, vol. 43, no. 3 (Summer): 8-9.

Pendleton, Thomas

1995   "From the Editors," *The Shakespeare Newsletter*, vol. 45, no. 2 (Summer): 26.

2003   "Alan H. Nelson's *Monstrous Adversary: The Life of Edward De Vere, 17th Earl of Oxford*," *The Shakespeare Newsletter*, vol. 53, issue 3, no. 258 (Fall): 65, 69, 95.

Perkins School for the Blind

2020   "Hellen Keller, Shakespeare Skeptic" (https://www.perkins.org/stories/helen-keller-shakespeare-skeptic, accessed August 22, 2020).

Philadelphia Public Ledger, The

1931   [review of *Hidden Allusions* by Eva Turner Clark]. [excerpt quoted in a Cecil Palmer advertisement in *Shakespeare Pictorial*, no. 46 (December).]

Phillips, Gerald M.

<u>Books</u>

1932   *The Tragic Story of "Shakespeare," Disclosed in the Sonnets* (London: Cecil Palmer).

1935   *Sunlight on Shakespeare's Sonnets* (London: Thornton Butterworth, Ltd.).

<u>Personal letters</u>

1933   Letter to J. Thomas Looney, September 28. [JTL papers]

Phillips, Robin

2020   *SHAKESPEARE: The Truth Behind the Name*. [film]

Plato

1990   *The Republic*, vol. 7 of *Great Books of the Western World, Second Edition*, pp. 295-441 (Chicago: Encyclopedia Britannica, Inc.).

Pollard, Alfred W.

1920   "Another 'Identification' of Shakespeare," *The Times Literary Supplement*, issue 946 (March 4): 149.

Porohovshikov, P. S.

Articles and reviews

1939   "Who Was Shakespeare?" *John O'London's Weekly*, January 27, pp. 657-661.

Personal letters

1931   Letter to J. Thomas Looney, January 7. [JTL papers]

Prechter, Robert R., Jr.

2005   "The *Sonnets* Dedication Puzzle, 1," *Shakespeare Matters*, vol. 4, no. 3 (Spring): 1, 12-19.

2005   "The *Sonnets* Dedication Puzzle, 2," *Shakespeare Matters*, vol. 4, no. 4 (Summer): 1, 18-27.

Price, Diana

Books

2012   *Shakespeare's Unorthodox Biography: New Evidence of an Authorship Problem*, published in paperback with corrections, revisions, and additions. (Shakespeare-authorship.com) [First published by Greenwood Press, Westport, CT, 2001]

Articles and published letters

1996   "Rough Winds Do Shake: A Fresh Look at the Tudor Rose Theory," *The Elizabethan Review*, vol. 4, no. 2 (Autumn): 4-23.

2003   [letter], *Skeptic Magazine*, vol. 11, no. 3 (Spring): 22.

2005   "Shakespeare's Authorship and Questions of Evidence," *Skeptic Magazine*, vol. 11, no. 3 (Fall): 10-15.

Prodromou, Luke

2019   "The Shakespeare Authorship Debate Continued: Uncertainties and Mysteries," *The Oxfordian 21* (September): 13-33.

Publishers' Circular, The

1920   "'Shakespeare' Identified in Edward de Vere," March 6, pp. 233, 237.

Punch, or the London Charivari

1920   "Bridging the Literary Gulf," May 19, p. 396.

Quiller-Couch, Arthur

1918   *Notes on Shakespeare's Workmanship, From Lectures by Sir Arthur Quiller-Couch* (London: T. Fisher Unwin).

1924   *Shakespeare's Workmanship* (London: T. Fischer Unwin, Ltd.).

R. H. C. [see Alfred R. Orage]

Raleigh, Sir Walter

1907   *Shakespeare* (London: Macmillan & Co., Ltd.). [Reprinted 1928]

Ranson, F. Lingard

Books

1937   *Lavenham, Suffolk* (printed privately).

Articles

1937   "Shakespeare Was an East Anglian," *East Anglian Magazine*, vol. 2, no. 7 (April): 292-300.

1937   "Correspondence," *East Anglian Magazine*, vol. 2, no. 9 (June): 422.

1937   "Lord Oxford and Shakespeare," *East Anglian Magazine*, vol. 2, no. 12 (September): 551.

1937   "Shakespearean Page," *East Anglian Magazine*, vol. 3, no. 3 (December): 148.

1938   "Shakespearean Page," *East Anglian Magazine*, vol. 3, no. 7 (May): 351.

1938   "The Trend of Shakespearean Thought Today," *East Anglian Magazine*, vol. 3, no. 11 (September): 520-521.

1941   "A Letter from Lavenham" [his October 31, 1940 letter], *Shakespeare Fellowship News-Letter* (American), vol. 2, no. 2 (February): 21.

Rascoe, Burton

1945   "The Battle Still Rages Over Who Was Shakespeare," *New York World-Telegram*, July 31.

Ray, William J.

2011   "Two Years after *Contested Will* or, How are the Stratfordians Doing?" *Shakespeare*

Matters, vol. 10, no. 4 (Fall): 24-30.

Reedy, William M.
    1920a   "Another Shakespeare," *Reedy's Mirror*, vol. 29, no. 24 (June 10): 474.
    1920b   "The Shakespeare Myth," *Reedy's Mirror*, vol. 29, no. 25 (June 17): 493.

Regnier, Thomas
    2003   "Could Shakespeare Think Like a Lawyer," *University of Miami Law Review*, vol. 57, no. 2 (January).
    2006   "Teaching Shakespeare and the Law," *Shakespeare Matters*, vol. 6, no. 1 (Fall): 1, 11-13.
    2011   "The Law in *Hamlet*: Death, Property, and the Pursuit of Justice," *Brief Chronicles*, vol. III (Fall): 109-134.
    2014   [Review of *Shakespeare Beyond Doubt: Evidence, Argument, Controversy* edited by Paul Edmondson & Stanley Wells], *Brief Chronicles*, vol. V: 193-204.

Reisz, Matthew
    2014   "Much Taboo, But Not About Nothing," *Times Higher Education* [weekly supplement to *The Times*], issue 2169 (September 11): 10.

Rendall, Gerald H.
    Books and pamphlets
    1930   *Shakespeare Sonnets and Edward de Vere* (London: John Murray).
    1931   *Shake-speare Handwriting and Spelling* (London: Cecil Palmer).
    1934   *Personal Clues in Shakespeare Poems and Sonnets* (London: John Lane).
    1939   *Ben Jonson and the First Folio of Shakespeare's Plays.* [pamphlet]
    1941   *Arthur Golding, Translator—Personal and Literary—Shakespeare and Edward de Vere* [pamphlet]
    1944   *Shakespeare in Essex and East Anglia.* [pamphlet]
    Articles, reviews, published letters
    1930   "Shakespeare Sonnets and Edward de Vere" [letter], *Times Literary Supplement*, issue 1478 (May 29): 457-58.
    1930   "Shakespeare's Handwriting and Orthography" [letter], *Times Literary Supplement*, issue 1495 (Sept. 25): 757.
    1932   "The Earl of Oxford as Shakespeare," *Everyman*, Aug. 25.
    1934   "The 'Mortal Moon' Sonnet" [letter], *Times Literary Sup.*, issue 1676 (March 15): 194.
    1937   "Shakespearean Page," *East Anglian Magazine*, vol. 3, no. 2 (November): 74-75.
    1939   "Notes and Comments on *An Enquiry*," Supplement 1, *SF Newsletter*, no. 14 (April): 1-5.
    1941   "Arthur Golding, Translator—Personal and Literary—Shakespeare and Edward de Vere," *The Essex Review*, April, p. 108. [reprinted as a pamphlet in 1941.]
    1966   "1930 Toast to Edward de Vere." [reprinted in *Shakespearean Authorship Review*, no. 15 (Spring): 3.]
    Personal letters
    1936   Letter to Katharine E. Eggar, November 23. [Eggar Archives]

Richardson, Friend W.
    1943   "Fighting a Man of Straw," *Hemet News* (March 16).

Robertson, J. M.
    Books
    1926   *The Problems of the Shakespeare Sonnets* (London: Routledge).
    1931   *The State of Shakespeare Study: A Critical Conspectus* (London: Routledge).
    Articles and reviews
    1920   "The New Shakespeare Claim," *Yorkshire Post and Leeds Intelligencer*, March 6, p. 6.
    1920   "The Identity of Shakespeare," *The Bookman's Journal*, vol. 2, issue 30 (May 21): 59.

Robinson, Joan
    1933   "Shakespeare and Mr. Looney," *Cambridge Review*, no. 54 (May 12): 389.

Robinson, W. Ringland [W. R. R.]
    1938   "Bacon-Shakespeare theory" [letter], *Northern Whig and Belfast Post*, January 13, p. 3.
    1938   "A Group of Authors?" [letter], *Northern Whig and Belfast Post*, January 27, p. 9.

Roe, Richard Paul
    2011   *The Shakespeare Guide to Italy: Retracing the Bard's Unknown Travels* (New York: Harper Perennial).

Rolland, Romain
    1920   "Shakespeare the Truthteller," *Dial*, August, pp. 109-121.

Rollett, John M.
    1997   "The Dedications to Shakespeare's *Sonnets*," *Elizabethan Review*, vol. 5, no. 2 (Autumn): 93-122.
    1999   "Secrets of the Dedication to Shakespeare's *Sonnets*," *The Oxfordian*, vol. 2: 60-75.
    2000   "Was Southampton Regarded as the Son of the Queen? Part 1," *De Vere Society Newsletter*, January, pp. 8-12.
    2000   "Was Southampton Regarded as the Son of the Queen? Part 2," *De Vere Society Newsletter*, July, pp. 19-27.
    2001   [Letter], *De Vere Society Newsletter*, January, p. 18.

Rollins, Hyder E. (editor)
    1927   *The Paradise of Dainty Devices* (Cambridge, MA: Harvard University Press).
    1935   *England's Helicon*, vol. II (Cambridge, MA: Harvard University Press).

Rubin, Don
    2015   "Spinning Shakespeare," *The Oxfordian*, vol. 17 (September): 63-77.

Rush, Peter
    2016   *Hidden in Plain Sight: The True History Revealed in Shake-speare's Sonnets*, second edition (Leesburg, VA: Real Deal Publications). [2015]

Rutherford, Forrest
    1946   "Daniel Frohman Introduces the Great Unknown," *Shakespeare Fellowship Quarterly*, vol. VII, no. 1 (January): 1-2.

S.
    1921   "Stratford and Stony Stratford," *The Bookman's Journal*, vol. 3, no. 71 (March 4): 335.

S. W.
    1931   "The Earl of Oxford Also a Candidate for Shakespeare's Crown," *Philadelphia Enquirer*, April 25, p. 14.

Saben, Mowry
    1939   Letter to George Frisbee, December 21. [JTL papers]

Saintsbury, George
    Publications edited
    1932   *The Cambridge History of English Literature* (Cambridge: University Press). [1910]
    Articles and reviews
    1926   "The Hundred Flowers," *The Nation and the Athenaeum*, vol. 39, no. 10 (June 12): 295.

Sammartino, Peter
    1990   *The Man Who Was William Shakespeare* (New York: Cornwall Books).

Sampson, George
    1928   "More About Shakespeare," *The Bookman*, vol. 75 (May): 113-115.

San Francisco Chronicle, The
    1920   "Shakespeare is Again Unmasked," August 29, p. E2.

Saturday Review, The [London]
    1920   "Shakespeare: A New Folly," vol. 129 (March 27): 308-310.
    1928   "The Elizabethan Earl of Oxford," vol. 145 (May 19): 634-636.
    1930   "Fiddlesticks," vol. 149 (May 10): 592.
    1931   "Seven Shakespeares," vol. 152 (October 31): 560.
    1932   "The Life-Story of Edward de Vere as 'William Shakespeare,'" vol. 152 (June 4): 569.

Saturday Review of Literature, The [New York]
    1937   "Prefatory Note," May 1, p. 11.

Schelling, Felix E.
    1927   *Shakespeare and "Demi-Science:" Papers on Elizabethan Topics* (Philadelphia: Press of the University of Pennsylvania).

Schoenbaum, S.
    1991   *Shakespeare's Lives* (New York: Oxford University Press).

Schumann, Howard
    2009   "Concordia Authorship Research Center Set to Open," *Shakespeare Matters*, vol. 8, no. 2 (Spring): 1, 6-10.

Schücking, Levin L.
>1937   *The Meaning of Hamlet* (Oxford: Oxford University Press).

Scientific American
>1940   "Who Was Shakespeare" [editor's introduction to correspondence], *Scientific American*, vol. 162, no. 5 (May): 299.

Scotsman, The
>1920   "Shakespeare Identified," March 4, p. 2.
>1920   "Shakespeare Identified," March 20, p. 11.
>1921   "Poetry," February 17, p. 2.
>1931   "Shakespearean Research," June 8, p. 2.

Sears, Elizabeth
>Books
>2003   *Shakespeare and the Tudor Rose* (Marshfield Hills, MA: Meadow Geese Press). [1991]
>Articles and published letters
>1992   [Letter], *Shakespeare Oxford Newsletter*, vol. 28, no. 1 (Winter): 12.

Seaton, James
>2014   *Literary Criticism from Plato to Postmodernism: The Humanistic Alternative* (New York: Cambridge University Press).

Shahan, John M.
>Books edited
>2011   *Exposing an Industry in Denial: Authorship doubters respond to "60 Minutes with Shakespeare," issued by the Shakespeare Birthplace Trust on September 1, 2011* (Shakespeare Authorship Coalition).
>2013   *Shakespeare Beyond Doubt?: Exposing an Industry in Denial* (Tamarac, Florida: Llumina Press). [edited with Alexander Waugh]
>Articles
>2007   "Is There a Shakespeare Authorship issue?" *Shakespeare Oxford Newsletter*, vol. 43, no. 3 (Summer): 17-21.
>2013   "General Introduction and Challenge to the Shakespeare Birthplace Trust," in *Shakespeare Beyond Doubt?* (2013), pp. i-x.
>Articles co-authored with Richard F. Whalen
>2006   "Apples to Oranges in Bard Stylometrics: Elliott & Valenza Fail to Eliminate Oxford," *The Oxfordian*, vol. 9: 13-125.
>2009   "Elliott and Valenza's Stylometrics Fail to Eliminate Oxford as Shakespeare," in *Discovering Shakespeare: A Festschrift in Honor of Isabel Holden*, edited by Daniel L. Wright, pp. 137-142.

Shakespeare Fellowship, The
>1923   *Circular*, December 14. [Col. Ward: Report on First Year's Work]
>1925   *Circular*, August 14. [Col. Ward: Need for historical setting in which Oxford wrote]
>1925   *Circular*, November 20. [Col. Ward: Annual Report for 1925]
>1926   *Circular*, September 7. [Col. Ward: Fourth Annual Report]
>1927   *Circular*, December 21. [Col. Ward: Fifth Annual Report]
>1928   *Circular*, January 5. [Col. Ward: Announcement of Edward de Vere's £11,000 annuity]
>1928   *Circular*, February 3. [Col. Ward: Additional announcement of the annuity]
>1928   *Circular*, March 27. [Col. Ward: Notice of Georges Connes's *Le Mysterie Shakespearien*]
>1928   *Circular*, July 5. [Col. Ward: De Vere Country]
>1928   *Circular*, October 29. [Col. Ward: Sixth Annual Report; and report that the effects of the War with Spain as severe as those of the recent Great War]
>1928   *Circular*, November 6. [Col. Ward: Sir George Greenwood's passing, with excerpts from his letter of October 20, 1928]
>1929   *Circular*, June 23. [Percy Allen: *Declaration of Faith/Manifesto of Conversion*]
>1932   *Circular*, June 30. [Col. Ward: Cecil Palmer bankruptcy]
>1933   *Circular*, November 1, 1933. [Col. Douglas: Objec[tive]s of the Fellowship]
>1935   *Circular*, April. [Capt. Ward: *"Shakespeare" Identified* available at St. Giles Bookshop]

Shakespeare Fellowship Newsletter (American)
>1939   "Origin and Achievements of the Shakespeare Fellowship, vol. 1, no. 1 (December): 5.
>1939   "Ernest Stirling Allen," vol. 1, no. 1 (December): 6.

1940   "Scientific Proof Given that Lord Oxford Posed for Ancient Portraits of the Bard," vol. 1, no. 2 (Feb.): 2-5.

1940   "Funds Needed for Exploration," vol. 1, no. 2 (February): 6.

1940   "Rapid Growth of Research Fellowship Means End of Pompous Obstructionists," vol. 1, no. 2 (Feb.): 7.

1940   "Best Wishes from Abroad," vol. 1, no. 2 (February): 10.

1940   "An Oxfordian's Happy Thought," vol. 1, no. 2 (February): 12.

1940   "Burt of Boston and the Globe," vol. 1, no. 3 (April-May): 8.

1940   "Shakespeare Fellowship Business," vol 1, no. 3 (April-May): 6.

1940   "Who Was Shakespeare?" vol. 1, no. 3 (April-May): 4.

1940   "Miss Book of Indiana," vol. 1, no. 3 (April-May): 13.

1940   "Oxfordian News," vol. 1, no. 4 (June-July): 4.

1940   "Baltimore Discovers Oxford," vol. 1, no. 4 (June-July): 8.

1940   "The Honor of Authorship," vol. 1, no. 4 (June-July): 12.

1940   "... Let No Dog Bark," vol. 1, no. 5 (August-September): 6.

1940   "Under the Stukas' Shadow," vol. 1, no. 5 (August-September): 6.

1940   "Resolute and Determined," vol. 1, no. 5 (August-September): 11-12.

1940   "First Play Presenting Oxford as 'Shakespeare,'" vol. 1, no. 5 (August-September): 12.

1940   "Oxfordian News," vol. 1, no. 5 (August-September): 6.

1940   "In the Army Now," vol. 1, no. 6 (October-November): 6.

1940   "Some of Our Speakers," vol. 2, no. 1 (December): 6.

1941   "The Annual Meeting," vol. 2, no. 1 (February): 19-20.

1941   "Books and Flames," vol. 2, no. 3 (April 1941): 30.

1941   "Growing Interest," vol. 2, no. 3 (April): 30.

1941   "Letters from England," vol. 2, no. 3 (April): 36.

1941   "Bénézet versus Campbell," vol. 2, no. 4 (June): 44.

1941   "Oxfordian News," vol. 2, no. 4 (June): 42.

1941   "News from England," vol. 2, no. 4 (June): 52.

1941   "Letters from Members: Brief Excerpts," vol. 2, no. 6 (October): 6.

1941   "Our Third Year," vol. 3, no. 1 (December): 8-9.

1942   "War and the Fellowship," vol. 3, no. 2 (February): 18.

1942   "De Vere in San Francisco," vol. 3, no. 4 (June): 33.

1942   "Mister V," vol. 3, no. 4 (June): 52.

1942   "London Letter," vol. 3, no. 4 (June): 53-54.

1942   "Carolyn Wells," vol. 3, no. 4 (June): 56.

1942   "Encouragement," vol. 3, no. 5 (August), p. 66.

1942   "Whitman Collection," vol. 3, no. 5 (August): 68.

1942   "From Letters Received," vol. 3, no. 6 (October): 78.

1942   "Our Fourth Year," vol. 4, no. 1 (December): 10.

1942   "From England," vol. 4, no. 1 (December): 11.

1943   "Stratford Relics" [Review of "El-Dorado-on-Avon," by Roderick L. Eagle, *Everybody's*, February 28, 1942], vol. 4, no. 3 (April): 38.

1943   "Reference Files," vol. 4, no. 3 (April): 40.

1943   "What Members are Doing" vol. 4, no. 4 (June): 46.

1943   "Letters from England," vol. 4, no. 5 (August): 67-68.

1943   "To Our Readers," vol. 4, no. 6 (October): 80.

Shakespeare Fellowship News-Letter (English)

1937   "Occasional Notes," no. 1 (January): 8.

1937   "Occasional Notes," no. 2 (March): 10.

1937   "Our President at Lavenham," no. 3 (May): 5.

1937   "Annual General Meeting," no. 6 (July): 1.

1937   "General Annual Meeting of the Shakespeare Fellowship," no. 6 (November): 1.

1938   "News from Holland," no. 10 (July): 2-3.

1938   "Annual General Meeting," no. 12 (November): 1.

1939   "Notes from America," no. 14 (April): 9.

1939   "Occasional Notes," no. 15 (July): 8.

1940   "Minutes of the General Meeting," April p. 2.

1940   "Mr. John Barrymore," April, p. 7.
1941   "Did Queen Elizabeth Bear a Child?" October, p. 3.
1942   "Editorial Notes," April, p. 1.
1942   "The Life of William Shakespeare," October, pp. 2-3.
1942   "Charles Wisner Barrell and Our American Branch," April, p. 3.
1943   "Editorial Notes," May 1943, p. 1.
1943   "Oxfordian News," May, p. 3.
1943   "Editorial Notes," October, p. 1.
1945   "The General Meeting," November, p. 2.
1952   "Cecil Palmer," March, p. 4.

Shakespeare Fellowship Quarterly
1944   "Introducing the *Quarterly*," vol. V, no. 1 (January): 1-2.
1944   "Editorial Policy," vol. V, no. 1 (January): 16.
1944   "Discoverer of the True Shakespeare Passes," vol. V, no. 2 (April): 17-23.
1944   "Progress and a Handicap," vol. V, no. 3 (July): 48.
1945   "Beginning Our Sixth Year," vol. VI, no. 1 (January): 1-2.
1945   "'Shakespeare' Identified," vol. VI, no. 1 (January): 10.
1945   "Incorporation of the Fellowship to Stimulate Oxford Research," vol. VI, no. 2 (April): 17.
1945   "President Bénézet's Lecture Tour," vol. VI, no. 2 (April): 18-20.
1945   "Death of Canon Rendall," vol. VI, no. 2 (April): 21.
1945   "Recognition of Merit," vol. VI, no. 2 (April): 21.
1945   "A London Worthy's Letters," vol. VI, no. 2 (April): 26.
1945   "Foster of Iowa Speaks Out," vol. VI, no. 2 (April): 32.
1945   "A Great Pioneer's Ideas on Intellectual Freedom," vol. VI, no. 3 (July): 33-34.
1945   "President Bénézet Lectures in Philadelphia," vol. VI, no. 3 (July): 35-36.
1945   "Oxford's Birthday Signalized," vol. VI, no. 3 (July): 36.
1945   "Oxford-Shakespeare Case Loses Brilliant Advocate," vol. VI, no. 4 (October): 49-50.
1945   "Our President Rings the Bell Again," vol. VI, no. 4 (October): 56-57.
1945   "National Circulation for Oxford-Shakespeare Story," vol. VI, no. 4 (October): 64.
1946   "The Oxford-Shakespeare Book that Charmed Mr. Folger: Esther Singleton's
        Shakespearian Fantasias," vol. VII, no. 1 (January): 14.
1946   "Radio Presentation of Oxford-Shakespeare Case," vol. VII, no. 3 (July): 33.
1946   "Truth from Texas," vol. VII, no. 3 (July): 34.
1946   "Shakespeare Authorship Fraudulent," vol. VII, no. 3 (July): 44-45.
1946   "Lord Oxford Among the Lambs," vol. VII, no. 4 (October): 54.
1946   "Thou Shalt Not Bear False Witness," vol. VII, no. 4 (October): 70-71.
1947   "Mrs. Eva Turner Clark: Founder of the Shakespeare Fellowship, U.S.A.," vol. VIII, no. 1
        (Spring): 1-3.
1947   "Shakespeare: Man of Mystery," vol. VIII, no. 1 (Spring): 3.
1947   "Philadelphia's New Shakespeare Society Points Way to Truer Understanding of the
        Dramatist," vol. VIII, no. 1 (Spring): 15-16.
1947   "The Fellowship's General Meeting Highly Successful," vol. VIII, no. 2 (Summer): 17-20.
1947   "Oxford-Shakespeare Talks," vol. VIII, no. 2 (Summer): 20.
1947   "What Do You Think," vol. VIII, no. 2 (Summer): 32.
1947   "Money is a Good Soldier," vol. VIII, no. 3 (Autumn): 33-34.
1947   "Progress During the Passing Year," vol. VIII, no. 4 (Winter 1947-48): 49-57.
1947   "Convincing Brief by Charlton Ogburn," vol. VIII, no. 4 (Winter 1947-48): 49-50.
1947   "Constructive Newspaper Publicity," vol. VIII, no. 4 (Winter 1947-48): 50.
1947   "Oxford in *Grolier Encyclopedia*," vol. VIII, no. 4 (Winter 1947-48): 50-51.
1947   "Tufts College then—and Now," vol. VIII, no. 4 (Winter 1947-48): 54-55.
1947   "Bénézet at Wedgewood Club in Boston," vol. VIII, no. 4 (Winter 1947-48): 55.
1947   "Dr. Bénézet's 'Shakespeare Hoax,'" vol. VIII, no. 4 (Winter 1947-48): 56.
1947   "The Bolton-Bénézet Debate," vol. VIII, no. 4 (Winter 1947-48): 57.
1947   "Our Secretary at Pennsylvania," vol. VIII, no. 4 (Winter 1947-48): 57.
1948   "Libel Suit Grows Out of Fellowship's Annual Meeting," vol. IX, no. 2 (Summer): 16.

Shakespeare Matters
2013   "*Shakespeare Beyond Doubt* or *Shakespeare Beyond Doubt?* You Decide," vol. 12, no. 3

(Summer): 1, 19, 38.

Shakespeare Oxford Newsletter
1993   "Burford Reaches 15,000 With the Case for Oxford," vol. 29, no. 2 (Spring): 14-15.
1994   "Information and Commentaries from Betty Sears, Our Past President," vol. 30, no. 1 (Winter): 19-20.
2014   "What's the News?" vol. 50, no. 2 (Spring): 7.

Shakespearean Authorship Review
1961   "Notice of Death of Bénézet," no. 6 (Autumn): 23.

Shapiro, James
    Books
2010   *Contested Will: Who Wrote Shakespeare?* (New York: Simon & Schuster).
    Articles and reviews
2011   "Hollywood Dishonors the Bard," *The New York Times*, October 16, 2011.

Showerman, Dr. Earl
2015   "The Rediscovery of Shakespeare's Greater Greek," *The Oxfordian*, vol. 17: 163-191.
2015   "*A Midsummer Night's Dream*: Shakespeare's Aristophanic Comedy," *Brief Chronicles*, vol. 6: 107-136.

Simonton, Dean Keith
1994   *Greatness: Who Makes History and Why* (New York: The Guilford Press).
1999   *Origins of Genius: Darwinian Perspectives on Creativity* (New York: Oxford University Press).

Simpson, H. B.
1917   "Shakspere, Bacon and a 'Tertium Quid,'" *The Nineteenth Century and After*, vol. 82 (December): 1248-1264.
1935   "Shakespeare's Sonnets" [Reviews of *Personal Clues in Shakespeare Poems and Sonnets* by Gerald H. Rendall *and Shakespeare's Sonnets* by Gerald W. Phillips], *The Shakespeare Pictorial*, no. 84 (February): 32.

Singleton, Esther
    Books
1929   *Shakespearian Fantasias: Adventures in the Fourth Dimension* (New York: William Farquhar Payson) [Repr. in 2019, edited by James A. Warren, Veritas Publications]
1930   *The Shakespeare Garden*, new edition, with introduction by Eva Turner Clark (New York: W. F. Payson).
    Articles and reviews
1928   "A Great Courtier," *Saturday Review of Literature* [American], July 21, pp. 1049-1051.
1940   "Was Edward de Vere Shakespeare? *Shakespeare Fellowship News-Letter* (American), vol. 1, no. 4 (June/July 1940), pp. 9-10. [published posthumously; MSS dated 1921]
    Personal Letters
1929   Letter to Col. Bernard R. Ward, May 6. [Reprinted in *The Shakespeare Pictorial*, September 1930, p. 16.]

Sisson, C. J.
    Books
1936   *Lost Plays of Shakespeare's Age* (Cambridge: The University Press).
    Articles and reviews
1934   "The Theatres and Companies," in *A Companion to Shakespeare Studies* edited by G. B. Harrison & Granville Barker, pp. 9-44.

Slater, Gilbert
    Books
1931   *Seven Shakespeares* (London: Cecil Palmer).
    Articles, reviews and published letters
1938   "The Rival Poet of the Sonnets" [letter], *Shakespeare Fellowship News-Letter*, no. 8 (March): 12.

Smart, John Temple
1928   *Shakespeare—Truth and Tradition* (Oxford: Clarendon Press).

Smith, G. C. Moore
1929   "The Seventeenth Earl of Oxford," *Review of English Studies*, vol. 5, no. 17 (January): 93.

Smith, Logan Pearsall
    1933   *On Reading Shakespeare* (New York: Harcourt, Brace).

Smith, Sarah
    2005   [Comment on *"Shakespeare" by Another Name* by Mark Anderson] (back cover of book's dust jacket).

Smithers, Ursula
    1924   "Oxford and Jonson," *The Hackney Spectator*, February 29, p. 4.
    1924   "Oxford and Jonson, II," *The Hackney Spectator*, March 14, p. 4.

Sobran, Joseph
    Books
    1997   *Alias Shakespeare: Solving the Greatest Literary Mystery of All Time* (New York: The Free Press).
    Articles and reviews
    1997   "Shakespeare's Disgrace: Is This the Key to Identifying and Understanding the Poet?" *Shakespeare Oxford Newsletter*, vol. 33, no. 2 (Spring): 1, 4-6.
    2000   "The End of Stratfordianism," *Shakespeare Oxford Newsletter*, vol. 36, no. (Spring): 12-13, 25, 31.
    2003   "Nelson's Flawed Life of Oxford," *Shakespeare Oxford Newsletter*, vol. 39, no. 4 (Autumn): 1, 9-10, 16.
    2005   "Before He was Shakespeare, Part 1," Shakespeare Oxford Newsletter, vol. 41, no. 1 (Winter): 1, 13-16.
    2005   "Before He was Shakespeare, Part 2," Shakespeare Oxford Newsletter, vol. 41, no. 2 (Spring): 1, 12-14.

Southland Times [New Zealand]
    1920   "A Literary Log," issue 18840, June 5.

Spectator, The
    1920   "A Sleepless Shakespeare," March 7, p. 416.
    1921   "The Poems of Edward de Vere," August 27, p. 278.

Squire, John C. [Solomon Eagle]
    Books
    1922   *Essays at Large* (New York: H. Doran Co.). [See especially "Shakespeare and the Second Chamber"]
    Articles and reviews
    1921   "Mr. Looney and Lord Oxford," *The Outlook*, March 12, p. 231. [as Eagle]
    1921   "The Critic at Large: A Voice from the Past," *The Outlook*, July 2, p. 15. [as Eagle]
    1923   "The Oxford Movement," *The Observer*, March 25, p. 4.
    1928   "Lord Oxford," *The Observer*, May 6, p. 6.

Spurgeon, Caroline
    1935   *Shakespeare's Imagery and What It Tells Us* (Cambridge, UK: Cambridge University Press).

Stage, The
    1931   "Shakespeare Fellowship," April 30, p. 15.
    1959   "Percy Allen," February 12, p. 17.

Standen, Gilbert
    1930   *Shakespeare Authorship: A Summary of Evidence* (London: Cecil Palmer).

Starner, Janet Wright & Barbara Howard Traister
    2011   *Anonymity in Early Modern England: What's In a Name* (Burlington, VT: Ashgate Publishing Company).

Steadman, Edmund C.
    1901   "Advice to English Schoolboys Who Want to Become Shakespeare," *The Literary World*, vol. 63: 327.

Steinburg, Steven
    2018   Renaissance of Lies: Part 2 of the Autobiography of Edward de Vere
    2019   *I Come to Bury Shakspere*, revised fifth edition (CreateSpace). [2011]

Stokes, Frederick A. [Frederick A. Stokes Co.]
    1920   Letter to J. Thomas Looney, October 29. [JTL papers]

Stoll, Elmer Edgar
    1937   "The Detective Spirit in Criticism," *Saturday Review of Literature*, May 8, p. 12-17.

Stone, Elliott
    1997   [Letter], *Shakespeare Oxford Newsletter*, vol. 33, no. 2 (Summer): 21.

Stone, Irving
    1971   *The Passions of the Mind* (New York: Doubleday and Co.).

Stopes, Charlotte Carmichael
    1922   *Life of Henry, Third Earl of Southampton* (Cambridge: The University Press).

Story, Ted
    2008   *Shake-speare's Treason: The True Story of King Henry IX Last of the Tudors.* [A one-man show based on Hank Whittemore's *The Monument*] [with Hank Whittemore]
    2016   *The Shakespeare Fraud: The Politics Behind the Pen* (Somerville, MA: Forever Press).

Strachey, Lytton
    1928   *Elizabeth and Essex: A Tragic History* (London: Chatto & Windus).

Streitz, Paul
    2001   *Oxford, son of Queen Elizabeth I* (Darien, CT: Oxford Institute Press).

Stritmatter, Roger A.
    Books
    2003   *The Marginalia of Edward de Vere's Geneva Bible: Providential Discovery, Literary Reasoning, and Historical Consequence* (Northampton, MA: Oxenford Press).
    2013   *On the Date, Sources and Design of Shakespeare's The Tempest* [with Lynne Kositsky] (Jefferson, NC: McFarland & Co.)
    2016   *The 1623 Shakespeare First Folio: A Minority Report* [A special issue of *Brief Chronicles*.] (Baltimore: Shakespeare Oxford Fellowship).
    2019   *The Poems of Edward de Vere, 17th Earl of Oxford . . . and the Shakespeare Question, Volume I: He that Takes the Pain to Pen the Book* (Shakespeare Oxford Fellowship).
    Articles and reviews
    2001   "From the Editors: Oxford is Shakespeare: Any Questions?" *Shakespeare Matters*, vol. 1, no. 1 (Fall): 1, 3, 20. [as editor, with co-editor Bill Boyle.]
    2002   "Tender Airs, Tudor Heirs," *Shakespeare Matters*, vol. 1, no. 2 (Winter): 3. [as editor, with co-editor Bill Boyle.]
    2003   "'Monstrous Animosity:' How Nelson's Oxford Bio Distorts Both Oxford and Oxfordians," *Shakespeare Matters*, vol. 3, no. 1 (Fall): 8-9.
    2004   "A Critique of *The Monument* Theory" [with Lynne Kositsky], *Shakespeare Matters*, vol. 4, no. 1 (Fall): 1, 10-14.
    2006   "What's In a Name? Everything, Apparently . . .." *Rocky Mountain E-Review of Language and Literature*, vol. 60, no. 2, pp. 37-49.

Sun, The (Sydney)
    1920   [notice of the Australian edition of *"Shakespeare" Identified* published by Angus and Robertson.], June 17.

Sunday Times, The
    1930   "The Shakespeare-de Vere Controversy," May 4, p. 10.
    1932   "Shakespeare's Rivals: Claims of 17th Earl of Oxford," September 18, p. 21.

Sutton, Graham
    1931   "Another Theory About Shakespeare," *The Bookman*, vol. 81 (November): 132.

Sydenham of Combe, Lord & H. Crouch Batchelor
    1924   "The 'Shakespeare' Myth: A Challenge," *The English Review*, August, pp. 221-229.

T. P.'s & Cassel's Weekly
    1928   "Renaissance Courtier and Patron of Letters," June 23.

Tattersall, Ian
    2015   *The Strange Case of the Rickety Cossack: And Other Cautionary Tales from Human Evolution* (New York: Palgrave Macmillan).

Teachout, Terry
    2010   "Denying Shakespeare," *Wall Street Journal*, April 17, p. W14.

Teggart, Frederick
    1977   *Theory and Processes of History* (Berkeley: University of California Press).

Thornley, H. E.
    1920   [letter], *Yorkshire Post and Leeds Intelligencer*, March 11, p. 4.

Tierney, J. W.
    1945   "In the Country and Out of It," *The Countryman*, Spring, p. 46. [excerpt reprinted in *Shakespeare Fellowship News-Letter*, May 1945, p. 4.]

Tillyard, E. M. W.
    1942   *The Elizabethan World Picture* (New York: Vintage).
    1962   *Shakespeare's History Plays* (New York: Collier Books). [1940: London: Chatto & Windus]

Times, The
    1945   "Canon G. H. Rendall," Jan. 6, p. 6.

Times Literary Supplement, The
    1919   [first mention of *"Shakespeare" Identified* in print], issue 934 (December 11): 735.
    1923   [review of Col. Ward's *The Mystery of "Mr. W. H."*], issue 1108 (April 12): 248-50.
    1923   "Shakespeare Through Oxford Glasses," issue 1116 (June 7): 389.
    1926   "Le Mystere Shakespearien," issue 1275 (July 8): 464.
    1928   "Edward de Vere, Earl of Oxford," issue 1282 (June 21): 461.
    1928   "Edward de Vere," issue 1379 (July 5): 504.
    1931   [review of Clark's *Shakespeare's Plays in the Order of Their Writing*], issue 1530 (May 28): 440.
    1932   [reviews of six books], issue 1563 (January 14): 29.
    1936   [review of Cairncross's *The Problems of Hamlet*], issue 1820 (December 19): 1053.

Times of India
    1920   "The Latest Shakespeare," May 26, p. 11.
    1931   "Who Wrote Shakespeare," February 25, p. 5.

Tomlinson, Philip
    1934   "Bottom's Dream," *Times Literary Supplement*, May 3, p. 2.

Towns, Vincent
    1937   "Human Riddles that have Vexed the World: The Mystery of Shakespeare," *Boston Globe*, Dec. 30, p. 14.

Traubel, Horace
    1908   *With Walt Whitman in Camden* (New York: D. Appleton and Company).

Trilling, Lionel
    2008   *The Liberal Imagination: Essays on Literature and Society* (New York: New York Review Books). [1950]

Truth, The
    1935   "In Vere Veritas," February 6, p. 224.
    1952   "Obituary" [of Cecil Palmer], January.

Turner, Frederick Jackson
    1976   *The Frontier in American History* (Huntington, HY: R. E. Krieger Pub. Co.).

Twain, Mark
    1909   *Is Shakespeare Dead?* (New York: Harper & Bros.).

Uncle Dudley,
    1938   "A Mystery Tale of Shakespeare," *Boston Globe*, July 10, p. C4.

Underwood, George
    1923   "Readers and Writers: Dethroning Shakespeare-Anti-Stratfordian Scepticism," *The Freethinker*, vol. 43, no. 20 (May 20): 316-17.

University of California, Berkeley
    2016   *Handbook for Graduate Study in English*. [Given to all Ph.D. candidates]

V. R.
    1928   "Biography," *The English Review*, June, pp. 735-36.

W. R. R. — See W. Ringland Robinson

Waldron, John
    1937   "Flying Trapeze: 'Shakspere' vs. 'Shakespeare,'" *Washington Post*, December 10, p. 13.

Wall Street Journal
    1953   "'Tis Neither Here Nor There," February 11, p. 12.

Ward, Capt. Bernard M.
  Books, pamphlets and circulars
  1926   *A Hundreth Sundrie Flowers: From the Original Edition of 1573, by George Gascoigne.* With an introduction by the editor (London: L. F. Etchells and H. Macdonald).
  1928   *The Seventeenth Earl of Oxford 1550-1604 from Contemporary Documents* (London: J. Murray).
  1935   *Shakespeare Fellowship Circular* (April). [re *"Shakespeare" Identified* available at St. Giles Bookshop]
  1936   *An Enquiry Into the Relations Between Lord Oxford as "Shakespeare," Queen Elizabeth and the Fair Youth of Shakespeare's Sonnets* (London: Percy Allen). [with Percy Allen]
  Articles, reviews and published letters
  1925   "The Authorship of *The Arte of English Poesie: A Suggestion*," *The Review of English Studies*, vol. 1, no. 3 (July): 284-308.
  1928   "Edward de Vere" [letter], *The Times Literary Supplement*, issue 1289 (June 28): 486.
  1928   "The Famous Victories of Henry V," *The Review of English Studies*, vol. 4 (July): 270-294.
  1928   "Edward de Vere" [letter], *The Times Literary Supplement*, issue 1383 (August 2): 568.
  1929   "Queen Elizabeth and William Davison," *The English Historical Review*, vol. 44 (January): 104-106.
  1929   "John Lyly and the Office of the Revels," *Review of English Studies*, vol. 5, no. 17 (January): 57-59.
  1929   "Shakespeare and the Anglo-Spanish War, 1585-1601, I," *Revue Anglo-Américaine*, vol. 6, no. 4 (April): 297-311.
  1930   "Shakespeare and the Anglo-Spanish War, 1585-1601, II," *Revue Anglo-Américaine*, vol. 7, no. 4 (April): 298-311.
  1932   "*The Merry Wives of Windsor* and the Order of the Garter," *The Shakespeare Pictorial*, no. 48 (February): 32.
  1932   "Obituary" [of Mr. L. J. Maxse], *The Shakespeare Pictorial*, no. 49 (March): 48.
  1932   "The Three Williams in Shakespeare," *The Shakespeare Pictorial*, no. 50 (April): 68.
  1932   "The Date of *Love's Labour's Lost*," *The Shakespeare Pictorial*, no. 55 (September): 148.
  1932   "Annual General Meeting," *The Shakespeare Pictorial*, no. 57 (November): 180.
  1933   "Annual Dinner," *The Shakespeare Pictorial*, no. 64 (June): 92-93.
  1933   "The Shakespeare Family in Contemporary Satire," *The Shakespeare Pictorial*, no. 65 (July): 112.
  1933   "These Late Eclipses" [letter], *The Times Literary Sup.*, issue 1661 (November 30): 856.
  1933   "Shakespeare, Oxford, and Elizabethan Times," *The Shakespeare Pictorial*, no, 70 (December): 192.
  1933   "These Late Eclipses" [letter], *The Times Literary Sup.*, issue 1664 (December 7): 878.
  1933   "These Late Eclipses" [letter], *The Times Literary Sup.*, issue 1664 (December 21): 909.
  1934   "Lecture on The Elizabethan Drama," *The Shakespeare Pictorial*, no. 71 (January): 4.
  1934   "The Other Side of the Atlantic," *The Shakespeare Pictorial*, no. 71 (January): 4.
  1934   "The 'Mortal Moon' Sonnet," *The Times Literary Supplement*, issue 1681 (April 19): 282.
  1934   "Shakespeare Fellowship Dinner, *The Shakespeare Pictorial*, no. 76 (June): 84.
  1934   "A Companion to Shakespeare Studies," *The Sh. Pictorial*, no. 79 (September): 144.
  1934   "Shakespeare's Pays as Dramatized History," *The Sh. Pictorial*, no. 80 (October): 149.
  1935   "Hamlet," *The Shakespeare Pictorial*, no. 85 (March): 48.
  1935   "Notices: The Late Canon A. K. Hobart-Hampden," *The Shakespeare Pictorial*, no. 93 (November): 176.
  1936   "The Original Order of Shakespeare's Sonnets," *The Sh. Pictorial*, no. 97 (March): 52.
  1936   "'Shakespeare' and the Homilies," *The Shakespeare Pictorial*, no. 103 (September): 18.
  1937   "Two New Oxford Discoveries," *Shakespeare Fellowship News-Letter*, no. 3 (May): 1.
  1937   "Shakespearean Page" [Review of *When Shakespeare Died* by Ernest Allen], *East Anglian Magazine*, vol. 3, no. 1 (October): 40-41.
  1937   "Correspondence," *East Anglian Magazine*, vol. 3, no. 3 (December): 141-142.
  1938   "Review of *The Man Who Was Shakespeare* by Eva Turner Clark," *Shakespeare Fellowship News-Letter*, no. 7 (January): 1-3.
  1938   "Correspondence" [response to Gilbert Slater's letter], *Shakespeare Fellowship News-Letter*, no. 7 (January): 7.
  1938   "Correspondence" [response to Gilbert Slater's letter], *Shakespeare Fellowship News-*

        Letter, no. 8 (March): 12.

1939   "Reply to the 'Refutations,'" *Supplement 1, Shakespeare Fellowship News-Letter*, no. 14 (April), p. 23.

Personal letters

1933   Letter to J. Thomas Looney, mid-Sept. 1933. [not dated]

Ward, Colonel Bernard R.

Books and Shakespeare Fellowship Circulars

1923   *The Mystery of "Mr. W. H."* (London: Cecil Palmer).

1923   *Circular*, December 14. [Report on First Year's Work]

1925   *Circular*, August 14. [Need for historical setting in which Oxford wrote]

1925   *Circular*, November 20. [Annual Report for 1925]

1926   *Circular*, September 7. [Fourth Annual Report]

1927   *Circular*, December 21. [Fifth Annual Report]

1928   *Circular*, January 5. [Announcement of Edward de Vere's £11,000 annuity]

1928   *Circular*, February 3. [Additional announcement on the annuity]

1928   *Circular*, March 27. [Notice of Georges Connes's *Le Mysterie Shakespearien*]

1928   *Circular*, July 5. [De Vere Country]

1928   *Circular*, October 29. [Sixth Annual Report; and report that the effects of the War with Spain were as severe as those of the recent Great War]

1928   *Circular*, November 6. [Sir George Greenwood's passing, with excerpt from his letter of October 20, 1928]

Articles and reviews and published letters

1922   "'Shakespeare' at Hackney," *The Hackney Spectator*, Oct. 27, p. 3.

1922   "'Mr. W. H.' and 'Our Ever-Living Poet," *The National Review*, vol. 80 (September): 81-93.

1922   "Shakespeare's Mysterious 'W. H.' a Hackney Man?" [letter], *The Hackney Spectator*, September 1, p. 12.

1922   "Edward de Vere and William Shakspere—A Dual Mystery," *The National Review*, vol. 81 (October 1922): 267-76.

1922   "'Shakespeare' at Hackney," *The Hackney Spectator*, October 27, p. 3.

1922   "'Shakespeare' at Hackney," *The Hackney Spectator*, November 3, p. 11.

1922   "'Shakespeare' at Hackney," *The Hackney Spectator*, November 24, 1922, p. 14.

1922   "Report of a Lecture," *The Hackney Spectator*, December 8, p. 11.

1923   "The Shakespeare Fellowship," *The Hackney Spectator*, Jan. 5, p. 11.

1923   "Shakespeare Through Oxford Glasses," *The Hackney Spectator*," September 21, p. 2.

1923   "Report of Our First Year's Work," *The Hackney Spectator*, December 14, p. 8, 18.

1924   "Recent Progress," *The Hackney Spectator*, July 25, p. 9.

1924   "Fellowship Notes," *The Hackney Spectator*, August 1, p. 10.

1924   "The 'Shakespeare' Myth," *The Hackney Spectator*, August 15, p. 11.

1924   "The Shakespeare Signatures and Sir Thomas More," *The Hackney Spectator*, November 7, p. 4.

1924   "The Annual Report 1923-24," *The Hackney Spectator*, November 21, p. 2.

1925   "Annual Report for 1925," *Hackney and Stoke Newington Recorder*, November 20.

1928   "Shakespeare and Elizabethan War Propaganda," *Royal Engineers Journal*, December, pp. 470-474.

1929   "1928: An Important Year," *The Shakespeare Pictorial*, no. 11 (January): 16.

1929   "Propaganda in Plays," *The Shakespeare Pictorial*, no. 12 (February): 16.

1929   "Elizabethan Secret Service," *The Shakespeare Pictorial*, no. 12 (February): 16.

1929   "Elizabethan Exchequer Figures," *The Shakespeare Pictorial*, no. 13 (March): 16.

1929   "Shakespeare and Chapman," *The Shakespeare Pictorial*, no. 15 (May): 24.

1929   "Queen Elizabeth's 'Parsimony,'" *The Shakespeare Pictorial*, no. 16 (June): 20.

1929   "Queen Elizabeth and Secretary Davison," *The Shakespeare Pictorial*, no. 17 (July): 19.

1929   "Presentation to Professor Lefranc," *The Shakespeare Pictorial*, no. 18 (August): 14.

1929   "What Lurks Behind Shakespeare's Historical Plays," *The Shakespeare Pictorial*, no. 19 (September): 16.

1929   "Shakespeare and Richard III: A Tudor Government Propaganda Department" [letter], *The Morning Post*, September 3, p. 5.

1929   "The Case for Oxford as Shakespeare," *The Shakespeare Pictorial*, no. 22 (December): 20.

1929   "Shakespeare and the Sonnets: A Suggested Interpretation," *Poetry and the Play*, Winter
            1929-30, pp. 10-13.
1930   "Annual Dinner," *The Shakespeare Pictorial*, no. 27 (May): 96.
1930   "The Case for Edward de Vere as 'Shakespeare,'" *The Shakespeare Pictorial*, no. 31
            (September): 16.
1930   "Henry Wriothesley and Henry de Vere," *The Sh. Pictorial*, no. 33 (November): 16.
1930   "A Challenge and Its Acceptance," *The Shakespeare Pictorial*, no. 34 (December): 16.
1931   "Facts Collected, Problems Unsolved," *The Shakespeare Pictorial*, no. 35 (January): 16.
1931   "The Oxford-Shakespeare Case Corroborated," *The Sh. Pictorial*, no. 37 (March): 48.
1931   "Oxford's Handwriting," *The Shakespeare Pictorial*, no. 38 (April): 63.
1931   "The Annual Dinner," *The Shakespeare Pictorial*, no. 40 (June): 96.
1931   "The Records of the Court Revels," *The Shakespeare Pictorial*, no. 42 (August): 132.
1931   "The Shining Possibilities of Anne Vavasour," *The Shakespeare Pictorial*, no. 43
            (September): 148.
1931   "The Original *Venus and Adonis*," *The Shakespeare Pictorial*, no. 44 (October): 194.
1931   "A Great Shakespeare Discovery," *The Shakespeare Pictorial*, no. 46 (December): 196.
1932   "Mr. Justice Shallow," *The Shakespeare Pictorial*, no. 47 (January): 16.
1933   "A Protest Addressed to the Editor of *The Review of English Studies*," *The Shakespeare
            Pictorial*, no. 59 (January): 12-13.

Personal Letters
1925   Letter to Katharine E. Eggar, March 26. [Eggar Archives]
1925   Letter to Katharine E. Eggar, April 4. [Eggar Archives]
1926   Letter to Gilbert Standen, October 9. [SAT Archives]
1925   Letter to Gilbert Standen, December 14. [SAT Archives]
1927   Letter to Katharine E. Eggar, March 23. [Eggar Archives]
1927   Letter to Katharine E. Eggar, April 13. [Eggar Archives]
1928   Letter to Katharine E. Eggar, May 17. [Eggar Archives]
1928   Letter to Gilbert Standen, June 7. [SAT Archives]
1928   Letter to Gilbert Standen, August 10. [SAT Archives]
1928   Letter to Gilbert Standen, December 7. [SAT Archives]
1928   Letter to Gilbert Standen, December 25. [SAT Archives]
1929   Letter to Gilbert Standen, March 22. [SAT Archives]
1929   Letter to Gilbert Standen, April 12. [SAT Archives]
1929   Letter to Katharine E. Eggar, June 21. [Eggar Archives]
1929   Letter to Katharine E. Eggar, July 2. [Eggar Archives]
1929   Letter to Katharine E. Eggar, September 4. [Eggar Archives]
1929   Letter to Gilbert Standen, December 2. [SAT Archives]
1930   Letter to Gerald H. Rendall, April 19. [SAT Archives]
1932   Letter to Gilbert Standen, November 18. [SAT Archives]

Warren, James A.
    Books and pamphlets written and edited
    2017   *An Index to Oxfordian Publications: Including Oxfordian Books and Selected Articles from
                Non-Oxfordian Publications*. Fourth edition. (Somerville, MA: Forever Press)
    2018   *"Shakespeare" Identified* by J. Thomas Looney [Centenary edition] (Somerville, MA:
                Forever Press; reissued in 2019 by Veritas Publications).
    2019   *Oxfordian Archives in England: Two Databases of Oxfordian Ephemera and Oxfordian
                Books in the Special Collections Holdings of Brunel University, the University of London
                & the University of Liverpool*. [draft]
    2019   *"Shakespeare" Revealed: The Collected Articles and Published Letters of J. Thomas Looney*.
                (Cary, NC: Veritas Publications).

    Articles
    2015   "The Use of State Power to Hide Edward de Vere's Authorship of the Works of 'William
                Shakespeare,'" *Brief Chronicles VI*, pp. 59-81.
    2015   "Oxfordian Theory, Continental Drift and the Importance of Methodology," *The Oxfordian*,
                vol. 17: 193-221.
    2016   "Literary Criticism and the Authorship Question," *The 1623 Shakespeare First Folio: A
                Minority Report*, pp. 117-132. [a special issue of *Brief Chronicles*]

2018   "J. Thomas Looney in *The Bookman's Journal*: Five Letters (1920-1921)" [introduction and annotated editions of Looney's five letters], *The Oxfordian*, vol. 20: 131-156.

2020   "Comparisons of Oxford's Poetry with 'Shakespeare's': Five Letters from J. Thomas Looney to *The New Age* (1920-1921) and *The Outlook* (1921)," *The Oxfordian*, vol. 22: 103-120.

Washington Post

1924   "A New Rival to Shakespeare," March 10, p. 6.

1928   "Terse Reviews of Latest Books on Our Shelves," July 1, p. S9.

1928   "A Noted Baconian," November 15, p. 6.

1934   "By Any Other Name," April 1934, p. 8.

1948   "Who Wrote What?" [Editorial], July 10, p. 4.

Watterson, Henry

1920   "The Shakespeare Myth," *Reedy's Mirror*, vol. 29, no. 25 (June 17): 498.

Waugaman, Elisabeth

2019   "A Reassessment of the French Influence in Shakespeare," *The Oxfordian*, vol. 21: 155-176.

2019   "Review of *Early Shakespeare* by Bronson Feldman and edited by Warren Hope," *The Oxfordian*, vol. 21 (September): 261-69. [with Richard Waugaman]

Waugaman, Richard

Books

2014   *It's Time to Re-Vere "Shakespeare": A Psychoanalyst Reads the Works of Edward de Vere, Earl of Oxford* (Oxfreudian Press).

2017   *Newly Discovered Works by "William Shake-speare, a.k.a. Edward de Vere, Earl of Oxford* (Oxfreudian Press). [2014-

Articles and reviews

2009   "The Sternhold and Hopkins' Whole Book of Psalms is a Major Source for the Works of Shakespeare," *Notes and Queries*, vol. 56, no. 4 (December): 595-604.

2010   "Maniculed Psalms in the de Vere Bible: A New Literary Source for Shakespeare," *Brief Chronicles*, vol. 2: 109-120.

2019   "Review of *Early Shakespeare* by Bronson Feldman and edited by Warren Hope," *The Oxfordian*, vol. 21 (September): 261-69. [with Elisabeth Waugaman]

2020   "Is Falstaff a Portrait of the Historical Henry VIII?" *The Oxfordian*, vol. 22 (September): 65-78.

Waugh, Alexander

Books

2014   *Shakespeare in Court* (Kindle single, available at Amazon.com).

Books edited with Mark Anderson and Alex McNeil

2016   *Contested Year: An Anthology of Critical Reviews and Corrections to Each Chapter of James Shapiro's The Year of Lear: Shakespeare in 1606.*

Articles and reviews

2014   "Sweet Swan of Avon," *The Oxfordian*, vol. 16: 97-103.

Webb, Judge Thomas E.

1902   *The Mystery of William Shakespeare: A Summary of the Evidence* (London: Longmans, Green).

Webster, Lewis Hammond

1946   "Those Authorities," *Warwick Valley Dispatch*, January 30.

Wells, Carolyn

Books

1937   *The Rest of My Life* (New York: J. B. Lippincott Co.).

Articles and reviews

1937   "The Oxford Theory," *Saturday Review*, June 5, pp. 9, 16.

1941   "Oxford's Pseudonym," *Shakespeare Fellowship News-Letter* (American), vol. 2, no. 6 (October): 71.

Wells, Stanley

Books edited with Paul Edmondson

2013   *Shakespeare Beyond Doubt: Evidence, Argument, Controversy* (Cambridge: Cambridge

University Press)

<u>Articles</u>

2013   "Allusions to Shakespeare to 1642," in *Shakespeare Beyond Doubt: Evidence, Argument, Controversy*, edited by Paul Edmondson and Stanley Wells, pp. 73-87.

Western Morning News

1932   "The Stratford Maze: Was 'Shakespeare' a Group of Writers?" January 11, p. 2.

Whalen, Richard F.

<u>Books</u>

1994   *Shakespeare—Who Was He? The Oxford Challenge to the Bard of Avon*. Foreword by Paul H. Nitze. (Westport, CT: Praeger).

<u>Articles and reviews and published letters</u>

1995   "Shakespeare/Oxford in 'Jeopardy,'" *Shakespeare Oxford Newsletter*, vol. 31, no. 2A (Spring): 12-13.

1995   "Before Looney, Did Anyone Know Oxford was Shakespeare? A Novel, a Song and a Portrait Inventory Suggest So," *Shakespeare Oxford Newsletter*, vol. 31, no. 4 (Autumn): 12-16.

2000   [Letter], *Shakespeare Oxford Newsletter*, vol. 36, no. 3 (Fall): 23-24.

2003   "Nelson's New Oxford Biography," *Shakespeare Matters*, vol. 3, no. 1 (Fall): 1, 20-21.

2006   "The 'Prince Tudor' Hypothesis: A Brief Survey of the Pros and Cons," *Shakespeare Oxford Newsletter*, vol. 42, no. 2 (Spring): 10.

2010   "Stratfordian Professor Takes Authorship Question Seriously," *Shakespeare Oxford Newsletter*, vol. 46, no. 1 (May): 7-11.

<u>Articles co-authored with John M. Shahan</u>

2006   "Apples to Oranges in Bard Stylometrics: Elliott & Valenza Fail to Eliminate Oxford," *The Oxfordian*, vol. 9: 13-125.

2009   "Elliott and Valenza's Stylometrics Fail to Eliminate Oxford as Shakespeare," in *Discovering Shakespeare: A Festschrift in Honor of Isabel Holden*, edited by Daniel L. Wright, pp. 137-142.

Whitman, Sidney

1903   *Personal Reminiscences of Prince Bismarck* (London: J. Murray).

Whitman, Walt

1888   "What Lurks Behind Shakspere's Historical Plays," *November Boughs*.

Whittemore, Hank

<u>Books</u>

2005   *The Monument*. (Marshfield Hills, MA: Meadow Geese Press).

2005   *The Monument: An Abridged Introduction to the 918-page First Reference Edition* (Marshfield Hills, MA: Meadow Geese Press).

2008   *Shake-speare's Treason: The True Story of King Henry IX Last of the Tudors* [A one-man show based on *The Monument*] [with Ted Story]

2010   *Shakespeare's Son and His Sonnets: An Expanded Introduction to The Monument* (Groton, MA: Martin and Lawrence Press).

2012   *Twelve Years in the Life of Shakespeare*, edited by William Boyle (Somerville, MA: Forever Press).

2016   *100 Reasons Shake-speare was the Earl of Oxford* (Somerville, MA: Forever Press)

<u>Articles, reviews, letters</u>

1999   "Abstract & Brief Chronicles," *The Shakespeare Oxford Newsletter*, vol. 35, no. 2 (Summer): 1, 10-14, 22.

2001   "Prince Hamlet, the 'Spear-Shaker' of Elsinore," *Shakespeare Oxford Newsletter*, vol. 37, no. 1 (Spring): 8-12.

Wikipedia

2020   "Elizabethan Era." (https://en.wikipedia.org/wiki/Elizabethan_era, accessed June 26).

Wilde, James (1st Baron of Penzance)

1902   *Lord Penzance on the Bacon-Shakespeare Controversy: A Judicial Summing-Up*. (London: S. Low, Marston & Co.).

Wildenthal, Bryan H.

<u>Books</u>

2019   *Early Shakespeare Authorship Doubts* (San Diego: Zindabad Press).

Articles, reviews and published letters
2012   [Letter], *Skeptical Inquirer*, March-April, p. 62.
2016   "End of an Oxfordian Era on the Supreme Court?" *Shakespeare Oxford Newsletter*, vol. 52, no. 3 (Summer): 9-13.

Wilkinson, Heward
    Books
    2009   *The Muse as Therapist: A New Poetic Paradigm for Psychotherapy* (London: Karnac).
    Articles and reviews
    2010   "James Shapiro and the Sources of Literary Imagination," *Shakespeare Matters*, vol. 10, 2 (Spring): 1, 24-26.

Williamson, Hugh R.
    1933   "Poor Will," *The Bookman*, vol. 84 (July): 83-84.

Willoughby, D.
    1931   "Who Was Shakespeare?" *Saturday Review*, May 2, pp. 53-54.

Wilson, J. Dover
    1932   *The Essential Shakespeare: A Biographical Adventure* (Cambridge: The University Press).
    1935   *The Manuscript of Shakespeare's Hamlet and the Problems of Its Transmission* (Cambridge: The University Press).

Wilson, Lisa
    2012   *Last Will. & Testament.* [film]

Wimsatt, Jr., William K. and Monroe C. Beardsley
    1946   "The Intentional Fallacy," *Sewanee Review*, vol. 54: 468-88. [Revised in 1954]
    1954   "The Intentional Fallacy," revised version, in *The Verbal Icon: Studies in the Meaning of Poetry*, pp. 3-18 (Lexington, KY: University of Kentucky Press). [1946] From http://letras.cabaladada.org/letras/intentional_fallacy.pdf, 9 March 2015.

Wolpert, Lewis & Alison Richards
    1997   *Passionate Minds: The Inner World of Scientists* (Oxford: Oxford University Press).

Wood, Clement
    1925   "The Shakespeare Riddle: Has It at Last Been Solved," *New Leader*, September 26, p. 9.
    1927   *The Outline of Man's Knowledge* (New York: Lewis Copeland Company).

Wright, Daniel L.
    Books edited
    2009   *Discovering Shakespeare: A Festschrift in Honor of Isabel Holden* (editor) (Portland, OR: Concordia University Bookstore).
    Articles and reviews
    2013   "'I am I, howe'er I was begot'" in *A Poet's Rage*, edited by William E. Boyle, pp. 153-196 (Somerville, MA: Forever Press).
    2000   "Vere-y Interesting: Shakespeare's Treatment of the Earls of Oxford in the History Plays," *Shakespeare Oxford Newsletter*, vol. 36, no. 1 (Spring, 2000): 1, 14-21.

Yorkshire Post and Leeds Intelligencer
    1920   "The Real Shakespeare: Edward de Vere, Earl of Oxford," March 4, p. 6.
    1921   "Mr. Looney's Solution of 'Shakespeare:' Edward de Vere's Poems," February 16, p. 4.

Index

Note: Index does not include text in textboxes.

D

E

P

About the Author

James A. Warren is the editor of the Centenary Edition of J. Thomas Looney's *"Shakespeare" Identified* and *"Shakespeare" Revealed: The Collected Articles and Published Letters of J. Thomas Looney*. He is also the creator and editor of *An Index to Oxfordian Publications*, now in its fourth edition, and the author of *Summer Storm*, a novel with an Oxfordian theme.

He has given presentations at several Oxfordian conferences and his articles have appeared in *Brief Chronicles*, *The Oxfordian*, *The Shakespeare Oxford Newsletter* and *Shakespeare Matters*. In October 2020 he was named the Shakespeare Oxford Fellowship's Oxfordian of the Year, and in 2013 the Shakespeare Authorship Research Centre at Concordia University conferred upon him its Vero Nihil Verius Award for Scholarly Excellence.

Mr. Warren was a Foreign Service officer with the U.S. Department of State for more than twenty years, serving in Public Diplomacy positions at U.S. embassies in eight countries, mostly in Asia. He later served as Executive Director of The Association for Diplomatic Studies and Training (ADST) and as Regional Director for Southeast Asia for the Institute of International Education (IIE). Since 2016 he has been a Fellow at the Center for the Study of the Great Ideas.

Made in the USA
Middletown, DE
15 August 2021